THE OXFORD HANDB

NIETZSCHE

The diversity of Nietzsche's books, and the range of his philosophical interests, have posed daunting challenges to his interpreters. This *Oxford Handbook* addresses this multiplicity by devoting each of its thirty-two essays to a focused topic, picked out by the book's systematic plan. The aim is to treat each topic at the best current level of philosophical scholarship on Nietzsche. The first group of papers treat selected biographical issues: his family relations, his relations to women, and his ill health and eventual insanity. In Part II the papers treat Nietzsche in historical context: his relations to other philosophers—the Greeks, Kant, and Schopenhauer—and to the cultural movement of Romanticism, as well as his own later influence on analytic philosophy. The papers in Part III treat a variety of Nietzsche's works, from early to late and in styles ranging from the 'aphoristic' *The Gay Science* and *Beyond Good and Evil* through the poetic-mythic *Thus Spoke Zarathustra* to the florid autobiography *Ecce Homo*. This focus on individual works, their internal unity, and the way issues are handled within them, is an important complement to the final three groups of papers, which divide up Nietzsche's philosophical thought topically. Part IV treats issues in Nietzsche's value theory, ranging from his metaethical views as to what values are, to his own values of freedom and the overman, to his insistence on 'order of rank', and his social-political views. The fifth group of papers treat Nietzsche's epistemology and metaphysics, including such well-known ideas as his perspectivism, his promotion of becoming over being, and his thought of eternal recurrence. Finally, Part VI treats another famous idea—the will to power—as well as two linked ideas that he uses will to power to explain: the drives, and life. This volume is a key resource for all scholars and advanced students who work on Nietzsche.

Ken Gemes is Professor of Philosophy at Birkbeck, University of London, and the New College of Humanities, London.

John Richardson is Professor of Philosophy at New York University.

THE OXFORD HANDBOOK OF

NIETZSCHE

Edited by

KEN GEMES

and

JOHN RICHARDSON

OXFORD

UNIVERSITY PRESS

OXFORD
UNIVERSITY PRESS

Great Clarendon Street, Oxford, OX2 6DP,
United Kingdom

Oxford University Press is a department of the University of Oxford.
It furthers the University's objective of excellence in research, scholarship,
and education by publishing worldwide. Oxford is a registered trade mark of
Oxford University Press in the UK and in certain other countries

© The several contributors 2013

The moral rights of the authors have been asserted

First published 2013
First published in paperback 2016

Published in the United States of America by Oxford University Press
198 Madison Avenue, New York, NY 10016, United States of America

British Library Cataloguing in Publication Data
Data available

Library of Congress Cataloging in Publication Data
Data available

ISBN 978–0–19–953464–7 (hbk)
ISBN 978–0–19–877673–4 (pbk)

CONTENTS

PART III PRINCIPAL WORKS

PART IV VALUES

PART V EPISTEMOLOGY & METAPHYSICS

PART VI DEVELOPMENTS OF WILL TO POWER

LIST OF ABBREVIATIONS

The following standard abbreviations are used throughout this volume. Note, while authors use these abbreviations they will be referring to specific editions and possibly translations of the relevant work. Each essay comes with a bibliography indicating what the relevant translations and editions are. Also note, some authors use these abbreviations but their bibliography contains only entries for the *KSA* and *KGW* (see below)—the most scholarly and widely referenced German editions of Nietzsche's collected works. In that case the relevant authors have translated from the relevant works as they are contained in either the *KSA* or *KGW*. In citing the *KSA*, the standard order is volume number: notebook number [note number], e.g., *KSA* 11: 25 [7]. In a few cases the page number is given after the note number, for quick reference; thus *KSA* 12: 9 [89].382. And in some cases the authors cite KSA by volume number: page number.

A	*The Antichrist*
BT	*The Birth of Tragedy*
BGE	*Beyond Good and Evil*
C	*Stiftung Weimarer Klassik Friedrich Nietzsche: Chronik in Bildern und Texten*
CW	*The Case of Wagner*
D	*Daybreak* (also translated as *Dawn*)
DW	'Die dionysische Weltanschauung'
EH	*Ecce Homo*
FS	*Frühe Schriften*
GM	*On the Genealogy of Morality* (also translated as *On the Genealogy of Morals*)
GS	*The Gay Science*
GTG	'Die Geburt des tragischen Gedankens'
HAH I	*Human, All Too Human*
HAH II	*Assorted Opinions and Maxims*
HAH III	*The Wanderer and His Shadow*
HC	'Homer's Contest'
KGB	*Nietzsche Briefwechsel: Kritische Gesamtausgabe*
KGW	*Kritische Gesamtausgabe*
KSA	*Kritische Studienausgabe*
NCW	*Nietzsche contra Wagner*
OS	'On Schopenhauer: Notes 1868'
PPP	*The Pre-Platonic Philosophers*

PT	'On the Pathos of Truth'
SL	*Selected Letters of Friedrich Nietzsche*
ST	'Sokrates und die griechische Tragödie'
TI	*Twilight of the Idols*
TL	'On Truth and Lies in an Extramoral Sense'
UM	*Untimely Meditations* (also translated as *Unmodern Observations* and *Unfashionable Observations*)
UM I	'David Strauss, the Confessor and the Writer'
UM II	'On the Uses and Disadvantages of History for Life' (also translated: 'On the Uses and Abuses of History for Life')
UM III	'Schopenhauer as Educator'
UM IV	'Richard Wagner in Bayreuth'
WC	'We Classicists' (also translated 'We Philologists')
WP	*The Will to Power*
WLN	*Writings from the Late Notebooks*
Z	*Thus Spoke Zarathustra*
ZVT1	'Zwei öffentliche Vorträge über die griechische Tragödie. Erster Vortrag: Das griechische Musikdrama'
ZVT2	'Zwei öffentliche Vorträge über die griechische Tragödie: Zweiter Vortrag: Sokrates und die Tragoedie'

LIST OF CONTRIBUTORS

Christa Davis Acampora is Professor of Philosophy at Hunter College and the Graduate Center, City University of New York. She is the author of *Contesting Nietzsche* (University of Chicago Press, 2013) and the editor of the *Journal of Nietzsche Studies*.

R. Lanier Anderson, Associate Professor at Stanford University, works on the history of late modern philosophy, focusing primarily on Nietzsche and Kant. He is the author of many papers on Nietzsche, including recently "Nietzsche on Truth, Illusion, and Redemption" (*European Journal of Philosophy*, 2005), "Nietzsche on Redemption and Transfiguration," in Landy and Saler, eds, *The Re-Enchantment of the World* (Stanford University Press, 2009), and "What is a Nietzschean Self?" in Janaway and Robertson, eds, *Nietzsche, Naturalism, and Normativity* (Oxford University Press, 2012). Current research interests include a book on Kant's theoretical philosophy (*The Poverty of Conceptual Truth*, nearing completion), as well as work on Nietzsche's moral psychology and special topics on the relations between philosophy and literature.

Keith Ansell-Pearson is Professor of Philosophy at the University of Warwick. In 2013/14 he will be a Visiting Fellow at the Humanities Research Center of Rice University, US.

Tom Bailey teaches philosophy at John Cabot University in Rome. His research focuses on Kant and post-Kantian philosophy of the nineteenth century, particularly Nietzsche, and on ethics and political philosophy.

Jessica N. Berry is the author of *Nietzsche and the Ancient Skeptical Tradition* (Oxford University Press, 2011). She is Associate Professor of Philosophy at Georgia State University in Atlanta.

Daniel Came is lecturer in Philosophy at the University of Hull. Previously he has held a College Lectureship in Philosophy at St Hugh's College, Oxford and a Junior Research Fellowship in Philosophy at Worcester College, Oxford. He is the author of *Nietzsche: The Problem of Existence* (Polity Press, forthcoming) and the editor of *Nietzsche on Art and Life* (Oxford University Press, 2014). His most recent research also includes articles on Schopenhauer and on the relationship between ethics and aesthetics, including "Moral and Aesthetic Judgments Reconsidered" (*Journal of Value Inquiry*).

Maudemarie Clark is Professor of Philosophy at the University of California, Riverside, and George Carleton Jr. Professor of Philosophy at Colgate University. She is the author of *Nietzsche on Truth and Philosophy* (Cambridge University Press, 1990) and (with David Dudrick) *The Soul of Nietzsche's "Beyond Good and Evil"* (Cambridge University Press, 2012). She is also translator and editor (with Alan Swensen) of Nietzsche's *On the Genealogy of Morality* (Hackett, 1998) and editor (with Brian Leiter) of Nietzsche's *Daybreak* (Cambridge

University Press, 1997). Many of her articles on Nietzsche concerning morality and politics will be published by Oxford in 2014.

Adrian Del Caro is Distinguished Professor of Humanities and Head of Modern Foreign Languages and Literatures at the University of Tennessee at Knoxville. In addition to numerous articles and books since 1980 on Nietzsche, Hölderlin, Hofmannsthal, and Celan, he is the translator of *Thus Spoke Zarathustra* (Cambridge University Press, 2006), *Beyond Good and Evil* and *On the Genealogy of Morality* (Stanford University Press, 2013, in press), and Schopenhauer's *Parerga and Paralipomena II* (Cambridge University Press, in progress). His last monograph on Nietzsche was the ecocritical *Grounding the Nietzsche Rhetoric of Earth* (Walter de Gruyter, 2004); a monograph in progress is on *Geist* and *Erdgeist* in Goethe's *Faust*.

David Dudrick is Associate Professor of Philosophy at Colgate University. He is the author (with Maudemarie Clark) of *The Soul of Nietzsche's "Beyond Good and Evil"* (Cambridge University Press, 2012) and articles on Nietzsche and on Foucault.

Sebastian Gardner is Professor of Philosophy at University College London. He is the author of books and articles on the philosophy of psychoanalysis, Kant, Sartre, and other figures in modern European philosophy.

Ken Gemes is Professor of Philosophy at Birkbeck College, University of London, and at the New College of the Humanities, London. He has published extensively on Nietzsche and topics in logic and the philosophy of science. With Simon May, he is co-editor of *Nietzsche on Freedom and Autonomy* (Oxford University Press, 2009).

Jacob Golomb is Ahad Ha-am Professor of Philosophy at the Hebrew University of Jerusalem and the philosophical editor of the Hebrew University Magnes Press. He has been a visiting professor of philosophy at the Penn State University and a member of Wolfson College, Oxford. His books include *Nietzsche's Enticing Psychology of Power* (1989), *In Search of Authenticity: from Kierkegaard to Camus* (Routledge, 1995), *Nietzsche in Zion* (Cornell U.P., 2004), *The Hebrew Nietzsche* (2009). He has also published extensively on Kierkegaard, Sartre, Camus and on the philosophy of Zionism.

Robert Guay is Associate Professor and Director of Graduate Studies in Philosophy at Binghamton University, State University of New York. He is currently working on a book project on Nietzsche's ethical thought.

Randall Havas is Professor of Philosophy at Willamette University. His academic writing focuses on Heidegger and Nietzsche.

Charlie Huenemann is Professor of Philosophy at Utah State University.

Nadeem J. Z. Hussain is Associate Professor of Philosophy at Stanford University. He specializes in metaethics and the history of late nineteenth-century German philosophy. He has written extensively on interpretations of Nietzsche's metaethics. Relevant publications include "Honest Illusion: Value for Nietzsche's Free Spirits," in B. Leiter and N. Sinhababu (eds), *Nietzsche and Morality* (Clarendon Press, 2007); "The Role of Life in the Genealogy," in S. May (ed.), *The Cambridge Critical Guide to Nietzsche's "On the Genealogy of Morality"* (Cambridge University Press, 2011); and "Nietzsche and Non-Cognitivism," in S. Robertson and C. Janaway (eds), *Nietzsche, Naturalism, and Normativity* (Oxford University Press, 2012).

Dylan Jaggard is an independent scholar.

Christopher Janaway is Professor of Philosophy at the University of Southampton. He has written extensively on the philosophy of Nietzsche and Schopenhauer and on aesthetics. His most recently published book is *Beyond Selflessness: Reading Nietzsche's "Genealogy"* (Oxford University Press, 2007). He is general editor of the *Cambridge Edition of the Works of Schopenhauer*, and in 2007–10 was principal investigator on the AHRC-funded project "Nietzsche and Modern Moral Philosophy" at Southampton.

Paul Katsafanas is Assistant Professor of Philosophy at Boston University. His recent publications include "Deriving Ethics from Action: A Nietzschean Version of Constitutivism" in *Philosophy and Phenomenological Research* (2011), "The Concept of Unified Agency in Nietzsche, Plato, and Schiller" in *Journal of the History of Philosophy* (2011), and *Agency and the Foundations of Ethics: Nietzschean Constitutivism* (Oxford University Press, 2013).

Brian Leiter is Karl N. Llewellyn Professor of Jurisprudence and Director of the Center for Law, Philosophy, and Human Values at the University of Chicago. He is the author of many books and articles, including *Nietzsche on Morality* (Routledge, 2002; 2nd edition forthcoming) and *Why Tolerate Religion?* (Princeton, 2013).

Paul S. Loeb is Professor of Philosophy at the University of Puget Sound. He is the author of *The Death of Nietzsche's Zarathustra* (Cambridge University Press, 2010). His current projects include a monograph on Nietzsche's theory of will to power and a collaborative translation of *Thus Spoke Zarathustra* and *Unpublished Fragments from the Period of "Thus Spoke Zarathustra"* (Vols. 7, 14, and 15 of *The Complete Works of Friedrich Nietzsche* from Stanford University Press).

Mark Migotti teaches in the Department of Philosophy at the University of Calgary, and has published on Nietzsche and Schopenhauer, Peirce and pragmatism, and the nature of promising. He is the co-author (with Richard Sanger) of *Hannah's Turn*, a play about the romantic liaison between Hannah Arendt and Martin Heidegger that premiered at the Summerworks Theatre Festival in Toronto, Canada in August 2011. His long-run projects include a book on Nietzsche's early philosophical development and a book on his critique of morality.

David Owen is Professor of Social and Political Philosophy at the University of Southampton. He has published nine books and numerous articles including, most recently, *Nietzsche's "Genealogy of Morality"* (Acumen, 2007), *Recognition and Power*, co-edited with Bert van den Brink (Cambridge University Press, 2007) and *Multiculturalism and Political Theory*, co-edited with Anthony Laden (Cambridge University Press, 2007). He is currently working on books on agonism, realism, and perfectionism in Nietzsche's thought and on the political theory of migration.

Graham Parkes is Professor of Philosophy at University College, Cork. He is the author of *Composing the Soul: Reaches of Nietzsche's Psychology* (University of Chicago Press, 1994) and of numerous papers on Nietzsche as well as on Japanese thought. He is also the editor of *Heidegger and Asian Thought* (University of Hawaii Press, 1987) and of *Nietzsche and Asian Thought* (University of Chicago Press, 1991).

Peter Poellner is Professor of Philosophy at the University of Warwick. He is the author of *Nietzsche and Metaphysics* and of numerous papers on Nietzsche. He also writes on phenomenology, especially on Husserl and Sartre. Thematically, his current interests center on issues in the philosophy of mind and the philosophy of value, especially nonconceptual content, self-deception, and the structure and ethical relevance of emotions.

Bernard Reginster is Professor and Chair in the Department of Philosophy at Brown University. His work focuses on ethics, moral psychology, and issues arising from psychiatry. He has published numerous articles on Nietzsche, Schopenhauer, and other nineteenth-century German philosophers and his book *The Affirmation of Life: Nietzsche on Overcoming Nihilism* (Harvard University Press, 2006). He has begun to publish articles on issues from psychiatry, and was recently an Erikson Fellow at the Erikson Institute at the Austen Riggs Center.

John Richardson is Professor of Philosophy at New York University. He is the author of *Existential Epistemology: A Heideggerian Critique of the Cartesian Project* (Oxford University Press, 1986), *Nietzsche's System* (Oxford University Press, 1996), *Nietzsche's New Darwinism* (Oxford University Press, 2004), and *Heidegger* (Routledge, 2012). He is a co-editor of *Nietzsche* (2001) in the series Oxford Readings in Philosophy.

Aaron Ridley is Professor of Philosophy at the University of Southampton. His books include *Nietzsche's Conscience: Six Character Studies from the "Genealogy"* (1998) and *Nietzsche on Art* (2007).

Simon Robertson is a lecturer in philosophy at Cardiff University. He works on and has published articles in a range of fields, including contemporary ethics (normative ethics, metaethics, practical reason), Nietzsche, philosophy of normativity, and philosophy of risk; and he is the editor of *Spheres of Reasons* (Oxford University Press, 2009) and, with Christopher Janaway, *Nietzsche, Naturalism, and Normativity* (Oxford University Press, 2012).

Richard Schacht is Professor of Philosophy and Jubilee Professor of Liberal Arts and Sciences (Emeritus) at the University of Illinois. He has written extensively on Nietzsche and other figures and developments in the post-Kantian interpretive tradition. His books include *Nietzsche* (in Routledge's Arguments of the Philosophers series), *Making Sense of Nietzsche, Hegel and After*, and *Finding an Ending: Reflections on Wagner's Ring* (with Philip Kitcher). He is editor of *Nietzsche: Selections*; *Nietzsche's Postmoralism*; *Nietzsche, Genealogy, Morality*; and a forthcoming Norton anthology, *After Kant: The Interpretive Tradition*

Robin Small is Professor of Philosophy of Education at the University of Auckland. His most recent book is *Time and Becoming in Nietzsche's Thought* (Continuum, 2010). He is also the author of *Nietzsche in Context* (Ashgate, 2001) and *Nietzsche and Rée: A Star Friendship* (Oxford University Press, 2005), as well as editor and translator of *Paul Rée: Basic Writings* (University of Illinois Press, 2003).

Ivan Soll is Emeritus Professor of Philosophy at the University of Wisconsin-Madison. He has also taught in Italy, Germany, England, Hungary, New Zealand, and Turkey. His philosophical work is principally concerned with figures in the Continental tradition, particularly Kant, Hegel, Schopenhauer, Nietzsche, Sartre, and Freud, and with issues in aesthetic theory, philosophical psychology, and the philosophy of life. He has also been active as an author, designer, and publisher of fine-press book art.

Gudrun von Tevenar is Visiting Fellow at Birkbeck College, University of London. She has lectured and published on the moral philosophies of Kant, Schopenhauer, and Nietzsche, as well as German Idealism.

Julian Young is W. R. Kenan Jr. Professor of Humanities at Wake Forest University. He is the author of ten books and many articles, most of them on Schopenhauer, Nietzsche, or Heidegger. They include *Nietzsche's Philosophy of Religion* (Cambridge University Press, 2006) and, most recently, *Friedrich Nietzsche: A Philosophical Biography* (Cambridge University Press, 2010).

INTRODUCTION

KEN GEMES AND JOHN RICHARDSON

WHILE no single volume can hope to cover all of Nietzsche's extremely wide-ranging interests, this one aims to offer papers on a principled list of his main philosophical topics, which we arrange under the three headings of 'values' (Part 4), 'epistemology and metaphysics' (Part 5), and 'development of will to power' (Part 6). We supplement these treatments of philosophical topics with sets of papers on a few biographical questions (Part 1), on Nietzsche's relations to certain other philosophers (Part 2), and on many of his individual works (Part 3). This results in a certain overlap, as a philosophical topic is treated within the context of a particular work, for example; we consider this a worthwhile reminder that Nietzsche's philosophical ideas are offered in works with distinctive characters and ambitions.

BIOGRAPHY

Nietzsche led a more interesting life than most philosophers, a life with striking romantic elements. The strong psychological turn of his thinking, and his insistence on viewing ideas in the context of a particular personality and life, license an attention to his own. Indeed he himself stresses the relevance of his life to his thinking. His autobiography *Ecce Homo* situates his ideas within his own psychology and presents his works as expressing his ongoing education not just about the world but about himself. The Prefaces he wrote in 1886 to several earlier works also emphasize this biographical context. Moreover, Nietzsche puts great stress on the question of what effect philosophical ideas have on one's 'living'. We may take his own life as showing what someone fully informed about his ideas would consider the way to live—and may partly judge them by this fruit.

If our interest is in connecting his thinking with his biography, the great range of the former means that there are many different aspects of his life and personality we might focus on. Few topics in the realm of human psychology escape his attention; many could be profitably considered in his personal case. We've picked a few: his relations to his family; his relations to women; his lifelong sickness and eventual madness. But there are many other points on which his life and ideas strikingly interact, including: his musicianship and its bearing on his views about art; his feelings about places and belief that ideas can be marked by their geographical provenance; his feelings about nature and scenic beauty; his relation to his friends (and theory of friendship); his attitudes and behaviour towards those 'low' around him, i.e. low by his own exacting standards. The three biographical aspects we've picked bear quite differently on his thinking: they affect it, if they do, by quite different causal mechanisms.

Family. Graham Parkes (Chapter 1) notes Nietzsche's belief in a kind of hereditary determinism: even (or especially?) in philosophy, thinking reflects what one's ancestors did. He often applies this to his own case—and invites us to interpret his ideas against this background. Given the great preponderance of Christian pastors in his own lineage, we see that this determinism needn't work in a straight line: his ancestry didn't determine him to be a Christian, though he might have thought it explained a hortatory and religious aspect in his thinking. Parkes introduces the religious and personal temperaments of Nietzsche's father and two grandfathers, which forms a striking background to his own radical thought about religion. A separate issue is the bearing on Nietzsche's thinking of his upbringing and family life. Parkes discusses the impact on Nietzsche of witnessing (at age four) the drawn-out and agonizing death of his father (from 'softening of the brain'). Parkes suggests that this was the beginning of Nietzsche's turn from the Christian faith; it also gave him great foreboding over his own later ailments. After his father's death (and the death of Nietzsche's younger brother soon after), he grew up in a household comprising six females (mother, sister, two aunts, grandmother, and housekeeper). This family experience is surely germane, throwing light on Nietzsche's infamous quips about women, on his claim to 'know women', and on his sometimes exaggerated masculinity. Nietzsche's longest-lasting connections were to his mother and sister, and Parkes shows in detail the shifts and complexity in these relationships.

Women. On this topic Nietzsche emphasizes the even greater relevance of his biography: he warns that his ideas on it may be 'just his', i.e. express his quite particular perspective. Since he thinks perspectivity holds quite generally, what does he mean by this more pointed alert? He is acknowledging, it seems, a narrowness in his own perspective on this topic, a lapse in his ability to incorporate and include other viewpoints, which he elsewhere touts as his great strength. And yet this acknowledgement doesn't prompt him to temper or moderate his views; he seems rather to use it to license an extra vehemence. Julian Young in Chapter 2 shows how Nietzsche's anti-feminism and misogyny first appeared only in 1883 with *Thus Spoke Zarathustra*; he argues that before this Nietzsche was even a 'cautious feminist'. What happened to change him, Young argues, was his disastrous experience with Lou Salomé; it was this biographical event, and not his philosophical thinking, that explains his 'turn' against women. The anti-feminism is not a consequence of Nietzsche's attack on 'levelling', for example; the latter can still less explain his outright hostility towards women. Young details Nietzsche's experience with Salomé and conveys the rage he felt towards her. What he writes against women in and after this period are acts of revenge, Young suggests. Surprisingly, this campaign did not damage Nietzsche's relations with his friends, most of whom were emancipated women. Young discusses why these and other feminists have so often found Nietzsche's writings congenial despite his misogynistic remarks: they have followed Nietzsche's own advice and treated these ideas as 'just his'.

Sickness and madness. Here we meet still other questions about the bearing of biography on thinking. Nietzsche's madness has often been taken to count against his ideas, and indeed it's easy to hear a note of exaggeration and shrillness in works immediately preceding his breakdown (in early 1889, at age 44)—for example in *Antichrist* and *Ecce Homo*. What was the cause and nature of his insanity, and does it have any bearing on the works he wrote before that break? Charlie Huenemann (Chapter 3) shows that the long-standard explanation for the dementia—syphilis—is almost certainly false. The cause is much more likely to have been a tumour, growing all his life on the surface of his brain and behind his right eye. This would explain the severe headaches and eye problems he suffered regularly beginning in childhood. Huenemann brings out vividly the extraordinary physical suffering this ailment subjected Nietzsche to—and how it was joined by other serious problems, especially digestive ones. His philosophical production in these circumstances is quite remarkable. But it is not surprising, as Huenemann points out, that Nietzsche puts such great weight on 'health', as even his principal value, and especially on the kind of health that overcomes sickness and suffering. Huenemann argues that when Nietzsche values 'madness', it is a healthy and philosophical madness exemplified in Zarathustra, and which Nietzsche tried to cultivate in himself. But he fell victim in the end, 'perhaps over most of 1888' Huenemann suggests, to the different kind of madness brought on by his tumour.

HISTORICAL RELATIONS

Nietzsche seems not to pay close and sustained attention to other philosophers, yet he is highly aware of his relations to them, and very eager to locate his own positions in contrast with theirs. He takes one characteristic stance towards them: he reads their writings as symptomatic of certain underlying values—values often quite different from those the philosophers explicitly endorse. This diagnostic approach shifts attention away from the arguments those philosophers give in defence of their views, suggesting that these arguments are not the factors really driving them to those views, and also not the factors we ourselves should most weigh in considering them. But although this move is characteristic of Nietzsche, he does not adopt it uniformly; he also often rebuts arguments in the more direct and traditional way, by exposing false premises and gaps in reasoning. A recurring theme in this part's papers is the interplay between these two very different ways Nietzsche responds to philosophers' views.

The Greeks. Jessica Berry's piece (Chapter 4) shakes up the received views about Nietzsche's career as a philologist and his relation to the Greeks. Against the common idea that he was a philologist first but then quickly came, forced by the vitriolic criticism of his first book *The Birth of Tragedy*, to abandon the field in favour of philosophy, Berry shows that from the beginning Nietzsche criticized philology from what he took to be a distinctly philosophical perspective. But he also, until the end of his intellectual career, continued to consider himself a philologist as well as a philosopher, and criticized philosophy from a philologist's perspective. Similarly, his relationship with the Greeks is more nuanced than usually perceived. Berry points out that Nietzsche's early work on Homer emphasized, against the established tradition that read the classics through the prism of Enlightenment humanist thought, that Homer in fact recognized the inevitable brutish and violent element in human nature, the 'delight in *drunkenness, delight in cunning, revenge, envy, slander, obscenity*'. Against the common perception that Nietzsche maintains an ontology of radical flux, allegedly inspired by his reading of Heraclitus, Berry points out that Nietzsche was well aware of, and even quoted, fragments from Heraclitus that emphasized order, necessity, and stability in the course of nature. For Nietzsche, ancient Greeks such as Heraclitus and Homer were interesting not because of any doctrines they suggested, but because of the example they themselves provided of certain psychological types. And Nietzsche, like the ancient sceptics following Pyrrho, whose relation to Nietzsche Berry examines in detail, was generally more interested in the psychological consequences of philosophical doctrines than in their content, and like those sceptics he often rejected any ambitions to limn the true nature of reality.

Romanticism. Adrian Del Caro in Chapter 5 examines Nietzsche's engagement with romanticism, contrasting his early romantic period, and the influence of Goethe, Hölderlin, and Richard Wagner, with his later attempts to 'cure himself' of all romanticism. A framing question here is to what extent Nietzsche shared Goethe's famous equation of the classical with health and the romantic with sickness—which Nietzsche most often calls decadence. Del Caro pays special attention to the figure of Dionysus who first functions in *The Birth of Tragedy* as a romantic figure of transcendence (a representative of the Schopenhauerian transcendent world of the primally unified will), and who then later reappears as a figure of affirmation of this the one and only world, the world of becoming. He shows how early Nietzsche takes over from Hölderlin a deep appreciation of nihilism—the loss of meaning—as the fundamental problem of modernity, but later comes to see himself as repudiating Hölderlin's insistence on the primacy of poetry over philosophy and what he takes to be Hölderlin's nationalistic notion of cultural renewal. Despite this repudiation Del Caro argues that there are deep programmatic, and even textual, affinities between Nietzsche's *Zarathustra* and Hölderlin's *Hyperion*. As to Goethe, while Nietzsche praised him as a 'European event' he also attempted, often through mistaken claims about Goethe, to carve out his own identity as the one true prophet of cultural regeneration in the face of the nihilistic challenges romanticism and idealism pose for modernity. Del Caro argues that it was fundamentally through his engagement with Wagner that Nietzsche first came to realize that romanticism actually embodied a life-denying repudiation of this world rather than a genuine path to cultural renewal.

Kant. Tom Bailey's chapter, the sixth in the volume, examines Nietzsche's intense and complex engagements with Kantian idealism and Kantian ethics. Bailey shows that Nietzsche's extensive early readings in neo-Kantianism resulted not in a theoretical endorsement of Kantian idealism, but rather in an exploration of both its therapeutic or cultural benefits and its theoretical difficulties. Bailey then distinguishes two main targets in Nietzsche's later attack on Kantian idealism—namely, the notion of a reality inaccessible to our perceptual and conceptual capacities and the notion of judgment as providing a priori determinations of reality. Bailey argues that in his later period Nietzsche strongly denied an inaccessible reality, but wavered on the Kantian notion of judgment: he shifted from accepting this notion, and the implication (drawn by the neo-Kantian, Afrikan Spir) that empirical judgments are impossible, to rejecting the notion and holding that we can indeed make judgments about the reality accessible to us. And with his notion of the 'will to power', he nonetheless persisted in exploring the idea that judgements give us a priori access to reality. Regarding Kantian ethics Bailey first argues that Nietzsche's explicit criticisms of it are unconvincing, primarily because they rest on misunderstandings of it. But Bailey argues that Nietzsche also developed a distinctively 'Kantian' ethics of his own—that is, an ethics which, like Kant's, affirms agency as the highest and unconditional value. Nietzsche differs from Kant in admitting different degrees of agency, and therefore moral significance, across agents and over time. For Bailey, this difference provides a more persuasive explanation of Nietzsche's consistent rejection of Kantian ethics than Nietzsche's own explicit criticisms of it.

Schopenhauer. Ivan Soll (Chapter 7) argues that Nietzsche's entire philosophical career can be seen as a response to Schopenhauer's pessimistic assessment of the value of existence. Indeed his first published book *The Birth of Tragedy*, argues Soll, basically rests on a Schopenhauerian metaphysical framework. Schopenhauer's principle of individuation applicable to the world of representations is the key element in Nietzsche's concept of the Apollonian; and Schopenhauer's principle of the undifferentiated nature of ultimate reality of the Will is the key element in Nietzsche's concept of the Dionysian. Similarly, Nietzsche follows Schopenhauer in rejecting the Kantian claim that we organize the world of experience in order to make it knowable, in favour of the claim that we organize our experience so that we may have objects of our willings. For Schopenhauer and Nietzsche the Kantian notion of a faculty of reason and knowledge separate from the will is a fantasy. Where we seek truth we seek it to serve our will. However Nietzsche takes this line a step further by emphasizing that often illusion and falsity can be the most productive for achieving the will's ends and therefore one should not reject them. Soll also sees Schopenhauer's fundamental posit of the will as taken up in Nietzsche's concept of the will to power: Nietzsche rejects Schopenhauer's contention that the will has no ultimate end, and posits power as that end. Soll shows how Nietzsche's normative and metaphysical views can be read as responses to Schopenhauer.

Analytical philosophy. The paper by Simon Robertson and David Owen (Chapter 8) explores Nietzsche's influence on analytic philosophy. They focus on his relationship to the field of analytic ethics since it is here that his influence has been most notable. After briefly commenting on Nietzsche's comparative neglect, they outline some key rationales motivating his re-evaluation of (ethical) values and, in particular, his critique of modern morality. To demonstrate his influence on the work of Charles Taylor, Alasdair Macintyre, and Bernard Williams, they consider the role of Nietzsche's genealogical method in his re-evaluative project. This raises the important questions of how genealogy can be relevant to morality, and on what basis Nietzsche carries out his critique of morality. Robertson and Owen show how Taylor uses his notion of hypergoods to explain how Nietzsche's genealogies might support a reassessment of moral values, and how Macintyre uses the notion of epistemological crises to explain Nietzsche's strategy of critique. Williams, by contrast, takes Nietzsche to be offering fictional stories in order to elucidate real psychological processes whose very existence undermines the motivation to be moral in the received sense of that term. This leads to a consideration of Nietzsche's criticisms of moral objectivity and authority as elucidated by Williams and by Philippa Foot. After considering Nietzsche's substantive critique of the value of moral values and its relation to some similar-looking objections developed by a range of more recent morality critics the piece concludes with some brief suggestions as to where further engagement with Nietzsche by analytic moral philosophers might fruitfully take place.

PRINCIPAL WORKS

Many of Nietzsche's books are strikingly unlike one another. They differ not just in style but in purpose; some indeed belong to distinct genres. The prevailing interpretive practice of juxtaposing extracts from many of his books to construe Nietzsche's position on a topic runs the danger of missing how the sense of each passage is affected by its context in a work. As a counter to this tendency we include articles on a number of Nietzsche's books, to bring out the specific problems, methods, and procedures that characterize them. These articles treat many of the topics covered later in this volume, but within the scope and project of particular works in which they are prominent.

The Birth of Tragedy. Nietzsche's first book develops his famous contrast between the Apollonian and Dionysian, the latter supplying a harsh truth about the world, the former a beautifying illusion that makes it bearable. Daniel Came in Chapter 9 argues, against Reginster in particular, that Nietzsche held essentially the same position in his late works as well: that illusion is necessary in order to affirm life—in order to tolerate seeing it to some extent as it is. In *The Birth of Tragedy* the Apollonian illusion is built into tragedy itself, fused with the Dionysian insight into the inevitability of suffering; this renders it healthier than either the purely Apollonian, or a Socratic optimism of rationality. And, though not well recognized, the *amor fati* that Nietzsche promotes in his much later works depends on illusion too, because it involves seeing the necessary as beautiful—an aesthetic judgment that must be false, Came argues, due to Nietzsche's general anti-realism about values. Similarly the project of self-creation that Nietzsche advocates involves a self-beautifying illusion, for example by 'standing back' from one's character and not scrutinizing it too closely. Nietzsche indeed has, Came suggests, a 'pretence theory of the self', so that any conception of one's self will have to involve illusion. Thus, he argues, the early position of *The Birth of Tragedy* on this crucial topic is much more stable in Nietzsche than it is typically regarded to be.

Unfashionable Observations. This set of four polemical essays was written 1873–6. As Keith Ansell-Pearson (Chapter 10) shows, they are principally attacks on several aspects of the prevailing (German) culture, but also have broader and more positive implications that give them a thematic unity. Ansell-Pearson focuses on one theme that unites them, along with other works of this early period: Nietzsche's commitment to the sublime as a standard for judging the present age. Nietzsche opposes this sublime to a philistine comfortableness; he thinks it is the role of philosophy to elevate a people, so that they aspire to greatness. In the first essay, on David Strauss, Nietzsche scorns German self-satisfaction after its military victory over France; this has nothing at all to do with great culture. Nietzsche diagnoses among the 'cultural elite' a merely mock culture, dependent on predecessors and creating nothing itself. In the third essay Nietzsche offers Schopenhauer as a genuine philosopher in his effort to rise above merely academic questions and to advise us on the art of living—an art that aims at greatness and so disregards the fashions of the time. Turning back to the second essay, on history, Ansell-Pearson shows how Nietzsche values history mainly for its power to restore life's 'possibilities' to us, in the example of the highest individuals, who live concurrently by virtue of history. This theme of greatness or sublimity will obviously preoccupy Nietzsche through his later works as well.

The Gay Science. As Christopher Janaway (Chapter 11) remarks, this is one of Nietzsche's most important books, reflected in the way he comes back to it—after his wrenching crisis over Lou Salomé, after *Zarathustra* and *Beyond Good and Evil*—to add not just a preface but an ambitious fifth book. *The Gay Science* introduces some of Nietzsche's most important topics; Janaway reviews and advances debate on several of these. The book's title reflects its ambition to handle painful truths, arrived at by some kind of science, in a cheerful and uplifting way. One such truth is the death of God, and the way this must pull down with it God's 'shadow', morality, as we find out the truth about its origins. Nietzsche focuses his critique of morality on its value of compassion; Janaway brings out the nuance and complexity to his assessment of it. The most sensational idea introduced in the book is the thought of eternal return; large puzzles arise about the use Nietzsche makes of this thought, and Janaway sorts them and offers his own proposal. He also points out how the challenge to will the return of one's life 'just as it is' seems at odds with Nietzsche's advocacy of artistically fashioning and falsifying one's life. Janaway suggests that Nietzsche was indeed 'troubled' over how to reconcile truth and art, rejecting efforts to resolve the tension by subordinating either to the other. This leads Janaway lastly to Nietzsche's critique of our usual scientific methods for seeking truth; rather than renouncing truth, Nietzsche anticipates a new 'science' better aimed at what truth there is.

Thus Spoke Zarathustra. Nietzsche proclaims this book as his greatest achievement, but his philosophical interpreters have often disagreed; it seems to lack the argument that would make it genuinely philosophical. Gudrun von Tevenar (Chapter 12) aims to rehabilitate the work for philosophical attention. She points out that although it has parodic elements its main purpose can't be parody. Nietzsche's assertion that it is 'tragedy' is initially confusing, but refers to the fearful 'overcoming' which Zarathustra accomplishes and von Tevenar undertakes to explicate. This overcoming is of, in particular, pity and disgust, directed at humanity in its smallness and pettiness. Von Tevenar examines the conflict in Zarathustra between this disgust at humanity and his love for it; he wants not to resolve this contradiction, but to find wholeness through it. We see this in his 'counter-ideal' to Christianity, which, von Tevenar argues, involves a new kind of love, with three components: a discrimination by order of rank, a replacement of God and Messiah with the *Übermensch*, and a love for self-sacrifice from one's need to 'go under'. Nietzsche also replaces the Christian notion of eternity with a sexualized, earthly analogue. Lastly von Tevenar examines the relationship between Zarathustra and Jesus: they are more akin than we might have thought, and indeed Nietzsche may mean Zarathustra's path as the one Jesus might have taken had he matured beyond thirty.

Beyond Good and Evil. Maudemarie Clark and David Dudrick (Chapter 13) argue that this book has best claim to be Nietzsche's most important philosophical work. Yet, they point out, the work's form and content pose problems for finding much philosophical significance in it. The first step is to recognize that Nietzsche intends the book to be capable of both an exoteric and an esoteric reading; in the former it articulates a crude naturalism, but in the latter he has normative aspirations that leave behind the methods of science. Clark and Dudrick begin with the Preface's famous comparison of truth with 'a female' and observe how his point echoes Kant's in his Preface to the first edition of the first *Critique*: Nietzsche too wants to diagnose the failure of dogmatic metaphysics, and learn from it a way to satisfy philosophy's original promise. The point, Clark and Dudrick argue, is to exploit the 'magnificent tension of the spirit' between the will to truth and the will to value. They pursue this point into a close reading of sections 3 and 4 of *Beyond Good and Evil*. They find the clue leading from the exoteric sense of these sections to their esoteric and genuine sense—the sense in which they speak Nietzsche's 'new language'—in *BGE* 3's reference to Protagorean relativism. When we realize that Nietzsche accepts this relativization of truth to humanity, we see that 'false' in his new language means not corresponding to a standard beyond man. Nietzsche's denial of such a transcendent standard means that these sections do not state a critique of truth, but rather his denial that our cognitive practices require (or are capable of) an external justification. Reading the rest of the book along these lines, and finding out its further esoteric senses, shows its philosophical sophistication and importance.

On the Genealogy of Morality. Probably this book has had the greatest recent influence and is most likely today to be read by students and treated by philosophers. This may be partly due to its format: Richard Schacht in Chapter 14 notes that, in its three essays, it is the only late exception to Nietzsche's usual 'aphoristic' style. Schacht brings out nuances in the very title, and points out that the term 'genealogy' is rarely used in the book itself; it isn't Nietzsche's title for a worked-out method, as often supposed. The book carries on a search for the origins or history of human values and practices, which Nietzsche had pursued in earlier works; Schacht shows how the latter anticipate its ideas, including even its famous distinction between master and slave moralities. The book's Preface sets the overall purpose of the essays, to examine the origins of current morality, as preparation for a 'revaluation' of this morality's value—a revaluation that *Genealogy* itself forgoes. Schacht then treats key issues regarding each of the book's three essays. The first essay presents slave morality as arising out of *ressentiment* against masters; Nietzsche thinks—in Lamarckian fashion, Schacht argues—that this resentful attitude or affect becomes ingrained, and is inherited in later generations. The second essay centres on the phenomenon of 'bad conscience'. Schacht shows how Nietzsche treats this not just critically, but also as making possible that 'artist's cruelty' which makes possible a new kind of human enhancement. The third essay tells still another story, this time about the 'ascetic ideal', a 'will to transcend' certain essential features of life—such as appearance, change, even willing—from which life suffers. Schacht argues that although Nietzsche finds this ascetic ideal present in the 'unconditional will to truth', this by no means implies that Nietzsche abandons truth as an aim. These three stories, Schacht suggests, should be understood as 'conjectures' and as examples of the kind of thinking we must do if we're to understand morality and values.

The Antichrist. Dylan Jaggard argues in Chapter 15 that we should read this work as supplying historical evidence for the diagnosis of Christianity, evidence that the *Genealogy* largely lacked. Nietzsche wants to find out the truth about Christianity and in particular how it denies or disvalues 'life'. He thereby turns truth into service of life, whereas previously it had mainly served the denial of life. Jaggard goes on to treat Nietzsche's account of the origins of Christianity in Judaism; Nietzsche relies here on the biblical scholar Julius Wellhausen's account of the early history of the Jews, and superimposes upon this a psychological reading of how the different historical situations are reflected in the different ideas of God layered into the Pentateuch. The overall character of the development is towards a moral and legal outlook in which relation to God is mediated by priests and laws. Jaggard shows how Nietzsche presents Christianity developing from this root; it is framed not so much by the historical Jesus as by the distortions of him imposed by the early Christians, Paul in particular. These early disciples mistake the quasi-Buddhist example Jesus meant to set. Motivated by resentment over his death, they interpret his 'kingdom of God', by which he meant an inner peace, into a realm after death in which sinners would be punished and the good rewarded. Finally Jaggard turns to the lessons Nietzsche draws from this history for today: although Christianity may be suited to many due to their sickness, some have the opportunity to abandon the idea of a moral world order and to give up some—though Jaggard argues far from all—of the Christian values.

Ecce Homo. Nietzsche's autobiography (if that's quite what it is), written at the very end of his productive years, is of obvious interest. Christa Acampora (Chapter 16) focuses on what the book says on the difficult topics of agency, fate, and freedom. She begins with the book's subtitle, 'How one becomes what one is': Nietzsche's account of his life will also clarify this famous expression for an ideal or favoured path of personal development. Acampora shows how Nietzsche thinks a person is really a set of drives ordered or ranked a certain way (which is the person's 'type'); there's no will or subject separate from these that could carry out the work of becoming. Nevertheless, as Acampora shows, Nietzsche thinks that work depends on the exercise of a certain 'selfishness', which includes, in part, careful attention to seeming trivialities like diet and climate. Moreover this selfishness needs to be expressed in a struggle and fight against 'objects of resistance' and indeed 'enemies'; Acampora suggests that the primary aim is to incorporate this opposition rather than to destroy it, though she notes that Nietzsche often speaks of destroying. By these fights one both expresses one's internal order of rank, and accomplishes it. Indeed it is even possible to change one's constitutive rank order, and so the 'type' to which one belongs; this happens by a reorganization of one's drives, carried out not by a separate will, but by those competing drives themselves. But what is most important is that the drives be pulled together into a more thorough unity, so that one becomes more fully a single thing. By all of these tactics, Acampora argues, Nietzsche holds that some of us can become what we are.

VALUES

Nietzsche's normative agenda is notoriously difficult to pin down. His denial of the objectivity of values, and insistence on their perspectivity, presses on us metaethical questions about the force with which he offers his values. One particular such question is whether he means them 'aesthetically', rather than morally or ethically, and if so just what this involves. As to what values he offers us, much recent work has argued that he values self-creation, autonomy, and a certain kind of free will. He also famously characterizes his ideal as of an 'overman'. But what exactly is involved in these notions of autonomy and the overman requires detailed development. Moreover these positive values raise questions about their implications for the values of equality and justice: does pursuit of Nietzsche's ideal require a kind of hierarchy and the dismissal or even subjugation of the weak by the strong?

Metaethics. Nadeem Hussain (Chapter 17) begins with a brief review of the major kinds of traditional metaethical theories which may be roughly divided into cognitivist theories which allow for genuine beliefs about morality and take moral claims to be truth-apt, and non-cognitivist theories which take the use of an indicative sentence such as 'Torture is wrong' not to express beliefs of any kind and take such sentences not to be truth-apt. While many passages in Nietzsche's texts can look initially as though they express metaethical positions, any attempt to ascribe some particular metaethical stance to Nietzsche must deal with the fact that the metaethical suggestions in these passages can easily seem to contradict each other. After considering the initial textual evidence for ascribing versions of various metaethical positions to Nietzsche, Hussain considers objections to such ascriptions. He first treats interpretations of Nietzsche as some kind of cognitivist, holding, respectively, an error theory, or some kind of revolutionary fictionalism, or some form of subjective realism. These interpretations are related to attempts to ascribe to Nietzsche a new set of ultimate values based on such notions as will to power or life. Hussain then treats interpretations which take Nietzsche to be some kind of non-cognitivist, but shows reasons to doubt such ascriptions of subjectivism and non-cognitivism. The chapter ends with serious consideration of the view that perhaps Nietzsche simply does not have a considered metaethical stance.

Aesthetic values. Starting from Nietzsche's observation that 'life without music would be an error', Aaron Ridley (Chapter 18) argues that aesthetic values permeate Nietzsche's philosophy from his earliest to his last books. Much of Nietzsche's work can be seen as creating an aesthetic theodicy, as heralded in his famous aperçu that it is 'only as an aesthetic phenomenon that existence and the world are eternally justified'. Ridley goes on to show that artistry is not confined to the creation of conventional works of art but occurs in the form-giving that is essential to all human forms of life. Since Nietzsche, despite his various animadversions on metaphysics, remained committed to the view that the world is in some basic sense chaotic and meaningless, he held that only by imposing forms can we create a cognizable world. This close association between the conditions of life itself and the aesthetic activity of giving form is shown to belie the Kantian conception, taken up by Schopenhauer, that any appreciation of aesthetic phenomena is essentially disinterested. The aesthetic activity of form-giving is further shown to be an essential part of self-creation. Ridley notes the tension between those passages such as the first part of *GS* 290 that suggest a deliberate conscious plan of self-creation and those such as *EH* 2, 9 that trumpet the importance of non-conscious subterranean forces. He argues that Nietzsche wants both, since he thinks both are aspects of artistry, which requires both conscious planning, but also subjection to laws that only emerge in the creative endeavour itself.

Autonomy. Lanier Anderson argues in Chapter 19 that the notion of autonomy is central to Nietzsche's philosophical concerns, and traces different interpretive construals of his notion back to differing views about the main philosophical work Nietzsche wanted it to do. Anderson distinguishes six main interpretive approaches, each with its own conception of autonomy: (1) autonomy as spontaneous self-determination, in the sense of traditional free will; (2) a 'standard model' interpretation counting actions as autonomous when they are caused by rationalizing beliefs and desires; (3) a view that traces autonomy to a Kantian transcendental subject; (4) constitutivist theories that seek to explain the source of normativity by 'deriving ethics from action'; (5) 'hierarchical model' interpretations arguing that complex, higher-order attitudes 'speak for the agent', and thereby constitute her autonomy; and (6) conceptions of autonomy as an ethical ideal. Nietzsche's own remarks about autonomy suggest that he construed it as a rare achievement, proper to a relatively few excellent lives, and this feature tends to support the interpretation of Nietzschean autonomy as an ethical ideal. The chapter explores the connection between that conception and Nietzsche's views on strength and weakness of will.

The overman. Randall Havas (Chapter 20) argues that the notion of the overman is strongly connected to Nietzsche's conceptions of agency and free will. Nietzsche thinks of human actions as commitments and of the latter as irreducibly temporal inasmuch as commitment requires both obedience to the past and responsibility for the future. More specifically, in making any possibility his own, the agent commits himself to certain outcomes in the face of contingencies beyond his control. The overman is someone who has overcome his aversion to the temporal character of action in this dual sense. He no longer has ill will towards the past as that which determines his current possibilities, nor does he have ill will to the fact that his plans for the future are nevertheless a hostage to fate—his best-laid plans may fail. In Nietzsche's view, such overcoming is achieved in the first place in the overman's relations to his 'peers'. This shows that the familiar picture of the Nietzschean overman as someone who lives out his life in indifference to others should be rejected in favour of an account that sees the highest form of human life as the achievement of a form of mutuality with others who are similarly capable of affirming the temporal character of human agency. This involves a sense of responsibility that is only possible when one has given up the notion of an external grounding such as God. Such a sense of responsibility is a constitutive condition of agency. Agency and free will, then, involve not the ability to escape the constraints of time and necessity but the ability to will those very constraints.

Order of rank. Robert Guay's paper (Chapter 21) argues for the importance of Nietzsche's conception of 'order of rank' for understanding his philosophical enterprise as a whole. He demonstrates that with the notion of order of rank Nietzsche means to positively advocate some form of hierarchy in opposition to what he sees as an unreflective modern consensus on egalitarianism. On this reading order of rank is as essential to Nietzsche's project as are the notions of will to power and revaluation of values. Guay identifies five interpretations of order of rank: Natural Aristocracy, Mythic Archaism, Political, Anthropological, and Transcendental, and then argues that it is the Transcendental that is fundamental for Nietzsche. He argues that only the Transcendental interpretation can account for several of Nietzsche's claims about order of rank: that it is 'problematic', constructed, processual, primarily important to 'the human type' rather than to various fixed types, and intrinsically social in nature. On this Transcendental interpretation, Nietzsche presents order of rank not substantively, as a recommended set of hierarchical values among persons, but as a condition for the availability of normative authority. Nietzsche employs 'order of rank', that is, precisely because the idea that human beings fall into fixed types is problematic, and he sees this as provoking a series of questions on how natural beings could sustain any normative order, what sort of social dynamic this would entail, how plastic our normative commitments might be, and how these commitments might potentially raise our status as human beings.

Promising. Mark Migotti in Chapter 22 aims to explain what we can learn about promising, and about Nietzsche's critique of morality, from his discussion of sovereign promising in the opening sections of the second essay of *On the Genealogy of Morals*. He begins by arguing that Nietzsche's philosophical focus is not on promising in the narrow sense of making a pledge to do something for someone else, but in the broader sense of pledging or committing oneself in general. Migotti contrasts Nietzsche's approach to promissory fidelity with what Migotti calls the moral obligation tradition of thinking on the subject, and argues that, in its focus on questions of what it means and how it is possible to bind oneself to a course of action, the Nietzschean approach is philosophically deeper than the moral obligation approach. A concluding section turns to interpretive debates about the role of the sovereign individual in Nietzsche's thought and shows that revisionist readings of *Genealogy*

II: 1–2, according to which Nietzsche is not really in favour of sovereign individuality and sovereign promising, are misconceived.

Peoples and races. Jacob Golomb in Chapter 23 argues that a balanced understanding of Nietzsche's attitude toward races, nationalism, and politics can be best reached by examining his anthropological philosophy with its pivotal principle of the will to power. Nietzsche's emphasis on sublimation rather than domination as the will to power's most genuine exercise argues against Nazi and fascist misappropriations of his thought. For Nietzsche the most sublime use of will to power is directed at self-overcoming rather than the subjugation of others. What Nietzsche prized above all was spiritual power (*Macht*) not the brute political force (*Kraft*) or the violent act (*Gewalt*) which he denounced with all the sarcasm at his command. By the same token, Nietzsche's *Übermensch* is one who has used this power to sublimate his naturally conflicting drives into a unified and authentic whole; he is one who has overcome his own 'human, all too human' nature; rather than one who tries to literally overcome other humans, as the most facile interpretations would have it. Nietzsche rejects the totalitarian state, whose severe demand for conformity precludes the very existence of the *Übermensch*, as 'a fearful tyranny, as an oppressive and remorseless machine' (*GM* II: 17) and calls such a totalitarian state (perhaps under Hobbes's influence) 'the coldest of all cold monsters' (*Z* I: 'On the New Idol'). Golomb concludes with the rhetorical question 'Can one imagine a Nazi, fascist, or even a proto-Nazi wearing a brown or black shirt (the *camicie nere* of Mussolini's time) saying such things of his or her *Vaterland*?'

EPISTEMOLOGY AND METAPHYSICS

These traditional philosophical rubrics are disputed by Nietzsche, and his views don't fit comfortably within them. Nevertheless he addresses issues 'in the neighbourhood' of the long-standing problems about truth and knowledge, being and time. At issue is just how deeply and thoroughly his critique of these notions goes. Does he still believe in truth, for example, or do his 'perspectivism', his 'aestheticism', and/or his diagnosis of truth as ascetic show that he quite rejects it (either its possibility or its value)? To what extent does he value science's truths, and model his own theories after it? And when he denies being in favour of becoming, how radically is he reconceiving things—if there still are things at all for him? Is this idea of becoming a theory about time, and how is it related to his famous thought of eternal recurrence?

Perspectivism. Ken Gemes (Chapter 24) argues that Nietzsche's perspectivism should be read as a 'psycho-biological' claim, and not as either an epistemological or semantic claim. He first examines and rebuts readings of it as a semantic claim about the nature of truth. These come in two versions: the first takes it as the thesis that true claims are 'only perspectivally true', which is taken to conflict with the correspondence theory of truth; the second takes it as the thesis that there are no facts, and no truth, at all. Gemes shows that these views run into severe problems of incoherence, and are also little supported in Nietzsche's texts. He turns next to readings of the perspectivism as an epistemological claim that all knowledge depends on interests or affects. To be interesting, the claim must be that interests play not just a causal but a constitutive role with respect to knowledge, but interpreters do not make clear how this constituting would work. And counting against both semantic and epistemological readings, Gemes argues, is Nietzsche's general focus not on theories of truth or knowledge, but on psychological diagnoses of the wills to truth and to knowledge. Those readings are also at odds with Nietzsche's attribution of perspectives to all living things, including things, e.g. plants, incapable of truth or knowledge. Gemes then turns to his positive suggestion, that the perspectivism is, in its overt and descriptive component, the claim that every drive has a perspective that it seeks to express, often against other drives. And perspectivism also has an implicit prescriptive component, the claim that the healthiest life involves the maximal expression of the richest set of drives, each with its own perspective. Gemes shows how Nietzsche stresses the synthesis of multiple drives, effected by not repressing but rather sublimating them, as illustrated in Freud's analysis of Leonardo. Here, rather than in questions about truth or knowledge, is the centre of Nietzsche's interest in perspectives.

Naturalism. Brian Leiter in Chapter 25 revisits his influential account of Nietzsche as a naturalist—both a 'Methodological Naturalist', holding that philosophical inquiry should model its theories on science's, as well as a 'Substantive Naturalist' holding that man doesn't have a different origin from the rest of nature. Leiter shows the sources of Nietzsche's position in the German naturalism of the mid-nineteenth century, in particular the work of Lange. His naturalism is, however, 'speculative', in that he postulates causal mechanisms not confirmed by science. Nietzsche's ambition to explain morality naturalistically coexists with a 'therapeutic' ambition to induce some readers to escape from morality; still, Leiter argues, we can separate out the positions he arrives at by his naturalism, from the rhetorical strategies he employs therapeutically. Leiter goes on to address several doubts that might arise against reading Nietzsche as a naturalist. First, his reference to cultural phenomena is no impediment to his naturalism. Second, Nietzsche's explanation by 'causes' is both strong enough to be interesting, and also not really at odds with passages (in the mature works at least) in which he seems to express doubts about causation. Third, Nietzsche's seeming reliance on the notion of will to power in his explanations does not militate against reading him as a naturalist, Leiter argues, because he relies only on a psychological version of this thesis, and not on a 'crackpot' metaphysical version. Leiter concludes by summing up some of Nietzsche's psychological theses that seem to have been confirmed by recent scientific findings.

Aestheticism. Sebastian Gardner's paper (Chapter 26) presents Nietzsche's 'philosophical aestheticism' as a position that extends from *The Birth of Tragedy* right through to the late writing, not abandoned even in the 'positivist' works (*Human, All Too Human* and *Daybreak*) in which Nietzsche is far more critical of art. Already in *The Birth of Tragedy* Nietzsche denies metaphysical truth to art, since he presents (Gardner argues) the Dionysian world—the Schopenhauerian 'artist's metaphysics'—not as real but as a necessary posit for fulfilment of our practical needs. And when Nietzsche criticizes art in those positivist works, his focus is on its modern, romantic form, and he leaves untouched whether it did (among the Greeks) or could in future play that favourable role. Central to Nietzsche's later aesthetic theory is the notion of an aesthetic state, which Gardner characterizes as a 'cycle of projection and introjection': we invest the object with properties that it then 'restores to us in a heightened form'. We view it as an Apollonian appearance imposed on a Dionysian ground, and judge that this view—and the way it shows the world generally—enhances our feeling of life. This aesthetic projection involves us in false beliefs, but we at least see them as false. And by this aesthetic state we mediate between our theoretical reason (with its commitment to truth) and our practical reason (committed to life) in a way that sustains the tension between these, 'so that the bow should not break'. Gardner notes, finally, that this great importance Nietzsche gives to the aesthetic state is not matched by extensive treatment of art, because he still has the doubts expressed in *Human, All Too Human* about contemporary artistic culture. Instead, Gardner suggests, he associates the aesthetic state with his own philosophical ideas of will to power and eternal recurrence: these give to the world the 'affective colouring' of, respectively, the Apollonian and Dionysian visions, so recapitulating *Birth of Tragedy*'s union of these.

Becoming. Robin Small in Chapter 27 points out how Nietzsche finds becoming—but also being—at odds with both knowledge and life. He examines Nietzsche's handling of this quandary, beginning with its historical part: Nietzsche's story of how the philosophical tradition first builds the concept of being, but then pulls it down by the stages described in the famous 'history of an error' chapter in *Twilight of the Idols*. This development culminates in the replacement of being with becoming, Small suggests. But to see what Nietzsche means by becoming we need to see its surprising relation to time. We arrive at a genuine sense of becoming only by stripping away our experience of time as succession, Small argues. Nietzsche thinks this happens in our dreams, whose 'time chaos' gives us a sense of becoming. We make this becoming into time by positing (falsely) both periods of non-change (rest) and discontinuities in what is really continuous change. By these posits we arrive at a distinction between the persisting substance and its successive states, which helps us to deal effectively with our environment, but at the cost of misconceiving the world in terms of being. We experience time as involving a conflict between future and past, and this is a temporal interpretation of a deeper conflict within becoming. Nietzsche's attempted solution to this conflict, and to the opening predicament about becoming and being, lies in his thought of eternal return, Small proposes: this joins future and past, and also 'stamps being on becoming' in a way that makes each individual life an 'image of eternity'.

Eternal recurrence. Paul Loeb in Chapter 28 runs emphatically against the grain of most recent interpretations of this idea, in taking Nietzsche to offer it not as a challenge or thought experiment, but as a cosmological truth: only this lets us see why he considered it his most important teaching. Loeb suggests that the broad recent failure to see the idea's meaning derives from the question-begging presumption that it is obviously false or absurd. He also blames the tendency to discount and disregard *Thus Spoke Zarathustra*, in which the idea is principally presented; interpreters focus instead on what is merely a preview, in *Gay Science* 341. And they usually misread even this section because they miss the context provided by *GS* 340; this identifies the 'demon' who announces eternal recurrence as Socrates' demon, and the time of the announcement as Socrates' death. *GS* 342 then introduces Zarathustra as the individual who will, in dying, react to eternal recurrence with joy, rather than Socrates' despair. Turning to *Zarathustra*, Loeb focuses on its 'Vision and Riddle' chapter, which he argues presents eternal recurrence as supported by 'direct mnemonic evidence'—memory of having lived certain moments before. Indeed, Loeb claims, it even presents Zarathustra as enjoying 'prospective memory' of events yet to come in his life. Although commentators claim that Nietzsche never offers any proof of cosmological eternal recurrence in his published texts, Loeb argues that in fact he does so in this *Zarathustra* chapter as well as in his first presentation of the doctrine in *GS* 109. In particular, Loeb argues, the *Zarathustra* proof makes clear that Nietzsche posits the recurrence of time itself, so that Zarathustra (e.g.) returns, when he dies, to the *past* moment when he began living. Finally, Loeb argues that the usual interpretation of eternal recurrence as a thought experiment cannot explain why we should carry out just this experiment. Why, in particular, should I 'affirm my *non-recurring* life by craving its eternal recurrence'? This would express life denial by wanting my life to be other than it is. So this prevailing interpretation can't even account for the practical role Nietzsche gives it.

DEVELOPMENTS OF WILL TO POWER

Although Nietzsche makes emphatic attacks on metaphysics he sometimes seems, especially in his notebooks, to develop and defend an ontology himself, expressing it especially in his idea of will to power. He attributes such a will to life generally, but mainly uses the notion to explain human experience and behaviour, where it plays a role in his 'drive psychology'. There are large challenges to explain just what Nietzsche means by 'will to power' and what status he gives it—and to reconcile these positions with his critiques of metaphysics. One particular issue is whether and how he uses the idea in support of his normative agenda—in support of his revaluation of values. And questions have also been raised as to how useful and plausible the notions of will to power and drives can be, even in their narrower applications to human psychology. The papers in this last Part address these questions.

Will to power and causation. Poellner's essay (Chapter 29) examines the extensive metaphysical reflections in Nietzsche's later writings, the great bulk of them in his notebooks. It argues that a large number of these reflections take their departure from his (plausible) rejection of regularity accounts of causation. Nietzsche thinks we cannot adequately understand causation without reference to causal powers, and he accepts a dynamist physics according to which the physical world is exhaustively constituted by powers, so that his ultimate ontology consists of a world of force-like rather than thing-like entities. It is shown how this metaphysics underwrites his claim of the primacy of becoming over being. His metaphysics of the will to power involves two further basic premises: first, that all causal powers we are directly acquainted with are essentially dependent on volition; secondly, that all conscious volitions (effective desires) are reducible to the will to power—desires for the experience of successful activity. Nietzsche concludes that, unless we are sceptical about the intrinsic nature of causal force, we need to understand it in terms of the will to power. The essay reconstructs the reasoning which leads Nietzsche, in the notebooks, to this metaphysics, and assesses some of its salient constituent claims. In the final section, it addresses the question of Nietzsche's commitment to these ideas, given his sceptical or dismissive thoughts on metaphysics in (most of) the mature published writings. Poellner proposes that there is a genuine conflict in his later thought, and that Nietzsche in his late period was alternately drawn towards metaphysical indifferentism and panpsychist metaphysics.

Will to power and values. Bernard Reginster in Chapter 30 argues that will to power is a desire for effective agency. As opposed to Richardson's claim that the will to power is a second-order phenomenon accompanying each first-order drive, Reginster's idea, put in terms of drive psychology, is that the will to power is an independent self-standing drive. He shows how this helps explain Nietzsche's psychology of the slave revolt in morality. The point of this revolt and its *ressentiment*-inspired revaluation is not that it allows the slaves to subvert and gain power over the masters, but that it provides an interpretation of the world that allows the slaves to see themselves as effective agents; as such it is an expression of their will to power. The main point of the invention of the notion of free will is not to facilitate the blaming and holding responsible of their oppressor, the masters, but to praise themselves for choosing to remain passive in the wake of the masters' provocations. Similarly, the ascetic ideal embraced by the powerless functions to heighten their feeling of power, since in conforming to the dictates of that ideal they gain power over themselves (their drives to be more active), and come to see their weakness—their inability to act on their natural aggressive drives—as strength—their claimed choice to refrain from acting on those drives. Furthermore, this account explains why Nietzsche takes morality to be *pathological*: under severe restrictions, the will to power is eventually induced to turn against itself—to become a 'will to nothingness'.

Drives. Paul Katsafanas (Chapter 31) treats what is arguably the most fundamental notion in Nietzsche's psychological analyses of human action and morality, the notion of a drive. Notoriously, Nietzsche talks of drives in terms usually ascribed to full-blown agents; thus he talks of drives valuing and interpreting and of drives having perspectives. Katsafanas notes that this may easily lead to the following dilemma: either drives are taken to be mere dispositions—in which case it is hard to accommodate Nietzsche's agential descriptions of them as interpreting and valuing and as having perspectives; on the other hand, drives may be seen as agent-like homunculi—in which case it appears that they cannot explain such phenomena as agency and selfhood since they already presume these very notions. Katsafanas proposes to solve this dilemma by arguing that drives are indeed dispositions but that they are dispositions that lead agents to affective orientations. The key point here is that it is not the drive by itself that is literally doing the interpreting or valuing—hence the drive is not a homunculus; nevertheless the drive is orienting the agent towards certain valuations and interpretations.

Life. John Richardson in Chapter 32 examines Nietzsche's idea of 'life', and in particular the use he makes of it in evaluating values and in justifying his own values. It distinguishes several different senses 'life' might have—biological, human, phenomenal, personal, poetic—and shows how the first four are joined together in Nietzsche's analysis of humans as complexes of drives deposited during the deep history of biological and cultural evolution. It tries similarly to clarify Nietzsche's idea of 'value': he 'naturalizes' values, and also disputes the prevailing conception of values, which makes them principles followed by agents; against these 'agent values' he argues for the efficacy of 'body values'. Given these accounts of what Nietzsche means by 'life' and 'value', the paper goes on to see how he intends the former to bear on the latter. What authority does life have, what criterion does it give for revaluing values, and what correction in our values does this criterion dictate? The paper shows how Nietzsche answers these questions, and does so in a way that addresses the obvious challenge to his argument from life to values, that this commits the naturalistic fallacy. It gives these answers in two stages: first presenting them as lessons learned from biological life—its will to power embedded deeply in us—and applied to correct our agent values, then presenting them as more radically revising the role of agent values in us, by restoring authority to our bodily taste and feeling (a change indicated in the way *Zarathustra* presents Life as the object of sexual love).

PART I

BIOGRAPHY

CHAPTER 1

....

NIETZSCHE AND THE
FAMILY

....

GRAHAM PARKES

> From his early utterances through to the last days of sanity Nietzsche exhibited
> an unusually deep feeling of connection with the ancestors, a feeling that corre-
> sponds, in spite of all subsequent conflicts, to an ultimately indestructible sense
> of family.

Curt Paul Janz[1]

NIETZSCHE's direct experience of family life was intense but somewhat one-sided, for he
never became a parent and his relations were generally with relatives older than himself.
Instead of fathering, like most males of the species, literal offspring, he chose the Platonic
way of giving birth to philosophical thoughts, which he embedded in books that he sometimes called his "children." Though one would hardly turn to Nietzsche for advice on parent-
ing, some of what he writes about children, and especially about how to educate them, is
well worth our attention. Similarly with his observations about marriage, another institution in which he declined to participate.[2] But limitations of space necessitate a narrower
focus, on the familial relationships that he did actually experience, and on his ideas about
the effects of such relationships on the individual who grows up among them.

Families tend to be intense complexes of relations—intense because determined by
fate: you can't choose your grandparents, parents, or siblings, nor effectively divorce them—
and the larger the family, the more relations, the greater the intensity. Nietzsche grew up
within a large extended family of relatives who lived within visiting distance, while the
immediate family in which he spent the first part of his youth consisted of six others, all of
them female: his mother Franziska, his sister Elisabeth, his aunts Rosalie and Auguste, his
grandmother Erdmuthe, and the live-in housekeeper, Miene. After the death of his father
when young Fritz was four, he grew up as a lone boy among six women. One might imagine

---

[1] Janz 1981: vol. 1, p. 23.
[2] For example, an aphorism with the title "Marriage as a long conversation": "When entering into
a marriage one should ask oneself: do you think that you can enjoy good discussions with this woman
into your old age? Everything else in marriage is transitory, but most of the interaction takes the form of
conversation." (*HAH* I: 406)

then that he lacked male companions and role models, even if in compensation he had a rich experience of the female psyche. But after his father's death he developed a close relationship with his maternal grandfather, David Ernst Oehler, and from the age of eight he formed firm friendships with two intelligent and creative boys, Gustav Krug and Wilhelm Pinder, with whose distinguished fathers he also enjoyed good relations.

The family is important for Nietzsche not only because it constitutes the world that conditions the individual's early development, but also because he thinks that the ancestors behind the grandparents continue to influence unconsciously one's present experience. He even claims to owe his becoming a philosopher to the ancestors and the capabilities they bequeath to later generations.

> One has a right to philosophy ... only thanks to one's line of descent, the ancestors: what is "in the blood" is decisive here. Many generations must have worked to prepare for the philosopher; each one of his virtues must be acquired, cultivated, handed down, incorporated. (*BGE* 213)

There's a distinctly Lamarckian tone to this, and although Nietzsche makes occasional mention of Lamarck, he remains vague about just how this kind of inheritance works, content to leave it as being simply through "the blood" in some sense.

Let us begin with this extended, less literal, sense of family and what Nietzsche thinks we inherit from our ancestry, as it continuously conditions our experience of the world through an influx of embodied energies from past worlds. This is especially worth considering because it continues to be a remarkably neglected aspect of Nietzsche's thought.[3]

ANCESTORS

> One can never erase from the soul of a human being the traces of what his forbears most liked to do and did most often.... It is quite impossible that a human being should *not* have the qualities of his parents and ancestors in his body, whatever appearances may say against it. (*BGE* 264)

In 1881 Nietzsche reports the realization of an archaic dimension to his experience, one that has drastically transformed his relations, he says, to "existence as a whole":

> I have *discovered* for myself that ancient humanity and animality, indeed the entire primal age and past of all sentient being continues in me to create, to love, to hate, to infer. I suddenly awoke in the middle of this dream, but only to the consciousness that I am indeed dreaming and that I *must* continue to dream in order not to perish. (*GS* 54)

The personal tone here—discovered *for myself*—is significant: he is reporting an experience and its consequences rather than asserting a universal truth or framing some kind of theory. The tone is "experimental" (in the spirit of Montaigne and Emerson) insofar as the idea is to be tried out and tested for the ways it might transform one's experience. This constant creating, loving, hating, and inferring Nietzsche calls a "dream"—an imaginative process always going on, of which we are mostly unconscious, but which keeps us going, saves us from

---

[3] For a discussion of the issue of ancestral inheritance in Nietzsche, see Parkes 1994: 305–34.

perishing. And yet also something to which we can awaken, and thereby perhaps discover the deep-level human and animal fantasies that underlie every moment of experience.

Nietzsche knows that commonsensical, realistic people are going to find this idea ridiculous, and he harangues the professional "realists" for naively supposing they can be unaffected by such atavism.

> You are still carrying around with you evaluations of things which have their origin in the passions and loves of earlier centuries!…In every feeling, in every sense impression there is a piece of this ancient love [of "reality"]: and so some phantasy, some prejudice, some unreason, some ignorance, some fear and heaven knows what else have always worked and woven their way into it. That mountain there! That cloud! What is "real" about those? Try taking away the phantasm and the whole human *contribution*, you sober ones! Yes, if you only could do *that*! If you could only forget your heritage, your past, and training—your entire humanity and animality! (*GS* 57)

We can't forget our entire humanity and animality, since this heritage induces in us a continuous dream that helps us survive. While such dreaming is unavoidable ("I must continue to dream if I am not to perish"), it's possible to wake up and recognize the dreaming for what it is, and so by imaginative correlation and subtraction develop a keener sense for what might be "real."

Indeed Nietzsche reserves the highest praise for those few human beings who are able to fully appropriate this archaic inheritance: one who "knows how to experience the history of humanity as his own history" can be considered "the heir of all the nobility of all previous spirit and an heir under obligation" (*GS* 337). The obligation is to be grateful for what one has inherited. Nietzsche was fascinated by "the tremendous abundance of gratitude" that flows from "the religiosity of the ancient Greeks" (*BGE* 49), and in keeping with this his Zarathustra praises "the way of noble souls" because

> …they want nothing *gratis*, and least of all life.
> Whoever is of the rabble wants to live gratis; we others, however, to whom life has given itself—we are always wondering *what* we can best give *in return!* (*Z* III: "On Old and New Tablets" 5)[4]

Since life has given itself to us all in the form of a body that bears with it a heritage of millennia, there is much to be grateful for—though also to be wary of, for as Zarathustra warns: "Not only the reason of millennia—but also their madness breaks out in us. It is dangerous to be an heir." (*Z* I: "On the Bestowing Virtue" 2) No wonder then that Zarathustra regards those who ignore this noble heritage as baser souls: "Whoever is of the rabble, his memory goes back to his grandfather—but with the grandfather time stops."

We were all "mayflies and rabble" until some of us acquired "the historical sense," which gives us "ancestors" and our "*noble* family tree" (*KSA* 9: 15 [70]). Rather than conducting research into one's personal family tree (a topic Nietzsche appears to have lost interest in after his childhood), exercising the historical sense means inquiring into "the dream" that's always going on in the deeper reaches of the soul.

---

4 Contrast the biblical injunction: "And whoever will, let him take the water of life gratis" (Revelation 22:17).

> Direct self-observation is not nearly sufficient for us to know ourselves: we need history, for the past flows on within us in a hundred waves; indeed, we ourselves are nothing but that which at every moment we experience of this continual flowing. (*HAH* II: 223)

This kind of experience enabled Nietzsche to situate his life, through imaginative engagement with psyche and history, within the larger matrix of Western culture.

This is not to say that an understanding of one's literal forebears is irrelevant: since Nietzsche thought that inherited nature outweighs environmental nurture, knowledge of one's more immediate heritage is also helpful.

> Given that one knows something about the parents, a conclusion concerning the child is permitted.... Even with the best upbringing and education one can do no more than manage some dissimulation concerning such an inheritance. (*BGE* 264)

What many of Nietzsche's "forebears most liked to do" was to read the Bible, pray, and preach. His family tree shows that his father, both grandfathers, and one great-grandfather were clergymen—one of them a bishop and one an archdeacon. Farther back on his paternal grandfather's side are six more clergymen, three of them bishops or archdeacons. Given Nietzsche's view of the power of heredity, it would be remarkable if his soul did *not* bear the traces of so much Bible reading and praying and preaching; and so even though he became unable to believe in the religion of his forefathers, it would be surprising if all traces of religiosity had vanished from his being.

There was a legend in the Nietzsche family, to which Friedrich was happy to subscribe, to the effect that they were descended from members of the Polish nobility by the name of "Nietzky," who had left their homeland to avoid persecution because of their Protestant faith. This gave the family a feeling of being different (and superior) in which Nietzsche indulged throughout his life. But subsequent genealogical research by one of his younger cousins has proved this legend to have no basis in fact.[5] What that research has revealed, however, is more interesting. On the Nietzsche side of the family he is also related to the Schlegel brothers, who played a major role in the beginnings of German romanticism at the turn of the eighteenth to nineteenth centuries, and further findings could show that he was even related to Goethe.[6] But he also turns out to be related, through his mother's side of the family, to the composer Richard Wagner (!) through a common ancestor named Spörel at the beginning of the sixteenth century.

GRANDPARENTS

> One is much more the child of one's four grandparents than of one's two parents: this is because at the time we were engendered, the parents had usually not yet established their own characters. The seeds of the grandfatherly type come to fruition in us, and in our children the seeds of our parents. (*KSA* 12: 9 [49])

---

[5] See Janz 1981: vol. 1, pp. 26–7. See *KSA* 9: 21 [2] for Nietzsche's own account of his Polish ancestry.
[6] See Janz 1981: vol. 1, p. 32, based on Oehler 1939.

So who were these grandparents whose child Nietzsche felt himself to be? He knew only three of them in person, since his paternal grandfather, Friedrich August Ludwig Nietzsche (1756–1826), died eighteen years before he was born.

Friedrich Wilhelm Nietzsche came into the world on October 15, 1844 in the tiny village of Röcken, some 35 kilometers west of Leipzig. His mother's family were the Oehlers, who lived in the nearby village of Pobles, where his grandfather, David Ernst Oehler, was the pastor. This grandfather was the son of a weaver, and having excelled at school he went on to study theology at the University of Leipzig. He arrived there in 1807, some thirty years after Friedrich August Nietzsche had studied in the same faculty. By that time theology at Leipzig had become more liberal, and David Ernst seems to have come away with a broad-minded and undogmatic view of the world, according to which all areas of human endeavor, from the natural sciences and history to music, poetry, and the other arts, are to be regarded as precious gifts from the Lord. He was thus not the kind of man to be attracted, as Nietzsche's father was, to the Pietist "Awakening" movement that was popular among the Lutheran clergy of the time. According to one of his grandsons: "Grandfather Oehler was no Pietist but rather lived in the era of rationalism, and as was customary he was a member of a freemasons' lodge."[7] With its openness to other systems of thinking and emphasis on a humanistic and cosmopolitan morality, freemasonry was quite compatible with the Enlightenment ideals of contemporary Lutheran Protestantism and the Prussian political system connected with it.

A year after receiving the pastorship of Pobles and surrounding villages, David Ernst Oehler married Wilhelmine Hahn, daughter of a landowning family in the region, so that the parsonage soon became a working farm. But since the Oehler family eventually grew to eleven children, their standard of living remained modest. An avid reader and very much concerned with education, David Ernst regarded teaching as an important component of his duties and expended a considerable amount of energy on educating the children in the village as well as his own offspring. He greatly enjoyed spending time in his study, which had a comprehensive library where works of theology by no means predominated. "His study was his own special realm. Books that he had opened and wanted to consult further would lie open, and pieces of paper on which he had made notes also had to be left where they were."[8] Unsurprisingly, young Fritz especially enjoyed spending time in his grandfather's study when he visited Pobles: "My favorite occupation was to be in grandpapa's study, and my greatest pleasure was browsing through all the old books and magazines there." (*KGW* I.1: 303) An indication of the breadth of his grandfather's intellectual interests is the fact that young Fritz found numerous works on such relatively occult subjects as magnetism and somnambulism in his library, including Justinus Kerner's well-known *The Seeress of Prevorst*, which appear to have influenced Nietzsche's later ideas about the multiplicity of the psyche.[9]

The grandfather was also a man of unusual physical vitality who enjoyed the work of running the farm as much as tending to the spiritual needs of his human flock. He was a keen huntsman and was by no means above enjoying a good game of cards, not to mention regular beer and occasional wine.[10] (He has thus been aptly compared to Laurence Sterne, a man

---

[7] Adalbert Oehler, "Erinnerungen meines Lebens" (unpublished manuscript), cited in Goch 1994: 79.
[8] See Goch 1994: 78, 76, 81.   [9] See Parkes 1994: 255–6.   [10] Adalbert Oehler, cited in Goch 1994: 81.

of the cloth with similarly secular inclinations, whose masterful *Tristram Shandy* would become one of young Nietzsche's favorite novels.)[11] In many ways quite a theatrical character, David Ernst had the ability "to deliver speeches in a masterful way" and possessed "a wonderful gift of being able to portray persons or events in a vivid and dramatic manner" (Janz 1981: vol. 1, p. 41). He was also a musical soul with some talent for the piano, and his large brood of children, sometimes supplemented by friends and guests, afforded him the opportunity of staging musical and theatrical performances. Life in the Pobles parsonage was thus a great deal livelier than in the Nietzsche household, and so Fritz and his sister Elisabeth always enjoyed staying with their grandparents, where there was fresh and wholesome food from the farm and its vegetable gardens, much opportunity to be in the open air, and within the house an abundance of entertainments in which to participate.

Writing about the educational aspects of the holidays that she and Fritz spent at the Pobles parsonage, Elisabeth remarks of her grandfather:

> In the background of it all stood the figure of our grandfather Oehler, who, despite his good nature, was an astute observer of people and things, and also, as I realized later in life, an exceedingly skeptical critic of the human comedy, especially when it assumed pathetic airs. Every kind of cant...was anathema to him. (Förster-Nietzsche 1912: vol. 1, p. 29; translation modified)

His daughter's biographer emphasizes David Ernst's psychological acuity and his consequent lack of patience with the morally narrow-minded and the intellectually lazy, quoting one of his sons on the topic of his father's short temper and a strategy he had developed for mitigating its effects.

> If Father was annoyed, he wouldn't say much about it but would simply write it down: he would discharge most of his anger and bitterness onto pieces of paper. He would often say, "The paper is patient, and can put up with anything." But he would then put away what he had written in a secret part of his writing desk. (Oscar Ulrich Oehler, cited in Janz 1981: vol. 1, p. 39)

His grandson Fritz clearly inherited this psychological acuity and became a past master of the technique of transmuting emotion into writing, often for himself but also for an audience. After Nietzsche's father died when the boy was only four, the genial and literate grandfather became the male figure he was closest to for the next several years. As Nietzsche later put it, in a note with the title "Correcting nature": "If one doesn't have a good father, one should get oneself one." (*HAH* I: 31)[12]

The matriarch of the Oehler family, Wilhelmine, was also temperamental, though some of her irritability could be ascribed to her physical handicaps: she had lost the sight of one eye during a bout of chicken pox, and one of her legs was shorter than the other owing to an accident in childhood. But these impediments in no way diminished her ability to run the household, even though, with eleven children to care for, she had no time to spoil any of them through excess attention. An extremely vigorous woman, she kept the whole family so healthy through her skills as a gardener, and as the main cook and preparer of the bounty

[11] The comparison with Sterne is made by R. J. Hollingdale (1965).
[12] Nietzsche's mentor in classics at the Universities of Bonn and Leipzig, Friedrich Ritschl, was also significant father figure for him, though this role was soon taken over by Richard Wagner.

from the garden, that her daughter Franziska (Nietzsche's mother) claims not to remember a doctor's ever having visited the Oehler home.[13]

Not much is known about grandmother Wilhelmine (with eleven children to take care of she can't have had time to write many letters), but the accounts of holidays that Fritz and his sister spent in Pobles suggest that his relations with her were warm, since her emotional outbursts were brief and interspersed with longer periods of calm. As one of her sons reported: "Sometimes she was like a keg of gunpowder that easily explodes; but after the explosion she would have an immediate feeling of relief and everything would be fine again." (Oscar Ulrich Oehler, cited in Goch 1994: 86) The grandmother's temperamental nature seems to have bypassed the Oehlers' daughter Franziska, to resurface again in *her* daughter Elisabeth (who was not so much inclined to rapid reconciliation). Nietzsche himself also seems to have inherited, in accordance with his idea that character traits skip a generation, the passionate natures of these grandparents. His parents and schooling tended to discourage displays of emotion during his youth, but in later life he often refers to his own "explosive" potential.

Although Nietzsche never knew his paternal grandfather in person, he was at least able to get to know him through the works he left behind, since Friedrich August Ludwig Nietzsche had been a prolific author. His books naturally held pride of place in the household of his widow, Erdmuthe, Nietzsche's grandmother. The family of Friedrich August's mother, the Herolds, had been Lutheran pastors for four generations, since the early seventeenth century, so it was taken for granted that the latest scion should become a man of the cloth too. Friedrich August studied theology at the University of Leipzig just ten years after Goethe had been a student there, and he was educated in a Protestant worldview that advocated a rational, historical, and philological approach to Holy Scripture, with the aim of critically filtering out what was "inauthentic" in the text of the Bible by trying to remove later interpolations from alien sources.[14] In choosing to study philology and history the grandson was to some extent following in his forbear's footsteps. Yet whereas the rational-critical method practiced by the elder Friedrich Nietzsche was by no means destructive of religious faith, but was intended rather to strengthen it by providing an authentic foundation, in the mature hands of the grandson it would serve an opposite aim.

Friedrich August Nietzsche published several books on theological topics, including a textual-critical study of the New Testament written in Latin. His most famous work was the profusely titled *Gamaliel, or the Everlasting Duration of Christianity, for Instruction and Tranquilization amidst the Present Ferment in the Theological World*, published in Leipzig in 1796. (The grandson would eventually arrive at a more modest appraisal of the "duration of Christianity.") The title of another of his books, *Contributions toward the Propagation of Reasonable Thinking about Religion, Education, the Duties of Subjects, and Human Love* (1804), conveys a further sense of his rationalist approach and the breadth of his scope as a writer. His works give a favorable picture of the human race as being endowed by nature with considerable powers of understanding which, if properly developed, can to a large extent replace divine revelation with human reason. Nevertheless, "religion is not merely a matter of the understanding, but must also be a matter of the heart," since even the most

---

[13] Franziska Nietzsche, "Mein Leben" (1895); printed in Goch 1994: 32–64, 47.
[14] See Pernet 1989: chapter 3.

highly developed human reason is incapable of understanding the totality of God and His creation. Friedrich August's theology is thus a kind of "rational supranaturalism," the goal of which is the progressive "enlightenment and ennoblement" of the whole of humanity and the "furthering of human happiness through the promotion of wisdom and virtue."

The seeds of Friedrich August's energetic rationalism, with its reverence for the indefatigable questioning powers of the human intellect, surely came to fruition in his grandson. But they were so well nurtured by the philological regimen to which the younger Friedrich was subjected at school and university that, when the equilibrating force of faith fell away, his intellectual acumen would be employed to undermine rather than support Christian belief. Literally prolific as well as literarily, the grandfather sired nine children in his first marriage before marrying Erdmuthe Dorothea Krause at the age of 53, a union that produced a further three offspring: Fritz's father, Carl Ludwig, and two sisters (Fritz's aunts), Rosalie and Auguste.

Erdmuthe Krause herself came from a family of pastors and was matriarch of the household in which young Fritz grew up. She had spent her youth in Weimar, in circles associated with Goethe, and there was speculation that her mother's name appears in the young Goethe's diary. Her brother, Johann Friedrich Krause, was a professor of theology who was ultimately appointed to a high official post in Weimar that had been occupied by Johann Gottfried Herder—a formidable thinker whose ideas about the human soul in many ways anticipated Nietzsche's (though he acknowledges Herder only cursorily).[15]

Erdmuthe married a lawyer to the Court of Weimar, but amidst the devastation of the country following the battle of Jena in 1806, where Napoleon defeated the Prussian army, her husband contracted a fatal disease and died. Her second husband was Friedrich August Nietzsche, twenty-two years her senior, who by the time of their marriage had reached the exalted rank of superintendent in the Lutheran Church. After his death, she did her best to keep alive the spirit of his theological worldview in the household of her three children, and especially after the arrival of her grandchildren. According to the younger grandchild, Elisabeth:

> The whole milieu in which we lived, especially thanks to the profound religiosity that pervaded it, must have had the most powerful influence on my brother. Although our grandmother Nietzsche had grown up in the rather sober period of the Enlightenment with its simplified ideals of God, virtue, and immortality, and so felt far from comfortable in the atmosphere of the Pietistic movement of the eighteen-fifties, when people became "awakened" and passionately and publicly declared themselves to be miserable sinners, her entire being and life were nevertheless permeated by a delicate and touching religiosity. (Förster-Nietzsche 1912: vol. 1, p. 32)

The contrast between sober Enlightenment and enthusiastic Pietism refers to a deep and widespread conflict in the religious life of Protestant Europe at the time, and one that caused a rift in the microcosm of the Nietzsche family. Erdmuthe's adherence to the rationalist ideals of her late husband appears to have been anything but delicate, and her consequent discomfort with the more emotional and fundamentalist outlook of the Pietistic "Awakening" movement set her at odds with her own son (Nietzsche's father) when his faith veered in that direction.

---

[15] See Förster-Nietzsche (1912: vol. 1, p. 4). See also the discussions of Herder in Parkes 1994.

Young Fritz's autobiographical writings exhibit great affection and respect for his paternal grandmother, and his attitude toward religion was much closer to hers than to his father's— another exemplification of his idea that inherited character traits tend to skip a generation.

PARENTS

> As my father I am already dead, while as my mother I am still alive and growing old. These dual origins, from the highest and lowest rungs of the ladder of life as it were, decadent and at the same time beginning—this explains, if anything does, that neutrality, that freedom from taking sides with respect to the entire problem of life, which is perhaps my distinctive feature. (*EH*: "Why I Am So Wise" 1)

Nietzsche's father, Carl Ludwig, was born in October 1813, when his own father was 57 years old and his mother 35. This was the year that Prussia declared war on France, and when Napoleon, after his victory at the Battle of Lützen (near Röcken), met defeat at the Battle of Leipzig some twenty kilometers farther on. The year 1813 also saw the births of the Danish philosopher Søren Kierkegaard, who developed a form of existentialism that bears striking similarities to Nietzsche's, and of the composers Richard Wagner and Giuseppe Verdi. After the Congress of Vienna in 1815, the several territories that comprised Saxony at the time came under the jurisdiction of the victorious state of Prussia, so that the soil from which Nietzsche's ancestors had sprung became known as Prussian Saxony.

In the Nietzsche household, as in the whole of Saxony at that time, the Lutheran catechism held sway, which stressed hard discipline, conscientiousness, and a dedication of one's person to serving the greater community. Not only did Carl Ludwig know as a 12-year-old that he wanted to become a preacher, but he actually wrote his first sermon at that tender age (Bohley 1980: 390). He did not, however, inherit his parents' physical robustness and was a somewhat hypochondriacal child. The death of his father when the boy was 13 increased his insecurity and sense of isolation from his peers, which in turn engendered an almost pathological dependence on his mother that would last for the rest of his life. A defensive reaction set in, whereby he rejected everything "worldly" and took refuge in a realm of the spirit. His pious and serious demeanor at school, and his eagerness to be a model pupil, further alienated him from his classmates and earned him the nickname "the little pastor"—a name his son's peers would apply to him in turn (Max Oehler, "Nietzsches Vater" (unpublished manuscript based on the extant correspondence); cited in Goch 1994: 367).

In his letters home from the seminary he attended during 1827 and 1828, he frequently complains of violent headaches and other pains, acute homesickness, and nocturnal anxiety, especially during thunder- and hailstorms (*GSA* 100/100).[16] As one commentator concludes: "Impression from the letters of the thirteen-to-fourteen-year-old boy: an extremely sensitive, pious, physically delicate boy, with a tendency toward hypochondria and an anxious concern over his health. Frequent complaints of violent headaches." (*GSA* 100/445 [2])[17] A fellow seminarian, who would later become the school doctor at the prestigious school at Schulpforta (and so have the occasion to treat young Fritz there for eye problems and

---

[16] Carl Ludwig Nietzsche, letters from October 1827 and March–April 1828.
[17] Ingeborg Krüger, "Notes for a Biography of Nietzsche's Father."

headaches), attributed the father's sickliness to the fact that he was engendered at a time when his own father was already ailing.[18] At 18, Carl Ludwig underwent prolonged medical treatment in Leipzig; two years later he was declared provisionally unfit for military service on grounds of "general physical weakness"; four years after that he was deemed unfit indefinitely (Goch 1994: 102).[19]

The valetudinarian father is a striking exception among Nietzsche's ancestors, most of whom were not only long-lived but also unusually prolific. Great-grandfather Gotthelf Engelbert Nietzsche, born in 1714, was one of eleven children and lived to be 90 years old. His son, Nietzsche's grandfather, was one of eight children and reached the age of 70, having sired twelve children in two marriages. His second wife, Erdmuthe (Nietzsche's grandmother), lived to be 77. The maternal grandparents had eleven children and died at 72 and 82. Nietzsche's mother lived to be 71 and his sister 89. For the most part the life force flowed strong and long in the immediate family—with the exception of Nietzsche's father.[20]

Carl Ludwig studied for four years at the University of Halle-Wittenberg (1833–7), when the theological faculty was in transition between traditional rationalism and the new "Awakening" theology that was revolutionizing Lutheran Pietism in Saxony. Pietism had the aim of infusing Protestantism with deeper religious feeling, and the Awakening movement sought to make the emotional elements in piety and faith even more central. By the end of his course of study Carl Ludwig had shifted most of his allegiance to the new movement, having come under the sway of the charismatic preacher Christian Couard. He was deeply influenced by this teacher's emphasis on the direct experience of sinfulness and grace. What is paramount is: "faith in the power of God through which the sinner is reborn and becomes a new creature in Jesus Christ. This new birth, or rebirth, is the indispensable condition for participation in the kingdom of heaven." (cited in Pernet 1989: 20)

Although Carl Ludwig was an industrious student, his teachers noted a weakness in his grasp of theoretical theology as a result of the time and energy he devoted to writing sermons. In this area he received the highest praise, not only for the eloquence of his language but also for his powers of memory—the sermons had to be given without a text—and the effectiveness of his gestures. Indeed his preaching would sometimes become so impassioned that he would be moved to tears by his own performances, so that some of his superiors complained of "too much pathos." But it becomes clear from his letters and from much of the content of the sermons themselves that the role of fervent preacher was to some extent a mask he was obliged to adopt in order to conceal the fragility of his personality. He himself admitted that the pulpit was the only place where he could avoid being plagued by "doubts and fears": "As soon as I begin to preach. . . I become peaceful, self-assured, courageous, and decisive."[21] Perhaps some of Nietzsche's later insights into the phenomena of actors, masks, and personae derive from early experience of the complex defensive strategies deployed by his father.

Another way of shoring up internal fragility is to attach oneself to strong external structures in the outside world. In Carl Ludwig's case he was happy to find refuge in a time of political turmoil at the court of Duke Joseph of Saxe-Altenburg, one of the small dukedoms

[18] C. A. Zimmermann, Krankenbuch Schulpforte 1862, reprinted in *GAB* 1: 340.
[19] See also Bohley 1987: 176 n. 73.   [20] See Volz 1994: 326.   [21] Cited in Bohley 1980: 392.

of which Saxony was composed at the time. Joseph was a conservative ruler who used a repressive force of soldiers and police to stifle any progressive or democratic movement that might threaten his hegemony. Carl Ludwig was given the post of tutor to the duke's three daughters, and through his employer's good graces he traveled to Berlin in 1841, where he eventually obtained a brief audience with King Friedrich Wilhelm. The fruit of this meeting was his being granted the pastorship at Röcken later that year. Though this was hardly the level of post he had hoped for—in a tiny village situated in flat and somewhat featureless countryside far from the city—he moved into the parsonage there with his mother and two unmarried sisters, whose presence would serve to allay his continuing "doubts and fears."[22]

Franziska Ernestine Rosaura Oehler, the sixth of the eleven Oehler children, was given names (as all her siblings were) that formed acrostics in Latin. "Our dear father," she wrote late in life, "loved giving us each a word to accompany us for the journey of life: so I received *FERO* (I bear, tolerate)." (Goch 1994: 34) The child's initials dictate the posture she is to adopt toward the world, and in view of the burdens that were to be laid upon her as a young woman, "I bear" was an apt adage indeed. David Ernst Oehler's concern for education did not transcend the customs of the time, which reserved thorough schooling for the boys in the family alone. And so Franziska, though possessed of native wit and practical good sense, received little in the way of a formal education. In a letter to her son written later in life, she remarks: "I feel that my education was insufficient and our energies were directed more toward practical and useful work."[23] In spite of the relatively secular atmosphere of the parsonage, the Oehlers' was another home in which the precepts of the Lutheran catechism held sway; and although the family's churchgoing habits were remarkably relaxed, Franziska's upbringing instilled in her an unshakable faith in the power of prayer, a practice that appears to have figured in every day of her adult life.[24] Three of her brothers eventually became pastors and two of her elder sisters married into the ministry. The next generation also tended to become or marry clergymen: there were seven pastors among Nietzsche's cousins on his mother's side. No wonder, then, that young Fritz should characterize himself in one of his autobiographical sketches as "the son of a Protestant country pastor."

Looking back on her childhood Franziska writes: "To grow up as the only girl in a series of five brothers surely contributed to my good health, since I had to participate in the wildest games if I didn't want to be exposed to their scorn." Being especially close to her brothers, the young girl was at first something of a tomboy. She eventually acquired a reputation as the most adept tobogganer in the family: "My brothers later teased me for being such an excellent steerer, since I often had two or three smaller siblings on board with me. On some of the steeper hills you could sometimes even take off into the air for a bit, but I would only attempt that trick when I was on my own."[25]

Since Pobles is less than an hour's walk from Röcken, it was natural for Carl Ludwig Nietzsche to introduce himself to his colleague David Oehler. By the time he visited the

---

[22] In a letter to a friend Carl Ludwig wrote: "Trembling with doubts concerning my abilities, I am often seized with such fear that I would rather not take up the post at all" (November 16, 1841; cited in Goch 1994: 110).

[23] Franziska Nietzsche, letter to Friedrich Nietzsche, March 3, 1877.

[24] On Franziska's churchgoing, see Goch 1994: 73 and 360; on prayer, see Pernet 1989: 28.

[25] Franziska Nietzsche, letter from October 1895, cited in Goch 1994: 30; "Mein Leben," cited in Goch 1994: 35, 46.

Pobles parsonage, Franziska had grown into a beautiful young woman of seventeen and a presence that even he, with his general lack of interest in "worldly" things, could not help noticing. In an account of a visit from the handsome young pastor (who was twelve years her senior), she writes:

> The company drank coffee amid gay conversation, after which Pastor Nietzsche, whom we already knew to be a piano player, was persuaded to improvise, which he did in an especially masterful way that day. We then went into the garden, where he asked me for a bouquet, and also for a sprig of dill since he loved the fragrance.

Overwhelmed by Carl Ludwig's handsome looks, courtly demeanor, and elegant attire, Franziska nevertheless knew from the start that he was not exactly "single," since she observed that "the young Pastor Nietzsche visited with his mother and two sisters...who live with him." Nevertheless, it wasn't long before Carl Ludwig asked his older colleague for the hand of his daughter in marriage. Franziska was overjoyed—but also anxious, since she was still so young and had little experience of the world beyond the village. But her mother encouraged her by pointing out that lack of life experience was something that "every day would help to remedy."[26]

Carl Ludwig pressed for an early wedding, since as a pastor approaching the age of 30 he needed a wife. Although his mother was at first less than enthusiastic about the prospect of having an unrefined country girl as a daughter-in-law, she apparently encouraged him to pick Franziska over her elder sisters.[27] Since the Oehler family was under some financial pressure to get their daughters married off, and none of the older sisters had received any proposals, David Ernst gave his consent. According to Elisabeth, he warned the bridegroom-to-be: "Our Fränzchen is a bit of a tomboy, and allow me as a horticulturist to tell you that you are taking a wild shoot into your family, from which you must rear a noble tree." The staid and proper Nietzsche clan must indeed have been unnerved by the young woman's spiritedness, though Elisabeth's report of grandmother Erdmuthe's saying, "Fränzchen is a magnificent savage, and her vigor and roughness are just delightful," makes the matriarch sound uncharacteristically gushing (Förster-Nietzsche 1912: vol. 1, p. 13).

A year after the wedding Franziska bore their first child, bringing into the world on the birthday of Friedrich Wilhelm IV, King of Prussia, the future philosopher Friedrich Wilhelm Nietzsche. Carl Ludwig was overjoyed at the arrival of a son on such an auspicious day, but for Franziska the labor and birth were so difficult that she was still bedridden when her son was baptised, ten days after the birth. Since she was a vigorous young woman of 18, such indisposition was unusual, and it appears that she had contracted some kind of inflammation in the chest, which must have made nursing her newborn a torture instead of a delight.[28]

However, the birth of the son served to secure for Franziska a determinate position in the Nietzsche household—that of second mother to grandmother Erdmuthe. Her status was further consolidated by the birth of another child, Elisabeth Therese Alexandra (one name from each of her father's former royal pupils), twenty-one months later, and a third, Carl Ludwig Joseph, nineteen months after that. Such a consolidation was much needed, since

---

[26] Franziska Nietzsche, "Mein Leben," cited in Goch 1994: 54–5, 50, 59.
[27] See the extract from Franziska's journal from August 1849 reprinted in Goch 1994: 151.
[28] See Goch 1994: 129–30 on Franziska's indisposition after giving birth.

when Franziska was brought into the Nietzsche household as a bride of 17, she was made to feel insignificant in relation to the matriarch Erdmuthe (65) and her two daughters, Rosalie (32) and Auguste (28). All the more so since the Nietzsches saw themselves as exalted socially far above the naïve young farm girl, pretensions that were to generate considerable tension between them and the down-to-earth Oehler family.

One of Nietzsche's most psychologically acute reflections on the parent-child relationship is to be found in a one-sentence aphorism in *Human, All Too Human* that bears the title, "The parents live on":

> The unresolved dissonances between the characters and dispositions of the parents continue to resound in the nature of the child, and constitute the history of his inner sufferings. (*HAH* I: 379)

A sense of the dissonances that set in early on between his parents is well conveyed by a passage from a letter that Carl Ludwig wrote to a friend shortly after the marriage.

> The longer I know my in-laws the less I am able to respect them; my mother-in-law in particular is a totally worldly and common woman. It oppresses and tortures me terribly sometimes that I have to be so ashamed of my in-laws, and I am astonished that my Fränzchen could have grown from this kind of soil! My bad relationship with her parents has led to many an hour of discord with my Fränzchen: it pains her so much that I cannot stand her parents, for they do not do anything against me. That is true, but our orientations toward life and faith are so different that when it comes to an expectoration, *which I am nevertheless careful to avoid*, I am afraid of a formal break with the Pobles parsonage, if I don't manage to put up with the whole thing for Fränzchen's sake, and let her see as little as possible of my aversion and disgust for her parents, in order not to hurt her, since she is so fond of her family—although she must have noticed that I have expressed myself definitely against mutual visits. (Carl Ludwig, letter of February 22, 1844; cited in Goch 1994: 127)

This letter is evidence of the considerable stresses generated by the largely unexpressed emotional life within the Röcken parsonage. There is no indication that Carl Ludwig's aversion was reciprocated by his in-laws, though they must have been aware of a cool distance on the part of their son-in-law. But even allowing for David Ernst's more liberal theological outlook, and the more secular home life that followed from it, Carl Ludwig's antipathy is remarkable in its intensity. It is probable that he sensed his father-in-law's ironic distaste for the Awakening movement to which he was so passionately committed, and he may even have suspected that David Ernst's psychological perspicacity could see through the mask of his own extreme piety.

In spite of her husband's efforts to suppress his antipathy toward her family, it was clearly a cause of deep distress to Franziska; yet she had no alternative but to resign herself to the situation. The natural consequence was a tendency to withdraw into herself, so as to minimize domestic discord. This must have been hard for her as a natural extravert, but she apparently put her trust in God that He would guide her through this trial. That she managed to negotiate the difficult transition from her carefree life in Pobles to the oppressive existence in the parsonage at Röcken at the age of only 17 attests to her robust and resourceful nature.

Considering what the mature Nietzsche says about parents in general, it becomes clear that the "nurture" counterpart to the "dual origins, from the highest and lowest rungs of the ladder of life" had its share of negative effects on him. In the context of discussing what it means for a man to possess a woman, Nietzsche invokes the parents.

Parents can't help making their child into something similar to themselves—they call this "education"—no mother doubts at the bottom of her heart that with the child she has borne herself a possession, no father disputes his right to subject it to his own conceptions and evaluations. (*BGE* 194)

FATHER AND SON

[In several respects] I am merely my father once again and, as it were, the continuation of his life after an all-too-early death. (*EH*: "Why I Am So Wise" 5)

In the numerous autobiographical sketches Nietzsche wrote during his youth, he always mentions his father with affection and respect, and often remarks on his love of music. "He occupied his leisure hours with study and with music. He had a distinct talent for playing the piano, especially in free improvisation." (*KGW* I.1: 282) Franziska corroborates with respect to her son's early years: "The boy always listens quiet as a mouse and refuses to take his eyes off his father when he begins to play the piano." So it became natural for Franziska to request some music from the father when her son started crying.[29]

But when the soothing powers of music failed, stricter measures were required. Carl Ludwig wrote to his friend: "Brother Fritz is a wild boy, and sometimes only Papa can bring him to reason, since he has the rod at hand." (Carl Ludwig, letter of December 15, 1846; cited in Bohley 1987: 171) In his enthusiasm for the Awakening movement, the father apparently subscribed to the Pietist educational maxim whereby "the child's willfulness has to be broken so that it may later be open to the will of God." The talk of bringing the child to reason suggests he also believed that this process can be effected at the tender age of 2. Whether the rod was actually employed or its nearness used as a threat cannot be determined, though physical punishments by parents at that time were the norm. In a letter Franziska wrote late in life, she says of her son: "When he was very small, and my husband was still alive, he would throw himself onto his back when things didn't go according to his will, but dear Papa's *manual* intervention soon cured him of this habit." (Franziska Nietzsche, letter of June 23–4, 1895, in *Der entmündigte Philosoph*: 38) Just as the Lutheran catechism, which had dominated Carl Ludwig's early childhood, was still widely in force, so the father recreated, as often happens, the conditions of his own upbringing for the benefit of the next generation.

A popular writer (Miller 1991) on the effects of overly severe discipline on young children has claimed that Nietzsche was badly abused as a boy and that this accounts for the harshness of the philosophy he developed as an adult.[30] But the biographical evidence adduced in support of this claim is minimal, and the case is made to rest instead on poorly understood quotations from Nietzsche's philosophical writings. Young Fritz's behavior, as well as the parental reactions and his responses to those reactions, hardly sounds unusual—let alone pathologically extreme—for a bright and headstrong two- to three-year-old. And considering the high tensions between Franziska and her in-laws that underlay daily life in the home,

[29] On Fritz's early fascination with the piano, see Oehler 1940: 42.
[30] On Fritz's good and bad behavior, see Bohley 1987: 169 and Goch 1994: 135–6.

together with all the unspoken as well as spoken judgments and the repressed reactions and feelings on the part of the adults, it's a wonder there are no reports of *more* difficult behavior on Fritz's part.

Although there are no other mentions of caning or spanking, it is likely, given the practices of the time, that both Nietzsche children were spanked for misbehaving when they were very young. Fritz certainly learned early to internalize parental discipline, and an incipient sense of pride (and fear of shame) soon came to inhibit punishable behavior, so as to avoid the embarrassment of being overtly disciplined. Such a regime leads naturally to a certain amount of repression, but it rarely proves traumatic, and Fritz seems to have passed through the process relatively unscathed. The "harshness" of Nietzsche's philosophy is a response to a culture and civilization that he sees as badly in need of improvement, rather than a product of childhood trauma from being continually beaten.

Nor does it seem that young Fritz was unduly thrown off by the arrival of two siblings, Elisabeth (when he was almost two) and Joseph (when he was three-and-a-half). What did upset him, profoundly, was the traumatic event of his father's succumbing to a fatal illness.

It was in the course of the revolutionary uprisings that shook the established political order in Europe during 1848 that Carl Ludwig's health had begun to deteriorate. As a staunch royalist loyal to King Friedrich Wilhelm, he wrote to his closest friend: "My nerves have been badly affected by the recent political disturbances: I am unable to sleep properly and have been having all kinds of strange visions." (Carl Ludwig, letter to Emil Julius Schenk, April 17, 1848, cited in Goch 2000: 376) Even the account from Elisabeth, who generally paints as rosy a picture of family life as possible, makes clear the dire effect on her father of the King's conciliatory response to the rebellion in Berlin: "He burst into tears, left the room, and was able to rejoin the company only after spending several hours alone. Nor were we permitted to speak of the event ever again." (Förster-Nietzsche 1912: vol. 1, p. 15)

In an autobiographical essay from 1858 the 14-year-old Fritz writes as follows:

> Up to this point happiness and joy had always shone on us, and our life had flowed by untroubled as a bright summer's day. But now dark clouds gathered, lightning flashed, and devastating blows fell from heaven. In September of 1848 my dear father suddenly became ill. (*KGW* I.1: 284–5)

The talk of "devastating blows from heaven" suggests the incredulity to which the boy must have been subject, at the tender age of almost four, at seeing his beloved, admired, and revered father be suddenly laid so low. By November Carl Ludwig's condition became serious enough to warrant his being taken to a clinic in the town of Naumburg, several hours' journey away, to undergo homeopathic treatment at the hands of a renowned practitioner. Toward the end of the month Fritz went with his mother to visit the invalid father, but his condition was worse than ever and they felt their presence was aggravating his mood rather than cheering him up. As Franziska wrote to a friend:

> The vomiting and then every day the most terrible headaches. . . cause my dear husband indescribable torment, and it becomes so bad on the days of vomiting that he says that he might lose his mind because of it. May our dear God in his mercy prevent that from happening. . . . We had hoped to bring him a little joy, but found him extremely sad and weeping a lot. . . . I forgot to say that unfortunately the doctor also said that it was a brain disease, but

promised a slow but sure recovery. (Franziska Nietzsche, letter to Emma Schenk, December 1, 1848; cited in Goch 1994: 141)

After the patient returned home from the treatment in Naumburg, his sister Auguste sent the doctor a report that suggests it had been ineffectual:

> Toward four in the morning on Sunday I gave him [a homeopathic powder] but half an hour later he vomited, felt more ill in the course of the day, and became very weak, lying mostly in bed with shortness of breath and screaming from the pain in his head whenever he had to move.... At midnight the terrible moaning began again. (Report to Dr Stapf in Naumburg; cited in Goch 2000: 381)

Given the modest size of the parsonage, young Fritz couldn't have avoided hearing the sounds of his father's agony. And even if the children were kept physically insulated from the scene of the sickness, the distress of the adults would have been palpable.

Early the next year a specialist from the city of Leipzig was brought in, who offered a grim diagnosis. As Nietzsche recounted several years later:

> We were horrified to learn that the doctor thought it was softening of the brain: not yet a completely hopeless case, but nevertheless very dangerous. My beloved father had to endure terrible pain, and instead of becoming better the illness grew worse from day to day. (*KGW* I.1: 285)

By April, Carl Ludwig had gone completely blind: "Eventually even the light from his eyes failed, and he was condemned to spend the rest of his suffering in eternal darkness" (*KGW* I.1: 285)[31] Franziska wrote to a friend that her husband was still able to think and, with great difficulty, to talk: "But this thinking and not being able to express it properly seems to be embarrassing and stressful for him: he always shakes with irritation when he hasn't spoken the way he wanted to." (Franziska Nietzsche, letter of April 4, 1849; cited in Bohley 1987: 179)

With the coming of spring and better weather, the young children were granted some respite from the misery of being cooped up in the house with a father who had gone blind and was almost mute, except for groans of pain. The son of a pastor friend of Carl Ludwig's visited the Röcken parsonage for a weekend in April and sent his parents a less than encouraging report.

> I found Pastor Nietzsche in very poor condition. He sits in a chair most of the time, for he is extremely weak but doesn't like staying in bed since he also can't sleep properly. . . . He is unable to see, though it's only a temporary condition according to the specialist from Leipzig, and that's why his eyes are always rolling from side to side. . . . They say he is now well on the way to recovery, but I can hardly believe that he'll be back to normal within half a year. (Gustav Karl Ferdinand Menzel, letter of April 12, 1849; cited in Goch 2000: 387–8)

It is harrowing to imagine the contrast for the four-year-old Fritz between the father he was used to seeing—preaching sermons from the pulpit of the church by the parsonage, reading and writing in his study, improvising at the piano—and this shell of the former person, sitting immobile, sightless, eyes rolling in his head. It must have been hard to reconcile the

[31] In a letter from April 4 Franziska writes of her husband's "not being able to see at all"; cited in Goch 2000: 387.

constant talk of the patient's being "well on the way to recovery" with his daily experience during that dismal period. Indeed Fritz's saying that his father spent "the rest of his suffering in eternal darkness" suggests that he knew that the blindness was not the "temporary condition" that he and the weekend guest had been led to believe.

> Even though I didn't fully comprehend the magnitude of the imminent danger, the sad and anxious mood must have made an unsettling impression on me. The suffering of my father, the tears of my mother, the worried expressions on the doctors' faces, and eventually the careless remarks of people in the village—all must have given me a premonition of a threatening misfortune. And this misfortune did eventually strike. (*KGW* I.2: 260)

The eventual "careless remarks" no doubt contradicted the consistently optimistic view of the situation presented by his mother. One must remember that although young Fritz wrote his autobiographical essays for his own enjoyment, they were also to be read by his mother and aunts and grandmother, and so he was unable to be totally candid or to contradict what he had been told during the ordeal of his father's decline.

For many weeks Carl Ludwig lay in bed, his energies unrestored, tormented by bed-sores and becoming weaker and weaker. On July 26, 1849, at the age of 35, he lapsed into a coma. Nietzsche recounts in retrospect:

> When I woke up the next morning [July 30], I heard nothing but weeping and sobbing all around me. My dear mother came in, in tears, crying mournfully: "Oh God! My dear Ludwig is dead!" Although I was still very young and inexperienced, I nevertheless had some idea of death. Overcome by the thought of being separated from my dear father for ever, I wept bitterly. The next few days were spent in tears and in preparing for the funeral. Oh God! I had become a fatherless orphan and my dear mother a widow! (*KGW* I.1: 285)

Not long after the event Carl Ludwig's step-sister, Friederike Dächsel, gave the time of death, with Prussian precision, as 5:49 a.m. "His skull was opened up and it was confirmed that he had died of softening of the brain, which had already affected one quarter of his head." (Janz 1981: vol. 1, p. 19) Max Oehler, a nephew of the deceased, stated that the surgical section performed during the autopsy had revealed some kind of "tumor." (Janz 1981: vol. 1, pp. 46–7) And the teenage Fritz's final comment about his father's death: "This was the first disastrous event, which changed the shape of the rest of my life for ever." (*KGW* I.2: 259) This death changed the shape of Nietzsche's life by initiating a gradual loss of faith in the religion of his father and forefathers: the death of the father thus anticipated the son's later ideas concerning the death of God.

Biographers and commentators tend to date Nietzsche's loss of faith much later, to his arrival at the University of Bonn, but careful study of the juvenilia, and especially the poems he began writing from the age of 12, suggests that the One Christian God became unbelievable much earlier.[32] His autobiographical essays had to remain silent on such a crucial matter. But imagine the context: a family life saturated with religiosity, in which the four-year-old's father is the most revered figure in the community, a paragon of the virtues, and God's representative on earth. When he gave his weekly sermon, he would appear in the pulpit high

---

[32] See Schmidt 1991 for a comprehensive discussion of the poems Nietzsche wrote during his youth, many of which suggest a loss of faith that he couldn't possibly acknowledge openly.

up on the wall at the end of the church's nave (the staircase to it being hidden) as if he had swung down from Heaven to preach. The young boy must have wondered why the Almighty had singled out his father for subjection to such an excruciating illness and death. Although what psychologists call childhood amnesia tends to prevent our remembering the experiences of our early years, it may also be true, as Fritz later writes, that "the early impressions the soul receives are enduring." (*KGW* I.2: 3)

Six months after his father's death, something else happened to further disrupt the daily activities of life: Fritz had a dream in which the dismal tones of mourning resound again.

> I heard the sound of the organ in the church as at a funeral. Then I saw the reason: a grave suddenly opened up and my father climbed out from it wearing a burial shroud. He hurries into the church and soon comes out again with a small child in his arms. The burial mound opens again, he climbs in, and the lid sinks back upon the opening. The thundering organ sounds fall silent and I wake up.—The next day little Joseph suddenly became ill, got cramps, and died within a few hours. Our grief was enormous. My dream had been fulfilled completely. The small body was laid in the arms of the father. —In this double misfortune God in heaven was our only consolation and protection. (*KGW* I.1: 286)

A double misfortune indeed, especially since Joseph was just a few weeks short of his second birthday. He had been intermittently ill during the preceding nine months, and although Franziska attributed his death to "teething cramps" it was more likely the result of an infection of some kind.[33] Since her special fondness for her youngest child had been intensified by the loss of his father, the burden of grief was especially crushing for her, but surely also "enormous" for her five-year-old son. No wonder that young Fritz should write that his exposure to deaths in the family had produced in him a tendency toward seriousness and sadness.

In view of these events, it is instructive to consider an aphorism from *Human, All Too Human* with the title "The tragedy of childhood."

> It is perhaps not uncommon that those who strive for noble and lofty goals have to undergo their hardest struggle during childhood: perhaps through having to maintain their attitude in the face of a low-minded father prone to illusion and lying, or else, like Lord Byron, to live in constant strife with a childish and irascible mother. If one has experienced such a thing, one will never as long as one lives get over knowing who one's greatest and most dangerous enemy has really been. (*HAH* I: 422)

If Nietzsche is writing here, as he so often does, about himself, one wonders what brought about this change of attitude toward his progenitor. The major factor is probably his reading of the writings that Carl Ludwig left behind, and especially the letters, since these paint a picture of the author that is considerable less flattering than the impression one receives from his widow, from Elisabeth, and from Fritz's autobiographical writings.

Under the circumstances one could well imagine Nietzsche wanting to deny the influence of heredity in matters of health and illness after the experience of witnessing his father's awful demise, even though his psychology emphasizes the importance of what is inherited by the

---

[33] Bohley (1987: 181) quotes a letter of Franziska's from April 1849 where she mentions little Joseph's illnesses; see also Volz (1994: 36) on the probable cause of death.

individual from parents and forebears.[34] And indeed his chronic headaches and eye trouble, which began in his mid-teens, later gave rise to the fear that the fate that befell his father would also befall him. Letters he wrote as he approached the age of 35 evidence considerable anxiety over this possibility: "Now at 'the midpoint of life' I am so 'surrounded by death' that it might seize me at any hour." (Letter of September 11, 1879, *KSB* 5: 441) And as he later commented in retrospect: "In the same year as his life declined, mine declined, too. In the thirty-sixth year of my life I arrived at the nadir of my vitality." (*EH*: "Why I Am So Wise" 1) But it is characteristic of Nietzsche that he made no attempt in his thinking to construct defensive rationalizations against the haunting fear—real, as it would ultimately turn out—of his own mental collapse.

In writing about this period of his life, during which he was moving away from the influence of Wagner (and his power as a father figure), Nietzsche explains how he turned the fateful legacy from his father to his advantage.

> Now that *bad* inheritance from my father's side came to my assistance in a way I cannot admire enough, and just at the right time—basically a predestination to an early death. Sickness *gradually liberated me, cleaning me out....* Sickness likewise gave me the right to a complete change in my habits...it bestowed on me the *compulsion* to lie still, to be idle, to wait and be patient...but all that means to think! (*EH*: "Human, All-Too-Human" 4)

This is a fine example of Nietzsche's technique of turning fateful necessity to his advantage, of creating value from what at first appears an utter liability. He owes his being the thinker he is to the sickness inherited from his father.

But if his father was in fact "prone to illusion and lying," to what extent was Nietzsche's mother "childish and irascible"?

MOTHER AND CHILD

Usually a mother loves herself in her son more than the son himself. (*HAH* I: 385)

At the age of 11, Fritz began the practice of presenting his mother with a collection of his poems for her birthday.[35] The first poem begins with effusive good wishes and ends with an ardent declaration of filial love:

> I love you oh so much that I want to squeeze you flat
> But perhaps I'd better not, since you might not relish that.
> Yet there's more I'd like to give you
> Which the last two lines will point to.
> Perhaps you'd like to know
> What else I want and how.
> I so much want to kiss you
> That I'll do it here and now.

---

[34] Some late remarks from *Ecce Homo* constitute a striking exception, though the hyperbole suggests that they are perhaps not to be taken at face value: "One is related least of all to one's parents...The higher natures have their origins infinitely farther back...I don't understand how, but Julius Caesar could be my father—or Alexander, this embodiment of Dionysos." (*EH*: "Why I Am So Wise" 4)

[35] The group of nine poems is in *KGW* I.1: 115–25.

The passion sounds genuine—if unusual for an 11-year-old to put in writing. The opening lines certainly made a powerful impression on Franziska, for her nephew reports that she remembered them until the end of her life (Oehler 1940: 59). Three years earlier she had remarked in a letter on Fritz's need for affection by saying: "Whenever he can he sits—just imagine—in my lap, or else stands behind me on a chair in order to hug me and kiss me." (Franziska Nietzsche, journal, cited in Goch 1994: 179–80; letter to Edmund Oehler, November 1, 1852, *GSA* 100/1110) The "just imagine" suggests that it was not customary for a boy just turned 8 to enjoy such physical closeness. At any rate, the lack of subsequent remarks on the topic probably indicates a gradual reduction of affectionate behavior on the part of the mother.

Along with the reasonable project of reducing his dependence on her, Franziska apparently began to impose her will on him with greater force. It was also to make up for the loss of the father, who could have exemplified the stern, manly virtues to which a son must aspire, that she concealed her maternal tenderness. Under pressure from the Nietzsche family to ensure that Fritz grow up to be a paragon among pastors, she found herself assuming more masculine postures in order to play the role of strict disciplinarian.[36] By withholding the natural expression of love in closeness and intimacy, she created a distance from which she could better keep the son's nose to the grindstone of schoolwork, music practice, Bible reading, and the refinement of proper manners.

A letter Franziska wrote while she was away visiting relatives indicates the extremity of her desire to exert control and ensure that order prevailed even—or especially—in her own absence.

> Be a good boy and take your umbrella when it rains and if you do happen to get wet then make sure to change your clothes as soon as you get home, for you know that it's not good for you if you don't. All your things are lying on the bed near the wardrobe, and for daily wear put on your *old jacket and light gray trousers*, which you have in Pobles with you, as well as your *waistcoat*, if it's *cold* wear the *thicker gray trousers* and on Sundays *the good coat as well* which you can get Frau Ludwig to clean for you with a piece of flannel and hot water, and make sure it's well brushed before and after wearing it; and for special occasions there's your good jacket and waistcoat [and so forth, concerning underwear, shirt collars, etc.]...Always be sure to shut whatever you've opened and lock the room when you go to school....Take this sheet of paper with you and put it in your desk and read it over now and then or check it to make sure that you're doing everything it says for these are "*rules of conduct*." (Letter to Fritz of June 10, 1857, *KGB* I.1: 321–2)

These instructions, so breathlessly punctuated and frantically over-underlined, are addressed to a boy of 12—yet since he was by all accounts remarkably mature, serious, and self-disciplined for his age, the nagging certainly seems excessive.

With no alternative but to tolerate her attempts to regulate his life down to its tiniest details, Fritz developed an obedient conformity on the outside while maintaining a private world of phantasy within, where he could enjoy a measure of autonomy and freedom. Emotional energy that had flowed toward the mother when she was more demonstrative of her affections was now, in this phase of withholding, being turned back onto the boy's

---

[36] There is an insightful discussion of Franziska's emotional attitude toward her son during the period in Goch 1994: 188–90.

own psyche. The reduction of maternal love, especially with the father absent, would feed the already anxious son's anxiety—though the increase in psychic energy as a result of the retroflection of his emotions would nourish his imaginative life. At the same time, lacking a father with whom to vie for the mother's love, Fritz still found himself confronted with "paternal" authority emanating from the formidable Franziska. But since he couldn't oppose this openly, he tended to turn his combative energies back upon himself in the form of harsh self-discipline.

In the summer of 1858 the family, now consisting of only Franziska and her two surviving children, moved again, to a larger house at Weingarten 18 in Naumburg, which would remain the Nietzsche family home until her death forty years later. The children spent most of the summer with the grandparents in Pobles, and Elisabeth reports that Fritz and their grandfather enjoyed especially frequent and intense conversations that year. But even though David Ernst Oehler, who was renowned for his pedagogical expertise, played such an important part in Fritz's intellectual development, his wishes concerning the grandson's further education were not to be fulfilled (Förster-Nietzsche 1912: vol. 1, p. 34).[37]

The grandfather had always thought that the best training for the pastorship was the illustrious Waisenhaus, a school in the city of Halle which gave full scholarships to boys who were orphaned. Franziska had been against this because it would mean "giving up the dear boy at the age of ten," which she thought was painfully early. She was able to prevail against her father by holding out the possibility that Fritz would win a scholarship at Schulpforta, which was one of the very best schools in Europe at the time, and was situated by fortunate happenstance just outside Naumburg, an hour's walk from the new family home (Franziska's journal, *GSA* 100/850, and letter to Adalbert Oehler, June 24, 1895; cited in Goch 1994: 187, 186).[38] And indeed, whether as a result of a visit from a Pforta inspector to the school Fritz was attending or general word-of-mouth reports of the boy's unusual abilities, Franziska received a letter announcing an award.

The abundant correspondence that has survived from Fritz's first months at Pforta exhibit intensely ambivalent feelings. In the first letter to his mother, written on his first day at school, he writes that he is feeling well so far but asks what "well" can mean "in a strange place." Five days later, he writes, "Just wait, the homesickness will soon come!"; and after a further month, "I almost have the impression that homesickness is catching up with me: there are already a few signs of it." (Letters of October 6, October 11, mid-November 1858, *KSB* 1: 16, 20, 29) He clearly thinks that he ought to be feeling homesick, but is very much immersed in the new world of the school. Nevertheless, these early letters are full of complaints that he is sending many letters but receiving hardly any in return: why isn't his mother writing more often—and Elisabeth, and Wilhelm, and Gustav? He feels abandoned and is afraid that they have forgotten him already. He even writes to his mother on the third day, "*Don't forget my birthday!*"—an inconceivable eventuality in the Nietzsche family. But then two days later he is more relaxed, and jokingly requests "around 40 letters and 20 boxes and packages full of presents."

---

[37] On David Oehler as a pedagogue, see Pernet 1989: 46 n. 12 and Goch 1994: 376 n. 244.
[38] See also Bohley 1987: 193–4.

But the most remarkable phenomenon is the bizarre game he and his mother play concerning things he needs her to send him urgently. As soon as he arrives at Pforta he writes listing numerous items that weren't in his trunk—"inkstand, pens, soap and several other small things"—and asks for, in addition, chocolate powder and a geography textbook. Three days later he adds to the list: a pair of strong eyeglasses, his boot-jack, a small brown jug, sewing kit, and scissors, ink, a dozen writing tablets, and dress-shoes. In a second letter written the same day, he sums everything up in a large list, adding "drawing pins" and an instruction to "see the first and second letters." (Letters of October 6 and October 9, 1858, *KSB* 1: 16–19)

After four weeks and several more letters, he is *still* requesting ink, sewing kit, and scissors. The situation is all the more strange because there was an efficient postal service between Schulpforta and Naumburg—hampers of laundry, a frequent topic in the letters, were sent back and forth every week—and Fritz even met his family in Altenburg (a village halfway to Naumburg) on the second Sunday after leaving home. One has to wonder whether Franziska, usually so efficient, was at some level intentionally forgetting to send things, as a way of maintaining her son's dependence on her. Fritz certainly seems, through his insistent and urgent demands, to be seeking confirmation of maternal love. (Letters of October 23, 1858; August 20, 1860; May 4, November 26, 1861; April 19, 1860; November 25, 1860; May–June 1859; *KSB* 1: 21, 120, 157, 186, 100, 131, 66)

In his second year at Pforta he begins to keep a journal, though he gives up after the first month. The notes and letters suggest that he is suffering more from homesickness this year than before. The first entry in the journal consists of a five-point plan developed by his tutor, Professor Robert Buddensieg, for dealing with this affliction. One point, naturally, is: "If we study hard, sad thoughts will melt away"; while the final recommendation reads: "If none of this works, then pray to God our Lord." (*KGW* I.2: 98) The homesickness seems more intense than would be expected in such a situation, which is that the now 15-year-old boy is only an hour's walk away from his family and friends, and that he often meets his mother and sister on weekends and always goes home for the holidays. Franziska finds him overly dependent on her, though she is at the same time glad to be loved by the most important man in her life. Fritz finds her emotional reserve disconcerting, yet at the same time he chafes at her possessiveness. Even after he moves away from home to university, this pattern persists in a less pronounced form.

Franziska's possessiveness was all the stronger for having a double origin. Having suffered from her husband's lack of love for her (by comparison with his loving dependence on his mother), she wanted to ensure that her one surviving son would always fully reciprocate her maternal love for him. Moreover, since she had undergone unusual pains to bring him into the world and sustain him during his infant helplessness, she would always consider him basically her own property—as Nietzsche himself eventually came to realize.

Anticipating Freud's ideas about the "mother imago" and Jung's ideas about the links between the image of the mother and the "anima," Nietzsche offers the following piece of psychological wisdom:

> From the Mother.—Every man carries in him an image of woman derived from the mother: this is what determines whether he will revere women or disparage them or else be in general indifferent toward them. (*HAH* I: 380)

In his own case, he tended to be attracted by, as well as attract, women older than himself, and especially women who were already married, and thus in some sense "safe."[39] He would be correspondingly awkward around women of his own age or younger. He also had a tendency, of which he was aware, to project his mother's possessiveness onto other women in his orbit, to whom he would then not want to get too close:

> The Golden Cradle.—The free spirit will always breathe more easily when he finally decides to shake off that motherly caring for and watching over that is practised by the women around him. (*HAH* I: 429)

Yet Nietzsche let himself be cared for by his mother, depending on her maternal kindness for as long as it suited him. And since he was the first son, whose genius was confirmed by his appointment as professor of classics at the age of only 24, Franziska deferred to his authority and indulged his whims.

Two events caused ruptures in their over-close relationship: first Nietzsche's explicit repudiation of Christianity (beginning with the publication of *Human, All Too Human* in 1878), and then his brief but ardent encounter with the beautiful Lou Salomé in 1882. Since Franziska remained resolutely devout until the end of her long life, she was never able to accept or understand her son's apostasy and regarded it as some kind of mental aberration. Despite his mother's once calling him in a fit of rage "a disgrace to [his] father's grave," they would always become reconciled after such ruptures, though at a lesser degree of closeness than before.[40]

In later life Nietzsche would express irritation at his mother's narrow range of experience, but her patient support of him, especially after his mental collapse, evidences a remarkable ability on her part to bear the burdens of life with competent tolerance—a virtue for which he was not as grateful as he could have been. Shortly before his mental collapse he put it most cruelly:

> If I look for the most profound opposite of myself, for a boundless commonness of instinct, I always find my mother and sister—to believe myself related to such rabble would be blasphemy against my divinity. [*EH*: "Why I Am So Wise" 3]

It turned out, of course, that in spite of the enormous drain on her energies that the task of taking care of him entailed, she prevailed in the end. A magnificent photograph from 1891 shows Franziska grasping with both hands the right arm of her debilitated son and wearing a wistful expression: "Here we are again, together, at long last."

BROTHER AND SISTER

> I must confess that the deepest objection to "eternal recurrence," my genuinely abyssal thought, is always mother and sister. (*EH*: "Why I Am So Wise" 3)[41]

---

[39] For example, Sophie Ritschl, Cosima von Bülow, and Ida Overbeck.

[40] Alluded to in a letter to Franz Overbeck, September 9, 1882, *KSB* 6: 256, and explained in *KGB* III.7/1: 278.

[41] The earlier English translations do not have this passage, which was suppressed by Elisabeth in earlier German editions.

Since Nietzsche's relations with his sister have been well discussed in the secondary literature in English, the treatment here can be brief.[42] His admirers love to hate the perfidious Elisabeth, who for her own nefarious ends sold her brother out to the fascists. But although she lacked his genius, Elisabeth Nietzsche was an extremely clever, capable, and astute woman, and the circumstances do not clearly warrant moral condemnation of her betrayal of his ideas and ideals.

Born in 1846, almost two years after her brother, Elisabeth lived much of her early life in his shadow. He was the first son, strong and bright, and she was the little sister, often permitted to accompany him in a subservient role—though generally not when he was with his two best friends, Gustav and Wilhelm, both of whom were bright and capable boys too. Her devotion to her elder brother had one very happy consequence: thanks to her habit of collecting every piece of paper to which Fritz applied a pen until he went to university, we have an unusually full record of Nietzsche's thoughts and feelings from an early age. She was also in a privileged position, when older, to write a biography: in fact she wrote several, though none of them is very reliable.

While Nietzsche came to dislike his home town of Naumburg intensely because of its pretentions to good, solid virtues and pursuit of bourgeois comforts, his sister liked the place for precisely those reasons. With almost proprietary pride she describes Naumburg as "a thoroughly Christian, conservative city, loyal to the King and a pillar of the throne and the church." (Förster-Nietzsche 1912: vol. 1, p. 22) But in fact Naumburg was fairly liberal politically at the time they were growing up there: the discrepancy points up Elisabeth's tendency to look on the conservative side and see what she wants to see.

Like her mother, Elisabeth was disappointed when Nietzsche decided to abandon the study of theology at the University of Bonn and switch to classical philology instead. By way of explanation he wrote to her, in a sentence that gives concise expression to the difference between religion and philosophy: "This is where the ways of human beings diverge: if what you want is happiness and peace of soul, then believe; if you want to be a disciple of truth, then search." (Letter of June 11, 1865, *KSB* 2: 61) She again followed her mother in deploring Nietzsche's attacks on Christianity in *Human, All Too Human*, though perhaps her greatest concern here was not to jeopardize her friendship with Richard Wagner and Cosima, with whom she had become quite close.

But the greatest break with her brother came as a result of the Lou Salomé fiasco, and indeed Elisabeth's devious machinations behind the scenes of this affair were responsible for the deepest hurt her brother ever experienced. Underestimating the intensity of his sister's dependence on him (just as he preferred to ignore his own dependence on her), Nietzsche naively supposed that he could get Elisabeth to befriend Lou and thereby improve his chances of successfully wooing the brilliant and beautiful 20-year-old from Russia. Instead Elisabeth became an implacable enemy and misrepresented, to her mother and others, her brother's plans for a Platonic *ménage à trois* with Lou and Paul Rée as a debauched project for living in sin. Nietzsche's letters from the period show him driven dangerously close to the edge emotionally, but he came through—in part because he managed to direct his energies into composing his masterpiece, *Thus Spoke Zarathustra*.

[42] See Peters 1977, Macintyre 1992, and Diethe 1996 and 2003.

A third ground of estrangement between the Nietzsche siblings was Elisabeth's choice of a husband: the anti-Semitic colonialist Bernhard Förster. Revolted by what the man stood for, Nietzsche tried his best to dissuade Elisabeth from associating with him and getting involved in his ill-conceived project for a "pure Aryan" colony in Paraguay. In 1885, around the time of their wedding, which Nietzsche declined to attend, he wrote to his sister:

> It is one of the puzzles I've thought about a number of times: how can it be possible for us to be blood relatives....
> If I was angry with you, it was because you forced me to give up the only people with whom I could speak without hypocrisy. Now—I am alone. (Draft of letter of March 1885, *KSB* 7: 24–5)

Beyond Nietzsche's concern for his sister's welfare, as well as the Nietzsche family's reputation, was the desire to retain some of the emotional closeness he and his sister had enjoyed. But Elisabeth was not to be deterred, and so Nietzsche eventually had to make the break: "Everything has deserted me in the meantime: even [my sister] has jumped away and gone off to join the anti-Semites (which is about the most radical way of 'finishing' with me that there is)." (Letter to Elisabeth, June 5, 1887, *KSB* 8: 83)

Bernhard Förster became embroiled in a scandal concerning the colony in Paraguay, went bankrupt, and committed suicide in a hotel room in June 1889. By this time Nietzsche had already undergone the mental collapse from which he would never recover. Elisabeth returned to Germany and began the project of making "the mad philosopher" famous. In her ruthless determination to turn her brother's legacy to her own financial advantage, she created a bogus book by Nietzsche, *The Will to Power*, that gave the impression that his philosophy was moving toward reactionary ideas that were close to her own. She lived long enough—to the age of 94—to become acquainted with Mussolini, whose politics were close to her own, and she even presented her brother's walking stick to Hitler when he visited the Nietzsche Archive that she had established in Weimar.

These acts of perfidy were no doubt motivated by a desire for revenge: this would pay him back for his lack of gratitude for all the sacrifices she had made for him over the decades. Harsh justice, but Elisabeth did sacrifice much of the first part of her life for his sake, and Nietzsche could certainly have expressed more thanks to her for that. She turned out to be (like the rest of us) human, all too human, and her example demonstrates the power of one sibling to injure another—even posthumously.

One of Nietzsche's last words on his family, written shortly before his mental collapse (though in a text that's deliberately rich in hyperbole), may not be representative of his feelings about the two women closest to him, but its vehemence is striking.

> The treatment I've been receiving at the hands of my mother and sister, up to this moment, fills me with unspeakable horror: here a veritable Hell-machine is at work, with unfailing certainty over the moment when I can be mortally wounded—in my highest moments...for there is no energy for defending against these poisonous worms....The physiological contiguity enables such a "pre-established disharmony." (*EH*: "Why I Am So Wise" 3)

His long-suffering mother surely doesn't deserve such harshness, for she always meant well and often did her son good. Elisabeth's case is more problematic, since she surely did mean her brother ill at times and often caused him deliberate harm.

She was especially effectual in destroying his reputation: to this day many people think they know that Nietzsche prepared the philosophical ground for Nazism, and was on top of that a misogynist. Had he expressed more gratitude for Elisabeth's care and attention early on, she might not have turned so vindictive and he could perhaps have escaped being so grossly misunderstood. It is sad that he turned out to be so inept in the familial relation that was to affect him the most, even after his death—and for at least a century.

BIBLIOGRAPHY

(A) Works by Nietzsche

GAB   *Friedrich Nietzsche, Historisch-Kritische Gesamtausgabe, Briefe*, ed. K. Schlechta (4 vols). Munich: Beck, 1933.

KGB   *Nietzsche Briefwechsel: Kritische Gesamtausgabe*, ed. G. Colli and M. Montinari (25 vols). Berlin: De Gruyter, 1967–2006.

KGW   *Nietzsche Werke: Kritische Gesamtausgabe*, ed. G. Colli and M. Montinari (24 vols + 4 CDs). Berlin: De Gruyter, 1967–2006.

KSA   *Sämtliche Werke: Kritische Studienausgabe in 15 Einzelbänden*, ed. G. Colli and M. Montinari (15 vols). Berlin: De Gruyter, 1988.

KSB   *Sämtliche Briefe: Kritische Studienausgabe*, ed. G. Colli and M. Montinari (8 vols). Berlin: De Gruyter, 1986.

Z   *Thus Spoke Zarathustra*, ed. and trans. Graham Parkes. New York: Oxford University Press, 2005.

(B) Other Primary Works

Friedrich Nietzsche: Chronik in Bildern und Texten, Stiftung Weimarer Klassik. Munich and Vienna: Hanser, 2000.

GSA   Goethe-Schiller-Archiv, Weimar.

(C) Other Works Cited

Benders, Raymond and Oettermann, Stephan. 2000. *Friedrich Nietzsche: Chronik in Bildern und Texten*. Munich: Deutscher Taschenbuch Verlag.

Bohley, Reiner. 1980. "Nietzsches Taufe," *Nietzsche-Studien* 9: 383–405.

Bohley, Reiner. 1987. "Nietzsches christliche Erziehung," *Nietzsche-Studien* 16: 164–96.

Diethe, Carol. 1996. *Nietzsche's Women: Beyond the Whip*. Berlin: De Gruyter.

Diethe, Carol. 2003. *Nietzsche's Sister and the Will to Power*. Urbana and Chicago: University of Illinois Press.

Förster-Nietzsche, Elisabeth. 1912. *The Life of Nietzsche*, vol. 1: *The Young Nietzsche*. New York: Sturgis & Walton.

Gabel, Gernot U. and Jagenberg, Carl Helmuth (eds). 1994. *Der entmündigte Philosoph: Briefe von Franziska Nietzsche an Adalbert Oehler*. Hürth: Gabel Verlag.

Goch, Klaus. 1994. *Franziska Nietzsche*. Frankfurt and Leipzig: Suhrkamp.

Goch, Klaus. 2000. *Nietzsches Vater*. Berlin: Akademie Verlag.

Hollingdale, R. J. 1965. *Nietzsche: The Man and His Philosophy*. London: Routledge.

Janz, Curt Paul. 1981. *Nietzsche Biographie* (3 vols). Munich: Carl Hanser Verlag.

Macintyre, Ben. 1992. *Forgotten Fatherland: The Search for Elisabeth Nietzsche.* London: Farrar, Straus & Giroux.

Miller, Alice. 1991. "Friedrich Nietzsche: The Struggle Against the Truth," in *The Untouched Key: Tracing Childhood Trauma in Creativity and Destructiveness.* New York: Anchor Doubleday, 71–134.

Oehler, Adalbert. n.d. "Erinnerungen meines Lebens." Unpublished manuscript.

Oehler, Adalbert. 1940. *Nietzsches Mutter.* Munich: C. H. Beck.

Oehler, Max. 1939. *Zur Ahnentafel Nietzsches.* Weimar: R. Wagner.

Parkes, Graham. 1994. *Composing the Soul: Reaches of Nietzsche's Psychology.* Chicago: University of Chicago Press.

Pernet, Martin. 1989. *Das Christentum im Leben des jungen Friedrich Nietzsche.* Opladen: Westdeutscher Verlag.

Peters, H. F. 1977. *Zarathustra's Sister: The Case of Elisabeth and Friedrich Nietzsche.* New York: Crown Publishers.

Schmidt, Hermann Josef. 1991. *Nietzsche Absconditus, oder Spurenlesen bei Nietzsche, Teile 1–3.* Berlin-Aschaffenburg: IBDK Verlag.

Volz, Pia Daniela. 1994. *Nietzsche im Labyrinth seiner Krankheiten.* Würzburg: Königshausen & Neumann.

CHAPTER 2

···

NIETZSCHE AND WOMEN

···

JULIAN YOUNG

ON 10 July 1874, the committee of the combined faculties of the University of Basle met in order to decide the question of admitting women to the university. The meeting was occasioned by the application of a Fräulein Rubinstein from Leipzig to enrol as a doctoral student in the classics department. Though the matter would normally have been decided by the humanities ('philosophical') faculty alone, it was felt that this was an issue of such moment that only the university as a whole could decide it. After a two-hour discussion the committee voted six to four against admission. The meeting must have been a heated one since the dissenting four demanded that their dissent be explicitly recorded (Janz 1978: vol. I, pp. 624–5).

In spite of his hero, the great historian Jacob Burckhardt, being on the other side, one of the dissenters was the then Dean of Humanities Friedrich Nietzsche. This suggests that Nietzsche's long-established reputation as one of philosophy's most virulent anti-feminists and misogynists—as the 'philosopher of the whip'—merits at least a second look.

The 'women's question', the demand for female equality, was much in the air during Nietzsche's productive life. And since a higher education was the avenue to both economic equality and convincing a sceptical male world of a woman's capacity to cast a meaningful vote, its focus was on access to university education.

In continental Europe, female emancipation first became an issue during the workers' uprising of 1848. For the women who supported the uprising, the demand for women's rights was inseparable from the demand for workers' rights. Among such women was the socialist and pioneering feminist, Malwida von Meysenbug. Meysenbug's account of her rejection of her aristocratic upbringing, her attempt to acquire an education and later to set up a women's university, recorded in her autobiography, *Memoirs of a Female Idealist*, became a seminal text for the next generation of feminists. Nietzsche first met her at the inaugural Bayreuth Festival of 1876. (On account of Wagner's early socialism—he, too, had been involved in the 1848 uprising—Meysenbug was a keen Wagnerian.) Nietzsche greatly admired Meysenbug's moral idealism. For the rest of his life, up until his mental collapse, she became his 'motherly friend', the most important of his several adopted mothers.

In the autumn of 1876 Meysenbug rented the second and third floors of the Villa Rubinacci in Sorrento. Nestling beneath pine-covered hills[1] and surrounded by lemon groves, the villa's front balconies opened out onto breathtaking views over the Bay of Naples and towards Vesuvius in

---

[1] 'Pines which listen, deepening further...the southern stillness and the midday quiet' (*KSA* 8: 32 [19]) as Nietzsche described them in those pre-Lambretta days.

the distance. Accompanied by his close friend Paul Rée and the Basle law student and aspirant novelist Albert Brenner, Nietzsche joined Meysenbug in this idyllic spot at the end of October for a six-month stay. Working, walking, eating, and reading together, the four friends established the prototype for Nietzsche's lifelong ambition: the creation of 'monasteries for free spirits' (*KGB* II.5: 471), communes of artists and thinkers who, rejecting the stuffy and outmoded conventions of Victorian morality, would create new and more successful ways of living. Exemplifying these forms of life and becoming thereby 'educators' of their generation, the inhabitants of these 'monasteries' were to be, in the language of *The Gay Science*, 'the seed bearers of the future, the spiritual colonizers and shapers of new states and communities' (*GS* 23). The 'monasteries' were intended to embrace both men and women. Meysenbug reports that the Sorrento experiment in communal living went so well that it led them to develop the idea of

> a kind of mission house for adults of both sexes to have a free development of the noblest spiritual life, so that they could then go forth into the world to sow the seeds of a new spiritualized culture...Nietzsche and Rée immediately offered their services as teachers. I was convinced I could attract many women students...in order to develop them into the noblest representatives of the emancipation of women. (Janz 1978: vol. I, p. 750)

Nietzsche's work-in-progress in Sorrento was *Human, All Too Human*, his first published work to make 'the women's question' an explicit topic. What made it an issue, of course, was that, living with Meysenbug, he was brought face to face with the aspirations of the emancipationists. Here are some of the things he says in that work: 'The perfect woman is a higher type than the perfect man' (*HAH* I: 377); it is a deplorable state of affairs that 'for so long, higher education was available to women only through love-affairs and marriage' (*HAH* I: 259); 'Women can, through...education,...acquire all the male strengths and virtues' (*HAH* I: 425); it is 'noble and free-thinking women who set themselves the task of the education and elevation of the female sex' (*HAH* I: 424).

The Wanderer and His Shadow, which became part of the second volume of *Human, All Too Human*, contains further remarks on women. 'Many a woman has the spirit of sacrifice and can no longer enjoy life when her husband refuses to sacrifice her' (*HAH* III: 272). 'What women now think of the male mind can be divined from the fact that when they adorn themselves, the last thing they have in mind is to emphasize the intellectual qualities of their face'. They prefer, rather, to present an appearance of 'lustful sensuality and mindlessness...Their conviction that men are terrified of intellectual women is so firm that they are even ready to deny they have any sharpness of mind and deliberately impose on themselves a reputation for *shortsightedness*' (of being a 'dumb blonde' in other words) (*HAH* III: 270). What women say among themselves, however, is 'stupid as a man'. And that indeed is where stupidity belongs: 'stupidity is, in woman, the *unwomanly*' (*HAH* III: 273).

The Wanderer and His Shadow appeared in December 1879, a year after the original *Human, All Too Human*.[2] On account of Nietzsche's poor eyesight, the preparation of a print-ready copy of the manuscript fell to his friend and former student, Heinrich Köselitz ('Peter Gast'). After reading through the manuscript in preparation for his task, Köselitz, as was his habit at the time, suggested some alterations:

---

[2] The second edition of *Human, All Too Human* appeared in 1886. The original work became Volume I, *Assorted Opinions and Maxims* and *The Wanderer and His Shadow* combined to form Volume II.

You write, 'The domestic animal which understood how to create itself a right within humanity is the woman'. The comparison of women with domestic animals is unworthy and unphilosophical; woman are as little animals as men are women. Women have, particularly in intellectual matters, advantages which men could do well to emulate. (*KGB* II.6/2)[3]

Nietzsche replies:

Many thanks for picking me up on that. I do not wish to present the appearance of diminishing women and have cut out the whole passage. What is true is that, originally, only men were held to be human beings… the recognition of women as human beings was a great moral advance. My— or our—view of women should not be brought into contact with the word 'domestic animal'.—I was judging according to [the travel writer, Sir Henry Veel] Huntley's description of the situation of women in primitive tribes. (*KGB* II.5: 900)

When we compare this with Schopenhauer's view, more representative of the age, that

women are qualified to be the nurses and governesses of our earliest childhood by the very fact that they are themselves childish, trifling, and short-sighted ['short-sightedness' again!], in a word, are all their lives grown up children; a kind of intermediate stage between the child and the man, who is the human being in the real sense, (Schopenhauer 1974: vol. II, pp. 614–15)

we can see that the exchange actually does considerable credit to both men.

Taking the above quotations as a whole, four things seem to be true of Nietzsche's attitude to women during his 'positivist' period. First, women are at least as intelligent, and probably more so, than men (a claim that may now be beginning to receive empirical support). Second, he has deep sympathy, indeed empathy, for the plight of women forced to appear 'short-sighted' by a paternalistic society and a corresponding contempt for a male culture unable to acknowledge the intelligence of women. Third, he has deep respect for emancipationists, for 'noble and free-thinking' women like Malwida von Meysenbug. And fourth, he respects women in general. There is no trace of misogyny in the works of the 1870s.

Can we, then, go so far as to describe the 'positivist' Nietzsche as a 'feminist'? It is clear that he supports equality of educational opportunity. And so he certainly *should* have supported economic and political equality, since a society which educates people to high achievement, but denies them the opportunity to exercise the capacities they have acquired, cultivates discontent and dissent. On the question of the vote Nietzsche is hesitant. There is, he says, 'no little danger' in entrusting politics to women since they are, by disposition, personal rather than objective. Yet he immediately emphasizes that, far from this being a comment on 'the eternal feminine' (a favourite topic, we shall see, in his later works), it is merely an observation on 'how things are at present' in a society where female dispositions are moulded by male chauvinism. In time, he says, 'all this may change' (*HAH* I: 416). It seems to me, therefore, that during his positivist period and indeed up until 1882 (neither *Daybreak* not *The Gay Science* reveals any major change in his attitude to women[4]), Nietzsche can reasonably be described—certainly by nineteenth-century standards—as not only an admirer of feminists but as himself an at least cautious feminist.

* * *

[3] 'To Nietzsche 1252'.

[4] Section 346 of *Daybreak* says this of 'misogyny': the man who says, 'among men', 'woman is the enemy' hates his own 'immoderate drive' and so hates his dependence on the 'means' of satisfying it. Misogyny, in other words, is really the sickness of *self*-hatred.

With the publication of the first part of *Thus Spoke Zarathustra* in August 1883, however, all this changes. In startling contrast to the earlier stance, we now get the 'whip' remarks—remarks, we shall see, deliberately designed to offend the emancipationists. Zarathustra (who often plays Mr Hyde to Nietzsche's Dr Jekyll) tells a 'little old woman' that 'Everything about women has pregnancy as its... solution', that 'a man should be brought up for war and a woman for the recreation of the warrior', that 'the happiness of a man is ' "I will" '... of a woman, ' "he wills" ' '. And so on. The old (and so, we are led to suppose, wise) woman replies with her infamous 'little truth': 'You are going to women? Then don't forget the whip'. (Z I: 'Of Old and Young Women') (This remark is often misunderstood. The allusion is probably to Wagner's Fricka, who has a literal whip with which to drive her chariot and holds the whip-hand over her husband, Wotan, supposedly the supreme god but actually thwarted and controlled by his wife. The remark is thus probably *not* intended to advise men to take the whip to their women. Whichever way it is read, however, actually makes little difference. If women are to be whipped that must be because they demand firm, manly discipline. But if we are being warned that, given half a chance, they will upset the natural order of things by seizing the whip-hand, then, again, they demand firm, manly discipline.)

Three years after *Zarathustra*, in *Beyond Good and Evil*, things get even worse. Four themes now emerge.

(1) 'Woman *as such*', the 'eternal feminine', lacks the capacity for 'manly' pursuits. Women have no concern for truth and so no capacity for 'science'—their great talent is in the (slavish) practice of lying. They have no capacity for 'enlightenment' (rational objectivity) and should hold their tongues on religion and politics—and on the question of 'woman as such'. Even women themselves admit that there has never been a female mind as profound as a man's. ('How come there have never been any great women composers or philosophers?', in other words.) Even women admit that the female heart can never be as just as a man's (and so women are unfit to rule either a nation or a family) (*BGE* 232). It follows from all this that the proper role for women is the traditional one of bearing and bringing up children (*BGE* 239). A woman scholar has something wrong with her sexuality (*BGE* 144).

(2) Women are terrifying and potentially barbaric. 'Woman' is 'the beautiful and dangerous cat'. Inside her glove are her 'tiger's claws'. In love and revenge women are terrifying ('Hell hath no fury like...') (*BGE* 239, 131).

(3) Women must be subject to tight masculine control. This follows immediately from their capacity for barbaric terrorism. The oriental treatment of women as 'property' is thus 'enormously rational'.[5] Woman must not lose her 'fear of man' (*BGE* 238).

(4) For all these reasons, the demands for 'female self-determination' are manifestly 'stupid' as are the emancipationists themselves: they fail to realize that setting forth Madame de Staël or George Sand as examples of how fine an emancipated woman can be is counter-productive since men simply find such women comical—*counter-examples* to the emancipationist's claims (*BGE* 233, 239).

---

[5] This affinity with Islam extends to Nietzsche's political theory. Inspired, like Ayatollah Khomeini, by Plato's *Republic*, Nietzsche's ideal state, I argue (Young 2010), resembles an Islamic state more closely than any other existing political structure.

What we see, then, is that by 1883 and even more strongly by 1886, Nietzsche has moved from a position of general support for emancipationist demands to violent, total, and *abusive* hostility: formerly 'noble and free thinking', emancipationists are, by 1886, 'pedantic, superficial and schoolmarmish, as well as narrow-mindedly arrogant, presumptuous, and lacking in restraint'. Once they emerge from their traditional role of servitude, ' "the eternal tedium of woman" (which they all have in abundance)' becomes unmistakable (*BGE* 232). The later Nietzsche is thus not only an anti-feminist but also, at least on paper, a misogynist. The question is, therefore: what happened between 1882 and 1883 to cause this dramatic change of attitude? One possible explanation has to do with his attack on what he calls 'the democratic enlightenment', an attack that first begins to appear in his notebooks in early 1883 (*KSA* 10: 9 [29]).

* * *

Christian ('slave') morality, Nietzsche holds, was a disaster. For in preaching the equality of all souls before God it elevated the 'sheep' or 'herd animal' to the ideal. The result was to undermine and eventually destroy the self-confidence of the exceptional individual, to make him feel ashamed of being a 'tall poppy'. Yet the very survival of our culture depends on such individuals: only the creative non-conformist who rejects existing morality and creates a new form of life, can enable us to thrive in an ever-changing environment. God, of course, is now 'dead': Christian metaphysics has become unbelievable for modern, educated Europeans. But this is by no means the end of Christian morality since that lives on (minus its metaphysics) in the disguise of those 'modern ideas' that constitute the 'democratic enlightenment' (*BGE* 10, 44, 202, 203, 242, 253, 260).

What Nietzsche calls the 'democratic enlightenment' stems from Rousseau and the French Revolution, so that he sometimes offers 'French ideas' as a synonym (*BGE* 253; *KSA* 11: 25 [178]). Under the term he includes political democracy, universal suffrage (*BGE* 202; *KSA* 11: 25 [174, 211]), 'utilitarianism' (conceived as a movement of social emancipation rather than a philosophical theory), trades unions and 'socialism' (a term that covers both social democracy and communism) (*BGE* 202). All these movements are applications of the doctrine of 'equal rights', which makes them the 'heirs' (*BGE* 202) to Christianity's doctrine of the equality of all souls before God (*BGE* 44). This being so, the democratic enlightenment is as damaging to the appearance of the exceptional individual as is explicitly Christian morality. Its effect is to destroy hierarchy, to 'level' everyone down to the same low mean. In the potential higher type, it produces a 'pathological enervation', kills the will to rise above the average (*BGE* 201, 202, 44). Democratization produces a society of herd animals, who, because the exceptional individual is nowhere to be seen, threaten to become the 'last men' of *Zarathustra*'s Prologue.

Beyond Good and Evil claims that the emancipationist movement, the demand for 'equal rights' for women, is a particular instance of the democratic enlightenment's demand of equal rights for everyone (*BGE* 239). It is, therefore, an aspect of the general destruction of the 'pathos of distance' (*BGE* 257) and hence of the excellence that is the life blood of any culture. This gives us one possible explanation of the transformation of Nietzsche's attitude to women: he changed his mind on the question of emancipation in 1883 because that was when he first saw that the demand for equal rights for women was an aspect of the general demand for equal rights and thus a disguised perpetuation of Christian morality. Nietzsche changed his mind because he saw that feminism was part of the general 'levelling' of European culture.

There are, however, three things wrong with this explanation of Nietzsche's 'turn'. The first is that the 1883 attack on the emancipationists in Part I of *Zarathustra* makes no attempt to connect itself to any general attack on 'levelling'. It is true that in Part II which appeared in the following year, there is a strident attack on the 'tarantulas' who 'preach equality' and thereby poison the body politic (*Z* II: 'Of the Tarantulas'). But no attempt is made to number emancipationists among the tarantulas, indeed the discussion is conceived in exclusively masculine terms: the driving force is the sons' 'envy' of the fathers. So it looks as though the absorption of the attack on feminism into the attack on the 'preachers of equality' first happens in *Beyond Good and Evil*—three years, that is to say, *after* the initial 'turn' against women.

The second point is that the rejection of democratization in all its forms does not, in fact, logically imply a rejection of feminism at all. This was realized by Nietzsche's friend, Meta von Salis. For, as we shall see, though a passionate feminist, the aristocratic von Salis was every bit as 'elitist' and anti-democratic as Nietzsche. Her only disagreement with him consisted in her insistence that exceptionality is not gender-specific, that there can be exceptional women as well as exceptional men. What von Salis saw, in other words, was that the demand for equal rights *for women* does not at all entail the demand for equal rights *for everyone*. If Nietzsche did not realize this for himself, von Salis, whom he first met in 1884, must surely have pointed it out to him. Yet it produced no change in his outlook.

The third deficiency in appealing to the critique of democratization to explain Nietzsche's turn against women is that it cannot easily explain the appearance of misogyny, the strong sense, much of the time, that women are the *enemy*. There is a venom in the later remarks on women, a will to demean (women such as George Eliot who venture into Nietzsche own preserve of letters are always 'little' (*TI*: 'Skirmishes of an Untimely Man' 5)) that is matched by nothing he says about trade unions, parliamentary democracy, or socialism. There is something uniquely personal in the attack on women. This suggests that one should turn to Nietzsche's biography and in particular his biography for the year 1882 to find the cause of his turn against women.

* * *

The salient biographical event of 1882 was the 'Salomé affair'.

Lou Salomé was beautiful, brilliant, 21 (sixteen years Nietzsche's junior), and highly attractive to men: starting with Pastor Hendrik Gillot, her supposed teacher in Moscow and twenty-five years her senior, almost every man she met wanted to get her into his bed.[6] The daughter of a Baltic German who had risen to the rank of general in the Russian army, she was the youngest of six siblings. Since the others were all boys, she developed characteristics—intelligence, resoluteness, and clarity of purpose—that were considered 'mannish' by the standards of the day. Lou had been permitted to come to Europe (chaperoned by her anxious mother Louise) in order to acquire an education. She did this in part by auditing lectures at Zurich University (at the time, the only German-speaking university to admit women)[7] but also by attaching herself to brilliant men. The trouble with this second strategy was that what she wanted from them was consistently at variance with what they wanted from her. Though she

[6] The one noble exception appears to have been Freud. In later life, Salomé qualified as a psychoanalyst and joined Freud's inner circle.

[7] It allowed women to attend lectures in the humanities as early as 1847 and to enrol as doctoral students in 1866. Thus when Basle refused women admission to its doctoral programme it was refusing to do what Zurich had been doing for eight years already.

told all of them, as she told Paul Rée, right from the start, that her 'love-life was closed for the duration of [her] life', sex kept rearing its ugly head. (Lou was by no means against sex as such: in later years she would have an ecstatic affair with the poet Rainer Maria Rilke, fifteen years her junior, as well as with many with other lovers. According to her biographer, Julia Vickers,[8] however, it was not until her maturity that she gained the confidence that she could give herself fully to a man without succumbing to the traditional female role of married submission that she was trying so hard to escape.)

To try to put the tangled and miserable events of the Salomé affair into a nutshell, what happened was this. Sometime in March 1882, Nietzsche received a letter (now lost)[9] from Paul Rée encouraging him to come to Rome where, staying with Malwida von Meysenbug, was a beautiful young Russian who showed great promise in philosophy and was dying to meet him. Rée proposed Lou partly as Nietzsche's disciple and, in view of his half-blindness, partly as his amanuensis. But he clearly also thought of her as a marriage prospect for his best friend since on 21 March Nietzsche replied:

> greet the Russian girl for me. I have been lusting (*lüstern*) after this kind of soul. Indeed I'm soon going on the hunt for it—in view of what I have planned for the next ten years I need it. But marriage is a completely different matter—I could at most agree to a two-year marriage, and this only in relation to what I have to do in the next ten years. (*KGB* III.1: 215)

On 26 April 1882, in St Peter's Basilica in Rome, Rée introduced his two friends to each other. Nietzsche greeted Lou with the clearly pre-prepared line 'What stars have brought us here together?' Falling instantly in love, he instructed Rée to present Lou with a marriage proposal on his behalf. Unbeknownst to Nietzsche, however, Rée had meanwhile lost all interest in a love match between Lou and his friend, since, subsequent to offering her to Nietzsche, he had fallen in love with her himself. He must, therefore, have been greatly relieved when his proposal on Nietzsche's behalf was gently rejected—as had been his proposal on his own behalf less than a month earlier. In spite of these setbacks and conflicting undercurrents, it was agreed on all sides that the three of them should seek out a place where, accompanied for sake of propriety by an older woman, they could live a communal life devoted to thinking and writing. Effectively, in other words, they agreed on a 'return to Sorrento'; to set up, once again, a 'monastery for free spirits' with Genoa as the most likely site.

At the beginning of May, chaperoned by Lou's mother, the troubled threesome set off from Rome on a slow journey to Lucerne. En route, they spent several days in Orta San Giulio, an ancient, peninsular town jutting out into the serene Lake Orta in north-west Italy. Here, Nietzsche somehow managed to prise Lou away from the jealous Rée and the anxious Louise in order to visit the devotional spiral of twenty little chapels, each depicting a scene from the life of St Francis of Assisi, that encircles the summit of Orta's Sacro Monte. Here, something of an intense nature occurred. Nietzsche may have revealed the secret of the 'eternal return of the same' or there may have been an embrace. Or both events may have occurred. Asked many years later whether Nietzsche (by now a world star) had kissed her, Lou nonchalantly replied that she 'couldn't remember'.

Arriving in Lucerne and realizing by now that Rée would not have presented his marriage proposal in the best possible light, Nietzsche repeated the offer in person in the city's

---

[8] Vickers 2008. See especially pp. 69–70, 98, 124.

[9] It was probably destroyed, like a great many others, by Elisabeth Förster-Nietzsche.

Lion Gardens—but unfortunately with the same result as before. The ill-matched trio then attended the photographic studio of Jules Bonnet where the famous 'whip' photograph was taken. It shows Lou standing in a small cart drawn by her two 'horses', Rée and Nietzsche, and brandishing a 'whip' made out of a sprig of lilac. The tableau vivant was arranged by Nietzsche and, under the guise of humour, seems intended as an ironic comment on both his own and Rée's enslavement to Lou. (Notice that since 'You are going to women? Then don't forget the whip' was written less than nine months after this episode, the nature of the photograph strongly supports reading the remark as warning one to remember *the woman's*—Lou/Fricka's—whip.)

On 16 May the visitors left Lucerne for separate destinations. Nietzsche and Rée now began to bombard Lou with letters designed simultaneously to express their own love for her and to undermine the other's credentials. It was arranged, however, that in August Lou would spend three weeks with Nietzsche in Tautenburg, a village near Jena just beginning to become fashionable as a summer retreat. The ostensible purpose of the visit was for her to receive the instruction in philosophy necessary to prepare her for the 'monastery for free spirits', a project to which, officially, all three were still committed. She was to be chaperoned by Nietzsche's sister Elisabeth.

Towards the end of July 1882, in Bayreuth for the first performance of Wagner's *Parsifal*, Elisabeth and Lou met for the first time. Unfortunately, it was loathing at first sight. Lou found little to admire in the dowdy, not very bright or educated, small-town spinster, fourteen years her elder, while Elisabeth (in addition to a quasi-incestuous hatred of any woman who threatened to supplant her in the affections of her brother) was furiously jealous of the beautiful girl. Elisabeth, moreover, was no longer quite *persona grata* in Bayreuth on account of her brother's public defection from the Wagnerian cause five years earlier.[10] Lou, on the other hand, waltzed effortlessly into the inner circle of the Wagnerian glitterati where she flirted with the attractive and engaged in philosophical dialectics with the clever, as well as displaying the 'amusing' whip photograph to all and sundry.

En route from Bayreuth to Tautenburg there was a furious argument, during which Elisabeth accused Lou of being a nymphomaniac in intellectual's clothing, to which Lou replied by demanding to know (as Elisabeth reports),

> Who first dragged our plan of a communal living into the dirtiest mud, who first thought in terms of marriage? That was your brother! And to emphasize it once more, she said: 'Yes, it was your noble, pure-minded brother who first had the dirty idea of a concubinage!'

Rée, it seems clear, in his effort to undermine Nietzsche, must have told Lou of the latter's 'two-year marriage' ('living in sin') proposal. Later on—the argument seems to have simmered on for some weeks—Lou said: 'Don't think for a moment that I am interested in your brother or in love with him; I could sleep in the very same room as him, without getting any wild ideas' (*KGB* III.7/1: 912–18).

In spite of all this, the visit to Tautenburg went ahead as planned. Lou had been profoundly impressed by Nietzsche's most recent book *Daybreak*, and knew she had the opportunity to pick the brains of one of the leading thinkers of the age. To keep Rée's jealousy at

---

[10] Basically, Nietzsche terminated personal relations with the Wagners in 1876. But it was the appearance of *Human, All Too Human* two years later with its public attack on the cult of (Wagnerian) genius that made him *persona non grata* in Bayreuth.

bay, however, she had to send him, day by day, a minutely detailed account of *everything* that went on.

In Tautenburg, Nietzsche and Lou basically ignored Elisabeth, reducing her to chaperone in name only. They alternated between quarrelling and having intense, day-long conversations, usually about how to find God in a post-Christian age. As a result of these conversations Nietzsche decided that Lou should become his 'heir' rather than 'pupil' since her mind, he felt, was as deep as his own.

After Tautenburg, Elisabeth devoted all her energies to systematically poisoning Nietzsche's mind against her arch-rival. She reported Lou as ridiculing him among his enemies in Bayreuth and accusing him of low egoism and even lower lechery. Later on, she convinced him that Rée had perpetrated the 'false' (but actually true) rumour that under a veneer of intellectualism, Nietzsche had had sexual designs on Lou. And she reported her version of events to their mother, Franziska, who was in any case completely scandalized by the proposed *ménage à trois*, Platonic or otherwise. This resulted in her telling her son, who, on leaving Tautenburg had travelled home to Naumburg, that he was 'a disgrace to his father's grave', upon which Nietzsche walked out of the house, slamming the door behind him.

In spite of all that had happened, the disintegrating trio assembled, one final time, at the beginning of October, for five tense weeks in Leipzig. Officially, the monastery for free spirits was still on the cards, Paris now being the proposed site. But after Lou and Rée departed to live together 'as brother and sister'[11] on his country estate, Nietzsche quickly realized that they had being paying no more than lip service to the monastery idea and that he had, in fact, been dumped.

He was devastated. In the space of six months he had lost the love of his life, his best friend, his mother, and his sister—who, he slowly realized, had manipulated his feelings with lies and half-truths and whom he began to hate along with everyone else. He fled to his customary winter retreat in Genoa but, finding his old lodgings rented, moved along the Ligurian coast to Rapallo where he spent the winter of 1882–3. From here, and later from his summer retreat in Sils Maria, he fired off a flurry of crazy letters. Sometimes they pretend he has risen above the whole Salomé business, sometimes they beg for reconciliation— 'Lou, dear heart, do create a clear sky above us' (*KGB* III.1: 335)—and sometimes they are swamped by abject self-pity: shortly before Christmas he writes Lou and Rée jointly that he can neither sleep nor work, that he has taken a huge dose of opium, and that they must just regard him as a crazy person 'driven half-mad by solitude'. They are, he adds, 'not to worry too much if he kills himself' (*KGB* III.1: 360). Mostly, however, the letters vibrate with anger and abuse, as well as the suppressed violence of injured, masculine pride. Sometimes the anger is directed against Rée: 'I would have a strong desire to give you a lesson in practical morality with a couple of bullets', he writes, but regrets that engagement in a duel could only be for 'clean hands, not oily fingers' (*KGB* III.1: 434). (That the, by now, strongly *anti*-anti-Semitic Nietzsche should take advantage of Rée's Jewishness to indulge in an anti-Semitic slur is one mark of how disturbed he was.) Most viciously, however, the anger, abuse, and violence are directed against Lou. She is 'a dried up, dirty monkey with bad breath and false breasts' (*KGB* III.1: 435), a woman who 'belongs on the lowest level of humanity [is a 'slut'] despite her good brain' (*KGB* III.1: 362), a 'masculine' (i.e. whip-wielding) 'pseudo girl'

---

[11] This was Georg Brandes' report (*KGB* III.6: 505).

(*KGB* III.3: 636). Repeatedly he calls her a 'cat'; referring, presumably, to her determination to pick his brains without offering a quid pro quo, he accuses her of a 'cat-egoism which cannot love' (*KGB* III.1: 348, 347). Reasserting, in other words, his damaged masculine authority, he writes that he always dislikes hearing her voice 'except when you beg' (*KGB* III.1: 352). A year or so later an entry in his notebooks reveals that the violence of Nietzsche's feelings towards Lou has spread so as to encompass women in general: 'Until now we have been very nice to woman. Sadly the time comes when, to be able to deal with a woman, one has first of all to slap her across the mouth' (*KGB* XII.1: 150).[12]

In spite of Nietzsche's theoretical and personal commitment to 'loving fate' and so embracing the 'eternal return' of everything that had happened to him (including, of course, the Salomé affair), I do not believe he ever managed to forgive, let alone love, either Rée, Lou, or Elisabeth. Still in 1887, in *On the Genealogy of Morals*, he finds himself (irrelevantly) claiming that, with women, 'asceticism' is 'at most, one more seductive charm, a little *morbidezza* (delicacy) on fair flesh, the angelic expression on a pretty, fat animal' (*GM* III: 1), a clear repetition of the accusation made against Lou five years earlier in one of the crazy letters that, in place of love, she has a 'cunning self-control when it comes to the sensuality of men' which she deploys to satisfy her 'powerful will' (*KGB* III.1: 351). And in his final work, *Ecce Homo*, he goes out of his way to deny *Human, All too Human*'s in fact considerable intellectual debt to Rée (*EH*: 'Human, All Too Human' 6), as well as claiming that Elisabeth cannot be his sister since that would be a 'blasphemy against my divinity' (*EH*: 'Why I Am So Wise' 3).[13]

Apart from his final insanity, the Salomé affair was the worst thing that ever happened to Nietzsche. Though he was marginally more scrupulous towards Rée than Rée was towards him, it reveals him at his worst, almost as much sinning as sinned against. The final, incisive word on the whole, sad affair may be given to Schopenhauer. Writing in 1844 he observes that, next to the 'will to live', sexual lust

> shows itself...as the strongest and most active of all motives, and incessantly lays claim to half the powers and thoughts of the younger portion of mankind. It is the ultimate goal of almost all human effort; it has an unfavourable influence on the most important affairs, interrupts, every hour, the most serious occupations, and sometimes perplexes for a while even the greatest minds. It knows how to slip its love-notes and ringlets even into...philosophical manuscripts. (Schopenhauer 1969: vol. II p. 533)

* * *

One such 'philosophical manuscript' was *Zarathustra* Part I. Though not published until August 1883, it was actually written in Rapallo the previous January—at exactly the same time as the abusive letters quoted above. Its remarks on women, in other words, are cut from the same fabric as those letters, are an act of revenge. Nietzsche more or less admits this, describing *Zarathustra* as a great 'bloodletting', by means of which he got the pain of the Salomé affair out of his system (*KGB* III.1: 403). The catharsis, however, was incomplete since he needed to make a second attempt in *Beyond Good and Evil*. Here, as we saw,

---

[12] The phrase here is *auf den Mund schlagen*. Nietzsche, of course, would never have slapped a woman and it is possible that the intention of this phrase is better captured by 'shut her up'. But however it is translated the verbal violence is unmistakeable.

[13] Elizabeth, of course, suppressed the passage for many years.

'woman' is described as 'the beautiful and dangerous cat' with 'tiger's claws' concealed inside her glove. Since he repeatedly described Lou as a 'cat' this is as good as naming names. To know Nietzsche's biography is to know exactly who the tiger was that had mauled his heart.

This, then, I submit, is the reason for the transformation of Nietzsche's attitude to women: pain of a kind and intensity he had never before known (*KGB* III.1: 403) finds a kind of release—a 'bloodletting'—in the chauvinism and misogyny of *Zarathustra* and *Beyond Good and Evil*. Not the critique of democratization but rather the Salomé affair explains the transformation. The cause of his 'turn' against women lies in his biography, not his philosophy.[14]

* * *

One of Nietzsche's weaknesses as a philosopher was his occasional inability to distinguish between the philosophical and the pathological. But in the case of *Beyond Good and Evil*'s remarks on women he had, I think, a shrewd suspicion that a personal pathology had invaded his philosophy. His remarks on 'woman as such', he admits in section 231 of that work, are personal and idiosyncratic: in them, he writes, 'an immutable "this is me" speaks up'. The 'truths' he offers are only '*my* truths', a 'spiritual fate', a 'great stupidity that . . . *will not learn*'. Because this most self-aware of men knows that he has not recovered from the Salomé affair, he warns the reader that his view on women may well be infected by pathology and prejudice.

This surprising self-undermining raises two questions. First, why, given his reservations, did he not simply excise the remarks from the work—as, earlier, he had excised remarks about women from *Human, All Too Human* (see pp. 47–8 above)? And second, given that they were not excised, why does he not leave it to the reader to sort the philosophical from the pathological? Why does he go out of his way to draw attention to a possible weakness in the work?

The answer to the first question has, I think, to do with Nietzsche's personal, intimate, buttonholing style of philosophizing. His books are written, in the first instance at least, not for a timeless audience located somewhere in outer space but for 'the very few',[15] five or six contemporaries, five or six actual or potential 'friends' (*GS* 381) he hopes to attract to his cause of cultural regeneration. *Beyond Good and Evil*, for instance, is written for, above all, Heinrich von Stein: its 'After-song' calling for 'new friends' to join him in the 'high mountains' of thought recycles a poem originally sent von Stein imploring him (in vain) to abandon Wagner and join him in the high mountains of Sils Maria (*KGB* III.1: 562). Since Nietzsche's proper readers may literally have to live with him in a monastery for free spirits—he had hoped von Stein would join him in Nice—it is important they should know who he is, warts and all.[16]

---

[14] As John Richardson (to whom I am indebted for many helpful comments on this essay) has pointed out to me, it would be interesting to consider to what extent this is true, not just of the remarks about women, but of the general 'macho' stance of Nietzsche's later philosophy.

[15] *The Antichrist*'s subtitle.

[16] *Ecce Homo* eliminates the warts. But here, I think, knowing that he is at the end of his journey, Nietzsche *is* addressing a timeless audience: the purpose is to mythologize himself, to turn himself into a model of spiritual development—in his own language, an 'educator'—for future generations.

The answer to the second question has to do, I believe, with the strange fact that, by 1884, nearly all Nietzsche's friends and nearly all the admirers he knew personally were not just women, but *feminist* women, women who were, by both example and ideology, emancipationists. Among the more prominent: Malwida von Meysenbug, the role model for all his other feminist friends; Meta von Salis, the rich, aristocratic, lesbian feminist who became, in 1887, the first Swiss woman to complete a PhD—not, she said, because she had much interest in the title for its own sake, but 'in the interest of the women's question';[17] Resa von Schirnhofer, an Austrian who obtained her PhD, also from Zurich, two years after Meta; Helen Zimmern, a London Jew of German parentage, author of the first philosophical biography of Schopenhauer in English and later translator of Nietzsche into English;[18] and Helene Druscowicz, an Austrian who obtained her PhD from Zurich in 1878 and would later write (from the psychiatric institution to which she became confined) a pamphlet entitled *The Male as Logical and Moral Impossibility and Curse of the World* (she had turned against Nietzsche by then).

Given that, for the last six years of his sanity, these were his immediate circle of friends and readers (increasingly he avoided men, particularly professors), Nietzsche must have recognized, I believe, that he had landed them with a serious problem of consistency: the problem of explaining how a 'Nietzschean feminist' could be anything other than a self-contradiction. And so, in the spirit of Zarathustra inviting his followers to scrutinize his teaching with a view to 'denying' some or all of it (a slavish and uncritical pupil 'repays a teacher poorly',[19] he observes) Nietzsche invites his feminist friends to scrutinize his view on women with an eye to separating the philosophical from the pathological.

* * *

The paradoxical fact of the later Nietzsche's friendships with feminists raises three questions. First, what was it about his writings that, in spite of their anti-feminism and misogyny, attracted feminist women to his philosophy? Second, how did such women deal with their problem of consistency, how did they render the idea of a 'Nietzschean feminist' coherent? And finally, what was it about feminist women which, in spite of their feminism, attracted Nietzsche to them?

The first of these questions is the easiest to answer. What attracted feminists to Nietzsche, it is clear, was the coincidence of his message of personal liberation and self-realization with their own. They, like him, wished to become 'free spirits', to throw off the oppressive constraints of Victorian morality. They, like him, wished to become 'who they were'.

This coincidence of message provided the basis of an explicitly Nietzsche-inspired brand of feminism that grew up in early years of twentieth century. To reconcile their

[17] It was von Salis who bought the Villa Silberblick in Weimar as a home for Nietzsche for the last three years of his life and site for the Nietzsche Archive.
[18] Nietzsche's attitude to Zimmern was ambiguous. On the one hand, he felt his masculine security threatened by this 'protagonist for women's rights' (*KGB* III.3: 750). 'Curious', he wrote to Köselitz, 'one had defended oneself well enough against women's emancipation: yet a paradigm example of the little literary woman has arrived here to join me' (*KGB* III.3: 724). On the other hand, he responded very positively to her Jewishness, in reference to which, and to his sister's recent marriage to the leading anti-Semite Bernhard Förster, he wrote to his mother: 'God help European understanding if one were to abandon Jewish understanding' (*KGB* III.3: 750).
[19] *Z* I 22; see too *GS* 335.

feminism with the apparently anti-feminist elements in Nietzsche's philosophy, these early feminists deployed one of two basic strategies:[20] they either held it to be superficial to read Nietzsche as an anti-feminist—his attack, Valentine de Saint Pont insisted in 1912, was not on women's aspirations but on 'the feminine', something which could appear as easily in men as in women[21]—or they admitted his anti-feminism and rejected it as a pathological error, but held that his basic, emancipatory message was nonetheless true and important.

For von Salis and von Schirnhofer and the other women who actually knew Nietzsche, the first of these strategies (the 'creative misreading' strategy, we might call it) was not available, since, in conversation and letters, *he went out of his way to thrust his anti-feminism under their noses, to insist that the remarks in the philosophical texts should not be understood as anything other than anti-feminism.* To Elisabeth he wrote gleefully in May 1885 that 'on all of those who rhapsodize about the "emancipation of women" it has slowly, slowly dawned that I am the "big bad wolf" for them' (*KGB* III.3: 613). (One of the Zurich feminists, Louise Röder-Wiederhold, who had the misfortune to have *Beyond Good and Evil*'s remarks on 'woman as such' dictated to her, he reduced to tears (Janz 1978: vol. II, pp. 392–3.) In Zurich, he continues in the letter to Elisabeth (Köselitz was his source of information), 'there is great fury against me among the female students'. Though this circle included his good friends Resa von Schirnhofer and Meta von Salis, he concludes the letter with an expression of gratitude that the feminists were beginning to get the point: 'Finally! And how many such 'finally's do I still have to wait for!' (*KGB* III.3: 600) And to Malwida von Meysenbug he proudly writes (quoting her back to herself), that 'as my friend Malvida [sic] says "I'm even worse than Schopenhauer"' (*KGB* III.5: 809).

Since the creative misreading strategy was not available to them, Nietzsche's feminist friends were thus forced, at least implicitly, to adopt the alternative (and much more sensible) strategy of treating his anti-feminism as a pathological quirk and error separable from his essential philosophy.

Helen Zimmern has left a report of how, with Sils Maria's summer season of 1884 drawing to a chilly close, it was time for the mentally deranged Countess Mansuroff to depart to warmer climes. She, however, refused to leave her hotel room. When, after several days of trying, her friends had still failed to dislodge her, Nietzsche, who had a soft spot for this Russian aristocrat, pianist, composer, and former pupil of Chopin, asked that the matter be put in his hands. And then, Zimmern continues,

> one day at noon…he suddenly appeared at the front entrance of the hotel [Alpenrose] with the sick lady, who followed him like an obedient dog, even though she had otherwise always gone into a fury if anyone spoke of a departure. None of us, however, had any idea of what Nietzsche had done. The famous whip had certainly not been used… (*C* 588–9)

The levity of this reference to the whip by a committed feminist surely indicates an implicit and indulgent subscription to the 'personal quirk' strategy.

That Resa von Schirnhofer took the same line is suggested by the way she reports and elaborates on a 'favourite thought' Nietzsche communicated to her in July 1884, the thought that

---

[20] See Aschheim 1992: 86.   [21] See Aschheim 1992: 62–3.

human beings know only the smallest part of their possibilities, which corresponds to aphorism 336 of *Daybreak* with its final sentence "Who knows to what we *could* be driven by circumstances!", aphorism 9 of *The Gay Science*, "We all have hidden gardens and plantations…",
and aphorism 274 of *Beyond Good and Evil*… "Fortunate coincidences are necessary… for the
higher human being 'to erupt'… Mostly this does *not* happen, and in every corner of the earth
people sit waiting…" (Janz 1978: vol. II, p. 300)[22]

One can see here, I think, von Shirnhofer reading Nietzsche's philosophy so as to emphasize his message of personal liberation and self-realization while quietly discarding the fact
Nietzsche himself addresses the message to 'men only'. Conspicuously absent is any attempt
to creatively misread the 'whip' remarks.

Meta von Salis deploys the strategy of separating the anti-feminism from the essential
philosophy most explicitly. Noting (as I have) Nietzsche's 'increasing sharpness of tone'
on the 'women question' in the post-*Gay Science* (i.e. post-Salomé) years, she says that it
never made her cross or indignant since 'a man of Nietzsche's breadth of vision and sure-
ness of instinct has the right to get things wrong in one instance'. Pointing out his mistake 'more on his behalf than on ours', she identifies its source as the 'shameful fact that
what he says is still accurate with regard to the majority of women'. Nietzsche, in other
words, she suggests, made a reasonable, but in fact false, inductive generalization from the
run of contemporary womanhood to 'the eternal feminine', and so failed to see that, while
'the woman of the future, who realises a higher ideal of power and beauty in harmonious coexistence, has not yet arrived', one day she *will*. 'God be praised', she concludes, 'for
the fate which allowed me to see and reverence, beyond the ephemeral significance of the
women question, elite human beings—men and women' (Salis-Marschlins 2000: 31–6).
As observed earlier, in short, the aristocratic von Salis, every bit as anti-democratic as
Nietzsche, makes just one adjustment to his philosophy: the future belongs to 'super-
women' as well as 'supermen'.

* * *

My final question was the question of why the chauvinist Nietzsche showed such a marked
predilection for the company of feminist women. To answer it one needs to attend, I think,
to *Zarathustra*'s conception of woman as man's 'playmate', the 'warrior's' 'recreation' when he
comes home from the serious and manly business of (intellectual) 'warfare' (see my second
section): someone, as they say, to 'bring out his inner child'.

Nietzsche was often uncomfortable and gauche with women. Not only Lou Salomé but
also the equally beautiful Mathilda Trampedach[23] received a marriage proposal when no
more than a couple of words (about Longfellow's 'Excelsior') had been exchanged. And neither, for all his fulminations against Christianity's turning sex into something sinful and
disgusting, was he comfortable with sex. To his notebooks he confides that

> The most touching thing in a good marriage is the mutual knowledge of the repulsive secret
> from which the new child is created and born. In the generative act one experiences the humil-
> iation of the beloved out of love. (*KSA* 8: 18 [39])

---

[22]   A translation appears in Gilman 1987: 160. In Gilman's index this passage is given the quaint but
appropriate title 'On *man's* potential' (my emphasis).

[23]   See Young 2010: chapter 12.

But when his relationship with women was free of distortion by unresolved sexual tension, 'play' became an important element. With his sister (in happier days) he spent hours making up silly verses on trivial everyday topics such as the purchase of a 'tea machine',[24] as he did with the extremely 'ugly' (*KGB* III.1: 528) Resa von Shirnhofer—after they had lubricated themselves with 'Vermouth di Torino' in a café on top of Nice's Mount Boron (*C* 581). One of Nietzsche's motherly and decidedly non-feminist friends was Emily Fynn, who with her daughter (also Emily) was a regularly summer visitor to Sils. A letter Emily wrote Nietzsche's mother in 1890, a year after his mental collapse in 1889, discloses the relaxed and charmingly playful relationship among the trio. Nietzsche, she recalls,

> was very graciously interested in my daughter's paintings, and always said that she ought to paint something ugly in addition, in order to heighten, even more, the beauty of her [alpine] flowers. And then, one morning, he brought her, as a model, a live, hopping toad, which he himself had caught; and he greatly enjoyed his successful prank! In return we sent him after a few days what looked like a jar of jam, but as he was carefully opening it, grasshoppers sprang out at him! (Gilman 1987: 213)

Charming though this unexpected side of Nietzsche's relations with women is, what needs to be remembered is that, right up until the end of his sanity, his ideal woman was none of the women we have met so far but rather Cosima Wagner (formerly von Bülow, née Liszt). Though all personal contact had ceased a decade earlier, as he was going mad, he wrote her love letters casting her in the role of Ariadne and himself in that of Dionysus (*KGB* III.5: 1241). It would seem, therefore, that his ideal marriage would have been with Cosima. One of the 'mad' letters suggests, indeed, that he is in fact her third husband (*KGB* III.5: 1244).

Between May 1869 and April 1872, Nietzsche, newly appointed as professor of classics in Basle, visited the Wagners in Tribschen, Lucerne, about three hours away by train, twenty-three times. He had his own bedroom and an open invitation to use it whenever he wished (*KGB* II.2: 6). Richard regarded him as a son and the gaggle of Wagner/von Bülow children as an older brother. He was intimately engaged in the selection of their Christmas presents and was one of the select few present at the bottom of the Tribschen stairwell for the first performance of the *Siegfried Idyll*, in celebration of Cosima's birthday, on the morning of Christmas Day, 1870.

While Richard was exactly the same age as Nietzsche's father, Cosima was a mere seven years older than himself. And so he fell in love with her. But it was, of course, an impossible love, modelled on the romantic archetype created by Rousseau's St-Preux,[25] Goethe's Werther,[26] and (in real life) by Nietzsche's 'favourite poet'[27] Friedrich Hölderlin. Each of these heroes was in love with the wife of an exemplary man. (Noel Coward's 1945 *Brief Encounter* is a reworking of the same theme.) Nietzsche fell in love with Cosima as earlier, while a student in Leipzig, he had fallen in love with Sophie, the young and vivacious wife of his beloved 'doctor-father', Friedrich Ritschl. With Cosima, as with Sophie, the love was impossible, and so entirely safe, and so relaxed.

---

[24] See Young 2010: chapter 20.   [25] The male lead in *Julie; ou la nouvelle Héloïse*.   [26] The male lead in *Die Leiden des jungen Werthers*.   [27] See *KGW* I.2: 12 [1]

With the intelligent, educated, and gifted Cosima, the possibilities of 'play' went far beyond toad jokes and silly verses. With her, play regularly included playing four-handed piano works—including Nietzsche's own compositions—as well as the play of ideas: she read all the works he produced prior to the rupture in their friendship and subjected them to detailed and often perceptive critiques. In dedicating his *Five Prefaces to Five Unwritten Books* to her in 1872, he wrote 'in deeply felt respect and as an answer to questions raised both by letter and in conversation' (*KSA* 1: 754). It is important to note here that for Nietzsche philosophy and play by no means exclude each other: 'taking matters seriously', he rightly insists in *The Gay Science*, should *not* be regarded as excluding 'laughter and gaiety'. Philosophy should be serious but not earnest. It should be the '*gay* science' (*GS* 327).

Putting these facts together one thing becomes obvious: for a man such as himself, or Wagner, a woman capable of being his *ideal* 'playmate' would have to possess a high level of intelligence and education. She would *have* be someone, like Cosima (or Lou), who *did* read his books, rather than like the decidedly non-intellectual, conservative Catholic, Emily Fynn, whom he begged not to since they would hurt her feelings.[28] The higher type of 'warrior's recreation' cannot consist *solely* of toad jokes and silly verses, since on a daily basis that would become boring.

One can surmise, therefore, that beneath his emotional and intellectual confusion, Nietzsche never really lost his initial disposition in favour of access to higher education for suitably gifted women. What terrified him was women's access to power, a monstrous regime of women such as Lou Salomé. 'Women are always less civilized than men', he believes. 'At the base of their souls they are wild' (*KSA* 11: 25 [92]). This deep-seated fear of, as one might be tempted to call it, 'castration' is what lies behind the often-repeated sentiment that 'One wants the emancipation of women and achieves thereby the emasculation of men' (*KSA* 10: 3 [1] 442). To be sure Nietzsche himself observes apropos 'the labour question' that 'If one wants slaves it is foolish to educate them to be masters' (*TI*: 'Skirmishes of an Untimely Man' 40). But it is a by no means unusual human failing for insights in one domain to fail to be carried over into another, particularly when strong emotions are involved.

BIBLIOGRAPHY

(A) Works by Nietzsche

BGE   *Beyond Good and Evil*, ed. Rolf-Peter Horstmann, ed. and trans. Judith Norman. Cambridge: Cambridge University Press, 2002.

EH   *Ecce Homo*, in *The Anti-Christ, Ecce Homo, Twilight of the Idols, and Other Writings*, ed. Aaron Ridley, trans. Judith Norman. Cambridge: Cambridge University Press, 2005.

GM   *On the Genealogy of Morals*, ed. Keith Ansell-Pearson, trans. Carol Diethe. Cambridge: Cambridge University Press, 1994.

GS   *The Gay Science*, trans. Josefine Nauckhoff and Adrian Del Caro. Cambridge: Cambridge University Press, 2001.

HAH   *Human, All Too Human*, trans. R. J. Hollingdale. Cambridge: Cambridge University Press, 1986.

---

[28] See Gilman 1987: 195.

KGB   *Nietzsche Briefwechsel: Kritische Gesamtausgabe*, ed. G. Colli and M. Montinari (25 vols). Berlin: De Gruyter, 1975–2004.

KGW   *Nietzsche Werke: Kritische Gesamtausgabe*, ed. G. Colli and M. Montinari (24 vols + 4 CDs). Berlin: De Gruyter, 1967–2006.

KSA   *Sämtliche Werke: Kritische Studienausgabe in 15 Einzelbänden*, ed. G. Colli and M. Montinari (15 vols). Berlin: De Gruyter, 1988.

TI   *Twilight of the Idols*, in *The Anti-Christ, Ecce Homo, Twilight of the Idols, and Other Writings*, ed. Aaron Ridley, trans. Judith Norman. Cambridge: Cambridge University Press, 2005.

Z   *Thus Spoke Zarathustra*, ed. and trans. Graham Parkes. New York: Oxford University Press, 2005.

(B) Other Primary Works

C   *Friedrich Nietzsche: Chronik in Bildern und Texten*, Stiftung Weimarer Klassik. Munich and Vienna: Hanser, 2000.

(C) Other Works Cited

Aschheim, S. E. 1992. *The Nietzsche Legacy in Germany 1890–1990*. Berkeley and Los Angeles: University of California Press.

Gilman, S. 1987. *Conversations with Nietzsche*, trans. D. Parent. New York: Oxford University Press.

Janz, C. P. 1978. *Friedrich Nietzsche: Biographie* (3 vols). Munich and Vienna: Carl Hanser Verlag.

Salis-Marschlins, M. 2000. *Philosoph und Edelmensch: Ein Betrag zur Charakteristik Friedrich Nietzsches*. Schutterwald: Wissenschaftlicher Verlag.

Schopenhauer, A. 1969. *The World as Will and Representation*, trans. E. Payne (2 vols). New York: Dover.

Schopenhauer, A. 1974. *Parerga and Paralipomena*, trans. E. Payne (2 vols). Oxford: Clarendon Press.

Vickers, J. 2008. *Lou von Salomé: A Biography of the Woman who Inspired Freud, Nietzsche and Rilke*. Jefferson, NC: McFarland.

Young, J. 2010. *Friedrich Nietzsche: A Philosophical Biography*. New York: Cambridge University Press.

CHAPTER 3

....

NIETZSCHE'S ILLNESS

....

CHARLIE HUENEMANN

1 CASE REPORT

....

FN, a right-handed 44-year-old former college professor, was referred to the psychiatric clinic at Basel for treatment in January 1889.[1] He had been troubled since childhood by severe headaches, often accompanied by acute eye pain and vomiting. His headaches were generally located above his right eye. They would typically last anywhere from two to nine days and occur about every two or three weeks. Other complaints over his life included various intestinal discomforts and rheumatic pains in his left arm. He had previously contracted and been treated for gonorrhea (twice), dysentery, and diphtheria in his twenties. Upon presentation at Basel, FN exhibited disorientation, grandiose delusions, megalomania, and loquacity. His right pupil was much larger than left (though this too had been noted since his childhood). His right eye was functionally blind and he could not swivel it to the right. Reflexes were generally good and speech was unimpaired; his tongue exhibited no trembling. His handwriting was unimpaired. He tended to pull up his left shoulder and lower his right when walking. His left foot, when pressed upward, would pulse back in rhythmic beats ("left ankle clonus"). He was diagnosed by the Basel physicians as having general paresis (or, in other words, tertiary syphilis).

FN was then transferred to the clinic at Jena, where doctors concurred with the Basel diagnosis. In subsequent weeks he continued to exhibit states of disorientation and dementia, along with hoarding of objects, smearing of stool and drinking of urine, and smashing windows and glass in states of heightened paranoid anxiety (he believed that Bismarck was trying to assassinate him). His ability to play the piano was unimpaired for at least one year after arriving at Jena. In 1890 he was released to his mother's care and over the next ten years showed increasing apathy, loss of activity, and diminished mental capabilities. FN died in August 1900 of a stroke, complicated by pneumonia.

---

[1] Yes, right-handed, despite many internet reports to the contrary, according to Marie-Luise Haase, Nietzsche editor at the Klassik Stiftung Weimar (personal correspondence, February 21, 2008).

2 THE DIAGNOSIS

It was fairly common for a middle-aged man suffering from some form of dementia to be diagnosed with syphilis in a late nineteenth-century German hospital (Sax 2003: 48). This is true for two reasons. First, syphilis was known to be "the great imitator," meaning that it can manifest itself in very different ways. Though some symptoms are more common than others, a physician could rarely be said to be obviously wrong when diagnosing syphilis in a broad range of very different cases. This made syphilis a handy "one size fits all" diagnosis for doctors practicing at a time when the science of mental illness was still very underdeveloped. Second, syphilis was known—or at least widely supposed—to be very common. In fact, this supposition was groundless since there was no sure test for syphilis until the Wasserman test was introduced in 1906. Once this test was introduced and applied, the number of patients thought to suffer from syphilis in at least one German clinic dropped dramatically from 30 percent to only 8–9 percent (Schain 2001: 73). So syphilis in fact was not as widespread as commonly believed and the advanced stage Nietzsche was supposed to have (tertiary syphilis) is rarer still, developing in only 2–4 percent of syphilitic patients. But all this was not known until much later.

So when Nietzsche arrived at the Basel clinic, it was natural to diagnose him as suffering from tertiary syphilis, though the diagnosis was a notably poor fit with his symptoms, even given the state of knowledge at the time. The telltale sign for syphilis (before the Wasserman test) was a trembling tongue. Nietzsche's tongue did not tremble and his speech was unaffected. People with tertiary syphilis also often present an expressionless face, though Nietzsche's face was, if anything, overly animated with excitement. Syphilitics typically suffer from headaches a few days, weeks, or months before their collapse, while Nietzsche's were nearly lifelong. Syphilis usually affects the body uniformly, but Nietzsche's symptoms were lateralized: his headaches were located on the right side, his arm pains (and his "ankle clonus") were on the left, and his peculiar gait was oriented toward his left. He did not show any of the general trembling or the seizures typically seen in people with tertiary syphilis and in fact was reported to play the piano well for a year or more after his collapse. But perhaps most tellingly: patients suffering from tertiary syphilis very rarely survive for more than a few months or two years at the most; Nietzsche survived in his condition for another *ten* years, which is practically unheard of in cases of tertiary syphilis.

In fact, the only specific symptoms supporting the syphilis diagnosis were his dementia and the fact that Nietzsche's right pupil was unusually large and unresponsive; but many illnesses can lead to dementia and his pupil asymmetry had been with him nearly all his life. During the examination in Basel he did claim that he "had infected himself twice," which was taken to be evidence for contracting syphilis. But Nietzsche made this claim while also claiming that he was the tyrant of Turin and that Bismarck was trying to kill him—so who knows? If the remark was meaningful at all, it could well have referred to his being treated twice for gonorrhea back in his student days (Schain 2001: 14, 82). Really, when all is said and done, the only reasons for diagnosing Nietzsche with syphilis were (1) the fact that syphilis is "the great imitator," and so can be stretched to diagnose a lot of disparate sets of symptoms, and (2) the fact that Nietzsche and his mother could not afford "first-class" medical attention and so had to content themselves with the most conveniently available diagnosis.

The diagnosis is almost certainly incorrect, as several recent psychiatric studies have shown.[2] No diagnosis will be definitive unless Nietzsche's remains are someday exhumed and analyzed, but meanwhile, from the available medical records, the evidence much more strongly supports an alternative diagnosis. In all likelihood, Nietzsche was suffering from a *retro-orbital meningioma*. A meningioma is a tumor on the surface of the brain which, when left untreated, can grow continuously over a lifetime, crowding the brain into the rest of the cranial cavity. If Nietzsche had one of these tumors growing just behind his right eye, we would expect to see a familiar list of symptoms: chronic intermittent headaches on the right side, acute eye pains in the right eye (with eventual blindness in it), visual disturbances, scattered impairments on the left side of his body, and—at some critical point, as the tumor displaced his right frontal lobe—dementia resulting from a *de facto* frontal lobotomy. Meningiomas can also lead to manic behavior and extremely anxious paranoia.[3] Nietzsche displayed all of these symptoms far more clearly than he evidenced the symptoms that are typical of the patient suffering from tertiary syphilis. Moreover, there are no symptoms typically presented by patients with meningiomas which Nietzsche did not present. So this recommends itself as the most plausible diagnosis of what caused Nietzsche's lifelong headaches, at least some of his eye problems, his collapse in Turin, and his deterioration afterwards.[4]

This is not to say that there were not other conditions he may have been suffering from as well, of course. His writings, both public and private, reveal the sort of extreme mood swings seen in patients suffering from some kinds of bipolar disorder (which also, by the way, have been linked by several studies to exceptional creativity).[5] His family included several cases of psychological or neurological ailments. We know also that two of his mother's sisters had psychiatric illnesses of some kind (one committed suicide); one of her brothers developed mental illness in his sixties, and another may have died in an asylum. Nietzsche's own father had *petit-mal*-type seizures for some years, and later displayed difficulties in speaking and blindness before dying at 35 years of age. An autopsy revealed that one quarter of his brain had become dysfunctional due to softening of tissue. To the extent that any of these illnesses, or more basic conditions giving rise to them, are inheritable, Nietzsche may have shared them. The cause or causes of the various intestinal problems which dogged him throughout his life are unknown, though they may have been due to the dysentery he contracted as a young man (we do not know how adequate the treatment he received was). He was once diagnosed with chorioretinitis (inflammation of the retina and its protective layer) and that certainly would have contributed to his vision problems. So there may have been many conditions from which he suffered simultaneously; but in all likelihood, it was a meningioma that brought on his dramatic collapse.

---

[2] See Schain 2001, Sax 2003, Orth and Trimble 2006, and Owen et al. 2007.

[3] See Owen et al. 2007: 629 and Ghadirian et al. 1986.

[4] The diagnosis was offered first by Leonard Sax 2003. Owen et al. 2007 come to the same conclusion. Orth and Trimble 2006 suggest frontotemporal dementia, which would account for much of the behavior Nietzsche exhibited after entering the clinic, but would not account for the laterality of the symptoms Nietzsche presented (nor the eye problems, nor the grandiose delusions). Richard Schain 2001 suggests schizophrenia, which is a cluster of symptoms that is quite compatible with the meningioma diagnosis.

[5] There is now a sizable scientific literature on this link; for a start, see Santosa et al. 2007.

This more accurate understanding of Nietzsche's illness puts into perspective its role in shaping his philosophical concerns. Nietzsche's father died when Nietzsche was four. His younger brother, after experiencing seizures, died a few months later. He must have learned, at some point, of the illnesses of his aunts and uncles. And he himself began experiencing crushing headaches and painful eye problems before he turned ten. It would have been impossible for him *not* to have suspected that whatever killed his father and brother, and otherwise debilitated his mother's relatives, lay also in his own future. And in all likelihood, he was *right*. As a boy, he began to carry in his skull the cause of terrible suffering and helpless madness. The question he faced, over the rest of his life, was what to do about it.

3 HISTORY OF THE DIAGNOSIS

But before turning to the philosophical issues connected with Nietzsche's illness, we should briefly recount the circus-like history of controversies over the syphilis diagnosis.[6]

As stated above, Nietzsche had been diagnosed with tertiary syphilis soon after his collapse in Turin. The doctors who subsequently examined Nietzsche had neither reason nor inclination to challenge this diagnosis. Apparently—as incredible as it may sound to modern ears—Nietzsche's mother and sister *were never informed of the diagnosis* while Nietzsche was alive, and Elizabeth learned of it only after her brother's death. Elizabeth was scandalized by this information and hired Dr Paul Julius Möbius to refute the claim that Nietzsche had syphilis. Möbius examined the evidence, but ended up siding with the doctors at Basel and Jena. Indeed, he published a book saying so, concluding it with the warning that no one should read Nietzsche's books, since their author had a syphilitic brain. Elizabeth, for her part, upon no real evidence whatsoever, claimed that Nietzsche's madness had been brought on by some mysterious "Javanese tea" he had been ingesting, along with the chloral hydrate he often used to help him sleep.

But Möbius's opinion went otherwise unchallenged until 1926, when Dr Kurt Hildebrandt published a book arguing that Nietzsche's several maladies were in fact psychosomatic, resulting from the tremendous emotional pressures present in his life (as well as Nietzsche's suppressed desires to avoid his academic work at Basel and avoid Wagner's adoring crowds at Bayreuth). *En route* to this conclusion, Hildebrandt noted many of the incongruities between the syphilis diagnosis and Nietzsche's symptoms, but ended up endorsing the syphilis diagnosis anyway, since he believed that clearly something had gone wrong physically with Nietzsche's brain, causing his collapse in Turin. He also raised the possibility that Nietzsche had contracted syphilis nonsexually, a possibility Walter Kaufmann later advertised in various works.

In 1930, Erich Podach, a philologist without any training in medicine, brazenly took on the medical establishment and argued that the syphilis diagnosis did not fit with Nietzsche's complete medical record. This touched off a dispute with Dr Wilhelm Lange-Eichbaum, a follower of Möbius's methods and ideas, who insisted vaguely that some doctor in Berlin had incontrovertible evidence that Nietzsche had contracted syphilis in a brothel in Leipzig and had been treated by two Leipzig physicians. Neither Lange-Eichbaum nor anyone else was

---

[6] This history is recounted in greater detail in Schain 2001: chapter 10.

able to track down these Leipzig physicians, and the Berlin doctor's evidence turned out to have been merely a communication from Möbius himself. Still—despite this evidentiary short-circuit—Lange-Eichbaum's standing in the medical community and Podach's lack thereof persuaded many scholars that the syphilis diagnosis was correct. (After World War II, Lange-Eichbaum published another book on Nietzsche, this time claiming that Nietzsche's syphilitic thought provided the moral and political self-justification for the Third Reich.)

Controversies over the diagnosis continued throughout the 1940s, 1950s, and into the 1960s, without any new light being shed on the matter. In the end, the more influential biographers either sided with the medical experts and perpetuated the syphilis diagnosis, or steered clear of any settled conclusion.[7] It was not until Sax (2003) that the syphilis diagnosis was creditably discredited.

4 Sickness, Health, and Philosophy

No philosopher ever suffered as Nietzsche suffered. His eye condition made reading and writing extremely difficult and painful; most of his books had to be dictated, at least in part. Still, he forced his eyes into use, which made his pains and difficulties all the more severe. His headaches would routinely lay him out, miserable and vomiting, for several days every two or three weeks. In 1875 he estimated, "Every two or three weeks I spend about thirty-six hours in bed, in real torment" (*SL* 137).[8] By 1879, these headaches were liable to spread out over nine days, and he estimated that he had lost about one-third of the year to them (referred to in Hayman 1980: 219).[9] On top of all this, he often suffered from assorted digestive problems, as well as from the nineteenth-century remedies for them (including chemical baths, enemas, leeches, and diets that were nothing if not creative). He traveled incessantly from 1879 onward, seeking exactly the right environmental conditions to allow him to even begin his work. Somehow, amidst all these painful episodes and so much disruptive motion, he managed to publish more than a dozen profound books and amass a mountain of notes.

All this just to make the point that Nietzsche's state of health was a critical concern for him at every waking moment. One small misstep, he believed, could immobilize him for days or weeks. He knew that his extraordinary caution might seem ridiculous to others, but his only hope, in the face of his terrible ailments, was to cultivate a lifestyle which gave him maximal control over his immediate environment so that he would have the chance to accomplish his life's work.[10] His illness, then, was something of an elephant in the living room: no matter where he looked, he saw it, and there was no avoiding it or getting around it.

It is then little wonder that the notion of *health* became so central to Nietzsche's philosophy. It is a value he never denigrates, abandons, or "revalues." Instead, it becomes something

---

[7] The former is exemplified by Blunck 1953, Hollingdale 1965, Kaufman 1974, and countless others drawing upon them; the latter by Hayman 1980 and Safranski 2002.

[8] Letter to Rohde, December 8, 1875.

[9] Letter to Elizabeth Nietzsche, December 29, 1879.

[10] Letter to Overbeck, November 1880: "The daily struggle against my head trouble and the laughable complexity of my distresses demand so much attention that I am in danger of becoming *petty* in this regard... Help me hold on to this hiddenness—tell people I am not living in Genoa; for a good long time I must live without people and live in a city where I do not know the language" (*SL* 174).

of his own replacement for "the good," or "knowledge," or "truth," or any of the other traditional values Nietzsche calls into question. His philosophy as a whole—and his life, come to
think of it—were aimed at regaining health after suffering debilitating sickness and finding
ways to maintain or enhance one's health when challenged with injury.

Health, as we ordinarily think of it, is the capacity of an organized entity to rebound
with strength when injured. The key question is, "How much can this thing suffer and still
rebound to its former state of stability, power, and influence?" A healthy human, animal,
plant, garden, economy, or corporation can withstand many assaults upon it and return,
under its own power, to its former state; unhealthy ones (the *décadents*, as Nietzsche later
calls them) tend to falter or die under lesser assaults. Of course, being healthy does not
imply anything about the entity's "goodness" in any traditional moral sense. A weed can be
as healthy as a rose and a cancer cell is all too often healthier than the cells around it. Health
is a measure of *resilience* or strength under opposition and it is a value which Nietzsche
thinks life itself endorses and promotes in us. "All naturalism in morality, that is, all *healthy*
morality, is ruled by an instinct of life," Nietzsche writes (*TI*: "Morality as Anti-Nature" 4).
That is, the instinct of life, when allowed to express itself, steers us toward the values that
are genuinely healthy for us, though these healthy values do indeed oppose what traditional
morality promotes.

We exhibit health when we are injured and are able to rebound. But it is also true that we
become healthier in this rebounding. Suffering, to a healthy individual, is like being inocu-
lated: we experience a certain kind of suffering and we learn and grow stronger through the
experience. In the preface to *The Gay Science*, Nietzsche recounts how injury and sickness
yield great returns upon recovery:

> In the end, lest what is most important remain unsaid: from such abysses, from such severe
> sickness, also from the sickness of severe suspicion, one must return *newborn*, having shed
> one's skin, more ticklish and malicious, with a more delicate taste for joy, with a tenderer
> tongue for all good things, with merrier senses, with a second dangerous innocence in joy,
> more childlike and yet a hundred times subtler than one has ever been before. (*GS* Preface 3)

The healthy ones become stronger through enduring sicknesses, and never more than
when those sicknesses are severe. Nietzsche does not explicitly provide an explanation for
this fact, that we can rebound with greater strength following injury, but it is not hard to
put together a plausibly Nietzschean explanation. Presumably, to fight off the sickness, the
healthy person needs to appropriate the strength in the sickness and turn it to the person's
own advantage: this is a case where one "will to power" co-opts another one and thereby
strengthens itself.[11] Hence the person ends up stronger (and also subtler and more sensitive)
in multiple respects.

That is what happens, at any rate, if we respond to sickness in a *healthy* way. We welcome
sickness and struggle, in anticipation of the greater health and strength that will come with
our recovery. But if we respond to sickness in a *sick* way, then we will seek to avoid sicknesses
and when we are afflicted, we will try our best to flee from our pain rather than incorporate
its strength. We may also try to drown out our pain (that is, redirect our attention away from
it) by pouring resentment upon whatever we imagine as the cause of our suffering:

[11] For further discussion of this, see Richardson 1996: 28–44.

...one wishes, by means of a more vehement emotion of any kind, to *anesthetize* a torment-ing, secret pain that is becoming unbearable and, at least for the moment, to put it out of con-sciousness—for this one needs an affect, as wild an affect as possible and, for its excitation, the first best pretext. "Someone must be to blame for the fact that I feel bad"—this kind of reason-ing is characteristic of all who are diseased. (*GM* III: 15)

And this passage continues, painting in vivid colors a portrait of the unhealthy ones making matters worse for themselves through blame-mongering:

Those who suffer are one and all possessed of a horrifying readiness and inventiveness in pre-texts for painful affects; they savor even their suspicion, their brooding over bad deeds and apparent curtailments; they dig around after dark questionable stories in the viscera of their past and present, where they are free to wallow in a tormenting suspicion and intoxicate them-selves on their own poison of malice—they tear open the oldest wounds, they bleed to death from scars long healed, they make malefactors out of friend, wife, child, and whatever stands closest to them.

The unhealthy sufferer is exactly like someone who trashes his own living room after hear-ing bad news. He "blames" the chair, the end table, and the bookshelf and punishes them, though of course what he is really after is the feeling that he is not a victim but a powerful aggressor. For the moment, anyway, the bad news is "put out of consciousness." Only later does he realize the damage he has done to himself—though he is still more likely to blame anyone other than himself.

Throughout Nietzsche's writings there are many detailed discussions of health and sickness, but this is not the right place for a full examination of them. For our purposes, what we should note in these twin passages is just how much personal experience is recorded in them. The first is an exuberant depiction of just how *good* it feels when one has recovered. The second is an equally astute portrait of way in which we desperately dig around for someone to blame when we are simply overwhelmed by pain. Nietzsche evi-dently knew both feelings most intimately. The first he knew as health, as convalescence, as *recovery*; the second he knew as continuing disease, as an attitude born of weakness, as *resentment*.

The task for Nietzsche, both personally and philosophically, was to compose one's attitude to make recovery more predominant than resentment. His personal task, specifically, was this: how shall I construe my experiences so that I am more inclined to see each injury as an opportunity for greater strength and health in this life rather than as one further incentive to hate my existence and dream of another one? His philosophical task was the essentially same, but now arranged for full orchestra: how can humanity gain strength from a clear knowl-edge of its own limitations, its natural origins, and the pointlessness of its existence, without lapsing into the illusions and superstitions of the past? This turned out to be the problem of nihilism.[12]

---

[12] For a full-scale discussion of this problem in Nietzsche's philosophy, see Reginster 2006.

5 Madness as Revelation

Among philosophers, madness is what happens when passion overpowers reason. As a rule, this has been viewed by the great philosophers as a very bad thing. So it comes as no surprise that, at least in his early works, Nietzsche reverses this verdict and sees "mad" frames of mind as indicative of something deep and important that reason is unable to access.

The Birth of Tragedy offers the most explicit discussion of this view. The work as a whole aims to explain the deeply powerful art of classical Greek tragedy through two organs of the human psyche: the Apollonian and the Dionysian. Through the Apollonian we are able to transform the world of ordinary experience, which is often hard to comprehend, into a world of beautiful illusion and fantasy. The sloppy disorder of experience is made intelligible through a poem, or through a painting, and we are thus able to reinterpret our experience and live in a simulacrum of it. The Apollonian is our ability to impose graceful measure, symmetry, and harmony on that which is inherently chaotic and confused; to render sane what is by itself insane. But we are not allowed to remain in this dream world. Every so often, reality itself punches through this veil of appearance and forces us to confront the beastlier, chaotic world beneath the illusion. Our openness to this violent reality is the Dionysian. Some event reveals to us the primordial pain at the root of the existence of the world: the brute fact *that it is*, and that there is no reason, purpose, or explanation behind it. In this moment of revelation, we are restored to nature and to reality. All illusion is dropped, as well as any rational or meaningful schema we have imposed upon the world. But along with terror and despair, this restoration also brings to us a deep joy, an intoxicated and ecstatic bliss that we celebrate in wine and song:

> Under the charm of the Dionysian not only is the union between man and man reaffirmed, but nature which has become alienated, hostile, or subjugated, celebrates once more her reconciliation with her lost son, man. […]
> In song and dance man expresses himself as a member of a higher community; he has forgotten how to walk and speak and is on the way toward flying into the air, dancing. His very gestures express enchantment. Just as animals now talk, and the earth yields milk and honey, supernatural sounds emanate from him, too: he feels himself a god, he himself now walks about enchanted, in ecstasy, like the gods he saw walking in his dreams. He is no longer an artist, he has become a work of art: in these paroxysms of intoxication the artistic power of all nature reveals itself to the highest gratification of the primordial unity. (*BT* 1)

The Greeks were experts in both Apollonian and Dionysian modes and they saw the task of their art to be a celebration of the Dionysian, but coupled and tempered by our equally strong need for Apollonian illusion. In the new preface to the work, written in 1886, Nietzsche draws attention to the key idea of the work: "that the existence of the world is justified only as an aesthetic phenomenon" (*BT*: "Attempt at Self-Criticism" 5)—that the senseless and absurd become meaningful by our making them beautiful. The world is redeemed by transforming its senseless understructure—best seen through an intoxicated madness—into beautiful illusion, principally through music, the aesthetic mode which is able to incorporate both primitive rhythms and soaring harmonies.

According to Nietzsche, the Greeks realized that our capacity for mad frenzy is in fact a *condition* for a fully human life and not an obstacle to it. Eventually, he says, it was Euripides who, under Plato's spell, sought to cure this frenzy with the medicine of cold dialectic; and this in turn led to the death of Greek tragedy and the great impoverishment of art and philosophy generally. Human beings need the passionate madness of Dionysus if they are to grow rich in insight and strength and gain mastery over life's incessant challenge. The Dionysian, in other words, can be seen as a key component to Nietzschean health; without it, we shrivel and grow timid and ineffectual. What the younger Nietzsche celebrated in Wagner was his almost Greek ability to draw out the primordial passions and put them in harness with music so as to produce the aesthetic sublime. For the first time in a long while, it seemed, humans were to become capable of becoming *fully* human once again, through art.

These notions of "Apollonian" and "Dionysian" are terribly murky, of course, and Nietzsche moved on to new projects before focusing them into anything more precise. The terms could name real noumenal entities, akin to Schopenhauer's *Wille*; or they could name psychological proclivities in human beings; or they could be free-floating metaphors meant only to capture some observable distinction among kinds of artistic efforts. But the key idea is that the intoxicated madness of the Dionysian—"*Rausch*"—is capable of revealing something important. "*Rausch*" is the intoxicating "rush" one experiences when swept up in music, in the savage beating of drums, in soaring crescendos, or in the thrilling anonymity of a mosh pit. The participant loses concern over her individuality and feels joined to greater forces within and without. *Rausch* could be taken to be merely a curious psychological phenomenon or it could be taken as an experience of prophetic significance. In *The Birth of Tragedy*, Nietzsche takes it to be the latter. Madness constitutes seeing through the illusions reason has made for itself and connecting with a profound condition for our being. It can be set aside only at the cost of stunting our spiritual engagement with the world.

The same attitude is present throughout the *Untimely Meditations*, though in the essays there is no explicit talk of "madness." Instead, in each one, Nietzsche berates his contemporaries for lacking the spiritual depth that is required to make great culture. It is not that the thinkers of his age are lacking in any rational capacities, intelligence, or skills. If anything, they are overly endowed with these. The problem is that they have failed to open their *hearts* to the deep perplexities, anguish, and joy that are at the core of our existence and the true subjects in great works of art. They lack precisely what *Rausch* is supposed to reveal. But instead of directing his fellows toward Dionysian madness, and to the primordial passions it occasions, Nietzsche instead directs them toward *nature*. In the final essay, "Richard Wagner in Bayreuth," Nietzsche claims that this is in fact what Wagner's art is saying to them:

> I lead you to a realm that is just as real, you yourselves shall say when you emerge out of my cave into your daylight which life is more real, which is really daylight and which cave. Nature is in its depths much richer, mightier, happier, more dreadful; in the way you usually live you do not know it: learn to become nature again yourselves and then with and in nature let yourselves be transformed by the magic of my love and fire. (*UM* IV: 6)

The fundamental idea of culture, as Nietzsche wrote earlier in "Schopenhauer as Educator," is "to work at the perfecting of nature" (*UM* III: 5)—meaning, the perfecting of the nature that lies at the ground of our existence, the condition with which we need to be reconnected before being transformed by a great artist's love and fire. The producers of culture need to be in touch with the violent and ecstatic conditions for human existence—"nature"—if their work is to successfully engage us. Thus the overall shape and function of both the Dionysian in *The Birth of Tragedy* and "nature" in the *Untimely Meditations* are very much the same: each is the irrational root of a meaningful human existence and getting in touch with it is required for rendering that existence meaningful.

6 THE FUNCTIONAL ROLE OF MADNESS

But later on, as Nietzsche abandoned the murky "artist's metaphysics" of *The Birth of Tragedy* and drifted away from Wagner, he adopted a more quasi-scientific and functionalist attitude toward madness. His focus was not on what *Rausch* reveals, since he had grown skeptical of any allegedly direct access to primordial truth. He was more interested in the functional role madness plays in the transformation of an individual from a mere beast of burden into a prophet, and the role it has played historically in getting populations to embrace new moral and religious ideas. But, as we shall see, he also continued to acknowledge that there is something vital about madness which is needed for any great cultural revolution. And to a certain extent, he even prescribed madness for himself and his own revolution.

Consider, for starters, this lengthy but all-too-revealing passage from *Daybreak*:

> Let us go a step further: all superior men who were irresistibly drawn to throw off the yoke of any kind of morality and to frame new laws had, *if they were not actually mad*, no alternative but to make themselves or pretend to be mad—and this indeed applies to innovators of every domain and not only in the domain of priestly and political dogma:—even the innovator of poetical metre had to establish his credentials by madness. [...] 'How can one make oneself mad when one is not mad and does not appear so?'—[...] The recipes [...] are essentially the same: senseless fasting, perpetual sexual abstinence, going into the desert or ascending a mountain or pillar, or 'sitting in an aged willow tree which looks upon a lake' and thinking of nothing at all except what might bring on an ecstasy and mental disorder. Who would venture to take a look into the wilderness of bitterest and most superfluous agonies of soul in which probably the most fruitful men of all times have languished! To listen to the sighs of these solitary and agitated minds: 'Ah, give me madness, you heavenly powers! Madness, that I may at last believe in myself! Give deliriums and convulsions, sudden lights and darkness, terrify me with frost and fire such as no mortal has ever felt, with deafening din and prowling figures, make me howl and whine and crawl like a beast: so that I may only come to believe in myself! I am consumed by doubt, I have killed the law, the law anguishes me as a corpse does a living man: if I am not *more* than the law I am the vilest of all men. The new spirit which is in me, whence is it if it is not from you? Prove to me that I am yours; madness alone can prove it.' (*D* 14)

Before turning to the philosophical implications of this passage, we would do well to note the biographically revealing ones. The "recipe" Nietzsche offers for inducing madness in oneself—the fasting, sexual abstinence, mountains, staring upon a lake—is not too far from Nietzsche's own mode of life, at least after 1879. The talk of overcoming the law ties in with Nietzsche's own observation, in *Ecce Homo*, that with *Daybreak* he began his project of revaluing all values. And as for the prayer to "the heavenly powers"—we know that *The Wanderer and His Shadow* and *Daybreak* were written under the most miserable physiological conditions Nietzsche ever experienced (1879–81); so it would appear that at least this part of his prayer to the heavenly powers was heard. We need to be aware that Nietzsche must have recognized his own living conditions in this passage.

The passage claims that for genuine innovation in any domain, some madness is needed. One needs at least the "mad" faith in one's own ability to overcome traditions and offer some new and viable alternative ("If I am not *more* than the law I am the vilest of all men"). *If* one is not mad already, and does not appear to be mad, then one needs a recipe for becoming mad. For Nietzsche, the critical ingredients in this recipe include social isolation, majestic scenery, and entertaining oneself with "wicked" thoughts. What are such conditions likely to do to a thinker? They will certainly bring him out of step with the social norm and lead him to make utterances and write books that are not typical fare. But beyond this, the hope is that such conditions will lead to *enthusiasm*, in the original sense of being inspired or divinely possessed. To be divinely possessed is to possess *genius*, and so, as Nietzsche writes just before the quoted passage, "all earlier people found it much more likely that wherever there is madness there is also a grain of genius and wisdom—something "divine," as one whispered to oneself" (*D* 14).

"Or rather," as Nietzsche then adds, "as one said aloud forcefully enough." For his explicit purpose in this passage is not exactly to recommend courting divine inspiration (he could not of course take such inspiration seriously), but rather to explain how it is that there come to be substantive changes in moral traditions. *A genius comes along*: that is to say, someone with a strange enough and lonely enough persona that other people take seriously his claims to inspiration. And *he* takes his own inspiration seriously as well; indeed, he is supremely confident in himself. Nietzsche's historical argument is quite nearly that people accept the new and even radical ideas of such asocial "geniuses" because, in the past, there has been just enough repayment to warrant further investment in them. It would seem, then, that someone need only spend a few months at the seashore or on the mountain, speaking with no one and thinking up strange thoughts, in order to become our next heralded guru, the one with the new answers to our old problems.

But it is not obvious that Nietzsche regards such opportunism as necessarily a bad thing. In *Human, All Too Human*, he notes that

> …when [the great spirits'] goal is the production of the greatest possible *effect*, unclarity with regard to oneself and that semi-insanity added to it has always achieved much; for what has been admired and envied at all times has been that power in them by virtue of which they render men will-less and sweep them away into the delusion that the leaders they are following are supra-natural. Indeed, it elevates and inspires men to believe that someone is in possession of supra-natural powers: to this extent Plato was right to say that madness has brought the greatest of blessings upon mankind. (*HAH* I: 164)

The end of this passage reads most naturally as an endorsement of at least some of the consequences of people believing their leaders are mad. Madness can be elevating and inspiring, and in that heightened sense of power, many extraordinary things can happen. Perhaps it is true, as Nietzsche had said in *Daybreak*, that anyone wishing to bring about any massive moral or religious change really does need either to be mad or become mad.

Again, it is impossible not to wonder where Nietzsche saw himself in this. We have already noted that Nietzsche, in his wandering years, seems to have followed (whether deliberately or not) his own recipe for madness and we have noted that he saw the utility of madness, in terms of bringing about significant spiritual revolution. When we start to think about *Thus Spoke Zarathustra*, the wonder about Nietzsche's own relation to madness deepens.

7 MADNESS OF ZARATHUSTRA

Madness, Nietzsche thinks, can be caused in two ways. It can be rooted in some form of *deficiency*, as when a profoundly sick individual is energized by some variety of resentment or illusory revenge and pursues it with wild abandon. Or madness can be caused by an *over-abundance* of powers, loves, and enthusiasms, as when an individual is so intoxicated by the opportunities of life that his or her ensuing behavior seems to be opposed to what the rest of us would regard as prudent and practical. This, at any rate, seems to be the distinction Nietzsche is trying to make in the following note from March–June 1888, though his central concern here is to understand how the madness born of deficiency is sometimes confused for the healthy madness born of overabundance:

> [...] history contains the gruesome fact that the exhausted have always been mistaken for the fullest—and the fullest for the most harmful.
> Those poor in life, the weak, impoverish life; those rich in life, the strong, enrich it. The first are parasites of life; the second give presents to it.—How is it possible to confound the two?
> When the exhausted appeared with the gesture of the highest activity and energy (when degeneration effected an excess of spiritual and nervous discharge), they were mistaken for the rich. They excited fear.—The cult of the *fool* is always the cult of those rich in life, the powerful. The fanatic, the possessed, the religious epileptic, all eccentrics have been experienced as the highest types of power: as divine.
> [...] To make oneself sick, mad, to provoke the symptoms of derangement and ruin—that was taken for becoming stronger, more superhuman, more terrible, wiser. One thought that in this way one became so rich in power that one could give from one's fullness.
> [...] On the highest rung of power one placed the most intoxicated, the ecstatic. (—There are two sources of intoxication: the over-great fullness of life and a state of pathological nourishment of the brain.) (*WP* 48)[13]

The back-and-forth quality of this note suggests that Nietzsche was still trying to make sense of the distinction himself. One can become intoxicated and appear full of strength and life, either from some kind of illness or from overabundant health. We can fill in some of the missing details by assuming that madness born of illness comes when something has gone wrong in an individual's psychology (the "fanatic, the possessed, the religious epileptic, all eccentrics"). Perhaps, for example, some deeply rooted fear of confrontation has manipulated a person's reason in such a way as to make the person blind to confrontation and to force them to see all things as agreeing in some invisible universal harmony and contributing to some comprehensive divine plan. In this case some groundless fear has skewed the person's perceptions and led to an apparently powerful, intoxicating superstition. To be sure, Nietzsche often accuses various human populations and historical movements of just

---

[13] A similar distinction is drawn between a lesser and a greater form of romanticism in *GS* 328.

this kind of madness; Christianity itself is a prominent example.[14] But intoxication can come as well from an overabundance of powerful drives which lead an individual to frenzied, celebratory behavior which is strikingly unusual ("stronger, more superhuman, more terrible, wiser") and which will seem mad to the rest of us. Indeed, it *is* mad, considered from any purely practical point of view.

We might alternatively characterize this distinction as between *psychological madness* and *philosophical madness*. The first is rooted in some cognitive shortcoming: perhaps some regulating feature in one's mind no longer functions as it should and the result is erratic or mad behavior. Philosophical madness, on the other hand, is supposed to be rooted in perfect health or overabundant health. The individual is so consummately healthy and strong that he or she is willing and able to take on the sort of risks and challenges that the rest of us regard as crazy. The two can be confused for one another, since in both cases individuals are propelled into abnormal behavior. But the difference, which is crucial for Nietzsche, is that only psychological madness is pathological; philosophical madness is the expression of health.

This, at any rate, seems to be the only way to distinguish the madness of Jesus, Paul, and Pascal from the madness of Nietzsche's own Zarathustra. Zarathustra is clearly supposed to be philosophically mad, out of an overabundance of health, "like a bee who has gathered too much honey", as he says to the sun (*Z* I: "Zarathustra's Prologue" 1). Indeed, Zarathustra's self-imposed mission is to coax his listeners toward a full affirmation of their origins (the earth) and their true capabilities—regardless of whether those capabilities lead to actions that should be called "good" or "evil" by the lights of some spurious ideology. Zarathustra's wisdom is a full embrace of *what is*, once *what is* is allowed to pursue its own ends freely and without corruption. It is a thorough affirmation of nature, of power, of tragedy, of triumph, and (finally) of the eternal return. "Man's greatest distance and depth and what in him is lofty to the stars, his tremendous strength—are not all these frothing against each other in your pot? Is it any wonder that many a pot breaks?" (*Z* IV: "On the Higher Man" 15). This frothing overfullness with the promise of each human and the promise of life is philosophical madness, which (it seems) is as fully able to produce a cracked pot as any psychological madness.

Thus Spoke Zarathustra is as much poetry as any kind of prose and is itself frothing with many exuberant and "mad" episodes and passages. It is for this reason that Nietzsche scholars tend to rely less on it than the works following it: it is simply too surreal, too poetic, and too maddeningly wild to yield much of anything when subjected to philosophical scrutiny. But these features are precisely what leads Nietzsche, late in 1888, to say of Zarathustra:

> He contradicts with every word, this most affirmative of all spirits; all opposites are in him bound together into a new unity. The highest and the lowest forces of human nature, the sweetest, most frivolous and most fearsome stream forth out of one fountain with immortal certainty. Until then one does not know what height, what depth is; one knows even less what truth is. [...] There is no wisdom, no psychology, no art of speech before Zarathustra. (*EH*: "Thus Spoke Zarathustra" 6)

This portrait of Zarathustra allows us to assemble a more complete picture of philosophical madness. Such madness entails an integration of the many disparate forces within an individual's

---

[14] For further discussion, see Huenemann 2010.

psychology. No drive is repressed, it seems; all are allowed full expression and development. The philosophical madman, we may speculate, affirms each element in his or her own psychology, and out of that turbulent froth of drives pours forth "one stream with immortal certainty"—perhaps what Nietzsche calls in *Twilight of the Idols* "a Yes, a No, a straight line, a *goal*" (*TI*: "Maxims and Arrows" 44). Zarathustra is able to harness his drives toward a single productive end (the production of wisdom, psychology, and speech, for example). He appears mad precisely because he is willing to give evidence to "the highest and the lowest forces of human nature, the sweetest, most frivolous and most fearsome." That may scare or bewilder the rest of us. But he does not suffer from psychological madness because of the *full* affirmation of his many drives: no drive is suppressed or unacknowledged and Zarathustra apparently can own up to all the forces animating him.

For Nietzsche, suffering as he was over the years 1879–85, Zarathustra was his own ideal, or the kind of philosophical madman he aspired to be in order to realign his various misfortunes into newfound strength. Lou Salomé, for her part, viewed the creation of the character Zarathustra as a self-transformation on Nietzsche's part, an attempt by Nietzsche to turn himself into something of a religious icon:

> The Zarathustra figure represents Nietzsche's own transformation, mirroring the transformation of his vitality into a godlike photograph; this is analogous to his dream about the birth of a superior man from the human. Zarathustra is, so to speak, Nietzsche's superior man; he is the superior Nietzsche. Consequently, the work possesses a deceptive double character: on the one hand, it is a work of literature in the aesthetic sense and it can be judged from that perspective exclusively; on the other hand, it is a work of literature only in a purely mystical sense—an act of religious creation through which the highest demands of Nietzsche's ethics find their fulfillment for the first time. (Salomé 2001: 123)

She knew as well as anyone the broad array of personal problems and strains Nietzsche was experiencing at the time, and knew of his resolve to overcome them and forge them into something positive (see his letter to Overbeck, December 25, 1882 (*SL* 199): "Unless I discover the alchemical trick of turning this—muck into gold, I am lost"). Zarathustra represents that transformation—not simply through its content as a work of fiction, but also through the fact that in creating it, Nietzsche also created for himself a means for overcoming the most miserable circumstances of his own life.[15]

---

[15] The conditions just prior to his writing *Thus Spoke Zarathustra* were especially miserable. In 1882 he suffered through the Paul Rée / Lou Salomé debacle, which by itself brought him to the brink of madness, as he confessed in his letters (see the letter to Overbeck, December 25, 1882; *SL* 198–9). And, to make matters worse, 1882 also brought to Nietzsche's awareness scurrilous rumors that had been circulating in Bayreuth about the nature of his illness and its connection to his alleged sexual misadventures. Wagner himself, in correspondence with Nietzsche's doctor in 1877, had speculated that Nietzsche's eye problems were caused by excessive masturbation. The content of this correspondence was then leaked in the summer of 1882, and by the time the rumors reached Nietzsche they had grown to include pederasty. See his letter to Gast, April 21, 1883. Needless to say, these rumors only added to the anguish Nietzsche was experiencing at this time. For more details, see Montinari 1988.

8 MADNESS OF NIETZSCHE

Certainly, by the time he wrote *Ecce Homo*, Nietzsche thought he had succeeded in acquiring a Zarathustra-like form of philosophical madness. The book is written in a thoroughly self-congratulatory mode, celebrating the great health he has gained through his various travails and the "good books" he has produced out of that consummate health. He holds nothing back, opining that "to take a book of mine into his hands is one of the rarest distinctions anyone can confer upon himself" (*EH*: "Why I Write Such Good Books" 1), and:

> Anyone who saw me during the seventy days of this autumn when I was uninterruptedly creating nothing but things of the first rank which no man will be able to do again or has done before, bearing a responsibility for all the coming millennia, will have noticed no trace of tension in me, but rather an overflowing freshness and cheerfulness. (*EH*: "Why I Am So Clever" 10)

Amidst these immodest declarations, he details his diet, his various likes and dislikes, his lifestyle, and so on. The work has just the sort of disjointed overabundance one would expect from a philosophical madman. But at the same time, knowing Nietzsche's advancing neurophysiological condition, one wonders whether a psychological madness was not also at work.

Indeed, one is led to wonder whether there really is any such thing as purely "philosophical" madness. To believe that there is would be to maintain that, sometimes, erratic or abnormal behavior (and even behavior that is dangerous to the self and others) issues from a mind that is in fact quite healthy. But the problem is that we typically gauge the healthiness of a mind on the basis of the behavior that it generates; so it is hard to see any possibility for philosophical madness, as Nietzsche describes it. We would need to have some independent account of mental health, perhaps one (like Nietzsche's) based on an ontology of drives, where we could individuate drives and determine when they are being fulfilled or frustrated. But since such an account would end up being so thoroughly tendentious and theoretical, it would be hard to place more confidence in it than we do in our ordinary judgments about the sanity or insanity of people's behaviors.

Despite these reservations, there are those unsettling moments when reasonable people wonder whether the alleged madman is saner than the science which condemns him. And the basic fact remains that, at least until the final days in Turin, Nietzsche did indeed manage to find a way to live through a horrendous set of circumstances. The fact that he did not kill himself is frankly impressive. And, of course, he did not merely endure his circumstances—he *embraced* them. If it took some sort of madness to achieve this result, we may be right in identifying it as a healthy form of madness—a philosophical madness, as opposed to a psychological madness.

How then are we to think of Nietzsche's mental state over his last year? Is there any reason for regarding his last philosophical works as issuing from a "healthy" sort of madness and his last postcards and ravings in the clinics as issuing from an illness? Or (and this seems much more likely) was there a gradual shift over 1888, as his system of beliefs, drives, and behavioral restraints moved from a more balanced state into a less balanced one? Was there always some degree of psychological madness at work in his writings, with a larger degree at work in the end?

It is impossible to provide any precise answer to this question. Here, for the sake of illustration, are four passages, two from *Ecce Homo*, and two from his last letters sent out in late 1888 and early 1889. Can anyone say which are which?

> One day there will be associated with my name the recollection of something frightful—of a crisis like no other before on earth, of the profoundest collision of conscience, of decision evoked against everything that until then had been believed in, demanded, sanctified.

> The unpleasant thing, and one that nags my modesty, is that at root every name in history is I; also as regards the children I have brought into the world, it is a case of my considering with some distrust whether all those who enter the "Kingdom of God" do not also come *out of* God.

> Wherever I go, here in Turin for example, every face grows more cheerful and benevolent at the sight of me. What has flattered me the most is that old market-women take great pains to select together for me the sweetest of their grapes.

> With every glance I am treated like a prince—there is an extremely distinguished air about the way people open the door for me or serve me food. When I enter a large shop, all the faces change.[16]

Anyone who has not already memorized these passages will find it difficult to sort out which passages came from a published work and which from the letters that caused Nietzsche's friends to fear for his sanity. We find the same thoughts balancing between profundity and nonsense, the same grandiose delusions, and the same misperceptions. Overall, the differences between *Ecce Homo* and the letters published in late December 1888 are differences in degree, not of kind. What he felt to be his great success is often hard to distinguish from the early signs of his mental collapse.

This is what may be sensibly said. Over his entire life, Nietzsche was, let us say, a *complicated* person. From early on, he saw himself as a kind of prophet, a destiny, who would leave an indelible mark upon cultural history. In order to fit this role, he often felt compelled to distance himself from others, though at the same time he felt despair over his loneliness. His health was complicated, as we have seen, and his personal relations were often intensely complicated. He may also have suffered from psychological disorders, which would have exacerbated the other problems. Out of this maelstrom of complications, he was able to effect a heroic strategy—his *philosophy*—for overcoming these various obstacles and establish for himself a meaningful, significant life in the face of them. In order to be effective, the strategy had to be employed sensitively and judiciously, as his conditions changed over time. But as his neurophysiological condition progressed, he began to lose control over the strategy. He was no longer able to clearly see what was happening around him or to see the changes in his own behavior. The applications of his strategy became odd, then more and more curious, and finally bizarre, perhaps over most of 1888. But—for whatever reason—at the same time his manic swings became more pronounced and he confused these swings for evidence of his own philosophical success. He thought he had solved the riddle of his own existence. But in fact he was being overcome by a malady that had been progressing over his whole life. And that is a tragic ending if ever there was one: for while Nietzsche was in ardent pursuit of one kind of madness, he fell victim to another.[17]

---

[16] *EH*: "Why I Am a Destiny" 1; letter to Jacob Burckhardt, January 6, 1889 (*SL* 347); *EH*: "Why I Write Such Good Books" 2; letter to Meta von Salis, December 29, 1888 (*SL* 343).

[17] I wish to thank Dr Thomas Schenkenberg of the University of Utah's Department of Neurology for his generous help in sorting through the possible diagnoses of Nietzsche's illness. He in turn discussed

Bibliography

(A) Works by Nietzsche

BT   he Birth of Tragedy, trans. Walter Kaufmann. New York: Vintage Books, 1967.

D   Daybreak, trans. R. J. Hollingdale. Cambridge: Cambridge University Press, 1997.

EH   Ecce Homo, trans. R. J. Hollingdale. New York: Penguin Books, 1979.

GM   On the Genealogy of Morality, trans. Maudemarie Clarke and Alan J. Swenson. Indianapolis: Hackett Publishing, 1998.

GS   The Gay Science, trans. Walter Kaufmann. New York: Vintage Books, 1974.

HAH   Human, All Too Human, trans. R. J. Hollingdale. Cambridge: Cambridge University Press, 1986.

SL   Selected Letters of Friedrich Nietzsche. Indianapolis: Hackett Publishing, 1996. Reprint of Selected Letters of Friedrich Nietzsche. Chicago: University of Chicago Press, 1969.

TI   Twilight of the Idols, trans. R. Polt. Indianapolis: Hackett Publishing, 1997.

UM   Untimely Meditations, trans. R. J. Hollingdale. Cambridge: Cambridge University Press, 1997.

WP   The Will to Power, trans. Walter Kaufmann and R. J. Hollingdale. New York: Vintage Books, 1968.

Z   Thus Spoke Zarathustra, trans. Walter Kaufmann. New York: Penguin Books, 1978.

(B) Other Works Cited

Blunck, Richard. 1953. Friedrich Nietzsche: Kindheit und Jugend. Munich and Basel: Ernst Reinhardt.

Ghadirian, A. M., Gauthier, S., and Bertrand, S. 1986. "Anxiety Attacks in a Patient with a Right Temporal Lobe Meningioma," Journal of Clinical Psychiatry 47: 270–1.

Hayman, Ronald. 1980. Nietzsche: A Critical Life. New York: Oxford University Press.

Hildebrandt, Kurt. 1928. Gesundheit und Krankheit in Nietzsches Leben und Werk. Berlin: Krager.

Hollingdale, R. J. 1965. Nietzsche: The Man and His Philosophy. Baton Rouge: Louisiana State University Press.

Huenemann, Charlie. 2010. "Nietzschean Health and the Inherent Pathology of Christianity," British Journal for the History of Philosophy 18: 73–89.

Kaufmann, Walter. 1974. Nietzsche: Philosopher, Psychologist, Antichrist. Princeton: Princeton University Press.

Lange-Eichbaum, Wilhelm. 1928. Genie, Irrsein, und Ruhm. Munich: Reinhardt.

Lange-Eichbaum, Wilhelm. 1946. Nietzsche: Krankheit und Wirkung. Hamburg: Lettenbauer.

Möbius, Paul. 1902. Über das Pathologische bei Nietzsche. Wiesbaden: J. F. Bergmann.

Montinari, Mazzino. 1988. "Nietzsche and Wagner One Hundred Years Ago: 1980 Addendum," in T. Harrison (ed.), Nietzsche in Italy. Saratoga, Calif.: ANMA Libri & Co., 113–18.

Orth, M. and Trimble, M. R. 2006. "Friedrich Nietzsche's Mental Illness—General Paralysis of the Insane vs. Frontotemporal Dementia," Acta Psychiatrica Scandinavica 114.6: 439–44.

the case with Dr Jim Poulton, Dr E. T. Ajax, and Dr Richard Gier, all of whom I hereby thank for their indirect guidance. None of them should be held responsible for any mistakes in this essay. Rob Sica provided helpful comments and directed me to some of the psychiatric literature. Also, I thank Dr Dave Christian for several discussions of the issues raised in this essay.

Owen, Christopher M., Schaller, Carlo, and Binder, Devin K. 2007. "The Madness of Dionysus: A Neurological Perspective on Friedrich Nietzsche," *Neurosurgery Online* 61.3: 626–31.

Podach, E. F. 1931. *The Madness of Nietzsche*, trans. F. A. Voigt. London and New York: Putnam.

Reginster, Bernard. 2006. *The Affirmation of Life.* Cambridge, Mass.: Harvard University Press.

Richardson, John. 1996. *Nietzsche's System.* New York: Oxford University Press.

Safranski, Rüdiger. 2002. *Nietzsche: A Philosophical Biography*, trans. Shelley Frisch. New York and London: W. W. Norton & Co.

Salomé, Lou. 2001. *Nietzsche*, trans. S. Mandel. Urbana and Chicago: University of Illinois Press.

Santosa, C., Strong, C. M., Nowakowska, C., Wang, P. W., Rennicke, C. M., and Ketter, T. 2007. "Enhanced Creativity in Bipolar Disorder Patients: A Controlled Study," *Journal of Affective Disorders* 100.1–3: 31–9.

Sax, Leonard. 2003. "What Was the Cause of Nietzsche's Dementia?" *Journal of Medical Biography* 11: 47–54.

Schain, Richard. 2001. *The Legend of Nietzsche's Syphilis.* Westport, Conn.: Greenwood Press.

PART II

HISTORICAL RELATIONS

CHAPTER 4

....

NIETZSCHE AND
THE GREEKS

....

JESSICA N. BERRY

"Oh, those Greeks!" Nietzsche gushes in the 1886 Preface to *The Gay Science*, "They knew how to live" (*GS* Preface 4). To take this exclamation as indicative of the highest praise, from a philosopher whose thought has often been captured—if somewhat superficially—in the contrast between what is "life-affirming" and "life-denying," would be entirely justified, with one *caveat*: Nietzsche's philosophical views are not so neatly bipolar and his relationship with Hellenic thought and culture not nearly so two-dimensional as such a gloss would suggest. On the whole, Nietzsche's attitude toward Greek antiquity was of course extremely positive, at times glowing: in a notebook entry from 1875, he heralds them as "the only people of *genius* in world history" (*KSA* 8: 59). But this claim, though not inaccurate, flirts with vapid generalization, since his interest in and affection for Greek figures were far from equally distributed. His estimations vary widely over the hundreds of references to Greek authors and ideas that appear in his work, both published and unpublished, from the beginning to the end of his productive career.

One conspicuous exception to the above claim that the Greeks "knew how to live" is of course Plato, whom Nietzsche found "deviated so far from all the fundamental instincts of the Hellenes, so morally infected, so much an antecedent Christian" that he is tempted "to describe the entire phenomenon 'Plato' by the harsh term 'higher swindle' " (*TI*: "What I Owe to the Ancients" 2). And more generally, Nietzsche's enthusiasm for thinkers in the sixth and fifth centuries BCE—what he called the "tragic age" of the Greeks—far outstripped his interest in the Hellenistic philosophers, about whom he was noticeably quieter and less effusive.[1] In keeping with the rigorousness and depth as well as the breadth of Nietzsche's training as a classical philologist, he would, quite rightly, have rejected the idea that "the Greeks" constitute a homogeneous category. Our approach here will be accordingly selective, focusing on some of the earliest Greek authors whose work helps illuminate Nietzsche's own work, rather than attempting any comprehensive overview of so complex

---

[1] Reflecting on *BT* in *EH* (*EH*: "The Birth of Tragedy" 3), Nietzsche singles out "those of the two centuries *before* Socrates" as "the *great* Greeks in philosophy."

a relationship.[2] In that respect, of course, the title of this contribution, "Nietzsche and the Greeks," is somewhat misleading. But it is crucial to appreciate that Nietzsche himself, though he would call time and again upon "our luminous guides, the Greeks" (*BT* 23) and though he would frequently allow himself the indulgence of referring to them collectively or to the Greek "character," was fully aware that no generalizations about a culture that spans the centuries from the Mycenaean to the Hellenistic era can be particularly accurate or instructive or completely free from distortion.

What we should hope to gain from an investigation into Nietzsche's fascination with Hellenic thought and culture is, rather, a keener sense of the sort of kinship Nietzsche purported to have felt with the Greeks and the extent to which his concerns were mirrored by theirs and gradually shaped by their framing of problems that already loomed large for him, as well as the way in which his approach to them, through their texts, lends us insight into his philosophical methodology. We will begin, then, with an examination of the methodological scruples Nietzsche developed in the course of his quarrelsome relationship with Classics as an academic discipline. Nietzsche's relationship with classical philology as a profession was a rocky one, but important for the development of his philosophy. Next, we will turn to three figures whose thought has influenced—or has been alleged to have influenced—Nietzsche's central projects and mature views. Foremost among these projects is his revaluation of values, and, as we will see, the concerns that animate it emerged early on and fueled Nietzsche's keen interest in the Homeric epics. In turn, his vision of pre-Archaic Greek civilization helped bring those concerns into even sharper relief and helped Nietzsche articulate his critique of contemporary and conventional moralities.

After considering briefly Nietzsche's singular interest in Homer, we will look toward the Greek philosophers, concentrating on two cases in point, Heraclitus and Pyrrho. The importance of the former figure has long been acknowledged by those with a professional interest in Nietzsche. He has been credited with informing not only Nietzsche's critique of

[2] Of the substantial—and growing—literature on Nietzsche's intellectual debt to the Greeks, the bulk reflects a similarly selective approach and thus comprises primarily article-length treatments focused on one or another ancient figure, text, or idea. *Die Antike in Nietzsches Denken: Eine Bibliographie* by Lindken and Rehn (2006) is a helpful field guide to this material. There are relatively few book- or monograph-length contributions to the field whose titles promise synoptic treatments of Nietzsche and antiquity, and all seem to aim at a more comprehensive treatment than they in fact provide: Hubert Cancik 1995 offers a very useful and historically sensitive account of Nietzsche's philological training and deals at length with Nietzsche's early philosophical reflections on the Greeks, but his series of lectures is weighted fairly heavily toward Nietzsche's early writings and is generally more informative than interpretive. The more recent Müller 2005 delivers a two-part account of Nietzsche's debt to the Greeks. The first, historical investigation of Nietzsche's early career pays special attention to his relationship with his Basel colleague Burckhardt and his study of Diogenes Laertius; the importance of both is now widely acknowledged. Sustained discussion of pre-Platonic thought, however, occupies only a brief chapter and is limited almost entirely to Heraclitus and Parmenides. The second part aims to be more philosophical and focuses on Nietzsche's struggle with Socrates and Plato. In the scholarship in English, Victorino Tejera 1987 endeavors primarily to reconstruct the historical Socrates in such a way as to defend him against Nietzsche's charges of decadence and decline, but his insistently poetic discussion saddles Nietzsche with an unfortunately sloppy composite Socrates, whom he is alleged to have violently misunderstood, and does so on the basis of some fairly idiosyncratic and liberal readings of the Platonic texts (1987: 102). Similar difficulties and a host of others plague Wilkerson 2006, on which see Mann 2008.

Platonic metaphysics, which he clearly does, but also with having contributed to positive metaphysical or ontological doctrines in Nietzsche; I shall argue, however, that Heraclitus has been miscast in the second of these two roles. Secondly, turning to the latter of these figures, Pyrrho of Elis, I will argue that his skeptical methods have largely been overlooked as an aid to making Nietzsche's views on truth and knowledge more comprehensible. In both cases, we will find that an independent working knowledge of the relevant Greek figures *on their own terms*, and not only through the lens of Nietzsche's works, can be decisive in forming a better or a worse, even a right or a wrong reading of his texts.

1 "*PHILOSOPHIA FACTA EST QUAE PHILOLOGIA FUIT*"[3]

The basic facts of Nietzsche's training and early career as a classical philologist are by now well known: he was educated at Pforta, the most prestigious school in Germany for the study of Classics, before entering the University of Bonn in 1864. There his talents greatly impressed Friedrich Ritschl, whom he followed to Leipzig and who helped secure his post as a professor of classical philology in Basel. By the age of 25, he attained the status of full professor and remained active in that role for the next decade. The work he produced during this period, unquestionably and soberly philological in character, is less well known: among other things, he published in the journal *Rheinisches Museum* a study of the poet Theognis and three lengthy studies on the Greek doxographer Diogenes Laertius, which collectively constitute half of Nietzsche's published philological work. He lectured publicly on the Homeric epics and on "rhythm" in Greek music and lyric poetry, read and wrote extensive notes for a series of courses on the pre-Platonic philosophers, and drew up notes and sketches for an authoritative commentary and authentication of the fragments of the atomist philosopher Democritus of Abdera. In 1868, he even compiled a comprehensive index of twenty-four years of *Rheinisches Museum*; never let it be said that Nietzsche did not pay his dues as a classicist. Yet the bulk of his efforts during this time, when he was most intensely absorbed with ancient thought and culture, went unpublished, and a good deal of this material is fragmentary, unrevised, and available only in German (or in the case of some of his student writings, of course, Latin or Greek).[4]

Nevertheless, some of the circumstances surrounding these early chapters of Nietzsche's intellectual biography are notorious. It is often asserted, for instance, that the publication

---

[3] "What was once philology has now been made into philosophy": Nietzsche concluded his inaugural lecture at Basel (May 28, 1869) with this reversal of a quote from Seneca's *Epistles* (108: 23), "*quae philosophia fuit facta philologia est.*" See "Homer und die klassische Philologie" (*FS* 5: 305).

[4] The five volumes of Nietzsche's *Frühe Schriften*, edited by Mette and Schlechta (Munich, 1994), cover comprehensively the years 1854–69 and include everything from Nietzsche's grammar-school essays to his early philological research. The fifteen-volume Colli and Montinari *Kritische Studienausgabe*, now the standard German-language edition of Nietzsche's collected work (correspondence aside), picks up where this leaves off. Although selections from Nietzsche's early notebooks are now beginning to be translated systematically into English, following the *KSA*, any similar volume-by-volume translation of Nietzsche's *Frühe Schriften* has yet to be undertaken.

of *The Birth of Tragedy* in 1872, which was savagely attacked by Ulrich von Wilamowitz-Moellendorff in his pamphlet *Zukunftsphilologie!*, effectively destroyed Nietzsche's reputation among respectable philologists and hopelessly compromised his future in the profession.[5] The reports of Nietzsche's demise as a philologist at the hands of the ill-tempered Wilamowitz, however, turn out to have been greatly exaggerated. It bears keeping in mind that although Wilamowitz would eventually become perhaps "the most celebrated Greek scholar of his time" (Lloyd-Jones 1976: 7), he was four years Nietzsche's junior, a student and young upstart not unlike Nietzsche himself, and had not yet secured this venerable reputation when he assailed Nietzsche's first major publication. Otherwise, the publication of *The Birth of Tragedy* was greeted with silence; the profession chose simply to ignore it.[6] That Nietzsche is not today counted among the towering figures in the history of classical philology is due more to the humble and marginal status of his positive contributions in the field than to any scandalous academic drama.

The received view, which informs scholarly work on Nietzsche even now, has it that he began his career as a philologist and eventually turned away from this vocation—even though accounts differ as to whether Nietzsche abandoned philology or was drummed out of the ranks. I propose, however, that the allegation of such a break has made it more difficult to interpret properly both Nietzsche's unique approach to the classical texts—an approach that was never philosophically neutral, even prior to his having much philosophical experience—and his persistent characterization of himself as a philologist—far beyond the posited "break" with philology. By his own estimation, if not by that of his colleagues, Nietzsche was a philologist to the end of his productive days, just as he was a philosopher from the very first. In Nietzsche's view at least, the line between these two areas of inquiry is itself far finer than it appears to us—if in fact it exists at all. Several considerations make this overlap clearer.

The first involves simply coming to terms with Nietzsche's insistence on self-applying the label "philologist" to the end of his days. In his mature works, his withering criticisms of *philosophers* are often advanced from the point of view of a *philologist*: "Forgive me," Nietzsche says in *Beyond Good and Evil*, "as an old philologist who cannot desist from the malice of putting his finger on bad modes of interpretation..." (*BGE* 22). Here and elsewhere, he observes a distinction between those whose drive to understand in some sense gets the better of them, such that they rush to judgment or make judgments far more ambitious than are sustainable, and himself, in whom the "metaphysical need" and desire for certainty does not compromise his judgment, or rather his holding back from judgment: "Whoever concerns himself with the Greeks," in particular, "should be ever mindful that an unrestrained thirst for knowledge for its own sake barbarizes men just as much as a hatred of knowledge. The

---

[5] Wilamowitz's infamous pamphlet, along with Wagner's and Rohde's defenses of Nietzsche and Wilamowitz's reply to those, are collected in Gründer 1969.

[6] This reaction is confirmed by Nietzsche's own outraged observation of it as entirely incongruous with the inflammatory nature of *BT*, captured in a letter to his own mentor Ritschl (January 30, 1872): "You will not grudge me my astonishment that I have not heard a word from you about my recently published book; and I hope you will also not grudge me my frankness in expressing this astonishment to you. For this book surely is by way of being a manifesto, and surely it challenges one least of all to keep silence" (*SL* 93). According to James Whitman (1986: 454) as well, "scholars continue to refer to the reception of *BT* within the philological community of Nietzsche's time as 'violent controversy'. No phrase could be less apt." See also Silk and Stern 1981: chapter 5.

Greeks themselves, possessed of an inherently insatiable thirst for knowledge, controlled it by their ideal need for and consideration of all the values of life" (*PTG* 30–1). A certain critical distance and a cautious, "ephectic" attitude are distinctive of philological practice and are exactly what he accuses most thinkers of failing to exhibit.[7] And to practice philosophy properly, as he clarifies in a later work, demands that we be skillful readers—not only of texts, but also of people and the world around us, approaching them with precisely the skills appropriate to the philologist:

> Philology is to be understood here in a very wide sense as the art of reading well—of being able to read off a fact without falsifying it by interpretation, without losing caution, patience, subtlety in the desire for understanding. Philology as *ephexis* in interpretation: whether it be a question of books, newspaper reports, fate or the weather. (*A* 52)

I shall have more to say about Nietzsche's ephectic stance in what follows. For now, though, we can say that philology, for Nietzsche, was not restricted to a particular subject matter (e.g., classical texts), nor was it defined exclusively by reference to its typical products (e.g., theories regarding the authenticity or inauthenticity of ancient writings). In addition, and importantly, Nietzsche thought of philology methodologically, as a kind of interpretive art or skill—one in which his contemporaries were too often deficient. Thus, while he may have resigned his post as a professor of classical philology, he in no way saw himself as having ceased its proper practice.[8] Indeed, it may not be an exaggeration to suggest that he viewed the *preservation* of its proper practice as hinging on his departure from the profession itself; it is for this reason that in the notes for the never-finished *Untimely Meditation* "We Philologists," Nietzsche describes "the classicist of the future as skeptic of our entire culture, and thereby destroyer of professional philology" (*WC* 357).[9] Even by his earliest estimations, the profession was irredeemably corrupt and inspired very little hope that it would accomplish all it could or should accomplish.

Classicists might find it tempting to characterize Nietzsche's scathing remarks about philologists as sour grapes, the expression of resentment over a career cut short, but to do so would neglect the damning things Nietzsche had to say about philology as an academic discipline, and indeed, about his professional colleagues *during* the years in which he occupied a professorship in the field. This critical attitude is latent even in Nietzsche's inaugural lecture on Homer at Basel and it is in evidence over the years in which he was principally engaged with the *Untimely Meditations*—particularly "On the Uses and Disadvantages of History for Life" and "We Philologists." These essays reveal Nietzsche's conviction that the dispassionate ("scientific") examination of ancient texts and the collection and preservation of facts about the past, done for its own sake and ostensibly irrespective of questions of value—*philosophical questions*—was not only an empty enterprise, but could even be injurious to a culture or

---

[7] The skeptical character of philological practice is well illustrated in the first chapter of Porter 2000, "Skeptical Philology."

[8] David Lachterman (1992: 14–18) also makes this point emphatically, when he calls this "tissue of biographical 'facts'... a convenient myth, alleviating or cancelling the need to encounter at first hand Nietzsche's own [philological] published texts, lectures, schemes and notes."

[9] I shall refer to this essay as "We Philologists" ["*Wir Philologen*"] in the text, although citations to it will be abbreviated "*WC*," referring to the Arrowsmith (1990) translation "We Classicists." Arrowsmith's translation comprises plans and sketches from Nietzsche's notebooks throughout 1875 (cf. *KSA* 8: 9–96).

a people: "We want to serve history only to the extent that history serves life: for it is possible to value the study of history to such a degree that life becomes stunted and degenerate…" (*UM* II: Preface). And these essays reveal his opinion that the majority of contemporary philological efforts were little more than shallow antiquarian work.

Thus, in his early writings, Nietzsche's withering criticisms of *philologists* are already being advanced from the point of view of a *philosopher*. Reflecting on his field only shortly after taking it up, Nietzsche declares: "Here too we see how countless men actually live only as forerunners of a real man; the scholar, for instance, as forerunner of the philosopher, who knows how to make use of the scholar's antlike labor in order to make his own statement on the *value of life*. Obviously, when it's done without *guidance*, the *greatest part* of the ant-work is simply nonsense, superfluous" (*WC* 340). In his diagnosis of the myopia and narrowness of his colleagues, Nietzsche distinguished himself from these mere scholars and their "antlike labor" precisely by collapsing the distinction between philosophical and genuine philological work, essentially declaring himself perhaps *the first philologist*, just as in his later writings he would provocatively claim the title of a "psychologist without equal," and perhaps even *the first psychologist* (*EH*: "Why I Write Such Good Books" 5, "Why I Am a Destiny" 6).[10]

It was Nietzsche's psychological insight, in fact, that led to his conjecture that the interpretations of ancient texts advanced by most of his philological contemporaries were in fact projections of their own, peculiarly modern, Enlightenment values—what Nietzsche called *humanistic* or *humane* values [*das Humane*]—onto antiquity. Under the sway of this projection, the classics were held to be indispensable tools for the building of culture and for the reinforcement of dogmas about the fundamental goodness of human beings and the naturalness of civility, democracy, and man's harmony with the natural world (*WC* 359). Nietzsche contrasts these sharply with the *human* [*das Menschliche*]—indeed, *all too human*, even "immoral" and shamelessly brutal—characteristics that he claimed the Greek world, and as we shall see in the next section the Homeric world in particular, pointed to: "The *human element* that the classics show us is not to be confused with the *humane*. The antithesis is to be strongly emphasized; what ails philology is its effort to smuggle in the humane" (*WC* 328).[11] Young though he was, Nietzsche was not beyond accusing his contemporaries of blinkered philistinism, sophistry, poor judgment, shallowness, even ignorance (*WC* 326, 332, 370). But their ignorance he qualified as a willful sort of ignorance: they busied themselves with minutiae and remained narrow, refusing to see a broader picture, all the more easily to vindicate their own (*humanistic* or *humane*) values. The methods employed by classical philologists were in large part, in Nietzsche's assessment, self-serving.

What Nietzsche claimed for his own part, by contrast, was a knowledge of Hellenic life, thought and culture superior to the other members of his profession, on the basis of a clearer vision, a better awareness of his own historical and cultural situation, and a unique, self-professed kinship with the Greeks: "Greek antiquity has not yet been assessed as a whole," he

---

[10] That Nietzsche's view of himself as a psychologist was at all times integral to his self-image is also in evidence at *BGE* 23, 45, 222, 269; *GS* Preface 2; *GM* III: 19, 20; and *TI* Preface and "What I Owe to the Ancients" 3.

[11] *KSA* 8:17: "*Das Menschliche, das uns das Alterthum zeigt, ist nicht zu verwechseln mit dem Humanen. Dieser Gegensatz ist sehr stark hervorzuheben, die Philologie krankt daran, dass sie das Humane unterschieben möchte…*"

remarks in notes from 1875, but "if [a classicist] has the *talent*, he can claim possession of his heritage—that is, undertake the *assessment* of the whole Hellenic mind. So long as scholarship puttered at details, *misunderstanding* of the Greeks prevailed" (*WC* 329).[12] On a similar note in the second *Untimely Meditation*, he says:

> it is only to the extent that I am a pupil of earlier times, especially the Hellenic, that though a child of the present time I was able to acquire such untimely experiences. That much, however, I must concede myself on account of my profession as a classicist: for I do not know what meaning classical studies could have for our time if they were not untimely—that is to say, acting counter to our time and thereby acting on our time and, let us hope, for the benefit of a time to come. (*UM* II: Preface)

Here, then, Nietzsche credits the "untimeliness" that conditions the possibility of his critique of morality to his study of the Greeks. In this arena, as his notes from this period reveal, Nietzsche went so far as to estimate himself as "the only competent man in the lot" (*WC* 331), and we have no reason to suppose that his opinion of himself changed significantly over the course of his career.

2 HOMER

In the late 1860s and early 1870s, Nietzsche devoted careful study to the Greek tragedians, Aeschylus, Euripides, and Sophocles, and to historians—especially Thucydides. But he remarked to himself in the notes for "We Philologists" that the "greatest event is still the precociously *Panhellenic Homer*. Everything good comes from him" (*WC* 375). As we have seen, Nietzsche's denunciation of classical scholarship focused in large part on the delusions modern scholars fostered about the civility of the Greeks—a false prejudice exposed in his distinction between the *human* values he found in Greece and the *humane* values he indicted as projections or distortions. Homer, to whom Nietzsche refers explicitly more times than to any other single Greek figure, became an important vehicle for the representation of these "human values" and consequently a crucial figure for his reassessment or revaluation of the values of the earliest Greeks. Thus, he became a corrective to what had been the imposition upon them of modern ideals—those captured in Winckelmann's formula of "noble simplicity and quiet grandeur" and in the notion that the Hellenes enjoyed a harmonious existence and oneness with nature that had subsequently been lost. Using the Homeric epics as a lens, Nietzsche claimed to have recovered evidence of a far longer and more brutal past than his contemporaries were pleased to admit. Wilamowitz especially contested this view, but in a letter to Rohde (July 16, 1872), Nietzsche defended his interpretation against Wilamowitz's objections: "That a tremendous, wild conflict, emerging from dark crudity and cruelty, precedes the Homeric era, that Homer stands as victor at the close

[12] In this declaration, Nietzsche took inspiration from Friedrich August Wolf. Throughout the material for "We Philologists," Nietzsche transcribes passages from Wolf's *Kleine Schriften* that capture the idea that only one with great creative talent can really grasp the Greeks and make anything valuable out of a study of antiquity. Scholarship requires artistic talent (*WC* 336).

of this long comfortless period—this is one of my most certain convictions. *The Greeks are much older than people think*" (*SL* 97).[13]

The deeply irreligious worldview as a window on this recovered past and Homer's "cheerful" and "healthy" immoralism became pivotal in the articulation of Nietzsche's critique of contemporary morality:[14]

> Homer is so much at home among his gods, and as a poet takes such pleasure in them, that he at any rate must have been profoundly unreligious; with that with which popular belief presented him—a paltry, crude, in part horrible superstition—he trafficked as freely as a sculptor with his clay...(*HAH* I: 125).

The "freedom" Nietzsche attributes to Homer is important here, since Nietzsche takes it to be characteristic of the Hellenic world as a whole (at least prior to Plato) and its "human values": "The delight in *drunkenness*, delight in *cunning, revenge, envy, slander, obscenity*—in everything which the Greeks *recognized* as human and therefore built into the structure of society and custom. The wisdom of their institutions lies in there being no gulf between good and evil, black and white.... Where did the Greeks acquire this freedom? Clearly from *Homer*" (*WC* 375).[15] Freedom, in this non-metaphysically loaded sense of a mere absence of constraint or even of never having known such constraint, is in Homer's case a *freedom from* superstition, *from* the crushing weight of moral convention, and *from* the systems of morality that tyrannize modern individuals; more accurately, perhaps, it might be characterized just as a flagrant indifference to the behaviors and attitudes that contemporary morality—and Christian morality in particular—would prize highly.

In Nietzsche's attribution to Homer of an artistic and passionate spirit and a childlike naïveté,[16] he identified those characteristics that gave the most ancient peoples their capacity for an innocent delight in cruelty that provides such a striking contrast to Christian morality and indeed to any morality to which compassion and an absence of suffering were central.[17] By treating their gods as the source of the injustices committed by human beings, the Greeks remained altogether above that quintessentially Christian sentiment, guilt, and the Christian tendency to denigrate everything human and worldly: "For the longest time these Greeks used their gods precisely to keep 'bad conscience' at arm's length, to be able to

---

[13] This thesis is echoed at *HAH* I: 219 and at *D* 195.

[14] The second chapter of E. R. Dodds' classic study *The Greeks and the Irrational*, "From Shame-Culture to Guilt-Culture," though it does not mention Nietzsche, is helpful in illuminating with vivid textual references a distinction that is one of Nietzsche's primary concerns (Dodds 1966: 28–63). See also, of course, Bernard Williams's *Shame and Necessity* (1993).

[15] See also *HAH* II: 220.

[16] "When I say the Greeks were generally *more moral* than modern man, what does this mean? The utter visibility of the soul in behavior shows that they were without shame; that they lacked bad conscience. They were more open, more passionate, like artists. There's a sort of childlike naïveté about them, which gives a touch of purity, something close to holiness, to everything they do. Their individuality, very marked; isn't there a higher morality in that?" (*WC* 337)

[17] Paraphrasing Burckhardt's *Griechische Kulturgeschichte* in the notes for "We Philologists," Nietzsche writes: "Childlike nature. Credulous. Passionate. They live unconscious of the genius they produce. Enemies of constraint and stupidity. Pain. Imprudent behavior. Their way of intuitively understanding misery, combined with a sunny temperament, genial and cheerful. Profundity in understanding and glorifying everyday things (fire, agriculture). Deceitful. Unhistorical.... The individual raised to his highest powers through the polis. Envy, competition, as among talented people" (*WC* 360).

remain cheerful about their freedom of soul" (*GM* II: 23).[18] Since we saw above Nietzsche's characterization of Plato as an "antecedent Christian," Nietzsche's formula "Plato *contra* Homer" should now come as no surprise: "that is the complete, the genuine antagonism— there the 'otherworldly one' with the best of wills, the great slanderer of life; here its involuntary deifier, *golden* nature" (*GM* III: 25). Ultimately, Homer appears to Nietzsche not only as the antithesis of Plato but also as the "greatest victory over Christianity and Christian culture" (*KSA* 11: 86).

Nietzsche's aim in his studies of Homer, elsewhere in his work on ancient texts, and even in his reflections on Homer in his mature writings, was forcefully and consistently to emphasize, to broaden and deepen rather than to diminish, the abyss between ancient and modern worldviews. Unlike his immediate forerunners, who dreamt of reviving classical Athens in the modern age, Nietzsche went so far as to declare at one point: "My aim is: to create complete hostility between our modern 'culture' and the ancient world. Whoever wants to serve the former must *hate* the latter" (*WC* 341). Nietzsche appreciated that the triumph of Christian morality over modern Western society has been so complete, so decisive, that it is difficult, if not impossible, even to visualize an alternative ideal. In the hands of the most talented philologist, the Homeric epics afford us just such a vision—a way of saying, " 'So this has existed—once, at least—and is therefore a possibility, this way of life, this way of looking at the human scene' " (*PTG* 23). This is in no way to claim that they afford us a vision of the way things could be or ought to be now or in the future, but they are a valuable antidote to what Nietzsche sometimes calls the "poison" of Christianity and conventional moralities, since a fundamental feature of those systems is that they present themselves not only as universally true but also as categorical. Ultimately, the task is not to resurrect antiquity, which is what Nietzsche accused his contemporaries of trying to do in order to vindicate their own modern liberal values; rather, the task is to overcome it: "To *surpass* Greek culture by action—that is the task. But to do that, we must first know it" (*WC* 382). As we saw at the close of the previous section, it was in virtue of the "untimeliness" cultivated by his study of the Greeks, and of Homer in particular, that Nietzsche found himself in a unique position to accomplish precisely this difficult "revaluative" task.

3 HERACLITUS

In addition to their having furnished the material for a decisive critique of Christian morality, Nietzsche credited the Greeks with nothing less than having "invented *the archetypes of philosophic thought*," adding: "All posterity has not made an essential contribution to them since" (*PTG* 31). By 1872, the work Nietzsche prepared for publication focused increasingly on philosophical texts and problems. While his approach remained philological in the sense clarified above, Nietzsche indicated in the unpublished *Philosophy in the Tragic Age of the Greeks* that philosophical figures had for him come to be representative of Hellenism more broadly:

---

[18] Andrea Orsucci (2000: 366) points out that this view owes a great deal to Leopold Schmidt's *Die Ethik der alten Griechen* (1882), an important source for many passages in *GM* and in *BGE*.

It seems to me that those ancient wise men, from Thales through Socrates, have touched in their conversation all those things which to our minds constitute typical Hellenism. In their conversation as in their personalities they form the great-featured mold of Greek genius whose ghostly print, whose blurred and less expressive copy, is the whole of Greek history. If we could interpret correctly the sum total of Greek culture, all we would find would be the reflection of the image which shines forth brightly from its greatest luminaries. (*PTG* 32)

Among the "luminaries" Nietzsche treated in this work is the notoriously obscure Heraclitus of Ephesus, who takes center stage in *Philosophy in the Tragic Age*, figures prominently in Nietzsche's lectures on the pre-Platonic philosophers, and continues to appear in positive remarks in the published work throughout Nietzsche's career. In *Twilight of the Idols*, Nietzsche says: "I set apart with high reverence the name of *Heraclitus*" (*TI*: " 'Reason' in Philosophy" 2) as a kindred spirit who resists the idolatry of reason and the worship of rational activity as such—a decadent instinct to which philosophers starting with Socrates succumb. Nietzsche's admiration for Heraclitus, with whom he even claims to identify in important respects and "in whose proximity," he says, "I feel altogether warmer and better than anywhere else" (*EH*: "The Birth of Tragedy" 3), has been rightly noted. But the significance of his attention to Heraclitus has suffered from persistent misinterpretation.

The scholarship on Nietzsche and the so-called "dark" or "riddling" Ephesian has tended to treat Nietzsche's critique of Platonic "being" and his complementary promotion of "becoming" as an endorsement of an ontological position—an ontology of radical flux, inspired by Heraclitus.[19] This reading has, in its turn, been pressed into the service of supporting even more radical readings of Nietzsche's critical philosophy: it has been taken to underwrite his "perspectivism" as a doctrine that entails a rejection of any privileged epistemic standpoint; and it has been linked to a wide variety of anti-essentialist, anti-rationalist, and anti-realist programs, as well as a thoroughgoing rejection of truth and (in the most extreme cases) even of the canons of logical reasoning. Fortunately for Nietzsche, however, none of these views is easily sustainable.

First of all, such interpretations encourage the impression that Nietzsche's interest in Heraclitus is driven by primarily metaphysical and ontological, or at least cosmological, concerns. However, as with Homer, in many of the early (mostly unpublished) texts in which Nietzsche deals at length with Heraclitus, we can see that he expressly subordinates his interest in the *content* of Heraclitus' thought and the reconstruction of his doctrines to his interest in reconstructing Heraclitus' *character*. Of Homer, Nietzsche had written early on that the important problem is "*the question of the personality of Homer*" (*FS* 5: 290);[20] in the midst of dispute about the personal identity of the author of *The Iliad* and *The Odyssey*—specifically, whether that "author" was one or many—Nietzsche issued a clarion call to his colleagues to consider the question from the standpoint of *psychological* integrity and unity. The same spirit

---

[19] Though their conclusions are subtly different; see, for example, Cox 1998 and 1999: 163, 184–93, Richardson 1996, Nehamas 1985: 70–105, Magnus 1978, and Danto 1965: 72. Exceptions to this general trend can be found, of course, but those with a less radical reading of Nietzsche's views of truth and knowledge too often present themselves as forced either to sidestep the issue of Nietzsche's enthusiasm for Heraclitus or else to handle it with caution, acknowledging the difficulty of reconciling our impressions of Heraclitus' flux doctrine with any more systematic philosophy (e.g., Richardson 1996 and 2004).

[20] Nietzsche's inaugural lecture at Basel appeared in print with the title, "Homer and Classical Philology," but was originally called, "On Homer's Personality."

animates Nietzsche's interest in Heraclitus. Indeed, he tells us in the Preface to *Philosophy in the Tragic Age of the Greeks* that even if he had wholly rejected Heraclitus' cosmological aims (his attempt to find a unifying principle for the cosmos) and views (that *logos* provides such a principle), it would do little to undermine his enthusiasm for the *personality* of Heraclitus or of any of the pre-Platonic philosophers with whom he was preoccupied. Thus he opens *Philosophy in the Tragic Age* with the following (uncharacteristically flat-footed) programmatic remark: "I am going to tell the story—simplified—of certain philosophers. I am going to emphasize only that point of each of their systems which constitutes a slice of *personality* and hence belongs to that incontrovertible, non-debatable evidence which it is the task of history to preserve" (*PTG* 24).[21] And, even more concisely: "The only thing of interest in a refuted system is the personal element" (*PTG* 25).

It is important to keep in mind that Nietzsche's task as philologist and intellectual historian is not, as it arguably is for us, to offer detailed rational reconstructions of the systems of individual thinkers, but to record the place of the contribution of individual thinkers along a particular narrative arc, the aesthetic unity of which he took to be the great achievement of Hellenic culture and which has as much to do with the characters of those thinkers as with their doctrines.[22] So in *Philosophy in the Tragic Age* in particular, the presentation of Heraclitus is highly selective and also constrained by Nietzsche's interest in the trajectory of that narrative arc: he illuminates Heraclitus' cosmological pronouncements only in order to show him as a predictable link in a chain of philosophical developments that he takes to have the same fundamental aim—"to simplify the realm of the many" (*PTG* 49). But in other of Nietzsche's works, entirely other features are brought into relief: Nietzsche's long discussion of Heraclitus in the fragmentary essay "On the Pathos of Truth," for instance, is almost entirely silent on his cosmology, physics, and epistemology. Instead, he focuses extensively on Heraclitus' flagrant misanthropy, his solitary habits, and his disdain for political life and social convention:

> …no one will be able to imagine such regal self-esteem, such boundless conviction that one is the sole fortunate wooer of truth. Men of this sort live within their own solar system, and that is where they must be sought.…Such a being might seem more comprehensible in a remote shrine, among images of the gods and amidst cold, sublime architecture. As a man among men Heraclitus was incredible. (*PT* 63–4)

In this section of the essay, Nietzsche's focus is on the philosophical character in general and on the psychological profile of the searcher after truth; Heraclitus simply suits him best as a vivid illustration of this profile.

So we should be more cautious than to conclude that the account in *Philosophy in the Tragic Age* is the only guide or even the best guide to what Nietzsche identifies with in Heraclitus, or that his selection of this or that feature for presentation is an endorsement of its literal truth.[23] *Philosophy in the Tragic Age* was to provide only a framework within which philosophical problems would be eventually analyzed and cultural criticisms offered; though highly polished as a draft, it was never intended for presentation as a stand-alone work. And elsewhere than this

---

[21] See also the end of the original preface (*PTG* 23).

[22] On the significance of this methodological principle as characteristic of a robust tradition in classical philology from the 1830s onward, see Whitman 1986.

[23] As to the claim that, "because Nietzsche does feel so close to Heraclitus, we can, with some caution, use his readings of the latter as statements of his own conception of becoming" (Richardson 1996: 78), I am more cautious than most.

essay (e.g., in *BT* 11), Nietzsche maintains his focus on Heraclitus' significance as a cultural force and an important representative of the tragic worldview, as well as on his untimeliness, his visionary insight, and his general disdain for the common run of humanity.[24]

There appears to be some support for the radical interpretation in the later works, but these cases demand closer examination. Leading up to the denunciation of the "true world" as a fable in *Twilight of the Idols*, for instance, Nietzsche singles out Heraclitus for praise because, "When the rest of the philosopher crowd rejected the evidence of the senses because these showed plurality and change, he rejected their evidence because they showed things as if they possessed duration and unity" (*TI*: "'Reason' in Philosophy" 2). Though Nietzsche takes issue with Heraclitus' having rejected the senses at all, he concludes that, "Heraclitus will remain eternally right with his assertion that being is an empty fiction. The 'apparent' world is the only one: the 'true' world is merely *added by a lie*" (*TI*: "'Reason' in Philosophy" 2). Here it is crucial not to lose sight of the *context* in which this claim is embedded: in this section on "'Reason' in Philosophy," the target of Nietzsche's attack is, unsurprisingly, not a single ontological or cosmological thesis, but the tendency among philosophers to posit some stable and enduring "reality" behind the appearances so as to satisfy an entirely personal need. The task of this section is to determine "which of the philosophers' traits are really idiosyncrasies" (*TI*: "'Reason' in Philosophy" 1), and Heraclitus is immediately held up as an exception to an otherwise unfortunate psychological rule among these types. To claim that Nietzsche's objective here is, even indirectly, to advance or develop an ontological agenda of his own is something of a distortion.

In addition, the weight of interpretive interest in Nietzsche's discussions of the theme of "becoming" in Heraclitus reflects a persistent tendency to overestimate Heraclitus' commitment to a "flux doctrine" and a sometimes almost willful blindness toward other, more prevalent, themes of necessity, stability, and regularity in Heraclitus. This is where a familiarity with Heraclitus independent of Nietzsche comes to be especially important.[25] If we look at the 120-odd fragments that constitute Heraclitus' extant work, we find not only slender evidence on which to base such a doctrine, but also ample evidence in support of ideas plainly in tension with the notion that nothing in the natural world persists. Before they are ascribed

---

[24] Hence the characterization of Heraclitus as a "magnificent hermit of the spirit" (*BGE* 204; see also *GM* III: 8).

[25] For an excellent case in point, see the analysis of "becoming" in Richardson (1996: ch. 2), with which the interpretation I offer here should be compared. Unlike many commentators, Richardson honestly acknowledges the controversy regarding the attribution to Heraclitus of a doctrine of flux (see n. 30); and he rightly observes that Heraclitus' concept of *logos* in fact suggests a far more conservative doctrine than the one he attributes to Nietzsche (1996: 85). Nevertheless, he argues that Nietzsche's emphasis on becoming is inspired by Heraclitus and that its importance "is reflected in the weight it bears for him—in the major further conclusions he takes it to imply. This claim, which I call his theory of Flux [*Fluss*] or becoming... supports certain hypercritical—skeptical and nihilist—lessons" (1996: 77). Among these are the lessons that all of our views, both commonsense and theoretical, distort reality and are therefore false; that we do not and cannot have knowledge; and that these distorted views are the result of an erroneous belief in enduring objects—*things* or *beings*—of which there are none (1996: 77). The problem here is not that Richardson fails to provide independent argument or textual support for these "hypercritical" consequences, because he certainly does. Indeed, this is the argument to which much of *Nietzsche's System* is devoted. The more local problem, for assessing Nietzsche's debt to Heraclitus, is the way in which Richardson allows his commitment to those consequences, established independently, to be reflected back upon and ultimately to shape his reading of Heraclitus. He worries aloud that "becoming [in Heraclitus] was supposed to rule out beings" (1996: 88), but it does not. Indeed, Heraclitus' theory of becoming "in this version we've detailed, seems neither sufficiently convincing

to Nietzsche, therefore, both the content of the so-called "flux doctrine" and its attribution to Heraclitus deserve some reconsideration.

Textual support for the flux doctrine (*Flusslehre*), as Nietzsche was well aware, rests almost entirely on the three or four so-called "river fragments," the authenticity of which, to say nothing of their correct interpretation and significance relative to Heraclitus' other writings, was actively in dispute.[26] Of these, only the cryptic Fr. 12 is widely recognized to be a probable record of Heraclitus' own words: "Upon those who step into the same rivers different and [still] different waters flow" (Robinson 1991: 17).[27] And this fragment hardly constitutes an endorsement of a radical process ontology. The more familiar fragment to us, containing the pronouncement that "it is not possible to step twice into the same river" (Fr. 91; Robinson 1991: 55), occurs in a longer passage from Plutarch. This is the only version of the fragment that clearly invites us to take Heraclitus' river image as a metaphor for all existing things. Yet no one now denies that this statement and its context constitute Plutarch's interpolation of "the Aristotelian form" of "Plato's paraphrase of the river-statement [Fr. 12]" (Kirk 1954: 381).[28] However, independently of Plutarch's uncritical acceptance of Plato's "everything flows" paraphrase and his own embellishment on Fr. 12, there is not a shred of uncontested evidence to suggest that Heraclitus expressed in his river observation the doctrine that all things are constantly changing like flowing rivers.[29] So the notion that Heraclitus did endorse a flux theory in the strong sense is not *utterly* without foundation, of course, but overemphasizing it and neglecting the controversy surrounding its

nor sufficiently strong to support all the claims Nietzsche bases on it" (1996: 89). The most radical readings that the fragments of Heraclitus can easily bear, unfortunately, "cannot capture the full force of Nietzsche's becoming, because then that theory would hardly support the denial of things, which he so emphatically roots in it. . . . To rule this out, *the theory of becoming must make some stronger point*" (1996: 82, emphasis mine; cf. 83, 85). My concerns with this argument are methodological: Richardson's approach seems to force upon him the task of *finding* a reading of Heraclitus appropriate to the views he attributes to Nietzsche, a move which would undermine the *evidentiary* status of Heraclitus' views for these doctrines in Nietzsche.

[26] The lively debate over this issue can be glimpsed, for instance, in the extensive notes in Eduard Zeller's *Die Philosophie der Griechen in ihrer geschichtlichen Entwicklung dargestellt*, which Nietzsche read in about 1867 (Brobjer 2008: 258). In the first major section in the second volume, Zeller presents the views of (among many other figures familiar to Nietzsche) Schleiermacher (*Herakleitos der Dunkle*, 1807), Bernays (*Heraclitea*, 1848), Lasalle (*Die Philosophie Herakleitos des Dunkeln*, 1858), and Teichmüller, whom Nietzsche read extensively and who claims, most conservatively, that Heraclitus' so-called flux doctrine is intended only to challenge Xenophanes' theological views. Zeller's own view is just about the most radical that the river fragments can reasonably be taken to support; namely, the idea that substances have a kind of "Ship of Theseus" existence. Zeller takes Heraclitus to be committed to the constant change of things, but neither he nor anyone he mentions takes this to imply that Heraclitus believes *there are no things*. More on Zeller's significance for Nietzsche's view below.

[27] Cf. Kirk 1954: 367. Charles Kahn (1979: 168) asserts that Fr. 12 "does *not* deny the continuing identity of the rivers, but takes this for granted. . . . Hence the point here concerns neither the irreversibility of the flow of time, the uniqueness of an individual event or experience, nor the general instability of things." See also Reinhardt 1942 against the very notion of a *Flusslehre* in Heraclitus.

[28] Of course *Plato* thought that Heraclitus held all things to be constantly changing like flowing rivers; this view comes in for his lighthearted derision, for instance in *Theaetetus* [152e] and *Cratylus* [402a], where it is hyperbolized in the claim that you cannot step even once into the same river, since the constant flux of things undermines the possibility of self-identity over time.

[29] There is one provocative fragment that differs significantly from Fr. 12 and from the Plutarch fragment(s), namely Fr. 49a: "We step and do not step into the same rivers; we are and we are

interpretation clearly does some injustice to the extant ancient texts and ultimately to Nietzsche as a student of Heraclitus.[30]

With that in mind, consider the only passage in *Philosophy in the Tragic Age of the Greeks* that troubles the more cautious reading with its announcement that, "[Heraclitus] altogether denied being" (*PTG* 51). As we might expect, a number of commentators have cited this passage in support of the radical reading, though generally not in full. The passage continues:

> For this one world which he retained—*supported by eternal unwritten laws*, flowing upward and downward in brazen rhythmic beat—nowhere shows a tarrying, an indestructibility, a bulwark in the stream. Louder than Anaximander, Heraclitus proclaimed: 'I see nothing other than becoming. Be not deceived. It is the fault of your myopia, not of the nature of things, if you believe you see land somewhere in the ocean of coming-to-be and passing away. You use names for things as though they [the things] rigidly, persistently endured; yet even the stream into which you step a second time is not the one you stepped into before.' (*PTG* 51–2, emphasis added)

With Nietzsche's mention of the "eternal unwritten laws" that govern change, this passage is not as unambiguous in favor of the radical flux reading as is sometimes suggested.[31] The reference to "the stream into which you step a second time," clearly drawn from the Plutarch fragment, is suggestive here, and Nietzsche does refer vaguely to this image in one other passage (*HAH* II: 223). But, although he alludes often to the pervasiveness of change and becoming and to Heraclitus' "negation of duration and persistence in the world" (in the lecture material on the pre-Platonic philosophers, for instance), he makes no use of this or any other river fragment in his otherwise very thorough scholarly material on Heraclitus.

What Nietzsche does draw upon, and heavily, in his lecture series on the pre-Platonic philosophers, is a contemporary sourcebook—one of the most complete treatments at the

---

not." The source is a first-century CE Stoic-minded anthologist of Homeric allegories known as Heraclitus Homericus or pseudo-Heraclitus. The statement is very cryptic and the Greek somewhat convoluted, so that even those commentators who accept the notion of a flux doctrine in Heraclitus seem reluctant to make the statement bear much weight. Geoffrey Kirk (1954: 373), for example, argues so vigorously about the outrageousness of taking this claim as authentic that he does not even devote a separate section of commentary to it, but instead appends it to his commentary on Fr. 12. Kahn (1979: 288) concurs, translating the fragment in an appendix of dubious quotations only "for the sake of completeness"; it seems to him, he says, merely a "thinly disguised paraphrase of the river fragments."

[30] Richardson (1996: 78) takes note of the fact that "interpreters sometimes dispute whether Heraclitus does have a theory of flux or becoming." In fact, he concedes: "It may be doubted that Heraclitus intended his image to convey so much content" (1996: 86). Christoph Cox (1999), by contrast, mentions only a half-dozen Heraclitus fragments, most of them fragments on opposite perceptions, and he nowhere draws attention to the controversy surrounding their interpretation. Rather, he uncritically accepts the interpretation of Guthrie 1962 that attributes a radical flux theory to Heraclitus, without mentioning the interpretations offered by the many scholars who categorically deny any firm basis for this attribution. Moreover, he rests his entire portrait of Nietzsche's Heraclitus on *PTG*, calling it "Nietzsche's most sustained treatment of Heraclitus" (1999: 186), which is at least misleading in light of the lectures, philological writings, and other material in which Nietzsche is concerned with Heraclitus.

[31] Proponents of that view seem to be aware of the tension; Cox (1999: 187), for instance, somewhat shockingly, simply replaces this short but inconvenient phrase with an ellipsis.

time—that packaged itself as a kind of systematic treatment of the early Greeks that could be of help precisely to scholars and pedagogues presenting work on those figures. Eduard Zeller's *Die Philosophie der Griechen in ihrer geschichtlichen Entwicklung* (1844–52, first edition) exerts a clear influence on Nietzsche's treatment of many pre-Platonic figures.[32] Zeller entertained an explanation of Heraclitean becoming that blended the emerging atomistic explanations offered by contemporary physicists with the notion that Heraclitus viewed becoming as dominant. "According to this interpretation everything is constantly changing by an invisible and as it were molecular addition and subtraction of fire, water, and earth" (Kirk 1954: 376). This interpretation helps explain how becoming could be constant in the natural world (i.e., by a neverending addition and subtraction at the microscopic level, such that no object of our experience genuinely endures or persists in the way we think it does), and how such change could be ultimately empirically verifiable, by all the ordinary methods employed by the natural sciences, in spite of the fact that it is not evident to immediate sense experience. On the interpretation most likely to have been adopted by Nietzsche, in light of his demonstrable reliance on Zeller,[33] Heraclitus can deny being in a narrow sense without in any way undercutting the notion that there is real stability somewhere—i.e., in the natural laws that govern change.

As Nietzsche's reference to "eternal unwritten laws" in the above passage suggests, he appreciates that there is a wealth of evidence in the extant fragments demonstrating that Heraclitus in fact insists upon the existence of stability or persistence in the natural world. To whatever degree the "flux" motif appears in Heraclitus, it is overshadowed by the theme of *logos*, and by themes of measure (*metron*), regularity, order, design, law, and necessity. Fr. 30 asserts the eternal existence of the cosmos and describes it as "an ever-living fire, being kindled in *measures* and put out in *measures*" (Robinson 1991: 25); and Fr. 94 claims that "*Helios* will not overstep his *measures*; otherwise, the avenging Furies, ministers of Justice, will find him out" (Robinson 1991: 57). "Wisdom," says Heraclitus, "is one thing: to be skilled in true judgment, how all things are *steered* through all [things]" (Fr. 41, Kirk 1954: 386). And one Heraclitean pronouncement particularly celebrated by Nietzsche emphasizes not only the pervasiveness of war and strife, but also of necessity: "One must know that war is common and right is strife and that all things [happen] by strife and *necessity*" (Fr. 80, Kirk 1954: 238). The "exchange" between opposites (another incarnation of measure in Heraclitean thought) is both temporally regular and logically necessary; that is the condition for there being a cosmos (an ordered, coherent world) at all. So Heraclitus' point is not simply that there is constancy in the cosmos because change is itself ever-present or permanent—which sounds sophistic at any rate. The idea is that natural change occurs in measured, regular cycles and that it is governed by an orderly principle, *logos*. "*Logos*" is the short answer to the question how, according to Nietzsche, Heraclitus fills out the insight (otherwise common to all pre-Platonic philosophers) that "all things are one."

In his notes and sketches from the winter of 1872, Nietzsche records a brief but telling observation about the centrality of *metron* and *logos* in Heraclitus: "The orderliness of the world—the most laboriously and slowly achieved result of terrible evolutions— grasped as the essence of the world: Heraclitus!" (*PT* 32) And even in *Philosophy in the*

---

[32] Porter 2000: 397–9 n. 112, n. 117.
[33] Again, see Porter 2000: chapter 5 and notes.

Tragic Age, the text that has been appealed to almost exclusively in support of the radical readings, Nietzsche's treatment of Heraclitus much more often sounds the notes of *regularity, measure, necessity,* and *stability within change* that suggest something reliable and persistent about the natural world—something, that is, to which we could rightly attach the notion of truth, something of which knowledge is possible. Consider the dramatic opening statement Nietzsche writes for Heraclitus' entrance onto the stage of pre-Platonic thought: " 'Becoming' is what I contemplate...and no one else has watched so attentively this everlasting wavebeat and rhythm of things. And what did I see? Lawful order, unfailing certainties, ever-like orbits of lawfulness, *Erinnyes* sitting in judgment on all transgressions against lawful order, the whole world the spectacle of sovereign justice and of the demonically ever-present natural forces that serve it" (*PTG* 50–1). Law and order; even if we read "becoming" as a continuous flux, it is far from being the kind of chaotic flux that could undermine the very concept of "thinghood" itself and leave us in a "featureless" world. Later in the same chapter, his enthusiasm for Heraclitus' insistence that everything happens in accordance with strife and necessity leads Nietzsche to observe that,

> It is a wonderful idea, welling up from the purest springs of Hellenism, the idea that strife embodies the everlasting sovereignty of strict justice, bound to everlasting laws. Only a Greek was capable of finding such an idea to be the fundament of a cosmology...[T]he qualities wrestle with one another, in accordance with inviolable laws and standards that are immanent in the struggle. The things in whose definiteness and endurance narrow human minds...believe have no real existence. (*PTG* 55)

The point of this last statement is that the ordinary run of mortals fail to locate "definiteness and endurance" in the appropriate place, not that it is nowhere to be found. In short, it would be irresponsible to draw from the observation that "what we suppose to have real existence does not" the conclusion that "nothing has real existence."

Finally, even if Nietzsche's claim that Heraclitus "altogether denied being" told the whole story about his appreciation of Heraclitus, it would still be clear that this view would do nothing to undermine either the possibilities of truth or knowledge.[34] There has been a persistent critical blindness to the spuriousness of the connection between any coherent "flux doctrine" and the radical metaphysical or epistemological consequences it has been taken to have. This is to say that, even if Heraclitus were an unrepentant "flux theorist," there is no reason why, on any reasonable and textually sustainable interpretation of that view, that doctrine need commit Nietzsche to the same doctrine or commit either Nietzsche or Heraclitus to a rejection of, say, truth, knowledge, or reason.

[34] In fact, Nietzsche frequently draws attention to Heraclitus *qua* seeker after truth and suggests strongly that he has a closer relationship with it even than his contemporary Hellenes, not to mention than modern philosophers: "For the world forever needs the truth, hence the world forever needs Heraclitus, though Heraclitus does not need the world" (*PTG* 68). See also *PTG* 69, *PT* 156, and *PPP* 55. And more generally in *PTG*, there are too many instances of Nietzsche's demonstrable respect for the truth and the pre-Platonic philosophers' relationship to it to sustain the interpretation that he denies truth; see, e.g., chapter 8.

4 Pyrrho

Though Nietzsche should not be read as having rejected the existence of either truth or knowledge, his remarks about these concepts are ambivalent, at times pessimistic enough that he has often been called a skeptic. Whether we pursue the charge of skepticism or defend him from it, however, depends heavily on what the term is taken to mean. Once again, a familiarity with some of the ancient sources available and familiar to Nietzsche can be of help. Though he seldom refers to any ancient skeptic by name in his published writings, his discussions of skepticism are frequent enough in both the published and the unpublished works to command our attention. Many of these remarks are strongly positive: Skeptics are "the decent type in the history of philosophy [while] the rest are ignorant of the first requirements of intellectual integrity" (*A* 12). "[G]reat intellects are skeptics. Zarathustra is a skeptic. The vigor of a mind, its *freedom* through strength and superior strength, is *proved* by skepticism" (*A* 54). And where Nietzsche clearly has the ancient skeptics in view, his comments exhibit a genuine admiration and respect for their methods. In the end, the affinities between them are substantial enough that an understanding of the ancient skeptics' positions can also help sharpen our understanding of Nietzsche's attitudes toward truth and knowledge, as well as the nature and value of philosophical inquiry.

Unlike Heraclitus, though, who appears dozens of times in Nietzsche's corpus, the mid-fourth- to mid-third-century BCE figure Pyrrho of Elis appears only once in the published work (though he appears many times in Nietzsche's notebooks), in a cryptic passage in *Human, All too Human* (*HAH* III: 213). Nietzsche's familiarity with the character—the personality—of Pyrrho goes back, unsurprisingly, to his work on Diogenes Laertius' *Lives and Opinions of the Eminent Philosophers* (*DL*). Originally, he endeavored to settle the question of how many sources Diogenes depended on in producing his doxographical treatise, probably compiled in the third century CE. Nietzsche posited only two sources initially,[35] but in the process of unearthing the evidence for his claim and arranging it for presentation, he eventually came to the conclusion that a third, skeptical source must be responsible for some of the material in Book IX—specifically, the biographical accounts of both Pyrrho of Elis (*DL* IX: 61–108) and one of his immediate followers, Timon of Phlius (*DL* IX: 109–116).[36] In the course of completing his *Laertiana*, Book IX commanded the lion's share of Nietzsche's attentive study; this chapter begins with the life of Heraclitus, includes the biographies of other of Nietzsche's favorite philosophers, Democritus and Leucippus, as well as Protagoras,[37] and ends with Diogenes' accounts of the lives of Pyrrho and Timon. Nietzsche's investigation afforded him a thorough familiarity not only with this material, but also with

---

[35] Specifically, Diocles of Magnesia, a first-century BCE historian, and Favorinus of Arles, a rhetorician, philosopher, and author of skeptical arguments who lived and was active around 100 CE. For a thorough account of Nietzsche's argument and an assessment of its contribution to philology, see Barnes 1986.

[36] Nietzsche tentatively identified this source as Theodosius, whom he supposed to be a skeptic. For more on Nietzsche's conjecture, which seems to have been at best hasty, at worst erroneous, see Barnes 1986: 22 and Bett 2000a: 66 n. 19.

[37] In a notebook entry from 1888, Nietzsche reflects that "our current way of thinking is still to a high degree Heraclitean, Democritean, and Protagorean" (*KSA* 13: 293).

a great deal of other relevant source material for the Pyrrhonian skeptical tradition.[38] His notes from the late 1860s are filled with references not only to Pyrrho and Timon, but also to Aenesidemus, Sextus Empiricus, and other central figures.

Later in his career, too, Nietzsche's enthusiasm for ancient varieties of skepticism is in evidence: It appears in his notebooks and other writings, just after the 1887 publication of Victor Brochard's *Les sceptiques grecs*, which, until very recently perhaps, was one of the best available works on the history of skepticism. Many of Nietzsche's notebook entries from the spring of 1888 and afterward indicate that he seized the book almost immediately upon its publication and read it with much interest.[39] This re-engagement with Pyrrho and his Hellenistic follower Sextus Empiricus (the main characters, as it were, in Brochard's study) prompted a number of reflections about Pyrrhonism in Nietzsche's late notebooks.[40] And in addition to the increased attention the Pyrrhonian tradition received in this unpublished material, Nietzsche also began to include positive reflections in his published work about the skeptics and skepticism in antiquity: in *Ecce Homo*, for instance, he makes explicit mention of Brochard's study and declares the skeptics "the only honorable type among the equivocal, quinquivocal tribe of philosophers!" ("Why I Am So Clever" 3) There is ample evidence, therefore, for Nietzsche's familiarity with the principal sources of Greek skepticism and his interest in Greek skeptical thought, both in his early years as a Classics scholar and toward the end of his career; but some of the best evidence we have in addition to this is Nietzsche's own attitude toward knowledge and toward the practice of philosophy.

The core of Nietzsche's philosophy, his critique of moral values, is fueled by his unrelenting criticism of dogmatism and "faith" in all its forms and by his perennial interest in psychological health and the conditions that hinder or promote it. Concern over the former is announced in the opening lines of *Beyond Good and Evil*: "Supposing truth is a woman— what then? Are there not grounds for the suspicion that all philosophers, insofar as they were dogmatists, have been very inexpert about women? That the gruesome seriousness, the clumsy obtrusiveness with which they have usually approached truth so far have been awkward and very improper methods for winning a woman's heart?" (*BGE* Preface) The latter concern helps set the agenda for the *Genealogy*. Framing his project in the preface as an inquiry into the origin and value of value judgments themselves, Nietzsche asks: "Have they inhibited or furthered human flourishing up until now?" (*GM* Preface 3). Both of these concerns, which are not independent of one another, but integrally linked, are also central to Pyrrhonism.

---

[38] Thus, in spite of the dearth of explicit remarks about the history of Greek skepticism in Nietzsche's published work, Richard Bett (2000a: 67) has also argued that "Nietzsche seems to have involved himself with skepticism to a greater degree than he would have had to do purely in his role as a scholar of Diogenes Laertius" and that overall "... the general impression to be derived from [Nietzsche's philological] material is of a scholar who knows the history of Greek skepticism very well, and who considers it an important episode in the wider history of Greek philosophy."

[39] As noted by Bett 2000a: 63–5; see also Brobjer 2001: 12–14.

[40] See, e.g., *KSA* 13: 264, 265, 276–8, 293, 311–12, 324, 332, 347, 378, 403, 446. Some of these late references, it must be admitted, are negative in tone; usually, Pyrrho is under indictment for his tranquil character (a feature of his personality that is emphasized by Diogenes). Many of these passages, for instance, refer to "*Pyrrho, ein griechischer Buddhist*" (*KSA* 13: 264; see also *KSA* 13: 347, 378) and associate him with decadence and exhaustion because of the tranquility (*ataraxia*) that is reported to be the result of skepticism. I will address this apparent tension later.

For the Pyrrhonists, in fact, the opposition to dogmatism—which they construe broadly as an opposition to those who hold and profess beliefs (*dogmata*) about the hidden or "unclear objects of investigation in the sciences" (*PH* 1: 13)[41]—is definitive of their skeptical practice: "Those who are called Dogmatists in the proper sense of the word think that they have discovered the truth.... And the Sceptics are still investigating. Hence the most fundamental kinds of philosophy are reasonably thought to be three: the Dogmatic, the Academic, and the Sceptical" (*PH* 1: 3).[42] Pyrrhonian skepticism thus takes dead aim at the results of all speculative reasoning and at those who have called a halt to their investigations because they take themselves to be in possession of the truth. Nietzsche argues strenuously that the systems of morality to which he is opposed, and not only Christian morality, are sustained by just such speculation—by a belief in responsibility that requires metaphysically free agents, for instance, or by belief in the existence of another world behind or beyond the appearances. His critical strategy is to arouse suspicion about these beliefs by demonstrating that they are held not because they enjoy rational support but because they serve a special sort of psychological need. They are symptomatic, in fact, of the type of thinking he so frequently characterizes as unhealthy.

Thus Nietzsche approaches philosophical systems and value judgments as diagnostic objects, regarding them in his capacity as a pathologist, a "philosophical *physician*": "All those bold insanities of metaphysics, especially answers to the question about the *value* of existence, may always be considered first of all as the symptoms of certain bodies" (*GS* Preface 2). This approach is one he shares with the Pyrrhonists, whose practice is explicitly diagnostic and therapeutic. As Sextus Empiricus, perhaps our most thorough source for ancient skepticism and a physician in his own right, states: "Skeptics are philanthropic and wish to cure by argument, as far as they can, the conceit and rashness of the Dogmatists" (*PH* 3: 280). While "philanthropic" may not be the most apt description of Nietzsche's project, his interest in the sickness and health of both individuals and their cultures and in human flourishing itself, prompts him similarly to home in not only on the metaphysical beliefs that underwrite conventional morality but also on the degree of conviction with which those beliefs are held—insofar as that indicates the presence of an unrestrained "will to truth"[43] and "metaphysical need"[44] that finds satisfaction in the ascetic ideal and may even lead to nihilism:

> In rare and isolated instances it may really be the case that such a will to truth...a metaphysician's ambition to hold a hopeless position, may participate and ultimately prefer even

[41] *PH* = Sextus Empiricus, *Outlines of Pyrrhonism* (*Purrhoneioi Hupotuposeis*).

[42] Note that the Academics turn out, on Sextus' account, to be negative dogmatists, in virtue of their assertion that nothing can be known. Really then, the most fundamental kinds of philosophy can be thought to be two—the Dogmatic (positive and negative) and the Skeptical.

[43] See also *GM* III: 24 for a discussion of the connection between "this unconditional will to truth" and "the *belief in the ascetic ideal itself*," and *GS* 347: "The demand that one wants by all means that something should be firm (while on account of the ardor of this demand one is easier and more negligent about the demonstration of this certainty)—this, too, is still the demand for support, a prop, in short, that *instinct of weakness* which, to be sure, does not create religious, metaphysical systems, and convictions of all kinds but—conserves them." We have seen a closely related concern emerge in Nietzsche's early work, too: "an unrestrained thirst for knowledge for its own sake barbarizes men just as much as a hatred of knowledge" (*PTG* 30–1).

[44] See, e.g., also *BGE* 12, *HAH* I: 37, and *GS* 151.

a handful of 'certainty' to a whole carload of beautiful possibilities; there may even be puritanical fanatics of conscience who prefer even a certain nothing to an uncertain something to lie down on—and die. But this is nihilism and the sign of a despairing, mortally weary soul…. (*BGE* 10)

If Nietzsche's diagnosis is correct, if (as he says elsewhere) "convictions are prisons" (*A* 54), and if the revaluation of values requires a distance from conventional morality, or rather the freedom from and indifference to it that Nietzsche discovered in the Homeric epics, then the significance of Nietzsche's insistence on "*ephexis* in interpretation," which we encountered earlier, can be better appreciated.[45] The Greek term *ephexis* means "a stopping or checking"; it comes from the verb *epechein* ("to hold back" or "to check"), which is the source of the skeptical *epochē*, or suspension of judgment, that is the distinguishing feature of Pyrrhonism.[46] Suspending judgment is what allows the skeptic to avoid maintaining beliefs; on their account, *dogmata* are the primary obstacles to psychological well-being.

It is in virtue of their concern with well-being that the skeptics' aims are said to be therapeutic: Sextus Empiricus calls *ataraxia*, commonly translated "tranquility" but better understood as "freedom from disturbance" (*PH* 1: 10), the "causal principle" of Pyrrhonism (*PH* 1: 12), in the sense that the desire for this untroubled state of mind is what motivates people to study natural philosophy in the first place. In the course of this study, the skeptics are those who demonstrate a talent (a *dunamis antithetikē*) for opposing one appearance to another, one argument to another, one judgment to another, in such a way as to neutralize any claim advanced by the dogmatist. The result of honing and exercising this talent is *epochē*, suspension of judgment on all matters the skeptic investigates. Strictly speaking, since Pyrrhonists suspend judgment on the nature of causality as well, they cannot guarantee or even recommend in any unqualified sense that their practice will result in *ataraxia*; the skeptics simply report that such a state reliably accompanies their suspension of judgment.[47] *Ataraxia* is often linked with psychological states like indifference and impassivity and appears on some accounts to be a flight from suffering and avoidance of strife and conflict. None of these states could name a goal Nietzsche finds respectable, of course; but he would surely agree that freedom from psychological disturbance and disease, like the "metaphysical need" we saw above and the kind of weltering *ressentiment* and biliousness Nietzsche finds again and again in priestly types (and indeed in the majority of human beings), is desirable, whether or not he takes it to be achievable in any given case.[48]

Recovering Nietzsche's positive estimation of the Greek skeptics, a task made all the more difficult by his having remained relatively quiet about them, and understanding his critique of the philosophical tradition against the backdrop of this estimation helps make sense of how he is able to retain the idea that philosophic inquiry is a goal-oriented enterprise, one

[45] At *GM* III: 9, Nietzsche lists among other "individual drives and virtues of the philosopher…his doubting drive, his negating drive, his wait-and-see ("ephectic") drive…." Elsewhere he calls the "*ability to defer decision*" the essence of all learning (*TI*: "What the Germans Lack" 6).

[46] According to Sextus, "Suspension of judgment (*epochē*) gets its name from the fact that the intellect is suspended (*epexetai*) so as neither to posit nor reject anything because of the equipollence of the matters being investigated" (*PH* 1: 196); Pyrrhonists in fact referred to themselves also as *aphektikoi*. For a more detailed discussion of Nietzsche's promotion of "*ephexis* in interpretation," see Berry 2005.

[47] "The end to be realized they hold to be suspension of judgment, which brings with it tranquility like its shadow: so Timon and Aenesidemus declare" (*DL* IX: 107); cf. *PH* 1: 29.

[48] On this issue see Berry 2004.

that aims at knowledge of the truth, even as he works tirelessly to promote suspicion about the "truths" advanced by others and even sometimes by himself. Importantly, neither Nietzsche nor the Pyrrhonists deny the existence of truth, though they never find themselves in possession of it; such a denial would be, after all, dogmatic.[49] If successful, their methods neither establish new systems nor do they prove that there are no viable systems to be established. They do not even constitute an epistemology.[50] The Pyrrhonist is as little interested in doing epistemology as is Nietzsche; neither sets out to vindicate, refute, or refine any theory about knowledge. They do not aim to define it, determine its scope, or to elucidate its justification conditions. And neither aims to demonstrate that knowledge is impossible.[51] Like the skeptics, who do not adduce views of their own but merely refute propositions advanced by others and undermine their convictions (*DL* IX: 74), and in keeping with the methodological scruples of the good philologist, Nietzsche's work is more critical than constructive.

5   CONCLUDING REMARKS

Naturally, the works collected together as Nietzsche's *Junge Schriften* are dominated by lecture notes, sketches for essays and drafts of others, and a variety of meditations on classical texts; this simply reflects his training and early professional career as a professor of philology. But the evidence that Nietzsche never abandoned his engagement with the Greeks and never questioned his high estimation of Greek culture and thought is abundant throughout his career. Among Nietzsche's final reflections in *Twilight of the Idols*, he acknowledges that he owes a debt to the ancients.[52] And in spite of his persistent reminders of the unparalleled originality of his own thought and the relative rarity of his unqualified praise of others, we can see that this debt is

[49] This point and Nietzsche's awareness of it can hardly be overemphasized. He captures it explicitly, for instance, in a passage from *Daybreak*: "You have just *ceased* to be a skeptic!" one voice says to another, "For you *deny*!" (*D* 477) Moreover, an aggressive denial of the possibility of truth is difficult to square with Nietzsche's enthusiasm for the methods and successes of the natural sciences, and it cannot be reconciled with the recurrent motif of Nietzsche's suspicion about metaphysics, with his complaint that otherworldly religions (Christianity in particular) perpetuate "lies" and are incompatible with intellectual honesty and with the admiration we have seen him express effusively for Heraclitus and other thinkers, whose thought is a path to truth if any can be.

[50] See Williams 1988.

[51] Bett 2000b, however, reads the early Pyrrhonists as more negatively dogmatic about knowledge.

[52] In view of what we have been considering as the profound and lasting influence of the Hellenic tradition on Nietzsche's thought, his remark in this passage that "not to mince words, [the Greeks] *cannot* be to us what the Romans are. One does not *learn* [*Man lernt nicht*] from the Greeks…" (*TI*: "What I Owe to the Ancients" 2) seems deeply puzzling. But this observation, with its emphasis on scholarly study [*lernen*], its discussion of "taste" and the value of "good French writers," and its following immediately a passage that finds Nietzsche reflecting explicitly on his experience as a pupil and his development as a writer, must be read in that narrower context. Perhaps Nietzsche's rhetorical style does not bear the stamp of Greek dialectics, then, and perhaps the whole phenomenon of German Philhellenism needs to be approached with caution and not uncritically (as Nietzsche's glancing blow at both Winckelmann and Goethe here would suggest (*TI*: "What I Owe to the Ancients" 4)). But as Nietzsche emphatically takes ownership in this chapter of his peculiar understanding of the Dionysian and its significance for the idea of "the eternal recurrence of life," and as he closes this chapter with a return to his own beginnings in *The Birth of Tragedy*, we can have no doubt about what Nietzsche owes to the ancients and to the Greeks in particular: "And with that I again return to the place from which I set

substantial and that a clear understanding of Nietzsche's "untimely" critiques of his contemporary culture and its morality demands a careful reconciliation of it.

In the notes for "We Philologists," Nietzsche observed that, "The Greeks are interesting and desperately important because they have so many great individuals" (*KSA* 8: 43). Here, of course, we have encountered only a few of those he had in mind: one whose exuberant immoralism awakened Nietzsche to the bare possibility that decadence and Christian morality could be overcome; another whose obscurity, misanthropy, and elective solitude lent him his own untimeliness and visionary insight, and gave him a vantage point from which to launch an audacious challenge to the rival systems of thought promoted by the Eleatics; and a third whose practices animated the methodological scruples adopted by Nietzsche as a young student and provided an ideal critical model for his later work. But the honor Nietzsche accorded these and other great Hellenic figures was no mean hero worship; not only would any wholesale adoption of their values and views be a fundamentally slavish act, it would also be in vain, as Nietzsche realized early on. These individuals were the products of a peculiar place and time. Their systems grew out of a particular "soil natural and native" to them, and out of conditions that no longer exist (*PTG* 23–4, 29). The reconciliation of Nietzsche's debt to the ancients is also a reckoning with these multifarious conditions and so with the whole Hellenic world as such—impossible to encapsulate neatly, but disastrous to neglect as an influence on the development of Nietzsche's thought.[53]

BIBLIOGRAPHY

(a) Works by Nietzsche

A   *The Anti-Christ*, trans. R. J. Hollingdale, in *Twilight of the Idols and The Anti-Christ.* Middlesex: Penguin, 1968.

BGE   *Beyond Good and Evil*, ed. and trans. Walter Kaufmann, in *Basic Writings of Nietzsche.* New York: Modern Library, 1966.

BT   *The Birth of Tragedy*, ed. and trans. Walter Kaufmann, in *Basic Writings of Nietzsche.* New York: Modern Library, 1966.

D   *Daybreak*, trans. R. J. Hollingdale. Cambridge: Cambridge University Press, 1982.

EH   *Ecce Homo*, trans. Walter Kaufmann, in *On the Genealogy of Morals and Ecce Homo.* New York: Vintage, 1969.

FS   *Frühe Schriften* (5 vols). Munich: C. H. Beck, 1994.
        Bd. 3: *Schriften der Studenten-und Militärzeit 1864–1868*, ed. Hans Joachim Mette and Karl Schlechta.

out—*Birth of Tragedy* was my first revaluation of all values: with that I again plant myself in the soil out of which I draw all that I will and *can*—I, the last disciple of the philosopher Dionysos—I, the teacher of the eternal recurrence..." (*TI:* "What I Owe to the Ancients" 5).

[53] I would like to thank the editors, especially John Richardson, for many helpful suggestions for improvement. The material on Heraclitus was presented in rudimentary form at the 15th annual conference of the Friedrich Nietzsche Society of Great Britain and Ireland (September 2005), "Nietzsche on Time and History," and I would like to thank the organizers of that conference and its participants, especially Tony Jensen, for their very constructive comments and questions. I have also profited a great deal during the development of this essay from conversations with Alex Mourelatos, Tim O'Keefe, and Greg Moore.

Bd. 4: *Schriften der Studenten-und Militärzeit 1864–1868 / Schriften der letzten Leipziger Zeit 1868*, ed. Hans Joachim Mette and Karl Schlechta.

Bd. 5: *Schriften der letzten Leipziger und ersten Basler Zeit 1868–1869*, ed. Carl Koch and Karl Schlechta.

GS   *The Gay Science*, trans. Walter Kaufmann. New York: Vintage, 1974.

HAH   *Human, All Too Human*, trans. R. J. Hollingdale. Cambridge: Cambridge University Press, 1986.

GM   *On the Genealogy of Morality*, trans. Maudemarie Clark and Alan J. Swensen. Indianapolis: Hackett, 1998.

KSA   *Sämtliche Werke: Kritische Studienausgabe in 15 Einzelbänden*, ed. G. Colli and M. Montinari (15 vols). Berlin: De Gruyter, 1988.

PT   *Philosophy and Truth: Selections from Nietzsche's Notebooks of the Early 1870s*, ed. and trans. Daniel Breazeale. New Jersey: Humanities Press, 1979.

PTG   *Philosophy in the Tragic Age of the Greeks*, trans. Marianne Cowan. Washington, DC: Regnery, 1962.

PPP   *The Pre-Platonic Philosophers*, trans. Greg Whitlock. Urbana: University of Chicago Press, 2001.

SL   *Selected Letters of Friedrich Nietzsche*, trans. Christopher Middleton. Indianapolis: Hackett, 1996.

TI   *Twilight of the Idols*, trans. R. J. Hollingdale, in *Twilight of the Idols and The Anti-Christ*. Middlesex: Penguin, 1968.

UM   *Untimely Meditations*, trans. R. J. Hollingdale. Cambridge: Cambridge University Press, 1986.

WC   "We Classicists," trans. William Arrowsmith, in *Unmodern Observations*. New Haven, Conn.: Yale University Press, 1990.

(b) Other Primary works

DL   Diogenes Laertius. *Lives of Eminent Philosophers* (2 vols), trans. R. D. Hicks. Cambridge, Mass.: Harvard University Press, 1925.

PH   Sextus Empiricus. *Outlines of Scepticism*, trans. Julia Annas and Jonathan Barnes. Cambridge: Cambridge University Press, 2000.

(c) Other Works Cited

Barnes, Jonathan. 1986. "Nietzsche and Diogenes Laertius," *Nietzsche-Studien* 15: 16–40.

Berry, Jessica N. 2004. "Nietzsche and the Origins of Ethical Eudaimonism," in Paul Bishop (ed.), *Nietzsche and Antiquity: His Reaction and Response to the Classical Tradition*. Rochester: Camden House, 98–113.

Berry, Jessica N. 2005. "Perspectivism and Ephexis in Interpretation," *Philosophical Topics* 33.2: 19–44.

Berry, Jessica N. 2011. *Nietzsche and the Ancient Skeptical Tradition*. New York: Oxford University Press.

Bett, Richard. 2000a. "Nietzsche on the Skeptics and Nietzsche as Skeptic," *Archiv für Geschichte der Philosophie* 82: 62–86.

Bett, Richard. 2000b. *Pyrrho, His Antecedents, and His Legacy*. Oxford: Oxford University Press.

Bett, Richard. 2005. "Nietzsche, the Greeks, and Happiness (with Special Reference to Aristotle and Epicurus)," *Philosophical Topics* 33.2: 45–70.

Bishop, Paul (ed.). 2004. *Nietzsche and Antiquity: His Reaction and Response to the Classical Tradition*. Rochester: Camden House.

Brobjer, Thomas H. 1995. *Nietzsche's Ethics of Character: A Study of Nietzsche's Ethics and its Place in the History of Moral Thinking*. Uppsala: Uppsala University.

Brobjer, Thomas H. 2001. "Nietzsche's Disinterest and Ambivalence Toward the Greek Sophists," *International Studies in Philosophy* 33.3: 5–23.

Brobjer, Thomas H. 2008. *Nietzsche's Philosophical Context: An Intellectual Biography*. Urbana: University of Illinois Press.

Cancik, Hubert. 1995. *Nietzsches Antike*. Stuttgart: J. B. Metzler Verlag.

Conway, Daniel and Rehn, Rudolf (eds.). 1992. *Nietzsche und die antike Philosophie*. Trier: Wissenschaftlicher Verlag.

Conway, Daniel and Ward, Julie K. 1992. "Physicians of the Soul: *Peritrope* in Sextus Empiricus and Nietzsche," in Daniel Conway and Rudolf Rehn (eds), *Nietzsche und die antike Philosophie*. Trier: Wissenschaftlicher Verlag, 193–223.

Cox, Christoph. 1998. "Nietzsche's Heraclitus and the Doctrine of Becoming," *International Studies in Philosophy* 30.3: 49–63.

Cox, Christoph. 1999. *Nietzsche: Naturalism and Interpretation*. Berkeley: University of California Press.

Danto, Arthur. 1965. *Nietzsche as Philosopher*. New York: Macmillan.

Dodds, E. R. 1966. *The Greeks and the Irrational*. Berkeley: University of California Press.

Gründer, Karlfried (ed.). 1969. *Der Streit um Nietzsches "Geburt der Tragödie."* Hildesheim: Georg Olms Verlagsbuchhandlung.

Guthrie, W. K. C. 1962. *A History of Greek Philosophy*, vol. I: *The Earlier Presocratics and Pythagoreans*. Cambridge: Cambridge University Press.

Kahn, Charles H. 1979. *The Art and Thought of Heraclitus*. Cambridge: Cambridge University Press.

Kirk, Geoffrey Stephen. 1954. *Heraclitus: The Cosmic Fragments*. Cambridge: Cambridge University Press.

Kirk, Geoffrey Stephen, Raven, John Earle, and Schofield, Malcolm. 1983. *The Presocratic Philosophers*. Cambridge: Cambridge University Press.

Lachterman, David R. 1992. "*Die ewige Wiederkehr des Griechen*: Nietzsche and the Homeric Tradition," in Daniel Conway and Rudolf Rehn (eds.), *Nietzsche und die antike Philosophie*. Trier: Wissenschaftlicher Verlag, 13–35.

Lindken, Theodor and Rehn, Rudolf. 2006. *Die Antike in Nietzsches Denken: Eine Bibliographie*. Trier: Wissenschaftlicher Verlag.

Lloyd-Jones, Hugh. 1976. "Nietzsche and the Study of the Ancient World," in James C. O'Flaherty, Timothy F. Sellner, and Robert M. Helm (eds), *Studies in Nietzsche and the Classical Tradition*. Chapel Hill: University of North Carolina Press, 1–15.

Magnus, Bernd. 1978. *Nietzsche's Existential Imperative*. Bloomington: Indiana University Press.

Mann, Joel. 2008. "Wilkerson's Nietzsche and Nietzsche's Greeks," *Journal of Nietzsche Studies* 35/36.

Müller, Enrico. 2005. *Die Griechen im Denken Nietzsches*. Berlin: De Gruyter.

Nehamas, Alexander. 1985. *Nietzsche: Life as Literature*. Cambridge, Mass.: Harvard University Press.

O'Flaherty, James C., Sellner, Timothy F., and Helm, Robert M. (eds). 1976. *Studies in Nietzsche and the Classical Tradition*. Chapel Hill: University of North Carolina Press.

Orsucci, Andrea. 2000. "Antike, griechische," in Henning Ottmann (ed.), *Nietzsche-Handbuch: Leben, Werk, Wirkung*. Weimar: J. B. Metzler, 365–79.

Ottmann, Henning (ed.). 2000. *Nietzsche-Handbuch: Leben, Werk, Wirkung.* Weimar: J. B. Metzler.

Porter, James I. 2000. *Nietzsche and the Philology of the Future.* Stanford: Stanford University Press.

Reinhardt, Karl. 1942. "*Heraklits Lehre vom Feuer*," *Hermes* 77: 1–27.

Richardson, John. 1996. *Nietzsche's System.* New York: Oxford University Press.

Richardson, John. 2004. *Nietzsche's New Darwinism.* New York: Oxford University Press.

Robinson, T. M. 1991. *Heraclitus: Fragments.* Toronto: University of Toronto Press.

Schmidt, Leopold. 1882. *Die Ethik der alten Griechen.* Berlin: W. Hertz.

Silk, Michael and Stern, Joseph. 1981. *Nietzsche on Tragedy.* Cambridge: Cambridge University Press.

Tejera, Victorino. 1987. *Nietzsche and Greek Thought.* Dordrecht: Martinus Nijhoff Publishers.

Whitman, James. 1986. "Nietzsche in the Magisterial Tradition of German Classical Philology," *Journal of the History of Ideas* 47: 453–68.

Wilkerson, Dale. 2006. *Nietzsche and the Greeks.* London: Continuum.

Williams, Bernard. 1993. *Shame and Necessity.* Berkeley: University of California Press.

Williams, Michael. 1988. "Scepticism Without Theory," *Review of Metaphysics* 41: 547–88.

CHAPTER 5

···

NIETZSCHE AND ROMANTICISM: GOETHE, HÖLDERLIN, AND WAGNER

···

ADRIAN DEL CARO

1 SILENCING ROMANTICISM, OR TO SPEAK OR NOT TO SPEAK

···

THANKS in part to Nietzsche's own efforts to unmask the ills of romanticism, which became one of his chief critical objectives beginning with his aphoristic phase, the issue of his relation to romanticism has become obfuscated by the lesser but more intriguing question as to whether he is a romantic—as if somehow answering this question instead would once and for all unmask Nietzsche or otherwise make it easier to deal with him. If Nietzsche can be labeled a romantic, it is reasoned (perhaps among the intellectually lazy) that one is spared the labor of actually engaging his texts; "romantic" is thus used as a pejorative and whatever one wishes to ascribe to it in a negative spirit, e.g., irrationalism, nostalgia, nihilism, etc. is used to tarnish Nietzsche by association. For polemic and strategic purposes, therefore, tagging Nietzsche with the romantic label, as opposed to critically engaging the issue of his relation to romanticism, is for many the preferred option. Not much is gained for humanities scholarship in this limited and disingenuous approach to explicating Nietzsche. Even those for whom romanticism is not a pejorative, notably scholars of the movement and of its proponents, expose themselves to the danger of tagging Nietzsche; their legitimate, academically rigorous findings on the relationship of Nietzsche to romanticism will be appropriated by the labelers whose intention is not to engage Nietzsche's thought but instead to dismiss it. If we agree with Staten that "Nietzsche is, with Rousseau, the writer who has been most susceptible to political/ideological appropriation" (Staten 1990: 216), then we can better understand how the twentieth century staked out positions on Nietzsche. Again, Nietzsche was complicit in this ongoing strategy by virtue of helping to identify romanticism as a chief ill of modernity, and we would be naive to ignore the power play underlying his strategic intentions as well as those of subsequent players who have entered the Nietzsche arena.

Defining romanticism is a challenging and fraught exercise because it is pervasive in the modern character and moreover a key dimension of the modern, which makes it difficult for us to sufficiently extricate ourselves from romanticism for purposes of dispassionately describing what is romantic. That said, a significant and compelling part of Nietzsche's romanticism, both in the early, self-avowed romantic period and in the later anti-romantic self-criticism and cultural criticism that animate the writings beginning with *Human, All Too Human* (1878), can be found in his elaboration and reworking of what he called *the Dionysian*. The properties of Dionysus, the art deity whom Nietzsche juxtaposes with Apollo in *The Birth of Tragedy* (1872), are quintessentially romantic in the sense suggested by two of Nietzsche's forerunners, namely Rousseau in his *Emile, or On Education* (1762) and Goethe in his *The Sorrows of Young Werther* (1774). Both forerunners of romanticism contributed in their works to an elevation of the embodied virtues, e.g., feeling, the passions, spontaneity, physical activity, and creativity associated with the unconscious or the irrational. The "good" characters in their respective novels are those who live close to nature, such as women (mothers especially), children, farmers, artisans, and artists; these natural types are capable of staving off the corrupting and enslaving tendencies of culture and society, both of which are too addicted to reason, rote learning, quantified knowledge, and subjugation of nature. Transferred to the stage of *The Birth of Tragedy*, constructed as it was with the help of Schopenhauer and Wagner, the pro-nature properties of Dionysus, god of wine, chaos, music, tragedy, sexuality, the unconscious, superabundance, resurrection, and fertility, combine with the pro-reason properties of Apollo, god of individuation, order, restraint, imagistic (plastic) art, the *logos*, consciousness, and lucidity, thereby creating the highest form of art—tragedy. In intellectual-historical terms, the Dionysian, consisting of the orgiastic, superabundant, and creative properties of Dionysus, come to stand for *Natur* in its agon with *Kultur*. When the romantics demonstrate an interest, indeed a longing for primitive forms of expression such as the folk song or the folk saga or generally anything relating to *folk*, they are seeking out the essential, natural vestiges of humanity least corrupted by culture and prior to the ascendancy of reason. Whereas young Nietzsche promulgated his Dionysianism as artistic metaphysics inextricably tied to the metaphysical worldview of Schopenhauer, the anti-romantic Nietzsche, abandoning not only Schopenhauer but hostile in the extreme toward metaphysics, recreated the Dionysian on a purely physical and physiological basis, foregrounding the notions of superabundance, flourishing vitality, disruptive chaos, strength, and capacity for life affirmation. These later Dionysian properties do not need defending on metaphysical grounds because they are self-evident; indeed, they are the nature of life itself, which Nietzsche infuses with his famous "will to power." The later "philosophical" Dionysus of Nietzsche becomes the spokesman for rediscovering the potential of bodied human being at a time in history when humans have shown a decided tendency to lead disembodied lives.

The value of investigating Nietzsche and romanticism lies in what the relationship can tell us about why and how he uses the romantic label, and why and how he attempts to dodge the label himself. This exploration should be revealing of the causes of Nietzsche's unease about modernity and about the depth of his modernity and ours. It is instructive to explore Nietzsche's positions on romanticism because, as with most issues he engaged, the findings reflect back upon us, upon humanity in the modern era, as opposed to simply reflecting back

upon the mere person Nietzsche. As for the other "mere persons" enlisted for my exploration, they too are fine lenses through which to study our modern selves: Goethe, Hölderlin,
and Wagner represent profound influences on Nietzsche, and in terms of romantic capital
they represent such superabundance of romantic wealth that they rise fittingly to Nietzsche's
challenge of spiritual agon. But in addition to the value these figures have as allies and opponents of Nietzsche, there is the often overlooked value of how they serve, from the reader's
point of view, as Nietzsche's physicians. In the 1886 preface to the second edition of *Human,
All Too Human*, he famously laid out the transition from "bound" spirit to "free spirit" that
characterized his emergence, indeed escape, from his romantic-Wagnerian past as a process
of healing, of recovery (*KSA* 2: 13–22), and he referred to his overcoming of romanticism
in medical terms, calling it his "anti-romantic self-treatment" (*KSA* 2: 14; *HAH*, Preface 1).[1]
Fond as he was of conflating his real sickness, which ultimately caused him to take early
retirement from the University of Basle, with the spiritual sickness he attributed to romanticism, Nietzsche typically credited himself with the successful "cure"; while this serves as a
partial accounting, we also need to give credit to Goethe, Hölderlin, and Wagner for illuminating the darker recesses of Nietzsche's psyche.

It has long been demonstrated that Nietzsche knew himself to be a romantic and
counted this trait among his greatest weaknesses. However, the all-important difference he
points out to his readers is that he *knew* of this weakness and fought against it, as a philosopher, thereby taking the appropriate action necessary to separate himself from the "incurable romantic" Wagner (Del Caro 1989a: 24, 30; *KSA* 2: 14; *HAH*, Preface 1). To Nietzsche it
makes a considerable difference whether one is fundamentally healthy enough to throw off
a disease like romanticism, as he claims to have done; the "incurable" romantics (observe
how even contemporary speech uses this locution) literally die of their affliction. Behler
formulated how Nietzsche's struggle with romanticism was conducted "counter to his own
inclinations, especially when one considers his profound statements on the significance
of illness and decadence" (Behler 1973: 241; Del Caro 1989a: 124). Typically Nietzsche
challenges the stability of any healthy state in order to inoculate it and thereby achieve
a more refined, even heartier state of health—it is no different in his relation to the "illness" romanticism which, properly treated and dispatched, results in a wiser and stronger
Nietzsche.

Accordingly the valiant efforts of Julian Young to distinguish among types of romanticism
as Nietzsche presents them are more amusing than edifying. Young settles momentarily on
the "psychological" conception of romanticism, after finding Nietzsche to be insufficiently
literal and absolute in his use of stylistic distinctions (i.e., classical vs romantic). The psychological litmus test asks whether hunger or superabundance is at work in creation. But
he insists on juxtaposing this kind of romanticism with the older and recurring distinction
between classical and decadent aesthetics, revealing his frustration with Nietzsche's flexible
use of these terms. Thus Young thinks he has provided us with his own psychological explanation of Nietzsche when he offers that "Nietzsche sometimes seduces himself into the view
that *nearly* all European art that is life-affirming comes from the classical or Renaissance
period in European history and *nearly* all art that does not (e.g. the medieval art of 'genuine

---

[1] See also the preface to *The Gay Science*, where N claims to have liberated himself from his "careless
spiritual diet and habits—one calls them romanticism…" (*KSA* 3: 346; *GS* Preface 1).

Christianity') is life-denying." Now referring to this Nietzschean position as a "school-boyish thesis" and a "simple-minded dichotomy of historical periods," Young continues to demand absolute linguistic accountability from Nietzsche, spinning out a third conception of romanticism which he calls "historical" (Young 1992: 142–3). There are basic flaws in the reasoning to which Young resorts. First, Nietzsche does not hold himself accountable to expressions and formulations he has uttered in such a way that his views remain fixed and rigid—especially in the case of romanticism where his criticism deepens and takes on tributaries over time. Secondly, Young fails to consider that Nietzsche is a self-avowed decadent, modern, and romantic, making his formulations on romanticism all the more complicated and contradictory. Instead, all we get from Young is a weak disclaimer in the general direction of Nietzsche's complicity in the problem: "By the time of *The Gay Science* Nietzsche realizes that he himself is vulnerable to the charge of psychological romanticism and warns himself to guard against it" (Young 1992: 144).

Goethe's equation of classical with healthy and romantic with sick should not be under-estimated for its importance to Nietzsche's views. Goethe himself went beyond Young's "simple-minded dichotomy of historical periods" when he qualified his formula; what is modern is not romantic because it is new, he claimed, but because it is weak, sickly, and ill, and what is ancient is not classical because it is ancient but because it is strong, fresh, cheer-ful, and healthy (Del Caro 1989a: 93). Nietzsche was the first to impart depth to Goethe's formulations (Del Caro 1989a: 97), and this he did both conceptually, by philosophically "diagnosing" romanticism, and empirically, by virtue of manifesting the illness of romanti-cism and studying its effect on his own body. Critics tend to read Nietzsche metaphorically where he is being literal on the question of illness serving as a stimulus; once this tendency is better understood, criticism will be in a better position to transcend the pejoratizing of romanticism. Theo Meyer reveals an early and influential source of the confusion when he describes Kaufmann's book of 1950 as having effectively substituted the productive enlightener for the Dionysian romantic (Meyer 1993: 11). Kaufmann was virtually tone-deaf to the Dionysian (Del Caro 1988: 130–3), and of course highly motivated to associ-ate Nietzsche with Goethe for purposes of rehabilitating Nietzsche's image. And Nietzsche himself played up his intellectual affinity for Goethe, at least up until the point where he discovered that Goethe lacked the Dionysian, prompting Nietzsche to coin for himself the term "Dionysian pessimism." But as Meyer cautions, it is possible to make a sharp dis-tinction between Goethe and Nietzsche, for while the former stresses objective beauty the latter proceeds subjectively (Meyer 1993: 91). Finally, try as he might to associate him-self with Goethe's image as the classically robust antipode of the sickly, weakly romantic, Nietzsche must have noted Goethe's introspective insight; for all the similarities in how Goethe and Nietzsche praise the ancients at the expense of fragmented moderns, "when these comparisons extend to himself, it becomes obvious that Goethe did not see himself as a happy Greek, but put himself into the camp of the moderns" (Behler 1993: 99). Which is to say, on balance, that Goethe no less than Nietzsche is in the camp of the romantics, even while Nietzsche siphons from Goethe's classical stature to fuel his own critique of romanticism.

Ernst Behler discovers a fully developed consciousness of modernity among the early German romantics who for the first time in history regard "fiction, literature and the arts to be in a process of constant progression and renewal" and who attribute to poetry (*Poesie*) "unlimited transformability and mutability" (Behler 1997: 72, 79). This embrace of the dynamic in art, with its attending empowerment of successive generations in terms of creativity, appears quite compatible with Nietzsche's needs. Behler underscores how *irony* is the distinguishing feature of romantic *Poesie*, marked as it is by alternating denial, affirmation, self-creation, by destruction, expansion, and contraction (Behler 1997: 88). One does not need to look hard to find these properties in Nietzsche's aphoristic writings, and they directly animate *Zarathustra*, Nietzsche's romantic triumph in performative terms. We better understand how *Zarathustra* affects us romantically, I think, when we view it as a symptom of "world irony" as defined by Behler. Such irony he sees in *The Gay Science* 344, where Nietzsche poses the hypothetical that God turns out to be our "longest lie," earlier dramatized in aphorism 125 (The madman) (Behler 1997: 250). I submit that *Zarathustra* can be read as an epic (or mock-epic) treatment of this colossal world irony, whose magnitude as a problem requires an ironic approach. But as Behler points out, Nietzsche was hostile to irony, perceiving it as a symptom of decadence common both to romanticism and to the Socratic method; though he studiously avoided the use of the term "irony" and purportedly avoided irony itself, in fact Nietzsche worked with the classical notion of *dissimulatio* which he preferred to translate as "the mask" (Behler 1997: 252–4). No one today would deny the significance of the mask to Nietzsche's voice, and though Nietzsche would argue against romanticism that his use of the mask is a device borrowed strictly from his divine "philosophical" mentor Dionysus, this mentor's presence in modern discourse is a *romantic achievement* executed by F. Schlegel, Hölderlin, Goethe, Creuzer, et al. and later sculpted into a worldview by Nietzsche.

A main reason why the Dionysian had to wait for Nietzsche to find its deepest expression and most vivid representation is because he engaged more boldly than the early romantics in that characteristically modernist phenomenon of transporting reflection, theory, and philosophizing into the territory of art, poetry, and literature, a phenomenon Behler refers to as "the consciousness of literary modernism," a " 'poetry of poetry' that blends critical, reflective discourse with its own creative invention" (Behler 1993: 5). Observe how Nietzsche in *The Birth of Tragedy* (11–14) condemns Socrates and Euripides for representing just such a fusion of criticism and art, yet *The Birth of Tragedy* is, ironically, itself a splendid fusion of criticism and art, with an even more Dionysian and genuinely, deliberately ironic invasion of art by philosophy to come in *Thus Spoke Zarathustra*.

We should recall at this point that when Nietzsche claimed to have cured himself of romanticism, he did so by embracing philosophy and giving himself over to the healing powers of philosophy, as expressed in the preface of *The Case of Wagner* (*KSA* 6: 11; *CW*, Preface) and the preface to *The Gay Science*, where philosophy is directly correlated to health and is celebrated as the voice of a sound body (*KSA* 3: 347, 349; *GS*, Preface 2). Clearly philosophy becomes Nietzsche's preferred activity, helping him to convalesce and to put distance between himself and his artist undertakings of the romantic phase. The priorities become reversed when Nietzsche no longer considers himself a romantic, such that the anti-Socratic, anti-theory bias of *Tragedy* morphs into an anti-poet bias as he sculpts himself into a philosopher. Even here, however, we must recall that despite Nietzsche's sometimes strident prosecution of the poet, he knew himself to be a poet at heart and celebrated himself in *Ecce Homo* on the grounds of poetry and expression. This classical feud between the poets and the philosophers breaks out anew in the modern, romantic era when Hegel parodies the romantic irony of the Jena School, condemning the romantics for foregrounding the ego, for simply letting themselves go and wallowing in vanity (Behler 1997: 121). And though Behler is quick to add that this posture amounts to mere denunciation, implying that the criticism is undeserved (Behler 1997: 124), observe how Nietzsche too engages in what can be called broad denunciation of romanticism.

Romanticism must be denounced, in the reckoning of both Hegel and Nietzsche, because of the stakes involved in allowing romanticism to go unchallenged. Hegel's own formulation of "God is dead," which according to Immelmann has not been sufficiently researched as a possible influence on Nietzsche's later formulation, was made in the context of the rise of early romantic *Poesie* and the danger posed by it to self-consciousness, namely "to no longer be able to speak authentically," resulting for Hegel in "unhappy self-consciousness" (Immelmann 1992: 77). The loss of authentic speech is an urgent concern to Nietzsche, who wrote "On Truth and Lie in an Extra-Moral Sense" in 1873 but in a rare show of restraint decided not to publish it. Behler argues that given the findings of this language-sceptical essay Nietzsche should have stopped writing entirely, and yet he did the very opposite (Behler 1997: 265, 268). When we ask ourselves why Nietzsche went on to become an extremely articulate philosopher, one who faced down issues in the history of philosophy with the stylistic nuance and creativity of an artist, we eventually come around to the understanding that he suppressed "Truth and Lie" because to have done otherwise would have been to capitulate to the inarticulate, to succumb to the nihilistic view that nothing of value can be said in the modern age. Instead, Nietzsche engaged language with a vengeance, so to speak, and for the dividends of his renewed investment in language (supposedly along anti-romantic lines), Erich Heller provides a cogent account.

According to Heller the contradictions of Nietzsche's thought are deliberate, arising from his deep-seated fear of curtailing articulation, as well as his hatred of Socrates and the lethal effect of Socratism on speech. "By winning a logical argument, Socrates exposed his partners to cheap ridicule. But, Nietzsche said, this plebian pursuit of dialectics and logic is the worst offense against the fullness of life, against its plenitudes of contradictions that nurture the sense of tragedy" (Heller 1988: 6). Thus on Heller's reasoning, Nietzsche would rather utter the basic, bold contradiction represented by the superhuman *and* the eternal recurrence of the same (there has never been an superhuman…) than to leave these concepts unstated, unarticulated (Heller 1988: 11). Moreover, in the grand scheme the enemy for Nietzsche is not contradiction, which mirrors the abundance and superabundance of life, but logic, which is a construct (Heller 1988: 13). Though he claimed to have become a philosopher who cured himself of the artistic malaise represented by romanticism, the chief means used by this "new" philosopher were the old means of romantic expressivism.

This expressivism (Charles Taylor's term) was also favored by Nietzsche's early favorite Hölderlin, who himself had to make a choice between poetry and philosophy, opting for poetry. Contrary to his friends and erstwhile schoolmates Hegel and Schelling, Hölderlin took the path of poetry, knowing that only the language of poetry is capable of speaking of the beautiful, of the sublime. In order to speak adequately of nature in particular, aesthetic and not philosophical discourse is needed (Bay 2003: 115). This reasoning aptly applied to Hölderlin's novel *Hyperion* appears to me to resonate strongly with Nietzsche's writing of *Zarathustra*, a work that shares more of Hölderlin's example than the mere fact that both Hölderlin and Nietzsche can be said to have practiced the vocation of poet "in paltry times" (*in dürftiger Zeit*, from "Bread and Wine").

2 Hölderlin, or the Love of the Living

When Hölderlin sings of the living (*das Lebendige*) in the poem "Socrates and Alcibiades" he exerts immediate and profound appeal on young Nietzsche, helping to engage him for classical studies, to formulate the life-affirming properties of the Dionysian in the early romantic period, and ultimately to ground the philosophical writings that later distinguish Nietzsche as the philosopher of life affirmation (*amor fati*, the Dionysian, the eternal recurrence of the same; Del Caro 1989a: 83–4). Of course Nietzsche will disavow Hölderlin and seem to "overcome" his reliance on him, but this gesture of repudiation is helpless to conceal the unmistakable imprint Hölderlin leaves on Nietzsche's creativity. The most basic expression of the relationship here lies in the concepts of love, vitality, and totality or wholeness of being (Del Caro 1989a: 43). These concepts and the two thinkers are so closely linked in the minds of Nietzsche's twentieth-century followers, moreover, that a well-established conflation of Hölderlin and Nietzsche takes place, such that Georg Heym evokes them simultaneously to elevate his own life affirmation (Meyer 1993: 272–3), while Thomas Mann carries on a dispute with Stefan George concerning whether Nietzsche would have been better off if he had stayed closer to Hölderlin's conception of the poet instead of having pursued a more philosophical approach in prose (Meyer 1993: 342). An even more famous conflation of Hölderlin and Nietzsche is perpetrated by Heidegger, who plunders both thinker-poets freely and simultaneously in his essays on Hölderlin's great hymns and Nietzsche's *Zarathustra* in particular. When Heidegger is sometimes credited with having "discovered" Hölderlin and having made him accessible for twentieth-century literary criticism and theory, it is often forgotten that any number of great German-language poets and writers of the first half of the twentieth century (Hofmannsthal, George, Hesse, T. Mann) were visibly influenced by both Nietzsche and Hölderlin, in effect responding to Hölderlin because they were responding to Nietzsche's energizing contact with romanticism.

A nihilistic tone is struck early in the novel *Hyperion*, with the hero lambasting the inertia and futility of the human condition (Del Caro 1989a: 242). Later in this section I will treat even stronger structural and philosophical convergences between *Hyperion* and *Zarathustra*, but for the moment, I am more interested in demonstrating that both writers took an interest in the threat of nihilism and constructed their works as a response to it. This is documented by Immelmann when he explains, in terms reminiscent of Hegel, that "in literature nihilism can be traced as the destruction of meaningful, communicative speech" (Immelmann 1992: 30). While Hölderlin responded to the vacuum of meaning with a "remythologizing of values," he predates Nietzsche in the use of a nihilistic aesthetics that regards art as a metaphysical activity (Immelmann 1992: 31). Insofar as Hölderlin himself was prone to melancholy, boredom, and inertia, he suffered from the root causes of nihilism (Immelmann 1992: 126). Though we cannot ascribe these exact afflictions to Nietzsche, there is still a striking resemblance between his overcoming of adversity (ill health, misplaced faith, unrequited love, decadence, etc.) and the uses Hölderlin made of his own obstacles. If we agree with Bay that Hölderlin's *Hyperion* represents the first German novel to engage the problem of the loss of a cultural center, and therefore stands at the threshold of modernity by virtue of illustrating the consequences of the loss of the absolute, then surely we can discern this same fundamental concern in Nietzsche's writings at a more advanced stage of modernity in which the conditions for nihilism's insidious ravages have become even more favorable.

There is clear evidence of Hölderlin's influence in *Zarathustra*, in some cases reflected in rhetoric that appears to borrow nearly verbatim from *Hyperion* (Del Caro 1989a: 44–5). Nietzsche knew Hölderlin's poetry and prose very well even as a *Gymnasiast* and in 1861 he penned an eloquent defense of Hölderlin in "Letter to My Friend" by emphasizing Hölderlin's incisive criticism of the philistine, his genuine longing for the ancient Greeks, his intellectual proximity to Hegel and Schiller, and the special power of the prose in *Hyperion* ("indeed, this prose is music") (Del Caro 1989a: 41–2; *Werke* III: 95–8). Some of the language Nietzsche uses in *Ecce Homo* to describe his own writings, such as *The Birth of Tragedy* and *Zarathustra* is remarkably similar to the manner in which young Nietzsche describes Hölderlin's skill in poems, hymns, the Empedocles fragment, and *Hyperion*. When Nietzsche began the long process of cutting his ties to romanticism, he conveniently forgot what Hölderlin had achieved and what this remarkably *modern* poet had meant to him early on. It is a typical strategy of Nietzsche to turn against those who meant most to him in terms of intellectual affinity, especially if he had developed a reliance on them.

Even more significant than the content and rhetorical delivery of passages critical of our modern human condition is the deeply catalyzing role played by both Hyperion and Zarathustra—they share the mission of prophecy reflecting their conviction that humanity has fallen into spiritual torpor. One is tempted to follow Nietzsche's carefully mapped-out trail to the original prophet Zoroaster for the source of his prophetic inspiration, and indeed there is no disputing that the new Zoroaster, i.e., Nietzsche's Zarathustra, is a remake of the original who comes back to revisit the problem of good and evil for which he himself was responsible. However, there are closer models whom Nietzsche had in mind during the Zarathustra period, as revealed in his notes for early 1884. Claiming that he and his kind are "too musically demanding" for simple, repetitive rhyme, he praises two modern masters of the lyrical:

> How the form of Platen and Hölderlin already does us good! But much too strict for us! The right way is playing with the most diverse meters and occasionally the unmetrical by itself: the freedom we have already achieved in music through Richard Wagner! Surely we may adopt it for poetry! Ultimately it is the only one that speaks robustly to the heart!—Thanks to Luther! (*KSA* 11: 59–60)

In this glimpse into Nietzsche's workshop we observe how the problem of language is couched in terms of form, freedom comparable to Wagnerian music, and robustness harking back to Luther's skill with the German language. Quite conspicuously both Hölderlin and Wagner are cited as modern manifestations of or at least signposts in the direction of a new speech that will rival Luther's. The very next unpublished note on the page (25[173]) reads:

> The language of Luther and the poetic form of the Bible as the basis of a new German *poetry*:— this is *my* invention! Antiquitizing, rhyming—all false and does not speak *profoundly* enough to us: or even worse Wagner's alliteration! (*KSA* 11: 60)

Nietzsche's achievement in *Zarathustra*, to which the immediate quote obviously alludes, has resulted in a breakthrough for German poetry (*Poesie* here). While Luther's robustness and the poetic form of the Bible (verses, parables, etc.) are retained and joined, notice that

Hölderlin's "antiquitizing" (*das Antikisiren*) and the convention of rhyme are discarded as false, as is Wagner's use of alliteration (*Stabreim*). Now when we focus our attention on the kind of figure represented by the speaking Zarathustra, we see Nietzsche elevating Luther's robust, biblical German, while simultaneously downplaying the imitation of Greek poetic forms (Hölderlin) and the entire romantic convention of rhyme (Goethe, Wagner, et al.). We also see that although Nietzsche claims in his notes to have surpassed Hölderlin and Wagner in these matters, they were clearly on his mind during the composition of *Zarathustra* and that work was written in agon with them.

For a final demonstration of the presence of Hyperion, the hero, in Zarathustra the prophet I turn to Hansjörg Bay's dissertation on *Hyperion*. This nuanced study, I wish to point out, is in no way interested in charting a parallel between Hölderlin and Nietzsche, and in fact Nietzsche is not discussed in this book of more than 400 pages. As mentioned previously, for Bay modernity breaks out circa 1800 when human beings begin to feel the loss of a center represented by God (Bay 2003: 25). On this reckoning, the respective missions of Hyperion and Zarathustra draw on the same negative energy or what Behler calls the "world irony" of God's death. Bay also explains why Hölderlin opts for *Poesie* over philosophy, despite the influence of his friends Hegel and Schelling, because only poetry can adequately speak of the sublime and of nature (Bay 2003: 115).[2] Here, too, we mark that Zarathustra's speaking frequently references the sublime and nature, spanning the ingenious nature metaphors of the Prologue and culminating in Zarathustra's formulation and affirmation of the eternal recurrence of the same.

Diotima in her second speech to Hyperion tells him he must *descend* to human beings like a ray of light, like the life-giving rain, bringing light like Apollo and shattering and animating like Jupiter. Enhancing the movement suggested by his name Hyperion, he must *go down* and accomplish a "turn to the earth" (Bay 2003: 297–8). Already in section 1 of the prologue Zarathustra adopts the role of the sun and begins speaking of his own *katabasis*, which in the Nietzsche literature is commonly discussed in the context of Socrates. In *Hyperion* the solar metaphors blend with rain and "flowing, over-flowing and pouring oneself" are joined with the "maternal substance of the earth" such that fructification and animation bring forth cultivation (Bay 2003: 299). Zarathustra's superabundance is also used to fructify, for he speaks of the superhuman as a shattering lightning that inoculates humanity. Hyperion learns that he has something to give needy humanity; his sun-god stature puts him in the role of Poros to express his superabundance (Bay 2003: 300), much as Zarathustra claims to need to go down in order to share his superabundance. While Hyperion is shy of human beings and therefore reluctant to interact with them politically (Bay 2003: 304), Zarathustra is suspicious of people and suffers from disgust for the pettiness of humans. The impure and increasingly dirty condition of humanity concerns Hyperion and his friends, such that they undertake a "highly aggressive program of purification" aimed at cleaning up the earth itself. Toward this end two mountain streams become one "majestic stream" that will wash away the impurities (Bay 2003: 306), reminiscent of Zarathustra's characterization of humanity as a polluted stream that needs the sea of superhuman in order to become clean. Hyperion resembles Mohammed as one who comes to proclaim not his personal teaching

---

[2] See Del Caro 1993: 1–27, where I argue for poetry as a more appropriate medium than philosophy for writing on life in the manner of Nietzsche's *Lebensphilosophie*.

but "the monologue of nature" that "sublimates the turn to the earth"; moreover, the radiating and flowing of this model of prophet culminates in "a speaking: What Hyperion has to 'sow' are words, and what is supposed to pour itself onto the 'slumbering land like the all-refreshing rain' is the stream of his speech" (Bay 2003: 310). Again, Nietzsche has unmistakably adopted these contours and strategies from Hölderlin, and without them the Prologue of *Zarathustra* and the effect of the work in general would be sorely diminished. Finally, Bay recounts how Hyperion has a series of experiences leading to his "becoming a human being" (*Menschwerdung*; Bay 2003: 312)—the precise operation that Zarathustra claims for himself in the Prologue section 1 when he speaks: "Behold, this cup wants to become empty again, and Zarathustra wants to become human again" (*Z* I: "Zarathustra's Prologue" 1).

Ulrich Gaier discusses the foundational importance of love for Hölderlin's vision of a new earth, for love is to be the binding element of a new national culture of the West, and while the gods themselves have retreated, their divinity remains and is manifest in the love moderns have for one another according to Hölderlin's "religious patriotism" (Gaier 1993: 34–5). Hölderlin's conception of the "fatherland" in his hymns is expansive, not exhausted by modern notions of nationalism and resembling more a "kingdom of God" (Gaier 1993: 2). What Gaier refers to as Hölderlin's "poesie on the basis of anthropology" (Gaier 1993: 203) bears strong resemblance to Nietzsche's project of a new earth, and the emphasis on anthropology and love are retained by Nietzsche as powerful motivations for Zarathustra's *katabasis* and his self-transformation into the ultimate affirmer of *amor fati*. The tradition represented by Hölderlin, Herder, and Novalis as it is inherited from Plato, namely the notion of the poet as a servant of nature whose function is to educate the earth (Gaier 1993: 203), breaks sharply with Nietzsche's sense of how our species is supposed to interact with the earth. When the poet becomes an instrument and resigns his autonomy in order to enter the service of his community (Gaier 1993: 402), the essential difference between Zarathustra and Hyperion is transacted, because Zarathustra cannot and will not function in the capacity of a servant, nor is there a vision of a community in *Zarathustra* beyond the projected arrival of "Zarathustra's children" or the superhuman. It is also quite plain that Zarathustra does not represent a poet, the lucid ironies of the chapter "On Poets" notwithstanding, and that poets tend to muddy the waters (to *invent*) more than they help. At this point the relationship between Nietzsche and Hölderlin defaults to the same kind of relationship Nietzsche has with Socrates and Christ, both teachers of love, to be sure, but teachers whose respective model of teaching is diametrically opposed by Zarathustra. This turning away from the teachers of Western tradition mirrors what Robert Gooding-Williams calls the transition from the German "body politic" to the healthy human body as symbolized by Nietzsche's abandonment of Wagnerian (national) ideals and his embrace of Dionysian (bodied) creativity (Gooding-Williams 2001: 18). In the final analysis Nietzsche throws Hölderlin overboard using the charge of metaphysics, unjustly and unfortunately in many ways because Hölderlin did entertain the notion of a non-metaphysical divinity,[3] a vision for the renewal of the species in its relation to the earth, a role for the Dionysian in earth affirmation, and a profound faith in love and creativity. As a youth Nietzsche had been motivated by Hölderlin's critique of the philistine and his insights into the German character, while as a young man

---

[3] As discussed by Gaier who stresses poetry on the basis of anthropology and a broad human community conceived as the kingdom of God (Gaier 1993); and as discussed by Del Caro 1991: 80–99.

caught up in the atmosphere of the founding years of the Reich and Wagner's romanticism, he conflated Hölderlin the patriot with Wagner (Del Caro 1989a: 41–3). Once the break with Wagner and romanticism takes places, Nietzsche dismisses Hölderlin as part of the dynamic of nationalism associated with Wagnerianism, but he performs a double repudiation by associating romanticism with mere art and mere poetry, which he throws over in favor of philosophy. Hölderlin is therefore rejected for a number of reasons including his status as a poet first (Del Caro 1989a: 44).

3 Goethe, or Dueling over Dionysus

In a discussion of the German character in *Beyond Good and Evil* Nietzsche found himself wondering out loud what Goethe might have thought about the Germans, because this is one issue on which he did not speak clearly and preferred to remain silent. What Nietzsche was certain of, however, was that Goethe "rethought" not only his Faust but "the whole problem of the human being" as a response to the rise of Napoleon (*KSA* 5: 185; *BGE* 244). This passage linking the greatness of Napoleon and Goethe helps to explain why these two more or less constant heroes are paired in Nietzsche's imagination. Goethe represents true nature, amorality, and life affirmation, while his lesser contemporaries such as Herder (and by association a host of romantics) represent the "anti-nature" that is morality (Del Caro 1989a: 38). In another juxtaposing formulation Nietzsche later described Napoleon as an example of "ascent to nature" versus Rousseau's notion of "return to nature"; ascending to nature was achieved by Goethe as well, whom Nietzsche also referred to as a "European event" in the same context. Meanwhile, Rousseau the arch-romantic skulks away branded by the invective "first modern man, idealist and scoundrel in *one* person" (*TI* 9: 49). The vivid and true representation of nature manifesting in Napoleon and Goethe generally presents itself in Nietzsche as an uncompromising rising up to nature, as opposed to foisting morality on it (Herder et al.) or idealizing it along democratic lines (Rousseau).

What impressed Nietzsche about Goethe and clearly influenced the language and direction of *Zarathustra* is well formulated by Gooding-Williams: "Goethe's sense that one could resist the exhaustion of one's creative capacity, by opening one's self to forces that subjective poets have disowned, prefigures Nietzsche's representation of Dionysian bodies as reclaiming and incorporating previously repressed and dying passions" (Gooding-Williams 2001: 130).[4] Here we have a theoretical, Dionysian-based formulation of what Nietzsche called "ascent to nature," insofar as Goethe's ability to harness nature's forces allowed him to express himself robustly, amorally, and creatively. Schiller had observed already in the 1790s that Goethe was somehow closer to nature in his genius than other creative individuals, for which he coined the term naive to describe Goethe's art (very influential later on Schopenhauer's conception of artistic genius) and sentimental to describe his own more analytical, self-conscious productivity. Let us bear in mind this extraordinary synergy of Goethe's with nature when Nietzsche at the end of his career begins to fault Goethe for not

---

[4] Later on Gooding-Williams discusses how Nietzsche favors the model of Prometheus not only in *The Birth of Tragedy*, but also in *Zarathustra* where again it is Goethe's poem "Prometheus" that affirms creativity in the face of those who practice only resignation (2001: 238–40, 246).

possessing the tragic and not embodying the Dionysian—he could only stretch to make such claims by willfully ignoring the Dionysian in Goethe and boldly recasting the Dionysian to resemble himself.

Goethe like Hölderlin was capable of perceiving the importance of creativity and maintaining a strong connection to the earth in the wake of the Enlightenment's unexamined celebration of the concept of progress. Rudolf Kreis speaks of a "morphic field" arising in the line of writers including Goethe, Hölderlin, Büchner, and Nietzsche, with Nietzsche representing its clearest contours; these figures draw our attention relentlessly to the earth and the wild and they oppose modernity's flight to the cities (Kreis 1995: 81). Due to Goethe's great stature he was a constant presence in Nietzsche's early essayistic writings, functioning for Nietzsche as a stand-in for the Greeks and a great individual in the manner of Schopenhauer and Wagner (Del Caro 1989a: 78–9). More specifically, it was Goethe's amorality that helped him to affirm life and thereby represent the classical aesthetic of ascending vitality (Del Caro 1989a: 80). In a most consequential way, Nietzsche adopted Goethe's stance on knowledge and elevated it to his own motto, drawing heavily from it to animate the pages of his most successful essay *On the Uses and Disadvantage of History for Living*: "Furthermore I despise everything which merely teaches me without increasing or directly animating my activity" (*UM* II, Preface). The desire to incorporate and thrive is a mainstay of Nietzsche's thought from *The Birth of Tragedy* to *Twilight of the Idols*; he never waivers from this earth-bound, biocentric focus, and its major proponent before Nietzsche had been Goethe.[5]

The more Nietzsche invested in defining his "Dionysian pessimism" as a new form of classicism, the more he felt he had to distance himself from Goethe, ostensibly because Goethe did not sufficiently possess a sense of the tragic or embody the Dionysian, but Nietzsche was seriously wrong about this. For the moment it is necessary to explore how Nietzsche attempts to carve out his own space in matters Dionysian. The distinction originally made by Goethe between the robust classical and the sickly romantic served Nietzsche well enough, but internal inconsistencies prompted him to dismiss the term *klassisch* in favor of Dionysian pessimism (Del Caro 1989a: 26–7). We recall that Behler characterizes Nietzsche's embrace of classicism as "against his inclinations," and it is Behler who begins to speak of "Dionysian classicism [which] brings Nietzsche into a direct intellectual affinity with the early German romanticists, whom he himself barely knew, while he held only cliché-like ideas of romanticism in general" (Behler 1973: 241; Del Caro 1989a: 124). What becomes clear is that Nietzsche appropriated the term "classic" in much the same manner that he appropriated the term "Dionysian," using them to describe his personal achievements in the realm of intellectual history.[6] This reworking of the Dionysian into a worldview, i.e., investing the concept with supposedly anti-romantic meaning and deepening it to the point where it comes to stand for "new philosophizing" is in fact one of the most historical

---

[5] Meyer also points out the primacy of life over knowledge based on Goethe's motto (1993: 34) and how creativity becomes increasingly associated with great individuals based on the example of Goethe (84). In joining vitality and classical restraint (Goethe), "Nietzsche now strives for a symbiosis of life-dynamics and intellectual discipline. Now a disciplined 'Dionysus' begins to speak" (90). Because he did not like narrative prose, according to Meyer, Nietzsche was primarily interested in biography and essayistic forms where prose blends with philosophy, as in *Conversations with Goethe* by Eckermann (135). This aversion to prose would not of course extend to Dostoyevsky and should not be accepted axiomatically.

[6] See Del Caro 1989b and 1998.

events in all of romanticism, so that ironically when philosophers today engage Nietzsche's writings they are engaging the very romanticism Nietzsche and they hold in contempt and continue to pejoratize.

Though Nietzsche used Goethe when advantageous to formulate his new Dionysian aesthetics, he did not wholeheartedly embrace Goethe as the ultimate alternative to nihilism and idealism (Del Caro 1989a: 77–8). If he had done so, Nietzsche's standing in intellectual history would have been diminished, and he was far too ambitious and self-promoting to allow any predecessor to eclipse him. In *Twilight of the Idols* Goethe is praised as a European event, an attempt to overcome the eighteenth century through an "ascent" to nature, and as an individual who drew on history, natural science, antiquity, and Spinoza to engage life through practical activity. He was according to Nietzsche the personification of totality, working constantly to bridge reason and sensuality; the antipode of Kant, a realist in unreal times, a yea-sayer whose greatest experience had been Napoleon, tolerant out of strength rather than weakness, a "spirit become free" and no longer capable of denying anything: "But such a faith is the highest of all possible faiths: I baptized it under the name *Dionysus*" (KSA 6: 151–2, TI 9: 49). Now in the very next aphorism, immediately after crowning Goethe with the highest glory, Nietzsche questions the gains of the nineteenth century and asks rhetorically: "Why is it that the end result is not a Goethe but instead chaos, a nihilistic sighing, an utter bewilderment, an instinct of exhaustion that in practice constantly drives us *to reach back to the eighteenth-century*? (—for example as emotional romanticism, as altruism and hyper-sentimentality, as feminism in taste, as socialism in politics)" (KSA 6: 152; TI 9: 50). Nietzsche explains this end result by describing even the nineteenth century as an "intensified *barbarized* [*verrohtes*] eighteenth century, i.e., a *décadence* century," such that Goethe was a mere interlude and a beautiful "in vain" for Germany and Europe; the missed opportunity he ascribes to how great individuals are commonly misunderstood, and when the public does not know how to make use of them, this uselessness itself testifies to the individual's greatness (ibid.). The lavishing of praise on Goethe cannot mask the lack of effect that he has had on the nineteenth century. By directly juxtaposing himself with Goethe in the context of this supreme praise, Nietzsche leaves open the possibility that he, not Goethe, will be the one to lead humanity into a robust and Dionysian future.[7] In order to set the hook deeper he invokes Goethe again at the beginning of aphorism 51: "Goethe is the last German for whom I have respect…" only to conclude this aphorism and this chapter of

---

[7] I think Nietzsche had already made this clear in 1887 in Book Five of *The Gay Science*, where he discusses romanticism in the aphorism "What is Romanticism?" (GS 370). At the point where he claims credit for christening superabundance with the name Dionysus, he also speaks glowingly of Rubens, Hafis, Goethe "spreading a Homeric light and splendour over all things," and it is here too that he refers to "romantic pessimism, the last *great* event in the fate of our culture. (That there *could* be a completely different pessimism, a classical one—this intuition and vision belongs to me as inseparable from me, as my *proprium* and *ipsissimum*; only the word 'classical' offends my ears; it has become far too trite, round, and indistinct. I call this pessimism of the future—for it is coming! I see it coming!—*Dionysian* pessimism)." Observe first that Rubens, Hafis, and Goethe "spread Homeric light and splendour," because the Homeric according to Nietzsche had been the triumph of the Apollinian in BT 3. Observe secondly that here, too, Nietzsche reserves a space for himself to surpass Goethe and lead us into the Dionysian future.

Twilight with the reminder: "I have given humanity the most profound book that it possesses, my *Zarathustra*: in a short time I shall give it the most independent—" (*KSA* 6: 153; *TI* 9: 51).

Attempting to characterize Goethe's writings as classical in the finest tradition of the Greeks, Nietzsche in *Human* made the strongest possible case for Goethe as having successfully resisted the tendency of "revolution in poetry" that had swept up so many in the modern era. The revolutionizing tendencies were resisted by Voltaire, Byron, and Goethe, by means of restraint and conformity with the classical conventions of drama, and such restraint, though it may appear absurd to moderns, is the only way to avoid naturalism in art (a replay of the argument from *The Birth of Tragedy* regarding the function of the chorus and the popularization of tragedy by Euripides). Consequently, Nietzsche stressed that Goethe left us "no new motifs and characters, but the old, long familiar ones in constantly enduring re-animation and restructuring" (*KSA* 2: 180–4; *HAH* I: 221). At this relatively early stage revolution is associated with romanticism in poetry and we note that Voltaire, Byron, and Goethe could be spoken of in one breath as classical spirits—this despite Byron's *Manfred* and Goethe's *Faust*—two works that can scarcely be claimed for classicism at the expense of romanticism. There is a hint here of how Nietzsche is beginning to position himself relative to Byron and Goethe; soon Byron will be thrown over as a hopeless romantic, while Goethe will be elevated as a robust classicist with the exception of *Faust*, toward which Nietzsche always maintained a certain suspicion despite his having quoted the work throughout his career.

There is something rather stretched and resembling backhanded praise in Nietzsche's observation that Goethe left us with nothing new. By relegating Goethe to classicism as strongly as he does, Nietzsche is able to typecast him, to reduce him to a singular role even as he elevates him for the strength and discipline required to adhere to classical standards. I summarized in 1989 how Goethe was faulted by Nietzsche for his hostility toward the Enlightenment and Newton, his concept of the eternal feminine, his excessively reflective dramatic characters, his elevation of the seduction of Gretchen by Faust to tragic material, his own "untragic" and conciliatory nature, and ultimately his failure to understand the Greeks (Del Caro 1989a: 98). Very pointedly Nietzsche claimed in *Ecce Homo* that Goethe, Dante, and Shakespeare would be unable to breathe in the rarified air of Zarathustra (Del Caro 1989a: 98), marking the completion of Nietzsche's dramatic self-promoting at the expense of erstwhile models.[8] While Goethe's adherence to classical norms may of course continue to be praised, observe that his skill in the vital area of tragedy is questioned and his supreme innovation in terms of creativity, namely *Faust*, is dismissed as idealistic feminism and failed tragedy. Meanwhile, and quite predictably, *Zarathustra* is touted as the greatest *innovation* and gift of all time—a work so peerless that one is almost tempted to call it "revolutionary."

When one considers the rich rhetorical apparatus of *Ecce Homo* as it designs to elevate *Zarathustra* to the highest creative achievement of all time, one notices how Nietzsche returns again and again to the notion that the writing of *Zarathustra* was Dionysian action, Dionysian deed. It is this unique ability to execute a Dionysian aesthetic that enables

---

[8] Others who have remarked on this turn away from Goethe are Young (1992: 165) and Gooding-Williams (2001: 191), who observes that Zarathustra's poetizing has more truth content than Goethe's.

Nietzsche to claim that he has surpassed Goethe and more specifically Goethe's *Faust*, since this is the work that sticks in his craw, so to speak. The strongest objection I have to Nietzsche's claiming sole possession of the Dionysian is that it arguably belongs to Goethe as demonstrated in *Faust*, indeed, the much-derided eternal feminine is powerful Dionysian material and it shapes and defines Faust every bit as much as does the earth spirit—another Goethean innovation that Nietzsche appears to ignore. Only by ignoring the feminine component of the Dionysian and the feminine component of creativity in general could Nietzsche deceive himself into thinking that Goethe somehow lacked tragic depth and Dionysian creativity. *Zarathustra* contains many secretive and disguised, veiled references to Dionysus, Ariadne, and feminine creativity, but they pale in comparison to Goethe's treatment of these ancient myths and themes in *Faust*. Finally, it is absurd for Nietzsche to claim that Goethe did not understand the Greeks, for in fact Goethe's understanding of the Greeks appears to be deeper and bolder than Nietzsche's, drawing on and elaborating the most ancient myths of creativity as they involve male and female figures (Gretchen as Medea, Ariadne, Medusa; the Mothers; Helen et al.), as opposed to reinventing a "Dionysian" world based on male values and reflecting only Nietzsche's taste.[9]

4 Wagner, or Resisting the Charms of Expression

What seems to have contributed most to Nietzsche's abandonment of his erstwhile mentor and friend is the company Wagner preferred to keep, figuratively and literally. As long as Nietzsche could uphold the image of an esoteric, tragically pessimistic spirit in Wagner, a potential continuator of tragedy in the highest tradition of Aeschylus and Sophocles, Nietzsche could sing his praises without compromising his own standards and inclinations—early Nietzsche was genuinely devoted to Wagner as a thinker capable of Dionysian pessimism. However, it eventually dawned on Nietzsche that although Wagner had shown occasional flashes of affinity with early Greek thought, ultimately Wagner was a Euripides figure as portrayed in *The Birth of Tragedy*, i.e., someone who panders to the common people and allows "the spectator" onto the stage (Del Caro 1989a: 120). By embracing the role of German hero, German composer, German-Christian animator of the Teutonic myths, and anti-Semite, Wagner showed his true colors as a populist, hyper-modern person; his wholesale representation of the worst aspects of the new German nationalism were genuinely incompatible with Nietzsche's elitist, esoteric, and anti-democratic sentiments. Wagner began to represent to Nietzsche what earlier nationalist thought had manifested as a reaction to Napoleon after the dissolution of the Reich in 1806, and at this point Wagner and patriotic, political romanticism are inextricably linked in his mind (Del Caro 1989a: 150–3).

Whereas the effect of tragic art in ancient times had been to elevate the Greeks as a cultural people for whom an aesthetic worldview was of paramount importance, indeed the defining

---

[9] For books treating Goethe's sources for *Faust* as they relate to feminine creativity see Bohm 2007, Ilgner 2001, and Jantz 1969, especially p. 53 where he discusses Goethe's standing in the anti-Platonic tradition.

characteristic of their lives according to Nietzsche, in Nietzsche's day, as Gianni Vattimo points out, art had become a relic and a means to entertain the exhausted, industrious spectator after a long day's work. In this role art necessarily becomes crude and debased in order to meet the needs of the people (Vattimo 1992: 33–4).[10] Of course Wagner's art is on Nietzsche's mind when he speaks like this, and Wagner becomes the poster child of artistic modernity, ably fulfilling the role of narcotic for a tired and bored audience in need of a little stimulation. We should recall that the attempt to appeal in a populist manner is anathema to Nietzsche and always had been— the lowering of art to a secondary, indeed debased role in order to reflect the views and needs of the people is a capitulation to naturalism, the worst tendency in modern art. For his part, and I would say despite the great experiment of *Zarathustra* which is supposed to be a book "for all and none," Nietzsche's art is rather monologic, capable of being social if the right audience is engaged, but in no way is it demagogic art as in the case of Wagner (Meyer 1993: 147; Del Caro 1989a: 165–72). When Geuss therefore cites the example of the architectural seating design of the *Festspielhaus* at Bayreuth as evidence of Wagner's egalitarian ideal, he addresses the major incompatibility that had always existed between Nietzsche and Wagner (*BT* xvi), an incompatibility that only becomes exacerbated by Wagner's unique brand of romanticism.

The attacks on Wagner are not limited to his works but conspicuously extend to Wagner's person, which Meyer appears to justify by explaining that the invectives are motivated by the tension between Nietzsche's paganism and Wagner's Christianity, and Dionysian vitality versus romantic weakness (Meyer 1993: 42). I would add that the *ad hominem* dimension of Nietzsche's critique of Wagner is typical and differs from other critiques only in intensity. When Nietzsche needed to cut his intellectual ties to Hölderlin, the person Hölderlin was depicted as weak and irresolute. In the opposite direction, when Goethe's works could not be sufficiently championed as Dionysian, it was Goethe's person that Nietzsche elevated. Similar patterns will be found in most of Nietzsche's writings, inasmuch as he kept a close eye on the kind of life one lived in relation to the thought one espoused. Thus for example Goethe was consistently praised for his strong stance against Christianity and his embrace of paganism.

Nietzsche dramatized the differences between himself and Wagner by recounting the story of how he mailed two copies of *Human, All Too Human* to Bayreuth while at the same time he received from Wagner a signed copy of the text for *Parsifal*: "This crossing in the mail of the two books—it seemed to me as though I heard an ominous sound. Did it not sound like the crossing of *swords*?" He concluded this section of *Ecce Homo* with the exclamation: "Unbelievable! Wagner had become pious…" (*KSA* 6: 327; *EH* 6: 5). The duel imagined here is between the Enlightenment and romanticism, with Voltaire, to whom Nietzsche had dedicated the first edition, serving as Nietzsche's second, while the book itself as a declaration of independence from Wagner serves as the glove in the face. Here in his autobiography of 1888 the further staging of their antagonism for one another serves to position the two men on the world stage. By this time of course *Zarathustra* has been richly extolled and glorified by Nietzsche, so the mention of *Parsifal* calls forth a juxtaposition of the two works and what they represent.[11]

---

[10] Indeed, while Vattimo discusses this debasement of art in the context of *Human, All Too Human*, see *GS* 80 and 86 as well, especially the latter where "culture" is associated with narcotics.

[11] Gooding-Williams discusses Book IV of *Thus Spoke Zarathustra* as a travesty of *Parsifal* (279), pointing to the dragon and dwarf figures as allusions to Wagner's *Ring* cycle (222, 235) and to Zarathustra as a messenger and teacher in the manner of Wotan who foresees Siegfried (234). Clearly Nietzsche drew on all manner of intertextuality for the composition of *Zarathustra*, but I caution against direct, specific linkages such as these because they seem reductionist.

A provocative account of *Zarathustra* contra *Parsifal* is provided by Rudolf Kreis, who argues that Nietzsche's writings increasingly become a "Siamese twin" of Wagner's works, functioning as a counterpoint while intertwining with them (Kreis 1995: 19–20, 40). Without stooping to the level of engaging Wagner's racism and anti-Semitism, Nietzsche instead engages Wagner's view that *Parsifal* was "the most Christian of all artworks," thereby opposing the historical constant that lies at the root of Wagner's art, namely the struggle against Judaism (Kreis 1995: 21). The scenario is broadened to global proportions when Wagner romanticizes the conquest and missionization of the Teutons, for with the arrival of Boniface among the early Germans a world-historical clear-cutting and ravaging of the forest lands takes place, symbolizing the earth-negating properties of colonizing Christianity (Kreis 1995: 62). Kreis reads Zarathustra as resembling the ancient prophets of Judaism who embrace the land, the physical earth; Nietzsche understood the profound anti-Judaism and anti-earth implications of *Parsifal* and saw this work as a fantasy of world domination, which he opposed in his own writings by drawing on Greek and Hebrew myths (Kreis 1995: 105). Thus for Kreis nothing less than the future of the earth is at stake when Nietzsche opposes Wagner, and Wagner is elevated to the position of earth's most formidable and insidious enemy, insofar as he crusades against the earth masquerading as a composer. I think Kreis's approach explains Nietzsche's aversion to Wagnerian "romanticism" in several respects, including why Nietzsche is never content to attack only Wagner's music, why Zarathustra speaks with such urgency regarding the meaning of the earth, and why the Dionysian, bodied life along with the eternal recurrence of the same become the counterpoint to Christian asceticism and the doctrine of the afterlife. Wagner becomes the personification and distillation of Christianity at a point in history when the earth's fortunes are tied to humanity's; Nietzsche's creative efforts are expended in the project to unmask Wagnerianism and to provide a sound, earth-affirming alternative to the suicidal "rapture."

There is a reductionist tendency in Kreis's thesis, compelling as it is in other respects, where it suggests that Nietzsche's earth affirmation corresponds one-to-one with Wagner's earth negation; the Nietzschean project is much broader and frequently conducted independently of Wagner, though we might concede that exposing and opposing Wagnerianism becomes one of Nietzsche's means. Nietzsche may well have feared that art would be decisive in the battle for bodies for earth versus souls for heaven, because he ascribed considerable power to Wagner's effect. The overwhelming effect of Wagnerian music, mingled as it is with rhetoric, drama, and suggestion, is hypnotic (Meyer 1993: 97–8). Nietzsche also ascribed narcotic effect to Wagner's art in particular and to how modern art is "enjoyed" in general. Questions arise as to how Nietzsche sets about to counter this "overwhelming" influence: can he offer a viable alternative in studied, ironic formulations that constantly alert the reader to potential or actual manipulation of their emotions by Nietzsche? Can he rely on the seductive, engaging effects of aphoristic and parabolic rhetoric, whereby he tells part of the story, so to speak, but allows readers to draw their own conclusions? And to what extent can we honestly claim that Nietzsche's writings in themselves do not strive for overwhelming effect, when in fact what characterizes these writings first and foremost is "effect"? Gooding-Williams reveals how Nietzsche is quite capable of using the overwhelming (lulling, suspending, suggesting) effect in a manner similar to Wagner's when he "inspires" the higher men to "lose themselves in the ecstasy of a drunken singing" (Gooding-Williams 2001: 290–1). Is this an isolated example or possibly a symptom of a greater, more pervasive effort in *Zarathustra* to overwhelm the reader? After all, since Nietzsche remained a champion of effect as an indicator of vitality, it is not the means of manipulation that he objects to in Wagner and in Christianity so much as the ends toward which they strive:

> Ultimately it depends on to what *end* lies are told. That in Christianity the "holy" ends are lacking is *my* objection to its means. Only *bad* ends: poisoning, slander, negation of life, contempt for the body, the denigration and self-violation of human beings through the concept of sin— *consequently* its means are also bad (*A* 56, *KSA* 6: 239—emphasis Nietzsche's).

Related to this dueling strategy of creative engagement is the very nature of the modern artist. Wagner is christened "the Cagliostro of modernity" because he is so powerfully histrionic, such an effective mime and confidence man (Del Caro 1989a: 155). The historical Count Cagliostro was an occultist, confidence man, alchemist, swindler, healer, and adventurer—he was a skilled actor and deceiver, such that Nietzsche associated his engaging, alluring effect with both Schopenhauer's "lesser" and charming (*bezaubernd*) aspects (*KSA* 3: 455; *GS* 99) and with Wagner.[12] Small wonder, then, that Wagner should be depicted in Book IV of *Zarathustra* as the Magician who sings the Magician's Song later retitled by Nietzsche in the *Dionysus Dithyrambs* to "Ariadne's Lament."[13] For that matter, the Wagnerian shadow looms even earlier in *Zarathustra* when the jester thwarts Zarathustra's enterprise by "leaping over" the tightrope walker and causing him to fall to his death—the jester actually threatens Zarathustra and warns that unless he departs, it is Zarathustra who will next be leaped over (*KSA* 4: 23; *Z* I: "Zarathustra's Prologue" 8). The enmity between Zarathustra the sincere teacher of the superhuman and the jester as the personification of randomness, acting, and lack of meaning is reiterated in the Prologue when Zarathustra says: "Uncanny is human existence and still without meaning: a jester can spell its doom" (*Z* I: "Zarathustra's Prologue" 7). This enmity can be regarded as the tension between the teachings represented by Nietzsche and Wagner, with Nietzsche striving for an unromanticized embrace of the earth and Wagner using all his wiles and histrionic talents (the jester) to ensure the failing of human beings to cross over from animal to superhuman.[14]

The problem of fanaticism as he was certain to have observed it in Wagner's followers and in Christians more generally occupied Nietzsche in *Human, All Too Human*, where he described the worst kind of teacher as "the moral fanatic who thinks that the good can only grow out of and on the good" (*KSA* 2: 584; *HAH* III 70). He reformulated this notion when he explained how the ability to weigh many things and draw from them a quick conclusion contributes to the making of great politicians, generals, and merchants, while looking

[12] Karl Gutzkow actually associated Wagner with Cagliostro before Nietzsche did (*KSA* 14: 404–5).

[13] The Magician is set upon by Zarathustra, beaten with a staff and upbraided for his performance as a mere actor here. Quite significantly, the Magician's Song is later more clearly linked to Dionysus when it is retitled "Ariadne's Lament," expressing that female figure's longing for the companionship of her lover-god. Thus in Nietzsche's mind from the time of *Zarathustra* all the way through to the final manuscript he prepared for publication (*Dionysus Dithyrambs*) in 1888, Wagner, acting, the feminine, and Dionysus are thought of in tandem. We must not overlook the obvious in Nietzsche's rejection of romanticism and Wagnerian romanticism/modernity, namely that Wagner was a musician and actor, a figure drawing together music and drama as the highest expressions of art. In embracing a "philosophical" Dionysus, can we really expect that Nietzsche would divest his favorite god of these two most compelling properties?

[14] See also Gooding-Williams's association of jesters with actors, with Wagner, and with the higher men (2001: 90).

at only one thing and elevating it to the single motivation of all action contributes to the making of a hero and a fanatic (*KSA* 2: 687; *HAH* II 296). When he speculated on the origins of Buddhism and Christianity in *The Gay Science* (Book Five, 1887), he described how both religions found a sick will harboring a desperate yearning for an unconditional "thou shalt": "[B]oth religions were teachers of fanaticism in times of a slackening of the will and thereby offered innumerable people support, a new possibility of willing, a delight in willing." But this special kind of willing takes the form of "hypnosis of the entire sensual-intellectual system to the benefit of the excessive nourishment (hypertrophy) of a single point of view and feeling which is now dominant—the Christian calls it his *faith*" (*GS* 347). Fanaticism on this account is a disease resulting from the imbalance of nourishing only one point of view, but observe that its power is drawn from willing, and its effect on a person is hypnotic. Now when Nietzsche discusses fanaticism in the works of 1888, he is more deliberate in underscoring its pathology. Christ himself was a decadent who vacillated between the Buddhist-like preacher and "that fanatic of attacking" who was the sworn enemy of priests and theologians (*KSA* 6:202; *A* 31). Later in *The Antichrist* we find: "The pathological conditionality of his optic makes the convinced person into a fanatic—Savonarola, Luther, Rousseau, Robespierre, Saint-Simon—the opposite type of the strong spirit who has become *free*" (*KSA* 6: 237; *A* 54). One more step and Nietzsche finds himself discussing the "delicatesse" required by Wagner's art and how one can only find it in Paris. The reason for this, he explains, is that Wagner's "closest relatives" are the late French romantics with their high-flying and uplifting art, "artists like Delacroix, like Berlioz, with a core of illness, of incurability in their essence, pure fanatics of *expression*, virtuosos through and through" (*KSA* 6: 289; *EH* 3: 5). Clearly a failing so detrimental to the autonomy of an individual as fanaticism was bound to draw Nietzsche's scrutiny, and in the above example one sees that fanaticism is alive and well in the modern character both in the form of Christian faith and in modernity's taste for art. The term "fanatics of expression" used to describe artists such as Wagner and the French romantics should not be construed as praiseworthy inasmuch as it gives voice to the "core of illness, of incurability in their essence" (*KSA* 6: 289; *EH* 3: 5). If the illness were not the core, but instead the inoculating effect lending strength to the stable and healthy artist, then one might construe the illness as a potentially positive force. In this case, however, the pathological fanaticism of Wagner and the French romantics appears to function in tandem with the pathological, narcotic effect of art on modern, tired sensibilities, such that Wagner's "delicatesse" notwithstanding (and the word *delicatesse* here is also meant ironically), Wagner's fanatic expressivism will ultimately anesthetize and stupefy exhausted modern audiences. *Expression* has always been regarded as a chief value of romanticism and Nietzsche shares certain practices and tendencies with the romantics in this regard (Del Caro 1989a: 252–8); however, insofar as fanaticism is the opposite of the free spirit, fanatic expression or fanatic expressivism as it manifests in Wagner and other quintessential moderns must be opposed.

The question that arises at this point and indeed so often in considerations of Nietzsche's relation to romanticism is whether such a hyper-romantic quality, in this case fanatic expression, can even be opposed. There is a pervasive nature to this fanatic expression, such that one of the twentieth century's greatest poets, Gottfried Benn, construed Nietzsche's phrase "fanatics of expression" as the quintessence of his philosophizing, leading us "to a language that wants and does nothing more than phosphorizing, luciferizing and anaesthetizing" (Behler 1997: 279). This may be a particularly nihilistic reading of what happens to expression in the wake of Nietzsche's philosophizing, and at the very least it is ironic that Benn and others who stand on the threshold to postmodernism would be resigned to see in language nothing but incendiary effects and numbness. In the face of this fanatic expression Nietzsche would claim that the free spirit must be able to recognize the phenomenon and not engage in it. While expression itself is a need of the free spirit, fanatic expression binds the spirit to a pathological ethos of expression for its own sake, hardly an improvement over the art for art's sake that Nietzsche also condemns in the modern condition. Still, this stance of independence from fanatic expression that the free spirit must maintain seems more a desire than an achievement in Nietzsche, especially since the chief means to maintaining expressive independence are those associated with romantic, modernist inclinations such as irony.

5 Antiromantic Self-Treatment, or The Art of Reining In and Letting Go

Though he spoke harshly of pity, Nietzsche was extraordinarily capable of it, leading Staten to remark on the "permeability of his boundary of individuation" (Staten 1990: 214). And lest we object that Nietzsche's mythologizing of humanity's suffering and passion and pain smacks of romanticism, Staten cautions that "Romanticism would not be something *external* to Nietzsche's project but something that works it from within, as what has to be opposed so strenuously because it is so intimate, so proper to Nietzsche's own economy" (1990: 215). Here we return to the understanding with which Nietzsche himself takes to the field in his critique of romanticism, namely that he too was a modern, a decadent, a romantic, but unlike Wagner he fought against it and unlike Wagner he was not incurable. If Nietzsche was actually successful in his self-treatment against romanticism, we would have to work with two Nietzsches, the first a romantic and the second a cured romantic turned antiromantic. But I suspect that with romanticism as with alcoholism, there is no "cure," only reforming—we might call Nietzsche a reformed romantic.

A true antiromantic, one who had never succumbed to the narcotic that is romanticism, would be able to counter the effects of the "romantic ideal of dissolving established limitations and determinations" (Schulte-Sasse 1997: 30).[15] Nietzsche proposed that Goethe had been such a spirit, toiling wisely and patiently within the venerable classical norms: "only the law can give us freedom" (Del Caro 1989b: 592). But we have seen that Nietzsche did not consider Goethe to be the winner in the struggle between romanticism and classicism, and we have Nietzsche's repositioning of himself relative to Goethe in essential points of the Dionysian. For that matter, only in Nietzsche's imagination (and perhaps in the mind of Germanist literary purists) does Goethe not qualify as a romantic.

Let us grant Nietzsche his coveted primacy in having deepened the concept of the Dionysian and now ask ourselves what it is that the Dionysian represents. *Rausch* is the

---

[15] Schulte-Sasse's excellent essay demonstrates again that the tools the romantics used for this *menstrum universale* were wit, irony, chaos, fantasy, etc.—how could Nietzsche or any modern not avail himself of these tools?

defining property of the Dionysian, rapture or frenzy, or intoxication, and this *Rausch* Staten correctly identifies as the "properly *Romantic* kernel out of which all his thought, early and late, unfolds" (Staten 1990: 194). The rapturous superabundance that Nietzsche holds up against weakness, exhaustion, declining health, degeneration has its cognate in the will to power, a force Nietzsche is unlikely to deny in himself. Just as he argued that the thrill of willing was pursued by Buddhists and Christians in their compulsion to become fanatics, it could be that *Rausch* and the power of willing assume various expressions in Nietzsche's writings, masked and veiled expressions to be sure, sometimes indicative of ascending, other times of declining vitality.

In *BGE* 208 he diagnoses "paralysis of the will" as the European disease and warns that it is deceptive: "This illness has the prettiest fancy-dress clothes and liar's outfits. And most of what presents itself in the shop windows these days as 'objectivity,' for instance, or 'scientific-ity,' '*l'art pour l'art*', or 'pure, will-less knowing,' is only dressed-up skepticism and paralysis of the will." The shop window disguise is a "characteristic sign of his times" according to Behler, in which Nietzsche "perhaps even [sees] his own manner of presentation" (Behler 1997: 211). To be sure, Nietzsche would argue that the shop window phenomenon is mere dressing up of a serious pathological condition, but exactly who is doing the dressing up and what provides the background energy to get it done? Nietzsche obviously thinks he has *discovered* this phenomenon or he wouldn't refer to his work here as "diagnosis" ("I will vouch for this diagnosis of the European disease"). What makes dressing up a symptom of disease, as opposed to a deliberate strategy of life affirmation, say, is that sickness masks itself as sublimation, i.e., the fundamentally sick society does not know it is sick when it lays claim to "objectivity" or "pure will-less knowing." Now if the society knew all along that it were sick, and undertook to transform this sickness into something higher, say "objectivity," Nietzsche would still have to argue that the basic sickness manifests "objectivity" as a symptom, because objectivity according to Nietzsche is either a delusion or a symptom of decline. Ultimately Nietzsche would argue that the sick society *invents* mechanisms for coping with its disease, and it calls its inventions "objectivity" or "*l'art pour l'art*." It is worth pointing out here that sickness in itself is no objection for Nietzsche, for the point is what one makes of that sickness, just as he claimed to master the practice of alchemy, making his own ill-ness and romanticism into "gold" by fighting and ultimately overcoming the adversity.[16] We also have the inoculation theory described by Nietzsche in *Human, All Too Human* (I: 224), whereby a people that becomes weak in part but maintains strength and health on the whole is able to absorb "the infection of the new and incorporate it to its advantage" (*KSA* 2: 188). Sickness in Nietzsche's view is part of nature's economy, and is frequently discussed in tandem with "evil" beginning in *Human* and especially in *The Gay Science*, as an under-explored, repressed, or misunderstood trait that actually contributes to the overall health of our species.

The notion of inventing a category or creating a euphemism, as a function of failing to dig-nify the legitimate and life-sustaining effects of traditionally negative traits, brings us back to an earlier aphorism in *Beyond* where Nietzsche discusses the atmosphere in Germany in the wake of Kant's *Critiques*. First he establishes that Kant never satisfactorily explained how synthetic judgments a priori are possible, because his answer begs the question: they are

---

[16] For references to Nietzsche's metaphorical use of "alchemy" see Del Caro 2004: 125, 152, 209.

made possible by virtue of a faculty. Suddenly, Nietzsche claims, all the budding theologians of the Tübinger Stift were out beating the bushes looking for "faculties," and the "malicious fairy" of romanticism was unleashed, and "German philosophy" celebrated its honeymoon. In this period, he explained, "people did not know how to tell the difference between 'discovering' and 'inventing'!" (*BGE* 11). Is this the decisive distinction according to which Nietzsche or anyone might assign romanticism (illness, decadence, declining vitality, shop window dressing) to someone or something? Does the operation of "discovering" redound to strength and superabundance, while the operation of "inventing" redounds to weakness that adopts window dressing?

In any case the highly inventive *and* discovering Nietzsche might not want to be too conclusive on this issue. He might instead "enjoy the ride" that is life affirmation, adopting some of his own advice in matters of style and living dangerously. This he even appears to do in *BGE* 224, where he offers some of the keenest insights into the European imagination, the European psyche, our attraction to Homer, our apotheosis in Shakespeare:

> *Moderation* is foreign to us, let us admit this to ourselves; our thrill is precisely the thrill of the infinite, the unmeasured. Like the rider on a steed snorting to go further onward, we let the reins drop before the infinite, we modern men, we half-barbarians—and *we* feel supremely happy only when we are in the most—*danger*.

Not surprisingly, an inventory of Nietzschean traits that could occupy either the romantic or the unromantic results in two columns of similar length, with occasional bleeding of one column into the other on issues he straddles. First, the romantic features of his thought would have to cluster around his cherished reworking of the Dionysian, a concept spanning his entire career, enabling him to foreground the virtues and values of corporeality, most notably sensuality and superabundance. His modernization of Dionysus, a philosophical paganism, instantiates romanticism's fondness for primitive, mythological culture, at the same time that it actualizes romanticism's elevation of the senses. It is clear as well that Nietzsche values closeness to nature, or an affinity with nature, that is stock romantic fare. When proto-romantics such as Rousseau and young Goethe condemn the corruption of human beings by society and their enslavement to utilitarian principles and mindless work, Nietzsche is often indistinguishable from them, as seen most clearly in *Thus Spoke Zarathustra*. On this score the German romantic cultural dichotomy of *Natur* versus *Kultur* is continued and deepened by Nietzsche. Prone as they were to explore and highlight illness, decadence, and exceptional types of human beings (artists, criminals, the insane, the ascetic, deviants, etc.), the romantics shared with Nietzsche an appetite for the extraordinary and a curiosity for deviance. A related romantic trait is the exploration of the unconscious, especially since the irrational was often perceived by romantics as a powerful, misunderstood force. The psychological acumen Nietzsche was justifiably proud of in himself is clearly traceable to romanticism and its preoccupation with the "dark" side of human being.

Irony as a rhetorical device elevated to a worldview is also evident in Nietzsche, though he rejected the word irony and the practice of irony as it is commonly ascribed to the Socratic dialectic. The dance of denial with affirmation, of creation with annihilation, was regarded by Nietzsche as Dionysian and though he preferred the terms *dissimulatio* and mask, their effect and their existence as Dionysian properties remain romantic. If Nietzsche's blending of art, theory, and philosophy marks him as a modernist and sometimes champion of postmodernists, this same blending is illustrative of romantic style. It is not by accident that the aphorism and the fragment are celebrated by Nietzsche, for these forms resonated power-fully with the early theoretical romantics whom Nietzsche knew least but with whom he shared the greatest affinity. As critics of the Enlightenment, the romantics tended to stress creativity, plenitude, and contradiction, all vital aspects of human being, and they were not enamored of logic. For all his sympathy for the Enlightenment, there is still too much of the poet in Nietzsche, as well as critic of the Enlightenment's unexamined elevation of progress, to not align him with romanticism. The romantic ideals of love, vitality, and wholeness of being so prominent in Hölderlin are also alive and well in Nietzsche, as are the sting of nihil-ism and the search for a new meaning in the face of the loss of the absolute. Quite notably, Hölderlin and Nietzsche both use metaphors of overflowing and insemination to describe the work of their respective heroes (Hyperion and Zarathustra) *vis-à-vis* a maternal, fructi-fied earth. Nietzsche can also be said to practice expressivism as it was a defining trait of romanticism, for as a celebrator and spokesman of life, it would be inconceivable for him to eschew expression. However, Nietzsche would rein in romantic expressivism where it tends to fudge the difference between "inventing" and "discovering."

On the unromantic side of the ledger are a series of traits that lend credibility to his claim of being an anti-romantic. His strident critique of metaphysics, including Platonism, Christianity, and the philosophy of Kant and Schopenhauer, positions him as the affirmer *par excellence* of the earth, the senses, and the closest things (the quotidian). As a consist-ent critic of the disembodied life, Nietzsche's radical immanence culminates in the anti-romantic doctrine of eternal recurrence of the same, which is the radical antidote to the notion of an afterlife. Despite and perhaps even because of his own frail health, Nietzsche championed strength, cheerfulness, lightness, and health, and his doctrines big and small support these traits. Irony was regarded by him as a base ploy whose master was Socrates, a base human being who used his dialectic to emasculate noble types. While romantics revel in irony, too much mixing and reducing ends up threatening the rank order that Nietzsche ascribed to all life; his position against Socrates reflects his position against the masses, against plebian instincts and egalitarianism. After *The Birth of Tragedy* there are few positive references to folk in Nietzsche's writings, because he no longer romanticizes the concept but instead rejects the folk (*das Volk*, common people) and their demands on art and culture as instigated already by Euripides. While romanticism tends to be inclu-sive, exoteric, and altruistic, celebrating the expressions of all peoples and men and women equally, Nietzsche is elitist, esoteric (though not consistently, as seen in *Zarathustra*), and on the surface antifeminist. In the ancient struggle between poetry and philosophy, where poetry aligns with romanticism, Nietzsche clearly states his preference for philosophy, then ironically cancels himself out by positing the existence of a new "Dionysian" philosophizing which draws heavily on irony.

Unromantic, at least in Nietzsche's estimation, would be his rejection of Greek metrical forms and European (romantic) rhyme, in favor of a robust, reinvigorated German prose not seen since Luther. But here, too, it should be pointed out that in his lyric poetry, of which there is a substantial body, Nietzsche favors the use of rhyme, with the *Dionysus Dithyrambs* constituting an exception. A deep and consequential difference between him and the romantics is the role of the poet; whereas for romantics the poet is a priestly type who minis-ters to his community as a servant, Nietzsche's Zarathustra, though a prophet, serves no one but humanity, and this he does ambivalently and without ever achieving a sense of commu-nity (hence *Zarathustra* as a "book for all and none" as indicated by the subtitle). Romantics contributed to the concept of nation and a people (*Volk*) at least since Herder in the eighteenth century, and clearly a long line of romantic patriots can be drawn from Herder to Wagner; however, Nietzsche clearly and consistently breaks with romantic patriotism and this must be regarded as one of his greater triumphs, especially given the emergence of virulent nationalism and anti-Semitism in the nineteenth and twentieth centuries. It is then an unromantic turn of events that Nietzsche rejects the body politic in order to embrace the body per se, but some might argue that Nietzsche's ecumenical, universal embrace of human beings empowered to dwell affirmatively on the Earth is a truly romantic "return" to nature, though Nietzsche would quibble here and call it an "ascent" to nature—the former requiring only nostalgia and idealism (i.e., weakness), the latter requiring effort and self-overcoming (i.e., strength).

When faced with the loss of the absolute, and especially in the wake of Kant's *Critique of Pure Reason*, the romantics tended to glorify infinite creativity and world irony, making them theoretical forerunners of today's postmodernists. Nietzsche's unromantic response to the crisis of values was romantic perhaps in its means, but not in its ends; he proposes new life-affirming values, and new meaning residing in the earth and the superhuman. Ultimately this rigor or discipline in the face of the value vacuum challenges relativism and distinguishes Nietzsche as a philosopher, and his strong championing of the hermeneutic method of philology, alongside his equally strong embrace of scientific method, mark him as an opponent of romanticism. Art cannot exist for its own sake according to Nietzsche, but instead art serves life by providing us with an urgently needed stimulus aimed at the higher life, the higher species. Creativity in the hands of a romantic would never attempt a project such as Nietzsche's, focused as it is on creating a meaning for the Earth—unless of course the scope of this project demanded the deployment of all possible means, including the romantic.

BIBLIOGRAPHY

(A) Works by Nietzsche

A   *The Antichrist*, in *The Portable Nietzsche*, trans. and ed. Walter Kaufmann. New York: Viking, 1968.

BGE   *Beyond Good and Evil*, trans. Judith Norman. Cambridge: Cambridge University Press, 2002.

BT   *The Birth of Tragedy*, in *The Birth of Tragedy and Other Writings*, ed. Raymond Geuss, trans. Ronald Speirs. Cambridge: Cambridge University Press, 2006.

CW   *The Case of Wagner*, in *The Basic Writings of Nietzsche*, trans. and ed. Walter Kaufmann. New York: The Modern Library, 1968.

EH   *Ecce Homo*, in *The Basic Writings of Nietzsche*, trans. and ed. Walter Kaufmann. New York: The Modern Library, 1968.

GS   *The Gay Science*, trans. Josefine Nauckhoff and Adrian Del Caro. Cambridge: Cambridge University Press, 2001.

HAH   *Human, All Too Human*, trans. R. J. Hollingdale. Cambridge: Cambridge University Press, 1986.

KSA   *Sämtliche Werke: Kritische Studienausgabe in 15 Einzelbänden*, ed. G. Colli and M. Montinari (15 vols). Berlin: De Gruyter, 1988.

TI   *Twilight of the Idols*, trans. Duncan Large. Oxford: Oxford University Press, 2009.

UM   *Untimely Meditations*, trans. R. J. Hollingdale. Cambridge: Cambridge University Press, 1984. Vol. II: *On the Use and Abuse of History for Life.*

Werke   *Werke in drei Bänden*, ed. Karl Schlechta. Munich: Carl Hanser Hanser Verlag, 1973.

Z   *Thus Spoke Zarathustra*, trans. and ed. Adrian Del Caro, ed. Robert Pippin. Cambridge: Cambridge University Press, 2006.

(B) Other Works Cited

Bay, Hansjörg. 2003. *"Ohne Rückkehr." Utopische Intention und poetischer Prozeß in Hölderlins "Hyperion."* Munich: Wilhelm Fink Verlag.

Behler, Ernst. 1973. "Die Kunst der Reflexion: Das frühromantische Denken im Hinblick auf Nietzsche," in Vincent J. Gunther et al. (eds), *Untersuchungen zur Literatur als Geschichte: Festschrift für Benno von Wiese*. Berlin: Schmidt, 219–48.

Behler, Ernst. 1993. *Germantic Romantic Literary Theory*. Cambridge: Cambridge University Press.

Behler, Ernst. 1997. *Ironie und literarische Moderne*. Munich: Ferdinand Schöningh.

Bohm, Arnd. 2007. *Goethe's Faust and the European Epic: Forgetting the Future*. Rochester: Boydell & Brewer.

Del Caro, Adrian. 1988. "Symbolizing Philosophy: Ariadne and the Labyrinth," *Nietzsche-Studien* 17: 125–57.

Del Caro, Adrian. 1989a. *Nietzsche Contra Nietzsche: Creativity and the Anti-Romantic*. Baton Rouge: Louisiana State University Press.

Del Caro, Adrian. 1989b. "Dionysian Classicism, or Nietzsche's Appropriation of an Aesthetic Norm," *Journal of the History of Ideas* 50.4: 589–605.

Del Caro, Adrian. 1991. *Hölderlin: The Poetics of Being*. Detroit: Wayne State University Press.

Del Caro, Adrian. 1993. *Hugo von Hofmannsthal: Poets and the Language of Life*. Baton Rouge: Louisiana State University Press.

Del Caro, Adrian. 1998. "Nietzschean Self-Transformation and the Transformation of the Dionysian," in Salim Kemal et al. (eds), *Nietzsche, Philosophy and the Arts*. Cambridge: Cambridge University Press, 70–91.

Del Caro, Adrian. 2004. *Grounding the Nietzsche Rhetoric of Earth*. Berlin: De Gruyter.

Gaier, Ulrich. 1993. *Hölderlin. Eine Einführung*. Tübingen: Francke Verlag.

Gooding-Williams, Robert. 2001. *Zarathustra's Dionysian Modernism*. Stanford: Stanford University Press.

Heller, Erich. 1988. "Nietzsche and the Inarticulate," in Volker Dürr, Reinhold Grimm, and Kathy Harms (eds), *Nietzsche: Literature and Values*. Madison: University of Wisconsin Press, 3–13.

Ilgner, Richard. 2001. *Die Ketzermythologie in Goethes Faust*. Herbolzheim: Centaurus Verlag.

Immelmann, Thomas. 1992. *Der unheimlichste aller Gäste: Nihilismus und Sinndebatte in der Literatur von der Aufklärung zur Moderne*. Bielefeld: Aesthesis Verlag.

Jantz, Harold. 1969. *The Mothers in Faust: The Myth of Time and Creativity*. Baltimore: Johns Hopkins University Press.

Kaufmann, Walter. 1950. *Nietzsche: Philosopher, Psychologist, Antichrist*. Princeton: Princeton University Press.

Kreis, Rudolf. 1995. *Nietzsche, Wagner und die Juden*. Würzburg: Königshausen & Neumann.

Meyer, Theo. 1993. *Nietzsche und die Kunst*. Tübingen: Francke Verlag.

Schulte-Sasse, Jochen. 1997. "General Introduction: Romanticism's Paradoxical Articulation of Desire," in Jochen Schulte-Sasse (ed.), *Theory as Practice: A Critical Anthology of Early German Romantic Writings.* Minneapolis: University of Minnesota Press, 1–44.

Staten, Henry. 1990. *Nietzsche's Voice.* Ithaca: Cornell University Press.

Vattimo, Gianni. 1992. *Nietzsche: Eine Einführung.* Stuttgart: Verlag J. B. Metzler.

Young, Julian. 1992. *Nietzsche's Philosophy of Art.* Cambridge: Cambridge University Press.

CHAPTER 6

···

NIETZSCHE THE KANTIAN?

···

TOM BAILEY

IT is perhaps understandable that Nietzsche is often supposed to have had little interest in Kant and Kantian questions or at most to have treated such Kantian notions as the 'thing in itself' and the 'categorical imperative' in his own, non-Kantian ways. For he reserves some of his most dismissive remarks for Kant—in *Twilight of the Idols*, for instance, he calls Kant the 'most deformed concept-cripple there has ever been'—and there no strong evidence that he ever read any of Kant's texts.[1] Yet, on closer inspection, Nietzsche turns out to have had an intense and complex relationship with Kant. He developed a range of Kantian concerns and commitments through intensive engagements, if not directly with Kant's texts, then at least with numerous commentaries on Kant and works in neo-Kantianism. And these engagements not only developed substantially over time, from his earliest writings to his last, but were often developed most sophisticatedly without explicit reference either to Kant or to Kantian sources. Furthermore, Nietzsche's ultimate conclusions are neither as decisive nor as applicable to Kant himself as his dismissive remarks about Kant would suggest. Rather than one of mere dismissal or indifference, then, Nietzsche's relationship with Kant was

---

[1] *TI* VIII 7. Translations from Nietzsche's and Kant's texts are my own. For other examples of Nietzsche's dismissive remarks about Kant, see *D* 481, *GS* 193, *BGE* 5 and 11, *TI* IX 1, 16, and 29 and *A* 61. Regarding his reading of Kant, Thomas Brobjer has claimed that Nietzsche read Kant's *Critique of Judgement* in 1868, while planning a dissertation to be entitled '*Über den Begriff des Organischen seit Kant*', and that his references to and enthusiasm for Kant in notes, letters, and lectures of the late 1860s and early 1870s also suggest a reading of Kant during that period. However, Brobjer admits that there is no strong evidence that Nietzsche owned or borrowed any text of Kant's in this period and that the references to Kant in his later notes probably derive from secondary readings. In particular, Brobjer argues that the quotations, summaries, and discussions of passages in Kant's texts that Nietzsche noted during his visits to the library at Chur, Switzerland, in mid-May and early June 1887 derive from a reading of Kuno Fischer's commentary on Kant, *Immanuel Kant und seine Lehre*. I would suggest that Fischer's commentary, rather than Kant's *Critique of Judgement*, was the probable source also of the numerous references to and quotations from Kant in Nietzsche's dissertation plan of 1868, on which Brobjer bases his claim about an early reading of Kant. See Brobjer 2008: 36–9, 48, 195, 202, 226–7, and 38 nn. 86, 87, 89, and 90. For examples of the use made of Fischer as a source for Kant references and quotations in the dissertation plan, see *KGW* I.4: 62 [3–57] (April–May 1868), esp. 62 [22–4, 27, 38, and 55] and the notes in Crawford 1988: 242–4, 245–6, and 252, and for references to the relevant passages of Fischer's book, see the notes in Nietzsche 1993. See also nn. 6 and 32.

broad and dynamic, mediated by secondary sources, often left implicit and undecided, and not always fair to Kant himself.

This essay explores two main themes in this intense and complex relationship with Kant. The first part focuses on Kantian idealism and shows how Nietzsche developed a critical treatment of some of its most basic presuppositions. The second part considers his relation to Kantian ethics and shows that, while criticizing it, he also affirmed a distinctively 'Kantian' ethics of his own.[2]

1 Nietzsche and Kantian Idealism

An Early Kantian Education

Nietzsche's engagements with Kantian questions began in the mid-1860s, and particularly with his enthusiastic discovery of a copy of Arthur Schopenhauer's *The World as Will and Representation* in a second-hand bookshop in Leipzig in 1865, when he was 21. This was followed by a period of extensive further readings in neo-Kantianism, lasting some ten years or so. These texts proposed various brands of Kant-inspired idealism, according to which human perceptual and conceptual capacities impose certain conditions on their objects, such that human beings cannot know objects as they may be 'in themselves', independently of these conditions. These positions were often presented as means of accommodating philosophy to the challenge of the developing natural sciences, and to the rejection of metaphysics and teleology in particular. For they offered to account for the sciences as applicable to knowable objects whilst also admitting a role for philosophy in the evaluation of basic scientific notions and the practical guidance of human life.

Particularly significant for Nietzsche was Schopenhauer's distinction between the world as it appears to us, subject to the conditions of space, time, and causality, and the world as it is 'in itself', that of the blindly striving 'will' to which we have a certain access in our experience of willing and in some moral and aesthetic experiences.[3] Nietzsche also engaged with Eduard von Hartmann's pessimistic metaphysics, according to which cognition and willing are manifestations of a single unconscious substance which leads the world towards a

---

[2] For reasons of space, this essay will not consider Nietzsche's less extensive treatments of Kantian aesthetics. For a discussion of this aspect of his relation to Kant, see Rampley 2000: esp. 156–65, 174–83, and 190–214. I thank Keith Ansell Pearson, João Constancio, Tsarina Doyle, Ken Gemes, Clare Kirwin, Mattia Riccardi, Sergio Sánchez, and Dennis Schulting and the participants at seminars and conferences in Galway, Leiden, Oxford, Pisa, and Southampton for their extremely valuable comments on earlier drafts of this essay.

[3] Nietzsche first read Schopenhauer's *Die Welt als Wille und Vorstellung*, in its second edition, either at the end of October or in early November 1865 and he reread it, along with *Parerga und Paralipomena* and possibly other works of Schopenhauer's, in the immediately following years. He also read various commentaries on Schopenhauer and works by Schopenhauerians between the late 1860s and mid-1870s. See, in particular, *KGB* I.2: 486 (5 November 1865) and 491 (12 January 1866) and also Janz 1979: vol. 1, 180 and Brobjer 2008: 29, 31–2, 47–9, 55, 66–70, 72, 191–8, and 211–12.

state of conscious non-willing, and with Afrikan Spir's postulation of a single non-empirical object of judgement, on the grounds that the temporal and manifold character of sensible experience contradicts the requirements of concept application.[4] But equally important for Nietzsche were the less metaphysically extravagant positions adopted by Friedrich Lange and attributed to Kant in commentaries by Kuno Fischer and Friedrich Überweg. Of particular significance in this regard was Lange's account of how human physiology and psychology impose certain idealist conditions, including the notion of an independently existing object itself, such that our knowledge does not extend beyond these conditions. For Lange, therefore, metaphysics is mere 'conceptual poetry', valuable only as a means of creating uplifting myths.[5] Fischer's and Überweg's commentaries provided Nietzsche with further idealist readings of Kant's treatments of space, time, imagination, the 'categories', and the 'ideas' and drew the consequent sceptical conclusions about our knowledge of the 'thing in itself'.[6]

At first sight, these neo-Kantian readings would seem to have led Nietzsche to endorse Kantian idealism in his first writings. For example, in a paragraph of *The Birth of Tragedy*, he writes that Kant and Schopenhauer explained 'the limits and the conditionality of knowledge in general', and refers in particular to 'the illusory notion which pretends to be able to fathom the innermost essence of things with the aid of causality' and to Kant's demonstration that, rather than 'entirely unconditional laws of the most universal validity', space, time, and causality 'elevate the mere appearance [...] to the sole and highest reality as if it were the innermost and true essence of things, and thus make any actual knowledge of this essence impossible'. In the same book he also presents 'Dionysian' experience as revealing 'empirical reality'—'a perpetual becoming in time, space and causality'—to be a mere 'appearance [or

[4] Nietzsche mentioned Hartmann's *Philosophie des Unbewußten: Versuch einer Weltanschauung* in a letter to Carl von Gersdorff of 4 August 1869 (*KGB* II.1: 19; see also *KGB* II.2: 37 (5 November 1869)) and on 16 June 1875 he sold a copy of the first edition, published in 1869. See Campioni et al. 2003: 284. Numerous notes of this period refer to this edition and it also includes the passages that Nietzsche quotes in *UM* II 9. On this and other texts of Hartmann's that Nietzsche read, see Brobjer 2008: 51–5, 196, 198, 206, and 208. As regards Spir, Nietzsche sold a copy of *Forschung nach der Gewissheit in der Erkenntniss der Wirklichkeit* on 16 June 1875 and borrowed the first edition of *Denken und Wirklichkeit: Versuch einer Erneuerung der kritischen Philosophie* from the library at the University of Basel five times between March 1873 and November 1874. See Crescenzi 1994: 420, 421, 425, and 428, Campioni et al. 2003: 582, and Brobjer 2008: 71–2, 203, and 207. In D'Iorio 1993: esp. 257–8 and 259–70, Paolo D'Iorio argues that the notebook evidence reveals a particularly intensive engagement with these two works of Spir's between the summer of 1872 and the spring of 1873.
[5] Nietzsche read the first edition of Lange's *Geschichte des Materialismus und Kritik seiner Bedeutung in der Gegenwart* by August 1866 and reread it in 1868 and 1873. See, in particular, the references in Nietzsche's letters to Carl von Gersdorff at the end of August 1866 and to Hermann Mushacke in November 1866 (*KGB* I.2: 517 and 526, respectively) and also Brobjer 2008: 33–5, 192, 195, and 206.
[6] Nietzsche read Fischer's commentary on Kant, *Immanuel Kant und seine Lehre*, the fourth and fifth volumes of Fischer's *Geschichte der neuern Philosophie*, by April–May 1868, as is indicated by the numerous references to and quotations from it in his dissertation plan of April–May 1868. See, for instance, *KGW* I.4: 62 [23, 24, 27, 28, 37, 38, 40, 46, 52, and 55] (April–May 1868) and the notes in Crawford 1988: 242–6, 249 and 251–2 and also Brobjer 2008: 37 and 49 and the relevant footnotes in Nietzsche 1993. His library includes a copy of Überweg's *Grundriß der Geschichte der Philosophie von Thales bis auf die Gegenwart*, which he bought on 5 October 1867. See Campioni et al. 2003: 641–2 and Brobjer 2008: 37, 49, 194–5, and 205.

illusion, *Schein*]', 'the true non-being', and only a manifestation of 'the true being and primal unity [*Ur-Eine*]' that lies beyond it.[7]

Yet there are also indications that the early Nietzsche was far from convinced by Kantian idealism. Closer inspection of *The Birth of Tragedy*, for instance, suggests that he endorses and employs idealist positions only for therapeutic or cultural reasons, rather than for strictly theoretical ones. In particular, when presenting his account of Dionysian experience, he describes the notion of a 'primal unity' as a 'metaphysical assumption' and a 'metaphysical comfort', an 'illusion' which makes the ephemeral nature of the world we know bearable to us, by treating this world as the 'artistic game' of a 'primal artist of the world' beyond it.[8] And rather than providing any theoretical examination or defence of idealist positions, he endorses them in the context of a critical discussion of the deleterious effect on 'art' of the modern belief in the possibility of genuine knowledge, in the hope that, by reducing human knowledge itself to a kind of 'art', idealism might succeed in reversing this cultural priority.[9] Furthermore, in his unpublished writings of this period he develops two substantial kinds of theoretical criticism of Kantian idealism. First, its preclusion of positive claims about objects as they might be independently of idealist conditions leads him to doubt that the 'thing in itself' has any epistemological significance and that it is even legitimate to assume its existence. And second, the idea that human knowers themselves are both the origins and the products of idealist conditions of human knowledge he presents as incoherent and as a reason for leaving Kantian idealist positions behind.[10]

It might be tempting to suppose that the early Nietzsche developed a more nuanced brand of Kantian idealism in the light of these therapeutic or cultural concerns and these theoretical criticisms.[11] But perhaps even this would be to underestimate the experimental

---

[7] *BT* 18, 4. See also *BT* 15, 17, and 19 and, on Dionysian experience, *BT* 1, 5–8, 15–19, 21, 24, and 25. Similar idealist claims can be found in *UM* I 6 and III 3. Nietzsche's claims about Dionysian experience of the 'true being and primal unity' would appear to contravene precisely the limits that idealism sets on human knowledge. Some commentators, like Stack 1980: 37–9, 1987: 7–11, and 1991: 33 and Clark 1990: 63–93 and 1998: 40–7, consider him to be simply inconsistent in this regard, while others, like Brown 1980: 40–5, read his account of Dionysian experience as intended precisely to justify his idealism.

[8] *BT* 4, 18, 24, 5. See also *BT* 1, 16, and 17.

[9] See *BT* 18. Similarly, in *UM* I 6 and III 3 Nietzsche does not endorse Kantian idealism as justified, but rather claims only that it has rarely been correctly understood and that its cultural implications have rarely been adequately grasped.

[10] See *KGW* I.4: 57 [51, 52, and 55] (Autumn 1867–Spring 1868), II.4: 241–2, 291–6, and 339–40 (Summer 1872), III.2: 301, 312–14, 338, 340–1, and 344–5 (1873) (PTG 1, 4, 10, 11, and 13) and 374 and 378 (Summer 1873) (TL 1) and III.4: 19 [125 and 153] (Summer 1872–beginning of 1873).

[11] For instance, Crawford 1988 and 1997 present the early Nietzsche as making a series of radical modifications to Schopenhauer's idealism on the grounds of certain criticisms and solutions offered by Hartmann and Lange, particularly regarding the determination and postulation of the 'thing in itself', the misleading influence of subject-predicate grammar on metaphysics, and the role played in cognition by unconscious thought and (on Lange's account) by psycho-physical structures. Stack 1980, 1983: esp. ch. 8, and 1987: 7–23 similarly present the early and later Nietzsche as criticizing Kantian idealism on grounds derived from Lange. Hill 2003: pt 1, on the other hand, argues that the early Nietzsche modifies Schopenhauer's position by appropriating Kant's notion of a supersensible intellect as the source of nature's systematic order and as posited not by a 'determinative' judgement about natural objects themselves, but by a merely 'reflective' judgement about how a mind subject to certain conditions must experience its objects as 'designed' for it. Thus, for Hill, the early Nietzsche comes to 'reflectively' posit a single transcendental mind as the ground upon which the knowable world and human knowers themselves depend and to extend such merely 'reflective' status also to the claims of mechanistic science and Darwinian biology. Doyle 2009: ch. 3 provides a similar reading. For criticism of Hill, see Bailey

and inconclusive nature of his early engagements with such idealism. For his failure to commit to any such position in his early published texts—in which he was, after all, primarily concerned with other matters—and his criticisms of such positions in his unpublished writings of this period strongly suggest that he was far from convinced by them. And while his unpublished writings display the intensity of his interest in Kantian idealist positions, in these writings he was also free to explore them without being constrained by requirements of coherence, argument, or commitment. Indeed, there his criticisms are accompanied by numerous endorsements of idealism. Rather than adopting or developing any particular position, then, it seems more plausible to consider Nietzsche's early engagements with Kantian idealism as a preliminary, experimental 'education' in certain contemporary Kantian positions and issues.

The Rejection of Kantian Idealism

Unlike his earlier writings, Nietzsche's writings from *Human, All Too Human* onwards are consistently critical towards Kantian idealism and in his last books he decisively rejects it. The precise objects, grounds, and consequences of this rejection are not immediately clear, however. He is perhaps most naturally read as claiming either that human perceptual and conceptual capacities inevitably 'simplify' or 'falsify' the real nature of things or that the notion of an objectively 'real' nature of things is itself incoherent. After all, in rejecting Kantian idealism he famously claims that there is '*only* a perspectival seeing, *only* a perspectival "knowing"' and that the 'real world' has become 'a myth'.[12] On such a reading, he would criticize Kantian idealism for claiming the opposite—namely, that we have some access to reality as this lies beyond our perceptual and conceptual capacities or that we can at least conceive of it, without having access to it.[13] But attributing such a position to Nietzsche raises notorious problems. In particular, it is paradoxical to claim to know that we can have no genuine knowledge and difficult to see how Nietzsche could make such a claim whilst also affirming the importance of empirical knowledge and making numerous knowledge claims of his own.

It is fortunate, then, that a closer reading of the relevant passages reveals that, in rejecting the notion of a reality beyond our perceptual and conceptual capacities, Nietzsche's interpretation and criticism of Kantian idealism is in fact precisely the opposite of what might first appear. That is, he defends against Kantian idealism the idea that reality is accessible to our perceptual and conceptual capacities. He is thus concerned not that Kantian idealism claims that we can have some access to or conception of the real nature of things, but rather that it denies this. Furthermore, these passages also reveal a second concern, one regarding less the accessibility of reality than how we make judgements about reality at all. This concern finds Nietzsche less decisive: he shifts from denying that we can make genuine judgements about the reality accessible to us to accepting this possibility, whilst simultaneously

---

2006: 231–3. Other commentators, such as Fazio 1986–9, D'Iorio 1993: 259–70, Sánchez 1999: 66–90 and 2000b, and Green 2002: esp. chs 2 and 3, emphasize Nietzsche's early endorsement of Spir's scepticism about empirical judgement, which I discuss below.

  [12] *GM* III: 12; *TI* IV.

  [13] See, for instance, Danto 1965: esp. ch. 3 and Nehamas 1985: ch. 2, esp. 48–52. Such readings allow for considering Nietzsche's position itself as a kind of 'Kantian' idealism. See, for instance, Stack 1983: esp. ch. 8 and Crowell 1999.

exploring the idea that judgements might give us a priori access to other aspects of ourselves and the world. Here I will consider these two concerns—with the accessibility and the judgement of reality—in turn, before considering their implications for Kant's own position.

The Accessibility of Reality

In his later texts Nietzsche makes three criticisms of the Kantian notion of a reality inaccessible to human perceptual and conceptual capacities—namely, that this notion is contradictory, that it is epistemologically superfluous, and that it is morally suspicious. Each criticism suggests that he does not hold that these capacities 'simplify' or 'falsify' reality or that the notion of reality is incoherent, and instead indicates that, in rejecting the notion of an inaccessible reality, he also admits a reality which is, at least in principle, accessible to our perceptual and conceptual capacities, while being ontologically independent of them.[14]

Nietzsche's first criticism of the notion of an inaccessible reality, that it is contradictory, is particularly clear in a section of *On the Genealogy of Morality* in which he rejects 'the Kantian concept of the "intelligible character of things"'. Noting that this concept makes reality '*completely and utterly incomprehensible*' to us, he rejects it on the grounds that there is no '"disinterested contemplation" (which is a non-concept and absurdity)', but '*only* a perspectival seeing, *only* a perspectival "knowing"'. What is significant here is how Nietzsche also calls the Kantian concept of reality a 'contradictory concept' and insists that 'perspectival "knowing"' may achieve a certain '"objectivity"', which he describes as the capacity 'to make precisely the *difference* in perspectives and affective interpretations useful for knowledge'.[15] In rejecting non-perspectival or 'disinterested' knowledge of reality, then, Nietzsche is not claiming that our 'perspective' of particular perceptual and conceptual capacities inevitably 'simplifies' or 'falsifies' reality or that it renders the notion of reality incoherent. He is simply denying the Kantian claim that

---

[14] Nietzsche continued to study Kantian idealist treatments of the notion of an inaccesible reality in the 1880s, with particular attention to Lange and, notably, also Otto Liebmann. Regarding his reading of Lange in this period, in notes of 1884 and 1885 he refers to the fourth edition of *Geschichte des Materialismus und Kritik seiner Bedeutung in der Gegenwart* (1882) and his library includes a marked copy of the 1887 reprint of this edition. See *KGW* VII.2: 25 [318 and 424] (Spring 1884) and VII.3: 34 [99] (April–June 1885), Campioni et al 2003: 346, and Brobjer 2008: 33–6, 221, 226–7 and n. 68 to 34. Liebmann was, like Lange, one of the first to propose a 'return' to Kantian idealism, understood as a sceptical denial of our knowledge of reality. However, although Nietzsche's library contains a copy of the book with which Liebmann became known, *Kant und die Epigonen: Eine Kritische Abhandlung*, it is unmarked and Nietzsche's reading appears to have concentrated on Liebmann's later books, *Zur Analysis der Wirklichkeit: Eine Erörterung der Grundprobleme der Philosophie* (in its second edition) and the first part of *Gedanken und Thatsache: Philosophische Abhandlungen, Aphorismen und Studien*, entitled *Die Arten der Nothwendigkeit—Die mechanische Naturerklärung—Idee und Entelechie*. The copies of these two books preserved in Nietzsche's library are both marked, the former particularly heavily, and notebook evidence suggests that he read the former between the spring and autumn of 1881 and the latter regularly from mid-1885 onwards. See Campioni et al 2003: 364–7 and Brobjer 2008: 76, 104, 221–2, and 229. Nietzsche's Kantian readings in this period also included various books by his friend Heinrich Romundt, Hartmann's *Phänomenologie des sittlichen Bewußtseins* between the spring and summer of 1883, and re-readings of Fischer's *Immanuel Kant und seine Lehre* and Hartmann's *Philosophie des Unbewussten* in the late 1880s. On the readings of Romundt, see Campioni et al. 2003: 346 and 517–19 and Brobjer 2008: 38–9 and n. 91 to 39; on the readings of Hartmann, see Brobjer 2008: 104 and n. 89 to 38; and on the re-reading of Fischer, see n. 32 below.

[15] *GM* III: 12.

this perspective precludes knowledge, such that reality must be inaccessible, or '*completely and utterly incomprehensible*', to perspectival knowers like ourselves. This Kantian claim is presumably 'contradictory' because it makes knowledge of reality impossible for us. His rejection of the notion of an inaccessible reality as contradictory thus involves his affirming rather than denying the accessibility of reality to our particular perceptual and conceptual capacities.[16]

Nietzsche's second criticism of the notion of an inaccessible reality is that it is epistemologically superfluous. In particular, in his account of 'How the "Real World" at Last Became a Myth' in *Twilight of the Idols*, the 'Königsbergian' step (a reference to Kant's home town) affirms an 'unreachable, indemonstrable, unpromisable' reality and is followed by the dawning realization that such a reality must be 'if unreached also *unknown*' and then by its rejection as 'an idea grown useless, superfluous, *consequently* a refuted idea'. Nietzsche concludes that the reality to which we have access therefore should be considered not as merely 'apparent', but as real, since the standard of a further, inaccessible reality is superfluous. Thus, in making the final step, he insists that '*with the real world we have also abolished the apparent world*'.[17] In the preceding chapter of *Twilight of the Idols*, '"Reason" in Philosophy', he also refers to Kant in affirming 'the evidence of the senses' and our knowledge of 'the actual world', or the 'apparent' world of 'becoming', against the postulation of a 'real world' and in concluding that '[t]he grounds upon which "this" world has been designated as apparent establish rather its reality—*another* kind of reality is absolutely indemonstrable'.[18] Like his first criticism, then, Nietzsche's second criticism of the notion of an inaccessible reality affirms, rather than denies, the possibility of our knowing reality.

Nietzsche's final criticism of the notion of an inaccessible reality consists of hypotheses regarding the psycho-physical and cultural functions of belief in such a reality. These hypotheses are intended to suggest that, rather than playing a necessary theoretical role in our knowledge of the world, this belief can be explained by other, decidedly more suspicious, purposes which it serves. Nietzsche refers particularly to a kind of sickness or frustration with the accessible world and to the prospect of defending traditional moral and theological ideas against empirical doubts. In 'How the "Real World" at Last Became a Myth',

---

[16] Anti-sceptical readings of this kind have been developed by various commentators. On Maudemarie Clark's influential reading, for instance, Nietzsche's criticism of the 'real world' is directed at the 'Kantian' sceptical claim that theories which satisfy our ordinary epistemological standards—such as simplicity, coherence, and explanatory and predictive power—need not capture things' true natures. Clark argues that, after oscillating in his early works between an endorsement of this claim and doubts about its demonstrability and conceptual coherence, the later Nietzsche rejects the notion of an inaccessible nature of things as conceptually contradictory, along with the idea that the objects of knowledge are not independently-existing things, but rather subjective sensations. According to Clark, he thus arrives at a 'neo-Kantian', even 'common sense', realism, according to which things exist independently of human knowledge of them and have natures which, although they may be beyond the possible determination of our particular cognitive capacities, are nonetheless not in principle beyond the grasp of theories which satisfy our ordinary epistemological standards. See Clark 1990: chs 1–5 and, replacing the conceptual criticism with an empiricist one, Clark 1998 and Clark and Dudrick 2004. For other anti-sceptical readings, see Anderson 1996, 1998, 1999, 2002, and 2005: 187–92, Hill 2003: pt. 2, and Doyle 2009: chs 1–2, esp. 56–65.

[17] *TI* IV. See also *HAH* I: 9, 16, 20, and 21 and *A* 10. It is notable that, at least in *HAH* I: 9 and *KGW* VII.2: 27 [68] (Summer–Autumn 1884), Nietzsche appears to accept that the epistemological insignificance of a 'real world' need not preclude its existence.

[18] *TI* III 2, 6.

for instance, he describes the 'Königsbergian' step as postulating a reality that is intended to be 'merely as thought a consolation, an obligation, an imperative' and in '"Reason" in Philosophy' he writes that '[t]o concoct stories about "another" world than this one is quite senseless, as long as there is no strong instinct for slandering, belittling, and suspecting life in us: in the latter case we *revenge* ourselves on life through the phantasmagoria of "another", a "better" life'.[19] Again, then, in criticizing the notion of an inaccessible reality, Nietzsche affirms rather than denies possible human knowledge of reality—in this case, knowledge of that reality which might sicken or frustrate us or threaten our traditional moral and theological ideas.

The later Nietzsche therefore criticizes the Kantian notion of an inaccessible reality not because it claims that we have access to or can at least conceive of reality, but precisely because it denies this: for Nietzsche, this notion makes reality inaccessible to us in a way that is contradictory, epistemologically superfluous, and morally suspicious and it ought to be rejected in the name of the reality that we can perceive and conceive.

Judgements of Reality

Nietzsche is clearly occupied with the notion of an inaccessible reality in such passages as the section in *On the Genealogy of Morality* on 'perspectival "knowing"' and the account of 'How the "Real World" at Last Became a Myth' in *Twilight of the Idols*.[20] But in other discussions of Kantian idealism in his later texts he is concerned with other, more distinctive Kantian notions. This is particularly evident in the chapter '"Reason" in Philosophy' of *Twilight of the Idols*. There, albeit without mentioning them by name, Nietzsche treats the positions of Spir and Gustav Teichmüller, positions which he studied particularly intensively in the late 1870s and 1880s and which led him to treat Kantian idealism less in terms of its notion of an inaccessible reality than in terms of how it considers us to make judgements about reality at all.

Indeed, before *Twilight of the Idols* Nietzsche found himself in the peculiar position of rejecting the notion of an inaccessible reality in the name of the reality that is accessible to us whilst also denying that we can make genuine judgements of that reality. For in his early unpublished writings and in his published works from *Human, All Too Human* until *Beyond Good and Evil*, he endorsed Spir's argument for the impossibility of empirical judgements, according to which a concept can be applied only to a self-identical object and no such object is manifested in sensible experience, while nonetheless not following Spir in postulating a further, non-empirical object of judgement. As he puts it in *Beyond Good and*

---

[19] *TI* IV, III 6. For other instances of Nietzsche's hypotheses regarding the psycho-physical and cultural functions of belief in an inaccessible reality, often with reference to Kant, see *HAH* I: 17, *BT* 'Attempt at a Self-Criticism' 5, *BGE* 2, 5, 6, 10, 59, 210, and 211, *GM* III: 25, *GS* Preface 2, 346, 347, and 370, *TI* IX 34, *A* 10, 15, 24, 38, 50, and 58, *EH* II 10, *BT* 2 and IV 3–8, and *KGW* VII.2: 25 [412] (Spring 1884), 26 [308] (Summer–Autumn 1884) and 27 [47] (Summer–Autumn 1884). See also *HAH* I: 9, 10, and 16 and *Z* I 3 for statements of the deflationary aims of such hypotheses and the other references regarding the suspicious functions of Kantian idealism in n. 33 below.

[20] Nietzsche also treats the notion of an inaccessible reality in, for instance, *HAH* I: 5, 8–10, 16, 20, and 21, *GS* 54, 58, 151, and 335, *BGE* 10 and 15, and *KGW* VIII.1: 7 [3] (end of 1886–Spring 1887) and VIII.2: 9 [3] (Autumn 1887).

Evil, although 'man could not live without accepting the fictions of logic, without measuring reality against the wholly invented world of the unconditioned and the self-identical, without a constant falsification of the world through numbers', these are nonetheless 'the falsest judgements'.[21]

In ' "Reason" in Philosophy', however, Nietzsche abandons Spir's argument for the impossibility of empirical judgements. His main concern in this chapter is to criticize claims that 'reason' gives us grounds for postulating 'unity, identity, duration, substance, cause, thinghood, being' of objects, despite the fact that our sensible experience of these objects does not exemplify these concepts. Spir clearly makes an a priori claim of precisely this kind, with his premise regarding the self-identity of the object of judgement. What is notable in this chapter is that in criticizing such claims, Nietzsche not only rejects the postulation of non-empirical objects and features, as he had done previously, but also denies that reality can be determined on logical grounds and affirms the possibility of empirical judgements. Thus in the following passage he affirms empirical 'science' and stresses that this is not only because he rejects non-empirical postulations, but also because he does not consider 'logic' to be a measure of reality.

> We possess science today precisely insofar as we have decided to *accept* the evidence of the senses,—insofar as we have learned to sharpen them, arm them, to think them through to their conclusions. The rest is deformation and not-yet-science: which is to say metaphysics, theology, psychology, epistemology. *Or* formal science, theory of signs: like logic and that applied logic, mathematics. In these reality does not appear at all, not even as a problem; just as little as does the question of what value such a convention of signs as that of logic may have.[22]

---

[21] *BGE* 4. For this position, see also *HAH* I: 1, 11, 16, 18, and 19, *HAH III* 11 and 12, *GS* 107, 110, and 111, *BGE* 2 and 36, and *KGW* III.2: 316–20, 324, 335–7, 351–2 (PTG 5, 7, 10, and 15), and 373–6 (Summer 1873) (TL 1), III.4: 19 [235, 236, and 242] (Summer 1872–beginning 1873) and 23 [11 and 39] (Winter 1872–3), VII.3: 34 [49 and 131] (April–June 1885), 35 [35, 56, and 61] (May–July 1885), 36 [23] (June–July 1885), and 40 [12, 13, 15, and 27] (August–September 1885), VIII.1: 2 [90] (Autumn 1885–Autumn 1886), and VIII.2: 9 [97] (Autumn 1887). D'Iorio argues that after engaging with Spir's *Forschung nach der Gewissheit in der Erkenntniss der Wirklichkeit* and the first edition of *Denken und Wirklichkeit* in 1872–3, Nietzsche engaged intensively with the revised, second edition of *Denken und Wirklichkeit* in 1877, the summer of 1881, and the summer of 1885. See D'Iorio 1993: esp. 257–9 and also Brobjer 2003: 222. For the extensive markings and annotations in Nietzsche's copy of the second edition of *Denken und Wirklichkeit*, see Campioni et al. 2003: 567–70.

[22] *TI* III 3. Notably, in *TI* III 4, Nietzsche also raises the problem of how 'being, the unconditioned, the good, the true, the perfect' could have its '[o]rigin in something else'. This is the problem also raised in *HAH* I: 1 and *BGE* 2, passages in which Nietzsche rejects the standard 'metaphysical' solution of postulating distinct ontological origins for basic opposites and proposes instead to simply affirm sensible experience, characterized in Spirean terms—that is, as a 'becoming' that contravenes the requirements of concept application, or 'being'. In contrast, *TI* III 4 he criticizes the postulation of distinct ontological origins without concluding that empirical judgements are impossible. See also *KGW* VIII.1: 6 [14] (Summer 1886–Spring 1887) and VIII.2: 9 [97] (Autumn 1887). Those commentators who treat the significance of Spir for the later Nietzsche generally consider his endorsement of Spir's argument against the possibility of empirical judgement to persist throughout his later works. See D'Iorio 1993: 277–94, Sánchez 2000a, and Green 2002: esp. chs 2 and 3. I criticize Green in this regard and provide further discussion of the passages referred to in the text above in Bailey 2006: 242–9. See also Clark 2005, Clark and Dudrick 2006, and Green 2005: 55–72.

In other words, only in *Twilight of the Idols* does Nietzsche reject the Spirean grounds on which he had previously denied that we can make empirical judgements—that is, the 'logical' grounds that a concept can be applied only to a self-identical object. Before *Twilight of the Idols*, these grounds had led him to deny that we can make judgements of the reality that is accessible to us. By rejecting these grounds in *Twilight of the Idols* he comes to accept that we can make judgements of this reality.

' "Reason" in Philosophy' is also significant for its expression of Nietzsche's treatment of Teichmüller, who also made a priori claims about the object of judgement. Having insisted that logic is no measure of reality, Nietzsche explains the idea that 'reason' gives us grounds for postulating 'unity, identity, duration, substance, cause, thinghood, being' of objects as a reflection of what he calls 'the basic presuppositions of the metaphysics of language', which, he claims, originated in 'the age of the most rudimentary form of psychology'. Of this psychology he writes, '[i]t is *this* which sees everywhere deed and doer; which believes in will as cause in general; which believes in the "I", in the I as being, in the I as substance and *projects* the belief in the I-substance onto all things—only thus does it *create* the concept "thing" [...] only from the concept "I" does there follow, derivatively, the concept "being" '.[23] Although this diagnosis is applicable to Spir's postulation of a self-identical object of judgement, it applies more closely to Teichmüller's postulation of the object of judgement as a substance. For Teichmüller maintains that the subject has 'immediate experience' of herself as a substantial being which unites the plurality of her sensations, affects, and willings, that this unifying activity is reflected in subject-predicate grammar, and that the subject can know an object only by extending this concept of substantial being to it.[24] Thus in ' "Reason"

---

[23] *TI* III 5. For similar attacks on the 'metaphysics of language', see *BGE* Preface, 16, 17, 19, 20, 34, and 54, *GM* I: 13, and *KGW* VII.3: 34 [46] (April–June 1885) and 40 [16] (August–September 1885), VIII.1: 2 [83, 84, 139, and 141] (Autumn 1885–Autumn 1886) and 4 [8] (beginning of 1886–Spring 1886), and VIII.2: 9 [98] (Autumn 1887). Nietzsche's account of 'the most rudimentary form of psychology' owes much to his extensive readings in Victorian anthropology. In particular, his library includes German translations of Walter Bagehot's *Physics and Politics, or Thoughts on the Application of the Principles of 'Natural Selection' and 'Inheritance' to Political Society*, W. E. H. Lecky's *History of European Morals from Augustus to Charlemagne*, John Lubbock's *The Origin of Civilisation and the Primitive Condition of Man: Mental and Social Condition of Savages*, a translation of the third edition of which Nietzsche bought on 28 July 1875, and Max Müller's *Essays on Mythology, Traditions and Customs*. See Campioni et al. 2003: 129–30, 344–5, 364, and 401, respectively, and also Brobjer 2008: 64, 65, 76, 221, 223, and 102 n. 69. See Thatcher 1982 and 1983 for useful expositions of Bagehot and Lubbock in relation to these elements of Nietzsche's thought.

[24] In his notebooks, Nietzsche refers explicitly to Teichmüller's *Die wirkliche und die scheinbare Welt: Neue Grundlegung der Metaphysik* at *KGW* VII.1: 7 [153] (Spring–Summer 1883), VII.2: 26 [416] (Summer–Autumn 1884), and VII.3: 40 [12, 24, and 30] (August–September 1885) and he refers to Teichmüller and to the claims and arguments of this text in numerous other notes of these and later years. Although he borrowed the first volume of Teichmüller's *Aristotelischen Forschungen* from the library at the University of Basel on 12 May 1870 and perhaps also read the second volume in this period, it would appear to have been Franz Overbeck who later introduced him to other works of Teichmüller's, by sending him the latter's *Über die Reihenfolge der platonischen Dialoge* in August 1879, followed by copies of *Neue Studien zur Geschichte der Begriffe* and *Die wirkliche und die scheinbare Welt*. See *KGB* 1217 (2 August 1879), 469 (22 October 1883), 470 (27 October 1883), 609 (2 July 1885), and 645 (12 November 1885), Crescenzi 1994: 400, and Brobjer 2008: 52, 96–7, 196, 223–6, 228, and 230–1. For interpretations of Teichmüller's significance for Nietzsche, see D'Iorio 1993: 283–94, Orsucci 1997: esp. 53–6 and 2001: 212–19, and Small 2001: 43–56.

in Philosophy' Nietzsche rejects not only his own previous Spirean claims about the self-identity of the object of judgement, but also Teichmüller's account of how the subject herself postulates the object of judgement as a substance.

The Will to Power

However, Nietzsche also attempts to reformulate precisely the kind of argument from primitive psychological premises that he diagnoses in Spir and Teichmüller. That is, while affirming an empirically accessible and judgeable reality, he also derives an ontology of causation as 'will to power' a priori from the causal power that primitive psychology attributes to conscious choice, or 'the will'—and that he consistently denies. In particular, in a section of *Beyond Good and Evil* he argues for what he calls 'the right to clearly determine *all* effective force as: *will to power*' on the basis of three hypothetical premises: first, that 'our world of desires and passions is the only thing "given" as real'; second, that 'we accept the will as, effectively, *effective*'; and third, that 'we account for our psychological experience in terms of 'one basic form of will', namely, 'the will to power'.[25] Were these premises to be accepted, he insists, the principle of parsimony would require that explanations not only of psychological events, but also of organic and inorganic ones, be given in terms of 'the will to power'.

In *On the Genealogy of Morality*, Nietzsche affirms this conclusion with regard to organic events—as the claim that 'all happening in the organic world is an *overwhelming, a becoming-master*'—and, extending the 'organic' to include human social practices, he also accounts for certain actions and practices in these terms.[26] But it is in his unpublished writings that he pursues his ontology of 'the will to power' most enthusiastically. There he emphasizes that, although he derives this ontology from the causal power of willing, he does not attribute willing to a substantial subject—he thus follows primitive psychology in the former respect, but not in the latter. The explanations of events in terms of 'the will to power' that he envisions consequently concern not causal relations between substantial 'things', but rather mere 'willings' or 'powers' or, at most, hierarchically organized composites of them. In a note of 1888, for instance, he writes of the substantial subject and the derivative notion of the 'thing' that if 'we eliminate these additions: what remains are not things but dynamic quanta in a relation of tension with all other dynamic quanta: whose essence consists in their relation to all other quanta, in their "effects" on these'. And in another note in the same notebook, he writes of his derivation of this ontology that 'life, as the form of being that is best known to us, is specifically a will to the accumulation of force' and that his ontology is a 'hypothesis which extends from this to the whole character of existence'.[27]

---

[25] *BGE* 36.

[26] *GM* II: 12. See also *GM* I: 13 and for the accounts of actions and practices, see the treatment of 'ascetic ideals' at *GM* III: 11 and 18 and also the general claims at *BGE* 23 and *A* 2.

[27] *KGW* VIII.3: 14 [79, 82] (Spring 1888). See also *KGW* VIII.2: 9 [91] (Autumn 1887) and VIII.3: 14 [121] in particular, and *KGW* VII.3: 34 [247] (April–June 1885), 35 [15] (May–June 1885), 36 [31] (June–July 1885), 37 [4] (June–July 1885), 38 [12] (June–July 1885), 40 [42 and 61] (August–September 1885), and 43 [1] (Autumn 1885), VIII.1: 1 [28, 30, and 58] (Autumn 1885–Spring 1886), VIII.1: 2 [69, 91, 142, 151, 152, and 158] (Autumn 1885–Autumn 1886), and 5 [9] (Summer 1886–Autumn 1887), VIII.2: 9 [98 and 106] (Autumn 1887), 10 [19, 138] (Autumn 1887), and 11 [72, 73, 83, 111, 113, and 114] (November 1887–March 1888), and VIII.3: 14 [122, 123, 173, and 174] (Spring 1888).

Insofar as he derives this causal ontology a priori from the causal power of willing, Nietzsche knowingly provides precisely what in criticizing Spir and Teichmüller he denies can be provided—that is, an a priori determination of reality—in precisely the way that in criticizing them he rejects—that is, by extending to reality a primitive psychological presupposition about agency that he considers erroneous. It is unsurprising, then, that in *Beyond Good and Evil* he emphasizes that an explanation of nature in terms of 'the will to power' is still 'only an interpretation' of it and that in presenting his argument for this ontology there he not only admits to merely 'assuming' his first and third premises, but also presents the second, that regarding the causal power of willing, in a similarly hypothetical manner. Indeed, as his parenthetical remark about the second premise being 'really just our belief in causality itself' indicates, he consistently claims that any supposed 'explanation' of an event in terms of causal powers reflects the mistaken belief that an agent's action is determined by the causal power of her conscious choice, just as any attribution of causal powers to a substantial 'thing' reflects the mistaken belief that choice and its power are to be attributed to a substantial 'will'. As he puts it in ' "Reason" in Philosophy', the primitive psychology reflected in the postulation of 'thinghood' and 'cause' of objects ultimately derives from 'the error that the will is something that *effects*'.[28]

Overall, then, it might be said that while in his early engagements with Kantian idealism Nietzsche was undecided between his theoretical doubts and his therapeutic or cultural enthusiasm, in his later engagements he was undecided between his more developed doubts about its denial that reality is accessible to and judgeable by our ordinary perceptual and conceptual capacities and his enthusiasm for his own Kantian-inspired ontology of 'will to power'.[29]

Kant

In concluding this discussion of Nietzsche's engagements with Kantian idealism, it is worth briefly considering how far they might be extended beyond his particular Kantian sources to Kant's own positions and arguments and contemporary readings of them. In

---

[28] *BGE* 22, 36, *TI* III 5. Thus Nietzsche bases his 'will to power' ontology neither on merely empirical evidence or normative commitments nor on basic metaphysical postulates, but rather on an empirical premise that he considers false. This tells against Tsarina Doyle's attempt to read Nietzsche's ontology as following from his epistemology and, in particular, as introducing causal powers into scientific and psychological explanations in response to Kantian idealism's relegation of causal powers to a supra-empirical reality. For Doyle's reading has Nietzsche deny only the substantial nature of 'the will' and a related conception of causality and not also the causal power of the 'will', and thus has him affirm rather than reject the consequences of the belief in causal power for scientific and psychological explanations. See Doyle 2004 and 2009: chs 4–5, esp. 115–21. Nietzsche elaborates on his criticism of causal 'explanations' in *TI* VI 3 and also in *GS* 112 and 127, *BGE* 12, 14, 17, and 21–3, *GM* I: 13, and *KGW* VII.3: 34 [53 and 124] (April–June 1885) and 35 [52] (May–July 1885), VIII.1: 1 [44] (Autumn 1885–Spring 1886), 2 [83, 84, 139, and 158] (Autumn 1885–Autumn 1886), and 4 [8] (beginning of 1886–Spring 1886), VIII.2: 9 [91] (Autumn 1887), 7 [1] (end of 1886–Spring 1887), and 11 [145] (November 1887–March 1888), and VIII.3: 14 [98] (Spring 1888). Notably, this criticism echoes claims made by Teichmüller and Liebmann, among other readings of Nietzsche's. On these claims, see Orsucci 1997: 57–63.

[29] For a discussion of the tensions that may arise between such speculations and Nietzsche's more realist strands, see Gardner 2009.

this respect, his criticisms of the notion of an inaccessible reality are not particularly promising. For it is highly debatable whether Kant affirms an inaccessible reality or, if he does, whether he argues for it in the ways that Nietzsche criticizes.[30] Kant takes pains to distinguish his 'transcendental' idealism from scepticism, such that 'transcendental' conditions of knowledge are intended as guarantees of an 'empirical' realism. To avoid problems such as those identified by Nietzsche, some Kant commentators even argue that he intends the 'thing in itself' to refer simply to the object of knowledge considered independently of the a priori conditions of knowledge and thus to express no commitments about the reality of the object considered in this way.[31] Furthermore, even if Kant's 'thing in itself' is equated with the inaccessible reality that Nietzsche rejects, Nietzsche's criticisms of its contradictoriness, superfluity, and suspiciousness have little to 'say' to, for instance, Kant's insistence on our being affected by the objects that we come to know or the necessity of an idealist 'Copernican Revolution' to avoid the inadequacies of realism. Thus Nietzsche's criticisms of the notion of an inaccessible reality would seem more applicable to the positions and arguments of Schopenhauer, Lange, or Fischer than to those offered by Kant himself.

Nietzsche's engagement with Kantian conceptions of judgement, on the other hand, concerns three significant issues regarding Kant's own account of judgement. First, like Spir, Kant considers a judgement to consist in the normative application of a concept to an object and thus raises the problem of how sensible experience could be admitted into a judgement, since such experience would appear to have a causal, rather than normative, role in explaining a judgement. Kant's solution, to claim that the imagination provides criteria for the application of concepts to sensible experience, is notoriously unsatisfactory and it might be more fruitful to reject the notion of judgement on which the problem rests, as Nietzsche does in ultimately rejecting Spir's faith in 'logic'. Second, like Teichmüller, Kant also claims that a judgement must refer to an 'I', understood as a non-empirical being, a claim that raises significant questions about the nature and role of the subject in knowledge of an object. Nietzsche's criticism of Teichmüller and his attempts to formulate an ontology without substantial subjects might be considered a response to such questions. Finally, Nietzsche's treatment of thinghood and causality relates to another of Kant's primary concerns, namely, to defend against empiricist objections the idea that the objects of judgement ultimately consist of substances in causal relations. By both criticizing such an idea as an error of 'reason' that reflects a primitive psychology and offering an alternative ontology in terms of 'the will to power', Nietzsche arguably responds to a very similar concern. By attending more closely to his treatment of conceptions of judgement than to his criticisms of the notion of an inaccessible reality, then, Nietzsche's engagements with Kantian idealism might be shown to be not only richer, but also more tellingly related to Kant's own idealism.

[30] Admittedly, Nietzsche commentators often take Kant to affirm an inaccessible reality and Nietzsche to successfully dispose of it. Besides the works referred to in n. 16 above, see, for instance, Brown 1980: 42–5, Stack 1991: esp. 30–3, Houlgate 1993: esp. 128–57, Conrad 2001: 25–33, and Ibáñez-Noé 2002: 132–4 and 144–7.

[31] See, in particular, Allison 1983/2004 and, on the significance of such interpretations for Nietzsche's critical relation to Kant, see Mosser 1993: esp. 73–6, Weiss 1993, and Riccardi 2010: 340–8.

2 NIETZSCHE AND KANTIAN ETHICS

Unconvincing Objections

Nietzsche's engagements with Kantian ethics are concentrated almost exclusively in his works and notes of the 1880s and are less marked by particular secondary readings than his engagements with Kantian idealism.[32] He generally treats Kantian ethics as symptomatic of a broader crisis of modern 'morality', and of the moral value of equality in particular. Indeed, his most common claims regarding Kantian ethics are that it uncritically affirms such modern moral values and that it exploits the notion of an inaccessible reality to protect them from empirical criticism. In *Beyond Good and Evil*, for instance, Nietzsche presents Kant as an uncritical moralist who, with his notion of a 'categorical imperative', wishes to show that ' "what is honourable about me is that I can obey,—and it *should* be no different for you than it is for me!" ', while in the 1886 preface to *Daybreak* he writes that Kant 'saw himself necessitated to posit an indemonstrable world, a logical "Beyond", to create room for *his* "moral realm" [. . .] to make the "moral realm" unassailable, better still incomprehensible to reason'.[33] However, it is not clear that Nietzsche's general criticisms of modern morality offer much prospect of a fruitful engagement with Kantian ethics. For even if Kantian notions of equality, freedom, and reason are 'moral' in Nietzsche's pejorative sense, his general criticisms of morality—for its '*ressentiment*' or asceticism, say, or its obstruction of 'higher' individuals—bear little relation to Kantian arguments and concerns.

Moreover, in the two published passages in which Nietzsche proceeds beyond such general claims about Kantian ethics and 'morality' to make more specific objections, his

---

[32] Besides the relevant parts of the texts by Fischer, Hartmann, Lange, Romundt, Schopenhauer, and Überweg mentioned in nn. 1, 3–6, and 20, Nietzsche's readings on Kant's ethics included Schopenhauer's *Über das Fundament der Moral/Über die Grundlage der Moral*, which he read in 1884, presumably in his copy of Schopenhauer's *Sämtliche Werke*. See Campioni et al. 2003: 554 and Brobjer 2008: 32, 38 and n. 89, and 226. In Nietzsche's notebooks, at *KGW* VIII.1: 7 [4] (end 1886–Spring 1887), there are also a series of quotations, summaries, and discussions of passages from Kant's *Grundlegung zur Metaphysik der Sitten*, *Kritik der praktischen Vernunft*, *Kritik der Urteilskraft* (*Critique of Judgement*), *Die Religion innerhalb der Grenzen der bloßen Vernunft*, *Die Metaphyik der Sitten*, and *Der Streit der Fakultäten*, which in *KSA* 14: 739 are attributed to Nietzsche's visits to the library at Chur, Switzerland, in mid-May and early June 1887. However, Brobjer provides evidence that these notes derive not from first-hand readings of these texts of Kant's, but from Nietzsche's re-reading of Fischer's *Immanuel Kant und seine Lehre*. See Brobjer 2001: 421, 2003: 65 and n. 42, and 2008: 38 and n. 87.

[33] *BGE* 187, *D* Preface 3. See also MS 27, *HAH* III 216, *D* 142, 197, 207, and 481, *GS* 193 and 335, *BGE* 5, 11, 186, 188, and 210–12, *GM* III: 12 and 25, W 7, *TI* III 6, IV, and IX 1, 16, 29, and 42, *A* 10, 12, 55, and 61, *EH* 'UB' 3 and 'W' 2–3, and, for examples of the relevant notes, *KGW* III.4: 19 [34, 53, and 136] (Summer 1872–beginning 1873), IV.2: 24 [39] (Autumn 1877), IV.3: 30 [188] (Summer 1878), V.1: 6 [135 and 347] (Autumn 1880), and 7 [21, 34, 216, and 217] (end of 1880), VII.1: 7 [21] (Spring–Summer 1883), VII.2: 25 [121, 351, and 437] (Spring 1884), 26 [75, 375, and 461] (Summer–Autumn 1884), and 27 [76] (Summer–Autumn 1884), VII.3: 30 [10] (Autumn 1884–beginning of 1885), VIII.1: 2 [190] (Autumn 1885–Autumn 1886), VIII.2: 10 [11, 118, and 205] (Autumn 1887), and VIII.3: 14 [107, 108, 116, 141, and 163] (Spring 1888), 15 [19 and 28] (Spring 1888), and 16 [25] (Spring–Summer 1888).

objections are unconvincing. In the first, a section of *The Gay Science* entitled, 'Long Live Physics!', he insists that to require that everyone do the same thing in the same circumstances is a 'blind, petty and undemanding' kind of 'self-centredness' and that it is impossible to judge our reasons for action, since experienced actions and circumstances are always more singular than those identified by reasons. In the other passage, a section of *The Antichrist*, he alleges that a Kantian moral judgement considers 'pleasure as an objection' and is therefore 'harmful' or '*dangerous to life*'. And in both passages he concludes that rather than making Kantian moral judgements, we ought to cultivate our own particularities and creativity: in 'Long Live Physics!' he claims that, unlike Kant, we '*want to become who we are,*—the new, the unique, the incomparable, those who give themselves laws, those who create themselves!', while in *The Antichrist* he insists that '[a] virtue must be *our* invention, *our* most personal self-defence and need' and that 'each should invent *his* virtue, *his* categorical imperative'.[34]

These objections are unconvincing primarily because they misrepresent the nature of a Kantian moral judgement. First, such a judgement does not hold simply that every agent should do or refrain from the same action in the same circumstances, a judgement which indeed could be made on 'self-centred' grounds or for the sake of any contingent need or want of any agent. Rather, it is supposed to be 'universal' in a stronger sense, one that would exclude such particular grounds by referring to specifically moral, unconditional ones, those which Kant often describes as the object of a distinctively moral kind of 'respect'.[35] Nietzsche displays a better appreciation of this sense of universality in the section of *The Antichrist*, where he describes the grounds of a Kantian moral judgement not as 'self-centred', but as the '"good in itself", good with the character of impersonality and universality' and as 'a feeling of respect for the concept "virtue"'.[36] But by insisting that a Kantian moral judgement thus considers 'pleasure as an objection' he misrepresents it in another way. For Kant allows that what is morally good might coincide with the satisfaction of contingent needs or wants, insists that such needs or wants be taken into account insofar as they are relevant to moral concerns, and even considers the achievement of moral goodness itself to provide its own kind of 'pleasure'.[37]

[34] *GS* 335, *A* 11.

[35] The difference between these two senses of 'universality' has much exercised Kant commentators, since Kant has been thought by some to succeed in justifying only the weaker sense. For discussion of this issue, see, for instance, Allison 1996: 143–7 and 150–4 and Wood 1999: 48 and 81–2. Nietzsche's objection here echoes one of Schopenhauer's, in Schopenhauer 1841: pt II, §7 and 1844: App.

[36] *A* 11.

[37] Although critics since Schiller have alleged that Kant makes the presence of countervailing inclinations necessary to the performance of one's moral duty, a more charitable interpretation would be that he simply considers to act 'from duty' to be to do what is morally required because it is morally required and thus irrespective of whether doing what is morally required also coincides with the satisfaction of inclination. See, in particular, Kant 1785: 397–9 and also my discussion in Bailey 2010b: 638–40. As regards the determination of what 'duty' requires, Kant's employment of his formulas to derive duties in *The Metaphysics of Morals* indicates that he considers the satisfaction of contingent needs or wants as morally significant insofar as they are relevant to the 'universal' concerns expressed by his formulas. See, for instance, his argument for a duty of beneficence in Kant 1797/1798: 453. Finally, while Kant initially restricted pleasure and displeasure to the satisfaction and dissatisfaction of inclination, from the *Critique of Judgement* onwards he simply distinguishes between (dis)pleasure at the (dis)satisfaction of an inclination and (dis)pleasure at the (lack of) fulfilment of moral requirements. See Kant 1790: 178–9 and 207–9, 1793: 283–4, and 1797/1798: 211–13, 378, and 399–400.

Nietzsche also misrepresents Kantian moral judgement in denying that our reasons for action can be judged. For Kant too admits that reasons are indeterminate and that we therefore cannot judge past actions by the reasons for which they may have been performed. But he insists that this indeterminacy does not preclude the prescription of future actions according to reasons and that, in this, a sufficient level of determinacy can be attained through the mutual qualification of different reasons for action.[38] Nietzsche simply does not consider this possibility.

Finally, Nietzsche's proposal that rather than making Kantian moral judgements, we cultivate our own particularities and creativity is as far from Kantian concerns as his general criticisms of 'morality'. For much as 'autonomy' is often considered a characteristically 'Kantian' concern, to consider it to preclude considerations of universality or equality in the name of an agent's particularity or creativity—so that we might thus *become who we are,—the new, the unique, the incomparable*'—is clearly quite alien to the Kantian conception of moral judgement.[39]

Nietzsche's Kantian Ethics

To reveal more persuasive grounds for Nietzsche's criticism of Kantian ethics, it is necessary to consider certain other passages in which, while not mentioning Kant and Kantian ethics explicitly, Nietzsche himself develops distinctively 'Kantian' notions of autonomy and equality. Particularly significant in this regard is a series of sections at the beginning of the second essay of *On the Genealogy of Morality*. There Nietzsche presents what he calls the 'sovereign individual' as an agent—that is, a being able to 'will' its actions—whose

[38] See, in particular, Kant 1785: 407–8 and 1797/1798: 390 and, for a reading that emphasizes this, O'Neill 1989a: 83–5, 1989b: 130 and 141, 1996: 89–97, and 2002: 331–43. Kant also admits that we do not always act for reasons, in his accounts of 'affects' and 'passions' at Kant 1792–3/1794: 29 n., 1797/1798: 407–8, and 1798b: 251–75 and also at 1790: 380 and 1789–90: 196. In later notes at *KGW* VIII.1: 7 [62] (end of 1886–Spring 1887) and VIII.2: 10 [57] (Autumn 1887), Nietzsche appears to recognize that Kant considers the reasons for which an agent acts to be indemonstrable. For some discussion of Nietzsche's presentation of the objection in *GS* 335, see Bailey 2006: 256–60.

[39] Arguably, the modern notion of 'autonomy' as an expression of an individual's particularity or singularity owes more to John Stuart Mill than to Kant and it is notable that in the 1880s Nietzsche engaged in particularly intensive readings of Mill's *Utilitarianism*, *On Liberty*, and *Civilisation* and his review of Alexis de Tocqueville's *Democracy in America*. On these readings, see Fornari 2006: 219–314. Nonetheless, it is often claimed that Nietzsche rejects Kantian notions of equality or universality in the name of the unequal or particular or the creative, generally understood in terms of the 'autonomy' of an individual's acting according to his or her particular or creative drives or qualities. See, in particular, Owen 1994: chs 1–4, 1995: 87–90, 1999: 3–11, and 2009: 210–19, Ridley 1998: 1–11 and 69–72 and 2009: 192–4, May 1999: 13, and Dudley 2002: 3–8, 123–212, and 227–30, and also Ansell-Pearson 1991a: 174–87 and 1991b: 273–80, Hunt 1991: chs 2 and 5–8, esp. 22–3, Gerhardt 1992: esp. 40–4, White 1997: esp. 36–44, Kerckhove 1997: 15–20, 24–6, and 28–30, Williams 1999: 206–12, Guay 2002: 310, and Hill 2003: pt 3. Similar readings of Nietzsche's ethics, albeit without reference to Kantian ethics, are given in Janaway 2007: 117–23 and 2009: 60–4 and Richardson 2009: 136–45. Another, now less common, approach is similarly alien to Kantian concerns—namely, that which holds that, with his criticism of 'other-worldly' entities and qualities, Nietzsche overcomes the dualisms of Kant's moral philosophy and urges the affirmation of what allegedly remains, a 'this-worldly' realm of drives or 'becoming'. See, for instance, Deleuze 1962: 102–8, Ansell-Pearson 1987: 310–39, Müller-Lauter 1995: esp. 25–7, and Simon 2000.

'*measure of value*' is agency itself, such that by 'looking out from himself upon others, he honours or he despises', distinguishing 'his equals' in agency from those of lesser agency and '*affirm*[*ing*]' himself as capable of a certain degree of agency. In this, Nietzsche claims, the 'sovereign individual' is distinctively 'autonomous'.[40]

It is plausible to consider this account of the 'sovereign individual' as a particular instance of the 'noble' ethics that Nietzsche presents in the first essay of *On the Genealogy of Morality* and in *Beyond Good and Evil*. Such an ethics identifies 'good' or 'bad' actions with those performed by exemplary 'good' or 'bad' agents and identifies 'good' or 'bad' agents by a distinguishing characteristic—such as their being 'blond-headed', a 'warrior', or 'truthful'—which is supposed to bestow 'goodness' or 'badness' on their actions. 'Good' and 'bad' actions are determined, and agents motivated to perform 'good' actions and not to perform 'bad' ones, by a constant, creative and mutual demonstrating and measuring of the relevant 'goodness'-bestowing characteristic, a practice that Nietzsche often refers to as 'requital [*Vergeltung*]'.[41] In his account of the 'sovereign individual', then, Nietzsche would appear to present agency itself as a goodness-bestowing characteristic that must be continually demonstrated in actions and judged to do so by others.

If this is so, then the 'autonomy' that Nietzsche affirms against the Kantian conception of moral judgement does not concern the cultivation of particularity or creativity, but is rather itself profoundly Kantian. For Nietzsche's 'sovereign individual' affirms agency as such and in general as the highest and unconditional value, and thus a sense of the equal or universal moral significance of agency that denies any fundamental moral significance to agents' contingencies or, indeed, to anything other than agency. A 'sovereign individual' therefore considers an action, whether his own or another's, as 'good' or 'bad' not according to whether it satisfies independent moral principles, achieves a substantial moral good, or manifests a moral disposition—all things that might also be achieved without agency—but rather according to whether the action demonstrates the ability to 'will' one's actions—and thus achieves something which *only* agency can achieve. Nietzsche's account of the 'sovereign individual' thus echoes the Kantian conception of 'autonomy' as an agent's treating agency, or 'will', itself as the highest and unconditional value—in the terms of Kant's formulas, moral value consists in willing what can be willed to be 'a universal law', taking will always as an 'end' and not merely as a 'means', and the 'autonomy' of a will's thus 'giving law to itself'.[42]

Crucially, however, while affirming the equal moral significance of agency the 'sovereign individual' is also sensitive to differences in degrees of agency across agents and over time, and consequently admits different degrees of moral significance among agents and over time. In determining the 'goodness' or 'badness' of an action according to its demonstration of agency, then, the 'sovereign individual' is also concerned with the degree of agency demonstrated by the agent, relative to that demonstrated by others. Nietzsche emphasizes this in

[40]   *GM* II: 2, 3.

[41]   For Nietzsche's account of the ethics of 'good and bad', see, in particular, *BGE* 259, 262, 263, 265, 272, and 287 and *GM* I: 10 and 11. Notably, of the ten sections of his earlier texts to which Nietzsche refers in *GM* Preface 4 as prefiguring claims made in *GM*, six present his notion of 'requital' in some detail and one of these is one of two successive sections of *D* which present lengthy analyses of 'requital' precisely in terms of agency. See *HAH* I: 45 and 92, *HAH* III 22, 26, and 33 and *D* 112 and also *HAH* I: 44 and *D* 113.

[42]   Kant 1785: 421, 429, 433, 431. In support of attributing this sense of 'autonomy' to Kant, see my reading of the first section of his *Groundwork of the Metaphysics of Morals* in Bailey 2010b.

the sections of *On the Genealogy of Morality* when he insists that the 'sovereign individual' is 'autonomous and supermoral (for "autonomous" and "moral" are mutually exclusive)', since there he equates the 'moral' with the treatment of agents as 'uniform, like among like'.[43] And it is precisely this sensitivity to differences in degrees of agency which makes necessary the constant, creative, and mutual demonstration and measurement of agency among 'sovereign individuals', by means of which their 'equals' are distinguished from others and the 'goodness' or 'badness' of actions is determined. Nietzsche's Kantian ethics thus differs from standard Kantian ethics, including Kant's own, in admitting different degrees of agency and therefore moral significance among agents and thus substantially modifying the egalitarianism or universality standardly required by a Kantian moral judgement.

The sections on the 'sovereign individual' thus provide an alternative explanation for Nietzsche's criticism of Kantian ethics to those given in 'Long Live Physics!' and the section of *The Antichrist*. That is, they suggest that for Nietzsche Kantian ethics rightly considers agency itself as the highest and unconditional value, but fails to appreciate that agency itself varies in degree and that the requirements of respecting this value and agents' success in fulfilling them must be determined among agents. Indeed, his proposal that we become 'those who give themselves laws' in 'Long Live Physics!' or that 'each should invent *his* virtue, *his* categorical imperative' in *The Antichrist* might be reread in this light—that is, as an appeal not to particularity or creativity as such, but to demonstrations of degrees of agency among 'equals' in agency.[44]

Against this explanation of Nietzsche's criticism of Kantian ethics, it might be objected that in his account of the 'sovereign individual' Nietzsche cannot mean 'agency' in a Kantian sense. For elsewhere he denies that actions can be explained or prescribed according to reasons, that an agent consists of a substantial 'will', and that her actions are caused by her conscious choice. He also rejects the contra-causal spontaneity of 'free will' and the overinflated sense of responsibility that he associates with it—namely, that which holds the agent alone responsible not only for all his behaviour, but also, as Nietzsche puts it in *Twilight of the Idols*, 'for [his] existing at all, or for being constituted as he is, or for living in the circumstances and surroundings in which he lives'.[45] Indeed, he often refers to Kant as affirming such senses of 'free will' and responsibility. Furthermore, in rejecting such senses of 'agency' Nietzsche tends to present actions as explicable in non-conscious, non-rational, or non-substantial terms.

However, Nietzsche nonetheless shares with Kant a basic conception of agency as action that is not determined by immediate experiences and desires. For, just as Kant defines agency as motivated action that is 'free' in the sense that it 'can […] be *affected* but not *determined* by impulses', Nietzsche presents the agency of the 'sovereign individual' as consisting of an ability to 'forget' and thus 'digest' experiences and desires which allows for 'a little

---

[43] *GM* II: 2. That Nietzsche uses the word '*sittlich*' rather than '*moralisch*' for 'moral' here need not imply that he considers the 'sovereign individual' to be free only of the primitive 'morality of custom [*Sittlichkeit der Sitte*]' under which he claims that agency develops and not also of modern morality, which he generally refers to as '*Moral*' or '*Moralität*'. For he considers the treatment of agents as 'uniform, like among like' to persist in modern morality and, indeed, often refers to Kantian equality as exemplifying this. See *HAH* I: 96–9, *D* 9, and *BGE* 187 and 188, for instance.

[44] I provide some further discussion of this 'Kantian' ethics in Bailey 2003: 14–21 and 2006: 254–6.

[45] *TI* VI 8. For Nietzsche's criticisms of the contra-causal spontaneity and overinflated responsibility associated with 'free will', see also *BGE* 21, *GM* I: 13 and II: 4, and *TI* VI 7 and 8.

tabula rasa of consciousness', and an opposing ability to make and keep a promise, or 'an active *willing*-not-to-be-rid-of, a continuous willing of something once willed, a real *memory of the will*'. This, he claims, constitutes a 'rare freedom' and 'the extraordinary privilege of *responsibility*'.[46] In endorsing this basic Kantian conception of agency, Nietzsche does not follow Kant in thinking that such 'freedom' also requires contra-causal spontaneity or hold the 'sovereign individual' responsible in the overinflated sense—he considers the 'sovereign individual' to be 'free' simply to will actions without being determined to them by immediate experiences and desires and 'responsible' simply for his willed actions. Nor does he follow Kant in focusing on reasons or contravene his own criticisms of the sufficiency of reasons or 'will' for prescribing or explaining actions—he presents the actions of the 'sovereign individual' as reflecting a particular hierarchy of abilities, including non-conscious and non-rational ones, albeit one that is organized such that it can determine its actions independently of its immediate experiences and desires and according to conscious reasoning and choosing, the subsidiary abilities that in his account Nietzsche refers to as those of being 'able to calculate, compute'.[47]

Nor is Nietzsche's account of the 'sovereign individual' an isolated or exceptional case. For the Kantian ethics that he expresses there also informs much of his ethics elsewhere. This is particularly clear in his treatment of justice in the second essay of *On the Genealogy of Morality*, where, after presenting the sovereign individual's consciousness of the ability to will actions as 'a true consciousness of power and freedom' and a 'consciousness of [. . .] power over oneself and fate', he accounts for the origins of 'justice' in terms of 'power' in precisely this sense. In particular, he writes that 'justice' originates in 'the good will among those of approximately equal power to come to terms with one another, to "understand" each other through a balance—and, regarding those of lesser power, to *force* them to a balance among themselves'.[48] For Nietzsche, then, justice consists of the 'balances' which demonstrate approximately equal degrees of agency among 'equals' in this sense and their inequality with respect to those of greater or lesser agency. Indeed, in *Twilight of the Idols*, his numerous remarks in praise of 'noble' social distinctions and against the modern political ideal of 'equality' are accompanied by the following explanation: 'The doctrine of equality! . . . But there exists no more poisonous poison: for it *appears* to be preached by justice itself, whereas it is the *end* of justice . . . "Equal for equals, unequal for unequals"—*that* would be the true voice of justice: and what follows from it, "Never make unequals equal"'.[49]

Another example of Nietzsche's emphasis on the demonstration of agency is provided by his treatments of love. For instance, two successive sections of *The Gay Science* present different kinds of love—benevolence, compassion, courtesy, sexual love, and friendship—as

---

[46] Kant 1797/1798: 213, *GM* II: 1, 2. For Nietzsche's conception of agency, see also *BGE* 19 and 230 and *TI* VIII 6 and for this particular aspect of Kant's, see also Kant 1797/1798: 211.

[47] *GM* II: 1.

[48] *GM* II: 2, 8. Besides the three passages referred to in *GM* Preface 4 in this regard, *HAH* 92, *HAH III* 26, and *D* 112, see also *HAH III* 22 and 33, *BGE* 259, *GM* II: 4–7 and 9–11, and *KGW* VIII.1: 5 [82] (Summer 1886–Autumn 1887).

[49] *TI* IX 48. See also *Z* II 7, *BGE* 202 and 272, *GS* 356 and 377, *TI* IX 37, *A* 43 and 57, and *KGW* VIII.1: 3 [13] (beginning of 1886–Spring 1886) and 5 [107] (Summer 1886–Autumn 1887) and VIII.2: 9 [173] (Autumn 1887) and 11 [127, 142, 148, and 156] (November 1887–March 1888), and the remarks on Kant at *KGW* VII.2: 25 [437] (Spring 1884) and 26 [84] (Summer–Autumn 1884). For a reading of Nietzsche's political philosophy in these terms, see Bailey 2012.

indicators of relative levels of dependence among agents and of their different preferences regarding these levels. In particular, benevolent kinds of love are presented as relations of dependency between those unequal in independence, and therefore as valued by those who depend on others or wish to maintain others' dependence on them, while other kinds of love are presented as relations of independence between approximate equals in independence. Of those who prefer the latter kinds of love, Nietzsche writes approvingly that 'they are often hard towards one who is suffering, for he is not worthy of their striving and pride,—but they are more obliging towards their *equals*, against whom it would be honourable to fight and struggle, *if* the occasion should arise'.[50] That the independence and equality with which Nietzsche is concerned here are matters of agency is indicated by a series of sections later in the book, in which he criticizes traditional love relationships for their subordination of women's 'wills'. In such relationships, he writes, 'the way of man is will; the way of woman is willingness', whereas 'the capacity [...and] the good will for revenge' are necessary if a woman is to 'be able to hold us (or "enthral" us, as they say)' and being 'capable of and ready for mastery over men' is necessary if women are to have 'lofty, heroic, royal souls'.[51] These remarks strongly suggest that it is precisely agency which Nietzsche thinks is approximately equal and demonstrated in ideal love relationships, such as to preclude dependent forms of love.[52]

The passages on the 'sovereign individual' in *On the Genealogy of Morality* therefore provide resources for a potentially more fruitful critical approach to Kantian ethics than Nietzsche's explicit objections, resources that also inform much of his ethics elsewhere. In particular, this approach implies that rather than rejecting Kantian ethics outright, Nietzsche shares its affirmation of the value of agency as such—its basic sense of 'autonomy'—but insists that it misconceives of equality among agents because it fails to appreciate that agency itself and therefore also agents' moral significance are a matter of degree. Nietzsche's best criticisms of Kantian ethics would thus appear to be both implicit and internal.

CONCLUSION

Nietzsche's dismissive remarks about Kant and his lack of reading of Kant's own texts therefore obscure sophisticated engagements with both Kantian idealism and Kantian ethics, engagements that are dynamic and often implicit, mediated by secondary sources, ultimately undecided, and applicable to Kant himself only in qualified or indirect ways. In particular, Nietzsche's intensive engagements with Kantian idealism from the mid-1860s to the mid-1870s combine an interest in its potential therapeutic or cultural benefits, emphasized in his published writings of this period, with an exploration of its theoretical difficulties, developed in his unpublished writings without drawing definitive conclusions. In his later published works, he proceeds to reject Kantian idealism explicitly, not only for the

---

[50] *GS* 13. See also *GS* 14.

[51] *GS* 68, 69, 70.

[52] For a more detailed presentation of this reading of the treatments of love in *GS*, accompanied by a corresponding reading of Zarathustra's meetings with 'higher men' in Z IV, see Bailey 2010a.

conceptual incoherence, epistemological insignificance, and suspicious psycho-physical and cultural functions of its notion of an inaccessible reality, but also for the unlicensed ontology and primitive psychology of its notions of judgement. Yet he nonetheless also reformulates precisely the argument from Kantian notions of judgement that he diagnoses, as the grounds for his own ontology of 'the will to power'. Indeed, in both its critical and reformative aspects, his treatment of Kantian notions of judgement appears more pertinent to Kant's own concerns than his criticisms of the notion of an inaccessible reality. In his later works, Nietzsche also engages with Kantian ethics, not only by airing some unconvincing objections to it, but also by developing a distinctively 'Kantian' ethics of his own—one that, while sharing the Kantian value of agency as such, or 'autonomy', insists on different degrees of agency and therefore moral significance among agents, and thus offers a more promising, internal criticism of Kantian ethics. Albeit often in indirect ways, then, Nietzsche offers a range of intense, developing, and subtle critical engagements with Kantian idealism and Kantian ethics.

Bibliography

(A) Works by Nietzsche

KSA   *Sämtliche Werke: Kritische Studienausgabe in 15 Einzelbänden*, ed. G. Colli and M. Montinari (15 vols). Berlin: De Gruyter, 1988.

KGW   *Werke: Kritische Gesamtausgabe*, ed. Giorgio Colli and Mazzino Montinari. Berlin: De Gruyter, 1967–.

(B) Other Works Cited

Allison, Henry E. 1983/2004. *Kant's Transcendental Idealism: An Interpretation and Defense*. London: Yale University Press.

Allison, Henry E. 1996. 'On a Presumed Gap in the Derivation of the Categorical Imperative', in *Idealism and Freedom: Essays on Kant's Theoretical and Practical Philosophy*. Cambridge: Cambridge University Press, 143–54.

Anderson, R. Lanier. 1996. 'Overcoming Charity: The Case of Maudemarie Clark's *Nietzsche on Truth and Philosophy*', *Nietzsche-Studien* 25: 307–41.

Anderson, R. Lanier. 1998. 'Truth and Objectivity in Perspectivism', *Synthese* 115: 1–32.

Anderson, R. Lanier. 1999. 'Nietzsche's Views on Truth and the Kantian Background of his Epistemology', in Babette Babich (ed.), *Nietzsche and the Sciences*, vol. 2: *Nietzsche, Epistemology and Philosophy of Science*. Dordrecht: Kluwer Academic Publishers, 47–59.

Ansell-Pearson, Keith. 1987. 'Nietzsche's Overcoming of Kant and Metaphysics: From Tragedy to Nihilism', *Nietzsche-Studien* 16: 310–39.

Ansell-Pearson, Keith. 1991a. 'Nietzsche and the Problem of the Will in Modernity', in K. Ansell-Pearson (ed.), *Nietzsche and Modern German Thought*. London: Routledge, 165–91.

Ansell-Pearson, Keith. 1991b. 'Nietzsche on Autonomy and Morality: The Challenge to Political Theory', *Political Studies* 39: 270–86.

Babich, Babette. 2002. 'Sensualism and Unconscious Representations in Nietzsche's Account of Knowledge', *International Studies in Philosophy* 34.3: 95–117.

Babich, Babette. 2005. 'Nietzsche on Truth, Illusion and Redemption', *European Journal of Philosophy* 13.2: 185–225.

Bagehot, Walter. 1874. *Der Ursprung der Nationen. Betrachtungen über den Einfluß der natür-lichen Zuchtwahl und der Vererbung auf die Bildung politischer Gemeinwesen*, trans. I. Rosenthal Leipzig: Brockhaus. (From the English Edition, *Physics and Politics, or Thoughts on the Application of the Principles of 'Natural Selection' and 'Inheritance' to Political Society*, 1st edn. London: King, 1872).

Bailey, Tom. 2003. 'Nietzsche's Kantian Ethics', *International Studies in Philosophy* 35.3: 5–27.

Bailey, Tom. 2006. 'After Kant: Green and Hill on Nietzsche's Kantianism', *Nietzsche-Studien* 35: 228–62.

Bailey, Tom. 2010a. 'La filosofia come pratica di comunità. Leggere *La Gaia Scienza* II e *Così Parlò Zarathustra* IV', in Giuliano Campioni, Chiara Piazzesi, and Patrick Wotling (eds), *Letture de 'La Gaia Scienza'*. Pisa: ETS, 55–67.

Bailey, Tom. 2010b. 'Analysing the Good Will: Kant's Argument in the First Section of the *Groundwork*', *British Journal for the History of Philosophy* 184: 635–61.

Bailey, Tom. 2012. 'Vulnerabilities of Agency: Kant and Nietzsche on Political Community', in Maria J. Branco and João Constâncio (eds), *As the Spider Spins: Essays on Nietzsche's Critique and Use of Language*. Berlin: De Gruyter, 107–27.

Brobjer, Thomas H. 2001. 'Nachweise aus Höffding, Harald: Psychologie in Umrissen u.a.', *Nietzsche-Studien* 30: 418–21.

Brobjer, Thomas H. 2003. 'Nietzsche as German Philosopher: His Reading of the Classical German Philosophers', in Nicholas Martin (ed.), *Nietzsche and the German Tradition*. Oxford: Lang, 39–83.

Brobjer, Thomas H. 2008. *Nietzsche's Philosophical Context: An Intellectual Biography*. Urbana and Chicago: University of Illinois Press.

Brown, Richard. 1980. 'Nietzsche and Kant on Permanence', *Man and World* 13: 39–52.

Campioni, Giuliano, D'Iorio, Paolo, Fornari, Maria Cristina, Fronterotta, Francesco, Orsucci, Andrea, and Müller-Buck, Renate. 2003. *Nietzsches persönliche Bibliothek*. Berlin: De Gruyter.

Clark, Maudemarie. 1990. *Nietzsche on Truth and Philosophy*. Cambridge: Cambridge University Press.

Clark, Maudemarie. 1998. 'On Knowledge, Truth and Value: Nietzsche's Debt to Schopenhauer and the Development of his Empiricism', in Christopher Janaway (ed.), *Willing and Nothingness: Schopenhauer as Nietzsche's Educator*. Oxford: Oxford University Press, 37–78.

Clark, Maudemarie. 2005. 'Nietzsche and Green on the Transcendental Tradition', *International Studies in Philosophy* 37.3: 5–28.

Clark, Maudemarie and Dudrick, David. 2004. 'Nietzsche's Post-Positivism', *European Journal of Philosophy* 12.3: 369–85.

Clark, Maudemarie and Dudrick, David. 2006. 'The Naturalisms of *Beyond Good and Evil*', in Keith Ansell Pearson (ed.), *A Companion to Nietzsche*. Oxford: Blackwell, 148–67.

Conrad, Mark T. 2001. 'Nietzsche's Kantianism', *International Studies in Philosophy* 33.3: 25–36.

Crawford, Claudia. 1988. *The Beginnings of Nietzsche's Theory of Language*. Berlin: De Gruyter.

Crawford, Claudia. 1997. '"The Dionysian Worldview": Nietzsche's Symbolic Languages and Music', *Journal of Nietzsche Studies* 13: 72–80.

Crescenzi, Luca. 1994. 'Verzeichnis der von Nietzsche aus der Universitätsbibliothek in Basel entliehenen Bücher (1869–1879)', *Nietzsche-Studien* 23: 388–442.

Crowell, Steven Galt. 1999. 'Nietzsche Among the Neo-Kantians; Or, the Relation Between Science and Philosophy', in Babette Babich (ed.), *Nietzsche and the Sciences*, vol. 1: *Nietzsche, Theories of Knowledge and Critical Theory*. Dordrecht: Kluwer, 77–86.

Danto, Arthur C. 1965. *Nietzsche as Philosopher*. Guildford: Columbia University Press.

Deleuze, Gilles. 1962. *Nietzsche et la philosophie*. Paris: Presses Universitaires de France.

D'Iorio, Paolo. 1993. 'La Superstition des Philosophes Critiques. Nietzsche et Afrikan Spir', *Nietzsche-Studien* 22: 257–94.

Doyle, Tsarina. 2004. 'Nietzsche's Appropriation of Kant', *Nietzsche-Studien* 33: 180–204.

Doyle, Tsarina. 2009. *Nietzsche on Epistemology and Metaphysics: The World in View.* Edinburgh: Edinburgh University Press.

Dudley, Will. 2002. *Hegel, Nietzsche and Philosophy: Thinking Freedom.* Cambridge: Cambridge University Press.

Fazio, Domenico M. 1986–9. 'Il pensiero del giovane Nietzsche e Afrikan Spir', *Bollettino di Storia della Filosofia dell'Università degli Studi di Lecce* 9: 243–62.

Fischer, Kuno. 1860–1. *Immanuel Kant und seine Lehre* (2 vols), 1st edn. Mannheim: Basserman.

Fornari, Maria Cristina. 2006. *La morale evolutiva del gregge. Nietzsche legge Spencer e Mill.* Pisa: ETS.

Gardner, Sebastian. 2009. 'Nietzsche, the Self and the Disunity of Philosophical Reason', in Ken Gemes and Simon May (eds), *Nietzsche on Freedom and Autonomy.* Oxford: Oxford University Press, 1–32.

Gerhardt, Volker. 1992. 'Selbstbegründung: Nietzsches Moral der Individualität', *Nietzsche-Studien* 21: 28–49.

Green, Michael Steven. 2002. *Nietzsche and the Transcendental Tradition.* Urbana and Chicago: University of Illinois Press.

Green, Michael Steven. 2005. 'White and Clark on *Nietzsche and the Transcendental Tradition*', *International Studies in Philosophy* 37.3: 45–75.

Guay, Robert. 2002. 'Nietzsche on Freedom', *European Journal of Philosophy* 10.3: 302–27.

Hartmann, Eduard von. 1869. *Philosophie des Unbewußten: Versuch einer Weltanschauung.* Berlin: Duncker.

Hartmann, Eduard von. 1879. *Phänomenologie des sittlichen Bewußtseins.* Berlin: Duncker.

Hill, R. Kevin. 2003. *Nietzsche's Critiques: The Kantian Foundations of his Thought.* Oxford: Oxford University Press.

Houlgate, Stephen. 1993. 'Kant, Nietzsche and the Thing in Itself', *Nietzsche-Studien* 22: 115–57.

Hunt, Lester H. 1991. *Nietzsche and the Origin of Virtue.* London: Routledge.

Ibáñez-Noé, Javier. 2002. 'Nietzsche and Kant's Copernican Revolution: On Nietzsche's Subjectivism', *New Nietzsche Studies* 5.1–2: 132–49.

Janaway, Christopher. 2007. *Beyond Selflessness: Reading Nietzsche's Genealogy.* Oxford: Oxford University Press.

Janaway, Christopher. 2009. 'Autonomy, Affect and the Self in Nietzsche's Project of Genealogy', in Ken Gemes and Simon May (eds), *Nietzsche on Freedom and Autonomy.* Oxford: Oxford University Press, 51–68.

Janz, Curt Paul. 1979. *Friedrich Nietzsche: Biographie* (3 vols). Munich: Deutsche Taschenbuch.

Kant, Immanuel. 1785/1910. *Grundlegung zur Metaphysik der Sitten*, in *Kants gesammelte Schriften*, vol. 4, ed. Königlich Preußische (now Deutsche) Akademie der Wissenschaften. Berlin: Georg Reimer (now De Gruyter).

Kant, Immanuel. 1788/1910. *Kritik der praktischen Vernunft*, in *Kants gesammelte Schriften*, vol. 5, ed. Königlich Preußische (now Deutsche) Akademie der Wissenschaften. Berlin: Georg Reimer (now De Gruyter).

Kant, Immanuel. 1789–90/1942. 'Erste Einleitung in der Kritik der Urteilskraft', in *Kants gesammelte Schriften*, vol. 20, ed. Königlich Preußische (now Deutsche) Akademie der Wissenschaften. Berlin: De Gruyter.

Kant, Immanuel. 1790/1910. *Kritik der Urteilskraft*, in *Kants gesammelte Schriften*, vol. 5, ed. Königlich Preußische (now Deutsche) Akademie der Wissenschaften. Berlin: Georg Reimer (now De Gruyter).

Kant, Immanuel. 1792–3/1794/1914. *Die Religion innerhalb der Grenzen der bloßen Vernunft*, 1st edn/2nd edn, in *Kants gesammelte Schriften*, vol. 6, ed. Königlich Preußische (now Deutsche) Akademie der Wissenschaften. Berlin: Georg Reimer (now De Gruyter).

Kant, Immanuel. 1793/1923. 'Über den Gemeinspruch: Das mag in der Theorie richtig sein, taugt aber nicht für die Praxis', in *Kants gesammelte Schriften*, vol. 8, ed. Königlich Preußische (now Deutsche) Akademie der Wissenschaften. Berlin: Georg Reimer (now De Gruyter).

Kant, Immanuel. 1797/1798/1914. *Die Metaphysik der Sitten*, 1st edn/2nd edn, in *Kants gesammelte Schriften*, vol. 6, ed. Königlich Preußische (now Deutsche) Akademie der Wissenschaften. Berlin: Georg Reimer (now De Gruyter).

Kant, Immanuel. 1798a/1917. *Der Streit der Fakultäten*, in *Kants gesammelte Schriften*, vol. 7, ed. Königlich Preußische (now Deutsche) Akademie der Wissenschaften. Berlin: Georg Reimer (now De Gruyter).

Kant, Immanuel. 1798b/1917. *Anthropologie in pragmatischer Hinsicht*, in *Kants gesammelte Schriften*, vol. 7, ed. Königlich Preußische (now Deutsche) Akademie der Wissenschaften. Berlin: Georg Reimer (now De Gruyter).

Kerckhove, Lee F. 1997. 'Nietzsche's Critique of Kantian Moral Autonomy', *Eidos* 14.2: 15–31.

Lange, Friedrich. 1866/1882/1887. *Geschichte des Materialismus und Kritik seiner Bedeutung in der Gegenwart*, 1st edn/4th edn/reprint of 4th edn. Iserlohn: Baedeker.

Lecky, W. E. H. 1879. *Sittengeschichte Europas von Augustus bis auf Karl den Grossen*, trans. H. Jolowicz, 2nd edn. Leipzig and Heidelberg: Winter. (From the English edition, *History of European Morals from Augustus to Charlemagne* (2 vols), 3rd edn. London: Longmans, Green & Co., 1877.)

Liebmann, Otto. 1865. *Kant und die Epigonen: Eine Kritische Abhandlung*. Stuttgart: Schober.

Liebmann, Otto. 1880. *Zur Analysis der Wirklichkeit: Eine Erörterung der Grundprobleme der Philosophie*, 2nd edn. Strassburg: Trübner.

Liebmann, Otto. 1882. *Gedanken und Thatsachen: Philosophische Abhandlungen, Aphorismen und Studien*, part 1: *Die Arten der Nothwendigkeit—Die mechanische Naturerklärung—Idee und Entelechie*. Strassburg: Trübner.

Lubbock, John. 1875. *Die Entstehung der Civilisation und der Urzustand des Menschengeschlechtes, erläutert durch das innere und äußere Leben der Wilden*, trans. A. Passow. Jena: Costenoble. (From the English edition, *The Origin of Civilisation and the Primitive Condition of Man: Mental and Social Condition of Savages*, 3rd edn. London: Longmans, Green & Co., 1875.)

May, Simon. 1999. *Nietzsche's Ethics and his War on 'Morality'*. Oxford: Oxford University Press.

Mosser, Kurt. 1993. 'Nietzsche, Kant and the Thing in Itself', *International Studies in Philosophy* 25.2: 67–77.

Müller, Max. 1869. *Essays*, vol. 2: *Beiträge zur vergleichenden Mythologie und Ethnologie*, trans. Felix Liebrecht and R. Fritzsche (3 vols, 1869–76), 1st edn. Leipzig: Engelmann. (From the English edition, *Chips from a German Workshop*, vol. 2: *Essays on Mythology, Traditions and Customs* (3 vols, 1867–70), 2nd edn. London: Longmans, Green & Co, 1867.)

Müller-Lauter, Wolfgang. 1995. 'Nietzsches Auflösung des Problems der Willensfreiheit', in Sigrid Bauschinger, Susan L. Cocalis, and Sara Lennox (eds), *Nietzsche heute: Die Rezeption seines Werkes nach 1968*. Stuttgart: Francke, 23–73.

Nehamas, Alexander. 1985. *Nietzsche: Life as Literature*. London: Harvard University Press.

Nietzsche, Friedrich. 1993. *Appunti filosofici (1867–1869). Omero e la filologia classica*, trans. Giuliano Campioni and Federico Gerratana. Milan: Adelphi.

O'Neill, Onora. 1989a. 'Consistency in Action', in *Constructions of Reason: Explorations of Kant's Practical Philosophy*. Cambridge: Cambridge University Press, 81–104.

O'Neill, Onora. 1989b. 'Universal Laws and Ends in Themselves', in *Constructions of Reason: Explorations of Kant's Practical Philosophy*. Cambridge: Cambridge University Press, 126–44.

O'Neill, Onora. 1996. 'Kant's Virtues', in Roger Crisp (ed.), *How Should One Live? Essays on the Virtues*. Oxford: Oxford University Press, 77–97.

O'Neill, Onora. 2002. 'Instituting Principles: Between Duty and Action', in Mark Timmons (ed.), *Kant's 'Metaphysics of Morals': Interpretative Essays*. Oxford: Oxford University Press, 331–47.

Orsucci, Andrea. 1997. 'Teichmüller, Nietzsche e la critica delle "mitologie scientifiche"', *Giornale critico della filosofia italiana* 17: 47–63.

Orsucci, Andrea. 2001. *La Genealogia della morale di Nietzsche. Introduzione alla lettura*. Rome: Carocci.

Owen, David. 1994. *Maturity and Modernity: Nietzsche, Weber, Foucault and the Ambivalence of Reason*. London: Routledge.

Owen, David. 1995. *Nietzsche, Politics and Modernity: A Critique of Liberal Reason*. London: Sage.

Owen, David. 1999. 'Nietzsche, Enlightenment and the Problem of Noble Ethics', in John Lippitt (ed.), *Nietzsche's Futures*. London: Macmillan, 3–29.

Owen, David. 2009. 'Autonomy, Self-Respect and Self-Love: Nietzsche on Ethical Agency', in Ken Gemes and Simon May (eds), *Nietzsche on Freedom and Autonomy*. Oxford: Oxford University Press, 197–221.

Rampley, Matthew. 2000. *Nietzsche, Aesthetics and Modernity*. Oxford: Oxford University Press.

Riccardi, Mattia. 2010. 'Nietzsche's Critique of Kant's Thing in Itself', *Nietzsche-Studien* 39: 333–51.

Richardson, John. 2009. 'Nietzsche's Freedoms', in Ken Gemes and Simon May (eds), *Nietzsche on Freedom and Autonomy*. Oxford: Oxford University Press, 127–49.

Ridley, Aaron. 1998. *Nietzsche's Conscience: Six Character Studies from the 'Genealogy'*. London: Cornell University Press.

Ridley, Aaron. 2009. 'Nietzsche's Intentions: What the Sovereign Individual Promises', in Ken Gemes and Simon May (eds.), *Nietzsche on Freedom and Autonomy*. Oxford: Oxford University Press, 181–95.

Romundt, Heinrich. 1882. *Antäus. Neuer Aufbau der Lehre Kants über Seele, Freiheit und Gott*. Leipzig: Veit.

Romundt, Heinrich. 1883. *Die Herstellung der Lehre Jesu durch Kant's Reform der Philosophie: Separat-Abdruck aus dem Deutschen Protestantenblatt*. Bremen: Roussell.

Romundt, Heinrich. 1885. *Grundlegung zur Reform der Philosophie: Vereinfachte und erweiterte Darstellung von Immanuel Kants Kritik der reinen Vernunft*. Berlin: Nicolaische.

Sánchez, Sergio. 1999. *El Problema del Conocimiento en la Filosofia del Joven Nietzsche. Los Postumos del Periodo 1867-73*. Córdoba: Editorial Universitas.

Sánchez, Sergio. 2000a. 'Logica, Verità, e Credenza. Alcune Considerazioni in Merito alla Relazione Nietzsche-Spir', in Maria Cristina Fornari (ed.), *La Trama del Testo. Su Alcune Letture di Nietzsche*. Lecce: Edizioni Milella, 249–82.

Sánchez, Sergio. 2000b. 'Linguaggio, Conoscenza, e Verità nella Filosofia del Giovane Nietzsche. I Frammenti Postumi del 1873 e le loro Fonti', *Annurario Filosofico* 16: 213–40.

Schopenhauer, Arthur. 1841. 'Über die Grundlage der Moral', in *Die Beiden Grundprobleme der Ethik*. Frankfurt: Hermann.

Schopenhauer, Arthur. 1844. *Die Welt als Wille und Vorstellung* (2 vols), 2nd edn. Leipzig: Brockhaus.

Schopenhauer, Arthur. 1851. *Parerga und Paralipomena: Kleine philosophische Schriften* (2 vols). Berlin: Hayn.

Schopenhauer, Arthur. 1873–4. *Sämtliche Werke* (7 vols). Leipzig: Brockhaus.

Simon, Josef. 2000. 'Moral bei Kant und Nietzsche', *Nietzsche-Studien* 29: 178–98.

Small, Robin. 2001. *Nietzsche in Context*. Aldershot: Ashgate.

Spir, Afrikan. 1869. *Forschung nach der Gewissheit in der Erkenntniss der Wirklichkeit*. Leipzig: Förster und Findel.

Spir, Afrikan. 1873/1877. *Denken und Wirklichkeit: Versuch einer Erneuerung der kritischen Philosophie* (2 vols), 1st edn/2nd edn. Leipzig: Findel.

Stack, George J. 1980. 'Nietzsche's Critique of Things-in-Themselves', *Diálogos* 15.36: 33–57.

Stack, George J. 1983. *Lange and Nietzsche*. Berlin: De Gruyter.

Stack, George J. 1987. 'Kant and Nietzsche's Analysis of Knowledge', *Diálogos* 22.49: 7–40.

Stack, George J. 1991. 'Kant, Lange and Nietzsche: Critique of Knowledge', in Keith Ansell-Pearson (ed.), *Nietzsche and Modern German Thought*. London: Routledge, 30–58.

Teichmüller, Gustav. 1867–73. *Aristotelischen Forschungen* (3 vols). Halle: Barthel.

Teichmüller, Gustav. 1879a. *Über die Reihenfolge der platonischen Dialoge*. Leipzig: Köhler.

Teichmüller, Gustav. 1879b. *Neue Studien zur Geschichte der Begriffe* (3 vols). Gotha: Perthes.

Teichmüller, Gustav. 1882. *Die wirkliche und die scheinbare Welt: Neue Grundlegung der Metaphysik*. Breslau: Koebner.

Thatcher, David S. 1982. 'Nietzsche, Bagehot and the Morality of Custom', *Victorian Newsletter* 62: 7–13.

Thatcher, David S. 1983. 'Nietzsche's Debt to Lubbock', *Journal of the History of Ideas* 44.2: 293–309.

Überweg, Friedrich. 1866–7. *Grundriß der Geschichte der Philosophie von Thales bis auf die Gegenwart* (3 vols). Berlin: Mittler.

Weiss, Steven D. 1993. 'Nietzsche and the Thing in Itself: Surviving Modern Kant Scholarship', *International Studies in Philosophy* 25.2: 79–84.

White, Richard. 1997. *Nietzsche and the Problem of Sovereignty*. Chicago: University of Illinois Press.

Williams, Garrath. 1999. 'Nietzsche's Response to Kant's Morality', *Philosophical Forum* 30.3: 201–16.

Wood, Allen W. 1999. *Kant's Ethical Thought*. Cambridge: Cambridge University Press.

CHAPTER 7

....

SCHOPENHAUER AS NIETZSCHE'S "GREAT TEACHER" AND "ANTIPODE"

....

IVAN SOLL

SCHOPENHAUER'S ANTIPODAL INFLUENCE
....

THE influence of one philosopher upon another is not to be measured *solely* by considering the *views* that the second figure *adopts* from the first, for philosophical influence is not manifested solely in areas of agreement. One should also consider the *issues* raised by the first that become important issues for the second. A philosopher's location and definition of issues and problems has often been at least as significant as his answers to them. Moreover, the influence that one philosopher exerts upon another is manifested in the disagreement as well as the agreement he provokes. In philosophy those ideas that provoke alternative views, even diametrically opposed views on the same issues, may be important influences on those who respond to them.

Of course, not all ideas with which we disagree, even all those with which we expressly and publicly disagree, influence us in any notable way, but some do. When we disagree, even strongly disagree, with figures we nevertheless respect and with views which we find at least plausible or even seductive on what we take to be issues of great import, we are arguably influenced by these figures and views, despite our disagreement with them, for they determine the focus and direction of our thinking. Views and figures we adhere to for a while and then come to reject, wholly or in part, may influence us, not just while we adhere to them, but also in our revolt against them. Nietzsche himself repeatedly makes the point that in philosophy, as in life in general, we are defined by the opponents we choose and thus it is important to choose worthy opponents. He repeatedly argues that we should be grateful to our most worthy and challenging opponents, for it is only against them and in competition with them that we can develop or that we can best develop our own ideas, powers, and selves.[1]

In Schopenhauer Nietzsche found not just the source of some of his most important ideas, but also one of his most worthy opponents. Nietzsche described Schopenhauer both as his "great teacher" and his "antipode."[2] Some have taken these two descriptions to be inconsistent and thus as representing two successive phases in Nietzsche's relation to Schopenhauer, an early one in which he was an adherent of Schopenhauer's philosophy and a subsequent one in which he came to reject Schopenhauer.[3] While it is undeniable that Nietzsche's view of Schopenhauer did evolve and that, as time passed, he did become more and more critical of Schopenhauer, this standard account does justice neither to the complexity of their relationship nor to Nietzsche's continued debt to Schopenhauer throughout his writings. It is crucial to realize that for Nietzsche, Schopenhauer was both his "great teacher" and his "antipode" simultaneously. For Nietzsche, given his agonistic view of learning and self-development, one's opponents are one's teachers and one's great opponents are one's great teachers.

To understand Nietzsche's relation to Schopenhauer we must understand how Nietzsche adopted some of his central ideas from Schopenhauer, how he further developed or adapted some of Schopenhauer's positions to suit his own purposes, and how Nietzsche developed some of his ideas as alternatives to Schopenhauerian positions. In pursuing this, we must consider not only what he explicitly says about Schopenhauer, but also those aspects of his philosophy that seem to be influenced by Schopenhauer even though he does not explicitly acknowledge the influence.[4] Schopenhauer was someone to whom and against whom Nietzsche often directed his arguments, often without mentioning him. He was thus one of Nietzsche's most constant partners in those only obscurely imagined ghostly dialogues that animate Nietzsche's solitary philosophizing, as they animate most solitary philosophizing.

In 1886, Nietzsche writes: "What was at stake was the *value* of morality and over this I had to come to terms almost exclusively with my great teacher Schopenhauer, to whom that book of mine [*Human, All Too Human*]…addressed itself as to a contemporary…" (*GM* Preface 5). Christopher Janaway has suggested that what Nietzsche here says about his treatment of morality in *Human, All Too Human* is also more broadly true of much of Nietzsche's philosophizing on a variety of topics in the period in which he wrote *Human All*

---

[1] In *Homer's Contest* (1873), Nietzsche argues that the idea that really challenging competition and hence worthy opponents were crucial for the development of human excellence was prominent in classical Greek culture, and he strongly suggests that it is true for all human beings in all cultures. In *The Gay Science*, he says "Better a wholehearted enmity than a friendship held together by glue" (*GS* Preface 14). Also see section 13 of the main text. Also see *Z* I: "On Friendship" and "On War and Warriors."

[2] Nietzsche refers to Schopenhauer as "my first and only educator, the great Arthur Schopenhauer," in the preface to *Human, All Too Human* II and as "*my great teacher*" in the preface to *On the Genealogy of Morals*, both written in 1886. He refers to Schopenhauer as his antipode in *Nietzsche contra Wagner*, in the section "Wir Antipoden" (We Antipodes), where he says of both Wagner and Schopenhauer: "they negate life, they slander it, say no to life, and in that they are my antipodes."

[3] See, for example, Kaufmann 1950.

[4] Nietzsche quite regularly did not acknowledge those who influenced his ideas or mention those against whom he was arguing. His failure to mention Schopenhauer when discussing topics on which he adopted Schopenhauer's ideas or on which he was arguing against Schopenhauer is to some extent similar to the way he treated other philosophers. However, it seems that he tended to do this more with Schopenhauer than with others for reasons outlined in note 7.

Too Human, Daybreak, and The Gay Science (1878–82).[5] I would like to suggest even more broadly and boldly that it is true of much of Nietzsche's philosophizing across his entire career. This passage epitomizes Nietzsche's entire antipodal, ongoing, and vital relation to Schopenhauer. Although Nietzsche's questioning of the *value* of morality is a radical departure from Schopenhauer, he still sees himself in developing this important theme in his work as addressing Schopenhauer as if he were "*a contemporary*".[6]

The Core Concern of Nietzsche's Philosophy: Schopenhauer as Nietzsche's Antipode

A clear conception of what constitutes the core concern of Nietzsche's philosophic project is not only important for understanding Nietzsche's work itself, but also crucial for assessing his debt to Schopenhauer. We cannot understand the nature and extent of Schopenhauer's importance for Nietzsche until we get clear about what Nietzsche took to be of the greatest importance in his own and anyone else's philosophical work. The fact that Nietzsche came to view Schopenhauer as his "antipode" reveals what lies at the heart of Nietzsche's own philosophical project, for it is only with respect to what constitutes the core of his project that he could define anyone else as his "antipode." To view someone as being one's antipode is not just to differ, even to differ radically, with that person on some issue or another; it is to view that person as one's opposite in what constitutes the very center of one's thought and being. We should not read Nietzsche's description of Schopenhauer as his antipode to indicate simply that he thought that there was so great a distance between them that Schopenhauer could not have had any real influence upon him.[7] Schopenhauer's relation to Nietzsche was indeed antipodal, and in an essential way, but that fact does not undermine the importance of their relationship. On the contrary, it shows rather how important that relation was. Nietzsche was able to view Schopenhauer as his antipode only because he saw him as having

---

[5] See Christopher Janaway's excellent essay, *Schopenhauer as Nietzsche's Educator*, in Janaway 1998.

[6] In this essay I shall not attempt to mention all of the areas in which Nietzsche's philosophy is a response to Schopenhauer's. Instead I shall trace of few of the major lines of influence in more detail.

[7] This simplistic and mistaken view of their antipodal relationship was encouraged by Nietzsche himself. After an initial period in which Nietzsche openly and consistently acknowledged his debt to Schopenhauer, he began to emphasize their differences and to neglect to mention Schopenhauer's influence where it existed. He seems to have embarked upon a campaign to distance himself, both publicly and in his own mind, from Schopenhauer, and to minimize and even deny the influence that Schopenhauer had exerted and continued to exert upon him. Nietzsche was probably motivated to do this by a combination of the following reasons: (1) Nietzsche was engaged in a long and difficult process of distancing himself from Richard Wagner, who was an avid admirer of Schopenhauer. Nietzsche tended to subject Schopenhauer to the same total rejection that was necessary to free himself from the domineering and oppressive influence of Wagner. (2) As time went on and Nietzsche did not receive the recognition that he believed he deserved, he began to call attention to his own groundbreaking originality more and more shrilly and acknowledge his debts to others less. (3) His conviction that Schopenhauer was his antipode on the core issue of his philosophy seemed to justify and call for unqualified rejections of him. I have traced the inaccurate and ungenerous nature of Nietzsche's comments regarding his debt to Schopenhauer and their misleading effect on some of the interpreters of Nietzsche in my essays "The Hopelessness of Hedonism and the Will to Power" (1986) and "Pessimism and the Tragic Sense of Life" (1988).

addressed the same central concerns as himself and as having taken diametrically opposed positions with respect to them. He also viewed him as being one of the most important and influential advocates of the view that Nietzsche wanted to oppose—not just an opponent but a worthy opponent.

In order to bring Nietzsche's antipodal relation to Schopenhauer into focus we must then locate that center of Nietzsche's philosophical project, the central issue in terms of which he could view Schopenhauer as his antipode. This, simply stated, is *the issue of whether life is worth living*. This is the issue that animates Nietzsche's entire philosophic project starting from his very first book, *The Birth of Tragedy* (1872). In that book Nietzsche approaches classical Greek culture—and by implication any culture—as being essentially defined by its struggle with what Nietzsche took to be the most fundamental problem confronting all human beings, namely, finding a way to tolerate and even to joyfully affirm and embrace life, despite the fact that it is essentially characterized by ineluctable suffering and frustration and does not seem to contain any obvious intrinsic meaningfulness or worth. In his prolonged struggle to find life tolerable and even desirable Nietzsche had to resist and oppose Schopenhauer's famous "*pessimism*," the view that life is essentially meaningless suffering and not worth living, and reject Schopenhauer's arguments for this view.

Schopenhauer's Influence on *The Birth of Tragedy*

While Nietzsche, who was a young professor of classics at the time he wrote *The Birth of Tragedy*, had found ample evidence in his study of classical Greek culture that the central concern of this culture was to come to terms with the suffering and meaninglessness of life, he had also found in his intensive study of Schopenhauer a powerful and influential modern voice articulating the same central concerns. It was the confluence of what Nietzsche took to be at the core of both Greek culture and Schopenhauer's philosophy that furnished a powerful impetus for his first book and the subsequent development of his philosophy.

Nietzsche acquired a copy of Schopenhauer's main work, *The World as Will and Representation*, in 1865, while he was a student in Leipzig, devoured it avidly, and became an enthusiastic admirer of Schopenhauer. Nietzsche's first book, published seven years later in 1872, seems to be greatly influenced by Schopenhauer in its central problematic, its language, and many of its fundamental ideas.

The problem of the value of life, given its inevitable suffering and lack of intrinsic meaningfulness, which leads Schopenhauer to espouse the pessimistic view that life is not worth living, becomes for Nietzsche the problem that gives impetus to the development of Greek art and culture and, by extension, to the development of all art and culture. To illustrate the centrality of this problem in Greek culture, Nietzsche cites the Greek myth of the wise satyr Silenus, who, when captured by King Midas and asked to reveal what is best for man, replies: "Oh wretched ephemeral race, children of chance and misfortune, why do you compel me to tell you what it would most expedient for you not to hear? What is best of all is utterly beyond your reach; not to be born, not to be, to be *nothing*. But the second best for you is—to die soon" (*BT* 3).[8] Nietzsche argues that this story exemplifies an important

---

[8] Nietzsche quotes this from Sophocles' *Oedipus at Colonnus*, lines 1224 ff.

aspect of Greek culture: "The Greek knew and felt the terror and horror of existence" (*BT* 3). This awareness comes to the fore, according to Nietzsche, notably in Greek tragedy, in which terrible and ineluctable fates are encountered by figures such as Oedipus, Orestes, Prometheus, and Antigone.

With all of this material concerning the "terror and horror of existence" to be found within Greek culture itself, what reason is there to think that Schopenhauer's pessimism played any significant role in shaping Nietzsche's views about the nature of Greek culture and the human condition in general? Could Schopenhauer have not represented for Nietzsche nothing more than a recent repetition of the already long established Greek view that in life suffering is inevitable?

There is ample evidence that Nietzsche had not only been deeply impressed by his reading of Schopenhauer's philosophy, but that his reading and his admiration had centered upon Schopenhauer's stark presentation of this problem and what Nietzsche, at least at first, took to be his courageous handling of it.[9] It would be unfruitful to speculate about which of these two sources of the idea that human existence is deeply and essentially problematic, that life may not be worth living, was more important for Nietzsche. They were both important in influencing the direction and focus of his overall philosophical project. The issue of which of them Nietzsche encountered first is of no great consequence. By the time Nietzsche began to write his first book, he was already well acquainted with and deeply influenced by both, and the two sources undoubtedly re-enforced each other.

Nevertheless, Schopenhauer's presentation of the existential problem arguably furnished a kind of support for Nietzsche's adoption of this problem as a central focus of his philosophy, which is not to be found in the Greek sources. First, the very fact that Schopenhauer was, roughly considered, almost a contemporary, and a prominent one, was significant. Schopenhauer's focus upon this problem and the great response that it had called forth provided Nietzsche with evidence that the problem was not historically or culturally limited, but of universal human concern and relevant to his own time.[10] Secondly, while Greek mythology and tragedy present the problem repeatedly and with great vivacity in unforgettable images and stories, they do not support it with anything like philosophical argument or analysis. Schopenhauer fills this gap by offering arguments for his pessimism, which in turn depend upon a philosophical theory of the essential nature of human beings, for which he also offers arguments.

In *The Birth of Tragedy*, Nietzsche does not explicitly use or cite Schopenhauer's arguments for the problematic nature of human existence and pessimism, but the language and concepts that he uses to analyze the various reactions to the difficulties of human existence in classical Greek culture show the unmistakable influence of Schopenhauer.[11]

---

[9] Nietzsche at first tended to see Schopenhauer as admirable, like the Greek tragedians, for openly confronting the essential suffering of human life and trying to figure out a way to embrace life nevertheless. But later he came to view Schopenhauer as having adopted, in response to his courageous confrontation with the ineluctable suffering of life, a negative attitude of rejection toward life—and thus as his antipode.

[10] Schopenhauer (1788–1860) had died only five years before Nietzsche encountered his work in 1865. Schopenhauer's work went ignored for most of his life, but from the publication of his *Parerga and Paralipomena* in 1850, his fame spread very quickly. By the time Nietzsche first read him, he was one of the most widely read philosophers in Europe. Nietzsche refers to Schopenhauer as "the most read German philosopher" in *D* 167.

[11] In this essay, for want of space, I shall follow Nietzsche example in *The Birth of Tragedy* and not present or evaluate Schopenhauer's main arguments for pessimism. These arguments appear in *The World as Will and Representation* (*WWR*) I: 37, 57, II: 46. But a detailed analysis of these arguments might

The Apollonian and Dionysian

Nietzsche's conceptions of the two fundamental and competing forces that, according to him, shaped Greek art and culture and, indeed, shape all art and culture, *the Apollonian* and *the Dionysian* are heavily indebted to Schopenhauer.

That Nietzsche presents them not just as phenomena peculiar to classical Greek culture, but as *universal human tendencies* and, moreover, as tendencies that address the fundamental problems of the suffering, insignificance, and intolerability of human existence, shows Schopenhauer's influence. Nietzsche begins the first section of the book with a claim about the usefulness of these categories in understanding not just Greek art, but all art: "We shall have gained much for the science of aesthetics, once we perceive...that the continuous development of art is bound up with the *Apollonian* and *Dionysian* duality." Contributions to "the science of aesthetics" clearly do not consist of insights limited to Greek culture, but of ideas about "the continuous development of art" in general. Similarly, when he talks of "*borrowing* these terms from the Greeks," he suggests that he is borrowing them to understand the art of other cultures as well.

The focus of *The Birth of Tragedy* wavers back and forth between a discussion of classical Greek culture and of art and culture in general. While Greek culture furnishes his immediate material, Nietzsche continually tries to mine it for more universal insights. This aspect of the book reflects a tension in Nietzsche between his need to prove himself as a young scholar of classical studies and his tendency to take positions of a more general psychological and philosophical nature.[12] This tendency toward general theorizing, which had to appear to other classicists inappropriate for the first scholarly work of a young colleague, was no doubt inspired to some extent by Schopenhauer. For the young Nietzsche, Schopenhauer was not just a philosopher whom he admired, but the paradigm of what a real philosopher, in contrast to the mere scholar, could and should be—a model which exerted a magnetic pull upon Nietzsche to become a philosopher himself.[13]

Nietzsche presents the driving impetus of what expresses itself as the Apollonian tendency in Greek culture to be a general human drive to create and enjoy "*beautiful illusions*," whose beauty and perfect "intelligibility" consist in an organic unity in which "there is nothing

be used to further explore Schopenhauer's influence upon Nietzsche, in that one could then see how many of Nietzsche's philosophical positions, developed throughout his works, seem to be addressed to specific aspects of these Schopenhauerian arguments, without mentioning Schopenhauer by name.

[12] The fact that one of the focuses of *The Birth of Tragedy* was professional—that Nietzsche wrote it, at least on one level of consciousness and concern—to demonstrate his competence as a classicist, may help to explain why in this work he does not explicitly cite or utilize Schopenhauer's *arguments* for the problematic nature of life and pessimism. In as much as Nietzsche's task as a classicist was to furnish an analysis of Greek culture, he was not obligated to furnish any arguments for the plausibility of this view. In retrospect, Nietzsche, who in time came to identify himself more clearly as a philosopher, expressed regret for the paucity of philosophical argumentation in this book, criticizing it as "disdainful of proof, mistrustful even of the propriety of proof" (*BT* "An Attempt at Self-Criticism" 3).

[13] In Schopenhauer Nietzsche had a model of a philosopher who, like himself after he retired from his university position in the late 1870s, was not a professor at a university. Schopenhauer had sharply distinguished real philosophers from professors of philosophy (see *WWR* I: xix, xxv–xxvii). Nietzsche adopts and further develops this Schopenhauerian distinction into a similar, also sharply drawn distinction between philosophers and scholars, particularly in Part I of *Beyond Good and Evil*, "On the Prejudices of the Philosophers."

unimportant and nothing superfluous" (*BT* 1).[14] The impetus for the creation of such *beautiful illusions* is the lack of such a perfect integration of parts, and thus the lack of beauty and perfect intelligibility, in the world of our everyday experience. He contrasts the "perfection" of these illusions with "the incompletely intelligible everyday world" (*BT* 1). We need such illusions of organic unity and thus of enhanced beauty and meaningfulness, according to Nietzsche, in order to "make life possible and worth living" (*BT* 1). This implies that the experience of life, as it is without any meliorating illusions, replete with its "horrors," "terrors," and suffering, and lacking any such redeeming unity, beauty, or intelligibility, is, as Schopenhauer had argued, intolerable.

Apollo as the God of Individuation

Nietzsche not only presents his notion of an Apollonian tendency as a response to the problem that was at the heart of Schopenhauer's philosophy, he develops it using distinctively Schopenhauerian ideas and language. Another essential trait of the organically unified illusions of the Apollonian is that they are characterized by clear demarcation and separation of their constituent parts, by what Nietzsche, clearly borrowing a term used by Schopenhauer, refers to as '*the principium individuationis*' (the principle of individuation)

Schopenhauer had accepted the central conclusions of the arguments that make up Kant's "Copernican Revolution in philosophy," namely, that in experiencing the world we do not just passively receive the data that the world presents to us, but that *we actively construct the world of our experience* by imposing structures upon any data we receive, and that we thus provide a unifying context in which all the data are brought into relation with each another.[15] Kant had argued that we impose these unifying structures upon our experience in order to organize and "synthesize" the chaotic mass or "manifold" of the myriad and unrelated individual data of experience into a unified experience of a world that is sufficiently coherent to be comprehensible and the foundation of our empirical knowledge of the world. Among these unifying structures Kant had listed space, time, and causality.[16] He had, moreover, argued that all of us always

[14] (1) The notion of a perfect organic unity actually requires not just the absence of superfluous parts, but also the presence of all required parts. Nietzsche's failure to mention this was probably just an oversight. (2) Note that in Nietzsche's conception of the Apollonian there is a confluence of what is "beautiful" and what is "intelligible." In the Apollonian organic unity in which every part has a part to play, there is *beauty*, because the parts form a perfectly balanced whole, and *intelligibility*, because the fact that every part has an essential function in the whole allows us to understand why it is there. This fusion of the notions of beauty and intelligibility mirrors a duality in the existential concerns which the Apollonian drive is supposed to address: to make the world tolerable we need to find it both beautiful and intelligible. In the Apollonian experience both needs are felicitously met.
[15] Kant develops this theory in *The Critique of Pure Reason*. I shall refer to this seminal idea of Kant's, which has been advocated subsequently by a wide range of thinkers in various fields as *the constructivist theory of experience* or simply as *constructivism*.
[16] Kant's complete list of these structures had included two "forms of pure intuition," space and time (which entail that we necessarily experience everything as existing or occurring at some location in space and in time), and twelve "pure categories of the understanding," among which were most notably causality (which entails that we necessarily experience every event as having a cause) and substance (which entails that we necessarily experience the world as made up of substances or things, which are somehow unified complexes of qualities and retain their identity through various processes of change). Schopenhauer, like many of Kant's early admirers and disciples, thought Kant's list of categories to be unnecessarily complex. So he reduced the necessary structures of experience to just three: space, time,

impose the same structures upon our experience, because only they are capable of successfully "synthesizing the manifold" of the overwhelmingly numerous and chaotic bits of information that we encounter into a coherent experience of a unified world.[17]

Indeed, Kant's argument for the thesis, that we *construct and impose these structures upon our experience* rather than simply *encounter them in our experience*, is actually based upon their *universal* and *necessary* presence in all of our experience. He claims that the space, time, and causality are not only present in all of the *experience we actually have had*, but that we cannot even imagine *any possible experience that we might have* without them. He argues that while their presence in all the experience we have had could be the result of their simply being universally present features of the world we encounter, this cannot explain how we can be certain they *would be present in any possible experience that we might have*. Since we cannot be sure of what we might encounter in our experience, we can only be sure that our experience of whatever we encounter will have these structures, if it is we who impose these structures upon anything we encounter.

Schopenhauer accepted Kant's major conclusion, that we construct our experience by imposing structures such as space, time, and causality upon whatever we encounter. However, he revised Kant's constructivist theory of experience in several significant and distinctive ways. Prominent among his revisions, was his pointing to a couple of universal and necessary features of our experience that Kant had not mentioned. First, he insisted upon the duality in all our experience between a subject, which experiences, and an object, which is experienced (*WWR* I: 1). Even with respect to one's experience of oneself, he argued that the self as the subject that knows is different from the self as the object that is known. Secondly, he argues that all of our experience is and has to be the experience of a world made up of a plurality of individual things, which we can distinguish even when we cannot distinguish them one from another qualitatively (*WWR* I: 23 and 25). The cogency of Schopenhauer's position can be illustrated by the example of seeing a group of beer bottles in a case. We easily see that there are twenty-four of them although we cannot perceive any difference among the appearance of the individual bottles. Our ability to see them as a plurality of individuals depends upon our somehow distinguishing them though they all look exactly alike to us. We can do this only because of their differing locations in the framework of space and time. Schopenhauer argues that we are able to experience the world as composed of pluralities of individuals only because we impose the structures of time and space upon our experience of it. Thus, he presents this feature of our experience as a direct consequence of the sort of construction of our experience Kant had mapped out, but as an important consequence that Kant had failed to mention, notice, or sufficiently appreciate. Schopenhauer repeatedly refers to this fundamental feature of our experience as "*the principium individuationis*."[18]

---

and causality. He also argued that these three formed an indissoluble whole, none of them being possible without the other two, and that they alone generated out of themselves the other fundamental structure of experience, substance (See *WWR* I: 1–5)

[17] On the constructivist views developed by Kant, Schopenhauer, and Nietzsche, we do not directly experience the chaotic manifold, which we, in some tricky sense, *encounter* or *confront* in the world, as a chaotic manifold. It first registers in our experience only in its constructed form, in which the manifold is unified and thus no longer just a manifold.

[18] For just some of the many references to the "*principium individuationis*" or "individuation" in Schopenhauer, see *WWR* I: 23, 25, 30, 43, 52, 54, 55. For references to the "*principium individuationis*" in Nietzsche's *BT*, see sections 1, 2, 4, 16, 21, and 22.

Nietzsche uses Schopenhauer's focus upon *individuation* to define the Apollonian. He says that the beautiful, complex, unified wholes of Apollonian art must be constituted by components that are clearly individuated one from another. He even refers to this fundamental feature of the Apollonian using Schopenhauer's term, *the principium individuationis*. He presents the clear individuation of constituent parts as an essential characteristic of all Apollonian illusions. Indeed, he takes it to be a defining characteristic of the Apollonian: "We might call Apollo himself the glorious divine image of the *principium individuationis...*" (*BT* 1).

He also relies upon the notion of individuation to define the entire pantheon of the Greek gods: "We should not be misled by the fact that Apollo stands side by side with the others as an individual deity, without any priority or rank. For the same impulse that embodied itself in Apollo gave birth to this entire Olympian world, and in this sense Apollo is its father" (*BT* 3). In what sense could Nietzsche possibly mean this? It is Zeus who is traditionally described as "the father of the gods" and Apollo is said to be his son. It is Apollo, precisely as the personification of individuation, who, in a metaphorical but clear sense, is the father of the entire pantheon of the Greek gods. It is the very fact that the Greek gods are pictured as "standing side by side," that is, as a plurality of clearly individuated individuals, that holds the clue to their Apollonian origins.[19]

As we have seen, Nietzsche presents us with two defining features of the Apollonian in art and culture: (1) it consists of wholes, which form organic unities in which there are no superfluous parts and which are therefore beautiful and intelligible; (2) these wholes are characterized by a clear individuation of their component parts. What, however, is the relation of these two requirements for the realization of the Apollonian in art? Are they separate but jointly necessary conditions for the Apollonian? Nietzsche never explicitly states what he takes their relation to be, but they do seem to be tied together in a manner that Nietzsche may have recognized but neglected to mention. The clear individuation of parts is arguably a necessary condition for the creation of organic unities. What characterizes organically unified wholes is not only that there are no superfluous and no missing parts, but that they are unities of distinguishable parts. If the unity is not experienced as a unity of clearly individuated parts, it cannot be experienced as an organic unity. Various pieces of fruit perfectly arranged in a bowl (in real life or in a still-life painting) may constitute a beautiful organic unity. But if the fruit is blended into a homogeneous mass, even if it has a beautiful color, it no longer presents us with an organically unified whole. Unity based upon homogeneity is not organic unity.[20]

In linking individuation with illusion Nietzsche draws upon the constructivist theory of experience discovered by Kant, but in the form developed by Schopenhauer.[21] Since,

[19] It might be argued that, in contrast to other polytheistic conceptions, the Olympian gods of the Greeks are notable for their well-defined individual identities. In some other polytheistic schemes, such as those found in Meso-America or India, there is a plurality of gods, but their identities sometimes merge and separate in ways that are hard to define or grasp. In contrast to the Greek conception, they could be considered to be pluralities of fuzzily defined individuals.

[20] Kant was probably moved by such considerations when he overstated the case and claimed that a single quality could not be beautiful. Clearly he was wrong; a single color or tone or texture can obviously be beautiful. But there is a certain aesthetic satisfaction to be derived from cohesive structures, which requires that these structures be composed of distinguishable parts. To recognize the organic unity of a structured whole one must be able to distinguish the parts that are united in that whole.

[21] There is evidence that Nietzsche was introduced to Kant's theory through his reading of Schopenhauer and continued to confront constructivism mostly in its Schopenhauerian rather than Kantian form. See Brobjer 2008.

according to Schopenhauer, individuation arises as a consequence of the spatio-temporal framework of experience and this framework is imposed upon experience by the experiencing subject, the individuality of particular things, like the spatio-temporal framework out of which it arises, is not a quality of the object of experience as it is "in-itself," apart from being experienced. Thus, it is, *in this sense*, illusory.[22]

Nietzsche became an adherent of the constructivist theory of experience principally through his reading of Schopenhauer's version of it and he remained an adherent of some form of constructivism throughout his philosophical writings. Nevertheless, just as Schopenhauer modified certain aspects of Kant's version of the constructivist theory, Nietzsche revised and further developed the Schopenhauerian version. To understand the extent and limits of his debt to Schopenhauer, we must understand which parts of Nietzsche's version of constructivism were directly derived from Schopenhauer, which represent further developments of Schopenhauerian positions, and which are clear deviations from them. We shall find that the way in which Nietzsche uses the notion of individuation and the constructivist theory of experience in his conception of the Apollonian reveals that he both he relied upon Schopenhauer's version of the theory and developed it in new directions.

What Motivates Us to Construct the World of our Experience: Three Views

First, Nietzsche's view of the motivation that leads us to construct our experience departs radically from the views of both Kant and Schopenhauer. Considering the negative consequence of our construction of experience, namely, our loss of the ability to know things as they really are in themselves, a question arises as to why we would want to do this. Kant had suggested that though the construction of our experience seems to entail certain cognitive limitations, we are nevertheless led to construct it by our cognitive interests and needs. Without the ordering and unifying structure created by our construction of experience, we would not be left with a knowledge of reality as it really is in itself, but only a chaotic awareness of a myriad of unrelated bits of sensory input, which would not constitute any sort of knowledge. In constantly constructing the world of our experience, we seem to cut ourselves off from the possibility of having metaphysical knowledge, that is, knowledge of

---

[22] One should distinguish this sort of "illusion," which may encourage errors only about the metaphysical status of certain aspects of our experience, from the sort that tend to lead to errors in our empirical beliefs about specific matters of fact in the world, such as that the stick half-submerged in water will continue to appear to be bent when removed from the water or that the apparently convergent railroad tracks really do come together up ahead. Unfortunately neither Schopenhauer nor Nietzsche clearly distinguishes between them. It important to keep this distinction in mind and to ask what sort of illusions Nietzsche is considering when he speaks about illusion, in order to understand and assess his claims that we do not object to the illusory nature of certain experiences. Many of the illusory experiences that Nietzsche has in mind, when he argues that we do not mind the illusory character of experience, do not tend to lead to specific mistaken empirical judgments, but only to mistaken meta-empirical judgments about the nature of our empirical experience in general.

reality as it is, without any changes and distortions incurred in the process of experience. We are motivated to do this, Kant seems to suggest, in order to create the only sort of experience that can yield an empirical knowledge of the world. Thus, we sacrifice only the empty dream of metaphysical knowledge of things as they are in themselves, in order to obtain an empirical knowledge of the world as we experience it, which is, after all, the only sort of knowledge we can have and the only sort that is needed to make science possible. We sacrifice the hollow hope of an ideal but unobtainable and impossible knowledge to achieve a more limited, but possible and crucial kind of knowledge. So it turns out to be not much of a sacrifice at all.

Schopenhauer, while accepting Kant's conclusion, that the construction of our experience cuts us off from the experience of things as they are in themselves, significantly modifies Kant's account of the human motivation for engaging in such a construction. Kant analyzes the problem and presents his solution in exclusively cognitive terms: the problem for him is to explain the apparently willing sacrifice of a kind of knowledge; his answer is to show that there are more than adequate cognitive compensations for this sacrifice and that the apparent sacrifice did not really amount to much, if any, real cognitive loss. The only human interests to which Kant appeals in stating and solving the problem are cognitive ones. There is no consideration of any other, noncognitive human interests that might have overridden or intersected with our cognitive concerns in this matter, and which might have supplied the impulse to construct our experience, even though this entailed cutting ourselves off from the experience and knowledge of things as they are in themselves. Kant develops his constructivist theory of human experience within an exclusively cognitive context.

Schopenhauer, on the contrary, held that human beings (and indeed all beings) are beings which are most essentially constituted by their will, and whose most fundamental activity is to will, not to know. He naturally tended to view our cognitive concerns and activities as ultimately serving the requirements and concerns of the will.[23] Instead of presenting our construction of experience as motivated by the necessity to create a world coherent enough to know, he presents it as motivated by the need to create a world in which we can exercise our will. In making his case, the notion of individuation plays a central role. What the will requires is not primarily a world composed of the sorts of objects that can be known, but a world which is composed of the sorts of objects that can constitute objectives that one can will (that is, desire or want). Schopenhauer argues that the will requires objectives made up of individual things—that the will needs to focus upon a goal that is an individual or involves individuals in order to will at all. On Schopenhauer's view, we construct the world of our experience, using the structures of space, time, and causality, primarily in order to produce individuated objects that can constitute the objectives of our desires.[24] On Kant's view we construct the world to fulfill what he calls the "transcendental" requirements for any possible knowledge of the world; on Schopenhauer's view, to use Kantian terminology, we do it to fulfill the "transcendental" requirements for any possible willing.

This Schopenhauerian modification of Kant's constructivism is important, for it reconsidered and reworked an aspect of Kant's theory that had tended not to receive much attention. Kant's limitation of the scope and quality of human knowledge, his denial of the possibility

---

[23] "Thus, originally and by its nature, knowledge is completely the servant of the will" (*WWR* I: 33).

[24] He claims that objects become "interesting to the individual, in other words ha[ve] a relation to the will" only through "their many different connexions in space, time and causality...in a word, *as particular things*" (*WWR* I: 33, my emphasis).

of metaphysical knowledge of things as they are "in themselves," had become the mesmerizing focus of philosophical inquiry in Germany in the period following the publication of his *Critique of Pure Reason* (1781). Philosophers had devoted their major energies to coming to terms with this limitation in the scope of our cognitive aspirations either by attempting to deny it in some way or to find exceptions to it. Many tried to work out ways of circumventing the limitation: some by recourse to a special "intellectual intuition" that was not warped by the normal structures we impose upon experience; others by recourse to a special "dialectical" method or logic that transcended the distortions and limitations of normal thought; still others (like Schopenhauer) through the putatively nondistorted (or relatively nondistorted) view we have in the uniquely privileged case of our awareness of ourselves. Thus, Schopenhauer's revision of Kant's account of the motivation for our construction of experience signaled a significant change of focus, and one which Nietzsche adopted, though with different conclusions.

In explaining the construction of consciousness as a response to the requirements of willing rather than knowing, Schopenhauer rejected the view that our consciousness primarily serves the ends of cognition, namely, the acquisition of truth and knowledge, and also the view that our cognitive interests are autonomous and irreducible, that is, not reducible to being just the means or instruments of noncognitive interests. While Kant had not explicitly argued that our cognitive interests were autonomous and irreducible, his analysis of the structuring of human consciousness solely in terms of cognitive concerns had implicitly suggested that. Schopenhauer's alternative analysis of the construction of consciousness rejects the primacy and autonomy of cognition as a human concern. Thus it provides a model of an explanation of the structure of consciousness—and thus of human cognition—in noncognitive terms.[25]

It is a model that Nietzsche follows in developing his notion of the Apollonian in *The Birth of Tragedy* and throughout his philosophy as a whole, but with certain crucial changes. Nietzsche, following Schopenhauer's lead, presents the structuring of experience that creates the Apollonian unities, which appear in certain works of art and in our dreams, as emerging from noncognitive concerns. Departing from Schopenhauer, however, he does not present this structuring as motivated by the transcendental needs of the will to have the sorts of objects that can serve as its objectives. He attributes the structuring rather to what might be considered an *aesthetic need* for experiences of beauty, which in turn serves a deeper *existential need* to make and our lives seem tolerable and even attractive.[26]

---

[25] David Hume had already famously maintained that "reason is and ought only to be the slave of the passions." Schopenhauer, who (along with Kant and Nietzsche) was an ardent admirer of Hume, was thus taking a position that Hume had already taken. But Schopenhauer developed Hume's rather briefly stated *prise de position* in ways that Hume had not. Schopenhauer applied it to the issue of the impetus for our active structuring of our experience, which does not arise as an issue until Kant had argued for the existence of this structuring.

[26] Since *the Apollonian* is a drive toward "intelligibility" as well as beauty, one might think that it is still governed by cognitive concerns. The desire for this sort of *intelligibility* is, however, not really cognitive in the usual sense, in that it is not a desire for knowledge of any sort or truth, but rather for a sense of the significance of every part of a complex, ordered whole. This sense of intelligibility is compatible, according to Nietzsche, with the awareness that we have constructed the order of the whole and thus the significance of its parts, and that they are in this sense "illusions." See note 22.

Nietzsche's theory of the Apollonian may at first not seem to be an alternative to Schopenhauer's theory of experience. While Schopenhauer offers an account of the genesis of the spatial-temporal-causal structure present in all of our everyday experience, Nietzsche's theory of the Apollonian, narrowly viewed, seems at first to be an account of the genesis of the organic unity that is present only in our experience of certain works of art and in our dreams, not in our everyday experience. But Nietzsche's theory of the Apollonian, considered in a somewhat broader context, clearly emerges from and also contributes to a more general theory of experience, one which combines elements adopted from Schopenhauer along with significant departures from Schopenhauer's views.

The individuation, which Nietzsche presents as the central precondition of the possibility of organic unity and thus of the Apollonian experience of beauty, is already a fundamental feature of everyday experience and, as Schopenhauer had cogently argued, a direct and necessary consequence of the spatio-temporal ordering of all experience. Thus, the structuring of our normal experience of the world, as presented by Schopenhauer, furnishes the *necessary preconditions* of the Apollonian creation of organic unity.

The unifying tendency of the Apollonian was most likely viewed by Nietzsche as an extension of the unifying forces and tendencies already present in our structuring of everyday experience. Nietzsche probably considered our construction of everyday experience to be the initial phase of the Apollonian drive toward an experience of redemptive unity.

If one believes, as Nietzsche did, that the deepest concern of every human being is to be able to experience one's life as beautiful, meaningful and thus tolerable and even desirable, and this depends, in turn, upon our being able to experience it as unified, then it is natural to view the construction of all of our experience, including our everyday experience, as motivated by the same desire. Moreover, it would be natural and easy for him to view it in this way, since all of the structures in question do seem to unify our experience. Space and time put all things and events into a single spatio-temporal framework, in which each of them has a position in relation to all the others. The notion of causality, which connects all the events in our experience in chains of cause and effect, appears to be a sort of glue that holds the world of our experience together. The notion of substance unites myriads of individual sensations together in the larger unities of physical things and allows us to see various sequences of flux as the change in objects that persevere over time. Thus, Nietzsche probably saw the impetus to an Apollonian organic unity in art and dreams to be the continuation of a drive to unify our experience that is already present in the construction of our everyday experience. Since he tends to see the final phase of this tendency to construct a unity in our experience as being driven by aesthetic and existential concerns, he probably saw the initial phase also as being driven by the same concerns.[27]

---

[27] For a discussion of the problem of the motivation of the construction of reality in Kant, Schopenhauer, and Nietzsche and an argument for Nietzsche's view that the construction of our everyday experience is continuous with our construction of the Apollonian organic unities in dreams and works of art, see my essay "Nietzsche on the Illusions of Everyday Life" in Schacht 2000.

Dionysus as the God of the transcendence of Individuation

Nietzsche's conception of the *Dionysian* as the basic drive which exists in opposition to the Apollonian is also heavily influenced by Schopenhauerian ideas.[28] In developing the notion of the *Dionysian* in *The Birth of Tragedy* Nietzsche uses Schopenhauer's idea that individuation is a fundamental though illusory feature of our experience, to interpret the phenomenon of the Dionysian cults, which were such a significant presence in the Greek world. Nietzsche locates the central aim and impetus of the Dionysian drive in a desire to achieve a state of consciousness in which all individuation is transcended. During the Dionysian rites, according to Nietzsche, the participants liberate themselves from the illusion that they are individuals separate from other people and from nature in general, an illusion which is imbedded in the very heart and structure of our everyday experience. Nietzsche conceives of Dionysus as the god of the transcendence of individuation in direct contrast to Apollo, the god of individuation. The Dionysian state, according to Nietzsche, is one in which we become conscious of the fundamental unity of all reality. It is a state in which we not only understand that the individuation and plurality that characterizes the world of our everyday experience is illusory, but in which we actually manage to tear away the "veil of maya" that usually covers and distorts our experience, and directly experience the "primordial unity," which is the true nature of the world. In his conception of the *Dionysian* Nietzsche draws directly on this conception of reality and some of this terminology is taken directly from Schopenhauer.[29]

Because Nietzsche presents the Dionysian consciousness as revealing the true nature of reality, which is hidden from us in normal experience, it is tempting to infer that he believes the Dionysian drive to attain this state is motivated by the prospect of having knowledge of things as they really are "in-themselves." However, Nietzsche actually proposes that it is not cognitive interests that motivate the Dionysian drive, but rather what might be described as *existential concerns*. This is consistent with his general view that cognitive concerns are never our ultimate concerns. The attraction of the Dionysian state, according to Nietzsche, is not its overcoming of illusion per se, but of the *alienation* that we necessarily experience in an individuated world, as a result of the separation of our selves from other people and nature: "Under the charm of the Dionysian not only is the union between man and man reaffirmed, but nature which has become alienated, hostile, or subjugated, celebrates once more her reconciliation with her lost son, man" (*BT* 1).

Nietzsche's treatment of the Dionysian drive, like his treatment of the Apollonian, utilizes Schopenhauerian metaphysical and epistemological ideas, but he uses them to construct accounts of human phenomena which do not appeal to any notion of a desire for knowledge or truth in explaining what motivates them. In doing this he both follows and surpasses Schopenhauer. When Schopenhauer had defended the view that human cognition

[28] Here I am analyzing only the notion of the Dionysian that Nietzsche develops in *The Birth of Tragedy*. Later he tends to use the notion of the Dionysian in a quite different way, namely, to represent his ideal of the affirmation of life despite a clear acceptance of its suffering and horrors.

[29] Schopenhauer had used the Indian notion of the "veil of Maya" to represent the illusory character of the world we experience repeatedly in *WWR*; Nietzsche uses it in sections 1, 2, and 18 of *BT*. The term "primordial unity" (see *BT* 4–6) is Nietzsche's, but the idea that it is the true nature of the world is taken from Schopenhauer.

ultimately serves the will by creating the necessary conditions for human action, he seems to have had in mind primarily normal, empirical cognition. He had argued that the fundamental spatial-temporal-causal structure of this sort of consciousness and the individuation of particulars that it produced was constructed primarily in order to serve the will. He also argued that this structure, because we impose it upon our experience, is illusory. Nietzsche accepts Schopenhauer's ideas that the world of our everyday experience is (1) *constructed,* (2) *constructed to serve interests that are ultimately not cognitive,* and (3) *illusory.* However, Nietzsche departs from Schopenhauer not only, as I have already argued, in his view of what these non-cognitive interests are, but also in his attitude toward the illusory character of our experience.

Schopenhauer, while accepting Kant's claim that the very structure our everyday experience is illusory, remains pretty much within the mainstream of the philosophical reaction to Kant's limitation of our knowledge. Like several other philosophers of the period, he accepts the illusory character of our everyday experience and the limitation of knowledge that is its consequence, but claims that one can circumvent these illusions and limitations in special sorts of experience. Schopenhauer argues that the illusions of our everyday empirical experience can be overcome and consequently an undistorted metaphysical knowledge of reality can be found in (1) one's experience of one's self and (2) one's aesthetic experience.

He claims that our experience of ourselves "as will" is different "*toto genere*" (in every way) from our experience of the rest of the world, including our experience of other aspects of ourselves, such as our bodies. While he is extremely vague about the justification for this dramatic and startling claim, he probably bases this claim on two considerations: first, in experiencing ourselves as will, that is, as beings who make decisions, who select goals and try to realize them, we experience ourselves as freely making these decisions and thus not as subject to the causal determinism that otherwise is a universal feature of the world we experience; second, that the will, not being a physical object, does not exist in space.[30]

If one believed (1) that our experience of ourselves differs in the basic ways just mentioned from our normal experience of other things as they appear to us, and also (2) that there are only two ways to experience things, either as they normally appear to us or as they are "in-themselves," then one might easily conclude, as Schopenhauer did, that in experiencing ourselves as will, we must be experiencing ourselves as we really are "in-ourselves." Since he holds that space, time, and individuation belong to the basic structure of the experience of things as they appear to us, he concludes that they do not apply to the realm of the will, and thus that there cannot be a plurality of individual wills, but only a single unindividuated world will in which all human beings are united.[31]

[30] (a) These two differences, while quite significant, would, even if they proved to hold, still not justify his claim that one's experience of oneself is different from one's experience of other people and things in every way. To show that one's experience of oneself is different from one's experience of normal other objects in the world in some ways is not to show it is different in every way. But it is not our task here to evaluate this claim. (b) In the second volume of *World as Will and Representation* (*WWR* II: 17), Schopenhauer retreats from this extreme view, but only very slightly, admitting only that we experience our own wills in time.

[31] Schopenhauer's thesis, that there can be only one will, is not at all based upon any introspective evidence, but is rather an inference based upon the conclusion that, as the reality of things in themselves, it cannot share the structures of the phenomenal world. He seems to assume uncritically that there are only two ways of experiencing anything, *as it appears* and *as it is*. This leads to the implausible idea that if we experience something that lacks some of the usual structures of appearance, it must lack all of them. His thinking about the possible ways in which we can experience things is much too limited and binary.

In *The Birth of Tragedy*, Nietzsche uses Schopenhauer's view that despite the appearance of plurality of things in our empirical experience, we are really all united with each other and with nature in a single will, to describe the state achieved in the orgiastic rites of the Dionysian cults. Again following Schopenhauer, he describes this will as the reality that is veiled and distorted in our everyday experience. But the one-world will's status as the undistorted metaphysical reality, while adopted from Schopenhauer, is not used to explain the attraction of the cult that leads to our realizing and embracing one's participation in it. The satisfaction of embracing this truth does not lie for Nietzsche in its truth. This is in conformity with Nietzsche's general position, that the satisfaction connected with embracing any truth never lies in the fact of its truth per se.

This general position furnishes the foundation for Nietzsche's claim that the redemptive satisfaction of the Apollonian state is not in the least undermined by the fact that it is still more illusory than the everyday experience of the world that it redeems, nor even by our realization that it is more illusory. Nietzsche's treatment of both the Apollonian and the Dionysian reflects his broader rejection of the fundamental philosophic attitude of generally valuing veridical experience above illusory experience, which had been assumed unquestioningly and unreflectively by most philosophers. Moreover, Nietzsche also rejects the corresponding psychological thesis, that we in fact always, or at least generally, value fact over fiction, truth over lies, and veridical over illusory experience. He argues that our desire for the organically unified experiences offered by Apollonian art and dreams and the satisfactions they provide are in no way diminished by our awareness that these experiences are illusory. Similarly, he holds that the attraction of the Dionysian state of consciousness is not constituted by any metaphysical truth that it may reveal.

Nietzsche's rejection of the traditional view, that illusory experience is inferior to veridical experience, is clearly expressed in his treatment of dreams. With respect to "the beautiful illusion of the dream worlds, in the creation of which every man is an artist" and which is "the prerequisite of all plastic art, and...of an important part of poetry too," he claims that "even when this dream reality is most intense, we still have, glimmering through it, the sensation that it is *mere appearance*... " (*BT* 1). Our usual reaction to this realization is, according to Nietzsche, is to say to ourselves, "It is a dream! I will dream on!" He claims that despite the realization that dreams are illusions, "our innermost being [nevertheless] experiences dreams with profound delight..." (*BT* 1). In these comments, Nietzsche obliquely addresses the traditional problem concerning dreams put forward by Descartes in his *Meditations*, which is: how do I know that any of my experiences of the world is not a dream and thus just an illusion? Nietzsche simply rejects Descartes' premise that while we are dreaming, we are unaware that we are dreaming. More importantly, he rejects the fundamental assumption which constitutes the context of Descartes' problem—that, since it is always in our interest to avoid being duped by illusion, we should distance ourselves as much as possible from reliance upon those sorts of experience that are illusory and thus misleading. This negative attitude toward illusion is part of the basis of the philosophical "rationalism" of the early modern period, which rejects reliance upon the evidence of the senses because it is vulnerable to illusion. Nietzsche is here arguing that, on the contrary, certain illusory experiences not only delight us, but are necessary for our survival and flourishing, in that only they allow us to tolerate and affirm our lives. A few sections later Nietzsche says: "If we conceive of our empirical existence, and that of the world in general, as a continuously manifested representation of the primal unity, we shall have to look upon the dream as a *mere appearance of a mere appearance,* hence as a still higher appeasement of the primordial desire for mere appearance" (*BT* 4).

Nietzsche is here clearly considering a view that he has woven together from Schopenhauer's doctrine of the primal unity of reality and Plato's doctrine of the forms, along with Plato's rejection of the value of art on metaphysical and epistemological grounds, which depends upon his theory of the forms. Plato rejects art as a mere imitation of an imitation (in Book X of *The Republic*). He uses the example of a painting of a bed, which is for him the copy of a bed which is a physical object, which in turn is a copy of the "form," "idea," or prototype of a bed. He argues the painting is thus "at two removes from reality," and consequently something that exists at a lower level of reality (and correspondingly furnishes a lower level of truth and knowledge) than either the form of the bed or its concrete exemplification, the real physical bed. Nietzsche is able to totally reject this Platonic view by shifting away from Plato's epistemological and metaphysical criteria for the value of an experience. He provocatively praises the dream and, by implication, all works of art, as supplying higher form of satisfaction for "the primordial desire for mere appearance" and thus for illusion. Despite the provocative and somewhat misleading formulation, Nietzsche does not mean that we have a desire for illusion per se, that is, for being deceived per se, but for the experience of beautiful and intelligible organic unities, which, given that the world is the way it is, happens to be found only in illusory constructions. Nietzsche's position, less provocatively put, is that in the pursuit and enjoyment of such Apollonian unities, we are *indifferent* to the question of whether they are illusory or not. Our most primordial desire, which is for satisfying experiences, is not limited to a desire for experiences that are veridical. Consequently, the value of experiences does not depend upon whether they are veridical or illusory.

Although Schopenhauer rejects the notion that our cognitive interests are autonomous and irreducible, he never rejects the value of truth and knowledge as radically as Nietzsche. Schopenhauer continues to treat them, like most philosophers, with an unquestioning assumption of their value. Even if he views all truth and knowledge as ultimately serving the will and action, he continues to treat them as if they were valuable as means to these ends. Nietzsche, following Schopenhauer's example of questioning and rejecting the prevalent view that truth and knowledge are valuable as ends in themselves, was able to go on to question and reject not just their intrinsic value, but the notion that they were nevertheless always valuable—if only as means to more important ends. Schopenhauer can be seen as opening up a process of critically questioning the usually unexamined value of truth and knowledge in human life, a process which Nietzsche was able to pursue with even more radical questions and to even more radical conclusions.[32]

---

[32] Nietzsche saw his questioning of the usually unquestioned value of the truth as one of his most important and original contributions. He begins the body of *Beyond Good and Evil*: "The will to truth which will still tempt us to many a venture, that truthfulness with which all philosophers so far have spoken with respect—what questions this truth has not laid before us! What strange, wicked, questionable questions! *What* in us wants 'truth'?... We asked about the value of this will. Suppose we want truth: why not rather untruth? and uncertainty? even ignorance?...and though it scarcely seems credible, it finally almost seems as if the problem had never been put so far" (*BGE* 1).

SCHOPENHAUER'S ONE-WORLD WILL AND NIETZSCHE'S WILL TO POWER

A striking point of similarity between the philosophies of Schopenhauer and Nietzsche is the prominent role played in each by the notion of *the will*. For Schopenhauer, the will constitutes the true nature of our mental life and of our very being. He argues that all other mental activities serve the will and can be seen as agents of the will. And he holds that all human beings, and indeed all other beings as well, are in their essential being just varying forms of the will—that "the world as will" is the world as it really is "in-itself."[33] One of the central motifs of Nietzsche's work is the *psychological theory* that a "*will to power*" is the basic motivation of all human behavior. He also explores, though perhaps more tentatively, the *cosmological* or *metaphysical hypothesis* that this will to power also constitutes the true inner nature of all being.

Some have argued that despite the superficial similarity that some sort of will plays a central role in both of their explanations of human beings and the world at large, their theories have little in common.[34] Others have simply treated Nietzsche's theory of the will to power without much discussion of Schopenhauer's influence. One's assessment of how much Schopenhauer's theory of the will influenced Nietzsche will obviously depend upon how much one thinks these theories have in common. And how much one thinks them to have in common will depend, in turn, upon one's view of the two aspects of Nietzsche's theory of the will to power, the psychological and the cosmological, and the relation between them. For it is the cosmological rather than the psychological aspect of Nietzsche's theory of the will to power which seems more clearly to be derived from Schopenhauer.

THE DUALITY OF NIETZSCHE'S THEORY OF THE WILL TO POWER: THE PSYCHOLOGICAL AND COSMOLOGICAL ASPECTS

There are basically two ways to approach the dual aspects of Nietzsche's will to power: one can take either the cosmological or the psychological aspect to be the more fundamental one. There has been a tendency to assume, usually without any argument or analysis, that the cosmological or metaphysical aspect of the theory—the thesis that the will to power constitutes the deepest and truest nature of absolutely everything in the world—is obviously the more fundamental thesis.[35] First, it has seemed more basic because of its greater scope or generality. If the cosmological thesis of the will to power is true, then the psychological

---

[33] See Book 2 of *WWR* I: "The World as Will, First Aspect."
[34] For example, Kaufmann 1950: 206–7.
[35] Examples of this approach are to be found in Martin Heidegger's *Nietzsche* and Richardson 1996.

thesis of the will to power seems to follow from it as just one of its more localized and limited consequences. If everything really is the will to power, then so are human beings—and of course their behavior will be principally motivated by what they essentially are. Secondly, it seems more basic because it tells us how things really are as opposed to the way things just seem to be, because it offers (or at least claims to offer) metaphysical rather than just empirical truth. This metaphysical thesis has tended to draw more than its fair share of attention among philosophers, who are usually more interested in pursuing metaphysical and epistemological issues than in discussions of psychological motivation. Some of them seem to hold the view that metaphysical issues are obviously deeper than psychological ones and should take precedence over them, and they assume that Nietzsche shares this view.

Despite these considerations, there are reasons to believe that in Nietzsche's philosophy the psychological aspect of the theory of the will to power is more fundamental than his extension of it into a theory of the true nature of everything in the world: (1) The very fact that the psychological thesis is just one local consequence of the more general cosmological theory also means that while the truth of the general thesis depends upon the truth of the psychological thesis, *the truth or plausibility of the psychological thesis does not depend upon the truth or plausibility of the general thesis.* (2) Nietzsche seems to have first developed the notion of will to power as a theory of the basic motivation of human behavior and only subsequently attempted to extend it to the nonhuman and nonorganic realms. (3) Nietzsche devotes vastly much more time and care in developing his psychological thesis of the will to power and arguing for it than he does in presenting his cosmological extension of this hypothesis. He advances the psychological thesis that the will to power is the ultimate motivation of all human behavior only after trying to show that many types of behavior can be better explained in terms of a will to power than in other ways. (4) The very notion of a will to power is originally drawn from the discourse of human behavior; its application outside that context seems problematic and possibly only a misleading metaphorical extension of its proper use.

Whether one considers the cosmological aspect of the will to power to be the foundation of the psychological thesis or merely a tentative extension of the psychological thesis, it is clear that Nietzsche considered it carefully and did not reject it out of hand. Because of Nietzsche's often expressed rejection of metaphysics, his proposal of such an apparently metaphysical thesis seems inconsistent and puzzling, and it has occasioned a great deal of commentary. Attempts to resolve this problem by arguing that he really did not propose it or that he clearly rejected it after considering or accepting it for a brief period seem forced and unconvincing. Even if one considers the psychological thesis of the will to power to be the foundation of his theory and the metaphysical thesis to be only a tentative and not fully endorsed experimental extension of it, Nietzsche clearly does repeatedly endorse, or at least seriously consider endorsing, the metaphysical-cosmological thesis of the will to power.

Both this thesis and the way that Nietzsche argues for it are clearly derived from Schopenhauer. Schopenhauer, having contrasted the experience one has of oneself as a will, that is, of oneself as creature who wills, who desires, who sets and attempts to achieve goals, to the empirical experience one has of oneself as a body in space and time and caught up in a web of causal relations with other such bodies, had proceeded to argue that this will is the true nature of the self as it is in itself. He then extended this metaphysics of the will not only to all other human beings and to all forms of life, but even to inanimate things. This extension does not, and cannot, depend upon one's experience of the will of others, for one cannot directly experience the wills of other people or other nonhuman beings. Nevertheless, Schopenhauer argues that it would be unreasonable for anyone to consider oneself to be *metaphysically unique*, that is, the only thing that has a real nature or being in-itself as well as an appearance. We must assume, he maintains, that other things are like us, at least in having a true nature that cannot be directly experienced by others, in addition to their nature as it appears to others. He argues that the only way we have to conceive of the inner nature of other things is by drawing upon the only experience we have of an inner nature, which is our own experience of ourselves as will. Thus we must, he argues, conceive of the true, inner nature of all things to be some form of the will. Schopenhauer is well aware that his position entails extending the notion of the will far past its normal domain of use, and that the will as it exists in some of the nonhuman realms must be conceived as existing without some of the basic characteristics of the human will, such as consciousness or the ability to deliberate among alternative courses of action.

Given the rather unusual and counterintuitive nature of this cosmological thesis, it is fairly clear that when it appears in Nietzsche's work, Schopenhauer is its source. Though it may be difficult to determine exactly how robustly or consistently Nietzsche advocated the thesis that the will is the true being of everything in the world, he certainly considered it seriously and seems to have supported it to some degree. The fact that he even considered it seriously for adoption shows that he was ruminating upon Schopenhauer's views as he developed his own theory of the will. And even if it turns out that he was less than wholehearted in his extension of the normal notion of the will to a notion of it as the fundamental nature of all being, he did unreservedly follow Schopenhauer in moving from the common notion of the will as just one part, aspect, or function of the human mind to a conception of the will as the central and dominant function of the human mind. It is this Schopenhauerian notion of the will as the primary function of the mind that underlies Nietzsche's psychological theory of the will to power as the deep motivation of all human behavior. But in this as in other matters, Nietzsche takes an idea from Schopenhauer and adapts it to his own purposes.

Nietzsche as Psychologist

One obvious way in which Nietzsche seems to substantially transform Schopenhauer's theory of the will is to furnish it with an ultimate goal: Schopenhauer tends to define the will as being essentially a striving after some goal or another; Nietzsche on the contrary defines the will as being essentially *a will to power*, that is, in terms of what he takes to be its essential and ultimate end. Schopenhauer had not devoted much time or attention to the question of what the ultimate end of willing might be, because he believed that the will has no *ultimate goal or goals*, but is rather a blind striving "without aim or end": "In fact, absence of all aim, of all limits, belongs to the essential nature of the will itself" (*WWR* I: 29, 164). Such claims may seem to be inconsistent with his thesis that every act of will must have an objective or goal, but they are not. Schopenhauer holds that every act of the will must have an objective or goal, but denies that these proximate goals are ever final goals or ends, in the sense that achieving them can never truly satisfy the will and allow it to rest: "Every individual act has a purpose or end; willing as a whole has no end in view" (*WWR* I: 29, 165). Schopenhauer's transcendental requirement for the possibility of willing, that each act of will must be directed toward some end, entails only that it be directed toward *some end or another*. Even his requirement, that this end must be composed of particular (that is, individual) things, entails only that the end be composed of *particular things of one sort or another*. All of this suggests that the will needs an immediate goal to focus upon in order to will at all, but that it is a matter of complete indifference as to what that goal happens to be. Moreover, accordng to Schopenhauer, the will cannot have an ultimate end or real and lasting satisfaction, because the very nature of the will as a dynamic striving forces it to immediately go on to new striving when it achieves any of its proximate goals. Nevertheless, Schopenhauer occasionally does propose that all willing has one goal, namely, *life*. "What the will wills is always life, just because this is nothing but the presentation of that willing for the representation, it is immaterial and a mere pleonasm if, instead of simply saying 'the will,' we say the will-to-live" (*WWR* I: 54).

Nietzsche responds critically to these aspects of Schopenhauer's theory of the will in a revealing entry to his notebooks written in 1888:

> Is 'will to power' a *kind* of 'will' or identical with the concept 'will'? Is it the same thing as desiring? or *commanding*? Is it that 'will' of which Schopenhauer said it was the 'in-itself of things'?
>
> My proposition is that the will of psychology hitherto is an unjustified generalization, that this will *does not exist at all*, that instead of grasping the ideas of the development of one definite will into many forms, one has eliminated the character of the will by subtracting from its content, its 'whither?'—this is in the highest degree with the case with Schopenhauer: what he calls 'will' is a mere empty word. It is even less a question of a 'will to live'; for life is merely a special case of the will to power;—it is arbitrary to assert that everything strives to enter into this form of power (*WP* 692).

Nietzsche here criticizes Schopenhauer's conception of the will as essentially striving without any specific ultimate aim as "a mere empty word" because it "eliminates the character of the will by subtracting from its content, its *whither*." In doing so, he seems unaware that he is appealing to the same thesis that Schopenhauer had already argued, that all willing must be the willing of a specific objective, a specific *whither*. Nietzsche's criticism seems grotesquely off the mark, since it was Schopenhauer who had emphatically insisted that having a specific, individual objective is a necessary condition for the occurrence of any act of the will. Indeed, he had argued that the fundamental structures of our consciousness, such as space, time, and causality, were constructed to fulfill this requirement of the will. Nietzsche seems to have misread Schopenhauer on this matter to be simply denying that the will has any specific aim or aims. As we have seen, what Schopenhauer actually denies is only that the will has any *ultimate aim*, any aim that would truly satisfy it in a manner that would bring it to rest, while he insists that it has to have immediate or proximate aims in order for it to will at all.

In as much as Schopenhauer requires each act of will to have only some specific, proximate aim or another, and these aims can and do change from one act of will to another, he seems to imply (or at least allow for the possibility) that there is no one general and ultimate goal of all human willing and action. And Nietzsche clearly wants to criticize him on this point. To deny that there is a single aim to all willing, which could be satisfied so completely as to bring it to rest, is not quite to deny that willing has a single final aim. Schopenhauer can at most be faulted for having invited this sort of misreading by carelessly describing the will as simply "aimless" because it has no ultimate aim that would put it at rest.

Moreover, as we have seen, Schopenhauer had argued that all will is necessarily the will to life. It is particularly puzzling that Nietzsche not only seems aware of this aspect of Schopenhauer's theory of the will, but actually refers to it and attacks it in the same notebook entry in which he criticizes Schopenhauer for failing to supply a "whither" to the will.

> It is even less a question of a 'will to live'; for life is merely a special case of the will to power; it is quite arbitrary to assert that everything strives to enter into this form of the will to power.

While it is certainly open to Nietzsche to disagree with this thesis and argue instead that the general and ultimate goal of all volitional behavior is power rather than life, how can he fault Schopenhauer for not having offered a theory of this sort at all and then reject it as an alternative to his own? Perhaps the answer to this puzzle lies in the question with which Nietzsche begins this note: "Is 'will to power' a *kind* of 'will' or identical with the concept 'will'? Is it the same thing as desiring? or *commanding*?" Nietzsche seems to be referring here to Schopenhauer's claim that it is "immaterial and a mere pleonasm if, instead of simply saying 'the will,' we say the will-to-live." Nietzsche may have wanted to assert that his theory, that the will is always a will to power, is not a mere pleonasm; that it does not merely unpack what is contained in the notion "the will"; that the will to power is indeed a "kind of will," indeed the kind of will that all will really is; that his theory (in contrast to Schopenhauer's) is not simply true by definition but empirically verifiable.

He suggests this when he criticizes all previous theories for failing to present the will as "the development of one definite will into many forms." If his own theory of the will to power does present the will as the development of *one definite form* into many forms, then he views the notion of a *will to power* as a definite form of the will and not as a mere pleonasm. Thus, he might think that Schopenhauer is not just offering a theory of the right sort that happens to be wrong, but a theory that is not of the right sort. He might think that Schopenhauer's thesis, that all will is the will to life, is not really a direct alternative to his own, which could be tested against it empirically. This would explain Nietzsche's claim that Schopenhauer did not supply the will with a "*whither*," with a general objective of the right sort.

Nietzsche, leaving this meta-criticism aside, also criticizes Schopenhauer's thesis that all will is the will to life, as if it were a meaningful but false thesis about the general aim of all willing. He argues that life is only a special form of the will to power and that it is only an arbitrary assumption that everything strives to enter into this form of the will to power— that all nonliving being strives to become living. These criticisms seem to be based upon the assumption that all things are manifestations of the will to power, and so they show that even in his last writings Nietzsche had still not fully rejected the Schopenhauerian idea that all things are manifestations of the will. He rejects Schopenhauer's thesis for suggesting without argument that all beings, including nonliving beings, strive to become alive, but he does not argue that they do not strive. However, this way of contrasting their views may be overly simplistic, for Schopenhauer's notion that the will is always a will to life played a significant role in the genesis of Nietzsche's theory of the will to power. In *Beyond Good and Evil*, the book in which Nietzsche first really develops the notion of the will to power as the basis of a general theory of the motivation of all human behavior, he treats the will to power as being "the will of life" and equates the will to power with life itself:

> Even in the body within which individuals treat each other as equals, ... if it is a *living* and not dying body, ... it will have to be an incarnate will to power, it will grow spread, seize, become predominant—not from any morality or immorality but because it is *living* and *because life simply is the will to power* ... 'Exploitation' does not belong to a corrupt or imperfect and primitive society; it belongs to the essence of what *lives*, as a basic organic function; it is the consequence of the *will to power, which is after all the will of life. (BGE 259)*

Although we should note that to claim that the will to power is *the will of life* is not quite the same as to claim it is *the will to life*, the two notions nevertheless have a close and complex relationship. To understand this relationship, we must examine the notion of *a will to life*. The idea that a will to life is the basic drive of all beings becomes problematic, as Nietzsche points out, with respect to nonliving beings. He interprets it to mean that nonliving beings have a drive to become living, which he rejects as unfounded. But the same problem exists for his thesis that a will to power is the basic drive of all beings: what reason is there to believe that nonliving beings strive for power any more than they strive for life? The problem lies not with the idea that it is life or power for which they strive, but with the idea that they strive at all. If we concentrate on these theories as they apply to living things and more specifically to human behavior, which is, as I have already argued, the true focus of Nietzsche's concerns and the heart and source of his theory of the will to power, these problems drop away for both theories.

It is more illuminating to ask, what are the implications of these two theories, and in what relation do they stand to each other, when considered as theories of the motivation of human behavior. With respect to human beings (or any living beings) the will to life cannot mean a will to *become* a living being or "*enter into*" life, because all human beings are already alive. What does it mean for an already living being to have a *will to life*?

This is a question to which Nietzsche devoted a good amount of thought. A will to life can mean a will to the preservation of life, a will to survival. Nietzsche, who was aware of Darwin's emphasis upon the importance of a drive to the preservation of the species, for a time seriously considers this interpretation of the notion of a will to life as the basic human drive.[36] He shows how important he considers this idea to be by beginning the main text of *The Gay Science* with the assertion that the basic human drive is for the preservation of the human race:

> *The teachers of the purpose of existence.* Whether I contemplate men with benevolence or with an evil eye, I always find them concerned with a single task, all of them and every one of them in particular: to do what is good for the human race. Not from any feeling of love for the race, but merely because nothing in them is older, stronger, more inexorable and unconquerable than this instinct—because this instinct constitutes the essence of our species, our herd. (GS 1)

He heartily embraces the Darwinian notion that this drive is directed toward the preservation of the species often at the expense of the individual, not just as being true, but also as a truth which, if it could be fully understood and accepted, would lead to a welcome transcendence of the tragic view of the human condition, which he had earlier treated as the highest possible attitude attainable, toward an even higher attitude of viewing human existence

---

[36] For an account of the history of Nietzsche's reading about Darwin, see the relevant sections in Brobjer 2008. For a full account of Nietzsche's relation to Darwin see Richardson 2004.

as comic, which would allow us to simply laugh about its negative aspects while embracing it: "Even laughter may have a future. I mean, when the proposition 'the species is everything, one is always none' has become part of humanity, and this ultimate liberation and irresponsibility has become accessible to all at all times. Perhaps laughter will then have formed an alliance with wisdom, perhaps only 'gay science' will then be left" (*GS* 74). This section represents a very important aspect and phase of Nietzsche's thinking about the major issue in his philosophy, the affirmation of life, but it does not represent his final position. In *The Gay Science* (1882) Nietzsche continued his already well-established practice of analyzing all sorts of human behavior, which we conventionally explain by appeal to hedonistic, altruistic, or cognitive motivations, in terms of power. However, he does not yet use the term "the will to power" and was not yet quite ready to venture the general thesis of the will to power as the basic motivation of all human behavior. Soon afterwards, in *Thus Spoke Zarathustra*, he first uses the term "the will to power," in a section titled "On the Thousand and One Goals," presenting it as the single source of those varying lists of what various cultures have considered to be virtuous. He then presents it in a more substantial and sustained manner in a section titled "On Self-Overcoming."[37] Here, he strongly suggests that our cognitive interests, the creation of values, and various acts of self-overcoming, such as self-criticism and self-discipline, are all motivated in the end by the will to power, which is our "whole will" and "the unexhausted and procreative will of life." In this section, he also mentions that aspect of his budding theory of the will to power which leads to his rejection of the Darwinian notion that the basic drive is a drive to sustain and preserve life, namely that "for the sake of power we are willing to risk life," that the will to power trumps the will to [the preservation of] life.

Thus, it may seem that for Nietzsche the will to power and the will to life are simply competing alternatives, but a more careful consideration of his views, particularly as expressed in his next book, *Beyond Good and Evil* (1886), shows that he really reincorporates the Schopenhauerian notion of a will to life into his theory of the will to power. This reintegration of the will to life into his theory of the will to power depends upon his opening up the notion of a *will to life* to include not only a *will to the preservation of life* (the Darwinian sense of a will to life), but also a *will to the enhancement of life*, not just a will to maximize its duration but also a will to maximize its quality He does this in one of his many rejections of the idea that we have autonomous cognitive interests:

> The falseness of a judgment is for us not necessarily an objection to a judgment; in this respect our new language may sound strangest. The question is to what extent it is life-promoting, life-preserving, species-preserving, perhaps even species-cultivating. (*BGE* 4)

Having recognized that a will to life includes that which promotes and cultivates the life of the individual and the species as well as that which preserves them, he goes on to argue: (1) that what we really desire is the enhancement, not just the preservation, of our lives; (2) that we are willing to risk or even sacrifice the duration of our lives for the enhancement of their intensity or quality; and (3) that what enhances the quality of our lives is the experience of power.

---

[37] These sections occur in parts I and II of *Zarathustra*, which were published in 1883, only one year after *The Gay Science*.

Psychologists should think before putting down the instinct of self-preservation as the cardinal instinct of an organic being. A living being seeks above all to *discharge* its strength—life itself is *will to power*; self-preservation is only one of the indirect and most frequent results. (*BGE* 13)

Thus the will to power is a will to the enhancement of life and, in this sense, also a will to life. Nietzsche's psychological theory of the will to power should be viewed as a significant refinement of Schopenhauer's theory of the will to life, not a complete departure from it.

BIBLIOGRAPHY

(A) Works by Nietzsche

BGE   *Beyond Good and Evil*, trans. Walter Kaufmann. New York: Vintage, 1966.
BT   *The Birth of Tragedy*, trans. Walter Kaufmann. New York: Random House, 1967.

(B) Other Primary Works

WWR   Schopenhauer, Arthur. 1969. *The World as Will and Representation*, trans. E. E. F. J. Payne (2 vols). New York: Dover.

(C) Other Works Cited

Brobjer, Thomas H. 2008. *Nietzsche's Philosophical Context: An Intellectual Biography.* Urbana: University of Illinois Press.

Janaway, Christopher. 1998. *Willing and Nothingness: Nietzsche as Schopenhauer's Educator.* Oxford: Oxford University Press.

Kaufmann, Walter. 1950. *Nietzsche: Philosopher, Psychologist, Antichrist.* Princeton: Princeton University Press.

Richardson, John. 1996. *Nietzsche's System.* Oxford: Oxford University Press.

Richardson, John. 2004. *Nietzsche's Darwinism.* Oxford: Oxford University Press.

Soll, Ivan. 1986. "The Hopelessness of Hedonism and the Will to Power," *International Studies in Philosophy* 18.2: 97–112.

Soll, Ivan. 1988. "Pessimism and the Tragic Sense of Life," in Robert C. Higgins and Kathleen Solomon (eds), *Reading Nietzsche.* Oxford: Oxford University Press, 104–31.

Soll, Ivan. 2000. "Nietzsche on the Illusions of Everyday Life," in Richard Schacht (ed.), *Nietzsche's Postmoralism.* Cambridge: Cambridge University Press, 7–33.

CHAPTER 8

....

INFLUENCE ON ANALYTIC PHILOSOPHY

....

SIMON ROBERTSON AND DAVID OWEN

THIS article explores Nietzsche's influence on analytic philosophy. Two prefatory comments on what we shall take this to mean. First, although there is a growing appreciation that many of his central concerns *connect* with those of analytic philosophy, here we focus on arguments advanced by analytic philosophers for whom Nietzsche is a significant philosophical presence and where we have good reason to see the arguments in question as provoked by or engaging with Nietzsche's own philosophical concerns. In presenting these philosophers as developing or responding to 'Nietzschean' arguments, we do not presuppose that they do so in ways entirely consonant with Nietzsche himself; although these arguments have a Nietzschean pedigree, it inevitably remains moot, given perennial difficulties in interpreting Nietzsche, whether they represent Nietzsche's decided views. Second, we won't here even begin to broach the (somewhat vexed) issue of how precisely to circumscribe 'analytic philosophy'. The writers we do focus on fall within the Anglo-American philosophical community and engage mainstream topics of enquiry in it; we trust they will be recognizably 'analytic'.

These remarks may suggest a rather short article. For while Nietzsche undoubtedly influenced much of so-called 'continental philosophy', his influence on its analytic counterpart may appear to be somewhat negligible. While it is the case that Nietzsche makes claims consonant with subsequent philosophy of language, mind, epistemology, metaphysics, and more, as practised by analytic philosophers, the explanation of such congruence rarely involves debt to Nietzsche. The notable exception is with ethics—which, plausibly, is what motivates Nietzsche's interest in those other areas of enquiry. It is therefore his ethics we focus on.[1] Even here, though, his express influence may seem minimal. Although he is occasionally mentioned, few analytic moral philosophers attend to the detail of Nietzsche's thought or present Nietzsche as any more than an esoteric point of minor historical interest. There are notable exceptions—Philippa Foot, Bernard Williams, Alasdair MacIntyre, and Charles Taylor among the most prominent—to whom we return below. But before doing so, it is worth commenting briefly on this comparative neglect.

[1] The other area we might have addressed is Nietzsche's aesthetics, but the analytic reception of this aspect of his thought, though real, is even more limited than in ethics.

Nietzsche's neglect is in fact raised as a topic in its own right by Philippa Foot. She writes:

> How is it, one may ask, that philosophers today do not even try to refute Nietzsche, and seem to feel morality as firm as ever under their feet? Why do we not argue with him as with other philosophers of the past? (Foot 2001a: 210–11)

And again:

> Why do so many contemporary moral philosophers, particularly of the Anglo-American analytic school, ignore Nietzsche's attack on morality and just go on as if this extraordinary event in the history of thought had never occurred? (Foot 1994: 3)

Foot's own response is to suggest:

> Part of the answer seems to be that a confrontation with Nietzsche is hard to arrange. We find it hard to know where we could meet him because of the intrinsically puzzling nature of a project such as his. Nietzsche had demanded a critique of moral values and announced that he was calling into question 'the value of those values themselves'... The idea of such a thing is enough to make one's head spin. (Foot 2001a: 211)

In addition to this consideration, we may also note that until recently and still only to a limited extent, analytic philosophy's own methodological commitments and related stylistic norms have left it unappreciative of forms of philosophy that involve historical and psychological approaches to ethical reflection or that, for reasons directly related to this, are expressed in highly rhetorical forms.[2]

The character and extent of Nietzsche's influence on analytic moral philosophy emerges through three interweaving strands in his work. The first is broadly meta-ethical and concerns the challenge that Nietzsche mounts to moral objectivity. (We do not suggest that Nietzsche's primary interests were meta-ethical; on the contrary, there are good reasons to take Nietzsche's guiding purpose to be a substantive ethical concern with human flourishing, the articulation of which involves commitment to various meta-ethical claims.) The second is his substantive criticism of morality. The third are the genealogical and comparative approaches through which he articulates these criticisms. In this article, we begin with some reflections on the influence of Nietzsche's project of a re-evaluation of values (§§1–2), before turning to his meta-ethical and substantive criticisms of morality (§§3–4).

1 THE IDEA AND PRACTICE OF THE RE-EVALUATION OF VALUES

Neither the neglect of Nietzsche's thought within analytic philosophy, nor Philippa Foot's attempt to explain this lack of engagement, would have surprised Nietzsche. On the contrary, he is thoroughly aware that his project is likely to appear barely intelligible, indeed

---

[2] For pertinent reflections on the relationship of Nietzsche's rhetorical styles to his substantive concerns, see Owen 2007: chapter 3. For some thoughts on why the analytic failure to attend to style is a significant limitation in relation to moral and political philosophy, see Williams 2006a: 205–7.

pointless, to his contemporaries. (He gives dramatic expression to this reaction in *GS* 125, 'The madman'.)[3] The response itself Nietzsche takes to reflect specific features of morality, namely, its claim to be *comprehensive* with respect to the domain of ethical value (i.e. as monopolizing that domain) and *normatively authoritative* with respect to that domain (*BGE* 202). Its supposed hegemony in turn renders unintelligible, and hence serves to suppress, the thought that there may be a viable ethical outlook distinct from morality. Nietzsche's approach to resolving this dialectical problem structures the way he engages in his project of the re-evaluation of values. However, before turning to that issue, we need to offer some prefatory remarks on re-evaluation.

It is central to this project that, at least from *Daybreak* on, Nietzsche is not arguing that there are no ethical values, nor that moral claims are disguised expressions of self-interest.[4] Head-spinning or not, the project of a re-evaluation of values is, at root, the project of ethical reorientation, a project which addresses both the form and content of ethics. Importantly, Nietzsche thinks that we already have an example of such a re-evaluation: the emergence of morality, as depicted in *GM*. Equally importantly, though, we have failed to acknowledge that it is a re-evaluation; a failure which Nietzsche identifies as itself a consequence of the triumph of morality.[5] Considered under this aspect, *GM* can be seen as an exercise in re-description designed to get us to see the emergence of morality as the product of a prior re-evaluation of values. It involved a transformation of (a) the dispositions of character held to be virtues or vices, that is, the nature of the good; (b) our understanding of ethical agency; (c) our view of the forms that ethical conscience does (and can) take, and with it the way we understand the ethical claims on us; and (d) our conception of the scope and authority of ethics. The importance of this re-description is that it makes clear that by the 're-evaluation of values' Nietzsche is not referring solely to the issue of whether or not we are right to regard particular evaluative claims characteristic of morality—for example, the claim that suffering is intrinsically bad—as justified. Rather this project also encompasses other features of morality considered as a specific kind of ethical outlook or orientation such as its claims to comprehensiveness and normative authority as well as its focus on obligations, willing, and blame and its related appeal to a particular kind of conception of ethical agency.

This work of re-description is important in a second respect and here we return to the ways in which Nietzsche's dialectical problem structures his approach to the project of re-evaluation. If it is compelling, the re-description makes intelligible the idea that morality is open to critical scrutiny: we can coherently ask whether the transition to and historical triumph of morality vindicates morality. Considered under this second aspect, *GM* may be seen as arguing that the transition to morality is *not* vindicatory, indeed if anything the reverse. Thus, *GM*'s first and second essays present accounts of various features that have become constitutive of morality, while the third essay elucidates the process by which these

---

[3] For discussion of this passage, see Owen 2007: chapter 3; and for contrasting readings, Pippin 1999 and Mulhall 2005: chapter 1.

[4] See *D* 103; see also on this point Ridley 2005.

[5] See *GM* I: 7. Nietzsche's point here is that, once morality has triumphed, internal features of morality support a historiography of ethics in which the salient historical developments are presented as the movement from pre-moral to moral conditions. Nietzsche's point is echoed by Bernard Williams when he remarks that we are susceptible to 'the powerful feeling that morality just is the ethical in a rational form' (1995d: 246).

became integrated in such a way that results in the institution we have today. In each essay, Nietzsche contrasts these features with aspects of the ethical orientation they superseded; and he attempts to explain this transition as a result of socio-psychological process. The critical thrust of these accounts is given, on the one hand, by what Nietzsche takes to be morality's constitutive refusal or inability to acknowledge that it may have arisen from immoral senti-ments and, on the other hand, by that fact that on the explanations Nietzsche advances, the transitions to morality are non-vindicatory. (Thus, for example, Nietzsche's account of the slave revolt in morals as an expression of *ressentiment* is an account of how our practical rea-soning succumbs to a form of wishful thinking which, in turn, reshapes the content of our practical reasoning.)

In addition to this genealogical approach, Nietzsche also deploys a comparative strategy which aims to undermine our attachment to morality. This consists in drawing attention to features of our ethical experience which are not easily accounted for or made intelligi-ble in terms of the outlook of morality—but which can, Nietzsche proposes, be helpfully addressed in terms of the ethical outlook superseded and suppressed by morality.[6] This sec-ond strategy also highlights a significant point for Nietzsche, namely, that although morality has triumphed over the preceding ethical outlook (essentially that of the Greek tragedians), this triumph is neither final nor complete.

Both of these strategies have been taken up by 'dissident' figures within analytical moral philosophy. The concern with the relationship of the historical triumph of an outlook and the vindication of an outlook exhibited in *GM* is one topic that has been central to the work of Taylor, MacIntyre, and Williams—each of whom acknowledges the importance of Nietzsche's genealogical approach, even if they reject its conclusions (Taylor) or ultimately advocate an alternative approach (MacIntyre). The critique of morality in terms of its claim to comprehensiveness has been further developed by Bernard Williams.

2 REORIENTATION IN ETHICS

2.1 Genealogy, Morality, and Vindication

One feature that unites the work of MacIntyre, Taylor, and Williams—beyond their differ-ently motivated and cast criticisms of morality—is a concern with practical reasoning, con-strued broadly as reasoning about how to live, what to do, etc., as 'reasoning in transitions' (to adopt Taylor's phrase (1989: 72)).[7] This phrase points to two claims. First, that consid-ering ethical outlooks is characteristically a matter of seeking to show that one outlook is superior (or inferior) to another in some specified sense. Second, that the mere fact that his-torically outlook B superseded outlook A does not vindicate outlook B. Thus, for example, Williams writes that if we reflect on how certain concepts rather than others have come to be ours and 'reflect on the relation of this story to the arguments that we deploy against the earlier conceptions':

---

[6] E.g., *D* 76 and relatedly *TI*: 'Morality as Anti-Nature' 3.   [7] See also Taylor 1995b.

we realize that the story is the history of those forms of argument themselves: the forms of argument…are a central part of the outlook we accept. If we consider how these forms of argument came to prevail, we can indeed see them as having won, but not necessarily as having won an argument. For liberal ideas to have won an argument, the representatives of the *ancient regime* would have had to have shared with the nascent liberals a conception of something the argument was about, and not just in the obvious sense that it was about the way to live or the way to order society. They would have had to agree that there was some aim, of reason or of freedom or whatever, which liberal ideas served better or of which they were a better expression, and there is not much reason, with a change as radical as this, to think that they did agree about this, at least until late in the process. (Williams 2006b: 190)

MacIntyre, Taylor, and Williams all endorse this view and relate it to Nietzsche's genealogical approach to morality.

The claim that Nietzsche is engaged in 'reasoning in transitions' is straightforwardly advanced by Charles Taylor. Having argued that practical reasoning attempts to establish that one outlook is superior to another—for instance, by showing that the movement from A to B resolves a contradiction in A—Taylor comments:

> The argument fixes on the nature of the transition from A to B. The nerve of the rational proof consists in showing that this transition is an error-reducing one. The argument turns on rival interpretations of possible transition from A to B, or B to A. (Taylor 1989: 72)

Deploying his preferred language of *hypergoods* (i.e., goods which are not only more important than others but which compose the standpoint from which other goods are weighed and judged in practical deliberations (Taylor 1989: 63)), Taylor goes on to make two points. The first concerns the idea of re-evaluation or, as Taylor has it, 'transvaluation':

> To have a hypergood arise by superseding earlier views is to bring about (or undergo) what Nietzsche called a 'transvaluation of values'. The new highest good is not only erected as a standard by which other ordinary goods are judged but often radically alters our view of their value, in some cases taking what was previously an ideal and branding it a temptation. Such was the fate of the warrior honour ethic at the hands of Plato, and later of Augustine, and later still in the eyes of the modern ethic of ordinary life. And as Nietzsche saw so well, a transvaluation is not necessarily a once-for-all affair. The old condemned goods remain: they resist; some seem ineradicable from the human heart. So that the struggle and tension continues. (Taylor 1989: 65)

From Taylor's standpoint, Nietzsche's project of re-evaluation involves two stages. The first is to demonstrate that the transition to morality, to the hypergood that Nietzsche labels 'the ascetic ideal' (*GM* III: 12), is not error-reducing. The second is to establish a new hypergood by demonstrating that the transition from morality to Nietzsche's favoured ethical outlook is error-reducing. The second point that Taylor makes is to identify the first of these steps with the practice of genealogy:

> If hypergoods arise through supersessions, the conviction they carry comes from our reading of the transitions to them, from a certain understanding of moral growth. This is always open to challenge: the attacks on hypergoods as repressive and oppressive constitute only the most virulent of such challenges. When Nietzsche wants to launch his out-and-out attack on morality, he does this by offering an account of the transition to it, the rise of slave morality. 'Genealogy' is the name of this kind of probing. No one can fail to recognise that, if true,

Nietzsche's genealogies are devastating. That is because genealogy goes to the heart of practical reasoning. A hypergood can only be defended through a certain reading of its genesis. (Taylor 1989: 72–3)

Thus, for Taylor, whether our commitment to morality can be vindicated is a question that should be addressed by adjudicating the clash of rival historical-cum-philosophical interpretations of the move from (aristocratic) ethics to (slave) morality. If it is the case that Nietzsche's genealogy offers our 'Best Account' of this transition, so much the worse for morality. It is, of course, importantly the case that Taylor does not take Nietzsche's genealogies to be true nor, consequently, does he take them to be devastating. Rather Nietzsche's importance is to illustrate a possible form of argument to which any hypergood can be exposed (Taylor 1989: 72).[8]

Nietzsche is famously situated as the rival to Aristotle in the central chapter of MacIntyre's *After Virtue*, albeit that Nietzsche's own ethical stance barely figures in the argument. Yet there is no doubt that Alasdair MacIntyre also takes genealogy to be an approach to evaluating transitions between outlooks and hence, at a very general and abstract level, the same kind of project as his own critique of morality (MacIntyre 1990: chapters 2 and 9).[9] Three common features link different approaches of this kind for MacIntyre.[10] The first is that they focus on epistemological crises, where this refers to a condition in which the system of judgements which are constitutive of and normative for intelligible action has broken down in some respect or other. The second is that that they acknowledge that insofar as others do not recognize the crisis which one is seeking to address, one is likely to 'be unable to render oneself intelligible' which 'is to risk being taken to be mad' (MacIntyre 1977: 455).[11] The third is that they advance the view that epistemological crises are resolved by the construction of a new narrative which enables the agent to understand both how he could intelligibly have held his original beliefs and how he could have been so drastically misled by them. MacIntyre's view of genealogy as falling into this general approach is confirmed by the attention paid to genealogy as a serious rival to his own favoured approach, a Thomist mode of enquiry predicated on the notion of tradition, as presented in his *Three Rival Versions of Moral Enquiry*. However, in this work, MacIntyre offers a highly controversial account of genealogy, claiming that it is subject to problems of incoherence or instability that arise from the fact that the genealogist is engaged in an incoherently radical rejection of the past, of continuities with the past, at the level of both society and self.[12] Hence MacIntyre claims that the 'function of genealogy as emancipatory from deception and self-deception thus requires the identity and continuity of the self that was deceived and the self that is and is to be' (MacIntyre 1990: 214). And, again: 'if the genealogist is inescapably one who disowns part of his or her own past, then the genealogist's narrative presupposes enough unity, continuity

---

[8] By 'genesis' Taylor is referring to the process of transition and the problem of authority that arises in relation to any such transition. For a good account of this topic in relation to Nietzsche's project of re-evaluation, see Ridley 2005.

[9] It should be noted that MacIntyre's concern with genealogy extends to its more contemporary form in the work of Michel Foucault and that, non-coincidentally, his reading of Nietzsche on genealogy is much informed by the interpretations of Foucault and Deleuze.

[10] We draw these features from MacIntyre 1977.

[11] Compare *GS* 125.

[12] The case is developed in MacIntyre 1990: chapter 9.

and identity to make such disowning possible' (MacIntyre 1990: 214). But MacIntrye insists that genealogy does not have, or has not yet shown itself to have, the resources to make sense of the idea of the self as possessing possible forms of unity, continuity, and identity through time (MacIntyre 1990: 215). Yet it is hard to see why MacIntyre should hold this view. Thus, for example, Nietzsche's rejection of 'soul atomism' is not a rejection of the idea of the self as possessing possible forms of unity, continuity, and identity through time; on the contrary, it represents such unity, continuity, and identity through time as an achievement.[13] While it is important to note that MacIntyre does acknowledge that genealogy may yet find the resources to meet his criticisms (and hence that the contest between genealogy and tradition as rival forms of moral enquiry is undecided), it is unclear on what grounds he takes it to lack these resources.

A third variant on the influence of genealogy on analytical moral philosophy can be found in the work of Bernard Williams. Williams agrees with Taylor and MacIntyre that genealogy is a way of addressing the issue of whether the transition from outlook A to outlook B is vindicatory. However, Williams departs from them in connecting Nietzsche's genealogy to the tradition of imaginary history or fictional developmental stories exemplified by Hume's account of the artificial virtue of justice (Williams 2000: 156).[14] On Williams's version, the character of Hume's type of account is one in which the story gives an explanation of how new concepts or values or institutions emerge and provide new reasons for action 'in terms of existing reasons for action which are taken as given', where 'the story provides a special function because the new reasons for action stand in a rational or intelligible relation to the original reasons or motivations, a relation which is not simply instrumental—or at least, it is not instrumental in giving individuals reasons for action which they could in principle acquire individually' (Williams 2000: 156). Nietzsche's genealogy is, Williams proposes, best seen as a special case of such accounts which involves the thought that the social processes involved in the emergence of (in this case) the institution of morality 'can be illuminatingly represented on the model of a certain kind of psychological strategy'(Williams 2000: 158). Consequently, Williams argues, the basic character of genealogy can be glossed thus:

> a fictional story which represents a new reason for action as being developed in a simplified situation as a function of motives, reactions, psychological processes which we have reason to acknowledge already. (Williams 2000: 159)

The question raised by such stories is whether the explanandum—in this case, morality—is stable under genealogical explanation, that is, 'whether one could understand the explanandum in terms of the fictional history and still (more or less) accept in their original terms the reasons for action which the explanandum provides' (Williams 2000: 159). Williams argues that while some ethical outlooks may well be stable under genealogical explanation,[15] morality

[13] See *BGE* 12. This is a matter of some controversy in Nietzsche scholarship; for contrasting views, see Gardner 2009 and Gemes 2009.

[14] For Williams's development of a Humean-cum-Nietzschean form of vindicatory genealogy, see Williams 2002 and for some salient reflections on genealogy in this form, see Craig 2007.

[15] One way to understand Williams's claim that Greek ethics is in better shape than morality is just as the thought that it is stable under this form of explanation. For the 'better shape' argument, see Williams 1993 and 2006c.

is not stable under the kind of explanation that Nietzsche provides. Indeed, this instability is a result of a special feature of morality:

> In the example of *GM*, the phenomenological fiction of *ressentiment* does not permit this [acceptance in their original terms of the reasons for action]: once again, this is a result of the special demands of the morality system, that it should present itself as separate from and higher than such motives. (Williams 2000: 159)

It is an important feature of Williams's interest in Nietzsche's genealogical approach, and one which stands in sharp contrast to the views of the significance of genealogy held by Taylor and MacIntyre, that he also takes it to provide an exemplification of a non-reductive approach to naturalizing ethics. The significance of this aspect of Nietzsche's work on Williams's view is that Nietzsche's concern with psychological realism and with, as far as possible, not invoking moralized aspects of psychology in explaining the development of morality offers an attractive route to addressing a general problem in stabilizing the notion of 'nature' in 'ethical naturalism', such that it neither collapses into physicalist reductionism nor encompasses everything and hence explains nothing (Williams 2000: 154).[16]

2.2 Comparison, Comprehensiveness, and Ethical Self-understanding

Nietzsche's second strategy for articulating the project of re-evaluation aimed at turning morality's claim to comprehensive monopoly over the ethical domain into a resource for the critique of morality. It does so by arguing that there are features of our ethical experience which morality makes obscure to us but which the ethical outlook superseded by morality can helpfully illuminate. This strategy has been taken up and developed by Bernard Williams.

Williams's argument involves three claims. First, that the ethical thought of the Greeks 'basically lacks the concept of *morality* altogether, in the sense of a class of reasons or demands which are vitally different from other kinds of reason or demand' (Williams 2006c: 44). Second, that there are features of the ethical experience of the Greek world, represented not in its philosophy but in tragic literature, 'which can not only make sense to us now, but make better sense than many things we find nearer to hand'(Williams 2006c: 46). Third, that in an important range of respects, 'the ethical thought of the Greeks was not only different from modern thought, particularly modern thought influenced by morality, but was also in much better shape' (Williams 2006c: 44). This argument is developed across a range of topics, but to illustrate its basic character we will focus on a single issue.[17]

It is a characteristic feature of morality, on Williams's view, that it combines the following two features: (i) an identification of practical necessity, *I must do X*, with the outcome of moral deliberation, *I categorically ought to do X*, and (ii) granting no special significance to the thought *I did it*, that is to the distinction between what I have done and what I have

---

[16] See also Williams 1995b for more specific discussion of how Nietzsche helps us on this issue, which is taken up in section 3.2.

[17] For an important critical appreciation of Williams's work in this vein, see Long 2007.

not done, but instead focusing wholly on the distinction between the voluntary and the involuntary (Williams 1985: 174–96).[18] Against this view, Williams argues that the distinction between what I have and what I have not done 'can be as important as the distinction between the voluntary and the non-voluntary' (Williams 1985: 177), a claim which he attempts to establish, first, by arguing for the non-identity of practical necessity and moral obligation—and, second, by illustrating the implications of this point for the significance of the thought *I did it*.

Williams's argument has two steps. The first notes that the identification of moral obligation with practical necessity fails to acknowledge that whereas obligation comes from without, from what people are reasonably entitled to expect of one, practical necessity comes from within, from commitments that are essential to one's identity (Williams 1985: 189, 191). The second points out that such identity-conferring commitments may involve other forms of value than moral value and, hence, practical necessity cannot be restricted to the moral realm (Williams 1981a, 1985: 174, 184). Williams illustrates the implications of this argument for the significance of the distinction between what I did and did not do with the example of Ajax following his goddess-deranged slaughter of a flock of sheep:

> Ajax then wakes up and shows that he has recovered his mind. There is a passionate lyric outburst of despair and, above all, shame: he has made himself, apart from anything else, utterly absurd. It becomes increasingly clear to himself that he can only kill himself. He knows that he cannot change his *ethos*, his character, and he knows that after what he has done, this grotesque humiliation, he cannot lead the only kind of life his *ethos* demands. . . . Being what he is, he could not live as a man who had done these things; it would be merely impossible, in virtue of the relations between what he expects of the world and what the world expects of a man who expects that of it. (Williams 1993: 72–3)[19]

Williams's point is not that we should endorse Ajax's suicide but that the ethical intelligibility and pathos of Ajax's response cannot be captured by morality. From the standpoint of morality, what matters is whether the slaughter of the sheep was voluntary or non-voluntary. If it is voluntary, then Ajax can be held accountable for it; he is guilty and can be justly blamed for his action. If it is non-voluntary, then Ajax is not culpable. What neither of these responses make intelligible, however, is the pathos of the tragic drama, the reasons that it moves us, since that depends on acknowledging that Ajax's suicide can be a practical necessity for him just because *he did it* despite the fact that he is not culpable for his actions and, hence, bears no guilt. More generally, this example suggests that morality's focus on other-regarding obligations, which it takes to comprise the whole sphere of practical necessity, deprives us of the resources by which to understand our experience of practical necessity (and hence also those aspects of agency connected to it). At the time, it also reveals a further way in which morality erroneously takes itself to be the comprehensive standpoint, since by conceptualizing phenomena like practical necessity in terms of categorical moral obligation, morality truncates our conception of ethical life, discouraging the thought that there is anything significant to ethical life that is not (or cannot be) captured in terms of morality and obligation.

---

[18] See also Williams 1981a.   [19] For commentary see Long 2007: 170–3.

3 CHALLENGING MORALITY'S FOUNDATIONS

Nietzsche's critique of morality's foundational presuppositions is comprehensive. On the one hand, he denies as erroneous a range of widely shared meta-ethical commitments, especially various manifestations of morality's claim to 'objectivity'. On the other, he rejects many conceptions of agency upon which traditional notions of responsibility, blame, and guilt rest. This section focuses initially on the meta-ethical errors; towards the end we draw some connections between these and the criticisms of agency and blame.

3.1 Normative Authority

'Moral objectivity' can mean many things, many of which Nietzsche denies. Here we shall focus on just one that has long been central to debates about practical reason, according to which morality is *normatively authoritative*. The generic idea is that morality represents an objective and authoritative normative standpoint because *compliance* with it is *categorically required*.[20] 'Compliance' can here be understood broadly to include doing whatever is required by, or appropriate in light of, moral norms, considerations, values, ideals, duties, prohibitions, and so forth. To say that compliance is 'categorically required' is to say that one *ought* to comply *irrespective* of whether doing so serves or conflicts with one's contingent subjective *motives*.[21] By 'motives' we mean a person's (occurrent and background) desires, aims, ends, interests, evaluative commitments, and the like—basically any item within one's existing psychological repertoire that could contribute to one's being disposed or motivated to perform a given action. Three further points about this normative authority thesis: First, it incorporates the traditional thought that particular moral obligations are categorical: if A has a moral obligation to φ, A ought to φ irrespective of A's motives. Second, it follows that morality is *universal* in jurisdiction in the sense, and to the extent, that a person does not fall outside its scope merely if or because compliance conflicts with

---

[20] This issue is orthogonal to debates about moral objectivity in recent realism–antirealism debates in meta-ethics, where the focus is the ontological bases of moral truths. Very roughly, moral realists hold that moral judgements can be objectively true and that when they are, this is because they pick out metaphysically robust moral values, facts, or properties; such items count as objective constituents of reality if their existence and character does not depend solely on individuals' thoughts about or attitudes towards them. Many passages indicate that Nietzsche, like contemporary error-theoretic moral antirealists, denies there are any such items (see especially *D* 103; *TI*: 'The "Improvers" of Mankind' 1; plus *HA* I: 39, 40, 56; *D* 3, 119; *Z* I: 'Of the Thousand and One Goals'; *GS* 301; *BGE* 108; *GM* Preface 3; *TI*: 'The Four Great Errors' 3; *WP* 590). And some commentators attribute to him standard antirealist arguments in support of that denial—for instance, arguments from ontological parsimony and best explanation. (see e.g. Leiter 2002: 146, chapters 5–8; and for classic arguments in mainstream meta-ethics, cf. Harman 1977: chapter 1, Mackie 1977: chapter 1). Whatever affinities Nietzsche shares with later antirealists, however, there is little evidence he influenced them. We therefore put these issues aside.

[21] We here treat *ought* as a normative concept in the specific sense that oughts (unmodified) entail normative reasons, such that if A ought to φ then A has a reason to φ (where 'A' stands for some agent and φ for a verb of action). Also, we will treat oughts as overriding whereas reasons need not be, and shall assume that if A ought categorically to φ then A has a reason to φ irrespective of A's motives. On these assumptions, morality's claim to normative authority entails a commitment to what is now often called 'reasons externalism' (see §3.3).

or fails to serve that person's motives. Third, different moral traditions offer contrasting accounts of the *source* of morality's normative authority (be it a transcendent metaphysics, pure practical reason, an impartial conception of value, intrinsically normative facts, or so forth); but they have in common that this is independent of or external to agential motives.

That Nietzsche denies morality's normative authority is evinced by a number of specific passages.[22] It also features throughout several more general themes to which we turn shortly. But it is first worth indicating why he must deny it. Central to Nietzsche's critique is the assumption that moral values and requirements can conflict with and be inimical to the highest forms of human flourishing and excellence. And he thinks that those 'higher men' whose flourishing or excellence morality does thwart ought *not* to comply with it.[23] Yet that would not be possible if morality were normatively authoritative. So he needs to deny that it is.

And it is here that Nietzsche's anti-objectivism about morality has had the most discernible impact on analytic ethics. Notably, Foot and Williams likewise deny morality's normative authority, and in somewhat Nietzschean spirit.[24] The rest of this section focuses on two themes in which this connection is most evident.

3.2   Foot's Challenge

The first emerges from Nietzsche's observation that the 'death of God'—the decline of faith in religious authority—has failed to prompt a corresponding weakening of faith in the authority of morality and its values.[25] Part of his point is that since morality has been thought authoritative in virtue of the authority of religion, and since the authority of religion is no longer accepted, we are no longer entitled to simply *assume* that morality is authoritative or that moral values should be retained.[26] That assumption has to be defended—or, in Nietzsche's

---

[22] E.g. *D* 103; *GS* 5, 345; *BGE* 46, 186–8, 198–202, 228, 263; *GM* II: 21–2, III; *A* 11; *EH*: 'Why I Am a Destiny' 7–8.

[23] Many questions arise concerning the source, scope, and normative force of such oughts that we won't be able to do justice to here. It should suffice to say, though, that they are relevantly non-moral and are bound up with the flourishing and/or excellence of Nietzsche's higher types.

[24] Links between Nietzsche, on the one hand, and Foot and Williams, on the other, have long been recognized of course—if for no other reason than the latter have both written on Nietzsche. Oddly, though, connections between their own and Nietzsche's views on morality's normative authority have been less widely noticed, perhaps because their articles on Nietzsche do not explicitly mention that theme. (Also, Foot and Williams often frame their discussions in more overtly and analytically more respectable Humean terms.) Nonetheless, given that their work on Nietzsche is contemporaneous with that on practical reason, it would be unlikely that the similarities we outline are coincidental. Foot's 'Morality as a System of Hypothetical Imperatives' and 'Nietzsche: The Revaluation of All Values' were first published in 1972 and 1973 respectively; while Nietzsche's influence on Williams is constant from at least the 1970s (for anecdotal evidence, see Clark 2001: 120–1 n. 3).

[25] See especially *GS* 108, 125, 343, 345, 357, 358; *TI*: 'Skirmishes of an Untimely Man' 5; and for further discussion Owen 2003: 253 ff., 2007: 2–5, 27 ff.; Robertson 2009: 70–1.

[26] As sometimes noted, there are similarities here (see especially *TI*: 'Skirmishes of an Untimely Man' 5) with Anscombe's (1958) claim that a law conception of ethics is insufficiently intelligible outside the theistic context from which it is derived, since it makes sense only in light of an authoritative lawgiver. Nonetheless, it is less obvious that Nietzsche assents to the conclusion Anscombe draws from it: that, if psychologically possible, we should jettison deontic concepts like *obligation* and *ought*, and reorient normative thought in terms of *virtue*. Arguably, more like Foot and Williams, Nietzsche does not deny

case, denied. And Nietzsche, increasingly bewildered that morality does continue to command widespread allegiance, comes to recognize the need to actively destabilize faith in it.

Hence in the *Genealogy*, one of Nietzsche's goals is to explain morality *away* in naturalistic terms. Although his official aim is to call into question the value of moral values (*GM* Preface 6), one way he does this is by showing that those values and the structural features like obligation holding them in place lack the objective grounding customarily supposed. Essay II, for instance, traces the origins and development of our modern concepts of moral *duty* and *guilt* (*GM* II: 21) back to a positivistic conception of obligation as material *debt* (*GM* II: 6). The earliest ethical schemes in which this conception figured—primitive 'ethics of custom' (*Sittlichkeit*)—were effectively systems of *hypothetical* (non-categorical) imperatives, obedience to which was conditional upon one's desires to avoid punishment and procure the benefits of society (*GM* II: 3).[27] These were gradually transformed, with the positivistic conception of duty becoming gradually moralized. The account culminates with the emergence of Christian morality: a system of categorical and universal duties, violation of which merits blame and guilt, justified through a deity whose commands are authoritative and unconditional (*GM* II: 19–22). Nietzsche accounts for this transformation in predominantly socio-psychological terms—as the result of various processes of *internalization* (*GM* II: 4–10, 16–18), whereby individuals developed dispositions to direct punitive emotions upon themselves, and *objectification* (*GM* II: 19–22), whereby debts become owed to increasingly more powerful (yet otherworldly and thereby unassailable) external authorities. With Essays I and III then explaining in naturalistic terms both how moral values acquired the content they did and how morality came to exercise the stranglehold it retains today—in terms, for example, of the specific drives and interests of particular socially-historically located groups—Nietzsche seeks to show that morality is neither the product of, nor justified by, some supra-human realm. It is rather just one possible form of ethical outlook among others—which, although it has helped to further socialize and to deepen human beings, is decidedly human in origin and serves (often pernicious) human drives and interests. Thus the account of morality's origins casts doubt on the supposedly objective (for instance: transcendently justified, interest-free) foundations of moral values and requirements. Indeed, Nietzsche thinks that modern morality is ultimately no more than a refined ethic of custom,[28] which, because ingrained through two millennia of internalization and objectification, we accept as authoritative.

Many similar themes find expression in Foot's classic paper 'Morality as a System of Hypothetical Imperatives' (1978): that morality is a scheme of socially entrenched norms; that it is just one amongst others; that it lacks any deeper authority; that whatever reasons we do have to comply with it are conditional on our possessing suitably moral motives; and that most of us probably do have suitably moral motives, due to the kinds of internalization that living in a social group produces. Although Foot concludes that morality consists of merely hypothetical norms and imperatives, her main argument effectively comprises a sceptical challenge calling on the moralist to show that morality instead possesses the authority traditionally claimed. Her argument runs as follows.

the intelligibility of deontic notions but seeks a demoralized, secularized interpretation of them (see e.g. *D* 103; *BGE* 272; *A* 11; cp. Foot 1978; Williams 1985: chapter 10).

[27] See e.g. Clark 1994: 26 ff., 2001: 107 ff. for this reading.
[28] See also *D* 9.

Foot begins by supposing that the truth of some ought judgements depends on the motives of the person they are about. If we claim *you ought to take the train*, believing you to be journeying home, that claim is false and we should retract it if taking the train would serve none of your motives. The ought is thus *escapable*: you escape it by lacking any motive that would be served by doing what it specifies.

Moral oughts, in contrast, are *inescapable*: you do not escape them if acting as they prescribe isn't ancillary to your motives. Foot observes, however, that many oughts are like this, including those we do *not* take to present categorical requirements. Her example is of requirements derived from frivolous norms of etiquette, as in 'women ought never to offer their hand when greeting a man before the man offers his'. She writes: 'the [ought] does not *fail to apply* to someone who has his own good reasons for ignoring this piece of nonsense, or who simply does not care about what, from the point of view of etiquette, he should do' (Foot 1978: 160). Legal requirements on positivist accounts provide another useful illustration: they apply to a person regardless of that person's subjective motives. The ought 'applies' in the sense that there are norms and conditions governing its correct and incorrect application. And it 'applies inescapably' if, *relative to some system of norms N*, there are conditions of application that determine its correct use, where the correctness of an ought judgement, relative to N, does not depend on the motives of the person it is applied to. Foot's point, however, is that the mere fact that some norm prescribes action in this inescapable sense does not *entail* a *true normative* claim. For it does not follow from the fact that 'according to some system of norms N, you ought to φ that you genuinely ought to φ'. Indeed, if N is a system of norms there is no reason to comply with in the first place, there may be no reason to do what it *claims* you ought. Therefore, if morality generates categorical oughts whereas etiquette (say) does not, morality and the oughts it generates must possess some additional quality besides being inescapable—they must be normatively authoritative.

Foot's challenge to the moralist, then, is to vindicate the assumption that morality is normatively authoritative, by showing that moral oughts, unlike (other) norm-relative requirements, do entail normative reasons for action and that these reasons do not depend on agential motives—a challenge she doubts can be met. There have subsequently been many responses to Foot's argument.[29] But even though some of her assumptions are certainly questionable—that morality is no more than a socially embedded set of practices with no further rational basis, say—it remains highly contentious whether moral demands, whatever their source, do entail normatively authoritative reasons for all agents; indeed, it is fair to say that no attempt to show they do has definitively succeeded.[30] This issue remains as pertinent today as it was for Nietzsche, who was one of the first moderns to articulate scepticism about morality's normative force.

[29] E.g. McDowell 1978; Brink 1997. Foot herself later recants—see her 1994.
[30] Nietzsche himself likens the age-old attempt to 'furnish the *rational ground* of morality' and thus reveal the 'foundation of ethics' to discovering the philosophers' stone (*BGE* 186).

3.3 Williams on Practical Reason, Agency, and Blame

Williams is likewise sceptical. He characterizes morality in terms (partly) of a commitment to what he calls 'reasons externalism', according to which at least some reasons satisfy the following schema:

(RE) A has a reason to φ even if A has no motive that would be served by φing

Since he attributes to morality the claim that moral obligations entail reasons satisfying RE, and since he denies that any reasons satisfy RE, he thereby denies morality's normative authority.[31] Work relating Williams to Nietzsche has focused mostly on their criticisms of free will and blame. But it is Williams's views on practical reason that in various ways unify his criticisms—views that are arguably informed as much by Nietzsche as the Humean framework from which he officially takes his lead. However, since any analysis of all these connections would require lengthy exposition, here we focus on just one. To do so, we organize our discussion around a style of question markedly Nietzschean in spirit: 'What is the point of morality's insisting that people do have reason to do what it demands?' To get to Williams's (Nietzschean) answer, we need first to introduce his plea for a 'psychologically realistic' model of practical reason.

Williams suggests that 'There is some measure of agreement that we need a "naturalistic" moral psychology' (Williams 1995c: 67). By 'moral psychology' he means an account of those capacities by which we come to the practical decisions and normative conclusions we do (not just narrowly *moral* decisions and conclusions), and which explains how we become motivated to act in light of them. Well aware of vexing issues about the ambit of 'naturalism', though eschewing any 'fiercely reductive' version of it, naturalism in Williams's hands plays the role of a guiding heuristic, by which, through piecemeal testing, one attempts to interpret human experiences in a way that is 'consistent with...our understanding of humans as part of nature' (Williams 1995c: 67).[32] In offering some further direction to this endeavour, Williams finds in Nietzsche 'a general attitude [...] that can be a great help' (Williams 1995c: 68). The attitude has two relevant dimensions. It manifests suspicion upon whichever aspects of moral psychology are at odds with psychological explanation more generally; and it calls on us to enquire whether 'what seems to demand more moral material makes sense in terms of what demands less' (Williams 1995c: 68). In response to the question 'How much should our accounts of distinctively moral activity add to our accounts of other human activity?', Williams replies:

> as little as possible [...] the more that some moral understanding of human beings seems to call on materials that specially serve the purpose of morality—certain conceptions of the

---

[31] Although Williams attributes to traditional *morality* a commitment to RE, he defends a demoralized *ethical* ideal consistent with its denial (1985: chapter 10). For more on Williams's 'moral-ethical' distinction, and its significance for Nietzsche, cp. Clark 2001: 101–5; Robertson 2012.

[32] Compare Nietzsche's well-known remark that we should 'translate man back into nature' (*BGE* 230). For contrasting recent accounts of Nietzsche's naturalism, cp. Leiter 2002: chapter 1 and Leiter's chapter in this volume ('Nietzsche's Naturalism Reconsidered'); Acampora 2006; Janaway 2007: chapter 3.

will, for instance—the more reason we have to ask whether there may not be a more illuminating account that rests only on conceptions that we use anyway elsewhere. (Williams
1995c: 68)

If we can understand human capacities in terms of psychological materials we use anyway
elsewhere—rather than appealing to models of deliberation and agency that resist such
integration—then we should.

This methodological heuristic in turn imposes a constraint on how to understand the
capacities by which people come to normative conclusions and act in light of them. Williams
himself endorses a common 'sentimentalist' thesis—attributable to Hume, for instance,
which there is also good evidence to think Nietzsche accepts in some form.[33] According to it,
practical reasoning—understood as deliberation the outcome of which is some pro-attitude
or disposition to act (a sincere normative judgement or intention, say)—must either start
from or otherwise engage one's antecedent motives. As a result, the contents of the practical conclusions one is motivated by are (necessarily) shaped and constrained by one's antecedent motivational repertoire—i.e. by those desires, aims, ends, interests, and evaluative
commitments familiar to the kinds of psychological explanation 'we use anyway elsewhere'.
In contrast, numerous moral theorists—for example rational intuitionists, moral sense theorists, Kantians—posit some additional faculty by which specifically moral truths may be
apprehended. Kant, for instance, held that the demands of morality are revealed through and
justified by reasoning that is *pure*—'pure' in that it need neither start from, nor otherwise
engage, one's subjective motivational repertoire but nonetheless arrives at substantive moral
truths which any rational agent could recognize and be motivated by. This requires not just a
capacity by which one can abstract from, and remain uninfluenced by, a specific motive at a
given time—but a capacity to abstract from, and remain sufficiently unmoved by, any and all
(subjective, non-moral) motives at any one time: a will that stands behind and is capable of
remaining uninfluenced by any such motive, yet a will that motivates one to act for the sake
of specifically moral duty. To make sense of this and to thereby justify the demands of morality as both motive-independent and universally applicable, Kant ended up *positing* (or *presupposing*) a radical conception of free will, one common to all rational beings, that stands
outside (but nonetheless causes action in) the natural world—a conception in tension with
even a very broad naturalism and about which, Williams therefore supposes, one should be
suspicious.[34]

Grounds for suspicion are amplified, however, by the thought that such conceptions
of agency may be far from ideologically innocent. As Williams puts it, a 'second helpful
thought to be recovered from Nietzsche is that such a peculiar account must have a purpose,
and that the purpose is a moral one' (Williams 1995c: 72). The *point* of positing some such
conception is to guarantee that people are capable of both recognizing moral reasons and
freely doing—or freely violating—whatever morality demands. And the point of *that* is to

---

[33] See *HAH* I: 39–40, 56; *D* 3, 103, 119; *GS* 5, 301, 345, 347; *Z* I: 'Of the Thousand and One Goals'; *BGE* 5,
6, 11, 46, 187, 199; *GM* Preface 3, II: 6, III: 12; *TI*: 'The Four Great Errors' 3; *A* 11; *WP* 590.
[34] Nietzsche's opposition to such conceptions of freedom is of course rife; see e.g. *D* 116, 129; *GS* 333,
335; *BGE* 15, 17, 21; *GM* I: 13; *TI*: 'The Four Great Errors'.

vindicate practices of moral *blame*.[35] Williams makes explicit several steps and assumptions Nietzsche doesn't. His thought goes as follows.[36]

Morality is committed to values like justice; so moral blame must also be just, such that those to whom it is attributed are legitimate targets of blame, i.e. *blameworthy*. For an agent A to be blameworthy for φ ing, it must be the case that (i) A had reason not to, and (ii) A could have not -ed. However, to ensure (i), A's reasons cannot depend solely on his motives, since he may lack suitably moral motives. Hence one pressure within morality to insist that people do have reason to do what it demands, whatever their motives—i.e. to present itself as normatively authoritative. Concerning (ii), the moralist who endorses RE faces a dilemma. On the one hand, if he accepts a naturalistic moral psychology in which deliberative possibilities are circumscribed by agential motives, he may be committed to an *unjust* conception of moral blame—since it would be unfair to blame A for φ ing if, given A's motives, A could not have become motivated not to φ or could not have reached the conclusion that he had reason not to φ. On the other hand, and to avoid that conclusion, the moralist may be tempted to represent the agent as someone who could indeed appreciate relevant moral reasons, whatever his motives, and who could have freely chosen not to do what he is blamed for doing. But this encourages the very conception of the will (like Kant's) that is in tension with a sensible naturalism and that Williams thinks problematic on theoretical grounds—a conception which, moreover, if indeed no one actually possesses such a will, does nothing to attenuate the *de facto* injustices of blame predicated on it. Either way, morality's commitment to an externalist view of reasons makes agents more susceptible to moral blame than they really are.[37]

Furthermore, though, Williams like Nietzsche thinks that moral blame may be objectionable aside from these theoretical misgivings. In particular, they both think that blame can function as a mechanism of control or power. There are many issues to explore here. But we shall conclude the section with one suggestion to which both Nietzsche and Williams seem sympathetic: that whatever legitimate applications blame may have, it can also be misappropriated—by promoting an unhealthy ethical outlook in which specifically moral considerations come to dominate a person's life at the expense of his realizing significant non-moral values.[38] For given that being blamed (by others or, as in the case of guilt, oneself) is typically

---

[35] Thus Nietzsche writes: 'the concept of "freewill" ... is the most infamous of all arts of the theologian for making mankind "accountable" ... that is to say for *making mankind dependent on him* ... Everywhere accountability is sought, it is usually the instinct for *punishing and judging* which seeks it ... the doctrine of will has been invented essentially for the purpose of punishment, that is of *finding guilty* ... Men were thought of as "free" so that they could become guilty: consequently, every action *had* to be thought of as willed, the origin of every action as lying in the consciousness ... Christianity is a hangman's metaphysics' (*TI*: 'The Four Great Errors' 7).

[36] On blame and free will, see Williams 1995a: 14–16 and 1995c: 72–4, and on their connections to reasons, Williams 1995b: 40–4.

[37] There have, unsurprisingly, been many responses to Williams's anti-externalist arguments, many of which are directed against the sentimentalist moral psychology he presupposes. See especially Korsgaard 1986, McDowell 1995, Millgram 1996, Parfit 1997, Scanlon 1998, and Skorupski 2007—the latter also providing a level-headed externalist defence of moral blame.

[38] Note that Williams doesn't disavow blame outright: he allows it an important role in disciplining ethical life and accepts that people may be legitimate targets of blame if they had reason—in his own preferred internalist sense—to do what morality demands. It is less clear whether Nietzsche affords blame or other punitive sentiments *any* positive role.

unpleasant, the desire to avoid blame may readily become internalized. And since a necessary means for avoiding moral blame is complying with morality, one way to ensure that one does avoid it is to internalize moral values. Hence blame may be used as a tool by which to 'recruit' people into morality. In turn, if moral values and the disposition to avoid blame come to govern one's thinking, one may come to neglect and thereby fail to pursue all sorts of non-moral goods constitutive of a flourishing life.[39] It is to these issues that we now turn in more detail.

4 ON THE DISVALUE OF MORAL VALUES

On a common reading, Nietzsche thinks morality disvaluable because it thwarts the realization of various non-moral goods constitutive of human flourishing. Similar looking worries were developed within mainstream analytic ethics in the latter quarter of the twentieth century. This section introduces the generic concern, as presented by recent morality critics, and then assesses an objection to assimilating their challenge too closely to Nietzsche's.[40]

Though they differ in detail, these morality critics argue that were we to comply with the demands of traditional moral theory, we would be required to systematically forego significant non-moral values—and this is a bad thing. Such non-moral goods include the sorts of relationships and personal projects that give our lives meaning and that contribute to our leading a good or flourishing life—friendships and emotional attachments, artistic and sporting pursuits, projects embodying personal excellence, and so on. One source of the worry emerges from the idea that morality represents an impartial standpoint which has priority over the partial and subjective interests of individual agents. Classical utilitarianism, for instance, requires each person to promote the good of all impartially, since the good of one person is as valuable as the good of any other; yet this may require an individual to sacrifice the sorts of personal project constitutive of his own good if promoting the good of others will have better overall consequences. Kantian theories are also susceptible to a version of the objection. For if a person is required to deliberate impartially by abstracting from his evaluative commitments and desires when considering what to do, his personal projects may become sidelined and ultimately eclipsed by the demands of morality. On either theory, if obligations derived from the impartial moral standpoint are not just categorical but also overriding, we may end up continually required to do as morality demands and hence not permitted to pursue our own personal good. This is one version or application of the objection that moral theories render morality too demanding.

---

[39] For other dimensions to Williams's Nietzschean criticisms of blame, especially the way in which the *act* of blaming can be an expression of *ressentiment* that produces in the blamer various misconceptions of both others and himself, see Williams 1995c: 72–4.

[40] The label 'morality critic' is Leiter's, which for convenience we appropriate here. Robert Louden (1988: 361) acknowledges the similarities, asking of the morality critics whether "Nietzsche's 'new philosophers' [have] finally arrived on the scene". The most likely influences are on Williams (e.g. 1981a, 1985: chapter 10) and Taylor (e.g. 1995b). Susan Wolf (1982: 433) mentions but distances herself from Nietzsche. For further references to other morality critics, probably not influenced directly by Nietzsche, see Leiter 2001.

[41] See esp. Leiter 2001, 2002: chapter 5; cf. Clark 2001: 107–14.

Brian Leiter, however, seeks to disassociate Nietzsche from this style of criticism, and for a number of reasons.[41] On the one hand, he reasonably claims, Nietzsche is concerned not with how morality might impede the *good* life for *many* of us but how it thwarts the *excellence* of the *few*. On the other, Leiter seems persuaded by various plausible responses moral theorists have subsequently made to the morality critics' objections. One such strategy is to amend one's moral theory and make morality less demanding, either by accommodating the legitimate pursuit of personal goods within an impartial framework or by setting aside space outside morality in which agents are permitted to pursue their own good.[42] We might then treat moral considerations as just one kind of reason alongside whatever non-moral reasons we have, both contributing to what, overall, we ought to do. Therefore, since moral considerations are not always decisive or overriding, they needn't generate an unremitting series of obligations. In which case, even if moral obligations are overriding, they need not be pervasive; thus they needn't preclude the pursuit of non-moral goods.

In light of such responses, Leiter argues that Nietzsche's objection is not directed specifically to the notion of moral *obligation* that Anglo-American morality critics find problematic—nor, moreover, is Nietzsche's principal critical target even moral *theory*. It is instead the moralized *culture* we actually inhabit; for a culture in which moral values predominate will *in practice* be inimical to the realization of the highest forms of human excellence. The crux of Leiter's reading of Nietzsche runs as follows.[43] Morality presents itself as universally applicable, such that moral values are supposedly good for all people. These values include, paradigmatically: happiness, the alleviation of suffering, altruism, equality, social utility, pity, harmlessness, extirpation of the instincts (their opposites being disvaluable) (Leiter 2002: 128). Since morality has succeeded in so presenting itself, Nietzsche's nascent 'higher types', whose flourishing and excellences morality thwarts, think that morality is also good for them; they thereby come to accept and internalize moral values (Leiter 2002: 28, 104–12, 176, 195). However, such 'values' are actually antagonistic to their flourishing and/or the realization of the excellences they are capable of (Leiter 2002: 113–36). Central to Nietzsche's conception of excellence is an ideal of creativity (Leiter 2002: 129–33), the pursuit and achievement of which requires a readiness to suffer, prioritizing one's own goals, standing apart from others, channelling one's instincts creatively, and so on. Most of us may be unable to achieve genuine excellence; but someone who is, if he has also internalized moral values (promoting the alleviation of suffering, altruism, equality, extirpation of instincts, say), will devalue and hence avoid the kinds of condition necessary for excellence. However, Leiter continues, Nietzsche's objection is *not* that 'morality is harmful [...] because its specific prescriptions and proscriptions explicitly require potentially excellent persons to forgo that which allows them to flourish' (Leiter 2001: 243). Nor is the objection that 'a conscientious application of [moral theory] would be incompatible with the flourishing of higher men' (Leiter 2001: 243). The objection is instead directed at a culture in which nascent excellent individuals internalize moral values, since such a culture will be one that *actually* thwarts excellence. Thus, Leiter concludes, morality 'is harmful because, in reality, it will have the effect of leading potentially excellent persons to value what is in fact not conducive to their flourishing and devalue what is, in fact, essential to it' (Leiter 2002: 133; 2001: 243). Thus even if undemanding moral theories avoid Nietzsche's objection, the objection retains its bite against moralized culture.

[42] Cf. Railton 1984; Brink 1986; Darwall 1987; Scheffler 1992.
[43] See especially Leiter 2001, 2002: chapter 5.

There is much to explore in Leiter's reading. Here we shall indicate just one line of enquiry. For without denying that Nietzsche is indeed a critic of moralized culture, we suspect that there may also be room for a Nietzschean critique of obligation-centred moral theories, even in their undemanding versions.

Note, firstly, that even relatively undemanding moral theories seem committed to the thought that moral considerations—those pro tanto considerations that *can* contribute to or generate moral obligation in its various guises—are pervasive. Even if such considerations do not generate an unremitting series of actual particular overriding obligations, they nonetheless remain continually relevant to what one ought (or ought not) to do. Secondly, all moral theorists agree that a person is morally permitted to pursue his non-moral personal projects only if he has no moral obligation to do something else. Thirdly, central to morality is the thought that, if a person fails to do what he has a moral obligation to do, he merits *blame* (an assumption shared by demanding and undemanding moral theorists). Then, however, there may emerge a residual pressure (both normative and psychological) to ensure that, when pursuing one's non-moral projects, one does not thereby violate a moral obligation, for instance by overlooking a moral obligation to do something else. (We might think of this as a 'meta-obligation', such that agents are morally required to ensure they do not overlook any (first-order) moral obligations.) However, because moral considerations are pervasive and remain continually relevant to what one ought (not) to do, agents may then be morally required to structure their deliberations in terms of the sorts of moral considerations that can contribute to moral obligations, so not to overlook any moral obligations. This remains the case even if their deliberative conclusion turns out to be that they are morally permitted to pursue their personal project, i.e. that there is no moral obligation not to.

This presents an analogue to the complaint Leiter levies against a moralized culture—but applied now to moral theory, including those undemanding models that seek to accommodate the legitimate pursuit of non-moral goods—according to which: the conscientious application of the theory may in practice make Nietzsche's nascent higher individuals more susceptible to moralization (especially if such individuals also mistakenly regard morality as normatively authoritative). For if, as Leiter himself suggests, Nietzsche's nascent higher types are 'more likely [than thoughtless brutes] to take seriously' moral considerations (Leiter 2001: 250), then in order to ensure they do not overlook any moral obligations, they will be more likely to internalize and/or structure their deliberations in terms of the moral values inimical to their flourishing or excellence.

This suggestion needs considerably more careful and detailed execution.[44] Nonetheless, our immediate point is that far from being peripheral to the concerns of analytic moral philosophy, there may remain room for a Nietzschean critique of moral theory—one which is not only akin to more recent morality critics but may offer further ways to develop their worries.

---

[44] For an attempt to deliver it, see Robertson 2011.

5 Concluding Remarks

Since Foot's earlier articles, Nietzsche has indeed received greater attention from both analytic moral philosophers and analytically minded Nietzsche specialists. Even so, as Foot has
more recently suggested, 'while Nietzsche's work now interests many analytic philosophers,
one finds few who actually try to confront him' (Foot 2001b: 99). One important respect in
which Foot's point has application concerns the fact that the recent morality critics' focus
is the *relation* between moral values and the good life—their objection being that morality
tends to *exaggerate* the value of the former. However, they do not typically object to the *content* of moral values as such; that remains untouched. Nietzsche, on the other hand, clearly
does object to, and seeks to re-evaluate, the content of at least some moral values—for example, pity and humility—on grounds that there is something inherent to their very nature that
is unhealthy or pathological and which can thereby be injurious to those who value or act
in light of them. Much work remains to clarify Nietzsche's worries here: it is likely to require
conceptual (and perhaps empirical) analyses of the psychological mechanisms that *valuing*
involves—the kinds of analyses we find not only in Nietzsche but also, nowadays, in various
branches of analytic philosophy. As a more systematic engagement with Nietzsche's work
emerges within analytic philosophy, it is likely that this issue will come to command greater
attention alongside those dimensions of his re-evaluation of values that are already being
developed.

BIBLIOGRAPHY

Other Works Cited

Acampora, C. D. 2006. 'Naturalism and Nietzsche's Moral Psychology', in Keith Ansell-Pearson
    (ed.), *The Blackwell Companion to Nietzsche*. Oxford: Blackwell Publishing, 314–33.
Anscombe, G. E. M. 1958. 'Modern Moral Philosophy', *Philosophy* 33: 1–19.
Brink, David O. 1986. 'Utilitarian Morality and the Personal Point of View', *Journal of Philosophy*
    83: 417–38.
Brink, David O. 1997. 'Kantian Rationalism: Inescapability, Authority and Supremacy', in
    G. Cullity and B. Gaut (eds), *Ethics and Practical Reason*. Oxford: Oxford University Press,
    255–91.
Clark, Maudemarie. 1994. 'Nietzsche's Immoralism and the Concept of Morality', in R. Schacht
    (ed.), *Nietzsche, Genealogy, Morality*. Berkeley: University of California Press, 15–34.
Clark, Maudemarie. 2001. 'On the Rejection of Morality: Bernard Williams' Debt to Nietzsche',
    in R. Schacht (ed.), *Nietzsche's Postmoralism*. Cambridge: Cambridge University Press,
    100–22.
Craig, Edward. 2007. 'Genealogies and the State of Nature', in A. Thomas (ed.), *Bernard Williams*.
    Cambridge: Cambridge University Press, 181–200.
Darwall, Stephen. 1987. 'Abolishing Morality', *Synthese* 87: 71–89.
Foot, Philippa. 1978. 'Morality as a System of Hypothetical Imperatives', reprinted in P. Foot,
    Virtues and Vices. Oxford: Blackwell, 157–74.

Foot, Philippa. 1994. 'Nietzsche's Immoralism', in R. Schacht (ed.), *Nietzsche, Genealogy, Morality*. Berkeley: University of California Press, 1–14.

Foot, Philippa. 1997. 'Recantation', in S. Darwall, A. Gibbard, and P. Railton (eds), *Moral Discourse and Practice*. Oxford: Oxford University Press, 322.

Foot, Philippa. 2001a. 'Nietzsche: The Revaluation of Values', reprinted in J. Richardson and B. Leiter (eds), *Nietzsche*. Oxford: Oxford University Press, 210–20.

Foot, Philippa. 2001b. *Natural Goodness*. Oxford: Clarendon Press.

Gardner, S. 2009. 'Nietzsche, the Self, and the Disunity of Philosophical Reason', in K. Gemes and S. May (eds), *Nietzsche on Freedom and Autonomy*. Oxford: Oxford University Press, 1–32.

Gemes, Ken. 2009. 'Nietzsche on Free Will, Autonomy, and the Sovereign Individual', in K. Gemes and S. May (eds), *Nietzsche on Freedom and Autonomy*. Oxford: Oxford University Press, 33–50.

Harman, Gilbert. 1977. *The Nature of Morality*. Oxford: Oxford University Press.

Janaway, Christopher. 2007. *Beyond Selflessness: Reading Nietzsche's Genealogy*. Oxford: Oxford University Press.

Korsgaard, Christine. 1986. 'Skepticism about Practical Reason', *Journal of Philosophy* 83: 5–26.

Leiter, Brian. 2001. 'Nietzsche and the Morality Critics', reprinted in J. Richardson and B. Leiter (eds), *Nietzsche*. Oxford: Oxford University Press, 221–54.

Leiter, Brian. 2002. *Nietzsche on Morality*. London: Routledge.

Long, A. A. 2007. 'Williams on Greek Literature and Philosophy', in A. Thomas (ed.), *Bernard Williams*. Cambridge: Cambridge University Press, 155–80.

Louden, Robert. 1988. 'Can We Be Too Moral?' *Ethics* 98: 361–80.

Mackie, John. 1977. *Ethics: Inventing Right and Wrong*. Harmondsworth: Penguin.

McDowell, John. 1978. 'Are Moral Requirements Hypothetical Imperatives?', *Proceedings of the Aristotelian Society* 52 (supp. vol.): 13–29.

McDowell, John. 1995. 'Might there be External Reasons?', in J. Altham and R. Harrison (eds), *World, Mind, and Ethics*. Cambridge: Cambridge University Press, 68–85.

MacIntyre, Alasdair. 1977. 'Dramatic Narratives, Epistemological Crises and the Philosophy of Science', *The Monist* 60: 453–72.

MacIntyre, Alasdair. 1985. *After Virtue*, 2nd edn. London: Duckworth.

MacIntyre, Alasdair. 1990. *Three Rival Versions of Moral Inquiry*. Notre Dame: University of Notre Dame Press.

Millgram, Elijah. 1996. 'Williams' Argument Against External Reasons', *Noûs* 30: 197–220.

Mulhall, S. 2005. *Philosophical Myths of the Fall*. Princeton: Princeton University Press.

Owen, David. 2003. 'Nietzsche, Re-evaluation and the Turn to Genealogy', *European Journal of Philosophy* 11: 249–72.

Owen, David. 2007. *Nietzsche's Genealogy of Morality*. Durham: Acumen Publishing.

Parfit, Derek. 1997. 'Reasons and Motivation', *Proceedings of the Aristotelian Society* 71: 99–130.

Pippin, Robert. 1999. 'Nietzsche and the Melancholy of Modernity', *Social Research* 66.2: 495–519.

Railton, Peter. 1984. 'Alienation, Consequentialism, and the Demands of Morality', *Philosophy and Public Affairs* 13: 134–71.

Ridley, Aaron. 2005. 'Nietzsche and the Re-evaluation of Values', *Proceedings of the Aristotelian Society* 105.2: 171–91.

Robertson, Simon. 2009. 'Nietzsche's Ethical Revaluation', *Journal of Nietzsche Studies* 37: 66–90.

Robertson, Simon. 2011. 'A Nietzschean Critique of Obligation-Centred Moral Theory', *International Journal of Philosophical Studies* 19.4: 563–91.

Robertson, Simon. 2012. 'The Scope Problem: Nietzsche—the Moral, Ethical, and Quasi-Aesthetic', in C. Janaway and S. Robertson (eds), *Nietzsche, Naturalism and Normativity*. Oxford: Oxford University Press, 81–110.

Scanlon, T. M. 1998. *What We Owe to Each Other*. Belknap: Harvard University Press.

Scheffler, Samuel. 1992. *Human Morality*. Oxford: Oxford University Press.

Skorupski, John. 2007. 'Internal Reasons and the Scope of Blame', in A. Thomas (ed.), *Bernard Williams*. Cambridge: Cambridge University Press, 73–103.

Taylor, Charles. 1989. *Sources of the Self*. Cambridge: Cambridge University Press.

Taylor, Charles. 1995a. *Philosophical Arguments*. Belknap: Harvard University Press.

Taylor, Charles. 1995b. 'A Most Peculiar Institution', in J. Altham and R. Harrison (eds), *World, Mind and Ethics: Essays on the Ethical Philosophy of Bernard Williams*. Cambridge: Cambridge University Press, 132–55.

Williams, Bernard. 1981a. 'Persons, Character and Morality', reprinted in Bernard Williams, *Moral Luck*. Cambridge: Cambridge University Press, 1–19.

Williams, Bernard. 1981b. 'Practical Necessity', reprinted in Bernard Williams, *Moral Luck*. Cambridge: Cambridge University Press, 124–31.

Williams, Bernard. 1985. *Ethics and the Limits of Philosophy*. London: Fontana.

Williams, Bernard. 1993. *Shame and Necessity*. Berkeley: University of California Press.

Williams, Bernard. 1995a. 'How Free Does the Will Need To Be?', reprinted in Bernard Williams, *Making Sense of Humanity*. Cambridge: Cambridge University Press, 3–21.

Williams, Bernard. 1995b. 'Internal Reasons and the Obscurity of Blame', reprinted in Bernard Williams, *Making Sense of Humanity*. Cambridge: Cambridge University Press, 35–45.

Williams, Bernard. 1995c. 'Nietzsche's Minimalist Moral Psychology', reprinted in Bernard Williams, *Making Sense of Humanity*. Cambridge: Cambridge University Press, 65–76.

Williams, Bernard. 1995d. 'Moral Luck: A Postscript', reprinted in Bernard Williams, *Making Sense of Humanity*. Cambridge: Cambridge University Press, 241–7.

Williams, Bernard. 2000. 'Naturalism and Genealogy', in E. Harcourt (ed.), *Morality, Reflection and Ideology*. Oxford: Oxford University Press, 148–61.

Williams, Bernard. 2002. *Truth and Truthfulness*. Princeton: Princeton University Press.

Williams, Bernard. 2006a. 'What Might Philosophy Become?' in Bernard Williams, *Philosophy as a Humanistic Discipline*. Princeton: Princeton University Press, 200–13.

Williams, Bernard. 2006b. 'Philosophy as a Humanistic Discipline', reprinted in Bernard Williams, *Philosophy as a Humanistic Discipline*. Princeton: Princeton University Press, 180–99.

Williams, Bernard. 2006c. 'The Legacy of Greek Philosophy', reprinted in Bernard Williams, *The Sense of the Past*. Princeton: Princeton University Press, 3–48.

Wolf, Susan. 1982. 'Moral Saints', *Journal of Philosophy* 79: 419–39.

PART III

PRINCIPAL WORKS

CHAPTER 9

THE THEMES OF AFFIRMATION AND ILLUSION IN *THE BIRTH OF TRAGEDY* AND BEYOND

DANIEL CAME

> That lies are necessary in order to live is itself part of the terrifying and question-able character of existence.
>
> Friedrich Nietzsche[1]

A unifying theme in Nietzsche's early works (1870–6) is the claim that 'illusion', 'deception' and 'lies' are necessary to make tolerable one's experience of the world. The central message of Nietzsche's first published work, *The Birth of Tragedy* (1872), is that the affirmation of life requires 'illusion' which allows us to cope with the 'insight into the horrible truth' of our condition (*BT* 7). In a recent book (Reginster 2006), Bernard Reginster argues that Nietzsche overcame this early position in his later works. The early position, in Reginster's view, fails to underwrite a genuine affirmation of life, which requires affirming life 'as it is', in its very 'terrifying and questionable character'. In the earlier works, Reginster contends

> Nietzsche has not yet developed the doctrine of will to power and has only the illusions of art to prescribe as an antidote for those who have 'looked boldly into the terrible destructiveness of so-called world history as well as the cruelty of nature, and [are] in danger of longing for a Buddhistic negation of the will,' that is to say, those who have achieved 'Dionysian wisdom' (*BT* 7). Tragic wisdom, at that early stage, thus prescribes eschewing the Dionysian depths and remaining at the Apollonian surface with its beautiful appearances—being, in other words, 'superficial—out of profundity' (*GS* Preface 4).
>
> In his later works, by contrast, tragic wisdom ceases to be (partly) Apollonian and becomes a fully Dionysian wisdom. The affirmation of life no longer requires that we avoid what *The Birth of Tragedy* characterizes as the 'insight into the horrible truth' of our condition (*BT* 7). We are now capable of contemplating this truth without being driven to nihilistic despair by it

---

[1] *WP* 853.

because the revaluation made possible by the doctrine of the will to power actually enables us to welcome and affirm it (Reginster 2006: 248–9).

In Reginster's account, it is the will to power that enables us to accept and affirm the horrors which in *BT* can be tolerated only by laying over them a structure of illusions. Reginster understands the will to power as 'the will to the overcoming of resistance', which more specifically 'has the structure of a *second-order desire*: [. . .] a desire for the overcoming of resistance in the pursuit of some determinate first-order desire' (p. 132). The will to power is to be the new standard of valuation. By evaluating things in terms of power we are enabled to positively value those things—suffering, impermanence, loss, nature's indifference to human needs and purposes— which had previously led to a negation of life. For Nietzsche, such 'resistances', rather than providing reason to "say No" to life, are in fact necessary for us to attain what we really desire— power. We experience a growth in power in relation to phenomena over which we previously lacked power, phenomena which previously obstructed our willing. The attainment of power therefore depends on the overcoming of resistance, and so what is disagreeable to our willing is not only consistent with what we positively value, but actually constitutive of it. Thus:

> if . . . we take power—the overcoming of resistance—to be a value, then we can see easily how it can be the principle behind a revaluation of suffering. Indeed, if we value the overcoming of resistance, then we must also value the resistance that is an ingredient of it. Since suffering is defined by resistance, we must also value suffering. (p. 177)

Reginster is right, I think, that Nietzsche finds in the will to power a way of assigning positive value to suffering and hence that the will to power plays a central role in Nietzsche's later understanding of affirmation. Moreover, a case could be made for such a position being proleptically articulated in *The Birth*, where a hallmark of the psychology of the tragic Greeks is a vitality and robustness which leads them actually to seek out confrontations with the 'harsh' and 'problematic' aspects of existence as a means to test and exert their strength—the Greeks, we are told, 'wanted truth at full strength' (*BT* 8). But at the same time, Nietzsche maintains that, despite their proclivity for the Dionysian depths, there was a limit to the amount of truth that the Greeks could bear: of human beings in general, Nietzsche tells us, 'not one whit more may enter [. . .] consciousness [. . .] than can be overcome again by the power of Apollonian illusion' (*BT* 25). But in respect of Reginster's claims concerning the will to power's capacity to underwrite an affirmation of life '*as it is*', the following difficulty arises: the value that can be derived from regarding suffering as a resistance to be overcome, and hence as an occasion for power, depends on the resistance in question being something which the agent perceives as something that he *could* overcome. If a resistance is something that would be physically or psychologically utterly destructive for the agent—or is merely perceived as such by the agent—then it cannot even in principle be revalued positively in the way that Reginster outlines. Rather than be an occasion for power, any such resistance would in fact destroy the agent's potential to gain power. In short, not everything can be seen as a resistance to be overcome and anything which cannot be seen in this way *cannot* credibly be justified or affirmed in terms of the will to power.[2] It follows that the will to power is not sufficient to underwrite a genuine affirmation of life.

---

[2] There are important differences between 'justifying' and 'affirming' life, which I shall not address here. For a characteristically adept account, see May 2008.

Simon May (2008) agrees with Reginster that Nietzsche's later position is that genuine affirmation of life is possible. May contends, however, that there are events that can destroy one's fundamental capacity to express power, and so affirmation of life as it is cannot be achieved in the way that Reginster envisages. But May argues that such events need not preclude affirming life as it is, since to affirm one's life is not the same thing as—and nor does it require us—to find everything good or beautiful about it. As a 'Yes-sayer' one can detest certain events of world history or of one's own individual life, while not wishing history or one's own life to be free of those events and experiences. What this overlooks, however, is that to affirm the terrifying and questionable character of life, for Nietzsche, is not simply to acknowledge and endure it, indeed not even to find it conditionally valuable—it is 'to perceive not merely the necessity of those sides of existence hitherto denied, but their desirability; and not their desirability merely in relation to the sides of existence hitherto affirmed (perhaps as their complement or precondition), but for their own sake' (WP 1041; cf. EH: 'Why I Am So Clever' 10; WP 1019). Existence must be affirmed not merely *in spite* of what seems most deniable about it—its terrifying and questionable character—but (at least in part) *because* of it.[3]

It is here perhaps that Reginster's account of affirmation in terms of will to power is most illuminating. If we are to affirm life not in spite of its horrors but because of them, the only Nietzschean foundation for such an affirmation seems to be the revaluation of suffering made possible by the will to power—that is, in terms of the experience of power to be derived from overcoming the resistance that such horrors represent. But how plausible is the notion that we can affirm life not in spite of the gas chambers of Auschwitz but because of them, not in spite of the rape and torture of children but because of it? In the end, it seems the only psychologically plausible—and recognizably human (but not all-too-human)—account of affirmation would require either the falsification, concealment, or evasion of such events, so that they are not included in the object of affirmation at all, or their repositioning at sufficient 'distance' from us so that they recede almost completely into the background.

The argument of this essay is that, *contra* Reginster and May, both in the early and the later works illusion is a necessary condition of the affirmation of life. The position of the later Nietzsche is basically the position of *The Birth of Tragedy*: one must falsify—whether by evasion or explicit falsehood—the horrors of life *to some degree* in order to affirm it. In section 1, I set out the core thesis found in *BT vis-à-vis* the relationship between affirmation and illusion, which I am suggesting provides a template for the position of the later phase; in section 2, I examine the role of illusion in one of Nietzsche's litmus tests of affirmation found in *The Gay Science* of 1882, '*amor fati*'—that is, the ability 'to see as beautiful what is necessary in things' (GS 276; cf. 107); in sections 3, 4, and 5, I turn to certain elements in Nietzsche's understanding of 'self-creation' and how, through the employment of 'distance' and 'pretence', it is intended to engender an affirmation of existence; and finally—if only very briefly—in section 6, I attempt a provisional assessment of Nietzsche's conception of affirmation as I interpret it here.

---

[3] Cf. *TI*: '"Reason" in Philosophy' 6: 'The tragic artist is not a pessimist—he says *yes* to the very things that are questionable and terrible, he is *Dionysian*...'.

1 THREE STAGES OF ILLUSION

All of Nietzsche's published works, not just *BT* as is widely supposed, were written under the spell of Schopenhauer's pessimism—the view that suffering is an essential and therefore ineradicable feature of life (*WWR* I: 56; II: xlvi, 573). In his major work, *The World as Will and Representation*, Schopenhauer argues that honest reflection on the world and human life shows, as he puts it, that 'it would be better for us not to exist' (*WWR* II: 605). This nihilistic judgement follows, Schopenhauer argues, primarily from his account of self-conscious beings as characterized by an incessant and inherently painful willing. According to Schopenhauer, willing is a sufficient condition of suffering, because all willing arises necessarily from a want or deficiency, and to experience a want is to suffer: to live is to will; to will is to suffer; therefore to live is to suffer.

But if all men are unhappy and will remain so until death, it is puzzling why suicide is so rare. Death is the obvious choice because it removes the misery. Schopenhauer's explanation seems to be that we are 'tricked' by 'the will to live' into continuing to exist. That is, we have an innate but ultimately irrational predisposition to exist—irrational because non-existence is what is really in our interest but we *deceive* ourselves that this is not the case, that happiness and fulfilment are attainable, that the future will be better, and so on. In a contemporary idiom, our hardwired survival instinct makes life seem positively valuable, when it is not.

Nietzsche, in effect, shares Schopenhauer's view that if we saw life as it really is, we would not be able to carry on, and that we continue to exist only because of the hold that various forms of illusion have over us:

> It is an eternal phenomenon: the insatiable will always finds a way to detain its creatures in life and compel them to live on, by means of an illusion [*Illusion*] spread over things. One is chained by the Socratic love of knowledge and the delusion [*Wahn*] of being able thereby to heal the eternal wound of existence; another is ensnared by art's seductive veil of beauty fluttering before his eyes; still another by the metaphysical comfort that beneath the whirl of phenomena [*Erscheinungen*] eternal life flows on indestructibly—to say nothing of the more vulgar and almost more powerful illusions which the will always has at hand. These three stages of illusion [*Illusionsstufen*] are actually designed only for the more nobly formed natures, who actually feel profoundly the weight and burden of existence, and must be deluded by exquisite stimulants into forgetfulness of their displeasure. (*BT* 18)

The first kind of affirmation depends upon the 'profound illusion' that 'thought, using the thread of causality, can penetrate the deepest abysses of being, and that thought is capable not only of knowing being but even of *correcting* it' (*BT* 15). That this claim is false has been shown, Nietzsche believes, by 'the extraordinary courage and wisdom of Kant and Schopenhauer' (*BT* 18). But illusion is what Socratism most explicitly opposes. This means that the Socratic justification must be unreflective as regards its basic practice, that is, it must suppress its essentially illusory nature.[4]

---

[4] As Reginster (2013) puts it, 'It is essential to this kind of illusion that its effectiveness in producing and sustaining an affirmative stance toward existence depends on its *not* being recognized as illusion, that is to say, on its inducing (false) *belief*.' I discuss this aspect of Nietzsche's critique of Socratic rationalism in detail in Came 2004.

What drives the Socratic project is the belief that by uncovering the truth about the world and our place in it, suffering can be 'eliminated' and 'the eternal wound of existence be healed' (*BT* 18). Nietzsche traces this optimism to Socrates' teaching that knowledge is the cause of virtue and virtue the cause of happiness. Additionally, the Socratic truth-seeking project enables us to affirm life by endowing it with *purpose*, which causes the Socratic inquirer to take delight in existence: 'Like the artist, theoretical man takes an infinite delight in everything that exists, and, like him, he is shielded by that delight from the practical ethics of pessimism' (*BT* 18). That truth-seeking endows purpose, though, isn't a claim that Socratism makes or would accept: Socratism conceives of itself as motivated *only* by an interest in truth—and it is because Socratism conceives of its project in this way that when 'Lessing, the most honest of theoretical men' came close to admitting that he valued the pursuit of truth more than truth itself, thereby revealing 'the fundamental secret of science', he aroused the 'astonishment and irritation of the scientifically minded' (*BT* 15). If Socratism is actually concerned more with truth-seeking than with truth, it follows that Socratism depends on illusion. But since illusion is what Socratism most explicitly opposes, in order to engage in the Socratic project, it is necessary to conceal from oneself one's basic motivation for doing so. This means that Socratism must be unreflective as regards its essential nature. But Socratism generates a demand for reasons, so the Socratic inquirer will ultimately need an argument or rational explanation as to why he affirms life. Such an individual would find inadequate the idea that he affirms life unreflectively. It follows that the *ideally* Socratic individual could not accept the true account of why he finds life bearable. Accordingly, Socratic affirmation can work only if one doesn't question *how* it works. But this goes against the Socratic obsession with rational explanation and so is ultimately untenable. The nature of Socratism entails that eventually it will call into question its own mode of affirmation. As a means of affirming life, then, Socratism is inherently unstable and finally self-defeating: it cannot survive the realization of its true nature.

Nietzsche identifies two other kinds of illusion which in different periods of history have protected humanity from the basic truth about its condition. In the Homeric age, the Greeks were spared insight into the horror of things by their 'Apollonian drive for beauty', which gave birth to the 'resplendent, dream-born figures of the Olympians' (*BT* 2) and the myths and artworks that glorified them. In Homer's depictions of the gods and heroes the Greeks saw images in which human nature and existence were transfigured. The 'Apollonian' drive is the source of the mimetic arts of painting and sculpture, as well as epic poetry, whose purpose is to provide us with beautiful, ennobling images of humanity in which the pain and suffering of our everyday lives is transfigured.[5] The Apollonian finds its natural expression in the 'image-making' (*bildende*) activity of dreaming, through which we represent the world to ourselves with greater clarity and beauty (*BT* 1). The images of dream are an instance of what Nietzsche calls *Schein* ('semblance'). The satisfaction of this drive requires that 'even while this dream-reality is most alive, we nevertheless retain a pervasive sense that it is *semblance*' (*BT* 1). If we mistake the images for 'crude reality', our condition becomes 'pathological' and their curative effect is lost. Dreaming heals, according to Nietzsche, because it allows us to experience even the 'grave, gloomy, sad' and 'dark' sides to life as beautiful.

---

[5] See *BT* 16: 'here Apollo overcomes the suffering of the individual by means of the luminescent glorification of the *eternity of the phenomenon*; beauty triumphs over the suffering inherent in life; pain is, in a certain sense, deluded away from amongst the features of nature.'

The Apollonian artist has the rare ability to harness the natural power of dreams and produce objects of semblance in the external world. The representational arts of sculpture, painting, and epic poetry provide us with illusions that perfect the ugliness and confusion of everyday existence, making our own lives seem worth living.

But the triumph of the Apollonian over the horrors of life was fleeting. Adapting the plot of Euripides' *Bacchae*, Nietzsche describes how the Greeks were confronted with a new religion and a new form of art, when the cult of Dionysus first reached their shores. With their terrifyingly primitive music and wild sexual abandon, the Bacchic revellers tore apart the 'artful edifice' of Apollonian culture, and revealed that the Greeks' 'entire existence, with all its beauty and moderation, rested on a hidden ground of suffering and knowledge' (*BT* 4).[6] In the throes of Dionysian ecstasy, the Greeks were exposed to the full force of nature's 'artistic violence' (*Kunstgewalt*), which 'kneads' and 'chisels' the stuff of mankind how it will (*BT* 1).[7] Faced with the truth of the human condition, the Apollonian illusions could no longer suffice to protect them.

In a striking passage in section 7, Nietzsche describes the state of mind of the Apollonian Greek after a night of Dionysian *Rausch* ('intoxication'):

> The ecstasy of the Dionysian state, abolishing the habitual barriers and boundaries of existence, actually contains, for its duration, a lethargic element into which all past personal experience is plunged. Thus, through this gulf of oblivion, the worlds of everyday and Dionysian reality become separated. But when one once more becomes aware of this everyday reality, it becomes repellent; this leads to a mood of asceticism, of denial of the will. This is something that Dionysian man shares with Hamlet: both have truly seen to the essence of things, they have *understood* (*erkannt*), and action repels them; for their action can change nothing in the eternal essence of things, they consider it ludicrous or shameful that they should be expected to restore order to the chaotic world. Understanding (*Erkenntniss*) kills action, action depends on a veil of illusion—this is what Hamlet teaches us [....].

The mood of Nietzsche's Greek parallels that of modern Socratic man, once the dream of enlightenment has been shattered. But the Greeks were saved from nihilistic despair by the third form of illusion—the art of tragedy, which has the power to transform 'those repulsive thoughts about the terrible or absurd nature of existence into representations with which man can live' (*BT* 7). The tragic represents the apex of artistic creation, largely because its foundation lies in a fusion of the Apollonian and Dionysian drives. The Dionysian seeks to release us from life's burdens through the ecstatic experience of *Rausch*. It is expressed in drunkenness and sexual frenzy and appears in more urbane forms as the arts of music and dance and in certain types of religious mysticism. The purpose of *Rausch* is to dissolve our individuality and provide a sense of oneness with the rest of existence. In a state of Dionysian ecstasy, the struggles of our ordinary lives appear to be merely a game played by nature.[8]

---

[6] Cf. *DW* 2: 'Things in the ambit of Dionysus became audible which had lain artificially hidden in the Apollonian world: all the shimmering light of the Olympian gods paled before the wisdom of Silenus' (p. 129).

[7] Cf. *DW* 2: '[*Rausch*] penetrates to the innermost thoughts of nature, it recognizes the fearful drive to exist and at the same time the perpetual death of everything that comes into existence' (p. 126).

[8] See *BT* 17: 'For a brief moment we really become the primal essence itself, and feel its unbounded lust for existence and delight in existence. Now we see the struggles, the torment, the destruction of phenomena as necessary, given the constant proliferation of forms of existence forcing and pushing their way into life, the exuberant fertility of the world will.'

The important point to note for present purposes is that the tragic is a subspecies of illusion, one that presents the content of the Schopenhauerian world view in a fashion that renders it (just barely) tolerable. Tragic art incorporates illusion in its character portrayal, symbolism, and in the clarity and beauty of its dialogue; and without that illusion it could not function. For Nietzsche is very clear that pure, undiluted Dionysian insight is strictly intolerable; it would produce in us a nausea that would literally kill us. Having defined music as the Dionysian art *par excellence*, he expresses this idea in *BT* 21 when he says that one could not survive listening to the music to the third act of *Tristan* without the accompanying Apollonian words and staging. While the literal claim about the putative effects of listening to *Tristan* is obviously false, it is clear that the psychological claim which it expresses—that a direct or unmediated confrontation with the naked reality of our existential situation would be psychologically devastating—is one that Nietzsche takes very seriously. But it is equally clear that Nietzsche thinks that the tragic is much closer to the truth than the Socratic is— that the basic horror of things is at least partially transmitted by tragedy. For in tragedy, the terrible aspect of life is presented to us. Tragedy paints a picture of a world in which there is a fundamental mismatch between the way things are and our basic needs and desires. The suffering that is meted out to the tragic protagonist is *unmerited*; everything he values and cares for can be destroyed by powers utterly beyond his rational control—Necessity, Fate, or the whims of merciless gods. In watching the drama unfold, we understand that these events depict the fate of a single human being, but we also grasp that this is the fate of all of us. On one level, what is happening on stage is happening to a *particular* individual. But on another level, tragedy represents the *general* truth about human life in the form of this individual's fate. Thus Oedipus's fate is a paradigm instance of human fate, as the verses of Sophocles' chorus intimate:

> Ah, generations of men, how close to nothingness I estimate your life to be! What man, what man wins more of happiness than enough to seem, and after seeming to decline? With your fate as my example, your fate, unhappy Oedipus, I say that nothing pertaining to mankind is enviable. (1186–95 [trans. Lloyd-Jones 1994])

Thus, in tragedy, Nietzsche clearly thinks,we find a significant cognitive insight as to the nature of the world and human life. But the fact remains that a veil of illusion is draped over this truth, and it is only in virtue of this illusion that the experience of tragedy is bearable at all. As Raymond Geuss succinctly puts it, 'tragedy brings us as close as it is is possible to come to the basic truth of things' (1999)—but not into direct contact with the truth itself. The affirmation of life that tragedy produces, then, is not really an affirmation of life at all— the object of affirmation is not unvarnished reality—but rather an affirmation of a diluted and hence falsified image of reality.

Nevertheless, Nietzsche clearly thinks that tragic illusion facilitates a more stable and durable form of affirmation than the illusions of the Socratic or the purely Apollonian. From a Socratic perspective, tragedy's involvement with illusion renders it deeply unsatisfactory. But tragic culture doesn't place the high value on truth that Socratic culture does, and this is why it isn't afflicted by the kind of internal instability that besets Socratism. Tragic culture finds nothing objectionable in falsehood, provided that it serves the affirmation of life. Accordingly, from the perspective of tragic culture, illusion is unobjectionable. On the contrary, the recognition that illusion is necessary for life is partly constitutive of the tragic world view. The purely Apollonian, on the other hand, is defined by illusion. But it is not healthy for an individual, or for a whole society, to become entirely absorbed in the rule of either the Apollonian or the Dionysian. The healthiest foothold (both for individuals and for cultures as a whole) is in both. Nietzsche's preference for the tragic is partly motivated by the thought that through the artistic weaving together of the Dionysian and Apollonian elements of the soul the Greek spectator became healthy, through experience of the Dionysian within the protective realm of Apollonian illusion.[9]

2 *Amor fati* and Illusion

Reginster maintains, as we have seen, that in the later works Nietzsche develops a conception of affirmation that no longer requires eschewing the Dionysian depths. Nietzsche's new ideal is said to be that of a tragic wisdom in which life's horrors can be confronted and endured, even welcomed and affirmed. Nietzsche's free spirits, on Reginster's interpretation, view reality as it is rather than how it appears to be. They have the ability to cope with the truth of reality without needing the 'healing balm' of the Apollonian.

In his later writings, Nietzsche does indeed seem to strive for an approach to affirmation that could move beyond all forms of illusion. He does so above all in his two litmus tests of an individual's capacity to affirm life: the 'eternal recurrence' and, especially, '*amor fati*.' In these doctrines, Nietzsche envisages a kind of affirmation that involves confronting as much truth as one can about life: 'the ideal of the most high-spirited, vital, world-affirming individual, who has learned not just to accept and go along with what was and is, but who wants it again and again *just as it was and is* through all eternity' (*BGE* 56), or someone who does not want 'anything to be different, not forwards, not backwards, not for all eternity. Not just to tolerate necessity, still less to conceal it [. . .], but to *love* it . . .' (*EH*: 'Why I Am So Clever' 10). But does this attitude of *amor fati* really consist in a courageous realism about human experience, in a 'triumphant Yes' to reality 'as it is'? One reason to think that it does *not* is that it is in tension with—if not explicitly contradicted by—Nietzsche's views concerning the intimate relation between honesty and strength: 'the strength of a spirit should be measured according to how much of the "truth" one could still barely endure—or more distinctly, to what extent one would require it to be thinned down, shrouded, sweetened, blunted, falsified' (*BGE* 39). What this key passage suggests is that human beings *in general* 'require' the truth to be falsified to some extent—and to what extent is a function of the individual's strength. The Christian—for Nietzsche, the paradigm of weakness—requires a wholesale falsification of existence in the form of extravagant metaphysical postulates. The Greeks, by contrast—the paradigm of strength—required only a minimal 'thinning down' of the truth in the form of a veil of illusion through which the basic truth of things could still be at least partially apprehended.

Recall also that Nietzsche characterizes his project of *amor fati* as precisely demanding that one 'learn more and more to see *as beautiful* what is necessary in things' (*GS* 276, emphasis added). The connection with artistry is this: it is the activity best suited to present

---

[9] Gemes and Sykes (2013) provide an interesting account of the role of illusion in Nietzsche's writings. What, according to Gemes and Sykes, is particular to both the early and later Nietzsche is the overt emphasis on the need for illusion in the construction of *meaning*.

'what is necessary in things' as beautiful. But presenting what is necessary in things as beautiful does not occur without artistic reconstruction and reinterpretation. As things are presented in nature they are chaotic and formless: 'Nature, artistically considered, is no model. It exaggerates, it distorts, it leaves gaps. Nature is *chance*' (*TI*: 'Skirmishes of an Untimely Man' 7). In Nietzsche's mature work, artistic representation remains essentially tied to illusion: its role is to present reality in a transfigured and idealized form which reshapes our thoughts about it and the evaluative attitudes with which we respond to it. And given his explicit 'anti-realism' about value—nothing has value 'in itself' Nietzsche tells us—it follows that the ascription of aesthetic value to necessity must involve illusion. Nietzsche thinks 'all claims of the form "X is valuable" are false'. No value judgements are ever true, so the role of valuing in our lives must be filled by fictions. The role of artistry suggests, à la *BT*, that achieving the attitude of *amor fati* still involves some kind of distortion of the less palatable aspects of experience.

3 SELF-ARTISTRY AND THE AFFIRMATION OF LIFE

As a means to achieving the attitude of *amor fati*, Nietzsche proposes, inter alia, the aim of 'giving style' to one's character—an art 'practiced by those who survey all the strengths and weakness of the nature and then fit them into an artistic plan until every one of them appears as art and even weakness delights the eye' (*GS* 290).[10] That is, he proposes the existentially motivated project of cultivating one's character into something that can be contemplated with aesthetic pleasure. Indeed, we are told that the one thing that 'is needful' is 'that a human being should *attain* satisfaction with himself—be it through this or that poetry or art' (*GS* 290). What this claim amounts to, I suggest, is that for the later Nietzsche self-affirmation is sufficient for life affirmation.

To say that we need to affirm ourselves if we are to affirm life is hardly radical. What *is* radical is the thought that to affirm oneself is also to affirm life *in general*. There are two senses in which this claim could be taken—a metaphysical and a psychological sense. May interprets the claim as metaphysical.[11] As a part of the whole you cannot affirm yourself in isolation. As an inextricable part of existence in general, to affirm oneself is to affirm all of existence. But if the claim is metaphysical, then it makes no difference whether the object of affirmation is oneself or any other aspect of existence. Given the essential interconnectedness of all things, to affirm any part of the whole is also to affirm the whole. Interpreted metaphysically, then, the object of affirmation could be literally anything. But Nietzsche clearly envisages a special connection between affirmation of oneself and affirmation of life. Accordingly, it seems to me that 'the one thing needful' passage is best interpreted as a psychological claim.

[10] See Nehamas 1985 for an exegetically questionable but philosophically interesting account of Nietzsche's doctrine of self-creation.

[11] May 2011a: 188–98.

It seems clear that Nietzsche conceives the project of 'giving style' to one's character as part of his guiding theme of affirmation. In its original biblical context,[12] 'the one thing needful' denotes attention to our salvation in Christ. In adopting this phrase, Nietzsche is provocatively suggesting that an alternative (secular) salvation is possible through the project of 'becoming the poets of our lives' and 'turning ourselves into works of art', that in conceiving of oneself as a work of art and remaking oneself in such a way one's existence will seem justified. What Nietzsche is after is an attitude of positive self-evaluation, a curative to two millennia of the internalization of sin and absolutizing of our sense of guilty indebtedness. This internalization of sin, in Nietzsche's account, leads to a different kind of subjectivity—and one that is inseparable from a pervasive sense of the evil of human life. Christianity has turned man 'into a great immortal criminal' (GS 78), and it is not only human beings that are impaired but the empirical world in general. 'Christianity', as Nietzsche says, 'painted the Devil on the world's wall' (HAH II: 78). Hence the roots of nihilism and Schopenhauerian pessimism have now been reassigned to a human origin. It is no longer the well of pain at the heart of things that is the source of life negation but the radical masochism and self-abnegation that lie at the core of Christian morality.

For Nietzsche, the achievement of self-creation is a unified and integrated self. Most of us are a disunity, a mass of conflicting desires and impulses that lack any overarching aim or direction. The self-created invidual, by contast, is an integrated whole.[13] On Nietzsche's view of the person, as in the Platonic conception,[14] the self or psyche is not a monadic unity, but is composed of several elements—the various instincts, drives, and passions—which may be more or less unified depending on their interrelations. These relations are determined by the relative proportions of the parts and by their conflict or harmony with one another (the degree to which the exercise or satisfaction of one frustrates the operations of another, and the affective by-products generated by such interference). Presumably, certain configurations of these elements will be simply pleasing in themselves, much as certain colours are. Furthermore, just as our tastes are gratified by certain compositional aspects of parts of the external world—a delicate musical cadence, the fine proportions of a statue—so our inner sense relays to the mind aspects of its own composition that please or displease.

The 'beautiful' self, like the beautiful painting, is one in which 'opposites are tamed', though without being suppressed or exorcized: rather, the instincts are not allowed to 'turn against each other', for there is, instead, 'power over opposites; moreover, without tension' (WP 803). The resolution of one broad 'contradiction' to which Nietzsche pays special attention—that between Rausch ('intoxication') and restraint—resembles the account

---

[12] Luke 10:42. The one thing needful evidently is that which Mary chose. Very roughly, this was to sit at Jesus's feet and hear his word.

[13] For particularly nuanced discussions of this theme, see Gemes 2001, 2006, and 2009.

[14] See Republic book IV. The correct relationship between the soul's three elements that is constitutive of justice and the other virtues is often described by Plato in terms that suggest its aesthetic appeal: 'once he [sc. the just man] has treated the three factors as if they were literally the three defining notes of an octave—low, high and middle—and has created a harmony out of them and however many notes there may be in between; once he has bound all the factors together and made himself a perfect unity instead of a plurality, self-disciplined and internally attuned: then and then only does he act...' (Plato 1998: 443d–e).

given in *BT* of how, in tragedy, the Dionysian and the Apollonian are reconciled. In the earlier work it was the chaotic and suffering nature of the Dionysian in-itself of things that was to be brought into a productive relation with the Apollonian drive to order, precision, and restraint. But now one is required to impose a 'form upon oneself as a hard, recalcitrant, suffering material' (*GS* 107). This means, above all, reconciling seemingly opposed or contradictory aspects of character. In particular, self-artistry combines the passionate and forceful energy of the Dionysian with the discipline, form, and obedience to rules of the Apollonian. And just as the tragic synthesis of Apollo and Dionysus represents 'the highest goal' of art, so the self is similarly enhanced when it learns to balance the instinctual passions and drives with the need for restraint. Unlike the Christian self which employs restraint only in order to inflict cruelty on itself, the 'aesthetic nature' takes a 'natural delight…in restraint, the enjoyment of the beauty of restraint' (*WP* 870). Thus the 'higher' type integrates his drives and impulses rather than seeking fruitlessly to extirpate them. The Christian rejects those drives which are constitutive of human nature, for instance, sexual and aggressive impulses—and this is one sense in which the Christian fails to affirm life. The 'higher' type, by contrast, fashions the constellation of drives that comprise the self into a coherent unity in which all drives and instincts receive expression, not in a wanton or anarchic manner, but in a way that is answerable to an organizing principle, a master drive, the 'law of one's own being' (*UM* III).

The achievement of self-creation, then, is fundamentally the achievement of psychological *health*. And from this perspective of health, it seems, affirmation naturally ensues. The core idea here, I think, is as follows: as self-conscious beings, each of us must endure the review of his own mind and actions just as much as that of his immediate surroundings, and the aesthetic sense is just as keen in its appraisal of the objects and relationships it finds within as it is of those in its environment. If the furniture of my house has the power to depress me then I have excellent existential reasons to change it if I can; likewise, if what I see of the furniture of my mind fills me with loathing and despair, I should require no further motivation towards reform. Freud once wrote: '[t]he moment a man questions the meaning and value of life, he is sick'[15]—implying that from the standpoint of psychological health questions pertaining to the meaning and value of life simply don't arise. This is strikingly close to the later Nietzsche's view, according to which the impulse to question the value of existence or search for the conditions of the affirmation of life is already to be involved in nihilism.[16] For Nietzsche, the life-enhancing effects of beauty and depressing effects of ugliness are such central and universal features of human nature as to provide our chief impetus towards self-creation, as well as our strongest defence against pessimism ('Whoever is dissatisfied with himself is continually ready for revenge…For the sight of what is ugly makes one bad and gloomy', *GS* 290). As naturally self-reflective creatures, the aesthetic qualities brought most often and most vividly to our attention are our own, so that if an exalted pleasure is to be derived from the contemplation of what is beautiful, and a depressing effect from surveying what is ugly, each of us has excellent reason to ensure that his own life and soul are in good aesthetic shape.

---

[15]   Letter to Maria Bonaparte, 13 August 1937, in Freud 1961: 436–7.   [16]   Cf. May 2008 and 2011b.

4 Self-Artistry, Illusion, and Distance

I have argued that the project of self-creation aims primarily at an attitude of positive self-evaluation, and that Nietzsche believes that such an attitude is sufficient for being well disposed towards life in general. But what form does the project of self-creation take? In particular, does it involve fictionalizing or confronting the truth about oneself? I suggest that the answer is both, for part of what honest self-assessment consists in is recognizing that among our most fundamental needs is the ability to cultivate and value illusion, and that to do so is necessary in order to defend against 'nausea and suicide' (GS 107). For '[e]very profound spirit needs a mask: more, around every profound spirit a mask is continually growing' (BGE 40);[17] and 'it is part of a more refined humanity to have reverence "for the mask" and not to practise psychology and inquisitiveness in the wrong place' (BGE 270).[18]

As we have noted, given his explicit 'anti-realism' about value—nothing has value 'in itself' Nietzsche tells us—it follows that the ascription of aesthetic value to the self must at some level involve illusion. Nietzsche thinks 'all claims of the form "X is valuable" are false'. No value judgments are ever true, so the role of valuing in our lives must be filled by fictions. Hence artistic illusions are just as essential for self-affirmation as honestly surveying one's strengths and weaknesses, and the important lessons about creation come from artists, who show us not only how to make things beautiful, but also how to endorse something illusory:

> What one should learn from artists.—What means do we have to make things beautiful, attractive, desirable for us when they are not? And I think that in themselves they never are. Here we have something to learn from . . . artists, who are really continually trying to bring off such inventions and feats. Moving away from things until there is much of them that one no longer sees and much that one must 'see into' them, in order still to see them; or seeing things around a corner and as cut out and framed; or placing them so that they partially obstruct one another and allow only perspectival glimpses through; or looking at them through coloured glass or in the light of the sunset; or giving them a surface and skin that is not fully transparent—all this we should learn from artists while being wiser than they are in other things. For with them, this subtle power usually comes to an end where art ends and life begins; but we want to be the poets of our life . . . (GS 299; cf. GS 78)

The artistic model, then, shows us not only how to 'make things beautiful', but also how to see beauty in things 'when they are not' beautiful 'in themselves'. That is, we assimilate our attitude to that of 'art as the good will to appearance' (GS 107), so as to clear our conscience about endorsing illusions. The specific tactics of self-artistry described in section 299 of The Gay Science make plain the fictionalizing implications of Nietzsche's position. By these means, artistic representation falsifies its object by depicting it as other than it is. But falsification is not supposed to apply only within the world of conventional artistic creativity. Hence Nietzsche emphasises that while artists may concern themselves with mere fictions and not real life, 'we want to be the poets of our life'. Thus, the conclusion is

---

[17] Cf. BGE 289: 'Every philosophy also *conceals* a philosophy; every opinion is also a hiding-place; every word also a mask.'

[18] Cf. Z IV: 'The Leech': 'Where my honesty ceases I am blind and want to be blind.'

clear: the conception of affirmation Nietzsche identifies as the true opponent of the ascetic ideal (*GM* III: 25) is in fact a 'counterforce' against our honesty (*GS* 107).The role of artistry in achieving this attitude is, as it was in *BT*, to obscure or veil the less palatable aspects of our experience.

In sketching this particular strategy for affirmation, Nietzsche freely endorses evasion of the truth—or even explicit falsehood—where it is necessary in order to achieve the goal of affirmation. Hence the same basic idea first broached in *BT* still guides Nietzsche's later thinking about the role of illusion in the affirmation of life. Compare section 78 of *The Gay Science* on artistic transfiguration:

> What should win our gratitude.—Only artists...have given men eyes and ears to see and hear with some pleasure what each man is himself, experiences himself, desires himself; only they have taught us to esteem the hero that is concealed in everyday characters; only they have taught us the art of viewing ourselves as heroes—from a distance, and as it were, simplified and transfigured...Only in this way can we deal with some base details in ourselves. Without this art, we would be nothing but foreground and live entirely in the spell of that perspective which makes what is closest at hand and most vulgar appear as if it were terribly vast, and reality itself.

Part of what it means to give style to one's character, then, is to stand back from one's character—one's given desires, dispositions, ambitions, values—rather as the painter stands back from his canvas. Like the artist, one uses this 'distance' to decide how one shall organize, arrange, and manipulate them according to an artistic vision.[19] Indeed, it seems a structural feature of Nietzschean self-affirmation that one must stand back from oneself: 'some greatness, like some goodness, wants to be beheld only from a distance' (*GS* 15); and in a similar vein: 'our dramatists have 'taught us the art of viewing ourselves as heroes—from a distance and, as it were, simplified and transfigured' (*GS* 78).

The importance of distance to the project of affirmation is clear: many things can be fully affirmed only by standing back and evading too coarse or realistic representations of the world and the human: Nietzsche thus enjoins us to 'move away from things until there is much of them that one no longer sees' (*GS* 299). But it is not only the horrors of life which might require concealment or distance but also the mundane, ordinary life and the mediocre—all clearly as much a feature of reality 'as it is'. In general, however, the motif of distance connotes 'retreat' from reality or the placing of space between oneself and something external for defensive purposes.

5 NIETZSCHE'S PRETENCE THEORY OF THE SELF

But what is the object of self-affirmation? Nietzsche famously rejects the notion of the unified Cartesian subject or singular self as a myth. Thus we have his famous dictum from the *Genealogy* that 'the doer is merely a fiction added to the deed' (*GM* I: 13), and his observation

---

[19] For a sustained discussion of the theme of 'distance', see Lovibond 2013.

in *Beyond Good and Evil* that 'our body is but a social structure composed of many souls' (*BGE* 26). The notion of a unifed self is thus a deception. So must the self-created individual participate in a deliberate pretence or make-believe that the self exists? Given Nietzsche's rejection of one's believing a proposition to be true as a necessary condition for one's endorsing that proposition, he could coherently hold such a view. For Nietzsche, one's believing in the truth of a given proposition is neither necessary nor sufficient for one's endorsing that proposition—instead, what matters is whether one's endorsement of that proposition promotes life. ('The falseness of a judgment is for us not necessarily an objection to a judgment... The question is to what extent it is life-preserving, species-preserving, perhaps even species-cultivating', *BGE* 4.) Consequently, Nietzsche can remain agnostic or even sceptical about the self as an ontological reality while still articulating his views in terms of apparently traditional notions of selfhood. Nietzsche could describe the self-created individual as endorsing the illusion that he is a self without claiming that he believes that he *really is* a self, in the sense that his knowledge that this belief was false would not affect the status of his belief. Such an attitude is possible on the basis of the interactions between one's believing that one really is a self and one's other beliefs. In particular, aesthetic beliefs seem particularly resilient, even when one holds additional beliefs which imply the falsity of that particular belief. This is true even when such additional beliefs concern matters of ontology. The classic example here is that one could convincingly believe—or at least appear to believe—that 'Sherlock Holmes lives on Baker Street' while also believing that 'Sherlock Holmes does not exist'.[20]

This explanation of how self-affirmation is possible in the absence of a self commits Nietzsche to a non-intuitive understanding of belief, which separates one's endorsing a proposition and one's believing that proposition to be true. This in turn results in worries about the practicality of such an approach, namely, that it seems to involve a contradiction to endorse a proposition while knowing (or believing) that proposition to be false. Usually in such cases we resort to self-deception to conceal the proposition's falsity from ourselves. Of course, even willing self-deception is extremely difficult.[21] Nietzsche needs to provide some convincing psychological explanation for how one can knowingly or even mistakenly endorse false beliefs, especially where such beliefs are as significant as one's belief in one's own selfhood.

Fortunately, Nietzsche has an ingenious solution to this worry. The reason why one's believing a proposition to be true appears to be such a powerful condition of one's endorsing that proposition is that it is difficult to conceive of other values which could possibly displace truth and other epistemic values. However, as Nietzsche suggests, there *are* alternatives. In particular, as we have seen, he exhorts us to look down upon ourselves from an 'artistic distance', that is, to approach the question of our selfhood from an aesthetic perspective (*GS* 107). From such an aesthetic perspective, it might be possible to endorse the illusion of one's own selfhood while simultaneously holding beliefs which deny or imply the denial of that proposition. Moreover, not only does an aesthetic framework provide us with an alternative, but it also provides an explanation for why one who adopts such a framework *would* believe in his self. Nietzsche claims that the self, taken as an aesthetic object, is

[20] See Lewis 1978.
[21] Nehamas's discussion of the 'problem of self-deception' is motivated by this particular worry. Cf. Nehamas 1983.

aesthetically pleasing since it can accommodate judgements of 'style'; that is, one's self when subject to the right conditions, can appear to incorporate elements which—like the formal elements of a work of art—leave the viewer with the impression that those elements were designed and organized by the 'constraint of a single taste' (GS 290). Of course, just as in the case of a work of art, the self might not lend itself to positive aesthetic judgement. In such circumstances, it might be necessary to shape one's concept of one's self until it conforms to one's standards of beauty. It might also be the case that this approach cannot be successfully adopted by everyone—as is well known, Nietzsche holds no commitment to egalitarianism.

All of the preceding suggests a pretence theory of the self, similar to the 'make-believe' views advanced by various philosophers of art concerning our response to fictional entities.[22] On this view, it might be possible to pretend that we have self-making properties or even that we are selves because of aesthetic pleasure that experiences of particularly cohesive examples of subjectivity produce. This pleasure explains why we could plausibly adopt an aesthetic approach to the self as well as why we could continue to maintain such an aesthetic approach even in the face of our belief that we lack anything like the self we appreciate.

6 CONCLUDING REMARKS

I have argued in this essay that the insight that a life without illusions is both psychologically impossible, and, as a goal, one that will lead to suicidal nihilism, is enunciated in BT and adhered to throughout Nietzsche's works. In Nietzsche's account, the various existential strategies humans have deployed in order to cope with the horrors of life—the religious, the Socratic, the Apollonian, and the Tragic—all to varying degrees depend upon illusion or evasion of the basic pessimistic truth about the world and human life. Nietzsche recommends a Dionysian approach to the question of affirmation because it brings us as close as it is possible to come reality. But the Dionysian too is itself inseparable from illusion.

Hence the suspicion remains that Nietzsche passes off what is in fact a further instance of life denial for life affirmation. For the Nietzschean stance still implicitly claims that the affirmation of our existence as it is cannot be achieved and must be sought, at least in part, in an illusory realm. This seems to be the charge levelled against Nietzsche by Julian Young, for whom Nietzsche's final position represents a cowardly retreat from his original ambition of life affirmation (Young 1992: 147). Specifically, Young accuses Nietzsche of abandoning the hard task of affirming existence and indulging instead in various forms of escapism. There might be something in this criticism. And indeed Nietzsche's pursuit of affirmation might in fact be self-defeating. For as May points out, the impulse to question the value of existence or search for the conditions of the affirmation of life is already to be involved in nihilism.[23] Adapting one of Nietzsche's own psychological insights ('No one talks more passionately about rights than he who in the depths of his soul doubts whether he has any', HAH I: 597), we might be tempted to make the following psychological claim: Nietzsche's affirmation is a mask for life-negating despair. But rather than characterizing Nietzsche as having inauthentically abandoned the project of affirmation we might equally say that he recognized

---

[22] Cf. Walton 1990.   [23] See May 2008 and 2011b.

that illusion just is among the conditions of the affirmation of life, that 'untruth is a condition of life' (*BGE* 6). Facing up to that would then count as an insight, albeit a decidedly gloomy one, rather than cowardly retreat. The accusation of abandoning the project would have force only if illusion were not necessary for affirmation.[24]

BIBLIOGRAPHY

(A) Works by Nietzsche

Reference edition of Nietzsche's works: *Sämtliche Werke: Kritische Studienausgabe in 15 Einzelbänden*, ed. G. Colli and M. Montinari (15 vols). Berlin: De Gruyter, 1988.

BGE   *Beyond Good and Evil*, trans. W. Kaufmann. New York: Random House, 1966.
BT   *The Birth of Tragedy*, trans. W. Kaufmann. New York: Random House, 1967.
DW   'The Dionysian Worldview', trans. Ronald Speirs, in R. Geuss (ed.), *The Birth of Tragedy*. Cambridge: Cambridge University Press, 1999.
EH   *Ecce Homo*, trans. W. Kaufmann. New York: Random House, 1969.
GM   *On the Genealogy of Morals*, trans. W. Kaufmann. New York: Random House, 1969. See also: *On the Genealogy of Morality*, trans. M. Clark and A. J. Swensen. Indianapolis: Hackett Publishing Company, 1998.
GS   *The Gay Science*, trans. W. Kaufmann. New York: Random House, 1974.
HAH   *Human, All Too Human*, trans. R. J. Hollingdale. Cambridge: Cambridge University Press, 1986.
TI   *Twilight of the Idols*, trans. R. J. Hollingdale. Harmondsworth: Penguin, 1968.
WP   *The Will to Power*, trans. W. Kaufmann and R. J. Hollingdale. New York: Random House, 1968.
Z   *Thus Spoke Zarathustra*, trans.W. Kaufmann. Harmondsworth: Penguin, 1978.

(B) Works By Schopenhauer

Reference edition of Schopenhauer's works: *Arthur Schopenhauer: Sämtliche Werke*. Wiesbaden: Eberhard Brockaus Verlag, 1949.

WWR   *The World as Will and Representation*, trans. E. E. F. J. Payne (2 vols). New York: Dover, 1969.

(c) Other Works Cited

Came, D. 2004. 'Nietzsche's Attempt at a Self-Criticism: Art and Morality in *The Birth of Tragedy*', *Nietzsche-Studien* 33: 37–67.
Came, D. 2013. *Nietzsche on Art and Life*. Oxford and New York: Oxford University Press.
Freud, S. 1961. *Letters of Sigmund Freud 1873–1939*, ed. E. L Freud, trans. T. and J. Stern. London: Hogarth Press.
Gemes, K. 2001. 'Post-Modernism's Use and Abuse of Nietzsche', *Philosophy and Phenomenological Research* 52: 337–60.

---

[24] I would like to thank Ken Gemes and Philip Donor Balliet for their very helpful comments on a draft version of this essay.

Gemes, K. 2006. 'We Remain of Necessity Stranger to Ourselves': The Key Message of Nietzsche's *Genealogy*', in C. D. Acampora (ed.), *Nietzsche's On the Genealogy of Morals: Critical Essays*. Lanham, Md: Rowman & Littlefield Publishers, 191–208.

Gemes, K. 2009. 'Freud and Nietzsche on Sublimation', *Journal of Nietzsche Studies* 38: 38–59.

Gemes, K. and Sykes, C. 2013. 'Nietzsche's Illusion', in D. Came (ed.), *Nietzsche on Art and Life*. Oxford and New York: Oxford University Press.

Geuss, R. 1999. 'Introduction', in Friedrich Nietzsche, *The Birth of Tragedy*, ed. R. Geuss and R. Speirs, trans. R. Speirs. Cambridge: Cambridge University Press, pp. viii–xxx.

Lewis, D. 1978. 'Truth in Fiction', *American Philosophical Quarterly* 15.1: 37–46.

Lloyd-Jones, H. 1994. *Sophocles, Ajax, Electra, Oedipus Tyrannus*, Loeb Classic Library. Cambridge, Mass.: Harvard University Press.

Lovibond, S. 2013. 'Nietzsche on Distance, Beauty, and Truth', in D. Came (ed.), *Nietzsche on Art and Life*. Oxford and New York: Oxford University Press.

May, S. 2008. 'Affirmation without Justification'. Unpublished ms.

May, S. 2011a. *Love: A History*. New Haven and London: Yale University Press.

May, S. 2011b. 'Why Nietzsche is Still in the Morality Game', in S. May (ed.), *Nietzsche's 'On the Genealogy of Morality': A Critical Guide*. Cambridge: Cambridge University Press, 78–100.

Nehamas, A. 1983. 'How One Becomes What One Is', *Philosophical Review* 92.3: 385–417.

Nehamas, A. 1985. *Nietzsche: Life as Literature*. Cambridge, Mass.: Harvard University Press.

Plato. 1998. *Republic*, trans. Robin Waterfield. Oxford: Oxford University Press.

Reginster, B. 2006. *The Affirmation of Life: Nietzsche on Overcoming Nihilism*. Cambridge, Mass.: Harvard University Press.

Reginster, B. 2013. 'Art and Affirmation', in D. Came (ed.), *Nietzsche on Art and Life*. Oxford and New York: Oxford University Press.

Walton, K. 1990. *Mimesisas Make Believe: On the Foundations of the Representational Arts*. Cambridge, Mass.: Harvard University Press.

Young, J. 1992. *Nietzsche's Philosophy of Art*. Cambridge: Cambridge University Press.

CHAPTER 10

'Holding on to the Sublime': on Nietzsche's Early 'Unfashionable' Project[1]

Keith Ansell-Pearson

The four *Untimelies* are thoroughly warlike. They prove that I was no daydreamer with his head in the clouds . . . (Nietzsche, *Ecce Homo*).

Introduction: Sublime Nietzsche

In this essay I aim to present a new argument about the early Nietzsche and focus largely on his *Unfashionable Observations*. I believe there is a neglected unifying theme to them and wish to claim that this centres on Nietzsche's commitment to the sublime. For Nietzsche it is imperative that we 'hold on to the sublime', and my essay is an exploration of just what he means by this. The concept of the sublime occupies a significant role in Nietzsche's thinking. It is surprising, therefore, that the topic, with the obvious exception of *The Birth of Tragedy*, has received scant treatment in the literature.[2] In this paper my focus is on Nietzsche's project in his early writings, which is a much wider project than simply *BT*, and I want to show how the sublime informs both Nietzsche's conception of philosophy and his ideas for cultural revitalization. I will illuminate how an appreciation of the sublime on Nietzsche's part is embedded in four contexts and problems: his exploration of what philosophy is in its beginnings; his attack on D. F. Strauss and cultural philistinism; his conception of culture

---

[1] This essay is a thoroughly revised and modified version of an essay first published as ' "Holding on to the Sublime": Nietzsche on Philosophy's Perception and Search for Greatness', in Herman Siemens and Vasti Roodt (eds), *Nietzsche, Power, and Politics* (Berlin and New York: Walter de Gruyter, 2008), 767–99. I am grateful to Christine Battersby and John Richardson for their helpful comments on earlier drafts of this essay and that have helped me to improve it.

[2] For treatments of the sublime in *BT* see Battersby 2007, Nabais 2006, and Rampley 2000.

as transfigured *physis*; and the critique of the science of history. Although Nietzsche is not, I think, saying anything especially new about the sublime, it is an important notion for him; what is novel in his early writings is his adoption of it as a category to define the very practice of philosophy and the way he employs it to set new horizons for life and culture. Nietzsche is attached to the sublime, I suggest, because it is the notion that best captures how we are able in human experience to push beyond certain limits. In Nietzsche the limits to be transcended are manifold and I highlight a number of them in what follows. They include: the limits of ordinary experience and understanding; the limits of reason; the limits of social conformism and conservatism; and the limits of scholarship and scholasticism. Indeed, his concern with the sublime manifests itself in the title of his early project where the chief task is to be 'unfashionable': the genuine thinker for Nietzsche is one who is able to go beyond the limits, both fashionable and timely, of his own time.

UNFASHIONABLE NIETZSCHE

Nietzsche published his four unfashionable observations between August 1873 and July 1876. Although each text was published as an independent treatise, Nietzsche indicated their interrelatedness by loosely joining them together under a collective title (Gray 1995: 395). At one time the ambition was for a much longer set of 'observations' (one plan gives thirteen titles; see *KSA* 7: 19 [330]). In part they were written as vehicles by which Nietzsche could expel everything that was polemically negative and rebellious inside him, but they should not be written off as mere negative polemics.[3] As Nietzsche later noted, in them he was making promises or pledges to himself concerning his future tasks and projects.[4]

In the four observations Nietzsche directs his gaze, as well as his polemical ire, at German culture, civilization, science, and art in the wake of the Prussian victory over France in 1871 which resulted in German political unification and the rule of *Realpolitik* under Bismarck. Until quite recently, and as a result of adopting an argument of Walter Kaufmann's, the four pieces of writing have been known in English as the 'untimely meditations' (Kaufmann 1974: 35). More recent scholarship has favoured the more literal 'observations' for *Betrachtungen* over the figurative 'meditations', and either 'unfashionable' or 'unmodern' for *unzeitgemässe*.[5] They contain an explicit disavowal of the age (*die Zeit*), above all the now or the present. They are not untimely in sense of inopportune or unseasonable but rather defiantly unfashionable. Neither are they reactionary or merely anti-modern: 'They aim at transcending the present, at superseding conventional notions

---

[3] Gray 1995: 410; see also Breazeale 1997: xxv.
[4] See letters to Georg Brandes dated 19 February and 10 April 1888 in Brandes 2002: 107–9 and 119–20 (cited in Breazeale 1997: xxvii). In the letter of 10 April 1888 Nietzsche writes: 'What you say about *Schopenhauer as Educator* gives me great pleasure. This little work serves me as a touchstone; he to whom it says nothing *personal* has probably nothing to do with me either. In reality it contains the whole plan according to which I have hitherto lived; it is a rigorous *promise*' (120).
[5] The first use in Nietzsche of the adjective '*unzeitgemass*' occurs in a letter to Erwin Rohde of 17 August 1869 and is specifically applied to Wagner. Wagner is said to stand above everything 'ephemeral'; he is 'unfashionable in the most beautiful sense of that word'.

of past, present, and future' (Arrowsmith 1990: xi). *Betrachten* means to look at, observe, or view, and only by extension to consider, meditate, or reflect: 'What Nietzsche intends by *Betrachtungen* is a persuasively discursive account of what he has *seen* and *considered...* '(Arrowsmith 1990: xi) Nietzsche's essays are an exercise in cultural criticism in which 'observation' is directed at the cultural and sociopolitical world. The focus of his attack is the German cultural elite—the cultural philistines, in Nietzsche's memorable phrase—and the adjective *unzeitgemäss* indicates that Nietzsche sees himself as belonging to an isolated critical minority that dares to attack the idols of the day. Nietzsche's antipathy is towards the cult of the present day or 'the modern', and one commentator has suggested that he is intensifying Schopenhauer's scathing attack on *Jetztzeit*, the 'Today' (Gray 1995: 397). At this point in time Nietzsche is influenced by Schopenhauer's concern over the allure of the temporal and of becoming.

Although the translation of 'untimely' has the merit of retaining the stem word 'time' (*Zeit*) from which the adjective Nietzsche uses derives, it 'implies something inept and inappropriate, something that occurs at the wrong time and hence is either premature or belated' (Gray 1995: 399). And yet, what motivates the kind of intellectual praxis Nietzsche carries out in the four observations is the need to speak the truth no matter how unpleasant it might be, and for Nietzsche this is an exercise that could not be more urgent or necessary. This commitment requires a careful calculation of the moment when one's interventions and actions will have their most profound and far-reaching impact (Gray 1995: 399), and is a feature of all of Nietzsche's polemics be they from his early period or from his late period, such as *GM* and *TI*. In some key respects the later writings represent a return to the early Nietzsche of the *Observations*, being polemical and unmodern. In the *Observations* Nietzsche's untimeliness consists in not paying obeisance to the sovereignty of popular opinion as an arbiter of taste, valuation, and truth. He who follows public opinion is always timely.[6] Nietzsche coins the term *Bildungsphilister* to describe the self-satisfied newspaper readers and consumers of culture. The 'cultivated philistine' is described in the second unfashionable observation on history as, 'the quickly dated up-to-date babbler about the state, the church, and art' and who has an insatiable stomach but knows little of genuine hunger and thirst (*UM* II: 10). The appreciator of genuine culture is unfashionable.

Today the observations are among Nietzsche's most neglected works and yet they are key documents for a proper understanding of his development. It is typically assumed that their ostensible subjects are so diverse that they seem to be connected by little beyond their collective title and common form (the traditional polemical essay divided into numbered, untitled sections). As Breazeale points out, a closer examination reveals a thematic unity that is not always evident at first. They contain important early treatments of essential Nietzschean topics such as the relationship between life, art, and philosophy, the cultivation of the true self, education, and the difference between genuine wisdom and mere knowledge or 'science' (Breazeale 1997: vii). To this I wish to add the claim that what unifies Nietzsche's early project, so strongly evident in the observations, is a commitment to the sublime.

---

[6] See Breazeale 1997: lxv–lxvi.

INTRODUCTION TO THE SUBLIME

The word 'sublime' is derived from the Latin 'sublimis', which is a combination of 'sub' (under), and 'limen' (a lintel or the top piece of a door, suggesting threshold); thus, in the *OED* the sublime is defined as 'set high up or raised aloft'. The treatise by Longinus, of uncertain date but typically ascribed to the first century CE, *Peri Hypsous*, translated as *On the Sublime*, *On Greatness*, or *On Eloquence* literally means 'On the Height', and the text is concerned with showing how our natural gifts can be led to states of elevation. The 'true sublime', says Longinus, which is to be found in 'the grand style' of poetry and literature, 'uplifts our souls', filling us with 'proud exaltation' and a sense of 'vaunting joy' (Longinus 1965: 107). The main German word for the sublime, '*das Erhabene*', linked to the adverb '*erhaben*' (raised, elevated), captures well this sense of elevation beyond the ordinary and the familiar.

Since the concept was introduced in the text attributed to Longinus, the sublime has stood for several things: the effect of grandeur or the grand style in speech and poetry; a sense of the divine or transcendent; the contrast between the limitations of human perception and the overwhelming majesty of nature; as evidence of the triumph of reason over nature and the imagination; and, most recently, as a signifier for that which exceeds the grasp of reason. As Philip Shaw notes in his guide to the subject, common to all these definitions is a preoccupation with struggle, so for Longinus the discourse of the sublime, be it in political oratory or epic verse, works to overcome the rational powers of its audience in an effort to persuade them of the efficacy of an idea by means of its sheer rhetorical force. We are ravished, as he notes, by the power of words (Shaw 2006: 18).

The word has multiple applications: a building or a mountain can be called sublime, as can a thought, some heroic deed, or a mode of expression. These are value judgements, though the sublime is not restricted to this, since it also describes a state of mind. Something majestic, such as the interior of a great cathedral, can fill us with awe. The sublime speaks of greatness or grandeur and sometimes we are literally lost for words in its presence. The failure of thought or words to capture the experience can often testify to its reality: a certain *je ne sais quoi* or the ineffable is at work. Often, and as noted, the word has the meaning of being lifted above or elevated, but the effect of the sublime can also be overwhelming and engulfing, something we find hard to resist. One writer, James Usher, writing in the nineteenth century, speaks of the power of the sublime in terms of taking possession of our attention and faculties, absorbing them in astonishment (Shaw 2006: 2). As Shaw notes, we have recourse to the feeling or experience of the sublime whenever our experience slips out of conventional understanding and the power of an object or event is such that words fail and points of comparison disappear. It thus marks the *limits* of reason and expression together with an indication of what might lie beyond these limits. It often has associations with the ultimate, the transcendent, the infinite, and descriptive failure raises a negative, even painful, presentation of the ineffable. Sublimity, therefore, refers to a moment when the ability to apprehend, to know, and to express a thought or sensation is defeated. In Kant the struggle at work in the experience of the sublime is between the evidence of the senses and the supersensible power of reason: the sublime ultimately involves for Kant the ascendancy of the rational over the real; the mind of man proves itself to be greater than anything we encounter or discover in nature. With Kant the emphasis shifts in thinking about the sublime away from empiricist and naturalistic theories, towards conceiving sublimity as a special mode of consciousness: through it, our higher vocation and human dignity are revealed to us (Kant 1790/1987: sections 23–9).

In her recent study *The Sublime, Terror and Human Difference* (2007), Christine Battersby maintains that: 'Nietzsche spent much of his philosophical career engaging with and seeking to resist the seductions of the sublime, and ended by reconfiguring sublimity in ways that are also radical and profound' (Battersby 2007: 160). For Battersby, Nietzsche provides us with a reconfigured 'bodily' sublime that gives depth to surfaces and to the moment. I wish to canvas two main insights so far as his early project is concerned: (a) The early Nietzsche does not resist the sublime but positively embraces it and becomes an advocate of it; (b) To properly grasp what this entails and means we need to read beyond *BT* and pay attention to the project of the Basel years as a whole. This would include materials such as the uncompleted and massively ambitious *Philosophenbuch*[7], *Philosophy in the Tragic Age of the Greeks* (prepared for publication but not actually published during Nietzsche's lifetime), essays such as 'On the Relation of Schopenhauer's Philosophy to German Culture', and the published *Unfashionable Observations*. When we do this, we find that the sublime and the exhortation to hold on to it define Nietzsche's early project. That's in essence what it is. This is not visible if we focus solely, as has been done to date in treatments on Nietzsche and the sublime, on *BT*. *BT* is an important part of the story, but it's only a part, and not I believe the most revealing.[8]

Nietzsche's deployment of the sublime harks back to Longinus and shares some of the classical features of the sublime from Longinus to Kant. In accordance with the tradition Nietzsche employs the sublime in connection with notions of elevation, exaltation, loftiness, ennoblement and the attainment of heights of experience. Nietzsche often follows the Longinian tradition in his thinking on the sublime, and it is in play in *EH* when he declares himself to be an artist of the grand rhythm and grand style.[9] As noted, a concern with the sublime also indicates a focus on the experience of awe, feelings of admiration, reverence, and astonishment, the expansion of our mental powers of comprehension, respect for our higher vocation (human-superhuman), and so on, and as we shall see, much of this is at work in Nietzsche's early thinking and his valuation of greatness. For Nietzsche it's not so much a question of the sublime providing us with access to some ideal of a rational and universal moral humanity, as it is in Kant and Schiller (Kant 1790/1987; Schiller 2001), but more that certain privileged and superior insights, perceptions, and moments become available to us. Ultimately, the importance of the sublime for the early Nietzsche is that it provides us with a mode of access into questions of value, enabling us to cultivate an appreciation of

---

[7] For insight into the history of 'The Philosophers' Book' see Breazeale 1979: xviii–xxiii.

[8] In *BT* Nietzsche works with a 'tragic sublime', in which nauseous thoughts about the dreadful and absurd character of existence, as human beings encounter it, are transformed into mental images with which it is possible to live, and in which the sublime represents the artistic taming of the dreadful and the ridiculous or the comic the artistic discharge of the dreadful.

[9] We typically construe Nietzsche as a philosopher of the tragic. Indeed, in *EH* Nietzsche says of himself that he is the *first* tragic philosopher (*EH*: 'The Birth of Tragedy' 3). However, in *EH* Nietzsche also reveals that 'The art of *grand* rhythm, the *grand style* of phrasing, as the expression of a tremendous rise and fall of sublime (*sublimer*), of superhuman (*übermenschlicher*) passion, was first discovered by me...' (*EH* 'Why I Write Such Good Books' 4)

what is important and significant and this resides in according positive value to what is rare, abnormal, and extraordinary. In essence, then, the sublime is being used by Nietzsche to indicate a dedication to that which is truly important and significant over the fleeting and fashionable. It also entails, as we shall see, valuing those instances of existence where the human being transcends the level of the animal.

The Sublime contra Philistine
Gemüthlichkeit

In some of his early writings Nietzsche appeals to the sublime as a way of drawing attention to the narrowness of life, of the discerning and judging that prevail in German scholarship, including its reliance on domestic and homely virtues, and he contrasts the elevation to greatness afforded by the sublime with what he calls 'Philistine homeliness'. This latter contrast is taken from the completed but unpublished short essay of 1872, and one of the five prefaces to five unwritten books sent as a Christmas gift to Cosima Wagner, entitled 'The Relation of Schopenhauer's Philosophy to a German Culture'. This unpublished essay of 1872 is important for anticipating in outline the three unfashionable observations Nietzsche will go on to write on Strauss and the cultural philistine, on the dangers of the historical fever, and on Schopenhauer as our educator, and for clearly indicating the extent to which Nietzsche relies upon a notion of the sublime to carry out his unfashionable critique of the present.

In this unpublished essay Nietzsche tells the Germans that they have their philosopher—Schopenhauer—and the task is to now search for and create the culture (*Kultur*) that is proper to him. Nietzsche begins the essay by warning his readers of the dangers of a fashionable and philistine relation to actuality and appeals directly to the sublime (he uses the word '*Grosse*' in this passage but '*Erhabene*' throughout the rest of the essay). Let me cite the opening of the essay in full in order to gauge its proper effect:

> In dear vile Germany culture (*Bildung*) now lies so decayed in the streets, jealousy of all that is great rules so shamelessly, the general tumult of those who race for 'fortune' resounds so deafeningly, that one must have a strong faith, almost in the sense of *credo quia absurdum est*, in order to hope still for a growing culture (*Kultur*), and above all—in opposition to the press with her 'public opinion'—to be able to work by public teaching. With violence (*Gewalt*) must those, in whose hearts lie the immortal care for the people (*Volk*), free themselves from all the inrushing impressions of that which is just now actual (*Gegenwärtigen*) and valid, and evoke the appearance of reckoning them indifferent things. They must appear so, because they want to think, and because a loathsome sight and a confused noise, perhaps even mixed with the trumpet-flourishes of war-glory, disturb their thinking, and above all, because they want to *believe* in the German character and because with this faith they would lose their strength (*Kraft*). Do not find fault with these believers if they look from their distant aloofness and from the heights towards their Promised Land! They fear those experiences, to which the kindly disposed foreigner surrenders himself, when he lives among the Germans, and must be surprised how little German life corresponds to those great individuals, works and actions, which, in his kind disposition he has learned to revere as the true German character. Where the German cannot lift himself into the sublime (*nicht in's Grosse erheben kann*) he makes an impression less than mediocre. (Nietzsche 1911: 65–6; *KSA* 1: 778–9)

The concern, then, is with greatness. As noted, the basic contrast Nietzsche is developing in this essay is between Philistine homeliness (*Gemüthlichkeit*) and the sublime (*das Erhabene*). German scholarship, Nietzsche argues, can be characterized in terms of a display of 'domestic and homely' virtues, such as industry, moderation, cleanliness, self-restriction, and so on. We can identify an unlimited knowledge drive at work in the practice of this scholarship, but when looked at closely it shows itself to be 'more like a defect, a gap, than an abundance of forces', the consequence of a 'needy, formless atrophied life' (1911: 66, 779). Even more damning, Nietzsche says that the Germans, as the 'true virtuosi of philistinism', are at home in life's narrowness, in narrow discerning and judging, with a submersion into detail, the minute, and the nearest. The contrast is clearly with the wide and the expansive, with the lofty and open horizon that Nietzsche associates with the sublime. If any scholars do manage to carry themselves into the sublime they make themselves as heavy as lead and 'as such lead-weights they hang to their truly great human beings, in order to pull them down out of the ether to the level of their own necessitous indigence' (1911: 66, 779). This attachment to 'Philistine homeliness', Nietzsche notes, is what is now supposed to guide the composition of poetry, the making of painting and music, and even philosophy. Today's educated person (*der Gebildete*) is to be educated historically (*historisch*), and 'by his historical consciousness he saves himself from the sublime in which the Philistine succeeds by his "homeliness"' (1911: 67, 780). The enthusiasm (*Enthusiasmus*) that history might inspire—for example, the lessons of great deeds and works—is to be blunted. Nietzsche protests that history (*Geschichte*) will disclose to us only those confessions which we are worthy to receive, and that the world has at all times been full of trivialities and nonentities (*Nichtigkeiten*), so that our hankering after history will reveal or unveil to us only these things and will become the enemy of the sublime, that is, of all that is great.

Let me now show how an appreciation of the sublime informs his early appreciation and conception of philosophy. I will then move on to discussing salient aspects of each of the first three unfashionable observations.[10]

Nietzsche on Philosophy: Origins and Tasks

The early Nietzsche has a fairly specific conception of what philosophy is in its origins. It is captured in some quite striking formulations. Philosophy for Nietzsche is bound up with the legislation of greatness, conceived as a 'name-giving' that elevates (*erhebt*) the human being, and has its origins in the legislation of morality (*Gesetzgebung der Moral*) (*KSA* 7: 19 [83]). The fact that the philosopher enjoys only a chance-like existence is the more reason to value this existence: 'The philosopher is the rarest form of greatness because human beings arrived at knowledge only by coincidence, not as an original endowment. But for this reason, also the highest type of greatness' ([195]). Philosophy is doing many things and has

---

[10]   Nietzsche, of course, also employs the sublime in the fourth untimely on Wagner in Bayreuth, but an analysis of this deployment lies beyond the scope of the present essay. See *UM* IV: 2, 3, 4, 7, and 9.

multiple tasks to perform, but one thing philosophy does for Nietzsche, and which makes it different from, say, science (*Wissenschaft*), is to lift or elevate us above the ordinary and the contingently empirical—the domains of the factual and actual—and show us things that are magnificent, stupendous, remarkable, abnormal, rare, and extraordinary. For Nietzsche the earliest philosophers, such as Heraclitus and Empedocles, are magnificent 'superhuman' types who come up with intuitions about existence that fill us with awe. Our confrontation with the Heraclitean insight into 'eternal becoming', for example, has something that is both terrifying and uncanny: 'the strongest comparison is to the sensation whereby someone in the middle of the ocean or during an earthquake, observes all things in motion'. Nietzsche then notes that it requires an 'astonishing power to transmit the effects of the sublime (*des Erhabenen*) and joyful awe to those confronting it' (*KGW* IV.2: 272). Heraclitus comes up with a sublime image (*erhabenes Gleichniss*) to do just this: 'only in the play of the child (or that of the artist) does there exist a Becoming and Passing Away without any moralistic calculations' (*KGW* IV.2: 278). Here we have philosophers who transcend the limits of experience through some profound intuition and arrive at sublime insights and disclose them for us.[11]

In the lecture course on the pre-Platonic philosophers he gave several times during his tenure at Basel, Nietzsche sought to resolve the riddle of defining the philosopher. Drawing on Aristotle's distinction between *phronesis* (prudence) and *sophia* (wisdom) in the *Ethics*, in which the former is concerned with common human goods and the latter with knowledge of what is most precious, Nietzsche points out to his students that the Greek word *sophos* does not simply denote 'wise' in the usual sense but is related etymologically to *sapio*, to taste. Suggesting nothing of quietude or asceticism, the 'wise' human being is the one who has 'sharp taste' as a 'sharp knowledge'; the aim is not to know how conclusions follow from principles but which branches and modes of knowledge contain those principles most worthy of knowledge (*KGW* II.4: 217–18; *PPP* 8).[12] For Nietzsche, this suggests the need for a discriminating taste, and his argument is that whilst philosophical thinking is of the same kind as scientific thinking, it differs from it in that it directs itself 'toward *great* things

[11] In *Philosophy in the Tragic Age of the Greeks* Nietzsche interprets Heraclitus as having an 'intuition' (*Intuition*) leading to two negations: first, a denial of the duality of two diverse worlds such as the physical and the metaphysical, one a realm of definite individuated qualities, the other a world of the indefinite that cannot as such be defined; second there is an even more bold negation, which is to deny 'being' (*Sein*) altogether. For Nietzsche, Heraclitus is a regal thinker who has the extraordinary power to think intuitively and who is hostile to reason or thinking in terms of concepts and logical combinations (Nietzsche notes that Aristotle accused him of sinning against the law of contradiction). Nevertheless, he defends Heraclitus' intuitive mode of thinking which embraces two things: one, the multicoloured changing world that crowds in upon us in all our experiences, and, two, the conditions that make our experience of the world possible (Heraclitus is a Kantian!). The fundamental conditions are time and space, including the pure, empty form of time: 'For they may be perceived intuitively, even without a definite content, independent of all experience, purely in themselves'. See *PTG* 5.

[12] Compare Aristotle, *Ethics*, book 6, vii: 'The wise men, then, must not only know all that follows from first principles, but must also have a true understanding of those principles'. Nietzsche repeats this lesson on taste in *HAH* II: 170 where he argues that taste makes one not only 'blessed' but also 'wise': 'which is why the Greeks, who were very subtle in such things, designated the wise man with a word that signifies the *man of taste*, and called wisdom, artistic and practical as well as theoretical and intellectual, simply "taste" (*Sophia*)'. See also *Z* II: 'On Those Who Are Sublime': '... all of life is a dispute over taste and tasting'.

and possibilities'. He duly notes that the concept of greatness is amorphous, being partly aesthetic and partly moral.[13] For Nietzsche, the great is that which departs from the normal and the familiar: 'We venerate what is *great*. To be sure, that is also the *abnormal*' (*KSA* 7: 19 [80]). Humanity, he further states, can only grow through admiration for what is rare and great in life and culture, and this is the domain of the sublime. For Nietzsche what is sublime is anything that lifts us beyond the everyday, the commonplace, the banal, the familiar, and the customary.

For Nietzsche, the most powerful and fruitful era for thinkers of ancient Greece is the time before and during the Persian wars (499–448 BC). This is the period when, he says, 'possibilities of life' are discovered, a time when philosophers appear who do not resemble deformed and ruined figures, scrawny desert hermits, theologizing counterfeiters, or depressed and pale scholars (*KSA* 8: 6 [48]). The 'tragic age' is thus something of a golden or flourishing and vital age for Nietzsche, with the Greeks on the point of discovering a type of human being higher than any previous type. According to Nietzsche, the early Greek philosophers had a degree of confidence in knowledge that will never be seen again. He calls this knowledge 'ultimate knowledge' and holds that the early Greeks at least believed they possessed it (*KSA* 8: 6 [7]). The early philosophers are not confronted with the danger and difficulty of knowing, which are later developments and shape the present day (Kant, for example). For them, the task is to free oneself from the power of myth and then to endure the darkness one falls into. One option is to embrace science (*Wissenschaft*) and to gradually augment knowledge; the other option is offered by philosophy and the 'ultimate knowledge' (*letzte Erkenntniss*). Nietzsche doesn't spell out what this consists in but I think we can take it to refer to 'decisive' knowledge on the most important matters, matters of value for example. According to Nietzsche's conception, the early Greek philosophers understood that the philosopher's right to existence is revealed when he gives focus to the limitless knowledge drive and controls it by giving it a unity.

A chief task for Nietzsche, then, is to determine the value and goal of the knowing of science (*Wissenschaft*). This is to be taken in the much wider sense than we conceive it in English as denoting the practice of rigorous, disciplined, and systematic inquiry, and as bound up with the so-called scholarly virtues of being value-free and objective. Nietzsche argues that the difference between the effect of philosophy and that of science, as well as their different genesis (*Entstehung*), must be made clear (*KSA* 8: 19 [23]). Science is dependent upon philosophical questions for all its goals and methods, though it easily forgets this (19 [24]). He poses the question: is philosophy an art or science? His answer is that in its aims and results philosophy is an art, but that it uses the same means as science (conceptual representation). He writes: 'Philosophy is a form of poetic artistry' (*Dichtkunst*). In fact, philosophy cannot be categorized, so it is necessary to invent and characterize a species for it (19 [62]). Philosophy has no common denominator, it is sometimes art and sometimes science (23 [8]). He commits himself to certain key positions, such as that philosophy is invention (*Dichtung*) beyond the limits of experience. Nietzsche does not mean this in a Kantian sense, although he has taken cognizance of Kant's transcendental turn by this point and accepted large parts of it. For Kant, although all our knowledge must have reference to

---

[13] Two important sources for Nietzsche's appreciation of 'greatness' are Schopenhauer (*The World as Will and Representation*, 1966, volume II, chapter 31) and Burckhardt's *Reflections on World History* (translated into English as *Force and Freedom* (New York: Meridian Books, 1955), 269–70.)

experience it does not follow that all of it arises out of experience. Something else is at stake for Nietzsche. The word Nietzsche uses is poetry or invention (*Dichtung*) and what he is getting at is the fact that philosophy continues and sublimates the impulse or drive (*Trieb*) of the mythic. The philosopher knows (*erkennt*) insofar as he invents or poeticizes (*dichtet*), and he invents insofar as he knows. There is, then, a union of poetry and knowledge in the philosopher (19 [62]). It is the continuation and refinement of the mythical drive and is essentially pictorial (thinking in terms of concrete images).

What does Nietzsche mean here when he credits philosophical thinking with 'poetry'? On one level he simply means that it makes imaginative and illogical leaps, which are also evident in science, for example in the form of conjectures ('Philosophical thinking can be detected at the core of all scientific thought'). This 'flight of imagination'—Nietzsche uses the word *die Phantasie*—involves leaping from possibility to possibility, with some possibilities being taken temporarily as certainties (19 [75]). This kind of 'possibility' is something like a sudden intuition ('it might perhaps...', for example), and this gives rise to a process of amplification. This leads Nietzsche to ask whether philosophical and scientific thinking are to be distinguished by their dosage or by their domain. Philosophy is close to art but it cannot exist without science: 'there is *no distinct philosophy separated from science*'. But then he argues: 'the reason why *indemonstrable* philosophizing retains a higher value than a scientific proposition lies in the aesthetic value of such philosophizing, in its beauty and sublimity (*Erhabenheit*)' (19 [76]). His idea is that a construction of philosophy cannot prove itself in the same way a scientific construction can. Such constructions of philosophy are best approached in terms of aesthetic considerations to do with artistic value. Heraclitus can thus never be obsolete.

Philosophy's value lies in its purifying tasks, such as cleansing muddled and superstitious ideas. To this extent it is a science, but to the extent that it is at the same time anti-scientific—for example in opposing scientific dogmatism (what today we would call scientism)—it is 'religious-obscurantist' (23 [10]). Nietzsche gives the example of Kant's discrediting of the theory of the soul and rational theology. Philosophy opposes the fixed value of ethical concepts and the hatred of the body. It shows us what is anthropomorphic: the translation of the world into the care or concern of the human being. Philosophy is harmful since it dissolves instinct, cultures, and customary moralities. In terms of the present, philosophy encounters the absence of a popular ethic, the absence of any sense of the importance of discriminating, a mania for history, and so on. The sciences are studied without practical application, whilst classical antiquity is studied in a way that fails to relate it to any practical attempt to learn from it. In the case of the philosopher we have a physician—the physician of culture—who must heal himself (29 [213]). This is because, according to Nietzsche, the philosopher must first become a thinker for himself before he can educate others. Schopenhauer provides the lesson needed here: the need to achieve genuine independence in relation to the present age. Nietzsche thinks this is an especially pressing task for the thinker today that is faced with the claims of a 'new age' (*Neuzeit*) (see *UM* II: 8).[14] So here a different limit is being transcended, namely, the limit of the prevailing world view.

[14] The composite concept *Neuzeit* was first used by the German poet Ferdinand Freiligrath (1810–76) in 1870, that is, around the time Nietzsche produces his reflections on history in the second untimely meditation, which commence in fact with *BT*. It can denote the 'modern' or the contemporary *Zeit* in the sense 'of today', and it can also assert a qualitative claim, such as being new, even better, than what has gone before, so attributing to the new an epochal character. Nietzsche has registered these meanings and is taking to task the pretensions of the modern to be something new, better, and epochal. For further insight into the concept of *Neuzeit* see Koselleck 1985: chapter 13.

Schopenhauer's greatness consists in the fact that he deals with the picture of life as a whole and interprets it as a whole. Moreover, he does so without letting himself become entangled in a web of conceptual scholasticisms. The problem with the present is that it is importunate (*zudring-lich*), being something that is always unintentionally overvalued. This is especially felt by the philosopher, says Nietzsche, whose peculiar task is to be the lawgiver of 'the measure, mint, and weight of things' (*UM* III: 3).

In relation to science, philosophy draws attention to its 'barbarizing effects', that is, the fact that it so easily loses itself in the service of immediate practical interests. This is another 'limit' that philosophy goes beyond. The *laisser aller* (let it go) attitude of modern science resembles the dogmas of political economy: it has a naïve faith in an absolutely beneficial result. The primary concern of philosophy is with the question of the value of existence, with what is to be revered. 'For science there is nothing great and nothing small—but for philosophy! The value of science is measured in terms of this statement' (*KSA* 7: 19 [33]). And then, he adds: '*Holding onto what is sublime! (Das Festhalten des Erhabenen!)*' (see also 19 [22]). For Nietzsche, the sublime refers to the (aesthetic) concept of greatness, and the task of philosophy is to educate people to this concept. To hold on to it is to keep in one's view, as a kind of superior perception or vision, the 'spiritual mountain range' that stretches across the centuries and thus to the 'eternal fruitfulness of everything that is great' (19 [33]).

In a later notebook from 1875 on the struggle between science and wisdom, Nietzsche claims that whilst science can probe the processes of nature it can never 'command' human beings: 'science knows nothing of taste, love, pleasure, displeasure, exaltation or exhaustion. Man must in some way interpret, and thereby, evaluate, what he lives through and experiences' (*KSA* 8: 6 [41]). Nietzsche claims that the sciences—natural science and history—explain but do not command; or where they do command it is always in the name of utility. By contrast, 'every religion and every philosophy has somewhere within it…a sublime (*erhabene*) *breach with nature*, a striking uselessness' (*KSA* 7: 29 [197]). He then asks whether this is all that there is to it. In short, how can value be given to that which exists outside of utility? Nietzsche considers this question in the context of several notes that bear the title 'The Afflictions of Philosophy (*Die Bedrängniss der Philosophie*)'. These 'afflictions' are both external (natural science and history) and internal (the courage to live according to a philosophy is breaking down). Nietzsche notes that the demands made on philosophy in the present age are greater than ever, and so are the attacks; and yet philosophers find themselves weaker than ever (29 [198]).

Nietzsche holds that philosophy is one of the preservatives of value and discrimination, but it has no specific existence of its own. With regards to the culture of his people, the philosopher seems to be an indifferent hermit, a teacher to a few select spiritual and abstract minds, or a destroyer of popular culture (*KSA* 7: 28 [2]). He is a hermit, or this is his appearance, owing to the fact that there is a lack of purposiveness in nature (he is not predestined to be). His work, however, remains for later ages. It is not that there is no purposiveness in nature, only a lack or deficit of it; nature cannot be relied upon as a result. It ruins countless seeds but also manages to produce a few great examples, such as Kant and Schopenhauer (the step from the one to the other, Nietzsche says, is a step towards a freer culture). Nature, Nietzsche says, is wasteful not out of extravagance but out of lack of experience (*KSA* 7: 29 [223]; see also *UM* III: 7). Thus, the artists and the philosopher both bear witness against teleology. Nevertheless, Nietzsche thinks it is legitimate for us to conceive of the philosopher as a kind of self-revelation of nature's workshop (19 [17]).

For Nietzsche philosophy is in search of a new 'people' and has the task of cultivating one that is equal to the concept of greatness or the sublime. But how can philosophy and the philosopher connect with a people—are not a people by definition something contingent and accidental (for example, when it finds itself in an accidental political situation)? Nietzsche's claim is that the people finds its uniqueness in this superior individual who, although he or she appears, is in fact 'timeless', not merely an accidental 'wanderer'. The philosopher exists in order to harness the 'unselective knowledge drive' by setting goals, determining measure, and making value judgements concerning existence (for example, defining what is great, rare, singular, even though these are mutable). Perhaps under modern conditions it is the philosopher's fate to be a wanderer that is looking for a people that is missing (this appears to be the narrative of *Thus Spoke Zarathustra*). If today there is an absence of noble popular philosophy, Nietzsche thinks this is because we have no noble concept of the people as a *publicum*; rather, our popular philosophy is for the *peuple*, not for the public (*KSA* 7: 19 [26]). The contrast being drawn here is between an indifferent and merely ordinary or everyday collective and a collective united and elevated by higher goals (perhaps between a mob and a genuine 'public'). In *BT* Nietzsche notes that 'public' (*publicum*) is merely a word that cannot be taken to denote a uniform and constant entity (*BT* 11). What he is resisting is the view that the artist and genuine philosopher should accommodate themselves to a force or power that is strong simply by virtue of its numbers or the loudness of its opinions. Public opinion should not be pandered to; rather, the task is to raise the public to a higher level of insight and being: 'Create for yourselves the concept of a "people" [*Volk*]: you can never conceive it to be noble and lofty enough' (*UM* II: 7). This idea that the public should be elevated in this way is an essential part of Nietzsche's early teaching on the sublime.

THE CASE OF STRAUSS

Let me now turn attention to examining how the sublime is put to work in the *Unfashionable Observations*, beginning with the first one on David Friedrich Strauss. In this observation Nietzsche aims to present a twofold challenge: first, a challenge to public opinion in Germany which equates victory over France in the war with the success of German culture; and second, to contest the idea that culture is the same as 'cultivatedness' (*Gebildetheit*). The need has arisen to distinguish between this and true cultivation. Nietzsche is here concerned with overcoming a different set of 'limits': not so much those of reason or experience, but rather the limits of social conservatism and conformism. Cultural philistinism is to be taken to task for Nietzsche because it stifles the appreciation of truly sublime art and culture.

For Nietzsche, a great victory is also a great danger. The delusion that German culture has also been victorious is a pernicious one, not simply, he stresses, because it is a delusion since delusions can be of the most salutary nature. It is rather that it has the potential to turn a victory into a defeat: 'the *extirpation... of the German spirit for the sake of the "German Reich"*' (*UM* I: 1). Germany has won the war not on account of the superiority of its culture but rather through its stricter military discipline, natural courage and perseverance, superior leadership, their more scientific conduct of war, and so on. None of this might matter except for the delusion that the finest seeds of culture have been sown in Germany:

> I perceive this delirium and this joy in the incomparably confident behaviour both of German journalists and of our fabricators of novels, tragedies, poems, and histories, for they obviously constitute a homogeneous group of people who seem to have conspired to take control of the modern human being's hours of idleness and meditation—that is, of his 'cultured moments'—and to drug him by means of the printed word. (*UM* I: 1)

Nietzsche claims that 'the pure concept of culture [*Kultur*] has been lost' (*UM* I: 1). What is culture for him? He provides one definition in the opening section of the text when he states that culture 'is a unity of artistic style that manifests itself throughout all the vital self-expressions of a people [*Lebensäusserungen eines Volkes*]' (*UM* I: 1). The appropriate contrast to be made is with 'barbarism', defined as the absence of style or the chaotic hodge-podge of all styles. His contention is that it is this hodgepodge in which the contemporary German dwells:

> The German amasses around himself all the forms, colours, products, and curiosities of all ages and climes and thereby produces that modern carnival motley which his scholars then can explore and define as 'the modern as such' (*UM* I: 1)

The Germans have an imitative culture, rather than a genuinely productive one (as the French have, Nietzsche claims). They have copied the French but for the most part without any great skill: '…up to the present day there has never been an original German culture' (*UM* I: 1).[15] For Nietzsche a culture will show that what is great in a people does not appear among them as a hermit or exile (*KSA* 7: 19 [37]). Its goal is not the greatest possible happiness of a people or the unhindered development of all its talents; rather, it should reveal itself in the correct proportion of these developments; its aim is the production of 'great works' and as such it points beyond mere worldly happiness. A 'mastering unity' needs to show itself among the drives (e.g. 'the Hellenic will'), and the attempt is made to construct a world from these drives: philosophy masters the knowledge drive, art controls ecstasy, and *agape* controls *eros* (*KSA* 7: 19 [41]).

The Germans live, then, under the illusion that they have a genuine culture, and Nietzsche's attack is focused on the contentment that so-called cultivated Germans feel about their situation. This is a contentment that since the war has repeatedly broken out in 'arrogant jubilation'. It is only the rare few, including Nietzsche himself, who notice the incongruity between the triumphant faith and the defect such jubilation conceals. For those who prefer to opine with public opinion such an incongruity ought not to exist. Nietzsche asks after the 'species' (*Gattung*) of human being that has risen to power in Germany that they feel themselves able to forbid, or at least prevent, the expression of such a concern, and he gives them the name of 'cultivated philistines' (*Bildungsphilister*). As Michael Bell notes, in contrast to the English term 'philistine' derived from the poet, Oxford professor of

---

[15] Nietzsche offers a number of definitions of culture in his early writings, including: 'Culture [*Cultur*] as a new and improved *physis*, without inner and outer, without dissimulation [*Verstellung*] and convention, culture as a unanimity of life, thought, appearance [*Schein*], and will' (*UM* II: 10); 'The culture of a people…defined as unity of artistic style in all the expressions of the life of a people…a people to whom one attributes a culture has to be in all reality a single living unity and not fall wretchedly apart into inner and outer, content and form' (*UM* II: 4); 'A single temperament and key composed of many originally hostile forces that now make it possible to play a melody' (*KSA* 7: 29 [205]); and, finally, as 'The aesthetic concept of greatness and sublimity: the task is to educate people to this concept. Culture depends upon the way in which one defines what is "great"' (*PT* 156).

poetry, and cultural critic Matthew Arnold (1822–88), which denotes a condition hostile to humane culture, Nietzsche's coinage 'culture philistine' denotes a decadent and banal spirit produced from within the circle of cultural knowledge (Bell 2007: 133). Nietzsche himself points out that it is well known that the word 'philistine', drawn from the vocabulary of university students, signifies in its popular sense the opposite of the son of the muses, the artist, and genuinely educated or cultured person. The cultivated philistine, however, takes himself to be the son of the muses and a cultured person. There is thus within such a person a total failure of self-knowledge and he is encouraged in this by public institutions and institutes of schooling, art, and education.

The cultivated philistine turns the genuine seekers of culture—those who created new vocabularies for art, literature, and music—into actual 'finders' and in the process reifies their creative quest, for example, by turning them into 'classical authors': 'We do indeed have a culture, they then claim, for after all, we have our "classical authors"; not only is the foundation there, but the entire edifice already stands erected upon it—we ourselves are this edifice' (*UM* I: 2). Nietzsche contends that there is only one authentic way of honouring the great artists of the past, which is to continue the search. What is wrong and misguided is:

> Merely to attach to them the provocative appellation 'classical', by contrast, and to feel 'edified' from time to time by their works—that is, to abandon oneself to those jaded and egoistic sensations that awaits each paying visitor at our concert halls and theaters, and to dedicate statues and initiate festivals and societies in their names—all this is only a small payment with which the cultivated philistine settles accounts with the classical authors so that in all the rest he no longer needs them, and above all so that he need not follow them and seek further. For the watchword of the philistine is: 'We should seek no further.' (*UM* I: 2)

In the early part of the century, Nietzsche notes, such a watchword made a certain sense. This was a time of romanticism and revolution with so much confused seeking, hoping, experimenting, and destroying that the German middle class was perhaps justified in fearing for itself. It thus rejected the 'brew of fantastic and language-perverting philosophies, that fanatical purposive view of history (Hegelianism), that carnival of all gods and myths that the Romantics put together, as well as those poetic fashions and insanities born out of intoxication' (*UM* I: 2). What this led to, however, was a general suspicion of the act of searching as such and a stress on having found culture: 'The joys of philistinism unfolded before his eyes: he fled from all that wild experimentation into the idyllic', opposing to the unsettlingly creative drive a contentedness with his own narrowness and limited intelligence (*UM* I: 2). As a way of reaching a compromise agreement with the troublesome 'classical authors' and their demand to search in art and greatness, this species of human invent the concept of 'the age of epigones' as a way of securing some peace for themselves, 'and so that they would be prepared to pass the impugning verdict "the work of an epigone" upon everything that was disquietingly modern' (*UM* I: 2). They also take control, Nietzsche observes, of the discipline of history (*Geschichte*), transforming fields of study, such as philosophy and classical philology, from which disruptions of contentedness can be expected, into historical disciplines (*historische Disciplinen*). The *raison d'être* given to this process was that of saving culture from the spirit of fanaticism. The attempt is made to understand everything historically so as to 'numb' the spirit and bring it back from the excesses of culture and the fostering of intolerance. For Nietzsche this is mere pretence: '…what they really hated was domineering genius and the tyranny of true cultural demands…' (*UM* I: 2).

The philistine expects no 'sublime masterworks' but rather only two things in art and culture: 'either imitation of reality to the point of apishly reproducing it in idylls or gently humoristic satires, or free imitations of the most recognized and famous works of the classical authors...' (*UM* I: 3) What the philistine values, then, is epigone-like imitation or iconic true portraiture of the present. From the latter he gains an exaltation that enhances his feeling of contentedness with the real, whilst the former is harmless and benefits his reputation as a classical judge of taste. Finally, Nietzsche notes, the philistine devises for his general taste, that is, his various likes and dislikes, a universally effective formula of 'healthiness' which serves to 'eliminate every disruptive troublemaker with the insinuation of being sick and eccentric' (*UM* I: 3). What gets Nietzsche's goat is the way in which Strauss, 'a true *satisfait* with the state of our culture and a typical philistine', approaches Schopenhauer's philosophy as unhealthy and unprofitable. Let me now turn to examining Nietzsche's early estimation of Schopenhauer in his (third) unfashionable observation on Schopenhauer as educator.

The Perfection of *Physis* and the Redemption of the Animal

For Nietzsche, Schopenhauer is the significant figure in modern philosophy after Kant because he sweeps away scholasticism and unlearns pure science. This is one 'limit' he transcends and that Nietzsche admires him for. The task is to employ his worldly wisdom for practical matters and thus fight for an improved *physis*. Schopenhauer has restored the antique conception of philosophy as the art of living.[16] In part he has done this by setting up a picture of life as a whole; because he has this picture he was able to regulate the sciences for himself and avoid becoming enmeshed in abstract scholasticism. The challenge of every great philosophy, Nietzsche says, is to provide a picture of life from which one can learn the meaning of one's own existence. A process of learning is at work here for Nietzsche: firstly, the individual gains insight into its own limited nature (its empirical limitedness, governed as it is by wants and the misery involved in their satisfaction); secondly, insight into this misery encourages the sacrifice of the ego and submission to the noblest ends such as justice and compassion. We are able to distinguish between those things that genuinely promote human happiness or fulfilment and those that only appear to do this such as honours, riches, and even erudition (what the ancient Stoics called 'external goods'). None of these can lift us out of the deep depression we feel in the face of the worthless character of our individual, empirical existence. Our striving after things can only acquire a meaning once they are subjected to a larger transfiguring goal. We should acquire power so as to aid the evolution of *physis*; for a while we feel we are capable of correcting its follies and basic ineptness. Initially this process concerns the individual itself but eventually it is for the benefit for everyone.

---

[16] This may be more evident if one focuses on *Parerga and Paralipomena* rather than *The World as Will and Representation*.

Although Nietzsche expresses his admiration for Schopenhauer there is no indication that in this early period he subscribes to his doctrine on the denial of the will to life. Schopenhauer purified himself of the opinions and valuations of his age, making himself unfashionable (*UM* III: 3). He can serve as a model (*Vorbild*) in spite of all his scars and flaws. The fact that the greatest human being can be dwarfed by his ideal does not serve to devalue it. Nietzsche astutely addresses the dangers of Schopenhauer's philosophizing, which consist in his pessimism and his disgust with becoming. What in fact interests Nietzsche about Schopenhauer is not his system or metaphysics but the man or the person. We profit from a philosopher insofar as they are able to provide an example, and this is proved by their visible life and not through their books. What distinguishes a genuine philosopher from a mere university professor is that the former attempts to live by his own philosophy. However, Nietzsche's conception of the task of the philosopher represents a departure from Schopenhauer: although Nietzsche follows Schopenhauer in construing the philosopher as a member of a trinity of genius, including the artist and the saint, the function assigned by him to such geniuses has a cultural and social dimension lacking in Schopenhauer (Breazeale 1998: 9). Although the task is said to be one of 'redeeming' nature this is not by raising self-knowledge to the point where the will to live is extinguished, but rather by holding up a picture of life as a whole, by giving us a new image of human being and by showing us 'possibilities of life'. The philosopher has a cultural role, even mission, to fulfil: he provides us with (a) an ideal image of existence itself and a new goal for humanity; (b) a table of values for judging the worth of specific forms of life and cultural ideals; (c) a critique of our age and cultural institutions in which the task is to be an unfashionable one (Breazeale 1998: 10).

Nietzsche notes that the powerful promoter of life longs for release from his own exhausted age and for a culture (transfigured *physis*); but this longing can result in disaffection and disappointment, encouraging the philosopher to become the judge of life who condemns it as unworthy of our attachment. The Greek philosophers had life before them in 'sumptuous perfection'; the same cannot be said of us moderns, where our sensibility is caught between the desire for freedom, beauty, and greatness of life and the drive for truth that asks only, 'Of what value is existence (*das Dasein*) at all?' (*UM* III: 3) In short, our danger is pessimism. Schopenhauer lacked belief in the future since it would bring only the eternal return of the same. For him, then, 'eternal becoming is a deceitful puppet play over which human beings forget themselves' and for whom the 'heroism of truthfulness consists in one day ceasing to be its plaything' (*UM* III: 4). If everything that 'is' finds itself caught up in the process of becoming, and this becoming is 'empty, deceitful, flat', worthy only of our lofty contempt, then the riddle presented to the human being to solve can be solved only in being (*UM* III: 4).

Given that Nietzsche also aspires to be unfashionable, to not be a thinker of his time, and given that meaning and value are not to be located for him in a process of history or evolution, how will he avoid the temptation of being and Schopenhauer's solution to the problem of existence? We tend to conceive this in terms of Nietzsche expressing an affirmation of life, and such an affirmation is indeed signalled in *UM* III as something 'metaphysical'. This is used not in a pejorative sense by Nietzsche (rightly so, I would maintain), but indicates the fact that the affirmation which is 'profound' is 'of another, higher life' and at the cost of the 'destruction and violation of the laws of this life': only in this way can the affirmation be unfashionable (*UM* III: 4).

Nietzsche recognizes that it is necessary to show how the Schopenhauerean-inspired ideal of the philosopher—the ideal that encourages purification and liberation from the fashions and idols of one's time—can educate and a new set of duties be derived from it (*UM* III: 5). Failure to do this leaves us only with a vision that enraptures and intoxicates. The 'lofty goal' of the philosopher must be brought near to us so that will educate us and draw us upward (*UM* III: 5). The challenge is this: how can the loftiness and dignity of the Schopenhauerean human being transport us beyond ourselves but not, in so doing, take us outside a community of active people in which the coherence of duties and the stream of life would vanish? Nietzsche's answer is the 'fundamental thought of *culture* [*der Grundgedanke der Kultur*]'. The new duties cannot be those of the solitary individual and they must enable us to get beyond the hatred that is at the root of Schopenhauer's pessimism, including the hatred of individuality and its limitations (*UM* III: 5). Let me show how he argues for this idea.

Nietzsche develops his thought of culture in the context of a discussion of the ends of nature and culture which seeks to contest rival conceptions of them that predominate in the modern period. The fundamental task for Nietzsche is the perfection of nature. What unites individuals and can hold them together in a community is the idea of culture conceived as the transfiguration of *physis*. The perfection of nature through culture entails fostering the production of philosophers, artists, and saints '*within us and around us*'. These three types or modes of being constitute a 'most sublime [*erhabensten*] order' (*UM* III: 5). Why is this to perfect nature? The philosopher bestows upon nature the idea of a 'metaphysical purpose', whilst the artist enables nature to attain 'self-enlightenment' by presenting an image in which it can recognize itself and which in the normal course of things—what Nietzsche calls 'the tumultuousness [*Unruhe*] of its own becoming'—it never has the opportunity to do (*UM* III: 5).

Nietzsche, then, is inviting us to value the rare and the unique, in which humanity works towards the production of great individual human beings as its most essential task (*UM* III: 6). We can reflect on species of animal and plant life and understand that what matters is the superior individual specimen—'the more unusual, more powerful, more complex, more fruitful specimen [*Exemplar*]' (*UM* III: 5).[17] Evolution, then, is to be valued in terms of an aesthetic judgment understood as a superior kind of perception of nature and its products: '…the point at which it [evolution] reaches its limit and begins the transition to a higher species' (*UM* III: 5). The goal is neither a large number of specimens and their well-being nor those specimens that are the last to evolve. Rather, it is 'those scattered and random existences that arise here and there under favourable conditions' (*UM* III: 5). Great human beings 'redeem' nature and evolution. Life, including an individual's life, can obtain the highest value and deepest significance 'by living for the benefit of the rarest and most valuable specimens, not for the benefit of the majority…' (*UM* III: 5). The individual may be a 'miscarried work of nature', but it can also bear 'testimony to the greatest and most amazing intentions of this artist' (*UM* III: 5). When thinking about individuals and the role they play in the 'circle of culture', Nietzsche's focus is on the longing for the 'whole' (*UM*

---

[17] James Conant has argued against translating *Exemplar* as 'specimen' and seeks to show that Nietzsche's argument is, in fact, about the nature of exemplarity and what it means for Nietzsche to be an exemplar. However, it is quite clear that 'specimen' is correct when one looks at the whole context of Nietzsche's treatment which is centred on a consideration of the evolution of species and on how we might plausibly construe the *significance* of evolution. See Conant 2000: 191–2.

III: 5). Our longing cannot simply be for our personal redemption but needs to turn outward in order to rediscover in the world the desire for culture which demands of us not only inner experiences, or even an assessment of the external world that surrounds us, but 'ultimately and primarily action; that is, it demands he fight for culture and oppose those influences, habits, laws, and institutions in which he does not recognize his goal: the production of genius' (*UM* III: 5).

Whilst there may be an 'unconscious purposiveness' at work in nature, the production of redeeming human beings cannot be left to chance and accident, to what Nietzsche at this time calls 'the dark drive [*jenes 'dunklen Drangs'*]' but must be replaced with a 'conscious intention' (*UM* III: 5). This is on account of the fact that today we are ruled by a culture of power (Nietzsche refers to 'the cultured state [*Kulturstaat*]' that misuses and exploits culture for perverted ends. The public, civil, or social life of the present age amounts to nothing more than equilibrium of self-interests. It does well what it does, namely, answering the question of how to achieve a mediocre existence that lacks any power of love, and it does this simply through the prudence of the self-interests involved. The present is an age that hates art and hates religion: it wants neither the beyond nor the transfiguration of the world of art (*KSA* 7: 19 [69]). Science has become a source of nourishment for egoism and state and society have drafted it into their service in order to exploit it for their purposes. In order to promote a new seriousness in the face of these lamentable developments Nietzsche states the need for a fundamental alteration of the world through 'images' that will make us shudder. The object of attack is 'the perversity of contemporary human nature' and its subjection to misguided notions such as ' "progress," "general education," "nationalism," "modern state," "cultural struggle" ' (*UM* III: 7).

Nietzsche comes up with a deeper explanation for this idea of a 'metaphysical' completion of nature, which centres on how we can think the human in its relation to the animal. On the one hand, the human feeds productively on the animal and its own animality (for example, animal vigour and the power of forgetting); on the other hand, it enjoys a supreme advantage over the animal in that it is able to understand its existence metaphysically. The animal by contrast is the site of 'senseless suffering' since it is subject to hunger and desires without having any insight into the nature of this mode of life:

> To cling so blindly and madly to life, for no higher reward, far from knowing that one is punished or why one is punished in this way, but instead to thirst with the inanity of a horrible desire for precisely this punishment as though it were happiness—that is what it means to be an animal. (*UM* III: 5)

Although it is a speculative claim to make, we can say that the human animal represents, at least potentially, the salvation of animal existence in which life itself *appears* 'in its metaphysical meaninglessness' (*UM* III: 5). Of course, in actuality it is difficult to know where the animal ceases and where the human begins, and many human beings do not transcend, for whatever reason, an animal existence. The salvation of the animal is also the salvation of the human animal. Nietzsche readily acknowledges that for the greatest part of our lives most of us live the way of the animal, desiring with more awareness what the animal craves out of blind instinct (we call this a life of 'happiness'). In a superior moment of perception or vision we witness the elevation of the human beyond the merely animal, when life rises itself up through the conquering and overcoming of need and makes 'the leap of joy' (*UM* III: 5). As he puts it in *UM* III:

...there are moments *when we understand* [*begreifen*] *this*; then the clouds break and we perceive how we, along with all of nature, are pressing onward toward the human being as toward something that stands high above us. (*UM* III: 5)

By contrast, in ordinary time and becoming, or what Nietzsche calls the 'tremendous mobility of human beings on the great earthly desert', which consists in the waging of wars, a ceaseless gathering and dispersing, an imitation of one another, as well as a mutual outwitting and trampling underfoot, we find only 'a continuation of animality', as if we were being cheated out of our metaphysical disposition and made to regress to the unconsciousness of pure animal instinct (*UM* III: 5).

It is a sublime vision of the human being, in the sense just outlined, that Nietzsche offers in contrast to other images of the human we find in modernity, such as the image that glorifies its descent into bestiality or the image that seeks to tells us that nothing more or other is operating in the human being than a robotic automatism (*UM* III: 4).

Nietzsche on History

A similar lesson on the sublime and the moment is provided by Nietzsche in the unfashionable observation on history entitled 'On the Utility and Liability of History for Life'. Unless history is given the grand treatment it will only create slaves, Nietzsche says, being nothing more than a fatal curiosity. Not every form of life or society that comes into existence can be considered worthy of existence, and yet the tendency of history is to make everything that does come into existence appear rational and purposive. History should speak of what is great and unique, of the exemplary model (*KSA* 7: 19 [10]). The current practice of history is part of our modern indiscriminate drive for knowledge and like all things that are unable or fail to discriminate, it is vulgar (19 [11]). In the realms of history and mathematics, Nietzsche notes, the most trivial matter is to count as more valuable than all the ideas of metaphysics taken together. The sole attachment, as that which determines value, is to the degree of certainty that can be acquired. Our attachment is to ever smaller objects of inquiry, focus, and value (19 [37]). In short, in this 'domesticated' form of history we become narrowly focused and lose sight of the sublime and the concern with higher vistas; so, here, we clearly see the key motif running through the different observations and that links them together.

As his plans show, Nietzsche had a clear idea of what he wished to demonstrate in the meditation (30 [1–2]). His starting point is to be a simple one: history (*Historie*) has its uses but it can also be detrimental. Nietzsche notes that it is possible for us to perish from any hypertrophied virtue (30 [2]). History can serve life in the three forms of the monumental, the antiquarian, and the critical. History is hostile to life when it has its source in a cult of inwardness, has a supposition of justice and claim to objectivity (for Nietzsche we only get the appearance of justice through the study of history), invites us to think of ourselves as mere latecomers (epigones), and places the meaning of individual existence within a world process. The remedies to the historical malady include the study of Plato (in which we find no history), and the powers of the ahistorical and the suprahistorical, including writing in 'praise of art' on account of its power to create atmospheres (29 [162]). The ahistorical (*unhistorischen*) refers to powers such as forgetfulness and illusion (*Wahn*). The suprahistorical (*überhistorischen*) refers to art and religion but also to nature, compassion (*Mitleid*), *and* philosophy (29 [194]). Art and religion are esteemed by Nietzsche as important instruments by which we can take possession of ourselves and organize the 'chaos' we are, so discovering what our genuine needs are. The aim is to do this in a way which does not make us fear cultivation or respond to the summons to become what are in a brooding manner: religion 'provides love for the human being', art the 'love for existence' (29 [192]).[18]

The power of forgetting, associated with the animal and named as part of the ahistorical, is what enables us to have confidence in our own being by limiting our horizon and without which we would be condemned to see everywhere in all things only a becoming (*Werden*), losing ourselves in the stream of becoming like pupils of Heraclitus (*UM* II: 1). This aspect of Nietzsche's argument has been well understood and is often emphasized. However, his argument on the role of the suprahistorical is of equal importance: not only is there the animal grace of forgetting, there is also a superior perception and a superior power of memory capable of inspiring human action and the task of becoming what one is. In *UM* III Nietzsche notes that haste is universal in modern times with people seeking to flee from themselves in order to avoid the confrontation with voices and demons that wish to speak to them and make them still. We live in a state of 'fear of memory [*Erinnerung*]' (*UM* III: 5): 'When we are quiet and alone we are afraid that something will be whispered into our ear, and hence we despise quiet and drug ourselves with sociability' (*UM* III: 5).

In essence, the suprahistorical is the attitude which holds that the past and the present are one and the same, and this means that history teaches us nothing new but only gives us the appearance of difference (*KSA* 7: 30 [2]). It is this attitude we find expressed in Schopenhauer's reflections on history.[19] Nietzsche, however, draws a different lesson from the suprahistorical from the one taught by his educator. In the meditation Nietzsche refers to the suprahistorical in two sections, in the opening section and then again in the essay's final section. The meaning he ascribes to it seems to change in the course of the essay. In section 1 it refers to a negating attitude to life that reflects a world-weariness and deep disgust; in section 10 it refers to 'eternalizing powers' that provide us with a point of stability and anchorage (*UM* II: 10). The key to understanding this shift in Nietzsche's argument, whereby he is able to make productive use of the suprahistorical, consists in appreciating the difference between the ahistorical and the suprahistorical: the former has the character of grace, but the latter, if is to be temporally effective (as Nietzsche desires), must be made to work as part of cultural training. Together the ahistorical and the suprahistorical enable us to divert our gaze from what is in the process of becoming and solely of empirical or natural value.

The history Nietzsche is keen to promote is that which requires the active human being and is written by the person with the richest experience:

> *Only from the highest power [Kraft] of the present can you interpret the past...* The voice of the past is always the voice of an oracle; only if you are seers into the future and familiar with the

---

[18] This should not be taken to mean Nietzsche does not entertain suspicions about art and religion at this time. In one sketch he notes that they stem from the desire to leap 'beyond this world by condemning it wholesale' and want only 'the peace of the One' (*KSA* 7: 29 [224]).

[19] See Schopenhauer 1966: vol. II, 439–47.

present will you be able to interpret the oracular voice of the past (*KSA* 7, 29 [96]; see also *UM* II: 6).

What is the future Nietzsche has belief in? It is a belief in the idea of the (eternal) return of the *possibilities* of life.[20] In section two of the meditation Nietzsche refers to the belief of the Pythagoreans that when the constellation of the heavenly bodies repeats itself so must the same events, down to the smallest, on earth. Nietzsche is not taking this as true, it should be noted, and so no licence can be given to the attempt to construct monumental history in the manner of an icon-like veracity. This will only happen, he notes, when astronomers once again become astrologers. Until this day comes history of this type must have recourse to artistic powers. In fact, Nietzsche says that the historian of the monumental will not examine the causes of what comes into being but rather focus exclusively on 'effects', that is, events (think of what a popular festival or a military anniversary does). An examination of the historical connexus of causes and effects would only demonstrate that the dice game of chance and the future 'would never again produce something wholly identical to what it produced in the past' (*UM* II: 2).

It is the task of the monumental or exemplary to occupy itself with the search for greatness and for these 'possibilities' of life; here the task is to study the sublime as it were. The great moments in the struggle of the human individual constitute a chain and this chain can unite humanity across the millennia 'like a range of mountain peaks'. It thus gives expression to a certain faith in humanity, the faith in the best and the highest exemplars. This provides the human being with a unique kind of memory. In his notes for the meditation Nietzsche insists that these individuals do not form and are not part of a process; instead, 'they live conjointly and concurrently, thanks to history, which permits such a collaboration' (*KSA* 7: 29 [52]). If the goal of humankind is not to be located in its end stage, but only in the highest specimens, those 'dispersed throughout millennia, conjointly represent all the supreme powers that are buried in humanity' (*KSA* 7: 29 [52]). It is this elevated conception of humanity that brings the monumental into conflict with another fundamental faith that dominates most easily and is the most widespread, namely the apathetic habit, everything that is base and petty and that says 'no' to the claims of the monumental. Life cannot be so extravagant, superfluous; rather, life has to be justified at its basest and lowest points only (the need for comfort and security, the need for the satisfaction of our basic animality at the expense of everything else, etc.). It is this base attachment to life that the exceptional or extraordinary human being treats with Olympian laughter and sublime derision (*erhabenen Hohne*; *UM* II: 2); they even descend to their grave with an ironic smile because they know that there is in fact nothing of them left to bury other than the dross, refuse, vanity, and animality that had always weighed them down whilst alive. What lives on is the signature of their most authentic being, such as a work, an act, or a creation. Fame denotes not the

---

[20]   This phrase 'possibilities of life' is used by Nietzsche with references to the modes of being introduced by the earliest Greek philosophers, such as Heraclitus and Empedocles. These 'possibilities of life' are not just of any kind. We encounter a rare and impressive resourcefulness, a daring that is both desperate and hopeful, and witness life pushing itself further and further upwards and more encompassing, as if the thinker possessed the spirit of one of the globe's great circumnavigators. This is what the great thinker is for Nietzsche, a circumnavigator of 'life's most remote and dangerous regions', *KSA* 8: 6 [48]. See also the posthumously published text of 1873, *PTG*, and *HAH* I: 261.

tastiest morsel of our egoism, as Schopenhauer thought, but the belief in the solidarity and continuity of the greatness of the ages and a protest against the passing away of the generations and the ephemeral quality of existence.

In the observation on history Nietzsche introduces the idea of the sublime in the context of a treatment of the problem of the 'weak personality' which refers to a human being that has developed the habit of no longer taking real things seriously.[21] What is real and existent makes only a slight impression on such a personality who becomes more and more negligent and indolent with respect to outward things. It is content so long as its memory is repeatedly stimulated anew, 'as long as new things worthy of knowing, which can be neatly placed in the pigeonholes of that memory, keep streaming in' (*UM* II: 5). The human being becomes a strolling spectator of life living in the midst of a cosmopolitan carnival of gods, arts, and customs. Great wars and revolutions can hardly detain such a human for more than a fleeting moment. Moreover, war seems to only exist for the sake of history and the journalism that consumes it. We want only more history and never real events. Nietzsche expresses it morally (*moralisch*): we are no longer capable of *holding onto the sublime* (*das Erhabene festzuhalten*) because our deeds are merely sudden claps (*Schläge*) of thunder and not *rolling* thunder. What is the point he is making in this lesson on the sublime?

I think it is the following: when we allow our deeds to become concealed or cloaked with the canopy of history we are unable to see ourselves as we should—with distance, delay, and echo and resonance—and art takes flight. We do not comprehend ourselves in our originality which can only take the form of the prolonged awe associated with the sublime conceived as the domain of the incomprehensible.[22] Nietzsche argues that whilst it is perfectly rational to assume we can comprehend and calculate in a moment (*Augenblick*), this is in fact short-sighted since under such conditions we in fact fail to see and hear many things. The rational person:

> ...fails to see some things that even a child sees; he fails to hear some things that even a child hears. And it is precisely these things that are important. Because he does not understand this, his understanding is more childish than a child, simpler than simple-mindedness—in spite of the many clever wrinkles in his parchment-like features and the virtuosity of his fingers when it comes to untangling what is entangled. (*UM* II: 5)

Nietzsche appeals to the 'incomprehensible' not only in order to indicate that something ineffable is at play, but also as a way of showing that the self we need to disclose to ourselves is quite different from the ordinary, habitual comprehension of ourselves produced for us by a false historical cultivation. Under modern conditions of cultivation and 'bourgeois universality' the individual sees itself not as an agent but as an actor:[23]

---

[21] Nietzsche borrows the notion of 'weak personality' from the Austrian dramatist and critic Franz Grillparzer (1791–1872) (see *KSA* 7: 29 [68]). He continues to deal with it in his late writings; see, for example, *GS* 365 and *KSA* 12: 10 [59] and 10 [145] (*WP* 886, *WP* 1009).

[22] See also *KSA* 8: 6[48]: 'I never tire of placing before my mind a series of thinkers in which each individual has within himself that incomprehensibility [*Unbegreiflichkeit*] which forces us to wonder just how he discovered this possibility of life'.

[23] The problem of the actor continues to occupy Nietzsche in his later writings. See, for example, from 1887, *GS* 36, 99, 356, 361, 368, *TI*: 'Maxims and Barbs' 38, *CW* 8, and *WP* 1009. See also *Z* I: 'On the Flies of the Market-Place': 'Little do the people comprehend what is great, which is: the creative. But they do have a sense for all showmen and play-actors of great matters'.

> The individual…can no longer believe in himself; he sinks into himself, into his interior, which in this case means into nothing but the cumulative jumble of acquired knowledge that has no outward effect, of learning that fails to become life. If we take a look at the exterior, we notice how the expulsion of the instincts by means of history has nearly transformed human beings into mere abstractions and shadows: no one runs the risk of baring his own person, but instead disguises himself behind the mask of the cultivated man, the scholar, the poet, the politician. (*UM* II: 5)

What would it mean to comprehend ourselves? For Nietzsche this takes place in a special kind of moment. The moment is, for him, the site of a contestation by the different forces or powers of life (base and noble, inferior and superior).[24] In *UM* III, for example, Nietzsche draws our attention to the haste and 'breathless seizing of the moment' (*Augenblick*) that characterizes the modern (the fashionable), namely, 'the rat race and chasing that now cuts furrows into people's faces and places its tattoo, as it were, upon everything they do' (*UM* III: 6). We moderns are becoming the 'tortured slaves' of three M's: moment [*Moment*], majority opinion, and modishness (*UM* III: 6). In *UM* IV Nietzsche says that we are 'mindlessly contemporary', 'spurred onward by the whip of the moment [*Augenblick*]!' (*UM* IV: 5) The other moment Nietzsche appeals to is the one where we hear something unfashionable about ourselves and communicate with ourselves in an untimely fashion. It is the moment where we seek to discover our genuine needs and give expression to a superior want, will, or desire. This is echoed in *Zarathustra*: 'If you believed in life more, you would throw yourselves away less on the moment' (*Z* I: 'On the Preachers of Death'). At present we are in the grip of a spurious cultivation in which the moment is caught up in a predatory striving, an insatiable acquisition, and a selfish and shameless enjoyment (*UM* III: 6). One kind of moment is overestimated whilst another kind is concealed from us.

CONCLUSION

In this essay I have attempted to demonstrate that the notion of the sublime is crucial for a full appreciation of Nietzsche's early project and as especially evident in the unfashionable observations. What happens in his thinking on the sublime after this point is another story. In addition to its essential sense of 'greatness', the sublime has other different senses and sometimes the later Nietzsche is a critic of our attachment to the sublime—for example, as a longing for transcendence and the otherworldly infinite or as an irrational desire for the overwhelming and the so-called profound (which in his late writings he locates in the music of Wagner)[25]—and at other times he can be an advocate of it and readily employ the different

---

[24] See *KSA* 7: 19 [196]: 'We should learn in the same way that the Greeks learned from their past and their neighbours—for *life*, that is, being highly selective and immediately using all that has been learned as a pole on which one can vault high—and higher than all one's neighbours. Thus, not in a scholarly way! Anything not fit for life is not true history. To be sure it depends on how high or how base you take this *life* to be…'

[25] See *CW* Postscript and 6.

German words for it.[26] The different contexts in which Nietzsche criticizes and employs the sublime have to be examined carefully in each case. Still, it cannot be doubted that Nietzsche continues to be preoccupied throughout his intellectual life with the question of greatness. Moreover, for the late Nietzsche philosophy is 'spiritual perception' (or vision) (*BGE* 252), that is, 'the *power* [*Macht*] of philosophical vision [*Blick*]' that is able to judge in all the most important matters and does not hide under the mask of 'objectivity' (*TI*: 'Skirmishes of an Untimely Man' 3). In *BGE* Nietzsche is concerned with how the enhancement or elevation of the human animal can best be secured, and he defines the philosopher as the one 'who is constantly experiencing, seeing, hearing, suspecting, hoping, dreaming extraordinary things' (*BGE* 292). Nietzsche also continues to be concerned with offering what he calls 'ecstasies of learning' in his later writing, and his thinking abounds with new images and new concepts designed to shock, disturb, and provoke us in our thinking, away from the habitual, the customary, and the conventional. One example is his conception of 'the Roman Caesar with the soul of Christ' (*KSA* 11: 27 [60]; *WP* 983), which, one might suggest, operates in the element of the incomprehensible—difficult to recognize—he is after with the sublime. The task is not only to elevate the human being but to do so in way that genuinely stretches human comprehension. This is why Nietzsche insists that thinking should not aim at a picturesque effect and 'beautiful feelings' cannot constitute an argument (*A* 12).[27]

So far as the early Nietzsche is concerned I think it is clear that he is working with a distinction between the merely empirical and the elevated supra-empirical, and as a thinker of the sublime this makes sense since the aim is to elevate us to superior vistas and to our higher, nobler self. I don't think this means we have to map onto Nietzsche Kant's problematic distinction between the sensibly conditioned self and the free and moral supersensible person since the conceptions of sublime 'morality' at work in the two cases are quite different, with Nietzsche, in contrast to Kant, advocating, and against the claims of moral conformism, what he calls 'immoral Epicureanism' (that is, a concern with one's noble self beyond the intrusions of the herd and moralistic humanity). I concur with James Conant who argues, contra the reading of Nietzsche as an aestheticist, that Nietzsche is seeking to transform our understanding of the categories 'aesthetic' and 'ethical', including our conception of them as resting upon distinct and mutually independent kinds of valuation (Conant 2000: 221–2). Indeed, we have seen that Nietzsche holds the category of greatness or the sublime to be an amorphous one, being partly aesthetic and partly moral.

Finally, the question arises: to what extent can this noble or aristocratic conception of philosophy inspire us today? It lies beyond the scope of this essay to address this issue but it can be noted that it does have a presence in contemporary philosophy. Deleuze and Guattari, for example, argue that the specific task of philosophy, as distinct from art and from science, is to *create* concepts and to concern itself not with truth, but with the singular, the remarkable, the extraordinary, and also that it is not populist writers who lay claim to this future of a new people and new earth but the most aristocratic ones (Deleuze and Guattari 1994: 108). And the work of Jean-Francois Lyotard on the sublime has, I believe, many resonances with

---

[26] Some important references to the sublime in the later Nietzsche include: *HAH* I: 130, 217; *D* 33, 45, 130, 169, 192, 210, 423, 427, 435, 449, 459, 461, 542, 553, 570; *GS* 290, 313; *BGE* 62, 229, 230; *GM* Preface 5, I: 8, 13, II: 24, III: 14, 21; *CW* 6.

[27] See *EH*: 'Why I Am So Clever' 10: 'Beware of all picturesque people!'

Nietzsche's valuation of it. For Lyotard the sublime is part of an avant-garde committed to its destabilizing power, its non-conformism, and with showing us the power and shock of the event (that there is something new or unpresentable) (Lyotard 1991).

BIBLIOGRAPHY

(A) Works by Nietzsche

A   *The Anti-Christ*, trans. Judith Norman. Cambridge: Cambridge University Press, 2005.
BGE   *Beyond Good and Evil*, trans. Marion Faber. Oxford: Oxford University Press, 1998.
BT   *The Birth of Tragedy*, trans. Ronald Speirs. Cambridge: Cambridge University Press, 1999.
EH   *Ecce Homo*, trans. Duncan Large. Oxford: Oxford University Press, 2007.
PPP   *The Pre-Platonic Philosophers*, ed. and trans. Greg Whitlock. Urbana: University of Illinois Press, 2001.
TI   *Twilight of the Idols*, trans. Duncan Large. Oxford: Oxford University Press, 1998.
UM   *Unfashionable Observations*, in Richard T. Gray (ed. and trans.), *The Complete Works of Friedrich Nietzsche*, vol. 2. Stanford: Stanford University Press, 1995.
Z   *Thus Spoke Zarathustra*, trans. Graham Parkes. Oxford: Oxford University Press, 2005.

I have relied upon vol. 11 of Gray's translation (1999) for English translations of the *Nachlass* from the time of the *Unfashionable Observations*.

(B) Other Works Cited

Ansell-Pearson, Keith. 2008. '"Holding on to the Sublime": Nietzsche on Philosophy's Perception and Search for Greatness', in Herman Siemens and Vasti Roodt (eds), *Nietzsche, Power, and Politics*. Berlin and New York: Walter de Gruyter, 767–99.
Arrowsmith, William. 1990. 'Foreword', in W. Arrowsmith (ed.), *Friedrich Nietzsche: Unmodern Observations*. New Haven: Yale University Press, xi-xix.
Battersby, Christine. 2007. *The Sublime, Terror and Human Difference*. London and New York: Routledge.
Bell, Michael. 2007. 'Nietzsche as Educator and the Implosion of Bildung', in *Open Secrets: Literature, Education, and Authority from J.-J. Rousseau to J. M. Coetzee*. Oxford and New York: Oxford University Press, 130–61.
Brandes, Georg. 2002. *Friedrich Nietzsche*. London: Living Time Press.
Breazeale, Daniel. 1979. 'Introduction', in D. Breazeale (ed. and trans.), *Philosophy and Truth: Selections from Nietzsche's Notebooks of the Early 1870s*. New Jersey: Humanities Press.
Breazeale, Daniel. 1997. 'Introduction', in R. J. Hollingdale (trans.), *Friedrich Nietzsche: Untimely Meditations*. Cambridge: Cambridge University Press.
Breazeale, Daniel. 1998. 'Becoming Who One Is: Notes on Schopenhauer as Educator', *New Nietzsche Studies* 2.3–4: 1–27.
Conant, James. 2000. 'Nietzsche's Perfectionism: A Reading of *Schopenhauer as Educator*', in R. Schacht (ed.), *Nietzsche's Postmoralism: Essays on Nietzsche's Prelude to Philosophy's Future*. Cambridge: Cambridge University Press, 181–257.
Deleuze, Gilles and Guattari, Felix. 1994. *What is Philosophy?* trans. Graham Burchell and Hugh Tomlinson. London: Verso.
Gray, Richard T. 1995. 'Afterword', in *Friedrich Nietzsche: Unfashionable Observations*. Stanford: Stanford University Press, 395–414.

Kant, Immanuel. 1790/1987. *Critique of Judgment*, trans. Werner S. Pluhar. Indianapolis: Hackett.

Kaufmann, Walter. 1974. *Nietzsche: Philosopher, Psychologist, and Antichrist,* 4th edn. Princeton: Princeton University Press.

Koselleck, Reinhart. 1985. *Futures Past: On the Semantic of Historical Time*, trans. Keith Tribe. New York: Columbia University Press.

Longinus. 1965. *On the Sublime*, trans. T. S. Dorsch. Harmondsworth: Penguin.

Lyotard, Jean-Francois. 1991. 'The Sublime and the Avant-Garde', in *The Inhuman: Reflections on Time*, trans. G. Bennington and R. Bowlby. Oxford: Polity Press, 89–108.

Nabais, Nuno. 2006. *Nietzsche and the Metaphysics of the Tragic*, trans. Martin Earl. London and New York: Continuum.

Nietzsche, Friedrich. 1911. 'The Relation of Schopenhauer's Philosophy to German Culture', in Oscar Levy (ed.), *The Complete Works of Friedrich Nietzsche*, vol. 2. London: T. N. Foulis, 65–9.

Rampley, Matthew. 2000. *Nietzsche, Aesthetics, Modernity*. Cambridge: Cambridge University Press.

Schiller, F. 2001. 'On the Sublime', in *Essays*, ed. Walter Hinderer and Daniel O. Dahlstrom. New York: Continuum, 22–45.

Schopenhauer, Arthur. 1966. *The World as Will and Representation*, trans. E. F. J. Payne (2 vols). New York: Dover.

Schopenhauer, Arthur. 1974. *Parerga and Paralipomena*, trans. E. F. J. Payne (2 vols). Oxford: Oxford University Press.

Shaw, Philip. 2006. *The Sublime*. London: Routledge.

Strauss, David Friedrich. 1862/1997. *The Old Faith and the New*, trans. Mathilde Blind, intro. and notes G. A. Wells. New York: Prometheus Books.

CHAPTER 11

....

THE GAY SCIENCE[1]

....

CHRISTOPHER JANAWAY

1 THE BOOK

....

DIE *fröhliche Wissenschaft*—called in English *The Gay Science*, in the sense of *Joyful, Joyous, Light-hearted*, or *Cheerful Science*—is one of Nietzsche's most important works. It lacks the stridency of some of his very latest productions and bridges a crucial period when his writing becomes exploratory, open-ended, and varied in style. The different parts of *The Gay Science* span the period of *Thus Spoke Zarathustra*, to which Nietzsche assigned distinctive significance among his books, and in *The Gay Science* itself we encounter the doctrine of eternal recurrence in stark form as a psychological test of one's ability to bear life, as well as the 'madman' who shouts out the death of God, and some of Nietzsche's most protracted mature reflections on art, deception, and truth. *The Gay Science* will never cohere into a single statable philosophical position and cannot be 'summed up'. But we may venture the following thoughts about the book's themes. An absence of values threatens the whole of European culture because of a lapse in the belief in God, but in Nietzsche's eyes the threat is also a massive opportunity for those able to seize it. He suggests that we might—if we are among their number—create new values that are truly our own, born out of a joyful stance towards our lives and a kind of aristocratic disdain for values that lament and seek to remove all suffering, negate the fullness we are capable of, and elevate what is weak and passive in humanity. To attain the new values we will need probing self-investigation, guided by an intellectual conscience that sees through our acquired habits of thought and feeling. But in alliance with this rigorous self-investigation we will require an artistic creativity towards ourselves that makes a confrontation with otherwise ugly truths bearable. In this book Nietzsche is troubled and arguably quite ambivalent about the value of truth: on the one hand he encourages us to be 'scientists' investigating and undermining with a probing conscience the origins of our own cherished attitudes; on the other hand, he questions whether all this truth-seeking will make life even bearable for us, let alone contribute to an ability to affirm its recurrence an infinite number of times. The crux is life and how we can 'say yes' to

---

[1] Some parts of sections 4–6 of this paper are modified versions of material that appears in Janaway 2007 and Janaway forthcoming.

it, and if there is an overarching theme it is that the traditional conception of dispassionate enquiry into truth will not serve toward that end.

The Gay Science began as a projected continuation of the preceding *Daybreak* (1881), then took shape as a separate work consisting of Books One to Four which were published as *The Gay Science* in 1882, with a 'Prelude in Rhymes' entitled 'Joke, Cunning and Revenge'. The supposedly light-hearted book ended not with a joke but with 'The tragedy begins' (*Incipit tragoedia*, the title of the final section 342), and in a narrative style not used in the rest of the book said the following of a previously unmentioned fictional character:

> When Zarathustra was thirty years old, he left his homeland and Lake Urmi and went into the mountains. There he enjoyed his spirit and solitude, and did not tire of that for ten years. But at last his heart changed—and one morning he arose with rosy dawn, stepped before the sun, and spoke to it thus: 'You great heavenly body! What would your happiness be if you did not have those for whom you shine! For ten years you have climbed up to my cave; without me, my eagle, and my snake, you would have become tired of your light and of this road; but we awaited you every morning, relieved you of your overabundance, and blessed you for it. Behold, I am sick of my wisdom, like a bee that has collected too much honey; I need outstretched hands; I would like to give away and distribute until the wise among humans once again enjoy their folly and the poor once again their riches. For that I must step into the depths, as you do in the evening when you go behind the sea and bring light even to the underworld, you over-rich heavenly body! Like you I must *go under*, as it is called by the human beings to whom I want to descend. So bless me then, you calm eye that can look without envy upon all-too-great happiness! Bless the cup that wants to overflow in order that the water may flow golden from it and everywhere carry the reflection of your bliss! Behold, this cup wants to become empty again, and Zarathustra wants to become human again.' Thus began Zarathustra's going under.

And thus Nietzsche had in truth begun writing his next book, because these words, with a few minor changes, became the opening of his unique literary experiment *Thus Spoke Zarathustra*, published between 1883 and 1885.

In the autumn of 1886 Nietzsche wrote a new Preface to *The Gay Science* (as he did to other previously published works[2]), and in 1887 the book appeared again with this added Preface, a new Appendix of verses called 'Songs of Prince Vogelfrei (or Prince Free-as-a-bird)', and an entirely new Book Five ('We Fearless Ones') which consists of forty sections and shares something of its subject matter and tone with the two works published immediately before and after it: *Beyond Good and Evil* (1886) and *On the Genealogy of Morality* (1887). So *The Gay Science* in its final shape straddles one of the most productive and creatively restless phases of Nietzsche's writing career. It was also the time of his deepest emotional troubles: a few months after the book was published in its first form he suffered a terrible personal blow when, having already alienated himself from his sister and mother, he was faced with the collapse of his close friendship and planned intellectual collaboration with Lou Salomé and Paul Rée. In a letter he wrote: 'This last *bite of life* was the hardest I have ever chewed on and it is still possible that I shall choke on it. . . . There is a duality of conflicting affects in all this that I am not equal to.' (*KSA* 6: 311–12)[3] This from the author who had just gone in print advocating gaiety in the pursuit of knowledge, and alluding in his book's penultimate section (341) to an idea he had been working on, the great test of

---

[2] *The Birth of Tragedy, Human, All Too Human* I and II, and *Daybreak*.
[3] Letter to Franz Overbeck, 25 December 1882.

being able to affirm one's life under the thought of its eternally recurring in every single detail.

2 *LA GAYA SCIENZA*

As well as its Preface, its 'free-as-a-bird' poems, and its substantial fifth Book, *The Gay Science* of 1887 also acquired a different title page, with a change of motto and a new parenthetical subtitle: ('*la gaya scienza*'). *La gaya scienza* is a version of *gai saber*, an old Provençal phrase that Nietzsche had already used briefly in *Beyond Good and Evil* 260:

> love *as passion* (our European specialty) must have had a purely noble descent: it is known to have been invented in the knightly poetry of Provence, by those magnificent, inventive men of the '*gai saber*'. Europe is indebted to these men for so many things, almost for itself.

Nietzsche is referring to those who are commonly known as troubadours: composers and performers of songs in southern Europe in the eleventh to fifteenth centuries.[4] The connotations of '*gai saber*' are of learning and knowledge (*saber*), song, artistry, and inventiveness, a light-hearted positive mood, passionate love, and distinctly aristocratic virtues. The passage just quoted from *Beyond Good and Evil* is from a section in which Nietzsche states the distinction between noble and slave moralities that later dominated the *Genealogy* in particular. The new subtitle of *The Gay Science* thus clearly evokes what Nietzsche calls 'an aristocratic way of thinking and valuing' (*BGE* 260). In his retrospect in *Ecce Homo*, Nietzsche remarks that the concept of *gaya scienza* is a 'unity of *singer, knight*, and *free spirit*' (*EH*: 'The Gay Science'), and in his 1883 notebooks he had explained: 'perhaps the Provençal was already...a high point in Europe—*very rich*, many-faceted human beings who nevertheless were masters of themselves, who were not ashamed of their drives' (*KSA* 10: 256). The ideas of self-mastery, attaining internal unity in complexity, and maximizing the operation of drives are all central notions in Nietzsche's conception of human greatness.[5]

What then of *Wissenschaft, scienza, saber*? What is this activity that one can pursue gaily? *Wissenschaft*, like the romance language terms Nietzsche juxtaposes it with, could almost be translated just as 'knowledge': *Wissen* on its own means knowledge or knowing. *Wissenschaft* is somewhat more, however: a systematic or disciplined form of investigation that yields or aims at yielding knowledge in some particular field. As has often been commented, Nietzsche and his contemporaries view his erstwhile discipline of classical philology as a *Wissenschaft*. So we should not restrict the term to the natural sciences; but even without that restriction it shares with 'science' an implication of systematicity, rigour, and commitment to dispassionate objectivity, and creates an immediate clash with 'Gay' or 'Joyful'.[6] In the text of *The Gay*

---

[4] In a notebook entry of 1881 Nietzsche lists under the heading *Gaya Scienza* several types of song: '*Albas*: morning songs; *serenas*: evening songs; *tenzoni*: polemical songs; *sirventes*: songs of praise and criticism; *sontas*: songs of joy; *lais*: songs of suffering' (*KSA* 9: 573). For other uses of *gai saber* and references to the Provençal troubadours in the notebooks, see *KSA* 10: 256; *KSA* 11: 423, 481, 494, 547, 549, 551, 669; *KSA* 12: 39, 94, 149.

[5] See Janaway 2012 on notions of greatness in Nietzsche.

[6] The notorious academic reception of *The Birth of Tragedy* (1872) included the following published remarks on Nietzsche by the classical scholar Wilamowitz-Moellendorff: 'He may gather tigers and

Science Nietzsche often gives us mixed signals concerning the mood in which disciplined knowledge or enquiry is to be pursued. In section 327 we hear what we might expect:

> The lovely human beast seems to lose its good mood when it thinks well; it becomes 'serious'! and 'where laughter and gaiety are found, thinking is good for nothing'—that is the prejudice of this serious beast against all 'gay science'. Well, then, let us prove it a prejudice!

But at the end of Book Five 'the tragedy begins' once again when a new, healthy ideal is said to 'place itself next to all earthly seriousness heretofore . . . as if it were their most incarnate and involuntary parody—and in spite of all this, it is perhaps only with it that *the great seriousness* really emerges' (*GS* 382). It is as if we can be serious only when not serious, just as we can be profound only when remaining at the surface of things (see *GS* Preface 1).

The Gay Science treats of tragedy and suffering, crisis and disorientation, loss of values and the 'terrifying' question: 'Does existence have any meaning at all?' (*GS* 357), yet it is equally fervent in its drive towards lightness and affirmation.[7] We should be alert for some attempted confrontation or rapprochement between art and science, or perhaps a kind of science that is an art or a kind of art that is a science ('How far we still are,' Nietzsche exclaims, 'from the time when artistic energies and the practical wisdom of life join with scientific thought so that a higher organic system will develop . . . !' (*GS* 113).) We may hope to find an approach to dark and painful truths that can face or finesse them in a satisfying way, as art perhaps can. But whatever the mood or manner in which Nietzsche wishes knowledge to be pursued, by the time we have finished reading Book Five of *The Gay Science* one thing at least that he hopes we shall learn is that for the tasks that concern him scientific selflessness—cold, impersonal enquiry conducted in no affective mood at all and from no personal point of view—is of no use, and is even a myth, the pursuit of which has surprising origins and deleterious consequences that reveal something profoundly awry with our values.

3 GOD IS DEAD

One of Nietzsche's most popularly known sayings occurs three times in *The Gay Science*. Book Three opens with this:

> *New battles.*—After Buddha was dead, they still showed his shadow in a cave for centuries— a tremendous, gruesome shadow. God is dead; but given the way people are, there may for millennia be caves in which they show his shadow.—And we—we must still defeat his shadow as well! (*GS* 108)

panthers around his knees but not Germany's philologically interested youth who are supposed to learn—in the asceticism of self-denying work—to look everywhere for nothing but the truth' (2000: 23). In a note from 1885–6 Nietzsche recounts how the title 'The Gay Science' is not understood by the learned of his day (*KSA* 12: 149). For wider discussion of the connotations and origins of the title see Williams 2001, Babich 2006, and Pippin 2010: 33–5.

7 Though it is worth noting the dissenting voice of Julian Young: 'the only kind of gaiety its author achieves is a kind of manic frivolity which is really no more than a symptom of desperation and despair' (Young 1992: 92). And right at the end of *GS* Nietzsche himself imagines the spirits of his own book complaining 'We can't stand it any more . . . stop, stop this raven-black music!' (*GS* 383).

Section 109 enlarges on the point: 'When will all these shadows of god no longer darken us? When will we have completely de-deified nature? When may we begin to *naturalize* humanity with a pure, newly discovered, newly redeemed nature?' Even if we no longer believe in God, in our pictures of the world we have not properly emancipated ourselves from that belief: we project on to the world our own ethical and aesthetic values, purposes and aims, lawlikeness, order, perfection, even cruelty or heartlessness, when all along 'the total character of the world... is for all eternity chaos... a lack of order, organization, form, beauty, wisdom, and whatever else our aesthetic anthropomorphisms are called'. If, for Nietzsche and those he imagines as his more sympathetic readers, the traditional belief in God has waned away, the disenchanted gaze upon the universe that should rightfully ensue is much harder to sustain.

The next occurrence of the death of God idea is the most striking and the most famous. In 'The Madman' (*GS* 125), a brilliantly crafted parable (reminiscent of Borges, perhaps, or Kafka) a madman shouts in the marketplace: 'God is dead! God remains dead! And we have killed him!' to an audience—an unhearing audience—of mocking unbelievers. Again the death of God is something that is assumed to have happened already, but only someone who appears mad realizes that it is a 'tremendous event' in which 'the holiest and mightiest thing the world has ever possessed has bled to death'. By ceasing to believe, we have committed a cosmic atrocity: 'who gave us the sponge to wipe away the entire horizon? What were we doing when we unchained the earth from its sun?' But the 'sane' unbelieving majority are in ignorance of themselves: 'This deed is still more remote to them than the remotest stars— *and yet they have done it themselves*'. The madman persona gives a vital dimension to *The Gay Science*: the double pain of facing both a disorienting vacuum of values and the alienation of sensing the vacuum when others do not. But, as we shall see, neither complacent unthinking atheism nor the 'heavy' desperation of the madman can be a final resting place for Nietzsche, the would-be light-hearted investigator.[8]

The later Book Five opens by recapitulating the same idea without the figurative punch of the parable, but with Nietzsche's literal diagnosis now laid bare:

> The greatest recent event—that 'God is dead'; that the belief in the Christian God has become unbelievable—is already starting to cast its first shadow over Europe. To those few whose eyes—or the *suspicion* in whose eyes is strong and subtle enough for this spectacle, some kind of sun seems to have set; some old deep trust turned into doubt... Even less may one suppose many to know at all *what* this event really means—and, now that this faith has been undermined, how much must collapse because it was built on this faith, leaned on it, had grown into it—for example, our entire European morality (*GS* 343).

A central theme of the *Genealogy*, published in the same year as these words, is that morality has been built on Christianity, and that it is nearsighted to expect morality either to be accepted as well-founded or eventually to survive at all, once belief in the Christian God has subsided.[9] Morality, then, is a 'shadow of God', a set of attitudes that persists with a ghostly life of its own, but which must be fought against, in Nietzsche's view, in order to reach higher and better-founded values. But finally in this section the death of God emerges as an

---

[8] See Pippin 2010: 49–51 n. 33.   [9] See especially *GM* III: 27.

opening or opportunity, evoking the thematic light mood of the book, when Nietzsche says that the immediate consequences of this event,

> the consequences *for ourselves*, are the opposite of what one might expect—not at all sad and gloomy, but much more like a new and barely describable type of light, happiness, relief, amusement, encouragement, dawn … Indeed, at hearing the news that 'the old god is dead', we philosophers and 'free spirits' feel illuminated by a new dawn; our heart overflows with gratitude, amazement, forebodings, expectation.

Nietzsche has already spoken of creating new values. In section 335 he advocates having 'an ideal of your very own' that 'could never be someone else's, let alone everyone's', urging upon his readers 'the creation of tables of what is good that are new and all our own' and the aspiration to be 'human beings who are new, unique, incomparable, who give themselves laws, who create themselves'. This call for the creation of new values comes at the culmination of a complex passage which speaks of unearthing the psychological and cultural provenance of our own moral attitudes, because in order to create new values, we have to attain some detachment from our existing values. For example, we have a belief in an internal voice of conscience that we heed, or a commanding voice that issues imperatives. What is the truth behind this idea of being commanded to do certain things because they are right? A central concern of *The Gay Science* is honesty (*Redlichkeit*) and the primacy of an 'intellectual conscience'.[10] Intellectual conscience is distinct from moral conscience, and can precisely infiltrate behind the latter, to investigate its origins and potentially disrupt our faith in it:

> But why do you *listen* to the words of your conscience? And what gives you the right to consider such a judgment true and infallible? For this belief—is there no conscience? Do you know nothing of an intellectual conscience? A conscience behind your 'conscience'? Your judgment, 'that is right' has a prehistory in your drives, inclinations, aversions, experiences, and what you have failed to experience; you have to ask, '*how* did it emerge there?' and then also, '*what* is really impelling me to listen to it?' … And, briefly, had you reflected more subtly, observed better, and studied more, you would never continue to call this 'duty' of yours and this 'conscience' of yours duty and conscience. Your insight into *how such things as moral judgments could ever have come into existence* would spoil these emotional words for you (*GS* 335).

Nietzsche here adumbrates a 'calling into question' of morality by discovering its origins, and implies that this process of discovery is a prerequisite for the acquisition of new values that the 'de-deification' of nature has made into a hopeful prospect. Our morality is a lingering 'shadow of God' whose banishment thus requires far more than the mere lapsing of our belief in God. Nietzsche more than hints here at the notion of genealogy as a precondition for a revaluation of values—and prefigures the strategy of his later *Genealogy*.

---

[10] See *GS* 2, 99, 107, 110, 319, 335, 344.

4 Problems with Compassion

In publications either side of *The Gay Science* Nietzsche focuses his critique upon 'the morality of compassion' (see especially *D* 132–8 and *GM* Preface 5–6), and a central target in both cases is Schopenhauer's conception of morality. The same trains of thought continue through *The Gay Science* itself. In section 99 Nietzsche condemns Schopenhauer's 'nonsense about compassion' as one of his regrettable and embarrassing doctrines. Schopenhauer's position is that a sympathetic feeling of pain at the suffering of another is the sole incentive to actions that have genuine moral worth. Their arising out of compassion is indeed, he argues, the necessary and sufficient condition of actions' having moral worth.[11] But such care for the well-being of another—the antithesis of the egoism that we normally expect from human beings—is explicable to Schopenhauer only if the caring agent has at least an inchoate metaphysical insight that individuality—the very distinction between self and other—is at bottom an illusion. It is this metaphysical aspect of Schopenhauer's account of the morality of compassion that Nietzsche scorns in section 99. But it is not his only problem with compassion (German *Mitleid*, also translatable as 'pity'). In the earlier parts of *The Gay Science* he seeks to impugn the credentials of compassion by way of an analysis of it in terms of drives:

> one should make a distinction in benevolence between the drive to appropriate and the drive to submit, depending on whether it is the stronger or the weaker who experiences it....Compassion is essentially the former, a pleasant stirring of the drive to appropriate at the sight of the weaker; however we must still keep in mind that 'strong' and 'weak' are relative concepts (*GS* 118).

Similar thoughts are expressed in sections 13 and 14: 'Compassion is the most agreeable feeling for those who have little pride and no prospect of great conquests; for them, easy prey—and that is what those who suffer are—is something enchanting'; 'When we see someone suffering, we like to use this opportunity to take possession of him; that is for example what...those who have compassion for him do'. So Nietzsche's analysis is that, while superficially selfless in motivation, compassionate behaviour expresses a self-interested drive towards power, or to the attainment of a feeling of power.

It is, however, only the 'relatively strong', in Nietzsche's conception, who will tend to use compassion in this possessive or conquering fashion. Those of greater strength, by contrast, will see compassion as a 'danger' (*GS* 271). Why? Section 338 of *The Gay Science* gives arguably Nietzsche's most sophisticated reflections on the questionable significance of our sensitivity to the suffering of others. Two questions are posed: 'Is it good for you yourselves to be above all else compassionate persons? And is it good for those who suffer if you are compassionate?' To the second question Nietzsche gives an interesting, if questionable, answer: if you are compassionate towards someone, you tend to rob them of what is personal to them and diminish their worth. Unhappiness or misfortune (*Unglück*) is as important to each individual as happiness or good fortune (*Glück*): they are 'two siblings and twins who either

---

[11] See Schopenhauer 2009: 196–203.

grow up together or—as with you—*remain small* together!' To whom is this last remark addressed? To adherents of the 'religion of compassion', who feel commanded to *help* anyone whom they detect to be suffering. Such people apply the general classification 'suffering' to an individual, unaware of the particularities of meaning that attend this suffering as part of the life of this individual. And anything categorized as 'suffering' they label as *eo ipso* something to be removed. If you applied this rule to yourself, you would, Nietzsche says, 'refuse to let your suffering lie on you even for an hour and instead constantly prevent all possible misfortune ahead of time' and you would 'experience suffering and displeasure as evil, hateful, deserving of annihilation, as a defect of existence'. But it is just this striving for safety from suffering at all costs that would produce a condition of growth-restricted happiness. The fundamental problem with the morality of compassion for Nietzsche is its assumption that all suffering is of the same nature, and that in virtue of this nature it is uniformly negative, uniformly to be removed or prevented.[12] Persistently to regard other human beings in this manner is, for Nietzsche, to betray their integrity:

> the one who feels compassion...knows nothing of the whole inner sequence and interconnection that spells misfortune for *me* or for *you*! The entire economy of my soul and the balance effected by 'misfortune', the breaking open of new springs and needs, the healing of old wounds, the shedding of entire periods of the past—...terrors, deprivations, impoverishments, midnights, adventures, risks, and blunders are as necessary for me and you as their opposites.

For Nietzsche, then, we need our sufferings in all their idiosyncrasy and any systematic motivation to deprive us of them tends to harm rather than benefit us as individuals. We may, however, see some sense in this last point while disputing Nietzsche's claim that an attitude of compassion inherently categorizes those who suffer in ways that diminish the personal significance of their suffering. While a kind of 'helping' compassion, bent principally on removing suffering per se, might be subject to such a charge, it is not impossible to feel a kind of compassion whose guiding motivation is precisely to understand what a particular suffering *is* for the sufferer in all their idiosyncrasy—though it must be said that the 'morality of compassion' and 'religion of compassion' that Nietzsche so strongly opposes are more likely to be systems of value which assign a generic character to suffering as such and enjoin us to accept universally binding prescriptions concerning it.

Nietzsche addresses the inverse question, 'Is it good for you yourselves to be above all else compassionate persons?' by imagining some examples (though he calls them 'bad examples', chosen for 'good reasons'):

> I know, there are a hundred decent and praiseworthy ways of losing myself *from my path*, and, verily, highly 'moral' ways! Yes, the moral teacher of compassion even goes so far as to hold that precisely this and only this is moral—to lose *one's own* way like this in order to help a neighbour. I, too, know with certainty that I need only to expose myself to the sight of real distress and I, too, *am* lost! If a suffering friend said to me, "Look, I am about to die; please

---

[12] A notable parallel passage is *BGE* 225: 'You want, if possible (and no "if possible" is crazier) *to abolish suffering*. And us?—it looks as though *we* would prefer it to be heightened and made even worse than it has ever been!... The discipline of suffering, of great suffering—don't you know that *this* discipline has been the cause of every enhancement in humanity so far?'

promise to die with me," I would promise it; likewise, the sight of a small mountain tribe fighting for its freedom would make me offer my hand and my life.

Here, then, is novel reason for finding compassion for others to be self-serving. For those who are only 'relatively strong' the suffering other is 'prey', an opportunity of affirming themselves at the expense of something weaker. But in this passage the character who is tempted to die with his friend or to offer his life for the mountain tribe is not necessarily someone who needs to assert his own power over others, rather he can be someone with the more subtle need to escape from the demand to care for himself, someone strong enough to give himself with genuine generosity to others, but in danger of thereby failing to be himself to the fullest of his strength.

5 The Heaviest Weight

Many questions are raised by Nietzsche's positive presentation of the demise of Christian belief and its associated moral values, by his attack on the assumed positive value of compassion and negative value of suffering, and by his sometime insistence that philosophers in future may create their own new values. One of the most pressing questions is: *what* new values might we have instead? There are two particular passages in Book Four of *The Gay Science* that have often been thought to provide clues towards answering this question. They are section 290, 'One thing is needful', and section 341, 'The heaviest weight'. Let us take the latter first:

> *The heaviest weight.* What if some day or night a demon were to steal into your loneliest loneliness and say to you: 'This life as you now live it and have lived it you will have to live once again and innumerable times again; and there will be nothing new in it, but every pain and every joy and every thought and everything unspeakably small or great in your life must return to you, all in the same succession and sequence—even this spider and this moonlight between the trees, and even this moment and I myself. The eternal hourglass of existence is turned over and over again, and you with it, speck of dust!' Would you not throw yourself down and gnash your teeth and curse the demon who spoke thus? Or have you once experienced a tremendous moment when you would have answered him: 'You are a god and never have I heard anything more divine?' If this thought were to gain power over you, as you are it would transform and possibly crush you; the question in each and every thing: 'Do you want this again and innumerable times again?' would lie on your actions as the heaviest weight! Or how well disposed would you have to become to yourself and to life *to long for nothing more fervently* than for this ultimate eternal confirmation and seal? (*GS* 341)

A way of reading this passage well represented in recent discussions is guided by two principal thoughts: (1) that the truth of the cosmological proposition that every event recurs eternally is not required for Nietzsche's purposes in this passage; (2) that the function of imagining the reaction one would have, if one were to entertain the idea of eternal recurrence, is that of testing one's attitude to one's actual life.[13] The coherence of this conception

---

[13] See, e.g., Clark 1990: 245–86; Nehamas 1985 (esp. 150–1). As Nehamas puts it, 'what [Nietzsche] is interested in is the attitude one must have toward oneself in order to react with joy and not despair to the

of eternal return (or recurrence) has often been questioned, as has the notion that the thought of eternal return can even serve, in the way Nietzsche believes, as a good test of the degree of one's self-affirmation.[14] But what is the attitude of self-affirmation itself, the state of 'being well disposed to oneself and to life' that Nietzsche proposes can be tested by this thought?

As we read 'The Heaviest Weight' we are apt to focus on the wide polarity of the possible reactions Nietzsche canvasses: despair versus elation. One can raise the question whether Nietzsche imagines the 'well-disposedness' he is interested in to be an all or nothing affair or a matter of degree (as perhaps suggested by the phrase '*how* well disposed...?'). But in addition it is worth noting that the extreme reactions are imagined in two distinct instantiations. In the first instance Nietzsche envisages someone struck all at once in a vulnerable and disoriented moment by the scenario of infinite repetition, which is announced so as to carry an air of authoritativeness, but comes into no intelligible connection with their overall rational understanding of the world.[15] The imagined reactions to the demon's scenario are immediate affective responses: an 'Oh Yes!' or an 'Oh No!' With this kind of reaction it is not relevant whether the scenario to which one reacts makes sense on critical scrutiny or whether one has good reason to react in any particular way to it. It is more that, suddenly taken off one's guard, one evinces one's true feelings. In the last two sentences of the section, however, Nietzsche is talking about a different instance: a huge transformation in one's life, a long-sustained attitude of joy or despair towards oneself. He asks: Would it be crushingly burdensome or fervently desirable if 'this thought were to gain power over you'? 'This thought' (*jener Gedanke*, more literally *that* thought or *the previous* thought) must refer back to what the demon first said: 'This life as you live it and have lived it you will have to live once again and innumerable times again'. The thought's gaining power over you suggests a persistent reliving of the imagined scenario of repetition, but also a prioritizing of the relived experience, its becoming vital to confront the thought as constantly as one can.[16]

possibility the demon raises' (151); and as Clark puts it 'A joyful reaction would indicate a fully affirmative attitude towards one's (presumably, non-recurring) life' (251).

[14] There are various conceivable positions here. One might hold (1) that the test of facing up to the thought of eternal return is essential to Nietzsche's conception of self-affirmation; or (2) that even though affirmation is characterizable without recourse to eternal return, confronting the thought of eternal return would be one way genuinely to test the degree of such affirmation. On the other hand, one might claim (3) that the eternal return scenario is not a coherent thought experiment and/or is a prospect one should remain indifferent to, and hence that it would not provide any good or worthwhile test of affirmation; or most negatively (4) that Nietzsche's trespassing on the ground of eternal return at all spoils and interferes with his conception of affirmation. Both negative challenges (3) and (4) are found in Ridley 1997. The more or less standard objection (3) is found, e.g., in Simmel 1986, Danto 1965, Soll 1973, Nehamas 1985, Clark 1990. For a fuller list—and a defence of the coherence and significance of eternal recurrence—see Loeb 2006; also Loeb's chapter in this volume.

[15] See Clark 1990: 251.

[16] If the thought of eternal return is itself an incoherent thought, as many allege (see n. 14 above), then its use as a test in a moment of vulnerable confusion may be defensible. But it is much less appealing to envisage that I should make it a matter of lifelong policy to keep on confronting myself with a thought and never reflect on its coherence, or that I should realize its incoherence and carry on regardless with the attempt to test myself against it.

The least obvious point in the passage is, arguably, in its last sentence. Something is *longed for* as an 'ultimate eternal confirmation and seal', but what? Is the object of my longing (1) *that my life repeat itself* again and innumerable times again? Or (2) *that I keep confronting the question* whether I would want each and every thing again eternally? Or (3) *that I should react with joy* every time the question comes to me? It is arguable that both (2) and (3) must come into play to make the 'longing' intelligible. The character addressed in this passage is portrayed as desiring to have something *confirmed*, and it is quite mysterious how (1) on its own could be a confirmation of anything at all. On the other hand, *my being apprised of* the fact that I would in all cases want my life again and again would provide me with strong evidence of my being well disposed to life and self in high degree. (2) and (3) coalesce, in fact, into one complex object of longing: I long *to confront myself repeatedly with the demon's scenario* and, whatever life may bring me, *always to react to it with joy*.

The attitude in question is scarcely imaginable if we take Nietzsche to mean that I might find each and every thing in my life equally good, equally pleasing, or equally meriting joy. To take Nietzsche's own case, he could no doubt imagine an alternative, counterfactual life without his crippling illnesses and disastrous personal involvements, without his sister's espousing the anti-Semitism (or the particular anti-Semite) that he detested. If we take him to mean that he could in principle want each of these misfortunes for its own sake, in just the way he wanted the exhilarations of mountain air, the fulfilments of writing, or the rare peace of an untroubled sleep, we border on an outlook that not only makes an inhuman demand but risks incoherence. But I would propose an alternative reading, the key to which is to distinguish pro- and con- attitudes of different orders. Numerous events in any life will be undergone, remembered, or anticipated with a negative first-order attitude; but that is compatible with a second-order attitude of acceptance, affirmation, or positive evaluation towards one's having had these negative experiences. If in some course of events one is, say, humiliated, one's experience is as such unwelcome, painful, and so on: obviously it could not be exactly a humiliation that one underwent, unless one's primary or first-order attitude were set against, rather than for, the course of events. But instead of asking fruitlessly whether you can undergo humiliation as something positive, Nietzsche poses a different question: would you be well enough disposed to want your life again, where that (second-order) wanting would embrace among its objects the particular hateful and excruciating humiliation from which you suffered? Facing this question is intelligible, indeed humanly possible. Answering 'Yes' to the whole of one's life in this way is scarcely easy for all human beings, but that is no objection for Nietzsche, who is searching for an extremely demanding ideal and looking to discriminate the rare few from the herd.

Nietzsche could, if he were strong enough,[17] wholly affirm his life whilst discriminating those of its contents that are against his will, negative, suffered, from those to which he has a first-order pro- attitude. So the question for Nietzsche is whether second-order affirmation can stretch to embrace everything to which one's first-order response is negative. Bernd Magnus has written that 'each of us would affirm the eternal recurrence of our lives only

---

[17] As Paul Loeb (2005: 74) points out, Nietzsche confesses that he would not be able to fulfil the ideal he sets up: '[A]s we know from his notes, letters, and published works, Nietzsche does not regard himself as strong or healthy enough to affirm his life's eternal recurrence: "I do not want life *again*. How have I borne it? Creating. What has made me endure the sight? the vision of the *Übermensch* who affirms life. I have tried to affirm it myself—alas!" (*KSA* 10: 4 [81]). In *GS* 276 he yearns to be only a Yes-sayer. See also *EH*: 'Why I Am So Wise' 3 for other biographical thoughts about the difficulty of affirming eternal return.

selectively'; 'Who among us', he asks, 'would not prefer some other possible life and world, no matter how content we may be with our present lot?... [N]o matter how content I may be with my life I can always imagine a better one.'¹⁸ But note that there are two distinct points here. The latter assertion is likely to be correct for most human beings: they can usually imagine a better life. But this does not answer the first question Magnus poses, whether any of us would *prefer* some other possible life and world. For it could be that someone able to *imagine* a better life nevertheless *affirms* and *loves* nothing other than his or her actual life. I argue that this is what Nietzsche has in mind—that one could be strong enough to love everything about one's single, actual life, not *wanting* or *wishing for* anything that is merely imagined or imaginable, however good that might have been.

6 Facing or Fashioning?

In the same Book of *The Gay Science* as 'The Heaviest Weight' a type of rare and valuable human being appears: a kind of artist, someone who forms, shapes, edits, or revises the details of his or her life and character in pursuit of 'satisfaction with himself—be it through this or that poetry or art'. *The Gay Science* 290 is the most extended and probably most discussed example of creative self-formation in Nietzsche's writings. Here a complex metaphor assigns multiple roles to the self: there are the natural strengths and weaknesses of character that are present as a given to be worked upon (the raw material), the form-giving agent (the artist) who creates beauty out of this material, the finished product itself (the artwork), and the locus of a satisfaction felt in contemplation of the product (the spectator).¹⁹ Nietzsche's conception of self-satisfaction here is dynamic: he emphasizes the *transition* from raw material to beautiful form, the active *work* that this requires, the *achievement* of satisfaction by one's own exertions.

> To 'give style' to one's character—a great and rare art! It is practised by those who survey all the strengths and weaknesses that their nature has to offer and then fit them into an artistic plan until each appears as art and reason and even weaknesses delight the eye. Here a great mass of second nature has been added; there a piece of first nature removed—both times through long practice and daily work at it. Here the ugly that could not be removed is concealed; there it is reinterpreted into sublimity. Much that is vague and resisted shaping has been saved and employed for distant views—it is supposed to beckon towards the remote and immense. In the end, when the work is complete, it becomes clear how it was the force of a single taste that ruled and shaped everything great and small [...] [O]ne thing is needful: that a human being should attain satisfaction with himself—be it through this or that poetry or art. (*GS* 290)

In the ideal of self-affirmation (or so we assumed above) things were different: the acceptance of the whole *truth* of one's life—what was and is—was to be embraced without flinching, without escape or erasure. But now the self-satisfaction to be attained through artistry consists in actively making one's character pleasing by falsifying it. We seem to have struck

¹⁸ Magnus 1988: 170, 172.
¹⁹ *BGE* 225 attributes a similar complexity to the self: 'in humans there is material, fragments, abundance, clay, dirt, nonsense, chaos; but in humans there is also creator, maker, hammer-hardness, spectator-divinity and seventh day.'

upon a deep-lying vein of ambivalence towards truth in Nietzsche. The ultimate test of being well disposed to oneself is to confront the whole truth and love it; but the one thing needful is to modify and dissimulate so as to find oneself satisfying and beautiful. How to address this tension, or apparent tension? First, one might argue that self-affirmation and aesthetic self-satisfaction do not after all exclude or oppose one another. Perhaps one is encompassed in the other. What is 'this life', whose recurrence the demon offers me as inviting affirmation or horrified recoil? One could read it as my actively created life-narrative, the self I tell myself I am and have been. From one point of view—one that can seem eminently Nietzschean ('there are no facts, only interpretations' (*WLN* 139, previously published as *WP* 481))—this is all the self I can have anyway. On this reading, I am asked to affirm my life under a construction in which it makes greatest sense to me—to construe it as, and thereby create it as, a whole in which I can take satisfaction. The 'tremendous moment' of self-affirmation would be one in which my narrative self-interpretation made the most complete sense to me as an artistic unity. Such a view is suggested by Alexander Nehamas, who elucidates the 'giving style' passage with the words:

> The value of everything depends on its contribution to a whole of which it can be seen as a part... But what is it to affirm the whole of which all these features and events *have been made* parts? [my italics—C. J.] The answer is provided by the thought of the eternal recurrence ... the thought that if one were to live over again, one would want the very life one has already had, exactly the same down to its tiniest detail, and nothing else. (Nehamas 1998: 142)[20]

This can be taken to imply that the life wanted again in its tiniest detail is a whole to which one has *artificially given* stylistic unity. However, we may doubt whether the constituent ideas in this picture can fit together so comfortably.

First, the presentation of the eternal return, with its invitation to affirm isolated momentary experiences such as that of the moonlight, the trees, and the spider, evokes not so much a crafted unity where every part makes sense in the whole, but rather a joyful acceptance of a different sort of wholeness: a total set of experiences whose connectedness amounts solely to their all being mine. Secondly, the eternal return scenario and the related notion of loving fate—'I want to learn more and more how to see what is necessary in things as what is beautiful in them—thus I will be one of those who make things beautiful. *Amor fati* [love of fate]: let that be my love from now on!' (*GS* 276)[21]—both emphasize confrontation with something that we might dare to call a real self, the necessary aspect of what one is and was, the unchangeability of one's life. And thirdly, in his frequent naturalistic mode Nietzsche is clear that what constitutes the individual is a composite of hierarchically related drives. That is what I *am*, whether I like it or not, indeed whether I know it or not, for '[h]owever far a man may go in self-knowledge, nothing [...] can be more incomplete than his image of the totality of drives that constitute his being' (*D* 119). The arrangement of drives that is myself is not typically conceived as something I have made into a whole, but rather as a unity (or in many cases a disunity) that has organized itself. What I must love if I am to affirm myself is the insuperable necessity of this unchosen self, and the one unalterable life trajectory I follow through having, or being, this self.

---

[20] For Nehamas's fullest account of these issues, see Nehamas 1985: chapters 5 and 6.
[21] On *amor fati* see also *EH*: 'Why I Am So Clever' 10.

A second way to address the tension between confronting the truth and fashioning the self is to collapse it in the other direction, on the grounds that self-fashioning *presupposes* truthfulness about oneself. The process of 'giving style to one's character' begins with something called 'surveying all the strengths and weaknesses that one's nature has to offer'. This implies not only that there is a 'pre-artistic' self, a raw material waiting to be given form, but that, in order to highlight or disguise the elements in one's character appropriately, one has to have apprehended a great deal (in principle everything) about one's nature, knowing it accurately enough to grasp whether some particular part is a strength or a weakness, attractive or ugly, and if ugly, whether it will respond best to removal, concealment, or viewing from a distance. On this reading, 'giving style to one's character' rides on the back of truthfulness. It is a kind of fulfilling game of pretence with the truth always in view, a response to the challenge of giving a pleasing aspect to something one already accepts as unchangeable. What may seem dubious and even repellent in this interpretation, however, is the degree of 'doublethink' it appears to demand of the person who attains self-satisfaction. I have to be fully apprised of my weakness and ugliness of character, while simultaneously revelling in a patent dissimulation in which I appear as something beautiful to behold.

A third approach is to acknowledge that truthful affirmation and artistic style-giving are distinct ideals pulling in opposite directions, but to hold that this very tension is a strength of Nietzsche's position. In Book Five of *The Gay Science* (as in *GM* III: 24–7) Nietzsche calls into question the ascetic ideal, whose most potent manifestation is our drive to assign unconditional value to being truthful. But why insist on his flipping over into an unconditional valuation of untruthfulness? A more Nietzschean position is that there is no 'one way' to value oneself: facing the truth about oneself has value in the quest for a positive meaning to individual existence, but so too does the fictionalizing or falsifying of self that can be learned from artists. The same duality accords well with Nietzsche's perspectivism: it is fitting that one should—to paraphrase the prime perspectivist thought of *GM* III: 12—have in one's power both one's ability to confront oneself full-on and one's artistry in falsifying oneself, and be able to shift them in and out.

7 ART AND ARTISTS IN *THE GAY SCIENCE*

The concepts of art and truth dance around one another repeatedly in *The Gay Science*, indeed from the title onwards. For example:

> *What one should learn from artists.*—What means do we have for making things beautiful, attractive and desirable when they are not? And in themselves I think they never are! Here we have something to learn from physicians, when for example they dilute something bitter or add wine and sugar to the mixing bowl; but even more from artists, who are really constantly out to invent new artistic *tours de force* of this kind. To distance oneself from things until there is much in them that one no longer sees and much that the eye must add *in order to see them at all*, or to see things around a corner and as if they were cut out and extracted from their context, or to place them so that each partially distorts the view one has of the others and allows only perspectival glimpses, or to look at them through coloured glass or in the light of the sunset, or to give them a surface and skin that is not fully transparent: all this we should learn from artists while otherwise being wiser than they. For usually in their case this delicate power

stops where art ends and life begins; *we*, however, want to be poets of our lives, starting with the smallest and most commonplace details. (*GS* 299)

Our ultimate gratitude to art.—Had we not approved of the arts and invented this type of cult of the untrue, the insight into the general untruth and mendacity that is now given to us by science—the insight into delusion and error as a condition of cognitive and sensate existence—would be utterly unbearable. *Honesty* would lead to nausea and suicide. But now our honesty has a counterforce that helps us avoid such consequences: art, as the *good* will to appearance. [...] As an aesthetic phenomenon existence is still *bearable* to us, and art furnishes us with the eye and hand and above all the good conscience to be *able* to make such a phenomenon of ourselves. (*GS* 107)

In Book Five too Nietzsche associates with the concept of the 'artist' such characteristics as 'falseness with a good conscience', 'delight in pretence', 'inner longing for role and mask, for an *appearance*' (361). In such passages Nietzsche again invites us to take the falsifying, distorting, and beautifying that occurs in the activity by which an artist produces an artwork and transpose it to the case of the self: we are the 'artists' who make a falsifying 'work' out of the raw material that is also ourselves—and without such falsification of ourselves by ourselves, it seems, existence could neither be borne nor even continued. But if we are to learn this from art proper, art proper must also be concerned essentially with making false appearances. How does this sit with another of the prominent concerns in *The Gay Science*, that of intellectual conscience and the virtue of honesty (see, e.g., *GS* 107, 335)?

A way of reconciling Nietzsche's talk of honesty with his talk of artistic deception is suggested by Aaron Ridley, who finds these preoccupations unified in the following way:

The artist's 'intellectual conscience', which insists on honesty, drives him—once he has honestly recognized the character of his and our most fundamental needs—to cultivate and value the false, but to do so to the minimum extent necessary to ward off 'nausea and suicide'...The creative spirit envisaged in *The Gay Science* is...one who, first, faces the truth as honestly as possible; second, tries to see as beautiful as much as possible of 'what is necessary in things' [see *GS* 276]...and then, finally, falsifies those conditions that defeat this attempt—that is, turns 'existence' into an 'aesthetic phenomenon'—to the least possible degree consistent with making life 'bearable' (Ridley 2007: 82, 84).

On this reading, when Nietzsche talks of art as a counterforce to honesty, he has in mind not a total or permanent self-deception or screening off of the truth; instead, as he says, 'We do not always keep our eyes from rounding off, from finishing off the poem;...At times we need to have a rest from ourselves by looking at and down at ourselves and, from an artistic distance, laughing *at* [*over*] ourselves or crying *at* [*over*] ourselves' (*GS* 107). Thus, for Ridley: 'it is a condition of the kind of creativity that Nietzsche is interested in that one first face the truth, and only then embark upon one's (modest) falsifications and rounding off of it' (2007: 83). One needs to falsify to some degree—and to which degree is a test of the limits of one's 'strength', as Nietzsche says in *Beyond Good and Evil*: 'so that the strength of a spirit would be proportionate to how much of the 'truth' he could withstand—or, to put it more clearly, to what extent he needs it to be thinned out, veiled over, sweetened up, dumbed down, or lied about' (*BGE* 39). But on this reading the ideal towards which art provides a helping hand is that of facing up to the truth of life as honestly as one can. Art's falsifications are no self-subsistent exercise in escaping from truth, but rather an employment of illusion in the service of the intellectual conscience, with its project of confronting the truth—a change of tactic when all other means take us to the limit of what we can bear.

Such an amicable settlement between the values of truth-telling and of producing illusions displays a Nietzsche apparently comfortable with himself. However, I think that for that very reason we should question Ridley's reading. Elsewhere Nietzsche paints the value of truth as poignantly troubling and problematic, as in 'what meaning would *our* entire being have if not in this, that in us this will to truth has come to a consciousness of itself *as a problem*?' (*GM* III: 27), and this remark from his notebooks: 'About the relation of art to truth I became serious at the earliest time: and even now I stand before this dichotomy [*Zwiespalt*] with a holy terror' (*KSA* 13: 550). Nietzsche is troubled, rather than settled, about the possibility of reconciling art with truth. And the unease increases with some of his later additions to *The Gay Science*, in Book Five and the second-edition Preface, which, as we shall see, raise more radical questions about the very nature of truth and the value of our pursuing it at all.

8 SELFLESSNESS, WILL TO TRUTH,
AND THE ALTERNATIVES

Section 344 in Book Five contains an important argument that brings us back to the nature of 'science'. Here is how Nietzsche poses the problem:

> We see that science, too, rests on a faith; there is simply no 'presuppositionless' science. The question whether *truth* is necessary must get an answer in advance, the answer 'yes', and moreover this answer must be so firm that it takes the form of the statement, the belief, the conviction: '*Nothing is more* necessary than truth; and in relation to it, everything else has only secondary value.' This unconditional will to truth—what is it?

Science (including the historical, interpretive disciplines practised by Nietzsche himself) not only seeks truth, but bases itself on a prior conviction or faith that seeking and attaining truth has a value that is not conditional upon anything else. 'Will to truth', as Nietzsche explains by paraphrase later in the section, is an attitude of desiring 'truth at any price'. So Nietzsche wants to know the nature of this demand that enquiry makes upon itself. Is it unconditionally valuable to hold true rather than false beliefs, unconditionally valuable 'not to let oneself be deceived'? Nietzsche suggests not. True beliefs could be regarded as unconditionally more valuable only if there were some guarantee that they brought greater benefit than false beliefs, but for Nietzsche this is not a safe assumption:

> Is it really less harmful, dangerous, disastrous not to want to let oneself be deceived? What do you know in advance about the character of existence to be able to decide whether the greater advantage is on the side of the unconditionally distrustful or the unconditionally trusting? But should both be necessary . . . then where might science get the unconditional belief or conviction on which it rests, that truth is more important than anything else, than every other conviction? Precisely this conviction could never have originated if truth *and* untruth had constantly made it clear that they were both useful, as they are.

The explanation Nietzsche offers instead is that, as 'scientific' enquirers, we unconditionally demand of ourselves *truthfulness*, i.e. the virtue of not being deceitful, even to ourselves. But this means, he argues, that the ground of our faith in truth is *moral*. Since the crafty flexibility and deceitfulness of an Odysseus[22] have at least as good a case for being useful strategies, where could the unconditional demand for truthfulness come from, other than from morality itself? So, Nietzsche contends that (unwittingly) we find ourselves morally bound into our unquestioning valuation of the pursuit of truth.

Then what is Nietzsche's alternative? Not the abandonment of all pursuit of truth, let alone the abandonment of the concept of truth. Rather, an attempt to see the value of truth acquisition as conditional—on the values of health, strength, affirmation, or the degree of viability, bearability, and self-satisfaction we can sustain. Can we put life first, and sacrifice truth-seeking to life if need be? The attempt (or experiment[23]) to do so will mean stepping away from the demand to seek truths at all costs, in two related senses: one (as we have seen) is to embrace the deliberate artistic reshaping of our experience as a way of enhancing it for ourselves; the other is to accept superficial appearances and see ourselves as under no constraint to delve beneath them. A resonant and much-quoted passage ends the Preface to *The Gay Science*, combining the related themes of artistic reshaping and the abandonment of any search for a hidden truth:

> Oh those Greeks! They knew how to live: what is needed for that is to stop bravely at the surface, the fold, the skin; to worship appearance, to believe in shapes, tones, words—in the whole Olympus of appearance! Those Greeks were superficial—*out of profundity*! And is not this precisely what we are coming back to, we daredevils of the spirit...Are we not just in this respect—Greeks? Worshippers of shapes, tones, words? (*GS* Preface 4).

Earlier in the same section Nietzsche teases us into reconceiving truth, using allusions to the female private parts:

> Today we consider it a matter of decency not to wish to see everything naked, to be present everywhere, to understand and 'know' everything. 'Is it true that God is everywhere?' a little girl asked her mother; 'I find that indecent!'—a hint for philosophers!...Perhaps truth is a woman who has grounds for not showing her grounds? Perhaps her name is—to speak Greek—*Baubo*? (*GS* Preface 4).

In Greek legend Baubo is a character who lifts her clothing and exposes herself to Persephone, making her laugh. The character is sometimes depicted as a lower female torso with a face and blatant genitalia. But the import of Nietzsche's words here is more enigmatic. How are we encouraged to feel about the prospect of truth's being revealed—is it desirable, undesirable, shocking, laughter-provoking? And what are we to think truth is? On the one hand it seems we are to think of truth as something hidden beneath appearances, but abandon any desire to unveil it. If truth is Baubo, on the other hand, is it not going to be self-revealing whether we like it or not? Then again Nietzsche has just said 'We no longer believe that truth remains truth when one pulls off the veil' (*GS* Preface 4), a remark suggesting that we should *not* after all think of truth as something that is hidden and waiting to be disclosed. If that is the import, it is reminiscent of a passage in the later *Twilight of the Idols* in which the conception of an 'unattainable' true world progressively transmutes into something

---

[22] Alluded to in *GS* 344 by the word *polytropoi*: Odysseus is described as *polytropos* in the opening line of the *Odyssey*.

[23] See *GM* III: 24.

superfluous and finally into something refuted: 'The true world is gone: which world is left? the illusory one, perhaps?...But no! *we got rid of the illusory world along with the true one!*' (*TI*: 'How the "True World" Finally Became a Fable').[24]

There is, finally, one other aspect of the (in the broad sense) scientific conception of truth-seeking enquiry that Nietzsche is out to undermine in Book Five; namely, its commitment to an ideal of selfless objectivity:

> The lack of personality always takes its revenge: a weakened, thin, extinguished personality, one that denies itself and its own existence, is no longer good for anything good—least of all for philosophy. 'Selflessness' has no value in heaven or on earth; all great problems demand *great love*, and only strong, round, secure minds who have a firm grip on themselves are capable of that. It makes the most telling difference whether a thinker has a personal relationship to his problems and finds in them his destiny, his distress, and his greatest happiness, or an 'impersonal' one, meaning he is only able to touch and grasp them with the antennae of cold, curious thought. In the latter case nothing will come of it, that much can be promised (*GS* 345).

Opposed to this is Nietzsche's model of interpretation through the affects, a model in which intellectual insight increases through multiplying affects as far as possible. In the *Genealogy* he speaks of

> the capacity to have one's pro and contra *in one's power*, and to shift them in and out: so that one knows how to make precisely the *difference* in perspectives and affective interpretations useful for knowledge...*the more* affects we allow to speak about a matter, *the more* eyes, different eyes, we know how to bring to bear on one and the same matter, that much more complete will our 'concept' of this matter, our 'objectivity' be (*GM* III: 12)

Nietzsche here urges 'philosophers' to practise a form of enquiry that engages as many personal feelings as possible and understands its subject matter more fully as a result. His own affectively engaged and rhetorically provocative investigation of the origins of our values stands as a good exemplar of such enquiry.[25] So, coming full circle, if we ask again what the 'science' is that Nietzsche thinks can be practised joyfully, we have at least learned some important negatives. For Nietzsche the best investigator is not a dispassionate 'pure subject', the object of investigation is not something mysterious and unattainable lurking behind our many experiences, and the exercise of investigation is not self-validating. Truth is multiple, located on the surfaces of things, best found through keeping alive our feelings, and best sought in the service of some values external to the activity of truth-seeking itself, values of health, flourishing, and life affirmation.

---

[24] Maudemarie Clark's influential account of Nietzsche on truth gives especial prominence to this passage (see especially Clark 1990: 109–17).

[25] See Janaway 2007 on this theme.

BIBLIOGRAPHY

(A) Works by Nietzsche

BGE *Beyond Good and Evil*, ed. Rolf-Peter Horstmann, trans. Judith Norman. Cambridge: Cambridge University Press, 2002.

D *Daybreak*, ed. Maudemarie Clark and Brian Leiter, trans. R. J. Hollingdale. Cambridge: Cambridge University Press, 1997.

EH *Ecce Homo,* in *The Anti-Christ, Ecce Homo, Twilight of the Idols, and Other Writings*, ed. Aaron Ridley, trans. Judith Norman. Cambridge: Cambridge University Press, 2005.

GM *On the Genealogy of Morality*, trans. Maudemarie Clark and Alan J. Swensen. Indianapolis: Hackett, 1998.

GS *The Gay Science*, ed. Bernard Williams, trans. Josefine Nauckhoff and Adrian Del Caro. Cambridge: Cambridge University Press, 2001.

KSA *Sämtliche Werke: Kritische Studienausgabe in 15 Einzelbänden*, ed. G. Colli and M. Montinari (15 vols). Berlin: De Gruyter, 1988.

TI *Twilight of the Idols*, in *The Anti-Christ, Ecce Homo, Twilight of the Idols, and Other Writings*, ed. Aaron Ridley, trans. Judith Norman. Cambridge: Cambridge University Press, 2005.

WLN *Writings from the Late Notebooks*, ed. Rüdiger Bittner, trans. Kate Sturge. Cambridge: Cambridge University Press, 2003.

WP *The Will to Power*, trans. Walter Kaufmann and R. J. Hollingdale. New York: Vintage Books, 1968.

(B) Other Works Cited

Babich, Babette E. 2006. 'Nietzsche's "Gay" Science', in Keith Ansell-Pearson (ed.), *A Companion to Nietzsche*. Oxford: Blackwell, 97–114.

Clark, Maudemarie. 1990. *Nietzsche on Truth and Philosophy*. Cambridge: Cambridge University Press.

Danto, Arthur C. 1965. *Nietzsche as Philosopher*. New York: Columbia University Press.

Janaway, Christopher. 2007. *Beyond Selflessness: Reading Nietzsche's* Genealogy. Oxford: Oxford University Press.

Janaway, Christopher. 2012. 'Nietzsche on Morality, Drives, and Human Greatness', in Christopher Janaway and Simon Robertson (eds), *Nietzsche, Naturalism and Normativity*. Oxford: Oxford University Press, 183–201.

Janaway, Christopher. Forthcoming. 'Beauty is False, Truth Ugly: Nietzsche on Art and Life', in Daniel Came (ed.), *Nietzsche on Art and Aesthetics*. Oxford: Oxford University Press.

Loeb, Paul S. 2005. 'Finding the *Übermensch* in Nietzsche's *Genealogy of Morality*', *Journal of Nietzsche Studies* 30:70–101.

Loeb, Paul S. 2006. 'Identity and Eternal Recurrence', in Keith Ansell-Pearson (ed.), *A Companion to Nietzsche*. Oxford: Blackwell, 171–88.

Magnus, Bernd. 1988. 'Deification of the Commonplace: *Twilight of the Idols*', in Robert C. Solomon and Kathleen M. Higgins (eds), *Reading Nietzsche*. Oxford: Oxford University Press, 152–81.

Nehamas, Alexander. 1985. *Nietzsche: Life as Literature*. Cambridge, Mass.: Harvard University Press.

Nehamas, Alexander. 1998. *The Art of Living: Socratic Reflections from Plato to Foucault.* Berkeley: University of California Press.

Pippin, Robert. 2010. *Nietzsche, Psychology, and First Philosophy.* Chicago: Chicago University Press.

Ridley, Aaron. 1997. 'Nietzsche's Greatest Weight', *Journal of Nietzsche Studies* 14: 19–25.

Ridley, Aaron. 2007. *Nietzsche on Art.* London: Routledge.

Schopenhauer, Arthur. 2009. 'Prize Essay on the Basis of Morals', in *The Two Fundamental Problems of Ethics*, ed. and trans. Christopher Janaway. Cambridge: Cambridge University Press, 113–258.

Simmel, Georg. 1986. *Schopenhauer and Nietzsche*, trans. Helmut Loiskandl, Deena Weinstein, and Michael Weinstein. Amherst: University of Massachusetts Press.

Soll, Ivan. 1973. 'Reflections on Recurrence: A Re-examination of Nietzsche's Doctrine, *Die Ewige Wiederkehr des Gleichen*', in Robert C. Solomon (ed.), *Nietzsche: A Collection of Critical Essays.* Garden City, NY: Doubleday, 339–42.

Wilamowitz-Moellendorff, Ulrich von. 2000. 'Future Philology! A Reply to *The Birth of Tragedy* by Friedrich Nietzsche', trans. Gertrud Postl, *New Nietzsche Studies* 4.1–2: 1–32.

Williams, Bernard. 2001. 'Introduction', in *The Gay Science*, ed. Bernard Williams, trans. Josephine Nauckhoff and Adrian del Caro. Cambridge: Cambridge University Press, vii–xxii.

Young, Julian. 1992. *Nietzsche's Philosophy of Art.* Cambridge: Cambridge University Press.

CHAPTER 12

....

ZARATHUSTRA: 'THAT MALICIOUS DIONYSIAN'[1]

....

GUDRUN VON TEVENAR

I am *not* at all surprised if one does not understand my Zarathustra and see no reproach in this: a book so profound and so strange, that to understand and *experience* just six sentences of it, is to be elevated into a higher order of mortals.

Friedrich Nietzsche[2]

1 INTRODUCTION

....

SYMPATHETIC summaries and commentaries on *Thus Spoke Zarathustra* (hereafter *Zarathustra* or *Z*) usually try hard to render its content acceptable or at least understandable by imposing some kind of order on it. They thereby invariably 'tame' *Zarathustra* and thus do not prepare us for the shock and bewilderment when actually reading the book itself. Shock at the language used: its relentlessly elevated style with its excesses and wild exaggerations, the fervent intensity, the tiresome sermons, the repetitions, and confusing contradictions. Yet hidden amongst that all too lush style are jewels of exquisite poetry! Then there is bewilderment as to the genre of book: is it philosophy? or literature? or maybe a joke? Bewilderment also as to its message, if indeed it has any.[3] Additionally, *Zarathustra* sits strangely amongst Nietzsche's other works which are (mostly) discursive and written in beautiful prose. While shock tends to ease in time, in as much as one eventually becomes

---

[1] *BT*: 'An Attempt at Self-Criticism' 7. Often translated as 'that Dionysiac monster'. Nietzsche uses *Unhold*, the negation—*un*—of *hold*, meaning fair, sweet, dear. 'Monster' seems rather harsh. Malice (*Bosheit*) is a key characteristic of *Unhold* and Nietzsche is quite partial to malice, particularly in *Thus Spoke Zarathustra* (see section 13). Note that Socrates is an *Unhold* too (*GS* 340). Please note that throughout this essay I have used my own translations of Nietzsche's works as they appear in the *KSA*.

[2] *KSA* 13: 541.

[3] Robert Pippin (2006) in his excellent introduction describes *Z* as 'more hermetic than Celan'!

accustomed to the shrillness of language and accommodating to the idiosyncracies of style, bewilderment as to the purpose of Z tends to remain, indeed, intensifies on realizing how greatly this work was valued by Nietzsche himself. Today, some scholars still regard *Zarathustra* as a regrettable oddity or an embarrassing misjudgement by an otherwise reliably great thinker, something best left idling in the background. Yet Nietzsche himself regarded *his Zarathustra*, as he affectionately or, maybe, protectively calls it, as his major achievement, the gift of overwhelming inspiration for which he cherished the highest hopes.

It is noteworthy that all eight works written after *Zarathustra* refer to it frequently and in *EH* Zarathustra's name appears *eighty times*, often with lengthy citations. Nietzsche was fiercely certain of *Zarathustra*'s potential to change the course of history and to inaugurate a new era (*EH* Preface 4 and *EH*: 'Thus Spoke Zarathustra' 6), and the unresponsive silence following publication must have been deeply hurtful despite his vociferous protestations to the contrary. True, late in 1888 his hopes are expressed in extreme language, perhaps a sign of his imminent mental collapse. In a letter to Deussen from 26 November 1888 Nietzsche writes:

> There [in *EH*] my Zarathustra will be shown for the first time in a clear light, the foremost book of millennia, the bible of the future, the highest expression of human genius which contains the destiny of humankind [...] my Zarathustra will be read like the bible. (*KSA* 15: 188)

Yet these outbursts should not stop one from engaging with *Zarathustra* as earnestly as with Nietzsche's others works, and this essay aims to rehabilitate the book as worthy of serious philosophical attention, taking philosophy in its widest possible connotation.

Prior to the ambitions of 1888, Nietzsche makes three claims regarding *Zarathustra*: it is a parody (*GS* Preface 1),[4] a tragedy (*GS* 342), a counter-ideal to the ascetic ideal (*GM* II: 25; *EH*: 'Genealogy of Morals').

2 PARODY

There is plenty of parody in *Zarathustra*,[5] as well as much irony and some gratuitous blasphemy. Amongst the more obvious instances of the latter are the 'Last Supper' and 'Ass Festival' of Part IV. Their slapdash compares unfavourably with Nietzsche's usual sophistication. But there are also refined parodies, such as the cave on the mountain top, as well as innumerable instances of well-crafted irony, amongst which the heading 'On Immaculate Perception' is surely one of the most deliciously apt. Irony has of course also more serious functions. It holds objects at a distance and makes judgements tentative or ambiguous by putting, so to speak, a question mark behind every statement, thus leaving matters amusingly or disconcertingly in the air. As such, irony is a useful subterfuge and hiding-place and so, perhaps, best seen as one of the many masks Nietzsche is known to employ.[6]

---

[4] Nietzsche refers in this passage to *GS* 342 and substitutes parody for tragedy. See also *KSA* 12: 313.
[5] Some scholars regard the whole of *Z* as a *New Testament* parody; others see Part IV as a satyr play.
[6] See Pippin 1988 and Behler 1998 for excellent discussions on the use of irony and parody in Nietzsche.

However, we still have an unexplained gap between Nietzsche's high hopes for *Zarathustra* and his designation of it as a parody, since it is implausible that these hopes could be seriously held if the sole or main purpose of *Zarathustra* lies in mocking and confusing us, or in making fun of those values Nietzsche wants rejected, or in testing our knowledge of Platonic philosophy and Christian narratives. All this is simply not weighty enough, for surely Nietzsche wanted more than just to entertain or dazzle us!

One can discern two main functions of irony in *Zarathustra*: firstly, as part of a pro-gramme of sanitation of what Nietzsche considered obsolete values. The ironic nudging and thus weakening and, hopefully, even dislodging of moribund values and traditions can then be seen as an initial probing offensive, as a preamble for a more forceful frontal attack towards their full destruction. Nietzsche thereby demonstrates what Zarathustra himself says innumerable times: that to be a creator one has to be a destroyer first (e.g. *Z* II: 'On Self-Overcoming'). Secondly, the countless instances of more or less easy to spot *New Testament* parodies in *Zarathustra* function as a mask or screen behind which the real, the esoteric message is developed.[7] And the esoteric message is a 'new' *New Testament*, Zarathustra's *Dionysian Testament*. This suggestion will be developed in the course of this essay and dis-cussed again in more detail in section 13.

Let us agree, then, that in *Zarathustra* parody and irony belong to the many masks employed by Nietzsche to simultaneously guide and lead astray, disclose and conceal, thus forcing us into a state of unease and the need to seek new orientations—Nietzschean orientations.

3 TRAGEDY

Nietzsche also claims that *Zarathustra* is a tragedy. Yet considering solely the storyline, it is difficult to see why. Granted that Zarathustra undergoes trials, suffers setbacks and illnesses, is unsure of himself and his mission, and struggles with nausea and abysmal thoughts, he is also given to much hope and delight, much 'Zarathustrian' laughter in song and dance. These trials and these delights, these ups and downs, seem altogether too commonplace, too much like our ordinary, often testing and often rewarding lives, to be deserving of that august designation 'tragedy'. Besides, tragedies usually end in calamity and grief. But no grievous end awaits Zarathustra! On the contrary, he embarks on his final descent full of joy and hope, radiant 'like a morning sun' (*Z* IV: 'The Sign').

Checking the *Nachlass* shows that Nietzsche did consider a variety of more dramatic inci-dents to take place. Incidents such as the burning of a city, Zarathustra suffering attacks by his very own animals, even Zarathustra's death. There are also events paralleling very closely (though not, it seems to me, ironically) those of Jesus' mission, such as healing a woman stricken with plague—who called Zarathustra *Heiland* (Saviour, Messiah) (*KSA* 10: 151),[8]

---

[7] Consider here *Z* III: 'On Apostates' 2, where Zarathustra almost laughs himself 'to death' when overhearing the common kind of doubt and parody about God.

[8] See also *KSA* 11: 409, where the 'ugliest man' of Part IV exclaims: 'You, our physician and saviour (*Heiland*)—oh Zarathustra, let us follow you.' For Socrates as healer-cum-saviour (*Heiland*), see *TI*: 'The Problem of Socrates' 11.

and, importantly, being sentenced to death (*KSA* 10: 454).[9] Note that to be sentenced to death is a fate Zarathustra would have shared with both Socrates and Jesus—a point to be discussed again below. For the moment we must simply be open to the fact that Nietzsche decided against more obviously dramatic events and also against paralleling Socrates' and Jesus' executions. Since Nietzsche did not close *Zarathustra* with a grievous calamity like a conventional tragedy, but chose to end it with Zarathustra striding towards a new, radiant, morning-glorious beginning, it follows that to nonetheless declare *Zarathustra* a tragedy must then rest on other considerations.

An obvious place to look for further insight is *BT*. Relevant for our investigation are aspects of Nietzsche's analysis of the opposing yet complementary characteristics of Apollo and Dionysus, and his distinction between tragic and theoretical world views and tragic and theoretical man. Much simplified, the tragic world view as expounded in *BT* is the adoption of an attitude of complete acceptance and affirmation of all of life's joys and all of life's pains. What facilitates this attitude is the contagion of Dionysian abandon to an intoxicated mental state that renders invalid common existential oppositions, such as joy and pain, life and death, thus allowing them to merge, once again, into their primordial, pre-rational unity and wholeness.

But why should that be tragic? Or, more precisely, why should emotional abandon to Dionysian intoxication make one a tragic hero? The answer is that Zarathustra is no mere spectator who succumbs passively to the performance of dramatic events, Zarathustra is on the stage and *actively* accomplishes the tragic Dionysian transformation. And this transformation is indeed a paradigm heroic task. The wholehearted embrace and affirmation of all of life's joys and all of life's pains is a very difficult thing to do, much more difficult than can be gleaned from the youthful and exuberant account given of it in *BT*, where joyous intoxicated primordial oneness is promised to Dionysian initiates almost by default. Yet later on, and particularly in *Zarathustra*, Nietzsche seems more alive to the difficulties that submersion into primordial oneness and unconditional affirmation entail, and he condenses these difficulties into the exceedingly mysterious notion of 'overcoming'—a central theme in *Zarathustra*.

The task of embracing and affirming all of life's joys is, of course, not difficult. Yet even the addition (potentially not actually!) of all of life's miseries in order to complete the Dionysian embrace will, I believe, be accepted without too much reluctance by many, particularly when it all happens in the heady atmosphere of intoxicated communal abandon. But this has little to do with true overcoming. What makes overcoming such a difficult, fearful, and truly heroic thing to do is the requirement of *actively* leaving behind all that is secure and familiar (including one's joys and pains), and all one is and values, thus seriously destabilizing one's very identity. Possibly more terrifying still, overcoming further requires the holding together of opposing and contradictory commitments and values—not their synthesis, nor their sublation, nor the repression or annihilation of the more uncongenial of them, nor yet their vanishing in temporary intoxication—but a holding together of their conflict and contradiction in one conscious and bold affirmation, one global yes-saying. And that demands, crucially, strength and courage (classic tragic virtues) to resist and withstand the natural tendency inherent in such contradiction-affirmation to perish through the very tension of their disparate elements.

---

[9] Zarathustra is sentenced to death as the 'seducer of the people'. Similarly Socrates and Jesus.

Nietzsche testifies to the dangers of overcoming by having Zarathustra fall ill repeatedly through anxiety and stress, including a week long coma when faced with the challenge of having to overcome his most abysmal thought (Z III: 'The Convalescent' 1–2). The fearfulness and sheer terror of Zarathustrian overcoming is further illustrated by multiple references in *Zarathustra* to *ashes*. 'Ashes' in *Zarathustra* refers both to the Phoenix[10] myth but owes even more, so I believe, to Goethe's celebrated poem *Selige Sehnsucht* ('blissful yearning'). There Goethe describes a secret yearning only the wise can understand: a yearning to perish, to perish by flames (*Flammentod*) so as to leave behind a debris of ashes and thus be purified for a new beginning.[11] Here, overcoming is a leap over a fearful abyss. Indeed, overcoming is nothing less than virtual death as expressed in the phrase 'Die and Become' (*Stirb und Werde*) of Goethe's poem.

Consider here also Zarathustra's anguish when conversing with his inner voice in 'The Stillest Hour' (Z II). It is barely possible to read this section without being profoundly moved and affected by the sheer terror expressed here by one unwilling to go where he knows he must go, one who feels utterly threatened and abandoned. What we witness here is Zarathustra's Gethsemane:[12]

> Do you know the terror of one falling asleep?—
> Down to his toes he is stricken because the ground is withdrawing and the dream begins. […]
> Yesterday, at the stillest hour, the ground withdrew from me and the dream began. […]
> never have I heard such a stillness surrounding me so that my heart was terrified.
> Then it spoke to me without a voice: '*You know it, Zarathustra?*'
> And I screamed in terror at this whispering, and the blood drained from my face, but I was silent. […]
> Then it spoke to me again without a voice: 'You do not *want* to, Zarathustra? Can this be true? Do not hide yourself in defiance!'—
> And I cried and trembled like a child and spoke: 'Oh, I wanted to, but how can I? Release me from this task! It is beyond my strength!'
> Then it spoke again to me without a voice: 'What do you matter, Zarathustra! Speak your word and perish!' … (Z II: 'The Stillest Hour')[13]

The following sections will offer a reading of *Zarathustra* which tries to make sense of *Zarathustra* as a tragedy by showing that Nietzsche here demonstrates the challenge of true tragic overcoming. Zarathustra is a tragic hero precisely because he has successfully met that challenge and has thereby elevated himself high above the usual passive Apollonian-Dionysian contradiction resolution.[14]

---

[10] For instance in Z I: 'On the Way of Creators'. 'You must want burning yourself in your own flame: how can you want to become new unless you become ashes first!'

[11] See Tevenar 2008.

[12] In the garden of Gethsemane, Jesus, alone and praying, struggled with doubt and fear about his mission and sacrifice, pleading with God to be relieved of it (Matthew 26).

[13] Regarding the sense of the 'uncanny' in Nietzsche, see also Gemes 2007: section 5 and Heller 1988: essay 10: 'Nietzsche's Terrors: Time and the Inarticulate'.

[14] Consider here the motto at the start of this essay.

4 A Tragic Overcoming: The Confrontation with *Ekel*

Before we can proceed two points require clarification. First, as mentioned, one would be much mistaken to take the narrative of Zarathustra's turbulent mission itself as the tragedy. A mistake easily made, indeed invited, by Nietzsche's consciously ambiguous use of the notion of *going down* or *going under* (*Untergang*). Admittedly, *Untergang* stands for descent, decline, and perishing, but it also stands for the sun going down (*Sonnenuntergang*) and for the submerging of a particular in a mass, as when an individual goes under (*geht unter*) in a multitude. Nietzsche uses *Untergang* in *Zarathustra* in at least three ways: Zarathustra's repeated descent from his mountain in pursuit of his mission. Next, Zarathustra's not too successful merging and submerging with messy humanity, well described in the prologue and elsewhere, with his subsequent struggle to surface again and reascend his mountain. Lastly, Zarathustra goes down like the sun goes down. This, to my view, is the most important function of Zarathustra's *Untergang* and Nietzsche draws particular attention to it in his rousing paean to the morning and evening sun at the beginning of *Zarathustra* (Z I: 'Zarathustra's Prologue' 1). Here Zarathustra emphatically declares that he will go down like the sun goes down, stating further that the sun goes down golden with bliss, bringing light even to the nether world. Hence it follows that not every *Untergang* is an end or amounts to a tragedy, since Zarathustra goes under repeatedly and the sun, indeed, does it daily, without either of them coming to any harm, though obviously the *Untergang* metaphor retains its link with decline and perishing.

Second, since, as suggested, the tragic challenge in *Zarathustra* is an overcoming, there must be something—some attitude, affect, or value—that needs overcoming. As is obvious from even a superficial reading, Zarathustra in his capacity as teacher-cum-preacher continuously challenges his followers to overcome numerous well-established attitudes and values. But there are also values and affects that are a direct challenge to Zarathustra himself. Prominent among them are his great nausea and disgust with man and his great pity for man. Nauseating disgust (*Ekel*) and pity (*Mitleid*) are of course major Nietzschean topics[15] and it is therefore not surprising that their temptation and their overcoming are defining features in the narrative and character of Zarathustra. In Part IV Zarathustra faces and overcomes the challenge of his last great temptation, the temptation of his pity for men, while in the following we will examine his equally successful overcoming of nauseating disgust.

As mentioned, nauseating disgust (*Ekel*) is a major Nietzschean topic and thus figures throughout his works, *Nachlass*, and letters. One can distinguish a positive aspect based on strong physical affects when confronted with sights and smells of bodily corruption, disease, putrefaction, and similar, to which we tend to react instantly with revulsion, aversion, and loathing, usually accompanied by violent bodily spasms like vomiting, shuddering, or turning away. These entirely instinctive reactions of *Ekel* are positive because they (1) signal

---

[15] See *GM* III: 14 on the dangers of 'great disgust with man and great pity for man'. Cf. *Z* III and *Z* IV. So great is Zarathustra's nausea (*Ekel*) that he often repeats it three times: *Ekel, Ekel, Ekel!* (for instance, in *Z* III: 'The Convalescent' 1).

danger and (2) protect us by either distancing us from or vehemently ejecting the offend-ing items. Nietzsche extends this positive physical aspect towards what he calls 'intellectual *Ekel*' whereby we reject and thus remove ourselves also from what he claims are dangers to our emotional and intellectual well-being, such as, for instance, contact with sick and weak members of the herd.[16]

However in *Zarathustra*, Nietzsche is mainly concerned with negative aspects of *Ekel* which, as we will see, he considers erosive of life affirmation. For evidence, consider Zarathustra's week-long coma after an attack of *Ekel* (*Z* III: 'The Convalescent' 1), also the doleful condition of the so-called 'higher men' in Part IV, many burdened with *Ekel* with one of the kings calling it 'the old illness' (*Z* IV: 'Conversation with the Kings' 1). Yet the persons most severely challenged by the negative aspects of *Ekel* are Zarathustra and Nietzsche him-self, who confesses in *EH*:

> *Ekel* with humans, with human rabble, has always been my greatest danger. (*EH*: 'Why I Am So Wise' 8)

Immediately following this confession Nietzsche cites Zarathustra's 'redemption' from it:

> What happened to me? How did I redeem myself from *Ekel*? Who rejuvenated my eyes? How did I fly to that height where no longer any human rabble sits by the fountain?
> Was it my *Ekel* itself that created wings for me and the strength to find pure water? In truth, into the highest height I had to fly to rediscover the well of joy!—
> Oh, my brothers, I found it! Here, at the highest height the well of joy gushes out for me! And here is a life that human rabble does not also drink.... (*EH*: 'Why I Am So Wise' 8, citing from *Z* II: 'Of the Rabble').

However, as 'redemption' this is very unsatisfactory. When escaping to the isolation of the 'highest height' it is not difficult to feel no nausea at humans as no humans are likely to be about. Moreover, such protection lasts only as long as the isolation itself as Zarathustra himself experiences when, according to the hermit's approving observation, he descends after ten years of mountain solitude 'with pure eyes and no *Ekel* round his mouth' (*Z* I: 'Zarathustra's Prologue' 2), only to become afflicted again when meeting up with humans once more. So what is it about humans that fills Zarathustra (and Nietzsche) with nauseat-ing disgust, and what makes this disgust so dangerous? Here is Zarathustra's own explana-tion of his abysmal thought and coma-inducing *Ekel*:

> —alas, humans recur eternally! The small human recurs eternally!—
> I once saw both of them naked, the greatest and the smallest human: all-too-similar to one another—all-too-human even the greatest ones!
> All-too-little even the greatest! That was my aversion [*Überdruss*] at humans! And the eter-nal recurrence even of the smallest!—That was my aversion at all existence [*an allem Dasein*]!
> Oh, *Ekel! Ekel! Ekel!* (*Z* III: 'The Convalescent' 2)

This citation answers both questions. It is the very smallness, the very human-all-too-humanness of humans which fills Zarathustra with nauseating disgust. And the disgust is

---

[16] For a more comprehensive analysis of nauseating disgust in Nietzsche, see my 'Nietzsche on Nausea' (Tevenar 2013).

dangerous because the resulting aversion does not stop at humans but is followed by the all-encompassing aversion 'to all existence'. Note that, unlike aversion to humans, one cannot escape from aversion to all existence by isolating oneself in solitude! Moreover, because aversion to all existence is incompatible with affirmation of life and global yes-saying, so passionately proclaimed by both Zarathustra and Nietzsche, there has to be a different and more effective solution to the problem of nausea as danger. And there is.

We can surely agree that the episode of the young shepherd choking with a heavy black snake in his throat is one of the most nauseating images possible (*Z* III: 'On the Vision and the Riddle' 2). Later, when identifying himself with the young shepherd, Zarathustra explains this episode as an attack of *Ekel*: it was my 'great aversion at men—that choked me and crawled into my throat' (*Z* III: 'The Convalescent' 2). And the solution? Well, after unsuccessful attempts to pull the snake out, the shepherd, on Zarathustra's advice, bites off its head and spits it out violently—a solution almost as nauseating as the problem itself! And this gives us a clue: violent ejection through spitting or vomiting is the paradigm reaction of positive basic physical *Ekel* which is here employed against intellectual *Ekel* with its alleged dangers of aversion to all humans and even existence itself. Thus, what we witness here is *Ekel*'s successful self-overcoming: it is by the application of *Ekel* that *Ekel* is overcome.[17] The success of this self-overcoming is amply demonstrated by the transformation of both shepherd and Zarathustra. The shepherd turns into a inspiring mirage of the *Übermensch*, while Zarathustra is subsequently praised as one 'without *Ekel*, as one who overcame great *Ekel*'— not, please note, whilst isolating himself from others in highest mountain solitude but while deeply engaged with a motley group of very demanding people (*Z* IV: 'The Voluntary Beggar', and throughout Part IV).

5 THE TRANSFORMATION OF THE TRAGIC HERO

Returning now to *Zarathustra* as a tragedy. A tragedy, according to *BT*, is the narrative of a process which illustrates both the inherent Apollonian-Dionysian conflict and its tragic resolution. *Zarathustra* is replete with metaphors of Apollo and Dionysus though it is noteworthy that neither god is actually mentioned by name. Apollo as sun god is present in the radiant light and sun-bathed clarity of Zarathustra's mountain top and he resides there also in his capacity as god of healing where Zarathustra returns to recover from his *Untergang*. Dionysus, in turn, stands for qualities opposed to Apollo. Hence we will find him wherever there are prominent contrasts to sunlit mountain solitude: that is, in wooded mountain glens, shaded valleys, and the throng of cities. Euripides' *Bacchae* confirms these locations and they are, furthermore, the very sites visited by Zarathustra during his mission. Additionally, the abysmal depth and chaos of the sea are Dionysian qualities, and

---

[17] Self-overcoming is also discussed in Nietzsche's other works, including *GM* III: 27 when describing 'Europe's longest and bravest self-overcoming' as: 'All great things perish through themselves, through an act of self-cancellation: thus the law of life wills it, the law of the *necessary* "self-overcoming" in the essence of life.'

Zarathustra frequently contrasts the boundless, formless sea with the elevation and solidity of mountains to highlight both their mutual dependence and the enormity and rigidity of their irreconcilable features.

> Oh, this black sad sea below me! Oh, this pregnant night moroseness! Oh, destiny and sea! To you I must now *descend!*
>
> I stand before my highest mountain and before my longest path: that's why I must first descend deeper than I ever climbed before:
>
> —descend deeper into suffering than I ever climbed before, down into pain's blackest flood! Thus wills my destiny: Well! I am ready.
>
> Whence come the highest mountains? This I asked once. Then I learned that they come out of the sea.
>
> This testimony is written into their very stone and into the sheer sides of their peaks. Out of the deepest the highest must come to its height.— (*Z* III: 'The Wanderer')[18]

The above metaphors establish contrast and conflict between Apollo's elevated, form-giving clarity and Dionysus's fluid darknesss. Conflict provides the dynamics whereby 'out of the deepest the highest must come to its height'. In other words, only by descending deeper than before—down into one's deepest, blackest Dionysian flood—can one climb higher than before, right up to one's highest Apollonian height. Yet, whilst contrast, conflict, and resultant cooperation is conducive to growth, tension between the opposites remains potent nonetheless, indeed, necessarily so, because of the ineliminable nature of their differences.

On reading *Zarathustra* one becomes aware of the profound and painful resonance of this tension within Zarathustra himself. This is so because Nietzsche locates Apollonian-Dionysian conflict and tension, in *Zarathustra* and elsewhere, not in external but in internal conflict. This fact enables us to recognize in Zarathustra's internal conflicts the familiar features of one of Nietzsche's most abiding themes, namely, the search for a path towards personal integration. Personal integration is achieved, according to Nietzsche, through the imposition of order, rule, hierarchy, over one's diverse and usually conflicting instincts and drives without repressing or annihilating any of them. If successful, such order results in the achievement of genuine personhood, what Nietzsche describes in *GM* as 'sovereign individuality' (*GM* II: 2).[19]

There are many Apollonian-Dionysian conflicts in Zarathustra. The following examines the conflict between Zarathustra's wisdom, ripened in mountain clarity and mountain solitude, and his love for humankind: befogged, contemptible, yet, possibly, redeemable humankind living below in the valleys and cities of ignorance. The painful and bruising nature of this conflict is evident every time Zarathustra, full of wisdom and love, leaves his mountain abode to descend and merge with humankind—only to return in due course, ill, dejected, and in need of healing. Note that descent from his mountain and submersion with humankind are two of the three kinds of *Untergang* discussed above, while the third, the *Sonnenuntergang*, illustrates the nature of the love which motivates this descent. Zarathustra's love will be discussed in detail in sections 8–10 below, for now it must suffice to stress the depth and abundance of this love, which yearns to overflow and spend itself just

---

[18] The German text is highly ambiguous here in its use of *steigen* and *hinab steigen* (climbing and descending respectively). Unlike Kaufmann, I have retained this ambiguity, justified by the 'paradox' that 'out of the deepest the highest must come to its height'.

[19] For an extended examination see Gemes 2006 and 2007 and Janaway 2006.

like his wisdom does (*Z* I: 'Zarathustra's Prologue' 1). Zarathustra specifies explicitly that his wisdom and love want to overflow in the same way and with the same abundance as the sun overflows when, on going down, it covers all in golden bliss (ibid.).

However, there are no suitable and appreciative recipients of Zarathustra's love and his yearning remains unfulfilled from the beginning. Remember how on his first descent Zarathustra confesses to the hermit, that he, in contrast to the hermit, *loves* humans. And so, full of love, Zarathustra preaches his wisdom (the *Übermensch*) to a multitude in the market place—a disastrous undertaking that leaves him ridiculed and humiliated. Undeterred, Zarathustra resolves not to speak to multitudes, not to be shepherd to a herd (*Z* I: 'Zarathustra's Prologue' 9),[20] but to seek companions and fellow-creators instead. And he does indeed find many disciples and loves them with a deep warm love. Such that, when a dream reveals to him that his teaching is besmirched in his absence, Zarathustra is appalled; yet the shock and distress at that reversal is as nothing compared to the anguish he experiences when hearing that his disciples are in danger. Now his love is activated and he prepares to help them with the eager anticipation and passionate determination of any lover hurrying to rescue his beloved (*Z* II: 'The Child with the Mirror'). But it will not last!

While Zarathustra wanders with his disciples and exhorts them with sermons and parables in an obvious similarity with Jesus wandering and preaching in the *New Testament*, and while in both settings the disciples follow with unquestioning devotion, with regard to Zarathustra's Apollonian-Dionysian conflict of wisdom and love the noteworthy contrast between him and Jesus lies in their respective love for their disciples. Jesus adheres unfailingly to his disciples in face of apostasy and even betrayal, while Zarathustra lets his wisdom persuade him that his disciples are not worthy of his love, are not what he seeks. No doubt it was wise of Zarathustra to conclude that his love is misguided because his disciples were not up to the task of becoming fellow-creators. They lacked the requisite freedom to create, a freedom only won through a painful process of conquest and self-authentication.[21] It is, then, the voice of wisdom we hear in Zarathustra's words:

> You say you believe in Zarathustra? But what matters Zarathustra! You are my believers: but what matter all believers!
> You had not began searching for yourself: and you found me. Thus do all believers, that is why all belief amounts to so little.
> Now I call upon you to lose me and find yourselves; ... (*Z* I: 'On the Virtue of Giving' 3)

Yet the parting with his disciples is a bitter blow to Zarathustra: his yearning to love is as deep as his grief at its loss, both painfully present throughout the sad and mournful reflections on returning home to his mountain refuge. During that journey he accepts that

> in the end one only ever experiences oneself. (*Z* III: 'The Wanderer')

And he chides himself for the folly of his love—his unwise, undemanding love:

> Oh, you fool Zarathustra, full of love and overfull of trust! But you have always been thus: always do you go full of trust towards everything terrible.

---

[20] Note the reference to Jesus, who is frequently described as shepherd.
[21] See Tevenar 2008.

> Every monster you want to stroke. A hint of warm breath, a soft something between the paws—: and straight away you want to call and love it.
> *Love* is the danger of the loneliest, love for everything, *if only it is alive!* Truly, my folly and my modesty in love are laughable!— (*Z* III: 'The Wanderer')

Amongst other similar conflicts in *Zarathustra* the one between love and contempt is worth mentioning briefly since it is often misunderstood. To speak of love and contempt in one breath is rather disconcerting. Hence the often-made attempt to ease its contradiction by postulating two intentional objects, such as love for the *Übermensch* and contempt for the 'last man'. But that cannot possibly be correct! Why would Nietzsche be interested in such a commonplace as loving one feature and feeling contempt for its opposite? What Nietzsche truly confronts us with is the challenging task of love and contempt for one and the same thing at one and the same time. It is love for oneself, he claims, which has to be both opposed and complemented by contempt for oneself before any possible ascent to greatness can take place. In Zarathustra's words:

> Oh my soul, I taught you the contempt that does not come like a gnawing worm, the great, the loving contempt, which loves most where it has most contempt. (*Z* III: 'On Great Longing')[22]

Consider further the absence of self-contempt in the presence of too much self-love that makes the last men so small, so very contemptible! Nietzsche is quite clear: it is not a question of either love or contempt but of holding and embracing within oneself the tension of their contradiction and using their alleged incompatibility for further progress; progress understood as individual growth and elevation achieved through the ordered affirmation of all of oneself.

In summary we can say that *Zarathustra* is a tragedy because it demonstrates the hero's successful transformation to a tragic world view. That for which no theory is adequate, which reason cannot explain, the tragic hero accomplishes by overcoming his own virtues and vices and by holding together in one affirming, inclusive, yes-saying what to untransformed, untragic, eyes are incompatibilities and paradoxes. Now the many and much maligned inconsistencies and contradictions in *Zarathustra* begin to make sense, so that now, when confronted with Zarathustra's provocative question about his own identity

> Is he a promiser? Or a fulfiller? A conqueror? Or an inheritor? An autumn? Or a ploughshare? A physician? Or a convalescent?
> Is he a poet? Or one who speaks the truth? A liberator? Or one who binds? Is he good? Or evil? (*Z* II: 'On Redemption')

it is no longer the case of deliberating and deciding on some qualities to the exclusion of others, for tragic Zarathustra is all of them, and all of them completely. Contradictions are now experienced as contributions to wholeness. On the way to greatness, Zarathustra claims, 'peak and abyss' (that is Apollo and Dionysus) are as one (*Z* III: 'The Wanderer').

---

[22] Also *Z* IV: 'The Ugliest Man', and *GM* II: 24. According to Nietzsche, Jesus too has both love and contempt for himself: *KSA* 8: 181.

6 TRAGEDY WITHOUT A CHORUS?

Let us now consider a possible objection to the claim that *Zarathustra* is a tragedy. It might be objected that no mere text could possibly function as a *BT* type tragedy because of the absence of what is there claimed as its most essential element and the very vehicle of the Dionysian transformation—the chorus with its music and dance. We may have a refutation to this objection when considering anew the style and language of *Zarathustra*. This language, irksome and incongruous as it is in philosophical discourse, may begin to make sense if we can assign a purpose to it.[23] And its purpose is, I suggest, to function as a substitute for the music of the chorus. In his *Beyond Selflessness* (2007), Christopher Janaway makes a convincing case that Nietzsche often uses language not to argue or explain but to arouse affective responses in readers. *Zarathustra* can be seen as a typical example of this, since Nietzsche's use of language for this purpose is maximally amplified in *Zarathustra* so as to elicit maximally affective responses. Moreover in *BT*, in line with the Schopenhauerian flavour of the book, Nietzsche emphasizes music's high capacity to arouse emotions. And in *EH* he explicitly links *Zarathustra* to music by proposing that 'one could, perhaps, count the whole of Zarathustra as music' (*EH*: 'Thus Spoke Zarathustra' 1).

My suggestion that in *Zarathustra* language and style are a substitute for the power of music in tragedy is further strengthened by the fact that there is, on the face of it, nothing in *Zarathustra* which appeals to 'theoretical man' or is indicative of a 'theoretical world view'. We have an almost total absence of arguments and explanations, and Zarathustra's so-called teachings, such as the *Übermensch* and Eternal Return, are rather underdeveloped and obscure—to put it mildly. But this absence is perplexing or annoying only if we approach *Zarathustra* as a philosophical treatise in a narrow analytical sense. If, on the other hand, we take Nietzsche's claim of *Zarathustra* as a tragedy seriously and remember that Nietzsche declared wisdom and not knowledge (*Wissenschaft*) to be the aim of tragedy (*BT* 18), then things begin to fall into place. If we define tragic wisdom as the unarticulated, unargued, unexplained sediment of tragic insights, then it follows that tragic wisdom so defined cannot possibly be taught or explained by rational means. Yet according to *BT*, it can be powerfully communicated via music-induced contagion of shared emotional experiences.

But here we must pause for a moment and consider what precisely it is that is thus communicated and to whom. Using the distinction of esoteric and exoteric wisdom, we can see that the transformational experience described in *BT* and invited in *Zarathustra* through its powerful language is for *all* spectators or readers. It is therefore *exoteric* and, crucially, *passive*, being simply the result of temporary emotional rapture. As such it cannot possibly bring about genuine tragic transformations but merely simulated ones. Simulated tragic experiences may still be uplifting or comforting, but since they are not the outcome of a genuine overcoming, they obviously cannot have genuine, deep-reaching transformative and redemptive power.[24] Esoteric wisdom, by contrast, is based on authentic tragic insights and is, by definition, available only to few, only to initiates.[25] We can say, then, that Zarathustra facilitates the possibility

---

[23] See Nehamas 1985, particularly chapter 1; also Shapiro 1989.
[24] Redemptive in the sense of *Z* II: 'On Redemption', which will make 'cripples' and 'fragments' whole.
[25] Though when remembering *Z*'s subtitle *A Book for All and None* and taking *All* to refer to his

of emotionally experiencing exoteric tragic insights by showing, enticing, and seducing us to become intoxicated spectators-cum-readers through his powerful language. *Zarathustra* can then be understood as a dramatic performance with Zarathustra as hero performing *his* transformation and inviting *all* to passively follow his progress. But behind the 'mask' of this performance is the esoteric Zarathustra who dismissed his disciples precisely because they were mere passive followers without authentic selves and therefore unable to find and walk their own way. Recall here Zarathustra's famous statement about *the way*:

> On many kinds of ways did I come to my truth; it was not on one ladder that I climbed to that height where my eyes sweep far.
> And ever reluctantly did I ask for ways,—that always goes against my taste! Much rather do I seek and try the ways myself [...]
> 'That—is *my* way,—where is yours?' Thus I answered those who asked me 'for the way'.
> For *the* way—does not exist! (*Z* III: 'The Spirit of Heaviness' 2)

Today we may query the suggestion that *Zarathustra*'s language functions like music in tragedy by pointing out that *Zarathustra*'s excessively emotional style often acts as a barrier to readers. But 125 years ago when *Zarathustra* was written, and 50–100 years ago when it was Nietzsche's most highly acclaimed and popular work, the sensibilities of even cultured readers were obviously significantly different. For part of the book's massive appeal then was precisely its language with its amazing capacity to arouse, to inspire, to summon—though, as to its what? or where? was usually not very clear.[26] During a seminar about *Thus Spoke Zarathustra* which he gave for several years, C. G. Jung discussed Nietzsche's demands for sacrifice and *Untergang* in preparation for the *Übermensch* and made this telling observation about the attitude of 'really serious people' in Germany at that time (1934):

> It is amor fati. This is the attitude now prevailing in Germany. It is the inner meaning of National Socialism. They live in order to live on—or die. [...] They praise the attitude of being ready, and naturally any rationalist asks, for what? That is just the point—nobody knows for what. Therefore, they have no programme, they have no mapped-out scheme which should be fulfilled. They live for the moment. They don't know where they are going. [...] but one thing is certain: they are going, there is no return, they must risk it. Then the rationalist asks: 'Risk what?' The answer is: 'Risk it.' They don't know what they are risking, they simply take it as a matter of course that they must take this attitude, that one risks it, whatever it is. (Jung 1988: vol. 1, p. 87)

This is an astute observation of communal emotional contagion at work. Note that these are, allegedly, 'really serious people' which are here swept away by emotional arousal and then, alarmingly, get stuck to a surface made up of slogans. They have no reasons or plans, no insights, tragic or otherwise, just an unarticulated commitment towards a common unknown 'fate'. Jung here exposes the amazing power of aroused affects, where through emotional intoxication and contagion a huge enthusiasm and also fatalism is generated and pitched high, ready to be exploited for any purpose.[27]

---

exoteric teaching, we may wonder whether Nietzsche believed or feared that his esoteric wisdom might ultimately be heard by *none*.

[26] When talking to educated, now elderly persons who read *Z* in the early twentieth century, all they usually remember is the elation they felt and being swept away, irresistibly, by sheer enthusiasm.

[27] See Aschheim 1992 for detailed discussions of the reception of Nietzsche and his works in twentieth-century Germany.

In summary we can say that *Zarathustra* is indeed a tragedy where Zarathustra performs a process we are meant to simulate by being emotionally aroused through the rhythm and poetry of his speeches and songs. By being emotionally affected and implicated we are to feel ourselves into the message and thus passively imbibe Zarathustra's teachings without being 'taught'—a process relevantly similar to responses of spectators to tragedies. Yet behind that tragic performance is Zarathustra's call to those few and rare individuals able to hear his summons to overcome themselves and thus be ready for their own way towards genuine, active, tragic transformation.

7 A COUNTER-IDEAL TO THE ASCETIC IDEAL

Next to calling *Zarathustra* a parody and a tragedy, Nietzsche also claims that Zarathustra provides a counter-ideal to the ascetic ideal. He makes this claim in two works, *GM* and *EH*, both written after *Zarathustra*. The first, *GM* II: 25, is just a few lines long and mentions Zarathustra by name and describes him as younger, stronger, of the future, and godless. The preceding section is important because it outlines the task ahead and the qualifications necessary to accomplish it, such as 'great health' and 'a kind of sublime malice'. Here we also meet again two of the contradictory Apollonian-Dionysian dualities: the destroyer-cum-creator in the statement 'so that a sanctuary can be erected, a sanctuary has to be broken' and love-cum-contempt in the prophecy that one day the 'redeemer of great love and great contempt' must come (*GM* II: 24). The second mention of Zarathustra as bringer of the counter-ideal is in *EH*'s discussion of *GM* III:

> The third treatise answers the question from whence the uncanny power of the ascetic ideal, the priestly ideal, derives. [...] *not* because a god is behind the priests [...] but [...] because it was up to now the only ideal, it had no competition. [...] Above all, a *counter-ideal* was missing—*until Zarathustra*. (*EH*: 'Genealogy of Morals')

The *Übermensch* and Eternal Return are generally taken as Zarathustra's greatest provocation and challenge to traditional beliefs and thus prime candidates for the counter-ideal. Both have been, and still are, much debated.[28] However, less spectacular alternatives to beliefs and values of a specifically ascetic Christian kind in *Zarathustra* have barely been considered by scholars so far. From the *EH* citation above it is clear that it is the ascetic ideal in its *priestly garb*, which, for Nietzsche, can only be *Christian garb*, that constitutes Zarathustra's main target. And Zarathustra is indeed singularly qualified to deal with priests and their ideals. He confesses:

> There was a time when Zarathustra too cast his delusions beyond humankind like all the otherworldly. The work of a suffering and tortured God seemed the world to me then. (*Z* I: 'On the Otherworldly')

[28] I agree with Simon May (1999) who considers the *Übermensch* and Eternal Return unsuitable candidates for what May calls the 'new ideal'. May favours 'to become what one is' as the replacement of the ascetic ideal.

And he cautions his disciples:

> Here are priests: and though they are my enemies, pass them by quietly and with sleeping swords! [...] Evil enemies they are: nothing is more driven to revenge than their humility. [...]
>   But my blood is related to theirs and I want my blood honoured even in theirs. (*Z* II: 'On Priests')

We can see now why Zarathustra is singularly qualified to deal with priests: he is related to them in blood and belief, in body and mind. Note also how much Zarathustra still values that relation, he wants it honoured: a rare, atypical request from the arch-destroyer! Let us therefore tap into the wealth of Zarathustra's insider knowledge and explore three topics with particularly rich Christian connotations: love, eternity (not Eternal Return), and Jesus, in order to test their suitability to replace or dislodge the ascetic ideal.

8 LOVE

There is perhaps only *one* coherent strand and abiding theme going right through *Zarathustra* and that is Zarathustra's love(s). Zarathustra is full, indeed, as we will see, over-full with love and one can distinguish at least three kinds. The first has been mentioned already: Zarathustra's longed for, tried, and ultimately rejected love for multitudes, disciples, and 'higher men'. It might seem odd to suggest that a failed love could contribute anything to a counter-ideal. Yet it does! This is best demonstrated by contrasting Zarathustra's with Jesus' love (as narrated in the *New Testament*) for multitudes, disciples, and the kind of bur-dened salvation-seekers called 'higher men' in Part IV. Without doubt, Jesus loved all and regarded all as equally deserving. Yet equality and particularly equalizing love was branded by Nietzsche as part of slave morality. Further, as told, Jesus searched for loving believers and unquestioning followers and described himself as *the way* to eternal salvation, while Zarathustra warned against salvation and dismissed followers, looking instead for fellow-creators free to find and walk their own way. Jesus as shepherd tending his flock is a potent Christian symbol[29] and a role Zarathustra emphatically rejects. Lastly, Jesus, moved by pity for the weak, healed the sick and crippled, while Zarathustra is deeply distressed only when confronted by the 'inverse cripples' of fragmented human beings (*Z* II: 'On Redemption'). The list could go on, but we have amassed enough evidence to make the by now obvious connection of Zarathustra's mature attitude with master morality and Jesus' with slave morality. Note that Zarathustra has undergone a development: in the prologue he loves all (*Ich liebe die Menschen*) (*Z* I: 'Zarathustra's Prologue' 2), yet right at the end he is still look-ing for those worthy of his love, for his equals, his 'children'. In other words, Zarathustra becomes more and more discriminating and increasingly aware of the need for an 'order of rank'. He thus moves from a Christian or slave morality position towards a noble one. This move echoes the one referred to above, namely that once, in the past, Zarathustra too was a believer in otherworldly values. We can conclude, then, that his failed loves are not fail-ures but rather corrections towards a stronger, healthier, nobler position, since loving with

---

[29] A shepherd's crook is still part of a bishop's regalia.

wisdom and discrimination creates and maintains the all-important order of rank, a pivotal aspect of a Nietzschean counter-ideal to Christian love.

9 Contra Christian Love

Next is Zarathustra's love as expressed in the litany of eighteen verses in the prologue each beginning with *I love* (Z I: 'Zarathustra's Prologue' 4) This litany is difficult to categorize since it could be a rather intense confession, or a manifesto, or a prayer. The content of the litany is remarkable too since there is *not one single verse!* which does not mention one or more of the following: going under (*Untergang*); crossing over; perishing (*zu Grunde gehen*); doom (*Verhängnis*); sacrifice; contempt; to waste oneself (*verschwenden*); and the piercing longing (*Pfeil der Sehnsucht*) to do so. These eighteen verses with their deeply ascetic tone and sacrificial appeal are preceded by the statement that 'what can be loved about man is that he is a going over and a going under' (an *Übergang* and an *Untergang*). A going over to what? A going under for what? Naturally, for the *Übermensch* as only he warrants such self-denying yearning and sacrificial giving.

Note the astounding similarity of this litany in form and content with Christian devotion and worship. Regarding form: because of their strong rhythm and strategic repetitions (thus easy to recite and learn by heart), litanies are much used for instruction and prayer in most religions including Christianity. Regarding the similarity of content, recall that Christianity praises and venerates those who give themselves over to God as the highest reality, spending themselves in love and devotion to him. Christian believers, especially ascetic ones, tend to view life on earth with contempt and yearn to sacrifice themselves for a pure and inestimably more valuable life 'beyond', as all meaning and value is located solely in that beyond. Because of this shared ascetic appeal some verses of *Zarathustra*'s litany would fit well into Christian liturgy despite their obvious Nietzschean tone:

> I love those who do not know how to live except by going under for they are the ones to go beyond.
> I love those of great contempt because they are the great venerators and arrows of longing for yonder shore. (Z I: 'Zarathustra's Prologue' 4)

Others require the substitution of Messiah for *Übermensch* and sacrifice for *Untergang* to make the similarity complete:

> I love him who lives to understand and who wants to understand so that the *Übermensch* (Messiah) will live one day. Thus he wants his *Untergang* (sacrifice). (Z I: 'Zarathustra's Prologue' 4)

Yet others, while remaining formally akin, state a new, earth-directed creed:

> I love those who do not first search behind the stars for a reason to go under and be a sacrifice: rather they sacrifice themselves for the earth so that the earth will one day belong to the *Übermensch*. (Z I: 'Zarathustra's Prologue' 4)

We can see, then, that Nietzsche utilizes Christian devotional language and inverts it: the *Übermensch* replaces God, Saviour, and Messiah, and yearning for a transcendent 'beyond' is turned into affirmation and love of earth. The longing to give oneself, to sacrifice oneself for something infinitely valuable and venerable, is channelled away from the divine into the here and now, into something human even if it is called superhuman. So, clearly, this love too provides a valuable component to the counter-ideal.

10   LOVE AS SUPERABUNDANCE

The third kind of love is more ambiguous. Parts of it we have discussed already and here is another version:

> Once more I want to go to humankind: I want to go under [*untergehen*] amongst them [*unter ihnen*], dying I want to give them my richest gift!
> This I learned from the sun when she goes down, the over-rich sun: when she pours gold into the sea from inexhaustible riches,—
> —such that even the poorest fisherman rows with *golden* oars! This, indeed, I saw once and did not tire of tears as I looked on.—
> Like the sun, Zarathustra too wants to go under [*untergehn*]: ... (Z III: 'Of Old and New Tablets' 3)

The theme of sacrifice is stronger here than in the prologue's *Sonnenuntergang* theme, though both speak of a love that wants to go under—an *Untergang* love—within that metaphor. Of course, *Untergang* and sacrifice are also main themes in Zarathustra's litany of love. But there is a difference! In the litany, Nietzsche talks of the inferior wanting to sacrifice itself to the superior, of the merely human to the superhuman, all clothed in a language of emptiness longing to be filled, of a yearning needing a goal. But that, importantly, does not describe Zarathustra's own love, merely what Zarathustra loves in others! Now, however, Nietzsche describes Zarathustra's own love: it is rich and ripe, indeed, it is burdened by its richness, needing to overflow like the sun overflows when spreading its golden abundance. Note the twist: sacrifice now flows from the superior to the inferior and love overflows from the full to the empty, a descending direction strongly suggested by the downward movement of 'going down' and 'overflowing'.

Yet one must ask what is the point of all these riches overflowing to their sacrificial *Untergang*? It's all very paradoxical, particularly when taking due note of the way Nietzsche emphasizes the neediness of the overfull to be relieved of their riches! This need of the overfull to give away their abundance we find already on the very first page of *Zarathustra* where Zarathustra questions the sun's happiness were it not for those to whom it can shine. And in Part III, in an extraordinary dialogue of Zarathustra with his soul, aptly named 'On Great Longing', this need is further explored:

> —should the giver not give thanks that the receiver received? Is gift-giving not a need? Is receiving not—mercy?
> Oh my soul, I understand the smile of your melancholy: your own over-richness now stretches out longing hands!

The dialogue also implies that this need longs to give all, longs for the vintner's knife:

> 'Is all weeping not a lamentation? And all lamentation not an accusation?' Thus you speak to yourself, and that is why you, oh my soul, would rather smile than pour out your suffering.
> —pour out in torrents of tears your suffering over your fullness and over the grapevine's aching need for the vintner and his knife! (Z III: 'On Great Longing')

From context it is clear that the vintner with his knife is Dionysus.[30] Because of this one could interpret Zarathustra's *Untergang* love as Apollo longing to spread his golden radiance (*Schein*) over Dionysian waters. While such an interpretation takes account of gift-giving longing, it fails to engage with the sacrificial theme. Hence a better interpretation, in my view, is to see it as an alternative to the divine love and sacrificial death of Jesus as described in the *New Testament,* where it was the means to redeem sinful and fallen humankind. Jesus' love is an overflowing and an *Untergang* too, but, crucially, it responded to a stated need in the recipients: their fall, their sin, their lack of goodness and worth required divine sacrifice. But when a debt (*Schuld*) is so great, when guilt (*Schuld*) is quite unredeemable, when wretchedness is utterly dependent on divine mercy, then, as Nietzsche eloquently describes in *GM* II and III, we have ripe conditions for the ascetic ideal. Compare this to Zarathustra's *Untergang* love: here, in utter contrast to Christian doctrine, it is the giver who is needy and not the receiver; here, as Zarathustra's soul intimates, it is the receiver who bestows mercy when receiving. But when this is indeed the case, then, please note, there is no guilt! Shifting need from receiver to giver removes from the former the stains of sin and guilt which underpin the ascetic ideal. While, admittedly, much ambiguity remains around the third love, we can nonetheless conclude that it too contributes much to a counter-ideal by undermining one of the ascetic ideal's greatest supports—guilt.

To summarize the three loves just described: The first is human (though of the rather exalted kind of Jesus and Zarathustra) love for other humans. Jesus loves all and, importantly, his love actually equalizes those it loves and thus does away with merit and distinction amongst them.[31] Zarathustra does precisely the opposite: his love is wise; it selects, honours, and thus raises distinctions. We can gloss the second love as love of the low and inferior for something higher, which seems to arise spontaneously from the deep human yearning to strive for more than the plain given in order to make that given meaningful. In Christianity, this is the love of creatures for their divine creator which, when not eased by various mystical experiences of nearness, emphasizes the essential otherness of humans and the divine and therefore tends towards a transcendent beyond. In *Z*, however, human yearning to rise above the plain given is directed towards the *Übermensch* and is now love from human to superhuman and no longer to the divine. Within a Christian context, the third is merciful divine love responding to creation's need for redemption, while Zarathustra declares that he himself is the needy one, requiring, like the sun, recipients into whose outstretched hands he can pour the overflow of his riches and wisdom, his 'honey' (*Z* I: 'Zarathustra's Prologue' 1). Thus, in contrast to Christian loves, Zarathustrian loves demonstrate a movement away from the otherworldly and its valuing of equality, its sin and guilt, its transcendence, aiming instead

---

[30] See the myth of Dionysus.
[31] This is particularly evident in many *New Testament* parables, such as 'The Lost Sheep' in Luke 15.

towards the earth and earthly values. And the seemingly ineradicable human striving with its readiness for *Untergang* is aimed and harnessed now for human and superhuman values.

11 ETERNITY

Let us turn now to eternity, other than Eternal Return, as the second possible component of Zarathustra's counter-ideal. Part III of *Z* was originally intended as the end of the whole book. It closes with 'The Seven Seals' or 'The Yes and Amen Song'. This song bears an obvious parallel and contrast to the *Revelation of St John* in the *New Testament*, which similarly functions as closure and end of revealed Christian teaching.[32] Among the many parallels are the symbolism of the number seven (there are seven times seven items in *Revelation*),[33] prophesy, the metaphor of 'seal', and the Alpha and Omega claim. Yet the contrast could not be greater. *Revelation* (also called *Apocalypse*) is hard to read without revulsion. It is a revengeful, bloodthirsty, horror story of the end of earth and time when at the advent of eternity all of mankind, except a small number of 'the chosen', is vanquished. Zarathustra's 'Seven Seals' song, by contrast, is a jubilant celebration of conquest, joy, lust, and desire. Each of the seven verses of his song concludes with this refrain:

> Oh how could I not lust [*brünstig sein*] after Eternity and the marriage ring of rings—
> the ring of recurrence!
> Never yet have I found the woman from whom I wanted children, unless it were this
> woman, whom I love: because I love you, oh Eternity!
> *Because I love you, oh Eternity!* (Z III: 'The Seven Seals (Or: The Yes and Amen Song)')

At first sight this looks like a love song, albeit a peculiar one. Peculiar first, because it lacks customary tenderness, and second, because of the term '*brünstig*', which in this context is somewhat offensive.[34] *Brünstig* is not a word usually used for human sexuality—it refers only to animals. Male animals during the rutting season are said to be *brünstig* and only for females which are 'on heat', that is, ready to conceive. As such, *brünstig* has little to do with either sexual desire or love; it is simply the entirely instinctive animal imperative to mate, and to mate only 'in season' when conception is possible. So *Brunst* is limited to the time of possible conception for that species, and *Brunst* is also, obviously, limited to animals within their own species: a ram is not *brünstig* for a dog, nor a stallion for a cow! Now, if Zarathustra as spokesperson and envoy of earth and time declares himself *brünstig* for eternity and wants to have children with her, then this declaration can only mean that time *can* have children with eternity, both because the time (as season) is right and because time and eternity are compatible, they are of the same kind.

This is in stark contrast to *Revelation*. As mentioned, the advent of eternity prophesied in *Revelation* is one of utter horror. The abyss between earth and eternity is such that it cannot be bridged; hence earth and time must be destroyed before eternity can reign. According to the theology of *Revelation*, earth, with its mess of sin and corruption (its 'abominations'),

---

[32] Though this can vary according to particular Christian denominations.

[33] The number 7 was sacred in many ancient middle-eastern religions.

[34] The English term 'lust' does not do justice to the animal mating aspect of *brünstig* and *Brunst*.

is totally and utterly incompatible with eternity. Yet Zarathustra with his song of primordial sexual urge brings eternity 'down to earth' and thus abolishes the abyss between time and eternity, being and becoming, and its particular Christian appendage of a pure timeless beyond set over against a sinful here and now. The contrast between a pure timeless beyond with earth's sinful and utterly worthless here and now is, of course, a major ingredient of the ascetic ideal. De-idealizing it is thus an eminently useful contribution to the counter-ideal.

12   ZARATHUSTRA AND JESUS

The last topic to be examined regarding its potential to contribute to the counter-ideal is the person of Jesus. Naturally, given the size of the task, our examination here must strictly limit itself to some of Nietzsche's remarks. Nietzsche makes a distinction, though not explicitly, between Jesus and Christ, and he regards Christ as a product of fabrication and falsification by the early church and particularly by Saint Paul. Nietzsche's relentless animosity and venom against institutionalized Christianity is well known, yet he treats Jesus himself with careful, gentle, delicacy, deploring the fact that there lived at that time no one with the sensibility of a Dostoyevsky to understand 'this mixture of sublimity, disease, and childlikeness' (*A* 31). In the *Nachlass* Nietzsche expressed the thought that Jesus might eventually have become the first renegade of his own teaching had he lived long enough (*KSA* 9: 66). Similarly in *Z* itself:

> In truth, that Hebrew, honoured by the preachers of slow death, died too early: and it has since become a doom for many that he died too early.
> He only knew tears and the melancholy of the Hebrews, together with hate of the good and just—the Hebrew Jesus, when longing for death overcame him.
> If only he had stayed in the desert and away from the good and just! Perhaps he would have learned how to live and how to love the earth—and also how to laugh!
> Believe me, my brothers! He died too early; he would himself have recanted his teaching if he had reached my age! Noble enough was he to recant!
> But he was still immature. Youth loves with immaturity and also hates with immaturity humanity and earth. (*Z* I: 'On Free Death')[35]

Two items are noteworthy here: (1) the mild tone adopted by Zarathustra towards Jesus; he speaks like an older brother regretting the follies and fate of a younger sibling; (2) the many parallels, actual and potential, that are outlined here between Jesus and Zarathustra. Both hate 'the good and just' and nothing profound or fundamental stops Jesus from learning how to live, love, and laugh—just immaturity! Note that Jesus was noble like Zarathustra. Indeed, had he reached Zarathustra's age, he would have recanted his youthful teaching and so avoided the doom of many, that is, avoided being turned into the founder of slave morality. And to love with maturity—something Jesus would have learned in time—implies loving like Zarathustra; that is, selectively, nobly, with wisdom.[36] All this leads to the surprising

---

[35]   This is the only instance in *Z* which mentions Jesus by name.
[36]   Recall the discussion in section 5 where Jesus, in contrast to Zarathustra, loves without wisdom. Also sections 8 to 10.

conclusion that Jesus and Zarathustra are of one kind, are perhaps kin, since there is nothing of note separating them—just maturity.[37]

This conclusion seems to upset our quest to substantiate Nietzsche's claim that Zarathustra provides the counter-ideal. When both are on 'the same side' how can one of them provide a counter-ideal to the other? But this is not a problem. In *EH* Nietzsche states that since (the historic) Zarathustra was the first to establish the opposition between Good and Evil, it is only fitting that Zarathustra should return to correct the negative consequences of his own legacy (*EH*: 'Why I Am a Destiny' 3). We could take this as a hint for something analogous regarding the ascetic ideal: i.e. Zarathustra with his priestly background and 'kinship' with Jesus has a similar task regarding the negative consequences of Jesus' legacy.

Jesus' legacy centres on his sacrificial death whereby he was turned into Christ the crucified, who then, Nietzsche claims, became the focus of dogmas involving sin, guilt, and redemption. This legacy, this 'doom for many', Zarathustra has to undo. How? We read in the *Nachlass*:

> To be redeemed from sin one used to recommend belief in Jesus Christ. But now I declare this remedy: don't believe in sin! This cure is more radical! The earlier cure wanted to make one delusion bearable through another. (*KSA* 9: 188)

The guilt of sin is indeed the key support of the ascetic ideal. Jesus' sacrificial death was meant to atone for guilt and thus save humankind for a possible blissful beyond. Yet the Christian dogma of redemption enshrines guilt and perpetuates it as a debt—eternally, inescapably. Nietzsche declares both guilt and redemption as delusions. And Zarathustra demonstrates this by replacing the love of Jesus as Christ, dogmatized by theology as atonement for guilt, with his own love which demonstrates, as argued above, that *there is no guilt*. Note that Zarathustra has not abolished guilt—one cannot abolish what is not there—he has merely exposed it as a delusion.

Another legacy of Jesus' early death was the missed opportunity to learn—and thus to teach—how to live, love, and laugh. Now, life, love, and laughter are very much Zarathustra's domain. He is, after all, the singing, dancing, laughing advocate of freedom, the lover of earth, the celebrant of life. That is his legacy! Consider here the end of the new preface to *BT* where Nietzsche introduces Zarathustra as 'that malicious Dionysian' (*Unhold*) followed by a long citation from *Zarathustra*:

> This crown of laughter, this rose-wreath crown: I crowned myself with this crown. I myself decreed my laughter holy. No one today found I strong enough for this.
>   Zarathustra the dancer, Zarathustra the light one, who waves his wings, poised for flight, wing-waving to all birds, poised and ready, blissfully, lightly poised and ready. [...]
>   This crown of laughter, this rose-wreath crown: my brothers, to you I throw this crown! I decreed laughter holy: you higher men, *learn*—to laugh! (*BT*: 'An Attempt at Self-Criticism' 7, assembled from *Z* IV: 'On Higher Men' 18–20)

Thus Zarathustra's legacy is one of joy and laughter which Jesus might also have reached had he lived long enough. We can conclude, then, that Zarathustra's attempt to undo the doom

---

[37] Jesus died when about 30 years old. *Z* begins with 'When Zarathustra was 30 years old' and tells how Zarathustra then spent ten years in solitude on his mountain before starting his mission: a strong hint that Zarathustra achieved what Jesus was unable to do—gain wisdom with maturity.

of Christian legacy by showing what Jesus might have become, makes a valuable contribution to a counter-ideal.

13 THE DIONYSIAN COUNTER-IDEAL

There are many other themes in *Zarathustra*, such as justice, punishment, free will, death,
which, when examined, will similarly offer a genuine alternative to prevailing Christian
ascetic ones. We can therefore agree that at least some of Zarathustra's teachings are a serious and philosophically sound attempt to replace the ascetic ideal with something Nietzsche
(and perhaps also we) would consider less pernicious. It is a different question altogether
whether the counter-ideal is successful. Does it work in practice? Can it give meaning to
suffering, provide wings for aspirations, offer fortification in pain, as religions, at their
best, are claimed to do? Naturally, this question cannot be answered by reference to philosophical coherence. Most likely the counter-ideal will work for some and not for others; a
fact Nietzsche would surely applaud given his thoughts about order of rank and pathos of
distance.

Two further questions need attending. First: why is the counter-ideal to the ascetic ideal
still so very ascetic? All this talk about overcoming, sacrifice, and yearning for *Untergang*
sounds frighteningly familiar. It is familiar but not frightening since Nietzsche considers
ascetic self-discipline necessary for self-creation and greatness. Asceticism is only harmful when aligned to life-negating contents and goals, such as those Christianity allegedly
imposes.

Second: accepting that Zarathustra, like any tragic hero, is a mask for Dionysus, why does
Nietzsche call him a *Dionysian Unhold*? Why is Zarathustra a wayward, malicious, monstrous Dionysian? Recall that in *GM* II: 24 Nietzsche stipulated 'a kind of sublime malice'
(*Bosheit*) as prerequisite for any attempt to reverse the ascetic ideal, and in *Zarathustra* malice figures prominently in Zarathustra's self-descriptions and is often combined with love
and especially with laughter:

> [If] my malice is a laughing malice, at home under rose-banks and lily-hedges:—since in
> laughter all evil is together, but holy and pronounced absolved by its own bliss: (Z III: 'The
> Seven Seals (Or: The Yes and Amen Song)' 6)
> Here laugh, laugh, my bright, feisty malice! From high mountains throw down your glit-
> tering mocking laughter! With your glitter bait for me the most beautiful human fishes! (Z
> IV: 'The Honey Sacrifice')[38]

This shows that malice—'sublime malice'—is not simply evil, though that stays, but also
mocking and mischievous, and, as we shall see, subversive and troublesome. Such malice
might indeed be a useful, perhaps even a necessary trait for someone bent on questioning
and undermining established values. Thus one can readily understand why Zarathustra
often bemoans the lack of malice in humans. Part of Zarathustra's nausea and abysmal
thought was precisely that everything was so small in humans, including their malice (Z

[38] Note that Jesus too is often portrayed as a fisher of men.

III: 'The Convalescent'). Malice, Zarathustra claims, is the best human power and humans must become both better and more evil (*Z* IV: 'The Higher Men').

In *GS* 340 Nietzsche describes Socrates as 'this mocking, love-sick monster' (*Unhold*) Nietzsche's relation to Socrates is highly complex and cannot be discussed here. But Socrates was certainly taken as subversive and troublesome by his contemporaries, and if Nietzsche calls him an *Unhold*, then he obviously had, like Zarathustra himself, plenty of that 'best human power'—malice! I suggest that Jesus belongs in this group too, though he was never called an *Unhold*, probably because too 'childlike' and hence lacking the sublimity of malice. Nonetheless, Jesus was, or was later portrayed as, subversive of establishment. He too was a troublesome agitator, just like Socrates, and Nietzsche states that both Athens and the Pharisees were right in their condemnation of them (*KSA* 11: 139). Both achieved, or it was achieved in their name, the remarkable and for Nietzsche most admirable and enviable feat of changing values, of actually bringing about a revaluation of values. Yet, while it is true that Socrates and Jesus succeeded in establishing new values, these were, for Nietzsche's life affirmation project, utterly harmful ones needing urgent revaluation in turn. And this is Zarathustra's task! Note how the sequence Socrates and Jesus followed by Zarathustra traces precisely the one described by Nietzsche in his wonderfully condensed 'The History of an Error', where, after a savage yet amusing debunking of Platonic and Christian values, comes the 'midday' moment of shortest shadow; end of longest error; high point of humanity; INCIPIT ZARATHUSTRA (*TI*: 'How the "True World" Finally Became a Fable').

Yet if part of Nietzsche's project was to stress Zarathustra's similarity with Socrates and Jesus as subversive value-creators, thus making Zarathustra eminently suitable to do likewise, why not make this similarity more obvious and complete?[39] Why the exoteric and esoteric layers of meaning and the ambiguities in teaching? Regarding these, one could of course reply that they were also used by Socrates and Jesus and thus perhaps part of their success. But then, why not proceed with Zarathustra's trial, condemnation, and execution as projected in Nietzsche's preliminary notes? When all three share the same kind of *Untergang*, thus making their commonality even more prominent, might this not vastly increase Zarathustra's appeal? Nietzsche obviously thought otherwise. Maybe because to share the same kind of *Untergang*, i.e. replace Zarathustra's radiant *Sonnenuntergang* with hemlock or the agony of the cross, might simply be too doom-laden, might possibly darken forever the gaiety and freedom of Zarathustra's message, and might therefore permanently obscure his essential identity with Dionysus. The essential identity of Zarathustra with Dionysus is *the* key for understanding *Zarathustra*. While classic life-affirming and life-regenerating features associated with Dionysus were a major theme for Nietzsche from *BT* onwards, and while in that early work we can already discern tentative moves by Nietzsche to articulate new values and a new mythology around this god,[40] in Nietzsche's later works, and pre-eminently in *Zarathustra*, Dionysus is the often unnamed masked figure in whose voice Nietzsche's strongest rhetorical and affective opposition to Socratic and Christian values are uttered. As an example, recall here the closing line of *EH*:—'Have I been understood?—Dionysus against The Crucified...'! Indeed, Nietzsche's rapturous praise of

---

[39] As envisaged in the *Nachlass*; see my notes 8 and 9.
[40] For Nietzsche's vision of Dionysus as the centre of a new mythology, see Gemes and Sykes (2013).

Zarathustra throughout *EH* is just rapturous praise for Dionysus, who is celebrated as the eternal yes to all things, 'the unbelievable, unbounded yes- and amen-saying' (*EH*: 'Thus Spoke Zarathustra' 6).

14 CONCLUSION

Zarathustra is a highly complex book and I have here only examined some of its many topics[41] in the hope of justifying my claim that *Zarathustra* is worthy of serious attention. The question remains why precisely Nietzsche chose to present his topics and teachings in just this peculiar dramatic form? For one could argue that his over-rich rhetoric only adds to the general obscurity and ambiguity of the book and that Nietzsche would have been well advised to present his thoughts in his usual style which, by any standard, is remarkable, beautiful, and extravagant enough. But Nietzsche didn't. Perhaps the silence of years and years of non-readers for his more openly philosophical books, where many of *Zarathustra*'s topics are discussed more soberly and systematically, finally persuaded him to try a different approach. And it has to be acknowledged that for more than half a century *Zarathustra* was indeed Nietzsche's most famous work, a gateway to his philosophy for many readers—though, I dare say, probably not a gateway today's academic philosophers are keen to use. However, if we take Nietzsche's designation of *Thus Spoke Zarathustra* as a tragedy seriously, as I think we should, and if we further accept that Nietzsche aims to change values at a deep psychological rather than intellectual level, then we have to admit that a rhetoric of inspiration, making full use of poetic and musical affective seductions, is more conducive to Dionysian intoxication as a necessary first step to self-overcoming and transformation to a tragic state, than any intellectual effort and philosophically sound argumentation. I suggest that an important part of Nietzsche's distinctive genius was to recognize and accept that tragic Dionysian transformations can only *begin* by way of simulation and identification (and even then only for a rare few) and not by way of philosophical and rational demonstrations.[42]

BIBLIOGRAPHY

(A) Works by Nietzsche

KSA *Sämtliche Werke: Kritische Studienausgabe in 15 Einzelbänden*, ed. G. Colli and M. Montinari (15 vols). Berlin: De Gruyter, 1988.

(B) Other Works Cited

Aschheim, S. E. 1992. *The Nietzsche Legacy in Germany 1890–1990*. Berkeley: University of California Press.

---

[41] For detailed comments on *Z* and step-by-step guidance see Lampert 1987 and Rosen 1995.
[42] I gratefully acknowledge my debt to Ken Gemes for his helpful discussions and comments.

Behler, E. 1998. 'Nietzsche's Conception of Irony', in S. Kenal, I. Gaskell, and D. W. Conway (eds), *Nietzsche, Philosophy, and the Arts*. Cambridge: Cambridge University Press, 13–35.

Breazeale, D. 1983. 'The Meaning of the Earth', in D. Goicoechea (ed), *The Great Year of Zarathustra (1881–1981)*. Lanham, New York, and London: University Press of America, 113–41.

Came, D. (ed.). 2013. *Nietzsche on Art and Life*. Oxford and New York: Oxford University Press. Forthcoming.

Gadamer, H.-G. 1983. 'Das Drama Zarathustras', with page-by-page English trans. by Z. Adamczewski, in D. Goicoechea (ed.), *The Great Year of Zarathustra (1881–1981)*. Lanham, New York, and London: University Press of America, 339–69.

Goicoechea, D. 1983. *The Great Year of Zarathustra (1881–1981)* Lanham, New York, and London: University Press of America.

Gemes, K. 2006. 'Nietzsche on Free Will, Autonomy and the Sovereign Individual', *Proceedings of the Aristotelian Society* 80 (suppl. vol.): 339–57.

Gemes, K. 2007. 'Strangers to Ourselves: Nietzsche on the Will to Truth, the Scientific Spirit, Free Will, and Genuine Selfhood', in G. von Tevenar (ed.), *Nietzsche and Ethics*. Oxford: Peter Lang, 19–54.

Gemes, K. and Janaway, C. (eds). 2013. *Nietzsche's Values*. Oxford: Oxford University Press. Forthcoming.

Gemes, K. and Sykes, C. 2013. 'Nietzsche's Illusion', in D. Came (ed.), *Nietzsche on Art and Life*. Oxford and New York: Oxford University Press. Forthcoming.

Gooding-Williams, R. 2001. *Zarathustra's Dionysian Modernism*. Stanford, Calif.: Stanford University Press.

Heidegger, M. 1977. 'Who is Nietzsche's Zarathustra?', in D. B. Allison (ed.), *The New Nietzsche*. New York: Dell Publishing, 76–9.

Heller, E. 1988. *Nietzsche: Ten Essays*. Chicago: University of Chicago Press.

Janaway, C. (ed.). 1998. *Willing and Nothingness: Schopenhauer as Nietzsche's Educator*. Oxford: Oxford University Press.

Janaway, C. 2006. 'Nietzsche on Free Will, Autonomy and the Sovereign Individual', *Proceedings of the Aristotelian Society* 80 (suppl. vol.): 339–57.

Janaway, C. 2007. *Beyond Selflessness: Reading Nietzsche's 'Genealogy'* New York: Oxford University Press.

Jasper, K. 1961. *Nietzsche and Christianity*, trans. E. B. Ashton. Chicago: Henry Regnery.

Jung, C. G. 1988. *Nietzsche's Zarathustra*, ed. J. L. Jarrett. Princeton: Princeton University Press.

Lampert, L. 1987. *Nietzsche's Teaching: An Interpretation of 'Thus Spoke Zarathustra'*. New Haven, Conn.: Yale University Press.

Mann, T. 1959. 'Nietzsche's Philosophy in the Light of Recent History', trans. R. and C. Winston, in T. Mann, *Last Essays*. London: Secker and Warburg, 141–77.

May, S. 1999. *Nietzsche's Ethics and his 'War on Morality'*. Oxford: Clarendon Press.

Montinari, M. 1982. *Nietzsche Lesen*. Berlin and New York: Walter de Gruyter.

Nehamas, A. 1985. *Nietzsche: Life as Literature*. Cambridge, Mass.: Harvard University Press.

Nussbaum, M. C. 1994. 'Pity and Mercy: Nietzsche's Stoicism', in R. Schacht (ed.), *Nietzsche, Genealogy, Morality: Essays on Nietzsche's 'Genealogy of Morals'*. Berkeley: University of California Press, 139–67.

Obholzer, A. 2007. *The Significance of Art in Nietzsche's Mature Thought*. Unpublished M.Phil. thesis, University of London.

Pippin, R. B. 1988. 'Irony and Affirmation in Nietzsche's Thus Spoke Zarathustra', in M. A. Gillespie and T. B. Strong (eds), *Nietzsche's New Seas*. Chicago: University of Chicago Press, 45–71.

Pippin, R. B. 2006. Introduction to *Nietzsche: Thus Spoke Zarathustra*, ed. R. B. Pippin and A. Del Caro, trans. A. Del Caro. Cambridge: Cambridge University Press, viii–xxxv.

Reginster, B. 2006. *The Affirmation of Life: Nietzsche on Overcoming Nihilism*. Cambridge, Mass.: Harvard University Press.

Rosen, S. 1995. *The Mask of Enlightenment: Nietzsche's Zarathustra*. Cambridge: Cambridge University Press.

Salaquarda, J. 1996. 'Nietzsche and the Judaeo-Christian Tradition', in B. Magnus and K. Higgins (eds), *The Cambridge Companion to Nietzsche*. Cambridge: Cambridge University Press, 90–118.

Salome, L. 1988. *Nietzsche*, ed. and trans. S. Mandel. Redding Ridge, Conn.: Black Swan Books.

Schacht, R. (ed.). 1994. *Nietzsche, Genealogy, Morality: Essays on Nietzsche's 'Genealogy of Morals'*. Berkeley: University of California Press.

Shapiro, G. 1989. *Nietzschean Narratives*. Indianapolis: Indiana University Press.

Siemens, H. 2007. 'The First Transvaluation of All Values: Nietzsche's *Agon* with Socrates in *The Birth of Tragedy*', in G. von Tevenar (ed.), *Nietzsche and Ethics*. Oxford: Peter Lang, 171–96.

Simmel, G. 1991. *Schopenhauer and Nietzsche*, trans. H. Loiskandle, D. Weinstein, and M. Weinstein. Urbana and Chicago: University of Illinois Press.

Staten, H. 1990. *Nietzsche's Voice*. New York: Cornell University Press.

Tanner, M. 1994. *Nietzsche*. Oxford: Oxford University Press.

Tevenar, G. von. 2007a. 'Nietzsche's Objections to Pity and Compassion', in G. von Tevenar (ed.), *Nietzsche and Ethics*. Oxford: Peter Lang, 263–82.

Tevenar, G. von (ed.). 2007b. *Nietzsche and Ethics*. Oxford: Peter Lang.

Tevenar, G. von. 2008. 'Zarathustra on Freedom', in J. Luchte (ed.), *Nietzsche's 'Thus Spoke Zarathustra': Before Sunrise*. London: Continuum, 129–40.

Tevenar, G. von. 2013. 'Nietzsche on Nausea', in K. Gemes and C. Janaway (eds), *Nietzsche's Values*. Oxford: Oxford University Press. Forthcoming.

Wilcox, J. T. 1983. 'Zarathustra's Yes', in D. Goicoechea (ed.), *The Great Year of Zarathustra (1881–1981)* Lanham, New York, and London: University Press of America.

Yovel, Y. 1994. 'Nietzsche, the Jews, and Ressentiment', in R. Schacht (ed.), *Nietzsche, Genealogy, Morality: Essays on Nietzsche's 'Genealogy of Morals'*. Berkeley: University of California Press, 127–38.

CHAPTER 13

....

BEYOND GOOD AND EVIL

....

MAUDEMARIE CLARK AND DAVID DUDRICK

Of Nietzsche's thirteen books, *Beyond Good and Evil* is most plausibly considered his most important. It is his most comprehensive, dealing as it does with all of the major topics of his later philosophy, and it makes the strongest impression of being intended as a major statement of that philosophy.[1] Many philosophers would choose *On the Genealogy of Morality* (*GM*) instead, on the grounds that it makes a more important and certainly a more accessible contribution to philosophy. Its form is more evident, making it much easier to determine its topic, claims, and arguments, and its content makes it seem to be at least an important and original book. Yet, on its facing title page, Nietzsche himself instructed that *GM* be "appended" to *BGE* "as a clarification and supplement," and it seems strange to accord the supplement more importance than the book it is meant to clarify and supplement. The solution might be to simply treat *GM* as a part of *BGE*, as Laurence Lampert does (Lampert 2001), which would make *BGE* the book to which Nietzsche referred a young American journalist as his most "far-reaching and important."[2]

[1] *Twilight of the Idols* may be almost as comprehensive, but it reads like a summary and simplified statement, its relationship to *BGE* analogous to that of Kant's *Prolegomena* to the first *Critique* or Hume's *Enquiries* to the *Treatise*. Nietzsche himself enthused over *Thus Spoke Zarathustra*, declaring that it "stands alone" not only in his own body of work but in the history of philosophy (*EH*: "Thus Spoke Zarathustra" 6). Yet he also said that *BGE* "says the same things as *Thus Spoke Zarathustra*, but differently, very differently" (letter to Burckhardt, September 2, 1886), the difference presumably being that *Z* says it poetically, whereas *BGE* says it philosophically, or at least much more philosophically than *Z* does. And if two books say the same thing but one of them says it more philosophically, that one should surely be considered the more important work of philosophy, which is our concern here.

[2] Nietzsche's actual claim was that *GM* and *BGE* counted as his "most far-reaching and important" books. This was in 1887, before he wrote his last five books. But none of these matches *BGE* as a candidate for Nietzsche's *Hauptwerk*, as we argue specifically about *Twilight* in the note above.

1 Problems for Interpreting *BGE*

BGE is such a complex work that it leaves us with far too many interpretative puzzles and controversies to even mention in an article of this length. Here we will focus on two problems concerning how to read the book as a whole. For whether or not it includes *GM*, there are two major problems facing those who accept the judgment articulated above concerning *BGE*'s importance, especially if they also judge Nietzsche to be an important philosopher. The first concerns its form. The book itself (i.e., apart from *GM*) contains nine major parts (plus a preface and concluding poem), each of which has a title and is subdivided into consecutively numbered sections or "aphorisms" (the traditional term), which vary in length from a sentence to a few pages. The problem is that little seems to hold these elements together. Rolf-Peter Horstmann's description of the book captures the impression *BGE* often makes on readers: "*Beyond Good and Evil*... looks like a collection of impromptu remarks... numbered and loosely organized into topic-related groups.... The impression is of an apparently arbitrary compilation of notes which are... presented in an artful though idiosyncratic way" (Horstmann 2002: xxii).[3]

No one who takes *Beyond Good and Evil* to be an important work of philosophy can remain content with this view of it. But although Walter Kaufmann warned us years ago against reading *Beyond Good and Evil* as a mere "collection of aphorisms for browsing," it has evidently been difficult to resist the temptation to do so. Interpreters tend to mine the book for whatever they can use for their own purposes, showing little concern with how to read the work as a whole. Alexander Nehamas's striking characterization of the book as a work of "dazzling obscurity" is meant to suggest an explanation: *BGE*'s memorable lines— e.g., "Christianity is Platonism for the people"—dazzle us with their brilliance, blinding us to the less striking surrounding material, hence to issues concerning how the book is organized and how its sections are interconnected. The upshot, according to Nehamas, is that "we still do not know how to read the book. We simply do not understand its structure, its narrative line. Indeed we do not even know whether it has a narrative line at all" (Nehamas 1988: 46). We deny below that his own interpretation of *BGE* rectifies this situation.

But there is a second problem as well, this time concerning *BGE*'s content, much of which seems both too crude and too badly supported to count as good philosophy. This includes, for instance, its derogatory comments about women (*BGE* 231–9), the English in general (*BGE* 252), and Darwin, Mill, and Spencer in particular (*BGE* 253). One might be inclined to dismiss these as peripheral to *BGE*'s main concern, especially if it were clearer what that concern is, but this is not possible in the case of its equally harsh criticism of democracy,

---

[3] Note that *BGE*'s title doesn't really tell us what it is about and its chapter titles often do not tell us what they are about either. In this sense, *BGE* differs substantially from Nietzsche's other nine-part work, *Human, All Too Human*. There the title does tell us what the book is about—as Nietzsche put it later: "where you see ideal things, I see what is human, alas, all too human" (*EH*: "Human, All Too Human"). And the titles of its parts inform us as to that part's subject matter. So the second part of *HAH* is about the moral sentiments, just as its title suggests. But *BGE*'s second part, "The Free Spirit," is not about free spirits. If the title is appropriate, it must be because it is addressed to free spirits. But this doesn't help give us a sense of its unity.

which runs throughout the book. Of course, one might sympathize with the criticism, but the sympathy is difficult to sustain when one recognizes that the critique is connected to a dream of philosophers who will "create" or "legislate" values (*BGE* 213), a denigration of ordinary human beings, who are said to exist and to be allowed to exist only for service and the general utility (*BGE* 61), and a criticism of religions for preserving too many of those who should perish (*BGE* 62). If similar-sounding points can be found in other writings Nietzsche published, it is almost always in much milder form.[4]

This is also true of *BGE*'s apparent assault on truth, which begins in *BGE*'s preface and continues at least throughout Part One and into Part Two. In no other published work do we find such strong denials of both the possibility of attaining truth and the value of doing so. But this seems to be the stuff of freshman relativism. Although it may now be accepted as obvious by postmodernists throughout the academy (though not as true, of course, once this concern is pushed), philosophers typically reject such postmodernist skepticism about truth, judging the arguments taken to ground it to be both wrongheaded and superficial. Clark (1990) claims that Nietzsche himself came to share this judgment, that he was the first to see through the postmodernist position on truth after having proclaimed it himself, but only in *GM*, written the year after *BGE*. That it seems marred by continuing commitment to a problematic and superficial position on truth that he overcame in later works adds to the difficulty of counting *BGE* as Nietzsche's most important work, much less as the work of an important philosopher.

2 Proposed Solutions

One therefore comes to *BGE* with the reasonable expectation that it is Nietzsche's most important work, only to find what appears to be a loosely connected set of thoughts, many of which range from the puerile to the nonsensical. What are the defenders of the book's status to do? One option is to accept the book's apparent features as its actual ones, but to argue that Nietzsche is putting them to an important philosophical *use*. This is the strategy taken most influentially by Alexander Nehamas and more recently by Rolf-Peter Horstmann. Nehamas and Horstmann both explain the form of *BGE* and at least some of its problematic content in terms of its helpfulness for communicating a philosophical position that cannot be presented effectively using more traditional philosophical resources, Nietzsche's notorious perspectivism. It has been interpreted in various ways, but the interpretation shared by these commentators is that truths are always "partial": claims can be true only *from* a particular perspective. Perspectivism consists not in a denial that one's beliefs are true, according to Nehamas, "but only in the view that one's beliefs are not, and need not be, true for everyone" (Nehamas 1985: 33). However, as Nehamas claims, this is a difficult position to defend.

---

[4] Likewise, the cutting comments about women that can be found in Nietzsche's other books (although, like the notorious comment about the whip, often not in Nietzsche's own voice) are no match for *BGE*'s extreme statement that a man of depth and benevolence "must think of woman as *Orientals* do: he must think of woman as a possession, as property that can be locked, as something predestined for service and achieving her perfection in that" (*BGE* 238).

The problem is that "simply by virtue of being offered," any view "is inevitably offered in the conviction that it is true. But then, despite any assurances to the contrary, it is presented as a view which everyone must accept on account of its being true." Nehamas concludes from this that "every effort to present a view, no matter how explicitly its interpretive nature is admitted, makes an inescapable dogmatic commitment," by which he means a commitment to the truth of the view "full stop" (Nehamas 1985: 131). Accordingly, Nietzsche must count as a dogmatist or anti-perspectivist anyone who puts forward a claim as true, or even puts forward the claim itself. But how can Nietzsche take a stand in favor of perspectivism and against dogmatism without turning his own position into a dogmatic one? Nehamas sees in *BGE* an "unprecedented solution" to this problem, for which traditional philosophical means—the presentation of views and argument—are unsuitable. If one tries to avoid dogmatism by simply *saying* "but this is only an interpretation," readers are likely to disregard either the view (since you have implied that you can give no reason for others to accept it) or the qualification (if they are independently attracted to it). Either way, one fails to communicate the perspectival (or interpretive, as Nehamas uses these terms) nature of the views one is putting forward. The alternative is to largely avoid "describing, supporting, and articulating" one's views and to exemplify them instead. According to Nehamas, this is the "main reason why *BGE*, like so many of Nietzsche's works, is so short on argument." Nietzsche embodies his views and attitudes towards life in the work itself (in the narrator he forces the reader to postulate), thereby offering them "for his audience's inspection," and "commending them, of course, simply in virtue of having chosen to offer them" (Nehamas 1988: 63). However, by not arguing for them, he avoids implying that they are to be accepted by everyone. And *BGE*'s apparent lack of organization is simply an absence of the strict logical connections between claims and ideas that we find in more traditional works of philosophy. But there are connections, Nehamas claims, precisely of the kind one finds in a good conversation, where one topic gives way to another not because it is logically connected but because of a looser kind of connection that reminds one of the participants of it. *BGE*'s form is therefore that of a monologue, which is perfectly suited to what Nehamas takes to be Nietzsche's project in *BGE*: that of presenting us with a person, a philosophical character, whose views he himself merely presents for our examination but for which he does not argue.

This is an ingenious reading but in the end it cannot claim to be a very plausible one. It attempts to salvage *BGE*'s status by putting it in the service of a philosophical position; but the position itself is a problematic one. It just isn't clear what sense can be given to the notion of a "partial truth," of a claim's being "true from a perspective." If this view immediately leads one into paradoxes of self-reference, as Nehamas admits, it isn't clear what reason Nietzsche would have had to accept it. And, in fact, Nietzsche actually never says that truth is perspectival, but only that knowledge is (e.g., *GM* III: 12).[5] At the very least, one wonders whether there is an alternative account of *BGE*'s philosophical importance. Laurence Lampert has supplied such an account. Whereas Horstmann and Nehamas see in *BGE* a repudiation of the task and methods of traditional philosophy, Lampert thinks that *BGE* aims to show that philosophy in this sense "is desirable and possible," hence "that there are plausible grounds for the mind's assent to a particular interpretation of the whole of things

---

[5] See Leiter 1994 and Clark 1998a for accounts of perspectivism as a claim about knowledge rather than as a claim about truth.

and plausible grounds for the mind's embrace of that interpretation as a teaching to live by" (Lampert 2001: 2). The book as a whole is "a coherent argument that never lets up: what is discovered about philosophy and religion, about what can be known and what might be believed, necessarily assigns to the philosopher a monumental task or responsibility with respect to morals and politics" (Lampert 2001: 7).

Now, Lampert admits that one cannot read this "coherent argument" off of *BGE*'s surface: to the uninitiated reader, the book seems characterized by disunity, even randomness, and lack of argument.[6] He explains the gulf between this appearance and the reality of Nietzsche's text by claiming that *BGE* is written in view of the distinction between the "exoteric and the esoteric," which *BGE* itself tells us was recognized by philosophers, "among Indians as among Greeks, Persians and Moslems, in short wherever one believed in an order of rank and *not* in equality and equal rights" (*BGE* 30). The view of the text as random and disorganized is the exoteric view, which Nietzsche writes so as to encourage. This is because "given the sway of the irrational, making a place for the rational in the midst of the irrational requires strategic finesse: it is a task for an artful writer who knows his audience and knows how to appeal to them" (Lampert 2001: 1). The text as viewed exoterically, Lampert thus implies, is one that will initially appeal to Nietzsche's readers. The text that is a "coherent argument that never lets up," on the other hand, is the text as viewed esoterically, the text that readers can begin to appreciate only once they have begun to be educated by *BGE* itself.

In the remainder of this essay, and even more so in Clark and Dudrick 2012, we offer support for Lampert's *general approach* to interpreting *BGE*. In particular, we provide evidence that *BGE* is deliberately written in view of the distinction between the exoteric and the esoteric, and the beginnings of a case for the claim that the problems we have discussed concerning the form and the content of *BGE* can be solved by recognizing that the problematic material belongs only to the text as exoterically interpreted and not to the esoteric text that appears as we begin to follow Nietzsche's plea to "learn to read [him] well" (*D* Preface 5). But we do not argue for this approach in the way that Lampert does, and our claims about the *content* of *BGE*'s esoteric text differ significantly from his.

Although mentioned by Nietzsche, esotericism has become part of contemporary intellectual culture by way of Leo Strauss and his followers. The main source of the differences between our approach to *BGE* and Lampert's is that the esotericism we find in Nietzsche has little in common with the Straussian variety and was not discovered under Strauss's influence (or Lampert's for that matter). More importantly, it does not share with the approach we associate with followers of Strauss two related features that make it seem objectionable, namely, that their approach seems designed to appeal to an "in-crowd" of those "in the know" at the expense of public disclosure of grounds for interpreting texts as they do, and that their attitude toward contemporary analytic (Anglo-American) philosophy, including its work in the history of philosophy, borders on contempt. In contrast, we offer no special

---

[6] Two of Nietzsche's letters suggest to Lampert that this cannot be the end of the story. One, to Georg Brandes (January 18, 1888), comments on readers' failure to recognize that "they are dealing [in Nietzsche's works] with a long logic of a completely determinate philosophical sensibility and *not* with some mishmash of a hundred varied paradoxes and heterodoxies": a second, to Jacob Burckhardt (September 22, 1886), tells us that *BGE* "says the same things as *Thus Spoke Zarathustra* but differently, very differently." It seems clear that no mere collection of aphorisms could express "a long logic of a completely determinate sensibility" or say differently what is said by the unified narrative of *Zarathustra*.

"method" or manual for cracking Nietzsche's "code." As far as we can tell, there is no such code, and the only "method" that we recommend—and attempt to practice—for appreciating the "esoteric Nietzsche" is that of trying to make the best sense of what he actually says in the most rigorous way. And we find analytic philosophers scorned by Straussians and modern philosophers ignored by them (especially Hume and Kant) particularly helpful for doing so.

Despite these differences, we agree with Lampert, as we have indicated, that it is necessary to distinguish an exoteric from an esoteric level on which *BGE* is written and can be read in order to read it well. We deny that the form and unity of the work, and therefore its philosophical content—much less its status as Nietzsche's masterpiece and a work of great philosophical depth—can be adequately appreciated without recognizing that its surface meaning differs substantially from what Nietzsche really believes, and that the latter is simply not accessible to most readers—perhaps any reader—without significant overcoming of their initial impressions.

In particular, we contend that the book is written so as to make it natural and very plausible to read it in a way we might characterize as crudely naturalistic, that is, in a way that supports naturalist and empiricist trends in philosophy at the expense of more traditional philosophical concerns, especially normative ones. This crudely naturalistic reading is the exoteric reading. The esoteric reading we defend in Clark and Dudrick 2012 grants that Nietzsche is a naturalist in an important sense, but insists that he does not turn his back on the normative aspirations of traditional philosophy, but attempts to satisfy them. In particular, contrary to the most powerful reading of Nietzsche as a naturalist in the literature (that of Brian Leiter), he does not claim that philosophy should follow the methods of the sciences. There is a long story about this that our book is designed to tell. Here we attempt to give some sense of that story by looking in some detail at two portions of *BGE*: its preface and aphorisms 3 and 4.

3 THE PREFACE

That *BGE* is much more like a philosophical treatise than it appears to be, contrary to Horstmann and Nehamas, and much more admiring of Kant than Lampert acknowledges, is suggested by the striking similarity between its preface and that of Kant's *Critique of Pure Reason*, almost certainly the greatest philosophical treatise in Nietzsche's native language. Although Nietzsche's preface certainly differs greatly from Kant's stylistically, its content is very similar. Each preface provides us with a story of the history of philosophy, these stories are quite similar, and each situates its author's own work as the culmination of that story.

Nietzsche's preface begins infamously: "Supposing that truth is a female—what?" The dash followed by the "what?" suggests that Nietzsche's supposition is intended to startle or jar.[7] As Burnham (2007: 2) rightly suggests, it is equivalent to a "double-take": Nietzsche portrays himself as startled by what he has just said. Unfortunately, many readers seem so startled by

---

[7] By omitting the dash and translating "*wie*" (a typical expression of surprise or puzzlement) as "what then?" Kaufmann's translation suppresses this suggestion and makes the line read much more smoothly, so that Nietzsche is asking us to consider the logical consequences of supposing truth to be, as Kaufmann translates it, "a woman." The latter translation choice helps to suppress the aspect of the line that would make it surprising or puzzling to readers, for the two words Kaufmann translates as "woman" in the passage, first "*Weib*" and little later "*Frauenzimmer*" (which Hollingdale translates as "wench"), are at the very least less respectful terms than the usual term for "woman" (*die Frau*). His translation therefore

it that they begin free-associating about women and/or truth and find it difficult to follow out the logic of the passage. Supposing truth to be a female has nothing to do with females and very little to do with truth. Although he pretends to be startled by the thought that truth is a female—perhaps because it seems to knock truth from her lofty perch—Nietzsche's concern here is what follows from this supposition about dogmatic philosophers, namely, that they are inept and inexpert when it comes to females. After several lines of mocking them on the grounds that the "gruesome seriousness and clumsy obtrusiveness with which they have tended to approach truth so far have been inept and inapt means for capturing a female," Nietzsche puts his point more literally:

> What is certain is that she has not allowed herself to be captured—and today every kind of dogmatism is left standing dispirited and discouraged. If it is left standing at all. For there are scoffers who claim that it has fallen, that all dogmatism lies on the ground, even more, that dogmatism is in its last throes. (*BGE* Preface)

We propose that Nietzsche is here using "dogmatism" in the Kantian sense, roughly, as a synonym for a commitment to metaphysics in the pre-Kantian sense.[8] It is then plausible to interpret the first theme of Nietzsche's preface as a familiar one concerning the failure and debased situation of metaphysics, a theme that was not new when Kant stated it almost a century earlier with a related (though belabored) set of metaphors.

Kant begins his preface to the first edition of the first *Critique* by characterizing metaphysics as the "battlefield of [the] endless controversies" to which reason is led because it is "burdened with questions which it cannot dismiss, since they are given to it as problems by the very nature of reason itself, but which it also cannot answer, since they transcend every power of human reason." This is followed by a (for Kant) poetic description of the hard times on which metaphysics has fallen: this "queen of the sciences," now "outcast and forsaken," "mourns like Hecuba" having fallen into a "worm-eaten dogmatism" (A viii–x). Although Kant makes metaphysics the woman, whereas Nietzsche's woman is the truth

---

tends to prettify the line, encouraging readers to think of it in more romantic terms than it warrants. Yes, it obviously suggests something erotic, and perhaps it foreshadows the complex and subtle eroticism with which Nietzsche aims to endow philosophy in this book. At this point, and in itself, however, the line is more crude than erotic.

[8] As we saw above, Nehamas assumes that Nietzsche means something very different by dogmatism than Kant did. For Nehamas, one is a dogmatist in virtue of one's commitment to the possibility of one's beliefs being true "full stop." For Kant, one is a dogmatist in virtue of one's uncritical assumption that substantive (synthetic) truth about the world can be gained using a priori methods. Kant himself thought a non-dogmatic or critical metaphysics was possible, but at least one of Nietzsche's contemporaries, who considered himself a neo-Kantian and had considerable influence on Nietzsche, did not. This is Afrikan Spir, and it seems likely that Nietzsche followed him on this point, as well as in his use of "dogmatisim." Nietzsche was influenced by Spir to embrace the falsification thesis in his early work, and it is clear from his notebooks that he was rereading and taking notes on Spir's *Denken und Wirklichkeit* while he was writing *Beyond Good and Evil* (Green 2002; Clark 2005). Here are the opening lines of Spir's two-volume work: "Since Kant the distinction between the dogmatic and the critical bent in philosophy has become familiar to all. The dogmatist wants to make decisions about the objects of cognition without first investigating the faculty of cognition itself and establishing its nature, laws, and limits. In contrast critical philosophy makes this latter investigation into the first and primary problem. One must of course observe that dogmatism is actually met with only in those doctrines that attempt to go beyond the limits of experience.... There is dogmatism only in metaphysics (Spir 1867: vol. I, p. 1).

metaphysics seeks, this really amounts to the same thing, in that metaphysics is a body of (purported) metaphysical truths.[9] In any case, when he rewrote the preface for the second edition, Kant largely discarded the metaphors and put his point directly: both logic and, much more recently, natural science have been "brought to the secure course of a science after groping about for many centuries" (B xii–xiv). In particular, natural science, "insofar as it is grounded on empirical principles," now carries with it the sense that it is on the right track, that progress has been and will continue to be made, and that its methods can be relied on for gaining knowledge of nature. Or, as Nietzsche puts the same point in *BGE* 204, "science is flourishing today and has its good conscience written all over its face." Metaphysics in contrast, Kant continues, has so far been unable "to enter upon the secure course of a science."[10]

Once we recognize that Nietzsche is using "dogmatism" as Kant did, the first theme of *BGE*'s preface emerges as simply a more brilliantly stated version of Kant's theme concerning the current situation of philosophy, namely, that its original hopes have gone unfulfilled because metaphysics, which aimed to fulfill these hopes, has been an abysmal failure, showing no signs of realizing its claim of attaining truth. The history of philosophy, for both philosophers, is the story of the conflict between dogmatism, with its commitment to a priori knowledge of reality, and empiricism, which denies that we have any such knowledge. And the other main themes of Nietzsche's preface can be seen as at least structurally similar to Kant's. Like Kant, Nietzsche will offer a diagnosis of metaphysics' failure and situate his own philosophy as the fulfillment of its original promise, hence as the hope for the future of philosophy. That is, the preface to *BGE* shows that, like Kant, Nietzsche stakes the future of philosophy on a diagnosis of dogmatism's failure, taking the right diagnosis of this failure as the key to recognizing how his own philosophy can fulfill philosophy's original hope. This is not to say that Nietzsche agrees with Kant's diagnosis. Kant considers the dogmatist's arguments a necessary, if necessarily unsuccessful, attempt to answer questions that arise from the nature of reason itself, until a critique of pure reason is undertaken and "the point at which reason has misunderstood itself" is discovered (A xi–xii). Nietzsche only hints at his diagnosis in *BGE*'s preface, but what he says makes perfectly clear that he rejects Kant's. This is implied by his claim concerning just how *little* it took "to furnish the foundation-stone for such sublime and unconditional philosophical edifices as the dogmatists used to build"—a

[9] For more on this, see the end of the following note.

[10] The situation of metaphysics as Kant presents it is similar to the view of philosophy held by the "young natural scientists" Nietzsche cites in *BGE* 204, who see "nothing in philosophy but a series of refuted systems and a wasteful effort that 'does nobody any good.'" And Kant's metaphors for describing this situation in his second-edition preface are in at least one respect now closer to Nietzsche's preface, insofar as his focus is no longer on the queen but on the inept combat among her suitors: "For in it reason continually gets stuck, even when it claims a priori insight (as it pretends) into those laws confirmed by the commonest experience. In metaphysics we have to retrace our path countless times, because we find that it does not lead where we want to go, and it is so far from reaching unanimity in the assertions of its adherents that it is rather a battlefield, and indeed one that appears to be especially determined for testing one's powers in mock combat; on this battlefield no combatant has ever gained the least bit of ground, nor has any been able to base any lasting possession on his victory. Hence there is no doubt that up to now the procedure of metaphysics has been a mere groping, and what is the worst, a groping among mere concepts" (B xiv–xv). Here it seems clear that the combatants are suitors of metaphysical truth, which makes it clear that this is how we should interpret the "Queen" in the earlier passage.

"superstition," "grammatical seduction," or "an audacious generalization on the basis of very narrow, very personal, very human, all too human facts" (*BGE* Preface). In contrast to Kant, then, Nietzsche clearly thinks that dogmatism's systems were based on bad arguments that are not required by the nature of reason itself.[11]

But there is another side to Nietzsche's attitude towards dogmatism. Although he dismisses its arguments in much harsher terms than does Kant, his hope that dogmatic metaphysics was simply an early stage of philosophy is expressed in even stronger terms.

> The dogmatists' philosophy was, let us hope, only a promise across millennia: as astrology was in an earlier age when perhaps more work, money, acuteness, and patience was lavished in its service than for any real science so far: we owe the grand style of architecture in Asia and Egypt to astrology and its "super-terrestrial" claims. (*BGE* Preface; cf. *GS* 300)[12]

Like Kant, Nietzsche suggests that the kind of knowledge desired by dogmatic metaphysics would be of a "superterrestrial" or non-natural kind, in any case, one that is impossible for human beings. But he thinks that just as astrology generated something of real value (i.e., the grand style of architecture in Asia and Egypt), so too may dogmatism. Even though his view of its initial upshot is more negative than Kant's, Nietzsche presents the desire behind dogmatic philosophy in more positive terms than does Kant, as the inspiration for something which has the potential to be great.

The positive or hopeful aspects of the second theme are given further specification as Nietzsche's preface moves into its third major theme, his hopes for the future of philosophy. Now that the error of Platonism "is overcome, now that Europe is breathing freely again after this nightmare and can at least enjoy a healthier—sleep, we *whose task is wakefulness itself*, are the heirs of all that strength which has been fostered by the fight against this error." There is much to figure out about this: who "we" are, what our "task" is, how and by whom Platonism was fought and overcome, and how to understand the "strength" inherited from this fight. The Preface provides little help with these matters. And then there is the pause, represented by the dash, between "healthier" and "sleep." What is it designed to do? First, the dash suggests that what comes after it is not what we might have expected. We might, for

---

[11] We note, however, that *GM*'s account of the relationship between philosophers and the ascetic ideal allows us to infer that Nietzsche agrees with Kant to the extent that he believes that the future of philosophy depends on philosophers' ability to recognize the "self-misunderstanding of philosophy" under which they have been operating (*GM* III: 10). But this self-misunderstanding has to do with the role of values in philosophy, which is why he calls it "ascetic," not with the nature of reason.

[12] This is a variation on Kant's suggested comparison of dogmatic metaphysics to alchemy. After claiming that he has resolved "to reason's full satisfaction" the questions that led to dogmatic metaphysics, Kant adds that "the answer to these questions has not turned out just as the dogmatically enthusiastic lust for knowledge might have wished; for the latter could not be satisfied except through magical powers in which I am not expert" (A xiii). Kant's formulation can also be compared to an important theme of *Beyond Good and Evil*, which is at best hinted at in its preface: the importance of the personal and "desiring" or lustful aspects of human life and thought, and the impossibility of the highest forms of either life or thought without them. Kant's reference to "lust for knowledge" that could only be satisfied by magical powers suggests that he recognizes the admixture of this "lower" element in dogmatic philosophy and views it as precisely the element that cannot be satisfied by a suitably "disciplined" philosophy—only the impersonal aspect is deserving of esteem and satisfaction. For Kant, philosophers must give up what they originally wanted in order to obtain the satisfaction of which philosophy is capable.

instance, have expected that the fight against dogmatism would make possible a healthier life. This fits with Nietzsche's view of the connection between dogmatism and the ascetic ideal, which we develop in our book. Second, it seems to be a joking reference to Kant's famous claim about Hume awakening him from his "dogmatic slumber," to which Nietzsche alludes more directly in *BGE* 209. Putting the two together, we have the suggestion that it is not enough for philosophy to get over dogmatism; it must overcome both its dogmatism and its *slumber*. What this involves is developed in terms of a new set of metaphors:

> But the fight against Plato or, to speak more clearly and "for the people," the fight against the Christian-ecclesiastical pressure of millennia—for Christianity is Platonism for "the people"—has created in Europe a magnificent tension of the spirit the like of which had never yet existed on earth: with so tense a bow we can now shoot for the most distant goals.

Here Nietzsche presents the task of those "whose task is wakefulness itself" as that of using the tension created by the fight against Platonism. He evidently thinks that the future of philosophy depends on maintaining the tension of the bow until it can be productive (until the arrow can be shot). But what exactly is this "'magnificent tension' of the spirit or bow"? This much is certain: it is the metaphor to which the entirety of the preface has been leading; as such, it is reasonable to suppose that it expresses what Nietzsche regards as a—if not *the*—central idea of *Beyond Good and Evil*.

Nietzsche does not unpack this metaphor for us, but a tense bow must involve two opposing forces. The preface suggests that the tension results from the fight against dogmatism—this fight has cultivated a strength that is one of the forces constituting this tension. We take this force, which is embodied in the anti-metaphysical movements of empiricism and naturalism, to be the will to truth. The other force must be that which animates dogmatism itself: the will that stands behind the tendency, e.g., to make "audacious generalizations on the basis of very narrow, very personal, very human, all too human facts." This is clearly not a will to truth, to see the world as it is. It is rather a will to see the world as one would have it be, to see it in a way that would support one's values. As such, we call this force "the will to value." In our book on *BGE*, we argue in detail for this reading of the two forces.

We will have more to say about Nietzsche's "magnificent tension of the spirit," in our discussion of *BGE* 3 and 4 below, and in Clark and Dudrick 2012. For now, it suffices to say that the preface that philosophy's future depends on the refusal of "we good *Europeans* and free, *very* free spirits" to collapse this tension, and perhaps even on our enhancing it so that it can be productive. This means not allowing the will to value to overwhelm the will to truth (as the "Jesuitism" would have it), nor permitting the will to truth to extinguish the will to value (as is threatened by the "democratic enlightenment"). That the world must be seen in terms of values is evidently among the "eternal demands" that dogmatic philosophy has "inscribed" in the "hearts of humanity."[13]

A reader who is attentive and educated in the history of philosophy will therefore take the preface to *Beyond Good and Evil* to be situating it in familiar philosophical terrain: it sounds the philosophical themes first struck by Kant in his preface to the first *Critique*. These themes concern the past, present, and future of philosophy. The history of philosophy

---

[13] Of course, if dogmatism has inscribed these demands in the human heart, they can be "eternal" only in relation to the future, not the past.

is the story of dogmatism (animated by the will to value) and the struggle against it by those skeptical of its claim to know reality by a priori means (led on by the will to truth). Just as Kant sought to do justice not just to "the starry stars above" but also to the "the moral law within," Nietzsche seeks a philosophy that will satisfy both the will to truth and the will to value. Such a philosophy is "the *target*" which the magnificent tension of the spirit may yet allow us to reach.

Our claim is that the rest of *BGE* follows the lead of the preface. *BGE* Part One provides a variation on Kantian themes by way of careful engagement with traditional philosophical issues and figures with the aim of showing how this target can be reached. As Julian Young writes, *BGE* is "really...two books of unequal size": the first part and the other eight (Young 2010: 411). In our view this makes perfect sense because the first part provides the philosophical or theoretical foundation for the practical philosophy, the claims about ethics, politics, and education, to which the rest of the book is largely devoted. Admittedly, a quick perusal of Part One of *BGE* makes this seem implausible. It seems to launch an attack on traditional philosophy. Its very title, "On the Prejudices of the Philosophers," seems to indicate that philosophers' biases render them incapable of coming to know the truth. And its very first section already appears suspicious of the desire to do so: speaking of the "will to truth," Nietzsche asks, "Granted we want truth: *why not rather* untruth?" (*BGE* 1). The suggestion appears to be that the truth of which philosophers are capable may not have the great value they have supposed.

As we suggested earlier, the key is to recognize that the text admits of two levels of meaning, the exoteric and esoteric—and, in this case, to see that Nietzsche's denigration of truth's value and of the possibility of attaining it belong only to the exoteric text. In what follows, we will give an example of how the esoteric text emerges by providing a close reading of *BGE* 3 and 4.

4   THE FUNCTION OF *BGE* 3 AND 4

BGE 3 opens with the claim that "the greater part of conscious thinking," including philosophical thinking, "must still be *counted* among instinctive activities," denying that " 'being conscious' is in any decisive sense *opposed* to what is instinctive." This opening seems designed to illustrate the thinking of the "new species of philosopher" introduced in *BGE* 2, philosophers who question the "faith in oppositions of values." This should alert us to the fact that, as Nehamas brings out, Nietzsche's writing often functions not merely to say something but also thereby to illustrate something else. We will argue that we are meant to put this lesson to use in interpreting *BGE* 3 and 4, that these two aphorisms illustrate something more than the thinking of new philosophers, namely, the magnificent tension of the spirit, from which that thinking will emerge.

Another important aspect of the opening of *BGE* 3 is Nietzsche's claim to have discovered the connection between philosophical thinking and instincts by "looking at philosophers long enough between the lines and at the fingers." This is a rather strange phrase, especially its ending, and we can presume that Nietzsche wanted to call the idea here to the attention of (careful) readers. This idea is presumably that he has arrived at the view in question by considering what is between the lines of philosophical writing and the source of this writing (the fingers, by extension, the philosopher). The suggestion is that in trying to understand philosophical writing, one should attempt to decipher not just what is said, but what is left unsaid, and what is going on with the philosopher *behind* the writing (this is illustrated in Nietzsche's own claims about philosophers in *BGE* 5–6). We regard this as a clue concerning how to read *BGE* in general, but especially aphorisms 3 and 4: one must read between the lines and try to decipher not just the strategy embodied in the writing (which all good reading requires) but also the strategy behind the writing.

We are in fact in need of such instruction in regard to these two aphorisms because they are among the most difficult in *BGE* to interpret. Their meaning is often unclear, and where it seems clear, it is difficult to see how Nietzsche's claims have minimal plausibility. Despite these difficulties, these are among the most frequently quoted passages from *BGE*. This is because they seem to provide clear evidence that Nietzsche denies both the possibly of gaining truth and the value of doing so. We will argue against so interpreting them by taking seriously Nietzsche's suggestion that we should read between the lines and figure out the strategy behind what he says. We will also be helped in this by taking seriously the suggestion that the purpose of what he says is sometimes to illustrate something he does not say. As we have indicated, we will argue that the main point of *BGE* 3 and 4 is to illustrate the magnificent tension of the spirit. This tension is found precisely in the falsification thesis that is present in Nietzsche's early work (Clark 1990: chapters 3 and 4). Nietzsche is trying to show us something that he does not say: that his early philosophy is the expression of a tension between the will to truth and the will to value. And once we see that, we can also catch a glimpse of the philosophy that is the target of the bow's arrow, a philosophical position beyond good and evil that has already emerged from that tension.

5 The Puzzles of *BGE* 3 and 4

We have a basis for reading between the lines of Nietzsche's text only if doing so is necessary to get clear on what he is actually saying and doing in it. So we begin by laying out puzzles for understanding *BGE* 4, which certainly seems to endorse the falsification thesis, that all of our purported truths are actually false. Claiming that even the judgments that we would normally regard as the most certain are actually false, it presents its author (and his peers, apparently) as "fundamentally inclined to claim that the falsest judgments (which include the synthetic judgments a priori) are the most indispensable for us." It then elaborates on this claim as follows: "without accepting the fictions of logic, without measuring reality against the purely invented world of the unconditional and self-identical, without a continual falsification of the world by means of numbers, mankind could not live" (*BGE* 4). So Nietzsche is apparently inclined to believe that judgments of logic and mathematics ("applied logic," according to *TI*: " 'Reason' in Philosophy" 3) are not only false, but more false than other false judgments. It is difficult to know what to make of this. By what standard could logic or mathematics be taken to falsify reality? If Nietzsche were simply denying that propositions of logic and math are true, one might take him to be treating them as "framework" principles that are neither true nor false. But he says that they are false. And, second, how are we to understand his claim that these are not only false, but *more false* than other judgments?

Now it may seem that we gain relief at least from the first of these problems if we consider *BGE* 4's opening claim that "the falsity of a judgment is to us not necessarily an objection to a judgment" (*BGE* 4). Evidently, when Nietzsche suggests that logic, mathematics, and other such "indispensable" judgments are false, he is not objecting to them. But then what *is* the point of calling them false? As the term functions in ordinary discourse, to call a judgment "false" is certainly to object to it as a candidate for belief or acceptance, and it is not clear in what other regard Nietzsche might be considering judgments here. This is undoubtedly why he goes on to suggest that his claim will sound "strange." Indeed, it seems ripe for parody: " 'Your judgment is false.' 'Yes, I know. What's your point?' " It is therefore difficult to disagree with Charles Larmore's reaction to Nietzsche's claim:

> This way of speaking is not simply strange and disconcerting. It is incoherent. The falsity of a judgment is so conclusive a mark against it that we cannot decide to endorse it nonetheless except by talking ourselves into regarding it as true. (Larmore 2008: 232)

It is problematic enough, as G. E. Moore made clear, to assert a proposition while claiming not to know if it is true (Moore 1942: 541). But if a person insists that a proposition is false and yet claims to believe it, that person is either lying or utterly confused. So Nietzsche's claim that falsity is not an objection is quite puzzling.

Interpreters who do not find it puzzling seem to think it follows from Nietzsche's critique of the unconditional will to truth in *GM* III. Brian Leiter implies that falsity is an objection only for those who have not overcome the belief in the absolute value of truth, which Nietzsche attacks in *GM* III (Leiter 2002: 159). Leiter takes *BGE* 4 to claim that "we ought to believe errors and falsehoods when they are necessary for our flourishing" (160), a claim he thinks follows from the denial of the absolute value of truth. But if this is Nietzsche's position, it is deeply problematic. The "ought" Leiter thinks Nietzsche recommends to us is not one on which we can act. This is because, as David Velleman argues, we do not even count as believing a proposition unless our acceptance of it has as its aim "getting the truth right with regard to that proposition." If our acceptance of a proposition lacks that aim, it can count as supposing that it is true (e.g., for the sake of argument), or entertaining it, or imagining or fantasizing that it is true, but it cannot be a matter of believing it (Velleman 2000: 184).

Yet, this in no way conflicts with Nietzsche's challenge to the unconditional will to truth which involves the belief in the absolute value of truth. At the first-order level, one must show a concern for truth, aiming to get the truth of one's belief right, as a condition of believing it at all. But, as Velleman makes clear, I can have "further, second-order goals with respect to this attempt" to get it right. I undertake a second-order attempt "to manipulate the outcome of a first-order attempt to accept what's true... when I try to get myself to hold a particular belief irrespective of its truth" (Velleman 2000: 185). It's at this second-order level that we locate Nietzsche's will to truth. It is a commitment to overcome the influence on belief of all of those factors that induce us to accept beliefs irrespective of what we have reason to believe. And one of those factors is clearly the will to value. Nietzsche's challenge to the unconditional will to truth in *GM* III is that the project of overcoming distorting influences on the attempt to form true beliefs can only be carried out in the name of some value. If that value is truth, then he takes the will to truth to be an expression of the ascetic ideal. We cannot go into this complicated issue here (see Clark 1990: 180–203). Our point is simply that Nietzsche's attack on the absolute value of truth is a very different matter from his claim in *BGE* 4 that falsity is not an objection to a judgment. For someone who does not consider falsity an objection to a judgment is not in a position to believe anything and therefore to think at all. If Nietzsche's basis for this opening claiming of *BGE* 4 is his critique of the absolute value of truth in *GM* III, then, he has conflated the two different levels on which truth can be our aim, which is basically Larmore's critique of him. We are not willing to concede this, however, until we see if there is some other way to understand what Nietzsche is saying and doing in *BGE* 4.

Another puzzling feature of this passage is that Nietzsche claims to be speaking a "new language," adding to his claim that falsity is not an objection "it is here that our new language perhaps sounds strangest." The problem is that he doesn't *seem* to be speaking a "new language" here. To speak a new language is to speak a different language than one spoke previously, and that would require, at a minimum, a different vocabulary and/or set of grammatical rules. Yet, to all appearances Nietzsche is continuing to speak ordinary German here. Readers unbothered by this must be assuming that he is simply referring to the new and unusual claims of his philosophy. But we have no reason just to *assume* that Nietzsche uses "language" as a synonym for "belief" or "claim." Surely it is necessary first to consider the possibility that he means what he says, that he actually is speaking a *new language* here. This would be the case if his words do not have the meaning they would have if he were speaking standard German, that his use of them in this context gives them a different meaning. In that case, the various claims in *BGE* 4 regarding falsity and its variants might only *appear* to be the problematic and puzzling ones that we have been discussing.

We will offer reason to think that this is actually the case by analyzing Nietzsche's argument in the aphorism that precedes *BGE* 4. Here is the second half of *BGE* 3:

> Behind all logic and its seeming autonomy of movement, too, there stand valuations or, more clearly, physiological demands for the preservation of a certain type of life. For example, that the definite should be worth more than the indefinite, and illusion [*Schein*] worth less than 'truth': such valuations might be, in spite of all their regulative importance for us, mere foreground appraisals, a particular type of *niaiserie*, which may be necessary for the preservation of just such beings as we are.

The argument seems to be this: first, valuations "stand behind"—in the sense that they induce us to accept and therefore explain why we accept—the demands imposed on us by principles of logic—e.g., to accept "q" if one accepts "if 'p,' then 'q'" and "p."[14] Second, the valuations that stand behind logic (because of the principles they induce us to accept)

---

[14] We have taken the "stands behind" relation to be one of *explanation* rather than of *justification*, although Nietzsche's choice of words leaves both options open. If it concerns explanation, Nietzsche's claim is about human psychology and perhaps physiology: human beings generally *do*, as matter of fact, endorse "q" when they endorse "p" and "if p then q," and the fact that they do so has an explanation, which, as the remainder of the passage suggests, is that evolution selected for beings whose thinking was so constrained. If it concerns justification, however, then the claim is about logic itself: human beings *are justified* in endorsing "q" when they endorse "p" and "if p then q" because doing so is demanded by their physiology, which was itself shaped by evolution. Such a position does psychologism one better (or worse): it would be "physiologism." Because to endorse such physiologism would be to take an exceedingly crude position concerning the nature of logical validity, the principle of charity weighs in favor of the explanatory reading. However, when we turn to the esoteric reading below, the argument is just as and probably more plausible if "stands behind" is given the justificatory reading.

are necessary for our preservation. Third, the fact that these valuations are necessary for our preservation does not ensure that they are not mere foreground estimates, a kind of "*niaiserie*." Therefore, (for all we know) these valuations, "their regulative importance for us notwithstanding," might be foreground estimates and a kind of "*niaiserie*." The main problem for understanding this argument concerns the meaning of "*niaiserie*," which in French means "silliness" in a sense close to "naivety." This makes the argument's conclusion puzzling. Whatever else it might be, it is not silly or naive to be guided by valuations that are necessary for our preservation. The best (and perhaps only) way to make sense of this conclusion is to suppose that it is elliptical, that we are to specify the meaning of "*niaiserie*" in terms of its context. In that context, it seems reasonable to take the conclusion of the argument to be that it may be silliness or naivety to take the valuations that stand behind logic to be conducive to truth. And from this it would follow that the principles of logic these valuations induce us to accept might not be true, indeed that they might be false. This not only makes sense of the argument of *BGE* 3, but also of the logic of *BGE* 4. If *BGE* 3 argues that the principles of logic might be false, *BGE* 4 opens by denying that calling them false is an objection to them. In fact, the falsest judgment (which include the synthetic judgments a priori) are "the most indispensable for us," for we "could not live" without "accepting the fictions of logic, without measuring reality against the purely invented world of the unconditional and self-identical, without a constant falsification of the world by means of numbers." Nietzsche thus implies that he is inclined to go further than *BGE* 3, claiming not merely that the principles of logic and mathematics might be false, but that they are false. The claims of *BGE* 4 still retain the puzzling character discussed above, but at least we can see how they are supposed to be related to the argument of *BGE* 3, a connection that would not be clear without a specification of "*niaiserie*" in terms of its context.

6 "MAN" AS THE MEASURE

But we haven't yet considered the crucial sentence of *BGE* 3, the one on which it ends: "Assuming, that is, that it is not just man who is the 'measure of things'…." In other words, *BGE* 3's argument to the conclusion that the principles of logic might be false presupposes the denial of Protagoras' claim that "man is the measure." Nietzsche is obviously urging the reader to consider whether he himself rejects this claim. If he doesn't, then he doesn't endorse *BGE* 3's argument. And since the problematic claim concerning truth not being an objection at the beginning of *BGE* 4 appears to be a way of dealing with the *fallout* from that line of argument, Nietzsche need not endorse *it* either.

The final line of *BGE* 3 is therefore a crucial sentence for understanding both the content and the rhetoric of *BGE* 3 and 4. In order to determine whether Nietzsche accepts Protagoras' dictum, we must clarify his understanding of it. One possibility is that he accepts Plato's interpretation: "that any given thing 'is to me such as it appears to me, and is to you such as it appears to you'" (*Theaetetus* 152a). In that case, it is clear why denying that man is the measure is a necessary assumption of *BGE* 3's apparent challenge to logic. If things simply *are* (to me) as they *appear* (to me), then the fact that principles of logic *appear* to me to be true implies that they are true, at least to me, and no challenge to my judgment can gain traction. Even if these same principles should appear false to you, this would give you no basis for challenging my judgment, but only for holding a different one. So *any* objection or challenge to *any* sincere judgment presupposes that "not just man is the 'measure of things' " in this sense, that how things appear to a person might not be how they actually are. Why, then, would Nietzsche even mention that presupposition here, much less go to the trouble of leading us to wonder whether he accepts it? Because the text seems so obviously designed to pose this question for the careful reader, it seems necessary to look for a different interpretation of Protagoras' dictum, one that gives it more relevance to the particular argument that Nietzsche claims presupposes it.

The obvious alternative to Plato's interpretation of Protagoras' claim, and one that makes it much more relevant to the argument of *BGE* 3, is that the measure of things is not the individual human being, but "man" in the sense of humanity in general, the human community. In that case, the point of *BGE* 3's final line—"supposing, that is, that not just man is the 'measure of things'... "—is that any claim that our most basic principles are or might be false can go through only if we suppose that the human community is not the measure of things. That is, the argument of *BGE* 3, which concludes that the principles of logic might be false, presupposes that there is some outside standard, one that stands above those that are or could come to be employed by human beings, to which these principles must correspond if they are not to falsify reality. The question posed for the reader by *BGE* 3's final line is whether Nietzsche actually accepts the existence and necessity of such a standard. If he does, the final line of *BGE* 3 serves merely to point out an important presupposition of the argument he endorses against logic. But this is not a very satisfying reading of its purpose. For we have to consider why Nietzsche would bother to point out this presupposition and follow it with an ellipsis, a clear indication to readers to continue the thought. A reader who does continue the thought should certainly wonder if Nietzsche actually accepts the presupposition to which he calls our attention. But why would Nietzsche prompt us to wonder if he actually accepts it? No good answer seems available if one believes that Nietzsche does accept it. It would make sense to point out the presupposition and encourage readers to think further about it if Nietzsche elsewhere (preferably in *BGE* itself) gave us some indication of what that outside or higher standard is supposed to be. But the only such standard that makes an appearance in Nietzsche's writing is the thing in itself. In his early writings he assumed that judgments must correspond to the thing in itself in order to be true, and followed African Spir in claiming that "things *are not in themselves* as they are *for us* and that we can only cognize them as they are for us" (Spir 1867: vol. I, p. 315).[15] This is why he followed Spir in accepting the falsification thesis, the thesis that all purported knowledge actually falsifies reality. In *BGE* 16, however, Nietzsche denies the very conceivability of the thing in itself. So he now rejects the only outside or higher standard he ever appealed to as judge of our cognitive practices. We therefore regard the final line of *BGE* 3 as an invitation to recognize that Nietzsche does not in fact deny that man is the measure.

The first reason in favor of doing so is that it gives us a satisfactory answer to why Nietzsche prompts us to consider whether he actually accepts the claim he cites as a presupposition of his own argument. The obvious answer is that he expects good readers to realize

---

[15] This is clearly the position of both "Truth and Lie in the Non-Moral Sense" and *Human, All Too Human* (especially *HAH* I: 9).

that he *doesn't accept it*, and therefore that he does not actually endorse the argument of *BGE* 3. This is the beginning of our esoteric reading of *BGE* 3 and 4. The exoteric reading, which does not require readers to overcome their initial impressions of these passages, is the one we have considered so far. Nietzsche argues that the principles of logic might be false, but then goes further, saying that they are false (along with the principles of mathematics and any other synthetic principles a priori) while at the same time insisting that this is not an objection to them. Our esoteric reading begins from the recognition that Nietzsche denies the presupposition of the argument in *BGE* 3 that the principles of logic might be false. If *BGE* 3 and 4 expresses what Nietzsche actually believes on these issues, we will have to figure out what that is by determining what he is committed to by denying that "not just man is the measure," and reading *BGE* 3 and 4 in the light of it.

The second reason in favor of reading Nietzsche this way is that doing so yields a much more satisfying interpretation of these two aphorisms than does the exoteric approach. As we will argue, it makes more sense of their otherwise puzzling rhetorical features, and it finds in them a much more sophisticated and compelling philosophical position than does the exoteric approach.

7 SOLVING THE PUZZLES OF *BGE* 3 AND 4

The first puzzle solved by our esoteric interpretation concerns why Nietzsche claims to be speaking a "new language" in the opening line of *BGE* 4. In the argument of *BGE* 3 for the conclusion that the principles of logic might be false, Nietzsche writes as if he endorses the argument and therefore its presupposition. And he continues to write this way in *BGE* 4. He writes as if he denies that "man is the measure," whereas he actually does not. But suppose he is not just trying to show us what he would believe if he accepted the presupposition, but is actually using these words to express what he believes. In that case, we cannot understand what he actually believes if we take his words to have the meaning they have in standard German. In this sense, even though his words look and sound like standard German, they are not (more accurately: some of them are not): Nietzsche is actually speaking a "new language," a language that differs from the one he was speaking previously in that some of his words do not have the meaning they would have—they are not being used to express the beliefs they would express—if he were continuing to speak standard German. The "new language" is, of course, only a variation on or dialect of German because many of the words retain their normal German meaning.

A second puzzle solved by the esoteric interpretation is why Nietzsche uses the French word "*niaiserie*" at a crucial spot in the argument of *BGE* 3, and in a way that requires us to fill in its meaning by relying heavily on its context. We suggest that this is because the word is literally in a "new language." It is French and it is the first use of French in *BGE*. We suggest that Nietzsche uses such a word here for two reasons: first, to signal that this is the first word in the "new language" he will soon tell us he is speaking, and second, to give us some indication of what is necessary to understand his new language. The word he chooses here seems designed to indicate that when he speaks in his "new language," we will not be able to discern his meaning simply by relying on dictionary definitions. We will have to decipher his meaning by determining what a word with that conventional meaning actually means in the context in which he is using it.

So what does "*niaiserie*" mean in Nietzsche's "new language"? When we were still interpreting the sentence in which it appears exoterically, we took it to mean (in context) that it was silly or naive to assume that the valuations behind logic were conducive to truth. And this entailed that the principles of logic might be false, a conclusion that Nietzsche takes further in *BGE* 4, claiming that they are false. So interpreted, however, these claims about the valuations that stand behind logic and the principles of logic presuppose that "not just man is the 'measure of things,'" a claim that Nietzsche does not accept. If he did accept that presupposition, he would be endorsing the claim that the principles of logic are or might be false. But because he does not endorse it, we can ascertain the meaning of what he says— i.e., what he stands behind, his commitments on the issues at hand—only by subtracting from the meaning of his claims everything that depends on accepting that "not just man is the measure of things." And when we do this subtracting, the claim that the valuations that stand behind logic might be *niaiserie*, that they might not be conducive to truth, means instead that they might not be conducive to establishing correspondence to an outside standard, a "measure" that is beyond "man." If the valuations that stand behind logic are *niaiserie* in this sense, it follows that they do not establish for the principles of logic a justification in terms of something beyond human purposes, a standard that lies outside of and above what is (in principle) available within human practices. Therefore, to call a principle "false" also has a different meaning in Nietzsche's new language. It means only that it does not correspond to an outside standard, a measure beyond man.

With this understanding of Nietzsche's new language in hand, we can solve other puzzles presented by *BGE* 4, one of which is its problematic denial that "falsity is not an objection to a judgment." Because Nietzsche makes explicit that this denial is written in his new language, we can take his point to be the unproblematic one that it is not an objection to a judgment that it fails to correspond to an outside or higher standard. This would be an objection only if "not just man" is the "measure," if there were some standard that transcends the standards available within human practices to which our judgments must correspond to count as true (in our ordinary language). And this, of course, is what we take Nietzsche to deny.

In further support of our esoteric reading, consider how it helps illuminate the next sentence of *BGE* 4:

> And we are fundamentally inclined to claim that the falsest judgments (which include the synthetic *a priori*) are the most indispensable for us; that without accepting the fictions of logic, without measuring reality against the purely invented world of the unconditional and self-identical, without a constant falsification of the world by means of numbers, man could not live—

If, as we propose, Nietzsche is speaking the "new language" here, then logic involves "fictions" and measures reality against a "purely invented world," and we falsify the world with our use of numbers, only in the sense that logic and math measure the world according to norms that lack any kind of outside justification. Consider, further, in what sense Nietzsche might mean that some judgments (including those of math, logic, and the synthetic a priori) are more false than others, and why he says that these same judgments are the "most indispensable" and ones without which "man could not live"? We suggest that he calls them "more false" (in his new language) because they are our basic norms, the ones that regulate our cognitive practices. Therefore, they are, in a sense, more lacking in outside or higher grounding than other judgments, which have grounding precisely in these higher norms or more basic judgments, judgments that are more central to our cognitive practices. That is why the latter are also "more indispensable" and required for our "life"—without them, there are no cognitive practices and therefore no "life" of the type with which we take Nietzsche to be concerned throughout *BGE* Part One.

The one account of what is meant by "life" offered in *BGE* Part One is the following: "Life [*Leben*]—is that not precisely wanting to be other than this nature [according to which the Stoics claim we should live] is? Is life not estimating, preferring, being unjust, wanting to be different?" (*BGE* 9) We take this to indicate (as we confirm in our book) that the "life" with which Nietzsche is concerned in *BGE* Part One should be understood not in biological terms but in normative ones. This "life" is a form of activity structured and guided by norms. Admittedly, *BGE* 4 might seem to be using "life" in a biological sense when it denies that falsity is an objection to a judgment, claiming that the only question is "to what extent it is life-promoting, life-preserving, species-preserving, even species-cultivating." The biological interpretation of "life" is also suggested by *BGE* 3's claim that the valuations that stand behind logic are "physiological demands for the preservation of a certain type of life," and they therefore might not be truth-conducive but only "precisely what is necessary for the preservation of beings such as us."[16] But we need not interpret it in this way; all of the relevant terms can be understood in a way that coheres with the normative interpretation of "life." "Beings such as us" need not be our *biological* counterparts, those who share merely our species membership, but could be our *normative* counterparts, those who share our form of life. This thought gives rise to the following interpretation: we would not be "beings such as us" if we were not engaged in reason-giving and thinking. Our practices count as reason-giving or thinking only to the extent that they are governed by the principles of logic, and our practices are governed by the principles of logic just to the extent that certain valuations stand behind them. Therefore, we could not be "beings like us" if we were not guided by the valuations that stand behind logic. In that case, Nietzsche's claim is that these valuations preserve not our biological being, but our human nature, our nature as normative beings. What is "life-promoting, life-preserving, species-preserving, even species-cultivating," then, is what promotes, preserves, and cultivates the normative practices that constitute our form of life.

This esoteric reading of Nietzsche's claim gains further support if we consider his examples of the valuations that stand behind logic: "that the definite should be worth more than the indefinite, and illusion [*Schein*] worth less than 'truth.'" That the second of these valuations "stands behind" logic seems obvious when we consider that it amounts to valuing truth over falsity and that logic is a normative system concerning how to preserve truth in inference. If we accept as true "*p*" and "'*p*' implies '*q*,'" then the principles of classical logic tell us that we must accept "*q*"—if we want to preserve truth. Of course, they don't tell us that we *ought* to preserve truth. But to the extent that we follow the principles of logic in our cognitive behavior, the commitment to preserving truth, hence to valuing truth over

---

[16] This sounds as if principles of logic were instilled in us by evolution, by the contribution they made to our ancestors' survival, which is what Nietzsche believed in his early works (e.g., *HAH* I: 18). In what follows, we argue in effect that this is no longer his view in *BGE*.

falsity, stands behind the principles that are embodied in that behavior. This suggests that Nietzsche fully recognized what Larmore believes he "fails to realize," that "thinking is in itself a norm-governed activity" (Larmore 2008: 234), that "the recognition of certain values such as truth [is] so deeply anchored in thought" that it constitutes a condition of its possibility (Larmore 2004: 172).[17] As we have already argued, this is not to say that to be a thinker one must have a will to truth. One can think without meeting the standards necessary to have a will to truth or even to value truth; one must, however, express a valuation of truth in one's inferential practices (cf. Velleman 2000: 184). That is to say that one must not only in general reason in accord with the principles of logic but must also express in one's behavior a recognition of them as justified. One must consider it an objection to a judgment that it is false or has marks that seem indicative of falsity, and to a piece of reasoning that it fails to abide by principles of logic.

Nietzsche's other example, that the definite is more important than the indefinite, is plausibly seen as the value that lies behind a particular logical principle, the law of bivalence, according to which every statement must be either true or false, and there is no other truth value. Some have claimed that Nietzsche denies bivalence (Hales and Welshon 2000: 51–2), but we need not take him to be doing so, at least not in this passage. Here he is simply pointing out that to the extent that we operate according to the law of bivalence, we are in effect taking it to be important to have definite (yes or no) answers to our questions. If definiteness were not so important, we would be open to recognizing truth values other than true and false (e.g., indeterminate, or neither true nor false).

But doesn't this suggest that there is a basis for questioning at least some of the valuations that Nietzsche claims stand behind logic? Perhaps. Nietzsche says of these valuations that "such estimates might be, in spite of their regulative importance for us, nevertheless mere foreground appraisals, a particular type of *niaiserie*, which may be necessary for the preservation of just such beings as we are." Because "*niaiserie*" is used in apposition to "mere foreground appraisals," it seems intended to specify or clarify it. If so, Nietzsche would seem to be insisting that regarding the valuation that stands behind bivalence as a "mere foreground appraisal" also implies that there is some outside standard to which our basic principles must conform. And this makes sense if we look at the rest of the sentence. Nietzsche is not just saying that this may be a mere foreground appraisal, but that it might be a foreground appraisal that is necessary for the preservation of beings like us. And this is what brings in the presupposition that there must be a higher standard. For if this valuation is necessary for the preservation of our form of life, thus for thinking itself (in the way in which the principle of non-contradiction is), then only the invocation of a higher standard will make sense of the claim that the principle prompted or justified by this value falsifies reality. But the question, then, is whether the valuing of the definite over the indefinite actually is necessary to preserve thinking. If it is not (and notice that Nietzsche does not say that it is necessary, only that it might be), then it could be a "foreground appraisal" (but probably not a "mere" one), or as Nietzsche puts it in *BGE* 2, a "provisional perspective," in the sense that definiteness

---

[17] We take this over from the original German version of Larmore's essay because he changed this formulation in the English version so that we could not use it without bringing up the somewhat sticky subject of whether the recognition of the value of truth puts us under obligation. Larmore argues that it does, and much of his argument against Nietzsche is based on this. The implication of Velleman's account is that that it does not (e.g., 186).

may well be important from the viewpoint of some particular cognitive interest (say, simplicity), but less important from a more inclusive perspective, one that takes into account other cognitive interests, such as information. The overall point, as Nietzsche makes clear when he begins speaking his "new language," is that the only standard for assessing our most fundamental cognitive principles is precisely how well they satisfy our various cognitive interests. We take this to be the point of Nietzsche's claim that the question in evaluating our most fundamental cognitive standards is how well they preserve and promote "life" in the normative sense: how well they preserve and further the practices that constitute our normative life.

We have not yet explained why Nietzsche calls the valuations that stand behind logic "physiological demands for the preservation of a certain kind of life," which sounds, again, as if being logical contributes to the preservation of our life in the biological sense. To see that we can interpret it instead in a way that aligns with the esoteric interpretation, consider that whether they have been shaped by nature or culture or by a combination of these, the dispositions that constitute our commitment to being logical are "inscribed" in our bodies, to use Foucault's phrase. Logical instincts are habits of response, and habits are necessarily embodied, established in our physiology. If they weren't, they wouldn't be habits, behaviors that we can engage in automatically without consciously directing ourselves to do so. And if the values that stand behind logic were not embodied in our cognitive/linguistic behavior, we wouldn't be thinking but only playing with words.

There is a final puzzle concerning *BGE* 4 that we have not yet mentioned. At the end of the aphorism Nietzsche tells us that "renouncing false judgments would mean renouncing life and a denial of life" and adds: "To recognize untruth as a condition of life: that certainly means resisting customary value feelings in a dangerous fashion; and a philosophy that risks this would by that alone already place itself beyond good and evil." Interpreted exoterically, without taking Nietzsche to be speaking his "new language" here, the claim is that one places one's philosophy "beyond good and evil" simply by recognizing that untruth—false beliefs, deception, and self-deception—is a "condition of life," meaning that it furthers life in the biological sense, and is perhaps even necessary for its preservation. But that's not really plausible, and it is difficult to see how Nietzsche could have thought it was. The problem is not the claim that untruth is a condition of life: it is certainly plausible that untruth often furthers biological life and we can, for the sake of argument, grant the stronger claim that it is a necessary condition of life in this sense. The problem is how simply recognizing *this* would by itself place one's philosophy beyond good and evil. One could, after all, recognize that untruth is a condition of life in this sense and yet still side with truth, condemning life precisely because it requires untruth. And Nietzsche clearly recognized that option in *HAH* I: 34. So it is difficult to see how he could not have recognized that taking untruth (in the normal sense) to be required for biological life would not be enough to place a philosophy beyond good and evil.

Can an esoteric reading of the passage solve this problem? We think it can. The first step is to recognize that Nietzsche is still speaking his new language here. It would be odd if he were not, given that, as we have argued, "false" and its variations are all in the new language in the earlier sentences of this aphorism. Recognizing "untruth as a condition of life" is then a matter of recognizing that there is no higher or outside justification for our "form of life," the normative form that human life takes. This is, of course, the point of what we have taken to be Nietzsche's affirmation of the claim that "man is the measure." And this is simply to say, as Simon Blackburn puts it, that when it comes to normative matters, "we stand on our own feet, and our feet are human feet" (Blackburn 1998: 310). But how would the recognition that we "stand on our own feet" in normative matters place a philosophy beyond good and evil?

We can find at least the beginning of an answer by reflecting on *BGE* 2. There Nietzsche claims that metaphysicians' "faith in the oppositions of values" leads them to "place their seal" on "popular evaluations and value oppositions" that set up distinctions between human beings. They did this precisely by claiming that things of the highest value must originate in some other, higher world, that they cannot be derived from this "transitory, seductive, deceptive, paltry world, from this turmoil of delusion and lust" (*BGE* 2). These metaphysicians thus "placed their seal" on these popular evaluations and value oppositions precisely by offering an ascetic interpretation of them, ones that implied the disvalue of the only world Nietzsche thinks there is, the natural world that human share with other animals. And in this way, distinctions between human beings were turned into what Nietzsche calls "gulfs," ones "across which even an Achilles of free-spiritedness would not be able to leap without shuddering" (*GM* I: 6). But it was precisely in this way that popular evaluations and value oppositions became "moralized," and "good and bad" was transformed into "good and evil." To reject the need for a standard outside of "man" in normative matters, to accept that man is the measure, is to recognize that that the gulf between man and man is not nearly as deep as the metaphysicians have claimed, and in doing so to place oneself beyond good and evil.

8 CONCLUSION

We are now in a position to say why, contrary to appearances, neither the form nor the content of the book need present problems for those who consider *Beyond Good and Evil* to be Nietzsche's masterpiece and a major work of philosophy. In both cases the solution is to recognize the distinction between an exoteric and an esoteric reading of Nietzsche's words. As to form, once we have a grasp of the book at the esoteric level, we can see that it is not a loosely organized set of reflections lacking in argumentation and justification, but a tightly organized argument concerning the nature and history of philosophy, and how best to realize its original aspirations. Of course, we have not been able to present a full case for this claim. But we have presented a detailed account of *BGE* 3 and 4 that shows these sections to be much more complicated and logically ordered than they first appear to be. We saw that, amidst provocative claims about truth, Nietzsche tells us that these claims *are conditional upon* the assumption with which *BGE* 3 ends. We also saw that there is good reason to think that Nietzsche rejects that assumption, casting his attitude toward the claims in *BGE* 3 and 4 in an entirely new light. To see the implications of these matters for understanding what Nietzsche himself endorses in *BGE* 3 and 4 requires no special code, only a sustained attempt to understand the logic of these passages, and a willingness to overcome one's initial impression of them. Those who are not willing to "learn to read [Nietzsche] well" (*D* Preface 5) will attain only a superficial (i.e., exoteric, rather than esoteric) and ultimately flawed interpretation of these passages. And if Nietzsche is engaging in such sophisticated and subtle communication in *BGE* 3 and 4, there is reason to be alert to the possibility that he is doing so throughout the rest of the book. In Clark and Dudrick 2012, we provide a detailed case that this is indeed so, at least in the first part of the book, which as we've said, provides the theoretical foundation for the practical philosophy of the other parts.

As to the content of *BGE*, our reading of the preface shows that Nietzsche is self-consciously locating this work in the philosophical tradition and, especially, in that of Immanuel Kant. While Part One of his book—and *BGE* 3 and 4 in particular—may seem to constitute an attack on both philosophy and truth, we've given reason to think that it is no such thing. Once the form of these passages is properly understood, the content turns out to be a sophisticated piece of metaphilosophy—one that involves a rejection of the philosophical foundationalism that has characterized the tradition. As Gary Gutting defines it, philosophical foundationalism is the view that philosophical knowledge is "required to legitimate the epistemic claims implicit [even] in well-established human practices" (Gutting 2009: 171). Gutting takes it to be "one of the most important recent pieces of philosophical knowledge" that this is not so. According to our interpretation, however, Nietzsche was already on board with this, before Kuhn, Lewis, and Wittgenstein and the other recent thinkers Gutting has in mind. That "not just 'man is the measure'" is precisely the idea that our cognitive practices— or more specifically, the claims to knowledge implicit in them—stand in need of philosophical justification.

When Nietzsche prompts us to recognize that he denies that "not just 'man is the measure,'" he is asking us to see that he no longer accepts the idea that our cognitive practices require justification in terms of a standard that transcends them. ("No longer" because Nietzsche's endorsement of the falsification thesis followed from his acceptance of the need for such justification and his belief that such justification was not forthcoming.) To hold that "man is the measure" is to hold that there is no non-circular, indubitable justification for the claims (e.g., that our senses are generally reliable) that form the basis of our cognitive practices, e.g., that our senses are generally reliable. It is also to hold that this in no way impugns these practices—while we may come to have reason to doubt aspects of these practices or even the practices themselves, and Nietzsche certainly has many criticisms of them to offer, the fact that they have no philosophical foundation is not such a reason. This being so, we should read the rest of the book in such a way that attempts to maximize coherence with this view, keeping in mind that its exoteric may differ from its esoteric meaning. And when we do so, we claim, it turns out that many of Nietzsche's other crude-seeming claims belong only to the exoteric text and give way to a much more philosophically interesting and sophisticated claim at the esoteric level.[18]

When we do this, we also find *BGE* not just to be informed by the history of philosophy, but also to express subtle and often surprising views on traditional issues. Among these issues are the limits of knowledge, the nature of the soul, and (at least some suggestion as to) how philosophy's traditional aspirations to seek both truth and value—aspirations that constitute what the preface calls "the magnificent tension of the spirit"—may be jointly fulfilled. We find, in sum, that *Beyond Good and Evil* is nothing less than a major work of philosophy and Nietzsche's masterpiece.[19]

---

[18] See, for example, Clark 1994 for an account of Nietzsche's apparent tirade against women in *BGE* that fits our claim here about the operation of the exoteric/esoteric distinction.

[19] Many thanks to John Richardson for very helpful comments on a previous version of this paper.

BIBLIOGRAPHY

(A) Works by Nietzsche

BGE   *Beyond Good and Evil* (1886), trans. R. J. Hollingdale. New York: Penguin, 2003.

Beyond Good and Evil (1886), trans. J. Norman. Cambridge: Cambridge University Press, 2002.

Beyond Good and Evil (1886), trans. W. Kaufmann. New York: Vintage, 1989.

D   *Daybreak: Thoughts on the Prejudices of Morality* (1881), trans. R. J. Hollingdale. Cambridge: Cambridge University Press, 1997.

HAH   *Human, All Too Human* (1878), trans. R. J. Hollingdale. Cambridge: Cambridge University Press, 1996.

Human, All Too Human I (1878), trans. G. Handewerk. Stanford: Stanford University Press, 1997.

GM   *On the Genealogy of Morality* (1887), trans. M. Clark and A. Swenson. Indianapolis: Hackett Publishing Company, 1998.

GS   *The Gay Science* (1882/1887), trans. W. Kaufmann. New York: Vintage Books, 1974.

The Gay Science (1882/1887), trans. J. Nauckoff. Cambridge: Cambridge University Press, 2001.

Z   *Thus Spoke Zarathustra* (1883–5), trans. W. Kaufmann, in *The Portable Nietzsche*, ed. W. Kaufmann. New York: Viking Penguin, 1982, 103–439.

(B) Other Works Cited

Blackburn, S. 1998. *Ruling Passions.* New York: Oxford University Press.

Burnham D. 2007. *Reading Nietzsche: An Analysis of Beyond Good and Evil.* Durham: Acumen Press.

Clark, M. 1990. *Nietzsche on Truth and Philosophy.* New York: Cambridge University Press.

Clark, M. 1998a. "On Knowledge, Truth and Value: Nietzsche's Debt to Schopenhauer and the Development of Empiricism," in Christopher Janaway (ed.), *Willing and Nothingness: Schopenhauer as Nietzsche's Educator.* Oxford: Clarendon Press, 37–78.

Clark, M. 1998b. "Nietzsche's Misogyny," in K. Oliver and M. Pearsall (eds), *Feminist Readings of Friedrich Nietzsche.* State College, Pa.: Pennsylvania State University Press, 187–98.

Clark, M. 2005. "Green and Nietzsche on the Transcendental Tradition," *International Studies in Philosophy* 37.3: 37–60.

Clark, M. and Dudrick, D. 2012. *The Soul of Nietzsche's "Beyond Good and Evil."* Cambridge: Cambridge University Press.

Clark, M. and Leiter, B. 1997. "Introduction," in *Daybreak: Thoughts on the Prejudices of Morality,* trans. R. J. Hollingdale. New York: Cambridge University Press, vii–xxxiv.

Green, M. S. 2002. *Nietzsche and the Transcendental Tradition.* Champaign, Ill.: University of Illinois Press.

Gutting, G. 2009. *What Philosophers Know: Case Studies in Recent Analytic Philosophy.* New York: Cambridge University Press.

Hales, S. and Welshon, R. 2000. *Nietzsche's Perspectivism.* Urbana: University of Illinois Press.

Horstmann, R. P. 2002. "Introduction," in Friedrich Nietzsche, *Beyond Good and Evil,* ed. R. P. Horstmann and J. Norman, trans. J. Norman. New York: Cambridge University Press, vii–xxviii.

Kant, I. 1781/1787/1999. *Critique of Pure Reason,* trans. and ed. P. Guyer and A. Wood. New York: Cambridge University Press.

Kaufmann, W. 1968. *Nietzsche: Philosopher, Psychologist, Antichrist.* New York: Vintage.

Larmore, C. 2004. "Der Wille zur Wahrheit," in O. Hoffe (ed.), *Nietzsche: Zur Genealogie der Moral.* Berlin: Akademie-Verlag, 163–76.

Larmore, C. 2008. *The Autonomy of Morality.* New York: Cambridge University Press.

Lampert, L. 2001. *Nietzsche's Task: An Interpretation of Beyond Good and Evil.* New Haven: Yale University Press.

Leiter, B. 1994. "Perspectivism in Nietzsche's *Genealogy of Morals*," in R. Schacht (ed.), *Nietzsche, Genealogy, Morality: Essays on Nietzsche's "Genealogy of Morals."* Berkeley: University of California Press, 334–57.

Leiter, B. 2002. *Nietzsche on Morality.* New York: Routledge.

Moore, G. E. 1942. "A Reply to My Critics," in P. A. Schilpp (ed.), *The Philosophy of G. E. Moore.* Evanston Ill.: Northwestern University Press, 535–677.

Nehamas, A. 1985. *Nietzsche: Life as Literature.* Cambridge, Mass.: Harvard University Press.

Nehamas, A. 1988. "Who Are 'The Philosophers of the Future'? A Reading of *Beyond Good and Evil*," in R. Solomon and K. Higgins (eds), *Reading Nietzsche.* New York: Oxford University Press, 46–67.

Nehamas, A. 1998. *The Art of Living.* Berkeley: University of California Press.

Schopenhauer, A. 1818/1969. *The World and Will as Representation*, trans. E. F. Payne. New York: Dover.

Spir, A. 1867. *Denken und Wirklichkeit: Versuch einer Erneuerung der kritischen Philosophie* (2 vols), 2nd edn. Leipzig: Förster und Findel. [All translations are Clark's.]

Velleman, J. D. 2000. *The Possibility of Practical Reason.* New York: Oxford.

Young, J. 2005. *Schopenhauer.* New York: Routledge.

Young, J. 2010. *Friedrich Nietzsche: A Philosophical Biography.* Cambridge: Cambridge University Press.

CHAPTER 14

···

NIETZSCHE'S *GENEALOGY*[1]

···

RICHARD SCHACHT

NIETZSCHE's *Zur Genealogie der Moral* (1887) was written at an important juncture in the final three-year period of his productive life between *Thus Spoke Zarathustra* (1883–5) and his collapse (in January 1889). Preceded by *Beyond Good and Evil* (1886), his "Prelude to a Philosophy of the Future" (as it was subtitled), appearing in the same year as the second edition of his *Gay Science* (1887) with its important new fifth part, and with but one (increasingly frantic and fraught) year of productive life remaining to him, we encounter Nietzsche at his philosophical "high noon," all too shortly before night abruptly fell.

The first modern translation of *GM* into English was Francis Golfing's *The Genealogy of Morals* (Doubleday, 1956, with *The Birth of Tragedy*). It was followed by Walter Kaufmann's and R. J. Hollingdale's *On the Genealogy of Morals* (Vintage, 1967, with *Ecce Homo*). Their translation had canonical status for decades, and still is the one most commonly used and cited. It is the version cited in this essay, but has been modified in places. Four new translations have appeared in recent years: Carol Diethe's *On the Genealogy of Morality* (Cambridge University Press, 1994), Douglas Smith's *On the Genealogy of Morals* (Oxford University Press, 1996), Maudemarie Clark's and Alan J. Swensen's *On the Genealogy of Morality* (Hackett, 1998), and Horace Barnett Samuel's *The Genealogy of Morals* (Courier Dover Publications, 2003). A volume of particular interest, in terms of the genesis of *GM* itself, is a translation of Paul Rée's two genealogical-psychological studies of morality that were very much on Nietzsche's mind (as he himself admits in his Preface to *GM*), *Paul Rée: Basic Writings*, edited as well as translated by Robin Small (University of Illinois Press, 2003).

GM has attracted considerable attention in the literature in recent decades, initially in essays, a considerable number of which may be found in my *Nietzsche, Genealogy, Morality* (University of California Press, 1994). Another such collection is *Nietzsche's 'On the Genealogy of Morals': Critical Essays*, edited by Christa Davis Acampora (Rowman and Littlefield, 2006). An essay that has influenced the post-structuralist reading of Nietzsche— and the "genealogy" of post-structuralism itself—is Michel Foucault's 1971 essay "Nietzsche, Genealogy, History," which may be found in translation in a collection of his writings

---

[1] Portions of this essay derive from a more extended discussion of some parts of *GM* in a previous essay of mine, "Nietzsche and Philosophical Anthropology," in Ansell-Pearson 2006.

entitled *Language, Counter-Memory, Practice*, edited by D. F. Bouchard (Cornell University Press, 1977). More recently a number of books on *GM* have appeared: most notably Christopher Janaway's *Beyond Selflessness: Reading Nietzsche's 'Genealogy'* (Oxford, 2007), David Owen's *Nietzsche's 'Genealogy of Morality'* (Acumen, 2007), and Lawrence J. Hatab's *Nietzsche's 'On the Genealogy of Morality': An Introduction* (Cambridge, 2008). Janaway's book is a particularly useful one.

Traditional readings of *GM* tended to focus—sometimes approvingly, sometimes not—on its treatment of morality in startlingly unconventional ways, and on the question of the historical plausibility (or implausibility) of the accounts given. Some subsequent readings have given more attention to the three essays as studies in moral psychology or the philosophical-psychological analysis of moral feelings, attitudes, and dispositions. Others have gone further, taking note of Nietzsche's frequent excursions into human psychological issues more generally and into matters relating to the broader task of the reinterpretation of human reality. On the other hand, a very different sort of reading has seized upon *GM* as a key text in the emergence of a post-structuralist, postmodernist, historicist, and deconstructionist subversion not only of morality but also much else in and about philosophy as we know it, from the concept of "man" (as well as of "God") to the very ideas of truth and knowledge. In what follows these various readings will be put to the test.

I

As will have been noticed, the title of the book has been translated variously. "*Genealogie*" is always translated as "Genealogy"; but "*Moral*" has been translated both as "Morals" and as "Morality." The "*Zur*" can be translated both as "On" and as "Toward," but is sometimes simply ignored. Since the book deals centrally with the "genealogy" of the morality that Nietzsche says is commonly considered to be "morality itself," "*Moral*" is perhaps best translated as "morality" rather than as "morals." However, he is by no means prepared to grant that status to it, having just written a year earlier (in *BGE*) that "Morality in Europe today is herd-animal morality [*Herdentier-Moral*]—in other words, as we understand it, merely one type of human morality [*eine Art von menschlicher Moral*], beside which, before which, and after which many other types, above all higher moralities [*höhere Moralen*], are, or ought to be, possible." (*BGE* 202) It might be best, therefore, to think of the word "morality" in the title as having scare-quotes around it, as a reminder that it is really only that particular "type of human morality" to which the term there refers.

This point is of no little importance, for Nietzsche has just been seen to take it to be the case that other "moralities" are possible, and in fact discusses two of them at length in the book—"master morality" and "slave morality." Both have their own "genealogies," as well as figuring in the "genealogy" of "morality in Europe today"; and neither is identical with it. The kind of morality Nietzsche calls "slave morality" may loom large in the genealogical family tree of what he calls modern-day European "herd morality," but it would be a mistake—and one that is often made—to equate them, as shall be seen. "Slave morality" may be a type of "herd morality," but for Nietzsche there can be "herd moralities" that do not share the particular pathologies he discerns in what he here calls "slave morality," and that have different genealogies.

With respect to the other problematic term in the title ("*Zur*"): since Nietzsche used it—rather than simply entitling the book "*Die Genealogie der Moral*" (as he could have done)—he must have had his reasons for doing so. One such reason may well have been that he considered the book's three "essays" to be contributions to the understanding of the "genealogy" of modern-day morality, but to be nothing like a complete and comprehensive treatise on the subject. "*Zur*" is a contraction of either "*Zu der*" (literally "to the," and to have the sense of "with respect to the") or "*Zu einer*" (literally "[with respect] to a").

Next: if "*Genealogie*" here means the study of the *Genealogie* of (modern-day) morality, then "Toward a Genealogy of [that] Morality" would be the best rendering of the title; while if it refers to that *Genealogie* itself, then "On the Genealogy" of it would be preferable. Since the latter construal would seem to be the more likely, the latter version of the title gets my vote. (In what follows, however, I shall refer to the book neutrally, simply as "Genealogy" or by its standard acronym in both German and English, "*GM*.")

The rendering of "*Genealogie*" as "genealogy" is unproblematic—but what does it mean here? Interestingly, Nietzsche hardly uses the term in connection with morality at all in the book itself (only twice, early on and very casually, in I: 2 and I: 4)—or anywhere else (as far as I know), for that matter. It is rather ironic, therefore, that much is made of it, as though it is a term to which he attaches some very special meaning. In the Preface he uses other quite ordinary terms in its place. In its second section, he uses—with emphasis—one of several words generally translated as "origin": "*Herkunft*." He writes (and says something significant about the relation of the book to his earlier work in doing so): "My ideas on the origin [*Herkunft*] of our moral prejudices [*moralischen Vorurtheile*]—received their first, brief, and provisional expression in the collection of aphorisms that bears the title "Human, All-Too-Human: A Book for Free Spirits." (*GM* Preface 2) And in its fourth section, he uses (without emphasis) another such equally common word generally translated in the same way: "*Ursprung*." There he writes: "The first impulse to publish something [further] of my hypotheses concerning the origin of morality [*den Ursprung der Moral*] ..." (*GM* Preface 4).

It would seem, therefore, that in speaking of the "genealogy" of modern-day morality in the title of the book, he means little (if anything) more than this, and is opting for the more unusual term "*Genealogie*" simply to give the book an intriguing name (as he sought to do in the cases of nearly all of his books). There is, however, one connotation of this term that he may have wanted to exploit here, though he did not attempt to get any further mileage out if it elsewhere. The term is normally used to invoke the idea of the "family tree" of ancestors from whom someone is descended. Nietzsche may have wanted to use the title to suggest to the reader that (modern-day) morality should be thought of similarly—as something human, to the character of which a multiplicity of (human and even all-too-human) ancestors has contributed.

This was not the first time that Nietzsche had given a book with a theme of this sort a title in which a term with similar connotations was used. He gave his very first book the title "The Birth [*Geburt*] of Tragedy"—and while the original edition bore the title extension "Out of the Spirit of Music," the actual burden of the book was that Greek tragic drama (and culture) had two parents, to each of which it owed something important: the two art forms and impulses he called "Apollonian" and "Dionysian." In this instance, the two types of pre-modern morality Nietzsche identifies in his exploration of the "origin" of modern-day morality are those that appear in the first of the three "Essays" of which the book consists: "master morality" and "slave morality." He conceives them to be and have been related to each other quite differently than were the two parents of tragedy; but the similarity is worth noting, as is this evidence of Nietzsche's interest in the "genealogies" or origins of things human from the very outset.

Further evidence of that interest, from a very different quarter, is provided by another of Nietzsche's early writings—in this case the unfinished manuscript (written at about the same time as *BT*) that bears the title "Truth and Lie in an Extramoral [*aussermoralischen*] Sense" (*TL*). In that essay it is "origins" again that are being considered—only in this instance the issue is the very human origin, under primitive and prehistoric conditions, of the ideas of "truth" and "knowledge," and of what they fundamentally (or at any rate primordially) amount to.

Nietzsche was not yet a philosopher when he wrote *BT* and *TL*; but he was on the way to becoming one during his years as a professor of classical philology at Basel University. He made what might be considered his philosophical debut with the publication of the first volume of aphorisms he entitled *Human, All Too Human* in 1878, while still on the faculty there in that capacity. In that book he does indeed (as he freely admits) anticipate at least some of the ideas he developed in *GM*, a decade later—most notably his "master morality and slave morality" concepts and distinction (*HAH* I: 45), and his conjecture with respect to the origin of justice (*HAH* I: 92). But he also had already arrived there at the basic conception of the importance of thinking "historically," or in terms of origins and development, in dealing with a great many matters of philosophical importance—up to and including our human reality itself.

That project—of reinterpreting our human reality and everything human naturalistically and historically—is announced prominently and programmatically at the very beginning of *HAH*. It is closely linked with his interest in the origin of morality in human life in *HAH* (the second part of which bears the heading "On the History of Moral Sentiments [*Zur Geschichte der moralischen Empfindungen*]." (This is a heading to which the title *Zur Genealogie der Moral* is strikingly and significantly similar.) So he writes, in a kind of manifesto for what he subsequently called "the philosophy of the future," and certainly for his own philosophical future:

> Lack of historical sense is the family failing of all philosophers; many...even take the most recent manifestation of man, such as has arisen under the impress of certain religions..., as the fixed form from which one has to start out. They do not want to learn that man has become.... But everything has become.... Consequently what is needed from now on is historical philosophizing, and with it the virtue of modesty. (*HAH* I: 2)

By "historical philosophizing" here Nietzsche clearly has in mind a kind of philosophical thinking that is attuned to the developmental character of human reality and of all things human. So, for example, extending the idea remarked upon above with respect to knowledge in *TL*, he suggests that "the steady and laborious process of inquiry [*Wissenschaft*]...will one day celebrate its greatest triumph in a history of the genesis of thinking [*Entstehungsgeschichte des Denkens*]" (*HAH* I: 16). And it is further notable that in the volume's very first section (immediately preceding this one), he puts more of his cards on the table, lauding "historical philosophy" as a kind of new philosophical thinking that "can no longer be separated from natural science, the youngest of all philosophical methods" (*HAH* I: 1). As he had already intimated in *TL*, human reality is for him a piece of nature through and through, however remarkably it may have developed; and that makes "natural science" highly relevant to its comprehension—even if not sufficient for its full understanding and appreciation. For the Nietzsche of *HAH*—and for the later Nietzsche as well—this is true of all things human, our "moral feelings" included.

This same project, of a "naturalizing" reinterpretation of our humanity, had been articulated four years earlier, in the first (1882) edition of *The Gay Science*, immediately following Nietzsche's proclamation of the death of God (*GS* 108):

> When will all these shadows of God cease to darken our minds? When will we complete our de-deification of nature! When may we begin to *naturalize* humanity in terms of a pure, newly discovered, newly redeemed nature [*uns Menschen mit der reinen, neu gefundenen, neu erlösten Natur zu **vernatürlichen***]! (*GS* 109; Nietzsche's emphasis)

Nietzsche shows that, here again, the kind of reinterpretation of human reality and of things human that he has in mind (and pursues in this book) is to be "historically" as well as naturalistically minded—and attuned to the "all too human" origins and development of human phenomena that are often not thought of as having "developed" at all, let alone in ways reflecting human circumstances, needs, and limitations. So the sections immediately following this one deal with such matters as the "origin [*Ursprung*] of knowledge" (*GS* 110); the "origin [*Herkunft*] of logic" (*GS* 111); the "many things" that had to "come together for scientific thinking to originate [*entstehe*]" (*GS* 113); and what accounts for the development of "very different moralities [*Moralen*]" in different communities (*GS* 116). *GS* is not organized by topic, as *HAH* is; but if it were, the part dealing with moralities and their origins would be one of the larger ones in the book.

When Nietzsche returned to prose publication in *BGE* (after the three-year hiatus in which he published only *Zarathustra*), he resumed consideration of moralities and their origins. He did so in a part of the book bearing the title "On the Natural History of Morality [*Zur Naturgeschichte der Moral*]" (coming even closer to the German title of *GM*). And he did so in conjunction with a reiteration of his call for a naturalistic reinterpretation of human reality more generally. He explicitly (on the title page, no less) considered *GM* to be a kind of "clarification and supplement" to *BGE*, which thus sets its immediate context—as a whole, but more specifically by his demand that beneath "the old mendacious pomp, junk and gold dust of unconscious human vanity..., the fearful basic text of homo natura [natural man] must again be recognized." He continues:

> To translate man back into nature; to become master over the many vain and overly enthusiastic interpretations and connotations that have so far been scrawled and painted over that eternal basic text of homo natura; to see to it that man henceforth stands before man as even today, hardened in the discipline of science, he stands before the rest of nature... —that may be a strange and crazy task, but it is a task—who would deny that? (*BGE* 230)

It is Nietzsche's evident intention in *BGE* that one should proceed in that same spirit when dealing with morality as a human phenomenon—and in particular, with the morality of "good and evil" that the very title of the book is used to convey he would have us get "beyond." So he begins the part of the book on the "Natural History of Morals" with the suggestion that the first order of business for moral philosophy ought to be to proceed as an anthropologist or zoologist would in dealing with a variety of cultures or creatures: "to prepare a typology of morals [*einer **Typenlehre** der Moral*]"—and to that end, in an analytical spirit, "to collect material, to conceptualize and arrange a vast realm of subtle feelings of value and differences of value that are alive, grow, beget, and perish" (*BGE* 186).

It is near the end of this part of *BGE* that Nietzsche proclaims "morality in Europe today" to be "herd-animal morality." Oddly enough, however, it is only later, in its final part—on what makes "higher" humanity "higher," and entitled "*Was ist vornehm?*" (literally, "What is foremost [outstanding]?")—that he gives a new version of his discussion in *HAH* of the distinction between "master morality" and "slave morality" and their genesis (*BGE* 260). His claim here to have "discovered" these to be the "two basic types" of morality (with "one basic difference") sits oddly with his assertion that a "typology of morals" is what is now needed—unless this is meant to be a major contribution to it. (The "one basic difference" is that "master moralities" are said to originate in a Yes of self-affirmation, whereas "slave moralities" originate in a No of antipathy to the very qualities that are affirmed by the "masters.")

In view of the use Nietzsche went on to make of this distinction in *GM* a year later, it is important to observe that he goes on to say: "I add immediately that in all the higher and more mixed cultures there also appear attempts at mediation between these two moralities"—since our culture (or cultures) in the modern Western world would presumably be among them. That would imply that the modern-day morality with the "genealogy" of which he is concerned in *GM* might well turn out to have a somewhat mixed pedigree. (In any event, for anyone interested in or about to read *GM*, these two parts of *BGE*—Five and Nine—should be required preparatory reading.)

II

It was with this combination of interests—in the development of both human reality and morality as we know them, among other things—that Nietzsche followed the publication of *BGE* with both *GM* and the new fifth "book" or part of *GS* (henceforth "*GS* V") in the following year. It is tempting to think that *GM* is a kind of sequel and supplement to Parts Five and Nine of *BGE*, while *GS* V stands in the same relation to the rest of it. In fact, however, *GM* is significantly related to much of the rest of *BGE* as well—and indeed has considerably more to say that pertains to the kind of naturalistic reinterpretation of human reality called for in *BGE* 230 than does *BGE* itself. Nietzsche had long been convinced that morals had played a key role in the "dis-animalization" of humanity. (See *HAH* II: 350.) Thus his project of a de-deified, naturalistic, and historically minded reinterpretation of our humanity quite understandably led him to think both about moralities in the perspective of their impact upon human reality, and about human reality in the perspective of the ways in which moralities have affected it. This is particularly true of the Second Essay; but the entire book can appropriately and fruitfully be read in this way.

GM consists of three "essays [*Abhandlungen*]"—which in itself is rather remarkable. What is remarkable about this is not so much the separateness of the essays—which Nietzsche makes no real attempt to relate, and which indeed give accounts that are rather difficult to integrate into a unified whole. It is rather the very fact that they are actually *essays*—notwithstanding that they have numbered sections, in the manner of his aphoristic works. Nietzsche's only book-length monograph (setting *Zarathustra* aside) was his first book, *The Birth of Tragedy*. His various "*Untimely Meditations*" (as he called them when he assembled them into a single volume), written during the next few years (1874–6), were not book-length; but they nonetheless were at least essays of a sort, in monograph form. After the last of them, however, Nietzsche abandoned that form altogether in his prose writings, in favor of the aphoristic style he came to prefer, from *HAH* to his final polemics and autobiographical *Ecce Homo*—with the single exception of *GM* and its three "essays." This may well have been because the monograph form to which he briefly returned here was better suited to telling stories—and he had three stories to tell, relating to the origin and development of modern-day morality.

Each of *GM*'s three essays tells a kind of story about a strand that Nietzsche believes to have become woven into the fabric of modern-day morality. The First Essay features the phenomenon that he calls by the French word *ressentiment*, and that might be thought of as a particular and especially virulent and pathological form of resentment, amounting to a kind of hatred of others to whom one is in thrall. The Second highlights the phenomenon of the feeling of guilt or what Nietzsche more frequently calls "bad conscience [*schlechte Gewissen*]." And the Third revolves around the phenomenon of a kind of profound aversion to everything fundamental to the kind of thing life in this world is, that amounts to a generalized hatred of life, and is manifested in asceticism (self-denial) and "ascetic (or life-denying) ideals." Each of these phenomena itself has its own "genealogy," to the understanding of which Nietzsche attempts to contribute in these essays, as a way of pursuing the larger goal of an understanding of the genealogy of modern-day morality. He also believes and suggests that some of the things involved in their genealogies had a significant impact upon the transformation of our proto-human animality into our attained human reality, with important implications for the future of humanity by way of both the possibilities and the vulnerabilities that this manifold transformation has had among its results.

Nietzsche gave *GM* the subtitle characterization "A Polemic." The book is certainly polemical at various points—even if considerably less consistently and unrelentingly than the three short books that followed it during the next and final year of his productive life (against Christianity, against Wagner, and against the philosophical tradition and idols of the age) were to be. But it is something more and different as well: some serious and thoughtful interpretation and case-making that is as sustained and substantive as Nietzsche ever gets. In his autobiographical *Ecce Homo*, written a year later (just prior to his collapse), Nietzsche says, with respect to *GM*'s three essays:

> Every time a beginning that is calculated to mislead: cool, scientific [*wissenschaftlich*], even ironic, deliberately foregrounding, deliberately holding off. Gradually more unrest: sporadic lightning; very disagreeable truths are heard rumbling in the distance—until eventually a tempo feroce [furious tempo] is attained in which everything rushes ahead in a tremendous tension. In the end, in the midst of perfectly gruesome detonations [i.e., thunderclaps], a new truth becomes visible every time among thick clouds. (*EH*: "Genealogy of Morals")

Nietzsche evinces his recognition of and interest in "truths" of a different order of magnitude with respect to morality in the very first section of the First Essay, when he refers to "English psychologists" who have "trained themselves to sacrifice all desirability to truth, every truth, even plain, harsh, ugly, repellent, unchristian, immoral truth.—For such truths do exist." (*GM* I: 1) Why they (or anyone else, such as himself) might want to do such a thing, and place such a value on truth, is another matter—with which Nietzsche is very much concerned, which he implicitly raises at the book's very beginning, and to which he explicitly returns at its end. But "such truths do exist"—and he plainly is intent upon bringing some of them pertaining modern-day morality to light.

GM begins with a preface that is of great importance to its understanding, and indeed to the understanding of the mature Nietzsche's philosophical sensibility and aspirations. The first section (*GM* Preface 1) makes a very striking beginning, the intended upshot of which is initially far from clear. It does not question the very ideas of truth and knowledge; indeed, it presupposes their meaningfulness. It raises a very different sort of question of an equally intriguing nature, however—a question of a more psychological nature, related to the question about the "will to truth" and the value of truth that Nietzsche had raised in the first section of *BGE*, and to which reference has just been made (in the previous paragraph). Its very first sentence is arresting: "We are unknown to ourselves, we knowers [*Erkennenden*]—and with good reason. We have never sought ourselves—how could it happen that we should ever find ourselves?" Nietzsche at least seems to go even further, concluding this opening section of the Preface with the assertion that we (as "knowers" or seekers of knowledge—of whom he readily admits to being one) not only "do not comprehend ourselves," but moreover "must [*müssen*] misunderstand ourselves"—perhaps in order to be able to remain motivated to carry on.

Yet Nietzsche certainly would appear to take this book (and its Third Essay in particular) to contribute to our self-understanding as "knowers"—as well as to an understanding of the "psychology of the priest" (*EH*: "Genealogy of Morals")—that is, of those who have exploited the susceptibility of much of humanity to "*ressentiment*" and "bad conscience" to make a religion as well as a morality revolving around "ascetic ideals." And even more importantly, it is also intended to shed light on ourselves as *Menschen*—as the kind of creature human beings have come to be—to the comprehension of which all three Essays are explicitly said to contribute.

Nietzsche concludes his reflection on *GM* in *EH* by characterizing it as consisting of "three decisive preliminary studies by a psychologist"—that is, by the kind of philosophical "psychologist" he takes himself to be—preparatory to something further: "a revaluation of all values" (*EH*: "Genealogy of Morals"). This "revaluation" is a task that Nietzsche had come at this point to consider the most pressing and important one on both his own philosophical agenda and that of the "philosophy of the future" he heralds in *BGE*.

In the second section of his Preface Nietzsche says something that is both interesting and significant on a number of levels. As has been observed, he grants that the ideas he is about to take up again in the three essays that follow are essentially "the same ideas" as those he had expressed on the matters in question in *HAH* (and presumably in *GS* and *BGE* as well). What he now says is that he actually takes this to count in their favor (as well as in his own favor as a philosopher), notwithstanding the question he had raised in the previous section:

> That I still cleave to them today...strengthens my joyful assurance that they might have arisen in me from the first not as isolated, capricious, or sporadic things but from a common root, from a fundamental will of knowledge [*Grundwillen der Erkenntniss*], pointing imperiously into the depths, speaking more and more precisely, demanding greater and greater precision. For this alone is fitting for a philosopher. (*GM* Preface 2)

This passage also says something important about Nietzsche's conception of philosophy and about what he takes it to be to think and express oneself philosophically—despite his penchant for vehement and hyperbolic rhetoric and for polemic.

Nietzsche states the general problem he is pursuing in *GM* in the Preface's autobiographical third section. His early interest in "where our good and evil really originated" is said to have been "transformed," in the course of his developing historical, philological and psychological sophistication, into other questions: "under what conditions did man devise these value judgments 'good' and 'evil'? and what value do they themselves possess?" He glosses this second question by the further questions with which he continues:

> Have they hitherto hindered or furthered human flourishing [*Gediehen*]? Are they a sign of distress, of impoverishment, of the degeneration of life? Or is there revealed in them, on the contrary, the plenitude, force, and will of life [*Wille des Lebens*], its courage, certainty, future? (*GM* Preface 3)

This is as good a statement as Nietzsche ever offers of the considerations in terms of which he proposes to carry out the "revaluation of values" he calls for. It is indicative of what he elsewhere (*WP* 1041) calls his "Dionysian value standard," deriving from the fundamental "affirmation of life" or "Yes about life" (*BGE* 205) that is the ultimate basis of his naturalistic value theory. And it is because the moral-psychological phenomena upon which he focuses in *GM*'s three essays fare badly by these criteria, on his analysis of them, that he rails polemically against them—and against the morality and religion he takes to have been built upon them and to sustain and promote them.

In the fifth and sixth sections of the Preface, Nietzsche makes it clear that this "revaluation" of the values associated with and promoted by modern-day morality—and with other phenomena that affect people's lives, such as various religions, types of art, social institutions and practices, and ways of thinking historically, scientifically, and philosophically—matters to him much more than "genealogical" inquiry pertaining to it per se. Even at the time of *HAH*, a decade earlier, he says,

> ...my real concern was something much more important than hypothesis-venturing [*Hypothesenwesen*]—whether my own or other people's—on the origin of morality. Or rather, more precisely: the latter [that is, the question of the origin of morality] concerned me solely for the sake of a goal to which it was only one means among many. What was at issue was the *value* of morality [*den* **Werth** *der Moral*]...What was especially at issue was the value of the "unegoistic," the instincts of pity, self-abnegation, self-sacrifice...(*GM* Preface 5)

This continued to be Nietzsche's more fundamental concern to the end of his productive life, even as he was engaged in a task "preliminary" to it in *GM*. When he speaks of "the value of morality," what he has in mind is the significance for (human) life of the various specific "moral values" associated with that morality, of which he here gives examples. The (higher-order) "value for life" of such (lower-order) traits or behaviors that have come to be "valued" in existing moralities and by those who embrace them is what needs to be ascertained, with a view to their "revaluation" (perhaps positively, perhaps negatively) accordingly. What matters most of all to Nietzsche, however, is not their "revaluation" per se, but rather that which it too is intended to serve: namely, the actual flourishing and enhancement of human life.

That highest concern is evident as Nietzsche goes on to observe that he had earlier seen, in the kind of morality (such as Schopenhauer's) that celebrates the "values" he mentions, "the great danger to mankind, its sublimest enticement and seduction—but to what? to nothingness?...to—*nihilism*?" For "it was precisely here that I saw the beginning of the end..., the will turning against life." (*GM* Preface 5) That continues to be his worry in *GM*—but now with respect to modern-day morality, and not just to that of Schopenhauer the arch-pessimist, of whose moral philosophy Nietzsche was specifically speaking here. So, in the next section, he states his fundamental worry more generally:

> What if a symptom of regression were inherent in the "good," likewise a danger, a seduction, a poison, a narcotic, through which the present was possibly living at the expense of the future? ... So that precisely [our revered modern-day] morality would be to blame if the *highest power and splendor* actually possible to the type man [*des Typus Mensch*] was never in fact attained? So that precisely [this] morality was the danger of dangers? (*GM* Preface 6)

This anxiety pervades the three essays that follow. But to repeat: *GM* is not itself offered by Nietzsche as his "revaluation of [modern-day] morality"—even though it is as close as he ever got to writing one before his lamentably brief productive life ended. As he knew full well, knowledge of the origins of things settles nothing with respect to their assessment. So he observes in *GS* V (written just prior to *GM*, in the same year) that "the history of the origins of these feelings and valuations" is "something quite different from a critique," and that "even if a morality has grown out of an error, the realization of this fact would not so much as touch the problem of its value" (*GS* 345). On the other hand, such knowledge may well provide insights into the character of things like "moral values" that are quite appropriately taken into account in assessing them; and so an awareness and understanding of them is to be sought, as part of the "due diligence" (as it were) that should be done preparatory to their revaluation. Putting these points together, Nietzsche writes:

> Let us articulate this new demand: we need a *critique* of moral values; *the value of these values themselves must first be called into question*—and for that there is needed a knowledge [*Kenntniss*] of the conditions and circumstances in which they grew, under which they evolved and changed (morality [*Moral*] as consequence, as symptom, as mask, as tartufferie, as illness, as misunderstanding; but also morality as cause, as remedy, as stimulant, as restraint, as poison), a knowledge of a kind that has never yet existed or even been desired. (*GM* Preface 5)

It is first and foremost to the attainment of that kind of knowledge that Nietzsche means to contribute in the three essays that follow. Yet he also takes the occasion to attempt to contribute to the reinterpretation and comprehension of "the type Mensch," in ways both suggested by and relevant to his inquiries. And he further avails himself of this occasion to provide at least a preview of his promised "revaluation" of the morality and associated moral phenomena he discusses.

III

"The truth of the first inquiry," Nietzsche tells us in *EH*, is "the birth of Christianity out of the spirit of ressentiment." (*EH*: "Genealogy of Morals") Here he is playing on the full original title of his first book, "The Birth of Tragedy Out of the Spirit of Music." As the title he gives to the First Essay itself indicates, however, he has something more in mind as well. Its title—"'Good and Evil' ['*Gut und Böse*'], 'Good and Bad' ['*Gut und Schlecht*']"—shows that his further purpose is to contrast the two fundamentally different types of morality he calls "slave morality" (the morality whose basic contrasting value concepts are "good" and "evil") and "master morality" (the basic contrasting value concepts of which are "good" and "bad").

It is the burden of the First Essay that the former of the two types is inspired and pervaded by "the spirit of *ressentiment*"—precisely in reaction to domination by those whose type of morality (the latter) has a radically different character: that of self-affirmation, on the part of those who are dominant, and tending to focus upon qualities associated with their dominance. Nietzsche considers the *ressentiment* that manifests itself in "slave morality" to be a (very understandable) reaction on the part of the dominated group to the dominant group. And he further suggests that its concepts of "good" and "evil" and their content are the negative images of the dominant group's self-affirming concept of "good" and its pejorative opposite "bad," supplemented by values associated with the dominated group's survival strategies.

It is noteworthy that Nietzsche makes no mention in this First Essay (or in *BGE* 260 or *HAH* I: 45 either, for that matter) of a very different type of normativity that he frequently discusses in his earlier writings and mentions again in the Second Essay. It is neither a "master morality" nor a "slave morality"—notwithstanding his contention (in *BGE* 260) that these are the "two basic types" of morality he has found to exist or have existed in the world. Rather, it is what is often referred to in English-language translations and discussions as "the morality of mores," in which the norms people live by are the "mores" or customs of their communities. Their communities may be "herd-like"; but they are not envisioned to have the structure of a self-affirming ruling group dominating a resentful ruled group. The reason for this seeming oddity may be that Nietzsche simply does not think of the so-called (in English) "morality of mores" type of normativity as a type of morality [*Moral* or *Moralität*] at all—considering it instead to be a type of ethic or ethicality, for which he uses the different word "*Sittlichkeit.*"

The Nietzschean German phrase commonly translated as "morality of mores" is "*Sittlichkeit der Sitte*"; and it would in any event seem appropriate to flag this terminological difference by translating this phrase as "the ethics of custom." We may tend to consider the terms "morality" and "ethics" to be more or less synonymous; but Hegel had distinguished significantly between "*Moralität*" and "*Sittlichkeit,*" as quite different types of normativity—and so, it appears, does Nietzsche, in his usage of "*Moral*" and "*Sittlichkeit,*" at least in this context.

Thus it would seem that Nietzsche's assertion in *BGE* that "European morality [*Moral*] today is herd-animal morality" (*BGE* 202) is making a different point about it than he is making when he emphasizes its kinship with "slave morality"—of which he clearly takes what he calls "Christian morality" to be an instance. Nietzsche nowhere claims that the three essays of *GM* give a complete account of the "genealogy" of modern-day morality, however; and it could well be that a more complete account of it for him would need to include significant mention of the "*Sittlichkeit der Sitte*" as well as of "master" and "slave" moralities.

Nietzsche argues in the First Essay, on etymological, historical, and psychological grounds, that the aristocratically self-affirmative concept of "good" (and its companion derisive counterpart concept of "bad," construed simply as the lack of "good"-making qualities) were prior in point of origin to the opposing conceptions of "good" and "evil" that have long been the rivals of the former, that triumphed over them in the "slave revolt in morality" two millennia ago, and that prevail in modern-day morality. The latter, he then contends, emerged as a *ressentiment*-charged reaction against the "masters" and everything associated with them—including their value judgments (*GM* I: 10).

But there is more than this to the First Essay. The morality of *ressentiment* is inseparable from the psychology of *ressentiment*, which Nietzsche believes to have been occasioned in a very understandable sort of way, but to have resulted in the emergence of a new type of human mentality—and therefore of a new type of human reality. "The man of *ressentiment*" is said to be a very different sort of human being from "the noble man"; and the secretive, furtive nature of the former, whose "spirit loves hiding places, secret paths and back doors," contrasts vividly with "the stronger, fuller nature" of the latter, "in whom there is an excess of the power [*Kraft*] to form, to mold, to recuperate and to forget" (*GM* I: 10–11).

Nietzsche thus is supposing, in a Lamarckian sort of way, that what presumably began as a form and manner of behavior that was forced upon the dominated group, was internalized and ingrained sufficiently not only to become "second nature" to its first generation, but moreover to be transmitted to subsequent generations and developed further in them. (What is Lamarckian here is the idea of the intensification through biological inheritance of intra-generationally acquired or heightened characteristics. The thought is: something one needs or chooses to do repeatedly and become good at, using some ability one already has, becomes an incrementally enhanced version of that ability and the beginnings of a disposition, which can become sufficiently ingrained in one's constitution to be passed on along with others of one's constitutional traits to one's offspring—a process which, if repeated often enough, can yield cumulatively significant results.) Lamarckism was scientifically respectable and commonplace at the time, and makes intuitive sense even today (even though we now know it to be mistaken).

Nietzsche seems to have taken this way of thinking for granted, and often avails himself of it. So, for example, he writes: "A race of such men of *ressentiment* is bound to become eventually cleverer than any noble race; it will also honor cleverness to a far greater degree: namely, as a condition of existence of the first importance." (*GM* I: 10) Some such subset of humanity is forced to be clever, then makes a virtue of the necessity, and this reinforcement results in further development of the trait, which is presumed to be biologically heritable in that more highly developed form. In this way, Nietzsche suggests, the seed of cleverness—and thus of intellect—was planted and grew in portions of humankind, along with the disposition to react with *ressentiment* when confronted with superiority.

The initial upshot of this set of developments, Nietzsche suggests, is that under the influence of the kinds of cultural developments through which these "instincts of reaction and *ressentiment*" were expressed, and through the heritability of acquired characteristics, the greater part of humanity was "domesticated" to the core. Thus he is prepared to suppose that it "really is true" that "the meaning of all culture," at least in the first place and with respect to its original function, "is the reduction of the beast of prey 'man' to a tame and civilized animal, a domestic animal"—not just a wild animal that has been broken, but a domestic animal as different from a "beast of prey" as a dog is from a wolf, and with psychological attributes that equip us from the outset for forms of life geared to the demands of the cultural reality that has displaced and "reduced" our erstwhile affective constitution (*GM* I: 11). On the other hand, it is part of the burden of his argument that humanity has come to consist of a considerable variety of different types, differently endowed as well as differently disposed, both by nature and by nurture; and that it is moreover a very open question how this or that particular configuration of human qualities and capacities will express itself.

Nietzsche couples this reasoning with a famous piece of his philosophical psychology, the point of which is to undercut the possibility of any objection to the account he is developing that would appeal to the idea of some sort of agent self within any of the types of human beings under consideration that is above the fray and ought to be capable of resisting any and all such dispositions. He does not attempt to make a case for it here, contenting himself with simply putting his cards on the table: "there is no 'being' behind doing, effecting, becoming; 'the doer' is merely a fiction added to the deed," he writes; and thus there is no "neutral substratum behind the strong man, free to express strength or not to do so." Further: "To demand of strength that it should not express itself as strength...is just as absurd as to demand of weakness that it should express itself as strength." (*GM* I: 13)

Problematic though certain of its underlying assumptions may be, the First Essay thus has a good deal to say about the origins and character of what Nietzsche variously calls our "psychology," our humanly attainable "spirituality," and our humanly realizable "soul." These developments are conceived not only to be fostered and reflected in the values and revaluations on which Nietzsche is commenting, but also to be gradually ingrained in the constitutions of the strands of humankind in which they have taken hold, with nature and nurture reinforcing each other in a manner the cumulative effect of which is a very different sort of human being than walked the earth before it all began.

IV

GM's Second Essay opens with the suggestion that "man"—or at any rate some part of humankind—has become something our proto-human ancestors were not: "an animal that may make promises [*versprechen darf*]." This ability—not merely to say the words but to have them mean something—is no mere fiction or illusion for Nietzsche. So he not only refers to this as "the paradoxical task that nature has set itself in the case of man" and "the real problem regarding man" (that is, regarding the shaping of our attained human nature), but also reflects on how "remarkable" it is "that this problem has been solved to a large extent." And he supposes this to have been done through a "breeding" process, in the course of which our prior nature—or at any rate, that of some among us—was altered, in a manner that can be (and therefore presumptively should be) understood naturalistically (*GM* II: 1). The question of what that process might have been is the central question of this Essay.

It is Nietzsche's contention that the "animal" man, which not only tends but also actually "needs to be forgetful" to be able to function well, "has bred in itself an opposing faculty, a memory, with the aid of which forgetfulness is abrogated in certain cases." It is no fiction, but rather a psychological reality. But this modification of our psychic constitution in turn required others: "The task of breeding an animal with the right to make promises evidently embraces and presupposes as a preparatory task that one first makes men to a certain degree necessary, uniform, like among like, regular, and consequently calculable." And this, Nietzsche contends, did in fact happen—at least to some significant extent, even if neither completely and perfectly nor irreversibly—through a process that he envisions (perhaps for lack of an alternative) in a Lamarckian manner. It is said to be "the tremendous labor...performed by man upon himself during the greater part of the existence of the human race, his entire prehistoric labor...", with the aid of the ethic of custom [*Sittlichkeit der Sitte*] and the social straitjacket."

Moreover, while this "long story" might seem to be the genealogy of nothing more admirable than the "herd mentality" of which Nietzsche is so contemptuous, he is quick to observe that it actually and ironically turns out also to have set the stage for a radical supersession of that very type of mentality and humanity; for its "ripest fruit" is said to be "the sovereign individual, like only to himself, liberated again from the *Sittlichkeit der Sitte*, autonomous and supra-ethical [*übersittlich*]." (*GM* II: 2) This type itself is far from being that about the possibility of which Nietzsche waxes so rapturously enthusiastic at the end of *GM* II: 16, and again near the end of the Second Essay itself (*GM* II: 24); but it is clearly a preliminary form of "higher humanity," well beyond that of the "pack of beasts of prey" we meet again in this essay (*GM* II: 17).

But the "long story" of that process is purported to have been a bloody as well as winding one, as Nietzsche immediately goes on to suggest. For it took more than "the *Sittlichkeit der Sitte* and the social straitjacket" as norms to bring about these changes in our nature. It took what he calls "mnemotechnics" or the "techniques of memory" in addition to the gentler persuasions of childhood socialization and acculturation; and he contends that "pain is the most powerful aid to mnemonics." Human memory is suggested to have begun as the unforgettability of great pain, burning in the consequences of not following the rules of the practice of promise-making and promise-keeping, and so providing a powerful incentive to do whatever it takes to avoid it. Eventually it may become "second nature" for one to do so; and in the longer run, the cumulative effect is suggested to have been that the elements of such a "second nature" have taken root (in a manner now familiar), as "the type Mensch" was transformed into a kind of constitutionally "domesticated animal," with the mental equipment and psychological dispositions needed to turn out "fit for society." So Nietzsche writes, of this longer process:

> With the aid of such images and procedures one finally remembers five or six "I will nots"...—and it was indeed with the aid of this kind of memory that one at last came "to reason"! Ah, reason, seriousness, mastery over the affects, the whole somber thing called reflection, all these prerogatives and showpieces of man: how dearly they have been bought! how much blood and cruelty lie at the bottom of all "good things"! (*GM* II: 3)

But the sort of "conscience" associated with the capacity to make and keep promises—at first under socially monitored circumstances and then on one's own, responsible only to oneself—is taken by Nietzsche to be very different from what he calls "that other [NB] 'somber thing,' the consciousness of guilt, the 'bad conscience' [*das 'schlechte Gewissen'*]" (*GM* II: 4). Strangely enough, it is this type of conscience, pathological though it may be, that he suggests to be of the greatest importance, not only in the context of the genealogy of our humanity to date, but also with respect to the further enhancement of human life, as a condition of the possibility of a significantly different sort of enhancement than the developments associated with the first sort of conscience alone could have made possible. It is that further development, and the human possibilities it has opened up, to which the rest of the Second Essay is largely devoted.

The "bad conscience" is not self-punishment as the internalization of the institution and practice of punishment Nietzsche associates in the first part of this essay with the creation of memory and reliability. Rather, he argues, it is self-torment, in which one does unto oneself a sublimated version of the violence one is unable to do unto others. And it is precisely the possibilities this opens up that he finds so fascinating and promising:

> ...the existence on earth of an animal soul turned against itself, taking sides against itself, was something so new, profound, unheard of, enigmatic, contradictory, and pregnant with a future that the aspect of the earth was essentially altered.... From now on, man is included among the most unexpected and exciting lucky throws of the dice... (*GM* II: 16)

The road to such a Zarathustrean *übermenschlich* higher humanity, Nietzsche is here suggesting, has the phenomenon of "bad conscience" as a condition of its possibility—not only negatively, as a price that must be paid to travel it, but also positively, as a kind of transforming ordeal of the spirit, upon which the very capacity to attain such a humanity depends. And this higher humanity even transcends the "sovereign individuality" celebrated earlier in the Second Essay—in a crucial respect for which again the phenomenon of "bad conscience" has been genealogically indispensable. For it is the key to the very capacity for creativity of the "creative spirit" to which Nietzsche looks with such fervent anticipation at its end (*GM* II: 24). The qualities of the "sovereign individual" are a part of the constitution and "great health" of this envisioned form of higher humanity; but they are not enough—for, admirable as they are, they are no recipe for creativity, any more than is the inventive cleverness that Nietzsche considers to be one of the traits we owe to the "slave" mentality.

V

Human reality had already been significantly altered in the ways Nietzsche discusses in connection with the use of punishment to "create a memory" in the human animal; but that line of development would not have led by itself to the emergence of this second kind of conscience, nor would it have sufficed to set the stage for the sort of higher humanity that is the focus of Nietzsche's highest hopes. "The 'bad conscience,' " he writes, "this most uncanny and most interesting plant of all our earthly vegetation, did not grow on this soil." (*GM* II: 14) He suggests how it may have originated—very differently from the "conscience" of the "sovereign individual," but once again, entirely naturalistically—in the extraordinarily important Section 16 of the Second Essay:

> I regard the bad conscience as the serious illness that man was bound to contract under the stress of the most fundamental change he ever experienced—that change which occurred when he found himself finally enclosed within the walls of society and of peace. (*GM* II: 16)

"In this new world," Nietzsche goes on to surmise, "these semi-animals, well adapted to the wilderness, to war, to prowling, to adventure," could no longer give free reign to "their former guides, their regulating, unconscious and reliable drives" that had served their kind so well prior to the advent of "society and peace." They were blocked by "fearful bulwarks" so daunting—"punishments belong among these bulwarks"—that even these aggressive "semi-animals" were deterred from doing so. With the stage thus set, Nietzsche introduces his theory of drive or instinct inhibition and "internalization": "All instincts that do not discharge themselves outwardly turn inward—this is what I call the internalization [*Verinnerlichung*] of man: thus it was that man first developed what was later called his 'soul.'" (*GM* II: 16) The consequence was that these aggressive drives, without losing their basic character, came to be turned upon the only available target: they "turned against the possessors of such instincts." And, Nietzsche continues, "that is the origin of the 'bad conscience.'"

But that is not all; for Nietzsche goes on to suggest that there is pleasure in cruelty (repugnant though this may seem to our modern sensibility)—and therefore also not only in the self-torment of "bad conscience," but also in something that it in turn makes possible, which is one of the greatest of gifts and boons to humanity: "This secret self-ravishment, this artists' cruelty, this delight in imposing a form upon oneself as a hard, recalcitrant, suffering material," he writes, is nothing less than "the womb of all ideal and imaginative phenomena, [which] also brought to light an abundance of strange new beauty and affirmation, and perhaps beauty itself" (*GM* II: 18). Nietzsche's very image in this passage is highly suggestive of how he conceives of this development: the "bad conscience" was not merely the impetus to this development, or even merely its catalyst; it was its "womb." And if this is so, it is something profoundly important with respect to the genealogy and future of humanity; for this would mean that it was the addition of the phenomenon of the "bad conscience" to the psychological make-up of humanity as it had previously been constituted that made possible the kind of sublimation process that has opened the way to all subsequent enhancements of human life, to date and to come.

It was only in just such a "womb," Nietzsche is contending, that the kind of transformation of our merely animal vitality into spirituality and myriad forms of creativity could occur that warrants the extravagant language of the conclusion of Section 16. For the key to all such transformation is a compulsion to turn oneself in to something other than one is. And this, he suggests, is a compulsion that, in its beginnings, had to take the form of a "war against the old instincts" and our "whole ancient animal self," yet impelled precisely by those "old instincts" and so involving the just-mentioned "delight in imposing a form upon oneself as a hard, recalcitrant, suffering material" (*GM* II: 18). Hence his startling suggestion that all of "higher culture," "higher spirituality," artistic creativity, and even intellectual integrity is rooted in cruelty, and in the disposition to take pleasure in it (*GM* II: 6). And hence also his concern that, were this disposition to be bred out of us, the motivational key to their difficult cultivation and pursuit would be lost.

The topic of the Third Essay is the phenomenon of the idealization of life-denying asceticism that is the dangerous flower of the strange plant of "bad conscience." It is not surprising, therefore, in light of the foregoing, that Nietzsche concludes the Second Essay by giving hopeful advance notice of a humanly possible antidote to it that the "bad conscience" itself also has made a human possibility: the "creative spirit" who will "redeem us not only from the hitherto reigning ideal but also from that which was bound to grow out of it, the great nausea, the will to nothingness, nihilism," affirming this life in this world in an unconditional way that "liberates the will again and restores its goal to the earth and his hope to man" (*GM* II: 24).

VI

With this impassioned rhetorical gesture, Nietzsche looks beyond genealogical inquiry, and beyond revaluation as well, not only to a "philosophy of the future," but also to a possible humanity of the future. In the Third Essay, however, he goes no further than to reflect upon the threat to it posed by "ascetic ideals," and to offer a further and more specific glimpse of the kind of alternative to them he envisions. Its title is in the form of a question: "What do ascetic ideals mean [*Was bedeuten asketische Ideale*]?" His question is not to be understood simply in the sense of asking what ascetic ideals say or "idealize"; for that is nothing particularly mysterious. Rather, he is interested in what they signify or reveal and what is to be made of them.

By "ascetic ideals" (plural) Nietzsche means such "ideals" as the three paradigm examples he cites in Section 8 and goes on to discuss: "poverty, humility, chastity"—the three things that Christian monks have long "taken vows of" in "renouncing the world." He further takes these "ideals" to be reflected in certain valuations associated with traditional Christian morality and its modern-day secular cousin: that there is something sinful or reprehensible about unabashed wealth, pride, and sexuality. By "the ascetic ideal" (singular) he means the general ideal of "renouncing the world"—condemning life and the world, assigning negative value to everything natural, and more. So, at the Essay's conclusion, he glosses it as:

> …this hatred of the human, and even more of the animal, and more still of the material, the horror of the senses, of reason itself…, this longing to get away from all appearance, change, becoming, death, wishing, from longing itself… (*GM* III: 28)

"The ascetic ideal," in short, is the ideal reflected in the "longing" of which Nietzsche here speaks—the ideal of somehow existing in a way that involves distancing oneself from all of these things, escaping them, rising above them, leaving them behind. This "longing" is a response to the "hatred" of which he speaks in the first part of the passage. And that "hatred," as he suggests earlier in this section, is owing to the "suffering" associated with those things in the experience of those who embrace some version of this "ideal"—not simply to that "suffering" per se, however, but rather to the sense that it might all be meaningless. "The meaninglessness of suffering, not suffering itself, was the curse that lay over mankind so far—and the ascetic ideal offered man meaning." (*GM* III: 28) It "placed all suffering under the perspective of *guilt*," which is already to give it (and one's existence) a kind of meaning. In doing so, it further signifies that the reality (both within oneself and in which one finds oneself) associated with suffering was to be hated, negated, rejected, and transcended—and that such repentance, denial, and transcendence endows one's existence with further meaning and worth, as the only way of mitigating one's guilt.

Such a suffering-prompted, meaning-craving, and guilt-fueled "will to transcendence" is so widespread, in one form or another, that Nietzsche suggests an extraterrestrial observer might conclude that "the earth was the distinctively ascetic planet, a nook of disgruntled, arrogant, and offensive creatures filled with a profound disgust at themselves, at the earth, at all life." (*GM* III: 11) It is commonly dressed up in positive interpretive clothing, but actually is a will to "nothingness," there being nothing beyond this life in this world to transcend to.

Even that recognition, however, is not enough to break the spell—and for deep human psychological reasons. For Nietzsche's answer to the question of "the meaning of ascetic ideals" and their grip on humanity—stated at the essay's outset, and restated at its conclusion—is that they are "an expression of the basic fact of the human will, its horror vacui ['abhorrence of a vacuum']: it needs a goal—and it will rather will nothingness than not will." (*GM* III: 1, 28)

Nietzsche recognizes and dreads one possible human future: a wasting away of "the human will" to the point of its actual, fatal extinction. The only other solution, he suggests, is for humanity to find its way to a genuine alternative to "the ascetic ideal" that would give "the human will" a "goal" of the sort that would satisfy that "need" inherent to it, but that would be as conducive to human flourishing as "the ascetic ideal" is detrimental to it. He dismisses "science [*Wissenschaft*]" as a candidate provider of such an alternative: "No! Don't come to me with science when I ask for the natural antagonist of the ascetic ideal, when I demand: 'where is the opposing will expressing the opposing ideal?'" For that requires "a value-creating power," which science lacks. Moreover—and worse still—he contends that "modern science" actually is "the best ally the ascetic ideal has at present," both because its fundamental effect is to "dissuade man from his former respect for himself" without repairing the damage, resulting in a "penetrating sense of his nothingness," and because its unconditional "will to truth" is in fact the ultimate and noblest but potentially fatal expression of the "ascetic ideal" (*GM* III: 24–5).

Interestingly, Nietzsche also has the same reservations about "the last idealists left among philosophers"—the very "free-spirited," kindred-spirited "Nay-sayers and outsiders of today…, these last idealists of knowledge in whom alone the intellectual conscience dwells and is incarnate today." (*GM* III: 24) A lively intellectual conscience, by itself, will not be enough. (Nor will the proud conscience of the "sovereign individual," admirable as it may be.) Something further is needed, of which his description of the "man of the future" he envisions as a "creative spirit" provides a hint. So it comes as no surprise when he writes parenthetically, toward the end of the essay: "*Art*—to say it in advance, for I shall some day return to this subject at greater length—art, in which precisely the lie is sanctified and the will to deception has a good conscience, is much more fundamentally opposed to the ascetic ideal than is science." (*GM* III: 25)

Nietzsche did not live to "return to this subject," but the general idea is clear enough. He contends that the "ascetic ideal" has prevailed precisely because "it was the only meaning offered so far"; but he was being uncharacteristically restrained, by not continuing: "until my Zarathustra." For in it his Zarathustra had already been made to proclaim "the Übermensch" to be the best available life-affirmative candidate for "the meaning of the earth" (*Z*: "Zarathustra's Prologue" 3), standing for the new anti-ascetic and anti-otherworldly ideal of the "enhancement of life" through "value creation." In that new dawn, this-worldly creativity emerges as the master-value, animated by an "artistic conscience" rather than a truth-obsessed "intellectual conscience" hostile to anything that does not pass its muster. For the latter, as a master passion, is as such (if not accompanied and animated by the former) hostile to life and its enhancement, and is thus the "ascetic ideal" once again—in yet another (and perhaps most insidious) guise.

It thus may seem that the Third Essay gives an answer to the question posed at the very outset of the book—with respect to what makes those tick who as "knowers [*Erkennenden*]" devote themselves to the pursuit of knowledge—that is rather grim. As such, Nietzsche writes, even those "hard, severe, abstinent, heroic spirits...are far from being free spirits: for they still have faith in truth [*sie glauben noch in die Wahrheit*]." However, upon closer examination, one sees that the kind of "faith" or "belief" he is talking about here is that which is akin to religious faith, and treats "truth" as a kind of God-substitute and new absolute value: "it is the faith in a metaphysical value, the absolute value of truth." Thus "this unconditional will to truth is faith in the ascetic ideal itself," even if it is no longer explicitly associated with the traditional idea of "God." The value of "truth" can be considered "absolute" if "truth" is associated and even fundamentally identified with that God. But "from the moment faith in the God of the ascetic ideal is denied, a new problem arises: that of the value of truth." (*GM* III: 24)

It by no means follows, however, that Nietzsche thereby gives up on the very idea of "truth," or abandons the further idea that a "will to truth" is possible—and may be worth having and cultivating. And in fact *GM* itself makes it quite clear that he is neither giving up on the former nor abandoning the latter. He most certainly believes that both of them must be significantly modified; but he also would appear to think that both, when so modified, will have important places in his (and our) "philosophy of the future." Neither truth and knowledge nor the value of truth and its pursuit (by would-be *Erkennenden* and "philosophers of the future") stand and fall with the idea of their unconditionality and absoluteness. And as Nietzsche makes clear in his Preface, they are actually required for the very idea of a "revaluation of values" to be undertaken, or even to make any sense. They do, however, need to be cut down to human size and shape.

Midway through the Third Essay, in what is almost an aside, Nietzsche steps out of his genealogical account for a few moments to say some things about truth and knowledge as he conceives of them. I suggest that he does so precisely here in an attempt to make it clear that he does not mean the things he is saying about them in their ascetic-ideal bondage to apply to their viability and value entirely. One does well to bear these remarks in mind when considering what to make of this Essay, the entire book, and his mature thought more generally:

> But precisely because we seek knowledge, let us not be ungrateful to such resolute reversals of accustomed perspectives and valuations with which the spirit has, with apparent mischievousness and futility, raged against itself for so long: to see differently in this way for once, to want to see differently, is no small discipline and preparation of the intellect for its future "objectivity"—the latter understood...as the ability to control one's Pro and Con and to dispose of them, so that one knows how to employ a variety of perspectives and affective interpretations in the service of knowledge....There is only a perspective seeing, only a perspective "knowing"; and the more affects we allow to speak about one thing, the more eyes, different eyes, we can use to observe one thing, the more complete will be our "concept" of this thing, our "objectivity." (*GM* III: 12)

VII

One may well ask: What is the status of the kinds of claims that I have been considering? Nietzsche professes, in his Preface to *GM*, to aspire to contribute in it to "a knowledge of a kind that has never yet existed or even been desired"—namely, "a knowledge of the conditions and circumstances in which [moral values] grew, under which they evolved and changed" (*GM* Preface 6). His actual contribution, however, may be something that is both less and more than that. I take him to be venturing a number of "conjectures" and "hypotheses"—as he explicit calls them in the Preface (*GM* Preface 5)—with respect to aspects of "the origin of morality" as we know it. He does so in an attempt to come up with plausible naturalistic accounts of certain phenomena that he believes to have been of crucial importance for the genealogy of modern-day morality—and also of the version and varieties of humanity that have come conjointly to exist.

In short, Nietzsche's aim—and his accomplishment as well, in my view—is less to establish the historical soundness of the particular "hypotheses" he proposes with respect to the unfolding of this genealogy, than to convince his readers that it could have been and probably was nothing grander than developments of the sort he relates in his rather imaginative accounts that shaped their development. He also draws upon and imports into his story certain biological and psychological ideas that he believed to be sound scientifically, independently of the account he offers, which influence his telling of the story.

Nietzsche proceeds by appropriating some ideas and coming up with others that seem plausible and promising, and running with them interpretively—mindful of the possibility that many of his proposed accounts are only hypotheses and conjectures, and that there may turn out to be good reasons to reconsider and revise them. He proceeds in this way because he thinks that this is the way to conduct one's "historical-philosophical" experiments. If one wants to think outside the box, one has no alternative—or at any rate, no better way to conduct such experiments. The results often may not deserve the name of "knowledge," historically speaking; and at times they may even go wide of the mark, not only historically but also psychologically and scientifically. But this for Nietzsche is the kind of thinking and interpreting that needs to be done if we are to advance our comprehension of moral phenomena or anything else about human reality, let alone position ourselves as best we can to undertake a naturalistic "revaluation of values."

Nietzsche thinks that these are some of the most interesting and important things a philosopher can and should be thinking about; and he tries to show us how he believes one might best go about doing so. He ventures his best guesses, and thereby challenges us and anyone else who might be interested to enter the fray and attempt not only to fault him but to improve upon his attempts and experiments. That, I suspect, is precisely what he would be doing if he were to return and join us today in reconsidering *GM* and its topics, and others of his texts and their topics—just as he himself did in his 1886 preface to his reissue of *The Birth of Tragedy* and on other subsequent occasions.

What would count as "knowledge" here—the kind of "knowledge" of which he speaks in *GM*'s Preface and to which he aspires to contribute in its three essays—may never be more than accounts of the kinds of moral-psychological and related human phenomena he is discussing that "ring true" as we consider them, and that continue to do so as we reconsider them. But where things human are concerned, that is often the best we can do. That's "knowledge" in the interpretation business for you—always an uncertain and even fallible work in progress, but still the name of the game.

BIBLIOGRAPHY

(A) Works by Nietzsche

GM *On the Genealogy of Morals*, trans. R. J. Hollingdale and Walter Kaufmann, in *On the Genealogy of Morals and Ecce Homo*, ed. Walter Kaufmann. New York: Viking Books, 1969.

(B) Other Works

Ansell-Pearson, Keith (ed.) (2006). *A Companion to Nietzsche*. Oxford: Blackwell.

CHAPTER 15

....

NIETZSCHE'S *ANTICHRIST*

....

DYLAN JAGGARD

INTRODUCTION

THIS article will offer an examination of *The Antichrist*. The importance of this work for understanding Nietzsche's critique of Christian moral values has been underestimated. In recent years Nietzsche's *Genealogy of Morals* is the work that has been given the most attention by Nietzsche scholars. Whilst this latter text is undoubtedly an important book, Nietzsche himself had always maintained that it was a preliminary study and part of a wider project to revalue Christian values. Readings of the *Genealogy* have recently fallen into two main camps. Some scholars, like Brian Leiter (2002), read the *Genealogy* as if it were supposed to be a factual account of the history of Christianity. Then there are those, like David Owen (2007), who argue that the value of this book lies not in its being a factual history but that it should rather be seen as a quasi-historical allegory that aims to free us from the hold that Christianity has on us. The problem with both approaches is the existence of *The Antichrist* itself. As history the *Genealogy* will not stand up on its own. But if we try to suggest that Nietzsche is not attempting to construct a factual historical account then the relationship between the *Genealogy* and *Antichrist* is something of a mystery. The psychological story given in the *Genealogy* needs to be read alongside the historical one given in *The Antichrist*. Nietzsche himself recommends this approach to his readers (A 24, 45). This article will begin by looking at the shift of emphasis towards truth and science from Nietzsche's earlier writings to *The Antichrist*. His account of the original Jewish revaluation of values which focuses on the creation of the notion of a moral world order will then be outlined. Following this, an account of Nietzsche's investigation into the origins of Christian ethical values will be given. Finally this article will look at what all this means for modernity as Nietzsche understands it.

I

Nietzsche consistently sought to question the value of truth. He writes in *Human, All too Human*, for example, 'There is no pre-established harmony between the furtherance of truth and the well-being of mankind' (*HAH* I: 517; cf. 109). In *The Gay Science* Nietzsche argues that if one were to weigh up the respective values of truth and untruth one would discover that truth is not by any means more useful or less harmful than untruth (*GS* 344). In the *Genealogy* he writes: 'Now that Christian truthfulness has drawn one conclusion after the other, in the end it draws its *strongest conclusion*, its conclusion *against* itself; this occurs, however, when it poses the question *"what does all will to truth mean?"* ... And here I again touch on my problem, on our problem, my *unknown* friends (—for as yet I *know* of no friends): what meaning would *our* entire being have if not this, that in us this will to truth has come to a consciousness of itself *as a problem?*' (*GM* III: 27).

Nietzsche's description of his ideal reader given in the Preface to *The Antichrist* is in stark contrast to this. To be one of Nietzsche's rightful readers, 'You need to have become indifferent, you need never to ask whether truth does any good, whether it will be our undoing' (*A* Preface). He requires of these readers 'A new conscience for truths that have kept silent until now' (*A* Preface). So here Nietzsche does not want to raise the question of the value of truth. The problem of the value of truth, the lack of a non-metaphysical foundation to support truth as a value, the self-overcoming of the will to truth thanks to its eventual realization of itself as a problem, none of this is given any consideration here. What is even more startling is what Nietzsche has to say concerning the relationship between aesthetic taste and truth. He raises the possibility that the reason why Christian truths have been dominant over those of science may come down to aesthetics. He writes, 'In the end, and in all fairness, people should ask themselves whether it was not really an aesthetic taste that kept humanity in the dark for so long: people demanded a *picturesque* effect from the truth, they demanded that the knower make a striking impression on their senses. Our *modesty* is what offended their taste for the longest time' (*A* 13). Nietzsche is often thought to favour the aesthetic over the true. But here he expresses the opposite sentiment.

Despite Nietzsche's lauding of the truth in *The Antichrist* he does not see truth as somehow unconditionally valuable. He discusses the law book of Manu and compares its teachings to that of Christianity. Both are founded on lies, on myths of the divine origin of their respective laws. Nietzsche writes, 'In the end, it comes down to the *purpose* the lie is supposed to serve. The fact that "holy" purposes are lacking in Christianity is *my* objection to its means. Only *bad* purposes: poison, slander, negation of life, hatred of the body, the degradation and self-violation of humans through the concept of sin,—*consequently* its means are bad as well' (*A* 56). Nietzsche believes that the goals of Manu are diametrically opposed to those of Christianity in that the former seeks the enhancement of life whilst the latter seeks to slander life (*A* 57). So for Nietzsche the enhancement of life takes precedent over the search for truth. Elsewhere he tells us, '[W]e are separated by the fact that we view the thing worshiped as God as pathetic, absurd, and harmful, not as "divine"; the fact that we do not treat it as a simple error but as a *crime against life*' (*A* 47). His primary objection to Christianity comes from its denial of life. The notion of life needs greater clarification. He writes, 'I consider life itself to be an instinct for growth, for endurance, for the accumulation of force, for *power*: when there is not will to power, there is decline' (*A* 6). Nietzsche connects weakness with the denial of reality. 'Who are the only people motivated to *lie their way out of* reality? People who *suffer* from it' (*A* 15). So there is a link between Nietzsche's valuing of truth and his emphasis on life enhancement. Those who are strong are generally those who are able to cope with reality and be honest with themselves. He writes of Christianity, 'the pietist, the priest of both sexes, is false *because* he is sick: his instinct *demands* that truth be denied at every point. "What makes things sick is *good*; whatever comes from fullness, from overfullness, from power is *evil*": this is how the faithful see things' (*A* 52).

The original subtitle of *The Antichrist* was supposed to be *The Revaluation of All Values*. In the end Nietzsche decided against this and chose *A Curse on Christianity* instead. I would surmise that this was due to his realization that revaluing values was something he had been undertaking for a considerable time prior to this. Indeed in *Twilight of the Idols* he claims that his first book *The Birth of Tragedy* was his first attempt at such a revaluation (*TI*: 'What I Owe to the Ancients' 5). Very early on in *Antichrist* Nietzsche offers us a summary of his revaluation of values:

> What is good?—Everything that enhances people's feelings of power, will to power, power itself.
> What is bad?—Everything stemming from weakness.
> What is happiness?—The feeling that power is *growing*, that some resistance has been overcome.
> *Not* contentedness, but more power; *not* peace, but war; *not* virtue, but prowess (virtue in the style of the Renaissance, *virtù*, moraline-free virtue).
> The weak and the failures should perish: first principle of *our* love of humanity. And they should be helped to do this.
> What is more harmful than any vice?—Active pity for all failures and weakness—Christianity...(*A* 2)

Nietzsche's high estimation of the value of truth is connected with his new estimation of the value of things. Something is good insofar as it enhances life, and life is will to power. Although Nietzsche regards life as trumping truth it is the case that truth has a central role to play in *Antichrist* in the service of life. The doubts about science raised in both *The Gay Science* and in the *Genealogy* are put to one side. The will to truth had previously served the denial of life but Nietzsche turns this will against the life-denying values of Christianity, and insofar as it serves life this will is valuable. Of course Nietzsche's new estimation of values cannot simply stand on its own. But Nietzsche is in no position to produce his own 'holy lie' about why the things he sees as valuable are indeed valuable. Instead what Nietzsche will attempt to do is undermine those values that have been previously taken as unconditionally valuable and he will try to do this by employing the truth. The truths that he uncovers take the form of a history of Christianity. A history that Nietzsche hopes will undermine our belief in Christian values.

Although critical of value systems that are life-denying, it is also the case that Nietzsche thinks that there are certain circumstances in which the adoption of such moralities may be essential for the continued existence of some human beings. Without these values they would not be able to go on living. Here it is fruitful to suggest that what the life-denying values do for these people is to enable them to make some kind of sense of their lives. The life that adopts a hostile stance towards the human condition can still be meaningful. Nietzsche argues that human beings attempt, if at all possible, to attain the circumstances that most enable them to flourish. This notion of flourishing is to be understood in the context of his notion of the will to power. All human beings try to gain as much power over their surroundings as possible. They wish above all things to be in control of their circumstances to as great a degree as possible. Those who are most able to do this are those who tend to adopt more life-affirming values. These values are an expression of their feeling of power and mastery over themselves and their environment (*A* 6). They are able to regard their existence in such a way that they can make sense of it whilst still being able to embrace it. In contrast there are some human beings who although they desire power, are unable to achieve it. These human beings are forced to adopt life-denying values. These values are an expression of their dissatisfaction with themselves and the world. These people will still want to feel as powerful as possible so that they invent values that make them feel important. In such a case, given that they need these values in order to make sense of, to giving meaning to, their existence, then even values that are essentially life-denying may have some value or worth. Without such values life would be entirely meaningless for such people. On the other hand Nietzsche wants to prevent those who do not need such values in order to make sense of their humanity from adopting them when they could instead adopt more life-affirming values.

When assessing the value of values Nietzsche needs therefore to assess not only the life-denying nature of the values themselves, but also the kind of people who are adhering to those values. If a group of people has no need of such life-denying values in order to make sense of existence then they ought to realize that they would be best to adopt more life-affirming values. He notes in *The Antichrist* itself 'I call an animal, a species, an individual depraved when it loses its instincts, when it chooses, when it *prefers* what is harmful to it' (*A* 6). When examining the value of Christian values Nietzsche will want to ask not only whether they are life-denying, which he undoubtedly believes them to be, but also if they are, whether or not we are able to live with more life-affirming values.

II

Nietzsche begins his history of Christianity by examining its origins in Ancient Judaism. Nietzsche will claim, despite the protestations of contemporary anti-Semites, that Christianity is a fundamentally Jewish phenomenon. To be anti-Semitic whilst claiming to be a Christian is to be a hypocrite. The essential factor in the tale Nietzsche has to tell about the Ancient Jews is how the notion of a moral world order emerged. This notion rests on the idea that the world is governed by moral laws emanating from God. Those who follow God's law are rewarded, whereas those who transgress his laws are punished. Nietzsche believes that this idea of a moral world order still continues to cast a spell over us today. Even those of an atheistic bent will often believe that there are objective moral values and that it is against these values that human beings ought to be judged.

Nietzsche's own source for his history of the Jews, although typically not acknowledged by him, is the biblical scholar Julius Wellhausen. The latter was a contemporary of Nietzsche's and Nietzsche is known to have copies of Wellhausen's works in his personal library and to have studied them in some detail.[1] So in order to get a better understanding of

---

[1] See Brobjer 1997 who offers a fascinating scholarly account of what Nietzsche was reading from 1885–9. See also Yovel 1998: 160–3 and Santaniello 1994: 124.

Nietzsche's history it will be essential to come to grips with the history of Israel that Wellhausen offers. Much of what Wellhausen says is based upon a close reading of biblical texts. Over the centuries various scholars, including philosophers like Hobbes and Spinoza, as well as members of the clergy, had questioned the received wisdom that Moses had composed the first five books of the Bible, known collectively as the Pentateuch.[2] It was during the nineteenth century that research into the problem of who did write the Pentateuch made real progress. Wellhausen's work is to some extent an attempt to draw together the strands of the works of other scholars into a coherent picture. He argues that the first five books of the Bible stem from four main sources. The first source identified is that commonly referred to as J. This was identified because it refers exclusively to God by the name Yahweh. The second source is known as the E source and it was identified because of its referring to God by the name Elohim. The third source, known as D, is responsible for the law book Deuteronomy. The final source, P, is known as the Priestly Code. It comprises the majority of the text of the Pentateuch and it treats of religious laws. It also duplicates many of the stories that are told in the JE source. The chronology for these sources is as follows. The J source and E source are thought to have been written around the time of the two kingdoms in the eighth century BCE. For the most part Wellhausen treats them as a single source. The D source is thought to date from the period just before the Babylonian exile towards the end of the seventh century BCE. The P source is supposed to date from the time of the second temple in the late sixth century BCE. Wellhausen divides the periods of the ancient Jews into a nature/fertility stage, represented by the texts of JE, a spiritual/ethical stage, represented in D, and finally a priestly/legal stage, which produced the P source. Nietzsche does not use these distinctions in his account, but his argument relies heavily on Wellhausen's idea that these biblical sources reflect the needs and values of the different circumstances of different generations. It must be noted that unlike Nietzsche, Wellhausen did not undertake his scholarly work on the Bible with the intention of undermining faith. So although Nietzsche's account owes more than a little to Wellhausen's scholarship, it is very different from Wellhausen's own account in terms of its aims and objectives. Wellhausen is also far more scholarly than Nietzsche. Where the latter takes some 362 pages to construct his arguments Nietzsche essentially covers the same ground in a little over three pages. The central difference between the two is the psychological input that Nietzsche adds. In many ways one can see *The Antichrist* as an attempt to give historical flesh to the psychological skeleton he first creates in the *Genealogy*.

Nietzsche begins his history of the Jews by remarking that, 'Originally, particularly in the time of the kings, Israel had a *correct*, which is to say natural, relation to all things' (*A* 25). The period of the kingdom refers to the time that begins with the appointment of Saul as the first king of Israel around the end of the eleventh century BCE.[3] The expansion of the kingdom into an empire was down to Saul's successor David, who conquered territories in the name of the Israelites. According to Nietzsche, the God of Israel at this time was just that: he was the national God of Israel. Nietzsche remarks, 'Their Yaweh was the expression of their consciousness of power, of their delight in themselves, their hopes of themselves: in him they anticipated victory and salvation, with him they trusted that nature would provide

---

[2] For a discussion of the historical development of the investigation into the question of who wrote the Pentateuch see Friedman 1988. Friedman also provides a useful appendix that shows which of the sources are responsible for which sections of the Pentateuch.

[3] For the historical details that Nietzsche misses out I rely on Armstrong 2007, Kamm 1999, and Wellhausen 1957.

what the people needed—above all rain' (*A* 17). So with their God these Israelites celebrated their own earthly existence. This God of theirs was not bound by any moral conventions. He most certainly was not a tolerant, philanthropic God (*A* 16). The early Jews, Nietzsche suggests, had no conception of sin or of guilt or of divine punishment. Sometimes their God would be vengeful or angry or jealous; he could be both a good God and a harmful God.

When we look at Wellhausen's account, we see that Nietzsche follows it closely. According to Wellhausen the early Jews' relationship to God was based around agriculture. He tells us that for the ancient Jews, 'The land is Jehovah's house' (Wellhausen 1957: 97). The Hebrew's relationship with God was intimately connected to the land and so to nature. Giving thanks to God was all about thanking him for the harvest. This is why the sacrifices at this time were always connected with a feast and also why they were always about celebration. Their festivals were all connected with the cycles of nature (cf. *WP* 152). Furthermore, Wellhausen tells us that, '[T]o Hebrew antiquity the wrath of God was something quite incalculable, its causes were never known, much less was it possible to enumerate beforehand those sins which kindled it and those which did not. An underlying reference of sacrifice to sin, speaking generally, was entirely absent. The ancient offerings were wholly of a joyous nature,—a merrymaking before Jehovah' (Wellhausen 1957: 81). So here the overall picture we have of the ancient Jews is of a race at harmony with nature whose religious practices are designed to celebrate their existence. Their God could sometimes be angry, but when he was there was no sense in which they attempted to give this anger some kind of legal status, whereby God was thought angry because specific sins had been committed. So here Nietzsche's account fits with Wellhausen's.

For Nietzsche then, Jews in the period of the kingdom were perfectly in tune with nature and in worshipping their amoral God they affirmed their own natural existence. They resemble the masters portrayed in the first essay of the *Genealogy*. Although Nietzsche does not make this explicit it is clear that their morality was a noble morality rather than a slave morality. The Jews of the *Genealogy* are forced to embrace a slave morality. *The Antichrist* offers an account of how this occurred.

The period of prosperity that the ancient Jews enjoyed was not to last. Nietzsche argues that with the decline of the kingdom the Jews came to be alienated from their human existence. In other words, they went from being life-affirmers to become life-deniers. Unfortunately, Nietzsche does not bother to supply some of the essential historical background to this change. He makes casual reference to historical events, telling us for example that the Jews were threatened by 'anarchy from the inside, Assyrians from the outside' (*A* 25). The single kingdom reigned over by David and Solomon was, after the latter's death, split into two separate kingdoms of Israel in the north and the much smaller Judah to the south. This occurred in 925 BCE. This did not by any means mark an immediate decline. There was relative prosperity during these years. However, establishing their legitimacy was a difficult thing to do for the new generation of kings, hence the anarchy from within that Nietzsche mentions. The political instability that this resulted in was eventually taken advantage of by the Assyrians. Around 733/2 BCE they invaded and conquered much of the northern kingdom. Samaria, the capital, fell in 721. The Assyrians demanded tribute from Judah in the south.

In 587 BCE the Babylonians, who had gained ascendancy over the Assyrians, destroyed the temple in Jerusalem. Much of the population of Judah was exiled to Babylonia, including some of its most important leaders and priests. The Jews found themselves in an almost impossible position. Yahweh had, it seemed, completely abandoned them. There were really only two ways of dealing with this crisis. One way was to suggest that God had not fulfilled his promises because he was simply not strong enough. If Israel had fallen it was Yahweh's fault because he was not as mighty as the gods of the Babylonians (Fox 1991: 71). Worshipping the gods of the conquering Babylonians would then have been sensible. The second option was to alter one's relationship to Yahweh. This according to Nietzsche is precisely what happened. He tells us that during this period of crisis, 'all hopes were left unfulfilled. The old god *could* not do the things he used to do. He should have been let go. What happened? His concept was *altered*, his concept was *denatured*: this was the price for retaining it' (*A* 25). God was punishing the Jews for their disobedience. It could then be said that God used the Babylonians to carry out his will.

The fact that Yahweh formed such an important part of the identity of the Jews meant that they really could not have given him up without effectively ceasing to exist as a people. The amoral national God of Israel was therefore transformed into a moral anti-natural God who sat in judgement of the Jews. The values of the noble Jews became obsolete because the exiled Jews could not now live up to the standards demanded by these values. Military action of any kind was no longer even an option for them. Their decline meant that they could not act with the same strength and assurance that they could in former times. Ultimately they became a people who were no longer at home in the natural world; hence they felt a psychological need to reject this world. This rejection was the only way that they could make sense of their lives in the light of all that had happened to them. Nietzsche tells us,

> The Jews are the most remarkable nation of world history because, faced with the question of being or not being, they preferred, with a perfectly uncanny conviction, being *at any price*: the price they had to pay was the radical *falsification* of all nature, all naturalness, all reality, the entire inner world as well as the outer. They defined themselves *counter* to all those conditions under which a nation was previously able to live; they made of themselves an antithesis to *natural* conditions—they inverted religion, religious worship, morality, history, psychology one after the other in an irreparable way into the *contradiction of their natural values*. (*A* 24)

The priests transformed the local God of Israel, through whom the Hebrews celebrated nature and power, into its opposite. Yahweh becomes a God who is universal in his reach. He becomes a transcendent deity who can only be accessed via the priest.

The Jewish exile lasted until 538 BCE when they were able to return home thanks to the decline of the Babylonian empire. This was caused by the ascendancy of the Persians. This event marks the beginning of the period of the second temple. In 398 BCE the ancient *Torah*, the law of Moses, was supposedly brought from Babylonia by Ezra (*A* 26). It is thought that this book was actually the Pentateuch as we now know it. The Israelites were told that they had failed to live according to the law that had been sanctioned by God. The way to make sure that God's anger would no longer be incurred was to make sure that in future they obeyed this law. The priests who composed much of this law, the Priestly Code, ensured that the priest was indispensable. Wellhausen notes that in the older JE source sacrifices are made without reference to priests. Anyone can make a sacrifice. In the Priestly Code it is only the priests that are able to make sacrifices. Moreover, the priest, and only the priest, was to be given part of the offering. (Hence Nietzsche's seemingly curious remark that 'the priest likes his steak', *A* 26.) It is also the case that in the earlier period there was no radical separation between holy and non-holy persons. Nor indeed was it the case that the holy was regarded as being strictly unapproachable (Wellhausen 1957: 131–2). Under the influence of the priests God became more and more distant from the people. As a result the priest becomes all-powerful.

Of course the laws enacted by the priests are dressed up as the word of God. These new laws had to be seen to have dated back to the time of Moses. This is how they are presented in the Bible as we now have it. But in order to make this seem plausible these priests had also to effectively rewrite much of the history of the Israelites. Nietzsche tells us, 'The whole *history* of Israel proved useless: get rid of it!—These priests performed a miracle of falsification and we have large portions of the Bible to prove it: in an unparalleled act of scorn for tradition and historical reality, they translated the history of their own people *into religion*, which is to say that they made it into an idiotic salvation mechanism of guilt before Yahweh and punishment, of piety towards Yahweh and reward' (*A* 26). What Nietzsche merely asserts here is something that Wellhausen painstakingly argues. Wellhausen shows that in the Bible, the Book of Chronicles is effectively a rewrite of the earlier Book of Kings (Wellhausen 1957: chapter 6). Historical events are reinterpreted so that they fit in with the laws and institutions enacted in the Priestly Code. The success or failure of any particular ruler is always accounted for in terms of the degree to which they can be said to obey this code. Of course, as Wellhausen himself notes, this means that a good deal of this history has to be fabricated in order to make everything fit this pattern.

In summary then the denaturing of values amounts to a revaluation of the value of the natural world. What is valuable about Yaweh is no longer that he offers a way of enhancing one's feeling of power in relation to how one prospers, whether that is as a warrior or as a farmer. God is no longer tied to the land of Israel; he has become what Nietzsche calls a cosmopolitan God. Yaweh will not now necessarily ensure the victory of the Jewish people in battle. Instead his power is tied to their obedience to his law. What has become crucial now is that one should obey God's will, which according to Nietzsche amounts in reality to obeying the will of the priest. For Nietzsche what takes place in this revaluation of values is the invention of a moral world and the demands of this world take precedence over the demands of the natural world.

III

Nietzsche's continues his history of Christianity by examining the historical Jesus. Nietzsche was by no means the first person to attempt to construct such an account. During the nineteenth century the fact that faith in God had diminished made it almost inevitable that questions should be raised about the Jesus of history. David Strauss, against whom Nietzsche's first *Untimely Meditation* was directed, wrote such an account. Nietzsche mentions Strauss's account in *The Antichrist* but he is mostly concerned to respond to that given by Ernest Renan (*A* 28–9).[4] The latter was an anti-Semite who argued that Christianity is fundamentally different from and superior to Judaism. This is something that Nietzsche especially seeks to challenge. He argues that Christianity grew out of Judaism and that it represents a radicalization of Judaism.

Nietzsche attempts to separate fact from fiction via a reading of the scriptures themselves. He begins by arguing that the Jesus who is portrayed in the scriptures bears little relation to

---

[4] For a discussion of Nietzsche's criticisms of Renan in *The Antichrist* see Santaniello 2000: 92–9.

the historical Jesus. He attempts to draw a portrait of the real Jesus, showing how the early Christians perverted his teachings. Nietzsche asserts that in fact, 'there has been only one Christian, and he died on the cross' (A 39). What is it that Nietzsche takes true Christianity as practised by Jesus to consist in? He argues that the most important element of Jesus's real message is the idea that one ought to overcome all feelings of resentment and enmity. Nietzsche believes that Jesus lacked the stomach for reality, so that what became important for him was the inner world wherein he believed the kingdom of God resided. Nietzsche holds that for the one true Christian, 'The "kingdom of God" is not something one waits for; it has no yesterday or tomorrow, it does not come "in a thousand years"—it is an experience within a heart; it is everywhere, it is nowhere' (A 34). He argues that for the historical Jesus, there was no eternal afterlife, rather, one attained heavenly bliss inwardly. What is more, Nietzsche thinks that when Jesus talked about himself as the Son of God, he considered everyone else to be a child of God also (A 29). Whereas Nietzsche asserts that Jewish morality was founded in resentment at and denial of the natural world, he believes that for Jesus, 'Denial is precisely what is totally impossible for him' (A 32). With Jesus, as he puts it, 'the incapacity for resistance itself becomes morality' (A 29). The example Jesus set was supposed to teach us how we are to live on this earth. For Nietzsche, Jesus's message was essentially one of passivity. He argues that in actual fact the life that Jesus taught us to lead has far more in common with Buddhism or Epicurianism than with Christianity as it developed under the auspices of the early disciples (A 31, 42; WP 167).

How is it that the message Jesus taught came to be perverted? Nietzsche argues that the first disciples did not and could not understand Jesus, who was 'a being awash in symbols and incomprehensibilities' (A 31). Because Jesus could only live within his own inner world, language, and indeed the outer world it referred to, was for him entirely metaphorical (A 32). In order to make sense of what he said, the disciples had to interpret Jesus's pronouncements in a crude literal manner. As a result the message he attempted to teach became corrupted. However, the most fateful misunderstanding of the original disciples was in the way they understood the significance of Jesus's death. Instead of learning the lessons taught by his dignified passivity on the cross, the disciples searched around for someone to blame for the death of their master. The origins of the early Christian movement lie in the resentment felt by these first Christians towards the upper orders of the Jewish Church whom they held responsible for the death of Jesus (A 27). Unlike Jesus, the disciples did not try to overcome their resentment, but instead pandered to these feelings. They blamed the upper class of Judaism for Jesus's death and sought revenge (A 40). Through Christianity the power of the Jewish priests became the focus of the resentment of the lower classes of Judaism. However, Nietzsche maintains that this movement was still a fundamentally Jewish movement.

Whereas Judaism is marked by the relative separateness of its community and its consciousness of the Jews as God's chosen people, Christianity sought to convert humankind as a whole to its creed. Christianity also altered the Jewish conception of God found in the Old Testament. In the Old Testament Yaweh had been portrayed as a wrathful God punishing those who transgressed his laws. Christianity marks a softening of the image of God so that he becomes a God of love. In spite of this however, there are undoubtedly hidden traces of the wrath of the old Jewish God. Where the Jews hoped for a kingdom of God on earth, whereby Yaweh would punish their enemies, the Christians abandon all earthly ambitions. The God of love will reward in Heaven those who convert to Christianity and repent of their sins. Those who do not repent are not to be punished by God on earth, but damned in the flames of Hell in the afterlife. Nietzsche notes that in Dante's *Inferno*, Hell itself is supposed to be a product of God's love (*GM* I: 15). He remarks of Christians, 'Do not be fooled: they say "judge not!" but then they send to hell everything that gets in their way' (*A* 44). Supposedly loving Christians would see all unrepentant sinners suffer eternal torment. Christianity also offers a radical new interpretation of the past to fit their religious outlook, just as the Jewish priests of the second temple had done. The history of Israel is now viewed in the light of its leading up to the coming of the Christian Messiah (*A* 42; *D* 84).

Christianity pretends that its God has decreed that its values are those that are valuable in themselves. In reality it is merely the case that these values are those which enable a certain form of life to bear its existence. Nietzsche writes,

> By letting God be the judge, they themselves are the judge; by exalting God, they exalt themselves; by *demanding* the very virtues that they themselves have—more, that they *need* to have to stay on top—, they give themselves the exalted appearance of struggling for virtue, of fighting to master the virtues. 'We live, we die, we sacrifice ourselves *for goodness*' (—the 'truth', 'the light', the 'kingdom of God'): in point of fact, they are just doing what they cannot fail to do. They act like sycophants, sit in corners, and live shadowy lives in the shadows, and then they make this their *duty*: as a duty, their lives seem humble, and this humility is one more proof of piety... Oh, this humble, chaste, charitable type of duplicity! (*A* 44)

The values of Christianity, such as humility, chastity, and pity, are those that enable weak resentful Christians to make sense of their existence. These are the kinds of values that are the opposite of those that the life-affirming Greeks and Romans consider to be of value.

How is it that the Romans, that noblest of all races, should succumb to the values of a slave morality such as that preached by Christianity?[5] In *The Antichrist* Nietzsche's central argument revolves around the notion of personal immortality. He attributes the power of Christianity to its preaching eternal damnation for non-believers. However this concept alone cannot account for the conversion of the Romans. One can get a more comprehensive account by looking not just at *The Antichrist* but at his other works also.

The early Christian movement, which for Nietzsche was essentially a revolt against priestly power, could not have succeeded without setting up its own priesthood. The figure at the heart of this development was Paul (*WP* 167). It is Paul who Nietzsche regards as primarily responsible for the spread of Christianity. Nietzsche argues that, '*His* requirement was *power*: with Paul the priest again sought power—he could employ only those concepts, teachings, symbols with which one tyrannizes over masses, forms herds' (*A* 42). The imposition of order and law by the Romans had secured trading routes between the different parts of the Empire. This meant that Christian ideas could be spread rapidly by Christian preachers. Most of the early converts were on the fringes of Roman society. The appeal Christianity had for such people can easily be seen by examining one of Nietzsche's favourite quotes from the writings of Paul: '*But God hath chosen* the foolish things of the world to confound the wise; and God hath chosen the weak things of the world to confound the things which are mighty; And base things of the world, and things which are despised, hath God chosen, yea, and things which are not, to bring to naught things that are: That no flesh should glory in his presence' (I Corinthians 1:27–9; *A* 45, 51). Christian practices also helped to foster feelings

---

⁵ For historical detail on the Romans and Christians I use both Barrow 1949 and Chadwick 1993.

of worth and a sense of belonging in these early converts. Nietzsche tells us, 'The happiness of the "smallest superiority," such as accompanies all doing good, being useful, helping, honouring, is the most plentiful means of consolation that the physiologically inhibited tend to make use of... When one looks for the beginnings of Christianity in the Roman world, one finds associations for mutual support, pauper, invalid, burial-associations, which sprung up from the undermost soil of the society of that time, and in which that principal medicine against depression, the small joy, that of mutual good deeds was consciously cultivated' (*GM* III: 18).

According to Nietzsche, it was Paul who first understood how powerful a tool the notions of eternal punishment and reward could be. Paul surmised, as Nietzsche puts it, 'that the concept "Hell" will master even Rome' (*A* 58). Nietzsche tells us,

> Christianity discovered the idea of punishment in Hell throughout the whole Roman Empire: all the numerous secret cults had brooded on it with especial satisfaction as on the most promising egg of their power. Epicurus believed he could confer no greater benefit on his fellows than by tearing up the roots of *this* belief: his triumph, which resounds the most beautifully in the mouth of the gloomy and yet enlightened disciple of his teaching, the Roman Lucretius, came too early—Christianity took the belief in these subterranean terrors, which was already dying out, under its especial protection, and it acted prudently in so doing! How, without this bold recourse to complete heathendom, could it have carried off victory over the popular cults of Mithras and Isis! It thereby brought the timorous over to its side—the firmest adherents of a new faith! (*D* 72)

The early Christians, who belonged to the lowest ranks of society, were able to gain a great deal of psychological comfort from the thought that those who belonged to the ruling orders were destined to be damned in Hell (*GM* I: 15). Nietzsche notes how the hatred of the Roman nobility by the early Christians is given fervent expression in St John's account of the Apocalypse, which he calls 'the most immoderate of all written outbursts that revenge has on its conscience' (*GM* I: 17). The psychological power of the notion of Hell lay not only in the imaginary revenge that it enabled the Christians to take upon the Romans, but also in the fear of eternal damnation itself. There was to be no rest for the wicked, and this proved a powerful incentive to convert to Christianity. Those who did not necessarily feel resentment towards the upper orders might still be motivated to become Christians by the fear of what might happen to them after death (*D* 72).

We have seen thus far some of the factors that led to the spread of Christianity. Many of those on the fringes of society were converted because of a sense of their own worthlessness. They found comfort in the values and practices of Christianity. They also had the satisfaction of believing that the nobles would be punished in the afterlife. Of course these factors are not the only ones. The Roman persecution of Christianity at different times, most notably under Nero, undoubtedly strengthened the resolve of the Christian community. The belief in martyrdom meant that many Christians actually welcomed persecution. Apart from the one passing comment quoted above (*HAH* I: 477), Nietzsche does not discuss the Roman persecution of the Christians in his published writings. However in his notebooks he gives this some consideration, arguing that the persecutions amounted to folly because this meant that Christianity was taken too seriously (*WP* 202).

All this tells us how Christianity was able to spread amongst the lower orders of the Roman Empire. It does not, however, tell us how it was that Christianity also came to dominate the lives of the upper-class Romans. Although Christianity grew as a cult, even by the beginning of the fourth century it was still by no means the chosen religion of the majority. Historians are generally in agreement that it was the conversion of the emperor Constantine in 312 AD that was the single most important event in the eventual conversion of the Empire as a whole.[6] Outnumbered by his rival Maxentius during a stand-off at the Milvian Bridge, Constantine prayed to the Christian God for victory and, greatly against the odds, defeated his opponent. It is said that from then on he became a Christian. Surprisingly, Nietzsche does not discuss Constantine in either published or unpublished writings. This would appear to be a rather astonishing omission from his genealogy of Christianity. All is not lost however, as the gap left in this account can be filled to some extent by examining Jacob Burckhardt's thoughts on Constantine. In his account of the conversion of Constantine, Burckhardt argues that it was for largely pragmatic reasons that he adopted Christianity. He tells us that, 'Constantine attentively observed how Christianity might contribute and be useful to a clever ruler' (Burckhardt 1949: 279, 292–306). When Constantine became Emperor, the Empire was in danger of breaking apart. What Christianity offered, with its characteristically passive values and its universal outlook, was the opportunity to stabilize and unite the Empire. It is also the case that when Constantine first prayed to the Christian God he, like many pagans after him, confused the monotheism of Christianity with the monotheism of sun worship. This latter form of monotheism was becoming increasingly popular in the Empire during this time. According to Burckhardt, the view of Constantine as a deeply spiritual rather than a politically pragmatic Emperor was encouraged by the distorted account of his life given by the Christian Eusebius.

Given Nietzsche's penchant for psychologically analysing historical figures it seems plausible to suggest that his lack of interest in Constantine might well stem from his not seeing anything other than political motives in his conversion. If Nietzsche had detected even a sniff of decadence or world-weariness, it seems likely that he would have pounced. The fact that Nietzsche does not ever discuss Constantine is puzzling, and it could perhaps be an indication that he accepts the kind of pragmatic story of the latter's conversion told by Burckhardt.[7] This is supported by a discussion in Nietzsche's notebooks concerning the motives that a ruler might have for converting to Christianity. Nietzsche notes that one advantageous thing about Christianity as a morality, from the point of view of the ruling classes, is that the kind of virtues it preaches, e.g. obedience, humility, passivity, etc., make Christians relatively easy to rule over (*WP* 216). His account echoes Burckhardt's explicit discussion of the pragmatic motives of Constantine. Nietzsche also notes at one point in the *Genealogy* that 'development toward universal empires is also always development toward universal deities' (*GM* II: 20). Although this comment is not placed in the context of a discussion concerning the Roman Empire, it does seem to indicate that Nietzsche understood that the political structure of such an empire, which gave such a dominant role to the

---

[6] Armstrong (2007: 102) notes that 'Before the conversion of Constantine . . . it seemed unlikely that Christianity would survive, as Christians were subjected to sporadic but intense persecution by the Roman authorities.' See also MacMullen 1984: chapter 5.

[7] Burckhardt, however, in contrast to Nietzsche's final views, sees a kind of inevitability in the eventual capitulation of the Romans. He remarks, 'Christianity was brought to the world by high historical necessity . . . The time was come for men to enter into a new relationship with things of the senses and things beyond the senses' (Burckhardt 1949: 124).

emperor, would tend also to infect the culture of religion with monotheistic tendencies. In *The Antichrist*, Nietzsche tells us, 'It is *not*, as is generally believed, the corruption of antiquity itself, of *noble* antiquity, which made Christianity possible...The period in which the morbid, corrupt Chandala classes of the entire *Imperium* were becoming Christian was precisely that in which the *opposing type*, the nobility, existed in its fairest and maturest form' (*A* 51). So clearly Nietzsche does not think that the triumph of Christianity was due to any sort of corruption on the part of the Roman nobility.[8]

All this helps us to understand some of the factors that enabled Christianity to get a foothold amongst the Roman nobility. However, there are still many unresolved issues. Given that according to Nietzsche, there are radical differences between the noble values of the Romans and those of Christianity, and that he believes that the former remained healthy, how is it even possible that the Romans did not reject Christianity outright once they understood what it really involved? In fact the conversion of Constantine by no means marked the wholesale capitulation of the Roman nobility. Quite a few of them did reject Christianity. Nonetheless, eventually Christianity came to be the dominant value scheme of the nobles also. Nietzsche's explanation for how this was possible lies in the affinities that can be detected between Christianity and the teachings of the Greek philosophers that circulated amongst the educated nobles. In particular, Nietzsche notes the connections between Christianity and Platonism. There are a number of beliefs that the Christian and the Platonist have in common. Both believe in the immortality of the soul, that the natural world is of little value, and that truth is to be found beyond this world. In the tenth book of the *Republic* Plato also discusses the notion that there may be punishments and rewards in the afterlife via Socrates' account of the Myth of Er. Nietzsche believes that both Christianity and Platonism are implicated in the ascetic ideal, and are essentially life-denying. In the Preface to *Beyond Good and Evil* he remarks that, 'Christianity is Platonism for "the people"' (*BGE* Preface). It seems that Nietzsche also thinks that Platonism is effectively Christianity for the nobility. He argues that it was Plato who opened the door of the Roman world to Christianity. Nietzsche tells us, 'In the great fatality of Christianity, Plato is that ambiguity and fascination called the "ideal" which made it possible for the nobler natures of antiquity to misunderstand themselves and to step on to the *bridge* which led to the "Cross"' (*TI*: 'What I Owe to the Ancients' 2). Nietzsche here suggests that the air of respectability that Plato gave to the ascetic ideal (Plato was himself a noble) contributed to the acceptance of Christianity by the Romans. He writes elsewhere, 'it was precisely in opposition to palpability that the charm of the Platonic mode of thinking, which was a *noble* mode of thinking, consisted—on the part of men who perhaps rejoiced in even stronger and more exacting senses than our contemporaries possess, but who knew how to experience a greater triumph in mastering them' (*BGE* 14).

Nietzsche notes that even before the birth of Christ, Roman Epicureans, such as Lucretius, had fiercely opposed ideas that would become the central doctrines of Christianity such as 'guilt, punishment and immortality' (*A* 58; cf. *D* 72). However the dominant philosophy for much of the Roman era was not Epicureanism but Stoicism. In contrast to the resistance

---

[8] Nietzsche's position in *The Antichrist* marks a shift from his earlier views. In section 224 of *Assorted Opinions and Maxims* in *HAH* he argues that the degeneration of the Roman world meant that it needed Christianity as a balm. In a note from 1884 he blames the triumph of Christianity on the corruption of the ruling classes (*WP* 874).

to the doctrines of Christianity represented by Epicureanism, in some respects Stoicism, like Platonism, facilitated the shift from the noble values of the Romans to the slave values of the Christians. As with much else, the Romans tended to appropriate only those aspects of a philosophy that suited their temperament. What was most valuable for them about Stoicism was not its pessimistic outlook upon existence, but its demand for self-discipline.[9] The Romans lived in dangerous times and so they had to learn to become hard enough to deal with whatever fate would throw at them (*GS* 306). The ascetic practices of Stoicism also provided the Romans with another outlet for their instincts of domination, but with the difference that they used these practices to dominate themselves (*D* 251). This form of asceticism, in contrast to that of Christianity, has earthly goals as its objective. Nietzsche points out that Julius Caesar employed ascetic practices such as 'tremendous marches, the simplest form of living, uninterrupted sojourn in the open air, continuous toil', as a way of protecting himself from illness (*TI*: 'Expeditions of an Untimely Man' 31). He further remarks of Caesar, 'One would have to seek the highest type of free man where the greatest resistance is constantly being overcome. This is true psychologically when one understands by "tyrants" pitiless and dreadful instincts, to combat which demands the maximum of authority and discipline towards oneself—finest type Julius Caesar' (*TI*: 'Expeditions of an Untimely Man' 38). However, those Stoics with a deeper philosophical interest in Stoicism tended to see the health of the soul as more vital than that of the body. Socrates and Plato were important influences on them. The most influential of these Stoics was Seneca. Certain of Seneca's texts bear a remarkable resemblance to parts of the New Testament, so much so in fact that letters between Paul and Seneca were forged by fifth-century Christians to account for this (Barrow 1949: 160–1). Nietzsche does not have much to say about Seneca, although he is listed in an aphorism entitled '*My impossibles*' as 'the toreador of virtue' (*TI*: 'Expeditions of an Untimely Man' 1). He also derides Seneca along with the Stoic Cicero in his notebooks for their 'didactic praise of philosophy' (*WP* 420). In his published works Nietzsche does not explicitly discuss the connections between Stoicism and Christianity, but there are places in his notebooks where he does so, although in a somewhat casual manner. At one point he connects Stoicism with Platonism and the 'preparation of the soil for Christianity' (*WP* 427; cf. *WP* 195). However it is worth remarking also that in another note he tries to draw a clear distinction between the two, arguing that Stoicism is a morality that enables the healthy to ward off decadence, and that in contrast, Christianity is a manifestation and defence of decadence (*WP* 268). In order to make sense of this apparent contradiction in Nietzsche's views of Stoicism I would suggest that Stoicism as a way of combating decadence is the kind of Stoicism that is manifested by Caesar and which focuses on the body. The kind of Stoicism that focuses on the soul, *á la* Seneca, is the kind that prepares the soil of Christianity.

Let us now sum up the various factors in the conversion of the noble Romans to Christianity. Monotheistic religious ideas had become increasingly important in the Roman Empire largely thanks to its size and political structure. The Romans thought that monotheistic Christianity would give them an opportunity to unite and stabilize the Empire. Sun worship had become a popular cult and many Romans confused this form of monotheism with Christianity itself. The kind of ascetic practices demanded by Christianity were

---

[9] Burckhardt remarks that Stoicism 'was... closely allied to the best aspects of Roman character' (1949: 189). See also Barrow (1949: 151–2) who writes, 'the Romans were natural Stoics long before they heard of Stoicism'.

by no means alien to the Romans. However, the majority of them used asceticism in order to achieve earthly goals. In contrast, Christian asceticism was demanded not as a means to the earthly enhancement of one's strength but rather for the purposes of actually weakening one's body. This asceticism was all in the name of the denial of life. Nonetheless, even this sort of asceticism was by no means entirely unknown in Roman culture. It was to be found in the writings of Plato and Seneca. Plato's nobility meant that doctrines like the immortality of the soul and the denial of the senses, which were common to Platonism and Christianity, were not thought by the noble Romans to be necessarily ignoble or decadent. As a result the Romans were hoodwinked into thinking that Christianity was a religion that would enable them to continue to flourish.

IV

But what are the lessons to be learned from this? What does Nietzsche think any of this really has to say to us? According to Nietzsche, modernity is about the clash of values. In one of his earliest works he tells us, 'In this oscillation between Christianity and antiquity, between an imitated or hypocritical Christianity of morals and equally despondent and timid revival of antiquity... modern man lives, and does not live very happily' (*UM* III: 2). He writes in *The Antichrist* ' "I don't know where I am; I am everything that doesn't know where it is"—sighs modern man' (*A* 1). He notes elsewhere, '[W]e all still have bad instincts, Christian instincts, in our bodies' (*A* 59). Yet at the same time he points out, 'Every practice at every moment, every instinct, every value judgment that people *act* on is anti-Christian these days: what *miscarriages of duplicity* modern people are, that in spite of all this they are *not ashamed* to call themselves Christians!' (*A* 38). Nietzsche's attack here is on those who mouth the doctrines of Christianity and live their lives in a manner that is fundamentally unchristian. The modern soul has, one might say, lost its ethical bearings. Nietzsche's task is to enable it to find its way.

Nietzsche still believes that Christianity is the value scheme that is the most suitable for many of his contemporaries. He tells us, 'Nobody is free to become Christian; nobody gets "converted" to Christianity—you have to be sick enough for it...' (*A* 51). There is no sense in which Nietzsche is able to persuade those for whom Christianity is needed that their belief in it is false. One of his most important works in terms of understanding his conception of modernity is *The Case of Wagner*. Here he writes of master and slave moralities that '[t]hese opposite forms in the optics of value are *both* necessary: they are ways of seeing, immune to reasons and refutations. One cannot refute Christianity; one cannot refute a disease of the eye' (*CW* Epilogue). In the Epilogue to this work Nietzsche states in plain terms what he understands by the term modern. He begins by describing the distinction between master morality and Christian morality. The former is a positive life-affirming force; the latter represents the morbid life-denying instincts of the sick. What the essence of modernity consists in, as Nietzsche sees it, is in the fact that the modern human being '*refuses* to experience these opposites as opposites' (*CW* Epilogue). He writes that 'Such *innocence* among opposites, such a "good conscience" in a lie is actually *modern par excellence*, it almost defines modernity. Biologically, modern man represents a *contradiction of values*; he sits between two chairs, he says Yes and No in the same breath' (*CW* Epilogue). The modern soul incorporates both master and slave moralities within. And it is Wagner himself that Nietzsche takes to be the quintessential modern soul in this respect: '[All] of us have, unconsciously, involuntarily in our bodies values, words, formulas, moralities of *opposite* descent—we are, physiologically considered, *false*' (*CW* Epilogue).

The first lesson to be learnt relates to Nietzsche's claim concerning the initial Jewish revaluation. Thanks to science we have at last been given the opportunity to become reconciled with the natural world again. The notion of a moral world order needs to be abandoned. Yet this idea will not go away. Kant is the philosopher who provides the main target in this respect for Nietzsche to fire his arrows of revaluation at. What Kant attempts to do is to reconcile the scientific world view with morality. He wants to acknowledge that the natural world operates according to the physical laws of science without giving up on the notion of moral responsibility. In order to do this Kant has to remove any naturalistic motivations from morality altogether. He has to make ethical motives entirely separate, so that morality itself becomes the motive for action. Freedom becomes a matter of obedience to a moral law one supposedly gives oneself and which is completely impersonal. Nietzsche writes, 'When the instinct of life compels us to act, pleasure proves that the act is *right*: and this nihilist with the intestines of a Christian dogmatist saw pleasure as an *objection* ... What could be more destructive than working, thinking, feeling, without any inner need, any deeply personal choice, any *pleasure*? As an automaton of "duty"?' (*A* 11). Kantian ethics thus represents a denial of our humanity. The notion of the thing-in-itself is really just a secularized version of Christian metaphysics. The death of God means the end of not only the Christian God but of any otherworldly authority. It is the natural world alone that we must look to from now on when we seek ethical guidance: 'We have changed our minds. We have become more modest in every way. We have stopped deriving humanity from "spirit," from "divinity," we have stuck human beings back among the animals' (*A* 14). The scientific world of the free spirit thus represents a revaluation of values in itself (*A* 13).

The second lesson relates to Christian morality itself. For Nietzsche the message of Christian morality is summed up in the words of Paul: 'Not many wise men after the flesh, not many mighty, not many noble, are called: But *God hath chosen* the foolish things of the world to confound the wise; and God hath chosen the weak things of the world to confound the things which are mighty; And base things of the world, and things which are despised, hath God chosen, yea, and things which are not, to bring to nought things that are: that no flesh should glory in his presence' (Paul, I Corinthians 1:27–9). Nietzsche believes that the values of Christianity are not those that enable us to embrace our earthly existence. It seems to make sense that deferring to a world beyond would mean that we somehow slander or devalue our earthly corporeal existence. However, surely one could adopt a naturalistic approach to ethics without necessarily having to abandon Christian moral values. Even if we accept Nietzsche's account of the origin of these values amongst resentful, weak, human beings it need not mean that these values are ones that it would somehow be detrimental to us if we continue to adhere to them. What reason do we have to abandon these values in favour of the kind of values that Nietzsche would have us adopt? Why should consideration for the needs and feelings of others be necessarily life-denying?

The Christian virtue that Nietzsche finds the most harmful is pity. If we take into account Nietzsche's thought that a philosophy is a personal expression of the philosopher's own psychological make-up and apply it to Nietzsche one could argue that his dislike of pity stems largely from the fact that he was often regarded as an object of pity himself (*BGE* 6). Santaniello discusses Nietzsche's first meeting with his brother in law Bernard Förster. He writes 'Forster was surprised and relieved at the contrast between Nietzsche's gentle disposition and the fierce tone of his writings. He regarded his half-blind, frail brother-in-law as an invalid to be pitied rather than feared.' (Santaniello 1994: 93) Could it be that Nietzsche's dislike of pity is simply a product of his own *ressentiment*? That being said, Nietzsche argues against the value of pity on the grounds that it is essentially life-denying. Nietzsche returns to the philosopher who had influenced his thinking more than any other, namely, Schopenhauer. He writes, 'Schopenhauer was right here: pity negates life, it makes life *worthy of negation.*' He continues, 'Schopenhauer was hostile to life: which is *why* he considered pity a virtue' (*A* 7). So Nietzsche is not claiming that the notion of pity as life-denying is unique to him. The difference between his view and Schopenhauer's is that for Schopenhauer it is precisely its life-denying qualities that make pity valuable. What is the connection between pity and life denial? For Schopenhauer the connection is that pity enables us to escape from the will to life that drives us constantly to seek our own advantage. Selfless actions are those that provide us with a temporary respite from the egotistical demands of our individual will. Nietzsche does not accept Schopenhauer's metaphysics and so his grounds for attributing life denial to pity are not the same as Schopenhauer's. Nietzsche has two arguments in *The Antichrist*. The first concerns what pity does to the agent who pities. The second is concerned with the consequences of pity. The first argument is based around what Nietzsche describes as the 'depressive effect' of pity (*A* 7). He believes that when we pity another we ourselves suffer as a result. Pity weakens us; it makes us less vital and less powerful. One might say that for Nietzsche pity takes the shine off life. His point is that our own suffering is hard enough to bear, so why suffer because others are suffering? The second argument he believes to be the more important. However, this argument is rather less easy to swallow than the first. Nietzsche is at his most uncompromising. 'By and large, pity runs counter to the law of development, which is the law of *selection*. Pity preserves things that are ripe for decline, it defends things that have been disowned and condemned by life, it gives a depressive and questionable character to life itself by keeping alive an abundance of failures of every type' (*A* 7). Here is the kind of quote that could easily be used to support a proto-fascist reading of Nietzsche. Indeed his whole tone here smacks of the very *ressentiment* that he condemns in Christianity.

Further on in the book however, Nietzsche says the following 'When an exceptional person treats a mediocre one more delicately than he treats himself and his equals, this is not just courtesy of the heart,—it is his *duty*' (*A* 57). Admittedly this passage itself, when read as a whole could also be used to support a proto-fascist reading, given that it advocates a hierarchical organization of society. Nonetheless one could argue that in his less resentful moments, there is room in Nietzsche, not for pity, but perhaps for kindness. It would seem that what he objects to is charitable deeds done out of a sense of guilt at the suffering of others. Such deeds carried out from a sense of one's own well-being, are acceptable for Nietzsche (*Z* I: 'Of the Gift-Giving Virtue'). Nietzsche thus advocates deeds that are motivated by the pleasurable feelings that attach to them rather than from an unpleasant feeling that can only be salved by the performance of a deed. What he also seeks to promote is not suffering with others but what he calls 'joying with' others (*GS* 338). What Nietzsche objects to is what he sees as the fundamental disparagement of life at the root of Christian values. An atheist who adheres to Christian values, ought, if they are consistent, to be a meek, humble, selfless, chaste, and largely joyless human being. Nietzsche does not want us to suddenly become heartless, uncaring, barbarians. He simply wants us to embrace life and to flourish to our full potential. As he notes in *Daybreak*, 'It goes without say that I do not deny—unless I am a fool—that many actions called immoral ought to be avoided and resisted, or that many called moral ought to be done and encouraged—but I think that one should be encouraged and the other avoided *for other reasons than hitherto*' (D 103).

Conclusion

In *The Antichrist*, Nietzsche uses the psychological insights of the *Genealogy* and constructs his own history of Christianity. His account of the original Jewish revaluation of values focuses on the creation of the notion a moral world order. The Jews created this moral world in order to slander the natural world that they had once been at home in. They needed to do this in order to survive as a people. Nietzsche's investigation into the origins of Christian ethical values shows that at the root of its revaluation of the values of antiquity lies a deep-seated desire for vengeance. The values of Christianity are suited to those who suffer from life because of the unpleasant conditions they find themselves in. Nietzsche argues that whilst there are many who still need these values to make sense of their lives, there are also those who are stifled by these values from attaining the most out of their existence. Nietzsche believes that for these people a more life-affirming set of values are required.

BIBLIOGRAPHY

(A) Works by Nietzsche

A	*The Anti-Christ*, in *The Anti-Christ, Ecce Homo, Twilight of the Idols, and Other Writings*, ed. Aaron Ridley, trans. Judith Norman. Cambridge: Cambridge University Press, 2005.
BGE	*Beyond Good and Evil*, trans. R. J. Hollingdale. London: Penguin, 1973.
CW	*The Case of Wagner*, in *The Birth of Tragedy and the Case of Wagner*, trans. Walter Kaufman. New York: Vintage.
D	*Daybreak*, ed. Maudemarie Clark and Brian Leiter, trans. R. J. Hollingdale. Cambridge: Cambridge University Press, 1997.
GM	*On the Genealogy of Morality*, trans. Maudemarie Clark and Alan J. Swensen. Indianapolis: Hackett, 1998.
GS	*The Gay Science*, trans. Josefine Nauckhoff and Adrian Del Caro. Cambridge: Cambridge University Press, 2001.
HAH	*Human, All Too Human*, trans. R. J. Hollingdale. Cambridge: Cambridge University Press, 1986.
TI	*Twilight of the Idols*, in *The Anti-Christ, Ecce Homo, Twilight of the Idols, and Other Writings*, ed. Aaron Ridley, trans. Judith Norman. Cambridge: Cambridge University Press, 2005.
WP	*The Will to Power*, trans. Walter Kaufmann and R. J. Hollingdale. New York: Vintage Books, 1968.
Z	*Thus Spoke Zarathustra*, trans. Walter Kaufmann. New York: Penguin, 1978.

(B) Other Works Cited

Armstrong, Karen. 2007. *The Bible: The Biography*. London: Atlantic Books.

Barrow, R. H. 1949. *The Romans*. Harmondsworth: Penguin.

Brobjer, Thomas H. 1997. 'Nietzsche's Reading and Private Library 1885–1889', *Journal of the History of Ideas* 58.4: 663–93.

Burkhardt, Jacob. 1949. *The Age of Constantine the Great*, trans. Moses Hadas. London: Routledge and Kegan Paul.

Chadwick, Henry. 1993. *The Early Church*. Harmondsworth: Penguin.

Fox, Robin. L. 1991. *The Unauthorised Version: Truth and Fiction in the Bible*. New York: Viking Press.

Friedman, Richard. E. 1988. *Who Wrote the Bible?* London: Jonathan Cape.

Kamm, Anthony. 1999. *The Israelites: An Introduction*. London: Routledge.

Leiter, Brian. 2002. *Nietzsche on Morality*. London: Routledge.

MacMullen, Ramsey. 1984. *Christianizing the Roman Empire*. London: Yale University Press.

Owen, David. 2007. *Nietzsche's 'Genealogy of Morality'*. Stocksfield: Acumen Publishing.

Santaniello, Weaver. 1994. *Nietzsche, God, and the Jews*. Albany: State University of New York Press.

Santaniello, Weaver. 2000. 'Nietzsche's Hierarchy of Gods in the *Antichrist*', *Journal of Nietzsche Studies* 19: 89–102.

Wellhausen, Julius. 1957. *Prolegomena to the History of Ancient Israel*, trans. J. Sutherland Black and Allan Menzies. New York: Meridian Books.

Yovel, Yirmiyahu. 1998. *Dark Riddle: Hegel, Nietzsche, and the Jews*. Oxford: Polity Press.

CHAPTER 16

BEHOLDING NIETZSCHE: *ECCE HOMO*, FATE, AND FREEDOM

CHRISTA DAVIS ACAMPORA

THAT *Ecce Homo*, with its subtitle "How One Becomes What One is," is Nietzsche's self-presentation of sorts seems rather easy to conclude. But why does Nietzsche do this? *What* is evident? What do we really learn from the work? Is it primarily a behind-the-scenes peek at Nietzsche's thought, the ideas that *truly* or *actually* motivated him? How complete is it as an autobiography, given that it seems devoted largely to his writings?[1] To what extent can we put much stock in the account at all given that Nietzsche would slip into madness not long after the first draft was complete and while still editing and revising it for publication?[2] I hope to shed some light on these common concerns about Nietzsche's *Ecce Homo* by focusing on how the text bears on his controversial and seemingly paradoxical ideas about agency, fate, and freedom in his presentation of the *type* he is and how he *evolved*. Ultimately, I think the presentation of himself that Nietzsche advances in *Ecce Homo* offers evidence that he

---

[1] It has often been noted that Nietzsche's autobiography focuses primarily on his literary and philosophical productions. *EH* has been read as a book about Nietzsche's books, about his assessment of his own writings, despite the title that announces the presentation of a life—*homo*, not *biblio*—and his profession that his life and his books should not be confused (*EH*: "Why I Write Such Good Books" 1). And there has been much attention given to the literary qualities of the text itself and what they indicate about Nietzsche's views about literature as a model for "giving style to one's character" (Nehamas 1985; cf. Sarah Kofman 1992).

[2] Walter Kaufmann's editorial introduction and notes claim Nietzsche collapsed before completing his revisions to the text. More extensive philological research has shown, in fact, Nietzsche continued to make alterations to the text, including its concluding poems, as late as January 2, 1889 (Montinari 2003: 111), though the scholarly opinion is still divided on the question of whether Nietzsche himself thought *EH* was finished and whether the text as it was published was that text or some near approximation. Compare, for example, Erich Podach's claim "What is certain is that Nietzsche did not leave behind a finished *Ecce Homo*, but we have one" with Mazzino Montinari's: "What is certain is that Nietzsche left behind a finished *Ecce Homo*, but we do not have it" (Montinari 2003: 120; Podach cited by Montinari 2003: 125 n. 35).

anticipates an achievable form of human freedom,[3] although it might be more limited than what the Nietzsche literature sometimes reflects.

How One Becomes What One Is

A host of questions arises from reflection on Nietzsche's citation and evocation of the Pindaric maxim, "become what you are." In the form in which it appears in the subtitle to *Ecce Homo—How One Becomes What One Is* (*Wie man wird, was man ist*)—no paradox need be evident: we could expect the book might have kinship with *Bildungsroman* literature, providing us with that sort of account of Nietzsche's maturation. But, as Nietzsche uses the expression in *Ecce Homo* and elsewhere, as for example in *The Gay Science*, it becomes more problematic and less clear what he intends. About himself and kindred spirits, he writes, "We want to become those we are" (*GS* 335), and in *GS* 270, he formulates it as an imperative: "you should become the one you are." Zarathustra, we are told, "once counseled himself, not for nothing, 'Become who you are'" (*Z* IV: "The Honey Sacrifice"). But how could we *become* what we *already* are in any ordinary sense of those terms? Must it be that Nietzsche is simply referring to what we (already) have the *potential to become* but which we have yet to realize or make manifest?[4] If we already *are* such selves, how could we *want* to become them, given that wants follow from lack or need? Moreover, if we already *are* such selves, how could it possibly be that things would turn out otherwise, that is, that we might *become* in any other way? And, just how does this curious imperative cohere with his other ideas, including the notion of self as subjective multiplicity and his repeated prioritizing of *becoming* over being?

To gain insight into what it means to become what one is and why and how it is necessary, we can consider an earlier account of the same that Nietzsche provides. Published nearly two decades prior, its subject was Wagner rather than Nietzsche.[5] In his fourth *Untimely Meditation* titled "Richard Wagner in Bayreuth," Nietzsche endeavors to provide an account of Wagner's development, his evolution: "*wie er wurde, was er ist, was er sein wird*" (*UM* IV: 1). He depicts Wagner's "powerful striving" (*UM* IV: 2), his great struggles to identify his

---

[3] Ken Gemes (2006) has recently argued that Nietzsche has an "achievement" conception of freedom, specifically, that one *becomes* free in becoming a full-fledged agent, which is something accomplished rather than a *de facto* human condition. In general, I agree, but puzzles remain about how such accomplishment is possible. For example, the account appears to presume some sort of agency for the *achievement* to occur (for it to be properly understood as an *achievement* rather than an *event* or *occurrence*), and thus it appears to require at least some of the very powers that are supposed to be lacking and serve as the basis for distinction. A similar concern is addressed by Robert Pippin (2009: 86; see also p. 79). The puzzle persists in John Richardson's (2009) analysis in which he explores agency as a capacity that arises in response to social demands and which acts like a drive and is capable of both acting upon and interacting with other constitutive (largely antecedent) drives (2009: 137, 140–2). This essay is my effort to contribute to this important discussion. See also the final chapter of my *Contesting Nietzsche*, which incorporates and slightly revises some of the material that follows.

[4] Alexander Nehamas (1985) discusses problems with this interpretation on p. 175.

[5] Although Nietzsche might be thought to minimize Wagner's significance when he writes in *Ecce Homo* that "Richard Wagner in Bayreuth" is really about himself rather than Wagner (*EH*: "The Birth of Tragedy" 4), it is nevertheless illuminating to explore the similarities and differences in these two works because they provide insight into the process Nietzsche envisions as well as its (and his) task.

life's task and reconcile multiple parts of himself that were in great tension (*UM* IV: 8). It seems clear that his struggle with and against himself is a significant part of what Nietzsche thinks constitutes his achievement and serves as an indication of his greatness; it is largely what Nietzsche discusses and what he ultimately praises. As we shall see, a curious feature of Nietzsche's account of his own development in *Ecce Homo* will be that he did *not* struggle, was *not* heroic in the way he depicts Wagner, although he does describe his development similarly in terms of unifying multiple, opposing drives.

In his earlier work, Nietzsche sums up the story of Wagner's development as follows: "The struggles that it depicts are simplifications of the real struggles of life; its problems are abbreviations of the endlessly complicated reckoning of human action and aspiration" (*UM* IV: 4). This gap between aspiration and action, and the necessary adjustment of aspiration to achieve reconciliation, mark an interesting contrast between Nietzsche's account of Wagner's development and the story Nietzsche later tells himself about himself (*EH*: Interleaf). For Nietzsche's story will have at least two features distinguishing it from Wagner's: Nietzsche "never struggled," as previously mentioned, and in contrast to Wagner's development, which was organized around his various ideas about cultural revolution and himself as its instigator, *becoming* (*Werden*) of the sort that Nietzsche finds interesting, requires that one *not have the slightest idea what one is*. This opens a complicated set of issues about how Nietzsche thinks one *becomes*—what constitutes becoming and how one goes about it. And it is relevant to a significant disagreement in the scholarly literature as to whether Nietzsche is a fatalist or an advocate of self-creation.[6] In the works under review here we find crucial clues to what Nietzsche has in mind, for becoming what one is appears to turn on *making oneself necessary*. Becoming what one is involves becoming "not just a piece of chance but rather a necessity" (*EH*: "Why I Am So Clever" 8). This is precisely what Wagner is supposed to have done in his heroic struggles (*UM* IV: 6). But by the time Nietzsche writes *Ecce Homo*, he sees himself as quite different from the man he clearly loved and admired, perhaps above all others (*EH*: "Why I Am So Wise" 3, "Why I Am So Clever" 5), even as he remained his harshest critic (e.g., *The Case of Wagner*). In understanding how Nietzsche's self-presentation of his development differs from that of Wagner, we also catch a glimpse of how Nietzsche endeavors to become "powerful *through* Wagner *against* Wagner" (*UM* IV: 7).[7] In *Ecce Homo*, against the backdrop of Wagner's exemplary evolution, Nietzsche depicts his

---

[6] Brian Leiter (1998) reads Nietzsche's anti-metaphysical comments about the soul and concludes that "there is [...] no 'self' in 'self-mastery,'" whereas Nehamas (1985) regards the self as something that *becomes* by virtue of some special activity one engages in that allows for self-transformation and transfiguration, self-becoming. Though these views seem at odds, perhaps it is a mistake to think that we must embrace only one or the other. A third option might grant subjective multiplicity while locating agency in the various powers of the contributors, claiming *multiple agencies*, as one finds in Parkes 1994 (e.g., pp. 320, 325), who claims Nietzsche presents a "a multiplicity [of subjective entities] behind which it is not necessary to posit a unity: it suffices to conceive the multiplicity as a regency" (Parkes 1994: 354; cf. *KSA* 11: 40 [38]). I find Parkes' account illuminating and supported by the text, but I think the *pattern* of the organization of the drives, which he claims is fated, is not fixed, and I think there is potentially greater unity than what his ultimate claim of the "play of masks" suggests, even though I recognize he thinks this occurs on the basis of what he calls "enlightened spontaneity" (Parkes 1994: 459 n. 74).

[7] The confines of this essay do not permit a fuller development of Nietzsche's relationship to Wagner, although I wish to point out that it is more complicated than often depicted. It is not an overstatement to claim that Wagner influenced Nietzsche from the beginning to the end of his career, and he appears by name or in the guise of a "type" in each and every work he wrote. While Nietzsche is immensely interested in the lives and works of other persons he thinks are greatly important (for better and for worse)—such as Homer, Socrates, Paul, Goethe, Beethoven, and Napoleon, to name just a few—only

own development in terms of a tense opposition between fighting and loving, which Nietzsche respectively links in *EH* to his wisdom and his cleverness.

Nietzsche begins *Ecce Homo* with reference to his "fatality" (*Verhängniss*), and he concludes the work with a section claiming himself as "a destiny" ("*Warum ich ein Schicksal bin*"). He uses this as an entry to explore his descent or ancestry (*Herkunft*), which includes what is both "highest and lowest," common and noble. Specifically, he focuses on what he inherited from his parents and his "dual descent" (*EH*: "Why I Am So Wise" 1); he describes his life as both ascendant and decadent (*EH*: "Why I Am So Wise" 1). This accounts for the fact that he is a "*Doppelgänger*" (*EH*: "Why I Am So Wise" 3).[8] His interest in inheritance includes consideration of acquired resources, capabilities, and capacities, and the intensification or diminution of powers, temperament, and inclinations. It includes intellectual, cultural, psychological, and physiological considerations relevant to his reception and criticisms of evolutionary theory[9] as well as his interest in atavism.[10] His first chapter, titled "Why I Am So Wise," focuses on the resources and liabilities he inherited from his parents. At the same time, he diminishes their role in determining him when he writes: "to be related to one's parents is the most typical sign of commonality. Higher types have their origins infinitely further back, on which at long last, an atavism must be unified, retained. Great individuals are the most ancient individuals."[11] This suggests that a higher type, as Nietzsche conceives it, is someone who somehow accesses and taps other, ancient characteristics, and is perhaps distinguished by virtue of the depth and reach of ancestral resources. Indeed, this is how Nietzsche describes himself earlier in the same section when he writes, "But as a Pole I am also an uncanny atavism. One must go back centuries to discover in this noblest race of men pure instincts to the degree that I represent them."[12] We find the same idea evident in his *UM* IV, in which he links Wagner with Alexander, much as he suggests in *EH* that

Wagner is analyzed in such detail in terms of his development. Wagner becomes increasingly important to Nietzsche after Wagner's death, at which time Nietzsche both writes his harshest criticisms and professes his deepest affection for Wagner.

[8] A preoccupation with genealogies, in terms of ancestry as well as the evolution and development of values and institutions, is evident throughout Nietzsche's works in his analyses of other cultures and types of individuals. It famously underlies his account of the emergence and conflict of noble and slavish morality and his examination of the modern European inheritance in Book VIII of *Beyond Good and Evil*, "On Peoples and Fatherlands" (see especially *BGE* 264 and 268). There is considerable discussion in the scholarly literature about Nietzsche's use of the terms *Herkunft*, *Ursprung* (origin), and *Entstehung* (emergence), particularly as it relates to Nietzsche's conception and practice of genealogy. The most famous, if not most illuminating, is Michel Foucault's "Nietzsche, Genealogy, History" (1977). See also Pizer 1990.

[9] See Moore 2002 and Richardson 2004.

[10] On Nietzsche's atavism, see Lingis 2000–1.

[11] Translated by Greg Whitlock in Montinari 2003. The passage cited is part of a replacement text he submitted for "Why I Am So Wise" 3, when he returned the first and second signatures of *EH* to the publisher on December 18, 1888. It does not appear in the Kaufmann translation on which I most often rely. This passage is somewhat at odds with *BGE* 264, mentioned above, which underscores that it is "absolutely impossible" not to embody the "qualities and preferences" of one's parents. These can be reconciled if one grants that Nietzsche holds that one is not *merely* what one inherits most immediately and that in higher types the ancient inheritances are enhanced and more pronounced.

[12] Translated by Greg Whitlock. "*Aber auch als Pole bin ich ein ungeheurer Atavismus. Man würde Jahrhunderte zurückzugehn haben, um diese vornehmste Rasse, die es auf Erden gab, in dem Masse instinktrein zu finden, wie ich sie darstelle*" (KSA 6: 268).

"Julius Caesar could be my father—*or* Alexander, that Dionysus incarnate" in (*EH*: "Why I Am So Wise" 3). This inheritance provides Nietzsche with a vast multiplicity of perspectives (*EH*: "Why I Am So Wise" 1); it does not simply *make* him great. What distinguishes the "well-turned-out person" is that "He instinctively gathers *his* totality from everything he sees, hears, experiences: he is a principle of selection" (*EH*: "Why I Am So Wise" 3). We might consider just what this multiplicity is and how it becomes something that approximates something singular, something capable of being choosy in the way he describes someone who is, as he puts it, "basically healthy" (*EH*: "Why I Am So Wise" 2) and has a hearty constitution, as I explore in the sections that follow.

It is not just sheer multiplicity that makes a person rich on Nietzsche's account. Having certain kinds of resources, particularly those that characterize opposing tendencies, so that the strength of their opposition might become a resource, seems to be important to him. Nietzsche identifies and elaborates the notion of subjective multiplicity throughout his writings. Consideration of those discussions allows us to see that he also distinguishes *orders of rank* and *orders of rule*. Those ideas can help us appreciate why he distinguishes these parts of himself in *Ecce Homo*, and how he thinks they became organized and productive in the life he presents in that work.

"Orders of Rank," "Types," and "Ruling Thoughts"

Nietzsche repeatedly offers the view that individuals are composites or conglomerates of multiple, competing drives, affects, and thoughts. These parts become organized, on his view, in terms of "orders of rank." Several "types" of such orders are discussed at length by Nietzsche, including the types of the "master," the "slave," and the "priest."[13] The "last man" might also be thought a type, and the *Übermensch* could be construed as an as-yet unachieved type (human, transhuman, or more-than-human).[14] We can consider "types" as distinguished by the general "orders of rank" constituting them.[15] What are ranked, as Nietzsche considers such cases, are "drives" (*Triebe*), and the rank ordering reflects the *relations* of the drives: which predominate, which serve the others, etc.

Orders of rank *characterize* individual human beings (*BGE* 6), on Nietzsche's hypothesis, such that he thinks *who* or *what* one is, strictly speaking, is this collection of drives in the particular order or relation they are. There is no self either *behind* (i.e., other than) the ordering, or *doing* the ordering (see *GM* I: 13). But if this is what we are, then it is hard to see how there can be anyone to appeal to in Nietzsche's Pindaric imperative to "become who you are." There should be no one "there" (*in* us) to answer a call to action, if indeed that is what Nietzsche's imperative is. Is there another way to make sense of Nietzsche's insistence that there

---

[13] See Richardson 2004 and 2009 for discussion of types as orders of drives.

[14] For the view that Nietzsche conceives the *Übermensch* as a future (or at least more-than-human) life form, see Loeb 2010. For the view that the *Übermensch* is neither a future life form nor a specific type of human being but rather a set of attributes or capacities, see Conway 1998.

[15] Brian Leiter attributes a "doctrine of Types" to Nietzsche (1998, 2002, 2007).

is nothing to "us" other than the competing drives of which we are constituted while he repeatedly appeals to some sense of agency? I propose we look for such in Nietzsche's accounts of how such drives are organized, how we are not merely a collection or group of drives but *drives organized in a certain way*, characterized by a political arrangement, and how such arrangements can change and take on different characteristics. Orders of rank can be examined from at least two related perspectives: in terms of their specific order, hierarchy, or relative rankings of the drives, as well as *the way in which* ruling or dominant drives relate to other drives. That is, there is a political character to such orders, and this allows us to consider *what* rules, *how* it rules, and how it *came to rule*. Indeed, in virtually all of his writings, we find Nietzsche exploring the nature and further implications of a conception of soul that follows from a notion of a "social structure of the drives and affects" (*BGE* 12).

Thus Nietzsche regards human psychology as a good bit more complex than often recognized by philosophers, particularly in their representations of subjectivity and willing. What philosophers have designated as "will" is, (*minimally*) for Nietzsche, a complicated and multidimensional process of interacting sensations, thoughts, and affects (*BGE* 19), which includes awareness of various states ("*away from which*," "*towards which*," "*from*" and "*toward*" more generally), thinking ("a ruling thought"), and affect (particularly "the affect of the command" insofar as "a man who *wills* commands something within himself that renders obedience, or that he believes renders obedience"). Another way of accounting for *willing* as Nietzsche depicts it is as shorthand for the *processes of organization* of an entity: what it senses as significant, its orientation, and the structure of ordering it achieves (*BGE* 19).

Suppositions about the status of human freedom more generally are unwarranted on the basis of this experience, because what is perceived here is not so much the condition of the whole organism in the world (an individual *agent* of activity) but rather *an aspect* or dimension of the interactions of the organism itself: "'Freedom of the will'—that is the expression for the complex state of delight of the person exercising volition, who commands and at the same time identifies himself with the executor of the order—who, as such enjoys also the triumph over obstacles, but thinks within himself that it was really his will itself that overcame them" (*BGE* 19). [16] Yet, we neither simply nor solely command or obey. Willing is complex. We experience ourselves as individual, atomic *willing* agents when actually we are a composite structure of wills and "under-wills," which is another way of speaking of drives seeking to master other drives: "we are at the same time the commanding *and* the obeying parties, and as the obeying party we know the sensations of constraint, impulsion, pressure, resistance, and motion [. . .] *we are accustomed to disregard this duality, and to deceive ourselves about it by means of the synthetic concept 'I'*" (*BGE* 19; italics mine). Thus, our best *evidence* of our freedom—the felt perception of freedom, our sense of ourselves as agents—is not indexed to our metaphysical or ontological status but rather to the perception of one aspect of a complex process of organization: "our body is but a social structure composed of many souls" in which some obey and others command (*BGE* 19). [17] These structures of *orders of rank* and their discernible patterns comprise one significant, but not exhaustive, aspect of what might be regarded as Nietzsche's interest in *types*.

[16] See the interesting debate about whether Nietzsche's discussion of the will in *BGE* 19 is an account of the *phenomenology* of willing (and linked with dismissal of the efficiency of the will) or an alternative account of what constitutes willing and the circumstances in which it occurs in Leiter 2007 and Clark and Dudrick 2009.

[17] Nietzsche repeatedly refers to the idea of the subject as a multiplicity; see also *GM* I: 13. For further

What constitutes a *type* in the sense discussed here is not only the particular drives that comprise the social structure distinguishing an individual but also *how* those drives are ordered and how their organization develops and is maintained—the ruling dynamic, the form of rule that achieves and seeks to preserve that arrangement or ordering of drives.[18]

Orders of rank themselves are also not absolutely fixed, not determined, and this is precisely what worries Nietzsche. Drives appear to be there from the start, and seem to be inherited and shaped historically. These can vary among different people and constitutions. Constitutive elements and inheritances are fixed, but their relative strengths and orderings are not. How, then, do they acquire their ordering? Nietzsche's account of himself as both a lover and a fighter in *Ecce Homo* offers some indications of how this might be achieved, and in the process (and in some cases) one becomes what one is by becoming a "necessity," rather than "a piece of chance" (*EH*: "Why I Am So Clever" 8).

NIETZSCHE AS A LOVER: SELFISHNESS VS SELFLESSNESS

In his chapter titled "Why I Am So Clever," Nietzsche, finally, directly provides "the real answer to the question, *how one becomes what one is*," and it entails what he calls "the masterpiece of the art of self-preservation or selfishness" (*EH*: "Why I Am So Clever" 9). Yet this is a curious art, because it does not include deliberate, conscious, active creation in the way that "self-creation" might be thought to require: Nietzsche claims that "to become what one is" "one must not have the faintest notion *what* one is" (*EH*: "Why I Am So Clever" 9). How can we become what we are if we don't even know what that is, if we *haven't the faintest notion* what that is? This clearly seems to support the fatalist interpretation that we simply become what we *already* are, that there is no conscious *planning* or *creating* at work, and thus there can be no imperative to action of self-creation and no special *kudos* to accrue if and when one happens to succeed.[19] There is, according to Nietzsche, an "organizing idea" that is "destined to rule," which "keeps growing deep down—it begins to command; slowly it

comments by Nietzsche on the aptness of political organizations as metaphors for the subject, see for example *KSA* 11: 40 [21], which is discussed briefly by Nehamas 1985: 181–2 (as *WP* 492).

[18] For example, strictly speaking, the master and the slave in Nietzsche's *On the Genealogy of Morality* reflect *different ways of ruling* and not simply different types of people. Missing from Leiter's account is discussion of "orders of rank," and this idea that is so important to Nietzsche seems more relevant to determining what one is than the "type facts" associated with such orders. The "type facts" themselves do not *determine* what one does; rather they are themselves *determinations* of the rank order of drives. What Leiter calls "type-facts" might be better understood as statements about conditions of a rank ordering (rather than particular features of such orderings). Each individual is a myriad of type facts, which are perhaps innumerable. They are fixed or determined *in relation to* the order of rank one is, not fixed or determined for the entire duration of the life of the organism. Type facts themselves do not determine but rather are themselves *determinations* of this ordering.

[19] One might also place the emphasis on an implied restraint against our tendency to *want* to know and to fabricate such answers that seek to unify conflicting and contrasting traits and characteristics. This is explored at length in Gary Shapiro's chapter on *Ecce Homo* (1989), which emphasizes the importance of the *Doppelgänger* in Nietzsche.

leads us *back* from side roads and wrong roads; it prepares *single* qualities and fitnesses that will one day prove to be indispensable as means toward a whole—one by one, it trains all *subservient* capacities before giving any hint of the dominant task, "goal," "aim," or "meaning'" (*EH*: "Why I Am So Clever" 9).

One way of understanding what is meant by "destined" here is to see it in light of Nietzsche's proposition of will to power (*BGE* 36): roughly, he proposes that all things seek the full expression of their capacities, the full measure of their powers. In this sense, what is "destined to rule" is simply whatever proves strongest, whatever succeeds in enabling the multifarious drives to be coordinated in a single entity. There is no separate faculty of will in itself that stands independent of the drives that comprise us, no *will* that adjudicates the inevitable conflict and contest of drives we are, such that it could be said to be within our power to have things turn out otherwise. "Destined," then, in this sense does not mean "predetermined," that is, decided already in advance of our becoming the particular organization of drives we are. Thus, in the particular instance in question, "destined" is a loose way of speaking about *eventual* outcomes and does not refer to any particular outcome that necessarily should come to pass (other than that what is strongest determines the order of the others, since that is how strength is expressed).

But Nietzsche invokes stronger senses of destiny elsewhere in his writings, including in his *Thus Spoke Zarathustra*, which is so central to his presentation and recounting of his life. In that context and others, he makes reference to *fate* and links his philosophical practice and axiological project of revaluation with *loving fate, amor fati*.[20] In *Ecce Homo*, Nietzsche writes: "My formula for greatness in a human being is *amor fati*: that one wants nothing to be different, not forward, not backward, not in all eternity. Not merely bear what is necessary, still less conceal it—all idealism is mendaciousness in the face of what is necessary—but *love* it" (*EH*: "Why I Am So Clever" 10). This important idea to Nietzsche receives a variety of treatments in the scholarly literature, and their consideration is beyond the scope of what can be treated in this essay; I wish to focus here on just one sense of love as a form of caring, which complements the general consensus in the scholarly literature that *amor fati* minimally entails a certain form of affirmation. In *Ecce Homo*, *love* and *fate* are united in Nietzsche's conception of selfishness and its role in his own development.

A major point of difference between Nietzsche's earlier account of Wagner's development and his own self-presentation of the type he is is found in Nietzsche's account of his own selfishness, or self-seeking (*Selbstsucht*).[21] Rather than engaging in heroic struggles, as he

[20] Contrasting positions on Nietzsche's views about fate are evident in the different accounts given by Brian Leiter (1999, 2007) and Robert Solomon (2003). For Leiter, what he calls "type-facts" play a "crucial role [...] in determining what one does, even what morality one accepts" (2007: 9). While events are not determined in advance for Leiter—and thus, there is no predestination in that sense—"facts" about a person, which limit and determine a range of possibilities, *are*. Thus Leiter regards his view as attributing a form of "causal essentialism" to Nietzsche (Leiter 1998: 225). Solomon emphasizes distinctions between fatalism and determinism, whereby determinism is focused on necessary causal connections and fatalism emphasizes the necessity of eventual outcomes without commitment to any specific causes that lead to such outcomes. Solomon thinks Nietzsche's fatalism is most closely related to ancient views, and that it is decidedly not a form of determinism in the contemporary sense.
[21] Kaufmann and others translate *Selbstsucht* quite reasonably as "selfishness," but I think self-seeking, conceived as part of a process of self-formation, is also appropriate. It resonates with the opening of Nietzsche's *On the Genealogy of Morality*, where he writes, "*Wir sind uns unbekannt, wir Erkennenden, wir selbst uns selbst: das hat seinen guten Grund. Wir haben nie nach uns gesucht,—wie sollte es geschehn, dass wir eines Tags uns* fänden?" (*GM* Preface: 1).

describes Wagner early on, Nietzsche claims he was particularly adept at self-preservation (*Selbsterhaltung*), characterized in this text as selfishness or self-seeking rather than simply self-perpetuation. This is the "ruling thought" he proposes in *EH* as an alternative to the ruling thought of morality and the ruling thought of Wagner, whom he saw as advocating *selflessness*. In *UM* IV, Nietzsche depicts Wagner as seeking *fidelity* (*Treue*) above all else. This loyalty was directed toward both the multitude (to be united as a "people," *UM* IV: 8) and the multiple and opposing parts of himself. It regards unity as a higher value than any individual needs or desires.

A long-standing concern in Nietzsche's works is what he regards as the morality of selflessness, which he thinks is ultimately life-denying and a symptom of decadence.[22] He attacks it repeatedly in *Ecce Homo*, as when he expresses his suspicion of the "so-called 'selfless' drives": "It always seems a weakness to me, a particular case of being incapable of resisting stimuli: *pity* is considered a virtue only among decadents [...] and sometimes pitying hands can interfere in a downright destructive manner in a great destiny" (*EH*: "Why I Am So Wise" 5).[23] But in his presentation of Wagner's evolution in *UM* IV, the realization of selflessness marks the pinnacle of Wagner's development: "we sense how the man Wagner evolved: [...] how the whole current of the man plunged into first one valley, then another, how it plummeted down the darkest ravines. Then, in the night of this half-subterranean frenzy, high overhead appeared a star of melancholy luster. As soon as he saw it, he named it *Fidelity, selfless Fidelity*! [...] Investing it with the utmost splendor he possesses and can realize—that marvelous knowledge and experience by which one sphere of his being remained faithful to another. Through free, utterly selfless love, it preserved fidelity. The creative sphere, luminous and innocent, remained faithful to the dark, indomitable, and tyrannical sphere" (*UM* IV: 2). This is echoed later when he writes: "For Wagner himself the event is a dark cloud of toil, worry, brooding, and grief; a renewed outbreak of conflicting elements, but all irradiated by the star of *selfless fidelity* and, in this light, transformed into unspeakable joy" (*UM* IV: 8). The kind of love he praises in his early text on Wagner is one that involves completely relinquishing oneself. In the "soul of the dithyrambic dramatist" (which Nietzsche claims for Wagner in *UM* IV and then for himself in *EH*), "the creative moments of his art" occur "when this conflict of feelings is taut, when his gloomy arrogance and horrified distaste for the world fuse with his passionate urgency to approach the world as a lover.

---

[22] Extensive discussion of Nietzsche's wrestling with and ultimate rejection of "selflessness" is found in Janaway 2007.

[23] Nietzsche repeatedly expresses the view that hostility to selfishness leads to decadence, declining life: "The best is lacking when self-interest begins to be lacking. Instinctively to choose what is harmful for *oneself*, to feel attracted by 'disinterested' motives, that is virtually the formula for decadence. [...] 'I no longer know how to *find* my own advantage.' Disgregation of the instincts! Man is finished when he becomes altruistic" (*TI*: "Skirmishes of an Untimely Man" 35). Cf. *NCW* 7; *TI*: "The Four Great Errors" 2; and for discussion see Müller-Lauter 1999a. Part of what is so problematic with pity is that it can motivate us to conserve what ought to perish, and in *Ecce Homo* he presents himself as a physiologist who is experienced in understanding organic degeneration and can apply those insights to psychological health. Nietzsche writes: "When the least organ in an organism fails, however slightly, to enforce with complete assurance its self-preservation, its 'egoism,' restitution of its energies—the whole degenerates. The physiologist demands *excision* of the degenerating part; he denies all solidarity with what degenerates; he is worlds removed from pity for it. But the priest desires precisely the degeneration of the whole, of humanity: for that reason he *conserves* what degenerates—at this price he rules."

When he now casts his eyes on earth and life, his eyes are like the rays of the sun which 'draw up the water,' collect mist, and accumulate towering thunderheads. *Cautiously lucid and selflessly loving* at the same time, his gazing eyes touch earth, and everything illuminated by this binocular vision is compelled by Nature with frightful rapidity to discharge all its powers, and to reveal its most hidden secrets" (*UM* IV: 7). Of course, Nietzsche takes a very different view on Wagner in his later works. In *The Case of Wagner*, for example, Nietzsche accuses Wagner of "disgregation," being fundamentally unable to bring unity to anything, offering only the superficial appearance of development and form (e.g., *CW* 7, 10), merely stoking up passions and emotions to achieve "effects" and overpower his audience; he seduces rather than creates (*CW*: Postscript 1). But we can't simply trust Nietzsche in *EH* when he implies that we might resolve the vast difference between his accounts of Wagner in *UM* IV and *CW* by substituting the name "Nietzsche" where the reader finds "Wagner" in the earlier work. Nietzsche offers readers a very different presentation of himself in *EH*, and it largely depends on the differences he identifies in *how* one evolves, what it amounts to, and what it entails.

In contrast to his portrait of Wagner, Nietzsche presents himself as cleverly *selfish*, a theme he treats repeatedly in works published after *UM* IV. Nietzsche highlights his "instinct of self-preservation [*Selbsterhaltung*]" (*EH*: 'Why I Am So Clever' 8), which he links with his "art of self-preservation": "In all these matters—in the choice of nutrition, of place and climate, of recreation—an instinct of self-preservation issues its commandments, and it gains its most unambiguous expression as an instinct of *self-defense* [*Selbstvertheidigung*]" (*EH*: "Why I Am So Clever" 8). This is affected by and engaged with seemingly insignificant matters of nutrition, place, climate, and recreation:

> [T]hese small things—nutrition, place, climate, recreation, the whole casuistry of selfishness—are inconceivably more important than everything one has taken to be important so far. Precisely here one must begin to *relearn*. What mankind has so far considered seriously have not even been realities but mere imaginings—more strictly speaking, *lies* prompted by the bad instincts of sick natures that were harmful in the most profound sense. [...] All the problems of politics, of social organization, and of education have been falsified through and through because one mistook the most harmful men for great men—because one learned to despise 'little' things, which means the basic concerns of life itself. (*EH*: "Why I Am So Clever" 10)

Looking after these "basic concerns of life" turns out to be important because we otherwise find ourselves expending immense amounts of energy fighting off harmful conditions, and any ruling thought that distracted our attention from such concerns, denigrated them as unimportant or inconsequential, would have potentially quite harmful effects. Thus, an important dimension of how one becomes what one is is by preserving oneself, conserving oneself from counterproductive resistance. Though our constitutions may be determined to a certain extent by the drives that we happen to have, and this is qualified below in important ways, we can nevertheless actively contribute to our development by taking care of ourselves in very basic ways, which greatly affect our capacities to act. In *Ecce Homo* and elsewhere, Nietzsche offers examples of a variety of relations and associations that are informative of the type we are, including: inheritance; sensory experiences of smells, touches, and tastes; tempo; experiences with art; diet and nutrition; biorhythms and times of day; conditions of climate, seasons, and weather; geography and topography; nationality; physiological constitution and states of health;

characteristics of dwelling places and domiciles; friendships and enemies; sexual relations; and forms of recreation.

The kind of selfishness he seeks to praise and revalue in *Ecce Homo* is not one that eagerly seeks or depends upon exploitation of others. What he links with his cleverness and good fortune in *EH* is much like what he describes as "ideal selfishness" in *Daybreak* 552, where he likens it to pregnancy and ripening. The same passage sheds further light on why it is important not to have the slightest idea what one is: "In this condition we avoid many things without having to force ourself very hard! We know nothing of what is taking place, we wait and try to be *ready*. At the same time, a pure and purifying feeling of profound irresponsibility reigns in us almost like that of the auditor before the curtain has gone up—*it* is growing, *it* is coming to light: *we* have no right to determine either its value or the hour of its coming. All the influence we can exert lies in keeping it safe." Nietzsche associates this with "a state of consecration" such that "if what is expected is an idea, a deed—towards every bringing forth we have essentially no other relationship than that of pregnancy and ought to blow to the winds all presumptuous talk of 'willing' and 'creating'. This is *ideal selfishness*: continually to watch over and care for and to keep our soul still, so that our fruitfulness shall *come to a happy fulfillment*." Such happy fulfillment, though, is not an end in itself that is merely self-serving and self-satisfying; it serves and benefits others, as Nietzsche imagines it: "Thus, as intermediaries, we watch over and care for to the *benefit of all*; and the mood in which we live, this mood of pride and gentleness, is a balm which spreads far around us and on to restless souls too."

The kind of self-preservation that Nietzsche describes aims not at preserving sheer existence or mere survival but rather achieving a certain "self-sufficiency that overflows and gives to men and things" (*GS* 55). Thus, *Selbstsucht* is not simply self-absorption or withdrawal, but rather is a form of storing up for the purpose of enhancing expressive capacities and sharing them with others. And just what might result that could be regarded as great? Nietzsche provides insight to this throughout his texts, including in *GS* 143, where he claims that the impulse "to posit [one's] own ideal and to derive from it his own law, joy, and rights" becomes creative rather than destructive, as in the case of polytheism: "The wonderful art and gift of creating gods—polytheism—was the medium through which this impulse could discharge, purify, perfect, and ennoble itself; for originally it was a very undistinguished impulse, related to stubbornness, disobedience, and envy." Morality is opposed to it, but the "invention of gods, heroes, and overmen of all kinds, as well as near-men and undermen, dwarfs, fairies, centaurs, satyrs, demons, and devils was the inestimable preliminary exercise for the justification of selfishness and self-rule of the individual."[24] He links this with freedom: "the freedom that one conceded to a god in his relation to other gods—one eventually also granted to oneself in relation to laws, customs, and neighbors." And in this respect self-creation is possible, not in making ourselves whole, but rather in cultivating and maximally expressing our creative powers, which allow us to project ourselves beyond what we presently are: "In polytheism the free-spiriting and many-spiriting of man attained its first preliminary form—the strength to create for ourselves our own new eyes—and ever again new eyes that are even more our own: hence man alone among all the animals has no

---

[24] Kaufmann's translation amended: "*Die Erfindung von Göttern, Heroen und Uebermenschen aller Art, sowie von Neben- und Untermenschen, von Zwergen, Feen, Centauren, Satyrn, Dämonen und Teufeln, war die unschätzbare Vorübung zur Rechtfertigung der Selbstsucht und Selbstherrlichkeit des Einzelnen.*"

eternal horizons and perspectives" (*GS* 143). Thus, Nietzsche regards selfishness as a means to free- and full-spiritedness. In this respect self-preservation is a form of nurturance.[25]

The idea of selfishness is so important to Nietzsche that he returns to it in his concluding chapter in which he declares himself a destiny. There, the most "severe self-love" is identified as "what is most profoundly necessary for growth" and is contrasted with "the 'selfless', the loss of a center of gravity, 'depersonalization' and 'neighbor love' (*addiction* to the neighbor)" and that which "would un-self man" in which "un-selfing […] negates life" (*EH*: "Why I Am A Destiny" 7). The evidence Nietzsche offers for this in this work is that Christian morality teaches that the basic conditions of life—"nourishment, abode, spiritual diet, treatment of the sick, cleanliness, and weather" are "small things," trivial matters rather than the most important. For Nietzsche, they are the most important, again, because when we find ourselves in unsuitable states of affairs (unsuitable relative to our constitutions), we are forced to expend great energy simply in *fighting off* what threatens our very existence rather than being able to *fight for* something else (*EH*: "Why I Am So Clever" 8). The nature of this *fighting for* and how and why it might matter are elaborated in Nietzsche's account of his *Kriegs-Praxis* in which he presents himself as a kind of fighter.

Nietzsche proposes to revalue the meaning of selfishness and present an account of its fruits in his presentation of himself in *Ecce Homo*. Self-seeking is proposed as a ruling thought that might have an organizing feature and could counter the ruling thought of morality. Orders of rule emerge in moralities in terms of the kinds of struggles they link with the way of life they advance, their interpretation of the struggles of human existence and their purposes, and the ways in which they encourage or discourage struggling more generally, including what they designate as *worthy* struggles. Both the *forms of struggle* and contest they promote and how they promote *action* within those contexts are relevant, and in *EH* Nietzsche distinguishes struggles that are enervating—"when defensive expenditures, be they ever so small, become the rule and a habit, they entail an extraordinary and entirely superfluous impoverishment […] energy wasted on negative ends" (*EH*: "Why I Am So Clever" 8)—from those that are invigorating. In reading Nietzsche's account of himself as a fighter as he presents his *Kriegs-Praxis*, we come to appreciate how he thinks about productive expenditures as well as how he thinks about our active participation in becoming who we are.

NIETZSCHE AS FIGHTER: *KRIEGS-PRAXIS*

Nietzsche's *Kriegs-Praxis* is an expression of the organization he *is*. It issues from an order of rule that organizes his various drives and is expressed in his engagements with others and their ideas. In articulating his *Kriegs-Praxis*, Nietzsche identifies *what* rules in him as well as *how* it does so. This provides another window on *how one becomes what one is*. One does not simply realize a potency that is already there, fully formed, from the start; nor does one make oneself into something other than what one already is. Rather, becoming what one is

---

[25] See also an earlier draft of the main concept for *EH* (1888), which focuses on the "problem of nutrition" [*Ernährung*]; *KGW* VIII.3: 24[1]; cf. *BGE* 36; *D* 171; *GS* 347.

is realized through an interactive process in which the constitutive rank ordering of drives is achieved by virtue of a form of ruling expressed in engaging others.

Nietzsche's *Kriegs-Praxis* is a particular manifestation of a phenomenon that he thinks is characteristic of all living things, namely that every "living thing seeks above all to *discharge* its strength" (*BGE* 13). This entails "Being *able* to be an enemy"—that is, being prepared to resist and engage combat and *in a certain way*, as we shall see—as well as "*being* an enemy"—that is, seeking out arenas in which such engagements can occur and participating in them (*EH*: "Why I Am So Wise" 7). Repeatedly, he links this with "*Natur*," which might suggest he thinks it is strictly the result of a particular type he already is. But that is not the whole story, for it was not necessary that Nietzsche turn out to be a fighter; he became one only because he sufficiently sought himself, sufficiently loved himself, realized his ideal selfishness, as described above.

In *Ecce Homo*, Nietzsche describes a strong nature as one that "needs objects of resistance." In such cases what is wanted is "what requires us to stake all our strength, suppleness, and fighting skill" (*EH*: "Why I Am So Wise" 7). The right sorts of fights provide conditions in which one potentially gathers and expresses one's strength. To achieve the conditions most conducive to this sort of activity, Nietzsche claims he applies four principles of engagement. A brief survey of these provides a more complex portrait of Nietzsche's "practice of war" and how it constituted him as an author who produced the works he did:[26] (1) he attacks causes or ideas and not individuals; (2) those ideas or causes have to be regarded as "victorious" such that the struggle against them is of monumental significance; (3) he attacks only that against which he lacks any personal grudges; and (4) his attacks are his alone and not something done as part of some mass movement.[27]

This gives some insight into what he thinks are healthy or invigorating kinds of fighting in contrast with sources of resistance that are merely draining, destructive, and diminishing. The second principle indicates the importance of taking on a worthy competitor. The engagement must truly test him if it is to bring out the best in him. It is important that he strives to surpass what he engages rather than simply destroy or denigrate it. This latter point is further advanced by the third principle, which prohibits utilizing these struggles to settle personal grudges. The fourth principle concerning his individual pursuit might be regarded as also contributing to the form of personal cultivation possible in agonistic encounters. Mass movements do not necessarily require the same sort of personal investment. Concerning the first and third principles, we might question whether Nietzsche, in fact, actually applied them. It is hard to see how Nietzsche's attacks on Strauss and Wagner are not directed at the individuals, despite his claim in *EH* that he uses the names of persons as indicative of types, as magnifying glasses for broader concerns; and it is hard to see how Nietzsche's lifelong and repeated engagement with Wagner does not take on the character of trying to settle a score. Nevertheless, in *Ecce Homo* as well as *The Case of Wagner*, Nietzsche clearly states that he is supremely grateful for Wagner, cherishes his relationship with him above all others, and he considers him a "windfall" for philosophy insofar as he provides

---

[26] I have listed these in an order that differs from Nietzsche's because I do not think his sequence indicates any particular priority.

[27] Whether or not Nietzsche *actually* put these principles into action is another matter. I discuss these concerns at some length in Acampora 2003b.

an exemplary psychological type that crystallizes the problems with modern human beings (*CW*: "Epilogue").

Although the confines of this essay do not permit extensive analysis of how, in challenging "problems [...] to single combat" (*EH*: "Why I Am So Wise" 7), Nietzsche became the philosopher he was and had the thoughts he did, we can note that this is precisely how Nietzsche *presents* himself in *Ecce Homo*. In defining his problems, Nietzsche establishes mammoth challenges that he sets out to surmount. He endeavors to show how these engagements required him "to stake all [his] strength, suppleness, and fighting skill," and summon all of his abilities. These struggles not only tested qualities and capacities Nietzsche already had but also facilitated his development of new or enhanced powers he would not have had otherwise.[28] It is hard to imagine how Nietzsche's views on the task of the creative affirmation of life, for example, could form without the contrast evident in his analyses of the moralization and denigration of human existence he finds in Platonic metaphysics, for example. Virtually all of Nietzsche's positive views are inseparable from the positions he battles such that his *Kriegs-Praxis* appears to play a significant role in shaping both *what* ideas he expressed and *how* he did so.

Throughout *Ecce Homo*, Nietzsche clarifies and qualifies these principles as he repeatedly makes reference to how his agonistic practice unfolds and is evident in his writings. He locates "the real opposition" he generates in *The Birth of Tragedy* in his effort to fight "the degenerating instinct that turns life against life," which he contrasts with "a formula for the highest affirmation, born of fullness, of overfullness, a Yes-saying without reservation" (*EH*: "The Birth of Tragedy" 2). He describes his *Untimely Meditations* as "warlike" (*EH*: "The Untimely Ones" 1) and makes frequent use of martial metaphors, describing himself as "quick on the draw," taking "pleasure in fencing," making "attempts at assassination" in which "paradise lies in the shadow of my sword" (*EH*: "The Untimely Ones" 2). He links *Human, All too Human* with war, but he qualifies and distinguishes it as "war without powder and smoke, without warlike poses, without pathos and strained limbs" (*EH*: "Human, All-Too-Human" 1). Concerning *Daybreak*, he writes that it is the beginning of his "campaign against morality," but we see further evidence of his agonistic ethos as he emphasizes his affirmative motivations and intentions when he claims he accomplishes his mission with "no negative word, no attack, no spite—that it lies in the sun, round, happy, like some sea animal basking among rocks" (*EH*: "Daybreak" 1).

It is possible to vanquish opposition by superseding it rather than destroying or committing violence against it, and this is what Nietzsche thinks he does: "morality is not attacked, it is merely no longer in the picture" (*EH*: "Daybreak" 1). Concerning his *Zarathustra*, he explains that while it inaugurates a "revaluation of values," which he also calls "the great war" (*EH*: "Beyond Good and Evil" 1), his goal is not simply defeating his opponent but rather creating a new entity, one in which "all opposites are blended into a new unity" (*EH*: "Thus Spoke Zarathustra" 6). In other words, Nietzsche's practice of his philosophical

---

[28] Promising cases to consider are his *agones* with Homer, Socrates, and Paul, which arguably affected Nietzsche's ideas about art and culture (the contest with Homer as the basis of his *The Birth of Tragedy*), philosophy and science (the contest with Socrates as the basis of his views on philosophy and science, particularly as evident in his *The Gay Science*, *Thus Spoke Zarathustra*, and *Beyond Good and Evil*), and morality and Christianity (the contest with Paul as evident in his *On the Genealogy of Morality* and *The Anti-Christ*). I discuss these at length in Acampora 2013.

martial art aims to incorporate his opposition and not only to destroy or incapacitate it.[29] And yet, despite what he represents as the overall affirmative project of his writings, he acknowledges that it is not solely creative and certainly not passive: "I know the pleasure in destroying to a degree that accords with my powers to destroy—in both respects I obey my Dionysian nature which does not know how to separate doing No from saying Yes. I am the first immoralist: that makes me the annihilator *par excellence*" (*EH*: "Why I Am a Destiny" 2). So, destruction is an inevitable dimension and consequence, if not a primary aim, of his agonistic practice. This is so not simply as a by-product, as his remarks about the overcoming of morality suggest, but as a necessary condition: "negating and destroying are conditions of saying Yes" (*EH*: "Why I Am a Destiny" 4). This makes it challenging to assess Nietzsche's *Kriegs-Praxis* both in terms of how well he applied his principles as he specified them in *EH* and in terms of how they square with his long-term project to analyze and assess oppositional structures and forms of organization, such as those evident in types.[30]

In addition to elaborating his agonistic principles and their evidence in practice in his writings, Nietzsche tries to account for the fitness necessary to engage his *Kriegs-Praxis*. Nietzsche emphasizes he is resistant without being reactive. Thus, he thinks his exposure to German decadence has the effect of strengthening him insofar as he resists it (*EH*: "Why I Am So Clever" 6), but he claims he is not merely oppositional and defiant and he repeatedly describes himself as "the opposite of a no-saying spirit" (*EH*: "Why I Am a Destiny" 1).[31] He describes himself as "full" of opposites, and believes a source of his strength can be found in what it takes to coordinate the expression of (rather than simply *unifying*) such great diversity; he repeatedly champions his diversity rather than singularity of type.[32] To be sure, this is not *sheer* diversity and individuality does not disappear. Nietzsche emphasizes how his diversity constitutes a plentitude by virtue of his *sublimation* of differing tastes (*EH*: "Beyond Good and Evil" 1). This sense of unity is more like a manifold than a synthesis. He directly links the potency he acquires with enhanced capacities: "For the task of a *revaluation of all values* more capacities may have been needed than have ever dwelt together in a single individual—above all, even contrary capacities that had to be kept from disturbing, destroying one another. An order of rank among these capacities; distance; the art of separating without setting against one another; to mix nothing, to 'reconcile' nothing; a tremendous variety that is nevertheless the opposite of chaos—this was the precondition, the long secret work and artistry of my instinct." And yet, he claims there is "no trace of struggle," no difficult challenge he sought to surmount ("I cannot remember that I ever tried hard"). In this activity,

[29] On the importance of affirming (even supporting and cultivating) one's opponent in Nietzsche's agonism, see Hatab 1995 and 2008, and Acampora 2002b and 2003a.

[30] The argument that Nietzsche progressively developed and applied such analyses throughout his career is advanced in Acampora 2013.

[31] See also *BGE* 31.

[32] Nietzsche also regards Wagner as a great mixture of types (*EH*: "Why I Am So Clever" 7). See also the discussion of mixture and hybridity in *BGE* "On Peoples and Fatherlands." The discussion in the latter text, particularly, shows that Nietzsche considers such a condition with ambivalence. On the one hand, he thinks it is a quintessential condition of modern human beings that they are great mixtures of types and tastes and that largely this is deforming and incapacitating. On the other hand, Nietzsche seems to think that such a condition might be potentially enhancing provided there is some way of yoking the multifarious tastes in such a way that allows them to be individually preserved and intensified.

he refers to himself as "the opposite of a heroic nature"; "there is no ripple of desire." But this is because he has successfully sought himself, preserved and defended himself through his practice of selfishness and self-protection. Thus, Nietzsche's account of his own *becoming* suggests that it did not entail becoming something other than what he already is, or at least that much was not his intent: "I do not want in the least that anything should become different than it is; I myself do not want to become different."

How One Becomes What One Is Redux

Nietzsche's presentation of himself as both a lover and a fighter suggests that becoming what one is is a process that involves both more and less action on our parts than what accounts of Nietzsche's philosophy sometimes suggest. It is less, because it is not a matter of us having a definite plan, a fixed notion of what we might become, or even sufficient will to bring about an alignment between our ambitions and our actions, as Nietzsche seems to have previously thought in his account of Wagner's development. It is more, because even though we can neither change the particular set of drives that constitute us nor deliberately arrange them as we might a bouquet of flowers or oil on a canvas, we can nevertheless influence whether our constitutive parts take a form capable of powerfully expressing the organization it becomes or whether we waste ourselves away through various forms of trivial and fruitless resistance, remaining nothing more than a bit of chance.[33] Becoming what one is involves becoming a necessity, and this is how Nietzsche depicts himself in his work.

How does one become a necessity rather than a piece of chance? And what light does this shed on Nietzsche's views about the human subject and its possibilities for freedom? It seems odd to think that necessity is somehow optional or at least contingent. How could necessity be anything other than—*necessary*? In *Ecce Homo*, Nietzsche repeatedly describes his development in terms of "self-preservation" rather than self-creation, and he characterizes the former as a way of conserving and harnessing energy so that it might be used for extraordinary tasks of the sort we find in his *Kriegs-Praxis*. Self-preservation consists in cultivation, including disciplining oneself to avoid what is enervating. Becoming necessary, for Nietzsche, is a form of freedom, perhaps the highest form achievable by human beings, because it entails becoming capable, becoming enabled, activated, and enlivened. This conception of freedom as being-capable allows us to see how Nietzsche's views about self-preservation and selfishness concern not sheer survival but rather a way of tapping creative powers. This allows us to see how both fatalistic and existential dimensions are evident in Nietzsche's works even though they are incomplete without their complement.[34]

We have seen that Nietzsche thinks individuals are characterized by both orders of rank and ruling orders that maintain them. Orders of rank are more than *arrangements*, because there are also abiding *relations* (i.e., various ways of holding together and maintaining such arrangements) that distinguish organizations. Constitutions are distinguished by the

---

[33] Cf. *EH*: "Why I Write Such Good Books" 4: "multiplicity of inward states is exceptionally large in my case, I have many stylistic possibilities—the most multifarious art of style that has ever been at the disposal of one man."

[34] See Nehamas 1985, especially pp. 177–86; and Leiter 1998: 255.

relative strength of the drive or drives that are dominant *and* its (or their) expressive efficacy and efficiency—that is how and how well it is able to order the other drives to pursue and achieve its ends.[35] Organizations form on the basis of the nature of their constituent parts (drives) and the kinds of possible relations that are thereby circumscribed. They are also constituted in and through their external relations.

Nietzsche's presentation of his *Kriegs-Praxis* shows that he not only *organizes* fights, but also, by virtue of that activity *becomes organized*; he becomes what he is.[36] His "practice of war" is both *expressive* of the order of rank he is and *effective* in rendering that ordering so that in the course of such activity he becomes ordered in a certain way. It is not, however, the only relation that has this sort of constitutional character, and in *Ecce Homo* Nietzsche identifies and refers to a variety of relations that are similarly (if not more so) constitutive, including nutrition, climate, geography, topography, friendship, and a variety of other associations and experiences. Nietzsche thinks that philosophical (particularly moral and religious) ideas can *literally* make us sick, physically decadent, and it is on this basis that he anticipates that a revaluation of the body and all related dimensions of what is "this worldly" (as opposed to *otherworldly*) might be reinvigorating, revitalizing. This is evident in Nietzsche's discussions of a wide range of physical and sensory experiences in *Ecce Homo* and other late writings and how they bear on psycho-physiological orders or constitutions. This sheds light on how he envisions the dynamic development of physio-psychology and how orders of rank emerge, develop, and change.[37]

For example, when describing "why he writes such good books," Nietzsche nearly always mentions the *places* where they were written (e.g., St Moritz, Naumburg, Genoa), and he frequently comments on the conditions of lighting and topography.[38] He mentions specific locations where ideas "come" to him, such as his famous declaration about the origin of the idea of eternal recurrence "6000 feet beyond man and time" in Silvaplana near Surlei (*EH*: "Thus Spoke Zarathustra" 1).[39] Nietzsche's Mediterranean experiences are virtually inseparable from his writing *Zarathustra*: the climate; the proximity to sea and mountains; the life-ways of the inhabitants, especially the fishermen; means of locomotion, health, vitality, particularly in terms of constitutional fitness; and the typography, which provided sweeping and vast "vistas" (*EH*: "Thus Spoke Zarathustra" 2). He associates these physiological and cultural experiences with his development of a capacity for *feeling* that he describes

---

[35] Maudemarie Clark and David Dudrick (2009) emphasize without elaborating the significance of what they call "political authority" in organizations of drives. They write, "the viewpoint of the person who experiences willing is constituted by, in the sense that it simply *is*, the viewpoint of the drives who use the trappings of political authority to get their way in conflicts with the other drives" (256). I certainly agree that "political authority" is an appropriate way to understand how Nietzsche conceives the relations of the drives, but it is more than "using" "trappings." The drives *are* successful on the basis of their participation in the political arrangements. This means that no drive gets its way by sheer strength alone; it is (and thus *we* are) inherently social and political all the way down, so to speak.

[36] See Siemens 2006 for discussion of Nietzsche's "socio-physiology," in which Siemens explores how agonistic social relations can be constitutive.

[37] For other discussions of how "small things" potentially influence and affect orders of relations such that we can see individuals as constituted *in relation* to their environments, see Domino 2002, Hutter 2006, and, in Nietzsche's own case, Krell and Bates 1997.

[38] Rich detail of Nietzsche's travels can be found in Krell and Bates 1997.

[39] Other examples in *EH* include his reference to the facts that "Songs of Prince Free Bird" was written in Sicily, *HAH* was written in Sorrento, and *D* was written in Genoa.

as the *pathos of distance*: feeling something below or beneath as part of a process of heightening that is characteristic of the pathos of distance, for example Christianity as beneath, "altogether unheard-of psychological depth and profundity" (*EH*: "Why I Am a Destiny" 6). Nietzsche claims this feeling gave him a particularly sharp sense of difference that facilitates rank ordering, it provides the conditions that make possible the exercise of judgment concerning what is higher and lower, nearer and further, and which allows one, at least potentially, to achieve a new order of relation "within" and "without," e.g., *BGE* 57.

Nietzsche appears to hold that there is a wealth of human resources, a trove belonging to humanity as such, to the "household of the soul" (*BGE* 20), which one may tap, educe, activate, and bring to life in the order one is. One of the ways in which we tap these resources and facilitate their development and organization is through seeking out a variety of experiences and other relations that can make it possible to cultivate what he calls a "second nature" early in his writings (*UM* II: 3). In *Ecce Homo*, Nietzsche presents himself as doing precisely this in his account of the dual (even triple) nature he heralds in *EH* ("Why I Am So Wise" 3). What is significant is that Nietzsche does not simply claim the distinction of *having* such a dual nature—much less willing it or simply creating or fashioning it for himself—he *acquires* it through experiences that access and cultivate resources that emerged through larger related historical, cultural, and physiological evolutionary and developmental processes.[40]

In his *Untimely Meditation* "The Use and Abuse of History for Life," Nietzsche describes a process of change in which we "plant in ourselves a new habit, a new instinct, a second nature, so that the first nature withers" (*UM* II: 3). This suggests a deep level of change is possible, but we should inquire into *how* it is possible, particularly given that we do not have recourse to a true self or orchestrating agent behind the scenes who could be "responsible" for such cultivation. Moreover, any desire for a second nature, for a reordering of the drives that we are, can be nothing other than the expression of yet another drive that longs to be dominant and thus we might wonder whether *deeper* is really the right way to think of it.[41] Wouldn't the dominant drive simply seek to reproduce itself albeit perhaps in a somewhat different pattern or taking on a somewhat different form of expression of what is essentially *the same* drive? If "nature" here refers simply to the nature of the dominant drive, then it does not seem to be the case that the second nature is a distinction that makes a difference. But if a being's "nature" is characterized by both the order of rank one is *and* the ruling order that abides in its constitution and preservation, then perhaps a genuine difference can be possible, not just because one wills it and not simply by force of accident or chance.

Acquiring a second nature or undergoing some sort of change in one's constitutive rank order, we might imagine, is something quite rare and is not easily accomplished. In the first place, rank orders are inclined to preserve themselves: they tend toward *Selbsterhaltung*, as noted above. Moreover, that to which one is drawn to interact or interrelate reflects preferences that accord with desires one *already* has on account of the order one *already* is.

[40] Nietzsche's works are replete with references to "what has been achieved in us," not by dint of our own will but rather "by nature." He uses this formulation in a frequently discussed passage on the "sovereign individual," who is "permitted to promise" (*GM* II: 2). Robert Pippin's discussion (2009) is particularly illuminating.

[41] This idea is most clearly reflected in *D* 109, which numerous commentators cite. See, for example, Parkes 1994: 290–2.

And yet, it does seem possible to change what it is that one typically wants, to develop new desires as well as new tastes, and thereby to be drawn into new relations. While the orientations of the drives might well be self-preserving, the effect of new relations among them is not entirely within any single drive's or collection's control. Organizations are constituted by their activities *in relation*, both internally and externally, and these relations potentially affect the ordering one is.

There are things we do that affect or influence the rank ordering we are, and these are deliberate without being deterministic: we select climates, foods, natural and constructed environments, friends, lovers, books, and music, etc., experiment with new and different relations, try to develop new tastes and new loves, and stubbornly and relentlessly cling to others. In sum, we *are* amidst a whole host of attachments, some of which can change and expand. But the "we" here should be regarded as shorthand for "the order of drives that constitutes us as agents, and the ruling order that abides therein."[42] That "we" that selects and experiments is itself an order that has come to rule and be powerful enough to do the selecting, and it will select in ways compatible with the orientation of the drive or drives that prevail. It is the result of a process in which some parts strengthen relative to others, and that ruling order henceforth interacts with others and potentially seeks to refine or refigure *the order one is*. In this respect we can see that change is possible, indeed likely, given the complexity of the constitutive elements, which Nietzsche characterizes as involved in a perpetual struggle for superiority over other drives and supremacy over the whole. In this respect, I think it is appropriate to regard Nietzsche's view of types as dynamic and fluid with considerable possibilities for change. This does not mean that any individual drive or the whole itself deliberately seeks fundamental change; rather the individual drives pursue only their further enhancement. The order is characterized by a certain *manner of ruling*: its organization is maintained in a certain sort of way, which has been briefly explored above. An important dimension to explore is how these constitutional characteristics can change, evolve, dissolve, or devolve. There is evidence in Nietzsche's texts that suggests he thinks they can and this explains his interest in more mundane, biologically material conditions such as climate, food, domicile, topography, and so on. Like Socrates in Plato's *Republic*, where we find the famous discussion of the different constitutions, Nietzsche is preoccupied with exploring how constitutional changes are possible and the role that philosophy might

---

[42] In his discussion of the sort of unity that is possible for the assemblages that Nietzsche thinks human beings are, Nehamas explores whether Nietzsche has in mind unity as coherence or unity as numerical identity. He sees a much greater fluidity than I would grant in what *rules* in such orders with the effect that they might be thought roughly to constitute some specific or distinctive collectivity. Here is where Leiter's emphasis on types could be instructive if modified to pertain not exclusively or even primarily to "type facts" but rather to orders of rank that consider both what is ordered *and* what rules so as to preserve that order. What I find missing from both accounts is an emphasis on the nature of the ruling that abides in the composite under consideration. See Nehamas 1985, especially pp. 181–2, and Leiter *passim*. There is also significant disagreement between the two concerning how unity is achieved in this multiplicity. For Nehamas, literature supplies an artistic creative model for producing the unity of the self. For Leiter, it is simply given. Also instructive is Richardson 2009 on unity as "that synthesis of a stable power-system of drives [...] accomplished by a single drive taking control, and imposing its single command" (135), though I do not see why it must be a single drive that does this rather than a regency or oligarchy. The political and agonistic character of the soul indicates greater possibilities.

play in bringing about such. In this context Nietzsche finds *necessity*, does not commit me to either essentialism or sheer affirmation.

It is through and within networks of interrelations that the particular perspectives and sets of orientations reflective of constitutive orders of rank come to be. As relations among drives change, relative to the strengthening or weakening of drives, so too can the orders of rank change relative to their more general *orientations* or how the more powerful drives maintain their strength. What we call "I" is constituted, takes on a specific character and form, and becomes individual rather than a diffuse mix of competing forces in these contexts. One can, Nietzsche thinks, amplify, heighten, and pique such relations through a variety of physiological, historical, and psychological experiences and relationships. Some people appear to do this more readily and more ably than others. Predisposition to seeking out such relations appears to contribute to the process while not determining it. In other words, whether one *becomes* in a certain way does not simply reduce to whether one was such a type from the start.

Thus, we can see that becoming what one is also involves becoming able to act as some *one* entity that draws resources and gathers strength from having a great variety of dimensions. Becoming what one is, then, is also from many things becoming one. This is a form of sovereignty, which for Nietzsche, at least in some contexts, refers to the form, efficiency, and efficacy of the activity of ruling that characterizes the organization of the constitutive drives, the order of rank one is.[43] At the same time that Nietzsche undermines the conception of the unitary, atomic, metaphysical substratum "I" (and in so doing emphasizes the multiplicity of drives and the potency of their *expression*), he nevertheless envisions orders or forms of ruling that give any particular organization integrity, durability, and expansive capabilities. This makes it more than a mere collection of multiple parts that might be properly called an individual. Nietzsche makes it clear he thinks persons are many things, that rather than a singular agent there are many, but in great individuals, particularly, they are able to achieve a certain form of coordination of that multiplicity that maximizes the expression of the diversity. Nietzsche expends great effort in examining effective and potent structures of ruling as well as various possible ways of educating the drives and effecting new possibilities for relations. It is an expressive activity that refers to the effective ruling of the order of rank that constitutes a person and allows us to "become what one is." An explicit appreciation for both orders of rank and means of achieving and maintaining such ruling orders is essential to understanding how Nietzsche thinks about moral psychology and related philosophical concerns. Fatalistic views conceived in terms of types are too rigid and too simplistic: we are both orders of rank and ruling orders. Self-creationist models can too easily dismisses the durability of orders of rank, and too readily overlook the fact that Nietzsche has undermined the very conceptual resources needed for the kinds of projects they envision. The highly interactive activity of ordering is dependent not simply on acts of will but also on the variety of relations of which we are a part, including "small things" that nurture us and the actions we are thereby able to take.

---

[42] This kind of sovereignty differs from that frequently attributed to Nietzsche on the basis of interpretations of GM II:2. See my discussion in Acampora 2006.

[43] This kind of sovereignty differs from that frequently attributed to Nietzsche on the basis of interpretations of GM II:2. See my discussion in Acampora 2006.

BIBLIOGRAPHY

(A) Works by Nietzsche

BGE   *Beyond Good and Evil*, trans. Walter Kaufmann. New York: Viking Books, 1966.
CW   *The Case of Wagner*, in *The Birth of Tragedy and The Case of Wagner*, trans. Walter Kaufmann. New York: Viking Books, 1967.
D   *Daybreak*, ed. Maudemarie Clark and Brian Leiter, trans. R. J. Hollingdale. Cambridge: Cambridge University Press, 1997.
EH   *Ecce Homo*, in *On the Genealogy of Morals and Ecce Homo*, ed. and trans. Walter Kaufmann. New York: Viking Books, 1969.
GM   *On the Genealogy of Morals*, in *On the Genealogy of Morals and Ecce Homo*, ed. Walter Kaufmann, trans. R. J. Hollingdale and Walter Kaufmann. New York: Viking Books, 1969.
GS   *The Gay Science*, trans. Walter Kaufmann. New York: Viking Books, 1974.
KGW   *Nietzsche Werke: Kritische Gesamtausgabe*, ed. G. Colli and M. Montinari (24 vols + 4 CDs). Berlin: De Gruyter, 1967–2006.
KSA   *Sämtliche Werke: Kritische Studienausgabe in 15 Einzelbänden*, ed. G. Colli and M. Montinari (15 vols). Berlin: De Gruyter, 1988.
UM   *Unmodern Observations*, ed. William Arrowsmith, trans. Gary Brown. New Haven, Conn.: Yale University Press, 1990.

In addition to the above works, I have also consulted Judith Norman's translation of *Ecce Homo* in Aaron Ridley and Judith Norman (eds) (2005), *The Anti-Christ, Ecce Homo, Twilight of the Idols, and Other Writings* (Cambridge: Cambridge University Press), 69–152.

(b) Other Works Consulted Cited

Acampora, Christa Davis. 2002a. "Nietzsche Contra Homer, Socrates, and Paul," *Journal of Nietzsche Studies* 24: 25–53.
Acampora, Christa Davis. 2002b. "Of Dangerous Games and Dastardly Deeds: A Typology of Nietzsche's Contests," *International Studies in Philosophy* 34.3: 135–51.
Acampora, Christa Davis. 2003a. "*Demos Agonistes Redux*: Reflections on the Streit of Political Agonism," *Nietzsche-Studien* 32: 373–89.
Acampora, Christa Davis. 2003b. "Nietzsche's Agonal Wisdom," *International Studies in Philosophy* 35.3: 205–25.
Acampora, Christa Davis. 2006. "On Sovereignty and Overhumanity: Why It Matters How We Read Nietzsche's *Genealogy* II:2," in Christa Davis Acampora (ed.), *Critical Essays on the Classics: Nietzsche's "On the Genealogy of Morals."* Lanham, Md: Rowman & Littlefield Publishers, 147–62.
Acampora, Christa Davis. 2013. *Contesting Nietzsche*. Chicago: University of Chicago Press.
Ansell-Pearson, Keith. 1991. "Nietzsche and the Problem of the Will in Modernity," in Keith Ansell-Pearson (ed.), *Nietzsche and Modern German Thought*. London and New York: Routledge, 165–91.
Babich, Babette E. 2003. "Nietzsche's Imperative as a Friend's Encomium: On Becoming the One You Are, Ethics and Blessing," *Nietzsche-Studien* 33: 29–58.
Clark, Maudemarie and Dudrick, David. 2009. "Nietzsche on the Will: An Analysis of *BGE* 19," in Ken Gemes and Simon May (eds), *Nietzsche on Freedom and Autonomy*. Oxford: Oxford University Press, 247–68.

Conway, Daniel W. 1998. "The Genius as Squanderer: Some Remarks on the *Übermensch* and Higher Humanity," *International Studies in Philosophy* 30.3: 81–95.

Domino, Brian. 2002. "The Casuistry of the Little Things," *Journal of Nietzsche Studies* 23: 51–62.

Foucault, Michel. 1977. "Nietzsche, Genealogy, History," in Donald F. Bouchard (ed.), *Language, Counter-Memory, Practice: Selected Essays and Interviews*, trans. Donald F. Bouchard and Sherry Simon. Ithaca, NY: Cornell University Press, 139–64.

Gemes, Ken. 2006. "Nietzsche on Free Will, Autonomy and the Sovereign Individual," *Proceedings of the Aristotelian Society* 80 (supp. vol.): 339–57. Reprinted in Ken Gemes and Simon May (eds). 2009. *Nietzsche on Freedom and Autonomy*. Oxford: Oxford University Press, 33–49.

Han-Pile, Béatrice. 2011. "Nietzsche and Amor Fati," *European Journal of Philosophy* 19: 224–61.

Hatab, Lawrence. 1995. *A Nietzschean Defense of Democracy*. Chicago: Open Court Press.

Hatab, Lawrence. 2008. *Nietzsche's "On the Genealogy of Morality": An Introduction.* Cambridge: Cambridge University Press.

Hutter, Horst. 2006. *Shaping the Future: Nietzsche's New Regime of the Soul and Its Ascetic Practices*. Lanham, Md: Lexington Books.

Janaway, Christopher. 2007. *Beyond Selflessness: Reading Nietzsche's "Genealogy."* Oxford: Oxford University Press.

Katsafanas, Paul. 2005. "Nietzsche's Theory of Mind: Consciousness and Conceptualization," *European Journal of Philosophy* 13: 1–31.

Kofman, Sarah. 1992. *De l'Ecce homo de Nietzsche*. Paris: Galilée.

Krell, David Farrell and Bates, Donald L. 1997. *The Good European: Nietzsche's Work Sites in Word and Image*. Chicago: University of Chicago Press.

Leiter, Brian. 1998. "The Paradox of Fatalism and Self-Creation in Nietzsche," in Christopher Janaway (ed.), *Willing and Nothingness: Schopenhauer as Nietzsche's Educator*. Oxford: Oxford University Press, 217–57.

Leiter, Brian. 2002. *Nietzsche's Moral Philosophy*. New York: Routledge.

Leiter, Brian. 2007. "Nietzsche's Theory of the Will," *Philosophers' Imprint* 7.7. Available at <http://quod.lib.umich.edu/p/phimp/3521354.0007.007/1>, accessed February 12, 2013.

Lingis, Alphonso. 2000–1. "The Return of Extinct Religions," *New Nietzsche Studies: The Journal of the Nietzsche Society* 4.3–4: 15–28.

Loeb, Paul S. 2010. *The Death of Nietzsche's Zarathustra*. Cambridge: Cambridge University Press.

Montinari, Mazzino. 2003. *Reading Nietzsche*, trans. Greg Whitlock. Urbana, Ill.: University of Illinois Press.

Moore, Gregory. 2002. *Nietzsche Biology Metaphor*. Cambridge: Cambridge University Press.

Müller-Lauter, Wolfgang. 1999a. *Nietzsche: His Philosophy of Contradictions and the Contradictions of His Philosophy*. Urbana, Ill.: University of Illinois Press.

Müller-Lauter, Wolfgang. 1999b. *Über Freiheit und Chaos*. Berlin and New York: Walter de Gruyter.

Nehamas, Alexander. 1985. *Nietzsche: Life as Literature*. Harvard, Mass.: Harvard University Press.

Parkes, Graham. 1994. *Composing the Soul: Reaches of Nietzsche's Depth Psychology*. Chicago: University of Chicago Press.

Pippin, Robert. 2009. "How to Overcome Oneself: Nietzsche on Freedom," in Ken Gemes and Simon May (eds), *Nietzsche on Freedom and Autonomy*. Oxford: Oxford University Press, 49–87.

Pizer, John. 1990. "The Use and Abuse of 'Ursprung': On Foucault's Reading of Nietzsche," *Nietzsche-Studien* 19: 462–78.

Richardson, John. 1996. *Nietzsche's System*. New York: Oxford University Press.

Richardson, John. 2004. *Nietzsche's New Darwinism*. New York: Oxford University Press.

Richardson, John. 2009. "Nietzsche's Freedoms," in Ken Gemes and Simon May (eds), *Nietzsche on Freedom and Autonomy*. Oxford: Oxford University Press, 127–49.

Shapiro, Gary. 1989. *Nietzschean Narratives*. Bloomington and Indianapolis: Indiana University Press.

Siemens, Herman. 2006. "Nietzsche contra Liberalism on Freedom," in Keith Ansell-Pearson (ed.), *Blackwell Companion to Nietzsche*. Oxford and Malden, Mass.: Blackwell, 437–54.

Solomon, Robert C. 2002. "Nietzsche on Fatalism and 'Free Will,'" *Journal of Nietzsche Studies* 23 (Spring): 63–87.

Solomon, Robert C. 2003. *Living with Nietzsche: What the Great "Immoralist" Has to Teach Us*. Oxford: Oxford University Press.

Stack, George. 1993. "Nietzsche's Earliest Essays: Translation of and Commentary on 'Fate and History' and 'Freedom of Will and Fate,'" *Philosophy Today* 37: 153–69.

PART IV

VALUES

CHAPTER 17

NIETZSCHE'S
METAETHICAL STANCE

NADEEM J. Z. HUSSAIN

In one of the first attempts to assess Nietzsche's views on foundational questions in value theory in the light of contemporary metaethics, John Wilcox writes:

> The term "metaethics" was coined after Nietzsche's time, but the issues were very much on his mind and figure prominently in his writings.... The difficulty is not that Nietzsche did not deal with such issues. The trouble rather is that on these issues, as on so many others, Nietzsche seems so contradictory—he seems to be on both sides, or on all sides, at once.... Consequently, a large portion of the present study... consists of an effort to show just how complex, just how apparently contradictory, Nietzsche's metaethical suggestions are. (Wilcox 1974: 5)

I plan to follow Wilcox's lead—at least initially. I will show how a wide range of apparently conflicting metaethical theories have been ascribed to Nietzsche on the basis of his writings. I will end, however, with serious consideration of the view that perhaps Nietzsche simply does not have what we would now regard as a metaethical stance.

I will first review the major kinds of contemporary metaethical theories. I will then consider the initial textual evidence for ascribing some version of each kind to Nietzsche. I will briefly consider objections to any such ascription that do *not* turn on the *relative* plausibility of ascribing this metaethical view as compared to others. I will then turn to pairwise comparative arguments in favor of claims of the relative plausibility of ascribing one metaethical interpretation to Nietzsche over another.

1 REVIEW OF KINDS OF METAETHICAL
THEORIES

It will help to begin with a brief review of the traditional kinds of metaethical theories even if we eventually conclude that Nietzsche's metaethical stance does not fit neatly into these categories—as, indeed, many contemporary theories do not—or that Nietzsche does not have a metaethical stance, let alone a theory.

The sincere utterance of an indicative sentence, say, "The Eiffel Tower is in Paris," is normally taken to be an expression of the speaker's belief that the Eiffel Tower is in Paris.[1] The belief, and the proposition that is its content, is either true or false depending on whether it is indeed a fact that the Eiffel Tower is in Paris. Such views are normally classified as forms of "cognitivism." The label is an odd one for several reasons. Cognition is a matter of knowledge and so one might think that all forms of cognitivism in metaethics involve claiming that there is moral knowledge. That is not, however, how the term is often used. Rather such views see moral language and thought as *purportedly* providing knowledge whether or not in fact they do.[2] "Error theories," for example, are cognitivist metaethical theories that deny that our moral practices succeed in giving us knowledge. One form of error theory proceeds by arguing that in fact, say, nothing is right or wrong because there are no such properties. Since nothing is right or wrong, or good or bad, or just or unjust, and so on, all moral beliefs are false.[3]

Within cognitivism, error theories are contrasted with forms of "realism." A realist thinks that torture really is wrong and so our belief that torture is wrong is true, and that, usually, our belief that torture is wrong is justified in a manner sufficient for knowledge. The nature of the fact that torture is wrong can still however be a matter of serious dispute between realists: is it part of some non-natural realm of truths? Can it be reduced to truths of history, psychology, or biology?

The possibility of the reduction to the psychological brings to the fore a related set of classificatory problems generated by certain philosophical connotations of the label "realism." For some philosophers, realism is a matter of the "objective" versus the "subjective." Consider an example. In cricket when the ball lands beyond the boundary, six runs are scored. In answer to the question, "Is it true that he just scored six runs?", one could sensibly answer, in such a situation, "Yes, it is true." It is natural to thus provide a cognitivist theory of cricket discourse: such utterances express beliefs and the beliefs are true or false depending on whether in fact the ball landed beyond the boundary and thus whether in fact he scored six runs. Given our earlier discussion, we should then be realists about cricket: he really did score six runs.

However the use of terms like "fact" and "realism" in this context will concern some. The laws of cricket are basically determined by the vote of two thirds of the members of the private Marylebone Cricket Club. This seems too "subjective" for terms like "fact" or "realism." We do not have sufficient "mind independence," as some would put it. Thus, for example, Alex Miller suggests treating realism as requiring that the relevant facts be constituted independently of human opinion in contrast with cases in which we may want to give what he calls a "judgement-dependent" account; the laws of cricket, and so the "fact" that someone scored six runs, depend essentially on our judgments about these matters (Miller 2003: 129). Thinking here, in contrast to cases where the label "realism" is really apt, does make it so.

---

[1] I borrow here from Hussain 2010: 336–7.

[2] Further problems with the label arise when we see that positions that are normally classified as noncognitivist turn out often to allow, in some sense, for moral knowledge.

[3] For a more careful attempt to state the varieties of error theory, see Hussain 2010.

Consider, however, utterances that apparently express beliefs about psychological states: "He wants an apple pie." What makes my belief that you want an apple pie true is a fact about your psychology. That fact is "subjective" in one sense, but not in the sense in which it is somehow up to me, the one with the belief. Thinking—someone's thinking—may make it so but my belief does not simply make it so. My beliefs are not somehow guaranteed to be true just because I have them and in this sense their truth is "objective" or at least relatively objective.

Much work would be needed to provide an exhaustive classification of cognitivist theories, and I have given no final solution to the labeling problems. However, these comments will set the stage for some of the difficulties involved in classifying Nietzsche's own position.

Before getting to Nietzsche we need to follow the other branch of our tree: not all utterances express beliefs. Commands are an obvious case. The command that the Eiffel Tower be in Paris does not express the belief that this is the case. Metaethical theories differ on whether they take utterances of sentences involving moral terms to be expressions of belief. Despite the use of an indicative sentence, perhaps the utterance "Torture is wrong" expresses a command not to torture rather than a belief of any kind. Traditionally theories labeled "noncognitivist" take moral utterances to express some attitude other than belief. For non-cognitivism it is not sufficient simply to posit that some attitude other than belief is directed at the proposition that torture is wrong. Any such view would still have to address the question of whether the proposition itself was true or not. Noncognitivism hopes to deny that there is anything here that is truth-apt, whether an attitude or a proposition that the attitude is directed at. The analogy with commands is thus instructive. It is not just a matter of not having beliefs; it is the matter of ensuring that there is nothing there to be true or false.

Contemporary noncognitivisms, as we shall see, add complexity to this picture by claiming that though at the most fundamental level the traditional noncognitivist starting point is essentially right, we can eventually both explain and vindicate our talk of moral belief and truth. We will be able to say that we have moral beliefs, that many of these beliefs are true, and even that we have moral knowledge; however, what we are doing when we say such things will turn out to be rather different than what we might have thought: it will still be a matter, underneath it all, of expressing noncognitive attitudes towards non-normative contents.

2 Error Theory

As I noted in the introduction, basically every kind of metaethical theory has by now been ascribed to Nietzsche. We will start though with the natural thought that Nietzsche's famous criticisms of Christianity and morality should be interpreted as presenting an error theory.[4] Nietzsche writes:

> My demand upon the philosopher is known, that he take his stand *beyond* good and evil and leave the illusion of moral judgment *beneath* himself. This demand follows from an insight which I was the first to formulate: that *there are altogether no moral facts*. Moral judgments

---

[4] I draw here extensively on Hussain 2007.

agree with religious ones in believing in realities which are no realities. Morality is merely an interpretation of certain phenomena—more precisely a misinterpretation. Moral judgments, like religious ones, belong to a stage of ignorance at which…"truth"…designates all sorts of things which we today call "imaginings." (*TI:* "The 'Improvers' of Mankind" 1)

A crucial feature of this passage is the analogy to religion. Presumably the problem with the relevant religious judgments is that they involve belief in God, angels, the divine, heaven, hell, the sacred, blessed, sin, etc.—"realities which are no realities." The failure of religious judgments is systematic in virtue of a systematic mismatch between the basic terms of the discourse and what is actually part of reality. Thus one problem with the judgment that God is triune is that "God" simply fails to refer to any part of reality. Whether to treat such judgments then as false or to deny them a truth value is of course an interesting matter—and indeed one could be tempted to see the fact that Nietzsche does not simply declare that such judgments are false as a recognition of this philosophical puzzle—but that we have an error theory of some kind for the discourse in question seems clear.[5] In the moral case what could the "realities" in question be? Perhaps there are no such properties as rightness or wrongness, good or bad, and so on. These are the "realities" which moral judgments believe in.

One can try to argue that this passage does not support an error theory of this kind by arguing that what Nietzsche is alluding to is the fact that moral judgments have certain presuppositions. To judge that what an agent did was morally wrong is, perhaps, to presuppose that the agent was, in some metaphysically problematic sense, free to choose otherwise. The reality that is not a reality is the reality of, here, free will. Rightness, wrongness, and so on, are not themselves under threat and thus we can accept Nietzsche's claims without ascribing to him a metaethical error theory since we do not have to ascribe to him the view that there is no such thing as rightness or wrongness.

There are three points to note here. First, depending on the kind of presupposition claim defended, the resulting difference in the basic metaethical stance ascribed to Nietzsche may not be much. If talk of rightness or wrongness necessarily presupposes, for example, free will, then any talk of rightness or wrongness in our world will indeed involve an error. It is not as though there is some way to avoid the error while continuing to talk in the same way. If, on the other hand, one tried to ascribe to Nietzsche the view that the presupposition failure does not always occur, then one has to provide some other explanation—or some appropriate interpretation—of the strength of Nietzsche's insistence that *"there are altogether no moral facts"* (*TI:* "The 'Improvers' of Mankind" 1).

Second, Nietzsche often does mention and appeal to the presuppositions of various practices, but here he claims that moral judgment itself believes in realities that are not realities. Despite one's inclination to insist that judgments, as opposed to the agents who make them, cannot have beliefs, the connection of the judgment to the belief seems to be stronger than that of presupposition.[6]

---

[5] Evidence that Nietzsche does perhaps see the philosophical puzzle about reference comes in the sentence following the passage quoted above: "Moral judgments are therefore never to be taken literally: so understood, they always contain mere absurdity" (*TI:* "The 'Improvers' of Mankind" 1).

[6] The German reads, *"Das moralische Urtheil hat Das mit dem religiösen gemein, dass es an Realitäten glaubt, die keine sind"* (*KSA* 6: 98).

Finally, this passage has to be read in the light of other similar passages, and these passages also seem to support ascribing to Nietzsche a metaphysical error theory rather than a presupposition or epistemic error theory. Thus Nietzsche writes:

> *Astrology and what is related to it.*—It is probable that the objects of the religious, moral and aesthetic sensations belong only to the surface of things, while man likes to believe that here at least he is in touch with the world's heart; the reason he deludes himself is that these things produce in him such profound happiness and unhappiness, and thus he exhibits here the same pride as in the case of astrology. For astrology believes the starry firmament revolves around the fate of man; the moral man, however, supposes that what he has essentially at heart must also constitute the essence and heart of things. (*HAH* I: 4)

Here in addition to the analogy with morality and religion we get the comparison to astrology, a domain whose claims Nietzsche would surely take as deserving an error theory. There are puzzles to which I shall return about whether this passage ultimately does support error theory at all, but to the degree that it does, it seems, for the reasons considered already, to support a metaphysical error theory.

Consider much later passages from the *Nachlaß*:

> All the values by means of which we have tried so far to render the world estimable for ourselves...all these values are, psychologically considered, the results of certain perspectives of utility, designed to maintain and increase human constructs of domination—and they have been falsely *projected* into the essence of things. (*WP* 12 [November 1887–March 1888])

Elsewhere he writes: "In the entire evolution of morality, truth never appears: all the conceptual elements employed are fictions" (*WP* 428 [1888]).

Nietzsche emphasizes the centrality of such thoughts in the following passage:

> It is only late that one musters the courage for what one really knows. That I have hitherto been a thorough-going nihilist, I have admitted to myself only recently: the energy and radicalism with which I have advanced as a nihilist deceived me about this basic fact. When one moves toward a goal it seems impossible that 'goal-lessness as such' is the principle of our faith. (*WP* 25 [Spring–Fall 1887])[7]

The nihilism here does seem to claim that there is nothing that gives any direction to life. If some realm of normative or evaluative injunctions were independent of these considerations, then talk of thoroughgoing nihilism would seem misplaced. In those limited domains, there would indeed be something we should do, or that would be good to do, and so the nihilism would be limited: in some domains there would indeed be goals.[8]

---

[7] Cf. "mankind has as a whole *no* goal." Nietzsche also writes here of the "ultimate goallessness of man" (*HAH* I: 33). "What does nihilism mean? *That the highest values devaluate themselves.* The aim is lacking; 'why?' finds no answer" (*WP* 2 [Spring–Fall 1887]). Note that, given the relevant dates—and like the passages from *TI*—these *WP* passages cannot be treated simply as the reflections just of an earlier "positivistic" Nietzsche, a point I will return to later.

[8] Here I repeat points made in my article "Nietzsche and Non-Cognitivism" (Hussain 2012b).

3 REVOLUTIONARY FICTIONALISM

Ascribing a global metaethical error theory to Nietzsche does face some serious problems, however. Famously Nietzsche himself regularly, and stridently, makes what certainly look like normative and evaluative judgments. He also regularly champions the creation of new values: "Toward *new philosophers*; there is no choice; towards spirits strong and original enough to provide the stimuli for opposite valuations and to revalue and invert 'eternal values'" (*BGE* 203). *Thus Spoke Zarathustra*, for example, is oriented around just such hopes for new values and the creators of new values.[9] If indeed Nietzsche thought that all evaluative and normative judgments involve serious error, then we need some story for why it makes sense to continue making such judgments.

One approach is to insist on a distinction between some domain of normative and evaluative judgments for which Nietzsche is proposing an error theory and another domain for which he is proposing some other account that would allow us to sensibly make value judgments. At the end of the previous section, we raised some textual worries about accounts that attempt to draw such a line.

However we could distinguish between the task of giving the correct metaethical account of current and perhaps past moral judgments, on the one hand, and giving the metaethical account of a proposed replacement practice, on the other. Elsewhere, I have argued that if we focus on the close connections drawn in Nietzsche's works between art, the avoidance of nihilism, and the creation of value, then we should see Nietzsche as suggesting a replacement practice for which the correct account would normally be considered a form of "fictionalism" (Hussain 2007). Understanding what fictionalism might involve requires returning to our earlier discussion of error theory. For many of us an error theory was presumably true of our childhood beliefs about Santa Claus. However, instead of simply no longer talking about Santa Claus, many of us end up replacing our belief in Santa Claus with a pretense involving imagining him coming down chimneys and living at the North Pole.[10] No general, automatic charge of inconsistency or incoherence applies to someone who both believes that a proposition is false and continues to pretend that it is true. We can knowingly pretend what we know is not the case.

I then argued that Nietzsche was concerned to avoid "practical nihilism" (Hussain 2007: 161, 166–7). Practical nihilism is the practical consequence in most agents of the belief, usually only a tacit belief, in valuelessness or goallessness—in an error theory for all our normative and evaluative judgments. This recognition of valuelessness emaciates the fundamental drives and desires that provide psychological unity and strength to the agent.[11] Nietzsche wants to create

---

[9] "Fellow creators, the creator seeks—those who write new values on new tablets" (*Z* I: "Zarathustra's Prologue" 9). Or see the discussion of how the lion cannot do what the child is needed for, namely, "[t]o create new values" (*Z* I: "On the Three Metamorphoses"). See also *GS* 55, 320, 335; *Z* I: "On the Thousand and One Goals"; *BGE* 211; *TI* Preface; *A*, in particular 13; *EH*: "Why I Am a Destiny" 1; *WP* 260, 972, 979, 999. See Schacht 1983: 466–9.

[10] Here I draw on Hussain 2010.

[11] One consequence of this can be the "last men" famously depicted in *Z* who retain some unity and ability to act but only in virtue, I suggest, of taking themselves to be pursuing a thin notion of the good that is somehow supposed to be unproblematic—one need here only think of many of our contemporaries who think that desire-satisfaction theories, in one form or the other, somehow avoid metaethical problems precisely because of such supposed thinness.

higher men who will somehow rise above this practical nihilism. However, part of what it is to be these free spirits and higher men, I suggested, is to "conceive reality *as it is*" (*EH*: "Why I Am a Destiny" 5).[12] Self-deception seems not to be a preferred option. What these higher men need to do is to find a way of regarding things as valuable while knowing that in fact they are not. The "honest illusions" of art provide a way forward by allowing us to create honest illusions of value:

> *What one should learn from artists.*—How can we make things beautiful, attractive, and desirable for us when they are not? And I rather think that in themselves they never are. Here we should learn something from physicians, when for example they dilute what is bitter or add wine and sugar to a mixture—but even more from artists who are really continually trying to bring off such inventions and feats. Moving away from things until there is a good deal that one no longer sees and there is much that our eye has to add if we are still to see them at all; or seeing things around a corner and as cut out and framed; or to place them so that they partially conceal each other and grant us only glimpses of architectural perspective; or looking at them through tinted glass or in the light of the sunset; or giving them a surface and skin that is not fully transparent—all that we should learn from artists while being wiser than they are in other matters. For with them this subtle power usually comes to an end where art ends and life begins; but we want to be the poets of our life—first of all in the smallest, most everyday matters. (*GS* 299)

This passage brings to the fore an essential feature of the view I wanted to ascribe to Nietzsche. What is essential is for the illusion of value to play the appropriate motivational role. This in turn requires that it engage agents. Part of this engagement is to recreate some simulacrum of the phenomenology of evaluative experience. Nietzsche emphasizes the ways in which evaluations "color" things: "The extent of moral evaluations: they play a part in almost every sense impression. Our world is *colored* by them" (*WP* 260 [1883–8]). It is some version of this phenomenology that needs to be recreated for the higher men.

This is where the label "fictionalism" can be misleading. It suggests that the fictions are easy to come by. "Just imagine for a moment that there is an elephant in the room," we say in the middle of concocting a philosophical example. However, I wanted to emphasize that the aim of Nietzsche's revaluations was to create honest *illusions* of value.[13] Illusions are different from mere pretenses. Merely pretending that the fork in the glass is bent is different from the illusion of a bent fork in a glass of water, an illusion that for most of us is an honest illusion, one by which we are not deceived. Creating an honest illusion of value thus requires much more than merely pretending that something is of value in some way. Passages like *GS* 299 are meant to suggest how one might achieve such illusions.

4 REJECTING METAPHYSICAL INDEPENDENCE[14]

In the discussion above of a revolutionary fictionalist reading of Nietzsche, I emphasized passages about our ability to create values. Consider again *GS* 299. The fictionalist reading focuses on the visual metaphors that suggest that one is not simply viewing the object in

---

[12] See also *GS* 2, 110, 283; *Z* II: "The Stillest Hour" 2; *BGE* 230; *A* 50; *EH* Preface 3, "Why I Am a Destiny" 3; *WP* 172 (Spring–Fall 1887).

[13] Here I repeat remarks made in my article "Nietzsche and Non-Cognitivism" (Hussain 2012b).

[14] I borrow talk of "metaphysical independence" from (Reginster 2006) though he is not the only one who uses it.

question as it actually is: "Moving away from things until there is a good deal that one no longer sees and there is much that our eye has to add if we are still to see them at all" (*GS* 299). The fictionalist sees this as suggesting that despite such maneuvers, the thing itself does not become "beautiful, attractive, and desirable." It just begins to look valuable even though it still is not actually valuable. The illusion of value is being generated by such maneuvers. Such a reading, one might argue, fails to take seriously the opening line of *GS* 299: "How can we make things beautiful, attractive, and desirable for us when they are not?" A straightforward interpretation of the passage, given that this question is placed right at the beginning, is that what follows the question are techniques that show how we can indeed "make things beautiful, attractive, and desirable" (*GS* 299). Post such maneuvers, we will count as having succeeded in making the thing *actually* beautiful, attractive, and desirable.

The fictionalist takes the presence of subjective elements as an indication that such maneuvers fail to transform reality—actually make things valuable. But our opponent wonders whether their presence really supports such a reading. Rather we should look for a way to take seriously the metaphor present in other related passages:

> We who think and feel at the same time are those who really continually *fashion* something that had not been there before: the whole eternally growing world of valuations, colors, accents, perspectives, scales, affirmations, and negations. . . . Whatever has *value* in our world now does not have value in itself, according to its nature—nature is always value-less, but has been *given* value at some time, as a present—and it was *we* who gave and bestowed it. (*GS* 301)

When a gift is given to someone, the recipient really does have the gift. Normally no fiction is involved.

The role of these passages, rather, is to reject the idea that values are, in some supposedly problematic sense, independent of us. Or at least to reject the idea that *all* values *are* this way or *need* to be this way: that some values are not independent of us in this manner is compatible with the thought that other values, or entire evaluative systems, do involve some kind of problematic claim of independence. Such views, then, reject an error-theoretic interpretation for at least some evaluative terms. This is compatible with taking Nietzsche to be committed to an error theory for some other evaluative or normative terms. A natural line of interpretation is to ascribe to him an error theory for distinctively moral, in some appropriately narrow sense, evaluative and normative terms.[15] For most of the discussion below, I will put aside the question of *which* subset of supposed evaluative properties are not problematically independent of us.

What then are the alternatives here? Start with the simplest point someone might make which is just that most things that have some value have it only because we have made them a certain way. The statue, perhaps as opposed to the lump of metal out of which it was made, is beautiful because it was shaped by us in certain ways. To put the point more technically, it is uncontroversial that many objects have whatever evaluative property they have, beauty say, in virtue of other non-evaluative properties, their shape. These other non-evaluative properties are ones that we are causally responsible for. It would indeed be controversial to claim that all cases of things having value are like this because that would be to deny, for example, that sunsets cannot be beautiful unless we are somehow responsible for the features that make them beautiful. The glows of some beautiful sunsets no doubt are the result

---

[15]   Cf. Leiter 2002: 146–47.

of dust clouds or pollution generated by humans, but surely it would be implausible to claim that something like this is necessary in order for sunsets to be beautiful.

In any case, such a view would not require some distinctive metaethical view about the property of beauty itself or about the nature of evaluative properties in general. One could add on such a commitment to any kind of metaethical theory. More importantly, for our purposes, this reading seems not to capture the apparent metaethical import that these passages have. As Nietzsche seems to emphasize, it is we who somehow make "the whole eternally growing world of valuations, colors, accents, perspectives...." It is not that we reshape things so that they now fall under an existing order of valuations. Rather, that there is value at all is what we are, surprisingly, responsible for. And this, indeed, sounds like metaethics.

Mentioning the implausible reading was important, though, because it allows us to see what we need to avoid if we are to give Nietzsche a distinctive metaethical stance here. Any interpretation that is compatible with a pre-existing, independent order of evaluative properties, even if we are sometimes, or always, responsible for the non-evaluative properties of things in virtue of which these evaluative properties get instantiated, is not a metaethically distinctive position.

Some examples will help. Reginster, in his book on Nietzsche and nihilism, *The Affirmation of Life*, takes the kind of metaphysical independence being rejected by Nietzsche in these passages as "most evident in the case of divine command theory and Platonic realism" (Reginster 2006: 57). As he puts it, "[i]f the value of compassion is a divine decree, or a Platonic Form, then its nature" (Reginster 2006: 57) is independent in the manner objectionable to Nietzsche. This instance of the view will help us get clear on a crucial matter. Presumably if compassion is valuable or good, then being compassionate is good. And presumably if being compassionate is good, then my being compassionate is good. Finally, if I am systematically compassionate, and am not bad in other ways, you might well be willing to conclude that I am a good person. Now consider the claim:

(1) Nadeem is a good person.

Since compassion is a matter of my having a certain kind of concern for others, it is a matter of something about my mind, of something subjective. And so *part* of what makes (1) true are my particular subjective mental states. Its truth thus does depend on my subjective mental states. Nonetheless, as this example should make clear, *this* kind of dependence on the subjective is hardly a denial of some pre-existing, independent, "metaphysical" order of evaluative properties since it is compatible with the supposedly most evident instances of such a view, namely, ones where compassion's goodness is a matter of a divine decree or a Platonic form. My motivational states may be part of what makes (1) true but crucially its truth also depends on a divine decree or Platonic form, properties or relations whose existence and whose rules of instantiation are not up to me.

Now we can see that just any old dependence of evaluative or normative truths on us will not be sufficient to constitute an interesting metaethical view. What we need is, in some sense or the other, for the very existence of the evaluative properties themselves to be a result of, or necessarily involve, us, our attitudes, or our activities.

There is a range of views that will attempt to do just this. We will start with what I will call forms of (naturalistic) reductive subjective realism. Such theories attempt to reduce evaluative properties to subjective, psychological, and usually, in some broad sense, naturalistic properties. Being valuable just is being the object, in one way or the other, of our actual or counterfactual motivational states.[16] These are not forms of eliminativist, error-theoretic reductions. Things really are valuable. They really do have, say, the property of being good. But that property is a naturalistic property, it is the property of being the object, in one way or the other, of our motivational states.

After considering various forms of subjective realism and the somewhat complex philosophical and interpretive issues surrounding which version, if any, to ascribe to Nietzsche, I will turn to a rather different kind of use of our subjective mental states for metaethical purposes, namely, an attempt to develop a noncognitivist interpretation of Nietzsche.

5 Reductive Subjective Realism

Recall that the problem with simply ascribing an error theory to Nietzsche was that he often does seem to make evaluative judgments. The motivation I gave above for considering forms of subjective realism was the role we supposedly play in the generation of values. The first form of subjective realism we will look at, though, begins by focusing on the first-order evaluative claims Nietzsche seems to make.[17]

5.1 Will to Power Interpretation

Nietzsche's own evaluative claims are often made in the context of rejecting other values. Nietzsche took as one of his central tasks something he called a "revaluation of all values." It is not exactly clear what this involves. But certainly part of what it involves is an assessment of the value of a range of traditional values. Often these are labeled as Christian values but it is relatively clear that the problematic values that play a central role in Christianity do indeed appear in the set of values he critiques. At times Nietzsche just seems to use the term "morality" ["*Moral*"] to identify his target.[18] Nietzsche's job is to assess Christian values for the purposes, or so it initially seems, of revaluing our values where this might well include demoting, in some sense, Christian values and replacing them with others. This all makes it sound as though there must be some fundamental evaluative standard that Nietzsche is using in order to assess the value of the values, the value judgments, of morality:

> [U]nder what conditions did man invent the value judgments good and evil? *and what value do they themselves have?* Have they up to now obstructed or promoted human flourishing [*Gedeihen*]? Are they a sign of distress, poverty and the degeneration of life? Or, on the contrary, do they reveal the fullness, strength and will of life, its courage, its confidence, its future? (*GM* Preface 3)

---

[16] Recall that this is to be contrasted with the non-metaethical view according to which evaluative properties are such that they are instantiated in virtue of, but are not reduced to, our motivations.

[17] The material that follows in this section draws extensively on Hussain 2011. It should be emphasized that there I avoid making claims about which metaethical view we should ascribe to Nietzsche. Nonetheless, much of the material used for the interpretive line run in that article can be used for the admittedly far more speculative metaethical interpretations developed here.

[18] In addition to *GM* in general, see *D* Preface 4 and *EH*: "Why I Am a Destiny" 1.

Later in the same preface he writes:

> [W]e need a *critique* of moral values, *the value of these values should itself, for once, be examined* [...] People have taken the *value* of these 'values' as given, as factual, as beyond all questioning; up till now, nobody has had the remotest doubt or hesitation in placing higher value on the 'good man' than on 'the evil', higher value in the sense of advancement, benefit and prosperity [*Gedeihlichkeit*] for man in general (and this includes man's future). What if the opposite were true? [...] So that morality itself were to blame if man, as species, [*des Typus Mensch*] never reached his *highest potential power and splendour?* (*GM* Preface 6)

One kind of assessment being made is relatively clear. We are to assess the values of morality instrumentally: do they promote human flourishing? What is less clear is precisely what is meant by human flourishing. Obviously it has something to do with power and splendour. Flourishing also seems to be connected to something called "life" where life is being conceived of as something that can be stronger or weaker, degenerating or growing, confident or in distress. Consider the focus in *GM* Preface 3 on the values of morality as symptoms of the condition of life.

The fundamental evaluative standard seems to be one which assesses systems of evaluations in terms of whether they allow the emergence of humans that are truly flourishing which then seems to be equated with achieving the "*highest potential power and splendour*" (*GM* Preface 6). What we need to get clear on then is what this way of being is like since that is what seems to be of fundamental value in Nietzsche's assessments of all other values.

It is, one must admit, not exactly clear what it is to flourish in Nietzsche's way, but a series of passages where Nietzsche talks about what he regards positively, gives us some clues:

> But from time to time grant me [...] a glimpse, grant me just one glimpse of something perfect, completely finished, happy, powerful, triumphant, that still leaves something to fear! (*GM* I: 12)

Nietzsche claims that "the plant 'man' has so far grown most vigorously to a height" not in the absence of suffering but in the "opposite conditions":

> his power of invention and simulation (his "spirit") had to develop under prolonged pressure and constraint into refinement and audacity, his life-will had to be enhanced into an unconditional power-will. (*BGE* 44)

Or here is another passage from *BGE* that, precisely because it focuses on compassion [*Mitleid*], an attitude that normally comes under withering criticism for the danger it poses to the development of humans, seems to give us insight into the kind of person that has succeeded in achieving splendour and power:

> A man who says, "I like this, I take this for my own and want to protect it and defend it against anybody"; a man who is able to manage something, to carry out a resolution, to remain faithful to a thought, to hold a woman, to punish and prostrate one who presumed too much; a man who has his wrath and his sword and to whom the weak, the suffering, the hard pressed, and the animals, too, like to come and belong by nature, in short a man who is by nature a *master*—when such a man has pity, well, *this* pity has value. (*BGE* 293)

We should also consider his condemnations of Christianity as a conspiracy "against health, beauty, whatever has turned out well, courage, spirit, *graciousness* of the soul" (*A* 62). The "true Christian" opposes "the beautiful, the splendid, the rich, the proud, the self-reliant, the knowledgeable, the powerful—in summa, the whole of culture" (*WP* 250).[19]

One can worry about how much of a substantive ideal emerges. After all he moves within a worryingly small cluster of concepts. The sustained discussions of all the ways of being that Nietzsche finds bad are perhaps more helpful. Those negative comments can raise the worry one has with "negative theology"—is there really a way of being that avoids all those criticisms? Nonetheless, I think that as long as we work hard to put aside our temptations to defang Nietzsche on the behalf of morality, we can, so to speak, go on: we can, that is, tell what Nietzsche would take to be instances of human power and splendour and, with some confidence, rank these instances.

Part of what comes through in the above passages is that for Nietzsche the cluster of evaluations in terms of power, vigour, self-reliance, health, creativity, intelligence, a strong will, and so on, hang together. We must understand why he thought this even if we eventually conclude that they do not hang together in the way Nietzsche thinks they do. One traditional way of seeing the unity in such lists is to think of "power" as the umbrella notion. Health, creativity, intelligence, and a strong will can be seen as part of what it would take for a human to have power over himself and his environment. This reading gets support from passages such as these:

> What is good? Everything that heightens the feeling of power in man, the will to power, power itself.
>   What is bad? Everything that is born of weakness. (*A* 2)

Or from the *Nachlaß*:

> What is the objective measure of value? Solely the quantum of enhanced and organized power. (*WP* 674)[20]

All this does suggest that power—understood as an "umbrella" notion for a range of related features of flourishing humans—is indeed the fundamental value or standard that Nietzsche uses for the purposes of assessing other values: whether something enhances or diminishes power determines its value. However, we do not yet have any reason to ascribe to Nietzsche any particular metaethical view. Indeed, though the view that Nietzsche's fundamental value or standard is that of power has been widely held, rarely has a metaethical position been developed from it.[21]

One can begin to think that there is a metaethical view lurking here, when one considers claims like the following:

> There is nothing to life that has value, except the degree of power—assuming that life itself is the will to power. (*WP* 55)

---

[19] See also *D* 201; *GM* I: 7; *WP* 873, 943, 936, 949.

[20] See also *WP* 858.

[21] "Power, then, is the standard of value which Nietzsche affirms with all the eloquence at his command" (Morgan 1965: 118). The "quantitative degree of power is the measure of value" (Kaufmann 1974: 200). There is "one standard about which Nietzsche does not take a relativist position. He evaluates the worth of persons on the basis of a single standard: the degree to which they have attained what he

Nietzsche does at least at times accept this assumption. Indeed, he seems to commit himself to an even stronger doctrine of the will to power:

> Physiologists should think before putting down the instinct of self-preservation as the cardinal instinct of an organic being. A living thing seeks above all to *discharge* its strength—life itself is *will to power*; self-preservation is only one of the indirect and most frequent *results*. (*BGE* 13)

Or, the most dramatically:

> *This world is the will to power—and nothing besides!* (*WP* 1067)[22]

All of life, or perhaps everything, is always striving for power. Once power appears as the central evaluative *and* ontological term, then it can hardly appear to be a coincidence that everything aims at power and that power also turns out to be what is good. Surely, one is tempted to think, Nietzsche believes that power is valuable somehow because everything aims at power.

It is the basic connection between life and power that will be essential to seeing how we might ascribe a metaethical view here to Nietzsche. Schacht writes that Nietzsche "takes 'life' in this world to be the sole locus of value, and its preservation, flourishing, and above all its enhancement to be ultimately decisive for determinations of value" (Schacht 1983: 359). "In the last analysis, value can only be 'value for life,' and can only be understood in terms of what life essentially involves" (367). Of course, for Schacht, "Life, as [Nietzsche] construes it, *is* 'will to power' in various forms—an array of processes all which are 'developments and ramifications' of this basic tendency" (367).[23]

The problem with morality, with other values, is that they contribute to declining, weakening life, to what Nietzsche labels "decadence":

> Nothing has preoccupied me more profoundly than the problem of decadence.... "Good and Evil" is merely a variation of that problem. Once one has developed a keen eye for the symptom of decline, one understands morality, too—one understands what is hiding under its most sacred names and value formulas: impoverished life, the will to the end, the great weariness. Morality negates life. (*CW* Preface)

This is to be contrasted with master moralities that do serve ascending life and power:

> In the [...] sphere of so-called moral values one cannot find a greater contrast than that between a *master* morality and the morality of *Christian* value concepts: the latter developed on soil that was morbid through and through [...], master morality ("Roman," "pagan," "classical," "Renaissance") is, conversely, the sign language of what has turned out well, of *ascending* life, of the will to power as the principle of life. (*CW* Epilogue)

calls power" (Hunt 1991: 131). "Nietzsche's advice: maximize power" (Richardson 1996: 148). See also Wilcox 1974: 194–6, Schacht 1983: 349, 398, and May 1999: 15. Contrast any metaethical view with the more straightforward normative view that the central good-making feature in the world is power: it is in virtue of power, or the lack thereof, that things are better or worse, good or bad.

[22]   Cf. *BGE* 22 and 36.
[23]   Cf. Schacht 1983: 396.

As Nietzsche puts it, "life itself" is the "instinct for growth, for durability, for an accumulation of forces, for *power*" (*A* 6). It is important not to think that there is some particular mental state like a desire that has power as its aim in each living creature. Rather a plausible will to power interpretation has to take talk of the will to power as a statement of the fundamental tendency, a tendency that is essential to life, towards expansion, domination, growth, overcoming resistances, increasing strength—shorthand: power. This becomes clear in passages such as the following:

> The democratic idiosyncrasy of being against everything that dominates and wants to dominate…has already become master of the whole of physiology and biology, to their detriment, naturally, by spiriting away their basic concept, that of actual *activity*. On the other hand, the pressure of this idiosyncrasy forces 'adaptation' into the foreground, which is a second-rate activity, just a reactivity, indeed life itself has been defined as an increasingly efficient inner adaptation to external circumstances (Herbert Spencer). But this is to misunderstand the essence of life, its *will to power*, we overlook the prime importance that the spontaneous, aggressive, expansive, re-interpreting, re-directing and formative forces have, which 'adaptation' follows only when they have had their effect; in the organism itself, the dominant role of these highest functionaries, in whom the lifewill is active and manifests itself, is denied. (*GM* II: 12)[24]

The real will to power doctrine, it seems, is a doctrine about what is essential to life.[25] To be alive is, in part, at least, to have a tendency towards expansion, growth, domination, overcoming of resistances, increasing strength, and so on. It is this picture of life, and the accompanying fundamental evaluative standard, that is present even where Nietzsche does not use the reductive-sounding locution of the "will to power."[26] To affirm life is to affirm this

---

[24] Cf. "Every animal […] instinctively strives for an optimum of favourable conditions in which to fully release his power and achieve his maximum of power-sensation; every animal abhors equally instinctively […] any kind of disturbance and hindrance that blocks or could block his path to the optimum (—it is *not* his path to 'happiness' I am talking about, but the path to power, action, the mightiest deeds, and in most cases, actually, his path to misery)" (*GM* III: 7). Also, "what was at stake in all philosophizing hitherto was not at all 'truth' but something else—let us say, health, future, growth, power, life" (*GS* Preface 2). Cf. *BGE* 259: "life itself is *essentially* appropriation, injury, overpowering of what is alien and weaker; suppression, hardness, imposition of one's own forms, incorporation and at least, at its mildest, exploitation […] life simply *is* will to power. […] 'Exploitation' […] belongs to the *essence* of what lives, as a basic organic function; it is a consequence of the will to power, which is after all the will of life." In a late note from the *Nachlaß*, he ascribes the will to power to an amoeba, hardly a case where it is plausible to think that a particular mental state is being ascribed (*KSA* 13: 14 [174]).

[25] I suggest that the passages from the *Nachlaß* and *BGE* that are often quoted to ascribe to Nietzsche a very strong form of the will to power doctrine should be interpreted as signs that Nietzsche was indeed occasionally tempted to a more reductive and extreme doctrine. The use though of the notion of life as involving some fundamental tendency towards growth, exploitation, domination, increase of strength is far more widespread as the rest of the passages quoted throughout this section show.

[26] Once we see the close connection between notions such as "life," "power," and "decadence," we also have the resources to allay Leiter's concerns about the textual support for any such will to power interpretation. Leiter writes: "Indeed, if, as the defenders of the strong doctrine of will to power believe, 'his fundamental principle is the *"will to power"*' (Jaspers 1965: 287), then it is hard to understand why he says almost nothing about will to power—and nothing at all to suggest it is his 'fundamental principle'— in the two major self-reflective moments in the Nietzschean corpus: his last major work, *Ecce Homo*, where he reviews and assesses his life and writings, including specifically all his prior books (*EH*: 'Why I Write Such Good Books'); and the series of new prefaces he wrote for *The Birth of Tragedy*, *Human, All-too-Human*, *Daybreak*, and *The Gay Science* in 1886, in which he revisits his major themes" (Leiter

fundamental tendency. The fundamental task is to assess evaluative systems according to whether they help the fundamental instincts of life or hinder them.[27]

For Nietzsche then there seems to be some connection between the descriptive claims about what is essential to life and the use of life as a fundamental standard for evaluating values:

> Every naturalism in morality—that is, every healthy morality—is dominated by an instinct of life; some commandment of life is fulfilled by a determinate canon of "shalt" and "shalt not"; some inhibition and hostile element on the path of life is thus removed. *Anti-natural* morality—that is, almost every morality which has so far been taught, revered, and preached— turns, conversely, *against* the instincts of life: it is *condemnation* of these instincts, now secret, now outspoken and impudent. (*TI*: "Morality as Anti-Nature" 4)

A naturalist morality is one that goes along with life's fundamental tendency to dominate. It affirms this tendency and looks for "shalts" and "shalt nots" that help life achieve these goals. Unlike the anti-natural morality, it does not fight, it does not revolt against, the fundamental instincts of life by condemning them. Nietzsche continues:

> Once one has comprehended the outrage of such a revolt against life as has become almost sacrosanct in Christian morality, one has, fortunately, also comprehended something else: the futility, apparentness, absurdity, and *mendaciousness* of such a revolt. A condemnation of life by the living remains in the end a mere symptom of a certain kind of life: the question whether it is justified or unjustified is not even raised thereby. One would require a position *outside* of life, and yet have to know it as well as one, as many, as all who have lived it, in order to be permitted even to touch the problem of the *value* of life: reasons enough to comprehend that this problem is for us an unapproachable problem. When we speak of values, we speak with the inspiration, with the way of looking at things, which is part of life [*unter der Optik des Lebens*]: life itself forces us to posit values; life itself values through us when we posit values. From this it follows that even that anti-natural morality which conceives of God as the counter-concept and condemnation of life is only a value-judgment of life—but of what life? of what kind of life?

2002: 142). Now this is not completely fair since *The Antichrist*, where the value monism gets, as we have seen, its strongest expression is from after these prefaces are written. In any case, once we focus on the term "life," life, and so power, do play the role one would expect of a fundamental evaluative standard in *Ecce Homo* and the new prefaces of 1886. See *EH*: "Why I Am So Clever" 10, "Why I Write Such Good Books" 5, "The Birth of Tragedy" 2–3, "Dawn" 1–2, "Why I Am a Destiny" 7–8; *BT* Preface 2, Preface 4–5; *HAH* I: Preface 1, Preface 6; *GS* Preface 2. See also *TI*: "Skirmishes of an Untimely Man" 33.

[27] We should briefly consider two objections. First, this interpretation should not be read as ascribing the kind of teleological view to Nietzsche that he would disapprove of. Indeed he clearly contrasts precisely this view with a teleological view. He writes: "[L]ife itself is *will to power*; self-preservation is only one of the indirect and most frequent *results*. In short, here as everywhere else, let us beware of *superfluous* teleological principles—one of which is the instinct of self-preservation . . . Thus method, which must be essentially economy of principles, demands it" (*BGE* 13). There are two ways of making sense of Nietzsche's view here. One is to interpret him as thinking of the claim that life is the will to power as teleological but not as a *superfluous* teleological claim. The second option is to ascribe to him the view that a general tendency to growth, domination, expansion, increase of strength, and so on, is simply too diffuse to count as having a *telos* in the relevant sense. The second objection involves *BGE* 9 where Nietzsche mocks the Stoics for the imperative "live according to life." As Nietzsche says, "how could you *not* do that? Why make a principle of what you yourselves are and must be?" As the discussion below should show, this in fact can be interpreted as eventually supporting this interpretation rather than undermining it.

404 NADEEM J. Z. HUSSAIN

I have already given the answer: of declining, weakened, weary, condemned life. (*TI*: "Morality as Anti-Nature" 5)

Such passages suggest a kind of naturalism about values that was quite widespread among late nineteenth-century thinkers and remains influential among contemporary naturalists.[28] Once we really see ourselves as natural creatures—once, to use Nietzsche's language, we "translate man back into nature" (*BGE* 230)—then we have to look for direction from nature. Where else could one look? And nature has constituted us, at the most fundamental levels, in certain ways. One would have reason to act against our natural constitution only on the basis of some set of commands or injunctions from beyond nature and that is precisely what we give up when we give up the idea of a metaphysically independent order of values. What we always are already in the business of valuing is, to use the shorthand, power.

This is true, Nietzsche crucially seems to think, even in cases where the values espoused by a particular group, or at a particular time, reject power or seem to hamper the enhancement of power. *GM*, for example, can be plausibly read as showing that even the occurrence of value judgments that condemn life, condemn life precisely by condemning tendencies to dominate, subjugate, grow, and so on, is to be explained by appealing to the fundamental tendency that is life to grow, to dominate, and so on. *GM* does this by providing an extended study of how this essential tendency to life, when it is in life forms that are relatively weak, that cannot directly dominate their environments, that are declining in strength—in short, to use Nietzsche's expression, in cases of decadence—this tendency of life itself generates value judgments according to which striving for power, dominating, expanding, and so on, are condemned. *GM* shows that the tendency toward power is, even in these extreme cases, inescapable.[29]

This then suggests the possibility of interpreting Nietzsche as having a form of subjective reductive realism. It helps here to remind ourselves of a central strategy followed by contemporary metaethical naturalists aiming at a form of reductive realism that does not rely on some problematic naturalistic analysis of normative or evaluative concepts.[30] Such a naturalist turns to other instances of a posteriori property identification, say that of water and H_2O. Such a reduction is defended by pointing to the range of things that we tend to call "water" and noting that what at the most fundamental level we seem to be in the business of tracking when we call things "water" is whether or not they have the chemical structure H_2O. Talk of "fundamental level" is essential here since, of course, most samples of what we call water have all kinds of things in them besides H_2O. Similarly, then, if one wants to know what the property of goodness itself is one looks to the things we call good and one attempts to figure out what it is at the most fundamental level that we are keeping track of. What gives unity, underneath it all, to our evaluative practices, to our practices of calling things good or bad, is, now to speak with Nietzsche, our pursuit of, to use his shorthand, power.[31] Continuing the analogy with the case

[28] I make some attempt to defend this claim elsewhere (Hussain 2011).

[29] See Hussain 2011 for a defense of this claim.

[30] Problematic because of classic Moorean worries about such analyses. See chapter 2 of Miller 2003 for a summary.

[31] *WP* 675: "To have purposes, aims, intentions, *willing* in general, is the same thing as willing to be stronger, willing to grow—and, in addition, willing the means to do this. The most universal and basic instinct in all doing and willing has for precisely this reason remained the least known and most hidden, because *in praxi* we always follow its commandments, because we *are* this commandment—. All valuations are only consequences and narrow perspectives in the service of this one will: valuation

of water and H_2O, we should identify the property of being good with that of being such as to enhance power.[32]

6 NONCOGNITIVISM

Finally, I turn to noncognitivist interpretations of Nietzsche. As I noted in the initial review of contemporary theories, it will be important to be clear about what we mean when we call a metaethical theory a noncognitivist theory. The most notable recent defense of such an interpretation is by Maudemarie Clark and David Dudrick, and I will follow their lead in taking the term "noncognitivism" to pick out the kind of theories that have come to be so identified in mainstream metaethics and that are defended by the likes of Simon Blackburn and Allan Gibbard.[33] Recall that the goal of such views is, roughly, to avoid ending up with an account according to which normative and evaluative language would express an attitude like belief that has an evaluative or normative proposition as its content. Such cognitivist views need to tell us what normative or evaluative facts are responsible for the truth or falsity of normative language and the propositions and beliefs expressed. Noncognitivism hopes to avoid all this. Thus the analogy with expressing commands. Noncognitivist theories of this kind are thus crucially theories about the semantics of normative and evaluative language. The meaning of such language is to be given by its role in expressing noncognitive

itself is only this will to power. A critique of being from the point of view of any one of these values is something absurd and erroneous. Even supposing that a process of decline begins in this way, this process still stands in the service of this will. To appraise being itself! But this appraisal itself is still this being!—and if we say no, we still do what we *are*. One must comprehend the absurdity of this posture of judging existence, and then try to understand what is really involved in it. It is symptomatic." See also WP 706; CW "Epilogue."

[32] For detailed discussions of contemporary versions of such views, see Miller 2003: 178–217. Whether or not such views, including any version ascribed to Nietzsche, can ultimately be made to work philosophically is another matter of course. The strategy followed here is thus different from the one Leiter ascribes to the proponents of the will-to-power interpretation, what he calls the "Millian Model" (2000: 282–86). For further discussion see Hussain 2011. Leiter himself uses a similar strategy (105–12) when he interprets Nietzsche as having a reductive subjective realism for prudential goodness and similarly appeals to strategies employed by contemporary metaethicists who attempt to defend such views, in particular the work of Peter Railton (see, for example, Railton 2003a and Railton 2003b). Crucially on Leiter's interpretation, there are only facts about what is good *for* different types of human. There is no account of what is good period, what is good for humans in general, or what is human flourishing in general as opposed to flourishing for a particular kind of person. Reginster, however, criticizes this line: "Nietzsche himself never relativizes the notion of flourishing, which is at the core of the prudential conception of the good, to one or another type of man. On the contrary, he always speaks of "*human* flourishing"—"the *highest power and splendor* actually possible *to the type man* (GM Preface 5–6; my emphases)" (Reginster 2003).Bernard Reginster and Harold Langsam also appear to articulate and defend forms of subjective realism. See Reginster 2006 and Langsam 1997. For a critical assessment, see Hussain 2012a. See also Richardson 1996.

[33] In what follows I draw extensively on Hussain 2012b. A more wide-ranging assessment of noncognitivist interpretations of Nietzsche would need to consider metaethical theories that perhaps differ quite a bit from the basic expressivist approaches of Blackburn and Gibbard but that still might deserve the label "noncognitivist." The logical space here is quite extensive. For obvious reasons of space, I do not attempt to do that here.

states, states that do not purport to represent the world as being a certain way and thus are not susceptible to either assessments of truth or falsity or questions about the nature of the states of affairs represented.

The notion of expression deployed in such theories is a distinctive one, or at least plays a distinctive role. It helps to draw a contrast with the way a cognitivist might use talk of expression—and, for our interpretive purposes, it helps in particular to draw the contrast with error theories. Take the error theorist who thinks that moral properties are metaphysically "queer," too queer indeed to exist (Mackie 1977: 38–42). We might challenge this error theorist: if these properties do not exist, then why do people go around calling things (morally) wrong? What is the point of this practice? Our error theorist might respond as follows: killing innocents causes suffering. It is hardly surprising, for all the obvious reasons evolutionary and otherwise, that humans have negative feelings towards killing innocents. These feelings partly explain why they call such killings wrong. Indeed, they *express* these negative feelings towards the killing of innocents by calling such killings wrong.[34]

When this error theorist uses "express" in this context she means it in a very straightforward, ordinary sense of the term. If you ask me whether Professor Smith is a good pedagogue and I reply by saying, "He's never around to help his students," then, in normal circumstances, I will have *expressed* a negative attitude towards Professor Smith. However this expression of a negative attitude is in addition to the expression of a straightforward, non-evaluative belief, namely, the belief that Smith is never around to help his students. The sentence is about a certain descriptive fact, the fact that Smith is never around to help his students. The semantics for judgments like this is *not* given by reference to the noncognitive attitude of disapproval that it can also be used to express. Thus that a claim is sometimes used to express emotions does not give us reason to give a noncognitive account of the semantics of that claim in the manner of contemporary metaethical noncognitivisms.

This is why the traditional emphasis has been on necessity: evaluative or normative judgments are *necessarily* accompanied by a noncognitive attitude. And *this*, so the noncognitivist argues, is best explained if the very role of the judgment is to express the noncognitive attitude. The judgment's meaning is to be given by reference to its role in expressing this *noncognitive* attitude. Thus we can only ascribe noncognitivism to a theorist if we think that she has these quite specific semantic commitments. Finally, it is these particular semantic commitments that give the noncognitivist distinctive tools to avoid error theory: since the state being expressed is not one that can be true or false we do not have to worry about some metaphysical threat to the truth of evaluative or normative claims.

I emphasize all this to identify the kind of textual evidence needed for ascribing noncognitivism to Nietzsche. As we have already seen, there do indeed seem to be passages that sound very error-theoretic and it may not be immediately obvious how they can support a noncognitivist interpretation of Nietzsche.[35] However, we have also seen the passages that seem to emphasize our role in the creation of values: for example, *GS* 301, with its insistence that we are the ones who have give value to a value-less nature.

---

[34] This is not to say that this strategy does not lead to further problems for the error theorist. See Hussain 2004b.

[35] I return to this problem in the next section.

A noncognitivist interpretation would take it as making the basic noncognitivist point—the point on which it agrees with error theory—that the fundamental ontology of the universe is one of natural, descriptive properties. There are no normative or evaluative properties out there in nature that humans have learnt, somehow, to track just as they have learned to track size and shape and mass: "nature is always value-less" (*GS* 301). When we call something good, for example, we are not—I simplify away from the complexity of contemporary noncognitivism—ascribing some property to the thing, not even a relational property to my psychological states as the subjectivist would have it. Rather I am expressing some noncognitive attitude of mine. Of course, once I am in the business of using normative or evaluative language—and thus in the business of expressing these attitudes—I can certainly say that such and such is good. However, again, all that is going on when I say this is that I am expressing some positive noncognitive attitude towards the object. My judgment is not about some evaluative fact independently out there in the world. In this sense, then, the noncognitivist might grant that we have "*given* value" to nature and "created the world" of valuations.

Why is this not subjectivism? The standard noncognitivist line is twofold: first, there is no reduction of normative or evaluative facts to subjective, psychological facts. The noncognitivist is simply doing away with normative facts and so can hardly be accused of reducing them.[36] Second, the forms of subjectivism that noncognitivism really wants to avoid are ones committed to the following:

(2) If S desires/approves of/likes *x*, then *x* is valuable/right/good.

Recall, that *GS* 301 is being read as making the grand *metaethical* noncognitivist point that nature is valueless. This is a descriptive claim and not a normative one and so the noncognitivist account does not apply. It is not using, as opposed to mentioning, normative language and so it is a matter of stating straightforward truths. (2) *does* use normative or evaluative language—see the "valuable/right/good" in the consequent—and so it *is* a normative claim and so the noncognitivist analysis does apply to it. Thus a sincere utterance of (2) is not the making of some descriptive claim. It is not reporting some truth let alone any truth entailed by the collection of descriptive truths that constitute the noncognitivist's metaethical theory. Rather it is the expression of some noncognitive attitude. Which noncognitive attitude? One option is some kind of higher-order, noncognitive attitude in favor of having the noncognitive state expressed by claims of the form "*x* is valuable" when one desires or approves of *x*.

Note that usually the noncognitive state of desiring *x* and the noncognitive state expressed by judgments of the form "*x* is valuable" are different. The second noncognitive state usually has a more complicated functional role. So, for example, it could include a tendency to avowal. It includes a tendency to extinguish a "conflicting" state, say the state expressed by claims of the form "*x* is not valuable."

Thus (2) does not follow just from the descriptive claims that comprise a noncognitivist theory—including the descriptive claim that nature is, in the intended sense, valueless. It is a matter of normative debate, not a matter of metaethics. Most contemporary noncognitivists—good, moral agents as they tend to be—will then proceed to take off their metaethical hats, put on their ordinary, moral agent hats, and happily reject (2).

---

[36] Again contemporary forms of noncognitivism are more complex; they allow for talk of normative facts, but they give a noncognitivist account of what one is saying when one says that it is a fact that murder is wrong.

Thus, says our noncognitivist, *GS* 301 expresses the general *descriptive* metaphysical worldview lying behind noncognitivism but there is no reason to read it as making anything like the *normative* claim (2). The kind of subjectivism we want to avoid, she continues, is the one expressed by the normative claim (2). That there is some sense in which a noncognitivist is committed to the fundamental ontology of the world being valueless is just part of the basic metaphysical commitments of the noncognitivist, but not, she would insist, a form of subjectivism.[37]

7 COMPARATIVE ASSESSMENTS

For reasons of space I have mostly been able merely to introduce several different metaethical interpretations. I have also had to leave aside several interpretations that could be understood as ascribing other metaethical views to Nietzsche but only with the kind of extensive development and critical discussion that is not possible here.[38] The real interpretive task facing us is that of deciding which metaethical position, if any, fits *best* with Nietzsche's texts as opposed to, for example, finding Nietzschean proof texts that might *suggest* any particular metaethical position. This task is comparative. Again, though, the kind of extensive comparisons that would be needed for a final ranking of interpretations would take far too much space. Instead, I will briefly mention some obvious comparative issues that are raised by the different interpretations.

Recall that I introduced revolutionary fictionalism, subjective realism, and noncognitivism all as ways of dealing with the passages, particularly the ones we have repeatedly seen

[37]   See Hussain 2012b for further discussion.
[38]   I am thinking of the interpretations of Nietzsche in Poellner 2007, 2009, 2012; Richardson 2004; Katsafanas 2010. Much of Poellner's rhetoric suggests that he may be ascribing some view similar to that of Wiggins and McDowell. Of course that in itself makes it hard to figure out whether Poellner is ascribing a distinctive metaethical position to Nietzsche since it is not completely clear what position either Wiggins or McDowell are themselves committed to. At other times he points to Dancy's work. All this might suggest some form of non-naturalist realism. When one focuses on the substantive content of Poellner's own remarks, it is unclear what he means by "*phenomenal objectivity*" and what ontological and semantic commitments are involved (Poellner 2007: 232). And thus it is unclear whether he intends to ascribe any particular metaethical view to Nietzsche. It is hard for me not to think that Poellner is confused about the space of logical possibilities for ways in which evaluative or normative truths could be dependent on subjective motivational states. Richardson seems, at least initially, to be self-avowedly presenting a metaethical view of Nietzsche since a major part of his most recent book is entitled "Metaethics." However, again, I find it quite hard to figure out if there is in fact a metaethical view being presented. Or, perhaps, since the view he presents seems, as far as I can see, to be compatible with either realism or noncognitivism, he must be using the term "metaethics" in a sense different from that of contemporary, mainstream discussions of these matters. Katsafanas's "constitutivist" position presents similar difficulties. Constitutivist positions like Korsgaard's or Velleman's seem, despite the widespread temptation to interpret them otherwise, neutral on metaethical issues; for all that seem to be the commitments of these views, they are compatible, again, with either realisms of various stripes or non-cognitivism. Katsafanas self-avowedly attempts to interpret Nietzsche in the light of constitutivist thinkers such as Korsgaard and Velleman, and, as far as I can see, then inherits the above-mentioned feature of their theories. For relevant discussions of Korsgaard and Velleman, see Hussain and Shah 2006, forthcoming; Hussain 2004a.

from *GS*, in which Nietzsche apparently claims that we *do* succeed in creating values. These were the passages that made *just* ascribing an error theory to Nietzsche implausible. The problem is that we still need to account for the error-theoretic passages we began with. We have seen revolutionary fictionalism's way of handling them; however, how should the subjective realist or the noncognitivist handle them? I have already discussed the possibility of claiming that Nietzsche intends the error-theoretic claims to apply only to some restrictive domain of normative or evaluative claims. Clark and Dudrick, in their defense of a noncognitivist interpretation, take up a version of the standard developmentalist strategy.[39] They grant that Nietzsche was an error theorist about all evaluative and normative judgments in *HAH* but they claim that by the time of the first edition of *GS*, he had given up his error theory because he gives up his cognitivism (Clark and Dudrick 2007: 193).[40] They thus posit a radical shift in Nietzsche's metaethical views from error theory to noncognitivism. This would account for the error-theoretic passages while allowing that Nietzsche's developed metaethical view was a noncognitivist one. One can imagine using a similar strategy for subjectivism.[41]

Unfortunately, it is not at all clear that the texts support such a radical shift. Furthermore, the specific passages which are supposed to have a noncognitivist flavor to them, do not, it seems to me, have such a flavor. They are either far more friendly to an error-theoretic or fictionalist reading or merely point to the kind of harmless everyday expression of noncognitive attitudes that I have already emphasized cannot use be used to support noncognitivism.

We have already seen the evidence from *HAH* for ascribing an error theory to Nietzsche (*HAH* I: 4, 32–3). I will return to the *GS* passages in a moment; however, we can see that the Clark-Dudrick thesis that there is a radical shift in Nietzsche's views is undermined by the presence of error-theoretic passages from *TI* written well after *GS* in 1888. Indeed, I began the section on error theory with one of the more dramatic of such passages, the one in which Nietzsche declares that he was the "first to formulate" the "insight" that "*there are altogether no moral facts.*"[42] This passage draws precisely the kind of parallel to religion that was drawn in, for example, *HAH* I: 4.[43] Again, one might try to read some restriction here to a narrowly conceived domain of specifically *moral* judgments. However, the context of the passage makes clear that a vast range of positions is included: Manu, Confucius, Plato, Judaism, and Christianity. And it is an interesting question whether Nietzsche too is included among the "improvers of mankind." Thus at least for all these normative and evaluative judgments Nietzsche is still a cognitivist and an error theorist. Therefore the purported change to noncognitivism must only have occurred for some subset of current evaluative terms.

However, first, no such restriction of domain by Nietzsche is actually defended on interpretive grounds by Clark and Dudrick. Second, there is evidence that no such restriction

---

[39] Oddly Reginster does not take up this particular puzzle in his book when he gives a subjective realist interpretation.

[40] In this section, I draw heavily on my Hussain 2012b.

[41] There are other possibilities that I will not consider here. Perhaps Nietzsche is a subjective realist about the good, reducing it to power, but thinks that achieving power requires false value judgments for some and perhaps honest illusions of value for others. Or perhaps Nietzsche could be interpreted as recommending revolutionary subjectivism or noncognitivism.

[42] Emphasis in the original.

[43] Similar passages occur, as we saw, from the *Nachlaß* well after *GS*.

existed in Nietzsche's mind. Consider the following passages from the *Nachlaß* which show no such restriction (note the dates):

> All the values by means of which we have tried so far to render the world estimable for our-selves…all these values are, psychologically considered, the results of certain perspectives of utility, designed to maintain and increase human constructs of domination—and they have been falsely *projected* into the essence of things. (*WP* 12 [November 1887–March 1888])

Or elsewhere: "In the entire evolution of morality, truth never appears: all the conceptual elements employed are fictions" (*WP* 428 [1888]).

Again, there is no sign in his notes of error theory being applied to most current evaluative and normative judgments, while the noncognitivism is restricted to some subset.

Now, finally, let us take a look at the *GS* passages Clark and Dudrick appeal to in their argument that Nietzsche came to accept noncognitivism. We have already seen *GS* 301. I take it that all hands agree that it is not at all obvious which metaethical view that passage supports. But let us take a closer look again at *GS* 299 which Clark and Dudrick do think attracts a noncognitivist reading (202):

> *What one should learn from artists.*—How can we make things beautiful, attractive, and desir-able for us when they are not? And I rather think that in themselves they never are. Here we should learn something from physicians, when for example they dilute what is bitter or add wine and sugar to a mixture—but even more from artists who are really continually trying to bring off such inventions and feats. Moving away from things until there is a good deal that one no longer sees and there is much that our eye has to add if we are still to see them at all; or seeing things around a corner and as cut out and framed; or to place them so that they par-tially conceal each other and grant us only glimpses of architectural perspective; or looking at them through tinted glass or in the light of the sunset; or giving them a surface and skin that is not fully transparent—all that we should learn from artists while being wiser than they are in other matters. For with them this subtle power usually comes to an end where art ends and life begins; but we want to be the poets of our life—first of all in the smallest, most everyday matters. (*GS* 299)

This passage does not seem to me to be an expression of noncognitivism, in the contempo-rary metaethical sense, at all. Notice one essential, dominant feature of this passage, namely, the crucial role that various kinds of concealment or deception play: making sure there are things we do not see, making sure we give them some kind of nontransparent covering and so on. Why would any of this be central to a noncognitive practice of valuing? After all the noncognitivist's point is precisely that there is *no* mistake, deception, or confusion involved in valuing—noncognitivists see themselves as saving us from having to posit errors.

Of course I suspect there is a reason for the emphasis on deception, and the best way to bring it out is to focus, in opposition to Clark and Dudrick, on the *continuity* between pas-sages such as these and what Nietzsche says in *HAH*. In his 1886 preface to *HAH*, Nietzsche reiterates the point he had made in the body of *HAH* about the "necessary injustice" involved in evaluative judgments. Nietzsche admits that his looking "into the world" with his uniquely "profound degree of suspicion"—the suspicion that makes one think that everything includ-ing of course our evaluations are human, all too human—was psychologically difficult:

> [I]n an effort to recover from myself, as it were to induce a temporary self-forgetting, I have sought shelter in this or that—in some piece of admiration or enmity or scientificality or

frivolity or stupidity; and...where I could not find what I *needed*, I had artificially to enforce, falsify and invent a suitable fiction for myself (—and what else have poets ever done? And to what end does art exist in the world at all?) (*HAH* I: Preface 1)

Note the connection between poetry and art and the generation of fiction. It is this connection that Nietzsche seems again to be harping on in *GS* 299. That is why we are learning from artists. That is why we need to be poets. And now it should come as no surprise that the passage I quoted already from *HAH* I: 33 continues as follows:

> [M]ankind as a whole has *no* goal, and the individual man when he regards its total course...must be reduced to despair. If in all he does he has before him the ultimate goal-lessness of man, his actions acquire in his own eyes the character of useless squandering. But to feel thus *squandered*...is a feeling beyond all other feelings.—But who is capable of such a feeling? Certainly only a poet: and poets always know how to console themselves. (*HAH* I: 33)

Poets can console themselves because they do what they have always done, as he says in the preface, namely, create fictions.

Clark and Dudrick take *GS* 299's message to be that we create value by evoking noncognitive reactions such as preferences and attitudes. Note first that in *GS* 299 there is hardly anything about noncognitive preferences and attitudes. All the metaphors, except for the first one about taste, are visual cognitive ones and Nietzsche clearly emphasizes that the latter metaphors, the ones involving artists, are the important ones. We could take the first one as emphasizing that generating a certain kind of noncognitive reaction is an important part of making something valuable. But, as I emphasized earlier, not any connection between noncognitive motivations and value judgments grounds noncognitivism. What we need evidence for is the specific semantic thesis that the noncognitivist is committed to.

Clark and Dudrick bring in *GS* 7 at this point as support. It starts as follows:

> *Something for the industrious.*—Anyone who now wishes to make a study of moral matters opens up for himself an immense field for work. All kinds of individual passions have to be thought through and pursued through different ages, peoples, and great and small individuals; all their reason and all their evaluations and perspectives on things have to be brought into the light. So far, all that has given color to existence still lacks a history. (*GS* 7)

Clark and Dudrick write that this passage "implies that the passions constitute 'all that has given color to existence'" (203). Talk of color is then taken, plausibly enough, as a metaphor for value. Would some such constitution claim support the noncognitivist reading? Again, it will not cut much ice against, say, the subjectivist unless you can defend the ascription of the specific semantic claim that is at the heart of noncognitivism. In any case, the passage does not give passions any such specific role. Evaluations, for example, and crucially, seem also to be part of what colors the world.

Furthermore, this passage actually plays against Clark and Dudrick. After emphasizing the vast amount of work that would be required for laying out the history and variation of "moral matters," Nietzsche writes:

> The same applies to the demonstration of the reasons for the differences between moral climates.... And it would be yet another job to determine the erroneousness of all these reasons and the whole nature of moral judgments to date. (*GS* 7)

The continuities with *HAH* and thus the continuing suggestions of systematic error are quite compelling.

Of course, this discussion only begins the comparisons needed for deciding which meta-ethical theory to ascribe.[44]

8 UNDERDETERMINATION

On the other hand, one may well think that we have accumulated compelling evidence for the conclusion that we do not have adequate textual grounds for ascribing *any* particular metaethical view or stance to Nietzsche. Leiter claims that "there are inadequate textual resources for ascribing to [Nietzsche] a satisfying answer" to questions about the semantics of moral claims (Leiter 2000: 278). Thus "there are simply not adequate grounds for 'assigning' to Nietzsche a view on such subtle matters as whether ethical language is primarily cognitive or non-cognitive" (279).

One reason for thinking that Leiter's position here is compelling is to remind ourselves of the kinds of arguments deployed in contemporary metaethics. Take, just as one example, appeals to judgment internalism as a basis for developing some form of noncognitivism. Standard forms of such arguments require claiming not just that motivations tend to accompany, or perhaps even stand in some lawlike relation to, the making of normative judgments. What judgment internalism requires is a form of conceptual necessity. It is such commitments that often drive contemporary metaethical debate. I would suggest that all extant metaethical theories—the kinds of theories which we have been trying to ascribe to Nietzsche—can account for contingent, even lawlike, connections between normative judgments, or even normative truths, and our motivations. A naturalistically inclined philosopher like Nietzsche tends precisely to focus on the contingent, on the kind of data that empirical investigation, in some broad sense, can provide. But such data does not really cut ice in metaethical debates, and thus correlatively, Nietzsche's assertions along such lines can be co-opted by differing metaethical interpretations. The fact that so many different, conflicting metaethical interpretations of Nietzsche exist can plausibly be seen as a symptom of just this feature of Nietzsche's texts.

The texts lack the granularity that would really be needed to resolve the claims of competing metaethical interpretations. Officially I have discussed reductive (naturalistic) subjective realisms, noncognitivism, error theory, and fictionalism. However, I have not discussed, for reasons of space, views that seem like constitutivist and non-naturalist realist interpretations of Nietzsche. It is hard not to have the feeling that in the face of this lack of resistance by the texts, we are seeing regular deployments of what I would call the "principle of hypercharity": if *p*, then Nietzsche believes that *p*. There comes a point where one should simply argue for the philosophical positions themselves, rather than engage in proxy wars by using historical figures. Of course, I have not given grounds that would justify any such attack *ad hominem*. The point is rather to urge caution on us all.

---

[44] See Hussain 2012a for a comparative assessment of subjective realist and fictionalist interpretations.

WORKS CITED

(A) Works by Nietzsche

A   *The Antichrist* (1895), in *The Portable Nietzsche*, trans. W. Kaufmann. New York: Viking Press, 1982, 565–656.

BGE   *Beyond Good and Evil* (1886), trans. W. Kaufmann. New York: Vintage Books, 1989

CW   *The Case of Wagner* (1888), trans. W. Kaufmann. New York: Vintage Books, 1967

D   *Daybreak* (1881), trans. R. J. Hollingdale. Cambridge: Cambridge University Press, 1982

EH   *Ecce Homo* (1887), trans. W. Kaufmann. New York: Vintage Books, 1989

GM   *On the Genealogy of Morality* (1887), trans. M. Clark and A. Swensen. Indianapolis and Cambridge, Mass.: Hackett, 1996

GS   *The Gay Science* (1887), trans. W. Kaufmann. New York: Vintage Books, 1974.

HAH   *Human, All Too Human* (1886), trans. R. J. Hollingdale. Cambridge: Cambridge University Press. 1986

KSA   *Kritische Studienausgabe*. Berlin: De Gruyter, 1980.

TI   *Twilight of the Idols* (1889), in *The Portable Nietzsche*, trans. W. Kaufmann. New York: Viking Penguin, 1982, 463–563.

WP   *The Will to Power* (1883–8), trans. W. Kaufmann and R. J. Hollingdale. New York: Vintage Books, 1968

Z   *Thus Spoke Zarathustra* (1891–2), trans. W. Kaufmann. New York: Penguin Books, 1966.

(B) Other Works Cited

Clark, M. and Dudrick, D. 2007. "Nietzsche and Moral Objectivity: The Development of Nietzsche's Metaethics," in B. Leiter and N. Sinhababu (eds), *Nietzsche and Morality*. Oxford: Clarendon Press, 192–226.

Gibbard, A. 1990. *Wise Choices, Apt Feelings: A Theory of Normative Judgement*. Cambridge, Mass.: Harvard University Press.

Hunt, L. H. 1991. *Nietzsche and the Origin of Virtue*. London and New York: Routledge.

Hussain, N. J. Z. 2004a. "The Guise of a Reason," *Philosophical Studies* 121: 263–75.

Hussain, N. J. Z. 2004b. "The Return of Moral Fictionalism," *Philosophical Perspectives* 18: 149–88.

Hussain, N. J. Z. 2007. "Honest Illusion: Valuing for Nietzsche's Free Spirits," in B. Leiter and N. Sinhababu (eds), *Nietzsche and Morality*. Oxford: Clarendon Press, 157–91.

Hussain, N. J. Z. 2010. "Error Theory and Fictionalism," in J. Skorupski (ed.), *The Routledge Companion to Ethics*. London and New York: Routledge, 335–45.

Hussain, N. J. Z. 2011. "The Role of Life in the *Genealogy*," in S. May (ed.), *The Cambridge Critical Guide to Nietzsche's "On the Genealogy of Morality."* Cambridge: Cambridge University Press, 142–69.

Hussain, N. J. Z. 2012a. "Metaethics and Nihilism in Reginster's *The Affirmation of Life*," *Journal of Nietzsche Studies* 43.1: 99–117.

Hussain, N. J. Z. 2012b. "Nietzsche and Non-Cognitivism," in S. Robertson and C. Janaway (eds), *Nietzsche, Naturalism, and Normativity*. Oxford: Oxford University Press, 111–32.

Hussain, N. J. Z. and Shah, N. 2006. "Misunderstanding Metaethics: Korsgaard's Rejection of Realism," in R. Shafer-Landau (ed.), *Oxford Studies in Metaethics*. Oxford: Oxford University Press, 265–94.

Hussain, N. J. Z. and Shah, N. Forthcoming. "Metaethics and Its Discontents: A Case Study of Korsgaard," in Carla Bagnoli (ed.), *Moral Constructivism: For and Against.* Cambridge: Cambridge University Press.

Jaspers, K. 1965. *Nietzsche: An Introduction to the Understanding of His Philosophical Activity,* trans. C. Walraff and F. J. Schmitz. Tucson: University of Arizona Press.

Katsafanas, P. 2010. "Deriving Ethics from Action: A Nietzschean Version of Constitutivism," *Philosophy and Phenomenological Research* 83.3: 620–60

Kaufmann, W. 1974. *Nietzsche: Philosopher, Psychologist, Antichrist.* New Jersey: Princeton University Press.

Langsam, H. 1997. "How to Combat Nihilism: Reflections on Nietzsche's Critique of Morality," *History of Philosophy Quarterly* 14.2: 235–53.

Leiter, B. 2000. "Nietzsche's Metaethics: Against the Privilege Readings," *European Journal of Philosophy* 8.3: 277–97.

Leiter, B. 2002. *Routledge Philosophy Guidebook to Nietzsche on Morality.* London and New York: Routledge.

Mackie, J. L. 1977. *Ethics: Inventing Right and Wrong.* London: Penguin.

May, S. 1999. *Nietzsche's Ethics and his War on "Morality."* Oxford and New York: Clarendon Press; Oxford University Press.

Miller, A. 2003. *An Introduction to Contemporary Metaethics.* Cambridge: Polity Press.

Morgan, G. A. 1941/1965. *What Nietzsche Means.* New York: Harper.

Poellner, P. 2007. "Affect, Value and Objectivity,, in B. Leiter and N. Sinhababu (eds), *Nietzsche and Morality.* Oxford: Clarendon Press, 227–61.

Poellner, P. 2009. "Nietzschean Freedom," in K. Gemes and S. May (eds), *Nietzsche on Freedom and Autonomy.* Oxford: Oxford University Press, 125–52.

Poellner, P. 2012. "Aestheticist Ethics," in S. Robertson and C. Janaway (eds), *Nietzsche, Naturalism, and Normativity.* Oxford: Oxford University Press, 52–80.

Railton, P. 2003a. "Facts and Values," in *Facts, Values, and Norms: Essays Toward a Morality of Consequence.* Cambridge: Cambridge University Press, 43–68.

Railton, P. 2003b. "Moral Realism," in *Facts, Values, and Norms: Essays Toward a Morality of Consequence.* Cambridge: Cambridge University Press, 3–42

Reginster, B. 2003. Review of Leiter, Brian, *Routledge Philosophy Guidebook to Nietzsche on Morality* (London: Routledge, 2002), in *Notre Dame Philosophical Reviews.* Available at <http://ndpr.nd.edu/news/23223-routledge-philosophy-guidebook-to-nietzsche-on-morality/>, accessed February 13, 2013.

Reginster, B. 2006. *The Affirmation of Life: Nietzsche on Overcoming Nihilism.* Cambridge, Mass.: Harvard University Press.

Richardson, J. 1996. *Nietzsche's System.* New York and Oxford: Oxford University Press.

Richardson, J. 2004. *Nietzsche's New Darwinism.* Oxford and New York: Oxford University Press.

Schacht, R. 1983. *Nietzsche.* London: Routledge.

Wilcox, J. T. 1974. *Truth and Value in Nietzsche: A Study of His Metaethics and Epistemology.* Ann Arbor: University of Michigan Press.

CHAPTER 18

....

NIETZSCHE AND THE ARTS OF LIFE

....

AARON RIDLEY

NIETZSCHE's thought developed rapidly during the brief period of his philosophical activity, and some of the changes were large. But on certain matters his views remained relatively constant. He was, for example, convinced from beginning to end that art was of great significance for life—not merely significant as a *part* of life, but as a model after which life should be led, understood, and evaluated.[1] As an enthusiastic poet and musician, he did of course also regard art as a significant part of life. But when he said, for example, that 'life without music would be an error' (*TI*: 'Maxims and Arrows' 33), he didn't just mean that life without it would be emptier or less enjoyable. He meant that life without music would have been robbed of a fundamental standard and vindication, of an ideal by which it might orient and celebrate itself. And the Nietzsche who made this remark in 1888 is entirely continuous with the Nietzsche who, in 1872, had famously declared that 'it is only as an *aesthetic phenomenon* that existence and the world are eternally *justified*' (*BT* 5). He may, in the intervening sixteen years, have lost some of his taste for talk of eternal justification (in the 1882 edition of *The Gay Science*, for example, the claim has become that 'As an aesthetic phenomenon existence is still *bearable* for us', *GS* 107). But the late Nietzsche remains committed, just as the early Nietzsche had been, to the view that life must, in some sense, be construed and conducted *as* an aesthetic phenomenon if it is not to be merely intolerable. My purpose in the present essay is to explore (at least parts of) what he might have meant by that and to do so in ways that highlight the fundamental continuity of this dimension of his thought.[2] For it may be that this very continuity provides an essential point of reference for an understanding of Nietzsche's thought more generally—for seeing how the sometimes quite dramatic developments in his other views might have been prompted by his enduring conviction that life is, in one way or another, to be regarded aesthetically.

[1] A claim that withstands, I think, the overt scientism of his third book, *Human, All Too Human*, in which the significance of art is officially downgraded. For, as will become clear in what follows, many of Nietzsche's main intuitions about the relation between art and life are present even in that work.

[2] For accounts of Nietzsche's thinking about art that have a more developmental emphasis, see Young 1992 and Ridley 2007a.

1 Aesthetic Phenomena

There are several sorts of aesthetic phenomenon that might be taken as models for life. There is, first, the phenomenon of aesthetic spectacle: life is pointful, one might hold, if it makes for decent viewing, as works of art and natural beauties do. Or there is the phenomenon, or alleged phenomenon, of aesthetic experience: one might hold, for example, that it is the lived quality of existence that settles its value, and that aesthetic experience provides the standard against which that quality is to be judged. Or, finally, there is the phenomenon of aesthetic creativity: one might hold that the worthwhile life is one that exhibits or is structured by a certain kind of artistry.

Nietzsche had a degree of investment in each of these thoughts. In section 2, I discuss the first of them; in section 3, I very briefly mention the implications of Nietzsche's thoughts about aesthetic spectacle for his thoughts about aesthetic experience; and I take up the theme of artistry in section 4.

2 Three Kinds of Spectator

Nietzsche was deeply interested in the notion of spectatorship; he returns to it repeatedly and from a variety of angles. Here, though, I will simply sketch in three sorts of perspective that he thinks might be taken on the spectacle that life presents.

2.1 Divine Spectators

In Nietzsche's later view, the pre-Socratic Greeks had consoled themselves for the sufferings of existence by reflecting that they were at least putting on a good show for the gods: 'With what eyes do you think Homer made his gods look down upon the destinies of men?', Nietzsche asks. 'What was at bottom the ultimate meaning of Trojan Wars and other such tragic terrors? There can be no doubt whatever: they were intended as *festival plays* for the gods' (*GM* II: 7). And this view, or one very like it, is already present in *The Birth of Tragedy*, where Nietzsche invites us to imagine that 'we are merely images and artistic projections for the true author', who, 'as the sole... spectator of this comedy of art' (indeed, as the 'primordial artist of the world'), 'prepares a perpetual entertainment for itself' (*BT* 5).

In both cases, Nietzsche's mortals apprehend life as fundamentally terrible—as filled with loss, destruction, and pain. And in this, or so Nietzsche almost invariably holds, they are quite right. His mortals are therefore faced with a choice: either confront the true character of existence, and despair—as Schopenhauer had thought one must; or confront it, and find a way of affirming life despite or even because of its terrible character. Nietzsche's admiration for the pre-Socratic Greeks is rooted in their genius, as he sees it, for making something of the latter alternative. And one of the ways in which they did this was to think of life as a spectacle for the gods (or for the 'primordial artist of the world'), a measure which allowed them to assign at least a certain sort of meaning to their mortal sufferings. For, as Nietzsche puts it, 'What really arouses indignation against suffering is not suffering as such but the senselessness of suffering' (*GM* II: 7). So suffering that is *enjoyed*—if only by a god who happens to catch sight of it—does at least have a certain point to it, and is, in that much, not wholly futile; and life is (partly) redeemed by that thought, even if not, one might imagine, quite so decisively from the mortal point of view as from the divine. This, then, is one way in which existence and the world might be thought to be 'justified', or at least made more bearable, when regarded as an '*aesthetic phenomenon*'.

2.2 Disinterested Spectators

The fact that Nietzsche's divine spectators are correctly to be thought of as engaging with existence as an '*aesthetic phenomenon*', however, might be obscured by a modern prejudice according to which aesthetic phenomena can only be contemplated as such when they are contemplated *disinterestedly*. All tastes and preferences must be suspended, on this conception, if the contemplated object is to be appreciated properly—that is, for its own sake. Whereas Nietzsche's divine spectators are far from disinterested in this sense: they have a distinct taste for mortal sufferings—even a preference for them, if, like the 'primordial artist', they are to be thought of as preparing the spectacle specifically for their own 'entertainment'.

Nietzsche has little patience with the cult of disinterestedness, however. It is, he holds, not only thoroughly *un*disinterested in its motivations (and hence dishonest), but is actively life-denying, indeed is an expression of the ascetic ideal. Its dishonesty lies in the pretence that the disinterested stance is demanded by the apprehension of beauty—whether as a precondition, as in Kant, or as a consequence, as in Schopenhauer—whereas the truth, according to Nietzsche, is that that stance answers to a hatred of life. One celebrates disinterestedness, on his view, precisely when one wants to get away from oneself, from the conditions of one's embodied existence, as if '*to gain release from a torture*' (*GM* III: 6). And the self-deception diagnosed here is, because motivated by the desire to escape from and deny our (human, animal) natures, ascetic through and through. In Schopenhauer, hatred of life engenders nihilism quite directly: Nietzsche quotes his paean to that 'painless', i.e. disinterested, 'condition' in which for a moment 'we are delivered from the vile urgency of the will', and remarks 'What images of torment and long despair!' (*GM* III: 6). In Kant, as in Christianity and Plato, the nihilism—and indeed the despair—are better disguised. But they are nevertheless what lurk behind and give point to the various fantasies—such as the noumenal realm, the *res fidei*, the world of the Forms—that have been offered as the 'reality' of which existence and the world are merely the 'appearances', each of these fantasies, in Nietzsche's view, invented only so as to denigrate life in favour of some non-existent 'other'. And this is very far removed from the undertaking in which he takes his pre-Socratic Greeks to be engaged. *Their* spectators were supposed to redeem life even in its darkest terrors and awfulnesses; whereas the disinterested spectator, on Nietzsche's reading of the matter, is the concoction of spirits who are in full—if often self-deceived—flight from precisely those terrors and awfulnesses.[3]

---

[3] For a fine discussion of Nietzsche on disinterestedness, see Janaway 2007: 188–91.

2.3 Genuine Spectators

Nietzsche contrasts the disinterested spectator with the figure of Stendhal, whom he calls 'a genuine "spectator" and artist'. In the event, however, although clearly approving of him, Nietzsche tells us rather little about Stendhal, except that, as an artist, with 'refined first-hand experience', beauty is for him 'a great *personal* fact, … an abundance of vivid authentic experiences, desires, surprises and delights', so that he approaches beauty in an unabashedly interested spirit—indeed, as '*une promesse de bonheur*' (a promise of happiness): 'to him the fact seems to be precisely that the beautiful *arouses the will* ("interestedness")'. Thus 'he *rejected* and repudiated the one point … which Kant had stressed: *le désintéressement*' (GM III: 6). Untainted as he appears to be, therefore, by any vestige of asceticism, we may take it that *his* kind of spectatorship is offered as some sort of mortal equivalent of the gods'—i.e. as something that would, if it took them as its purview, vindicate life and the world rather than deny and denigrate them.[4] Nietzsche gives us nothing else to go on here. But I shall return briefly to the genuine spectator in section 6, where I'll try to indicate his place in the larger structure of what I take to be Nietzsche's aesthetic ideal.

3 AESTHETIC EXPERIENCE

So, existence and the world might be justified or made bearable as an '*aesthetic phenomenon*' if viewed as a spectacle, although not, according to Nietzsche, if viewed as such in a disinterested spirit. And this tells us most of what we need to know about his views concerning aesthetic experience as a model for life. For the proponents of disinterested spectatorship are united in the claim that properly formed aesthetic experience consists in pleasure without interest—that is, in pleasure taken impartially in something beautiful for its own sake. Construed, therefore, as an ideal against which the lived quality of existence should be gauged, the proponents of this form of aesthetic experience hold up a state of disengagement—of radically non-partisan contemplation—as the model to which life should aspire.

Nietzsche, not surprisingly, rejects this contention.[5] Its attractions, such as they are, derive from a conception of spectatorship that he regards as the opposite of what the justification of life requires; and the mode of experience enjoined strikes him as correspondingly ascetic, if not indeed as paradoxical (see, e.g., GM III: 12). He is, I think, sympathetic to the idea that aesthetic experience, properly construed, might be taken as a model for the lived quality of life. But the proper construction of that experience he regards as lying in quite other regions. At its mildest, Nietzsche's version consists in Stendhal's apprehension in beauty of a promise of happiness; rather more heatedly, in what one imagines to be his gods' relish at the sight of mortal suffering. The early Nietzsche had thought of aesthetic experience as a matter of transported ecstasy (see, e.g., BT 1); the late Nietzsche thought of it in terms of sublimated

---

[4] Nietzsche's attitude towards Stendhal on beauty and happiness is in fact more complicated than this: for discussion, see Ridley 2011.

[5] Even if he had, very briefly, flirted with a picture rather like it in *Human, All Too Human*: see, e.g., *HAH* I: 34.

'sexual excitement, the oldest and most primitive form of intoxication' (*TI*: 'Skirmishes of an Untimely Man' 8). There are, then, perhaps slightly different conceptions of aesthetic experience in play in Nietzsche's writings.[6] But they have it in common that each is a mode of thoroughly *interested* engagement with life—with life as something to be embraced rather than stepped back from; even as something to be lusted after, whatever its terrors. And in this much, Nietzsche's version of aesthetic experience, if taken as a model for the lived quality of life, offers another kind of possible justification of existence as an '*aesthetic phenomenon*'— or, perhaps better, of existence as an exercise in aesthetic phenomenology. I won't, however, pursue the matter further here: the topic is large, and, except to the extent that it once again underlines Nietzsche's opposition to ideals of disinterestedness, it lies to the side of the main issues that I want to discuss.

4 ARTISTRY

Artists, according to Nietzsche, create their work in the sort of state that he regards as characteristic of aesthetic experience.[7] And the kind of creativity that they show, he thinks, offers another model after which life and the world might, as an '*aesthetic phenomenon*', be justified or made bearable. In order to make sense of this aspect of his thought, however, it will be helpful to begin by asking what artistry, for Nietzsche, consists in. For I think that it is quite easy to go wrong here (and also quite important not to).

4.1 Form-giving

Nietzsche's most basic conception of artistry is that it is a matter of giving form; it is a matter of imposing form upon something that had been formless (or in some other way unsatisfactory: formlessness, for Nietzsche, is one way of *being* unsatisfactory: it implies meaninglessness). A central statement of the view, revealingly not once invoking artists ordinarily so-called, is this: those who create states, says Nietzsche, lay their 'terrible claws upon a populace... still formless and nomad' and go to work 'until this raw material of people and semi-animals [is] at last not only thoroughly kneaded and pliant but also *formed*'. Their work, he continues,

> is an instinctive creation and imposition of forms; they are the most involuntary, unconscious artists there are—wherever they appear something new soon arises, a ruling structure that *lives*, in which parts and functions are delimited and coordinated, in which nothing whatever finds a place that has not first been assigned a 'meaning' in relation to the whole... [T]hey

---

[6] The differences shouldn't be overstated, however. The conceptions of *The Birth of Tragedy* and *Twilight of the Idols* are clearly very similar (both are forms of '*Rausch*'); the full discussion of *GM* III: 6 strongly suggests that Stendhal's variety of experience is not without an erotic dimension; and it would be a bold person who insisted that the relish of Nietzsche's gods must be *altogether* divorced from considerations of a parallel kind.

[7] See, e.g., *BT* 1, 2; *TI*: 'Skirmishes of an Untimely Man' 8, 9.

exemplify that terrible artists' egoism that has the look of bronze and knows itself justified to all eternity in its 'work' . . . (*GM* II: 17).

This conception of art and artistry is also pertinent to artists ordinarily so-called, and it may indeed be that these latter exemplify that conception in an especially clear and direct way. But Nietzsche's state-creators are, in his view, just as properly to be called artists—not in some extended, metaphorical sense, but in the fundamental sense that they, too, are imposers of form. And this equation of form-giving with artistry, which is explicit in Nietzsche's writings from at least the later 1870s onwards, almost certainly underpins his understanding of the matter from the start.[8]

To be an artist, on this construction, just *is* to impose form. And form, as the quoted passage shows, is conceived by Nietzsche along traditional (perhaps Romantic) organicist lines: because parts acquire their 'meaning' from their 'relation to the whole', the resultant structure '*lives*'. This is important to Nietzsche. His metaphysics changed considerably during the course of his life, but he remained committed throughout to the view that existence and the world are, in some basic sense, chaotic and meaningless—at any rate when considered in their *ur*-character. He also remained committed to the view that this fact, however interpreted metaphysically, constitutes the principal terror and awfulness of existence (it 'is not suffering as such but the senselessness of suffering . . .', etc.). So form-giving—artistry—strikes him as indispensable. In transmuting chaos into order, the artist creates living structures which, because they confer meaning upon their constituents, offer at least the prospect of redemption for a life and a world that threaten otherwise to be devoid of sense; and 'any meaning', as Nietzsche puts it, 'is better than none at all' (*GM* III: 28).

But of course some meanings are better than others. '[W]hat does all art do?', Nietzsche asks—referring to *all* art, to the art of state-makers just as much as that of sculptors or poets: 'does it not praise? does it not glorify? does it not select? does it not highlight? By doing all this it *strengthens* or *weakens* certain valuations' (*TI*: 'Skirmishes of an Untimely Man' 24)—which is to say that, in imposing form, the artist creates meanings whose patterns are already evaluatively charged. So, for example, in imposing *his* chosen form upon existence and the world—in his treatment of 'life as a wrong road on which one must finally walk back' (*GM* III: 11)—the ascetic priest sets up a field of meaning which encourages the devaluation of ordinary worldly existence in favour of a (non-existent) beyond.[9] Naturally the priest's art is not to Nietzsche's taste: he would prefer an art whose valuations are life-affirming. But the important point, for present purposes, is that, on Nietzsche's understanding of the matter, valuations of one sort or another are an integral dimension of the patterns of meaning that form-giving or artistry creates: they come for free, as it were, with artistry in what he takes to be its most fundamental sense.

---

[8] Or perhaps—at the very beginning, in *The Birth of Tragedy*—of his understanding of 'Apollonian' art; 'Dionysian' art may have to be understood somewhat differently.

[9] Nietzsche expressly refers to the priest's 'distinctive art', to his 'essential art': see *GM* III: 15.

4.2 Falsification

It is quite common, however, to come across readings of Nietzsche on these matters that construe him as claiming that what is fundamental or essential to artistry is not form-giving, but falsification or deception.[10] In a moment, I shall consider some of the passages that might appear to gesture in this direction. First, though, let me point out how very implausible such a position would be (whether held by Nietzsche or not).

Take, to begin with, Nietzsche's artists of the state: what do *they* falsify? They start out with a material that is formless, and they impose form upon it. But to give form to something that had lacked it is not to falsify it: it is to *change* it into something of which it is now true that it has form.[11] Or, if it is felt that it would be better to stick with artistry ordinarily so-called, take a potter or a sculptor of abstracts. Again, we have nothing more here than change (does the potter deceive us as to the nature of clay?). Or, if the thought is that we should focus instead on *representational* artistry, how plausible is it to think that a portrait, say, *must* falsify its subject? Not very, surely. Of course, a portrait *might* falsify its subject: a queen, for example, might be portrayed as less regal than she is, or a courtier as more handsome. But it is hardly essential to something's being a portrait that it should portray its subject deceptively. Or—as I had perhaps better put it—it is hardly essential that that should be so, unless, possibly, on some unrescuably crude conception of representational truth. So, I suppose, someone might insist that paintings inevitably falsify three-dimensional objects by rendering them in only two dimensions; or that caricatures or cubist portraits always deceive us about the appearance of their subjects (people don't *really* look like that!). But this would be to ignore or to misunderstand the essential role of medium- and/or genre-specific conventions in making sense of pictures—and hence of being in a position even to raise the question whether or not this or that representation falsifies what it is supposed to represent. Once we're at home with the relevant conventions, we have no difficulty in distinguishing between a caricature that captures its subject to a tee, say, and one that doesn't.

Of course, as I have said, artistry (whether ordinarily so-called or not) *may* be falsifying. For example, Nietzsche regards the priest's as an art of falsification: it is just a lie, in his view, to paint the world in the colours of guilt and sin[12]—and part of his critique of the priest is intended to get us to see that, like a bad caricature, the priest's art misses its mark. Falsification is thus possible only in the context of things taken as true—for instance that a given queen is more intrinsically regal than this, or that the concepts of guilt and sin misrepresent, or are unhelpful in navigating, the salient features of human psychology. But there is no reason to doubt, still less to deny, that artistry *can* be faithful to these and other (putative) truths, even if it sometimes isn't. So the idea that artistry is *essentially* a matter of falsification looks like a non-starter. And this is so even if it is the case, as it surely is, that much artistry proceeds—as Nietzsche reminds us—by means of selection and highlighting, by giving prominence to certain features at the expense of others.[13] For something that is less than the *whole* truth need not thereby be a falsification of

---

[10] For example, proponents of the view that Nietzsche subscribes to so-called 'fictionalism' about meta-ethical issues construe him in this way—see, e.g., Hussain 2007.

[11] Of course, there may be falsification at another level—if, for instance, the form-giver claims merely to be drawing attention to the form that was there *anyway*. But the possibility of such (meta-)deception hardly shows, or even begins to suggest, that form-giving is, per se, falsifying.

[12] See *GM* III: 15.

[13] See—apart from *TI*: 'Skirmishes of an Untimely Man' 24, already cited—*TI* 'Skirmishes of an Untimely Man' 8 or *GS* 299 for examples. Also cf. Nehamas 1985: 55–6 for related reflections.

the truths that it passes over or soft-pedals (which is why we distinguish between representations that, although simplifications, cut deep and representations that are merely simplistic—or sentimental).

There are, however, passages in Nietzsche that might seem to pull in a different direction. For example, there is the famous unpublished note in which he announces that 'we possess *art* lest we *perish of the truth*' (*WP* 822), a remark that might suggest that art saves us from perishing by deceiving us. But the suggestion is resistible. We possess seat belts lest we perish of car crashes, parachutes lest we perish of skydiving; yet neither of these countermeasures succeeds by being anything other than open-eyed to the nature of what is to be averted. And as with parachutes and skydiving, why not with art and truth?[14] Or take Nietzsche's characerization of 'art' as that 'in which precisely the *lie* is sanctified and the *will to deception* has a good conscience' (*GM* III: 25). Again, this might seem to suggest a peculiarly intimate relation between art and falsification. But the appearance is skin-deep at most: for while it may be true, perhaps, that *when* art lies its lies are 'sanctified' or that *when* art deceives it does so with 'a good conscience', it clearly does not follow from this that art always or essentially does either. (Actually, Nietzsche doesn't take even the more restricted claim to be true: he regards the lies and deceptions of the priest's art, for example, as neither sanctified nor aligned with the good conscience; and he came to think the same about, e.g., Wagner's art. At most, Nietzsche means that, in art—and perhaps only there?—falsification *can* be a good thing—on which more in a moment.) It is entirely consistent with Nietzsche's remark, in other words, that art might be mostly or nearly always truthful. Nor, finally, does the following claim establish an essential connection in Nietzsche's thought between artistry and falsification: 'Honesty', he says, 'would lead to nausea and suicide. But now there is a counterforce against our honesty that helps us to avoid such consequences: art as the *good* will to appearance' (*GS* 107). Assuming that the 'honesty' (*Redlichkeit*) that Nietzsche has in mind here isn't about, say, when I got up this morning or where Guatamala is, but is instead about large, unpalateable existential truths, the passage—again—implies nothing more than that art *may* traffic in deception and that it *may* be a good thing when it does. It certainly doesn't imply that art is, of its very nature, falsifying.

So what is the point of Nietzsche's remarks? The answer is that he thinks that *some* attempts at artistry—at form-giving—must, sooner or later, resort to the lie. These are attempts in which honest, truthful form-giving runs up against a feature or dimension of existence that is too terrible to accommodate within whatever patterns of meaning have been, perhaps can be, set up—at which point artistry reaches for the false. And Nietzsche's approbation of this recourse—his talk, with respect to it, of sanctification, good conscience, good will—is predicated on two commitments. First, he is committed to the value of truthfulness; he insists on it repeatedly;[15] and so, in this much, he likes his artistry honest. But, at the same time, he is committed to the view that life must be affirmed, however awful it unavoidably is. And this latter commitment licenses falsification in the face, as it were, of the unfaceable. He sums the matter up neatly in *Beyond Good and Evil*: 'it might be a basic characteristic of existence', he says, 'that those who would know it completely would perish, in which case the strength of a spirit should be measured according to how much of the "truth" one could still barely endure—or to put it more clearly, to what degree one would *require* it to

14 For elaboration of these points, see Ridley 2010.
15 See, e.g., *GS* 2, 335; *A* 50–6; *EH* Preface 3, etc.

be thinned down, shrouded, sweetened, blunted, falsified' (*BGE* 39). A strong spirit—Nietzsche admires strong spirits—will be able to face and affirm a very great deal; but even such a spirit, if honestly pressing the limit, will sooner or later find itself at a place where it must either lie or despair—and here, Nietzsche would prefer it to tell the saving lie. This is the place at which artistry and 'the *will to deception*' with 'a good conscience' come together.[16] Many instances of artistry, on the other hand, because not remotely engaged in pressing the limits of the bearable, simply do not have a (good) reason to reach for the false; and these, presumably, should go about their business of form-giving in a suitably truthful spirit (bearing in mind that such truthfulness may involve, as I have noted, selection and highlighting, giving prominence to certain features at the expense of others, etc.).[17]

In what follows, then, I shall take form-giving to be the essential characteristic of artistry as Nietzsche understands it; and falsification to be a recourse that it can, with a good conscience, take if the *only* alternative is to despair of the value of life.

5 The Art of the Self

Nietzsche regards art, ordinarily so-called, as tremendously important. If beautiful, it offers the 'genuine' spectator a promise of happiness; indeed it is 'the great stimulus to life' and hence a bulwark against despair (*TI*: 'Skirmishes of an Untimely Man' 24). Great art also acts as a spur to other artists, and so, at least in principle, fosters more beauties by which the genuine spectator's interests might be aroused. But Nietzsche is at least as inclined to celebrate art (in the ordinary sense) as a model for living: 'As an aesthetic phenomenon', he says, 'existence is still *bearable* for us, and art furnishes us with the eyes and hands and above all the good conscience to be *able* to turn ourselves into such a phenomenon' (*GS* 107). And this idea—that we should exercise artistry on our own lives—is a constant theme in his thought. In *Human, All Too Human*, he chides the (ordinary) artist for being too busy at his labours, for these 'prevent him from becoming better and more beautiful as a person, that is to say from creating *himself*' (*HAH* II: 102).[18] A little later, we are told that 'One can dispose of one's drives like a gardener and...cultivate the shoots of anger, pity, curiosity, vanity as productively and profitably as a beautiful fruit tree on a trellis' (*D* 560). In *The Gay Science*, it is said that we should learn form-giving from artists 'while being wiser than they are in other matters. For in them this subtle power usually comes to an end where art ends and life begins: but we want to be the poets of our life' (*GS* 299). Rather more portentously, we hear, in *Beyond Good and Evil*, that 'In man *creature* and *creator* are united: in man there is material, fragment, excess, clay, dirt, nonsense, chaos; but in man there is also creator, form-giver, hammer hardness, spectator divinity, and seventh day' (*BGE* 225).[19] And, in *Ecce Homo*, his late and rather wonderful autobiography, Nietzsche presents his own life as a

---

[16] This may explain Nietzsche's occasional tendency to to speak as if artistry and falsification were the same thing; for it might be true of great, courageous, affirmation-stretching art—which is to say of 'art' in *the most honorific sense*—that it always, in the end, resorts to the lie. But this tells us nothing about artistry in general.

[17] For a somewhat different take on these issues, see Janaway forthcoming.

[18] See also, e.g., *HAH* II: 174.

[19] Note the reference to 'spectator divinity': this ties back to the discussion of section 2.1, and will be explored further in section 6.

triumph of self-creation—that is, as a (perhaps more than) '*bearable*' aesthetic phenomenon, which he has achieved by giving himself form. The present section is devoted to some of the themes relevant to this dimension of his thought.

5.1 Exemplars

Just as one composer might inspire another, for example, so already accomplished feats of form-giving might prompt a person to become the poet of his life; and Nietzsche gives this idea some weight. Works of art in the ordinary sense might be the spur to this. Perhaps part of the happiness promised to the 'genuine' spectator by the sight of the beautiful lies in the prospect of realizing that beauty in himself. Or, again, because artists 'have taught us to esteem the hero that is concealed in everyday characters', they 'have taught us the art of viewing ourselves as heroes—from a distance and, as it were, simplified and transfigured' (*GS* 78): in such a case, the artist's characters act as a '*signpost to the future*', exciting 'envy and emulation' (*HAH* II: 99). But artistry in the wider sense, of form-giving in general, might equally serve. We might learn from history, for example, that 'in earlier times someone passed through this existence infused with pride and strength, someone else sunk in profound thoughtfulness, a third exhibiting mercy and helpfulness', and so surmise that since 'the greatness that once existed was in any event once *possible*', it may 'be possible again' (*UM* II: 2). Or we might be inspired by any of the exemplary characters whom Nietzsche himself holds up to us—perhaps most obviously by his well-known portrait of Goethe, who, he says, 'disciplined himself to a whole' and '*created* himself' (*TI*: 'Skirmishes of an Untimely Man' 49).

Throughout his life—in the early essay, 'Schopenhauer as Educator' (*UM* III), in the middle-period figure of Zarathustra, and, ultimately, in the figure of himself as he draws it in *Ecce Homo*—Nietzsche was committed to the value of exemplars in prompting an artistry of the self.[20] And he seems to have thought of this artistry as taking two possible forms (although in the end these may not be fully separable): a backward-looking form, in which one attempts to make a work of art of one's past; and a forward-looking form, in which one attempts, as he famously puts it, to ' "give style" to one's character' (*GS* 290).[21] I shall briefly treat these in turn.

5.2 Narrative Self-creation

The first three chapters of *Ecce Homo* are devoted, in large part, to substantiating what is expressed in the inscription placed between the preface of that book and its opening chapter: '*How could I not be grateful to my whole life?*', Nietzsche asks.[22] And he answers this rhetorical question by recounting his past in such a way that even the most awful events turn

---

[20] For a fine discussion of the importance of exemplars in Nietzsche's thought, see Conant 2001.

[21] For excellent and influential discussion of both forms, see Nehamas 1985.

[22] The inscription begins: 'On this perfect day, when everything is ripening and not only the grape turns brown, the eye of the sun just fell upon my life: I looked back, I looked forward, and never saw so many and such good things at once…'

out to have been for the best. Indeed, he says, if we are 'strong enough', then 'everything *has to* turn out best' for us (*EH* 'Why I Am So Wise' 2). So, for example, the early loss of his father, the excruciating catalogue of his illnesses, even his inability to withstand particular climates and diets—each of these is presented as having contributed to his having arrived at a fully achieved life. As he notoriously puts it, the strong person 'uses mishaps to his advantage; what does not kill him makes him stronger' (*EH* 'Why I Am So Wise' 2); and in his presentation of himself, Nietzsche paints an exceptionally strong person for whom everything has, indeed or therefore, turned out for the best.

In writing these autobiographical chapters, Nietzsche is, in effect, putting into practice a precept concerning the past that he had first recommended some years earlier. At what he calls 'a certain high point in life', it is possible for us to

> see how palpably always everything that happens to us turns out for the best. Every day and every hour, life seems to have no other wish than to prove this proposition again and again. Whatever it is, bad weather or good, the loss of a friend, sickness, slander, the failure of some letter to arrive, the spraining of an ankle... —either immediately or very soon after it proves to be something that 'must not be missing'; it has a profound significance and use precisely for *us*. (*GS* 277)

The idea, in other words, is that when 'our own practical and theoretical skills in interpreting and arranging events has...reached its high point' (*GS* 277), we can give form to our past, and can do so in such a way that the resultant meanings express a fundamentally affirmative valuation of life.[23] And this, of course, is artistry of the sort that Nietzsche commends— even if, for the reasons given in section 4.2, its form-giving may occasionally (ideally only *in extremis*) be less than fully honest. So here is one way in which one might engage in self-creation: one might impose a narrative form upon one's past that makes it not merely meaningful, but deserving of *gratitude*.

5.3 Substantive Self-creation

The best-known place at which Nietzsche advocates self-creation, however, enjoins something more meaty-sounding, a project in which one seeks to shape one's *future* self:

> *One thing is needful.*—To 'give style' to one's character—a great and rare art! It is practised by those who survey all the strengths and weaknesses of their nature and then fit them into an artistic plan until every one of them appears as art and reason and even weaknesses delight the eye. Here a large mass of second nature has been added; there a piece of original nature has been removed—both times through long practice and daily work at it. Here the ugly that could not be removed is concealed; there it has been reinterpreted and made sublime... It will be the strong and domineering natures that enjoy their finest gaiety in such constraint and perfection under a law of their own...For one thing is needful: that a human being should *attain*

---

[23] Notice that nothing in this conception requires that past sufferings or misfortunes lose their character *as* sufferings and misfortunes ('bad weather', for example, remains *bad* weather). The point is only that these episodes are woven into a narrative whole that can itself be affirmed. This claim contrasts, I think, with the view defended in Reginster 2006: 222–7.

satisfaction with himself, whether it be by means of this or that poetry and art...For the sight of what is ugly makes one bad and gloomy. (*GS* 290)

Despite its relative transparency, this passage has been much discussed, and there is indeed a good amount that one might say about it.[24] Here, though, I shall confine myself to two remarks. First, the need to '*attain* satisfaction' with oneself aligns this kind of artistry with Nietzsche's more general priority that despair should be steered off in favour of affirmation. Second, there is no reason to think of self-stylization as a matter of self-falsification: the process begins with a (presumably honest) 'survey [of] all the strengths and weaknesses of [one's] nature'; and the closest that Nietzsche comes to recommending deception is in his mention of the ugliness that had to be 'concealed'—and even this sounds, as it should in a 'strong' (and hence truth-bearing) spirit, like a last resort. Otherwise, the passage can simply be read as an exhortation to be Goethe-like, to discipline ourselves to wholeness, and hence to create ourselves.

5.4 An Apparent Tension

In the self-stylization passage, the process that Nietzsche envisages appears to be wholly conscious and deliberate. It begins with a survey of one's strengths and weaknesses, which are then fitted into an 'artistic plan', the execution of which requires 'long practice and daily work'. The conception of artistry that seems to be in play here—in which the artist engages in hard, premeditated labour—is one that we find elsewhere in Nietzsche's writings. In *Human, All Too Human*, for instance, he tells us that the artist 'does nothing except learn first how to lay bricks then how to build'; he has the 'seriousness of the efficient workman which first learns how to construct the parts properly before it ventures to fashion a great whole'; he possesses 'undiminishing energy, resolute application to individual goals' and 'the good fortune to receive an upbringing which offered in the early years the finest teachers, models and methods' (*HAH* I: 162–4). The artist, on this picture, is a highly skilled craftsman who applies himself assiduously to his work. And the self-stylist, it would seem, takes this picture as his model.

But in other places we come across an apparently very different picture. Here, for example, is Nietzsche's description of his own self-creation: to begin with, he says, 'one must not have the faintest notion *what* one is' to become. Indeed, 'the whole surface of consciousness...must be kept clear of all great imperatives': then,

> the organizing 'idea' that is destined to rule keeps growing deep down—it begins to command; slowly it leads us *back* from side roads and wrong roads; it prepares *single* fitnesses and qualities that will one day prove to be indispensable as means towards a whole—one by one, it trains all *subservient* capacities before giving any hint of the dominant task, 'goal', 'aim', or 'meaning'. Considered in this way, my life is simply wonderful...[—a triumph of] the long, secret work and artistry of my instinct. (*EH*: 'Why I Am So Clever' 9)

---

[24] See Leiter 2002: chapter 3 for some alleged difficulties concerning Nietzsche's conception of self-creation. For discussion of Leiter's view, see Owen and Ridley 2003.

On this conception, it would seem, there is no conscious deliberation, no 'artistic plan', no application of hard-won technique, indeed nothing that could be counted as *intentional* self-creation at all. Nor is the passage unique. So it would appear that Nietzsche is committed to the view that giving form to oneself is not, after all, a matter for consciousness, but is rather something of which one should remain, as far as possible, unaware. And this view would certainly seem to be in tension with the (equally explicitly defended) picture of the self-stylist as assiduous craftsman. (Actually, a hint of the same apparent tension crops up in the '*One thing is needful*' passage itself. For, together with talk of surveys, plans, hard work, and practice, Nietzsche also remarks that 'In the end, when the work is finished, it becomes evident how the constraint of a single taste governed and formed everything large and small'. That this singleness of taste should only reveal itself 'when the work is finished'—rather, say, than being already evident in the 'artistic plan'—would certainly seem to suggest, against the main thrust of the passage as a whole, an absence of premeditation.)

So which picture does Nietzsche mean us to accept? Is self-stylization a matter of conscious deliberation or not? The answer, in my view, is 'both'—i.e. is 'both' to both questions. And the reason for this emerges if we turn to an important discussion of artistry (ordinarily so-called) that I have not so far cited:

> Every artist knows how far from any feeling of letting himself go his most 'natural' state is—the free ordering, placing, disposing, giving form in the moment of 'inspiration'—and how strictly and subtly he obeys thousandfold laws precisely then, laws that precisely on account of their hardness and determination defy all formulation through concepts (even the firmest concept is, compared with them, not free of fluctuation, multiplicity, and ambiguity). (*BGE* 188)

Nietzsche's thought here depends upon an implicit distinction between two sorts of laws: those that *can* be formulated 'through concepts' and those that can't be. And in this he is, essentially, following Kant.

The idea that they share is that while there are some perfectly formulable laws which any artist worth his salt must learn and assimilate, there are also laws (or constraints or imperatives) that only declare themselves, as it were, in the artistic act itself, and which cannot be stated independently and in advance of that act. So, for example, any minimally competent composer must be *au fait* with the laws of harmony or with those of voice-leading in counterpoint. Such laws can be, and are, formulated and taught: they form part of the basic compositional toolkit. But the mere deployment of these will never take one further than competence. To go further requires what Kant calls 'genius'—the ability to see just which of the alternatives permitted by these laws (or even forbidden by them) is demanded by the concrete compositional circumstances of the moment. And to have such an ability is, as Kant puts it, to be one through whom 'nature gives the rule to art'[25]—such rules being neither stateable in advance, nor (hence) teachable. These are Nietzsche's laws that 'precisely on account of their hardness and determination defy all formulation through concepts'.

On one model of conscious deliberation—to which Kant was certainly attached—deliberation is a matter of deciding which (formulable) law applies to the case at hand; and if one takes that model seriously, as Nietzsche, I think, did, the genius's obedience to the (unformulable) rule given by 'nature' cannot be understood as a question merely of conscious deliberation,

---

[25] Kant 2007: §46. For an excellent discussion of Kant on the products of genius, see Guyer 2003.

even if such deliberation is involved (the genius is also, after all, a competent practitioner of his art). Which means that more than merely competent artistry requires both conscious deliberation and whatever it is that allows the genius to go further. It is this 'whatever it is', I suggest, that Nietzsche not implausibly glosses as the 'secret work and artistry of [his] instinct'.

My claim, then, is this. The tension in Nietzsche's position *is* only apparent. At some places and for some purposes, he highlights the conscious, craftsman-like dimension of artistry, in which notions such as planning, hard work, and practice have a place; at other times and with other priorities in mind, he emphasizes the dimension of artistry that is special to the genius, the dimension that consists in obedience to unformulable laws. Perhaps—in keeping with the generally hyperbolic tone of that book—he over-eggs the latter dimension in *Ecce Homo*, especially in his insistence that 'the whole surface of consciousness' must be kept free of imperatives. But the basic idea, it seems to me, is clear enough: Nietzsche is simply reminding us of the Kantian point that conscious deliberation, construed as in the previous paragraph, cannot account for (all of) what the genius achieves. And, as with (first-rate) artistry in general, so, one must suppose, with the artistry of one who succeeds in giving style to his character.[26] Indeed, Nietzsche goes further than Kant, not only in extending the range of materials properly to be thought of as artistic media to include the self, but in regarding artistic agency of the genius's kind as exemplary of free, autonomous agency as such.[27] As he puts it a little later in *Beyond Good and Evil*, although I cannot pursue the point here, artists know 'only too well that precisely when they no longer do anything "voluntarily" but do everything of necessity, their feeling of freedom, subtlety, full power, of creative placing, disposing, and forming reaches its peak—in short, that necessity and "freedom of the will" then become one in them'. And he attributes the artists' knowledge of this to their having 'more sensitive noses in these matters' than others have (*BGE* 213): what they know 'only too well' is not true of them alone.

6 NIETZSCHE'S IDEAL

In section 2, I quoted a pair of closely similar passages from *The Birth of Tragedy* and the *Genealogy*, in which mortal sufferings are regarded as entertainments for the gods. The

---

[26]   This way of resolving the tension is deliberately minimalist: it appeals to nothing that we shouldn't all be able to agree is present in what Nietzsche says, and to nothing that wasn't readily available to him as someone living after Kant. The resolution survives being made less minimalist, however. For example, I make it less minimalist in one direction in the remainder of the paragraph to which this note is appended. Another, slightly different direction, in which one might make it less minimalist would be to hook it up more vigorously, perhaps in the spirit of *Ecce Homo*, to the side of Nietzsche that insists that we systematically *overstate* the influence of conscious deliberation (at the expense of the 'instincts' and perhaps also of the drives) on the things that seem most important to us about ourselves and our undertakings. This emphasis would be consistent with Nietzsche's general hostility to Cartesianism, including its manifestation in Kant, and should, I think, be taken seriously—but only so long as a place of the right kind is reserved in the picture *for* conscious deliberation. Otherwise we have no resolution of the tension, and a plausible account of artistry is lost amid the slew of one or another sort of epiphenomenalism.

[27]   In this his thought is reminiscent of Hegel. As Robert Pippin puts it: Hegel's conception of agency is 'expressive' and his 'most frequent example . . . is an artist and his art work. In some sense of course, the artist causes the statue to be made, but what makes it "his" is that it expresses him and his artistic

similarities between those passages extend further, however, for both go on to assign a spe-cial position in the picture to the artist. The later Nietzsche puts it like this: tragic terrors 'were intended as *festival plays* for the gods; and, insofar as the poet is in these matters of a more "godlike" disposition than other men, no doubt also as festival plays for the poets' (*GM* II: 7). The early Nietzsche is more fulsome: 'Only insofar as the genius in the act of artistic creation coalesces with [the] primordial artist of the world, does he know anything of the eternal essence of art; for in this state he is... at once subject and object, at once poet, actor, and spectator' (*BT* 5). These remarks—which appear to be of a piece with the reference to the 'spectator divinity' of the self-creator (*BGE* 225)—seem to me to hint at a larger ideal than I have so far attributed to Nietzsche, even if it must be admitted that the indications are, as it stands, sketchy.

We can start to flesh them out, though, if we ask what the relatively ' "godlike" disposi-tion' of the poet might amount to. The answer, presumably, is that the poet, like the gods, is not only a keen observer of human living, but is also, in a sense, an author of it: he arranges human affairs in his art as gods do in the world. Unlike the gods, however, he is also himself an actor in the spectacle laid on for their delectation; but unlike the other actors, he knows what it is to have a ' "godlike" ' perspective on such things and so what it is to take a wholly undisinterested pleasure in them. His relation to himself as 'actor', that is, involves a kind of self-distancing that is special to him as a poet. This is not, one must suppose, a version of the self-disavowal characteristic of the disinterested spectator. It must, rather, be a version of the distance whose pathos Nietzsche so often celebrates—the distance of which, perhaps, no one has yet achieved enough to 'laugh at [himself] as one would have to laugh in order to laugh *out of the whole truth*' (*GS* 1); or the distance—six thousand feet, say—by which one must stand above 'man and time' (*EH*: 'Thus Spoke Zarathustra' 1); or—perhaps even more—the inward distance, 'ever widening... within the soul itself', which makes possible 'the development of ever higher, rarer, more remote, further-stretching, more comprehen-sive states' (*BGE* 257), and in which is played out 'This secret self-ravishment, this artist's cruelty, this delight in imposing a form upon oneself' that brings 'to light an abundance of strange new beauty and affirmation, and perhaps beauty itself' (*GM* II: 18). It is, I suggest, a self-relation defined by distance in something like this sense that marks the poet's 'disposi-tion' as ' "godlike" ', and, indeed, that marks (the artist) Stendhal as a 'genuine spectator' (*GM* III: 6).

This has the effect of establishing a certain unity between 'poet, actor, and specta-tor': because he is an artist, the poet's self-distancing allows him to be a ' "godlike" ' specta-tor of himself as actor. But recall that 'spectator divinity' is the prerogative not merely of the artist in the ordinary sense, but of the creator who is his own raw material—that is, of the self-stylist, of one who is the poet of his life.[28] And if we add *this* to the picture, the unity steps up to another level. For now the actor that the poet spectates is the poet's own work-in-progress; and to the extent that the work goes well—i.e. in free, autonomous obedience to the unformulable laws of his art—the poet of his life must see himself as beautiful, indeed as '*une promesse de bonheur*'. I think that this must be at least close to what Nietzsche meant by

intentions adequately' (Pippin 2000: 158). For discussion of the significance of artistic agency for Nietzsche's wider understanding of free, autonomous agency, see Ridley 2007b.

[28] Where the poetry in question may be, as I put it earlier, either narrative or substantive—although most likely it will be both.

his early talk of 'the genius in the act of artistic creation' coalescing with the 'primordial artist of the world'; and close, too, to what he must have meant by his late and rather hectic talk of the man who 'transforms things until they mirror his power—until they are reflections of his perfection. This *compulsion* to transform into the perfect is—art. Even all that which he is not becomes for him none the less part of his joy in himself; in art, man takes delight in himself as perfection' (*TI*: 'Skirmishes of an Untimely Man' 9). In any case, what we have in such a picture is not merely a unity of 'poet, actor, and spectator', although we do have that, and to a high degree. We also, and surely significantly, have a unity of aesthetic creativity, aesthetic spectacle, and aesthetic experience—in short, the perhaps maximal attempt to imagine how, as an '*aesthetic phenomenon*', existence and the world might be made bearable, even be thought 'justified'.

Does any of it make sense? I don't know. But it does seem to me that an ideal having something like this shape must have underpinned Nietzsche's attempts—early, middle, and late—to offer a kind of aesthetic theodicy that would ward off the temptations of nihilism and despair, and so, in a broadly pre-Socratic spirit, would say 'yes to life even in its most strange and intractable problems' (*TI*: 'What I Owe to the Ancients' 5), indeed say '*yes* to everything questionable and terrible in existence' (*TI*: ' "Reason" in Philosophy' 6).

Conclusion

However hazily I have been able to sketch it, this ideal or a close relative appears to be a constant in Nietzsche's thought from beginning to end. It may also, as I suggested at the outset, be an essential point of reference for an understanding of the otherwise quite dramatic developments in his views. I doubt, for example, that the mature positions on truth (as one value among others), on freedom (as possible for a lover of fate), on autonomy (as obedience to unformulable laws), or on the self (as an almost freakish achievement) would have assumed the forms that they did had it not been for Nietzsche's settled insistence that life must be led, understood, and evaluated after the model of art, if it is not to be a merely senseless horror. I can't defend these claims here. They are large and contentious. But they follow, I think, from a claim that I do take myself to have defended—namely, that when Nietzsche said that 'life without music would be an error' he meant it. Without music—without art—life would be formless, meaningless, an objection to itself: it would not just promise no happiness, it would warrant despair. Was he right about this? Again, I have no idea. But it is hard, at least, not to feel the pull of the thought that art is, as Nietzsche puts it, 'the great stimulus to life' (*TI*: 'Skirmishes of an Untimely Man' 24), and hard, too, if such is the case, not to wonder what might follow from that. Nietzsche seems to have thought that quite a lot followed.[29]

---

[29] My thanks to Chris Janaway, David Owen, and John Richardson for comments on earlier versions of this essay.

BIBLIOGRAPHY

(A) Works by Nietzsche

A   *The Anti-Christ*, trans. Judith Norman. Cambridge: Cambridge University Press, 2005.
BGE   *Beyond Good and Evil*, trans. Walter Kaufmann. New York: Vintage Books, 1966.
BT   *The Birth of Tragedy*, trans. Walter Kaufmann. New York: Vintage Books, 1967.
D   *Daybreak*, trans. R. J. Hollingdale. Cambridge: Cambridge University Press, 1997.
EH   *Ecce Homo*, trans. Judith Norman. Cambridge: Cambridge University Press, 2005.
GS   *The Gay Science*, trans. Walter Kaufmann. New York: Vintage Books, 1974.
GM   *On the Genealogy of Morals*, trans. R. J. Hollingdale and Walter Kaufmann. New York: Vintage Books, 1969.
HAH   *Human, All Too Human*, trans. R. J. Hollingdale. Cambridge: Cambridge University Press, 1986.
TI   *Twilight of the Idols*, trans. Judith Norman. Cambridge: Cambridge University Press, 2005.
UM   *Untimely Meditations*, trans. R. J. Hollingdale. Cambridge: Cambridge University Press, 1997.
WP   *The Will to Power*, trans. Walter Kaufmann. New York: Vintage Books, 1968.

(B) Other Works Cited

Conant, James. 2001. 'Nietzsche's Perfectionism: A Reading of *Schopenhauer as Educator*', in R. Schacht (ed.), *Nietzsche's Postmoralism*. Cambridge: Cambridge University Press, 181–257.
Guyer, Paul. 2003. 'Exemplary Originality: Genius, Universality, and Individuality', in B. Gaut and P. Livingstone (eds), *The Creation of Art*. Cambridge: Cambridge University Press, 116–37.
Hussain, Nadeem. 2007. 'Honest Illusion: Valuing for Nietzsche's Free Spirits', in B. Leiter and N. Sinhababu (eds), *Nietzsche on Morality*. Oxford: Oxford University Press, 157–91.
Janaway, Christopher. 2007. *Beyond Selflessness: Reading Nietzsche's 'Genealogy'*. Oxford: Oxford University Press.
Janaway, Christopher. Forthcoming. 'Beauty is False, Truth Ugly: Nietzsche on Art and Life', in D. Came (ed.), *Nietzsche on Art and Aesthetics*. Oxford: Oxford University Press.
Kant, Immanuel. 2007. *Critique of Judgement*. Oxford: Oxford University Press.
Leiter, Brian. 2002. *Nietzsche on Morality*. London: Routledge.
Nehamas, Alexander. 1985. *Nietzsche: Life as Literature*. Cambridge, Mass.: Harvard University Press.
Owen, David and Ridley, Aaron. 2003. 'On Fate', *International Studies in Philosophy* 35.3: 63–78.
Pippin, Robert. 2000. 'What is the Question for Which Hegel's Theory of Recognition is the Answer?', *European Journal of Philosophy* 8: 155–72.
Reginster, Bernard. 2006. *The Affirmation of Life: Nietzsche on Overcoming Nihilism*. Cambridge, Mass.: Harvard University Press.
Ridley, Aaron. 2007a. *Nietzsche on Art*. London: Routledge.
Ridley, Aaron. 2007b. 'Nietzsche on Art and Freedom', *European Journal of Philosophy* 15: 204–24.
Ridley, Aaron. 2010. 'Perishing of the Truth: Nietzsche's Aesthetic Prophylactics', *British Journal of Aesthetics* 50.4: 427–37.
Ridley, Aaron. 2011. 'Une Promesse de Bonheur? Beauty in the *Genealogy*', in S. May (ed.), *Nietzsche's 'On the Genealogy of Morals': Critical Essays*. Cambridge: Cambridge University Press, 309–25.
Young, Julian. 1992. *Nietzsche's Philosophy of Art*. Cambridge: Cambridge University Press.

CHAPTER 19

···

NIETZSCHE ON AUTONOMY[1]

···

R. LANIER ANDERSON

NIETZSCHE hardly ever leaves himself open to criticism for burying the lead; on the contrary, his works consistently aim for the brutally frank, unequivocal pronouncement of uncomfortable truth. Despite their directness, however, the texts generate unending puzzles for commentators because on a wide range of issues, Nietzsche's blunt claim in one context stands in apparent tension—or even seems flatly to contradict—some equally outspoken counterclaim in another. Nowhere is this more true than in his writing about freedom. Nietzsche was always keenly concerned to *liberate* us (or at least, some of us) from various fetters of traditional culture, and these efforts to promote freedom of spirit provide much of the motivation for the widespread classification of Nietzsche as a paradigm radical, alongside Feuerbach, Marx, and other critics of conventional nineteenth-century culture. At the same time, Nietzsche saves up some of his choicest vitriolic complaints to level against the notion of freedom. He treats freedom of the will with the most extreme impatience, as a gross fraud perpetrated on willful believers by a priestly class determined to make people feel guilty, responsible, and thereby dependent upon them (*TI*: "The Four Great Errors" 7, *et passim*). But if claims to freedom are fraudulently motivated and freedom itself is impossible in principle, then why did Nietzsche spend so much time and energy apparently promoting it himself?

This quandary has gotten close attention in the recent secondary literature.[2] Among several reasons for that development, two are especially salient for my purposes. First, Brian Leiter (1998, 2002, 2007) has lately championed a powerful *naturalist* reading of Nietzsche's

[1] The ideas in this paper have benefitted from conversations over the years with many colleagues, notably including Michael Bratman, Maudemarie Clark, Rachel Cristy, Ken Gemes, Nadeem Hussain, Chris Janaway, Paul Katsafanas, Joshua Landy, Brian Leiter, Alexander Nehamas, Katherine Preston, Bernard Reginster, John Richardson, and Aaron Ridley. I am especially indebted to Hussain's insights and to Pippin, Nehamas, and Ridley for illuminating conversations about the expressivist account of action. Rachel Cristy provided very helpful comments on the last draft. Some of the material included here was also aided by feedback from audiences and co-panelists during events at the University of California, Riverside, a NANS session at the 2007 Eastern Division Meetings of the APA, and at the University of Southampton. Special thanks to Clark, Janaway, Katsafanas, and Reginster for sharing their unpublished work, from which I have learned much. Thanks to Richardson and Gemes for the invitation to write this chapter and for their patience in seeing it through to completion.
[2] A good example of the wide range and philosophical diversity and interest of recent discussions can be seen in the papers collected in Gemes and May 2009.

philosophy, which returned the issue to the center of scholarly debate by emphasizing his fatalism and minimizing the role of freedom. Second, in the aftermath of Bernard Williams's engagement with Nietzsche, a number of scholars have sought to deploy recent insights from contemporary *philosophy of action* to help uncover and explain basic insights of Nietzsche's moral psychology, which they take to be crucial to his philosophical contribution and a key presupposition of his famous critiques of traditional morality and religious thought.[3]

This chapter maps the logical space of interpretive options in the recent debate, focusing on the concept of *autonomy*. One of the primary moves made by those seeking to vindicate a Nietzschean notion of freedom has been to distinguish different senses of freedom. They insist that Nietzsche's attacks on freedom of the will are restricted to a specific "metaphysical" type of freedom—perhaps "agent causation"[4] or the traditional idea of freedom of indifference—that is tied to the thought that the free agent could have acted otherwise (the so-called "principle of alternate possibilities"). Nietzsche's positive interest in the free spirit's liberation from tradition is supposed to appeal, instead, to a separate notion of autonomy, conceived as a power of self-governance or agential self-legislation. Thus, autonomy is the conception of freedom with the most relevance to recent discussion. But a broader, more important reason for focusing on autonomy is that, at least since the time of Rousseau and Kant, philosophers have treated autonomy not just as one conception of what human freedom comes to, but as an *ideal* with far-reaching philosophical consequences: autonomy is widely supposed to have implications for the proper conception of the self or the right social order, for the basis of normative claims in general, and it is even sometimes taken to be the central feature of the ideal human life. These broader philosophical consequences turn out to structure much of the recent debate over the place of the notion in Nietzsche's thought.

As I will show, recent scholars have defended different conceptions of what autonomy amounts to. These different interpretations proceed from differing commitments about what philosophical purposes the notion is supposed to serve in Nietzsche's wider project. That is, the weight-bearing work that autonomy is taken to do within his project directs commentators' thoughts about what autonomy is supposed to be, according to him. In this sense, the notion of autonomy cuts to the heart of far-reaching interpretive disagreements.

1 AUTONOMY AS SPONTANEOUS SELF-DETERMINATION VERSUS AUTONOMY AS SELF-RELATION

Literally and etymologically, autonomy is the power to give the law to oneself or set the rule for one's own activity. One quite natural way to interpret the idea is to assimilate it closely to the conception of spontaneous action that is central to the traditional problem of free will.

---

[3] The *locus classicus* for Williams's views on Nietzsche's moral psychology is of course Williams 1993a, but the depth and range of his engagement can also be seen in Williams 2002 and Williams 1993b.

[4] See Chisholm 1978. For further discussion relevant to the notion, see also Chisholm 1966 and 1976.

If a person is to be held morally responsible for her action, the thought goes, then the action must have been under her own control, such that she could have acted otherwise, had she so chosen. That is, the responsible person must have been *self-determining*—she must have given rise to the act through the operation of her own will, rather than being determined to act through some other causes. So understood, autonomy is a matter of spontaneous self-determination.

This is the conception of autonomy driving Brian Leiter's work on Nietzsche's conception of freedom (Leiter 2002: 81–104; see also Leiter 1998 and Leiter 2007). He holds that Nietzsche understands freedom in terms of an "Autonomy Condition" (Leiter 2002: 87), which can be met only when a person's action is spontaneously self-determining in the sense of lacking any determining causal antecedents outside the will. Such a conception of freedom has often been taken as a necessary condition for moral responsibility. But Nietzsche himself notoriously takes a dim view of both the legitimacy and the value of that notion of responsibility, so its connection to the idea of spontaneous free action provides motivation for him to *reject* freedom, rather than endorsing it. Nietzsche can be at his most blunt on this theme: "Today we no longer have any pity for the concept of 'free will'; we know only too well what it really is—the foulest of all theologians' artifices, aimed at making mankind 'responsible' in their sense, that is, *dependent on them*" (*TI*: "The Four Great Errors" 7).[5] So Nietzsche denies not only the actuality but also the possibility and indeed even the conceptual coherence (see *BGE* 21) of any such power of spontaneous self-determination. Since Leiter takes this notion to represent autonomy (or freedom) *as such*, he concludes that Nietzsche rejects autonomy in favor of a thoroughgoing fatalism governing all action. For Leiter's Nietzsche, everyday actions *appear* to arise out of spontaneous self-determination, but in fact, the apparent causal power of conscious thought or will to determine action is illusory. At least when it comes to the production and direction of action, conscious thinking and willing are wholly epiphenomenal (Leiter 2007).

Leiter is correct to insist that Nietzsche was skeptical of traditional claims to spontaneous self-determination and particularly so in connection with moral responsibility and the principle of alternate possibilities for action. Relatively early in his career, Nietzsche occasionally frames this stance in ways that flirt with the standard determinist position that we lack freedom because every event (and hence, every human action) is fully necessitated by exceptionless natural laws, together with determinately specified initial conditions. For example, in *Human, All-too-Human* he writes, "At the sight of a waterfall we think we see in the countless curvings, twistings, and breakings of the waves capriciousness and freedom of will; but everything here is necessary, every motion mathematically calculable. So it is too in the case of human action" (*HAH* I: 106; see also *HAH* I: 39, 107).[6] *Human, All-too-Human* (1878) is Nietzsche's most clearly naturalist-influenced book and it may be the case, as Leiter

---

[5] I note in passing the irony involved in the fact that Nietzsche's complaints about "responsibility" and "free will" in this passage apparently rest on the way they have been deployed precisely to deprive people of their freedom (i.e., to make us "*dependent on them*").

[6] Nietzsche also seems to rely on Schopenhauer's thought that "'insight into the strict necessity of human actions is the boundary line that divides *philosophical* heads from the *others*'" (*HAH* II: 33). In Schopenhauer's case, of course, this "insight" rests explicitly on classical determinism applied to the domain of phenomena—a domain he takes to be strictly structured by the a priori concept of cause such that every event is determined by causal natural law.

suggests (2002: 68–9), that at this stage he associated his rejection of free will with the sort of determinism typical of German materialism.

In later works, however, Nietzsche combines an equally uncompromising fatalism with clear *rejections* of classical determinism. For instance, in *GS* 127 he joins a complaint that "the faith in the will as the cause of effects is the faith in magically effective forces" (*GS* 127) to a more far-reaching criticism aiming to debunk the motivating theses of determinism itself as instances of the very same magical thinking: "The propositions, 'no effect without a cause,' 'every effect in turn a cause' appear as generalizations of much more limited propositions: 'no effecting without willing'; [etc.] ... [I]n the pre-history of humanity both sets of propositions were identical" (*GS* 127).[7] Perhaps the most famous case in point is the complex treatment in *BGE* 21, where Nietzsche combines the charge that "freedom of the will in the superlative metaphysical sense" is conceptually incoherent (because it requires the will to cause its own actions as a kind of *causa sui*—a "pulling oneself up into existence by the hair, out of the swamps of nothingness") with a parallel insistence that a mechanistic/materialist deterministic theory of "'unfree will'" is sheer "mythology" that "amounts to a misuse of cause and effect" (*BGE* 21).

In the face of such passages, Leiter is careful to concede that Nietzsche rejects standard determinism (Leiter 2002: 81–3). Instead, he regards Nietzsche as a "causal essentialist," holding that every substance has a causal essence that tightly constrains the possible pathways it can travel, without completely determining the actual path. Thus, a person's causal essence leaves open a narrow range of possible "life trajectories," but nevertheless, the essence remains "*causally primary*," in that it strongly circumscribes what the person can become and the actual trajectory is a product of its causal powers together with the effects of various environmental circumstances, in much the way the body shape of a plant is a product of the joint operation of its (plastic) internal developmental program plus environmental conditions (Leiter 2002: 81–2). As other scholars have shown, however, this form of fatalism is liable to textual objections in the same way a standard determinist interpretation is, for Nietzsche is just as skeptical about causal essences as he is about determinism itself.[8]

In fact, if we restrict our attention to the metaphysical underpinnings, Nietzsche's grounds for attraction to fatalism seem to be quite a bit stranger, from our current point of view, than any of the alternatives considered by Leiter (2002). As I have argued elsewhere (Anderson 2006), in his fatalistic pronouncements, Nietzsche seems to be committed to the *super*essentialist view that *every single one* of a person's actually existing (i.e., past and present) properties (whether they are actions or not) is necessary.[9] The remarkably modest reason advanced to support this radical claim is the mere fact that things are what they are

[7] Even at the end of Nietzsche's productive career, *Twilight of the Idols* shows the same combination of views (fatalism plus antideterminism): see, for example, *TI*: "The Four Great Errors" 8 and "'Reason' in Philosophy" 5.

[8] See, e.g., *KSA* 13: 14 [122] = *WP* 625 and *KSA* 12: 2 [149–52] = *WP* 556. For additional texts and extensive discussion of the antiessentialist strand in Nietzsche, see Poellner 1995: 79–136. In Anderson 2006, I offer further argument on this point and a detailed reading of the famous "lightning/flash" passage in *GM* I: 13, showing that it, too, cuts against any reading of Nietzsche as a causal essentialist, *sensu* Leiter.

[9] For him, "The individual is a piece of *fatum* from the front and from the rear, one law more, one necessity more for all that is to come and to be. To say to him 'Change yourself!' is to demand that *everything* alter itself, even retroactively" (*TI*: "Morality as Anti-Nature" 6, my ital.; see also *TI*: "The Four Great Errors" 8).

and not anything else: "*'necessity'*—this is only an *expression* for the fact that force is not also something else" (*KSA* 12: 9 [91] = *WP* 552, see also *KSA* 13: 14 [79] = *WP* 634); or again,

> To demand of strength that it *not* express itself as strength...is just as nonsensical as to demand of weakness that it express itself as strength. A quantum of power is just such a quantum of drive, will, effect—more precisely, it is *nothing other than just this* driving, willing, effecting itself... [*GM* I: 13, second ital. mine]

That is, strong things express strength, and *must* do so, *merely* because they are what they are: strength *just is* this expression, "this driving, willing, effecting itself." Likewise, the weak cannot express strength, but that is *simply* because they are (and so, *equivalently*, because they act) weak. Nietzsche generalizes this view in his doctrine that "a 'thing' is the sum of its effects" (*KSA* 13: 14 [98] = *WP* 551), which entails that a thing would not preserve its identity across any counterfactual change in properties (where properties = "effects"; see *KSA* 12: 2 [85] = *WP* 557), and thus, that *every one* of these properties is necessary to its identity.[10]

As a result, Leiter's causal essentialism is simultaneously too weak and too strong to capture Nietzsche's actual view. It is too weak in that it permits genuinely accidental properties; by contrast to Nietzsche's view, Leiter's causal essence affords a core set of properties that can (and given plasticity, do) preserve identity across counterfactual change in other properties (which count as the accidental ones). Conversely, it is too strong, since Nietzsche apparently draws superessentialist consequences precisely from his *skepticism* about there being anything like causal essences. The strong *must* act strongly exactly because *there is no* "substratum behind" the act itself that is responsible for their acting one way rather than another. Just as there is no lightning separate from the flash, so there is supposed to be no essentially "strong one" separate from the acts that express strength (*GM* I: 13).

In this sense, Nietzsche's view can be described as a kind of *inverse* superessentialism, by contrast to Leibniz's version of the thesis. Leibniz held that an individual like Adam has a complete essence which "contains" all Adam's properties, so that the properties could only have been different had God created a different essence (hence, a different Adam), but as we saw, Nietzsche arrives at the superessentialist result by just the opposite reasoning. He holds that there is *no* complete concept or essence of a thing separate from its properties and effects, so the thing itself is nothing but their collection. Each property is thus necessary in the degenerate sense that without it, the *collection* of properties would be different.

This unusual version of fatalism has strange consequences for the question of freedom. For note, if Nietzsche rejects both deterministic laws of nature and causal essences, the striking upshot is that in spite of his fatalism about the past and present, there is nothing left to determine the future, and it remains *open*. For all the radical universality of Nietzsche's fatalism in the dimension of past and present events, the *sort* of necessity he attributes to

---

[10] The relevant inference is just this: (1) A thing is nothing over and above the collection of its effects or properties; (2) But a counterfactual change in properties would remove one or more properties from the collection, replacing them with others; (3) But then the new collection would not be the same as the original one; and so (4) The remaining thing would not be the same as the original either, given the conception of thinghood asserted in (1); Thus, (5) A thing cannot preserve its identity across counterfactual change in properties. This reasoning forms the basis for Nietzsche's conclusion that every property is necessary to a thing's being the thing that it is. For detailed discussion, see Nehamas 1985: 74–105. The point is also treated in Anderson 2006.

events is remarkably weak. For him, "event and necessary event is a *tautology*" (*KSA* 12: 10 [138] = *WP* 639). The point cuts both ways. If the concepts <event> and <necessary event> are really just *identical* (tautologous), then it follows that all events are necessary—but also that necessary events are just events (construed as lacking any core essential features that could preserve their identity across counterfactual change). That is, things are necessary *only* in the degenerate sense that they are what they are and not something else: apparent necessity is "only an *expression* for the fact that a force is not also something else" (*KSA* 12: 9 [91] = *WP* 552). But the future *is* not anything (yet). Therefore, Nietzsche has no grounds for insisting that it *necessarily be* one way or another.[11]

The strangeness of this metaphysics, coupled with its unusual consequences for standard ways of thinking about freedom, makes it tempting to follow the many commentators who deny that Nietzsche's real position about autonomy was driven by metaphysical considerations at all. Such readers tend to locate the motivations of Nietzsche's thought about freedom in practical or evaluative commitments instead,[12] and this strand is dominated by a tendency to treat Nietzsche as some sort of compatibilist—a move which simultaneously seems to afford resources to resolve the tensions among his various remarks on freedom. Ken Gemes (2009), for example, orients his interpretation around an influential distinction between what he calls "deserts free will" and "agency free will." Gemes's characterization of these two notions rests on their practical and ethical role. Deserts free will is the concept of spontaneous freedom—rooted in the alternate possibilities idea—that is thought to be presupposed if it is to be fair to hold people morally responsible for their actions. Agency free will, by contrast, is tied to special conditions on genuine agency; Gemes's Nietzsche holds that these conditions are much more demanding than we typically think, so that most of our ordinary activity does not even count as true action at all, precisely because it does not exhibit the right sort of agency free will. Gemes then explains the apparently conflicting texts about freedom by proposing that Nietzsche's denials of free will all concern "deserts free will" and are of a piece with his criticisms of moral responsibility and the practice of blame as unjustified expressions of *ressentiment*, whereas his positive pursuit of freedom of spirit, his praise for the autonomous "sovereign individual" (*GM* II: 1–3), and the like, all concern agency free will, which is simply a different notion.

---

[11] It might be thought that this interpretation still makes *too much* of Nietzsche's fatalism, by doing insufficient justice to that strand in his texts (much emphasized in the French reception) which emphasizes the fluidity or multiple interpretability of *all* things, including even the present and past events I treat as fixed. In my view, though, the open future introduces all the indeterminacy needed to account for the textual evidence. Nietzsche does hold that the world is multiply *interpretable* (see, e.g., *GS* 58; *BGE* 22). But if that claim is the basis for any "ontological relativity" in Nietzsche, then an open future can do all the needed work by itself. Through the differential support they lend to such alternative interpretations, different *future* developments may have a kind of effect on the shape of the past (i.e., later events can change the *significance* of what has happened or affect what count as the appropriate categories under which to interpret past events). See Anderson 2005: 200–3, 207–11 for discussion. (Thanks to Nehamas (pers. comm.) for pressing this objection.)

[12] Müller-Lauter (1999) is something of an exception at this point. Although his detailed textual interpretation does belong broadly in this camp, which strives to reconcile Nietzsche's fatalistic rejection of libertarian free will with his defense of freedom in some other sense, Müller-Lauter gives quite substantial weight to metaphysical considerations *both* in his investigation of Nietzsche's fatalism and rejection of traditional free will *and* in his account of the kind of freedom he takes Nietzsche nevertheless to endorse (see Müller-Lauter 1999: 24–129).

Maudemarie Clark and David Dudrick pursue a related line by treating Nietzsche as a Humean compatibilist who attacks libertarian spontaneous willing not, as Leiter would have it, in the spirit of rejecting claims to freedom altogether, but instead as an incorrect conception of what our real freedom amounts to (Clark forthcoming; Clark and Dudrick 2009). Clark centers her compatibilist readings on two basic moves. First, she finds in Nietzsche an empiricist-inspired deflation of the metaphysical weight attached to the notion of causation; at times, she seems ready to reduce causality all the way to Hume-style regular conjunction of events (Clark forthcoming), but in any case, this move is supposed to remove the implication that causes are linked to effects by strong, objectively necessary connections. With this deflation in place, she insists, second, (in a standard compatibilist move) that free actions, so far from being impossible within causal networks so understood, are instead completely dependent on having a place in a causal structure. After all, an event cannot count as *my action* in unless it was suitably caused by my intentions or other psychological attitudes like drives (Clark and Dudrick 2009: 263, *et passim*).

To its credit, such a compatibilist interpretation can point to Nietzsche's clear rejection of the libertarian conception of spontaneous freedom. When coupled with his simultaneous charge that the contrary notion of " 'unfree will' " is also just "mythology" (*BGE* 21), it can seem that the real target of Nietzsche's underlying attack is not *freedom*, but the *incompatibilist* assumption, common to the partisans of both "free will" and "unfree will," that freedom is inconsistent with the natural causal order.[13]

But there are some compelling considerations on the other side of the ledger. It must be conceded in Leiter's favor that it is prima facie odd to think of Nietzsche as a compatibilist in our (or in a Humean) sense. Compatibilism takes its philosophical motivations from the effort to reconcile moral responsibility with conventional wisdom about the requirements of our best scientific picture of the world. It is hard to see the pull of that project for Nietzsche. As a first point, he is perfectly willing to reject *both* of the motivating premises. As we saw, Nietzsche is not a standard determinist, and for him, conventional moral responsibility counts not as a central feature of practical life to be vindicated at almost any theoretical cost, but as a gross (or even despicably motivated) ideological mystification that needs to be exploded.[14] More generally, second, it is at least *sometimes* the case that Nietzsche simply *dismisses* the apparent value-degrading consequences of scientific naturalism instead of taking them on as some fundamental challenge to our practical identities in the way the

---

[13] This is how Clark interprets the argument of *BGE* 21 in Clark forthcoming.

[14] Clark forthcoming argues heroically that *GM* II aims to recapture and vindicate a compatibilist notion of moral responsibility much along the lines of Strawson's expressivist account. While creative, her interpretation faces enormous countervailing textual evidence, since one of Nietzsche's main projects in the late writings, including not least the main strand of argumentation in *GM* II itself, was to discredit precisely the reactive attitudes (resentment, indignation) whose expression lies at the center of our practices of holding morally responsible for Strawson and his followers. It is not that Nietzsche denies that our conventional practices involve the expression of these affects or attitudes. On the contrary, he very much insists that they do. But for Nietzsche that is supposed to be *among the very worst things* about those practices. I concede that the late Nietzsche in general and *GM* II in particular simultaneously aim to recuperate some notion of responsibility—a kind of *taking* responsibility for oneself and one's actions—but this kind of responsibility is explicitly supposed to be a "privilege" earned only by a few (*GM* II: 2, *et passim*), and for that very reason completely inappropriate as a ground of any practice of holding accountable those who simply do not manage to be "responsible" in that sense. Thus, I remain unconvinced by Clark's efforts to find any nascent form of Strawsonian *moral* responsibility in *GM* II.

compatibilist program does.[15] Finally, even where Nietzsche does recognize a salient conflict between beliefs demanded by our epistemic norms and those answering to our practical and emotional needs, the basic "reconciling" impulse exemplified by compatibilism is not his typical philosophical response. Instead, he either emphasizes the conflict and takes the willingness to renounce one's practical needs for the sake of the truth as the measure of a spirit's strength (e.g., *BGE* 39; *GS* 347; *EH* Preface 3) or else he frankly accepts the need for saving *illusions* that would enable us to cope with the terrible truth (*BT*; *GS* 107, 344; *GM* III: 24). Thus, the entire *spirit* of contemporary compatibilism seems quite foreign to Nietzsche's assumptions, concerns, and basic intuitions. For these reasons, the version of compatibilism attributed to Nietzsche by Gemes is more persuasive, since it concedes from the outset that "deserts free will" and the whole question of moral responsibility are *not* meant to be rendered compatible with the natural order, and simply holds that for Nietzsche the true question about freedom is wholly orthogonal to questions about the order of nature in general (Gemes 2009: 37–9).

In fact, Aaron Ridley (2007) has argued convincingly that in *Beyond Good and Evil* 21—arguably the key text about the metaphysical side of our question—Nietzsche had no ambition at all to stake out his own position on the metaphysics of freedom, but aimed rather to *change the question*, turning our attention away from the standard debate about free will to a completely different issue. For Ridley, too, Nietzsche's question about freedom is located on an ethical rather than a metaphysical plane; the question is not even about the patterns of causal relations pertaining to our thoughts and actions, but about how those thoughts and actions relate to one another within the ethical *character* of the person.

It is true that *BGE* 21 is the *locus classicus* for Nietzsche's rejection of the conceptual coherence of spontaneous libertarian freedom, and Nietzsche does immediately thereafter turn to reject a deterministic conception of "unfree will" as well, as a "misuse of cause and effect" (*BGE* 21). So Nietzsche dismisses both "free will" and "unfree will," just as Clark and others have noted. But he does *not* go on to draw standard compatibilist-type conclusions—e.g., that we can therefore save our notion of moral responsibility, and the like. (Again, he lacks any of the motivations leading to that sort of compatibilism.) Instead, he writes this: "The 'unfree will' is mythology; in real life it is only a matter of *strong* and *weak* wills." This relatively cryptic comment is followed, as Ridley notes, by two compressed genealogical analyses directed against types of people who cannot get past worrying about the "unfreedom of the will"; these two types are criticized *on first-order ethical grounds* as being afflicted, in turn, by vanity (first type) and by a lack of self-esteem begetting gross irresponsibility (second type). The vain types feel threatened by the lack of libertarian freedom, despite its incoherence, because of their attachment to a fantasy of radical, self-generated independence that excludes any causal dependence on the world. The irresponsible are relieved by the thought of determinism, since it allows them to lay the blame for themselves elsewhere.

Nietzsche clearly takes a dim view of both types, so the broad illocutionary force of his cryptic remark is more or less legible. The point of criticizing libertarianism and determinism was never to advance a novel solution to the traditional problem of free will, but to suggest that there is something wrong with the whole question and with the underlying

---

[15] See, e.g., *GS* 373, where the sort of mechanistic worldview that generates the conception of universal determinism is simply dismissed as "the most stupid of all possible interpretations," in that it captures "precisely the most superficial and external aspect of existence" and is "poorest in meaning."

attitudes that are manifested by taking it seriously. The right question is not whether we are free or unfree, but whether we are strong, or weak like those vain and irresponsible types. So our own interpretive question should be: how is the question about strength and weakness related to freedom at all?

Ridley's focus on the question of character already suggests an important first step. What goes wrong in both of Nietzsche's cases—the weakness of vanity and the weakness of irresponsibility—concerns a flaw of character touching the way the person *relates to her self*: "It is…a symptom of what is lacking in himself when a thinker senses in every 'causal connection' and 'psychological necessity' something of constraint, need, [etc.]…; it is suspicious to have such feelings—the person betrays himself" (*BGE* 21).

Nietzsche's focus should remind us that the basic idea of a *self-relation* has arguably been just as central to historical and recent thinking about autonomy as any thought of libertarian self-determination. Giving the law to oneself is a way of establishing a particular kind of relation to oneself, such that one's overall psychology is self-controlled, or self-governing, or even, in a more Nietzschean direction, self-creating. Many broadly compatibilist thinkers about freedom have construed autonomy as one or another form of self-relation precisely so as to sidestep the whole question of determinism. For them, the question is not about whether the agent's intentions, plans, and actions do or do not find a place in certain causal patterns, but instead about what *structural interrelations* the agent's various attitudes bear *toward one another*, and what it would take for those self-relations to constitute a self-governing or self-controlled system. Of course, many different positions are available on this last question about what sort of self-relation counts as self-governance. I turn now to describe several of these proposals for understanding autonomy as a self-relation in Nietzsche, and to explore how they are related to the philosophical work that claims about autonomy are taken to do in his thought overall.

2 FIVE CONCEPTIONS OF AUTONOMY

I will discuss five different conceptions of autonomy as a self-relation that have been considered in the secondary literature on Nietzsche. Many of the commentators treated here exploit conceptual innovations from recent philosophy to make sophisticated moves going beyond anything Nietzsche makes explicit, so in important respects, these interpretations are not forced by the details of the text. Instead, commentators defend one or another specification of Nietzsche's broad comments about autonomy based on philosophical claims about the basic theoretical and ethical purposes the notion is meant to serve. Thus, contestation over what Nietzsche meant by autonomy turns out to be rooted in debate over the basic shape of his philosophical commitments, projects, and aims.

A. The "Standard Model"

One philosophical issue often tied to questions about autonomy is the *nature of agency*. Since the mid-twentieth century, philosophy of action has concerned itself centrally with the problem of what separates genuine actions from other kinds of events. One very natural thought is that an event counts as an action exactly when it is caused (in the right way) *by the agent herself*. So autonomy, in the sense of *self*-determination, is what separates actions from mere events. We have already seen reasons for compatibilist readers of Nietzsche to be attracted to this broad approach; recall, for example, Gemes's (2009) insistence that Nietzsche's concern with freedom is focused on *agency* free will rather than "deserts free will." However natural, though, this widespread thought works not so much to solve the central problem of philosophy of action as to sharpen its focus. For the suggestion itself raises two difficult questions: (1) What is it for an activity to be caused by the agent herself (and indeed, what *counts* as "the agent herself"); and (2) What is it for the person's activity to be caused "in the right way" by her internal states, so as to count as an action?

A standard approach to these questions in the recent literature descends from the field-shaping work of Donald Davidson.[16] On this "standard model" (Velleman 2000: 5–7), some happening is "caused by the agent herself" in the right way when she *wants* it to happen and *believes* that some behavior of hers would bring it about, and then that desire and belief combine to produce the behavior in virtue of their contents together with their characteristic psychological functioning as desire and belief. As Velleman points out, the last clause—demanding that the belief and desire cause the behavior *in virtue of* the way they represent the result (as something *to be brought about*, or desirable, and as a result that can be produced by the behavior, according to the person's belief)—is intended to ensure that the behavior is not only caused but also *justified* by the attitudes that participate in bringing it about, and thus that the "behavior eventuates not only *from causes* but *for reasons*" (Velleman 2000: 5–6). When activity is produced in response to reasons, it is thought to issue from the agent herself, who is identified with her rational capacities. Thus, for example, if I want to have a birthday gift for my friend Joshua, and believe that he would appreciate some suitably irreverent and useless plaything of the sort they carry at the funky shop called "Therapy" down on Castro Street, and if this belief and desire join forces to cause me to walk out to Therapy this afternoon, credit card in tow, so as to shop, then the activity of going shopping in the afternoon will count as an action of mine.

Nietzsche scholars often cite one noteworthy similarity between his basic mode of psychological analysis and this "standard model" in the philosophy of action. Both rely centrally on explanations of human behavior that appeal to the causal roles of subpersonal attitudes that represent the world in a certain way. There are differences in detail, of course. The standard model deploys interacting beliefs and desires, whereas Nietzsche speaks of a wide array of different attitudes, including beliefs, imaginings, thoughts, instincts, desires, wills, feelings, moods, valuations, and many others—but most especially *drives* and *affects*. Still, at a general level, there remains a similarity in approach, resting on the broadly naturalistic ambition to explain how subpersonal psychological states might work together to produce personal-level phenomena like action. Some scholars, like Clark and Dudrick (2009: 263), take Nietzsche's moral psychology of action to have more detailed parallels to the standard model, as well. For them, Nietzsche uses his psychological apparatus to draw a systematic distinction between mere desiring and valuing: Nietzschean drives, they insist, always stand in an "order of rank" (*BGE* 6) based on normative *authority* and not merely *strength*. The

---

[16] See, for example, the essays collected in Davidson 1980, especially chapters 1–5: "Actions, Reason, and Causes," "How is Weakness of the Will Possible?" "Agency," "Freedom to Act," and "Intending."

thought is then deployed to explain autonomy. When the whole person behaves in accordance with the drive that has authority, that counts as full-fledged *action* that is reflective of the person's values and hence of her will and her self—action which is thereby autonomous or self-determined (Clark and Dudrick 2009: 260–7, 263). This position is Davidsonian in spirit, in that the influence of what an agent has *reason* to do, based on her values, is what allows a particular subpersonal attitude to speak for the agent herself, such that its guidance of behavior amounts to *self*-governance by the agent.[17]

Precisely that feature, though, may give us reason for pause, from Nietzsche's standpoint. After all, one of the most distinctive features of his drive-based psychological reflections is that they afford compelling *nonrationalizing* explanations of behavior. Paul Katsafanas (2011) has shown just how widespread this mode of explanation is in Nietzsche. He points out further that one core form of such nonrationalizing explanation depends crucially on one of the basic differences between Nietzschean drives and standard-model desires. The difference in question concerns the relative *complexity* of the representational complements assumed for the two attitude types. A desire takes a one-place complement: for example, I desire an object (that fig, say), or I desire some propositionally structured state of affairs (e.g., that I exercise twice on the weekend). By contrast, drives take a *two-place* complement; a drive not only has a particular (propositional or individual) *object* that it tracks, but it also *separately* pursues a more abstract *aim*—a characteristic pattern of activity, of which the pursuit of this or that current object is merely an instance. Thus, my drive for food can take any number of objects (e.g., the fig, or the whole meal I am planning tonight, or simply that I am no longer hungry), but all these are merely particular occasions for the expression of the drive's broader aim, viz., eating. This structure makes drives especially well suited to the explanation of nonrational behavior. In the case where I am a compulsive eater, for instance, I naturally cannot do without appropriate *objects* for my drive—indeed, seeking them is the main focus of my compulsive attention—but at the same time, no such objects actually satisfy me; as soon as I have eaten them, the drive reasserts itself (i.e., its pursuit of its *aim*), and I am off in search of a new object. The aim/object distinction thereby makes drive-based explanation apt for exactly those cases where the conative state in operation is *not* activated because the circumstances are appropriate (e.g., because of the presence of an appropriate *object* of desire), but instead is "pushing the agent around"—activating itself in pursuit of its aim whether circumstances are favorable or not, and indeed whether *I*, the agent, find that aim valuable or not.

This feature of Nietzsche's drive-based psychology merely makes salient a broader and philosophically deep problem for the standard model's account of autonomy. As we saw, the standard model counts the agent as self-governing when her behavior is caused by subpersonal attitude(s) operating in their characteristic roles as beliefs and desires. The plausibility of that judgment rested on the idea that when beliefs and desires cause behavior in virtue of their representational contents, they *justify* the behavior, which can thereby be seen (by the agent) as called for by reasons. But of course, it is all too easy for a person to be deeply

[17] My formulation here is influenced not only by the explanation of the standard model in Velleman 2000, already cited, but also by Michael Bratman's formulation of the key problem faced by the standard model—that of identifying what subpersonal structure is such that "when it guides, the *agent* governs" action, and justifying why *that* structure has the right to speak for the agent. See the papers collected in Bratman 2007 for discussion.

alienated from her own desires or beliefs, with the result that the effectiveness of their normal causal influence offers no justification at all for the resulting behavior (at least to her), and indeed feels like the incessant pressure of an outside force rather than an expression of her own agency. If I am a compulsive shopper, for example, then my desire to get the gift for Joshua appears not as a reason-generating psychological state that justifies my trip to Therapy, but instead as a manifestation of the disorder that prevents me from controlling myself. In such circumstances, the characteristic causal operation of my desire is precisely the thing that renders me unfree. What I need then is not Therapy (the store), but therapy (the treatment) that is capable of *preventing* the effective operation of the desire.

The recent literature is replete with examples of the many ways agents can become alienated from their desires and other attitudes,[18] and as we will see below, it is not at all easy to explain what it takes for the agent to be identified with her subpersonal attitude in a way that rules out such alienation. For purposes of Nietzsche exegesis, however, it creates enough trouble for the standard model simply to make the obvious point that Nietzsche himself is an unusually rich source for examples of this sort of alienated self-relation, the diagnosis of which he clearly took as one of the primary targets for his psychological acumen. He is ever on the watch for the ways we are playthings of our drives or deeply self-deceived in our cherished values.[19] The characteristic operation of *that sort* of attitude (e.g., an unacknowledged desire for self-torture masquerading as guilt, an overwhelming *ressentiment* motivating moral indignation, etc.) cannot make its subject into an agent in the full sense or render her autonomous; on the contrary, the subject is typically unaware of such drives and desires, and would in any case be deeply invested in denying their legitimacy as well as their effectiveness. Since Nietzsche is *especially* sensitive to our potential alienation from drives and other attitudes—and to its autonomy-undermining consequences—a standard-model interpretation which makes their normal operation sufficient for self-governance can hardly capture his thought about autonomy.

B. A transcendental self?

I presented the main objection to the standard model in negative terms, as a matter of the agent's *incapacity* to identify with the attitudes motivating her behavior. But the same basic idea can also be seen in a positive light, as an agential *capacity* that underwrites our autonomy in the first place. What is at stake, after all, is the ability to detach from one's desires and other attitudes—a capacity which many have placed at the very center of our agency. Kantians, for example, posit a fundamental difference between two types of motivational incentives—those of reason and those of inclination—and they insist that reason has the

---

[18] Some nice examples are provided by Velleman (2000: 2–14), who focuses on Freudian slips, where unconscious conative attitudes do *motivate* the subject's activity in virtue of their contents, but in ways that are inaccessible to the agent and cannot provide any justification that she could or would acknowledge.

[19] Indeed, Katsafanas (2012a and 2012b) shows how powerful the resources of Nietzsche's drive theory are for uncovering cases where even the agent's *reflective deliberation and judgment* themselves are not in fact her own, but are in fact largely expressions of drives she does not endorse. For instance, he brings forward examples of jealousy, where the underlying, unendorsed, or even unacknowledged passion warps the way the agent perceives all of her evidence and even her reasoning itself.

basic capacity to "stand back" from the biddings of inclination and decide independently whether the inclination is to be endorsed or not.[20] Our autonomy depends on this capacity to "stand back" from desires and assess them, so that the self can follow reason's law even when it stands completely athwart the demands of all inclinations.[21] On the basis of this power's importance to moral and cognitive life, Kantians are willing to postulate a strong form of transcendental subjectivity, in which it resides. For them, genuine autonomy could only belong to this transcendental self, and never to any particular component psychological attitude, as in the standard model.

This Kantian view underlines one of the difficult questions that was immediately provoked by the natural thought at the heart of the standard model: even if we concede that a person would act autonomously if her behavior were caused in the right way by "the agent herself," what can count as "the agent herself"? What *is* this self that is capable of separating itself from all drives and desires and then endorsing or rejecting them?

The very question can generate Nietzschean skepticism, for it calls to mind numerous passages in which Nietzsche expresses grave doubt about any such pure self.[22] Precisely such skepticism about a self separate from subpersonal drives counts among the considerations leading naturalist readers—Leiter 2002, 2007, Leiter and Knobe 2007, Risse 2007, and others—to a deflationary reading of his positive remarks about autonomy. On their view, whenever it appears to us that our conscious self or intellect has taken some basic decision against a drive or other conative attitude within us, in reality what occurs is merely that *another drive*, which is opposed to the first and more dominant, has seized the place of speaking for

[20] Of course, Kant need not and does not deny that reason and inclination may interact in the same attitude—e.g., to form passions in which our inclinations are informed by influence from our power of choice. The key point for my purposes is just that the separation of two sources of motivation allows Kantians to claim that it is always (motivationally) possible for an agent to "stand back" from inclinations altogether, assess them from the standpoint of reason alone, and act in a way that is motivated by pure reason. See Reginster for additional discussion. (Thanks to Allen Wood for clarifying exchanges.)

[21] The basic form of argument, which posits an autonomous self as a precondition of practical agency quite generally, is a widespread move in the Kantian tradition. For a classic example, see the well-known response to Parfit in Korsgaard 1996: 363–97.

[22] Just to provide a hint of the domain, here is a quick and dirty, radically incomplete selection of Nietzsche's comments in this vein:

We suppose that *intelligere* must be...something that stands essentially opposed to the instincts, while it is actually nothing but a *certain behavior of the instincts toward one another*. (*GS* 333)

I shall never tire of emphasizing a small terse fact...namely, that a thought comes when "it" wishes, and not when "I" wish, so that it is a *falsification* of the facts of the case to say that the subject "I" is the condition of the predicate "think." *It* thinks; but that this "it" is precisely the famous old "I" is, to put it mildly, only a supposition, an assertion, above all no "immediate certainty." (*BGE* 17)

But there is no such substratum [the "doer"]; there is no "being" behind doing, effecting, becoming; "the doer" is simply fabricated into the doing—the doing is everything. (*GM* I: 13)

To indulge the fable of "unity," "soul," "person," this we have forbidden: with such hypotheses one only covers up the problem. (*KSA* 11: 577)

We enter a realm of crude fetishism when we summon before consciousness the basic presuppositions of the metaphysics of language...Everywhere it sees a doer and doing; it believes in will as *the* cause; it believes in the ego, in the ego as being, in the ego as substance...that calamity of an error. (*TI*: "'Reason' in Philosophy" 5)

And as for the ego! That has become a fable, a fiction, a play on words: it has altogether ceased to think, feel, or will! (*TI*: "The Four Great Errors" 3)

the self (see *D* 109). So far from there being a self capable of standing back from all the drives, what speaks for "the self" is nothing but the strongest or dominant drive itself.[23] Nietzsche is thus supposed to have renounced the philosophical resources that would be necessary to defend any substantial conception of autonomy, and the principle of charity is then taken to indicate that he must have meant to deny the possibility of autonomy altogether.

But of course, the principle of charity is an extremely powerful interpretive tool for extending the philosophical commitments of a text beyond its inescapable, directly asserted claims into a coherent overall system, and Kantian readers of Nietzsche have been no less inclined to use it. They insist, conversely, that Nietzsche's broad claims about self-mastery, autonomous self-governance, and related notions in fact commit him ineluctably to a much stronger, Kantian-style transcendental self than he was officially inclined to countenance. Sebastian Gardner (2009), for example, focuses on the preconditions for the "creation of values" central to Nietzsche's value theory, claiming that that they imply "a buried transcendental dimension" (Gardner 2009: 19) in his moral psychology. In order for the individual to create values of her *own*, the thought goes, she must have a conception of herself as a unified practical agent who is the source of those values. Even if the values are influenced by the drives within her, the agent must (first-personally) *think* of them as her own—and not merely the demands of some dominating drive—on pain of a "profound self-alienation" (Gardner 2009: 9) which would undermine the very autonomy Nietzsche sought to secure by appealing to the creation of values.

This argument appears to beg the question against the Leiter-style naturalist. As we saw, the naturalist will be inclined simply to deflate the autonomy Nietzsche is supposed to have sought right along with the notion of selfhood, insisting that when "I" speak the values of the dominant drive in the voice of my (more or less illusory) self, that is all the autonomy and all the "first-personalism" that Nietzsche wants or needs. The resulting interpretive impasse reveals one limitation of charity as an interpretive principle in the history of philosophy. It is impossible, of course, to respond to the philosophical claims of a historical text without making substantial use of our own best philosophical judgment, but where the substantive philosophical theses we use to precisify and clarify the text are themselves matters of deep and enduring controversy, charity will simply suggest opposing interpretive choices to those on opposed sides of the underlying philosophical debate.

Gardner does offer a second argument for his transcendentalist conclusion, which focuses on whether a collection of drives could even generate the requisite *idea* of a unified "I" without actually *amounting to* a unified transcendental self of the sort in dispute. Gardner writes,

> So the question arises, how, except in the perspective of an I, of something that takes itself to have unity of the self's sort, can a conception of unity sufficient to account for the fiction of the I be formed? (As it might be put: How can the 'idea' of the I *occur* to a unit of will to power or composite thereof—or to anything *less* than an I?) (Gardner 2009: 6)

I am puzzled by Gardner's puzzlement here. Three ideas suggest themselves, but none seems satisfying on Nietzschean grounds. The first thought proposes some difficulty about how a

---

[23] This last interpretive position—that the Nietzschean self is just the strongest drive—is widely endorsed by commentators even outside the naturalist and post-structuralist camps; see, e.g., Reginster 2003.

collection-self could successfully represent a particular *content*, the "I." But if that is the suggestion, it strikes me as being parallel to Descartes' Med. III proof of God's existence, and subject to similar problems. Some content of representation (the concept <God>, <I>) is supposed to be so special that a representational system could not reach it by any extrapolation or invention, so we must conclude that the *object* of the representation really exists, and provided the representation's content itself. But what is so special about the content <I>—the concept of a unified subject? Supposing that a Nietzschean bundle-self could represent at all, why couldn't it manufacture for itself an illusory "synthetic concept 'I'" (*BGE* 19) and think of itself under that concept? As a second thought, perhaps Gardner is worried that the bundle-self *cannot* represent at all, because of a general problem about the unity of consciousness. Here the worry does not concern the special content of "I," but rests on skepticism that a collection of subpersonal attitudes could give rise to *any* unified, reflective conscious state. Just that fact, however, raises doubt about its force from a Nietzschean point of view. Nietzsche assumes fairly robust representational capacities for his drives and affects, so he need not rely on central consciousness as the source of all representational content or power. (In this respect, Nietzsche is perhaps better positioned to respond than other radically naturalistic positions.)

A deeper and more authentically Kantian line of thought may capture Gardner's real motivation—the claim that all representation as such, or at least all *reflective* representation, necessarily presupposes a transcendental ego that *produces* it, by actively unifying it.[24] Kant himself insisted, for example, that representations can come together in a *judgment* only by being *synthesized* and thereby brought into a unity through the activity of a single, reflectively conscious cognitive agency. Perhaps Gardner's argument means to make an analogous point for representation generally, including (in an echo of Kant's "Transcendental Deduction") even "the fiction of the I," which must still connect the contents of many representations that appear to belong to me, if it is to play its role in the psychological economy. But if so, the point strikes me as more *Gardnerian/Kantian* than *Nietzschean* in flavor. Nietzsche himself exhibits strong skepticism against such arguments from the unity of judgment to the postulation of an underlying, strongly unified self (see *BGE* 17). So if some claim like Gardner's is true, why should we receive it as an interpretation of Nietzsche, rather than as a *criticism* that he has overlooked a deep insight of transcendental philosophy?

Elsewhere (Anderson 2012a), I have argued that both textual and philosophical considerations do militate in favor of postulating some Nietzschean self over and above its constituent subpersonal attitudes; others have also made a strong textual case for such an attribution (e.g., Janaway 2009). But the self envisioned in these accounts is often dramatically more limited than a Kantian transcendental ego. In particular, it does not *automatically* carry with it autonomous agency as an essential and defining capacity. These more modest conceptions of the self, if they could be suitably developed, would fit much better with the tenor of Nietzsche's remarks about autonomy, which treat it as a rare achievement made by a few people, rather than as an essential characteristic which comes as "standard equipment" built into our humanity as such (see. e.g., *GM* II: 1–3; *TI*: "Skirmishes of an Untimely Man" 38, 41).

---

[24] Thanks to Christine Lopez and Allen Wood for extremely helpful conversations about the basic argument at work in this paragraph.

C. Constitutivism

Kantians take an interest in a postulated transcendental self in no small part because they see it as the necessary basis of autonomous agency, but autonomy itself is of interest independently, as a repository of *value*. Rational, autonomous agency is what carries worth beyond any price, demands respect in our dealings with others, and is the basic value that morality strives to protect through the principle that we must respect humanity. What is more, for many philosophers in the post-Kantian tradition, autonomy also provides the key to solving a crucial problem about the *source of normativity*: in virtue of what standing, what features, what credentials, can any claim legitimately be *binding* on us? Kantians famously hold that neither concepts of perfection or objective value, nor appeals to the agent's own happiness or pleasure could provide this source of normativity, for both kinds of claim confront us from "outside" the will, as pressures or facts that are external to our power of choice, and can be binding for it only through some independent rational authority. Such authority, Kantians believe, can only arise from the will itself: the only truly binding constraint upon choice is the *self*-binding power of giving the norm or law to oneself (see Reginster 2012).

Some non-Kantians have been attracted to a similar strategy for grounding normative claims in the constitutive conditions necessary to make something an action at all (e.g., Velleman 2000). In its most general form, the basic move is often called a "constitution/ commitment argument." The approach begins by identifying some aim that is constitutive of action as such, so that nothing counts as an action in its absence. The argument then insists that any *agent* is ineluctably committed to that aim, on pain of her activities not counting as actions at all, and infers that the aim must have value for the agent. Constitution/commitment arguments thus ground the normative force of values in the *inescapability* of some aim, due to its contribution to the constitutive conditions for action itself. The strategy is thereby closely connected to our question about autonomy. Values are binding on us, the constitutivist argues, insofar as we ourselves undertake commitments to them and thereby impose them on ourselves. This self-binding amounts to a genuine constraint, despite the fact that we put it upon ourselves, because the inescapability noted above entails that any failure to undertake the relevant commitment would undermine the person's claim to genuine *action and agency*, as opposed to mere activity. Thus, any would-be escape from the commitment cannot count as anything the agent has *done*.

Constitutivism of this stripe has received sustained attention in the recent ethics and metaethics literatures, but neither the details of various proposed views, nor the difficult objections that have been raised against them, need detain us. For present purposes, we can focus on the proposals of Paul Katsafanas (2011), who has recently offered an intriguing extension of the constitutivist strategy to Nietzsche exegesis. Following Reginster's powerful interpretation of the will to power doctrine (Reginster 2006: 103–47), Katsafanas argues that for Nietzsche, the constitutive aim of action is power, construed as the aim of encountering and overcoming resistance to our activities. Katsafanas then exploits his compelling account of drives (rehearsed above) to argue that Nietzsche takes all action to be drive-motivated. Such drive-motivated action implicitly or explicitly strives to express the drive's *aim*, taking its *objects* as "chance occasions for [that] expression" (Katsafanas 2011: 637). But now, since what one strives for is the continuous pursuit of the aim and not any final attainment of the object, one is committed to having always more resistance to overcome, against which one's pursuit of the aim can gain expression. Thus, for drive-motivated creatures like us, over-coming resistance is a constitutive aim of action. According to the constitutivist reasoning, we are thereby inescapably committed to valuing the overcoming of resistance—that is, to valuing power—insofar as we pretend to act at all. Nietzsche thereby gains a constitutivist basis for the fundamental value of power in his value theory. Insofar as the view rests pow-er's value on the fact that *agents themselves* commit themselves to it, it connects Nietzsche's basic value (power) to the notion of autonomy as well, and this might be taken to explain Nietzsche's praise for autonomy in a number of prominent contexts (*GS* 335; *GM* II: 1–3; *TI*: "Skirmishes of an Untimely Man" 49, etc.).[25]

I doubt that Katsafanas's (2011) argument makes good on its claim to "derive ethics from action" in a Nietzschean spirit. Space prevents adequate treatment of the subtleties, but my main worry centers on the core constitutivist intuition that *inescapability* can serve as an adequate explanation for normative bindingness. To put the point in quick and crude form, Nietzsche himself was keenly aware of the force of *pessimism* as a normative stance, and with pessimism on the table, the inescapability (for agents) of the constitutive conditions on action fails to settle the open question of the *value* of being in the action business at all (or indeed, of being in any business whatsoever). Conceding Katsafanas's main premises for the sake of argument, perhaps I am ineluctably committed, qua agent, to aiming for power, but that is no reason that I cannot stand back from my life of incessant action, as a pessimistic *evaluator*, and conclude that exactly that fact is what makes the world such a terrible place. Since Nietzsche's doctrine of will to power is developed in constant dialogue with the challenge of Schopenhauer's value theory, the possibility of this move is highly salient in the context, and I do not see any device in Katsafanas's constitutivist strategy for disarming it.

But for our purposes, the more crucial question concerns whether we should extend Katsafanas's view by drawing the connection I suggested to the notion of autonomy. I think we should not. As we have seen, Nietzsche's own praise for autonomy repeatedly emphasizes that it is an *achievement*, rather than an essential feature of humanity as such, and indeed, he regularly goes out of his way to underline the *rarity* of the achievement: we who "give ourselves laws" are to be "*new, unique, incomparable*" (*GS* 335, my ital.); the sovereign indi-vidual is "*like only to himself*" in his autonomy and "aware of his superiority over all those who are not permitted to promise" (i.e., the right, or permission, that expresses his freedom) (*GM* II: 2, my ital.); and so on. This fits poorly with the basic spirit of constitutivism, where the inescapability of our commitment to the constitutive aim of action does the key work to secure the value of that aim. That commitment to the aim of action can hardly be the sort of "giving the rule to oneself" that Nietzsche meant to praise under the guise of autonomy, for it is utterly ubiquitous (indeed, inescapable!) and not at all the rare achievement he is trying to characterize. In fact, the specific conception of agency at work in Katsafanas 2011 seems particularly ill-positioned in this respect. After all, according to the will to power doctrine, the domain of drive-motivated processes encompasses not only full-blooded human action, but all human activity whatsoever—no matter how unconscious, weak-willed, or otherwise

---

[25] Katsafanas (2012b) offers a nicely developed account of Nietzsche's moral psychology of willing, but it does not explicitly make this connection between autonomous willing and the constitutivist program developed in Katsafanas 2011. It is not clear to me whether Katsafanas would endorse the connection suggested in the text.

alienated—and indeed, further, even nonhuman and *nonsentient* activities (*BGE* 36).[26] Insofar as Katsafanas's (2011) core argument works, therefore, all of these processes are implicitly committed to the aim of power, so that aim *cannot* serve to identify a highly select subset of human actions and character traits as uniquely valuable, in the way that Nietzsche's remarks about the achievement of autonomy seem designed to do. Nietzsche's core conception of autonomy, therefore, belongs not with the constitutivist notion of agency explored by Katsafanas, but elsewhere.

It is worth noting in conclusion that this result reveals a general trade-off between different kinds of evaluative work that the notion of autonomy might be thought to do. Insofar as it is meant to serve as part of the basis of normative bindingness in general or of moral obligation in particular, we will need a notion of autonomy that applies without question to a very wide swathe of our intentional activities, and subjects them to normative guidance. By contrast, insofar as autonomy is meant to distinguish a special class of actions and expressions of character that are difficult of achievement and special sites of distinctive value, we will need a notion of autonomy that is highly demanding and rarely attained. These two roles will thereby push us toward very different conceptions of what autonomy is supposed to be.

D. The Hierarchical Model and Identification

Much recent work in philosophy of action seeks a simpler solution to the problem of alienation faced by the standard model. The problem was that if an agent is alienated from one of her desires, then her behavior might well be caused by the desire's normal operation, just as the standard model requires for autonomy, without thereby providing any expression of her agency or autonomy at all; on the contrary, in such cases the person rightly feels herself to be *at the mercy* of her own desires and therefore deeply unfree. The proposed simple fix is to add more powerful resources to the standard model, while retaining its basic strategy of explaining agent-level phenomena (including full-fledged action) by appeal to the causal roles of subpersonal attitudes. The additional explanatory resources typically come from introducing new, more complex attitudes into the psychology hypothesized for the agent.

For forty years, this approach has centered around the influential proposals of Harry Frankfurt (1988a, 1999, 2004, 2006). Frankfurt's initial suggestion was straightforward: what separates the autonomous agent from the person being pushed around by her own desires is that the free agent *wants* to have the desire that she has, and wants that desire to be effective in action. Thus, to explain autonomous agency, all that needs to be added to

---

[26] A further problem for Katsafanas's constitutivism arises here. Katsafanas (2011) insists that we ineluctably value power because it is a constitutive condition of *action* and we are committed to being agents. But drive-motivated processes are not restricted to full-fledged action in the way this argument seems to assume; at the very least, they extend to the sort of mere activities (e.g., behavior out of repressed drives, Freudian slips, etc.) that Velleman (2000: 1–31) is at pains to *distinguish* from full-fledged action for the purposes of the constitutivist argument. And on this point, Velleman seems to be making the right move. After all, mere activities that do not rise to the level of genuine action are (at least very often) *not* the sort of behaviors that we are *committed* to, and they will include many activities that "the agent herself" would *reject*. But without that commitment, we cannot get the "constitution/commitment" reasoning off the ground, for there is nothing to suggest that the resulting activity or its aim need have any value for the agent.

the standard model psychology is the capacity to have *second-order* desires, through which the agent favors the effective first-order desire itself (Frankfurt 1988b/1971). The desire to have her effective first-order desire is supposed to distinguish the free agent from both the akratic who cannot control her rejected desire and the wanton who "does not care about his will" (Frankfurt 1988b/1971: 16), in the sense that he is not concerned one way or the other about whether his first-order desires are desirable ones to have.[27] This approach became known as the "hierarchical model," because of its crucial appeal to higher-order attitudes. But as Gary Watson (1975) pointed out, these higher-order desires are still fundamentally just desires, so an agent could be alienated from *them* in the same ways she can be alienated from first-order desires; she could (wantonly) not care about their desirability, or feel herself their akratic victim. In response, advocates of the hierarchical model have proposed a number of further psychological structures designed to guarantee that the agent is *identified* in an appropriate way with her positive attitude toward her effective desire, including rational values, and Frankfurt's technical notions of wholeheartedness, satisfaction (Frankfurt 1988c/1987), volitional necessity (Frankfurt 1999), love (Frankfurt 2004), and care (Frankfurt 2006).

Michael Bratman's (2007) proposal even integrates something parallel to constitutivist ideas about the agent's ineluctable commitment into the broadly hierarchical picture. What is needed in the face of Watson's objection is some psychological structure that is not just one more element in "the psychic stew" (Bratman 2007: 23), but plausibly constitutes the *agent's own* endorsement of the effective desire, such that (as he often puts it) when that structure guides, *the agent* governs. The proposal extends Bratman's planning theory of intention (Bratman 1987, 1999) to claim that *self-governing policies* are the attitudes that secure the agent's identification with her effective desire. Policies are *general* plans that commit the agent to some *type* of action in specified circumstances, and they are *self*-governing when they are higher-order policies aimed at regulating which of her own attitudes and motivations should be effective: for example, my self-governing policies might include a policy to cultivate my interest in music by seizing chances to hear performances, or a policy to support my concern for my nephew by making time to play the games we both love. Such policies plausibly play a significant role in constituting the cross-temporal continuity of a person's life: plans in general structure activity over time by including attitudes that make cross-temporal reference to one another, and self-governing policies further involve commitments to norms of stability and to the sort of self-management through higher-order attitudes typical of the hierarchical model. Building on a broadly Lockean theory of personal identity, Bratman (2007) then argues that such cross-temporal structure is what constitutes the agent as a person in the first place, and thus, the attitudes that produce and sustain it have a special claim to speak for her. When they guide behavior, it is the agent herself who governs, thereby attaining *self*-governance or autonomy.

Nietzsche scholars have been attracted to the hierarchical model of agency in its various guises, because of its apparent fit with other Nietzschean commitments. As we saw, one of the main features differentiating Nietzsche's psychology from that of the standard model

---

[27] In the extreme (and most naturally imaginable) case, a wanton would have no second-order desires at all; nevertheless, strictly speaking, what defines the category of wantons for Frankfurt is not the lack of second-order desires altogether, but the lack of "second-order volitions" construed as desires that (some relevant) first-order desire be *effective* (see Frankfurt 1988b/1971: 16–17).

is the range and complexity of the attitudes he posits,[28] and some of the attitudes that are most central to his explanations have the higher-order structure envisioned in the hierarchical model. In particular, as both Clark (1990: 205–44) and Reginster (2006: 103–47, *et passim*) point out, the *will to power* itself is best understood as a higher-order attitude which "wills power" in the sense that it aims to shape our other attitudes so that they express themselves in a particular manner (e.g., that they strive to overcome resistance, as Reginster would have it).[29] But it is far from clear, as we will see in a moment, that the hierarchical aspects of Nietzsche's psychological theorizing are the ones he himself deploys in explaining what makes an agent *autonomous*. The Bratman proposal, by contrast, has aspects that are intriguing from a Nietzschean point of view. After all, one of Nietzsche's most prominent treatments of autonomy—the famous "sovereign individual" passage from *GM* II: 1–3— *does* emphasize the individual's ability to coordinate his agency across time: he "is *permitted* to promise" and has the "privilege of *responsibility*" (*GM* II: 2) precisely because he has developed the capacity for a genuine "*memory of the will*" (*GM* II: 1) that coordinates a present intention or promise across time with a future act even in the face of adverse intervening circumstances, and conversely also matches future act to past intention.[30]

Despite the suggestive parallels, however, Bratman and Nietzsche are seeking basically and importantly different philosophical mileage from the notion of autonomy.[31] Bratman aims to characterize a broad notion of autonomy that addresses the basic question of philosophy of action—separating genuine, full-fledged *actions* from mere events, unconscious or absent-minded activities, akratic behavior, and the like. As such, his notion nicely complements a notion of an agent's *moral responsibility* for the actions that can be traced back to her intentions (in some suitably specified and qualified way). By contrast, as Gemes (2009: 36–7, 45–7) has reminded us, Nietzsche means to sketch a notion of autonomy that is quite rarely attained and implicates the person's entire character, rather than attaching simply to this or that action, considered separately. That notion is wholly inappropriate for co-deployment with claims about moral responsibility, since a great many interventions in the world that we conventionally count as actions (and subject to praise or criticism) are by no means autonomous in such a highly demanding sense; consider, for example, the myriad actions of slavish types and "last men" which Nietzsche routinely criticizes (and thereby treats as intentional in Bratman's sense), but which are by no means supposed to express the demanding sort of autonomy he holds up as ideal. This is as it should be for Nietzsche, since as we have seen, the relevant notion of moral responsibility is also one he is keen to reject (*TI*: "The Four Great Errors" 7–8; *GM* II, etc.). Instead, Nietzsche's conception of autonomy fits together with

---

[28] For further discussion on this point, see Anderson 2012a and the sources cited there.

[29] As Clark makes clear, interpretations in this general family owe a good deal to Kaufmann's (1974) influential presentation, and Richardson (1996) also deserves credit for emphasizing the importance of the will to power's shaping of more specific drives through pushing them to express themselves in a particular *manner*. For accounts that extend these important treatments, see Katsafanas's chapter in this volume, Katsafanas 2011, and Anderson 2012b.

[30] Hussain (1999) offers a detailed and sophisticated exploration of the philosophical possibilities opened up by interpreting Nietzsche's views along Bratmanian lines, along with some discussion of the differences between Nietzsche's and Bratman's concerns and the limitations of the parallel.

[31] My emphasis on these limits should not be taken to deny that the parallels are suggestive; some aspects of Nietzsche's psychology that fall short of the full theory of autonomy may well be fruitfully seen along Bratman-style lines. Again, see Hussain 1999 for illuminating discussion.

a stronger conception of responsibility—related in some ways to what Susan Wolf (1990) calls "deep responsibility"—which is typical of the way an artist is responsible for a work, or friends have responsibility for their friendship, or the way the sovereign individual can *take* responsibility for the future by her promise (even in cases where, from a moral point of view, it would not be fair to *hold* her responsible).[32] These narrower and more demanding notions of autonomy and responsibility lead Nietzsche to different conclusions than the Bratman view would entail about when an agent counts as autonomous.

Asceticism is a good case for bringing out the difference. The ascetic ideal certainly works to coordinate an agent's actions over time, and inevitably involves many self-governing policies implementing the ascetic's control over all the desires she is resolved to deny. More, Nietzsche would surely agree with Bratman that *who the ascetic is* must be closely tied to the plans and policies through which she imparts this powerful structure to her life—and since asceticism is a paradigm instance of the exercise of will to power (*GM* III: 11, *et passim*), we can also conclude that insofar as Nietzsche was committed to a hierarchical agent psychology, the ascetic clearly manifests that hierarchical structure. Ascetic practices would thus count as instances—indeed, *paradigm* instances—of autonomous, self-controlled agency, according to the hierarchical and Bratmanian interpretations. But of course, for Nietzsche himself, the ascetic ideal is precisely that from which we stand in need of liberation, and the sort of autonomy he aims to cultivate is supposed to be fundamentally incompatible with it, because of the internal self-dissociation it involves. For Nietzsche, precisely that self-dissociation prevents the ascetic from being *identified* in a fully autonomous way with *any* of her attitudes—either her (rejected) first-order desires or her apparently endorsed higher-order ascetic commitments.

Nietzsche scholars have also exploited non-Frankfurtian strands from recent philosophy of action in efforts to explicate the special sense in which the full-fledged agent is identified with her action. Robert Pippin (2010, 2009), for example, builds his interpretation on an expressivist theory of action derived proximally from Charles Taylor and ultimately from Hegel. On this view, what makes a behavior into an action, in the fullest sense, is not that it is *caused by* a separate intention, with which the agent herself then identifies, but instead that the action *gives expression* to the agent's intention and indeed her whole character, in a distinctive way that renders act and intention inseparable from one another. Space prevents full exploration of the details,[33] but an example can bring out the kind of identification between agent and action the idea envisions. Say I set out to write a poem.[34] Of course, I do have a relevant intention about writing and naturally I want to write a *good* poem. But as we all know to our pain, the intention with that content (viz., to write beautifully, etc.) lacks the causal power to bring about a poem that is in fact good. In cases like this, we do not look to a person's intention to predict what kind of poem she is going to write; on the contrary, we instead adjust our characterization of what the intention's content was all along to match the poem that is eventually produced. Thus, when my poem turns out badly, my readers rightly reject the lame excuse that *this* was not the good poem I intended to write. The content

---

[32] See Ridley 2009 for intriguing discussion of these issues surrounding the sovereign individual's distinctive form of responsibility.

[33] See Anderson forthcoming for discussion of further aspects of Pippin's version of the view. Aaron Ridley (2007) defends a version of expressivism that differs from Pippin's in some important details.

[34] The example here is based on Pippin 2010: 78.

my intention deserves to receive is exactly the one made manifest (*expressed*) in the *actual* poem, and in that sense, the intention's content depends on its eventual expression, rather than straightforwardly determining the outcome in action, as we assume in more standard cases of intentional action (like my execution of the intention to go shopping).

The important upshot for autonomy is that in such expressive cases, there is an extremely tight connection between the expressive content of the action and the meaningful content of the intention it expresses. In Pippin's terms, the action's content is "non-isolable" from the intention's, and the intention itself is "inseparable" from the action, in the sense that it is not rightly construed as an independent prior cause.[35] As a result, the meaningful intention and expressive action are supposed to forge a seamless whole. That tight connection between inner intention and outer expression can then be thought to capture the agent's "identification" with the action that is crucial to autonomy: thus, as Pippin would have it, "Nietzsche clearly considers freedom to consist in some sort of affirmative psychological relation to one's own deeds, a relation of identification, finding oneself in one's deeds, experiencing them as genuinely one's own" (Pippin 2009: 85), and expressive action meets these conditions.

Pippin seems inclined, further, to treat this expressivist account as a perfectly general answer to the founding problem of philosophy of action, so that expressing the character of the agent is what separates genuine actions from mere events. If that were true,[36] then

---

[35] For discussion, see Pippin 2010: 75–82. For Pippin, these two ideas (the "inseparability thesis" and the "non-isolability" thesis) spell out the notion of expression itself—the meaningful relation between the properly interpreted action and the inner content of the intention that speaks for the agent. The non-isolability thesis is a form of meaning holism applied to the action's proper description and thereby to its identity. What makes an event into an action is that it expresses something. A genuine action thus has a content. But *what* content? Non-isolability insists that neither the intrinsic features of the action by itself, nor any effort to stipulate some content via my intention, is sufficient to fix the content, which can happen only in a wider sociocultural hermeneutic context, in which the meanings of other actions and the interpretive standards of my fellows, as well as my intentions and the way they play out in the actual action, all help to determine what it means. Taking a step forward out of line counts as volunteering for the dangerous mission only given a social practice in which "stepping forward" is rightly so interpreted, etc. The inseparability thesis complements non-isolability by holding that the agent and her intention are not separate from the action, standing behind it as its previously existing causes, but exist as such *in* the action itself. My initial, subjective take on the meaning of the action, as embodied in my intention, has no privileged position in constituting the action. I myself might not accept my initial thought about the matter, once all is said and done. Pippin invites us to think of action as a continuous process in which my first intention is a provisional stab, which governs my initial steps toward my end but which is itself transformed in the face of circumstances and social interpretive norms as the process of acting goes forward. In the process, I gradually *figure out* what it was that I really intended all along. In the end, the expressivist claims, the actual truth of what I intended can only be captured by the completed action itself. Therefore, the intention is best understood not as a prior state "behind" the action, but as inseparable from the very content bound up "in" it. Action is "a continuous ... everywhere mutable translation or expression of inner into outer," where "what I end up with, what I actually did, is all that can count fully as my intention realized or expressed" (Pippin 2010: 78).

[36] I should note that it seems to me *not* to be true. The expressive theory gives an intriguing and plausible analysis of certain complex, deeply culturally imbedded actions, like artistic and cultural production, but its advocates overstate their case, I think, when they advance it as a general theory of action as such. For simple actions, like opening a door, walking over to get into the shade, and the like, the resources of the standard model or the hierarchical model give a much more straightforward and compelling account of the action and of what separates it, qua action, from mere activity or non-agential events.

anything that counted as a genuine action at all would meet these expressive conditions, and any would-be agent would thereby be committed to valuing autonomy as Nietzsche construes it. This consequence is directly parallel to the constitutivist result discussed above, and in my view, ought to have similar consequences for Nietzsche interpretation. If "finding oneself in one's deed" is construed broadly enough to capture the distinction between true action and mere events, then clearly the willful ascetic will end up counting as an agent who finds herself in her deeds. Even the "last men," whom Pippin is particularly keen to exclude as genuine agents in the Nietzschean sense, must sometimes accomplish expressive actions and thus "find themselves in the deeds" that express their small-mindedness—indeed, who could be more satisfied with themselves than they are!

Thus, the version of expressivism advanced by Ridley (2007) seems a more plausible account of Nietzsche's views on freedom than the more ambitious story suggested in Pippin 2009. Ridley's account of what the expressivist insight amounts to is similar to Pippin's: the successfully expressive agent finds herself in her deed in a strong sense because the guidance provided to activity by her intention, as well as the norms governing her intention formation and act execution, are *internal* to the process of carrying out the action itself, and cannot be informatively specified independently of the result, in the way suggested by the poem-writing example.[37] But Ridley is careful to concede that for Nietzsche himself (and in philosophical truth, in my view), such action is a relatively rare and highly special accomplishment, and cannot be predicated of any action whatsoever (Ridley 2007, esp. at 217–19). Precisely this restriction allows the resulting conception of autonomy to play the actual philosophical role Nietzsche seems to intend for it— namely, serving as a (rarely attained) *ethical ideal*.

E. Autonomy (Strength of Will) as an Ethical Ideal

A number of scholars have focused, like Ridley (2007) and Gemes (2009), on Nietzsche's suggestions that autonomy is a distinctive accomplishment of the character types he most admires, and these include some of the most compelling accounts of Nietzsche's thinking about autonomy in the recent literature.[38] These accounts can cite in their support many of the passages in which Nietzsche most clearly promotes freedom, as opposed to criticizing it: some of the more famous examples include:[39] "We, however, want to become *those we are*—human

[37] Ridley (2007: 211–17) nicely connects the expressivist insight to Nietzsche's powerful observation (see *BGE* 188, 213; *TI*: "Skirmishes of an Untimely Man" 41) that within the process of artistic creation (or, I would add, other creative activity that is nonroutine, in the sense that its specific success conditions cannot be fully specified in advance), the normative constraints that implicitly guide the activity and enable us to assess the success of our attempts are *not* rightly construed (as the weak characters criticized in *BGE* 21 would do) as *limiting* conditions that restrict our ability to act as we would, but are instead the very *enabling* conditions that permit the action to count as our own, and hence autonomous (self-controlled, self-governed) at all.

[38] In addition to Ridley (2007), readers should consult Janaway (ms) and, for a distinctive and highly developed interpretation that also belongs within this broad strand, Richardson (2009, 2004: 153–71, *et passim*). I have also contributed to this line of interpretation; see Anderson (2006) and Anderson (2012a).

[39] See also, along similar lines, *HAH* Preface; *GS* 347; *BGE* 29, 41, 44, 188, 203, 213; *TI*: "Skirmishes of an Untimely Man" 38, 41; etc.

beings who are *new, unique, incomparable* [my ital.], who give themselves laws, who create themselves" (*GS* 335); Nietzsche's claim that the "autonomous" "*sovereign individual*" is the "ripest fruit" of the self-disciplining morality of custom (*GM* II: 2); his praise of Goethe as a self-created "spirit who has *become free*" (*TI*: "Skirmishes of an Untimely Man" 49); the praise of Shakespeare's Brutus, "Independence of the soul!—that is at stake here. No sacrifice can be too great for that: one must be capable of sacrificing one's dearest friend for it, even if he should also be the most glorious human being, an ornament to the world…" (*GS* 98); and of course, these ringing lines from *Richard Wagner in Bayreuth*:

> A free human being can be good as well as evil, but…the unfree human being is a blemish upon nature and has no share in any heavenly or earthly comfort;…[and] everyone who wishes to become free must become free through his own endeavor,…[for] freedom does not fall into any man's lap as a miraculous gift. (*UM* IV: 11; quoted in *GS* 99)

In all these passages, autonomy is characterized as a kind of ethical ideal, which is rightly conceived *not* as standard equipment that is part and parcel of our humanity or our agency, but as an *achievement* that may occasionally be attained in the most excellent lives.[40]

But in what does this achievement consist? Space precludes adequate treatment of the question, or of the interpretive differences among commentators like Ridley (2007), Richardson (2004, 2009), Reginster (2003, 2006, 2012), or Janaway (ms). In lieu of a fuller account, I will close with a suggestion that this exegetical tack should take its bearings from that cryptic sentence in *BGE* 21 where Nietzsche announces his effort to change the subject from the traditional question of free will to something else: "The 'unfree will' is mythology; in real life it is only a matter of *strong* and *weak* wills."

As I read it, the fundamental suggestion of this remark is that in Nietzsche's view, the real problem about freedom has to do with an ethical problem of weakness of will. Nietzsche clearly believes that this ethical problem is both much broader and more widespread than we commonly think. It is broader in that the basic psychology of inner conflict behind standard-issue weakness of will has analogues in a great many cases where we are not akratic, strictly speaking, and these further cases, as well, deserve to be counted as ethico-psychological weakness, by extension. And it is more widespread, in that *very* many of our ordinary actions (including even clear instances of intentional agency, ordinarily construed) are really weak-willed in the extended sense even if we do not know it, because we are merely "following along" into the activities and pathways suggested for us by our social and motivational environment, rather than forging a path for ourselves autonomously, out of true independence of spirit (see Gemes 2009).

As I have argued elsewhere (Anderson 2006 and 2012a), the ubiquitous emphasis on strength and weakness throughout Nietzsche's writing is fruitfully interpreted in just this spirit, as a matter of ethical weakness of the will—crisply defined by Nietzsche as "the inability *not* to respond to a stimulus" (*TI* "Morality as Anti-Nature" 2)—and a corresponding notion of strength of will, which fundamentally amounts to a capacity for self-control or self-governance: "strong will: the essential feature is precisely *not* to will—to *be able* to suspend decision" (*TI*: "What the Germans Lack" 6). On this view, Nietzsche's claims about weakness and strength have a relatively clear moral psychological basis and a clear relation to autonomy.

---

[40] This important point gets distinct expression already in Nehamas 1985 and Schacht 1983, but it is now very often made; for example, it is one of the most broadly held themes sounded in the papers collected in Gemes and May 2009.

456   R. LANIER ANDERSON

Weakness amounts to a characteristic form of inner division that makes us vulnerable to being pushed around by our drives—and pulled around by external stimuli, because the drives and affects responsive to those stimuli are insufficiently integrated with the rest of our attitudes, and so elude the kind of control by the whole self that would enable us to resist the stimuli. Strength amounts to the converse form of inner unity, affording an integrated self that can control its constituent drives and so has the ability "*not* to will" even in cases where some drive is demanding it.

Thus, if the view broached here is correct, Nietzschean strength *in general* is a matter of the integration of the self's drives and desires so that they cohere to form a genuine self, or individual. In the strong self, the integrating order (which I take to *be* the self) settles the place of component drives within it and exploits their tendencies for its own larger ends. In this sense, we are justified in treating the strong individual as something over and above the constituent drives, and in understanding her strength as a matter of *her* control over those drives (see Anderson 2012a). For Nietzsche, this commanding self even identifies with the drives and their activities, just as in a successful commonwealth the governing class identi-fies with the whole (*BGE* 19). It thereby represents the drives (along with their "triumph over obstacles," *BGE* 19) as belonging to *it* and endorsed by it. Thus, the well-ordered, self-con-sistent, fully individual person follows the rule as she gives it to herself; she is autonomous.

So Nietzsche's views about the value of autonomy are nicely illuminated by appeal to this moral psychology of strength and weakness, just as the cryptic remark from *BGE* 21 suggested. Failures of autonomy or self-control are plainly cases of psychological weak-ness in the extended sense, traceable to some inner conflict among the agent's attitudes in which the whole or the core subset of the agent's drives and affects is unable to exert proper control over some recalcitrant drive. Such inner conflict can be understood by *analogy* to the conflicted motivational structures present in central cases of akrasia, even when we also include the extended cases, like asceticism or *ressentiment*-based valuation (*sensu* Reginster 1997), where the agent's behavior may not be akratic strictly speaking, but where she languishes in the grip of a self-defeating pattern of valuation or is hopelessly stuck with fundamentally inconsistent values or practical commitments. The achievement of autonomy, by contrast, is a distinctive form of self-relation that amounts to the converse state of strength—a harmonious integration and unity among the attitudes, in which each is governed by its place in the whole self. Such is clearly Nietzsche's conception of Goethe's achievement, for example:

> What he wanted was *totality*; he fought the mutual extraneousness of reason, senses, feeling, and will (preached with the most abhorrent scholasticism by *Kant*, the antipode of Goethe); he disciplined himself to wholeness, he *created* himself. (*TI*: "Skirmishes of an Untimely Man" 49)

As the last clause indicates, part of what makes such a unity count as *one's own* is precisely its having been *self-generated*—that is, that the unity among the drives and affects arises from regulating control over them that is exercised by and through the attitudes proper to the unified self that emerges from their interaction. In Nietzsche's view, it is not just autonomy but also the selfhood at its basis, making it possible, that must be achieved through a kind of self-creation.[41] And when it is most successful, such self-creation realizes

---

[41] Thus, the self that operates as the source of autonomous self-governance need not be construed as a transcendental subject that is a fundamentally different kind of thing than the subpersonal attitudes (as

a recognizable form of autonomy: the self here follows values and laws it gives to itself in producing its own integration and unity. From this standpoint, we can put some additional flesh on the bones of Ridley's (2007) suggestion that autonomy serves Nietzsche as an ethical ideal, for we can see it as the Nietzschean version of that widespread ideal of antiquity—"harmony of soul."

3 CONCLUSION

As we have seen, scholars have construed Nietzsche's conception of autonomy in widely divergent ways—from a libertarian notion of spontaneous freedom of will that he impatiently rejects, to an ethical ideal that he not only accepts, but takes up as his own and places at the center of his cultural and philosophical project. What I have tried to show throughout is that commentators' *interpretation* of Nietzschean autonomy is strongly driven by the deep-going *philosophical* agenda that they attribute to Nietzsche and/or accept themselves. Those for whom Nietzsche represents a valiant champion of hard-headed naturalism focus on the conception of autonomy as spontaneity in action and find plenty of Nietzschean ammunition for exploding our metaphysical fantasies about free action. Kantians insist that he was committed (like it or not) to a strong notion of the autonomous self—detached from the drives. Those who aim to find an adequate source of normative bindingness are tempted to read Nietzsche as a constitutivist, and those impressed by the standard model or its hierarchical descendants focus on Nietzsche's compelling treatment of psychological attitudes and their complex inner structure. Those inspired by an ethical ideal of self-affirmation (Janaway ms) or of psychological integration which leaves "no room . . . for my willing that the action were otherwise" (Ridley 2007: 216) connect those ideals to Nietzsche's thinking about autonomy.

One might worry, as a result, that Nietzsche's remarks on autonomy are hopelessly muddled or mutually inconsistent. But that would be overhasty. What this variation shows, to my way of thinking, is not any internal contradiction in Nietzsche, but the intrinsic richness and philosophical power of the notion of autonomy or self-governance itself. The core idea can be precisified in several different ways and developed in quite different directions, and our aim as commentators must be to discover which of those pathways follow the leading thread of Nietzsche's own philosophical concerns.

REFERENCES

(A) Works by Nietzsche

BGE   *Beyond Good and Evil* (1886), trans. W. Kaufmann. New York: Vintage, 1966.

in the Kantian accounts canvassed in section 2.B), but could be something more like an emergent order among the attitudes themselves, which can become self-reinforcing and in that sense self-creating. Space precludes any detailed articulation of such a conception of the self (which has some important features in common with the Bratman approach discussed in section 2.D), but I offer the beginnings of this sort of account in Anderson 2012a.

BT   *The Birth of Tragedy* (1872), trans. W. Kaufmann. New York: Random House, 1967.
D   *Daybreak* (1881), trans. R. J. Hollingdale. Cambridge: Cambridge University Press, 1982.
EH   *Ecce Homo* (1888), trans. W. Kaufmann. New York: Random House, 1967.
GM   *On the Genealogy of Morality* (1887), trans. M. Clark and A. Swensen. Indianapolis: Hackett, 1998.
GS   *The Gay Science* (1882, 1887), trans. W. Kaufmann. New York: Vintage, 1974.
HAH   *Human, All too Human* (1878–9), trans. R. J. Hollingdale. Cambridge: Cambridge University Press, 1986.
KSA   *Sämtliche Werke: Kritische Studienausgabe in 15 Einzelbänden*, ed. G. Colli and M. Montinari (15 vols). Berlin: De Gruyter, 1988.
TI   *Twilight of the Idols* (1888), trans. W. Kaufmann. New York: Viking, 1954.
UM   *Untimely Meditations* (1873–6), trans. R. J. Hollingdale. Cambridge: Cambridge University Press, 1983.
WP   *The Will to Power*, trans. W. Kaufmann and R. J. Hollingdale. New York: Vintage, 1967.

(B) Other Works Cited

Anderson, R. Lanier. 2005. "Nietzsche on Truth, Illusion, and Redemption," *European Journal of Philosophy* 13: 185–225.
Anderson, R. Lanier. 2006. "Nietzsche on Strength, Self-Knowledge, and Achieving Individuality," *International Studies in Philosophy* 38: 89–115.
Anderson, R. Lanier. 2012a. "What is a Nietzschean Self?" in Christopher Janaway and Simon Robertson (eds), *Nietzsche, Naturalism, and Normativity*. Oxford: Oxford University Press, 202–35.
Anderson, R. Lanier. 2012b. "The Will to Power in Science and Philosophy," in Helmut Heit, Günther Abel, and Marco Brusotti (eds), *Nietzsches Wissenschaftsphilosophie*. Berlin: Walter de Gruyter, 55–72.
Anderson, R. Lanier. Forthcoming. "Love and the Moral Psychology of the Hegelian Nietzsche: Comments on Robert Pippin, *Nietzsche: moraliste français*," *Journal of Nietzsche Studies*.
Bratman, Michael. 1987. *Intentions, Plans, and Practical Reason*. Cambridge, Mass.: Harvard University Press.
Bratman, Michael. 1999. *Faces of Intention: Selected Essays on Intention and Agency*. Cambridge: Cambridge University Press.
Bratman, Michael. 2007. "Reflection, Planning, and Temporally Extended Agency" in Michael Bratman, *Structures of Agency: Essays*. Oxford: Oxford University Press, 21–46.
Chisholm, Roderick. 1966. "Freedom and Action," in Keith Lehrer (ed.), *Freedom and Determinism*. New York: Random House, 11–44.
Chisholm, Roderick. 1976. *Person and Object: A Metaphysical Study*. London: Allen and Unwin.
Chisholm, Roderick. 1978. "Comments and Replies," *Philosophia* 7: 597–636.
Clark, Maudemarie. 1990. *Nietzsche on Truth and Philosophy*. Cambridge: Cambridge University Press.
Clark, Maudemarie. Forthcoming. "Nietzsche on 'Free Will,' Causality, and Responsibility." *Nietzsche on Ethics and Politics*. Oxford: Oxford University Press.
Clark, Maudemarie, and Dudrick, David. 2009. "Nietzsche on the Will: An Analysis of *BGE* 19," in Ken Gemes and Simon May (eds), *Nietzsche on Freedom and Autonomy*. Oxford: Oxford University Press, 247–68.

Davidson, Donald. 1980. *Essays on Actions and Events*. Oxford: Oxford University Press.

Frankfurt, Harry. 1988a. *The Importance of What We Care About: Philosophical Essays*. Cambridge: Cambridge University Press.

Frankfurt, Harry. 1988b/1971. "Freedom of the Will and the Concept of a Person," in *The Importance of What We Care About: Philosophical Essays*. Cambridge: Cambridge University Press, 11–25.

Frankfurt, Harry. 1988c/1987. "Identification and Wholeheartedness," in *The Importance of What We Care About: Philosophical Essays*. Cambridge: Cambridge University Press, 159–76.

Frankfurt, Harry. 1999. *Necessity, Volition, and Love*. Cambridge: Cambridge University Press.

Frankfurt, Harry. 2004. *The Reasons of Love*. Princeton, NJ: Princeton University Press.

Frankfurt, Harry. 2006. *Taking Ourselves Seriously, Getting it Right*. Stanford, Calif.: Stanford University Press.

Gardner, Sebastian. 2009. "Nietzsche, the Self, and the Disunity of Philosophical Reason," in Ken Gemes and Simon May (eds), *Nietzsche on Freedom and Autonomy*. Oxford: Oxford University Press, 1–31.

Gemes, Ken. 2009. "Nietzsche on Free Will, Autonomy, and the Sovereign Individual," in Ken Gemes and Simon May (eds), *Nietzsche on Freedom and Autonomy*. Oxford: Oxford University Press, 33–49.

Gemes, Ken, and May, Simon (eds). 2009. *Nietzsche on Freedom and Autonomy*. Oxford: Oxford University Press.

Hussain, Nadeem. 1999. *Creating Value: Appropriating Nietzsche for a Fictionalist Theory of Value*. PhD dissertation, University of Michigan.

Janaway, Christopher (ed.). 1998. *Willing and Nothingness: Schopenhauer as Nietzsche's Educator*. Oxford: Oxford University Press.

Janaway, Christopher. 2009. "Autonomy, Affect, and the Self in Nietzsche's Project of Genealogy," in Ken Gemes and Simon May (eds), *Nietzsche on Freedom and Autonomy*. Oxford: Oxford University Press, 51–68.

Janaway, Christopher. Ms. "Nietzsche on Morality, Drives, and Human Greatness." Unpublished manuscript.

Janaway, Christopher and Simon Robertson (eds). 2012. *Nietzsche, Naturalism, and Normativity*. Oxford: Oxford University Press.

Katsafanas, Paul. 2011. "Deriving Ethics from Action: A Nietzschean Version of Constitutivism," *Philosophy and Phenomenological Research* 83: 620–60

Katsafanas, Paul. 2012a. "Nietzsche on Agency and Self-Ignorance," *Journal of Nietzsche Studies* 43.1: 5–17.

Katsafanas, Paul. 2012b. "Nietzsche and Kant on the Will: Two Models of Reflective Agency." Available online at Philosophy and Phenomenological Research, DOI: 10.1111/j.1933-1592.2012.00623.x.

Kaufmann, Walter. 1974. *Nietzsche: Philosopher, Psychologist, Antichrist*, 4th edn. Princeton, NJ: Princeton University Press.

Korsgaard, Christine. 1996. "Personal Identity and the Unity of Agency: A Kantian Response to Parfit," in *Creating the Kingdom of Ends*. Cambridge: Cambridge University Press, 363–98.

Leiter, Brian. 1998. "The Paradox of Fatalism and Self-Creation in Nietzsche," in Christopher Janaway (ed.), *Willing and Nothingness: Schopenhauer as Nietzsche's Educator*. Oxford: Oxford University Press, 217–57.

Leiter, Brian. 2002. *Nietzsche on Morality*. London: Routledge.

Leiter, Brian. 2007. "Nietzsche's Theory of the Will," *Philosopher's Imprint* 7: 1–15. Reprinted in Ken Gemes and Simon May (eds) (2009). *Nietzsche on Freedom and Autonomy*. Oxford: Oxford University Press, 107–26.

Leiter, Brian and Knobe, Joshua. 2007. "The Case for Nietzschean Moral Psychology," in Brian Leiter and Neil Sinhababu (eds), *Nietzsche and Morality*. Oxford: Oxford University Press, 83–109.

Leiter, Brian and Sinhababu, Neil (eds). 2007. *Nietzsche and Morality*. Oxford: Oxford University Press.

Müller-Lauter, Wolfgang. 1999. *Über Freiheit und Chaos: Nietzsche-Interpretationen II*. Berlin: Walter de Gruyter.

Nehamas, Alexander. 1985. *Nietzsche: Life as Literature*. Cambridge, Mass.: Harvard University Press.

Pippin, Robert B. 2009. "How to Overcome Oneself: Nietzsche on Freedom," in Ken Gemes and Simon May (eds), *Nietzsche on Freedom and Autonomy*. Oxford: Oxford University Press, 69–87.

Pippin, Robert B. 2010. *Nietzsche, Psychology, and First Philosophy*. Chicago: University of Chicago Press.

Poellner, Peter. 1995. *Nietzsche and Metaphysics*. Oxford: Oxford University Press.

Reginster, Bernard. 1997. "Nietzsche on Ressentiment and Valuation," *Philosophy and Phenomenological Research* 57: 281–305.

Reginster, Bernard. 2003. "What is a Free Spirit? Nietzsche on Fanaticism," *Archiv für Geschichte der Philosophie* 85: 51–85.

Reginster, Bernard. 2006. *The Affirmation of Life: Nietzsche on Overcoming Nihilism*. Cambridge, Mass.: Harvard University Press.

Reginster, Bernard. 2012. "Autonomy and the Self as the Basis of Morality," in Allen Wood (ed.), *Cambridge History of Philosophy in the Nineteenth Century (1790–1870)*. Cambridge: Cambridge University Press, 387–433.

Richardson, John. 1996. *Nietzsche's System*. Oxford: Oxford University Press.

Richardson, John. 2004. *Nietzsche's New Darwinism*. Oxford: Oxford University Press.

Richardson, John. 2009. "Nietzsche's Freedoms," in Ken Gemes and Simon May (eds), *Nietzsche on Freedom and Autonomy*. Oxford: Oxford University Press, 127–49.

Ridley, Aaron. 2007. "Nietzsche on Art and Freedom," *European Journal of Philosophy* 15: 204–24.

Ridley, Aaron. 2009. "Nietzsche's Intentions: What the Sovereign Individual Promises," in Ken Gemes and Simon May (eds), *Nietzsche on Freedom and Autonomy*. Oxford: Oxford University Press, 181–96.

Risse, Matthias. 2007. "Nietzschean 'Animal Psychology' versus Kantian Ethics," in Brian Leiter and Neil Sinhababu (eds), *Nietzsche and Morality*. Oxford: Oxford University Press, 53–82.

Schacht, Richard. 1983. *Nietzsche*. London: Routledge.

Velleman, David. 2000. *The Possibility of Practical Reason*. Oxford: Oxford University Press.

Watson, Gary. 1975. "Free Agency," *Journal of Philosophy* 72: 205–20.

Williams, Bernard. 1993a. "Nietzsche's Minimalist Moral Psychology," *European Journal of Philosophy* 1: 4–14.

Williams, Bernard. 1993b. *Shame and Necessity*. Berkeley, Calif.: University of California Press.

Williams, Bernard. 2002. *Truth and Truthfulness: An Essay in Genealogy*. Princeton, NJ: Princeton University Press.

Wolf, Susan. 1990. *Freedom within Reason*. Oxford: Oxford University Press.

CHAPTER 20

....

THE OVERMAN

....

RANDALL HAVAS

> Man is not order of nature, sack and sack, belly and members, link in a chain, nor any
> ignominious baggage, but a stupendous antagonism, a dragging together of the poles
> of the Universe.
>
> Emerson, "Fate"

The Gay Science 347, entitled "Believers and their need to believe," ends with these lines:

> Once a human being reaches the fundamental conviction that he *must* be commanded, he
> becomes "a believer." Conversely, one could conceive of such a pleasure and power of self-deter-
> mination, such a *freedom* of the will that the spirit would take leave of all faith and every wish
> for certainty, being practiced in maintaining himself of insubstantial ropes and possibilities and
> dancing even near abysses. Such a spirit would be the *free spirit* par excellence. (*GS* 347: 289–90)

THESE remarks convey a familiar picture of an isolated, "heroic" Nietzschean individual, who,
having renounced all traditional hopes of finding firm foundations on which to live, stands
apart from others and imposes values of his own creation on an inhuman world. Nietzsche's
overman in particular appears at first blush to be such a person. But the familiar picture, I will
argue, stands on its head much of what Nietzsche actually thinks about getting "over" man.
Indeed, as I will try to show, the way of life embodied by the overman grows out of the very traditions on whose rejection it is premised and can be properly understood only as the achievement of a relationship to others that, perhaps paradoxically, that tradition itself makes possible.

Who, then, is the overman? What, in particular, makes him different from his predecessors? That Nietzsche holds out hope for a human form of life not at odds with itself in the
ways ours have been seems relatively uncontroversial, as does the thought that in his view,
the achievement of that hope depends on our ability to come to terms with the *temporal*
character of our lives. I contend, however, that Nietzsche believes it is specifically the temporality of human *agency* that has been most difficult for us to bear.[1] An overman is someone who has, by contrast, overcome his aversion to time; my aim in this paper is to make

---

[1] Among commentators with whose work I am most familiar Harold Alderman, Martin Heidegger,
and Tracy Strong stand out as readers most keenly aware of the centrality of temporality in Nietzsche's

clear what such overcoming involves. Our lives are, in a sense, spread out in time and as such subject to contingencies beyond our control. The unavoidable presence of such contingency offends a deep-seated sense of ourselves as in charge of the meaning of our lives. In response, we have traditionally sought to remove the threat of contingency either by means of a fantasy that our actions are somehow dictated by an authority higher than our own or, despairing of that, by renouncing the demand for meaning altogether. But the picture of autonomy that drives these strategies is, in Nietzsche's view, incoherent.[2] Whatever else it requires of us, becoming an overman demands that we overcome what *Beyond Good and Evil* calls this "worst of tastes, the taste for the unconditional" (*BGE* 31: 43). But in insisting on the conditional nature of agency, Nietzsche's point is not that we have no authority with respect to our actions but rather that we misunderstand the nature of the authority that we do have. Indeed, he holds that we have a vested interest in that misunderstanding. In affirming the conditional character of action, the overman does not deny that authority, but rather establishes it.

In this paper, then, I develop and defend an interpretation of Nietzsche's idea of an overman from the perspective of agency. The paper is in five sections. In the rest of my introductory remarks I offer a sketch of the reading as a whole. I suggest that actions, for Nietzsche, should be thought of as *commitments*. A person must, therefore, meet two conditions to count as acting in Nietzsche's sense: responsiveness to the past and responsibility for the future.[3] I discuss the first condition in some detail in section I and section II, and make clear there the sense in which commitment in Nietzsche's sense is itself a historical possibility, something he considers us capable of only once we've given up belief in God. The agent's responsibility for his future is the subject of section III. Although a person can of course make commitments to him- or herself, I argue there that responsibility is, in the first instance, responsibility to another. The notion of commitment therefore suggests that in Nietzsche's view, agency must be conceived in the light of the agent's relationships to others. Such relationships are likewise possible only in the wake of the death of God. The conclusion situates this reading in the context of the teaching of the overman in *Thus Spoke Zarathustra*. Of course, the view I attribute to Nietzsche is by now perhaps less surprising than the suggestion of its centrality to his thinking as a whole, but it provides a helpful way to make sense in particular of the idea of an overman as someone whose life embodies an affirmation of those features of human finitude to which Nietzsche believes we most object, and, I will argue, it allows us to see that the overman cannot be a *solitary* figure in the way the familiar picture portrays him to be.

I do not, however, aim to provide an interpretation of the use Nietzsche makes of the idea of an overman in *Thus Spoke Zarathustra*. In particular, I will have nothing to say about the overman being "the meaning of the earth" or of humanity as presently constituted as a "bridge" to the overman. Nor will I have anything to say about the concept of eternal

thinking in something like the sense that interests me here. See Heidegger 1962, Alderman 1977, and Strong 2000.

[2] I defend this interpretation below and, at greater length, in Havas 2005.

[3] This reading emphasizes Nietzsche's continuity with his "existentialist" successors—most notably, with Heidegger, though it locates the centrality of temporality in Nietzsche's thinking in a different place than Heidegger himself does. Indeed, Nietzsche's notion of temporality figures more or less exactly where Heidegger locates it in his *own* thinking: namely, in Nietzsche's account of what Heidegger would call "authenticity."

recurrence beyond suggesting here that whatever the fate of that concept in Nietzsche's thinking overall, it seems to me most useful to see it as a response to the difficulty he believes we
experience being agents at all.[4] My reading here is meant to defend one interpretation of that
difficulty. It should be possible to defend an interpretation of eternal recurrence along these
same lines, but that is a task for another paper. In any case, as we will see in a moment, the
role the idea of overcoming our humanity plays in the context of *Thus Spoke Zarathustra* is
also rather more complicated and, above all, indirect than anything I say here. I would like
instead to try to understand in a very general way how the idea of being an "overman"—
of overcoming our human, all-too human revulsion at the finite, temporal character of our
lives—functions in Nietzsche's thinking *überhaupt*. As I see it, the term "overman" designates
a way of life, not a particular person. I will therefore speak of *being übermenschlich* as well as,
in a more conventional vein, of *the* or *an* overman. The question is what change in our form
of life does being in this sense *übermenschlich* demand of us. But however we conceive of the
change in question, it is less a change in our *views* about things than in our way of living.

As I noted above, the suggestion that Nietzsche advocates some such change in the lives of
his readers hardly seems controversial. What may seem more so, however, is the idea I defend
here that we affirm the *temporal* character of life by living in a particular way. On my reading,
the term "overman" is simply one name he gives to *that* idea. The function of that name—the
actual *use* to which he puts the idea—in the books he wrote varies from one context to another.
However, I propose to postpone until the end of this paper questions about the function of that
idea in *Thus Spoke Zarathustra* and focus for the most part on its content more generally.

Very roughly, then, someone who is an overman has conquered his or her sense of offense
at time. To put the point in the terms I will defend here, to get "over" human being—to live
differently than we have lived thus far—demands that we affirm life's temporal character
where we once sought to deny it. We see best what that comes to by understanding how
Nietzsche thinks of the temporal conditions of agency. But Nietzsche holds that the possibility of a way of life that affirms those conditions is itself historically specific, inasmuch as
we—with our Platonic/Christian past—are the human beings whose denial and affirmation
of life are in question. As we will see, then, there are, in his view, at least *two* senses in which
we can speak of the temporality of agency. First, what we do is temporal in that it demands
both *obedience to the past* as the source from which we derive our present possibilities for
action and *responsibility for the future* in that, in making any of these possibilities our own,
we commit ourselves to certain outcomes in the face of contingencies beyond our control.
But second, there is, for Nietzsche, a sense in which the very possibility of possibility itself—
put less paradoxically: the possibility of possibilities *of our own*[5]—becomes available to us
only now in the present age. To put the point in perhaps more properly Nietzschean terms,
possibility itself (in the sense that interests Nietzsche) becomes possible only with the death
of God. As long as we rely in one way or another on God as the guarantor of our authenticity,
we are less than agents in the sense that interests Nietzsche. Being the overman is nevertheless
not a necessity, for nothing insures that we will in fact make this particular past our own. Indeed,

---

[4] That thought does not by itself rule out a "cosmological" reading of recurrence, but I will proceed as
though Nietzsche's main interest in the notion of recurrence is practical, not theoretical. This assumption
is, of course, controversial. See Loeb 2006b and Richardson 2006.

[5] As opposed, in other words, to those we formerly took in one way or another to be handed down
from on high.

we might very well just go on living, as Nietzsche fears, in our herd-like, last man-ish ways. As Tracy Strong puts the point, genealogy is not dialectics.[6] That is to say, there is, for Nietzsche, no guarantee that we will in fact become what he elsewhere calls animals with the right to make promises.[7] Before I begin, however, I need to address a doubt one might have about approaching the notion of the overman independent of its context in *Thus Spoke Zarathustra*.

In general, one is of course well advised not to take the concepts Nietzsche deploys out of context. Thus, however central to his thinking is the idea of "overcoming" what has so far passed for our humanity, it has not escaped the notice of commentators that in work Nietzsche himself published he gives the actual term "overman" a significant role to play *only* in *Thus Spoke Zarathustra*, and there—although he has Zarathustra refer in passing to the idea elsewhere in the book—most explicitly only in the "Prologue." That Nietzsche accords so little space in *Thus Spoke Zarathustra* to the idea of the overman and in fact claims that *another* concept—that of eternal recurrence—is that book's "fundamental conception" has led readers to wonder just how attached he was to the idea after all. Indeed, that the real drama of *Thus Spoke Zarathustra* seems to focus mostly on Zarathustra's *own* difficulty coming to terms with the thought of eternal recurrence invites one to wonder whether Zarathustra's hopes for a fundamental transformation of what it has meant so far to be a human being—his hopes, that is, for an overman—might not itself be a function of a wish for escape from his *own* past. As such, Zarathustra's thought of human life as a means to something more than merely human would be an expression of the same "spirit of revenge" he finds at the heart of the ways of life he rejects. And indeed insofar as we think of such a transformation as a radical *rejection* of the past, it is hard to avoid this conclusion. As Nietzsche sees it, however, the trick is not to *break* with the past, but instead to learn to make of it something of one's own, and nothing forces us to ascribe to Nietzsche himself a notion of overcoming humanity so utterly divorced from its own historical conditions. We may follow Robert Pippin here and conclude that this is one of the lessons Zarathustra learns in the course of that book without concluding that the notion more broadly of is no use to Nietzsche himself.[8]

---

[6] Strong 2000: 253.

[7] The thought—on which I elaborate below—that the *Genealogy*'s sovereign individual is a version of the Nietzschean overman has been challenged by, among others, Lawrence Hatab and Christa Davis Acampora. See Hatab 2005 and Acampora 2006. Simon May accepts the equation, but rejects it as a defensible ideal. See May 1999. These readings seem to me to ascribe to the sovereign individual some version of the form of radical autonomy I have argued elsewhere Nietzsche *denies* him as a condition of the kind of free will he or she in fact possesses. See Havas 2000 and 2005. For a very different approach to the one I take here, see Loeb 2006a. Like Acampora, Loeb rejects the idea that the sovereign individual is an overman, though not because the traits ascribed to the sovereign individual aren't properly *übermenschlich*, but rather on the ground that the sovereign individual cannot in fact possess those characteristics. The price Loeb pays for this reading is that everything Nietzsche says, in apparently approving terms, about the sovereign individual's "power over fate" and so on must be read ironically. His reading depends above all upon his taking seriously in ways I find I cannot the idea of the doctrine of eternal recurrence as a *cosmological* theory according to which in a quite literal sense everything recurs and has always recurred (though, Loeb stresses, without a starting point in time).

[8] For examples of readings challenging the importance traditionally accorded the notion of the overman, see Lambert 1986, Pippin 1988 and 2006a, and Clark 1990. Clark dismisses outright the notion of the overman as an alternative to life denial on the grounds that his alleged break with the past is at odds with a life-affirming insistence on the eternal recurrence of that same past. Thus, insofar as Zarathustra "appears to value human life only as a means to a superhuman life,... the overman ideal expresses Zarathustra's own need for revenge" (Clark 1990: 273–5). Pippin's reading is more nuanced in concluding only that Zarathustra must abandon his "vengeful" hopes of a radical break with the

I think, therefore, that rather than signal Nietzsche's rejection of the concept of an overman, the fact that Zarathustra gets nowhere with it as a teaching device and that Nietzsche himself does not develop the idea under that name suggests only its *pedagogical* uselessness. The idea of overcoming humanity cannot by itself turn itself into an ideal or goal for people who are otherwise indifferent to it. Nietzsche does indeed mean to help his readers come to find the idea of a certain kind of human life appealing that they presently experience as appalling. But, as Zarathustra learns rather quickly, simply *announcing* the concept of an overman cannot do that.[9] This does not mean, however, that we cannot try to understand better the idea itself. It is, in ways I will try to make clear, absolutely central to his thinking.

I

My aim in this paper is to interpret the idea of the overman in terms of Nietzsche's conception of agency.[10] In his view, part of what makes agency challenging for the likes of us is that it involves an affirmation of our indebtedness to the past. This is the first condition on agency. It is in such terms, I will argue, that we can best understand Zarathustra's claim that we experience the past as a *threat* to the will. But Nietzsche couples this emphasis on the past with a sense that the future looms as at least as large a difficulty for us. Nietzsche says that a *"memory of the will"* (*GM* II.1: 58) is required for action so that

> between the original "I will," "I shall do this" and the actual discharge of the will, its *act*, a world of strange new things, circumstances, even acts of will may be interposed without breaking the long chain of will. (*GM* II.1: 58)

To act is thus, as he puts it there, "to ordain the future" (*GM* II.1: 58), whence the demands of *responsibility*—what I am calling the second condition of agency. But he contends that we everywhere resist those demands. In the end, they prove as challenging to us as does time's "it was."

---

particular philosophical tradition that—as I will argue here—makes him possible. He nevertheless retains a "radically deflated" (Pippin 1988: 54) version of an overman as a historically specific ideal. This last suggestion seems basically right to me.

⁹ See, again, Pippin 2006a.

¹⁰ I am not alone in thinking of these matters in terms of the notion of agency. David Owen and Robert Pippin defend related readings. See, in particular, Owen 2007 and Pippin 2006b. Owen and Pippin attribute to Nietzsche what they consider to be an "expressivist" conception of agency according to which an agent bears an unalienated relationship to what she does if her actions "express" her character. This interpretation proceeds largely on the basis of Nietzsche's suggestion in the *Genealogy* that the masters' actions are "expressions" of their masterly strength. But it is harder to find the expressivism in Nietzsche's conception of the overman who is, I will argue, supposed to be the one who inherits his past in the ways that matter most to Nietzsche. The masters are not *historical* in the sense that interests Nietzsche most. Unlike the masters, in other words, the overman does not embody an expressivist conception of agency, but rather, in its emphasis on responsibility, what we might call an existentialist one. For a reading of Nietzsche as a compatibilist, see Gemes 2006. Gemes sees correctly that Nietzsche conceives of freedom of will in terms of responsibility, but he does not emphasize that the appeal to responsibility implies a notion of community at the heart of Nietzsche's conception of agency. See also Jenkins 2003.

Action, on this view, is possible only on the basis of the past *and* as extended into the future. By belittling as a "fiction" the idea of an agent simply *causing* his or her actions—the infamous doer behind the deed—the *Genealogy* takes aim not at the possibility of action as such but rather at what Nietzsche considers an especially tempting misinterpretation of it. In insisting on the temporality of agency, his point is thus not that no one ever does anything, but rather that who one is a function of what one does. The one cannot be identified without the other. But such identification is possible only insofar as agency is temporal in the sense at stake here. I am not a "doer behind my deeds," a disembodied ego trying to effect changes upon the world. I am *this* one (so-and-so) insofar as I do what one does in these circumstances, but I am this *particular* one (the one I am) insofar as I take responsibility for what I have done. These two conditions are combined in the thought that I make the past my own precisely by—in taking responsibility for my choices—extending it into the future. The evasion of responsibility is, in effect, the evasion of my identity as this particular agent. Or so I mean to argue.

That we should think of the overman in terms of agency and of the latter in specifically temporal terms is suggested, among other things, by the emphasis Nietzsche has Zarathustra place on the idea of the *will*. In "On Redemption," we find, famously, a diagnosis of what Nietzsche elsewhere refers to as the ascetic ideal as an expression of what Zarathustra calls "the will's ill-will [*Widerwille*] toward time and time's 'it was.'" And whatever else it is, the affirmation of eternal recurrence is presented as an alternative to the will's aversion to the past. Now Nietzsche inherits from Kant and others the notion of the will as a way of talking about what I am calling agency. His suggestion seems therefore to be that the agent experiences the past as an obstacle or embarrassment of some sort, as some kind of check on his or her power.

> 'It was': thus is called the will's gnashing of teeth and loneliest misery. Impotent against that which has been—it is an angry spectator of everything past.
>   The will cannot will backward; that it cannot break time and time's greed—that is the will's loneliest misery. (Z: "On Redemption" 111)

The inability to "will backward" and thereby "break time and time's greed" encourages a picture of the will as driven to try to assert *control* over what it has done. As Maudemarie Clark puts it, "our problem with time is our complete powerlessness with respect to the past."[11] But what kind of power over the past does the will seek? What kind of limitation does the will experience the past to be? Nietzsche suggests that the will encounters the past as a mortal threat of some sort, as a challenge to its very possibility. More specifically, the undoability of the past somehow makes willing anything at all seem pointless. But why? As what kind of challenge is the past perceived? A number of possible explanations suggest themselves. Perhaps the problem is that one is never truly in a position to "take back" what one has said or done. Call that the problem of regret. Or is the problem rather that things are always changing, that nothing lasts? Call that the problem of transience. Or, as it seems to me, is the problem instead that one feels that the past has one in *its* control, so that one feels, so to speak, doomed to repeat it? Call that the problem of originality. This last interpretation suggests that

---

[11] Clark 1990: 259. Nietzsche does indeed speak of the will's experience of itself as "*[o]hnmächtig gegen Das, was gethan ist*" (*KSA* 4: 180).

the challenge the past presents to our will is our unavoidable *indebtedness* to it. On this read-ing, the problem of the past is the problem of how to make one's actions one's own in the face of the fact that one cannot claim responsibility for the conditions that make doing what one does count as doing *that* possible. The will objects to not being in charge of its possibilities for action.

There are certainly suggestions that Nietzsche thought of the problem of the past in each of these terms and probably in others as well. Thus, Paul Loeb writes, "Because time is con-stantly flowing, and flowing in a forward direction only, the will sees that it cannot undo any deed and that it is powerless against that which is done and in the past."[12] This way of putting the point suggests fairly naturally the thought that the will suffers from its inability to *change* the past, so that controlling the past would be a matter of erasing or at least altering it. And one might indeed suffer from the past in that sense. Regret that one has said or done this or that would be a common form of such suffering. If we could undo what we have said or done (or, what will come to the same thing for Nietzsche, undo the consequences of what we said or did), the suffering expressed in regret would dissolve.

Some readers have accordingly found it helpful to think of affirming eternal recurrence as, in effect, a way to remove the possibility of regret. For example, one might find a life in which one was, like Nietzsche, unlucky in love to be regrettable and therefore not worthy of affirmation. The problem of the past becomes one of understanding one's life in such a way that regret over the way things turned out no longer makes sense. Readings that stress our ability not to change but to *reinterpret* the past in the light of the future (by coming, for example, to see an otherwise regrettable solitude as in fact permitting one to do work that one would otherwise have been unable to do) see the "it was" as an obstacle to the will in this sense. On Alexander Nehamas's version of this interpretation, for example, someone who affirms eternal recurrence overcomes his ill will against events in the past that are *not* under his control by seeing their significance as a function of a future that *is*. As an "art-ist" of one's life, one makes an otherwise "accidental" past necessary (specifically, to whom one is becoming). In this way, one may live without regret, even though one cannot actually *retract* what one has said or done.[13] Maudemarie Clark's interpretation of eternal recurrence similarly treats the problem of the past as one of regret. She understands the challenge of the thought of recurrence more "naively" to involve asking oneself whether, knowing, as it were, what one knows now, one would be willing to live one's life all over again—even without aes-thetic embellishments of Nietzschean "style." On this account, the thought of eternal recur-rence would appear unbearable to someone who had much to regret about his life but not to someone who did not.[14] While elegant and appealing, such readings do not seem to me to

[12] Loeb 2001: 28.
[13] See Nehamas 1985. The overarching project of this book is to show how Nietzsche might be serious—that is, say what he means and mean something by what he says—without being dogmatic. In this sense, Nehamas's interpretation may be read as addressing what I am calling the problem of originality. His account of one's ability to interpret the past must make clear what makes any interpretation of what happens to one—what becomes one's "style"—one's *own* (and not something dictated by the culture at large). Unlike the reading I propose here, however, Nehamas does not think of Nietzsche as settling that problem in relation to others.
[14] See her account in Clark 1990. The idea that Nehamas's and Clark's accounts treat the problem of time as one of regret is explored by Reginster 2006.

make clear enough in what sense the past is an obstacle to the *will*, a challenge, as I put it, to the possibility of agency itself.

Nietzsche suggests elsewhere that the problem the past presents for the will is that of transience. Zarathustra, for example, says that the fact that all things are *in flux* is a "stone" for the will. In other words, what the will finds unbearable is, roughly, life's impermanence. The thought is that because nothing we do truly endures, everything we do is worthless. The idea is familiar. For example, the kind of Buddhism to which Nietzsche objects takes some such view for granted. And Nietzsche himself certainly held that although there are no eternal, self-identical substances, the illusion that there are such things functions as a metaphysical comfort for those who feel the need for them.[15] That everything changes seems, according to "On Redemption," to be what, at least in Zarathustra's view, many traditional philosophers and religious teachers have cited as their grounds for rejecting life and seeking something metaphysically better. Thus, he says,

> And now cloud upon cloud rolled in over the spirit, until at last madness preached: 'Everything passes away, therefore everything deserves to pass away.
> And this itself is justice, this law of time that it must devour its own children'—thus preached madness. (*Z*: "On Redemption" 111)

Zarathustra seems pretty clearly to have in mind here philosophers who have held that the transience of things undermines their value.[16] And philosophers have not been alone in thinking this so. But again, although it is not hard to see how transience might intuitively be thought of as an objection to *life* in some general sense, it's not clear what sort of obstacle it presents to the *will*. Why should permanence be a desideratum for our accomplishments? That is, in what sense is impermanence a threat to the *possibility* of action? Why should the fact that my accomplishments are impermanent seem to make action itself impossible? "On Redemption" does not make this clear.

What, then, of the problem of originality? That problem, we said, was the problem of how to make one's actions one's own. The coherence of this suggestion depends on there being a sense in which, as they stand, my actions are somehow *not* my own. By itself, this thought is familiar enough. We can speak of someone making his actions he own where he is otherwise *alienated* from what he does. Nietzsche puts it this way in "Schopenhauer as Educator,"

> on account of their laziness, men seem like factory products, things of no consequence and unworthy to be associated with or instructed. The man who does not wish to belong to the mass needs only to cease taking himself easily; let him follow his conscience, which calls to him: 'Be yourself! All you are now doing, thinking, desiring, is not you yourself.' (*UM* 127)

Thus, my actions are not my own if they "belong" to someone else, if someone else has authority for them. But Nietzsche follows Emerson in the passage at hand in insisting that the someone else in question is no one in particular, but rather the "mass"—those he elsewhere refers to as "the herd." My suggestion about the past is simply that the will sees it as an obstacle to originality in something like this sense: if I feel that my options are, as it were, dictated by my history, I will fail to see them as truly *mine*. After all, *I* do not determine

---

[15] Platonism is an obvious example of this, but see *GS* 110 for a more general account.
[16] See Strong 2000: 225–31 for an interesting interpretation of these passages.

what counts as what. Indeed, as we will see, *Beyond Good and Evil* 188 makes clear that in Nietzsche's view, that much is settled *before* I arrive on the scene. This, I submit, is what the will finds problematic about time's "it was." A conditioned action seems to one who is in the grip of this picture of, in effect, free will to be action in name alone, nothing that one has *done*. Nietzsche insists, on the contrary, that only as conditioned is action possible at all.

My suggestion, then, is that we see more clearly how the past might appear to be an obstacle to the will (might seem to threaten the possibility of agency) if we see the problem of the past as that of our feeling under *its* control rather than of its failure to be under *ours*. In other words, the will seeks power over the past to counteract what it feels is the past's power over *it*. As I indicated above, the idea that the past is an obstacle to originality is not at all unfamiliar: the will does not feel in control of the past in the sense that it does not feel free of it. In short, the story Zarathustra tells of the will's ill will against time is part of Nietzsche's account of what is usually considered the problem of freedom of will. In the end, Nietzsche believes that what has seemed to a certain sensibility to make willing impossible is in fact what makes it possible at all. But we really see what this last claim comes to only by looking more closely at how Nietzsche thinks of the conditions of action.

None of this is obvious, however, from the passages we've been looking at in *Thus Spoke Zarathustra*, and I suggest that we look elsewhere for elucidation of the conditioned character of agency: specifically, to a pair of well-known passages from *Beyond Good and Evil* about free will and what I am calling the problem of originality—namely, *BGE* 21 and 188. These passages make clear, I think, that the past appears as an obstacle to the will to the degree that the will wants to be in control of its *options*. In other words, it is, as I said, the will's *indebtedness* to the past that is the subject of its "best reflection" (*bestes Nachdenken*) so far. That, in Nietzsche's view, is what philosophical fantasies of being unconditioned are really about. It is what philosophers are talking about when they talk, in particular, about free will. And when the will seeks revenge against time, it seeks it against time's control over *it*.

Both passages from *Beyond Good and Evil* that I want to discuss reject the idea of unconditioned action as incoherent. The second makes more explicit than the first what the conditions of action might actually be. But even the first passage makes clear that the will's sense of powerlessness is a sense of its powerlessness to put itself in charge of all its possibilities for action. This is why we can speak in this context of one's *indebtedness* to the past.[17] Somehow such indebtedness comes to seem a burden.[18] This is the feeling, the need that lies behind our search for timeless truth. The Platonist about morality, for example, feels that unless we have access to timeless moral truths, our moral judgments are no more than chatter. But this suggests in turn that Zarathustra finds behind such philosophical views a fantasy of absolute autonomy. On this account, our past philosophical and religious traditions are the expression of a fantasy of being unconditioned by time. In other words, for someone whose will is in the grip of this need for radical autonomy nothing for which one does not "bear the entire and ultimate responsibility" (*BGE* 21) is worth anything. As we will see, however, Nietzsche considers this picture of "ultimate responsibility" a supreme "self-contradiction" (*BGE*

---

[17] Pretty obviously, Heidegger's conception of existential guilt and of "thrownness" more generally is itself as indebted to Nietzsche's thinking about agency as it is to Kierkegaard's understanding of sin. See Heidegger 1962, especially §58.

[18] Nietzsche does not think it was always thus, but as far as I can tell, he has no account at all of *how* the past comes to be experienced in this way.

21) that makes hash of so much as the idea of agency. Whence, he will argue, its appeal: it helps to distract us from the demands responsibility actually makes upon us.

II

An agent, then, is someone with what Zarathustra calls a "will" and actions are what such a one "wills." Properly understood, action can be seen to constitute the agent by situating him between his past and his future, allowing him, in Zarathustra's words, to "create and piece together into one, what is now fragment, riddle, and dreadful accident" (Z: "On Redemption" 110). As I claimed above, this reading encourages us to connect what Zarathustra says about the will with what Nietzsche elsewhere offers as an interpretation of the problem of freedom of will. Three points should be borne in mind. The first is to see that, far from history's being an obstacle to agency, action, in Nietzsche's view, is possible only on the basis of the past. Second, however, because the past does not dictate what one makes of it and hence what, if anything, makes it one's own, Nietzsche makes clear that agency also demands that one make choices and take responsibility for them. Finally, we need to see that the problem of free will understood along these lines is historically specific: the possibility presented by *our* past is precisely the possibility of possibility itself (that is, the possibility of having possibilities of one's own, rather than ways of life supposedly dictated by transcendent metaphysical, religious, or moral authorities). As Nietzsche sees it, our long training in truthfulness has made it possible to see the sense in which it is impossible to evade being conditioned by the past. In other words, the very tradition an overman overcomes makes the overcoming of that tradition possible. In this way, an overman is one who makes his Platonic/Christian past his own by taking responsibility for what he says and does.

Let us start, then, with Nietzsche's attack on the traditional problem of free will. Although his argument in this passage is relatively familiar, what he ultimately makes of it may seem less so. His basic strategy is to make room for freedom construed as responsibility for action by questioning the intelligibility of the notion of freedom presupposed by both libertarianism and determinism. The former view is, in his view, conceptually unsustainable, while the latter depends upon a dogmatic insistence on the primacy of one form of justification over all others. Once we see this, however, we can begin to appreciate that the problem of free will is in fact not an abstract philosophical conundrum about how to square the realm of causal law with the space of reasons, but rather what Nietzsche calls the "profoundly personal" problem of responsibility for action. "In real life," Nietzsche says, "it is only a matter of *strong* and *weak* wills" (BGE 21: 29). The strong will experiences the past as a condition of originality, whereas the weak will endeavors to use it to evade the demands of responsibility. As we will see, *Beyond Good and Evil* 188 expresses Nietzsche's *own* strength of will in the telling of this very story.

The first prong of Nietzsche's argument is to reject as nonsense the conception of freedom that underwrites the idea of a disembodied, ahistorical understanding of agency. He writes:

> The *causa sui* is the best self-contradiction that has been conceived so far, it is a sort of rape and perversion of logic; but the extravagant pride of man has managed to entangle itself

> profoundly and frightfully with just this nonsense [*Unsinn*]. The desire for "freedom of will" in
> the superlative metaphysical sense…the desire to bear the entire and ultimate responsibility
> for one's actions oneself, and to absolve God, the world, ancestors, chance and society involves
> nothing less than to be precisely this *causa sui* and, with more than Münchhausen's audacity,
> to pull oneself up into existence by the hair, out of the swamps of nothingness. (*BGE* 21: 28)

The idea of acting from no point of view whatever makes as little sense in Nietzsche's estimation as any other version of the "dangerous old conceptual fiction" of an

> eye turned in no particular direction, in which the active and interpreting forces, through
> which alone seeing becomes seeing *something*, are supposed to be lacking; these always
> demand of the eye an absurdity and a nonsense [*Widersinn und Unbegriff*] (*GM* III.12: 119).

Like every other way in which we encounter the world, our actions are, in a word, *perspectival*. The thought of an *agent* turned in no particular direction is, therefore, just as absurd
and nonsensical as its ocular counterpart. The point is easier to appreciate if we bear in mind
Nietzsche's rejection of the fiction of a doer behind his or her deeds and consider as examples of actions not mere bodily movements supposedly caused by intentions but human
"doings" like voting, sealing an agreement, teaching a class on Nietzsche, and so on. "God,
the world, ancestors, chance and society" provide the background against which such
actions are possible. Without such a horizon of possibilities, teaching, say, would be impossible for the simple reason that where nothing counts as doing anything, nothing counts as
teaching in particular.

In other words, what surpasses even Münchhausen's audacity is the thought that anything the individual himself can do can make it the case that, say, pumping one's joined
hands up and down counts as a greeting or as sealing an agreement. Such practices must
already be in place before one's doing *this* can count as doing *that*. They are in this way
prior to this or that particular action; they lie in its "past." In a similar vein, the *Genealogy*
insists that

> Man himself must first of all have become calculable, regular, necessary, even in his own image
> of himself, if he is to be able to stand security for *his own future*, which is what one who prom-
> ises does! (*GM* II.1: 58)

Nietzsche's talk of becoming "calculable" (*berechenbar*) here is his way of insisting on what
some philosophers call "normativity." Normativity in this sense makes possible what the
Genealogy calls "standing security" for oneself. On this view, that there are appropriate and
inappropriate ways to respond to the demands of a given situation is nothing for which the
individual himself could intelligibly be held responsible. Responsibility is restricted to the
actions normativity makes possible. The metaphysical wish to be *causa sui* balks at *this* fact.
In effect, someone in the grip of this picture of freedom seeks incoherently to become the
source of the normativity of his own actions. To use a familiar analogy from games, nothing
I do determines that doing *this*—e.g., getting there before the ball does—counts as stealing
a base; the rules of baseball do that. Nietzsche's argument is that a metaphysically free agent
would in fact be unable to *do* anything, and, he suspects, that is ultimately what the metaphysician wants here: not freedom but passivity.

But to deny that I can be the source of normativity is obviously not to deny that I can
be held responsible for my actions. As we have seen, Nietzsche holds that far from being
a hindrance to agency, the situated, perspectival character of action is in fact a necessary

condition of it.[19] Traditionally, philosophical worries about determinism stand in the way of our seeing how this could be so. The second prong of Nietzsche's argument therefore asks that we extend our "enlightenment" about the nonsensicality of the notion of unconditioned choice to the notion of an unfree (i.e., causally determined) will as well. Nietzsche rejects in particular what he takes to be determinism's conflation of condition with causation as mere "mythology" born, ultimately, of what he thinks of as weakness of will. In Nietzsche's view, the thought that there is a determinist threat to the possibility of action rests on the dogmatic insistence that one kind of explanation (in this case, causal explanation) is the *only* kind. On his account, that it is sometimes appropriate to speak of the past as mitigating one's responsibility for this or that does not mean that it is always appropriate to do so. This is because our causal vocabulary does not reach beneath phenomena in such a way as to render otiose other ways of talking about things. "Cause and effect," he writes, are "conventional fictions for the purpose of designation and communication" and he admonishes us not to "project and mix this symbol world into things as if it existed "in itself" (*BGE* 21: 29)—which, by confusing context with cause, is what the determinist does. Insofar as the traditional problem of freedom of will rests upon these confusions, then it fails in Nietzsche's view to get off the ground. As he sees it, however, the problem of freedom of will is more than an expression of philosophical confusion. It conceals another problem altogether: namely, a practical—and, as such, "profoundly personal"—problem of responsibility. We avoid confronting *that* problem by turning it into an intellectual puzzle. As we will see presently, this is what he is getting at in saying that "in real life it is only a matter of *strong* and *weak* wills."

As we have seen, Nietzsche's argument in *BGE* 21 in favor of the view that all action is situated is meant above all to undermine our confidence that sense can be made of the idea of a literally and historically disembodied agency. As with perspectives more generally, we can see how the past makes freedom possible rather than being an obstacle to it only if we appreciate that disembodied agency is a contradiction in terms.[20] The argument is straightforward: something counts as *doing* something only where what it counts as doing is fixed beforehand. It makes no sense to try to do something where nothing counts as doing anything (or, alternately, where anything counts as doing something). This is why Nietzsche speaks in this context of a "rape and perversion of logic." But then why do we remain attached to the idea of disembodied agency? Why is belief in freedom of will in this sense one of those articles of faith that one considers true no matter how often it is refuted?[21]

To make further headway here, we need to see how *BGE* 21 joins to Nietzsche's rejection of determinism a diagnostic claim about the appeal (to some) of that view. Nietzsche writes:

> It is almost always a symptom of what is lacking in himself when a thinker senses in every "causal connection" and "psychological necessity" something of constraint, need, compulsion to obey, pressure, and unfreedom. (*BGE* 21)

Certainly, one can acknowledge that one's choices are made from a particular standpoint without thereby disowning one's responsibility for them. Nietzsche means to remove

---

[19] Compare Owen and Ridley 2003. See also Ridley 2007. For a reading that, by contrast, takes Nietzsche to be denying freedom of will in a sense that appears to accept the intelligibility of the usual debate, see Leiter 2001.

[20] Indeed, he calls it *"der beste Selbst-Widerspruch, der bisher gedacht worden ist."*

[21] See *GS* 347.

intellectual obstacles to our seeing how this can be so. In "real life," however, taking responsibility for what one says and does is easier for some than it is for others. It is, in Nietzsche's
view, a wish not to "be answerable for anything, or blamed for anything" (*BGE* 21) that typically underlies philosophical worries about determinism. "Owing to an inward self-contempt," those who are subject to this wish, "seek to *lay the blame for themselves somewhere
else*" (*BGE* 21). Weakness of will, here, is expressed as a wish in this way to evade responsibility for one's actions. It is in this sense, then, that the problem of freedom is a "personal"
problem of responsibility.[22]

According to *Beyond Good and Evil* 21, someone who experiences the past as an obstacle to agency actually wants just about the opposite of freedom. The desire for metaphysical freedom of will—the thought that the past represents an obstacle to action—reveals
itself instead to be a wish to avoid having to take responsibility for oneself. Thus, for all
Zarathustra's talk in "On Redemption" of the will's gnashing its teeth at the unrevisability of
the past, *Beyond Good and Evil* 21 suggests that ultimately the will can experience the past
as a *relief* from the pressures of responsibility. In other words, the person whose will is weak
in this sense tries to make an *excuse* of the past. Nietzsche contrasts such weakness with the
strength of people "who will not give up their "responsibility," their belief in *themselves*, the
personal right to *their* merits at any price" (*BGE* 21). Even those he calls the "vain races" feel
this way. Before we look more closely at this notion of responsibility, however, let us turn our
attention to *Beyond Good and Evil* 188, for Nietzsche speaks there specifically of the past as a
horizon that makes the future possible. We can then see more clearly how in particular cases
responsibility makes the future, as it were, actual.

In §188 Nietzsche refers to the conditions of agency as a "limited horizon" of possibilities
achieved by means of what he calls "discipline and cultivation" (*Zucht und Züchtung*) (*BGE*
188: 101), and he famously suggests that freedom may be thought of along the lines of artistic creation. Let us begin with the first point. He writes, "what is essential and inestimable
in every morality is that it constitutes a long compulsion" (*BGE* 188: 100). As did Aristotle,
Nietzsche thinks of such compulsion as a form of "training" (*anzüchten*) (*BGE* 188: 101).
And indeed, a little further on, he reiterates, "what is essential...seems to be that there
should be *obedience* over a long period of time and in a *single* direction" (*BGE* 188: 101).
"Slavery" in this sense makes intelligibility itself possible. Thus,

> the curious fact is that all there is or has been on earth of freedom, subtlety, boldness, dance,
> and masterly sureness, whether in thought itself or in government, or in rhetoric and persua-
> sion, in the arts just as in ethics, has developed only owing to the "tyranny of such capricious
> laws" (*BGE* 188: 100).

The point appears to be quite general. And Nietzsche's emphasis on, in effect, the cultural
context of choice is indeed a helpful corrective to the disembodied conception of agency
he rejects: "*every* morality is...a bit of tyranny against 'nature'; also against 'reason'" (*BGE*
188: 100; my emphasis). "Nature" is in quotation marks here because Nietzsche considers
the possibility of intelligibility achieved by means of training what is truly natural, what we

---

[22] Nietzsche is, of course, quite fond of this sort of diagnosis generally. See *BGE* 6. The reader who
finds such diagnoses too reductive is not likely to be reassured by the distinction Nietzsche draws there
between what he takes to be a properly *philosophical* commitment to such problems and the interest in
them shown by the mere scholar.

call "second nature." He puts "reason" in quotation marks as well to emphasize the fact that what training makes possible cannot be explained outside the context training achieves. Justification is internal to practices of justification that cannot themselves be justified in terms other than their own. Nietzsche's claim is that autonomy demands this kind of obedience to the past; freedom is possible only in context.

This last claim must be handled carefully, because it can be tempting to think that just because our ways of making sense of things make no sense from outside those very same ways of making sense of things, the latter are somehow arbitrary or, as Nietzsche ironically puts it here, "capricious." From the outside, in other words, the necessary "narrowing of our perspective" and the long compulsion that makes "virtue, art, dance, reason, spirituality" possible at all seems "forced, capricious, hard, gruesome, and anti-rational" (*BGE* 188: 101). Thus, what Nietzsche calls the "condition of life and growth" appears from the outside as "in a certain sense stupidity" (*BGE* 188: 101). But the point of qualifying "stupidity" in this way—as of putting "capricious" (*willkürlich*) in quotation marks or in the mouths of "anarchists"—is to steer us away from a careless philosophical inference from something's being the result of training to the conclusion that it is somehow arbitrary or ungrounded. What a practice makes possible is not undermined by its being a practice, but rather, if at all, by what the practice makes possible. This is why Nietzsche insists that without the "limited horizons" achieved by training, "you will perish and lose the last respect for yourself" (*BGE* 188: 102).

It is precisely the weak-willed—the metaphysicians and determinists of §21[23]—who find the idea of an external vantage point on their practices particularly tempting. From there, they will say, one's training is seen as an *arbitrary* imposition on nature, something that hinders one's ability to express oneself rather than what makes such self-expression possible in the first place. In other words, as before, a condition of agency seems to a "pure, will-less, painless, timeless knowing subject" (*GM* III.12) to make freedom impossible. But the view from nowhere does not support the lives we actually lead. Freedom demands context.

Nietzsche appeals to the experience of artists to clarify what freedom in context looks like.

> Every artist knows how far from any feeling of letting himself go his "most natural" state is—the free ordering, placing, disposing giving form in the moment of "inspiration"—and how strictly and subtly he obeys thousand-fold laws precisely then, laws that precisely on account of their hardness and determination defy all formulation through concepts. (*BGE* 188: 100)

Although Nietzsche himself does not do so in the passage at hand, it may be tempting to think in this context of musical examples, and the practice of improvisation may seem especially attractive in this regard. Success in improvisation depends upon doing the right thing at the right time, no more and no less, yet there seem to be no rules that guarantee success. Indeed, the fact that at a certain level of playing, the injunction to do "the right thing" may be all the conceptual precision available is exactly the point of the distinction Nietzsche draws here between concepts (*Begriffe*) and laws (*Gesetzen*). A law, in this sense, is a particular *kind* of necessity: the specific timbre or pitch contour required just here. As should be clear to anyone who has tried to learn how to do this, however, such necessities cannot be *deduced* from anything. Concepts and rules, in contrast to the laws the improviser obeys, are "not

---

[23] Those he calls "anarchists" and "utilitarians" in *BGE* 188.

free of fluctuation, multiplicity, and ambiguity" (*BGE* 188: 100–1). Any rule must, after all, be applied. This is part of what is meant when one is told to try to *hear* the right notes before playing anything. The activity of creation demands this form of passivity. The only concepts or rules to follow will be the "of-thumb" variety that demand the kind of musical interpretation they cannot themselves dictate. The exercise of such passivity is possible, however, only in the context provided in large part by one's past experience and training. The more experience of this sort, the more one can hear. By contrast, silence reigns in a vacuum.[24]

The demand either for concepts from which to *deduce* what one will do (determinism) or for freedom from "the tyranny of capricious laws" ("freedom of will in the superlative metaphysical sense") is, Nietzsche believes, driven by a wish not to have to stake oneself to anything. It is ultimately the expression of a wish for a kind of anonymity. As Nietzsche makes clear in *The Gay Science* 290, the results are rarely pretty. So far, however, the point seems quite general: *any* way of making sense of the world demands the context provided by long training. And the case of musical improvisation seems an apt illustration of this general point.

As I suggested, however, the appearance of generality is deceptive. Indeed, Nietzsche himself quickly zeroes in on a very different sort of example: his own training in Christian truthfulness.

> The long unfreedom of the spirit...the long spiritual will to interpret all events under a Christian schema and to rediscover and justify the Christian God in every accident...has shown itself to be the means through which the European spirit has been trained to strength, ruthless curiosity, and subtle mobility (*BGE* 188: 101).

The strength, curiosity, and mobility of spirit in question are pretty clearly Nietzsche's own, and the whole passage amounts in effect to a little genealogy of what *The Gay Science* calls the "subtler development of honesty and skepticism" (*GS* 110: 170) characteristic of his own philosophical "caution and care" (*GS* 109: 168). In other words, it is the "rigorous and grandiose stupidity" of *his* Christian past that "has *educated* [*erzogen*] the spirit" (*BGE* 188: 101) that guides his own work.

A well-known passage from *The Gay Science* quoted in the *Genealogy* makes the point even more explicitly.

> *What* in all strictness has really *conquered* the Christian God? The answer may be found in my *Gay Science* (section 357): "Christian morality itself, the concept of truthfulness taken more and more strictly, the confessional subtlety of the Christian conscience translated and sublimated into the scientific conscience, into intellectual cleanliness at any price. To view nature as if it were proof of the goodness and providence of a God; to interpret history to the glory

---

[24] This line of thought may make improvisation seem more like taking *dictation* than it often is. Thus, frequently enough, a musician must actually try out various things—say, by playing or singing them or by seeing them written down—to find out which is "right." In some sense, trial and error appear to have played an extremely important role in Beethoven's composing, and certainly the same also occurs in successful jazz improvisation and even more so in so-called new music. It is also worth noting that an improviser's situatedness involves more—say, at a *somatic* level (which would obviously include *limitations* on his or her technical facility (one can hear notes one cannot play))—than just training. Moreover, different musicians have different kinds and levels of devotion to practice. And so on. For a different but not incompatible treatment of these same issues, see Aaron Ridley 2007. I am grateful to Joel Taylor for instruction here.

of a divine reason, as the perpetual witness to a moral world order and moral intentions; to interpret one's experiences, as pious men long interpreted them, as if everything were pre-ordained, everything a sign, everything sent for the salvation of the soul—that now belongs to the *past*, that has the conscience *against* it, that seems to every more sensitive conscience indecent, dishonest, mendacious, feminism, weakness, cowardice: it is this rigor if anything that makes us *good Europeans* and the heirs of Europe's longest and bravest self-overcoming." (*GM* III.27: 160–1)

But this says, among other things, that *Nietzsche* himself—that is, the activity that constitutes him as this particular person—would have been impossible without this particular past. It is, in other words, his training in truthfulness that allows him to appreciate the truth about...his training in truthfulness. Genealogy—even the genealogy of genealogy itself—does not happen in a vacuum. But genealogy, as I noted above, is not dialectics: although Nietzschean truth-telling is a legitimate "heir" of its Christian ancestor, it cannot be *deduced* from it. Nothing about the Christian will to truth *compels* its self-overcoming.[25] This is why Nietzsche speaks of a "*fight*" (*Kampf*) in this connection:

> A thinker is now that being in whom the impulse for truth and those life-preserving errors clash for their first fight...Compared to the significance of this fight, everything else is a matter of indifference: the ultimate question about the conditions of life has been posed here, and we confront the first attempt to answer this question by experiment. To what extent can truth endure incorporation? That is the question; that is the experiment. (*GS* 110: 171)

The notion of an experiment here—one conducted in the very pages of Nietzsche's book—helps to temper the quasi-Hegelian tones of his talk of self-overcoming. The past does not *dictate* the future. One has a say in what one makes of it. And this is once again both a general and a specific point. Nietzsche is himself his own best example of making something of the past, but it is—indeed, Nietzsche himself is—something that must be "made." Being Nietzsche does not, as it were, happen by itself.

III

I turn now to the second temporal condition on agency: namely, the *übermenschlich* agent's relationship to his future. This is the other half of the problem of originality: the problem of how, in the face of one's dependence on the past, to say or do anything of one's own. To put the point in the terms of "On Redemption," it is the problem of how to transform "all 'it was' into 'thus I willed it!'" (*Z*: "On Redemption" 110) As our reading of *Beyond Good and Evil* 21 already indicates, an *übermenschlich* relationship to the future is achieved by taking

---

[25] It is true that Nietzsche speaks at the end of the *Genealogy* of "law" and "necessity" in this connection: "All great things bring about their own destruction, through an act of self-overcoming: thus the law of life will have it, the law of the necessity of 'self-overcoming' in the nature of life—the law-giver himself eventually receives the call: '*patere legem, quam ipse tulisti*'" (*GM* III.27: 161). But Nietzsche speaks of an "act" (not an event) of self-overcoming, and there is no reason to saddle him with a Hegelian conception of necessity here when he has available to him the notion of artistic necessity at stake in *BGE* 188. "Calls" can, after all, be ignored, and the experiment in question might turn out a failure.

responsibility for what one says and does. An overman is distinguished from his weak-willed and would-be timeless counterpart in that he takes the demands of such responsibility seriously. In doing so, he extends his life into the future in a way that the herd member does not. This is how he *becomes* historical, and it is in this way that he has a say in the meaning of what he does. In doing so, however, he makes himself accountable in the first place to others. Consequently, as we will see, *übermenschlich* individuality must be thought of as a form of *community*.[26] In other words, one becomes an overman by establishing a certain kind of relationship to others. It is in relationship to others that the temporality of agency is, as it were, lived out.

Nowhere does Nietzsche make this point as baldly as he does at the beginning of the second essay of the *Genealogy*, where he ascribes to the so-called sovereign individual qualities that make him *übermenschlich* in the sense that interests me here.[27] Such a person has in particular what Nietzsche calls "the right to make promises" (*GM* II.1: 57) and is thereby the "master of a *free* will" (*GM* II.2: 59). He is said, moreover, to possess a "memory of the will" thanks to which he is able to "stand security for *his own* (or as the German has it: [*als*] as) *future*" (*GM* II.1: 58). Of course, sovereign individuality "as future" is possible only on the basis of the past, but Nietzsche emphasizes the importance of forgetfulness in this context to warn against a kind of hypertrophy of the memory that binds one to the past in such a way that no future (and hence no present) is possible. By contrast, a healthy memory more or less *constitutes* the individual as someone oriented toward the future: he remembers not so much where he was, but rather where he is going.[28]

The sovereign individual's ability to "ordain the future" thus presupposes but is not reducible to a "preparatory" background of training that, as Nietzsche puts it, "*makes* [him] to a certain degree necessary, uniform, like among like, regular, and consequently calculable" (*GM* II.2: 59). Again, the distinction Nietzsche draws between training and the normativity training makes possible must be handled with care lest we conclude from the fact of the former the metaphysical arbitrariness of the latter. As we saw above, his point is that there is no standpoint from which to complain in *philosophical* tones about "the severity, tyranny, stupidity, and idiocy involved in" (*GM* II.2: 59) this kind of training, for it is the training itself that makes standpoints possible in the first place. This is why he speaks of "prehistory" in this context. Training—what he calls "the morality of mores"—makes being historical in the sense of being able to stand security for the future possible at all. Indeed, in his view, "the labor performed by man upon himself during the greater part of the human race, his entire

---

[26] Robert Pippin emphasizes this element of community in Zarathustra's search for an audience. See Pippin 2006a: p. xxvii.

[27] I have defended this reading at length in Randall Havas 1995. See also Randall Havas 1996, 2000, and 2005. A similar account has been defended in Owen 2007 and in Strong 2006.

[28] Nietzsche does not commit himself to the existence of such individuals. He does say that the problem of "breeding" such an animal has been "solved," but only "to a large extent" (*GM* II.1). We easily go astray if we think of the sovereign individual as a kind of Kantian moral agent slavishly devoted to bringing his actions into accord with the moral law. Nietzsche is clear that it is not the presence or absence of rationality that distinguishes the sovereign individual from the rest of us, but rather his willingness to take responsibility for what he says, to honor those commitments. Certainly, nothing prevents there being such individuals as Nietzsche values. A person may well make use of his past by guaranteeing his future in this way, but such a way of life remains, in Nietzsche's view, the exception to a general rule of last man-ish conformity and herd morality.

pre-historic labor" (*GM* II.2: 59) is justified *only* to the degree that it makes such autonomy possible. Without the autonomy it makes possible, the past is meaningless and in this sense *pre*historical.

As I stressed above, however, nothing *guarantees* the transition from prehistory to history (from the morality of mores to responsibility). This is why Nietzsche speaks of *responsibility* in this context: nothing *forces* the individual to take responsibility for himself. Indeed, in a sense, I *cannot* be forced to take responsibility for myself. The point is familiar from Kant: the result of force is always something other than responsibility. Whence, I submit, Nietzsche's apparent hedging of bets at the beginning of the second part of the *Genealogy* about whether in fact there are any such individuals. Our training has done all it can do to make this way of life possible; the rest is, so to speak, up to us. Thus, in insisting that such prehistorical training is a "means" (*das Mittel*), a presupposition of the way of life characteristic of "the man who has his own independent, protracted will and *the right to make promises*" (*GM* II.2: 59) he does not mean to suggest that as we stand, we are ourselves such individuals. Indeed, his challenge to us is precisely that we are *not*.[29]

Nietzsche emphasizes above all the *linguistic* dimension of individuality in these pages: the sovereign individual's "promises" are acts of speech, and he demonstrates his "right" to those acts to the degree that he takes responsibility for them. By contrast, those who do not take responsibility for their promises are "feeble windbags" and "liar[s]" (*GM* II.2: 60), "not," as Emerson has it, "false in a few particulars, authors of a few lies, but false in all particulars."[30] These are the weak-willed people of *Beyond Good and Evil* 21, those "Schopenhauer as Educator" refers to as lazy "factory products," mere copies of one another. But talk of promising is meant to emphasize that speech acts are, in the first instance, commitments made to those to whom one speaks. "Promising" is thus the name of a certain kind of human relationship: the kind that those Nietzsche calls metaphysicians, utilitarians, and anarchists seek to avoid. The sovereign individual thereby distinguishes himself from the "mass" of irresponsible speakers, but not from his "peers" (*die ihm Gleichen*) (GM II.2: 60). The solitude he seeks is thus from the herd, not from fellow members of his "mighty community" (*UM* 160).

Where speakers fail to honor their obligations to one another, the result is something less than community. Because no one in the herd takes responsibility for what he says, nothing said there has any value. "Nihilism" is Nietzsche's name for the herd's devotion to keeping things this way. In this sense, nihilism is evasion of the responsibility that is constitutive of the form of human freedom expressed in genuine community. The sense of community at stake here can appear quite abstract, divorced as it is from any particular set of values that might be expressed by this or that social hierarchy. But use of a definite or indefinite article in this context is bound to mislead. For it can be tempting to ask *which* community might be at stake here, when in fact Nietzsche does not have in mind community in this sense at all (e.g., the sense in which one speaks, for example, of the "academic community"). Thus, neither Nietzsche's masters nor their slavish counterparts count as communities in the sense that interests us here. Instead, like the overman, community in this sense is possible, if at all, only in the wake of the death of God. Roughly: only when one ceases to believe that

---

[29] For more on the idea that we are not animals with the right to make promises, see Havas 1995, especially the last chapter where I discuss this claim at length.

[30] Emerson 1983: 264.

one's actions are dictated by a higher power can one enter into the kind of mutuality constituted by the exercise of responsibility. That is why nothing Nietzsche says about the kind of person who occupies the herd suggests that he believes that participation in community is to be restricted to members of some social class or other. Nietzschean community is, as it were, simply what happens whenever two or more speakers make themselves responsible to each other.

According to the *Genealogy*, then, the individual exists *essentially* in relationship to others. That is why Nietzsche insists that the individual

> possesses his *measure of value*: looking out upon others from himself, he honors or he despises; and just as he is bound to honor his peers [*die ihm Gleichen*] ... he is bound to reserve a kick for the feeble windbags who promise without the right to do so and a rod for the liar who breaks his word even at the moment he utters it (*GM* II.2: 60).

In saying that praise for his peers and contempt for the rest is *necessary* ("*nothwendig*") for the individual, Nietzsche is saying that community achieved by individuality is both fundamentally *different* from and *better* than life in the herd. Community and herd do not, that is, represent two competing ways of life: the latter is instead the failure of the former. The individual is thus not free to be tolerant toward the herd or to consider himself—his individuality—in some way optional. This is how the notions of pathos of distance and order of rank are expressed in this context.

As we have seen, however, in the broader context of Nietzsche's conception of agency in general, *any* action has the character of a promise. All actions are, in this sense, commitments. It is only when we forget this point that the picture of a disembodied doer behind his or her deed begins to seem to make sense, and we end up with the philosophical picture of actions as bodily movements caused by intentions. Once the usual problem of free will obtrudes on our philosophical attention, we begin to wonder what *kind* of causation might be at stake here or whether our sense of freedom is perhaps an illusion. We wonder, that is, whether we ever really are in control of what happens to us, whether we are, in a word, the *origin* of what we do. Nietzsche's thought, however, is that in "real life" (*im wirklichen Leben*) (*BGE* 21: 29) it is in honoring our commitments that we settle the question of our originality. It is our failure to live up to them that makes us factory products. As he sees us, in other words, we are—as a matter of *fact*, not of necessity—mostly *not* in control of what happens to us. But this claim does not amount to a philosophical solution to a philosophical problem. The problem of originality is instead the "profoundly personal" problem of responsibility to be solved case by case by each of us, none for the other. But, again, because the commitments of agency more generally are, like promises, commitments to others, Nietzsche characterizes those with the right to make promises as, above all, *trustworthy* (*die Zuverlässigen*). Unlike the majority of people, they can be relied upon—whence the importance to Nietzsche of the sovereign individual's "peers" (*GM* II.2: 60).[31]

As was the case in *Beyond Good and Evil* 188, the appearance that Nietzsche is advancing a general account of agency to replace the disembodied account he rejects is deceptive. For the point about responsibility is, in the end, a point about *us*: we are the ones who, in his view, fail to take responsibility for what we do. This means that we are the ones whose

---

[31] See, for example, *BGE* 260 and 265, "What is Noble." I discuss the importance for Nietzsche of peers/equals in a well-lived life in more detail in Havas 2005.

lives represent, in effect, a failure of community. We are, in a word, a herd, and not just any herd, but rather the particular herd that fails to make something of its particular Platonic/Christian past. All it takes to get us out of these straits, however, is what the *Genealogy* styles an "act of will" (*GM* II.1: 58): namely, the assumption of the burdens of accountability. That seemingly slight difference, it turns out, makes all the difference in the world.

Responsibility might seem too thin a notion on which to ground Nietzsche's distinction between a well-lived life and the dismal alternative Nietzsche thinks we mostly live; it is true that it is unclear at best how one might derive specific content from the notion of responsibility alone. But we must bear in mind the *kind* of content Nietzsche thinks our lives lack. It is tempting to think that Nietzsche means to be providing here a kind of existentialist categorical imperative: do only what you are prepared to take responsibility for. But this does not mean that he thinks there is, as it were, a *procedure* according to which any responsible agent may derive the actions that are permitted from that standpoint. In the abstract, of course, "just about anything" might seem like a plausible answer to the question "for what may one take responsibility?" And so, in the abstract, the question seems empty. But Nietzsche does not mean the question to be asked in the abstract. He does not offer it as a rule from which an agent's conduct may be *deduced*. Taking responsibility is rather the means by which the question of the agent's originality may be settled. Answering the question, "for what am I responsible?" is how we redeem our past and its "it was," transform it into "thus I willed it." Moreover, as we have seen, Nietzsche believes that the ability to ask that question is itself possible only now that belief in God has become unbelievable, because in the past that belief was thought, in one way or another, to disburden the agent of his responsibility for what he did. Thus, in distinguishing us from the herd, responsibility distinguishes us from our past and thereby makes it our own. And, as we have also seen, without our willingness to assume that burden, that past remains all it has ever been: namely, a "grandiose stupidity."

This last point is, I think, obvious, and as such it is easy to miss. The "pre-historic labor" to whose "severity, tyranny, stupidity, and idiocy" the *Genealogy* refers is the very same Christian "tyranny,...caprice,...rigorous and grandiose stupidity" *Beyond Good and Evil* §188 credits with having "*educated* the spirit" and with fostering its—that is to say, Nietzsche's—"strength, ruthless, curiosity, and subtle mobility" (*BGE* 188: 101). It is that "two thousand years of training in truthfulness that finally forbids itself the *lie involved in belief in God*" (*GM* III.27: 160). Thus, the training that makes Nietzsche possible makes us possible as well.

On this reading, then, by telling the truth about, among other things, our ability to tell the truth, Nietzsche himself turns out to be the kind of *übermenschlich* individual heralded in the *Genealogy* and elsewhere. But his truth telling *qua telling* is told to his readers. And the question of the nature of that relationship turns out to provide the context for the introduction of the notion of the overman in *Thus Spoke Zarathustra* to which I turn in conclusion.

IV

An overman, then, is someone who has overcome his human, all-too-human resistance to the temporal character of agency by taking responsibility for the choices he makes. In this sense, his way of life is, in being historical, nevertheless unprecedented. No one has or could have been this particular individual. It is in this way that individuality is both historical and original. "No one," as Nietzsche puts it, "could have promised its appearance, although everything... was preparing for and growing toward it!" (*GM* II.3: 60).

As an agent in this sense the overman is spread out in time by taking up possibilities made available to him by his training and projecting them into the future. And in doing so, the overman is a member of "a mighty community" of his peers. But an *übermenschlich* way of life is, we saw, historical in a further sense as well. In this second sense of "historical," Nietzsche is his own best example of making something of the past. And this points us to the possibility of a future for Nietzsche's *readers* as well. To desire a future in this way is, in effect, to desire oneself. But how can Nietzsche make their future appeal to them in this sense, if they do not already to some degree desire it?

Nietzsche's difficulty finding appropriate readers is just what Plato says he should expect. A philosopher who has "seen the madness of the majority... and just like a man who has fallen among wild animals and is neither willing to join them in doing injustice nor sufficiently strong to oppose the general savagery alone" but who "seeing others filled with lawlessness... is satisfied if he can somehow lead his present life free from injustice and impious acts"... has nevertheless not accomplished the "greatest [thing] since he didn't chance upon a constitution that suits him. Under a suitable one," Plato goes on, "his own growth will be fuller, and he'll save the community as well as himself" (*Rep.* 496c–497b).[32] In other words, a true philosopher must both "go down" and expect the hostility of those he meets there. His "growth" and that of his peers depend upon his overcoming that hostility. Which of course does not mean that it *will* in fact be overcome. Indeed, everything would seem to point Nietzsche in the direction of hopelessness.

Certainly, Zarathustra finds that simply *announcing* the overman is pointless. He says to those assembled in the marketplace of the Motley Cow:

> *I teach you the overman.* Human being is something that must be overcome. What have you done to overcome him?... The overman is the meaning of the earth. Let your will say: the overman *shall be* the meaning of the earth! I beseech you, my brothers, *remain faithful to the earth* and do not believe in those who speak to you of extraterrestrial hopes! (Z: "Prologue" 6)

Predictably, however, those within earshot of Zarathustra's initial attempts to impart the wisdom he has gained in his mountaintop cave have no more use for it than do the crowd in *The Gay Science* 125 for the madman's claim that God is dead.[33] And their dismissal of his "teaching" on being told that "the greatest thing you can experience... is the hour of your great contempt" (Z: "Prologue" 6) is comprehensible enough, for they are not interested in their lives in what Zarathustra considers the right way. What would it take for them to become so?

The problem, in Nietzsche's view, is not that the people in the marketplace want the *wrong* things, but that in another sense, they want *nothing*. This is not to say that there is nothing they want, but rather that nothing they want truly matters to them. Indeed, in wanting nothing, they seem to Nietzsche to want precisely that nothing matter to them. That nothing matters is, in fact, what matters most to them. Nietzsche calls this condition "nihilism." The problem is

---

[32] Nietzsche himself makes the point explicitly in *BGE* 26.

[33] For more on the figure of the madman and the question of Nietzsche's audience, see Havas 1995. Compare David Owen 2007: 50–9.

thus worse than their not being able rationally to rank their desires. In having, as Zarathustra puts it, no "goal" (*Ziel*) of their own[34] (Z: "Prologue" 9), they have only such desires as "factory products" can have. They are copies, not originals. But being in this sense an original is not one goal among others. It is instead a condition of having any goals of one's own at all.

Convincing someone to value something he does not already value is, at best, deeply problematic. A person's desires can indeed be manipulated, but, as Hume emphasized, it is not clear that one can be *argued* into wanting something one does not already want. But, as we have seen, the problem for Nietzsche is subtly different. Thus, when he has Zarathustra say that the last men have no goal, that they lack a goal of their own, his point, as I said, is not that they have no desires at all—whatever that might mean. Nor is the difficulty that they have no higher order goals by reference to which to rank the desires they do have. That would indeed be a problem for them, but it is not the problem on which Nietzsche focuses his attention. Their problem is rather that they have no desire *for themselves.*

According to Zarathustra, our "highest hope" (Z: "Prologue" 9) should be the overman— that is, to be over man. But that does not mean that we are to become someone *other* than who we are. The goal, as Nietzsche puts it elsewhere, is to become what one is. This is the idea I have tried to explain in terms of the temporality of agency: the *übermenschlich* individual becomes who he is to the degree that he takes responsibility for what he says and does. "Hope" is thus another name for what the *Genealogy* calls "ordaining the future." Such hope is indeed "for" the future, but specifically for *having* a future at all. In this sense, the would-be overman is his own best hope. Zarathustra's difficulty finding an audience suggests that we might be, in this sense, hopeless.[35]

BIBLIOGRAPHY

(A) Works by Nietzsche

BGE   *Beyond Good and Evil*, trans. Walter Kaufman. New York: Vintage, 1966.
GS   *The Gay Science*, trans. Walter Kaufmann. New York: Vintage, 1974.
GM   *On the Genealogy of Morals*, trans. Walter Kaufmann. New York: Vintage, 1967.
UM   *Untimely Meditations*, trans. R. J. Hollingdale. New York: Cambridge University Press, 1977.
Z   *Thus Spoke Zarathustra*, trans. Adrian Del Caro. New York: Cambridge University Press, 2006.

(B) Other Works Cited

Acampora, Christa Davis. 2006. "On Sovereignty and Overhumanity: Why It Matters How We Read Nietzsche's *Genealogy* II:2," in Christa Davis Acampora (ed.), *Nietzsche's On the Genealogy of Morals: Critical Essays*. New York: Rowman & Littlefield Publishers, 147–61.
Alderman, Harold. 1977. *Nietzsche's Gift*. Athens: Ohio University Press.

---

[34] Nietzsche's German makes the point explicitly: "*Es is an der Zeit, dass der Mensch sich sein Ziel stecke*" (my emphasis).

[35] I am grateful to David Cerbone, Anthony Coleman, Ken Gemes, Tim Gould, Robert Guay, Melissa Weissberg, and especially Ed Minar for helpful discussion of the ideas in this paper.

Clark, Maudemarie. 1990. *Nietzsche on Truth and Philosophy*. Cambridge: Cambridge University Press.

Emerson, Ralph Waldo. 1983. "Self-Reliance," in Joel Porte (ed.), *Emerson: Essays and Lectures*. New York: Library of America, 257–82.

Gemes, Ken. 2006. "Nietzsche on Free Will, Autonomy and the Sovereign Individual," *Proceedings of the Aristotelian Society* 80.1 (supp. vol): 321–38.

Hatab, Lawrence. 2005. *Nietzsche's Life Sentence*. New York: Routledge.

Havas, Randall. 1995. *Nietzsche's Genealogy: Nihilism and the Will to Knowledge*. Ithaca: Cornell University Press.

Havas, Randall. 1996. "Nietzsche and Ordinary Language Philosophy," *International Studies in Philosophy* 28.3: 133–46.

Havas, Randall. 2000. "Nietzsche's Idealism," *Journal of Nietzsche Studies* 20 (Fall): 90–9.

Havas, Randall. 2005. "Nietzschean Equality," *Philosophical Topics* 33.2: 89–117.

Heidegger, Martin. 1961. *Nietzsche*. Pfullingen: Verlag Günter Neske.

Heidegger, Martin. 1962. *Being and Time*, trans. John Macquarrie and Edward Robinson. New York: Harper and Row.

Jenkins, Scott. 2003. "Morality, Agency, and Freedom in Nietzsche's Genealogy of Morals," *History of Philosophy Quarterly* 20.1 (January): 61–80.

Lambert, Lawrence. 1986. *Nietzsche's Teaching: An Interpretation of "Thus Spoke Zarathustra."* New Haven: Yale University Press.

Leiter, Brian. 2001. "The Paradox of Fatalism and Self-Creation in Nietzsche," in John Richardson and Brian Leiter (eds), *Nietzsche*. New York: Oxford University Press, 281–321.

Loeb, Paul. 2001. "Time, Power, and Superhumanity," *Journal of Nietzsche Studies* 21: 27–47.

Loeb, Paul. 2006a. "Finding the *Übermensch* in Nietzsche's *Genealogy of Morality*," in Christa Davis Acampora (ed.), *Nietzsche's "On the Genealogy of Morals": Critical Essays*. New York: Rowman & Littlefield Publishers, 163–76.

Loeb, Paul. 2006b. "Identity and Eternal Recurrence," in Keith Ansell Pearson (ed.), *A Companion to Nietzsche*. New York: Blackwell, 171–88.

May, Simon. 1999. *Nietzsche's Ethics and his War on "Morality."* New York: Cambridge University Press.

Nehamas, Alexander. 1985. *Nietzsche: Life as Literature*. Cambridge, Mass.: Harvard University Press.

Owen, David. 2007. *Nietzsche's "Genealogy of Morals."* London: Acumen Publishing.

Owen, David and Ridley, Aaron. 2003. "On Fate," *International Studies in Philosophy* 35.3: 63–78.

Pippin, Robert. 1988. "Irony and Affirmation," in Michael Allen Gillespie and Tracy B. Strong (eds), *Nietzsche's New Seas*. Chicago: University of Chicago Press, 45–71.

Pippin, Robert. 2006a. "Introduction," in Adrian Del Caro and Robert B. Pippin (eds), *Thus Spoke Zarathustra*. Cambridge: Cambridge University Press, pp. viii–xxxv.

Pippin, Robert. 2006b. "Lightning and Flash, Agent and Deed," in Christa Davis Acampora (ed.), *Nietzsche's On the Genealogy of Morals: Critical Essays*. New York: Rowman & Littlefield Publishers, 131–45.

Plato. 2004. *Republic*, trans. C. D. C. Reeve. Indiana: Hackett.

Reginster, Bernard. 2006. *The Affirmation of Life*. Cambridge, Mass.: Harvard University Press.

Richardson, John. 2006. "Time and Becoming" in Keith Ansell Pearson (ed.), *A Companion to Nietzsche*. New York: Blackwell, 208–29.

Ridley, Aaron. 2007. "Nietzsche on Art and Freedom," *European Journal of Philosophy* 15.2: 204–24.

Strong, Tracy. 2000. *Nietzsche and the Politics of Transfiguration* (expanded edition). Chicago: University of Illinois Press.

Strong, Tracy. 2006. "Genealogy, the Will to Power, and the Problem of a Past," in Christa Davis Acampora (ed.), *Nietzsche's On the Genealogy of Morals: Critical Essays*. New York: Rowman & Littlefield Publishers, 93–108.

CHAPTER 21

··

ORDER OF RANK

··

ROBERT GUAY

1 INTRODUCTION

THE renown of "order of rank" (*Rangordnung*), as a term of art, suffers in comparison to some of Nietzsche's more famous locutions. Nietzsche nevertheless makes two intriguing claims about order of rank: that it is the key to the very task of philosophy and that we inevitably misunderstand it.

This conjunction of claims presents us with at least three reasons why an inquiry into Nietzsche's notion of "order of rank" should be fruitful and thus worth pursuing. One is that although the term does not appear often, it appears more often than many more famous notions and is very well represented in Nietzsche's work. Nietzsche invokes "order of rank" from the early unpublished essays, such as "On the Future of Our Educational Institutions,"[1] to the very end of his career. Indeed, Nietzsche's usage of the term is most concentrated in what is arguably his decisive post-Zarathustra period: "order of rank" was even, along with "will to power" and "revaluation of values," among the titles that Nietzsche sketched out for his projected masterpiece.[2] Another reason to inquire into "order of rank" is that it marks off where Nietzsche's position is most untimely. Nietzsche means to advocate some form of hierarchy in opposition to what he sees as an unreflective modern consensus on egalitarianism. Attention to this distinctive aspect of Nietzsche's thought thus affords us a rare opportunity to confront what is, at least in Nietzsche's view, an otherwise unexamined set of commitments. A third reason to inquire into order of rank is that Nietzsche identifies doing so with his philosophy as a whole. In his notebooks, Nietzsche writes, "my philosophy is directed at order of rank" (*KSA* 12: 280). And at about the same time in the published writings, Nietzsche characterizes himself, "free spirits," and the future task of philosophers as concerned with order of rank. Understanding order of rank is essential to understanding Nietzsche's philosophical enterprise.

---

[1] See *KSA* 1: 699.
[2] On this see Janz 1978: vol. II, p. 380 and vol. II, p. 426. For some title sketches, see, for example, *KSA* 11: 692 and *KSA* 13: 196.

In what follows, I shall attempt to clarify and explain Nietzsche's notion of order of rank by presenting features of Nietzsche's discussion and a series of rival interpretations of it. I shall present Nietzsche's notion in terms of its "problematic" character, its sphere, its ground, and its social character. In doing so, I shall explicate Nietzsche's position by drawing a number of contrasts with the interpretations that I refer to as Natural Aristocracy, Mythic Archaism, Political, and Anthropological. I shall have to present these interpretations somewhat schematically, in some abstraction from the positions of particular individuals. I nevertheless hope to show the superiority of my own favored interpretation, which I refer to as Transcendental. On this interpretation, Nietzsche presents order of rank not substantively, but as a condition for the availability of normative authority. In any case I intend to illuminate the importance and centrality of order of rank in Nietzsche's thought.

2 The Problem

One typical feature of Nietzsche's discussions of order of rank is that Nietzsche identifies it as a *problem*. Nietzsche, that is, typically provides neither a specific ranking of things nor a principle of ordering,[3] but rather uses "order of rank" to identify something indeterminate or unresolved. The "problem" that Nietzsche thus identifies could arguably be one that the order of rank has, such as with application, or it could be that order of rank is itself problematic. The most basic formulation of this is simply "the problem of order of rank" (*HAH* I: Preface 6, 7), but Nietzsche alternately discusses "the *problem of value*, the determination of *the order of rank among values*" (*GM* I: 17), which seems to be equivalent.[4] Even where Nietzsche does not specifically discuss the general problem of order of rank, he alludes to its problematic character, either with such a phrase as "the question of rank" (*BGE* 265), or more indirectly, such as when he concludes a discussion of height and rank by posing the question, "Is greatness *possible*?" (*BGE* 212). Just as this question remains unanswered, so Nietzsche consigns the "solution" of the problem to "the future task of philosophers" (*GM* I: 17). Nietzsche even treats recognizing the problem as an accomplishment unto itself:

> Given that it is the problem of order of rank about which we may say that it is *our* problem, we free spirits: only now, in the midday of our life, do we understand what sorts of preparations, detours, tests, experimentations, disguises the problem needed before it was *allowed* to rise up before us … (*HAH* I: Preface 7)

Here, since the depicted agency is enigmatic, it is perhaps unclear whose accomplishment the recognition of the problem is. But Nietzsche seems not only to identify "order of rank" as a problem, but also to identify *with* it.

---

[3] Nietzsche occasionally offers an ordering in a specific domain: for example, *D* 446 seems to classify thinkers as "superficial," "deep," and "the dear underground." And he occasionally reports a ranking without affirming it himself, such as at *GS* 115. But in general, rankings seldom appear either with the term "order of rank" or otherwise.

[4] There is also an "order of rank of problems" (*BGE* 213), which might suggest that there is a problem of order of rank of problems, which would presumably itself have a ranking, but I will leave that aside.

I wish to suggest two initial interpretive possibilities for what the "problem of order of rank" is. The first can be called "Natural Aristocracy." According to this interpretation, the problem is determining the correct or suitable classification. There are natural, categorical differences among persons, and thus philosophers must identify both these categories and their relative rankings.[5] Once this identification is accomplished, there could then be tasks of implementation: for example, consolidating the type-groupings, supporting the higher-ranked types, or making the rank distinctions socially meaningful or enforced. But the implementation problem presupposes, in any case, the prior identification of types. So on this reading, Nietzsche is relatively unconcerned with how or why there should be categorical differences, but rather interested in figuring out roughly who belongs in which category. The second possibility for interpreting the problem of order of rank can be called the Normative. On this interpretation, the problem is not identifying the correct classifications, but explaining the very possibility of rank distinction and what such distinctions amount to. The problem that Nietzsche confronts, that is, is about the normative: how there can be normative authority at all, such that some things are better (or "higher") than others, at least. This interpretation accords a higher level of generality to the problem than the previous interpretation: whereas the Natural Aristocracy interpretation would locate Nietzsche's aim in saying that x is better than y (after, of course, identifying the correct categories), the Normative interpretation would locate Nietzsche's aim in explaining or possibly furnishing the conditions under which such authoritative comparative evaluations obtain or make sense. This of course is not to say that Nietzsche is somehow free from substantive judgments, but merely that his explanatory focus is the picture into which substantive judgments fit. The Normative interpretation, incidentally, is a component of the interpretation that I shall later identify as "Transcendental."

I now want to present five sets of considerations in support of the Normative interpretation over the Natural Aristocracy interpretation. My reason for devoting so much attention to this interpretive conflict is that the Natural Aristocracy interpretation is the most basic of those that differ from my own preferred interpretation: to a great extent, one can understand the other competing interpretations as variations on Natural Aristocracy. So my hope is that the considerations presented here will contribute to clarifying the full range of possibilities.

The first respect in which the Natural Aristocracy interpretation fails is by offering a version of order of rank that is incompatible with there being a genuine "problem" of the sort that Nietzsche suggested. According to Natural Aristocracy, the various ranks are natural kinds and the values associated with them are either noncognitive or also natural.[6] The only possible problems, then, are epistemic ones, such as how to accurately discern the natural kinds, or are practical ones peculiar to particular ranks, such as harms sustained by the higher ranks in a rank-averse society. In Nietzsche's account, however, the relevant problem

---

[5] I associate this interpretation with writings by Brian Leiter and Thomas Hurka, although neither is specifically concerned with "the problem of order of rank" and each introduces significant complications into his interpretation. For example, for Leiter, the types are natural kinds, but the evaluations of them are neither true nor false (at least at Leiter 2002: 152). Hurka sees Nietzsche as not supporting any clear metaethical position, but asserts "that he at least takes his claims to be factual" (Hurka 2007: 12). But I take these differences, and even whether these writers in particular advocate some form of the Natural Aristocracy interpretation, as unimportant for the present enterprise.

[6] This, of course, does not exhaust the metaethical possibilities, but I do not think there is another metaethical option that both fits with Natural Aristocracy and makes a difference for the present point.

is inherent in order of rank itself, not pursuant to an unproblematic order. For example, Nietzsche writes,

> ...a philosopher, in case there could be a philosopher today, would be compelled to posit the greatness of humanity, the concept "greatness," precisely in its range and multiplicity, in its unity in diversity: he would even determine rank and worth according to how much and how many things someone takes upon himself and bears, how *far* someone could extend his responsibility. (*BGE* 212)

The issues here are not ones of discovering what the rankings are or how to manage their reception, but whether philosophy, greatness, and the determination of both value and rank are possible at all.[7] This is left an open question, even as Nietzsche specifies conditions for a partially successful resolution. Nietzsche does not present the problem of order of rank as epistemic and further suggests that in the absence of epistemic limitations the problem would be seen all the more distinctly rather than resolved: "...finally we could say, we free spirits: here—a *new* problem! Here a long ladder whose rungs we have sat upon and climbed...an order of rank that we *see*: here—*our* problem!" (*HAH* I: Preface 7) A clear, unobstructed view of order of rank reveals it as a problem, one that even experience of the ladder fails to address.

Another aspect of this difficulty for the Natural Aristocracy interpretation is that this interpretation misplaces the role of science. Since, on this interpretation, rankings apply to categories that are, as natural, themselves unproblematic, science would presumably have a role in identifying the categories. This role, indeed, would be the whole research program: beyond that identification, there would be little else to accomplish in addressing order of rank. Nietzsche, by contrast, characterizes the role of science as a subsidiary or "preparatory" one:

> From now on all sciences have to prepare for the future task of the philosophers: this task understood as the philosopher having to solve the problem of value, having to determine the order of rank of values. (*GM* I: 17)

Here Nietzsche does not even identify science as particularly important: his claim is not that science is significant, but that it should be subordinated to philosophy, from which it is clearly distinguished. Nietzsche additionally claims that the problem of order of rank is not even accessible from the standpoint of science: "'*Science*' *as prejudice.*—It follows from the law of order of rank that scholars...may never catch sight of the *great* problems and question marks..." (*GS* 373; cf. *BGE* 204). The Natural Aristocracy interpretation seems to call for precisely the sort of inquiry that according to Nietzsche misses the point.

The next four sets of considerations are related to the previous one, that the Natural Aristocracy interpretation is not compatible with the sense in which Nietzsche takes order of rank to be problematic: one could, that is, see these considerations as additional ways of filling out what Nietzsche means by "problem." The second set of considerations, for example, is that order of rank is something indeterminate, unstable, and constructed. Whereas according to Natural Aristocracy the categories are fixed and stable, for Nietzsche

---

[7] Nietzsche here distinguishes between value and rank; perhaps this distinction is between the categorization and the value assigned to the categories (or their members). But even here they have the same status: neither value nor rank is more natural or less problematic than the other.

the very possibility of such categorical distinctions seems perpetually unresolved. There is a particularly clear albeit qualified statement of this in *Daybreak*: "The order of rank of greatness for all past humanity is always not yet determined" (*D* 548; cf. *WP* 999).[8] More generally, Nietzsche suggests that order of rank is something that needs to be carried out rather than merely discovered. The most primitive example of this is the most famous in Nietzsche's work:

> On the contrary it was "the good" themselves, that is, the noble, powerful, high-stationed, and high-minded who felt and posited themselves and their activity as good, that is, of the first rank, in contradistinction to all that is low, low-minded, common, and vulgar.... What does utility have to do with them! The viewpoint of utility is, with regards to such a fiery eruption of the highest rank-ordering, rank-distinguishing value judgments, precisely as alien and inappropriate as possible. (*GM* I: 2 ; cf. *BGE* 260)

Here the "rank-ordering value judgments" *enact* the relevant distinctions, and the way they do so leaves the rankings open to revision. Additional outbreaks of rank-ordering and rank-distinguishing would presumably transform the judgments of the past and establish new norms, themselves subject to further revision. There can be no fixed standard by which to measure such transformations, since the availability of standards is just what the rank-ordering is meant to explain. The standards that Nietzsche invokes are accordingly variable and contingent: so, for example, "there are countless healths of the body" (*GS* 120), "master morality" is merely "the sign language of what has turned out well" (*CW* Epilogue), and, lest anyone think that this is predetermined, "success has always been the greatest liar" (*BGE* 209).

The third consideration that speaks against the Natural Aristocracy interpretation is that Nietzsche characterizes the problem of order of rank as processual: that is, the problem takes shape only within a particular dynamic. The naturalness of Natural Aristocracy implies that its rank distinctions obtain prior to any manifestation of them: even though the ranks can of course be socially manifest, such manifestations would only represent distinctions that already obtain. In Nietzsche's depictions of the relevant dynamic, by contrast, the distinctions only emerge out of the ongoing actualization of "the will to be oneself":

> ...the cleavage between human being and human being, status and status, the plurality of types, the will to be oneself, to stand out—what I call the pathos of distance—is typical of every *strong* age. The force of tension, its breadth between extremes, today becomes ever smaller... (*TI*: "Skirmishes of an Untimely Man" 37)

Here even "being oneself," or at least the will to be oneself, is dependent on status differentials, which in turn depend on "standing out," which depends on the tension between extremes—all of this suggests that the basic categories are not extricable from the dynamic as a whole. Personhood and status arise within a social framework that supports distinction. Elsewhere Nietzsche characterizes the relevant process as even more broadly encompassing:

> You should above all see with your own eyes where injustice is always greatest: namely, where life has developed at its smallest, narrowest, neediest, most inchoate and nevertheless cannot help but take *itself* as the end and meaning of things, and out of self-preservation secretly,

---

[8] I discuss Nietzsche's reason for insisting on indeterminacy in Guay 2007: 170.

contemptibly, and incessantly crumbles away and puts into question the higher, greater, richer—you should see the problem of *order of rank* with your own eyes and how power and right and extensiveness of perspectives grow with one another into the heights. (*HAH* I: Preface 6)

Here Nietzsche does not specify what the problem is or how it relates to the other terms, but it is invoked in a process of preservation and growth that includes not only ethical distinction but "extensiveness of perspective," among other things.

The fourth set of considerations that speak against the Natural Aristocracy interpretation relate to Nietzsche's overriding concern with "the human type." On the Natural Aristocracy interpretation, Nietzsche's preliminary task would be to distinguish the range of human types: by identifying the basic, fixed psychological underpinnings of different sorts of persons, one could then both group them into categories and assess which ones are better. Nietzsche, however, expresses his interest in order of rank not primarily in terms of various fixed types being better or worse than others, but in terms of what order of rank means for the possibility of "the human type." Nietzsche, that is, primarily takes an interest in human diversity: in the distinction among types rather than in promoting particular well-defined types. And the basis of this interest is not the particular types of human identity and affiliation for their own sake, but because they affect what it means to be human. These passages from *Beyond Good and Evil* demonstrate this interest:

> With one look he grasps everything that, given a favorable collection and augmentation of powers and tasks, could still be cultivated from the human being, he knows with all the knowledge of his conscience how the human being remains unexhausted for the greatest possibilities, and how already the type "human" has confronted mysterious decisions and new paths—he knows still better...what sort of wretched things have so far usually shattered someone of the highest rank who is still becoming...(*BGE* 203)
>
> Every heightening of the "human" type has so far been the work of an aristocratic society—and so will it always be: as a society that believes in a long ladder of order of rank and difference in worth between person and person...(*BGE* 257)

In these passages, Nietzsche shows no interest in the particularities of rank. Indeed, he cannot: the point that he wishes to make is a structural one, which covers many "aristocratic" societies and possibly human development in general. Since these societies presumably have different rankings, Nietzsche can neither claim to have identified fixed categories nor endorse all their rankings. Instead, Nietzsche's interest lies in claiming that the human type is mutable, that some potential changes in the human type represent improvements or heightenings, and that these changes depend in some way on observing or "believing in" order of rank. Of course, in making the structural point about rank, Nietzsche is committed to there being something that occupies the structure. But Nietzsche is less interested in arriving at a particular ranking than he is in identifying the role that rankings play in the different ways that there could be of being human.[9]

---

[9] Heidegger makes a similar observation when he remarks that "the question of 'the order of ranks' " does not belong to "the question of 'values' in general in themselves" but rather to "the question of *humanness*." See Heidegger 1999: §114.

Another way of considering the distinctiveness of Nietzsche's position on this matter is to contrast it with that of Herder, or at any rate the one that Herder ascribes to the natural scientist:

> The natural scientist presumes *no order of rank* among the creatures that he considers; to him all are equally dear and valuable. So, too, with the natural scientist of humankind. The Negro has just as much right to take the Caucasian for a deviant as does the Caucasian to take him for a beast. . . . In that period when everything was taking shape, nature cultivated *the human type* as variably as her workshop required and allowed. (Herder 1971: vol. II, p. 262 [10th Collection, Letter 116])[10]

In one respect Herder's and Nietzsche's concerns are close to one another. They are both concerned with discovering a common humanity within human diversity and moreover with the advancement or heightening of this shared humanity. But in another respect they are polar opposites. For Herder, the starting condition for his inquiry is that there is a range of natural human kinds, but there is *no* order of rank among them: to see them as natural in the relevant sense is precisely to set inter-typical value judgments aside and instead see advancement in terms of something like breadth of diversity. For Nietzsche, by contrast, the very distinctiveness of "the human type" crucially depends on order of rank. Human beings set themselves apart from the rest of nature by establishing rank distinctions, and presumably raise the status of the human type by doing so in better ways. So now we can reassert the contrast with the Natural Aristocracy interpretation. Natural Aristocracy adopts Herder's standpoint of the natural scientist by taking the basic typological distinctions as natural, but then combines it with an insistence on order of rank. Herder takes those two elements to be incompatible. And Nietzsche insists on order of rank, but does not approach rank-ordering from the standpoint of the natural scientist. Indeed, he cannot, since what he wants to explain is human self-separation from merely natural status of the sort that the scientist could adequately explain.

The fifth and final consideration that speaks against the Natural Aristocracy interpretation is that it views rank atomistically, whereas Nietzsche views rank as inherently social. On the Natural Aristocracy interpretation, that is, any individual's rank status, as a natural fact, can be isolated from every other individual's rank status. And since it is accordingly a contingent natural fact that rank is distributed in the way that it is, it is possible, at least in principle, for it to be distributed in any other way. It is possible, for example, for everyone to belong to the same rank, if only many accidents of birth had been different: if the world were luckier, everyone could be high-ranking at the same time. On Nietzsche's view, by contrast, this is not an unlikely possibility, but something nonsensical. Rank, for Nietzsche, crucially depends on relations with others, such that one achieves differential status by attaining some kind of socially derived authority.[11] Here is one of Nietzsche's typical examples:

---

[10] Nietzsche was of course familiar with this work: Colli and Montinari cite it as one of Nietzsche's sources for the idea of a "*gai saber.*" See *KSA* 11: 337.

[11] See *KSA* 11: 638, where in discussing the unity of the subject, Nietzsche refers to "the dependence of the ruler on the ruled and the conditions of order of rank and division of labor as making possible the individual and at the same time the whole."

Giving rank to one's people.—To have many great inner experiences and to rest upon and beyond them with a spiritual eye—that makes up the persons of culture, who give rank to their people. In France and Italy the nobleman does this, whereas in Germany, where the nobleman has so far belonged to the poor in spirit (perhaps not for much longer), priests, teachers, and their descendents do this. (*D* 198)

Rank, here, is rooted in something arguably private: having and acknowledging "inner experiences" in a certain way. These private experiences only translate into rank, however, with at least three subsequent steps. The bearers of such experiences need to occupy socially constituted roles: "nobleman" is a possibility, and so is priest or teacher, depending on circumstances. These roles, further, have to shape a culture, and this culture must represent the life of a people. The rank of a people, at least, could not exist outside of a complex structure of social relations. And this example illustrates another feature of the sociality of order of rank. In Nietzsche's account, the establishment of order of rank raises some above others, but at the same time brings everyone up: culture, for example, introduces hierarchies that contribute to a shared unity.

To recapitulate, Nietzsche characterizes order of rank as in some way a problem, and there are five sets of considerations that speak against the Natural Aristocracy interpretation of what this could mean. Nietzsche characterizes order of rank as intrinsically problematic, indeterminate, processual, especially relevant to "the human type" rather than to the diversity of human types, and social rather than atomistic; the Natural Aristocracy interpretation takes the opposing side in each of these matters. If we reject that interpretation, that the categories are naturally given and their relative rankings are themselves unproblematic, then we might turn to the Normative interpretation. On this alternative, the very idea that human beings, who distinguish themselves in part by what they believe in and care about, fall into fixed types is problematic for Nietzsche, and this provokes a series of questions such as how natural beings could sustain any normative order at all, what sort of social dynamic this would entail, how plastic our normative commitments might be, and how these commitments might affect and potentially raise our status as human beings. Most generally, Nietzsche is inquiring into the possible authority of normative distinction. The considerations that speak against the Natural Aristocracy interpretation support such a reading: that order of rank is indeterminate and problematic, that it develops through a social process, and that the way in which order of rank is sustained contributes to what human beings make of themselves.

We can confirm some features of the Normative interpretation by looking at three more passages. The first is one of Nietzsche's earliest and strangest uses of the notion of order of rank. He has not settled on his vocabulary yet, but the notion is clearly present despite the different terminology, which is all the more jarring in its context:

Whoever is breathed upon by this cool draft will hardly believe that even the concept…remains only as the *residue of a metaphor*, and that the illusion in the artistic transference of a nerve stimulus into images is, if not the mother then the grandmother of every concept. Within this dice game of concepts, "truth" means—using each die as indicated, counting its pips exactly, setting up the right headings, and never violating the order of caste and the sequence of rank-classes. (*KSA* 1: 882)

Here, from the "Truth and Lies" essay, is an early account of concepts that ends with what I take to be the preliminary version of order of rank, "order of caste and the sequence of rank-classes." Order of rank seems incongruous in a theory of concepts, but Nietzsche makes a distinction that gives it a place to fit in. Nietzsche divides his account into two parts, one concerning concept formation and the other concerning concept usage. The account of concept formation is vaguely neo-Kantian with some rhetorical flourishes: we receive information through the nervous system, these stimuli are translated into images, and concepts are the metaphorical residue left by the illusion that this process generates. The account of concept usage is very different, however. Rather than a physiological account of mental representations, the account of concept usage is an account of correctness according to standards. Such a split between formation and usage is probably untenable, but Nietzsche brings order of rank into play in the latter, to characterize linguistic practice as a rule-governed activity that is to be assessed by its own standard of rightness.[12] Order of rank conveys categorization and hierarchy, and Nietzsche accordingly uses the notion to characterize linguistic practice in terms of social authority and correctness rather than causal dispositions to respond. To invoke order of rank as Nietzsche does in this early passage, then, is to bring normative criteria to bear.

A similar passage about morality suggests another feature of the Normative interpretation. In *Human, All Too Human*, Nietzsche writes, "The order of rank of desirable things, which depends on whether a low, higher, or highest egoism wants one thing or another, decides, once accepted, what is moral and what is immoral" (*HAH* I: 42; cf. *BGE* 265). Here there are some similarities to the account of concepts. Nietzsche proposes a split between private psychology and social authority and places morality under the regulation of the latter. The additional element here, however, is that Nietzsche also proposes a split between order of rank and substantive norms. This might indeed have been present in Nietzsche's discussion of truth: there, order of rank was likely a background condition rather than a direct prescription for what to count as true. With morality, in any case, Nietzsche makes explicit that order of rank is not a set of substantive values, but the normative background that makes moral distinction possible. This normative background is not unnatural: it has a psychological history and requires a social process of acknowledgement. But it is prior to moral distinction and problematic in that its acceptance and ability to guide action is a contingent social circumstance. Since order of rank is the sort of thing that has a history, it could fail altogether.

We can turn back to the 1886 writings to find a third and final passage that confirms the Normative interpretation. In the Preface to the second edition of *Human, All Too Human*, Nietzsche employs the unsurprising metaphor of the ladder and offers a couple of surprising claims about what it means to be human:

> ... we first had to experience the most multiple and contradictory conditions of crisis and happiness in soul and body, as adventurers and circumnavigators of that inner world called "human," as ones who size up that "higher" and "over another" that is also called "human"— penetrating everywhere, almost without fear, spurning nothing, losing nothing, enjoying everything to the fullest, cleansing and as it were sifting everything from that which is accidental—until finally we could say, we free spirits: "here—a *new* problem! Here a long ladder whose rungs we have sat upon and climbed—that we ourselves have at some point *been*. Here is a higher, a deeper, an under-us, a monstrously long order, an order of rank, that we *see*: here—*our* problem!" (*HAH* I: Preface 7)

---

[12] Cf. Charles Taylor on Herder's criticism of Condillac on the origin of language in Taylor 1995.

There are three observations that I wish to make about this passage. First, although Nietzsche recounts a need for a preliminary experience of "crisis and happiness in soul and body," or more simply of "everything," "everywhere," the problem of order of rank cannot come into view until everything "accidental" has been cleansed away or sifted out. This would seem to exclude natural contingencies, chance events, and causal relations. So I take Nietzsche to be acknowledging that order of rank has physiological and historical conditions, but insisting that it concerns a normative order that is in some sense separable from actual circumstances or effects. Nietzsche is interested in possibilities of normative status that can become detached from their developmental history. Second, Nietzsche identifies a rich "inner world" and a "higher and over another" with the human as such. To be human, then, is not to occupy a specific rank in the great chain of being, but something that Nietzsche expresses primarily in terms of the height relation. That is, what Nietzsche takes as significant is not the placement in a hierarchy of types, but the very concern with the recognition of difference. To be human, then, is to be receptive to considerations about "height," where this is also equivalent to having an "inner world." This suggests that Nietzsche's interest in order of rank does not involve laying out a sequence but human responsiveness to normative distinction. Third, Nietzsche writes of free spirits that they are both seated on and sometimes identical to the ladder. This I think reinforces the previous points. There are not stable types or rankings, because one is mobile on the ladder. In fact, the free spirits seem to be permanently mobile on the ladder, since the ladder extends "monstrously" far in either direction. And persons are not placed in types: they are identified not with the rungs, which they sit upon, but with the ladder as a whole. Nietzsche's point once again is not that persons fall into rankings but that one becomes who one is in relation to a normative order that supports ascent and that one can sometimes identify with.

Some illustrations of the relevant contrasts might be helpful here. One way of thinking about what order of rank might mean is to imagine an archaic society. In this world, that there are ranks and the identity of those in the highest ranks are the most basic and apparent social facts. Everyone recognizes the status differentials, not only explicitly but also implicitly in the way that every economic and symbolic formation organizes itself around the hierarchy of rank. For the inhabitants of this world, then, there is simply no question of what rank means: the meaning is played out, even if begrudgingly, in countless interactions. Among other things, rank entails wealth, power, authority, prestige, and various culturally specific prerogatives, and no one contests the offices of rank because no one ever imagines that these things could be separated. This is the Natural Aristocracy interpretation, with two main differences. One is that Natural Aristocracy might assign different occupants to the positions, and thus epistemic problems might arise. The other is that if you were to ask someone in the archaic society for a justification of rank privileges, the response would be either befuddlement or a recitation of the familiar relationships by which rank positions are most likely transmitted. If one were to question the Natural Aristocracy reading for a justification, the response would be either befuddlement or the claim that rank distinctions have been identified by the natural sciences.

By contrast, one might think of what it might mean in a contemporary society to think about what being a "higher type" might amount to. There are no recognizable roles, except perhaps some vestiges of archaic ones, and even the language to describe such a status is lacking: one can imagine oneself to be "above the fray" or to have an "elevated sensibility," but all other language of height is entangled in notions of class or wealth, which is not what one means in thinking of someone as somehow special or "higher." (No one imagines that wealth or power entails superiority. There are too many obvious counterexamples and too many other things to aspire to be.) In this situation, it is not clear what it could possibly mean to be exceptional or "higher." The category does not come with social prerogatives or economic or political advantages; in fact, such a status might go generally unrecognized. And there are no identity conditions for a higher status: one can doubt about whatever qualities seem to set one apart whether they are indeed significant. The problem here is not merely epistemic. Given that both criteria and social implications are unclear, the very category itself is problematic. The status itself may be empty or meaningless, and indeed one could tell a long story, passing through Greek notions of heroism, Christian notions of inwardness, and Romantic notions of individuality, among other places, about why someone might come to think that there is an important status to occupy here. But one might be aware of all this, see the very questions as historically or causally determined, and still wonder whether it is possible to be in some sense "higher." Someone with these concerns—what substantive goods, whether internal or external, are genuinely worthwhile, how to make something exceptional of one's life and oneself, whether or not such an aspiration even makes sense—is, I think, close to what I have been calling the Normative interpretation. The main difference is that Nietzsche is not interested only in the substantive ends in terms of which one makes sense of one's aspirations to be somehow higher. At least as important for Nietzsche is that the very concern with possible rank is something that contributes to making us fully human.

What I have been trying to show in this section is that there are two main interpretive options with respect to "order of rank," and that these options reflect not only the textual evidence with respect to the "problem" of order of rank, but also a fundamental choice about how to understand Nietzsche's philosophical enterprise. On one alternative, Nietzsche is advocating a substantive picture of how life should be arranged for everyone. This picture is characterized by privileges or subordinations that some types of persons have in relation to others. The type differences are fully natural, where this entails being pre-social, unalterable, and amenable to discovery by the natural sciences. And the relative superiority of some types, along with their attendant privileges, would be beyond dispute for Nietzsche—not something that requires explanation or defense in any way. "Order of rank," on this interpretation, is both the basic character of human nature and the desired form of social life; its "problem" is that this basic character is disguised by false ideals. On the other alternative, Nietzsche is not advocating a substantive way of life—he has no such picture in mind—but offering reflections on the possibility of normative authority in general, where this is problematic both because it is unclear what it would mean for such authority to obtain among natural beings such as ourselves and because the status of the human being as such depends on a contingent social success. On the Normative interpretation that I have argued for, this second view of Nietzsche's philosophical enterprise is the correct one. Nietzsche, in discussing order of rank, means to question the possibility of normative authority, and in doing so to connect this matter to the structure of social life and what it means to be human.

3 Its Sphere

My aim in this section is to clarify what Nietzsche takes to be the sphere of order of rank. A typical understanding of this is that Nietzsche is writing about differences in rank among persons and perhaps other things only indirectly or derivatively. I shall suggest, by contrast, that Nietzsche takes order of rank to apply to everything, but primarily to values and thence to persons. This suggestion will of course require some explanation and might even seem like a small difference. It will further illuminate Nietzsche's conception of order of rank, however, and in doing so will help to eliminate two more rival interpretations, Mythic Archaism and the Political.

To clarify what I mean by the "sphere" of order of rank, it helps to start with an example. A widespread assumption, I think, is that *persons* are the primary sphere of order of rank. Natural Aristocracy, at least, adopts such a position: what is above all else subject to a ranking is either character types or the persons who instantiate them. Then one could presumably say that other things derivatively partake in rank status, according to their association with the relevant persons: so we might say that private jets or philosophy books or fancy uniforms are subject to ranking, depending on what the ranking of persons is and how such things relate to it. These derivative things could be either incidentally or intrinsically related. According to Natural Aristocracy, for example, jets, books, and uniforms would presumably be only incidentally related to the relevant ranks, since a person belongs to a rank independent of anything else; someone might disagree, however, and believe that without jets, books, and uniforms, each rank status simply would not obtain. In any case, the ranking of persons is fundamental.

One could, of course, rank anything: football teams, wines, vacuum cleaners, philosophy departments, and so on. So the sphere of order of rank could conceivably be any of those things. But none of those things would be philosophically interesting in the way that persons are, and Nietzsche does make reference to "higher persons" and "higher types." This, by itself, shows little: superiority in (even metaphorical) height is not equivalent to superiority in rank, and even if it were, this would not establish that persons are specifically relevant to Nietzsche's discussion of order of rank, or that there are not other things that are more importantly so. Presumably, however, a focus on persons as falling within the sphere of order of rank comes not only from the textual evidence, but also from a judgment about philosophical importance. Nietzsche's project is fundamentally an ethical one and his interest in human personality stems from this. And a significant feature of his project is his argument against what I earlier referred to as unreflective egalitarianism. The focus on persons as within the sphere of order of rank comes, then, from a consideration of Nietzsche's criticisms of Christian, democratic, or Kantian versions of universal equality, and viewing order of rank as a counterproposal to these.

I do not doubt that Nietzsche takes persons as falling importantly within the sphere of order of rank. But this is only a part of Nietzsche's position and not one that can be understood in isolation. This passage, for example, suggests a picture in which a worldly process produces a more expansive sphere:

> I would much rather flatter [the spiritually challenged but vigorous opponents of atheism] with my proposition that a high spirituality itself only exists as the final offshoot of moral qualities; that it is a synthesis of those conditions that are attributed to "exclusively moral" persons after they have been acquired, one at a time, through long discipline and practice, perhaps in whole chains of generations; that the high spirituality is precisely the spiritualization of justice and the kindly severity that knows itself to be charged with the maintenance of the *ordering of rank* in the world, among things themselves—and not only among persons. (*BGE* 219)

There are several interpretive challenges with respect to this passage, but the most obvious one is what Nietzsche intends in locating such an extensive "ordering of rank" in the world. Any response will need, perhaps surprisingly, to explain how morality and justice relate to order of rank. But however one meets that challenge, Nietzsche clearly and indiscriminately places "things themselves" within the sphere of order of rank.[13] The Natural Aristocracy interpretation cannot, I think, accommodate the processual nature of order of rank depicted here: its maintenance is a task that one is charged with, following a multigenerational practice. But no reading that focuses exclusively on persons can accommodate what Nietzsche suggests here about its sphere.

The interpretive challenge remains: whether we can make sense of Nietzsche's position if it both accords great significance to order of rank and places everything within its sphere. Without an explanation we could arguably dismiss such an expansive sphere as an aberration. My suggestion is that this aspect of Nietzsche's position makes the most sense as an account of the relationship between values and ends on one hand and persons on the other.[14] There are three main elements of this account. The first is that a hierarchy of values is essential to what Nietzsche refers to as "Life": "Living—is that not precisely a wanting-to-be-different from this nature? Is living not evaluating, preferring, being unjust, being limited, wanting to be different?" (*BGE* 9; cf. *KSA* 11: 167 and Richardson 2004: 30). Here Nietzsche invokes a biological notion and claims that what distinguishes the living being as such is having a priority of ends. Nonliving nature, by contrast, is merely moved by external causes. Living beings at least want to be otherwise and thus have preferences, make value judgments, and set ends for themselves. To be alive, then, is to set oneself up in opposition to the rest of nature by taking a position on how things will turn out, and this requires a hierarchy of ends.

The second main element of this account is Nietzsche's claim that what one is and what ends one sets are interdependent. This passage, for example, offers a characterization of their interrelationship:

> Whichever groups of sensations inside a soul awaken the fastest... that decides as to the entire order of rank of its values, that ultimately determines its table of goods. The value-estimations of a person betray something of the *construction* of his soul, and wherein it sees its conditions of life, its very own need. (*BGE* 208; cf. *D* 326, *D* 552; *GM* Preface 1, *GM* I: 13; *A* 13).

"Betray" here could mean something minimal: that value estimations just provide evidence for what sort of a person one is. The relationship seems much closer, however: although Nietzsche distinguishes between psychological responses, order of rank, and table of goods, there does not seem to be much else to the soul besides having a hierarchical structure of preferences. Then the value estimations would be of more than epistemic import; they would "construct" the soul by providing the view of its "conditions of life." In either case, to be a person depends crucially on an "order of rank of values" (cf. *WP* 886).

---

[13] I suspect that Nietzsche's phrasing in calling for a rank-ordering of things themselves is in some way an allusion to Plotinus, who liked to rank persons, parts of souls, and all things: see, for example, Plotinus 1989: 155 (iii.4). I cannot see what interpretive difference this would make, however. Another possible source is perhaps Schopenhauer, for whom things exhibit themselves as "grades of the will's objectivity" (Schopenhauer 1969: 131).

[14] The following few paragraphs are a modified version of Guay 2007: 164–6.

The third main element of this account is a derivation of order of rank of persons from the preceding considerations. These considerations already suffice to generate an *intraper-sonal* order of rank: if a hierarchy of ends distinguishes the living as such, and one's self is a function of the ends that one sets, then there are distinctions of rank among one's actual or potential selves. Internal complexity and the conceivability of self-transformation make rank distinction internal to what one is. Thus Nietzsche writes in early works of addressing one's "higher self" or later of "in which order of rank the innermost drives of one's nature are aligned in relation to one another" (*BGE* 6).

This intrapersonal elitism involves a claim that Life demands that one adopt a hierarchy of ends and thus generate, from one's own standpoint, a hierarchy of selves. It thus remains far from what would be expected from rank distinction among persons. Nietzsche also seems to advocate what might be called personal indifference, however: that from one's first-person standpoint, evaluative commitments hold independent of their association with any particular individuals, even oneself. Merely numerical differences among persons do not matter with respect to evaluating them. This passage, for example, advocates personal indifference, and from there moves directly to *interpersonal* elitism:

> ...that what is appropriate for one absolutely *cannot* be for another, that the demand for one morality [*Moral*] for everyone is precisely the impairment of the higher persons, in short, that there is an order of rank between person and person and thus also between morality and morality. (*BGE* 228)

This passage might seem to advocate the opposite of what I am suggesting: that Nietzsche offers a kind of relativism about morality, and no more general standpoint obtains. But Nietzsche is appealing to order of rank here in order to show that there is such a standpoint, even if it is not widely recognized. The designation of "higher men" and the rank differences between moralities indeed only make sense given such a general standpoint. Nietzsche is not claiming, against universal morality, that there is no suitably impersonal view of things; he is claiming that in the suitably impersonal view of things there is, against universal morality, an order of rank between persons.

My aim at present is not to give a full account of the dynamics of the various elements in the sphere of order of rank. Such an account would have to be hopelessly contentious, as Nietzsche leaves many matters irredeemably obscure and underdetermined. At present I only wish to show that, if one takes part of Nietzsche's project as that of connecting val-ues and ends with persons or selves, then one can understand why Nietzsche would attrib-ute such an extensive sphere of order of rank. In the picture that I am suggesting, order of rank between separate persons requires order of rank among distinct intrapsychologi-cal elements, which in turn requires order of rank among various value commitments. For someone to be the person that she is, then, there needs to be order among all the potential objects of interest or concern. Things in the world must have their order of rank. Indeed, on this account, the order of rank among persons is the most derivative and tenuous. Whereas an interpretation such as Natural Aristocracy makes persons primary, on this account inter-personal order of rank can only be sustained in the context of worldly and intrapsychic relations.

I now wish to review two additional interpretations of order of rank, and suggest that they each presume a far too limited sphere. The first is Mythic Archaism. On this interpretation,

ORDER OF RANK   499

order of rank is part of an attempted "arousal of mythic pasts" (Habermas 1987: 87).[15] That is, on this reading Nietzsche advocates a future that is characterized by prehistorical patterns of authority, a mythic consciousness, and practices that are insulated from any dynamic of change. Unquestioned authority of certain individuals over everyone else is part of such a mythic past, and thus represents what Nietzsche means by "order of rank." This interpretation is structurally similar to that of Natural Aristocracy, in that it identifies basic distinctions between persons and claims that Nietzsche advocates reproducing these rank distinctions in social life. What is different with Mythic Archaism, of course, is that the rank distinctions are not natural in any obvious sense and indeed are not grounded in any way. The basis of distinction is not rooted in nature but in a mythic sensibility that avoids any question of grounds.

This interpretation finds its support in passages such as this one:

> In the first case, when those ruling are the ones who determine the concept "good," the lofty, proud conditions of the soul are experienced as conveying distinction and determining order of rank. The noble human being separates himself from those beings amongst whom the opposite of such elevated, proud conditions find expression: he despises them. One immediately notes that in this first kind of morality the opposition "good" and "bad" signifies just as much as "noble" and "wretched." (*BGE* 260)

This account has two distinguishing features. The first is *immediacy*: rank authority is established not by a process or a justification but by a particular kind of felt experience on the part of the superior, what Nietzsche elsewhere calls a "pathos of distance" (*GM* I: 2). The second distinguishing feature is what might be called *value compression*. In archaic Greek thought, for example, "good," "noble," "powerful," "rich," "brave," "truthful," and a host of other positive qualities are almost conceptually connected: one cannot conceive of one in the absence of the others. And the "bad," "poor," "wretched," "petty," "cowardly," on the other hand, are conceived of, at least by the ruling group, not as a set of groups with contingently overlapping membership, but as a single unfortunate lot.

Others have discussed the general interpretive shortcomings of Mythic Archaism.[16] Here I wish to focus on the way in which it restricts the sphere of order of rank. What the Mythic Archaism interpretation does is generalize from Nietzsche's imagined primal case to all rank distinction. The consequence of taking this initial step as paradigmatic is that both immediacy and value compression are adopted without qualification. This limits the sphere of order of rank to those who feel themselves to be noble and those who are subject to them: persons are accordingly fundamental and there is a narrow range of ranks. Nietzsche, by contrast, insists that things fall within order of rank, as discussed above, but also that there is a complex and pluralistic order of persons. So, for example, the primal case cannot accommodate a distinction between "higher," which Nietzsche is typically concerned with, and "better," the concern of the archaic noble; but according to Nietzsche, "the higher the kind of

---

[15] I do not claim that Habermas offers a Mythic Archaism reading; indeed, Habermas does not offer an interpretation of order of rank per se. As with Natural Aristocracy, in this case I am less interested in representing particular authors' interpretations than in isolating a position that takes its cues from familiar lines of interpretation. See also, for example, the reference to the "persistently archaic character of [Nietzsche's] politics" in Wolin 2005: 485.

[16] On Habermas's reading of Nietzsche see, for example, Wellbery 1988 and Geuss 1999.

type a person is, the greater the improbability that he turns out well" (*BGE* 62). More generally, Nietzsche suggests that the process of enhancement of the human type has produced a
"diversity of persons" (*BGE* 194) and a "plurality of types" (*TI*: "Skirmishes of an Untimely
Man" 37), so that all of these need to be accounted for within order of rank, not just a few
types along a single dimension of better and worse. This is why Nietzsche promotes a wide
range of elites: higher persons, geniuses, nobles, free spirits, attempters, legislators, the profound, the healthy, the manifold, the great, the strong, the virtuous, and so on. Order of
rank is part of Nietzsche's attempt to better understand, not to deny, the diversity of human
possibility.[17]

The other interpretation of order of rank that I wish to discuss is the one that I call the
Political.[18] On this interpretation, Nietzsche's basic commitment is the superior worth of
certain types of individuals, and this commitment generates the prescriptive project of
organizing political life so that this superior worth is somehow respected or cultivated. This
interpretation is thus similar to the previous ones in one respect: Nietzsche's notion of order
of rank is taken to apply primarily to persons. What distinguishes this interpretation is that
the question of what grounds this view is relatively unimportant—or does not go beyond an
appeal to the superiority of the superior—and the superiority is taken as specifically political in nature. "Political" here could mean a number of things: having authority to rule, meriting institutional privileges, or serving as the organizing focus of social life. But however
one understands the political, order of rank is taken as specifically appropriate to that.

Taking order of rank as specifically relevant to the sphere of the political presumably
comes from a belief in the importance of political authority or in the pervasive importance
of institutions in modern life, and an understanding of "ranks" as corresponding to something like public offices. Nietzsche, however, does not privilege the political with respect
to order of rank; in fact, he does just the opposite, distinguishing the political as especially
uninteresting because order of rank has little to do with it. The latter position is suggested,
for example, at *GS* 358: "Finally let us not forget what a church is, precisely in contrast to
every 'state': a church is above all a ruling-structure that secures the highest rank for the
more spiritual persons and believes so much in the power of spirituality that it forbids itself
all cruder means of force—by that alone the church is in all circumstances a nobler institution than the state." (*GS* 358) Here Nietzsche treats nonstate institutions as nobler precisely
because they, unlike the state, make room for order of rank. Politics' distinctive means, the
potential use of coercive force, is too "crude" to be suitable for sustaining rank distinction.
Nietzsche accordingly focuses not on the political but on "*spiritual* order of rank" (*HAH*
I: 362; *GS* 290), "order of rank among artists and philosophers" (*BGE* 59), "order of rank in
the sphere of the intellect" (*KSA* I: 699; cf. *D* 446), "societal order of rank" (*HAH* III: 30),
and so on.

---

[17] I take one of Nietzsche's criticisms of morality to be that it interferes with such an understanding,
because it submits all human values to a single dimension of assessment. See, for example, *KSA*
12: 507: "Moral values were till now the highest values: does someone want to cast that into doubt?... As
we distance these values from that position, we alter all values: the principle of its heretofore order of
rank is thereby overturned." Part of Nietzsche's criticism here is that moral values in particular, by virtue
of the way in which they subordinate all other values, interfere with a diversity of values that would be in
some way superior.

[18] Here again I do not have a specific commentator in mind, but elements of the interpretation that
I describe can be found, for example, in Appel 1998 and Detwiler 1990.

There is another problem with the Political interpretation that is relevant to the sphere of order of rank. As a consequence of assigning order of rank such a narrow sphere, the Political interpretation generates a prescriptive project. If order of rank is taken specifically as an intervention in the political, then there is not much for it to be about other than a view about what should be realized in the world. Nietzsche, by contrast, insists that order of rank is something that is present in any social formation and thus cannot be the basis of a distinctive prescriptive project, as each of these passages show: [19]

> ...an order of rank of goods is continually present to every society, to every individual, according to which he determines his actions and judges those of others. (*HAH* I: 107)
>   Wherever we encounter a morality, we find an estimation and order of rank of human drives and actions. (*GS* 116; cf. *WP* 988)
>   The *historical sense* (or the capacity quickly to assess the order of rank of evaluations according to which a people, a society, a person has lived) ... (*BGE* 224)
>   ...basic psychological inclination to set up orders of rank (*GM* II: 20)

Nietzsche employs order of rank to characterize something much more general than a particular desirable political formation: order of rank, for Nietzsche, explains how the human world always works.

In this section, I have tried to show that Nietzsche's notion of order of rank has a much wider sphere than is typically recognized and that this feature of Nietzsche's account runs against some commonly held interpretations. Order of rank encompasses just about everything, and does not accord primacy of place to the differential status of persons. The Mythic Archaism and Political interpretations in particular thus misdirect their focus: by attending primarily to persons they are mistakenly narrow and thereby lose sight of the broader picture in which order of rank functions.

4 ITS GROUND

In this section I shall discuss what Nietzsche takes to be the ground of his views on order of rank. In doing so, I shall introduce and criticize the Anthropological interpretation and present my own favored interpretation, which I call "Transcendental." On my view, Nietzsche presents order of rank not as reflecting a natural or mythic order, but as a condition for the availability of normative authority. There are thus two main elements to the Transcendental interpretation. One element is the one that I previously discussed: that Nietzsche's account of order of rank is meant to contribute to an explanation of normative authority rather than to offer substantive values. The second element is that Nietzsche provides this explanation by way of an argument concerning the constitutive conditions for the phenomenon of Life, and thus human self-overcoming, to be possible.

---

[19] Here one might compare order of rank with the dynamic, hierarchical, and transcendental account of power in Foucault 1990: 93: "Power's condition of possibility ... must not be sought in the primary existence of a central point ... it is the moving substrate of force relations which, by virtue of the inequality, constantly engender states of power, but the latter are always local and unstable."

Order of rank is grounded in its contribution to human self-enhancement. That is to say, we have a reason to acknowledge order of rank, according to Nietzsche, because the process by which human beings transform human identity for the better involves order of rank. We have already seen this in Nietzsche's discussion of the "human" type:

> Every heightening of the "human" type has so far been the work of an aristocratic society— and so will it always be: as a society that believes in a long order of rank and difference in worth between person and person and needs, in some sense, slavery. Without that pathos of distance ... that other, more mysterious pathos could not have arisen at all, that desire for always-renewed widening of distance inside the soul itself, the development of always higher, rarer, more distant, greater in tension, more comprehensive states, in short, the very heightening of the "human" type, the constant "self-overcoming" of the human, to take a moral formula in a supramoral sense. (*BGE* 257; cf. *GS* 377)

Order of rank seems to be a necessary condition for this heightening and self-overcoming, since it is a "need" that will be present in every case. This heightening, Nietzsche explains, can only proceed by a kind of self-activity that depends on a prior, social order of rank. Social distance makes possible the desire for internal distinction, which motivates transformative activity on oneself. Once again, then, Nietzsche's claim seems to involve the role of the evaluative in the phenomenon of Life. Life involves active transformation of the world, including oneself as a part of the world, and this activity depends on evaluative commitments underwritten by order of rank.

There are many ways in which we could thereby think of Life and the heightening of the human type as furnishing a ground. The most basic would be to consider order of rank instrumentally: as if heightening of the human type were an end that someone could initially have, and acknowledging order of rank were a necessary means to achieving that end. In that case, of course, the authority of order of rank is entirely contingent on having the relevant end. I would like to show that, in two respects, Nietzsche's case here is *not* merely instrumental. Order of rank is not an instrumental condition but a *constitutive* one: order of rank constitutes possibilities that would not otherwise obtain, rather than merely providing an efficient means to an end that could be independently identified. Nietzsche's case is also not instrumental by virtue of its *generality*. Order of rank, I take Nietzsche to be claiming, does not furnish one end among many, but something more like self-relating activity in general: in accordance with Nietzsche's characterization of Life, by taking on evaluative commitments one becomes the sort of being who sets ends and thereby actively generates self-transformation. Nietzsche offers a suggestion of how he makes this point in his discussion of the ascetic ideal:

> it rejects, denies, affirms, confirms according only to the meaning of *its* interpretation (—and has there ever been a more thoroughly thought-out system of interpretation?); it submits to no power, rather it believes in its privilege before every power, in its unconditional *distance of rank* in relation to every power—it believes that there is no power on earth that does not receive its meaning, its right to exist, its value from it alone, as a tool for *its* work, as way and means to *its* goals, to One Goal ... (*GM* III: 23)

This is only a single example of "distance of rank," but here Nietzsche identifies a content-dependency of all power and all goals. Nietzsche, of course, is not endorsing the ascetic ideal's interpretation here, but locating its generative possibility. Order of rank is a precondition for the determinate "meaning" of power and goals as such, or, as in this passage, it is that from which meaning is "received."

Before I develop this point, that Nietzsche sees the *content* of everything, and in particular power and goals, as dependent on order of rank, I wish to consider the final rival interpretation. This interpretation, the Anthropological, has to my knowledge only one exponent, John Richardson (see Richardson 2004), so I shall try to remain faithful to his account. In Richardson's view, Nietzsche accepts a Darwinian explanation of some of our instincts. That is, he explains certain human drives and values in terms of natural selection. But Nietzsche departs from Darwin by claiming that natural selection is inadequate to explain all human drives and values. A second form of selection, *social selection*, is required to explain "drives and practices that serve the survival or expansion of the social group (and not the individual or species)" (Richardson 2004: 85). Nietzsche further proposes a third form of selection, *self-selection*, which builds upon but overcomes the prior forms. Whereas the prior forms—in particular social selection—"design" tame, homogeneous individuals, self-selection aims at individuals who are defined by their degree of difference and distinction from others. Nietzsche's "breeding" cultivates escape from dominant social instincts, and accordingly "crucially pursues a 'rank order' or *hierarchy*, which he thinks is indispensable to making the strong and free individuals he advocates" (Richardson 2004: 201).

In light of the considerations that I have previously advanced, there is much to be said for the Anthropological interpretation. Richardson characterizes order of rank as integral to a dynamic, social-historical process rather than merely reflecting a pre-given evaluative order. Order of rank is furthermore central to self-relating activity, or as Richardson writes, "freedom" (Richardson 2004: 201). In particular, on Richardson's reading, self-transformative activity is involved: there is a "breeding" by which one makes oneself into the kind of being with one's own values. I nevertheless have three main objections to the Anthropological interpretation, of which the third is directly related to the ground of order of rank. The first objection is historical: the Anthropological interpretation places order of rank as a late offshoot in historical development, whereas Nietzsche insists that it is present at the very beginning. At the least, the mythic-archaic sense of distance arrives early, and more recent history presents a suppression or obscuring of order of rank rather than a new opportunity for it. Although, on the Anthropological reading, natural selection instills aggressive drives that could support some form of hierarchy, order of rank is a prescriptive notion concerning self-selection that only arises in response to social selection. My second objection is structural: the Anthropological interpretation characterizes order of rank as a kind of self-separation from the social, whereby individuals make themselves distinctive from others. Nietzsche, by contrast, characterizes order of rank as deeply social. Richardson suggests that society could be "engineered" (Richardson 2004: 203) for order of rank, but this would entail organizing social life for nonsocial persons, rather than, say, changing the social meaning of the "human" type. Third and most relevant to present purposes, the Anthropological interpretation understands Nietzsche as offering a causal-explanatory account of how various forms of selection bring about certain human drives and values; on the topic of why Nietzsche values the ideal ascribed to him, this interpretation is mostly silent.[20] Any justification it provides must rely on claims about what values are already "built

---

[20] See Richardson 2004: 200: "It is hard to say, I think, whether Nietzsche values this kind for its intrinsic character, or because of that difference and distinction from others."

into us" (Richardson 2004: 119) and what differences among persons are merely natural, and then take these claims as inherently justifying. What I have been suggesting, by contrast, is that the main function of order of rank in Nietzsche's enterprise is to contribute to an explanation of the availability of normative authority.

I have already discussed, in section 2, the reasons why one should adopt the Normative interpretation, and thus understand order of rank as contributing to an explanation of normative authority. If we adopt the Normative interpretation, then it is hard to see how a causal explanation of the development of human drives has much to contribute; but on the other hand, it remains unclear what could serve as the ground of order of rank, if not the appeal to developmental anthropology. My suggestion here is the interpretation that I call "Transcendental":[21] one that supplements the Normative interpretation of Nietzsche's aims with the claim that order of rank is grounded as a constitutive condition. This interpretation is "transcendental," then, in that it responds to a question of right by offering the conditions for the phenomenon of Life to be possible; I take this to be the basis of Nietzsche's claims such as "order of rank merely formulates the highest law of Life itself" (A 57). Order of rank makes possible the evaluative, self-relating activity distinctive of Life as such, not as a causal condition, but by contributing to the content by which persons distinguish themselves from the rest of nature.

We can find an example of this contribution of content in Nietzsche's claim, "one must compel moralities to bow first before the order of rank" (BGE 221).[22] Nietzsche is suggesting that we should think of morality as subject to that which is prior: our setting up of distinctions and making of comparative assessments. Without this prior order of rank, morality would be an empty "seduction under the mask of philanthropy" (BGE 221): it would have no content other than the attractive but deceptive surface of human kindness. Nietzsche's preferred picture apparently does contain moralities, but only if they take on nonsuperficial sense though engagement with an order of relative importance and value.

Nietzsche makes this point about substantive content not just about morality as a whole, but in many more specific contexts, in particular love of neighbor (BGE 216; GM I: 10), passion (D 27), and, as here, equality:

> [The noble soul] concedes, under circumstances that make it hesitate at first, that there are those who are equally entitled; as soon as it has cleaned up this question of rank, it moves among these equals and equally-entitled with the same security in shame and tender awe that it has in its dealings with itself. (BGE 265)

Nietzsche's critique of equality is familiar, but he is not opposed to equality per se. He objects to versions of equality that do not amount to anything: for example, "that everyone as an 'immortal soul' has equal rank" is a kind of "nothingness" (A 43). In the above passage, however, equality is a desirable form of social relations: it allows for a combination of self-assurance and awe. Nietzsche's general point seems to be that equality in any desirable form has to be equality in specifically meaningful ways; the problem with the

---

[21] I do not claim, of course, that this interpretation involves all or only things that could be called transcendental. Even with reference to Kant's understanding of "transcendental," there is much that is absent: a set of uniquely necessary conditions, priority to experience, and derivation from the logical form of judgments, for example.

[22] I discuss this passage, and the general issue of content, in Guay 2005.

democratic-socialist-Kantian-Christian form of equality is that it is granted independently of any particular quality at all. The provision of meaningful ways in which there can be (or fail to be) equality is the constitutive role of order of rank and how it thereby makes ethical distinctions possible.

Nietzsche makes a series of parallel points about the values and conditions he associates most closely with order of rank: responsibility (*BGE* 252, 272), reverence (*GS* 100; *BGE* 263, 287), faith (*BGE* 287), and suffering (*BGE* 270). His complaint is typically that the prominent forms are empty of content and interfere with the ways in which similar but more substantive values might be available. And what, for Nietzsche, makes the difference between the substantive and empty forms is order of rank; this is the point of the present section. Nietzsche's notion of order of rank is meant to contribute to an explanation of the possibility of normative authority, and does so as a constitutive condition for the phenomenon of Life. My preferred "Transcendental" interpretation is meant to capture these features of Nietzsche's approach.

5 SOCIALITY

One thing that I have tried to show in the preceding sections is that order of rank is not primarily a substantive notion: Nietzsche is interested in the availability of normative authority rather than prescribing a specific hierarchy. Even such a "transcendental" view must have some substantive implications, however, and in this section I wish to discuss some of them. Since it is difficult to identify any of Nietzsche's substantive views, let alone trace them back to order of rank, I shall focus on two matters that are most directly related: the role of order of rank in communities and the reasons why order of rank is not more widely acknowledged. Here I hope to indicate some of the reasons for thinking that there is a necessary public role for order of rank and that we are doomed to misunderstand it.

Order of rank stands somewhat awkwardly between individual and group, as this passage shows:

> "You shall obey someone and for a long time: otherwise you perish and you lose your last respect for yourself"—this seems to me the moral imperative of nature which is surely neither "categorical"—nor addressed to the individual, but rather to peoples, races, ages, classes, but above all to the entire animal "human," to human beings. (*BGE* 188)

This "moral imperative of nature," which I take to be derivative of order of rank, is both personal and collective. On one hand it calls for the obedience of each to another as the condition for warding off the loss of personal integrity. On the other hand, it is addressed especially to humanity as a whole or the human animal as such. Together these two aspects suggest that there must be standards that are not based in anyone's particular interest or allegiance, but nevertheless command authority. Without such standards, there is no basis for respect for individuals, even self-respect. And even less can there be any kind of community, let alone a "human" type, without such a common basis for social relations. Subjection to the authority of general standards makes a shared form of living possible.

Nietzsche thus comes to think that order of rank is necessary for the integrity of communities and individuals. The resulting need for obedience, although not itself conducive to any public justification, is not arbitrary or irrational, however, and it is not imposed by force. The most extensive discussion of order of rank appears in the chapter of *Beyond Good and Evil* called "We Scholars," and there Nietzsche suggests that the source of obedience depends on the quality of ideas:

> The greatest events and the greatest thoughts—but the greatest thoughts are the greatest events—are the last ones to be understood: the generations that are contemporary with them do not *experience* such events—they live right by them. It happens just as in the starry realm. The light of the farthest stars comes last to human beings … "How many centuries does a spirit need before being understood?"—that is also a standard, by which one also makes an order of rank and manners, as is needed: for spirit and star. (*BGE* 285)

Of course, it is not the best ideas that ultimately command obedience, but the "greatest" ones. And this greatness not only cannot be explained, it cannot even be recognized.

Nietzsche characterizes this failure in recognition as itself an inevitable and interesting feature of our social world. There are four explanations that Nietzsche offers for this failure and each points to a different aspect of his analysis of modernity. The first is antipathy. We are antipathetic to order of rank because it undermines the modern sense of individuality in which every person is a unique, completely independent source of value: thus, "One no longer has class-rank! One is an 'individual'!" (*D* 203). Order of rank is ignored in part, then, because it implies that everyone's identity depends on others in a way that no one would like to acknowledge. Another explanation that Nietzsche offers is the one closest to the passage about spirits and stars: we are simply not good enough to see order of rank. Nietzsche writes that the "spiritual middle-class … may never catch sight of the *great* problems and question marks" (*GS* 373) and that there are "persons not noble enough to see the abysmally different order of rank and cleft in rank between person and person" (*BGE* 62). The third explanation is that our commitments in distinctive spheres are confused or conflated, most typically the political and the existential. The failure to acknowledge order of rank is thus the "catastrophe that has crept out of Christianity to politics" (*A* 43) and diffused itself further from there.

The fourth explanation that Nietzsche offers for the failure to acknowledge order of rank is perhaps the most interesting. The explanation is that it stems from repression: a concealment from ourselves of what we are really doing. In the modern version of this, no form of order of rank is credible—all authority claims have come to seem implausible—even as we cannot live without order of rank. The result is that we sustain the patterns of authority that support our shared ways of life, but always represent ourselves as doing something much different. Nietzsche thus identifies the "moral hypocrisy of those commanding," in which they "know no other way to protect themselves against the bad conscience than to pose as the executors of more or higher commands" (*BGE* 199). This repression has an older source, however: Christianity's permanent institution of guilt about order of rank in general, so that it cannot be avoided or reduced, except by creating more guilt. This inheritance endures in the operation of order of rank in the modern world, whereby we misunderstand and thus make unavailable the conditions of our own flourishing.

6 CONCLUSION

I have not been able to present anything like a developed theory of order of rank because Nietzsche did not have one. Whether this absence is best explained by the inherently "problematic" character of order of rank or by Nietzsche's shortcomings as a philosophical writer, I leave aside. I hope nevertheless to have shown that, even in the absence of such a theory, order of rank has an important place in Nietzsche's thought and that it includes a range of concerns and applications that are not typically noticed. Order of rank connects the availability of normative authority to the structure of social life and thus, for Nietzsche, is central to the very enterprise of philosophy.

To be sure, order of rank has a natural basis, involves rank disparity between persons, contributes to an anthropological account of the development of certain drives, and has substantive social implications. But in Nietzsche's thought these are small pieces of a much broader account of how the authority of rank distinctions sustains the phenomenon of Life. And here, perhaps, is where Nietzsche's deepest philosophical interests lie.[23]

BIBLIOGRAPHY

(A) Works by Nietzsche

All quotations from Nietzsche are my own translation, with original emphasis. Works are cited by section number except for the *KSA*, which is cited by volume and page number.

KSA   *Sämtliche Werke: Kritische Studienausgabe in 15 Einzelbänden*, ed. G. Colli and M. Montinari (15 vols). Berlin: De Gruyter, 1988.

(B) Other Works Cited

Appel, Fredrick. 1998. *Nietzsche Contra Democracy.* Ithaca: Cornell University Press.

Detwiler, Bruce. 1990. *Nietzsche and the Politics of Aristocratic Radicalism.* Chicago: University of Chicago Press.

Foucault, Michel. 1990. *The History of Sexuality: An Introduction*, trans. Robert Hurley. New York: Vintage Books.

Geuss, Raymond. 1999. *Morality, Culture, and History.* New York: Cambridge University Press.

Guay, Robert. 2005. "Our Virtues," *Philosophical Topics* 33.2: 71–87.

Guay, Robert. 2007. "Transcendental Elitism," *International Studies in Philosophy* 39.3: 163–77.

Habermas, Jürgen. 1987. *The Philosophical Discourse of Modernity*, trans. F. G. Lawrence. Cambridge, Mass.: MIT Press.

Heidegger, Martin. 1999. *Contributions to Philosophy*, trans. Parvis Emad and Kenneth Maly. Bloomington, Ind.: Indiana University Press.

[23] I wish to thank Anna Gebbie, Randall Havas, and my students for their help in thinking about this topic, and Christine Swanton for explaining "Tall Poppy Syndrome" to me. I have also profited immensely, even if insufficiently, from a set of comments from John Richardson.

Herder, J. G. 1971/1797. *Humanitätsbriefe.* Berlin: Aufbau-Verlag.

Hurka, Thomas. 2007. "Nietzsche: Perfectionist," in Brian Leiter and Neil Sinhababu (eds), *Nietzsche and Morality.* New York: Oxford University Press, 9–31.

Janz, Curt Paul. 1978. *Friedrich Nietzsche.* München: Hanser.

Leiter, Brian. 2002. *Nietzsche on Morality.* New York: Routledge.

Plotinus. 1989. *Ennead I*, trans. A. H. Armstrong. Cambridge, Mass.: Harvard University Press.

Richardson, John. 2004. *Nietzsche's New Darwinism.* New York: Oxford University Press.

Schopenhauer, Arthur. 1969. *The World as Will and Representation*, trans. E. F. J. Payne. New York: Dover.

Taylor, Charles. 1995. "The Importance of Herder," in *Philosophical Arguments.* Cambridge, Mass.: Harvard University Press, 79–99.

Wellbery, David. 1988. "Nietzsche—Art—Postmodernism: A Reply to Jürgen Habermas," in T. Harrison (ed.), *Nietzsche in Italy.* Calistoga: ANMA Libri, 77–100.

Wolin, Sheldon. 2005. *Politics and Vision: Continuity and Innovation in Western Political Thought* (expanded edition). Princeton: Princeton University Press.

CHAPTER 22

....

'A PROMISE MADE IS A DEBT UNPAID': NIETZSCHE ON THE MORALITY OF COMMITMENT AND THE COMMITMENTS OF MORALITY[1]

....

MARK MIGOTTI

IN a much-noted passage in *On the Genealogy of Morals*, Nietzsche portrays human civilization and morality as originating in an abrupt and drastic process of domestication. 'All at once' a lusty, fierce, daring, dangerous creature had 'its instincts devalued and "disconnected"' (*GM* II: 16 56/322);[2] all of a sudden, this remarkable, self-transforming animal had to learn how to behave, had to delay gratification, curb reckless impulse, forego wanton vengeance, submit to authority, and generally contribute to the maintenance of a functioning social order. At the heart of this momentous transition from a proto-human life in the wild to an unprecedented life 'in the spell of society'[3] is the triumph of custom over instinct. 'The first principle of civilization,' Nietzsche declares in *Daybreak*, is that 'any custom is

[1] I would like to thank audiences at Hamilton College, the Universities of Calgary, Alberta and British Columbia, the Western Canadian Philosophical Association, the Canadian Philosophical Association, and Nietzsche in New York for helpful questions and comments on earlier versions of this paper.
I would like to thank Richard Zach, Jörg Esleben, and Ulrike Sturm for helpful observations on points of translation; Dennis McKerlie, Leonard Kahn, and Ken Gemes for helpful comments on draft versions of the paper; and Susan Haack for her usual care and acuity in discussing and improving draft after draft after draft.
  [2] In my references the first page number refers to the translation I used, the second to the *KSA*.
  [3] I have translated Nietzsche's '*in den Bann der Gesellschaft*' more literally than Walter Kaufmann or Maudemarie Clark and Allen Swensen. Kaufmann translates 'within the walls of society', Clark and Swensen 'within the sway of society'.

better than no custom' (*D* 16 15/29). And the chief principle of morality is that it is 'nothing other … than obedience to custom' (9–10/21–2).

In another much-noted passage from the same book, Nietzsche portrays the dominion of custom and morality as culminating in their transcendence:

> if … we place ourselves at the end of [this] enormous process, … where society and its morality of custom finally brings to light that to which it was only the means: then we will find as the ripest fruit on its tree the *sovereign individual*, the individual resembling only himself, free again from the morality of custom, autonomous and supramoral … (*GM* II: 2 36/292).

Having freed himself from the tyranny of socially enforced custom and habit, this sovereign individual has become able 'to vouch for himself as future, as a promisor does' (36/294). The aim of the present paper is to explain what we can learn about promising and about Nietzsche's critique of morality from his discussion of sovereign promising in *GM* II, sections one and two.

The paper is divided into four parts. In part one, I contend that the philosophical focus of *GM* II: 1–2 is not the nature of promising in the narrow sense of making a pledge to do something for someone else, but the nature of pledging or committing oneself in general. In part two, I set out the root difference between a moral obligation and a Nietzschean account of promissory fidelity: when the obligation to keep promises is understood in moralistic terms, the focus is on what promisors owe to promisees; when it is understood in Nietzschean terms the focus is on what promisors owe to themselves. In part three, I argue that in its focus on the difficult questions of what it means and how it is possible to bind oneself to a course of action, the Nietzschean account is philosophically deeper than the moral obligation account; and in part four, I turn to interpretive debates about the role of the sovereign individual in Nietzsche's thought, and show that revisionist readings of *GM* II: 1–2, according to which—distinct first impressions to the contrary notwithstanding—Nietzsche is not really in favour of sovereign individuality and sovereign promising, are misconceived.

1 VOLUNTARY RELIABILITY

The ability to 'vouch for oneself as future, as a promisor does', requires the ability to identify oneself across time in a practical way. When I promise to do something I thereby, *now*, lay practical claim to the *future* self who, when the time comes, will be responsible for doing what was promised. When that time arrives, the formerly future self is put to the test—and must either honour this claim or renege on it. The burden of the first section of *GM* II is to point up the importance of 'a true memory of the will' for this double identification of promise-maker and would-be promise-keeper. If, at the time appointed for keeping it, I forget my promise altogether—or, more usually and of greater philosophical and practical interest, 'forget' that my having promised *then* constitutes a decisive reason for undertaking the promised course of action *now*—I will not keep my promise.

When a sovereign individual makes a promise, he keeps it; he 'gives his word as something on which one can rely because he knows himself to be strong enough to uphold it, even against accidents, even "against fate"' (37/294). A sovereign individual, Nietzsche says, becomes *entitled* to promise (36/293);[4] and this entitlement is not easily earned. Nietzsche's sovereign promisor resembles the athlete who wins the privilege of competing for her national team, not the citizen who becomes eligible to vote simply by turning eighteen. Fair enough, one might remark: but in extolling the faithfulness of sovereign promisors entitled to promise, by contrast with the faithlessness of 'feeble windbags who promise without being entitled to' (37/294), is Nietzsche not simply urging that you make only promises you can keep? And did we really need *him* to tell us this?

To see that Nietzsche is doing something other than dressing up a piece of trite moral advice in racy new robes, it is helpful to ask what might be meant by the idea of a promise which *cannot* be kept, as opposed to one which simply *is not* kept. Promises might prove to be unkeepable for reasons that are circumstance-relative, agent-relative, or neither. Promises that can't be kept for reasons independent of particularities of agent or circumstance are promises to do what nobody could ever do, promises to do the logically or physically impossible. Promises that can't be kept for circumstance-relative reasons are promises to do things that nobody could do under the circumstances that obtain at the time appointed for performance. And promises that can't be kept for agent-relative reasons are promises that could be kept by *some* people under these circumstances, but can't be kept by *this* person *now*, the promisor himself under the circumstances presently obtaining.[5] Thus far, the spirit of the injunction against making promises you can't keep seems consonant with the spirit of Nietzsche's admiration for sovereign promisors strong enough to keep their word regardless of what it costs them. The main idea in either case is to commend the policy of making (and keeping) only keepable promises, and disparage the foolishness or weakness responsible for making (and breaking) promises unkeepable for any reason.

In the hands of ordinary moral thinking, however, the admonition not to make promises you can't keep is itself a moral precept, and has no bearing at all on the making of idle threats or vows. But Nietzsche's sovereign individual who has earned the right to promise is a paragon, not of morality, but of its transcendence; and his disdain for windbags who promise without being entitled to applies no less to makers of idle vows or threats than to idle promisors in a narrow moral sense. In fact, the true philosophical theme of *GM* II: 1–2—'the paradoxical task which nature has set itself with respect to man'—is not promising in the strict sense of a commitment made to a recipient, who thereby acquires certain rights, and which is generally welcomed by him, but rather the very idea of a voluntarily binding commitment as such, a deliberate refusal of future options and opportunities which conflict with the conduct to which one has committed oneself. It is here, in the possibility of a robust in-advance practical commitment, a principled rejection of otherwise desirable prospects if and when they conflict with the 'predefined' course of action, that Nietzsche finds 'the real problem of man'.

A capacity for self-generated commitment requires what I shall call 'voluntary reliability'. When Nietzsche makes much of the obstacle that a healthy tendency to 'active forgetfulness' poses to the possibility of successful promising and of the successful promisor's need

---

[4] For remarks on the translation of '[*jemand*], *der versprechen darf* as 'someone entitled to promise', see footnote 19 below.

[5] The notion of being unable for deeply personal reasons to keep a certain promise at a certain time raises philosophical issues which cannot be broached here. For an illuminating discussion of some of them, see Harry Frankfurt's 'Rationality and the Unthinkable' in Frankfurt 1988.

to 'distinguish the accidental from the necessary and to think in causal terms' (36/292), he indicates, I suggest, that his chief subject is this idea of voluntary reliability. For, on the one hand, a tendency to forget makes for either diminished or involuntary reliability; and on the other, the concept of *voluntary* reliability has purchase only by contrast with reliability in virtue of laws of nature or other necessities. If I rely on the strength of rope, knots, and a tree to prevent you from leaving this spot before I return, I am counting on the workings of nature to *keep* you in place; if I take your word for it that you will not leave, I am counting on *you* to *stay* in place. One of the ways in which the opening two sections of *GM* II serve to introduce the essay as a whole is via the thesis that a long history of involuntary and unwitting training—the subject of sections 3 to 15 of the essay—is required before voluntarily reliable individuals with an entitlement to promise can emerge.

A promise, normally so-called, is a voluntarily binding commitment made to a witting and willing promisee, one aware of and in agreement with the terms of commitment. When I promise something to someone, I thereby cede my otherwise standing right to change my mind about what to do: before I promise Jones that I will Φ, my Φ-ing or not Φ-ing is up to me; after I have promised it is up to him, as he can either release me from my promise or hold me to it. By contrast, a threat is a commitment made to a witting but *un*willing recipient, one aware of but not in agreement with the terms of commitment. When I threaten you with something, I warn you that I am unilaterally revoking my standing option of changing my mind about doing what I have threatened to do should the need arise. And when, incoherently but pungently, I confirm the seriousness of my intention with the words 'and that's a promise, not a threat', what I am actually saying is that this threat is real, not idle. By contrast with threats and promises, private vows are made to and for oneself.

We have, then, a genus concept of a pledge, or voluntary commitment, with three species: threats, promises, and vows. Unlike vows, promises and threats are addressed to recipients distinct from their issuers; unlike promises, vows and threats are fundamentally unilateral commitments which bind the issuer, but involve no 'normative transfer' from issuer to recipient. More compendiously, a pledge of any kind involves (i) a pledger, the subject *who* pledges, (ii) *what* is pledged, the action or course of action to be undertaken by the pledger, (iii) a recipient *to whom* the pledge is addressed, and (iv) a focal object *for* or *at whom* the pledge is directed. For present purposes, I assume that the recipient and the focal object of a pledge are the same. In the case of a private vow, the recipient-*cum*-focal object is also the pledger himself, so that the fourfold relation reduces to a twofold relation between a pledging agent and a pledged action. Being interpersonal acts, promises and threats need the pledger and the recipient to be distinct individuals. But whereas the focal object of a threat, the person *at whom* the threat is directed, is treated as a *mere* object, the focal object of a promise, the person *to whom* it is made, is treated as an object who is another subject—a reciprocal partner in a complex transaction, entitled as such to (re)act upon the promisor in various ways.[6]

Against this background, it is not surprising that the moral obligation tradition of thinking about promising has been preoccupied with the distinctive features of promissory

---

[6] The discussion of practical commitment in Heath 1995 bears in a number of interesting ways on the concerns of this paragraph. Heath's observations, in part derived from ideas of Thomas Schelling's (Schelling 1960) on the normative or 'action-theoretic' commonalities between genuine, credible threats and genuine, sincere promises, are particularly germane.

obligation, rather than the wider topic of voluntary reliability as such. It is one thing to inveigh against making promises you can't keep, quite another to inveigh against making idle threats or vows. Threats can be morally improper, in which case one will be morally obliged *not* to do what one pledged to do; and the question whether the makers of idle threats to commit moral wrongs are thereby morally better off than the makers of serious ones would be is surely a thorny one from the moral obligation perspective. For its part, the obligation to fulfill a private vow is thought to be less substantial and serious than that incurred in making a promise. When I make a private vow, it is thought, I can release myself without harm or impropriety or wrongness, whereas when I have promised something to another, unilateral 'release' from the obligation to perform is but a euphemism for refusing to perform, i.e. for breaking my promise.

Whether they make threats, vows, or promises, Nietzsche's sovereign individuals will do what they say. So, in particular, when they make promises in the narrow sense they keep them. In fact, the standards of promissory fidelity upheld by sovereign promisors are substantially more exigent than those assumed by most exponents of the moral obligation tradition.[7] Precisely because they 'know themselves to be strong enough to uphold [their word], even against accidents, even "against fate"' (37/294), sovereign promisors entitled to promise will in the nature of the case be deliberately sparing in the use they make of this entitlement: they promise 'reluctantly and rarely'. One reason for this is that sovereign individuals take themselves to honour those to whom they condescend to make promises—and here promising must be intended in its specific sense. 'Stingy with his trust, [one who promises like a sovereign] conveys a mark of distinction when he trusts' (37/294, emphasis deleted), and promiscuous promising would cheapen the currency. Another, perhaps deeper, reason is that sovereign individuals, correctly taking themselves to be strong enough to keep their word in the face of whatever comes at them, recognize that it would be foolish to put this strength to the test needlessly or frivolously. Knowing that you are presently strong and committed enough to keep your word 'in the face of accidents [and] even...of fate' is compatible with acknowledging that this strength is not impervious to misuse and that it would be dangerous to leave yourself open to superfluous accidents. It is one thing to 'take on' fate on carefully chosen occasions, it is another to tempt it pointlessly.

2 Moral Obligation

Because they promise rarely, sovereign promisors will refrain from making trivial promises, promises to do unimportant things for uninteresting reasons. From a moral-obligation perspective, the prospect of trivial promises is thought to put pressure on the stringency of promissory obligation. For it seems obvious to many that breaking a trivial promise in order to do something significantly more important and beneficial than what would be accomplished by keeping it is not only always morally permissible, but sometimes even morally required. Thus Pall Àrdal, for example, is disinclined to give 'an inflated status to faithfulness

---

[7] Kant being a conspicuous exception.

to promises *as such* compared with other virtues', in part because of the 'little obligation' that attaches to trivial promises (Àrdal 1968: 234).[8]

From the perspective of one entitled to promise in Nietzsche's sense, the possibility of trivial promises testifies only to the existence of trivial promisors, the pathetic windbags whose sad habit of breaking their word demonstrates that they don't really know what it means to give it 'for keeps'. Sovereign promisors recognize that they should exercise their entitlement to promise only on those occasions on which they want to make it perfectly clear that they really mean it. Their contempt for those who promise without being entitled to is not the moralist's dismay in the face of people taking unfair advantage of a just and beneficent social practice, or illegitimately harming people by foiling expectations which have been deliberately engendered, or ... [fill in what you take the correct explanation of the moral wrong of breaking a promise to be]; it is contempt for those who fool themselves—and perhaps others also—into thinking that they are committed when they are not.

The root difference between Nietzsche's approach to promising and that of the moral-obligation tradition can be further illuminated by examining the related questions: first, why moral-obligation theorists need, as Nietzsche does not, to worry about determining the conditions under which promissory language functions as the vehicle of a genuine promise (as opposed, for example, to forming part of the script of a play, or being used in evident jest, or ...); and second, why Nietzsche invokes, as moral-obligation theorists do not, the unexampled concept of an '*entitlement* to promise'?

Philosophers in the moral-obligation tradition need to worry about the conditions of genuine promising because only genuine promises are thought to give rise to a moral obligation to fulfill them. Since it is patently absurd to take the actor playing Romeo to be morally obliged to carry out the promises of lifelong love he makes to the actress playing Juliet, it is concluded that when the actor on stage says 'I promise to Φ' his words are not functioning in the way required to constitute the undertaking of an obligation on his part, and similar reasoning is applied to the cases of evident jest, to words uttered while asleep, to learners of a language etc., etc. To see why Nietzsche has a reason of principle for neglecting this issue, it will be useful to turn to the second point of difference mentioned above and proceed by imagining what a defender of the moral-obligation tradition might say in criticism of the moral-theoretic utility of the concept of an entitlement to promise.

A moral-obligation theorist will want to ask Nietzsche whether or not someone who lacks an entitlement to promise, but nevertheless 'promises', i.e. says to someone in all seriousness 'I promise you to Φ', has made a genuine promise. If the Nietzschean answers in the affirmative, the moral-obligation theorist will insist that he is making an acceptable point in a needlessly hyperbolic way. After all, he really means only to say that only the voluntarily

---

[8] John Searle takes the fact that promises can be made about 'matters that are morally trivial' (Searle 2001: 194) to be decisive evidence for the claim that 'there is nothing in the practice of promising as such that guarantees that every obligation to keep a promise will be grave enough to be considered a moral obligation'. In contrast, according to Tim Scanlon, 'the kind of reason that a promisee has for believing that [a] promisor will perform' must have a distinctively '*moral* force' (Scanlon 1998: 306, emphasis in the original); while Neal Tognazzini (2007), for all his searching criticism of Scanlon's theory of promissory obligation, shows no sign of demurring on this cardinal point. The mutually incompatible 'intuitions' of Searle on the one hand and Scanlon and Tognazzini on the other call to mind a remark of Nietzsche's from *Daybreak* (published in 1881): 'Nowadays,' he writes, 'sensibilities in moral things are "all over the place" [*kreuz und quer*]' (*D* 230 226/199); evidently they still are!

reliable have any business making promises, and he is quite right to say this: Don't make promises you can't keep! But the point speaks in favour of the moral-obligation outlook, not Nietzsche's; because the reason that the infirm of purpose should refrain from promising in the first place is that, *ex hypothesi*, when they do promise they run a great risk of violating their moral obligation to be as good as their word. If the Nietzschean decides to brazen it out and deny that promisors not entitled to promise really can succeed in doing something other than utter a form of words whenever they say 'I promise', it will be pointed out that he thereby saddles himself with the absurd thesis that feeble windbags can wriggle out of the obligation to keep their promises (or rather 'promises') altogether—simply by being too feeble to be entitled to make promises in the first place! For if only the voluntarily reliable are able to make genuine promises, and only genuine promises generate moral obligations, then no unreliable 'promisor', however much he is believed in good faith, will be obligated to keep his promise; it will always turn out not to have been a genuine promise—because it was made by an impostor, someone pretending to be entitled to do what they are not in fact entitled to do.[9]

Nietzsche might retort: Of course the friends of moral obligation, as embarrassingly earnest philosophically as they are naïve historically, will have trouble understanding the point of my notion of an entitlement to promise. Whether feeble windbags who promise without being entitled to really succeed in promising, as opposed to mouthing some words, simply doesn't matter here. I can, if you like, grant that this question might matter in various other contexts and for various other purposes; and that 'the practice of promising' would probably not survive without a reasonably accurate and accepted means of deciding when an utterance of 'I promise to Φ' counts as the making of a *bona fide* promise to Φ; and finally that the question of whether promisees have or have not been led in good faith to believe that they have been promised something will now loom large. But my notion of an entitlement to promise is not meant to be a mark of genuine promise-making across the board by just anyone; it is instead the mark of a genuine promisor, a sovereign individual who earns his entitlement to promise by dint of relevant abilities, not mere convention; and the philosophical point of this concept is to bring into focus how remarkable this ability really is.

Very well, the moral-obligation theorist might reply, if it is not a sense of moral obligation, what *is* it that accounts for the fidelity of sovereign individuals to their promises? Nietzsche's answer is found in the closing sentences of *GM* II 2:

> The proud awareness of the extraordinary privilege of responsibility, the consciousness of this rare freedom, this power over oneself and over fate, has in [the] case [of the sovereign

---

[9] It is worth remarking that Nietzsche's text tacitly endorses the 'common-sense' view that promises can be made by those not entitled to make them; after all, feeble windbags are said to '*promise* although they are not entitled to'! And it is also worth remarking that Tim Scanlon's ingenious example of 'the Profligate Pal' shows that moral-obligation theorists can in fact acknowledge the theoretical need for something like the concept of an entitlement to promise. Suppose that the profligate Pal, a notoriously *un*reliable promisor, promises something to a sympathetic friend of his. The friend does not take the promise seriously, but 'accepts' it nevertheless. According to Scanlon's theory of promissory obligation, in such a case it becomes something of a conundrum to decide whether and/or how the Profligate Pal has put himself under an obligation to perform as he had promised to perform; which is to say that it is something of a conundrum to decide whether he has made a genuine promise. Cf. Scanlon 1998: 312; and see Owens 2006: 72 for discussion of the thesis that 'promises are valid only if accepted'.

individual] penetrated to the profoundest depths and become instinct. What will he call this dominating instinct, supposing he feels the need to give it a name? The answer is beyond doubt: this sovereign man calls it his *conscience*. (37/294)

So the root difference between Nietzsche's account of promissory fidelity and that of the moral-obligation tradition is that whereas the latter holds that one is morally obligated to keep promises because, in virtue of having promised, one *owes it to the promisee* to perform, Nietzsche maintains that sovereign individuals are committed to keeping their promises because, in virtue of having given *their* word, they *owe it to themselves* to live up to it. For Nietzsche, one might say, promissory fidelity is demanded only of those who demand it of themselves.

3 PERSONAL INTEGRITY

Nietzsche's sovereign promisors are faithful to their word because not to be would reveal a particularly contemptible weakness—a weakness of will, and of the memory of the will that is required of an animal entitled to promise. According to Nietzsche, there cannot be a truly *fundamental* distinction between the ultimate grounds of obligation of a unilateral commitment such as a private vow or a threat and the ultimate grounds of obligation of the distinctively bilateral commitment constitutive of a promise narrowly so-called. A moral-obligation theorist is likely to object that this betokens insufficient respect for the claims of others and amounts to just the kind of moral self-indulgence you might expect from a pernicious individualist like Nietzsche. For those to whom promises are made by sovereign individuals this objection will seem groundless. As we have seen, anyone promised something by such a promisor can count on fulfillment, or can at least rest assured that non-fulfillment will not be through any fault of the promisor; moreover, sovereign promisors show respect to their promisees in the very act of choosing them as suitable recipients of a promise.

What, then, of the benighted windbags deemed unworthy of the respect of a sovereign individual? While the very idea of dismissing the run of humanity as hopelessly *infra dig* will, perhaps rightly, raise egalitarian hackles, I don't think that it is Nietzsche's assimilation of promises to vows and threats with respect to the ground of obligation that causes the trouble. One can prefer Nietzsche's account of promissory fidelity to any on offer from the moral-obligation tradition, grant that to promise promiscuously is to tempt fate foolishly, and agree that one does in an important sense 'distinguish' those to whom one is prepared to give one's word in the form of a promise, without saying that those to whom one is not prepared to make promises are a pack of miserable *Heerdenmenschen*.

In drawing attention to the voluntary reliability required of all who pledge in any form, as opposed to dwelling on the requirements of promissory fidelity in particular in the manner of the moral-obligation tradition, Nietzsche draws attention to the philosophically searching problem of understanding what it means to bind oneself. Hobbes thought this an impossible feat: '[it is not] possible for any person to be bound to himself, because he that can bind can release; and therefore he that is bound to himself only is not bound' (Hobbes

2002/1651: vol. II, pp. 26, 198); Nietzsche thinks it an improbable, indeed 'paradoxical' feat, the achievement of which marks an important advance in our moral consciousness.

We saw that Nietzsche makes much of the power of forgetfulness. 'That this problem [of breeding an animal entitled to promise] has been solved to a high degree,' he writes, 'must appear all the more amazing to one who can fully appreciate the force working in opposition, that of forgetfulness' (35/291). The idea that what Hobbes thought to be a flat impossibility—being bound to oneself—has been achieved 'to a high degree' would appear to be doubly foreign to Hobbes's way of thinking. For Hobbes's denial that one can be bound to oneself alone clearly presupposes that 'being bound' contrasts simply with 'not being bound', rather than contrasting also with something like 'being weak, chaotic, and capricious'.

The concept of a *binding* commitment contrasts with the concept of something which, though a commitment of sorts, is nevertheless not binding. Ordinary decisions to act are, I take it, commitments of this latter, 'flexible' sort, revisable, *pro tem* commitments. Insofar as deci-sions are deliberate acts, they commit you to what you have decided. For when you Φ or do not Φ *in virtue of having decided so to act*, your Φ-ing/not Φ-ing is importantly normatively differ-ent from *just finding yourself* Φ-ing or not Φ-ing. Here I am sitting on the couch and therefore not going to the store. I ask myself whether perhaps I shouldn't do my shopping and answer 'no, I'll not go to the store just yet', i.e. I decide not to go to the store. I am now committed, *pro tem*, to doing something other than shopping; I have *rejected* the possibility of present shopping, as opposed to making an alternative possibility actual for sheer lack of attention to the shopping option. But this decision doesn't bind me for any longer than I care to let it. Noticing the time and realizing that the store will soon close, I may recant my recent rejection of present shopping and head out the door.[10]

A binding commitment explicitly revokes the openness to future dismissal that characterizes those mundane decisions 'which a minute can reverse'. Hobbes seems to think that while I can-not effect such a revocation all on my own, I can do so in partnership with another: if I cede to him the power of holding me to or releasing me from my commitment, I am bound; if I retain this power myself I am not. But this runs together the question of whether my right to change my mind has been handed over to someone else with the question whether that right has been revoked in the first place. If I promise something to you, I am bound to you to do what I prom-ised to do; if I renege, I let you down by breaking the bond that I had established. In just the same way, if I vow to myself to do something (or threaten to do something to you), I am bound to myself to do what I vowed (or threatened) to do; if I renege, I let myself down by breaking the bond that I had established. Since the two cases seem to parallel each other in the relevant respects, Nietzsche gets the better of Hobbes on this point.

Nietzsche's key idea about sovereign promising weaves together the conceptual and the his-torical in his characteristically fruitful and provocative fashion. The conceptual point is that from the fact that one can *un*bind oneself it does not follow that one is *not* bound; the historical point is that resolute individuals have existed. And it is in crucial part because of their example that we have developed a workable idea of what it is or would be like to demand of oneself that in some particular respect—say, in seeing to 'a pal's last need'[11]—one will remain committed *to*

---

[10]   This example was used to make a similar point in a different context in Migotti 2003: 85.
[11]   This phrase and that used as my title are from Robert W. Service's *The Cremation of Sam McGee*. The couplets from which the phrases are taken read: 'A pal's last need is a thing to heed, so I swore I would not fail; | And we started on at the streak of dawn; but God! he looked ghastly pale' and 'Now a promise made

the end and would choose to perish rather than not see the job done: for to change one's mind about this would betray and thus annihilate the very person that one is, in the act of promising, setting out to be.

By contrast with the Nietzschean approach, the moral-obligation tradition of thinking about promissory fidelity, sooner or later, is bound to attenuate the sense in which promissory obligations is truly *self*-generated. For sooner or later, moral-obligation theorists can be counted on to ground the obligation to keep promises, in whole or in part, in the obligation not to abuse the trust of others; and *this* obligation is wider in scope than the obligation to keep promises and logically independent of it.[12] On background obligation views of this sort 'promising involves,' as Rüdiger Bittner puts it, 'not *creating* but *assuming* an obligation that addresses all persons meeting a certain condition' (Bittner 1989: 59, emphasis added). All persons must keep their promises: this means that anyone meeting the condition of having promised to Φ has thereby put him or herself under an obligation to Φ. True, in promising to Φ I create an obligation to Φ where none existed before; but I can only create this new obligation because I take for granted the obligation not to abuse trust. Unlike the obligation to Φ, this latter obligation is not one I am supposed to be morally at liberty to accept or reject as I see fit.

Nietzsche's sovereign promisors fulfill their promises and other pledges from a sense of personal integrity rather than a sense of moral obligation. In respect of stringency, personal integrity is no less demanding than moral obligation. The difference between these two grounds of fidelity is that the one binds only those who bind themselves, while the other yields obligations that are taken to apply more generally. Fidelity which is rooted in integrity differs from fidelity which is rooted in moral obligation, therefore, not chiefly in how it is experienced by those who take themselves to be bound, but in how those who do take themselves to be bound regard those who do not. If promise-breaking violates a moral obligation, it violates an obligation under which promisors already stand; if it violates an obligation of personal integrity, promise-breakers are worthy of condemnation as feeble windbags precisely because they do *not* take themselves to be really bound at all. Not that the feeble are under any obligation to take themselves to be obliged to be as good as their word—which would amount to an obligation to be strong and sovereign; it is just that their feebleness consists in and is constituted by this lack of self-command.[13]

---

is a debt unpaid, and the trail has its own stern code. | In the days to come, though my lips were dumb, in my heart how I cursed that load.'

[12] For a careful, thorough elaboration of this point, see Scanlon 1998: chapter 7.

[13] Cf. *BGE* 272: 'Signs of nobility: never thinking of degrading our duties into duties for everybody; not wanting to delegate, to share, one's own responsibility; counting one's privileges and their exercise among one's *duties*.' Remarkably, Kant agrees with Nietzsche that there cannot be an obligation to recognize our obligations. The faculty by which we are able to do this, according to Kant, is that of conscience, and conscience, along with moral feeling, love of one's neighbour (*Liebe des Nächsten*), and self-esteem or respect, is an 'aesthetic precondition (*Vorbegriff*) of the receptivity of the mind (*des Gemüts*) for the concept of duty as such'. There cannot be a duty to acquire these preconditions, Kant argues, because, since they are preconditions, if they were not in place, the duty to acquire them would, so to speak, fall on deaf ears. What there is, according to Kant, is a duty to cultivate these qualities and capacities, which, he assures us, are always present in some measure in all people. See Kant 1996/1785: part 2, introduction, chapter 13.

So the first 'immoralist' thesis at which Nietzsche arrives is that *no one* is under a moral obligation to keep his promises; for if the promisor is strong he is above morality and if weak beneath it. And the second is that the true source of genuine promissory fidelity is the felt need and well-honed ability of sovereign individuals to 'vouch for themselves as future'.

4 REVISIONISM REPUDIATED

So much for Nietzsche's account of promissory fidelity. When it comes to the question of how this account—and in particular the crucial figure of the sovereign individual—bears on the rest of his thought, we are confronted with proliferating controversy. According to a burgeoning revisionist school of interpretation, the apparently glowing colours in which Nietzsche paints the sovereign individual are a feint. Nietzsche's true aim, we are told, is not to praise, but to call into question; when he 'celebrates' the sovereign individual he does so, it is said, in 'overblown', even 'ridiculously hyperbolic' (Leiter 2011: 108, 103). I disagree. Indeed, while *GM* II: 1–2 is certainly replete with rhetoric requiring due hermeneutical care, it is thoroughly wrong-headed to suppose that Nietzsche here is in the business of conveying something quite other than what he seems clearly to be saying.

Revisionists think that Nietzsche cannot really hold the sovereign promisor of *GM* II: 1–2 in high esteem; for, they argue, the self-aggrandizing pretensions of this figure are immediately seen to be false when it is recognized that they presuppose belief in the metaphysical fiction of the freedom of the will. Spelled out in a little more detail, the core revisionist argument is this: Nietzsche describes the sovereign individual as 'Lord of the *free* will' and as revelling in 'the privilege of *responsibility*', but Nietzsche doesn't *believe* in free will or moral responsibility. So this 'self-important' (Leiter 2011: 108) sovereign individual entitled to promise is not, in Nietzsche's view, really free, but in the grip of an illusion; his 'proud consciousness of freedom and power' betokens wishful thinking on a grandiose scale. A comprehensive reckoning of the shortcomings of this line of reasoning would be out of place here; so I will focus only on those distortions and distractions which bear directly on present concerns.[14]

To begin with, revisionists are notably inclined to conflate promise-*making* and promise-*keeping*. Christa Davis Acampora, for example, takes it upon herself to 'reformulate' Nietzsche's question about the paradoxical task of breeding an animal entitled to promise as the question: 'What must have happened…in order for us to be able (for nature to have granted us the ability) to make promises?' (Acampora 2004: 204, emphasis deleted). But merely making promises is not the point; even feeble windbags can do *that*. Nietzsche's question is about what must have happened for "the tree of the morality of custom" to yield its ripest fruit, the sovereign individual able to live up to his word from a sense of personal integrity—as opposed to lesser creatures able, when they are able, to manage not to break their word only out of weakness, out of mindless habit or congenital timidity, for example. As far as merely making promises is concerned, sufficient comment is provided by Henry

[14] Thomas Miles (2006) ably exposes weaknesses in the revisionist line of thought which I do not consider here, and Randall Havas (2000) and Aaron Ridley (2007) offer interpretations of the sovereign individual which, I suspect, mesh fairly well with the interpretation presented here.

Hotspur in dialogue with Owen Glendower in *Henry IV, Part One*: When, as discussion among these rebel leaders becomes fractious, Glendower warns Hotspur 'I can call spirits from the vasty deep', Hotspur justly retorts: 'Why, so can I, or so can any man, but will they come when you do call for them?' (Act III, Scene 1).

When Nietzsche describes the sovereign individual as 'resembl[ing] only himself,...autonomous and supramoral (for "moral" and "autonomous" are mutually exclusive)' (36/293), he is, of course, poking fun at Kant, according to whom 'moral' and 'autonomous' are not mutually exclusive, but mutually entailing. Lawrence Hatab, however, takes this quip to apply much more widely. As he sees it, Nietzsche invokes the figure of the autonomous, sovereign promisor, not in order to put him on a pedestal, but to knock him off one; 'the sovereign individual,' writes Hatab, 'names...the modernist ideal of subjective autonomy, which,...Nietzsche *displaces*' (Hatab 1995: 37). He finds evidence for this claim in *GM* I: 13, where Nietzsche allegedly 'traces [autonomy] to the inversion of master morality' (Hatab 1995: 37).

In *GM* I: 13, a much debated proof-text for Nietzsche's ideas about free will and human agency, Nietzsche declares that the distinction between deeds and doers, assumed by ordinary language and common morality, is illusory: 'there is no "being" behind the doing, effecting, becoming; "the doer" is simply fabricated into the doing—the doing is everything' (25/279). This is heady and debatable stuff, the connection of which to an 'ideal of subjective autonomy' is not obvious. Presumably, Hatab thinks that the ideal of autonomy presupposes the allegedly mistaken separation of doer from deed, just as common morality does. Perhaps so, but the questions raised by *GM* II: 1–2 are first, do we need to read more into the use of the word 'autonomy' there[15] than is required to understand the mischievous allusion to Kant, and second, does the figure of the sovereign individual need to be interpreted in terms which run afoul of anything claimed in *GM* I: 13? The natural reading of the only other occurrence of the word 'autonomous' and its cognates in the Colli–Montinari collected works, in an unpublished note from the end of 1880, indicates that both questions are to be answered in the negative.

The lapidary first sentence of that note reads: 'Autonomous people are very rare' (*KSA* 9: 331). So too, manifestly, are the sovereign individuals of *GM* II: 1–2. It won't be everybody who can honestly say that, 'twitching in all his muscles' he is aware of 'a feeling of the completion of man himself'.[16] In his superb autonomy, the sovereign individual is a *rara avis*—thus *GM* II: 2; in their miserable need for self-preservation and justification, the majority of mortals self-deceptively seek to pass off inveterate weakness as virtuous choice—thus *GM* I: 13. The two ideas fit together in an obvious way: autonomous, sovereign individuals have become genuinely free; most of us have not.

As noted above, revisionists make much of Nietzsche's talk of the sovereign individual as 'lord of the free will'. For Nietzsche, they remind us, is a notorious foe of the very idea of 'free will' in a metaphysically freighted, contra-causal sense. He thinks that the idea of a '*causa sui*' or an uncaused cause, which is what a will would have to be to be free in this sense, is a sheer impossibility (*BGE* 21 50–2/35–6). Accordingly, argues Acampora, since 'the kind of freedom associated with the sovereign individual who would be "master of *free* will"' is in clear tension

---

[15] And it is striking that this one-liner contains the sole occurrence of the word 'autonomous' or its cognates *in Nietzsche's entire published corpus*.

[16] Here, I think, it is evident that Nietzsche is going 'over the top' for effect.

with Nietzsche's hostility to the possibility of free will in the philosophically traditional sense, we read Nietzsche charitably and restore consistency to his *oeuvre*, by denying that he is in favour of the sovereign individual. That philosophical straw man is now deemed 'free' by his overweening self alone; he is, as Brian Leiter bluntly puts it, 'delusional' (Leiter 2011: 109).

But there is no reason to believe that when Nietzsche calls his sovereign individual 'lord of the free will' he means 'free will' to be taken in its traditional, supernaturalist sense. He means what he says: that the sovereign individual is in possession of a 'long and unbreakable will' (*GM* II: 2 37/294), strong enough to withstand 'a world of new strange things, circumstances, even acts of the will…placed…between the original…"I will do", and [its] actual discharge' (*GM* II: 1 36/292). *Strength* of will in Nietzsche's sense brings *freedom* of will because of its capacity to liberate its possessors from the dominion of external pressure and circumstance. Because, as Ken Gemes observes, 'the type of freedom Nietzsche… invok[es]…does not involve freedom from the causal order' (Gemes 2006: 327), Nietzsche's sovereign individual can be eminently free, even though neither he nor anyone else enjoys 'freedom of the will' in its technical, metaphysically superlative sense.

The last revisionist argument I will consider turns on an allegedly fatal incongruity between Nietzsche's considered views on agency and the priority of becoming over being and the capacities of will ascribed to the sovereign individual. As we have seen, the sovereign individual's unflagging 'memory of the will' enables him, *when he has promised*, to *counteract* his natural, healthy tendency to forget what is best forgotten. Acampora is of the opinion that a true memory of the will can be developed at the expense of the more primordial power of forgetfulness: 'the kind of willing that is had in promise-making came with a price—the diminution of forgetting' (Acampora 2004: 203); and, she adds, "we allow [forgetting] to wither at our peril" (ibid.). But I can find nothing in the text that supports this view.

In Nietzsche's own (German) words, the phrase which needs to be interpreted here reads: '…*mit Hülfe dessen für gewisse Fälle die Vergesslichkeit ausgehängt wird,—für die Fälle nämlich, dass versprochen werden soll*'. Clark and Swensen translate 'with whose help forgetfulness is disconnected for certain cases—namely for those cases where a promise is to be made'. There is no suggestion here that an ability, *ad libitum*, to 'disconnect'[17] one force or capacity, healthy forgetfulness, by means of another, a memory of the will, should be attainable only on condition that the (locally, temporarily) disconnected powers have atrophied (Acampora 2004: 205), diminished (p. 203), or withered (p. 203). On the contrary: the strength of the ongoing, healthy capacity for forgetfulness *needed by all* is precisely the measure of the unprecedented kind of strength—of will—*enjoyed by sovereign promisors alone*. This is why Nietzsche distinguishes a true memory of the will from 'a passive no-longer-being-able-to-get-rid-of [an] impression once it has been inscribed,…[an] indigestion from a once-pledged word over which one cannot regain control' (35–6/292).

---

[17] The verb is *aushängen*: literally 'to unhinge, as a door; to unhook'. Significantly, this is the same verb Nietzsche uses in *GM* II: 16, in a phrase quoted at the beginning of this paper, to describe the abrupt change from proto-humans operating on animal instinct to primitively civilized humans forced to conform to social norms. The line of thought is clear: long in the prehistoric past, animal instincts *en bloc* were *ausgehängt* 'instinctively' in favour of the morality of custom; much later, our instinctually rooted *forgetfulness* can be selectively and deliberately *ausgehängt* in virtue of the memory of the will needed for getting beyond the morality of custom.

GM II: 1 begins and ends with a modal verb: in the first sentence, *dürfen*, roughly 'may', and in the last, *können*, 'can'. The normative burden of this section can be obtained by stitching together these opening and concluding sentences: in German we have *Nur die **dürfen** versprechen, die für sich als Zukunft gut sagen können;*[18] in different English renderings: only those able to 'vouch for themselves as future' (Clark and Swensen) or 'stand security for their own future' (Kaufmann) have a right, or permission, or prerogative, or entitlement to promise.[19] To repeat the main point one more time: sovereign, Nietzschean promising is the business only of those 'strong and reliable' enough to live up to the task.

Appealing once again to *GM* I: 13, Acampora asks whether

> the Nietzsche who so emphasizes becoming, and who is suspicious of the concept of the subject... [could] think that it is desirable—let alone possible—that a person could ensure his or her word in the future? How could one promise to do something, to stand security for something, that cannot be predicted and for which one is, in a sense, no longer the one who could be responsible for it? (2004: 209)

The reason Nietzsche can and does admire the ability to stand security for oneself as future is that its emergence signals the presence of people who have become something other than

---

[18] According to the native speakers of German I have consulted on the subject, the phrase '*für sich als Zukunft gut sagen*' is not now idiomatic German and is quite possibly a coinage of Nietzsche's own.

[19] As noted above, for many purposes the English modal verb 'may' translates the German modal verb '*dürfen*' without difficulty; for example, in questions of the form 'May I ... ?', which are straightforwardly rendered as '*Darf ich ... ?*'. But in the crucial phrase from the opening line of *GM* II: 1—'*ein Tier heranzüchten, das versprechen darf*—it has been clear to all translators that 'may' will not do. Like Douglas Smith, I have chosen to render the crucial verb '*durfen*' into English as 'entitled to'. Unlike Smith, I translate Nietzsche's German infinitive '*versprechen*' with the English infinitive 'to promise', so that '*versprechen darf*—which occurs four times in the four pages of *GM* II: 1–2—comes out as 'entitled to promise' (as opposed to Smith's 'entitled to make promises'). With the exception of Smith 1996 and Diethe 2007, translators of the *Genealogy* into English have gone wrong enough in their attempts to put this phrase into English as to be worthy of comment.In 1918, Horace B. Samuel had Nietzsche speaking in the opening sentence of 'an animal who can promise', and then switched to the notion of being 'competent to promise' for two of the remaining passages. In his 1956 translation, Francis Golffing rendered the first occurrence of the phrase as 'with the right to make promises', anticipated Smith's 'entitled to make promises' for the second occurrence, and changed again to the very free 'dares to make promises' for the remaining two occurrences. In her 1994 translation, Carol Diethe chose 'able to make promises' for the opening sentence, and then changed to 'with the right to make promises'. Independently of the merits of these various forms of English words, it needs to be said that there is no reason to use different English idioms for Nietzsche's repeated German phrase. And Samuel's 'can promise' and Diethe's 'is able to promise' treat '*durfen*' as if it were '*können*', thus obscuring the crucial contrast and interplay between these two concepts.Walter Kaufmann (1968) and Maudemarie Clark and Alan Swensen (1998) translate the phrase uniformly but differently. Kaufmann chooses 'with the right to make promises', a phrase which unfortunately calls to mind a host of moral and juridical connotations foreign to Nietzsche's untechnical German; while Clark and Swensen choose 'permitted to promise', a phrase which misleadingly suggests a person, or institution, or custom, or rule, or law responsible for giving the relevant permission. Nietzsche's sovereign promisors arrogate to themselves their entitlement to promise; it is they alone, who, to use an English phrase which comes close to the mark, 'have any business' promising. In 2007, Diethe published a revised version of her translation, in which 'the prerogative to promise' is used throughout, a choice perhaps close enough in meaning to 'entitled to promise' (or 'entitled to make promises') as to make dispute between these alternatives less than profitable.

the 'merely passive conduits for various disparate forces already existing and operating around them' (Gemes 2006: 332). Precisely because we are not, any of us, metaphysically simple, divinely sustained substantial souls, the task of *becoming* a self-unifying, truly individual subject becomes urgent for some of us—indeed precisely those for whom Nietzsche writes his books.

A final nail in the revisionist coffin is found in the language Nietzsche uses to speak about himself and his philosophical vocation. In August 1885, about a year before he would begin writing the *Genealogy*, Nietzsche writes to an unidentified recipient:

> To me, my *Untimely Meditations* signify *promises*: what they signify to others, I do not know. Believe me, I would have stopped living long ago if I had taken a single evasive step with respect to these promises. Perhaps someone will yet come along who discovers that, from *Human, All Too Human* onwards I have done nothing but fulfill my promises. (*KSA* 11: 671)

More tellingly yet, at around the same time, in a draft preface to an envisaged second edition of the *Untimely Meditations*, we read:

> He who reads these writings with a young and fiery soul will perhaps divine the heavy vows with which I bound myself for life at that time,—with which I bound myself to my life: may such a one be one of the few who are *entitled* to bind themselves to such a life and such vows. (*KSB* 7: 75)[20]

So when Nietzsche hazards the bold hypothesis that breeding an animal entitled to promise is the real problem of man, he is, *sotto voce* and with an inward chuckle, talking to and of himself.

BIBLIOGRAPHY

(A) Works by Nietzsche

BGE   *Beyond Good and Evil* (1886), trans. R. J. Hollingdale. London: Penguin Books, 1973.
D   *Daybreak* (1881), trans. R. J. Hollingdale. Cambridge University Press, 1997.
GM   *The Genealogy of Morals* (1887), trans. Horace B. Samuel. New York: Boni and Liveright, 1918.
The Genealogy of Morals (1887), trans. Francis Golffing. New York: Doubleday, 1956.
On the Genealogy of Morals (1887), trans. Walter Kaufmann. New York: Vintage, 1968.
On the Genealogy of Morality (1887), trans. Carol Diethe. Cambridge: Cambridge University Press, 1994, revised 2007.
On the Genealogy of Morals (1887), trans. Douglas Smith. New York: Oxford University Press, 1996.
On the Genealogy of Morality (1887), trans. Maudemarie Clark and Alan J. Swensen. Indianapolis: Hackett Publishing, 1998.

---

[20] In German, the parallel phrasing is perhaps more striking than in English translation. In *GM* II: 2, the strong and reliable are described as '*die welche versprechen dürfen*'; in the draft preface, the reader able to divine the 'heavy vows' with which Nietzsche, in writing the *Untimely Meditations*, 'bound himself to his life' is described as: '... *Einer jener wenigen...*, *die sich zu ... [solchen] Gelöbnissen entschliessen—dürfen*'

KSA   *Sämtliche Werke: Kritische Studienausgabe*, ed. Mazzino Montinari and Giorgio Colli. Berlin: Walter de Gruyter, 1980.
KSB   *Sämtliche Briefe: Kritische Studienausgabe*, ed. Mazzino Montinari and Giorgio Colli. Berlin: Walter de Gruyter, 1986.

(B) Other Works Cited

Acampora, Christa Davis. 2004. 'On Sovereignty and Overhumanity: Why It Matters How We Read Nietzsche's GM II:2', *International Studies in Philosophy* 26.3: 201–19.
Àrdal, Pall. 1968. 'And That's a Promise', *Philosophical Quarterly* 18: 225–37.
Bittner, Rüdiger. 1989. *What Reason Demands*, trans. Theodore Talbot. Cambridge: Cambridge University Press.
Frankfurt, Harry G. 1988. 'Rationality and the Unthinkable', in *The Importance of What We Care About*. Cambridge: Cambridge University Press, 177–90.
Gemes, Ken. 2006. 'Nietzsche on Free Will, Autonomy and the Sovereign Individual', *Proceedings of the Aristotelian Society* 80 (suppl. vol.): 321–38.
Hatab, Laurence. 1995. *A Nietzschean Defense of Democracy*. Chicago: Open Court.
Havas, Randall. 2000. 'Nietzsche's Idealism', *Journal of Nietzsche Studies* 20: 90–9.
Heath, Joseph. 1995. 'Threats, Promises and Communicative Action', *European Journal of Philosophy* 3.3: 225–41.
Hobbes, Thomas. 2002/1651. *Leviathan*, ed. A. P. Martinich. Peterborough, Ont.: Broadview Press.
Kant, Immanuel. 1996/1785. *The Metaphysics of Morals*, trans. and ed. Mary Gregor. Cambridge: Cambridge University Press.
Leiter, Brian. 2011. 'Who is the "Sovereign Individual"? Nietzsche on Freedom', in Simon May (ed.), *Nietzsche's 'On the Genealogy of Morality': A Critical Guide*. Cambridge: Cambridge University Press, 101–19.
Miles, Thomas. 2006. 'On Nietzsche's Ideal of the Sovereign Individual', *International Studies in Philosophy* 38.3: 5–25.
Migotti, Mark. 2003. 'All Kinds of Promises', *Ethics* 114: 60–87.
Owens, David. 2006. 'A Simple Theory of Promising', *Philosophical Review* 115.1: 31–77.
Ridley, Aaron. 2007. 'Nietzsche's Intentions: What the Sovereign Individual Promises'. Unpublished manuscript.
Scanlon, T. M. 1998. *What We Owe to Each Other*. Cambridge, Mass.: Harvard University Press.
Schelling, Thomas. 1960. *The Strategy of Conflict*. Cambridge, Mass.: Harvard University Press.
Searle, John. 1969. *Speech Acts*. Cambridge: Cambridge University Press.
Searle, John. 2001. *Rationality in Action*. Cambridge, Mass.: MIT Press.
Tognazzini, Neal. 2007. 'The Hybrid Nature of Promissory Obligation', *Philosophy and Public Affairs* 35.3: 203–32.

···

CHAPTER 23

WILL TO POWER: DOES IT LEAD TO THE "COLDEST OF ALL COLD MONSTERS"?

···

JACOB GOLOMB

MANY scholars have examined the intriguing issue of Nietzsche's so-called fascistic philosophy. This issue became especially poignant after the Second World War and the cynical Nazification of his thought by Hitler's professors. Most of these studies dealt with this subject in isolation from the main corpus of his philosophy.[1] However, a balanced understanding of his attitude toward races, nationalism, and fascism can be most adequately attained from within Nietzsche's general philosophical framework. I am referring here mainly to his anthropological philosophy and to its central notions, since for the issues that concern us here we do not need to dwell on the metaphysical ramifications of his thought which are rather remotely relevant to the question of racism, especially as Nietzsche's anthropology was the main focus for falsifications by Nazis philosophers who were ordered by Hitler to mobilized the authority of this famous philosopher.

IN THEORY: THE PHILOSOPHICAL–ANTHROPOLOGICAL BACKGROUND

···

Many Nazi readings of Nietzsche's thought justify their acts of misappropriation by referring to his key notion of the will to power in terms of a violent, overpowering, and physical force which, if one uses it effectively and efficiently, will secure a military victory and material conquest.[2]

---

[1] See the "Select Bibliography" appended to Golomb and Wistrich 2002.

[2] Read the notorious Nazi "interpretation" of Nietzsche by Bäumler (1931), the Nazi authority on Nietzsche, who uncritically endorsed Elisabeth Förster-Nietzsche's edition of her brother's *Nachlass* and referred to the will to power as to a political notion

In opposition to this gross misrepresentation of his position, this essay, in tune with Nietzsche's philosophical anthropology, will show that what Nazis referred to when using the so-called Nietzschean idea of a military and physical "*Macht*" was actually what Nietzsche understood by "*Kraft*" and "*Gewalt.*" Moreover, even within the conceptual domain of *Macht*, its violent and aggressive manifestations were confined by him, in most cases, to the behavioral patterns of persons who suffered from and expressed the psychological phenomenon of "negative" power.

The key to the meaning of the will to power is Nietzsche's notion of self-overcoming. "*Selbstüberwindung*" is a concept originating in Nietzsche's recognition of the psychological role of sublimation. Sublimation, as the mental mechanism that orders and subdues instinctual drives, is responsible for the attainment of one's "self-mastery" (D 109).[3]

As a perpetual willing, the will to power negates the already formulated forms and replaces them with other creations. Dialectical self-overcoming is the clue, then, to Nietzsche's mature philosophizing.[4] It can be construed partly as a "confession" (BGE 6) and partly as his triumph over the negative (in his eyes) elements of his character and culture.[5] Certain parts of Nietzsche's personal and intellectual biography are transformed by his mature philosophy; some are preserved intact, others are eliminated, while still others are elevated beyond the merely human, all too human biographical traits. Thus, Nietzsche's notion of self-overcoming also contains the meaning of maturity and spiritual growth. In the later stages of character development one should overcome whatever elements are alien to the inner, organic personality—the elements precluding authentic creativity and freedom. If one were to ask Nietzsche, "What is the purpose of this self-overcoming?" he could have succinctly answered: "to achieve maturity and power." In this respect the will to power is similar to the will to selfhood—namely to become an autonomous person capable of devising and effectuating values. The optimal will to power is realized in the ideal *Übermensch*. On the other hand, if this will is diminished in quality, one's tendency to escape from one's individual self and to identify with the "herd" will intensify. Individuals with a sound psychic make-up and personal authenticity[6] are endowed with a will to power of higher quality and more intense vitality. Hence their will tends to manifest the master morality, in contrast to the slave morality which is more typical of those possessing lesser power or *Macht*,

---

[3] For a fuller discussion of Nietzsche's notion of sublimation see chapter 1 in Golomb 1989.

[4] Thus it is not a sheer coincidence that the first detailed discussion of this notion is found in Z II in a chapter entitled "On Self-Overcoming," where Nietzsche discusses it in terms of an unceasing will to overcome oneself: "and life itself confided this secret to me: 'Behold,' it said, 'I am *that which must always overcome itself*... I must be struggle and a becoming and an end and an opposition to ends.'" This essential relation between Nietzsche's concept of the "will to power" and his notions of "*Selbstüberwindung*" and "opposition" is also stressed by Wolfgang Müller-Lauter's interpretation (1971: 10–33) regarding "*Gegensätzlichkeit*" as a fundamental feature of the will to power.

[5] As Nietzsche admits: "my writings speak *only* of my overcomings: 'I' am in them, together with everything that was inimical to me" (HAH II: Preface 1). We may assume that these "inimical" elements include the strong religious sentiments that Nietzsche inherited from his Lutheran father and pious surroundings, his metaphysical-transcendental inclinations (Schopenhauer), his romantic predilections (Wagner), and the nihilist-pessimistic world outlook prevalent at that time in European culture, inspired by the "death of God" and Darwinian doctrine. We should add to these cultural trends, Nietzsche's own initial racial and nationalistic prejudices, so widely shared at the time of his youth.

[6] On Nietzsche's ideal of authenticity (the existential *Wahrhaftigkeit* as opposed to the cognitive *Wahrheit*) see Golomb 1995: chapter 4 and Golomb 1990.

although the latter may be endowed with greater physical force or *Kraft*. The conceptual distinction between *Kraft* and *Macht* is crucial to any understanding of Nietzsche's mature doctrine of power: it represents his philosophical emphasis on the transition from physical force to mental and spiritual power. It also helps us understand more closely the ideal figure of the modern *Übermensch* who has managed to sublimate most of his or hers competing driving forces (*Kräfte*) into a unified and authentic powerful whole.[7]

POWER (*MACHT*) VERSUS FORCE (*KRAFT*) IN NIETZSCHE

By the notion of *Kraft* Nietzsche refers to a primitive energy, to a latent and indefinite state that only functions when activated within a concrete situation.[8] The transition from *Kraft* to *Macht* is thus a transition from the potentiality of force to its actualization. Blind "*Kraftquellen*" (*HAH* II: 226; *KSA* 2: 481–2) are transmuted and become "*Mächtig*" (powerful) through a concrete expression in a specific cultural and historical context. The transition from a primal, inchoate driving force into a rationally formulated power is essential to Nietzsche's original characterization of the process of sublimation already found in his first major composition, *The Birth of Tragedy*. The Apollonian principle shapes and sublimates the "Dionysian-barbarian" drives, thereby endowing them with cultural value and esteem. The distinction between "force" and "power" is based on the assumption that *power is a sublimated force*.[9] The *Naturtrieb* is simply the primordial, brute force; only its sublimated cultural manifestations are endowed with effective and actual power. Nietzsche later calls this sublimation "victory over strength" ("*Der Sieg über die Kraft*," D 548; *KSA* 3: 318). Contrary to the slaves' worships of brute force, only a force sublimated by rational Apollonian elements and thereby elevated to a culturally valuable level should merit our admiration. This is a qualitative power and its most intense expression can be found in the "genius"[10] in whom this force is inwardly directed towards creating a genuine selfhood.[11]

[7] I write "modern *Übermensch*" since I concur with John Richardson's (1996) exposition to the effect that the *Übermensch* is actually attained (if at all; see Golomb 2006) by a synthesis of slave and master in the framework of a higher culture. The point Richardson convincingly makes is that historically the masters (as depicted in the first essay of *GM*) have achieved unity through simplicity, and such simplicity is no longer available to us moderns. The slaves, on the other hand, are seriously disunifed (being no more "*individuum*" but "*dividuum*," *HAH* I: 57) since they cannot form that complexity into a coherent whole (cf. also *HAH* I: 137). I owe this footnote to the helpful comment of the editors of this *Handbook*.

[8] See, e.g., *HAH* II: 1–226; *KSA* 2: 481–2. This connotation of *Kraft* actually agrees with current everyday German usage, as in the expression "*schlummernde Kräfte im Menschen wecken*." S.v. "*Kraft*" in *Duden: Das grosse Wörterbuch der deutschen Sprache* (Mannheim: Bibliographisches Institut, 1978).

[9] See, e.g., *HAH* II: 1–220; *KSA* 2: 473.

[10] *HAH* I: 263; *KSA* 2: 219; and witness Nietzsche's claim in *UM* III: 5 that "the saint," "the philosopher," and "the artist" best exemplify this self-control and overcoming of one's self.

[11] And thus accomplishing the "spectacle of that strength which employs genius *not for works* but for *itself as a work*," D 548; *KSA* 3: 319.

Special mental resources are required to achieve the "victory over strength" through this process of self-sublimation. But with this "triumph" we become a supreme work of art—an actualized *Macht*. The authentic selfhood of the *Übermensch* is achieved by one's ability to bring about a "transfiguration of nature," a purification of the primitive, coarse element of force into refined, creative power. Those who give vent to brute force or naked aggression do not belong within the category of the *Übermensch*, in spite of the desperate efforts of the Nazis to claim for Hitler precisely such a title.[12] Nietzsche valued the mental and the spiritual more highly than the physical and the biological. This is evident even in those few passages that have sometimes been abused to give a distorted reading of Nietzsche's attitude towards physical strength, thereby suggesting that he worshipped pure violence.[13]

Triumph over blind nature and basic instincts, including the drive toward aggressive supremacy, is a sign of the powerful person. Nietzsche's discovery (in *D* and later works) that current morality was simply an artful disguise of the drive toward domination led him to reject it, for it was not a genuine manifestation of power.

Macht, with its connotations of determination and freedom, is better suited to the notion of power as a sublimated and creative force than is *Kraft*, with its implications of undefined potentiality. This point is further amplified in *Nachgelassene Fragmente*, part of which was posthumously compiled and illegitimately published as *The Will to Power*.[14] In many aphorisms Nietzsche rejects the "mechanistic" interpretation of the world in favor of a dynamic one, and expresses dissatisfaction with the concept of force, for it lacks the connotations

[12] Attempts that had already been incisively refuted and ridiculed in 1942 by Martin Buber in a Hebrew article published by a literary magazine in Palestine: *Moznayim* 14: 137–45. An abridged version, "People and Leader," is found in Buber 1957: 148–60. Analysis of this essay and Buber's view on "Nietzsche and the Nazis" is given in Golomb 2004: 185–7.

[13] E.g. BGE 257; KSA 5: 206: "the noble caste was always the barbarian caste: their predominance did not lie mainly in physical strength [*physisichen Kraft*] but in strength of the soul [*in der seelichen*]." Consider also Nietzsche's famous slogan that was adopted and distorted by Mussolini: "*Live dangerously*" (GS 283, *vivere pericolosamente* in Italian). However, Nietzsche speaks here not about warriors wearing black shirts (the *camicie nere*) but about the "seekers of knowledge! [*die Erkennenden*]," who are "more fruitful *human* beings, happier beings." This is one of the first descriptions of Nietzsche's ideal of "the *free spirit par excellence [freie Geist]*" that he extols in the same book (GS 347). They are persons who decline any dogmas, may they be scientific, metaphysical, political, or religious. They uphold the view that our cognitive horizon is open to an infinite number of perspectives from which one may view oneself—one's life, culture, and all that matters—without being afraid to "face any danger and to enter the open sea" (GS 343) of free convictions and creations. They are freethinkers who courageously embrace the immanent world devoid of gods and create their original perspectives while experimenting (not only intellectually but also existentially) with many modes of life and thought. Do such persons seem to be fascists?

[14] My occasional references to this unauthorized collection do not imply that I accept the Nazi professor Bäumler's (1930) description of this highly selective compilation of Nietzsche's notebooks of 1883–8 as his final "systematic work." On the other hand, I do not fully agree with the view of Karl Schlechta (1977: 55) who, trying to cleanse Nietzsche of the Nazi elements ascribed to him by Bäumler, maintains that "in Der Wille zur Macht nichts Neues steht" and thus suggests that the book is hardly worth reading. See also Strong's (1975: 220) view that "at best, the book serves an indexing function." I am not using uncritically this collection of Nietzsche's notes as representative of his final or mature philosophy, but am rather referring to it to get a closer look at his process of thinking in the making, where various ideas and notions were tested, refined, or rejected. Hence I am treating this collection much as Walter Kaufmann suggested when publishing the English translation of *The Will to Power*— namely, as a "thought laboratory." See the elaborated discussion of this whole issue by Bernd Magnus (1988).

of intentional, deliberate, creative direction.[15] Nietzsche is not satisfied with the notion of "force" because it is a quantitative concept derived from descriptive mechanistic physics, which fails to account for qualitative processes, such as sublimation (*WP* 660) and overcoming (*WP* 661).

A concept of sheer force derived from the natural sciences is inappropriate to philosophical anthropology. Nietzsche's notion of the will to power, however, unifies under one heading a large number of psychological observations and intuitions. It is a term that grows out of many specifically psychological phenomena, such as sublimated creation, self-overcoming, will, drives, intentional activity conscious of its own goals, moral praxis, or ascetic religious patterns. This unifying notion became the core of Nietzsche's mature psychology.[16]

Another reason why Nietzsche rejects the concept of physical force (apart from its psychological inappropriateness) is that it lacks intrinsic dynamic intensification. Force cannot be used to explain the basic psycho-biological phenomena of growth and maturation by means of overcoming (*WP* 643). Self-overcoming and sublimation require an indefinite investment of energy for the cancellation, preservation, and elevation of a given activity. The concept of force, however, is associated with the preservation of a certain amount of energy within a closed system (*WP* 1062 and 1064). This renders it unsuitable to a dynamic approach, one that generalizes the biological notion of continuous growth into a comprehensive psychological theory. Put differently: the concept of force obeys the dictum *ex nihilo nihil fit*, in that the effect contains nothing which did not already exist in the cause. Sublimation, self-overcoming, and the effort of the human being to intensify oneself cannot be bound by such mechanistic principles. Causal explanations do not apply in the mental domain of the human will, and one is quite justified in speaking of the phenomenon of the dialectical intensification of life, due to the operation of the will which elevates it to a qualitatively higher level and "degree" of power (*WP* 688). Mere preservation of being leads to stagnation. The will to power strives to overcome anything that curbs the being's intensification or affirmation. Thus, Nietzsche comes to realize that this dynamic growth is incompatible with the laws of the conservation of energy of classical physics (*WP* 689).

The aspects of force imbued with the element of power are manifest in the will to power. The substratum upon which the process of sublimation operates is the force, and the element that forms and molds this force is the will. Force is the necessary but not the sufficient condition for the display of power. The ("Dionysian") force together with the ("Apollonian") forms provide the essential conditions. This synthesis of Nietzsche's earlier dualistic principles into the monistic will to power shapes his mature "new psychology."[17]

According to various notes it appears that Nietzsche was not at all content with a psychology that had only become "the morphology and *the doctrine of the development of the will to power*" (*BGE* 23) but wished to revise Schopenhauer's formula and generalize the

---

[15] See, e.g., *WP* 619 where he states: "the victorious concept force [*Kraft*], by means of which our physicists have created God and the world, still need to be completed: an inner will must be ascribed to it, which I designate as 'will to power', i.e. as an insatiable desire to manifest power; or as the employment and exercise of power, as a creative drive, etc."

[16] Thus in his 1888 declaration of intentions—partly realized in his writings in this and the previous year—Nietzsche testifies to the centrality of the will to power in the "*Unitary conception of psychology*" (*WP* 688). For a concise exposition of this psychology see Golomb 1999.

[17] Cf. *BGE* 12, 45; *BT* Preface 2; *HAH* Preface 8; *GS* Preface; *A* 24, 28, 29, etc. Most notably, see Nietzsche's remarks in *EH*: "Why I Am a Destiny" 6.

psychological phenomenon of the will into a comprehensive metaphysical cosmology. This stands in sharp contrast to his basic intuition that viewed any metaphysical system as another redundant "shadow" of the dead God (*GS* 108). It also contrasts another of his published writings where he objects to Schopenhauer's cosmology of "the will in itself" as "a primeval mythology" (*GS* 127). This aphorism (and others) indicate that Nietzsche could not subscribe to a cosmological and metaphysical doctrine of the will to power; first, because he limits willing to "intellectual beings" only, and second, because he renders the concept of "substance" as an advantageous fiction (*GS* 111). Hence, in contrast to Schopenhauer, Nietzsche does not identify "being" with "willing." In his view, the latter is solely "a mechanism" (*GS* 127), a functional psychological system, within which the will is not an entity but a function—merely another action. In Nietzsche's authorized writing, then, the will to power is based upon distinctly psychological and anthropological principles. For our purposes here, this is what really matters in issues pertaining to racism, nationalism, and fascism.

Furthermore, even the Nazis (with the exception of Heidegger) did not deal professionally and theoretically with the metaphysics of the will to power or with its ontological ramifications. Nazism was mainly interested in the anthropological manifestations of this principle and its derivative typological implications which were conductive to various distortions, biases, and falsifications. Hence the main thrust of this essay is directed toward the exposition of Nietzsche's psychological typology.[18]

The preeminence of psychology's role in Nietzsche's thought is exemplified even in his famous entry published as *WP* 1067—an entry, so we are informed, that "Nietzsche jotted down in July 1885 but had set aside by February 1888 as material for which he had no further use" (Magnus 1988: 226). The entry describes "this world" as "a monster of energy [*Kraft*]", in which every element consumes the other in a perpetual struggle for dominance and control. Just as the human "monster of energy" (*WP* 995) sublimates tremendous force to create the *Übermensch*, so the entire "*Dionysian world*" creates itself "out of the play of contradictions back to the joy of concord," thereby becoming "*the will to power—and nothing besides!*" (*WP* 1067).

This unofficial cosmology entails Nietzsche's view that the will to power also manifests itself in the wish to impose interpretative perspectives on nature in order to control it through a set of cognitive projections (*WP* 643). One, capable of molding oneself and overcoming one's surroundings, is not only conscious of that fact, but immediately attempts to project and generalize this insight (or self-interpretation) on the entire cosmos. This projection should be understood as a heuristic-didactic clarification of the fundamentally psychological consequences of the will to power that Nietzsche played with in his notebooks. Presumably, because such a clarification lends no philosophical legitimacy to Nietzsche's official philosophy and stands in opposition to some of his main writings, he did not include such cosmological speculations in his published works.

---

[18] Nietzsche's attempt to locate humanity and culture within a metaphysics of the will to power is expressed mainly in the posthumous unauthorized collection *The Will to Power* (especially in sections 618–715 "which has no parallels"—as Kaufmann rightly says in his translation—"in Nietzsche's books" (*WP* 332 n. 53). Presumably, Nietzsche was not satisfied with these notes and ideas that stood in stark opposition to his published opinions. Aware of the contentiousness of such generalized speculations, he did not include them in any of his self-authorized books with the possible exception of *BGE* 36, where he conducts a speculative "experiment" ("*den Versuch*," *KSA* 5: 54) regarding the entire world as the "will to power and nothing else" (*KSA* 5: 55).

POWER (*MACHT*) VERSUS VIOLENCE (*GEWALT*)

The second volume of *HAH* places even greater emphasis on the spiritual and qualitative characteristics of power, establishing more clearly the distinction between power and force. Nietzsche describes humans in terms of creative powers, organizing the world around them in their own image and in accordance with their own uniquely human categories. We are assisted in this project by an intellectual capacity to construct theoretical perspectives,[19] which enable us to cope with nature by anthropomorphizing it. Thus, intellectual activity serves the psychological need for power. These needs are met even if we do not achieve victory in the practical arena of the history of force (*HAH* II: 50). Be that as it may, there is a growing tendency in Nietzsche's thought to spiritualize the notion of power as part of his attempt to distinguish power from the tangentially related concepts of *Kraft* and *Gewalt*.

Nietzsche's first writings already portrayed humans as a complex of instinctual drives, each of which strives continually to dominate the others. Such a depiction naturally suggested acts of violence as inherent in all life activities—including those manifesting power. The internal logic of this early psychology required Nietzsche to distinguish acts of brute violence (*Gewalt*) from those elements of power included in the sublimated concept of *Macht*. The criterion of self-overcoming is crucial in this spiritualization of power.

> Writing ought always to advertise a victory—an overcoming of *oneself* which has to be communicated for the benefit of others; but there are dyspeptic authors who write only when they cannot digest something... Through their anger they try unconsciously... to exercise violence (*Gewalt*) upon the reader—that is, they too desire victory but over others. (*HAH* II: 152; *KSA* 2: 441, my translation)

Here, as elsewhere (e.g., *BGE* 259), Nietzsche identifies the use, manipulation, and exploitation of others with violence (*Gewalt*), contrasting this external manifestation of gross force with power which is directed towards an internal expression of self-overcoming.

Nietzsche emphasizes the development of selfhood and the intrinsic use of the energy provided by the will to power for creation of one's self (*HAH* II: 366). While the process of self-overcoming is (by definition) free of violence directed toward others, other processes of assimilation and internalization do manifest it to a degree, particularly those which employ force against an object external to the self. Recognizing this, Nietzsche imposes three important constraints on the violent ramifications of the will to power.

First, Nietzsche maintains that a genuine process of assimilation does not entail sheer negative destructiveness; the will is constrained insofar as the external object must not be entirely obliterated, but rather preserved in part by being creatively sublimated. For this reason Nietzsche placed creativity in opposition to rejection and negation: "all rejection and negation... point to a lack of fruitfulness" (*HAH* II: 332). The violent implications of the creative assimilation of external entities only challenge their relative autonomy—but do not obliterate them.

---

[19] Almost from the beginning of his treatment of power phenomena, Nietzsche identifies perspectivism with power; see, e.g., *HAH* 1: Preface 6.

A second constraint limiting the violence of assimilative acts follows from Nietzsche's insistence that these acts are not concerned with physical violence directed against concrete objects: what is used and assimilated is not the object as such, but one's own mental impression or experience of it. Consequently, power is not identified as the ability of an individual to master others by force in acts of confrontation (*HAH* II: 228).

The most important constraint, however, derives from the purpose or goal of the affirmation of power. The point is not to change or reform the external object with the intent of destroying it, but ultimately to transfigure the agent of assimilation. Acts of violence may be typically instrumental in forcibly changing or transforming others but the instrumental use of others within a context of self-transformation and self-overcoming must be manifest in *sublimated* expressions of the will to power. These sublimated expressions were exactly what even the "strong individual" in the primitive society lacked. Because of his existential insecurity and the negative uncultured social circumstances such an individual:

> originally treated not only nature but societies and weaker individuals too as objects of plunder: he exploits them as much as he can and then goes on. Because his life is very insecure, alternating between hunger and satiety, he kills more animals than he can eat . . .

Unlike the refined person who in modern culture tends to sublimate his basic instincts, in case of the person who lived in a uncivilized society,

> His demonstrations of power are at the same time demonstrations of revenge against the painful and fearridden state of his existence: then again, he wants through his actions to count as being more powerful than he is. (*HAH* III: 181)[20]

The actions of insecure individuals who are lacking the inner sense of self-importance and power are mostly preoccupied with regaining or fortifying their fragile sense of selfhood. Hence, their acts of revenge cannot be properly motivated by the attitude of *amor fati*; he or she therefore lacks the truly genuine spiritual power which Nietzsche's psychology extols. Genuine power seeks an autonomous overcoming of the self, while revenge evades self-responsibility and only attempts to augment one's power ("*Machtzuwachs*") by exploiting and mistreating external objects. The actual exploitation of others—or even the disposition to do so[21]—signifies the absence of both autarky and authenticity attaching to a personal genuine power. It can only result in an anarchistic and counterproductive process *of bellum omnium conra omnes*—a perpetual chain of vengeful and aggressive acts.

On the other hand, a social contract that structures group relations in accordance with the principles of justice and equality is incompatible with the mental "instinct for dominance" ("*Triebe nach Übergewicht*," *HAH* III: 31; *KSA* 2: 563). Yet this drive differs essentially from the will to power which is defined precisely in contrast to the desire to control and dominate others, being sublimatory and inwardly directed. It is noteworthy that Nietzsche does not object to social organization in principle, and regards it as a necessary condition—if at times

---

[20] This passage actually represents one of the first portraits of the type of person who exhibits "negative" power patterns (Golomb 1989: chapter 6). See also the discussion in the next section.

[21] Nietzsche's rejection of human exploitation leads him even to qualify his known objection to socialism: "The *exploitation* of the worker was . . . a piece of stupidity, and exhausting of the soil at the expense of the future, an imperiling of society" (*HAH* III: 286; cf. also *HAH* III: 285).

a necessary evil. He describes the sublimatory processes as appearing only when the "state of nature" is transformed by the necessary establishment of a social order (*HAH* III: 31; *KSA* 2: 563). The instinct for dominance is sublimated in the process. Even so, this particular sublimatory act is not to be identified with the emergence of the will to power: the former follows from the coercions of an extrinsic social order, while the latter is spontaneously generated out of the dynamic interaction of the Apollonian-Dionysian components of the inner personality.

One must conclude that Nietzsche distinguishes between two types of sublimatory process: the autonomous (expressing the spontaneous self-overcoming of the will to power) and the heteronomous (deriving from external exigencies and operating on those instincts incompatible with social coexistence). The heteronomous processes provide a kind of safety valve preserving culture and social organization (see, for example, *HAH* III: 226). Ultimately, however, they only work to displace certain drives rather than spontaneously directing them. And it is only through sublimation, Nietzsche maintains, that culture will develop creatively and fruitfully. Nietzsche's conclusions at the historical level thus parallel the distinction drawn earlier at the level of the individual: just as the will to power provides the motivating force for forming and determining the individual, so too it does not merely preserve culture, but continually creates and regenerates it.

Moreover, Nietzsche claims that "in every healthy aristocracy" consisting of equally powerful individuals it is a sign of "good manners" to refrain "from injury, violence [*Gewalt*], and exploitation," looking instead to place "one's will on a par with that of someone else's" (*BGE* 259; *KSA* 5: 207). This is the background for Nietzsche's insistence that justice is "the good will among parties of approximately equal power to come to terms with one another, to reach an 'understanding' by means of a settlement—and to compel parties of lesser power to reach a settlement among themselves" (*GM* II: 8; *KSA* 5: 306–7).

Powerful persons may at times spontaneously manifest the power at their disposal, but the desire for power is more clearly evidenced in the behavior of those in whom precisely power is wanting and who require some kind of external affirmation. But where do such individuals find the power to exploit their weakness through such manipulative dynamics? It cannot be the case that the weak person starts without any power at all: the very need for power indicates the existence of some primary source of power. So conceived, "power" in Nietzsche's anthropological philosophy cannot be quantitatively variable from one person to another; the difference between the weak and the powerful is not one of quantitative magnitude. Power is a feature of every individual's constitution, and the variations are to be accounted for in terms of qualitatively distinct ways of its expression. For Nietzsche, the main characteristic of power is its insusceptibility to any quantitative assessments in terms of force. The nature of the difference between the "man of power" (*HAH* I: 44) and the "powerless" (*HAH* I: 45) is a contrast in the qualities or forms through which a constant resource is manifest. Hence, Nietzsche's powerful persons make no attempt to acquire more power, but wish to be conscious of and to enjoy the free expression of their power through its spontaneous reactivation (see, e.g., *WP* 661).

Furthermore, if the notion of "powerful master" and "powerful slave" had been quantitative and relative, Nietzsche would have been unable to explain how the historical domination of weak slave morality over the masters could have occurred.[22] Moreover, if the value

---

[22] *GM* III: 13 and see Golomb 1989: chapter 7.

of power depended on an estimation of quantitative degree, Nietzsche would clearly have committed a naturalistic fallacy, analyzing the specifically ethical value of a property (what ought to be) in terms of its natural characteristics (what naturally is). However, Nietzsche was conscious of such a fallacy and deliberately avoided it. He is clearly opposed to naturalization of morality which is to him not something given and delivered but something created and constructed:

> Every morality is, as opposed to *laisser aller*, a bit of tyranny against 'nature'; also against 'reason'; but this in itself is no objection. (*BGE* 188)

And again:

> What the philosophers called 'a rational foundation for morality' and tried to supply, was, seen in the right light, merely a scholarly variation of the common *faith* in the prevalent morality; a new means of *expression* for this faith. (*BGE* 186)[23]

At this point one might pose the obvious question: why, after all, does Nietzsche disapprove of the weak who do their best (according to their inherent nature) to acquire power from others by means of their weakness, while approving of the powerful individuals who cannot help but manifest their power—even at the expense of others?

Nietzsche recommends a direct struggle with external (social and economic) or internal (psychological) distress as the most reliable solution; in the long term it is the only way to ensure and affirm the inherent power of the individual personality. A character that develops exclusively through the formation of dependent relations with others can never become genuinely mature: it will not have developed its own power to its maximum potential. The affirmation of the self cannot be completed without the overcoming of its weak and regressive elements.

Nonetheless, Nietzsche's extensive discussions of ascetic morality required a third concept of force in addition to *Kraft* and *Macht*: the concept of *Gewalt* (violence):

> For certain men feel so great a need to exercise their strength [*ihre Gewalt*] and lust for power that, in default of other objects or because their efforts in other directions have always miscarried, they at last hit upon the idea of tyrannizing over certain parts of their own nature ... In every ascetic morality man worships a part of himself as God and for that he needs to diabolize the other part. (*HAH* I: 137; *KSA* 2: 131)

The notion of power as *Macht* is thus located between two extreme poles: quantitative, static *Kraft*, devoid of rational and creative sublimation, and the excessively dynamic and brutal *Gewalt*, suppressing and annihilating all other vectors of force. *Macht*, however, contains the meaning of cancellation as well as creative assimilation. Put differently, creative power is a compromise between an unrestrained and destructive play of the instincts and their hostile repression. By describing ascetic attitudes in terms of violence, Nietzsche emphasizes that they actually constitute a violence performed on power itself. The ascetic does finally achieve a kind of tranquility by choosing one drive to dominate the others until they are all eradicated. However, this tranquility is achieved at the expense of annihilating the sublime creative energy. The genuinely powerful individuals, by contrast, are continually readjusting

---

[23] See also *D* 100, 248, 428; *BGE* 9, etc.

the forces of their personality, calling on different drives to motivate positive action; using instinctual chaos as the material for a productive life (*GS* 277). The essential difference between the *Übermensch* and the ascetic saint, then, may be formulated in terms of the distinction between *Macht* and *Gewalt*, sublimation and repression. It should be noted, however, that repression is also an operation requiring a kind of force in the overcoming of drives, and so it is accompanied by a subjective experience similar to that characteristic of sublimation (*HAH* I: 142).

The portrait of the powerful personality emerges which depicts it as more vulnerable in direct confrontation with brute force, precisely because of its spiritual and rational elements. This feature clarifies an apparent paradox in Nietzsche's doctrine of the will to power: if Christianity (whose exemplar is the ascetic saint) represents a suppressed and declining will to power and a decadent system of instinctual drives, how did it defeat and overwhelm the elements that express an authentic will to power? If Nietzsche had been a pragmatist, the successful manifestation of power might have been his central criterion of power. But he is clearly not pragmatic in this way. A genuine power is not always obliged to show itself in terms of success in a world where force typically dominates spirit. Spiritual power, which is the only one that creates culture, is often vulnerable to the pressures of brute physical force. This is often the case on both the individual plane (the *Übermensch* versus the *Untermensch*) and the historicalcultural plane (the ancient Greeks versus the barbarians; the superior "pagans," i.e., ancient Greeks, versus Christianity). When the religious personality redirects its intense force outward, away from repressive self-tyranny and toward the domination of others, he intentionally sets out to suppress and destroy (*HAH* I: 114) precisely those others engaged in self-formation, not self-denial. These others retain their superior power despite the fact that they exercise less force (*HAH* I: 68).

Although the qualitative power of the individual or society is no guarantee of its material success and victory, it nonetheless ensures a spiritual and cultural superiority. For this reason Nietzsche is careful to distinguish between the history of power (spiritual and intellectual progress) and the history of force (physical and material domination). It is precisely those who have been in the weaker position relative to the history of force who are responsible for cultural advances relative to power: "It is the more unfettered, uncertain and morally weaker individuals upon whom *spiritual progress* depends."[24]

The strength of the powerful is not due to a greater degree of force, just as the weakness of the powerless is not simply represented in lower magnitudes of energy. Power and weakness do not signify different *quanta* but a different *direction* of the operation of power and distinct modes of derivation and intensification. It is useful here to recall the Kantian distinction between autonomy and heteronomy.[25] Nietzsche himself employs this distinction implicitly in his analysis of those individuals who use their power hypocritically. He observes this same pattern in the wider historical-cultural context of religion and morality. A weak and

---

[24] *HAH* I: 224; *KSA* 2: 188. It should be pointed out in this context that this position does not entail a renunciation of Darwinian doctrine, for the latter refers primarily to the material domination assured by the survival of the strongest (those possessing *Kraft*). Nietzsche rather offers a complementary perspective, treating "spiritual progress" as a function of agents who are wanting in force: "to this extent the celebrated struggle for existence does not seem to me to be the only theory by which the progress or strengthening of a man or race can be explained" (*HAH* I: 224; *KSA* 2: 188).

[25] On Kant's impact on Nietzsche's philosophy, read Berkowitz 1995.

persecuted social group or sect may attempt to subjugate the powerful by indirect means, just as the weak person extorts pity from the powerful as a means of absorbing some of their strength and undermining their autonomy. If religious and moral values emphasizing pity and justice are internalized by the powerful personality, they will inculcate feelings of guilt and humiliation. In this way the weaker persons obliquely draw the powerful "down" to their own level and so avoid the challenge of elevating themselves through self-development. What authority the weak may obtain is not, then, internally located. The powerful personalities, by contrast, autonomously legislate their *own* values and laws, becoming models for others. If they prescribe laws to others as well, it is not because they need to dominate them to enhance their own authority; it is only the spontaneous expression of their power. Thus Nietzsche says that "to be a lawgiver is a more sublimated form of tyranny" (*HAH* I: 261); that is, the lawgiving of the powerful is a natural creative expression—not a direct intentional act of violence (*Gewalt*) or an indirect, heterony-mous tyranny.

But why does the strong autonomous agent internalize certain corrupting values and yield to the *ressentiment* of the weak? Why does their power not guarantee a self-legislating creativity which would be resistant to such internalizations?

Nietzsche recognized the seriousness of this question and tried hard to respond to it. In *HAH* he suggests that the highly developed spiritual and intellectual component of power may in some sense weaken even the most superior personality. Because they are genuinely free and independent, they are unlikely to adhere to any rigid and inflexible complex of norms: the values they possess are open to examination and susceptible to being "overcome." They will, then, be more vulnerable to the surreptitious indoctrination which the weak use against them. Their freedom from any given tradition induces a kind of frailty, for it allows them to oscillate perpet-ually between whatever possibilities they may encounter. In historical praxis, this dynamic may produce an impressionable personality, susceptible to manipulation and exploitation:

> Compared with him who has tradition on his side and requires no reasons for his actions, the free spirit is always weak, especially in actions; for he is aware of too many motives and points of view and therefore possesses an uncertain and unpracticed hand. What means are there of nonetheless rendering him *relatively strong*? How does the strong spirit come into being? (*HAH* I: 230).

The problem may be recast as that of turning spiritual power into a concrete historical force: is it possible to preserve the spirit of a Hamlet in the body of a Faust? Nietzsche's solu-tion focuses on the social fabric woven with religious and moral dogmas that produce a psychological pattern of guilt, vengeance, and bad conscience. These are the weakest threads of culture, responsible for the corruption of spiritual power and intellectual pro-gress. In emphasizing these elements, Nietzsche implicitly admits that there can be no abso-lute psychological autonomy: even the most powerful are not impervious to influence by the environment with which they interact. The revaluation of prevalent cultural norms is essential to the evolution of the psychology of the *Übermensch* because even the arena of the "authentic legislator" may be penetrated by environmental values and forces. The absolutely autonomous will to power is, therefore, no more than a regulative idea—one that provides the model for approximation, but which can in principle never be fully realized.[26] Indeed, Nietzsche always refers to the will to power as something that is never absolutely satisfied. It is a perpetual movement of the whole person in relation to everything it encounters, a

---

[26] For an elaboration of this point, see Golomb 2006.

movement to assimilate, overcome, and mature with it. By nature, this activity is incessant, for its range of operation is infinite and in principle inexhaustible. Although Nietzsche wished to approximate the ideal will to power as closely as possible by translating power into a concrete historical force, he did not aim at exhausting or fully realizing its potential. There can be no final conclusion to this dialectic of power.

The creative and spiritual dimensions of genuine power make it more vulnerable in the "battlefields" of life governed by the rules of crude force, and in which victory is conferred upon those who possess material strength. But for Nietzsche, for whom "life is no argument" (*GS* 121), it is not paradoxical to consider *Macht* superior to *Kraft* and *Gewalt*. In his own way he aspires to the Socratic value of encouraging only the good life, rather than preserving life as such. This "good life" has nothing to do with the biological ideal of the Aryan race and the aggressive Third Reich, but actually it clearly negates them. This will become even further apparent once we explicate Nietzsche's basic anthropological typology between negative versus positive power patterns.

"Positive" Versus "Negative" Power Patterns

Negative power is symptomatic of a weak personality, lacking in power but incessantly attempting to obtain it. In Nietzsche's view this pattern was characteristic of the early Christians, who formed their religion out of a desperate need for power:

> There are recipes for the feeling of power, firstly for those who can control themselves and who are thereby accustomed to a feeling of power [*einem Gefühle der Macht*]; then for those in whom precisely this is lacking. Brahminism has catered for the men of the former sort, Christianity for men of the latter (*D* 65).
>
> In a sense, Christianity reconstructed the concepts of sin, bad conscience and guilt, and used them as instruments of cruelty and vengeance; these concepts have often justified the abuse, even the torture, of others, thereby intensifying the Christian's own feebleness (*D* 53).

Clearly, no positive power is exhibited in the satisfaction derived from abusing and dominating one's fellow beings. Disguised cruelty and its attendant (perverse) pleasure are called upon only to reinforce an unstable character. Negative power does not express itself spontaneously, but derivatively: it is fundamentally deficient and defective, striving to enhance its feeble "feeling of power" and shattered self-image by enjoyment obtained from abuse and cruelty.

Nietzsche applies this anthropological typology for his moral considerations. He does not posit power against morality, but proposes an active morality of positive power against the traditional passive type, opting for courageous creativity and autonomy based on the acquired selfhood of the moral agent. He contrasts the characteristic features of these two moralities:

> All actions may be traced back to evaluations, all evaluations are either *original* or *adopted*— the latter being by far the most common. (*D* 104)

The transmitted "morality of tradition" which mechanically and arbitrarily conditions us is in fact antiindividualistic, repressing the genuine personality, making it into a "*dividuum*."[27] Nietzsche proposes instead a "healthy" egoistic morality which springs out of positive power. The violence of the traditional morality against the individual explains its impoverishment, pessimism, and depression. As a result, vitality withers away, leaving a feeling of weakness, discontent, and "the profoundest misery" (*D* 106). This moral wretchedness and other expressions of the traditionally accepted ethos are manifestations of the will to power. However, this is only the limited expression of negative power, characterized by fear and weakness. The power impelling traditional morality is not sufficiently strong or independent, thus creating a perpetual anxiety that it may be undermined. This brings us to develop defense mechanisms against our doubts and instabilities which merely intensify them. Nietzsche therefore maintains that the supporters of official morality are directed by "an obscure anxiety and awe" (*D* 107) of losing their influence and authority. In consequence, their "moral commands" attempt to enhance and reinforce power by exploiting other human beings.

Nietzsche portrays in detail the cunning, devious, moral mechanisms that persons of negative power reinforce and use to affirm themselves. Their strategy is to establish the morality of duty, thus assuring "self-regard" (*D* 112). They achieve this by shrewdly and insidiously assuming sovereignty over individuals. Certain "rights" are granted which signify their recognition of others' powers, but in return others are required to comply with certain duties and to concede them their rights in return. Thus all are trapped within a network of duties and rights, which eventually reinforces and reaffirms the defective power of the moralists of duty.

But why do those who supposedly possess positive power still fall into the circle of moral duty? Nietzsche says that powerful persons do not need to accept any rights—since these would be a superfluous token of recognition. Whoever accepts the concept of "rights" as externally conferred has only a "feeble sense of power" (*D* 112).

The willingness to accept certain rights indicates that one is not at the top of the power hierarchy. By granting rights and demanding certain duties in exchange, the "sovereign" of negative power succeeds in controlling others. It follows that a traditional morality based upon a system of duties and rights is impelled by the "striving for distinction," especially pronounced in "weak" people moved by "the psychical extravagance of the lust for power!" (*D* 113). In contrast to this morality of duty, one who has successfully overcome oneself attains rights autonomously and freely: "they generously confer them upon others—not as part of manipulative negotiation, but out of a *surplus* of personal power" (*D* 437, 449). In effect, Nietzsche claims that only the truly powerful person who experiences "the feeling of fullness...the consciousness of wealth that would give and bestow, the noble human being...helps the unfortunate, but not, or almost not, from pity, but prompted more by an urge begotten by excess of power" (*BGE* 260).

Persons who love and esteem their selves are in psychological better position to express unconditionally their love to others without being afraid that by this act they might weaken their own power and selfhood. Similarly, genuine gifts generally come from persons who

---

[27] And see Nietzsche's exclamation: "In morality man treats himself not as *individuum* but as *dividuum*" (*HAH* I: 57).

experience their own selves as gifts while the genuinely altruistic acts are performed by egoists endowed with a strong sense of positive power. Their inherent and abundant richness overflows and is offered gratis to others.

Nietzsche draws an ideal picture of an entire culture driven by powerful individuals—generous, independent, unprejudiced, endowed with the ability to perform a creative sublimation of instincts. Such persons have "the ability to accept contradictions," possess dynamic vitality and self-control, are devoid of bad conscience, have adopted the attitude of *amor fati*, and exhibit self-acceptance. These are the "we free spirits"[28] with the attitude of "*la gaya scienza*," people who embody intellectual tolerance and existential integrity. They are noble and courageous, rejecting the desire for expansion or domination as ultimate goals in themselves (*D* 163, 164, 546). This picture could not be more opposite to that of the Nazi Aryan Reich, which sought to suppress such positive power patterns and deliberately wiped out so many of its living models.

In Practice

Nietzsche's basic distinction between persons endowed with positive versus negative power stands beyond eugenic and racial distinctions. Clearly, his long list of predicates of persons endowed with positive power includes no biological values.[29] His teaching is directed toward helping us activate or uncover the resources and origins of our ability to create and manifest positive power patterns. Nietzsche supposes that these origins are rooted deeply within us, but because of various psychological handicaps (cowardice, for example) and/or social-religious ethos and conditioning, we have repressed them and have prohibited their free operation. These handicaps have been projected as an ideological network with patterns of negative power, and Nietzsche uses his "hammering" method to shatter the prohibiting "idols" while freezing our faith in them. The very process of "freezing" our belief in most of the prevalent values of negative power is founded on the assumption that the "frozen" personality will reject certain values and accept other norms, which already exist both in our social surroundings and within our own selves.[30] The enticing psychological arguments for the morality of positive power, therefore, are not presented directly and prescriptively. Instead, the "freezing" process is employed indirectly by means of a *genealogy*, revealing the negative origins of prevalent norms and arguing that the effects of our accepting these norms are psychologically and existentially destructive. However, in order to evoke positive

---

[28] On the important qualitative distinction between "we free spirits" ("*wir freien Geister*," *BGE* 44) and the almost unattainable "free spirit par excellence" (*GS* 347) see Golomb 2006.

[29] For elaboration see the table of negative versus positive power patterns in Golomb 1985.

[30] There is a striking similarity between the procedure of "coolly placing on ice" (*EH*: "Human, All Too Human" 1) and the tactics employed by Socrates. Socrates "froze" by logical means, whereas Nietzsche does so by means of genealogical analyses. In his dialogues, Socrates seeks to freeze the listeners' belief in X, for example, by showing that this logically entails a belief in Y. The listeners are not ready to endorse belief in Y because of their belief in the set of values: p, s, t . . . which they share with Socrates. Nietzsche employs almost the same method. He shows his readers that their most "sacred" values have negative roots and the "effects" of their endorsement are stagnation, repression, inhibition of creativity, depression, regression, and so on. Obviously, most of us consider these effects undesirable and wish to freeze our beliefs in the values that are responsible for them.

power one must first overcome the inhibiting forces. Both the positive enticement and the negative freezing assume that men possess an implicit set of values that drive them to reject negative patterns. Therefore, along with his enticing anthropology, Nietzsche must explicate these implicit norms and elaborate them.

This explicatory feature of Nietzsche's discussion of power phenomena appears in a crucial passage, where he says he has "finally discovered two basic types of morality and one basic difference":

> There are *master morality* and *slave morality*—I add immediately that in all the higher and more mixed cultures there also appear attempts at mediation between these two moralities, and yet more often the interpenetration and mutual misunderstanding of both, and at times they occur directly alongside each other—even in the same human being, within a *single* soul. (*BGE* 260)

The two moral phenomena presented are actual cultural patterns, and are far from being a priori constructions of our "minds." "Master morality" and the pattern of the *Übermensch* are historical phenomena which Nietzsche defines more closely to avoid confusion with "slave morality." It is important to note that by these misleading idioms of "slaves versus masters" Nietzsche does not mean any socioeconomical status, such as aristocracy of blood and/or property, but only the high or low quality of mental resources of individuals and their fundamental power patterns.

Nietzsche, observing the cultural history of morality, discovers "the interpenetration and mutual misunderstanding of both." Moreover, history discloses the slow, gradual progression from the "morality of the herd" to a morality that increasingly stresses the value of the individual. According to Nietzsche, the gradual emergence of the morality of positive power is already taking place in the history of humankind (*GS* 117–20). Thus the main goal of his explications is to speed up this process. It follows that we must understand his "transfiguration of all values" not as an abolition but as a transfiguration of negative power into positive morality. It is, of course, not a radical change *ex nihilo*: in order that significant change takes place, the modifying element must already contain, at least implicitly, the seeds of this alteration. The process of "transfiguration," therefore, is well established both in our cultural history and also "within a single soul"—fluctuating between the opposing vectors of constructive and destructive powers.

The ideal of transfiguration of our nature and the sublimation of our drives and psychological makeup, which provide the necessary and sufficient conditions of the morality of positive power, distance Nietzsche from Nazi eugenics or racism based on a given or preferred set of biological traits. This is evident even in those few passages mentioning the "blond beast" that were appropriated by the Nazis who strove to endow it with racial, i.e., Nordic and Aryan, connotations to give a distorted reading of Nietzsche.[31] As a matter of fact, the first appearance in Nietzsche's writings of this notorious concept of the "blond beast" (*GM* I: 11) that actually refers to a lion as a metaphor of the processes of self-overcoming for "creation of freedom for" an authentic "self" (*Z* I: "Of the Three Metamorphoses") is far from denoting any specific racial notion but represents an amalgam of races and fictive

[31] For example, Alfred Bäumler, in the second part of his treatise (1931), tried to present Nietzsche as the philosopher of the Nordic race.

mythological figures: "the Roman, Arabian, Germanic, Japanese nobility, the Homeric heroes, the Scandinavian Vikings" (*GM* I: 11). Actually, the only idea of race that Nietzsche ever looked upon with favor was that of a mixed race (as mixed as possible)—a European race sprung from innumerable intermarriages between "the best aristocracy of Europe" and the Jews (*D* 205; *HAH* I: 475). This was his sarcastic attempt to counter the racial anti-Semitism that had begun to spread with Wagner and his zealous followers and a way to get even with the Germans, a nation he came to intensely dislike.

Furthermore, it is quite revealing that his own historical examples of societies that approximated "the essential characteristic of a good and healthy aristocracy" (*BGE* 258) were the ancient Greek *polis* and Venice (*BGE* 262)—in his view classic representations "of the morality of the powerful" (*BGE* 262). He also refers in this context to the historical examples of Rome and of the Renaissance—namely to cultural patterns that never made racial supremacy the cornerstone of their non-nationalist ideals or regarded the genetic features of particular persons as an a priori mark of superiority.

It should be also noted that the notion of sublimation in Nietzsche's teaching always involves a rejection of the damaging processes of repression. Thus, we must first restore to mankind its reservoir of repressed drives, unduly and harshly repressed by culture. But the choice is not simply between culture and raw barbarian nature. *BT* had already opposed the "Dionysian barbarian" (no less nihilistic than the excessively Apollonian or Christian anti-sensuality). The problem in Nietzsche's eyes was more one of culture versus civilization[32]— the former being based more on sublimation and vital creation than on repression and overspiritualization. Nietzsche never endorsed the prospect of chaotic turbulence and the uncontrolled release of the "blond beast" of prey in mankind. Thus, Thomas Mann (1959) was quite mistaken in accusing Nietzsche of calling for the massive and anarchic release of repressed instincts. The "blond beast" was at best a stage but not the final aim of Nietzsche's thought. His philosophical anthropology—in contrast to that of fascism—never "heroized the instincts" but only their creative sublimation.

NIETZSCHE THE GODFATHER OF FASCISM?

We might ask, then, how Nietzsche came to acquire the "honor" of being considered the philosopher of the Third Reich and whether such claims have any justification.[33] On account of what was presented above it seems that Nietzsche was more a herald of the crisis of values out of which Nazism emerged, rather than a godfather of the century's fascist movements per se. As we have seen, what Nietzsche prized above all was spiritual power, not the brute political force which he denounced with all the sarcasm at his command. Nietzsche is no less political than he is an "immoralist"—in a very moral and political sense.

---

[32] It might be worth noting here that the rhetoric of culture versus civilization was one that was fundamental to anti-Semites as in "*Wir haben Kultur, Sie (die Juden) haben nur Civilization*" (I owe this comment to the editors of this *Handbook*).

[33] Of course, as Hans Sluga (1993) has shown, Nietzsche was not the only German philosopher invoked as a spiritual forerunner of the Nazi regime, but his "Nazification" is a historical fact that cannot be denied, one that is the most poignant and criminal.

The crucial question that poses itself here is: what can Nietzsche have in common with fascism? The central ideal of Nietzsche's philosophy was the individual and his freedom to shape his own character and destiny. He was, from the beginning of his fame and onward frequently described as the "aristocratic radical" of the spirit because he abhorred mass culture and strove to cultivate a special kind of human being, the *Übermensch*, endowed with exceptional spiritual and mental qualities.[34] What can such a thinker have in common with National Socialism's manipulation of the masses for chauvinistic goals that swallowed up the life of the individual? What was it in Nietzsche that attracted such a Nazi appropriation in the first place? How far is it legitimate to view Nietzsche as a proto-fascist thinker? These are not such clear-cut issues as they may seem and though they have attracted much polemical heat they have not received so far any truly systematic treatment.[35]

Nietzsche's life and thought will never be reducible to a single constituency or political ideology. The ambiguities and contradictions in his work as well as his elusive, aphoristic style lend themselves to a wide range of meanings and a multiplicity of interpretations. Nevertheless, he was clearly an elitist of the spirit who believed in the right to rule of a "good and healthy aristocracy," one which would, if necessary, be ready to sacrifice untold numbers of human beings; he sometimes wrote as if nations primarily existed for the sake of producing a few exceptionally great men, who could not be expected to show consideration for "normal humanity." Not surprisingly, in the light of the cruel century which has just ended, one is bound to regard such statements with grave misgivings. One has to ask if there is not something in Nietzsche's philosophy with its uninhibited cultivation of a heroic individualism and the will-to-power, which may have tended to favor the fascist ethos.[36]

Many commentators have raised the question as to whether the vulgar exploitation of Nietzsche by militarists and Nazis could indeed be altogether arbitrary. While almost any philosophy can be propagandistically abused (Kant and Neo-Kantians were particular favorites among academic philosophers of the Third Reich as Sluga 1993 has shown), Nietzsche's pathos, his imaginative excesses as well as his image as a prophet-seer and creator of myths, seems especially conducive to such abuse by fascists. The radical manner in which Nietzsche thrust himself against the boundaries of conventional (Judeo-Christian) morality and dramatically proclaimed that God (meaning the bourgeois-Christian faith of the nineteenth century) was dead, undoubtedly appealed to something in Nazism that wished to transgress and transcend all existing taboos. The totalitarianism of the twentieth century (of both the Right and Left) presupposed a breakdown of all authority and moral

[34] See Georg Brandes' (Morris Kohen's) 1888 essay "Friedrich Nietzsche: Eine Abhandlung über aristokratischen Radikalismus" in Brandes (1895). In this second edition Brandes adds in a footnote a passage from a letter from Nietzsche dated December 2, 1887, in which Nietzsche states: "*Der Ausdruck 'aristokratischer Radikalismus' dessen Sie sich bedienen, ist sehr gut. Das ist, mit Verlaub gesagt, das gescheuteste Wort, das ich bisher über mich gelesen habe*" (p. 137).

[35] Recently, attempts to answer these questions were undertaken by some distinguished historians and philosophers who contributed to the collection of Golomb and Wistrich (2002). Here I would only deal with certain crucial motifs of this vast issue.

[36] Musssolini, for example, raised the Nietzschean formulation "live dangerously" (*vivere pericolosamente*) to the status of a fascist slogan (see note 13). His reading of Nietzsche was one factor in converting him from Marxism to a philosophy of sacrifice and warlike deeds in defense of the fatherland. In this mutation, Mussolini was preceded by Gabriele d'Annunzio, whose passage from aestheticism to the political activism of a new, more virile and warlike age, was greatly influenced by Nietzsche.

norms, of which Nietzsche was indeed a clear-sighted prophet, precisely because he had diagnosed nihilism as the central problem of his society—that of *fin-de-siècle* Europe. For him there was no way back to the old moral certainties about "good" and "evil." Nietzsche was convinced that there was no escape from the "nihilism" of the age, except to go forward into a more "perfect nihilism."[37] Nietzsche believed that only by honestly facing the stark truth about the sheer immanency of our universe (*GS* 108–11), i.e., that there is no absolute truth, no transcendent goal, no value or meaning in itself, could we pave the way for a real intellectual liberation and a revaluation of all values. Thus Nietzsche was, at worst, the unholy prophet of the crisis of values out of which Nazism emerged, rather than a godfather of fascist movements per se.

It seems that much of the confusion identifying Nietzsche with National Socialism can be traced back to the disastrous role of his sister Elisabeth Fürster-Nietzsche who took control of his manuscripts in the 1890s, when he was mentally and physically incapacitated. Already in the 1920s she promoted her brother as the philosopher of fascism, sending her warmest good wishes to Benito Mussolini as "the inspired re-awakener of aristocratic values in Nietzsche's sense"; similarly, she invited Hitler several times to the archive in Weimar, even giving him the symbolic gift of Nietzsche's walking stick in 1934. Nazi propaganda encouraged such (mis)appropriation, for example, by publishing popular and inexpensive anthologies and short collections of Nietzsche's sayings which were then misused in their truncated form to promote militarism, hardness, and Germanic values.

Not everyone shared the increasingly broad consensus before 1939 which saw Nietzsche as the spiritual godfather of fascism and Nazism. Opponents of Nazism like the German philosophers Karl Jaspers and Karl Löwith also sought to invalidate the official Nazi appropriation of Nietzsche in the 1930s. Together with a number of French intellectuals, they contributed to a special issue of *Acéphale* published in January 1937 and entitled "*Réparation à Nietzsche.*" The most prominent of the French anti-fascist Nietzscheans was the left-wing existentialist thinker Georges Bataille, who sought to rescue Nietzsche by demonstrating his abhorrence of pan-Germanism, racism, and the rabid anti-Semitism of Hitler's followers. In America, the most eminent postwar advocate of a "liberal" Nietzsche was Walter Kaufmann, an American scholar in Princeton who provided many of the most authoritative translations into English of Nietzsche's writings. His *Nietzsche: Philosopher, Psychologist, Antichrist* (1950) became a standard work in the critical rehabilitation of Nietzsche in the postwar English-speaking world, seeking to dissociate him from any connection with Social Darwinism and the intellectual origins of National Socialism.

At first sight, Nietzsche's unequivocal rejection of anti-Semitism might seem enough to answer the question concerning Nietzsche's responsibility for Nazism decisively in the negative. Certainly, a thinker who held a high opinion of Jewish people, looked to them as a spearhead for his own free-thinking Dionysian "revaluation of all values," and sought their full integration[38] could hardly be blamed for the Nazi Holocaust. On the other hand, we have his sweeping rejection of Judeo-Christian values (as they were mirrored in German Protestantism) and his reference to their origin in the sublime "vengefulness" of Israel and its exploitation of so-called movements of "decadence" to ensure its own self-preservation

[37] To use the term of Müller-Lauter in his 2002 essay.
[38] Consult majority of the essays in Stegmaier and Krochmalnik 1997 and Golomb 1997b. Cf. also Yovel 1998.

and survival. Even though Nietzsche's prime target was clearly Christianity—which he also blamed for the suffering of the Jews—the source of the infection ultimately lay in that fateful transvaluation of values initiated by priestly Judaism two millennia ago. Moreover, even when describing the "jewification"[39] of the world in terms that mixed admiration with disapprobation, Nietzsche seemed inadvertently to be feeding the myth of Jewish power, so beloved of Christian and racist anti-Semites. Though his intentions were profoundly hostile to anti-Semitism, this provocative technique was undoubtedly a dangerous game to play.

Actually Nietzsche had foreseen that horrible things would be done in his name and that his writings were liable to criminal misappropriations. Nietzsche collapsed mentally in 1889, the year in which Adolf Hitler was born, and thirty-three years before Mussolini, who originated the term "fascism". Hence naturally, terms like "Nazism" and "fascism" do not appear as such in Nietzsche's *oeuvre*. But this does not preclude the possibility of applying these terms retrospectively to Nietzsche's thought or to its many distortions. It is true that Nietzsche could not know that the Nazis would grant him the dubious honor of proclaiming him the "Great Godfather of Fascism" but he was deeply aware of this imminent danger. I will quote here only three passages, among many others, as certain evidences to this effect.

The first one is from *Beyond Good and Evil* 30:

> There are books that have opposite values for soul and health, depending on whether the lower vitality, or the higher and more vigorous ones turn to them: in the former case, these books are dangerous and lead to crumbling and disintegration; in the latter, herald's cries that call the bravest to their courage.

This saying reminds one of Georg Christoph Lichtenberg's brilliant aphorism: "A book is a mirror: If an ape looks into it an apostle is hardly likely to look out." Be that as it may, as the beginning of the above-quoted section testifies, Nietzsche foresees the danger of misinterpretation, should his writings fall into the wrong hands. To this he adds his warning:

> Our highest insights must—and should—sound like follies and sometimes like crimes when they are heard without permission by those who are not predisposed and predestined for them.

And indeed many pseudo-intellectuals without permission had applied themselves to Nietzsche's work and turned it into a travesty.

With amazing clarity of foresight, in *BGE* 40 Nietzsche again predicts the future falsification of his books:

> Around every profound spirit a mask is growing continually, owing to the constantly false, namely shallow, interpretation of every word, every step, every sign of life he gives.

His sense of misgiving at this prospect is voiced again in a letter to his sister, Elizabeth Förster-Nietzsche: "I am terrified to think about the kind of people who might one day rely on my authority."

The bitter irony of history saw to it that it was precisely his sister who was one of the most influential persons in this dreary affair of the falsification and Nazification of her brother's legacy.

---

[39] Actually (and here I agree with my editors) "*Verjudung*" is better translated as the more negative "jewification" than as "judaization" (the translation preferred, for instance, by Kaufmann).

Now the most crucial question remains: could Nietzsche, who had foreseen the imminent falsifications of his writings, have written differently? To demand from Nietzsche a more balanced, cool, rational, objective, emotionally detached writing style would mean demanding that he renounce his self-adopted role as a heuristic "*Versucher*" (enticer) of his readers.[40] But since Nietzsche persisted in writing for effect, especially to shock, despite his well-grounded fears that his writing might lend itself to misinterpretation—he cannot be held entirely blameless for the misuse of his works.[41]

Generally speaking, the case of Nietzsche is a good illustration of the pitfalls in an overly schematic approach to intellectual history which takes particular strands in a thinker's *oeuvre* and seeks to fit them into more general constructs like fascism or National Socialism. On the basis of Nietzsche's declared hostility to Christianity, liberal democracy, and socialism, it is possible to see him as a precursor of the fascist synthesis. Some aspects of his admiration for ancient Greek culture and for "Romanitas" were used by both fascists and Nazis while thoroughly distorting his philosophical intent. Indeed, all forms of xenophobia were profoundly alien to Nietzsche's outlook, no less than the hot-headed nationalistic rivalries so typical of the European nation state system into which he was born. This explains his revulsion from the German nationalism which had come into vogue with the success of Bismarckian power politics. In fact, in many respects Nietzsche was the least patriotic and least German of his philosophical contemporaries in the Second Reich.

Far from relating to nationalist obsessions, Nietzsche had asserted a life-affirming outlook that sought to empower individuals to overcome their limitations by questioning all our assumptions concerning truth, logic, beliefs, culture, values, and history. This spiritual power emancipated the individual, who has become "master of a free will"[42] after being involved a long and difficult process of sublimation. It was a vision fundamentally antithetical to the totalitarian collectivism of the Right and Left.

The break with Wagner is especially illuminating because the Wagnerian ideology and the cult that developed in Bayreuth was a much more real precursor of *völkisch* and Hitlerian ideas. Once Nietzsche had thrown off the romantic nationalism of his early days, his devastating critique of Wagner—prophetic in many ways of what was to come—reveals with what penetrating insight he saw through its dangerous illusions. National Socialism could plausibly derive inspiration from Wagner but it could only use Nietzsche by fundamentally twisting his philosophy.

Still, other crucial questions hover over this issue. Was Nietzsche not trying to manipulate an entire culture and society to cultivate a new kind of man and mode of life (as the Nazis were trying to do)? Has not the fact that he has refrained from drawing any normative, rational ethics facilitated his criminal misappropriation? Should we not consider his attempt to overthrow the values of the Enlightenment and eradicate the foundations of Christian morality an extremely dangerous maneuver?

To tackle this question as soberly and objectively as possible requires going beyond a common defense of Nietzsche in postwar scholarship. Walter Kaufmann and others tried to

[40] See Golomb 1986 and 1989 on this cardinal function of Nietzsche's philosophy and on its essential relation to his idiosyncratic literary style.

[41] At this point I tend to agree with Berel Lang's incisive article (2002).

[42] And read the excellent discussion by Gemes 2006.

severe Nietzsche altogether from Nazi ideology by stressing the fact that he was fundamentally an apolitical thinker who rejected pan-Germanism and anti-Semitism. But it does not necessarily follow that since Nietzsche detested German and other nationalistic attitudes, his teaching was essentially a nonpolitical one. Tempting as it may be to cleanse his thought from the taint of any political ideology, especially that of fascism, it is in fact a misguided strategy. For it is precisely by emphasizing the political import and content of Nietzsche's philosophy that one can throw into sharper relief his "antifascist" orientation.

The argument that presented Nietzsche as a staunch opponent of the nation state was especially prevalent among his advocates during the first twenty years after the Second World War. They wished to rehabilitate his reputation by denying any trace of resemblance between his writings and those who did almost everything to make them sound compatible with *Mein Kampf*. As a result, these apologists performed a sweeping depoliticization of Nietzsche's thought.[43] Against the generalizing accusations of Crane Brinton (1940 and 1941) and others, that Nietzsche was the godfather of Nazism, Kaufmann presented the leitmotif of Nietzsche's life and thought as that of "the antipolitical individual who seeks self-perfection far from the modern world" (Kaufmann 1950: 412, 418).[44]

It is noteworthy that much contemporary research—which has been less vulnerable to the atmosphere of suspicion that loomed over Nietzsche by the end of the Second World War—has tended instead to emphasize the significance of politics in his philosophy. Such scholars[45] have sensibly conceded that even if one cannot find in Nietzsche's antisystematic writings any definite political thought, his radical discussions of morality and concept of the "modern man" had a far-reaching political significance. It was in a certain cultural and political context that Nietzsche sought to attain his ideal of perfectly authentic individual—the *Übermensch*. Nietzsche did however reject the view that one can justify or rationally derive a political order from certain universalistic principles. It is also true that during his life Nietzsche did not publish anything comparable to Spinoza's *Tractatus Politicus*, which was specifically dedicated to political issues. Of course, there were always political implications in writings like his *Genealogy of Morals* which examined critically the moral values prevalent in modern society. Moreover, there is an early unpublished composition by Nietzsche (from 1872) that analyzes the "Greek State," and we also have many long passages from his published works which squarely deal with politics.[46] Possibly because of Hegel, whom Nietzsche criticizes in his writings, and who regarded

---

[43] For bibliographical details see Detwiler 1990: 1–9.

[44] This characterization of Nietzsche as an "antipolitical" thinker who is solely interested in cultivating the individual life does not prevent Kaufmann from dwelling at length on the bitter (mainly political) struggles in which Nietzsche was deeply involved with his ex-mentor Wagner and against German imperialism and anti-Semitism. These struggles placed Nietzsche well within the political framework of his times. However, one should not see here any contradiction on Kaufmann's part since Nietzsche's antipolitical attitude stemmed organically from his political and cultural interests and drives.

[45] See among many others Conway 1997a and b; Ansell-Pearson 1994; Strong 1988 and 1996; Waite 1996; Berkowitz 1995. Berkowitz writes: "It is tempting to conclude that Nietzsche does not practice or contribute to political philosophy... Yet Nietzsche moves within the domain of moral and political philosophy... [since] the question of human perfection lies at the heart of Nietzsche's inquiries" (1995: 1–2). See also Rorty 1989 where Nietzsche is portrayed as an "ironic liberal" and serves Rorty as a heuristic means to promote his postmodern liberalism.

[46] "Der griechische Staat," *KSA* 1: 764–77. See also *HAH* I: 8 entitled "A Glance at the State."

the Prussian state of the nineteenth century as the highest rational manifestation of the Universal *Geist*, Nietzsche felt particularly driven to attack this idea of statehood that had attracted his contemporaries.

One could say that Nietzsche was an antipolitical thinker for political reasons and a political thinker for philosophical reasons, among them his attempt to foster the existential ideal of personal authenticity. In other words, Nietzsche had adopted an antipolitical attitude for reasons that had to do with the future of human culture, an issue which he called "*grosse Politik.*" For Nietzsche, politics becomes "grand" when it sustains and assists in cultivating human greatness and cultural grandeur.[47] This "great politics" is fundamentally a politics of culture. And if we broadly define politics as an organized and orchestrated mobilization of human resources for the sake of group or nation, Nietzsche was indeed deeply engrossed with a politics that would embark on the cultural engineering of the entire society. We ought to recall that Nietzsche saw in a genuine philosopher the creator of values for future society. Like Plato, Nietzsche envisaged the philosopher as a legislator. Hence Nietzsche is no less political than he is an "immoralist"—in a very moral and political sense.

Consequently, it is hard to find in Nietzsche's writings a devastating criticism of the state as such, namely of a state which is a *means* "among other means" for promotion and fostering of the exceptional and authentic individuals. Most of his critique is directed against the nationalistic and militaristic state, "the New Idol" in his language,[48] that sees in its political might and strength the highest value and objective. In most cases, this criticism is solely directed against the German *Reich* founded by Bismarck. And read his famous exclamation:

> The Germans—once they were called the people of thinkers; do they think at all today? . . . politics swallows up all serious concern for really spiritual matters. *Deutschland, Deutschland über Alles*—I fear that was the end of German philosophy (*TI:* "What the Germans Lack" 1)

Nietzsche fought the idea of statehood and extreme nationalism from the time they became "the New Idol" and the highest value, namely from the instant they embraced the fascistic meanings. In counter-opposition to this fascistic view, the "new man" and the "good European" of Nietzsche's vision does not see and does not wish to see in the state in itself a main and final goal. In contrast to Bismarckian *Machtpolitik*, which aspired to shape aggressively a national identity, the new man of Nietzsche, that "free spirit" who believes in *Geist*, *Geist über Alles*, is free from any blind loyalty and attachment to the highest interests of the state. He does not seek to revive his personal identity either from transcendent religion or from the totalitarian and individual-consuming state. For such an individual, the state does not function as the origin, content, and objective for new personal identities and modes of life but solely as their cultivating haven and shelter.

Nietzsche explicitly engages the state in the service of personal authenticity and as such it is not just a legitimate political framework but even a necessary means in carrying out his philosophical program as far as the unique individual is concerned. According to him "one lives in a community, one enjoys the advantages of communality (oh what advantages!) We

---

[47] For this see also Nietzsche's "Schopenhauer as Educator" and "Der griechische Staat," *KSA* 1: 764–77.

[48] See *Z* I "On the New Idol."

sometimes underrate them today" (*GM* II: 9). Nietzsche holds that the project of cultivating genuine life and Dionysian-authentic culture beyond the sphere of society is doomed to fail and lacks any viability. When Nietzsche speaks about "community" or a "society" he refers also to its political arrangements and orders, among them the most vital one—the State. This we can figure out by reading his "genealogical" analyses of the "origin" of "society," of "the political organization," and of the "state" (*GM* II: 16, 17).

In short, due to reasons inherent in his general philosophy, Nietzsche does not reject the national-political social framework since, among many others, it too is one of the legitimate (and even vital) manifestations of human spirit and its creative power (*Macht*). This is what he claims in *A* 26 where he contrasts the unnatural "kingdom of God," its "Jewish priesthood," and their "moral world order" to the Kingdom of Men and to its "often very bold figures in the history of Israel." After drawing this contrast, Nietzsche refers to the "state" and to "judicial order, marriage, care of the sick and the poor" as a "natural custom... natural institution" that is "inspired by the instinct of life" (*A* 26). And since life and its enhancement are the highest values in Nietzsche's teaching, the state which is conducive to life's aspirations is quite a vital element in Nietzsche's philosophy.

However, once this legitimate (and "natural") creation changes its nature and instead of a means becomes a goal—becoming, instead of an expression of human creativity that purports to ensure and secure other human creations (especially self-creation or the creation of authentic selves), the manifestation of an extreme nationalism that seeks to hinder this free and spontaneous creativity—Nietzsche vehemently opposes it and wishes to curb its destructive effects: the fact being that he rejects the totalitarian state which function as "a fearful tyranny, as an oppressive and remorseless machine" (*GM* II: 17) and calls such a totalitarian state (perhaps under Hobbes's influence) "the coldest of all cold monsters" (*Z* I: "On the New Idol"). Can one imagine a Nazi, fascist, or even a proto-Nazi wearing a brown or black shirt (the *camicie nere* of Mussolini's time) saying such things of his or her *Vaterland*?

BIBLIOGRAPHY

(A) Works by Nietzsche

A   *The Antichrist*, in *The Portable Nietzsche*, trans. and ed. Walter Kaufmann. New York: Viking, 1954, 565–656.
BGE   *Beyond Good and Evil*, trans. Walter Kaufmann. New York: Vintage, 1966.
BT   *The Birth of Tragedy*, in *The Birth of Tragedy and The Case of Wagner*, trans. Walter Kaufmann. New York: Vintage, 1967, 15–144.
D   *Daybreak*, trans. R. J. Hollingdale. Cambridge: Cambridge University Press, 1982.
EH   *Ecce Homo*, in *On the Genealogy of Morals and Ecce Homo*, trans. Walter Kaufmann. New York: Vintage, 1969, 217–335.
GM   *On the Genealogy of Morals*, trans. Walter Kaufmann and R. J. Hollingdale. New York: Vintage, 1969.
GS   *The Gay Science*, trans. Walter Kaufmann. New York: Vintage, 1974.
HAH   *Human, All Too Human*, trans R. J. Hollingdale. Cambridge: Cambridge University Press, 1986.

KSA   *Sämtliche Werke: Kritische Studienausgabe in 15 Einzelbänden*, ed. G. Colli and M. Montinari. Berlin: De Gruyter, 1988.

TI   *Twilight of the Idols*, in *The Portable Nietzsche*, trans. and ed. Walter Kaufmann. New York: Viking, 1954, 463–563.

UM   *Untimely Meditations*, trans. R. J. Hollingdale. Cambridge: Cambridge University Press, 1986.

WP   *The Will to Power*, ed. Walter Kaufmann, trans. Walter Kaufmann and R. J. Hollingdale. New York: Vintage Books, 1968.

Z   *Thus Spoke Zarathustra*, in *The Portable Nietzsche*, trans. and ed. Walter Kaufmann. New York: Viking, 1954, 103–439.

(B) Other Works Cited

Acéphale: Réparation à Nietzsche. 1937. Double issue with contributions by Georges Bataille, Pierre Klossowski, Jean Rollin, and Jean Wahl. Paris. 21 January.

Ansell-Pearson, Keith. 1994. *An Introduction to Nietzsche as Political Thinker*. Cambridge: Cambridge University Press.

Bäumler, Alfred. 1930. "Nachwort," in *Kröners Taschenausgabe*, vol. 78. Leipzig: Alfred Kröner.

Bäumler, Alfred. 1931. *Nietzsche der Philosoph und Politiker*. Leipzig: Reclam.

Berkowitz, Peter. 1995. *Nietzsche: The Ethics of an Immoralist*. Cambridge, Mass.: Harvard University Press.

Brandes, Georg (Morris Kohen). 1895. "Friedrich Nietzsche: Eine Abhandlung über aristokratischen Radikalismus," in *Georg Brandes, Menschen und Werke: Essays*. Frankfurt am Main: Rütten & Loening, 137–213. English edition: *Friedrich Nietzsche: An Essay on Aristocratic Radicalism,* trans. A. G. Chater. London: William Heinemann, 1914, 3–56.

Brinton, Crane. 1940. "The National Socialists Use of Nietzsche," *Journal of the History of Ideas* 1.2: 131–50.

Brinton, Crane. 1941. *Nietzsche*. Cambridge, Mass.: Harvard University Press.

Buber, Martin. 1957. *Pointing the Way: Collected Essays*, trans. and ed. Maurice Friedman. New York: Harper.

Conway, Daniel W. 1997a. *Nietzsche and the Political*. London and New York: Routledge.

Conway, Daniel W. 1997b. *Nietzsche's Dangerous Game*. Cambridge: Cambridge University Press.

Detwiler, Bruce. 1990. *Nietzsche and the Politics of Aristocratic Radicalism*. Chicago: University of Chicago Press.

Gemes, Ken. 2006. "Nietzsche on Free Will, Autonomy and the Sovereign Individual," *Proceedings of the Aristotelian Society* 80 (suppl. vol.): 321–39.

Golomb, Jacob. 1985. "Nietzsche on Jews and Judaism," *Archiv für Geschichte der Philosophie* 67: 139–61.

Golomb, Jacob. 1986. "Nietzsche's Enticing Psychology of Power" in Yirmiyahu Yovel (ed.), *Nietzsche as Affirmative Thinker*. Dordrecht: Martinus Nijhoff, 160–82.

Golomb, Jacob. 1989. *Nietzsche's Enticing Psychology of Power*. Jerusalem and Ames: Hebrew University Magnes Press and Iowa State University Press.

Golomb, Jacob. 1990. "Nietzsche on Authenticity," *Philosophy Today* 34: 243–58.

Golomb, Jacob. 1995. *In Search of Authenticity from Kierkegaard to Camus*. London and New York: Routledge.

Golomb, Jacob. 1997a. "Nietzsche and the Marginal Jews," in Jacob Golomb (ed.), *Nietzsche and Jewish Culture*. London and New York: Routledge, 158–92.

Golomb, Jacob (ed.). 1997b. *Nietzsche and Jewish Culture*. London and New York: Routledge.

Golomb, Jacob. 1999. "Introductory Essay: Nietzsche's New Psychology," in Jacob Golomb, Weaver Santaniello, and Ronald Lehrer (eds), *Nietzsche and Depth Psychology*. Albany: State University of New York Press, 1–19.

Golomb, Jacob. 2004. *Nietzsche and Zion*. Ithaca: Cornell University Press.

Golomb, Jacob. 2006. "Can One Really Become a 'Free Spirit Par Excellence' or an *Übermensch*?" *Journal of Nietzsche Studies* 32: 22–40.

Golomb, Jacob and Robert S. Wistrich (eds). 2002. *Nietzsche, Godfather of Fascism? On the Uses and Abuses of a Philosophy*. Princeton: Princeton University Press.

Kaufmann, Walter. 1950. *Nietzsche: Philosopher, Psychologist, Antichrist*. Princeton: Princeton University Press.

Lang, Berel. 2002. "Misinterpretation as the Author's Responsibility (Nietzsche's Fascism, for Instance)," in Jacob Golomb and Robert S. Wistrich (eds), *Nietzsche, Godfather of Fascism? On the Uses and Abuses of a Philosophy*. Princeton: Princeton University Press, 47–65.

Magnus, Bernd. 1988. "The Use and Abuse of *The Will to Power*," in Robert C. Solomon and Kathleen M. Higgins (eds), *Reading Nietzsche*. New York: Oxford University Press, 218–35.

Mann, Thomas. 1959. "Nietzsche's Philosophy in the Light of Recent History," in Thomas Mann, *Last Essays*, trans. R. E. C. Winston and T. E. J. Stern. New York: Alfred A. Knopf, 141–77.

Müller-Lauter, Wolfgang. 1971. *Nietzsche: Seine Philosophie der Gegensätze und die Gegensätze seiner Philosophie*. Berlin: De Gruyter.

Müller-Lauter, Wolfgang. 2002. "Experiences with Nietzsche," in Jacob Golomb and Robert S. Wistrich (eds), *Nietzsche, Godfather of Fascism? On the Uses and Abuses of a Philosophy*. Princeton: Princeton University Press, 66–89.

Richardson, John. 1996. *Nietzsche's System*. New York: Oxford University Press.

Rorty, Richard. 1989. *Contigency, Irony, and Solidarity*. New York: Cambridge University Press.

Schlechta, Karl. 1977. "Philologischer Nachbericht," in Karl Schlechta (ed.), *Friedrich Nietzsche Werke*, vol. 5. Frankfurt am Main: Ullstein, 35–84.

Sluga, Hans. 1993. *Heidegger's Crisis: Philosophy and Politics in Nazi Germany*. Cambridge, Mass.: Harvard University Press

Stegmaier, Werner and Daniel Krochmalnik (eds). 1997. *Jüdischer Nietzscheanismus*. Berlin: Walter de Gruyter.

Strong, Tracy B. 1975. *Friedrich Nietzsche and the Politics of Transfiguration*. Berkeley: University of California Press.

Strong, Tracy B. 1988. "Nietzsche's Political Aesthetics," in M. A. Gillespie and T. B. Strong (eds), *Nietzsche's New Seas: Explorations in Philosophy, Aesthetics, and Politics*. Chicago: University of Chicago Press, 153–74.

Strong, Tracy B. 1996. "Nietzsche's Political Misappropriations," in Bernd Magnus and Kathleen M. Higgins (eds), *The Cambridge Companion to Nietzsche*. Cambridge: Cambridge University Press, 119–47.

Waite, Geoffrey. 1996. *Nietzsche's Corpse: Aesthetic, Politics, Prophecy, or the Spectacular Technoculture of Everyday Life*. Durham: Duke University Press.

Yovel, Yirmiyahu. 1998. *Dark Riddle: Hegel, Nietzsche, and the Jews*. Cambridge: Polity Press.

PART V

EPISTEMOLOGY & METAPHYSICS

CHAPTER 24

LIFE'S PERSPECTIVES

KEN GEMES

INTRODUCTION

NIETZSCHE's perspectivism is typically taken to be an epistemological thesis about the nature of knowledge or justification, or a semantic claim about the nature of truth. Occasionally it is taken to have metaphysical ramifications. For instance, those who take perspectivism to entail a denial of the correspondence theory of truth sometimes take it to entail a denial of metaphysical realism. It is often taken to be Nietzsche's most significant contribution to epistemology and/or the theory of truth, and hence to current philosophical debates. Maudemarie Clark, who interprets perspectivism as a claim about justification, begins her chapter on perspectivism in her important and influential book *Nietzsche on Truth and Philosophy* by noting that his "perspectivism regarding knowledge...constitutes his most obvious contribution to the current intellectual scene" (Clark 1990: 127). Part 1 of this essay considers various epistemological and semantic interpretations of perspectivism and presents philosophical and textual considerations against those interpretations. Part 2 argues that in fact Nietzsche's perspectivism is best interpreted as a kind of psychobiological claim. As such it serves as an extension of his claim that all life is will to power. On this reading, perspectivism has no semantic significance and little epistemological import.

PART 1

1.1 Semantic Perspectivism I: Perspectival Truth

According to a popular interpretation Nietzsche's perspectivism is essentially a semantic claim about the nature of truth. Typically this is glossed as

Any true claim is only perspectivally true.

Of course what this actually means, what perspectival truth involves, is far from clear. This kind of semantic perspectivism is typically taken to conflict with the correspondence theory of truth.[1] Thus Schacht says

> A fundamental idea underlying his [Nietzsche's] analysis of all such 'truths' [what Schacht calls 'man's truths'] is that none of them can plausibly be regarded as holding true in virtue of standing in a relation of correspondence amounting to a picturing, representing or modeling of a reality which is as it is independently of our experience of it. They are inextricably bound up with the *domains of discourse* (and associated forms of life) in which they occur, and in terms of which the standards or conditions are set by reference to which they may qualify as 'truths'. This idea, of what I shall call their *D-relativity*, is at the heart of his celebrated doctrine of 'perspectivism', according to which they may be considered to hold true only from some particular perspective, and thus only within the context of some particular 'language game'. (1983: 61)

It is not clear that semantic perspectivism, even allowing Schacht's claim on Nietzsche's behalf that truth is domain-relative, clashes with the correspondence theory of truth. After all, the claim that a statement is only true given a certain interpretation of its constituent terms need not be incompatible with a correspondence account of truth. For instance, one might hold that the claim "Athens has an opera house" is correspondence-true where "Athens" is interpreted as referring to Athens in Greece and correspondence-false where "Athens" is interpreted as referring to Athens, Georgia. Schacht's talk of domains of discourse might suggest that the alleged perspectival relativity of truth is in some way akin to the benign language relativity of truth indicated above. While Schacht does in fact claim that perspectives are not to be construed as mere vocabularies but as "forms of life" (1983: 63), this is not particularly instructive in telling us how this vitiates the correspondence account of truth. Indeed when he goes on to say

> The 'truth' of a given proposition thus is a matter of its conformity to the linguistic-conceptual scheme within which it functions, together with its appropriateness in relation to some state of affairs holding among the objects that are fixed and constituted in accordance with this scheme (1983: 63)

and further tells us that this notion of truth may be given both a "'coherence' characterization" and a "'correspondence' analysis" (1983: 63), we lose much of our sense that a genuine conflict with the correspondence theory is being joined.[2]

However, perhaps Schacht's talk of objects being fixed and constituted in accordance with a scheme is to be given a strong reading according to which these schemes fully determine

---

[1] Peter Poellner takes Nietzsche's perspectivism, on one reading, to entail both a denial of correspondence truth and a denial of realism:

> He [Nietzsche] declares that 'there are only interpretations', none of which can be said to be 'objectively' better or to be more 'fitting' than any other, since it is not coherent to suppose that there is anything for any interpretation to fit to in the required way. (1995: 282).

Poellner, to his credit, finds this view very puzzling.

[2] There are passages in Schacht's text that suggest that what he sees Nietzsche as rejecting with perspectivism is not so much the correspondence theory of truth but a certain version of realism. In particular, Schacht's Nietzsche objects to the idea that truth involves correspondence with "a reality that has an intrinsic structural articulation and ordering, since there is no such reality for propositions to correspond to" (1983: 61–2). Developing this claim Schacht says that, for Nietzsche, the world is not a world of

the nature of said objects. If, in line with this claim, perspectives are somehow full determiners of truth, so that what is true from perspective A may be false from perspective B, then there are serious worries that perspectivism leads to some kind of unpalatable relativism about truth. Nehamas, like Schacht, takes perspectivism to rule out correspondence accounts of truth and sometimes seems to endorse the claim that perspectives are somehow full determiners of truth: "every interpretation creates its own facts" (Nehamas 1985: 2).[3] However, he allows that some perspectives are better than others. The better is presumably not to be measured in terms of truthfulness. Again, how this position escapes the charge of relativism or incoherence is far from clear since it seems to allow that conflicting interpretations create their own facts. Presumably facts created by conflicting interpretations are conflicting facts, whatever that might mean. Furthermore, the claim that interpretations create their own facts, prima facie, leads to the dilemma that either no interpretation is false or there are false facts, being the facts created by false interpretations. Finally, consider the claim that there are no facts. Does this claim then create its own facts? And if so do those facts make the claim false or is that claim somehow true of those facts?

1.2 Semantic Perspectivism II: The Denial of Facts and the Denial of Truth

Interestingly, Nehamas, after suggesting that perspectivism involves the claim that perspectives create their own facts, goes on to suggest that perspectivism involves the denial of the existence of any facts. He notes that some have paradoxically expressed this idea in such formulations as that it is a fact that there are no facts but only interpretations (cf. Nehamas 1985: 65). Danto, like Schacht, takes Nietzsche to reject the correspondence theory of truth, but also claims that Nietzsche rejects the notion of true perspective: "We cannot speak of a true perspective but only of a perspective that prevails" (1965: 77). These interpretations suggest the following version(s) of semantic perspectivism:

> There are no facts/no truths, only interpretations.

Let us consider the no-truths version first. On this reading, semantic perspectivism, as Danto himself acknowledges (1965: 80, 230), raises the specter of facile refutations: semantic perspectivism is not true from my perspective.[4] Or, specifically against Danto, perspectivism is not a perspective that has prevailed. Compounding Danto's problems is that he attributes a pragmatic theory of truth to Nietzsche according to which "p is true and q is false if p works and q does

___

being but becoming. Now this in itself does not rule out correspondence truth since there may be correspondence between certain claims and the world of becoming. For instance this presumably holds, according to Schacht's Nietzsche, for the very claim that the world is a world of becoming. Whether realism is really incompatible with a world of becoming is a matter we cannot here enter into.

[3] I say Nehamas seems to endorse this metaphysical/semantical claim as in his text he says perspectivism "seems to claim" that "every interpretation creates its own facts." Below we shall consider the possibility that Nehamas is not endorsing this metaphysical/semantical reading of perspectivism but is in fact endorsing a more benign epistemological reading. While in this work I am critical of these semantical and epistemological readings I should add that Nehamas (1985) has been one of the chief sources and inspiration for much of my work on Nietzsche.

[4] Indeed, the no truth version entails that perspectivism is not true from any perspective!

not" (1965: 72). These pronouncements seem to yield the position, assuming perspectivism itself counts as a perspective, that perspectivism is not true ("we cannot speak of a true perspective") but if it works it is true ("p is true... if it works"). This entails that perspectivism does not work, which, according to Danto's pragmatic theory of truth, entails that perspectivism is false ("q is false if... q does not" work). Perhaps Danto's denial of truth to perspectives and his advocacy, on Nietzsche's behalf, of a pragmatic account of truth can be reconciled by claiming that in denying that perspectives are true he is simply denying that they are correspondence-true. This would allow that they can be true in the pragmatist's sense of the term, according to which a perspective is true if it prevails. But until we are given a firmer grip on what it means for a perspective to prevail, given the general hostility to perspectivism and hence its own apparent failure to prevail, Danto's version of perspectivism will be threatened with the consequence that it is by its own lights false. Most Nietzsche scholars now reject Danto's attribution of a pragmatist account of truth on the strength of such passages as *BGE* 5:

> The falseness of a judgment is for us not necessarily an objection to a judgment; in this respect our new language may sound strangest. The question is to what extent it is life-promoting, life-serving, species-preserving.

Here it seems that what is in question is not the equation of usefulness and correspondence truth but the equation of any kind of truth with usefulness.

The no-facts version of semantic perspectivism, as Nehamas's text suggests, leads to the paradoxical position that it is a fact that there are no facts. In addressing this problem Nehamas (1985: 66) suggests we characterize the no-facts version of perspectivism as the claim

(P) that every view is an interpretation.

Now the curious thing is that this, on the most obvious reading, is simply a tautology, for presumably views and interpretations are the same things. It is hard to imagine an interpretation which is not a view and a view which is not an interpretation.[5] A stronger reading would have it that every view is **only** an interpretation. This of course would raise the question of what it means to say that something is only an interpretation. A natural reading is that to say something is only an interpretation is to say that it is not true.[6] So on the strong reading the denial of facts claim seems to take us back to the denial of truth claim with all its paradoxical consequences.

The general conclusion to be drawn from the above arguments is that semantic versions of Nietzsche's perspectivism, or at least those that have been offered so far, saddle Nietzsche with an incoherent view. A well-known principle of interpretative charity admonishes interpreters not to ascribe incoherent views to interpretees. *Pace* Davidson, that principle is best

---

[5] Hard, but not impossible. Elijah Milgram has pointed out in conversation that one could take an interpretation to be not something propositional, but something practical, something like a form of life, or what is at work in Heidegger's notion of the ready-to-hand. But this is clearly not what Nehamas takes to be an interpretation. Furthermore, given this understanding of interpretation, it is simply false that every view is an interpretation, where a view is taken to be something cognitive such as a coherent set of beliefs. On the other hand, if a view itself is interpreted noncognitively to mean something like a form of life then we are back to a reading that makes the claim in question a tautology.

[6] Nehamas's text suggests that he interprets this claim in a weaker sense according to which to say that something is an interpretation simply means that it could be false (1985: 66). In this case perspectivism would boil down to a fairly trivial garden variety fallibilism.

seen as a general interpretative heuristic, rather than as an inviolable rule. However, if there is no probative textual evidence to back up the attribution of an incoherent view then one has good grounds for applying the heuristic of charity. In the case before us what is particularly striking is that in the passages in his published works where Nietzsche talks of perspectives and perspectivism there are few direct mentions of truth and none of facts. Furthermore, those published passages that do mention both perspectivism and truth do not particularly support the semantic interpretations of perspectivism considered above. For instance, perhaps the most notable published passage where Nietzsche directly connects truth and perspectivism is the following from *BGE* 34:

> Let us concede at least this much: there would be no life at all if not on the basis of perspectival evaluations and appearances; and if, with the virtuous enthusiasm and awkwardness of some philosophers, one wanted to abolish 'the apparent world' altogether, well, assuming you could do that—at any rate nothing would remain of your 'truth' either.

Prima facie, this passage lends no weight to those interpretations that take Nietzsche's perspectivism to be a denial of the correspondence theory of truth, or the proposal of a pragmatic theory of truth or a blanket denial of the existence of truth. Rather, it implies that the "apparent world" disdained by the philosophers (who presumably pine for some fanciful world of things-in-themselves) is the only truth-maker there is; abolish the apparent world and you abolish truth. If anything, this is a claim that sits well with the correspondence theory of truth.[7] The canonical passage on perspectivism in Nietzsche's published works, namely the passage in *GM* III: 12 (see section 2.2 of this essay), mentions neither truth nor facts.

There is only one passage in his notebooks which mentions both facts and perspectivism together:

> Against positivism, which seeks to stay with the phenomena saying "There are only facts," I would say: *No, facts are precisely what there are not, only interpretations.* We cannot establish any facts "in themselves": perhaps it is nonsense to want such things...As far as the word "knowledge" has sense, the world is knowable: but it is interpretable otherwise, it has no meaning behind it, but countless meanings—"Perspectivism". (*KSA* 12: 315, my italics)[8]

Often references in the secondary literature to this passage only include the italicized fragment (e.g., Danto 1965: 76 and, regrettably, Gemes 1992: 54). However, taken in its wider context, this is best read not as denying facts *tout court*, but only as denying the kind of brute facts posited by certain positivists. These would be facts analogous to Lewis's Given, that is, facts free of all interpretation; Nietzsche in this passage specifically rejects such "facts 'in themselves.'"

---

[7] This interpretation echoes that of Clark (1990: 109–17). Clark argues that the passage in *TI* entitled "How the 'Real World' became a Myth" is a repudiation of the notion of a world beyond the apparent world and an endorsement of the idea that all truth pertains to the apparent world. Clark makes the further claim that Nietzsche positively endorses the correspondence theory of truth. Gemes (2001) argues against the claim that Nietzsche really endorsed any particular theory of truth.

[8] In section 2.1 of this essay the second part of this notebook passage is given. That wider context also bolsters the reading that in denying facts Nietzsche is rejecting the idea of noninterpretive understanding, rather than rejecting the notion of facts *tout court*.

The sheer implausibility of the semantic versions of perspectivism and the lack of pro-bative textual evidence, especially in Nietzsche's published work, weigh decisively against Schacht's, Danto's, and Nehamas's attribution of semantic versions of perspectivism to Nietzsche.[9] Moreover there are more general reasons to think that Nietzsche was not par-ticularly concerned with such things as a theory of truth or the metaphysics of facts. These give additional reasons for being suspicious of interpretations that treat perspectivism as a semantic thesis. For more on this see sections 1.6, 1.7, and 2.2 of this essay and Gemes 1992.

1.3 Epistemological Perspectivism I: Knowledge, Interests, Affects

Another type of reading of perspectivism has it not as a claim about truth, but as a claim about knowledge:

> All knowledge is interest/affect-dependent and the more interests/affects we entertain the more complete our knowledge will be.

This is a view recently forwarded with respect primarily to interests by Brian Leiter in his *Nietzsche on Morality* and with respect primarily to affects by Chris Janaway in his *Against Selflessness*. There is a fairly banal reading of the alleged interest/affect dependence of knowledge according to which what interests or, in the terminology of *GM* III: 12, what "affects" we have will to some degree determine the knowledge we have. For instance, one with a strong interest in test cricket or one whose affects are aroused by cricket is more likely to have knowledge of Bradman's test average than one who has no interest in or no affects aroused by cricket. Here the claim that the more interests/affects we have the more knowl-edge we (are likely to) have has the implication, for instance, that one whose only interest/affects concerning London are wholly focused on London's tourist attractions is likely to have less knowledge of London than one who is interested in/has an affective response to multiple facets of London (tourist attractions, history, politics, transport network, etc.).[10] This makes perspectivism a fairly trivial thesis. Indeed it seems so trivial that one wonders

---

[9] We have noted that the published works do not generally put together the term "perspective" ("*Perspektiv*") and its cognates with "truth" ("*Wahrheit*") or "facts" ("*Tatsachen*") or their cognates. We have seen that the most notable exception, if anything, supports an attribution of the correspondence theory of truth to Nietzsche, rather than any skepticism towards truth. We saw above that the one passage from the notebooks that puts together "perspective" and "facts" is, in its full context, not conducive to the "no facts" semantic reading of perspectivism. There are various notebook passages that put together the terms "truth" and "perspective" or their cognates. Some of these might *possibly* be construed as backing the semantic interpretation of perspectivism. This is a thin thread on which to hang such contentious readings. Unfortunately considerations of space do not allow a full reading of those passages. There are several passages in both the published and unpublished work, and, notably, the unpublished early essay "Über Wahrheit und Lüge im aussermoralischen Sinne" (*KSA* 1: 875–92), which might suggest that Nietzsche at various times held certain skeptical positions about truth. Similarly there are passages that suggest that at various times he held skeptical positions about the notions of facts or a real world. However such texts are not specifically linked with perspectivism.

[10] Having more interests is not by itself sufficient for having more knowledge since aptitude for finding truth is also required.

why Nietzsche, a philosopher who does not seem generally to deal in such trivialities, would give it any emphasis at all.[11]

1.4 Epistemological Perspectivism II: The Constitutive Claim

There is a strong reading of the relation between interests/affects and knowledge according to which

> Our interests/affects play a constitutive role in our knowledge.

Leiter, apparently acknowledging that the mere claim that what knowledge we have is causally dependent on our interests is not a particularly substantive claim, says

> That the "affects" play a causal role in the genesis of knowing would not, by itself, be sufficient for perspectivism, however. What is necessary is that the affects also play a constitutive role in knowledge. What Nietzsche says of philosophers—"most of the conscious thinking of a philosopher is secretly guided and forced into certain channels by his instincts" (BGE:3)—applies quite generally to knowing: knowers and inquirers are moved by their desires, their passions, their affections, to ask certain kinds of questions, look into certain kinds of topics, pursue certain directions of research. So just as seeing an object from a certain angle plays a constitutive role in what is seen…so too interests or affects play a constitutive role in knowledge: you come to *know* about the aspects of the phenomena in question that answer to your particular interests and desires. (2002: 273)

Now being "guided," "forced," and "moved" are causal notions, and being told that one comes to know about aspects of phenomena that answer to one's interests does not in any way tell us how those interests are somehow constitutive of our knowledge of said phenomena. So while Leiter invokes an alleged constitutive relation between interests and knowledge, his examples give us no real idea of what this means.[12]

---

[11] Nehamas at times seems to be endorsing a fairly benign epistemological reading of perspectivism which stresses the interest relativity of knowledge. Thus his chapter on perspectivism concludes with the seemingly innocuous claim that perspectivism is "the view that all efforts to know are also efforts of particular people to live particular kinds of lives for particular reasons." (1985: 73). At other times, Nehamas seems to interpret perspectivism to be the thesis that all interpretation involves falsifying simplifications—a view he, I believe rightly, sees Nietzsche as illegitimately embracing (1985: 56). He also seems to take perspectivism to entail that every "system of thought and action includes within itself the premise that it is the only possible such system" (1985: 57). Note that this itself entails that every perspectivist system is itself inconsistent since, presumably, a perspectivist system besides containing the premise that it the only possible system also contains the claim that there are other possible systems. Without the latter claim it could not, after all, be a perspectivist system.

[12] Moreover, the claim that seeing an object from a certain angle plays a constitutive role in what is seen is highly dubious. What is seen can here refer to either the actual object under view or to the visual experience of said object. Presumably, on pain of falling into subjective idealism, Leiter means the latter. But while the angle one views an object from may be a causal factor in one's visual experience of that object, it is not clear that it plays a constitutive role in that experience. Arguably, a brain in the

Janaway gives an account of perspectivism that at first seems to be of the banal variety that claims that the affects, which he equates with feelings, play a causal role in determining what and how much knowledge we have:

> So Nietzsche's perspectivism about knowledge must involve the two claims: (1) that *there is only knowledge that is guided or facilitated by our feelings*, and (2) that *the more different feelings we allow to guide our knowledge, the better our knowledge will be*. (Janaway 2007: 206)

"Guided" here seems to suggest a merely causal relation between affects and knowledge. But, like Leiter, Janaway claims perspectivism involves more than such claims about the causal relation between affects and knowledge:

> For him [Nietzsche], feelings make knowledge *possible*. They are not ineliminable occupational hazards for the knower, but constitutively necessary conditions of the knower's knowing anything at all. (2007: 212)

Note this is a very strong and hence implausible claim. It entails, for instance, that a highly developed but unfeeling robot, or a person who due to brain bisection has lost the ability to have feelings, would be incapable of having any knowledge. Moreover, like Leiter with respect to interests' alleged constitutional role in knowledge, Janaway does not explain in what way feelings are constitutively necessary for knowledge.

1.5 Epistemological Perspectivism III: Anti-foundationalism

Another epistemological reading takes perspectivism to be a claim about the justification of beliefs. Maudemarie Clark, after rejecting accounts of perspectivism that take it to involve the falsificationist thesis, that every perspective involves falsification of reality or a denial of correspondence truth, argues that perspectivism is essentially the antifoundationalist thesis. To summarize her view:

> Beliefs are not justified through a comparison with a mind-independent reality or by reference to some indisputable foundational truths.

Clark attributes a "minimal correspondence theory of truth" to Nietzsche.[13] However, like many careful modern epistemologists she distinguishes between correspondence as an account of truth and correspondence as an account of justification. On her view Nietzsche rejects only the latter; we do not check whether our beliefs are correspondence-true by comparing them to an unconceptualized reality. Perspectivism for Clark is an epistemological thesis which rejects both correspondence and foundationalist accounts of justification of belief:

vat appropriately stimulated could be having the same visual experience I am having now even though there is no angle from which it is seeing any object, and hence such angles cannot be constitutive of its experience.

13 Clark's so-called minimal correspondence theory merely involves acceptance of all Tarski type T sentences of the form "S is true iff p," where p is replaced by a declarative sentence of the language in question and S is replaced by a name of p. In fact, this minimal correspondence theory is perfectly compatible with redundancy, coherentist, and even pragmatic accounts of truth.

Perspectivism amounts to the claim that we cannot and need not justify our beliefs by paring them down to a set of unquestionable beliefs all rational beings must share. This means that all justification is contextual, dependent on other beliefs held unchallengeable for the moment, but themselves capable of only a similarly contextual justification. (1990: 130)[14]

This reading, though having a strong air of anachronism to it, would not be attributing to Nietzsche a thesis that either in the nineteenth century or today would count as banal; antifoundationalist, holistic accounts of justification count as philosophically substantive. Below are some more general grounds, beyond its anachronistic air, to be suspicious of such a reading.

1.6 Nietzsche's Hostility to Accounts of Truth and Knowledge

Nietzsche does not explicitly mention truth or justification in any of the passages dealing with perspectivism in his published texts. While he does in the key passage which contains his most detailed discussion of perspectivism in his published work (*GM* III: 12) mention "objectivity" and "knowledge" he puts quotation marks around both terms. Indeed it is not clear that Nietzsche was really interested in such things as a theory of truth or an account of knowledge or justification. He typically tends to strongly denigrate such traditional philosophical projects—"Theory of knowledge is the love affair of the clever heads that have not learnt enough" (*KSA* 9: 63).[15] He is more likely to give a psychological diagnostic account of the will to truth or the will to knowledge than actual accounts of truth and knowledge. For instance, the second essay of his *Untimely Meditations*, "The Use and Abuse of History for Life," is largely a diagnostic account of why we are obsessed with the pursuit of knowledge and the dangers of that obsession. Similarly, a diagnosis of why we put such a high value on the pursuit of truth is central to the third essay of *GM*.[16] While references in Nietzsche's notebooks do in fact provide material for construals of perspectivism as epistemological, semantical, and even metaphysical theses, when looking at the work he actually published one does well to keep in mind his observation in *Ecce Homo*: "[t]hat a psychologist without equal speaks from my writings, is perhaps the first insight reached by a good reader" (*EH*: "Why I Write Such Good Books" 5).[17] This provides grounds for concurring with Chris

---

[14] While this may suggest that Clark is attributing a coherence account of justification of belief to Nietzsche it is worth noting that she only says that justification is dependent on other beliefs and not that justification is *wholly* dependent on other beliefs.

[15] See also *BGE* 208 where he diagnoses the obsession with skepticism, epistemology, and objectivity as a "paralysis of will." In particular he refers to skepticism, which is the engine behind so much epistemology, as "the most spiritual expression of a certain many-sided physiological temperament, which in ordinary language is called nervous debility and sickliness."

[16] For more on the theme that Nietzsche was more interested in the psychological meaning of the will to truth than actual theories about the nature of truth, see Gemes 1992.

[17] It is important to keep in mind that in the notebooks Nietzsche is often just experimenting with possible lines of enquiry. It is also striking that the notebooks contain a large amount of epistemological and metaphysical reflections that are often devoid of the larger evaluative/normative considerations that generally seem to govern the epistemological and metaphysical reflections that appear in his published works. If one were to give heavy emphasis to the notebooks' references to perspectivism and follow their lead in the decoupling of perspectivism from Nietzsche's wider normative agenda, one

Janaway's observation that "The notion that we have in *GM* III 12 a 'general theory of knowl-edge' is perhaps somewhat inflated...the whole section does not, in all honesty, read as if its first purpose is to make some authoritative contribution to epistemology" (2007: 211). While, as we have seen above, in the final analysis Janaway does in fact interpret perspectivism as having a significant epistemological bearing, the preferable conclusion is that it is not attempting to make any contribution to epistemology.

1.7 The Epiphenomenality of Much Conscious Belief

Related to Nietzsche's suspicion of such traditional philosophical projects as giving theories of truth, knowledge, and justification, Nietzsche, following Schopenhauer, tends to claim that the thoughts we consciously entertain are largely epiphenomenal. Now knowledge, and certainly evidential justification of the type Clark is concerned with, typically concern thoughts we consciously entertain, for those are the kinds of things that meet the eviden-tial requirement of knowledge.[18] Yet if conscious knowledge is largely epiphenomenal it is strange that Nietzsche should be giving an account of it or of the justification of belief, espe-cially in *GM* III where he is concerned to lay bare the inner nature of a phenomenon he takes to be of central importance in our lives and values—namely, the ascetic ideal, an ideal Nietzsche claims we unconsciously embrace.

Here is a selection of passages where Nietzsche advances claims that entail that conscious beliefs are largely epiphenomenal:

> Finally, why could a "purpose" not be an *epiphenomenon* [*Begleiterscheinung*] in the series of changes that brings about the purposive action—a pale image sketched in consciousness that serves to orient us concerning events, even as a symptom of events, *not* as their cause?...Are not all phenomena of consciousness merely terminal phenomena, final links in a chain? (*KSA* 12: 247)
> The "inner world" is full of phantoms...: the will is one of them. The will no longer moves anything, hence does not explain anything either—it merely accompanies events; it can also

could come up with a fairly epistemological and/or metaphysical reading of perspectivism that would indeed reflect much of the tenor of the unpublished work. The best of such readings, giving a heavy emphasis to the notebook materials, is in Poellner (2001). I would suggest that the notebooks are best used to augment themes that occur in Nietzsche's published texts. Admittedly what those themes are is a matter of contention. At this point it behoves me to mention *GS* 354, notably entitled "The Origin of our Concept of 'Knowledge,'" where Nietzsche does indeed present perspectivism as the semantic/epistemic claim that "the world of which we can become conscious is only a sign-world" and involves "a great and thorough corruption, falsification, reduction to superficialities, and generalization." Clark argues that this commitment to the falsification thesis is a leftover from Nietzsche's commitment to the Schopenhaurian notion that all our representations are false of the world of things-in-themselves, a commitment which by the time of *GM* and *TI* he came to repudiate (Clark 1990: 149). While I am not sure that Nietzsche ever fully gave up the falsificationist thesis (see, for example, *GM* III: 24 where falsifying is listed as part of "the essence of interpretation"), I believe that it plays little, if any, part in the normative agenda which is central to his later works. On the other hand, as argued below, perspectivism, as a nonepistemic, nonsemantical view, is central to that normative agenda.

[18] To anachronistically ascribe to Nietzsche an externalist account of knowledge which would omit the customary evidential requirement on knowledge would be to press his texts with an interpretative weight they could not bear.

be absent. The so-called *motive*: another error. Merely a surface phenomenon of consciousness—something alongside the deed that is more likely to cover up the antecedents of the
deeds than to represent them...What follows from this? There are no mental [*geistige*] causes
at all. (*TI*: "The Four Great Errors" 3)

Even allowing that the thesis of the epiphenomenality of belief, inasmuch as Nietzsche
embraced it, is an instance of hyperbole on Nietzsche's part, it is fairly clear that Nietzsche,
like Schopenhauer, generally treated consciously espoused beliefs more as symptoms pointing to deeper causes below the level of consciousness than as original springs of action. This
being so, it is particularly perplexing to think of him giving an account in *GM* III: 12 of how
such beliefs can constitute knowledge or be justified in the middle of a discussion of what he
takes to be one of the deepest springs of our actions, the ascetic ideal.[19]

1.8 Perspectivism Applied to All Life

Many of Nietzsche's references to perspectivism make it clear that he attributes perspectives
to all organic phenomena, all life:

> *perspective*, the basic condition of all life (*BGE* Preface)
> There would be no life at all if not on the basis of perspectival evaluations and appearances.
> (*BGE* 34)
> With the organic world a perspectival sphere is given. (*KSA* 11: 701)

Now perspectives for Nietzsche clearly involve interpretation. So if Nietzsche gives a broad
range to perspectives, allowing that all life, including nonsentient life, has perspectives,
then one would equally expect him to say that all life involves interpreting. This in fact he
explicitly says:

> All happening in the organic world is an *overpowering, a becoming-lord-over*; and...in turn,
> all overpowering and becoming-lord-over is a new interpreting... (*GM* II: 12)
> The will to power *interprets*... (The organic process constantly presupposes interpretation)
> (*KSA* 12: 139)

Now life forms that are not sentient—for example, plants—clearly do not have any mental life, and so are incapable of entertaining truths or knowledge and clearly incapable of

---

[19] Like Leiter, I take the *TI* passage to be a denial of the causality of conscious mental processes, not
of all mental processes. In fact, all these strong claims of the complete epiphenomenality of conscious
mental processes I take to be hyperbolic, overly strong statements by Nietzsche which do not represent
his considered position. There are a myriad of places where Nietzsche attributes causal powers to such
processes—for more on this see Katsafanas 2005. Nietzsche's considered position is not that conscious
mental processes have no causal powers, but rather that they themselves are largely a reflection of deeper,
typically hidden causes. It is these deeper causes that are of primary interest to Nietzsche. Thus, a more
considered view would see our conscious abstract musing on, for instance, the nature of fairness, as part
of a causal chain leading from, for instance, the unconscious desire to have power to the consciously
espoused love of justice. The point I want to make is that Nietzsche's strong emphasis on the fundamental
causal role of the unconscious drives in the phenomena that concern him (e.g., the genesis of our values)
militates against the claim that Nietzsche is deeply interested in giving accounts of how conscious beliefs
can be knowledge or of the justification or truth conditions of such beliefs.

878f

having, let alone justifying, beliefs. Those who take perspectivism to be a claim about truth or knowledge or justification do not explain why Nietzsche attributes perspectives to all life, including nonsentient life.

PART 2

2.1 The Psychobiological Reading of Perspectivism I: The Descriptive Component

In light of the above-detailed failures of epistemological and semantical readings on both philosophical and textual grounds, I now want to advance a reading which I think better fits Nietzsche's texts, better fits his overall philosophical project, and does not attribute to him banal or unacceptable epistemological or semantic theses.[20] This reading partially takes perspectivism to be a psychobiological claim. I say "partially" because it sees perspectivism as having both an overt descriptive and a hidden normative component. Let us first consider the descriptive component:

> Descriptive Component of Perspectivism: Each drive has its own perspective/ interpretation of the world and seeks to express that interpretation of the world, often at the expense of other drives.

The clearest direct textual evidence that this is (part of) what Nietzsche is getting at with his perspectivism comes from the following passages from his notebooks:

> As far as the word "knowledge" has sense, the world is knowable: but it is interpretable otherwise, it has no meaning behind it, but countless meanings—"Perspectivism."
> It is our needs that interpret the world: our drives and their for and against. Every drive is a kind of attempt to dominate; each has its own perspective, which it wants to force as a norm on the other drives. (*KSA* 12: 315)

What does it mean to say our drives have perspectives, that our drives interpret the world? Let us consider an example. Imagine a middle-sized animal (a hyena) that sees a similarly sized animal (say a small boar) not too far away. His drive for sustenance may incline him to attack the distant animal, thus interpreting it as prey, as a source of food; his drive for survival may at the same time incline him to flee, thus interpreting the distant animal as a potential predator. Thus we have the renowned fight or flight syndrome as an expression of

---

[20] This is not to imply that Nietzsche had exactly the same philosophical project clearly in mind throughout his intellectual career. Elsewhere (Gemes 2008) I have argued that while in his early work Nietzsche was largely focused on the Romantic project of helping to create a genuine German culture, by the time of his later works he had come to be strongly pessimistic about the possibility of a genuine culture, and merely hoped to inspire certain individuals to break through the shackles imposed by Judeo-Christian values. Perspectivism, especially in its prescriptive component, as described in this section, belongs largely to the later project.

the conflict between two competing drives. The example of the hyena explains how animal life can be said to have drives that interpret.[21]

Now it might be objected here that drives are not actually doing the interpreting but are merely playing a causal role in getting the hyena to interpret the boar in one way rather than another. In fact, the question about what exactly does the interpreting is a difficult question even in the case of human interpretation, especially for a philosopher such as Nietzsche who does not have a transcendental I that is the locus of judgments. Where a Kantian typically opposes the bodily drives and the I of judgment that may choose to ignore or indulge those drives, Nietzsche strongly rejects such a notion of an I separate from the drives, going so far as to talk of "the totality of drives which constitute one's being" (D 119—my translation). On the textual point it is worth establishing that Nietzsche himself in his published works talks of the drives interpreting. Thus in D 119 he says:

> Waking life does not have this freedom of interpretation possessed by the life of dreams... but I do add that when we are awake our drives likewise do nothing but interpret nervous stimuli...

Of course this talk of drives interpreting may grate on some philosophical sensibilities. But it raises an important question for all those who reject the Kantian I. Where is the locus of interpretations? On the Nietzschean picture what one has is various natural causal apparatus, including drives, perceptual apparatus, and other functional apparatus. What exactly does the interpreting in this case? Interpreting itself now is just a complex causal/functional event and so claiming the drives are a fundamental cause in a given interpretation is just to say they are fundamental to that interpretation. Note the hyena does not interpret the boar as food by explicitly making the judgment that it is food, rather it interprets it by interacting with it in a certain way, e.g., attacking it. Even in beings that make judgments, for Nietzsche, much interpreting is of this sort. The Christian interprets the world as being of little value not by making the explicit judgment "the world is of little value"—indeed many Christians would think it sacrilege to make such a judgment since the world is God's creation. Rather they interpret it as being of little value through their interactions with the world.

Applying this type of analysis to nonsentient life forms, such as plants, is more difficult. However, when one considers the movements of various nonsentient life forms—for instance, the tropisms whereby a sunflower moves to directly face the sun, or even the processes whereby a tree grows taller, thereby obtaining more light for photosynthesis—we gain an idea of how Nietzsche's notion of drives and interpretation can be applied to nonsentient life forms.[22] If

---

[21] The idea of drives interpreting is echoed in Freud. Drives for Freud and Nietzsche are the equivalent of Descartes's pineal gland, a site where the intentional and the physical-somatic meet. While this notion of a meeting of the intentional and the physical is problematic, it is no less so for all philosophy faced with the mind–body problem. Inasmuch as drives are functionally defined, one can see that placing intentionality in the drives fits in with modern functionalist accounts of intentionality.

[22] That Nietzsche entertained such notions of drives and perspectives, applicable to all organic life, is demonstrated in various passages from his published works and the notebooks; for instance, see the quotations in section 1.8 of this essay. Moreover, the idea that the entire organic world contains wills, drives, or instincts was common in the nineteenth century. The claim of ubiquity of will was of course championed by Schopenhauer, and hence was well known to Nietzsche. The ubiquity of all three in the organic world is argued for by G. H. Schneider in his Der Thierische Wille, a work explicitly referred to in Nietzsche's notebooks of 1895 (cf. KSA 10: 314–15). Wilhelm Roux in his Der Kampf der Theile im Organismus,

we make use of notions such as Gibson's notion of affordances (cf. Gibson 1977), according to which a given environment comes with things that afford various possible interactions and interpretations, we can see that plants in reacting to various such affordances are in some sense interpreting their environment. In this vein it is not unusual for scientists, for instance, entomologists, to say such things as that certain proteins "represent a communication channel by which both animals and plants interpret and react to their environment" (Raloff 1992: 45).[23]

2.2 The Psychobiological Reading of Perspectivism II: The Prescriptive Component

The notion of health is central to Nietzsche's writings, especially those of the later period. Indeed he often gives indications that he sees himself as a kind of physician who might bring a great health:

> I am still waiting for a philosophical *physician* in the exceptional sense of that word—one who has to pursue the problem of the total health of a people, time, race or of humanity—to muster the courage to push my suspicion to its limits and to risk the proposition: what was at stake in all philosophizing hitherto was not at all 'truth' but something else—let us say, health, future, growth, power, life. (*GS* Preface 2)

The notion that we have become sick, and hence are in need of physicians, is central to *GM* and especially the third essay of *GM*.[24]

> For man is sicker, more unsure, more changing than any other animal, of this there is no doubt—he is the *sick* animal. (*GM* III: 13)

Now what has made us sick, according to Nietzsche, is that we have dealt poorly with conflicts in our drives:

> In an age of disintegration that mixes races indiscriminately, human beings have in their bodies the heritage of multiple origins, that is opposite and not merely opposite drives and value

which Nietzsche also refers to in his notebooks, attributed drives to organs, tissue, and cells (cf. Moore 2002: 77–82). The motif of cells having drives is alluded to in several passages in Nietzsche, for instance:

> If we translate the characteristics of the lowest living being into terms comprehensible to our 'reason', they become *moral* drives. Such a being assimilates its neighbor, transforms it into its property (property is originally nutrient and accumulation of nutrient); it seeks to incorporate as much as possible, not only in order to compensate for loss—it is greedy. In this way, it grows alone, and thus finally becomes reproductive—it divides into two beings. (KSA 9: 490)

[23] This section has greatly benefited from the input of Ram Neta, who, among other things, suggested the use of Gibson's notion of affordances.

[24] In Gemes 2006 I argue that *GM* is really an attempt to provide a kind of therapy to us moderns who, through 2,000 years of self-vivisection under the influence of Judeo-Christian values, have become, in Nietzsche's words of *GM* Preface 1, "strangers to ourselves" and hence pathologically divided in our selves. That Nietzsche's fundamental complaint against Christianity is that it promotes such ill health is made clear in such passages as the following from *The Antichrist*:

> At the bottom of Christianity is the rancor of the sick, instinct directed *against* the healthy, *against* health itself. (*A* 51)

standards that fight each other and rarely permit each other any rest. Such human beings of
late cultures and refracted lights will on the average be weaker human beings. (*BGE* 200)

In particular, the priest, the supreme advocate of Judeo-Christian values, teaches us to deal
with conflicting drives by suppressing some of our strongest drives; our sexual drives, drives
to dominate, drives to excel, etc. In section 11 of the third essay of *GM* Nietzsche introduces
the priest as the prime mover behind this ascetic ideal. Later he characterizes the priest as a
would-be physician who in fact makes the sick even sicker (*GM* III: 16). In section 12 of *GM*
III right after his first introduction of the priest as the principal advocate of the sickly ascetic
ideal he seemingly abruptly introduces his notion of perspectivism:

> There is *only* a perspective seeing, *only* a perspective "knowing"; and *the more* affects we allow
> to speak about one thing, *the more* eyes, different eyes, we can use to observe one thing, the
> more complete will our "concept" of this thing, our "objectivity" be. (*GM* III: 12)[25]

Where this passage is, in the traditional matter, interpreted as a discourse on the nature of
knowledge and objectivity or as a thesis about truth or justification, its function in *GM* is totally
obscure. Why after having in section 11 finally identified the priest as prime mover behind the
ascetic ideal, the focal point of the third essay of *GM*, does Nietzsche turn to epistemological/
semantical concerns, after which, in the remainder of the essay, he concentrates on the effects of
the priest as a failed physician who only serves to make the sick sicker? I suggest that it is really
functioning here to surreptitiously give Nietzsche's countermodel of and injunction towards
genuine health.

[25] It is worth noting that this version of perspectivism explicitly mentions affects rather than drives,
whereas the passage about perspectivism from the *Nachlass* quoted in section 2.1 of this essay makes
reference to drives rather than affects. There are several points to be made here. Arguably, Nietzsche
often uses the terms "affect" and "drive" interchangeably, so that the degree of difference between affects
and drives in any single passage is a difficult matter of interpretation. If, following Janaway (2007: 206),
we take the talk of affects to be talk of feelings rather than drives, so that perspectivism is a thesis about
feelings, then we will have serious problems making sense of the claim that all life, all of the organic
world, has perspectives. While it is a little stretch to say, for instance, that plants have drives—clearly
they have dispositions that facilitate their survival and growth—it is a giant stretch to say they have
feelings. Generally drives, more than feelings, have the temporal spread required for the interpreting that
seems central to Nietzsche's perspectivism. Relatedly, intentionality, or at least basic aboutness, seems
to be more a property of drives than feelings. Furthermore, feelings seem for Nietzsche to be largely a
product of the drives and their interactions with reality—e.g., it is the conflict between the slave's drive to
dominate and his lowly and impotent position in the world that gives rise to his feeling of resentment. So
talk of affects speaking can be read as a reflection of the interpretative drives' interactions with the world.
Then why in *GM* III: 12 does Nietzsche specifically speak of affects rather than drives? I think part of
the basis for this is that this allows more direct contact with Schopenhauer's philosophy which is clearly
one of the targets of Nietzsche's critique in *GM* III and throughout *GM*, as Janaway also emphasizes
(2007: 202–3). Thus just before the passage cited above Nietzsche says:

> For let us guard ourselves better from now on, gentlemen philosophers, against the dangerous old concep-
> tual fabrication that posited a "pure, will-less, painless, timeless subject of knowledge[.]"

Schopenhauer in his account of the, for him, all-important knowledge of the world beyond appearances
emphasizes the notion of the quieting of affective elements and the escaping of the will. Similarly,
the notion of a timeless subject of knowledge is very much Schopenhauer's. So by emphasizing the
affective element in his account of perspectivism in *GM* III Nietzsche brings out his rejection of
the Schopenhaurian ideal of escaping the affects, will, and time. Schopenhauer is of central interest

Prescriptive Component of Perspectivism: The healthiest (highest) life involves the maximal expression of the richest set of drives, each of which has its own perspective, interpretation of the world.[26]

Where the priest of section 11 advocates suppression of the drives, Nietzsche in section 12 is advocating their fullest expression.

Why then does Nietzsche present perspectivism as a thesis about knowledge in both the notebook passage quoted above and the passage from *GM* III: 12? First it is worth noting that he puts quotation marks around the term "knowable" in the notebook passage and around both "knowledge" and "objectivity" in *GM* III: 12, thereby suggesting these notions may not be his real concerns. The greater context makes clear that one of his targets in *GM* III: 12 is indeed Schopenhauer's idea of a certain form of alleged disinterested knowledge that Schopenhauer claims, in aesthetic contemplation at least, allows us to escape the world of willing. Yet here again, arguably, the target is not Schopenhauer's actual account of disinterested knowledge; rather it is Schopenhauer's valorization of an ascetic injunction to escape the world of the will, or what Nietzsche calls the drives, through aesthetic contemplation. Finally, given that Nietzsche takes his audience to be laboring under the modern form of the ascetic ideal which puts an extreme value on truth and knowledge (this is a key point of emphasis in *GM* III: 23) it is not surprising that Nietzsche should disguise his anti-ascetic injunction in terms such as "knowledge" and "objectivity" which he takes to be

for Nietzsche's analysis of the ascetic ideal because, like much of Nietzsche's intended audience, Schopenhauer, as a confirmed atheist, appears to have escaped the influence of the Judeo-Christian worldview. In fact, according to Nietzsche, in his acceptance of asceticism, his desire to escape affects, Schopenhauer shows he is really still thoroughly dominated by that worldview. Maudemarie Clark (1998) also emphasizes the degree to which perspectivism, as presented in *GM* III: 12, is a response to Schopenhauer. Clark (1998) repudiates the account of perspectivism she gave in Clark 1990, now glossing perspectivism as the thesis that knowledge is "focused" by the interests, emotions, and the like (1998: 74). Again (cf. section 1.3 of this essay), this makes perspectivism a fairly anodyne doctrine—one's interests (help) determine what matters one has knowledge of. Perhaps more to the point, the claim that interests focus our knowledge is a doctrine that Schopenhauer himself embraced (cf. *WWR* I: 176–7; *WWR* II: 176, 372–3, 284–5) as, interestingly, Clark herself points out (1998: 42). Of course, for Schopenhauer this only concerns empirical knowledge, not the transcendental knowledge that Schopenhauer so highly valued. But that empirical knowledge is exactly what is of fundamental interest to Clark's Nietzsche. So, the only substantial difference between Clark's version of perspectivism and Schopenhauer's view is that Schopenhauer took empirical knowledge to be knowledge of mere appearances, whereas for Clark, Nietzsche's perspectivism concerns knowledge of the empirical world qua the one and only world. It is hard to see how this difference fits in with the general concerns of *GM* III. It is only by focusing on the normative rather than on any alleged epistemological import of Nietzsche's perspectivism that we find a point of conflict with Schopenhauer that explains the place of perspectivism in *GM* III.

[26] Maximal expression involves coherent expression of the drives. Note this allows that the masters of *GM* I even if they have a relatively simple set of drives can still count as healthy in that they achieve coherent expression. However, they would represent a lower level of health than one achieved by those such as Goethe who had both complexity of drives along with coherent expression of those drives:

What he [Goethe] wanted was totality...he disciplined himself to wholeness, he created himself....Goethe conceived of a person, strong, highly educated, accomplished in all corporeal matters, self-controlled, self-respecting, who can dare to allow himself the whole range and richness of naturalness. (*TI*: "Skirmishes of an Untimely Man" 49—my translation)

What the masters, the blond beasts, of *GM* I lack is this range and richness (of drives).

overly valued by his audience. Nietzsche in his summary of *GM* in *Ecce Homo* explicitly refers to the essays' calculated propensity to mislead readers and also refers there to their deeply uncanny nature (cf. *EH*: "Genealogy of Morals"). I take the disguising of his perspectivist prescription as a seeming epistemological thesis to be wholly in line with this deceptive, uncanny nature of *GM*.

2.3 Nietzsche's Normative Agenda: Sublimation Not Repression

Nietzsche's corrective to the repression and subsequent splitting-off of the drives, fostered by the ascetic ideal, is their reintegration into a coherent whole.

> The multiplicity and disgregation of drives and the lack of any systematic order among them results in a "weak will"; their coordination under a single predominant impulse results in a "strong" will: in the first case it is the oscillation and lack of gravity; in the latter, the precision and clarity of direction. (*KSA* 13: 394)
>
> Overcoming of the affects? No, if that means their weakening and annihilation. But instead employing them; which may mean a long tyrannizing of them…At last they are confidently given freedom again: they love us as good servants and happily go wherever our best interests lie. (*KSA* 12: 39)

Indeed this notion of a multiplicity of drives forming a controlled coherent whole is Nietzsche's prescription for his much vaunted "higher men":[27]

> The highest man would have the greatest multiplicity of drives, in the relatively greatest strength that can be endured. Indeed, where the plant "man" shows himself strongest one finds instincts that conflict powerfully (e.g., in Shakespeare), but are controlled. (*KSA* 11: 289)

In *Ecce Homo*, where Nietzsche elaborates the subtitle of that work "How One Becomes What One Is," Nietzsche tells the story of how one of his favorite heroes, namely Nietzsche, achieves a higher unity through the action of an unconscious master drive that sublimates weaker drives:

> To become what one is, one must not have the slightest notion of what one is…The whole surface of consciousness—consciousness is a surface—must be kept clear of all great

[27] Richardson argues persuasively that the same is true for Nietzsche's account of the overman:

> The overman is that very rare person who can form a wealth of conflicting parts into a system in which they all find expression[.] (Richardson 1996: 69)

The emphasis on conflict here is important. The account of sublimation given above does not emphasize the importance of the continuation of agonal struggle as part of Nietzsche's ideal. However, sublimation need not be understood as a static situation with a single drive forever in the ascendancy. On Nietzsche's picture of health the drives are always competing with each other for ascendancy, and while one ascendant drive may for some time co-opt the other drives, eventually—ideally when it has achieved its fullest expression—it will be overcome by some now more needy, more vigorous drive that will give new direction to the organism. This is part of Nietzsche's claim that all great things lead to their own self-overcoming.

imperatives...Meanwhile the organizing "idea" that is destined to rule keeps growing deep down—it begins to command; slowly it leads us back from side roads and wrong roads; it prepares single qualities and fitnesses that will one day prove to be indispensable as a means towards the whole—one by one, it trains all subservient capacities before giving any hint of the dominant task, "goal," "aim," or "meaning." (*EH*: "Why I am So Clever" 9)

According to Nietzsche, repression of the drives leads to a pathological condition while sublimation is the means to health.[28] The Nietzschean solution to the problem of differentiating sublimation from pathological symptoms, a problem that Freud never really solved, may be summed up in the slogan that sublimations involve integration or unification, while pathological symptoms involve splitting-off or disintegration, as we might call it.[29] What is disintegrated is, of course, the (possibility of a) unified self. For Nietzsche the difference between repression and sublimation is that in sublimation the stronger drive co-opts a weaker drive as an ally and this allows the weaker drive expression, albeit to an end that contains some degree of deflection from its original aim. For example, consider Freud's paradigm example of sublimation presented in his essay on Leonardo da Vinci (Freud 1961: vol. 11, pp. 57–137). According to Freud, Leonardo had a lifelong unconsummated homosexual drive which was partially transformed into a drive towards artistic and scientific investigations and creativity.[30] On Nietzsche's account, this counts as a case of sublimation because Leonardo's erotic drive is co-opted by what Nietzsche actually takes to be Leonardo's master drive, the drive towards artistic and scientific investigations and creativity. That erotic drive is then expressed in, for instance, Leonardo's lifelong endeavors to create and possess idealized representations of perfect male bodies. This new aim is a deflection from his homoerotic drive's original aim, namely the literal sexual possession of male bodies. By contrast, in repression the stronger drive attempts to stifle any expression of the weaker drive, so that its expression is either fully stifled or can only be achieved in a heavily disguised and conflicted

---

[28] Simon May is particularly acute on the importance of sublimation for achieving Nietzsche's version of health:

> Sublimation...can therefore be so life-enhancing because it enables us to harness to creative ends drives...whose violence might annihilate or paralyze us, and moreover, to accommodate a wide variety of opposing drives...whose co-existence might otherwise be impossible. By contrast, traditional 'ascetically ideal' morality deals with such drives simply by extirpating or crushing them. Thus it is only by sublimation that Nietzsche's highest man—the one who integrates the maximum number and variety of drives—is possible. (May 1999: 29)

[29] As Laplanche and Pontalis conclude in their entry on sublimation in their seminal *The Language of Psychoanalysis*:

> The lack of a coherent theory of sublimation remains one of the lacunae in psychoanalytic thought. (Laplanche and Pontalis 1973: 433)

For more on the relation of sublimation to pathological symptoms and repression and the advantages of Nietzsche's account of sublimation over Freud's, see Gemes 2009.

[30] Freud's account of Leonardo is implausible in a number of ways. For instance, recent studies suggest that, contra Freud, Leonardo had an active sexual life, and, notoriously, a central part of Freud's account crucially rests on a faulty interpretation of one of Leonardo's recollections of his dreams. Freud's interpretation of the relevant dream is vitiated by a mistranslation of Italian into German which at a crucial point takes Leonardo's recollection to be referring to an eagle where in fact he is referring to a kite. The accuracy of Freud's account is not germane to its use here as an illustration of the notion of sublimation.

form which often represents the inverse of the original aim. For instance, the Christian's hatred and envy of and desire for power over his fellow man are expressed as professions of brotherly love and disinterest in power.

2.4 The Advantages of the Psychobiological Reading over the Traditional: The Connection between Perspectivism and Will to Power

We have seen above some of the advantages of the psychobiological reading of perspectivism over traditional epistemological or semantic readings:

(a) It does not saddle Nietzsche with implausible semantic claims about truth, or banal or implausible claims about knowledge.
(b) It does not have Nietzsche trafficking in the type of speculations, theories of truth, and accounts of knowledge or justification which he generally so strongly rails against.
(c) It fits in with his claims about the largely epiphenomenal nature of consciousness.
(d) It fits in with his claim that all life, all the organic world, has perspectives.
(e) It makes clear the connection between perspectivism and Nietzsche's wider normative project.
(f) Unlike the epistemological or semantical readings, it specifically and explicitly explains the function of perspectivism in the third essay of *GM*.

A further advantage not mentioned above is that it allows for a deep connection between perspectivism and Nietzsche's notion of will to power, at the same time showing how Nietzsche's posit of the will to power need not be seen as metaphysical extravagance. Nietzsche continually emphasizes that all life is will to power:

> life itself is *essentially* appropriation, injury, overpowering of the foreign and weak, suppression, severity, imposition of one's own forms, incorporation, and at the least, putting it mildest, exploitation . . . life *is* simply Will to Power. (*BGE* 259)[31]

The drives are for Nietzsche the physical embodiment of the will to power and in emphasizing the (explanatory and causal) primacy of the will to power, Nietzsche is expressing the (explanatory and causal) primacy of the drives, and hence the importance of the interpretations, the perspectives, those drives embody. That is to say, the descriptive component of perspectivism, the claim that every drive has its own perspective and seeks to express that perspective, often at the expense of other drives, fits in with Nietzsche's claims that drives are the essence of all life and that life is essentially will to power.[32] Thus we have the Nietzschean equation life = will to power = the drives striving for expression.

---

[31] The identification of life and will to power also occurs in *BGE* 13: "life itself is *will to power*" and again in *GM* II: 6 and 12.

[32] In his notebooks Nietzsche explicitly expresses the connection between perspectivism and will to power in the following passage

This connection between drives and will to power is most forcefully presented by John Richardson:

> drives are 'will to power' in that they essentially pursue the continual enhancement of their distinctive activities, enhancement that consists in their mastery of others. So the level of a drive's activity, its strength, is measured by 'how much' it rules over others. (1996: 33)

The prescriptive component of perspectivism, the claim that a healthy life involves the maximal expression of the richest set of drives, fits in with Nietzsche's normative account of healthy life as the fullest expression of the will to power.[33] That this interpretation places both perspectivism and his notion of the will to power within the wider normative agenda that is central to his philosophy while stripping them of much of their seeming philosophical extravagance, in terms of semantic, epistemological, and metaphysical implications, must be seen as a large bonus of the psychobiological interpretation.

2.5 The Limited Epistemological Implication of the Psychobiological Account

Now it may be argued that by emphasizing the prescriptive content of perspectivism the psychobiological interpretation is in fact allowing some epistemological relevance to perspectivism. In particular, while the psychobiological account has no direct implications for accounts of propositional knowledge—accounts of knowing that—it arguably has implications concerning knowing how.[34] If the full and coherent expression of the drives is constitutive of a healthy life then it may be claimed that being able to so express one's drives is constitutive of knowing how to live healthily. In the case of one who achieves sublimation without any knowledge of the original nature of the redirected drives (e.g., allegedly Freud's Leonardo) such knowledge, such know-how, may occur without propositional knowledge about those drives.[35] However, in *GM* Nietzsche seems to be taking the position that modern man has become so repressed and sick through the domination of Judeo-Christian morality, has

---

> Perspectivism is only a complex form of specificity. My idea is that every specific body strives to become master over all space and extend its force (—its will to power) ... (*KSA* 13: 373, *WP* 636)

The extension of will to power and perspectivism beyond the domain of the organic to all bodies is, thankfully, largely confined to his notebooks.

[33] It is in this vein that Nietzsche says:

> I consider life itself to be an instinct for growth, for continuance, for an accumulation of forces, for *power*: where the will to power is lacking there is decline. (*A* 6)

[34] This point was brought to my attention by Peter Railton. Even here one might argue that inasmuch as epistemologists are in fact interested in general accounts of knowing how—in fact, typically, epistemologists are fixated on accounts of propositional knowledge to the near total exclusion of accounts of know-how—rather than particular cases of knowing how, perspectivism, with its account of the know-how necessary for a healthy life, is not relevant to epistemology. Similarly, while knowing how to wedel may be a partially constitutive of knowing how to ski well, this hardly seems relevant to a general epistemological account of knowing how.

[35] There are many places where Nietzsche expresses the idea that consciousness is a weak disruptive force:

internalized those values so deeply, that the only way the split-off drives can be reintegrated into a coherent whole is through a certain kind of therapy which arguably includes gaining explicit propositional knowledge of one's state.[36] Even granting this claim would not commit one to the position that perspectivism has implications for our account of propositional knowledge. It would be simply granting a causal claim to the effect that certain propositional knowledge is needed to achieve certain ends, to achieve certain know-how.

2.6 An "Axiomatic" Summary of Some of Nietzsche's Positive Claims and a Concluding Evidentiary Remark

The following claims are central to the positive account of Nietzsche's perspectivism, will to power, and his normative project presented above:

> Life is an embodied collection of drives.
> Will to power is the tendency/disposition of the drives to seek domination of the environment and of the other drives, often at the expense of other drives.
> Perspectivism is the descriptive claim that each drive has its own perspective/interpretation of the world and seeks to express that interpretation often at the expense of other drives; and the prescriptive injunction to let as many drives as possible be coherently expressed—that is an injunction towards what Nietzsche regards as health.
> Ascending life, healthy life, is a collection of drives that through sublimation has achieved concerted, maximal expression.

> in all productive men it is instinct that is the creative-affirmative force and consciousness acts critically and dissuasively. (*BT* 13)

There are also places where he emphasizes that unity is achieved through an unconscious master drive taking hold of lesser drives (for instance, the passage from *Ecce Homo*: "Why I am So Clever" 9, cited in section 2.3 of this essay, and also his famous description of the unity created by Wagner's ruling passion in *UM* III:2). Perhaps his most succinct expression of this is the following:

> The multiplicity of drives—we must take on a lord, but he is not in consciousness, rather consciousness is an organ, like the stomach. (*KSA* 11: 282)

[36] I say "arguably" because it is not clear exactly how Nietzsche intends the therapeutic effects of *GM* to be delivered. One can argue that Nietzsche, like Freud with his patients, intends that his audience first achieve explicit propositional knowledge of their state so that a deeper kind of knowledge, a certain know-how involved in the release of pent-up drives, can be achieved. Alternatively, one might argue that Nietzsche intends his work to somehow affect us at a level below full conscious apprehension, so that our drives are aroused more through emotional responses to his text than through conscious cognitive apprehension of propositional contents. It is worth noting that Nietzsche himself says of the three essays of *GM*:

> Regarding expression, intention, and the art of surprise, the three inquiries, which constitute this *Genealogy*, are perhaps uncannier than anything else written so far. (*EH*: "Genealogy of Morals")

The very first section of the preface of *GM* paints a picture of a dumbstruck audience who ask "utterly surprised and disconcerted, 'What was that that we have just experienced?'" This arguably adds some weight to the idea that Nietzsche is aiming at a therapeutic effect through influencing us at some level below consciousness.

Nietzsche approves of ascending life, healthy life, and seeks to promote it in those (few) who are capable of achieving it.

Interestingly, there is a passage in the *Nachlass* where Nietzsche actually expresses, or at least implies, some of the themes that have been central to this essay, namely, that it is drives that have perspectives; that wills to power are to be identified with drives; that conscious thinking of the kind that is emphasized in traditional accounts of perspectivism is largely epiphenomenal; and that Nietzsche has no real interest in a theory of knowledge:

> From all of our basic drives [*Grundtriebe*] come different perspectival evaluations of all happenings and experience...Man as a complexity of "wills to power"...thoughts are merely symptoms...The reduction of philosophy to a will to a theory of knowledge is comical. (*KSA* 12: 25–6)[37]

The sense that perspectivism is for Nietzsche an alternative to, and not a means of pursuing, epistemology is also contained in the following *Nachlass* passage:

> A plan: In place of moral values, rather natural values. The naturalization of morals....In place of "Theory of Knowledge," a theory of the perspectivism of the affects (to which a hierarchy of affects belong). (*KSA* 12: 342)

Presumably Nietzsche's notion of health as a full expression of the drives, a full expression of the will to power, counts as part of such natural values and part of his naturalization of morals.

BIBLIOGRAPHY

(A) Works by Nietzsche

BGE   *Beyond Good and Evil*, trans. W. Kaufmann. New York: Vintage, 1966.

EH   *Ecce Homo*, in *On the Genealogy of Morals and Ecce Homo*, trans. W. Kaufmann and R. J. Hollingdale. New York: Vintage, 1969.

GM   *On the Genealogy of Morals*, in *On the Genealogy of Morals and Ecce Homo*, trans. W. Kaufmann and R. J. Hollingdale. New York: Vintage, 1969.

GS   *The Gay Science*, trans. W. Kaufmann. New York: Vintage, 1974.

KSA   *Sämtliche Werke: Kritische Studienausgabe in 15 Einzelbänden*, ed. G. Colli and M. Montinari. Berlin: De Gruyter, 1988.

TI   *Twilight of the Idols*, in *Twilight of the Idols and The Antichrist*, trans. R. J. Hollingdale. New York: Penguin, 1968.

UM   *Untimely Meditations*, trans. R. J. Hollingdale. Cambridge: Cambridge University Press, 1983.

[37] This essay has benefited from input from Gudrun von Tevenar, Simon May, Chris Janaway, Maudemarie Clark, Peter Railton, John Richardson, Brian Leiter, Ram Neta, and Elijah Milgram, and input from participants at a Southampton University workshop "Nietzsche and Biology" in April 2008, from participants at an NYU in Florence workshop, "Skepticism," in June 2008, and from responses from members of the Cambridge Moral Sciences Club in January 2010.

(B) Other Primary Works

WWR   Schopenhauer, Arthur. 1969. *The World as Will and Representation*, trans. E. F. J. Payne (2 vols). New York: Dover.

(C) Other Works Cited

Acampora, C. (ed.). 2006. *Nietzsche's On the Genealogy of Morals: Critical Essays.* Lanham, Md: Rowman & Littlefield Publishers.

Clark, M. 1990. *Nietzsche on Truth and Philosophy.* Cambridge: Cambridge University Press.

Clark, M. 1998. "On Knowledge, Truth, and Value: Nietzsche's Debt to Schopenhauer and the Development of his Empiricism," in C. Janaway (ed.), *Willing and Nothingness: Schopenhauer as Nietzsche's Educator.* Oxford: Clarendon, 37–78.

Danto, A. 1965. *Nietzsche As Philosopher.* New York: Columbia University Press.

Freud, S. 1961. *The Standard Edition of the Complete Psychological Works of Sigmund Freud*, ed. and trans. J. Strachey (24 vols). London: Hogarth Press.

Gemes, K. 1992. "Nietzsche's Critique of Truth," in *Philosophy and Phenomenological Research* 52: 47–65.

Gemes, K. 2006. "'We Remain of Necessity Strangers to Ourselves': The Key Message of Nietzsche's *Genealogy*," in C. Acampora (ed.), *Nietzsche's "On the Genealogy of Morals": Critical Essays.* Lanham, Md: Rowman & Littlefield Publishers, 191–208.

Gemes, K. 2008. "Nihilism and the Affirmation of Life: A Review of and Dialogue with Bernard Reginster," *European Journal of Philosophy* 16: 459–66.

Gemes, K. 2009. "Freud and Nietzsche on Sublimation," *Journal of Nietzsche Studies* 38: 38–59.

Gibson, J. J. 1977. "The Theory of Affordances," in R. Shaw and J. Bransford (eds), *Perceiving, Acting, and Knowing: Toward an Ecological Psychology.* Hillsdale, NJ: Lawrence Erlbaum, 67–82.

Janaway, C. (ed.). 1998. *Willing and Nothingness: Schopenhauer as Nietzsche's Educator.* Oxford: Clarendon.

Janaway, C. 2007. *Beyond Selflessness: Reading Nietzsche's "Genealogy."* New York: Oxford University Press.

Katsafanas, P. 2005. "Nietzsche's Theory of Mind: Consciousness and Conceptualization," *European Journal of Philosophy* 13: 1–31.

Kaufmann, W. 1974. *Nietzsche: Philosopher, Psychologist, Antichrist*, 4th edn. Princeton: Princeton University Press.

Laplanche, J. and Pontalis, J. 1973. *The Language of Psychoanalysis.* New York: Norton Press.

Leiter, B. 2002. *Nietzsche on Morality.* London: Routledge.

Leiter, B. and Richardson, J. (eds) 2001. *Nietzsche.* Oxford: Oxford University Press.

May, S. 1999. *Nietzsche's Ethics and his "War on Morality."* Oxford: Clarendon.

Moore, G. 2002. *Nietzsche, Biology, Metaphor.* Cambridge: Cambridge University Press.

Nehamas, A. 1985. *Nietzsche: Life as Literature.* Cambridge, Mass.: Harvard University Press.

Poellner, P. 1995. *Nietzsche and Metaphysics.* Oxford: Oxford University Press.

Poellner, P. 2001. "Perspectival Truth," in Brian Leiter and J. Richardson (eds), *Nietzsche.* Oxford: Oxford University Press, 85–117.

Raloff, J. 1992. "Garden-Variety Tonic for Stress," *Science News* 141.6: 94–5.

Richardson, John. 1996. *Nietzsche's System.* Oxford and New York: Oxford University Press.

Schacht, R. 1983. *Nietzsche.* London: Routledge & Kegan Paul.

CHAPTER 25

....

NIETZSCHE'S NATURALISM RECONSIDERED

....

BRIAN LEITER

ACCORDING to one recent scholar, "Most commentators on Nietzsche would agree that he is in a broad sense a naturalist in his mature philosophy" (Janaway 2007: 34). This may come as a surprise to those who think of Martin Heidegger, Walter Kaufmann, Paul DeMan, Sarah Kofman, and Alexander Nehamas, among others, as commentators on Nietzsche. And yet there are indeed clear signs that in the last twenty years, the naturalist reading of Nietzsche has come to the fore, certainly in Anglophone scholarship.[1] In *Nietzsche on Morality* (Leiter 2002), I set out a systematic reading of Nietzsche as a philosophical naturalist, one which has attracted considerable critical comment, including from some generally sympathetic to reading Nietzsche as a philosophical naturalist.[2] I should like here to revisit that reading and, more importantly, the question of whether and in what sense Nietzsche is a naturalist in philosophy.

I. NIETZSCHE'S NATURALISM

....

Christopher Janaway claims that most Nietzsche scholars now accept that Nietzsche is a naturalist in what Janaway calls the "broad sense":

> He opposes transcendent metaphysics, whether that of Plato or Christianity or Schopenhauer. He rejects notions of the immaterial soul, the absolutely free controlling will, or the self-transparent pure intellect, instead emphasizing the body, talking of the animal nature of human beings, and attempting to explain numerous phenomena by invoking drives, instincts, and affects which he locates in our physical, bodily existence. Human beings are to be "translated back into nature," since otherwise we falsify their history, their psychology, and the nature of their values—concerning all of which we must know truths, as a means to the all-important revaluation of values. This is Nietzsche's naturalism in the broad sense, which will not be contested here. (Janaway 2007: 34)

---

[1] See, e.g., Bittner 2003; Clark 1990; Hussain 2004; Richardson 2004; Schacht 1988.

[2] See, e.g., Gemes and Janway 2005; Acampora 2006; Janaway 2007.

This is less a "broad sense" of naturalism, however, than it is "Laundry List Naturalism." Why are *these* a set of views a philosophical naturalist *ought* to hold? What is it that makes them the views of a philosophical naturalist at all?[3]

My aim in the 2002 book was to make some philosophical sense of why something like Janaway's Laundry List Naturalism seems, in fact, to be descriptively adequate to some of what Nietzsche says in a naturalistic spirit. I suggested that underlying this kind of Laundry List Naturalism was, in fact, a kind of familiar "Methodological Naturalism" (hereafter "M-Naturalism"), according to which "philosophical inquiry...should be continuous with empirical inquiry in the sciences" (2002: 3). Many philosophers are and have been Methodological Naturalists, but to understand Nietzsche, everything turns on the precise *kind* of M-Naturalism at issue. I emphasized two commitments of Nietzsche's M-Naturalism. First, I claimed that Nietzsche is what I called a Speculative M-Naturalist, that is, a philosopher, like Hume, who wants to "construct theories that are 'modeled' on the sciences...in that they take over from science the idea that natural phenomena have deterministic causes" (Leiter 2002: 5). Speculative M-Naturalists do not, of course, appeal to *actual* causal mechanisms that have been well confirmed by the sciences: if they did, they would not need to *speculate*! Rather, the idea is that their speculative theories of human nature are informed by the sciences and a scientific picture of how things work. Here, for example, is Stroud's influential formulation of Hume's Speculative M-Naturalism:

> [Hume] wants to do for the human realm what he thinks natural philosophy, especially in the person of Newton, had done for the rest of nature.
>
> Newtonian theory provided a completely general explanation of why things in the world happen as they do. It explains various and complicated physical happenings in terms of relatively few extremely general, perhaps universal, principles. Similarly, Hume wants a completely general theory of human nature to explain why human beings act, think, perceive and feel in all the ways they do....
>
> [T]he key to understanding Hume's philosophy is to see him as putting forward a general theory of human nature in just the way that, say, Freud or Marx did. They all seek a general kind of explanation of the various ways in which men think, act, feel and live....The aim of all three is completely general—they try to provide a basis for explaining *everything* in human affairs. And the theories they advance are all, roughly, deterministic. (Stroud 1977: 3, 4)

So Hume models his theory of human nature on Newtonian science by trying to identify a few basic, general principles that will provide a broadly deterministic explanation of human phenomena, much as Newtonian mechanics did for physical phenomena. Yet the Humean theory is still *speculative*, because its claims about human nature are not confirmed in anything resembling a scientific manner, nor do they even win support from any contemporaneous science of Hume's day.

Nietzsche's Speculative M-Naturalism obviously differs from Hume's in some respects: Nietzsche, for example, appears to be a skeptic about determinism based on his

---

[3] Janaway tells me that he thinks opposition to "transcendent metaphysics" is what unites the elements on the list, though it is hard to see how skepticism about that kind of metaphysics commits one to thinking "drives, instincts, and affects...in our physical, bodily existence" are explanatorily primary. Even if it were sufficient, it would simply push the question back one level: why is opposition to transcendent metaphysics the mark of naturalism? What motivates that opposition itself?

professed (if not entirely cogent) skepticism about laws of nature.[4] Yet Nietzsche, like Hume, has a sustained interest in explaining why "human beings act, think, perceive and feel" as they do, especially in the broadly ethical domain. Like Hume, Nietzsche proffers a speculative psychology, though as I have argued elsewhere (Leiter 2007; Knobe and Leiter 2007) and will return to below, Nietzschean speculations seem to fare rather well in light of subsequent research in scientific psychology. And this speculative psychology (as well as the occasional physiological explanations he offers in passing) appears to give us causal explanations for various human phenomena, which, even if not law-governed, seem to have a deterministic character (cf. Leiter 2002: 5).

But I also emphasized a second aspect of Nietzsche's M-Naturalism. As I noted, *some* M-Naturalists demand a kind of "results continuity" with existing science: "philosophical theories" should, they believe, "be supported or justified by the results of the sciences" (Leiter 2002: 4). I argued, however, there is only one kind of "results continuity" at work in Nietzsche, namely, the result that the German materialists of his day thought followed from advances in physiology, "that man is not of a "higher... [or] different origin" than the rest of nature" (Leiter 2002: 7).[5] Arguably, Nietzsche's main bit of *Substantive* Naturalism—meaning "the (ontological) view that the only things that exist are *natural*" (Leiter 2002: 5)—is a consequence of this "results continuity." We should perhaps pause to recall how profound an impression the discoveries about physiological influences on conscious experiences and attitudes had on Nietzsche.

The influential German materialism of the 1850s embodied a naturalistic worldview, well articulated by one of its leading proponents, the medical doctor Ludwig Büchner in his 1855 best-seller *Kraft und Stoff* (*Force and Matter*), as follows: "the researches and discoveries of modern times can no longer allow us to doubt that man, with all he has and possesses, be it mental or corporeal, is a *natural product* like all other organic beings" (1870: lxxviii). "Man is a product of nature," declared Büchner, "in body and mind. Hence not merely what he is, but also what he does, wills, feels, and thinks, depends upon the same natural necessity as the whole structure of the world" (1870: 239). German materialism may have had its origins in Feuerbach's works of the late 1830s and early 1840s, but it really exploded onto the intellectual scene in the 1850s, under the impetus of the startling new discoveries about human beings made by the burgeoning science of physiology. After 1830 in Germany, "Physiology... became the basis for modern scientific medicine, and this confirmed the tendency, identifiable throughout the whole of the nineteenth century, towards integration of human and natural sciences" (Schnädelbach 1983: 76). In his 1843 *Philosophy of the Future*,

---

[4] See, e.g., *BGE* 21–2.

[5] Janaway (2007: 37) says: "the status of this as a 'result' is perhaps debatable: it is hard to say whether the exclusively empirical nature of humanity was a conclusion or an assumption of scientific investigation in the nineteenth century or at any time." I find this quite surprising. If one discovers that conscious experiences have a neurophysiological explanation, or an explanation in terms of the biochemistry of the brain, hasn't one adduced some evidence that bears on whether man is of a "higher or different origin" than the rest of nature? Our consciousness and our capacity for self-reflection, for spirituality, for "inwardness" are all among the typical phenomena appealed to as evidence of our "higher" or "different" nature, perhaps as glimpses of an immaterial "soul" even. If, in fact, they are explicable through processes and mechanisms that are operative in other parts of the natural world, is that not evidence that we are not of "a higher or different origin" than other natural things? If not, what would be?

Feuerbach could write that, "The new philosophy makes man, along with nature as the basis of man, into the one and only universal and highest object of philosophy: anthropology, including physiology, becomes the universal science" (§54). The 1850s saw an explosion of books drawing on the new sciences, and articulated the German materialist's naturalistic view. As one scholar has written: "[T]he German materialists...took the German intellectual world by storm during the 1850s" (Vitzthum 1995: 98). A critic of materialism writing in 1856 complained that, "A new world view is settling into the minds of men. It goes about like a virus. Every young mind of the generation now living is affected by it" (quoted in Gregory 1977: 10). We know from Thomas Brobjer's research (Brobjer 2008: 44, 123, 133–4) that Nietzsche, as a young man, had read Feuerbach and was also a regular reader of the journal *Anregung für Kunst, Leben und Wissenschaft* which, in the early 1860s, published many articles about materialism, including by Büchner.

Yet the crucial moment for Nietzsche was his discovery in 1866 of Friedrich Lange's recently published *History of Materialism*, a book which opened up for him the whole history of philosophical materialism up to and including German materialism, as well as introducing him to the profound developments in modern natural science, especially chemistry and physiology (cf. Brobjer 2008: 32–6). As with Schopenhauer, the impact on the young Nietzsche was dramatic. "Kant, Schopenhauer, this book by Lange—I don't need anything else," he wrote in 1866 (quoted in Janz 1978: vol. I, p. 198). He viewed the work as "undoubtedly the most significant philosophical work to have appeared in recent decades" (Janz 1978: vol. I, p. 198), and called it in a letter of 1868 "a real treasure-house," mentioning, among other things, Lange's discussion of the "materialist movement of our times" (quoted in Stack 1983: 13). Lange himself was one of a number of "neo-Kantian" critics of materialism who held first that modern physiology vindicated Kantianism by demonstrating the dependence of knowledge on the peculiarly human sensory apparatus (Lange 1950/1865: 322, discussing the "confirmation from the scientific side of the critical standpoint in the theory of knowledge," and third section, chapter IV: "The Physiology of the Sense-Organs and the World as Representation"); and second, that the materialists were naive in believing science gives us knowledge of the thing-in-itself rather than the merely phenomenal world (cf. p. 84 "the physiology of the sense-organs has...produced decisive grounds for the [epistemological] refutation of Materialism"; pp. 277 ff.; p. 329). Yet Lange's general intellectual sympathies were clearly with the materialists as against the idealists, theologians, and others who resisted the blossoming scientific picture of the world and of human beings. Thus, for example, Lange remarks: "if Materialism can be set aside only by criticism based upon the [Kantian] theory of knowledge...in the sphere of positive questions it is everywhere in the right..." (1950/1865: 332).

While a reaction to German materialism did set in by the 1870s and 1880s, Nietzsche's youthful engagement with the materialists made a profound and lasting impression on him. In early 1868, he briefly contemplated switching from the study of philology to chemistry, and starting in the late 1860s, he began an intensive reading of work on natural science (Brobjer 2008: 35), readings which continued into the 1880s (Janz 1978: vol. II, pp. 73–4). He admits that in the late 1870s, "A truly burning thirst took hold of me: henceforth I really pursued nothing *more* than physiology, medicine and natural sciences" (*EH*: "Human, All too Human" 3). This impression is evident even in his mature work of the 1880s. In *Ecce Homo*, he complains of the "blunder" that he "became a philologist—why not at least a physician or something else that opens one's eyes?" (*EH*: "Why I Am So Clever" 2). Even in the often misunderstood Third Essay of the *Genealogy*—in which Nietzsche attacks only the *value* of truth, not its objectivity or our ability to know it—Nietzsche refers to "there being so much useful work to be done" in science and adds, regarding the "honest workers" in science, that "I delight in their work" (*GM* III: 23). As Clark notes, Nietzsche's mature works—the *Genealogy*, *Twilight of the Idols*, *The Antichrist*, *Ecce Homo*—"exhibit a uniform and unambiguous respect for facts, the senses, and science" (Clark 1990: 105).[6]

---

[6] Hussain (2004) makes an interesting and complicated argument to the effect that we should understand Nietzsche's naturalism through the lens of Ernst Mach, in order to understand how Nietzsche "could simultaneously reject the thing-in-itself, accept a falsification thesis, *and* be an empiricist" who is also "science-friendly" (2004: 327–8). For Mach, on this account, is an empiricist who believes "we do have direct access to all the reality there is, namely, the world of sensory elements," but at the same holds that "any attempt to have a thought that represents something about the world of sensory elements uses concepts that falsify" the sensory elements (2004: 353, 351). Yet Mach is still "science-friendly" since he holds that "ordinary empirical claims could still convey information about the flux of sensations despite being literally false" (2004: 354). It is a bit puzzling, though, how a Machian Nietzsche remains "friendly" to science in the sense emphasized by Clark (in the text) and undisputed by Hussain. Hussain contends that a Machian Nietzsche thinks causal claims "falsify" reality, even though they "are of course still useful for communicating information about relatively stable complexes of sensations and their relations." But how can they be "false" *and* communicate "information"? Lies, when recognized as such, communicate information, even though they are "literally false," but that is because of inferences one can draw about the motives and intentions of the liar, yet that does not seem to help in this instance. The idea must be, rather, that the statements, though literally false, are *partially* true in some sense. But how is this latter proposal going to help with Nietzsche? After all, it is "causal" claims that are "literally false" and causal claims are the ones Nietzsche needs. *Ressentiment*, he says in the *Genealogy* (to take but one example), has an "actual physiological cause" (I: 15): if that is *literally false*, then what remainder is left over that is true and that commends Nietzsche's causal/explanatory account against the moral and religious accounts he wants to displace? The philosophical difficulties with the proposed reading become more urgent given some of the historical and textual questions that arise. Did Mach really have any impact on Nietzsche? The major work by Mach in question didn't even appear until 1886, the same year as *Beyond Good and Evil*, on which it is supposed to have had an impact. Hussain admits that explicit evidence of influence is hard to come by. His more ambitious interpretive claim is that the Machian Nietzsche helps us make sense of crucial sections of a late work (of 1888), *Twilight of the Idols*. In particular, it is supposed to help us explain what Nietzsche means by his talk of the "apparent" world as being the *only* world. Hussain (2004: 345) invokes a passage from Mach's *Analysis of Sensations* (1886) which he says evokes Nietzsche's views in *TI*, especially in the famous section of *TI* on "How the 'True World' Finally Became a Fable." This passage, of course, has been interpreted by Clark, John Wilcox, and others as Nietzsche describing the trajectory of his own thinking about the appearance/reality distinction. Yet apart from both Nietzsche and Mach describing the thing-in-itself as "superfluous," I fail to see any interesting similarity between this *TI* passage and the one from Mach that Hussain calls to our attention. Indeed, the dissimilarities are more striking. There is nothing in the *TI* passage, for example, to suggest Nietzsche's affinity with the Machian view that "the world" is "*one coherent mass of sensations, only more strongly coherent in the ego.*" Moreover, the argument in the *TI* passage seems to suggest, rather clearly, that "positivism" is only the fourth stage in Nietzsche's thinking, one he leaves behind by the final sixth stage, when the "apparent" world is also abolished (on the grounds that there is no contrasting "true" world). Hussain's Machian reading may fare somewhat better with *parts* of the " 'Reason' in Philosophy" section of *TI*, though even here I am worried that the *actual* points of reference by Nietzsche are to Heraclitus and Democritus, not any contemporaries, and that Nietzsche's own summary of the argument (in section 6 of " 'Reason' in Philosophy") has no discernible Machian elements. Indeed, this last section (which Hussain ignores) fits rather better, I think, with Clark's interpretation of the passage (1990: 106–8).

By introducing Nietzsche's naturalism within a broader typology of *kinds* of naturalism, I appear to have sowed confusion among some scholars. Christopher Janaway's recent critique of my naturalist reading is illustrative. He complains that:

> [N]o scientific support or justification is given—or readily imaginable—for the central explanatory hypotheses that Nietzsche gives for the origins of our moral beliefs and attitudes. For a prominent test case, take Nietzsche's hypothesis in the *Genealogy*'s First Treatise that the labeling of non-egoistic action, humility, and compassion as "good" began because there were socially inferior classes of individuals in whom feelings of *ressentiment* against their masters motivated the creation of new value distinctions. This hypothesis explains moral phenomena in terms of their causes, but it is not clear how it is *justified* or *supported by* any kind of science, nor indeed what such a justification or support might be. (2007: 37)

This challenge, of course, simply ignores my claim that Nietzsche, like Hume, was a *Speculative* M-Naturalist, as Nietzsche had to be, given the primitive state of psychology in the nineteenth century. A Speculative M-Naturalist simply does *not* claim that the explanatory mechanisms essential to his theory of why humans think and act as they do are supported by existing scientific *results*. To be sure, what Nietzsche does do is appeal to psychological mechanisms—such as the seething hatred characteristic of *ressentiment*— for which there seems to be ample evidence in both ordinary and historical experience, and weave a narrative showing how these simple mechanisms could give rise to particular human beliefs and attitudes. It is, moreover, quite easy to see what empirical evidence would bear on this: e.g., evidence that a psychological state usefully individuated as *ressentiment* serves diagnostic or predictive purposes. Even in the First Essay of the *Genealogy*, Nietzsche elicits a variety of kinds of evidence of his own in support of the existence of this psychological mechanism: for example, the facts about the etymology of the terms "good" and "bad"; the general historical fact that Christianity took root among the oppressed classes in the Roman Empire; and the rhetoric of the early Church Fathers. Here we see Nietzsche arguing for a characteristically scientific kind of inference: namely, to believe in the causal role of a particular psychological mechanism, for which there is ample independent evidence, on the basis of its wide explanatory scope, i.e., its ability to make sense of a variety of different data points.

Janaway, it bears noting, in fact endorses a weaker version of my reading of Nietzsche as an M-Naturalist, though the weakening seems to derive from his misunderstanding of the role of "results continuity" in my interpretation of Nietzsche's M-Naturalism. He writes that "Nietzsche is a naturalist to the extent that he is committed to a species of theorizing that explains X by locating Y and Z as its causes, where Y and Z's being causes of X is not falsified by our best science" (2007: 38). Janaway prefers this account, because of his doubts about whether there are actual scientific *results* supporting Nietzsche's actual causal explanations. Since my reading of Nietzsche's naturalism, however, emphasized its *speculative* character, Janaway's formulation may serve instead as a way of stating a pertinent constraint on *speculative* explanations: namely, that they not invoke entities or mechanisms that science has ruled out of bounds. But even so, it may seem an unnecessarily weak criterion: why not expect, instead, that a good speculative naturalist will rely on explanatory mechanisms that enjoy some evidential support, or that enjoy a wide explanatory scope, of the kind we expect genuine explanations in the sciences to exemplify? I do not think there is text in Nietzsche that settles this matter, and so this is more a matter of giving the most philosophically appealing reconstruction of his actual explanatory practice. We shall return to that practice in the next section.

II. Two Nietzsches: Humean and Therapeutic

In my reading of Nietzsche as a philosophical naturalist, I emphasized two respects in which naturalism was either surbordinated to or displaced by other philosophical concerns. Even though, as I argued, "the bulk of [Nietzsche's] philosophical activity is devoted to variations on this naturalistic project" (Leiter 2002: 11)—that is, to explaining morality in naturalistically respectable terms—it is equally clear that Nietzsche's "naturalism is enlisted on behalf of a 'revaluation of all values'"—that is, the project of trying "to free...nascent higher types from their 'false consciousness,' i.e., their false belief that the dominant morality is, in fact, *good for them*" (Leiter 2002: 26, 28; cf. 283). That means, of course, that even when Nietzsche's texts are informed by his M-Naturalism, he has important reasons to employ a variety of rhetorical devices aimed at unsettling readers from their existing moral commitments.

In addition to the fact that Nietzsche's M-Naturalism is an instrument in the service of the revaluation of values, there is also the important point that he actually uses the term "philosopher" as an honorific to designate those who "create" values (Leiter 2002: 11). That activity is *not* part of the naturalistic project, except in two relatively weak senses: first, in presumably observing the stricture of "ought implies can," i.e., not valorizing any capacities and achievements that are, in fact, beyond the ken of creatures like us; and, second, in thinking that the sciences can illuminate the *effects* of different kinds of value on different kinds of people (*GM* I: Note is a striking example).[7]

Let us call "the Humean Nietzsche" the Nietzsche who aims to explain morality naturalistically (in the senses already discussed) and contrast him with the philosopher we will call "the Therapeutic Nietzsche" who wants to get select readers to throw off the shackles of morality (or MPS, as I have called it, 2002: 78–9). The "revaluation of values" involves enlisting the Humean Nietzsche for the Therapeutic Nietzsche's ends, though the Therapeutic Nietzsche has (as I argued in Leiter 2002: 159, 176) a variety of other rhetorical devices at his disposal beyond the Humean Nietzsche's understanding of morality: for example, exploiting the genetic fallacy (leading his readers to think that there is something wrong with their morality because of its unseemly origin) or exploiting their will to truth (by showing that the metaphysics of agency on which their morality depends is false). That the Therapeutic Nietzsche should avail himself of such nonrational devices is hardly surprising, indeed, follows from the Humean Nietzsche's understanding of persons. As I noted in Leiter 2002: 155:

> Nietzsche's naturalism, and the prominent role it assigns to non-conscious drives and type-facts, leads him to be skeptical about the efficacy of reasons and arguments. But a skeptic about the efficacy of rational persuasion might very well opt for persuasion through other rhetorical devices.

[7] I should note that I take the doctrine of eternal return to be an ethical doctrine and thus part of the project of "creating" new values, and so it has only a tangential connection to Nietzsche's naturalism.

And Nietzsche does precisely this, again and again, in the *Genealogy* and elsewhere. As I wrote, since "the ultimate goal of the *Genealogy* ... is to free nascent higher human beings from their false consciousness about MPS ... Nietzsche has no reason to disown fallacious forms of reasoning [such as the genetic fallacy] as long as they are rhetorically effective" (2002: 176).

Now Janaway (2007) has recently laid considerable emphasis on the Therapeutic Nietzsche, arguing plausibly that Nietzsche wanted to engage his readers emotionally or "affectively," because such engagement was a necessary precondition for altering the reader's views about evaluative questions. As Janaway puts it: "without the rhetorical provocations, without the revelation of what we find gruesome, shaming, embarrassing, comforting, and heart-warming we would neither comprehend nor be able to revalue our current values" (2007: 4; cf. 96–8).

Janaway, however, wants to conclude from this that it is wrong to treat "style"—that is, the rhetorical devices central to Nietzsche's therapeutic aims—as "mere modes of presentation, detachable in principle from some elusive set of propositions to which his philosophy might be thought to consist," since to do so, "is to miss a great part of Nietzsche's real importance to philosophy" (2007: 4). "Nietzsche's way of writing," Janaway explains, "addresses our affects, feelings, or emotions. It provokes sympathies, antipathies, and ambivalences that lie in the modern psyche below the level of rational decision and impersonal argument." This, Janaway says, is "not some gratuitous exercise in 'style' that could be edited out of Nietzsche's thought" (2007: 4).

These and similar passages in Janaway's book[8] seem to conflate the Humean and Therapeutic Nietzsches. There can be no doubt that Nietzsche's practical objective is to transform the complacent consciousness of (at least some of) his readers about the received morality, and it seems equally clear that he thinks the only way to do that is by engaging them emotionally. Yet the proposition that readers will only change their most basic moral commitments if their underlying affective states are aroused and altered is itself a philosophical position that can be stated unemotionally. What Janaway fails to establish is that one cannot, in fact, separate out the Humean Nietzsche's philosophical positions (about agency, motivation, the origins of morality, etc.) from the mode of presentation that is essential to the Therapeutic Nietzsche's aims.

Consider the analogous case of Freudian psychoanalysis. Unlike Nietzsche, of course, Freud's books had no therapeutic aim: therapy took place in the psychoanalyst's office. Freud's books, by contrast, expressed the cognitive content of his philosophical or theoretical positions: about the structure of the mind, the interpretation of dreams, the course of human psychic development, and—most importantly for our purposes—the centrality of the mechanism of transference to therapeutic success. Yet a correct theoretical description of transference is no substitute for the patient's actual *experience* of transference in the therapeutic setting, when he projects onto the analyst the heretofore repressed feelings that had been the source of his suffering, thus permitting the patient to recognize the reality of those feelings at last.

---

[8] See especially p. 212, where Janaway claims, without any support, that "it is beyond question that Nietzsche regards the *Genealogy* as providing greater *knowledge* [emphasis added] about morality than any combination of the traditional *Wissenschaften* could have attained unaided," which would only be true if one conflates the therapeutic aims with Nietzsche's philosophical theses about morality.

I assume no one denies that one can separate the theoretical account of transference as a therapeutic mechanism from the actual experience of cure via psychoanalysis culminating (more or less) with the moment of transference. Nietzsche differs from Freud in many respects, but only one that matters in this context: his books are both the expression of the theoretical position *and* the therapeutic method. The Humean Nietzsche's theoretical positions—e.g., what he thinks explains the genesis of our current morality, how he understands the mechanisms of human psychology, what he takes to the causal consequences of moral beliefs, and so on—are both explicit and implicit in a text that also aims to produce a therapeutic effect on certain readers, i.e., to free them from their false consciousness about the dominant morality. Just as successful therapeutic transference requires the patient to experience the repressed feelings directed at the analyst, so too a successful revaluation of values requires engaging the reader subconsciously at the affective level, so that he feels revulsion, disgust, and embarrassment about his existing moral beliefs. From none of this, however, does it follow that one cannot separate out philosophical or cognitive content from the therapeutic technique, that we cannot separate the Humean and Therapeutic Nietzsches.

In this connection, we should remind ourselves how prevalent the Humean Nietzsche's project is—not just in the *Genealogy*, but in *Daybreak*, in *Beyond Good and Evil* (the "Natural History of Morals" chapter most obviously), in *Twilight of the Idols*, and elsewhere. In a footnote from my book (Leiter 2002: 6 n. 10) that Janaway invokes more than once, I describe Nietzsche's M-Naturalism as reflecting "Nietzsche's actual philosophical practice, i.e., what he spends most of his time doing in his books." To this, Janaway objects that, "Nietzsche's methods, on the evidence of 'what he spends most of his time doing in his books,' are characterized by artistic devices, rhetoric, provocations of the affects, and exploration of the reader's personal reactions, and show little concern for methods that could informatively be called scientific" (2007: 52). Yet this criticism just betrays Janaway's conflation of the Humean and Therapeutic Nietzsches. The Therapeutic Nietzsche does indeed depend on "artistic devices, rhetoric, provocations of the affects, and explorations of the reader's personal reactions," and much of the corpus is given over to the therapeutic project; but this does not change the fact that the therapeutic project is pursued within and informed by the framework of the Humean Nietzsche's picture of persons and morality, which also permeates the corpus. The latter is a recognizably naturalistic conception, one which, in fact, explains why rational discursiveness—in contrast to the stylistic devices Janaway emphasizes—is an ineffective therapeutic technique.[9]

---

[9] Janaway pursues the same line of critique, involving the same confusion between the Humean and Therapeutic Nietzsches, in a different way as well. He suggests that Nietzsche could not have been an M-Naturalist because he rejects the "disinterested, impersonal, and affectively detached" posture of the scientific inquirer: Nietzsche "champions a literary, personal, affectively engaged style of inquiry that deliberately stands in opposition to science as he thinks it tends to conceive itself: as disinterested, impersonal, and affectively detached" (2007: 39). His evidence for this consists in the claim that Nietzsche's "most fundamental" objection to his friend Paul Rée's "results and methods" is that Rée assumes that "selflessness ... is constitutive of morality," that "selflessness has positive value" (2007: 40). That is certainly Nietzsche's *substantive* objection to Rée's position, but I do not see any evidence that it constitutes Nietzsche's objection to Rée's *methodology*. *GM* I: 1 starts by wondering about the motives of the "English psychologists" (of whom Rée is the exemplar), but then *GM* I: 2 moves to a genuine methodological objection, namely, treating the current use or meaning of something as warranting an inference about its origin (see Leiter 2002: 198–9 for discussion). To create a connection between Nietzsche's opposition to altruism as a moral ideal and his views about epistemically reliable methods

III. Culture, Causation, and Will to Power

Even if we agree that the Humean Nietzsche is an M-Naturalist, and that his M-Naturalism explains, in turn, why something like Janaway's Laundry List Naturalism seems a correct description of Nietzsche's expressed views, we are still left with three further obstacles to reading Nietzsche as a philosophical naturalist: first, though least importantly, whether there is a role for "culture" in the kinds of naturalistic explanations Nietzsche proffers; second, how to understand the notion of causation central to my M-Naturalist reading and whether Nietzsche is even entitled to help himself to such a concept; and third, and perhaps most worrying, whether Nietzsche's doctrine of will to power is really compatible with the idea that the Humean Nietzsche takes himself to be working "in tandem with" the empirical sciences rather than displacing and transforming them. In this section, we shall take up each issue in turn.

A. The Role of Culture in Naturalistic Explanations

On my reading of the Humean Nietzsche, he aims to offer theories that explain various important human phenomena (especially the phenomenon of morality), and that do so in ways that both draw on or are at least constrained by actual scientific results, but are mainly *modeled* on science in the sense that they seek to reveal the causal determinants of

---

of inquiry, Janaway appeals (2007: 40–1) to *GS* 345 in which Nietzsche says that " 'Selflessness' has no value in heaven or earth; all great problems demand great love." Yet this passage actually says nothing at all about methods of inquiry, though Janaway glosses it as follows: "adherence to the conception of morality as selflessness left Rée, unwittingly, trapped in a sterile mode of investigation that could bring only philosophical failure" (2007: 41). If this were really what was at issue, one might expect some textual evidence from *GM* expressing this worry. But other than a throwaway line in which Nietzsche calls the English psychologists "old, cold, boring frogs" (*GM* I: 1) in the context of querying their motives, the only apparent *GM* evidence Janaway can adduce is this:

> [I]n the epigram of *GM* III wisdom is a woman who loves only someone "carefree, mocking, violent," the opposite of the [type described in *GS* 345]. That epigram introduces Nietzsche's essay on the meanings of the ascetic ideal, and points forward to the essay's culminating claim that contemporary objective, scientific method . . . is but another version of an originally Christian, metaphysical faith in ascetic self-denial before something absolute and quasi-divine, namely truth. (2007: 41–2)

Tellingly, Janaway doesn't actually cite any text from *GM* III, and his characterization of the argument there seems to be inaccurate, in particular, in characterizing Nietzsche's objection as being toward "objective, scientific method" as opposed to science's overvaluation of truth (cf. Leiter 2002: 265 ff.). Science may, as Janaway claims, be "committed to a vision of itself as affect-free, disinterested, and impersonal," but apart from a few clock-like scholars, Nietzsche denies that *Wissenschaft* is really like this—even the English psychologists have concealed motives, as he tells us in *GM* I: 1! That science, like almost every other inquiry, is not really disinterested has no bearing on the methodological virtues of science, about which Nietzsche is clear. In sum, Janaway seems to confuse the motives for engaging in science with the *methods* of the sciences. One can *care deeply* about the subject of one's inquiry (as, e.g., Nietzsche does) and think causal explanation and naturalistically respectable causal mechanisms are the right way to understand how the world really works.

these phenomena, typically in various physiological and psychological facts about persons. More precisely, I have argued that Nietzsche embraces a view I call the "Doctrine of Types," according to which:

> Each person has a fixed psychophysical constitution, which defines him as a particular *type* of person.

I call the relevant psychophysical facts "type facts." It is type facts, in turn, that figure in the explanation of human actions and beliefs (including beliefs about morality). One of Nietzsche's central undertakings, then, is to specify the type facts—the psychological and physiological facts—that explain how and why an essentially ascetic or "life-denying" morality should have taken hold among so many people over the past two millennia.

One particular type fact is of central importance for Nietzsche: what he calls "will to power." Its central explanatory role is articulated in the *Genealogy* as follows:

> Every animal...instinctively [*instinktiv*] strives for an optimum of favourable conditions in which fully to release his power [or strength; *Kraft*] and achieve his maximum feeling of power; every animal abhors equally instinctively, with an acute sense of smell "higher than all reason," any kind of disturbance and hindrance which blocks or could block his path to the optimum...(*GM* III: 7)

If it is a natural fact about creatures like us that we "instinctively" maximize our strength or power, then this fact, together with other type facts and facts about circumstances, must figure in any explanation of what we do and believe. So, for example, those who are essentially weak or impotent (e.g., the slaves of *GM* I) express their will to power by *creating* values that are favorable to their interests; those who are *strong*, by contrast, express their power through physical action, and so on.

Christopher Janaway has objected that

> If Nietzsche's causal explanations of our moral values are naturalistic, they are so in a sense which includes within the "natural" not merely the psychophysical constitution of the individual whose values are up for explanation, but also many complex cultural phenomena and the psychophysical states of past individuals and projected types of individual (2007: 53).

More precisely, Janaway, relying on some passages from *Daybreak* (see Janaway 2007: 45–7), wants to emphasize Nietzsche's interest in the role of "inclinations and aversions" in an agent's moral judgments, where, as Janaway puts it, "my inclinations and aversions are acquired habits inculcated by means of the specific culture I find myself in" and "this culture inculcates just these habits because it has a guiding structure of value beliefs, and...this structure of value beliefs became dominant through answering to certain affective needs of individuals in earlier cultural stages" (2007: 47). As Janaway observes in a footnote (2007: 47 n. 24), my account of M-Naturalism has no reason to "deny" any of this. First, an important virtue of M-Naturalism is that it does not purport to settle a priori questions about ontology, deferring instead to whatever works in the explanatory practices of the sciences. It is striking, for example, that the best recent naturalistic work in moral psychology—I am thinking especially of Prinz's *The Emotional Construction of Morals* (2007), which tries to update the Nietzschean project of genealogy—explicitly incorporates cultural factors, via anthropology, as a central part of the relevant cognitive science that should figure in our understanding of morality. But second, an important theoretical desideratum for the naturalistic philosopher is, as Stroud puts it in explaining Hume's view, to explain via "general, perhaps universal, principles." The sciences explain not by emphasis on particulars, i.e., on tokens, but by subsuming the particulars under *types*. These *types* may, as Prinz shows, turn out to be cultural in character, but in Janaway's example, it is unclear whether it is cultural *types* that figure in explaining moral beliefs or whether cultural factors simply fix the particular content of phenomena explained by psychophysical types. In the end, I doubt very much turns on this. There is no reason to deny that Nietzsche the naturalist is interested in culture, but that should not lead us to lose sight of the role that psychophysical causes play in the explanation of morality he proffers.

B. Problems of Causation

On my reading of M-Naturalism, the Humean Nietzsche emulates the methods of science by trying to construct causal explanations of the moral beliefs and practices of human beings. Even on Janaway's (weaker) account of Nietzsche's naturalism, causation is central. As he puts it, Nietzsche "is committed to a species of theorizing that explains X by locating Y and Z as its causes, where Y and Z's being causes of X is not falsified by our best science" (2007: 38).

We do well to remember how important causal explanation is to Nietzsche's philosophical project. When he says in *Daybreak*, for example, that "[O]ur moral judgments and evaluations...are only images and fantasies based on a physiological process unknown to us" (*D* 119), so that "it is always necessary to draw forth...the *physiological* phenomenon behind the moral predispositions and prejudices" (*D* 542), he is making a causal claim, i.e., the claim that certain physiological processes *cause* moral judgments through some presumably complicated process that yields them as "images" and "fantasies" brought about by these causes. When he says in the *Genealogy* that *ressentiment*, and the morality that grows out of it, has an "actual physiological cause [*Ursache*]" (*GM* I: 15) his meaning is, of course, unmistakable. When he devotes an entire chapter of *Twilight of the Idols* to what he calls "the four great errors," errors that almost entirely concern causation—"confusing cause and effect," the "error of false causation," the "error of imaginary causes" he calls them—it is clear that he wants to distinguish *genuine causal relations* from the mistaken ones that infect religious and moral thinking. When he returns to the same theme in *The Anti-Christ*, he again denounces Christianity for trafficking in "imaginary causes" and for propounding "an imaginary *natural* science," one that depends on anthropocentric concepts and lacks, as Nietzsche puts it, "any concept of natural cause" (*A* 15; cf. *A* 25)—science consisting, on his account, of "the healthy concepts of cause and effect" (*A* 49). Causation and causal explanation are central to Nietzsche's naturalism, much as causation has returned to a central place in philosophy of science over the past thirty years (cf. Cartwright 2004). Without belief in some notion of causation, it is hard to see how any of these passages from Nietzsche make any sense.

I want to consider two different kinds of objections to making causation central to Nietzsche's M-Naturalism. The first kind of objection involves no skepticism about causation, but worries that "causation," and the work it does in Nietzsche's M-Naturalism as I describe it, is not adequate to define an interesting theoretical position. The second kind of objection takes issues with Nietzsche's belief in causation itself. The second challenge is, needless to say, the more radical in light of the evidence we have rehearsed so far.

Ken Gemes and Christopher Janaway (2005) have pressed the first kind of objection in a critical study of my book. They make three key objections to my account of M-Naturalism: first, that "there is much in science that does not involve causal accounts, as for instance Kepler's three laws of planetary motion" (2005: 731); second, that seeking causal explanations is not enough to establish methods continuity with the sciences—as they put it, "Just because astrology seeks to give causal explanations we would not say it shares a continuity of methods with the sciences" (2005: 731); and third, the actual causal role I claim Nietzsche assigns "type facts"—the essential psychophysical facts about persons to which Nietzsche appeals in explaining moral beliefs and attitudes—is too weak to state an interesting naturalistic thesis.

We may dispense with the first objection rather quickly. It is true enough that much that is characteristic of scientific practice and methodology does not concern causation at all, though even Kepler's three laws of planetary motion—which are mathematical *descriptions* of the motion of the planets—are deducible from Newtonian laws of motion and gravitation, and so hold true because of the causally effective forces described by those laws. But the claim at stake, in both my characterization of Nietzsche's naturalism and, for that matter, Stroud's characterization of Hume's, was *not* that science is exhausted by its interest in causal explanation, but rather that *a* characteristic feature of science is that it aims to provide true general causal or deterministic explanations of phenomena by appeal to a few general principles or mechanisms. That is obviously consistent with the fact that parts of this scientific enterprise are purely descriptive.

Relatedly, however, Gemes and Janaway worry that trying "to give causal explanations" is not enough for methods continuity. After all, astrologists and (we might add) Intelligent Design theorists can claim to offer *causal* explanations, but that hardly makes them M-Naturalists. Of course, on my account, the search for deterministic causes was only one feature of M-Naturalism; Nietzsche, as I noted, accepts some S-Naturalist constraints on viable causal mechanisms, though, in my view, he takes those substantive constraints themselves to follow from scientific findings. The problem with astrologists and Intelligent Design theorists is that their concepts of what can cause what run afoul of substantive findings of the sciences themselves (e.g., there is no empirical evidence in support of supernatural interventions in natural phenomena, or the causal power of the planets on human affairs).

More interesting, I think, is the objection Gemes and Janaway lodge against the naturalist view I call "causal essentialism" which I attribute to Nietzsche. On this view, as Gemes and Janaway note (2005: 733), "for any individual substance...that substance has 'essential' properties that are causally primary with respect to the future history of that substance, i.e., non-trivially determine the space of possible trajectories for that substance" (Leiter 2002: 83). They then write:

> The gloss [Leiter] gives on natural facts being causally primary with respect to some effect is that such facts are necessary but possibly not sufficient for the relevant effect. But this is an extraordinarily weak gloss; our having heads is a necessary but not sufficient condition for our becoming philosophers, but we would not want to say that our having heads is causally primary with respect to our becoming philosophers. And, while Leiter puts 'essential' in scare quotes, one worries that in as much as essential properties are typically taken to be unchangeable this saddles Nietzsche with a view that weights the causal role of nature rather heavily over that of nurture. (2005: 733)

In my book, I document the many places where Nietzsche, in fact, embraces the idea of an "unchangeable" or "essential" nature,[10] but the important point here is that an M-Naturalist, whether Nietzsche or Hume, *ought* to emphasize the causal role of nature over that of nurture, precisely in order to—as Stroud puts it in describing Hume's view—"explain various and complicated…happenings in terms of relatively few extremely general, perhaps universal, principles" (Stroud 1977: 3). This is why Hume seeks "a completely general theory of human nature," since one of the features that marks it as aspiring to the scientific is precisely its *generality*, namely, its attempt to transcend real and vivid cultural particulars to see what all these disparate cultural artifacts have in common, namely, their genesis from tendencies rooted in the nature of the human.[11]

The other part of Gemes and Janaway's critique—concerning the "weakness" of the necessary but not sufficient characterization of what it is for an explanans to be "causally primary"—simply exploits a familiar problem about empiricist analyses of causation, from Hume to Mackie: namely, that they flounder on the problem of picking out the regular "correlations" that count for purposes of causation or, in the case of Mackie, in specifying the conditions that are merely noncausal "background" conditions when we pick out the INUS cause of an event (where the INUS cause is "an insufficient but necessary part of an unnecessary but sufficient condition" for the event happening). Having a head does not cause anyone to be a philosopher (even if it is a necessary condition), but having the genetic make-up of a tomato is surely a key part of the best causal explanation of why a particular seed grows into a tomato plant. It would be astonishing—or simply gross anachronism—to think Nietzsche has a good explanation of how we mark this difference, especially when so many philosophers who have thought systematically about the problem do not. But that does not change the fact that ordinary and scientific practice recognizes the distinction. Indeed, Nietzsche gives every sign of being a sensible M-Naturalist on this score, and not a disreputable metaphysician, when he describes "science" as simply "the healthy concepts of cause and effect" (*A* 49). Let science and the application of scientific methods decide what is a cause and what is not; we may then help ourselves to whatever kinds of causes work. We may at least be confident that no interesting theory will develop around an explanation of philosophers in terms of their having heads, while *every* sensible scientific explanation of plants growing tomatoes will appeal to the genetic make-up of tomato plant seeds. If Nietzsche is right (an issue to which we will return), then the same will be true about the correct naturalistic account of moral beliefs and attitudes.[12]

<hr/>

[10] Nietzsche calls on us "to complete our de-deification of nature…[and] to 'naturalize' humanity in terms of a pure, newly discovered, newly redeemed nature" (*GS* 109). More strikingly, he makes claims about *essences* with frequency: for example, concerning "the *essence* [*Wesen*] of what lives" (*BGE* 259), "the essence [*Wesen*] of life" (*GM* II: 12), or "the weakness of the weak… —I mean [their] *essence* [*Wesen*]" (*GM* I: 13). The mistake of most antiessentialist readings of Nietzsche is to conflate Nietzsche's opposition to nonempirical or nonnaturalistic claims (which he does, indeed, repudiate) with an opposition to any and all claims about a thing's essence or nature. But the latter claims are quite colorable within a naturalistic framework (for example, Quine's), as long as we understand them as *empirical* or *naturalistic* claims made from within our best-going theory of the world.

[11] Of course, Nietzsche thinks that different kinds of moralities operate, in effect, as "nurture types," i.e., *types* of value systems that have predictable effects on certain natural *types* of persons. Yet it is always the natural-type facts that are explanatorily prior in understanding what effects any type of morality will have. (Thanks to John Richardson for pressing me on this point.)

[12] Perhaps we can finesse the difficulty by emphasizing that type facts are *explanatorily* primary, thus

Gemes and Janaway, both in their critique of my book and in their individual scholarship, are comfortable with the idea that Nietzsche believes in causal relations, however they are to be understood. But some critics of my presentation of Nietzsche's M-Naturalism purport to be skeptical on this score. I shall treat the recent critique by Christa Acampora (2006) as representative.

In my book (2002: 22–3), I noted Nietzsche's flirtation in some earlier work with Neo-Kantian skepticism about causation, as in passages like this one from *Beyond Good and Evil*:

> In the "in-itself" [*An-sich*] there is nothing of "causal connections," of "necessity," or of cause.... It is *we* alone who have devised cause, sequence, for-each-other, relativity, constraint, number, law, freedom, motive, and purpose; and when we project and mix this symbol world into things as if it existed "in itself," we act once more as we have always acted—*mythologically*. (*BGE* 21)

This kind of criticism would have been familiar to Nietzsche from the Neo-Kantian Friedrich Lange, who had criticized scientists precisely for their false belief that science gives us knowledge of the noumenal world, when in fact science only concerns the phenomenal world. "Cause" and "effect" are "pure concepts" Nietzsche says in this same passage (obviously echoing Kantian language), imposed by the human mind upon a world that, in-itself, contains "nothing of 'causal connections'" and the like. Notice, of course, that even in the Kantian perspective, this point does *not* undermine the objectivity of claims about causes; it simply confines their objective truth to the world as it appears to us. But since, as Clark has argued most systematically (1990: 103–5), Nietzsche ultimately repudiates the intelligibility of the noumenal/phenomenal distinction, it is unsurprising that his mature works should show none of the Neo-Kantian skepticism about causation.

Acampora claims, however, that this is "simply mistaken" (2006: 329 n. 5), and that skepticism about causation infects the mature works as well. Here, I take it, is the heart of her critique, which, it bears noting, includes an enormous concession to the reading of Nietzsche as an M-Naturalist that I have defended:

> Nietzsche is clearly a naturalist in seeking a focus on natural, observable phenomena for garnering our understanding of the world and our place within it. Empirical science is admirable for Nietzsche because of its rigorous method and its concern to free itself of supernatural and mythological presuppositions. The latter motivation reflects a kind of mental hygiene that for a long time has been recognized as important in philosophy but is rarely achieved, namely to avoid the use of hidden or unjustified assumptions. The problem with science, for Nietzsche, is that it quite often sneaks in principles or articles of faith that smack of the very metaphysical and theological conceptions that it seeks to overcome. Two such ideas that were crucial to the science of his day, and one of which remains the bedrock of scientific inquiry, are the teleological conception of nature and the concept of causation. (2006: 316–17)

shifting the status of the claim from the metaphysical to the epistemic domain. The claim, in other words, would be that in order to *explain*, e.g., the slave revolt in morals, the causal role of the type facts about slavish types—e.g., their propensity to *ressentiment*—is necessary, but not sufficient for explaining the event. That allows for the possibility that other causal factors—such as the social environment in which the slavish types find themselves—are important. But on this account, no explanation of the slave revolt that failed to make reference to the psychophysical type of "slaves" would be epistemically adequate. This might, however, weaken the claim beyond what Nietzsche seems to have in mind.

We can bracket the first point, and not only because teleology dropped out of scientific practice with the scientific revolution's triumph over Aristotelianism several centuries before. The question is whether Nietzsche really thinks that causation involves "metaphysical and theological conceptions" that Nietzsche rejects.

Acampora briefly cites (2006: 319) one of the Neo-Kantian passages from *Beyond Good and Evil* dealt with already, so we may put that to one side. She also relies, alas, on a passage from *The Gay Science* (*GS* 112), which arguably reflects the same Neo-Kantian skepticism and is not, in any case, a passage from Nietzsche's "mature" works, the domain where she claims my view that Nietzsche is no longer a skeptic about causation is "simply mistaken." The really crucial passage—the only one from Nietzsche's mature works she adduces—is from "The Four Great Errors" chapter of *Twilight of the Idols*, the section on "the error of false causality," according to which we falsely believe that our conscious mental states *cause* our actions. But, for Acampora's purposes, the crucial part of this section is its conclusion (I quote more than she quotes):

> There are no mental [*geistigen*] causes at all! ... [W]e really botched this 'empiricism'—we used it to *create* the world as a world of causes, wills, and minds. The oldest and most enduring psychology was at work here, doing absolutely nothing but this: it considered all events to be deeds, all deeds to be the result of a will, the world became a multitude of doers, a doer ('subject') pushed its way under all events. People projected their three 'inner facts' out of themselves and onto the world—the facts they believed in most fervently, the will, the mind, and the I. They took the concept of being from the concept of the I, they posited 'things' as being in their own image, on the basis of their concept of I as cause. Is it any wonder that what they rediscovered in things later is only *what they had put in to them in the first place*?—Even the 'thing,' to say it again, the concept of a thing, is just a reflex of the belief in the I as cause ... and even your atom, my dear Mr. Mechanist and Mr. Physicist, how many errors, how much rudimentary psychology is left in your atom! Not to mention the 'thing-in-itself' ...! The error of thinking that mind caused reality! And to make it the measure of reality! And to call it *God*!

That we are mistaken in thinking the conscious will is *causal* in action—which is, as I have argued elsewhere, Nietzsche's view (Leiter 2007)—clearly entails no skepticism about the reality of causation, which is what is supposed to be at issue in Acampora's critique of my reading of Nietzsche's M-Naturalism. What *is* supposed to motivate skepticism about causation from this passage is glossed by Acampora as follows: "the empirical world of the scientist is populated by a host of 'spirit-subjects' in the form of 'doers' or agents. This is the framework in which the concept of causation operates" (2006: 320). Suppose it is true that our belief in "atoms" resulted from our (false) belief that our wills are causal. How does this lead to skepticism about *causation*? It might warrant skepticism about the atomistic metaphysics of physics, but causation seems intact. Indeed, in the very next section of *Twilight*, Nietzsche quickly returns to his confident distinguishing of *real* from *imaginary* causes, consistent with the entire tenor of this chapter.

Acampora herself apparently realizes there is a problem with her reading, because—buried in a footnote oddly—she acknowledges, "This is not to say Nietzsche rejects causation altogether, only that our current way of conceiving it is hampered by these other conceptual presuppositions or 'errors' as [Nietzsche] calls them" (2006: 330 n. 8), and she goes on to note that the passages in *Twilight* that are concerned with critiquing "false" or "imaginary" notions of causality "suggest that Nietzsche endorses some kind of causation," but rejects the "framework organized around various metaphysical abstractions such as subjects and doers"

(2006: 330 n. 8). I take it, then, by Acampora's own admission, Nietzsche, in fact, believes in causation, but simply denies that some purported causes—for example, "subjects" or the conscious will—are, in fact, causal. But this was never at issue in my reading of Nietzsche's naturalism, which spent considerable time examining precisely this critique of his (Leiter 2002: 87–101). What Acampora promised, but has failed to deliver, is any evidence that it is "simply mistaken" to point out that Nietzsche believes in causation in his mature works. Rather than being "mistaken," Acampora, in her footnote, admits that it is correct!

Acampora's critique nonetheless raises an important issue: namely, whether Nietzsche is not a skeptic about what he takes to be the underlying *metaphysics* of modern science? And, if that is true, how could he then be a naturalist who takes science seriously? It is to a version of that more worrisome critique that we now turn.

C. The Metaphysics of the Will to Power

Once again, Janaway poses a sharp version of the pertinent challenge. He writes:

> Nietzsche's commitment to continuity of results with the sciences is put in some doubt by some of his statements about the fundamental explanatory notion of will to power, which may essentially import notions of overpowering and interpretation into the biological realm. (2007: 52)

Indeed, some of Nietzsche's discussions of will to power—especially in *GM* II: 12—raise doubts even about ascribing M-Naturalism to Nietzsche. As Janaway writes:

> The problem is that Nietzsche presents will to power as a *counter* to what he sees as the dominant paradigm in science, the "democratic idiosyncrasy against everything that rules and desires to rule," a prejudice about method which has "become lord over the whole of physiology and the doctrine of life—to its detriment [...] by removing through sleight of hand one of its basic concepts, that of true *activity*" (*GM* II: 12). Nietzsche says that the scientific explanation of organisms' behavior in terms of reactive adaptation to the environment must be rejected in favor of the view that at all levels of the organic world there is spontaneity, active appropriation, interpretation, and the imposition of form and meaning... (2007: 38)

Section 12 of the Second Essay of the *Genealogy* does indeed seem like a very strange passage for a philosophical naturalist to write, for the reasons to which Janaway calls attention. How can it be squared with the reading of Nietzsche as an M-Naturalist that is otherwise so well supported by the texts?

Maudemarie Clark has made a powerful case, partly following Walter Kaufmann, that "the theory of will to power originated in attempts to account for various human behaviors" (1990: 210), and certainly its most prominent role in the *Genealogy* is through the psychological principle articulated in *GM* III: 7, according to which "every animal...instinctively strives for...its maximum feelings of power," which then figures, as I have argued, in Nietzsche's explanation of the appeal of ascetic ideals (Leiter 2002: 255–63).[13] As Clark has also shown

---

[13] I disagree, however, with Clark's critique of will to power as an empirical hypothesis on a par with psychological hedonism (Clark 1990: 210–11). It is true, of course, that if a desire for the feeling of power is

(1990: 212–18), the published arguments for the more ambitious and metaphysical versions of the doctrine of will to power—according to which all matter, or at least all organic matter, is "will to power"—depend on premises (e.g., the causality of the will) that Nietzsche rather explicitly rejects, so he cannot mean them to be serious or persuasive arguments. Indeed, the bad arguments Nietzsche gives for the metaphysical doctrine of will to power are, Clark argues (drawing on *BGE* 5, 6, and 9), an ironic illustration of a tendency of philosophers Nietzsche so often critiques, namely, that they present their metaphysical doctrines as rational discoveries, rather than "attempts to construct the world, or an image of the world, in terms of the philosopher's values" (1990: 221).

Against that backdrop, we should recall that *GM* II: 12—the passage on which Janaway focuses—has as its real focus the correct way to do a *genealogy*, for example, of punishment. Nietzsche argues (cf. Leiter 2002: chapter 5) that a genealogy must distinguish between "the cause of the genesis of a thing and its final usefulness," since the former does not warrant any reliable inference about the latter. Nietzsche writes that he

> emphasize[s] this key point about historical methodology all the more because it basically goes against the currently ruling instincts and taste of the times, which would rather learn to live with the absolute randomness, indeed the mechanistic senselessness of all happening than with the theory of a *power-will* playing itself out in all happening.

This reflects, says Nietzsche, "the democratic idiosyncrasy against everything that rules and desires to rule" (*GM* II: 12), and this is followed by the short polemic against that idiosyncrasy which concludes with him affirming that "the essence of life" is "its *will to power*" which involves essentially "spontaneous, attacking, infringing, reinterpreting, reordering, and formative forces" (*GM* II: 12). The next section begins "To return to our topic"—namely the practice of genealogy as illustrated through the case study of punishment—and not a further word is said about the metaphysics of the will to power in the book, as opposed to will to power as a psychological hypothesis.[14]

Notice, then, that Nietzsche's apparent metaphysics of the will to power enters *only* in order to hammer home a point about correct historical methodology, one that stands quite independent of the truth of the metaphysics: it looks, in other words, precisely like an attempt to utilize metaphysical claims for rhetorical ends, i.e., to persuade his readers of the correctness of his approach to genealogy by associating it with a different, more "noble" value system. And having served its rhetorical purpose here, the metaphysics then vanishes

---

to be explanatorily illuminating, we need an account of that feeling that is both concrete and *conceptually* distinct from other feelings that might be thought to play a motivational role (e.g., pleasure). But that need for conceptual discreteness and distinctness is compatible with the empirical thesis that other apparent motivations are really instances of motivation by a desire for the feeling of power. That being said, the thesis that *all* behavior is motivated by a desire for the feeling of power is as implausible as psychological hedonism, but that is compatible with the important thesis that the feeling of power is a significant motivation for humans, and figures in the best explanation of central aspects of human action and values.

   [14] A third possibility is that will to power is to be construed as a kind of *biological* hypothesis, as Richardson (2004) tries to do. This strikes me as fraught with difficulties, both interpretive and scientific. As Forber (2007) shows, it is unlikely that Richardson's version of a Nietzschean power biology is compatible with Darwin, which is to say, it is not compatible with *real* biology, which puts it in the same boat as what I call the "crackpot" metaphysics of will to power. See the discussion in the text.

from the book, in favor of the psychological version of the doctrine made explicit in *GM* III: 7. It is tempting to conclude, given this context and given what Clark has demonstrated about the role of will to power in the published works, that *GM* II: 12 should not be taken too seriously at all.

In this connection, it probably bears remembering how unimportant Nietzsche himself ultimately views the idea of will to power. In the two major self-reflective moments in the Nietzschean corpus—*Ecce Homo*, where Nietzsche reviews and assesses his life and work, including specifically all his prior books, and the series of new, synoptic prefaces he wrote in 1886 for all his books pre-dating *Thus Spoke Zarathustra*—Nietzsche nowhere makes the case for the centrality of will to power, or a metaphysics of will to power, to his work. In light of Nietzsche's own appraisal of his philosophy, it seems particularly misleading to read passages like *GM* II: 12 too literally.

A concluding reflection on questions of interpretive method, however, may be in order here. My own interest in Nietzsche is not simply antiquarian, and continued interest in any philosophical naturalist, like Nietzsche, should be, at least in part, a function of the extent to which he gets nature and the facts right, and thus teaches us important things. If it turns out that Nietzsche, the man, really is committed to what seems entailed by the most flat-footed literalism about a bare handful of published "will to power" passages (such as *GM* II: 12), then so much the worse for Nietzsche we might say. We may do Nietzsche *the philosopher* a favor, however, if we reconstruct his Humean project in terms that are both recognizably his in significant part, and yet at the same time far more plausible once the crackpot metaphysics of the will to power (that all organic matter "is will to power") is expunged. I am inclined to Clark's hopeful view that the crackpot metaphysics is really presented in an ironic spirit, and that Nietzsche, the otherwise sound naturalist, knew better. The fact that none of his actual moral psychology depends on the crackpot metaphysics, and that he assigns the crackpot metaphysics no significance in his own appraisal of his corpus, is additional reason to be hopeful on this score. But Nietzsche was a mere mortal like the rest of us, and even being a genius cannot compensate for the dangers of being self-taught about so much. Perhaps Nietzsche really did believe he had some deep insight into the correct metaphysics of nature, one missed by the empirical sciences. If he had that thought—one wholly inconsistent with the rest of his naturalism—so much the worse for him. Those of us reading him more than a century later should concentrate on his fruitful ideas, not the silly ones, especially when they are not central to his important work in moral psychology.

IV. Is Nietzsche a Successful Naturalist . . . and How Could He Be?

Philosophical naturalists incur an evidential burden that most philosophers do not: their claims must answer to the facts as they unfold in the course of systematic empirical inquiry. Kantians can make up their moral psychology from their sanctimonious armchairs, invoking an interest only in the "concept" or "possibility" of moral motivation, but naturalists actually care about how human beings *really* work.

Hume, of course, does not fare that well by this more demanding evidential standard, since some of his speculation about human nature seems to involve wishful thinking about human moral propensities. Nietzsche is certainly not prone to wishful thinking, but does he actually fare any better? How does his speculative M-Naturalism look more than a century later?

As I have argued in recent work (Leiter 2007; Knobe and Leiter 2007), one important reason that philosophers should take Nietzsche seriously is because he seems to have gotten, at least in broad contours, many points about human moral psychology *right*. Consider:

(1) Nietzsche holds that heritable type facts, as I call them, are central determinants of personality and morally significant behaviors, a claim well supported by extensive empirical findings in behavioral genetics (Knobe and Leiter 2007).

(2) Nietzsche claims that consciousness is a "surface" and that "the greatest part of conscious thought must still be attributed to [nonconscious] instinctive activity" (*BGE* 3), theses overwhelmingly vindicated by recent work by psychologists on the role of the unconscious (e.g., Wilson 2002) and by philosophers who have produced synthetic meta-analyses of work on consciousness in psychology and neuroscience (e.g., Rosenthal 2008).

(3) Nietzsche claims that moral judgments are post hoc rationalizations of feelings that have an antecedent source, and thus are not the outcome of rational reflection or discursiveness, a conclusion in sync with the findings of the ascendant "social intuitionism" in the empirical moral psychology of Jonathan Haidt (2001) and others.

(4) Nietzsche argues (Leiter 2007) that free will is an "illusion," that our conscious experience of willing is itself the causal product of nonconscious forces, a view recently defended by the psychologist Daniel Wegner (2002), who in turn synthesizes a large body of empirical literature, including the famous neurophysical data about "willing" collected by Benjamin Libet.

If Nietzsche were more widely read by academic psychologists—too many years of Heideggerian and Derridean misreadings appear, alas, to have put them off Nietzsche—then he would be recognized as a truly prescient figure in the history of empirical psychology.

Naturalists, to be sure, are hostages to empirical fortune, and Nietzsche's remarkable track record may turn out to be less impressive in fifty or a hundred years. But prophecy about the empirical sciences is not my interest here. For Nietzsche's remarkable psychological insight raises a new and different kind of puzzle about the M-Naturalism I have ascribed to him and which I have defended here against various critics. To put it simply: Nietzsche seems to have been *right* about much of human moral psychology, notwithstanding his failure to employ any of the *methods* of the empirical psychology that has confirmed much of his work. What kind of *methodological* naturalism is that?

Scott Jenkins poses a succinct version of this objection in commenting on the empirical evidence that Joshua Knobe and I adduce in support of Nietzsche's moral psychology. Jenkins writes (2008):

Knobe and Leiter examine a wide range of psychological studies (including studies of twins' behavior, the effects of child-rearing practices on personality, and the relation between moral behavior and reports of moral attitudes) and argue that a person's behavior in moral contexts can be explained primarily through appeal to heritable "type-facts," while moral upbringing (the Aristotelian view) and conscious decision-making (the Kantian view) quite surprisingly play almost no role in such explanations. This empirical evidence, they argue, demonstrates that Nietzsche's theory of different psychological types, with their characteristic moral and theoretical commitments, at the very least deserves serious attention from philosophers interested in moral psychology. Knobe and Leiter do a very good job of making their case, and their work suggests an interesting question concerning Nietzsche's work—How, exactly, did he arrive at a theory that is confirmed by recent empirical investigations if not by way of considering the data that support the theory?

We need to distinguish, in this context, between what counts as *confirmation* of a theory from what might lead a genius like Nietzsche to have perceived a possible truth about human moral psychology. Empirical psychology has evolved methods for testing and confirming hypotheses that were not in use in the nineteenth century—hence the need for a naturalistically minded philosopher like Nietzsche to *speculate*. But by the same token, it is not as though Nietzsche lacked *evidence* on which to base his speculative moral psychology. His evidence appears to have been of three primary kinds: first, his own observations, both introspective and of the behavior of others; second, the personal observations recorded by others, in a wide array of historical, literary, and philosophical texts over long periods of time, observations which, in some respects, tended to reinforce each other (consider, e.g., the realism about human motivations detailed by Thucydides in antiquity and, in the modern era, in the aphorisms of La Rochefoucauld, both authors whom Nietzsche admired); and third, his reading about contemporaneous scientific developments, most of which—even if amateurish or simply wrong by today's standards—did represent systematic attempts to bring scientific methods to bear on the study of human beings and which, in some of their broad outlines, have been vindicated by subsequent developments. By the standards of contemporary methods in the human sciences, we would not deem insights arrived at based on this evidence to be well confirmed, but that certainly does not mean it is not, in the hands of a genius like Nietzsche, adequate for insights that survive scrutiny by our contemporary methods. This is precisely one of the reasons why Nietzsche is a great *speculative* M-Naturalist in the history of philosophy: with unsystematic data and methods he could nonetheless arrive at hypotheses that turn out to be supported by more systematic data and methods. Of course, unlike our contemporary social scientists, Nietzsche is not just a Humean, but a Therapist, and so weaves these hypotheses into a powerful critical project that aims to transform consciousness about morality. Some of our contemporary naturalists in moral psychology (e.g., Prinz 2007 and Haidt 2001) perhaps have similar aims, but nothing like Nietzsche's rhetorical talent or his fearless readiness to abandon conventional wisdom about morality. Contemporary cognitive science should lead us to have a renewed appreciation for the penetrating insight of Nietzsche's Speculative M-Naturalism, but cognitive science is no match for the rhetorical power of the Therapeutic Nietzsche, who sees not only how human beings actually work but also how to exploit these facts in a way that upsets the complacent moral consciousness of some of his readers.[15]

[15] Discussion with students in my spring 2008 seminar on "Nietzsche, Naturalism, and Moral Psychology" at the University of Texas at Austin was extremely helpful to me in working on this paper; I am especially grateful to Christopher Raymond for several important insights. I was also helped

Bibliography

(A) Works by Nietzsche

BGE   *Beyond Good and Evil: Prelude to a Philosophy of the Future,* ed. Rolf-Peter Horstmann. Cambridge: Cambridge University Press, 2002.

GM   *On the Genealogy of Morality,* trans. Maudemarie Clark and Alan J. Swensen. Indianapolis: Hackett Publishing, 1998.

GS   *The Gay Science,* trans. W. Kaufmann. New York: Vintage, 1974.

(B) Other Works Cited

Acampora, Christa Davis. 2006. "Naturalism and Nietzsche's Moral Psychology," in K. Ansell-Pearson (ed.), *A Companion to Nietzsche.* Oxford: Blackwell, 314–33.

Bittner, Rüdiger. 2003. "Introduction," in F. Nietzsche, *Writings from the Last Notebooks.* Cambridge: Cambridge University Press, ix–xxxiv.

Brobjer, Thomas. 2008. *Nietzsche's Philosophical Context: An Intellectual Biography.* Urbana: University of Illinois Press.

Büchner, Ludwig. 1870. *Force and Matter,* trans. J. G. Collingwood. London: Trubner.

Cartwright, Nancy. 2004. "From Causation to Explanation and Back Again," in Brian Leiter (ed.), *The Future for Philosophy.* Oxford: Oxford University Press, 230–45.

Clark, Maudemarie. 1990. *Nietzsche on Truth and Philosophy.* Cambridge: Cambridge University Press.

Forber, Patrick. 2007. "Nietzsche Was No Darwinian," *Philosophy and Phenomenological Research* 75: 369–82.

Gemes, Ken and Christopher Janaway. 2005. "Naturalism and Value in Nietzsche," *Philosophy and Phenomenological Research* 71: 729–40.

Gregory, Frederick. 1977. *Scientific Materialism in Nineteenth-Century Germany.* Dordrecht: D. Reidel.

Haidt, Jonathan. 2001. "The Emotional Dog and its Rational Tail: A Social Intuitionist Approach to Moral Judgment," *Psychological Review* 108: 814–34.

Hussain, Nadeem. 2004. "Nietzsche's Positivism," *European Journal of Philosophy* 12: 326–68.

Janaway, Christopher. 2007. *Beyond Selflessness: Reading Nietzsche's "Genealogy."* Oxford: Oxford University Press.

Janz, Curt P. 1978. *Friedrich Nietzsche: Biographie* (3 vols). Munich: Hanser.

Jenkins, Scott. 2008. Review of Brian Leiter and Neil Sinhababu (eds), *Nietzsche and Morality* (Oxford University Press, 2007), *Notre Dame Philosophical Reviews* 01.03. Available online at <http://ndpr.nd.edu/news/23289-nietzsche-and-morality/>, accessed February 28, 2013.

Knobe, Joshua and Brian Leiter. 2007. "The Case for Nietzschean Moral Psychology," in Brian Leiter and Neil Sinhababu (eds), *Nietzsche and Morality.* Oxford: Oxford University Press, 83–109.

Lange, Friedrich. 1950/1865. *History of Materialism,* trans. E. C. Thomas, 2nd edn. New York: Humanities Press.

by discussion at the conference on "Nietzsche, Naturalism and Normativity" at the University of Southampton in July 2008; I can recall particularly helpful comments or questions on that occasion from Ken Gemes, Christopher Janaway, Peter Kail, and David Owen. I also want to thank the commenters on the paper at my Nietzsche blog <http://> for several useful points. Finally, thanks to John Richardson for comments on the penultimate version.

Leiter, Brian. 2002. *Nietzsche on Morality*. London: Routledge.

Leiter, Brian. 2007. "Nietzsche's Theory of the Will," *Philosopher's Imprint* 7: 1–15.

Leiter, Brian and Neil Sinhababu (eds). 2007. *Nietzsche and Morality*. Oxford: Oxford University Press.

Prinz, Jesse. 2007. *The Emotional Construction of Morals*. Oxford: Oxford University Press.

Richardson, John. 2004. *Nietzsche's New Darwinism*. Oxford: Oxford University Press.

Rosenthal, David. 2008. "Consciousness and its Function," *Neuropsychologia* 46: 829–40.

Schacht, Richard. 1988. "Nietzsche's *Gay Science*, or, How to Naturalize Cheerfully," in R. C. Solomon and K. M. Higgins (eds), *Reading Nietzsche*. New York: Oxford University Press, 68–86.

Schnädelbach, Herbert. 1983. *Philosophy in Germany: 1831–1933*, trans. E. Matthews. Cambridge: Cambridge University Press.

Stack, George. 1983. *Lange and Nietzsche*. Berlin: De Gruyter.

Stroud, Barry. 1977. *Hume*. London: Routledge.

Vitzthum, Richard C. 1995. *Materialism: An Affirmative History*. Amherst, NY: Prometheus Books.

Wegner, Daniel. 2002. *The Illusion of Conscious Will*. Cambridge, Mass.: MIT Press.

Wilson, Timothy. 2002. *Strangers to Ourselves: Discovering the Adaptive Unconscious*. Cambridge, Mass.: Harvard University Press.

CHAPTER 26

NIETZSCHE'S PHILOSOPHICAL AESTHETICISM

SEBASTIAN GARDNER

Amongst artists rather than philosophers must be reckoned Friedrich Nietzsche, whom we should wrong (as we said of Ruskin) by trying to expound his doctrines in scientific language and then holding them up to the facile criticism which, so translated, they would draw upon themselves. In none of his books, not even in his first, *The Birth of Tragedy*, in spite of the title, does he offer us a real theory of art; what appears to be theory is the mere expression of the author's feelings and tendencies. He shows a kind of anxiety concerning the value and aim of art and the problem of its inferiority or superiority to science and philosophy, a state of mind characteristic of the Romantic period to which Nietzsche was, in many respects, a belated but magnificent representative. To Romanticism, as well as to Schopenhauer, belong the elements of thought which issued in the distinction between Apollonesque art (that of serene contemplation, to which belong the epic and sculpture) and Dionysiac art (the art of agitation and tumult, such as music and the drama). The thought is vague and does not bear criticism; but it is supported by a flight of inspiration which lifts the mind to a spiritual region seldom if ever reached again in the second half of the nineteenth century.'

Croce, *Aesthetic*[1]

1 INTRODUCTION

AT a very early point in his philosophical development, in *The Birth of Tragedy*, Nietzsche famously introduces the concept of 'aesthetic justification', by which he means not the

---

[1] Croce 1972: part II, chapter 18, pp. 411–12.

justification *of* aesthetic judgement—the familiar object of traditional aesthetic enquiry in, for example, Hume and Kant—but rather justification *by* the aesthetic: 'our highest dignity lies in the meaning of works of art—for it is only as an *aesthetic phenomenon* that existence and the world are eternally *justified*' (*BT* 5). And though the boldest statements of this out-look fade from Nietzsche's writings shortly after *BT*, the suggestion that in the final instance justification can *only* be aesthetic—that the aesthetic in some sense provides the normative bottom line—reappears throughout Nietzsche's writings.

Commentators have puzzled over this captivating but opaque notion, and the majority view is that it signals Nietzsche's intention to *oppose* art and the aesthetic to philosophi-cal reflection as such—the aesthetic is regarded as subverting the fundamental premises or defining objectives of philosophical enquiry, as taking the place of reason. Aesthetic jus-tification belongs, on this view, to a radically anti-realist, anti-rationalist philosophical programme, in which reality becomes equivalent to a work of art, a creature of rationally unconstrained subjectivity, the residue of fictionalizing aesthetic operations, always open to revision. This is the interpretation of Nietzsche given by Habermas, for example, and it has the status of a commonplace in much deconstructive and postmodernist discussion of Nietzsche.[2]

The view that I wish to defend, by contrast, understands Nietzsche's notion of aesthetic justification in terms of a lateral relation of *rational integration* between aesthetic conscious-ness and philosophical reflection, so that it is more accurate to speak of philosophical reason as *mandating* the aesthetic, and as *taking an aesthetic form*, than of the aesthetic as under-mining or displacing reason.

The conception of art and the aesthetic as playing a necessary, internal, privileged role in the task of philosophy—a position which I will call 'philosophical aestheticism'—is not original to Nietzsche: it goes back to Schiller, the early German Romantics, and the German Idealists.

However, it is also true that if Nietzsche belongs in this camp, then he privileges art on terms quite different from those of other members of this tradition. If a metaphysical or transcendental cognitive claim for art and the aesthetic were made by Nietzsche, then Nietzsche would fit squarely into the post-Kantian mould. Some commentators do think that the 'artist's metaphysics' which Nietzsche elaborates in *BT* show him to be thinking of art and the aesthetic as cognitive in the same sense as do the German Idealists and German Romantics—they suppose that Nietzsche thinks that reality *really is* a work of art, in the same way that Hegel thinks it is the Idea. My view—in agreement with the bulk of more recent commentary—is that this is not correct: Nietzsche denies that art is metaphysically or transcendentally cognitive. But if this is right, then a puzzle surrounds the suggestion that

---

[2] According to Habermas, for Nietzsche the aesthetic is 'reason's absolute other', 'metaphysically transfigured irrationality' (1987: 94): it comprises mere 'placeholders for the other of reason' (1987: 306) and lacks all connection with theoretical or practical validity claims (1987: 93–4). Other instances of this broad type of interpretation include Ferry 1993: chapter 5; Hammermeister 2002: 136–50; Megill 1985: part I; Porter 2000; and Schaeffer 2000: 208–36. It is of course not necessary to embrace, nor even to be critically engaged with, deconstruction or the postmodern turn in order to interpret Nietzsche in this way. Thus Benjamin, decades before the neostructuralist development, finds in *BT* an unrestricted intellectual 'nihilism': all concepts disappear and 'all sane reflection is at an end' in Nietzsche's 'abyss of aestheticism' (1998: 102–3).

Nietzsche's position is an instance of philosophical aestheticism as just defined: how can art be rationally integrated with philosophy, if art lacks cognitive significance?

My aim in this paper is to answer this question. I will first give an overview of the discussions of art and the aesthetic in Nietzsche's writings, concentrating on his early theory of tragedy, since this lies at the basis of almost everything that Nietzsche has to say about aesthetic issues at all periods of his thinking. I will then try to show in the main part of the paper how Nietzsche's position allows itself to be reconstructed as a distinctive and coherent form of philosophical aestheticism, which in addition holds interest from the standpoint of a traditional philosophical conception of what aesthetic theory should provide. I conclude with some brief remarks about the convincingness of Nietzsche's aesthetic strategy and its connection with the broader issue of Nietzsche's situation in the history of philosophy.

2 THE BIRTH OF TRAGEDY

In the opening sentence of *BT*, Nietzsche claims that through his new theory of the Apollonian and the Dionysian, the book will gain 'much for the science of aesthetics', adding that the 'continuous development' of art in general will receive its explanation (*BT* 1 [III.1: 21]).

To the extent that this raises the expectation of a conventional treatise on aesthetics, it is misleading. A more accurate account of the overarching project in *BT* is that it represents Nietzsche's attempt to describe and recommend certain *existential strategies* which are centred on art, and which in Nietzsche's view offer an alternative and a correction to Schopenhauer. While accepting Schopenhauer's view of the ubiquity and necessity of suffering, Nietzsche aims to show that Book III of *The World as Will and Representation* takes a false view of the nature and limitations of art, and that, in consequence of this, its Book IV, in which Schopenhauer sets out his pessimism, circumscribes too narrowly the existential options.

The convoluted structure of *BT*, and its emphasis on tragedy as a fusion of Apollonian and Dionysian principles, tend to obscure the fact, but it is important to see that Nietzsche already, in the basic, mutually independent conceptions of the Apollonian and the Dionysian introduced in the early sections of *BT*, makes significant progress in countering Schopenhauerian pessimism.

The Apollonian and Dionysian comprise in the first instance two forms of experience, which different forms of art cultivate out of natural functions of the human mind (the capacities for dream and intoxication respectively), and which each supply a different and individually sufficient way of 'justifying existence'.

The Apollonian, aligned with epic poetry, painting, and sculpture, and music qua its rhythm, consists in a beautifying selective representation of reality, elaborated through the projection of this representation into the consciousness of the Olympian gods, the reinternalization of which allows the Homeric Greeks to experience themselves as they suppose themselves to appear to their divine spectators.[3] This strategy, Nietzsche claims—hereby

---

[3] This conception may owe something to—and is at any rate continuous with—Schopenhauer's notion of man's 'double life' (*WWR* I: 16).

rejecting Schopenhauer's claim that the aesthetic attitude can be realized only in transient form, as a holiday from life—constituted the essence of Homeric, pre-tragic Hellenic culture, which (until destabilized by external factors) was entirely successful.

The Dionysian, aligned with music (qua the acoustic power of melody and harmony) and with lyric poetry, consists in *Rausch* (intoxication, rapture), ecstatic immersion in a primordial unity, a form of experience not considered possible by Schopenhauer, and which grants an experiential recovery of unity with nature and other men, and allows pain to be experienced with joy.[4]

This raises the question: if the Apollonian and Dionysian each on their own perform the necessary existential work, why do they need to be combined, and in view of their heterogeneity, how is their combination possible? Put another way, if Nietzsche is right that Greek tragedy exhibits a combination of the antithetical Apollonian and the Dionysian principles, how is this fact to be explained?

Nietzsche's answer to this question shows that the possibility and necessity of combining the Apollonian and Dionysian is of key importance for his claim for the extra-historical, contemporary, and philosophical significance of tragedy, and hence for his argument with Schopenhauer. What forced the Apollonian and Dionysian into marriage, Nietzsche claims, is the peculiar existential circumstance of the Greeks at a specific historical juncture, where the incursion of Asiatic Dionysus worship threatened the Homeric-Apollonian world view with destruction. Because Homeric-Apollonian culture was itself founded on an apprehension of one central plank of Dionysian truth—Silenus's Schopenhauerian wisdom, that life is essentially suffering—the new god could not be repudiated;[5] but assent to Dionysian truth had the effect of *exposing as illusory* the serene Apollonian vision which had previously kept Dionysian reality under wraps.[6]

The Homeric Greeks could not, however, simply switch existential tracks and convert to Dionysianism, because their greater innate sensitivity meant that Dionysian realization induced in them a degree of suffering much greater than that experienced by the Asiatic Dionysians (*BT* 3 [III.1: 32]) and they, unlike the Asiatic Dionysians, were habituated to living in Apollonian comfort—what worked for the 'barbarian' Asiatics could not, therefore, work for the more sensitive, Apollonized Homeric Greeks.[7] Tragedy arose from this situation of being unable to either reject or live with Dionysian truth: not as a new existential

---

[4] *BT* 2 [III.1: 29]: '*jene Erscheinung, dass Schmerzen Lust erwecken*'. It is significant that in the very earliest of the 1870 essays (viz. ZVT1 and ZVT2), as Sweet observes (1999: 356–7), Nietzsche ascribes the regenerative effects of tragedy to the Dionysian alone.

[5] *BT* 2 [III.1: 30]: the Apollonian Greek's 'astonishment' at the Dionysian dithyramb 'would have been intensified by its combination with the terror, not in the end so strange to him, that his Apollonian consciousness alone, like a veil, hid that Dionysian world from his view'; and *BT* 4 [III.1: 36]: the Apollonian Greeks were 'unable to conceal from themselves the fact that they themselves were awkwardly akin to' the Dionysian.

[6] Nietzsche also suggests a weakness in the Dionysian strategy: post-ecstatic re-entry into quotidian reality issues in lethargy, repugnance towards life, a 'mood of asceticism, of denial of will'. See *BT* 7 [III.1: 53–4], where comparison is drawn of Dionysian man with Hamlet. This mood finds its remedy in the Apollonian. But Nietzsche does not regard the Dionysian strategy as crippled by this limitation and treats it as only a subsidiary factor in the development of tragedy, which he grasps primarily from the perspective of the Homeric Greeks.

[7] Relevant here are the remarks at *BGE* 193, on forms of happiness irreversibly conditioned by dream experience.

strategy (since it merely combined, through an ingenious superimposition, the two pre-existent strategies), but as a new form of art which, by sharing the honours between the two deities, supplied the Greeks with a creative resolution of their quandary. And the relevance of this to Nietzsche's intention to address his own cultural situation is, of course, that, on his account, we too find ourselves in the position of Greek Apollonian culture in its encounter with Dionysian truth, insofar as we too are caught in an increasingly acute contradiction of theoretical with practical reason, of truth with the conditions of life.[8]

How, though, does tragedy 'hold together' Dionysian truth with Apollonian illusion? Why does the former not simply cancel out the latter? This is where *BT*'s 'artist's metaphysics' play an essential logical role:[9] Nietzsche advances the speculative hypothesis—which he must suppose the Greeks to have grasped in at least inchoate implicit form, and which is in any case necessary for tragedy to be re-embraced in the present day—that the '*Natur*' or 'primal Oneness' [*Ur-Eine*] which lies at the ground of Dionysian experience has its own, supra-personal telos, which realizes itself though us, initially in the 'symbolic expression' which it receives in Dionysian cult festivals and their musical forms[10] and then more profoundly, in tragic representation, through which it receives 'its constant redemption' (*BT* 4 [III.1: 34]). With this simple and brilliant move—supplying the Apollonian with a (Dionysian) ground, which it lacked previously in Homeric culture, and the Dionysian with a(n Apollonian) teleological realization, which it lacked previously in Asiatic culture—Nietzsche *validates* Apollonian representation, on *non-epistemic* grounds: indeed, it is precisely *because of* the epistemically negative character of the Apollonian, its status as '*illusion of illusion*', that it can play its necessary metaphysical role. By means of tragedy's Apollonian symbolic representation of Dionysian reality, Nature (the One) finds, Nietzsche says, satisfaction of its 'original desire for illusion', an 'even higher satisfaction' than that provided by empirical reality.

It is true, therefore, that a sizeable, modified portion of Schopenhauer's metaphysics is presupposed in some sense in *BT*, and it should be agreed also that Nietzsche fully intends his artist's metaphysics to resonate with his readers in such a way as to bring to mind the rich history of such proposals in Romantic post-Kantian philosophical aestheticism. What does not follow, however, is that Nietzsche's attitude to the metaphysical propositions in question is the same as that of his post-Kantian predecessors, and I think that the right view of this much-discussed issue is to be gleaned from the passage in *BT* 4 where he, in carefully chosen words, sets out the grounds for our acceptance of his artist's metaphysics.

In what reads like a rehearsal, with appropriate substitution of terms, of Kant's moral argument for the theological postulates, Nietzsche argues in explicitly first-personal terms from the felt '*longing*' for '*redemption by illusion*', not to the *truth* of Schopenhauer's

---

[8] We 'need art [specifically: Wagner's tragic art] precisely because we have evolved *looking into the face of reality*' (*UM* IV: 7 [IV.1: 41]). 'Our *art* is the reflection of desperate knowledge', *Nachlaß* 1872, N3, no. 124, p. 44 [III.4: 64].

[9] Nietzsche prepares the idea at the end of *BT* 1 [III.1: 26], where he talks of 'the artistic power of the whole of nature'. At the beginning of *BT* 2 [III.1: 26], he describes the Apollonian and Dionysian as 'artistic powers which spring from nature itself, *without the mediation of the human artist*, and in which nature's artistic urges are immediately and directly satisfied'. The 'metaphysical' character of the assumption becomes explicit in *BT* 4 [III.1: 34–5]. In *BT* 5 [III.1: 39], Nietzsche uses the phrase '*aesthetischen Metaphysik*'; '*Artisten-Metaphysik*' is introduced only in the later prefatory '*Versuch einer Selbstkritik*', *BT* 2 [III.1: 7].

[10] See the end of *BT* 2 [III.1: 29–30].

metaphysics, but to his *feeling himself compelled* to make the '*metaphysical assumption*' of a 'primal Oneness' that 'needs' the Apollonian vision (*BT* 4 [III.1: 34–5]; italics added ['*um so mehr fühle ich mich zu der metaphysischen Annahme gedrängt*']). What Nietzsche advances, therefore, is a *practically* or *axiologically* grounded argument, which delivers only a *necessity of representation*, not metaphysical truth.[11]

Our difference from the Greeks, then, is that we know that what needs to be postulated as a condition of the fulfilment of our axiological-practical needs cannot be taken in an unreservedly realistic spirit: it can have only the status of, in Kantian language, an 'object of practical cognition', which Nietzsche regards as an alternative to, not a form of, metaphysical truth.

One important reason for thinking that Nietzsche's stance towards his artist's metaphysics should not be interpreted realistically derives from his commitment to the inexplicability of tragedy. If Nietzsche's understanding of his metaphysics were the same as Schopenhauer's,

---

[11] On the historical connection here with Kant, see Hill 2003: 13–20, documenting Nietzsche's exposure to Kant's ideas. What Hill calls Nietzsche's 'first reading' of Kant runs from the early and mid-1860s to the early 1870s, and focuses on the *Critique of Judgement*—Nietzsche's initial reading of which Hill dates as in 1868—in which Kant's moral theology is presented at length. Also relevant is the influence of Lange, whose *History of Materialism* (1873–5) endorses Kant's conception of the regulative role of ideas of reason ('Ideals', in Lange's terminology), extends the Kantian regulative-postulative to the sphere of aesthetics, and even requires the aestheticization of Kant's ideas of reason; their 'value', Lange claims, is grounded in 'longing' and so indifferent to the lack of a relation to empirical reality and immune to logical attack ('Who will refute a Mass of Palestrina, or who will convict Raphael's Madonna of error?', 1950: 360). While the sceptical naturalist influence of Lange on Nietzsche's epistemology is well known, the importance of Lange's theory of 'The Standpoint of the Ideal' (1950: book II, section 4, chapter 4), as a midway station between Kant and Nietzsche, is much less explored. One exception is Vaihinger, who gives it much emphasis (1924: 341–2): Vaihinger refers to a letter from Rohde confirming the impression made on Nietzsche by Lange's theory of 'Metaphysics as a justified form of "poetry"', and asserts that 'in regard to Illusion Nietzsche must definitely be set down as a disciple and successor of Lange' (1924: 341). Also relevant is the *Nachlaß* material from summer 1872 to early 1873, showing Nietzsche to be highly interested in Kant's strategy of limiting *Wissen* to make room for faith, and offering artistic culture in place of Kant's religion: III.4: 14, III.4: 24, III.4: 27, III.4: 41, III.4: 105. Nietzsche's text of 1868, OS, already gives a deep critique of Schopenhauer's identification of will and the thing in itself, rendering it virtually inconceivable that Nietzsche could have accepted the truth of Schopenhauer's metaphysics at any later date. But there is in any case plentiful indication in *BT* of Nietzsche's wish to distance himself from, while making strategic use of, Schopenhauer's metaphysics. In the opening sections, Nietzsche sets '*Wille*' in inverted commas (*BT* 3, [III.1: 32–4]), casts his first explicit references to Schopenhauerian ideas in terms of mental states and phenomenological features (*BT* 1 [III.1: 22–5]), and deflects the briefly intimated metaphysical grounding of the Apollonian and Dionysian by referring these back to empirical psychology-cum-physiology. So rather than suggesting in *BT* 1, as a committed Schopenhauerian would, that Schopenhauer's metaphysics need to be assumed *ab initio* and the Apollonian and Dionysian extrapolated from them, Nietzsche offers the metaphysical parallel only as an illuminating *gloss* on the Apollonian/Dionysian contrast—his ulterior purpose being to prepare for the introduction, shortly to come, of his 'artist's metaphysics'. Nietzsche first shows an interest in relating his account of tragedy to Schopenhauer's metaphysics in the summer of 1870, in DW, thus some time *after* his first statement of his main thoughts about tragedy in ZVT1 and ZVT2 in January–February 1870, and in DW the connection with Schopenhauer is pursued, not in order to endorse Schopenhauer's metaphysics, but in order to show how retrieval of the insight in tragedy allows the conclusion Schopenhauer draws in Book IV of *The World as Will and Representation* to be turned on its head—Nietzsche's point being that *even if* one embraces Schopenhauerian metaphysics, still it does not follow that Schopenhauerian salvation is the only option.

then the discursive representation of the experience of tragedy by means of the artist's met-aphysics could be regarded as making that experience rationally transparent, in the way that Schopenhauer's account of tragedy as showing the self-antagonism of the will makes the meaning of tragedy rationally accessible (*WWR* I: 51). In that case, tragedy would give Nietzsche an *argument* for life affirmation, just as Schopenhauer thinks it argues for resigna-tion. But Nietzsche insists repeatedly on the inexplicability of the life-affirmative dimension of tragedy and its Dionysian component.[12] That is why tragic art has priority over any cor-responding tragic theory or structure of thought—the experience of tragedy is a condition on the communicability of 'tragic philosophy', 'the tragic idea'[13]—and why tragedy is strictly impossible without the spirit of music.[14] The discursive articulations of the Dionysian-tragic experience that Nietzsche offers in *BT* are not intended to *account for* the life-affirmative upshot of tragedy: his claim that Dionysian subjects cognize their noumenal identity with fecund self-delighting nature is not meant to *explain* how pain can be experienced as an occasion for joy, and grasping the artist's metaphysics is neither necessary nor sufficient for understanding why authority should be accorded to the experience of tragedy.[15]

Additional reason for thinking that Nietzsche does not regard his artist's metaphysics as giving the *ratio essendi* of the experience of tragedy derives from *BT* 9. Here Nietzsche dis-cusses the moral metaphysics of Aeschylus and Sophocles, i.e. the views implied by their works of the relation of human action to cosmic justice. Sophocles, Nietzsche tells us, con-ceives Oedipus as the 'noble man' whose actions, though they destroy the moral world, yet exert 'a magical and beneficial power', which founds 'a new world on the ruins of the old'. Nietzsche then explains that '[t]his is what the poet, *in so far as he is also a religious thinker*, wishes to say to us' (*BT* 9 [III.1: 61–2]; italics added), and adds, crucially, that this 'whole vision of the poet is nothing but that light-image that healing nature holds up to us after we have glimpsed the abyss' ['*jenes Lichtbild, welches uns, nach einem Blick in den Abgrund, die heilende Natur vorhält*']—'light-patches, we might say, to heal the gaze seared by the terrible night', like the flashes of light that dance around our eyes after we turn away from staring at the sun (*BT* 9 [III.1: 61, 63]).

The particularized vision of the poet Sophocles does not, however, Nietzsche explains, exhaust the tragic myth of Oedipus. Its full content, he claims, concerns the

---

[12] See *BT* 2, p. 21 [III.1: 30] on the votary of Dionysus; *BT* 3, p. 22 [III.1: 31] on the 'inexplicable cheerfulness' of the Greeks; *BT* 22, pp. 108–9 [III.1: 140] on the 'utterly unintelligible', 'incomprehensibly different' effect produced by *Lohengrin*; and above all *BT* 24, p. 115 [III.1: 148–9], where Nietzsche tells us that the phenomenon of musical dissonance alone can give us an inkling of how the aesthetic pleasure of tragedy, and so aesthetic justification, are possible. Nietzsche insists on the distance between the 'tragic myth' and its necessarily inadequate 'objectification in the spoken word' (*BT* 17, p. 81 [III.1: 105–6]; and see ZVT2, III.2: 31 and III.2: 32), and readily applies the term 'mystical' to the Dionysian (*BT* 2, p. 18 [III.1: 26]; *BT* 5, p. 30 [III.1: 40]; *BT* 16, p. 76 [III.1: 99]; *BT* 17, p. 82 [III.1: 107]; *BT* 20, p. 97 [III.1: 127]).

[13] E.g. *Nachlaß* 1875, N3, no. 193, p. 133 [IV.1: 179].

[14] We need to reconstruct the 'power of musical effect' if we want to grasp the meaning of tragedy: *BT* 17 [III.1: 105–6]. This dependence of tragedy on the spirit of music would make no sense, if Dionysian life affirmation were discursively intelligible.

[15] The inexplicability of tragic affirmation is connected closely, for Nietzsche, with tragedy's liberation from theodicy—its refusal to tell us that we should affirm how things are because they are as they *ought* to be. See Nietzsche's consideration of the attitude of the spectator of pre-Euripidean tragedy towards the question of the explicability of events in the plot of tragedy and the issue of the hero's desert in ZVT2, and later remarks on the topic of guilt and misfortune in *D* 78, and *GM* II: 23.

Schopenhauerian 'dissolution of nature' into a transphenomenal will (*BT* 9 [III.1: 63]). In similar fashion, Aeschylus' *Prometheus*—which, Nietzsche acknowledges, reflects Aeschylus's 'longing for *justice*'—rests on an 'unshakeable substratum of [Greek] metaphysical thought': it provides an 'ethical background to pessimistic tragedy and the justification of human evil' (*BT* 9 [III.1: 63–6]). *Prometheus* is thus interpreted in terms of the complex meaning carried by individuation according to Nietzsche's artist's metaphysics.

The moral metaphysics of Sophocles and Aeschylus are regarded by Nietzsche, therefore, as derived logically, through the interpolation of independent religious and ethical elements, and the mediation of the artist's individual personality, from Nietzsche's artist's metaphysics. What Nietzsche intends his artist's metaphysics to amount to is not an extraction of *metaphysical truth* from tragic myth, but a *restatement of tragic myth* in its highest, most comprehensive, maximally universal (and in that sense 'philosophical') form, one that allows all particular tragic myths (of Oedipus, Prometheus, etc.) to be grasped as instances of a single schema, variations on a theme, or partial realizations of an archetype; and since these particularized representations of the human condition are ultimately just 'light images', so too must be Nietzsche's revised Schopenhauerian metaphysics. Nietzsche is, therefore, regarding Schopenhauer's metaphysics as *myth suitable for modernity*—as a mythic content which we moderns will find it intelligible to postulate and which will serve for us as a discursive reflection of the experiential meaning of tragedy, related to that experience in a quasi-metaphorical but non-arbitrary way. In summary, then, Nietzsche's artist's metaphysics are determined jointly from two directions, as (1) conceptual after-images of the experience of tragedy, (2) capable of playing a logical role, as postulates, answering to the subject's concern to rationalize and validate that experience.[16]

3 AFTER *THE BIRTH OF TRAGEDY*

Nietzsche's writings on art and the aesthetic after *BT* may be divided into two phases. The first corresponds to *Human, All Too Human*, especially Part IV of the first volume, 'From the Souls of Artists and Writers', with its pro-science and polemically anti-art stance, up to *Daybreak*.[17] The second includes the remarks on art and the aesthetic in Book II of *The Gay Science*, where the aesthetic seems to regain its importance for Nietzsche, and in later

---

[16] All of these elements are present in Nietzsche's restatement of the artist's metaphysics in *BT* 24 [III.1: 146–7]; again Nietzsche emphasizes that it is the experience of a need and longing which sponsors tragic myth.

[17] The main lines of criticism here are specifically of art as: (1) illusion and deception, opposed to 'truth' (*HAH* I: 145–6, 149, 151, 153, 159–60, 215; *D* 255 and 324); (2) sapping the orientation to action and dissipating energies which might have led to genuine improvements in man's condition, instead effecting only transient alleviations of suffering (*HAH*: I: 148; *D* 41 and 269); (3) perpetuating religious attitudes to existence, arousing and pandering to the 'metaphysical need' which free spirits have otherwise quelled (*HAH* I: 150, 153). Nietzsche's 'scientific aesthetics' is now a hermeneutics of suspicion: see *HAH* I: 145, and III: 123 [IV.3: 243], where Schiller is said to provide a 'model of how *not* to tackle scientific questions of aesthetics'. One recurring object of Nietzsche's attack is the doctrine of genius and inspiration, a motivated illusion correlated with the false idea that the artist enjoys higher cognition (*HAH* I: 145, 162–5). Features of art which from the perspective of *BT* would appear minor and incidental, if not negligible—e.g. the comic function (*HAH* I: 169) and our capacity for taking 'pleasure in nonsense' (*HAH* I: 213)—gain significance in a context where it is hard if not impossible to see 'what influence *of*

writings of the 1880s, in particular the *Nachlaß* from the final years of Nietzsche's creative life.[18] In all of these writings, *BT* remains clearly visible in the background, but a new range of themes and issues opens up, and consideration is given to forms of art other than tragedy, Nietzsche's interest in which would seem to have faded.

Given my claim that Nietzsche does not abandon his philosophical aestheticism, what is most in need of comment is the treatment of art in the first of these phases. The crucial point is that Nietzsche's guiding concern in *HAH* is with a quite different object of investigation from *BT*, namely the role and meaning of art *as we encounter it under modern cultural conditions*.[19] According to Nietzsche in *HAH*, art as we actually find it, infected as it is with romanticism, fails to counter and to some extent promotes the tendency to nihilism, fundamentally because it is no longer grounded in and made to serve a tragic conception of human life. In this respect, Nietzsche declares, in a way that has some overlap with Hegel's famous thesis, that art has in a sense come to an end.[20]

HAH signifies, therefore, abandonment of *BT*'s claim for the cultural sufficiency of art, along with its prophetic Wagnerianism. Philosophically this involves several things: a downward estimate of the potency of art as a means of transformation; a recognition that aesthetic consciousness fails to incorporate and may be at odds with the newly appreciated virtues of scientific consciousness;[21] and above all a recognition that the existential significance of art is not single and not necessarily positive, i.e. that art allows itself to be put in the service of a variety of existential orientations, some of which are decadent.[22] But it entails no retraction of the claims made in *BT* concerning what art meant to the Greeks, and nothing

any kind' art exercises among us (*HAH* I: 212). Nietzsche suggests that the audience for contemporary works divides into a public which attends only to the representational content, to which it responds in rudimentary emotional ways, and the artistically informed, for whom art affords only technical pleasure (*HAH* I: 166).Of particular interest is an ingeniously constructed section in *Daybreak* (*D* 255), where Nietzsche (i) executes what appears to be a denunciation of music's romantic power, by exposing its structure as a carefully plotted series of deceptive devices, (ii) draws a distinction between 'innocent' and 'guilty' music, the criterion for which is the degree to which music genuinely 'believes in itself', and then (iii) issues an ironical invitation to his readers to claim that the music which affects us is indeed 'innocent' music—loading us with the burden of squaring our aesthetic attachments with our intellectual consciences.

[18] Especially the notes from 1883–8 (but mostly from 1887–8) assigned by Nietzsche's editors to Part IV of Book III of *The Will to Power*, 'The Will to Power as Art' (*N4*, §§794–853, pp. 419–53).

[19] *HAH* II: 169: People at present either have no artistic need or it is so small as to be easily satisfied; a more extensive artistic need exists in the higher social rank, but here it belongs to those who cannot do without the consolations of religion and yet find religion insufficiently sensually attractive; only in 'exceptional' men does there exist a need for art 'of an exalted kind'.

[20] Hegel 1975: 9–11 and 102–3. Notwithstanding major differences as to what this consists in, there are some striking parallels. See *HAH* III: 170 and in particular *HAH* I: 217 [IV.2: 179–80] on the 'desensualization of higher art' and the dissociation of sensual and intellectual elements within it as incompatible with its full integrity. See also *HAH* I: 218 and 221 on the development of architecture and music: 'art moves towards its dissolution [*ihrer Auflösung entgegen*] [...] in going down to its destruction [*im Zu-Grunde-gehen*] it interprets its birth and becoming' ([IV.2: 186]); 'the magic of death' plays around art (*HAH* I: 223 [IV.2: 188]). The issue which separates Hegel and Nietzsche is that of whether or not art's going-beyond sensuality represents a comprehensively *rational* development.

[21] See e.g. *HAH* II: 206.

[22] As acknowledged in a late note (*Nachlaß* 1888, *N4*, §816, p. 432 [VIII.3: 56]): artists of both 'ascending' and 'declining' life 'belong to all phases'.

said in *HAH* about the nature of art, when read in the terms I have suggested, contradicts the possibility in principle, whether or not it is actualizable under modern conditions, of art's regaining that meaning.[23]

If this is right, then Nietzsche's resumption of philosophical aestheticism after *HAH* does not involve a double volte-face, but merely the reactivation of a set of ideas which *HAH* had put to one side, without contradicting.

The interesting question concerns the differences between Nietzsche's philosophical aestheticism before and after *HAH*. In *HAH*, Nietzsche recognizes the value of the *pathos* of scientific truth-seeking, carries over from *BT* the opposition of art to science, rejects contemporary art, and sides with science against art. In *GS*, Nietzsche's confidence in the existential sufficiency of science has vanished,[24] but what, it seems, must stand in the way of a return to the aesthetic is the problem which *HAH* has shown that *BT* failed to solve, of how the *transition* to aesthetic consciousness can be made from the standpoint of a Socratic or 'theoretical' culture. The section which concludes Book II of *GS* nevertheless reaffirms unequivocally that art has an essential existential function: art, Nietzsche says, is the 'counterforce' which allows us to avoid 'nausea and suicide'—'As an aesthetic phenomenon existence is still *bearable* for us' (*GS* 107 [V.2: 140]). The kind of art that Nietzsche has in mind here—'exuberant, floating, mocking, childish, and blissful'—is, if not exactly Apollonian, at least no longer tragic.[25]

The task, then, is to rearticulate the philosophical aestheticism of *BT* in terms which relate to our problem situation rather than that of the Homeric Greeks, and which yield a broader account of art, less focused on the specific case of Greek tragedy, allowing us to understand why the aesthetic should continue to be of central importance for Nietzsche's thinking in the 1880s. Later I will offer a reconstruction designed to address these issues. But before proceeding with this, it will help to get a clearer view of Nietzsche's relation to traditional aesthetic theory.

---

[23] In fact Nietzsche's change of estimate regarding the prospect of a Wagner-led cultural rebirth involves less than might be thought: in his Wagnerian period Nietzsche was already clear that the great art-consuming public is aesthetically beyond redemption. See *UM* IV: 5 [IV.1: 31–3]. As Breazeale notes, one of Nietzsche's earliest expressions of dissatisfaction with the aestheticism of *BT* dates back to 1873: 'Hypertrophy of the aesthetic viewpoint for considering greatness and life' (*Nachlaß* N3, no. 68, p. 116 [III.4: 349]). Another early (scathing) attack on art and the artist, closely modelled on Plato, is in the *Nachlaß* 1875, N1, 'On the Poet', 243; here it is crucial, in order to grasp Nietzsche's target correctly, that one note the passage's heading: '*How the poet adopts religious sentiments and ideas and preserves them in times of decay*'.

[24] In *HAH* I: 222 [IV.2: 187–8], Nietzsche claims that we have absorbed the lesson of art, viz. its teaching to take delight in 'human life as a piece of nature', which has reemerged as an 'almighty requirement of knowledge'; we 'could' therefore give up art, having absorbed its capacity for life enhancement; the 'scientific man is the further evolution of the artistic'. This notion is exactly what Nietzsche has relinquished by the time of *GS*.

[25] Though in *GS* Nietzsche appears to think that we lack susceptibility to the Dionysian in art, he continues to believe that men of the higher type will 'want a Dionysian art': see *GS* 370 [V.2: 302] and the references in *GS* 342 and 382 to a (new) beginning of tragedy.

4 NIETZSCHE AND THE CONCERNS OF
TRADITIONAL AESTHETIC THEORY

As noted previously, *BT* was not constructed with the intention of addressing questions of aesthetic theory in the late eighteenth-century or Kantian sense. To a high degree, Nietzsche's thoughts about art in *BT* are driven by and downstream from certain axiomatic root convictions, whose *formulation* owes a great deal to the experience of art, but which are essentially convictions *concerning* existential strategies, not art as such. Examination of the sequence of early drafts of *BT* in the *Nachlaß* puts it beyond doubt that the Apollonian/Dionysian distinction derived from reflection, not on the nature of the arts or aesthetic experience, but on what is required for a very particular form of aesthetic experience, tragedy, to function as an existential strategy.[26] Only at a late point in recomposing his ideas did Nietzsche gloss his theory as a contribution to *der aesthetischen Wissenschaft*.

If we nonetheless look to either *BT* or Nietzsche's later writings for a set of views answering to the traditional concerns of aesthetic theory, we find ourselves attributing to Nietzsche a position which, though highly original, seems no less problematic. In *BT* Nietzsche appears to centre the whole of aesthetic theory on the single case of (Greek) tragedy, a methodological decision which hardly seems justifiable, while the Apollonian/Dionysian distinction itself appears to simply cut the sphere of art down the middle, implying as it does that Apollonian art and Dionysian art are essentially different classes of phenomena, contingently joined in Greek tragedy and thereafter merely confused in artistic practice and mistaken for two species of a single genus.[27] Furthermore, though Nietzsche openly repudiates traditional conceptions of the aesthetic,[28] he nowhere addresses in any depth the familiar themes of a Kantian analytic and deduction, even while appearing to wish to retain traditional aesthetic tenets concerning the differentiation of beauty from the merely agreeable and the aesthetic's presupposition of contemplativeness.[29]

Despite his failure to engage with the task of securing objectivity for aesthetic judgements and qualities, Nietzsche gives no sign that he understands his own first-order assessments of works of art as having merely subjective or private validity. If we pose the question

---

[26] ZVT1 and ZVT2 (Jan.–Feb. 1870), DW (Summer 1870), GTG (June 1870), and ST (June 1871).

[27] Nietzsche affirms a 'yawning abyss between the Apollonian plastic arts and Dionysian music' (*BT* 16 [III.1: 99]).

[28] On the Kantian doctrine of disinterestedness, see Nietzsche's remarks in the *Nachlaß* 1883 [VII.1: 251], *Nachlaß* 1886–7 [VIII.1: 225], *Nachlaß* 1888, N4, §812, p. 430 [VIII.3: 90], and the fuller discussion in GM III: 6. See also Nietzsche's criticism, in *Nachlaß* 1872, N3, no. 155, p. 53 [III.4: 153–4], of Schopenhauer's theory of the contemplation of 'ideas'. In *BT* 5 [III.1: 39], Nietzsche writes that 'we cannot imagine a truly artistic creation [. . .] without a pure and disinterested contemplation [*ohne reines interesseloses Anschauen*]', which as Tanner observes (*BT* 120 n.16) must be regarded as a lapse (though only at the level of terminology, since what Nietzsche has in mind, the context shows, is simply the sublation of the empirical will of the individual artist in Nietzsche's artist's metaphysics). The following section will cite further instances of Nietzsche's departure from and criticism of eighteenth-century and Kantian aesthetic orthodoxy.

[29] *Nachlaß* 1886–7 [VIII.1: 225–6]: the contemplative state is 'a presupposition' of the aesthetic.

of how Nietzsche wishes to understand aesthetic judgement, the answer strongly invited by Nietzsche's repeated use of baldly causal imagery—his characterizations of the aesthetic object–subject relation in terms of physiological stimulation, intoxication, sexual arousal, etc.[30]—is that it is a judgement of the causal capacity of an object to modify subjective states, specifically, to strengthen a subject's life force, raise its quantum of will to power, or increase its degree of 'health'. And for obvious reasons, such an analysis holds on the face of it limited interest: it fails to distinguish objects that engender aesthetic responses from other stimulative sensory objects which charge up desire, such as erotic and exhortative images, and it does not address the key question of how the causal relation comes to be normatively inflected.[31] Even if our general interpretation of Nietzsche is as a philosophical naturalist, it will be hard to see how he avoids lagging far behind Hume on the present score.

That Nietzsche should wish to affirm central elements of the traditional conception of the aesthetic, while rejecting wholesale the theories that have been offered of them in favour of a reductive naturalistic construal, makes his position very puzzling.[32] Ultimately it may seem that Nietzsche has his eye trained so exclusively on the question of the *point* of the aesthetic, of what art is *for*, in neglect of the more basic question of what art and the aesthetic *are*, that he ends up with a crudely functional conception of art and the aesthetic.[33] Croce's negative verdict on Nietzsche's contribution to aesthetics—that it does not bear serious scrutiny—accordingly looms.

There is no quick solution to the puzzle of Nietzsche's relation to traditional aesthetic theory. The same difficulty reveals itself, of course, in his relation to traditional epistemology and moral theory, and in what follows I hope to show that, just as Nietzsche's discussions of truth and value can be shown to have bearing on traditional understandings of those concepts, the same is true of Nietzsche's conception of art and the aesthetic: though in part Nietzsche wants to decline the questions which the traditional positions in aesthetics are intended to answer, his aesthetic outlook is not completely dissociated from traditional concerns.

---

[30] Such passages are numerous. See, e.g., *Nachlaß* 1872, N3, no. 52, p. 18 [III.4: 24]: advanced physiology will 'certainly comprehend the artistic powers', and *Nachlaß* 1887, N4, §805, p. 424 [VIII.1: 336]: the 'demand for art is an indirect demand for the ecstasies of sexuality communicated to the brain'; and §815, p. 432 [VIII.3: 410]: the force expended in artistic conception is 'the same as that expended in the sexual act'.

[31] Menke (1998: 149–51) affirms that the model of bare causal connection can be found in Nietzsche. Heidegger emphasizes how uninteresting Nietzsche's position becomes on a bald naturalist construal (1991: 92–3), and takes this as a reason for construing 'biology' and 'life' as terms of metaphysics (1991: 114, 219). Faas 2002 offers a strongly naturalistic construal of Nietzsche's aesthetics.

[32] See Hill 2003: 107–8. Nietzsche's account of the creation of beauty is strikingly negative—making things beautiful, Nietzsche says time and again, involves selection, exclusion, deletion of features. It involves also addition and fabrication (*GS* 299), but nothing is said about the particular character of the supplements.

[33] As Schacht puts it (2001: 192): 'Nietzsche in *The Birth of Tragedy* thinks of what art *is* in terms of what art *does* and how art *does it*.'

5 Reconstructing Nietzsche's Aesthetic Theory: Preliminaries

The reconstruction which I am going to sketch in the rest of this paper is designed to complete the two tasks which the preceding discussion has brought to light: Nietzsche's philosophical aestheticism needs to be explained in terms which prescind from *BT* and show it to be present in all phases of Nietzsche's development, and his conception of the aesthetic should be shown to stand in an intelligible relation to the concerns of traditional aesthetic theory. I begin in this section with some basic points concerning Nietzsche's aesthetic outlook.

In the first instance, we should remind ourselves of Nietzsche's non-traditional conception of philosophical enquiry.

On Nietzsche's view, the agenda of philosophical reflection is properly determined by a practical-existential imperative, which circumscribes what counts as a philosophical explanandum. In this light, Nietzsche may be regarded as in the first instance setting aside enquiry that pursues the traditional question of what constitutes and makes possible the 'judgement of taste', on the grounds that it lacks direct connection with our (true, proper) practical-existential interests and, more strongly, that the orientation which it expresses runs counter to those interests. The traditional problem of the objectivity of aesthetic judgement arises from a wish to be able to regard our aesthetic assessments as *object-tracking*, as exhibiting a judgement-to-world direction of fit. This concern presupposes, however, a stance towards our aesthetic judgements which, on Nietzsche's view, occludes their practical significance—it amounts to an attempt to relieve ourselves of a normative burden, to remove ourselves from the equation, by laying aesthetic responsibility on the object.[34] This means, not that notions of objectivity are without application to aesthetic matters, but that the senses of correctness of judgement which should matter to us in aesthetic contexts are ones that are strictly internal to our practically determined first-order engagement with works of art.[35] What Nietzsche rejects, in other words, is the eighteenth-century and Kantian idea that the contribution of the aesthetic to man's vocation can be elucidated by rendering theoretically perspicuous its distinctive rationality through second-order reflection: Nietzsche denies that there exists some set of special principles governing aesthetic judgement and reason-giving which philosophical reflection can bring to light by bracketing our practical orientations; there is, on his account, no universal, decontextualized, non-local conception to be formed of what it is to 'get it right' in the aesthetic sphere.

The next set of points bears on Nietzsche's view of the *locus* of the aesthetic. We find in Nietzsche's writings, particularly after *BT*, disparate remarks on the identity of works of art,

---

[34] More generally, Nietzsche rejects the existential orientation which underlies epistemology: 'The demand that one wants by all means that something should be firm [. . .] that *instinct of weakness*' (*GS* 347 [V.2: 264]). See also *HAH* III: 16 [IV.3: 188].

[35] *GS* 370 [V.2: 303]: 'Regarding all aesthetic values I now avail myself of this main distinction: I ask in every instance, "is it hunger or superabundance that has here become creative?"'. To get an understanding of what critical disputes look like when understood pursued in this practical light, see how Nietzsche conducts his argument with Wagnerians, in *CW*, esp. §11 and the First and Second Postscripts—'the best among Wagner's admirers [. . .] are simply right to admire Wagner. They share the same instinct' (*CW* 11 [VI.3: 32])—and in *GS* 368.

the relation of the work to the artist, and the artist's relation to the spectator/auditor, the cumulative force of which is to imply an unfamiliar view of *what it is*, fundamentally, that is aesthetic.

To begin with one of Nietzsche's more easily comprehended claims: Nietzsche insists repeatedly on the importance of the standpoint of the artist, saying in criticism of Kant and Schopenhauer that they accord a false primacy to that of the spectator.[36] This methodological point is accompanied by explicitly ontological claims. In a section of *HAH* titled 'Against the Art of Works of Art [*Gegen die Kunst der Kunstwerke*]', Nietzsche distinguishes (i) art in the sense of a 'great, indeed immense task [*übergrossen Aufgabe der Kunst*]', which is undertaken with respect to oneself and consists of a transformation of one's powers, and (ii) the quite distinct sense of 'what is usually termed art, *that of the work of art* [*die sogen-annte eigentliche Kunst, die der Kunstwerke*]'. Nietzsche adds that we usually, misguidedly, direct our attention to the latter, although it is in fact a 'mere *appendage* [*nur ein Anhängsel*]' (*HAH* II: 174).[37] The two are connected since, Nietzsche allows, one who has completed the 'task' of art in the first sense will 'seek to discharge' their subjective state in the creation of a *Kunstwerk*, but a clear distinction is made.

In other places—drawing the same line, but using different labels—Nietzsche veers towards a Collingwoodian ontology whereby the (real) 'work of art' is a *state* of the artist, or a construction within the artist's subjectivity.[38] This coheres with Nietzsche's remarks on how the appreciation of a work of art involves a reproduction, recapitulation, or retrieval of the artist's subjectivity: the spectator should 'become' the artist.[39]

The reason why these points are so important for Nietzsche is that he wants to think of the creation and reception of art in terms of a *real*, *extra*-imaginative activity of self-trans-formation, and of what it is to *grasp* a work of art, not as a matter of processing sensible form and representational content—this 'appreciative' activity belongs for him to a merely pre-liminary, strictly *pre*-artistic stage—but as an existential operation.[40] There is, connectedly, a sense in which for Nietzsche the true protagonist of every tragic work of art—the one who

---

[36] *Nachlaß* 1873, *N3*, no. 48, pp. 108–9 [III.4: 320]: the artist is first of all (like the philosopher) 'for himself': 'every work of art is first turned toward the artist and then toward other men'. See also the criticism of Schopenhauer as excluding the artist's experience, *Nachlaß* 1885–6, *N5*, no. 2 [110], pp. 80–2 [VIII.1: 113–14], and *Nachlaß* 1888, *N4*, §811, p. 429 [VIII.3: 149]: 'Our aesthetics hitherto has been a woman's aesthetics to the extent that only the receivers of art have formulated their experience of "what is beautiful?" In all philosophy hitherto the artist is lacking'.

[37] In *HAH* I: 221 [IV.2: 185], Nietzsche identifies 'the actual artistic deed' ['*die eigentlich künstlerische That*'] with 'the harnessing of the powers of representation', 'the mastering of all the expedients of art and their organization'. See also *D* 548.

[38] In the *Nachlaß* 1872, *N3*, no. 106, pp. 38–9 [III.4: 55], Nietzsche compares the existence of the work of art to the (as he here understands it) intrasubjective existence of the world in Kantian idealism: the work of art exists for a spectator 'only to the extent that he is himself an artist as well and contributes the forms [to the work]. He could boldly assert, "the work of art has no reality outside of my brain"'. Nietzsche again detaches the aesthetic from its traditional moorings in the aesthetic object when he reconceives scientific knowledge and the world qua object thereof as beautiful: see *D* 550.

[39] *Nachlaß* 1876–7, IV.2: 561: 'Will man über *Kunst* Erfahrungen machen, so mache man einige Kunstwerke, es giebt keinen anderen Weg zum aesthetischen Urtheil'. And the *Nachlaß* 1888: 'the effect of works of art is to *excite the state that creates art* [*die Wirkung der Kunstwerke ist die Erregung des kunstschaffenden Zustandes*]' (*N4*, §821, p. 434 [VIII.3: 33]).

[40] E.g., *Nachlaß* 1885–6, *N5*, no. 2 [110], p. 81 [VIII.1: 114].

overcomes and affirms—is *the tragic poet* himself.[41] And this in turn is connected closely with Nietzsche's redetermination of the *subject*—the artist and/or spectator—as the real aesthetic 'object': how we take the object to be aesthetically, as beautiful or whatever, is at the same time or really, according to Nietzsche, a way in which we take *ourselves* to be (a reflexive notion which goes back to *BT*'s artist's metaphysics: the One desired to behold *itself* in the form of beautiful illusion, and the Greeks experienced *themselves* as viewed from Olympus).[42]

6 THE AESTHETIC STATE

We come now to the concept which occupies the central position in Nietzsche's aesthetic theory: the idea of what Nietzsche most often calls, harking back to Schiller and perhaps borrowing the term consciously from him, *der ästhetische Zustand*, the *aesthetic state*—condition, constitution—of the subject.[43] This is what, on Nietzsche's view, is fundamentally and intrinsically 'aesthetic', its primary locus.[44]

In a note in the *Nachlaß* for autumn 1887 (thus at a notably late point in his development), under the heading '*Aesthetica*', Nietzsche gives one of his clearest and most explicit descriptions of the Aesthetic State:

> The states in which we put a *transfiguration and plenitude* [*eine **Verklärung und Fülle***] into things and work at shaping them until they reflect back to us our own plenitude and lust for life [*unsere eigene Fülle und Lebenslust*]: [. . .] *Three* elements above all: sexual drive, intoxication [*Rausch*], cruelty: all part of man's oldest *joy* in *festival*: all likewise predominant in the original 'artist'.
>
> Conversely: when we encounter things that show this transfiguration and plenitude, our animal existence responds with an *arousal of the spheres* where all those states of pleasure [*Lustzustände*] have their seat—and the mixture of these very delicate nuances of animal well-being and desires is the *aesthetic state* [*der **ästhetische Zustand***]. This state occurs only in natures capable of that generous and overflowing plenitude of bodily vigour; the primum mobile is always to be found there. The sober man, the weary man, the exhausted, the desiccated (e.g. a scholar), can receive absolutely nothing of art, because he does not have the

---

[41] *TI*: 'Expeditions of an Untimely Man' 24 [VI.3: 121–2]: the tragic poet displays 'the condition of *fearlessness* in the face of the fearsome and questionable'; what he communicates is '*of himself*' ['*von sich*'].

[42] See *Nachlaß* 1881, V.2: 358; *GS* 78, 107, 290; *TI*: 'Expeditions of an Untimely Man' 19–20; and *HAH* I: 149.One way of describing Nietzsche's innovation is to say that he, eschewing the object-attributive model of Kant's judgement of taste, applies to the aesthetic sphere as a whole the structure that Kant ascribes to the sublime—'true sublimity', Kant says, 'must be sought only in the mind of the judging person', as an attribute of the human subject qua 'mental attunement' or vocation (2000: Ak. 256, 245, and 264); and that, just as Kant's Analytic of the Sublime is intended to correct the 'subreption' whereby sublimity is (mis)attributed to the object in nature, so Nietzsche corrects the subreption whereby aesthetic value is (mis)attributed to objects other than ourselves. The connection of Nietzsche's theory of tragedy with Kant's dynamical sublime—noted by Hill (2003: 112)—deserves fuller exploration.

[43] See the use made of the '*ästhetischen Zustand*' in Schiller 1982: letters 20–1 and 23–4. Schiller also talks, equivalently, of the '*ästhetischen Verfassung*' or '*Stimmung*'.

[44] Heidegger (1991: 97–123) emphasizes the basicness for Nietzsche of the concept of the Aesthetic State.

primordial artistic force, the pressure of wealth: whoever cannot give, will equally receive nothing.

[…] Art reminds us of states of animal vigour; it is on the one hand a surplus and overflow of flourishing corporeality into the world of images and wishes; on the other, a rousing of the animal function through images and wishes of intensified life [*gesteigerten Lebens*]—a heightening of the feeling of life [*eine Erhöhung des Lebensgefühls*], a stimulus for it. (*Nachlaß* 1887, *N*5, no. 9 [102], pp. 159–60 [VIII.2: 57], translation modified)[45]

Though rooted in natural functions of the human organism, the Aesthetic State is not an immediate effect of our corporeal animal nature, rather it is taken up into the subject's self-determination—it is, Nietzsche goes on to say, directed towards 'perfection', defined as 'extraordinary expansion' of the 'feeling of power', the status which beings in their 'upward movement' strive to attain.[46]

The Aesthetic State is constituted by a cycle of projection and introjection: we invest the object with certain powers and properties, which it then restores to us in a heightened form. This sort of reciprocal structure again recalls *BT*'s account of the structure of Homeric consciousness, in which a point of view—the gods' vision of us from Olympus—is projected outwards in order to be reinternalized. The crucial difference is that in the Aesthetic State as Nietzsche now conceives it, the structure has been brought down to earth and requires no conceptual step outside the orbit of subjectivity. The Aesthetic State comprises a self-enclosed dynamic structure in which the two terms of the relation, the state of the subject and the appearance of the object, reinforce one another directly and in a manner which is normative as much as causal—the subject's aesthetic pro-attitude to the object and the object's aesthetic appearance, which is sponsored by and refers back to the subject, rationalize and *validate* one another, and it is because they do so that the Aesthetic State is able to carry conviction for the one who occupies it. The further robustness of the Aesthetic State is owed to the fact that it conditions the reflection which takes place within it, and thereby determines a form of normative self-consciousness. Consequently it presupposes no descent into pre-normative animality and is not undermined by reflection. Because it is self-supporting, the Aesthetic State satisfies, or at any rate allays, our need for categorical, unconditional normativity, identified by Nietzsche as a source of otherworldly, life-negating conceptual hallucinations.[47]

The second key dimension of the Aesthetic State lies in the tension maintained within it between, on the one hand, Apollonian appearance and on the other, the Dionysian reality which has been extruded but which persists as an object of subliminal awareness: a 'tremendous *expulsion* [*ungeheures Heraustreiben*]' is involved in idealization (*TI*: 'Expeditions of an Untimely Man' 8 [VI.3: 110]), and 'appearance is given the most profound significance,

---

[45] See also *TI*: 'Expeditions of an Untimely Man' 9. On what Nietzsche's notion of 'overflowing' amounts to, see Richardson 1996: 113–15.

[46] *Nachlaß* 1887, *N*5, no. 9 [102], p. 160 [VIII.2: 57].

[47] See *GM* II: 19–22. Regarding unconditional normativity, see the parable of the camel and the 'great dragon' of 'Thou shalt', in *Z* I: 'Of the Three Metamorphoses' [VI.1: 23–6]. That the Aesthetic State takes its place is implied by *EH*: 'Thus Spoke Zarathustra' 6 and 8, where Zarathustra is defined by a *'supreme deed'* compared to which all the rest of human activity seems 'poor and conditional' ([VI.3: 341]), and is identified with the Dionysian.

through Dionysus' (*Nachlaß* 1885–6, N5, no. 2 [110], pp. 80–2 [VIII.1: 114]). The compelling quality of aesthetic appearance thus derives from what it excludes, in something like the way that Freud conceives conscious representatives of repressed contents, such as symbols, as recruiting their force and significance from the repressed. The Aesthetic State thus demands a form of double vision.[48] What makes it coherent and stable is the subject's abiding awareness of the contribution made by its own aestheticizing activity, its sense of itself as overflowing into and shaping things, hence as exercising 'power' over them.

This allows us to see that, although Nietzsche's interest in art and the aesthetic after *BT* might seem to have become independent of tragedy, this is not really the case. Nietzsche ceases to focus and pin his hopes on (Wagner's) tragic drama, but he continues to regard the structure which is explicit in the experience of tragedy as the *implicit form* of aesthetic experience in general. In this way it becomes intelligible that Nietzsche should have supposed in *BT* that tragedy supplies the archetype of the aesthetic as such. The beginnings of a Nietzschean account of what distinguishes the beautiful from the agreeable, and of what aesthetic disinterestedness amounts to, can also be seen here: beautiful objects are invested with a particular complex kind of self-relation which objects of mere sensational gratification do not exhibit, and their apprehension involves a mode of satisfaction which requires that the object be held at a mirroring distance, rather than appropriated or consumed. Finally, the normatively substantial Aesthetic State offers an interpretation of the cryptic formula concerning aesthetic world justification employed in *BT*: for the world to be 'justified as an aesthetic phenomenon' just *is* for us to be in the Aesthetic State.

Earlier we noted Nietzsche's indifference to the problems set by the traditionally conceived judgement of taste. It may now be observed that what for Nietzsche most deserves the title 'aesthetic judgement' is in fact the life-affirmative judgement which he thinks stands at the core of the Aesthetic State, mediating the connection between the object and the subjective increase of life force. Though Nietzsche is of course not an aesthetic cognitivist, it is very important to grasp that he considers that our experience of art is necessarily *taken* by us as an experience or representation of *how the world is*: aesthetic response to a work of art is directly—i.e., without any need for inference or extrapolation through relations of 'verisimilitude', and not necessarily by virtue of anything pertaining to its representational content—an awareness *of the world* as being thus-and-so in relation to possibilities of life. Works of art construct 'art worlds', *Kunstwelten*.[49] Nietzsche is thus opposed to any view of the aesthetic as an autonomous formal domain, and the judgement at the heart of the Aesthetic State is quite different from any Kantian '*Beurtheilung des Gegenstandes*'. Aesthetic judgement in that traditional sense, viz. an estimation (*Schätzung*) of an object, is for Nietzsche a judgement of the object's capacity to modify *by means of the cognitive*

---

[48] Nietzsche's model for which is 'waking dream', the original condition of the Homeric Greeks, or willing to 'dream on'. See *BT* 1 and 4 [III.1: 23, 34] and also *UM* IV: 7 [IV.1: 42] and *GS* 59.

[49] E.g. *BT* 1 [III.1: 22]. *HAH* III: 156 [IV.3: 255] provides an illustration: 'music is taken to be an image of all human life and action'. On this point I differ from Schacht, who proposes that Nietzsche's *Kunstwelten* involve no strictly cognitive projection, but merely 'experiential character' (2001: 193, 207). In support of the cognitive construal, see *Nachlaß* 1887, N4, §804, p. 424 [VIII.2: 221]: 'To experience a thing as beautiful means: to experience it necessarily wrongly [*nothwendig falsch*]', and Nietzsche's affirmation that valuation presupposes 'a great deal of *belief*' (*Nachlaß* 1887, N4, §507, p. 276 [VIII.2: 16]).

claim we take to be projected by it—and so in a way that involves some thought of our being *in the right*—the subject's degree of interest in life, its *Lebensgefühl*. Nietzsche accordingly describes aesthetic judgements as (backward-looking) *'residues [Überreste]'* of judgements of happiness (*Nachlaß* 1881, V.2: 483),[50] and endorses Stendhal's definition of beauty as a (forward-looking) *'promesse de bonheur'.*[51]

The Aesthetic State stands therefore at the interstice of theoretical and practical reason: it contains a sort of rudimentary cognition, one which is independent of theoretical reason, and it ignites certain practical orientations, though without itself comprising any determinate practical judgement; it is proto-cognitive and pre-practical.[52] Regarding the means by which works of art achieve this effect, Nietzsche's view is that the process resists rational reconstruction: we know that art talks us into life, but—as when we are exposed to powerful rhetoric—the trick eludes us whereby a state of mind which it would previously have seemed impossible for us to enjoy is successfully induced in us. Hence the inexplicability of tragedy.

7 VALIDATION OF THE AESTHETIC STATE

The Aesthetic State, we have said, appears on its inside self-validating and substantial, by virtue of the reciprocal authorization of object and subjective state. But more is needed if it is to be integrated with philosophical reflection in the way that, I suggested, Nietzsche envisages. Nietzsche has made the attractiveness of the Aesthetic State sufficiently plain for it to be recommended as a psychological instrument, a prophylaxis for those who feel the threat of nihilism and perhaps a mood-altering treatment for those who have fallen victim to despair. The problem lies in the fact that, for as long as our estimate of the value of human existence remains the same as Schopenhauer's, the life-affirmative world characterization of

---

[50] Note that Nietzsche refers to happiness, *Glück*, not pleasure, *Lust*.

[51] *GM* III: 6 [VI.2: 365]. Also *D* 433 [V.1: 270]: 'beauty in art is always to be understood as the *imitation of happiness*'. Aesthetic normativity thus pertains primarily to the aesthetic response (e.g., *UM* IV: 5 [IV.1: 28]: what is audible in German music is *'right feeling [die richtige Empfindung]'*). What Nietzsche does not bother with philosophically is rightness as a property of the *relation* between the response and the object that elicits it (the feeling's being *right for that particular object*).

[52] Though in this sense 'primitive', the Aesthetic State is not envisaged by Nietzsche as taking on a properly *foundational* role. When Nietzsche talks of uncovering 'aesthetic judgements' at the root of moral values (e.g. *Nachlaß* 1881, V.2: 369 and V.2: 372), this usually pertains to his diagnostic-critical project. It is true, however, that Nietzsche also formulates the idea of a '*Reduktion der Moral auf Aesthetik*' and talks of aesthetically justified value judgements as the 'measure of things' for an individual (*Nachlaß* 1881, V.2: 369). What this amounts to is a question concerning Nietzsche's metaethics, and all that needs to be observed here regarding the connection of the Aesthetic State with moral valuation and valuing per se is that, though it is an implication of my account that the Aesthetic State *conditions* the valuations of one who has achieved it—in particular: it will engender appreciation that valuing is *itself* valuable, 'is itself the value and jewel of all valued things' (*Z* I: 'Of a Thousand and One Goals' [VI.1: 71])—it does not follow that Nietzsche *collapses* moral into aesthetic values or intends to provide a new, aesthetic basis for determining values. Showing that the relation Nietzsche envisages of morality with the aesthetic is in any case highly complex, see the highly idiosyncratic use of the notion of 'taste' in *EH*: 'Why I am So Clever' 8 [VI.3: 289–90]. For relevant discussion, see Hussain 2007 and Poellner 2007.

the Aesthetic State lacks *truth*. We can bring the problem into focus if we return to the artist's metaphysics of *BT*.

The logical point of Nietzsche's art-metaphysical story, I argued, was to provide a *warrant* for assent to tragic and, more generally, Apollonian representation, in view of the Apollonian violation of epistemic norms. The warrant was supplied in *BT* by Nietzsche's metaphysical conception of the telos of Nature—the primal One longs to behold itself in beautiful illusion. Nietzsche's account of the Aesthetic State provides a radical simplification of this story: the end which Nietzsche's artist's metaphysics attributes to the supra-personal One is reattributed to *ourselves*. On the face of it, this has a clear justification: if there was reason for us to aid and abet the *One's* realization of the desire for illusion which stems from its 'longing'—if we could share in its motivation—then by parity of argument there must be reason for us, directly on the basis of our *own* longing, to entertain and inhabit the illusory representations that are needed to make life possible for us; the supra-personal middle man can be eliminated through a Copernican shift of viewpoint.

This contraction of a neo-Schopenhauerian metaphysics into an account of our authorization to occupy the Aesthetic State achieves greater economy, but it gives rise to the problem that if we assume for ourselves the One's *right* to redemption through illusion, then we also assume the *problem* of the self-deceptive intention which the desire for illusion entails. So long as the desire for illusion was attributed to a third party, we could regard ourselves as merely put in its service, but we are now required to avow the intention to embrace an illusion as our own. In other words, we seem to be back with the original problem of Apollonian culture faced with Dionysian truth. Since, from outside the Aesthetic State, it continues to seem to us that the truth of our situation is recorded in the verdict of Silenus, how we can regard the Aesthetic State as legitimate?[53]

In order to see how Nietzsche may be thought to have dealt with this problem—which preoccupied him intensively—we need to examine Nietzsche's view of the epistemological significance of the aesthetic.

Nietzsche's assertions concerning the relation of art to 'truth', 'lies', 'illusion', 'deception', and so on are numerous and striking, and it can seem that Nietzsche entertains a range of conflicting views concerning the epistemological significance of the aesthetic, his real position on this matter being as hard to pin down as his real position on general questions of epistemology. As I observed in the introduction, for some commentators the writings of the *BT* period promote a view of art as grasping a deep metaphysical truth inaccessible to science,[54] while the apparent proximity in Nietzsche's writings of a high valuation of art with sceptical pronouncements has

---

[53] Megill puts it well: 'Perhaps we *could* enter the particular interior space that Nietzsche has constructed for us, just as we can enter the interior space that is offered to us by almost any work of art. But why *should* we?' (1985: 101). Megill considers that Nietzsche has no good answer to this question— 'though we may visit the aesthetic world, we cannot live in it' (1985: 102)—but his verdict turns on the point that the Aesthetic State is not grounded in theoretical reason: Nietzsche's aestheticism would succeed, according to Megill, only if 'it could be shown that the world really is an aesthetic phenomenon' (1985: 102). What I will go on to argue is meant to reply to Megill.

[54] For the reading of *BT* as advancing metaphysical or 'ontological' truth, see Schaeffer (2000: 213–17), Fink (2003: 9–10, 13, 22–3), Hammermeister (2002: 143–4), and of course Heidegger (1991). According to Heidegger, Nietzsche's final aim is to 'ground anew the manner in which values are posited', which requires that it first be made clear 'what constitutes Being', a task which leads to Nietzsche's conception of will to power as art (1991: 31, 215–17).

led others to think that the crux of Nietzsche's philosophy as a whole consists in a conjunction of aestheticism with radical anti-realism, his perspectivism amounting to an equation of cognition in general with artistic creation.[55] The interpretative situation is perplexing, but I think that, if we work through Nietzsche's comments on the relation of art to truth, we discover a consistent view which corresponds to neither of those just described, involves no extreme epistemological claims, and remains unchanged between *BT* and Nietzsche's later writings.

Nietzsche does regard his promulgation of the artist's metaphysics as presupposing a criticism of science, but his reservations about science are neither exclusively nor ultimately epistemological, and the epistemological limitations of science that he does assert, and that are needed for his argument, are highly restricted.

Nietzsche's view in *BT* is that it is necessary, in order for art to acquire the authority that it requires in order for it to be able to perform its function, that the value of science be circumscribed in two ways. Nietzsche's *existential* criticism of science is that its Socratic optimism has ended in disappointment.[56] His *epistemological* criticism is that science cannot achieve its goal of knowing the world *through and through*—one cannot, he says, dig to the antipode, and the (Kantian-Faustian) 'noble, gifted' man of science reaches the present peripheral boundary of human knowledge only to find that it 'twists around itself and finally bites itself in the tail' (*BT* 15 [III.1: 94, 97]). This epistemological criticism involves, however, nothing more drastic than the familiar Kantian, Critical idea that empirical knowledge has necessary limits. As the imagery of cognitive 'boundary' and antinomial tail-biting suggests, it is only the metaphysical *reach* of scientific cognition, its pretension to transcendental reality, that is in question; scepticism regarding the truth of scientific claims is not the issue.

How are the two criticisms of science connected? And why does Nietzsche need to enter any epistemological reservations at all about science? Epistemological reservations would obviously be needed if the artist's metaphysics were intended as metaphysical truth, but I have argued that this strategy, explicit in Schopenhauer, is not Nietzsche's—his metaphysics of Dionysian Oneness are only light-images in the form of practical postulates. And in any case, it might be suggested, the incapacity of science to sponsor values sufficient for human flourishing, emphasized later in *GM*'s Third Essay, entails that science, whether epistemologically successful or not, fails to supply an effective existential strategy, and so suffices to make room for art.

---

[55] See the references in note 2 above. Though I have described the metaphysical and anti-realist interpretations as opposed, in some accounts the two lines of thought rather strangely run into one another. This twist is found in Heidegger, insofar as he interprets Nietzsche's perspectivism ontologically rather than epistemologically: 'Reality, Being, is *Schein* in the sense of perspectival letting-shine. But proper to that reality at the same time is the multiplicity of perspectives' (1991: 215). A similar identification of the relativity of truth with an ontological thesis occurs in Ferry's interpretation of Nietzsche: in the aestheticism of Nietzsche's maturity, where art is conceived as 'the will to power's only adequate expression' (1993: 176), 'art continues for Nietzsche to maintain a direct link to *truth*. The true has [...] become the pure *difference* that is the multiplicity of vital forces' (158); Nietzsche's 'classicism of *difference*' is 'an invitation to think of art as the expression of a "reality", no longer of Being, but of Becoming' (188). Also involved, according to Ferry, is Nietzsche's radical individualism, which makes 'of the individual an absolute value, and first of all an ontological principle' (1993: 159).

[56] See *BT* 14–15 [III.1: 88–98], where the 'sublime metaphysical illusion' of Socratic optimism is exposed. See also *Nachlaß* 1872, N3, pp. 61–6 [III.2: 249–54].

The epistemological criticism of science is, nonetheless, of high importance for Nietzsche. In the first place, even when the artist's metaphysics are understood as practical postulates rather than metaphysical truths, some epistemological restriction of science is required: if the domain of human knowledge were filled entirely by science, then there would be, so to speak, no empty cognitive space for us to postulate the artist's metaphysics into. Second, and more importantly, epistemological reservations are necessary for Nietzsche's existential criticism, or at least for that criticism to be presented in the strong form that he wants, because on his full story, the *final* aim of science is not to gain unrestricted knowledge of reality, but to *thereby* 'correct being': Socrates's mission was 'to make existence appear intelligible and *consequently* justified', and science aimed to do this by demonstrating the 'lawfulness' of the world (*BT* 15 [III.1: 95–6]; italics added). The ultimate epistemological failure of science thus guarantees its existential failure.

Discrediting science's aim of achieving complete cognition is necessary, therefore, not in order that a case can be made for art's *cognitive* significance, but in order that the case can be made that art fulfils the *real, existential aim of science itself*. This explains why Nietzsche should say, in discussion of whether there is any hope of tragedy holding its own in contexts, such as our own, where the Socratic theoretical stance prevails, that this is possible '*only after* the scientific spirit has been taken to its limits, and has been forced by the demonstration of those limits to renounce its claim to universal validity' (*BT* 17 [III.1: 107]; italics added).

In *BT* Nietzsche is, we have just seen, far from collapsing scientific knowledge or truth as such into artistic creation, or deriving the authority of art from global scepticism, and nor does he affirm there the epistemological superiority of art. When Nietzsche does talk in *BT* of a deep truth inaccessible to science, he is referring to the Silenus–Schopenhauerian *existential* truth of the suffering-filled, *sinnlos* character of human life, and when 'science' appears to be criticized in *BT*, the target is Socratic optimism, belief *in* science, not scientific beliefs.[57]

This attitude is maintained throughout Nietzsche's writings.[58] Nietzsche consistently regards art as illusion in the sense that, even though aesthetic representations themselves are non-doxastic, they nonetheless *induce* beliefs which are either contradicted or not supported by the deliverances of our theoretical reason.[59] What distinguishes art from plain

[57] E.g. *BT* 7 [III.1: 53], regarding the shared knowledge of Dionysian man and Hamlet: 'True understanding, insight into the terrible truth' ['*die wahre Erkenntniss, der Einblick in die grauenhafte Wahrheit*'].

[58] Which is not to deny that Nietzsche also experiments with other views, including the association of aestheticism with epistemological nihilism. For example: 'Where one can know nothing that is true, there the lie is permitted', *Nachlaß* 1872, N3, no. 70, p. 27 [III.4: 40]. And *Nachlaß* 1873 (notes for the 'Truth and Lies' paper), N3, no. 187, p. 97 [III.4: 241]: 'Truth cannot be recognized. Everything which is knowable is illusion. The significance of art as truthful illusion'. Clark (1990: 95–6) connects Nietzsche's view of art in *BT* with the denial of truth, but this is because she reads into *BT* the view of truth found in Nietzsche's 'Truth and Lies' essay; the two texts differ, she says, 'only in relation to *BT*'s claim that Dionysian experience alone gives access to things-in-themselves' (1990: 90). Cf. Richardson 1996: 254–5 on the covert 'priority' of the will to truth in *BT*.

[59] That Nietzsche thinks that art *does* involve belief is quite clear: see, e.g., ZVT1, III.2: 11–12; *GS* 81 and 106, on how art makes ideas be believed. *CW* 8 [VI.3: 25]: 'Wagner's music is never true. But *it is taken for true*'.

theoretical falsehood, and allows it to achieve the status of non-deceptive or 'truthful' illusion, is simply the fact that art presents itself explicitly *as* illusory: art induces false belief, but it also expresses a compensating second-order truth, for it 'says' of the beliefs that it engenders that they are false.[60]

Now it may be asked: If this is Nietzsche's position on the epistemology of the aesthetic— if he neither ascribes higher truth to art, nor denies truth to science—how then can he resolve the problem of the self-deceptive intent which, once the artist's metaphysics have been Copernicanized into the Aesthetic State, his account seems to require: since, after all, even knowing that art is illusion and that art is truthful in telling us that its representations are false, it seems that we still need to go ahead and *believe* or somehow *assent to* those representations, if art is to fulfil its existential function.

The answer, I suggest, is that Nietzsche leaves the formal doxastic contradiction *unresolved*,[61] and instead constructs a view of our situation which allows us to self-deceive with a 'good conscience', i.e., which allows the necessary *normative* condition for our being able to enter the Aesthetic State to be fulfilled.[62] If theoretical reason had a monopoly on rationality, this would be impossible, but Nietzsche denies this. The relevant question for Nietzsche is instead: what, if anything, could make it rational (in a broad, not purely theoretical sense) for us to enter the illusory Aesthetic State? I suggest the following as Nietzsche's view.

In ways that have emerged, Nietzsche follows traditional practice in situating the aesthetic between the theoretical and the practical. And it is Nietzsche's view, I suggested earlier, that for all that we (as presently constituted) can determine, practical and theoretical reason are locked in an irresolvable conflict—for Nietzsche it is a final fact about our (present) philosophical horizon, that we can see no way of squaring the demands of our will to truth with those of life, even while it is not an option for us to give up on either truth or life.[63] In this contradictory situation, the aesthetic may be thought to assume a preeminent value. If theoretical and practical reason are in deadlock, and if this deadlock *must* be broken, then whatever we can do to keep going (meaning: to prevent the deadlock from stultifying life) has a rational warrant, a quasi-transcendental sanction. And one thing that we can do is to permit ourselves the Aesthetic State, which, according to the account suggested earlier, consists essentially in the non-theoretical, pre-practical projection of a liveable world and as such is fitted, perhaps uniquely, to play this crucial facilitative role. Moreover, having made this move, it will become possible for us to take up an affirmative attitude towards

---

[60] We find Nietzsche preoccupied with these distinctions in notes for the 'Truth and Lies' paper (*Nachlaß* 1873, N3, nos. 183–4, pp. 96–7 [III.4: 240–1]), where he sets out all the relevant considerations in an attempt to nail down the doxastic ambiguity of art.

[61] Nietzsche's model of 'waking dream' and willing to 'dream on' takes care of the question of psychological possibility: see note 60.

[62] *GS* 107 [V.2: 140]: 'art as the *good* will to appearance' ['**guten Willen** zum Scheine'], art furnishes us with 'the good conscience to be *able* to turn ourselves into such a[n aesthetic] phenomenon' ['*das gute Gewissen dazu gegeben, aus uns selber ein solches Phänomen machen zu* **können**']. See also *GM* III: 25 [VI.2: 420]: art is 'much more fundamentally opposed to the ascetic ideal than science is' because in art '*lying* sanctifies itself and the *will to deception* has good conscience on its side' ['*die Lüge sich heiligt, der* **Wille zur Täuschung** *das gute Gewissen zur Seite hat*'].

[63] As stated in *BT* 7 [III.1: 53]: 'something that Dionysian man shares with Hamlet: both have truly seen to the essence of things, they have *understood*, and action repels them […] Understanding kills action, action depends upon a veil of illusion'.

our situation: rather than regretting our conflict of truth with life, we will be in a position to celebrate being the peculiar kinds of creatures that we are, because in our new aesthetic self-apprehension, we will be able to see how the tension between our theoretical and practical reason makes us dynamic, experimental, creative, and—as if viewing ourselves from Olympus—aesthetically rewarding.

To summarize, Nietzsche's departure from the Kantian tradition inaugurated by the third *Critique* with regard to the role of the aesthetic as a mediator between theoretical and practical reason, consists in his employment of the aesthetic, not to effect a unification of freedom and nature within the subject (Schiller), nor to disclose the deep underlying unity of theoretical and practical reason and of freedom and nature (Schelling), but to *compensate* for its irremediable *disunity*. As Nietzsche puts it, employing his image of the post-Christian, post-Platonic free spirit as a taut bow: 'Art exists *so that the bow should not break* [***Damit der Bogen nicht breche, ist die Kunst da***]'.[64] In invoking the needs of practical reason to sanction the aesthetic, Nietzsche preserves its conflict with theoretical reason, the tension in the bow.

This comprises the first function envisaged by Nietzsche for the Aesthetic State in relation to theoretical and practical reason. But there is another, stronger ambition which Nietzsche also has for the aesthetic, and which is *therapeutic* rather than merely palliative.

The original problem which gave rise to the conflict of theoretical and practical reason, requiring aesthetic mediation, is the problem with which *GM*'s Third Essay concludes, and which Nietzsche there describes as driving the whole development of man—the problem of our need to find '*Sinn*', meaning, in our suffering; the existential problem described in *BT* as confronting the Greeks.[65] Nietzsche's view of the nature of this problem is not easily stated, but one thing which is clear is that, according to Nietzsche, the problem of *Sinn* needs to be reconceived, in a mode different from that in which the Platonic-Christian tradition has conceived it—that is, as we conceive it according to one or other version of the 'problem of evil', as requiring theodicy or some form of world 'correction'. Nietzsche's recasting of the problem of *Sinn* involves its *dissociation from theoretical reason*: it needs to be grasped anew in such a way that we cease to think of it as calling for or as being susceptible to a solution in theoretical reason. In terms of the formula of aesthetic justification employed in *BT*, the task is to reinterpret our need for *Sinn*— not merely reflectively, but at the deepest level at which we experience our needs as orientating us one way rather than another—in such a way that 'existence' is no longer felt to either require or be capable of receiving any justification other than an aesthetic justification.[66] If Nietzschean

[64] *UM* IV: 4 [IV.1: 24–5]: 'The greater grows the tension between general knowledge of things and the individual's spiritual-moral capacities [...]'; 'the greatness and indispensability of art lie precisely in its being able to produce the *appearance* of a simpler world, a shorter solution to the riddle of life. No one who suffers from life can do without this appearance, just as no one can do without sleep'. *BGE* Preface [VI.2: 4–5]: we exhibit a 'magnificent tension of the spirit the like of which had never yet existed on the earth: with so tense a bow we can now shoot for the most distant goals'. The metaphor is reemployed at *BGE* 206, 262 and in the Epode [VI.2: 138, 226, 254]. See also *HAH* II: 131. Nietzsche also uses a parallel musical image: 'If we could imagine dissonance becoming man—and what else is man?' (*BT* 25 [III.1: 151]).

[65] As made clear in *GM* II: 7 and 23, where *BT*'s account of the Apollonian existential strategy is recapitulated.

[66] Or no longer felt to require any justification at all—evidently, the notion of justification begins here to lose purchase. The important point in any case is that aesthetic 'justification' would not amount to an aesthetic *theodicy*, since it would not have *solved* the (theoretically construed) problem of evil, but rather left it behind.

aesthetic education could achieve this, then it would have got us *beyond* the deadlock of theoretical and practical reason, insofar as our practical life interests would no longer demand from theoretical reason anything that theoretical reason would find itself unable to supply. We would have educated ourselves out of the interpretation of our needs which originally made the aesthetic necessary for us, and the aesthetic sphere would have made itself self-sufficient, for it would now determine and fulfil its own end: the problem of discovering *Sinn* would have been converted wholesale into the task of realizing and sustaining the Aesthetic State, the self-justifying absoluteness of which would characterize the lives of aesthetically potent subjects. From such a perspective, the complaint that 'existence lacks *Sinn*' would do nothing but report a state of aesthetic impotence.[67]

8 The Aesthetic Significance of Philosophical Conceptions

On the account I have given, there is no abandonment of Nietzsche's early philosophical aestheticism after *BT*, merely a shift in its formulation and grounding. Now it may be asked why, if Nietzsche's view is as I have described it, he does not show himself to be more enthusiastic about art in his later writings, at least after the period of scientific hopefulness in

---

[67] If the Aesthetic State could become properly substantial in this way, then art would be strictly redundant (which is not, of course, to say that it would cease to exist). That Nietzsche has this in his sights is implied by the following passage: 'What if existence were nothing but an aesthetic phenomenon! [...] Whether we would then have such a thing as art? Whether the artist would ever have originated if man himself were a work of art? Whether the very existence of art does not prove that existence is an unaesthetic, evil, and serious phenomenon? Let us consider what a real thinker, Leopardi, says: It would truly be desirable for men not to need art' (*Nachlaß* 1875, N1, 'On Rhythm', 245). This element of contingency in the relation of art to the Aesthetic State is relevant to the point made in the following section. The issue of what precisely the therapeutic upshot of Nietzsche's aesthetic strategy comprises deserves further comment and involves a somewhat fine distinction. On my account, practical reason's success in wrenching itself away from theoretical reason and reconstruing its own needs, though it (causally, functionally) leaves the *deadlock* behind, still does not (normatively) *dissolve* its conflict with theoretical reason: the original (normative) *conflict* persists, insofar as the strategy employed by practical reason has no theoretical authorization—it has not proceeded by way of any *insight* to the effect that it is a *mistake* concerning the very *nature* of values or *Sinn* to require their reality in a (metaphysical) sense recognizable to theoretical reason; and because theoretical reason has not relinquished its claims on practical reason, the 'resolution' of the conflict is one-sided, asymmetrical, and non-reciprocal, and philosophical reason as a whole has not achieved unity. Put differently, practical reason effects through its aesthetic self-education a kind of change of identity, which philosophical reason must endorse insofar as it serves the interests of practical reason, but what cannot be claimed (as I read Nietzsche) is that this development is *rational* in any further, more comprehensive sense, since it does not issue from a realization that practical reason's earlier self-conception was *erroneous*. On this point I differ from Poellner (2007), who tends to suggest that Nietzsche considers that the primacy of practical reason can be invoked as a direct and sufficient ground for (comprehensively rationally justified) indifference to questions of the metaphysical reality of values. On my account, it is because Nietzsche does not think that appeal to the primacy of the practical can be expected to deliver such a result, that he considers the aesthetic turn necessary.

HAH had passed, whereas what we in fact find, notwithstanding the reaffirmation of the aesthetic in *GS*, is an attitude towards art which remains very muted in comparison with *BT* and even includes some reiteration of *HAH*'s depreciation of art.[68]

The answer is that a distinction needs to be drawn between Nietzsche's conception of the Aesthetic State and his view of what can effect its realization. In the 1880s Nietzsche maintains the reservations articulated in *HAH* regarding the real possibility of the emergence and appreciation of forms of art that will discharge their required existential function: he continues to regard our artistic culture as irremediably corrupt. This disenchantment with contemporary artistic practice and sensibility implies that a new 'home' should be found for the Aesthetic State, and this leads Nietzsche to cut loose the Aesthetic State from art to a large extent and to associate it instead, at least experimentally, with *philosophical* conception. The composition of *Zarathustra*, a poetico-philosophical hybrid, gives evidence of this, but the development is visible also, I suggest, in Nietzsche's doctrines of will to power and eternal recurrence. Nietzsche is firmly of the view that ideas themselves have, non-accidentally, an aesthetic character: theories, for Nietzsche, are things that we, as well as 'holding true', also *experience* in a rich sense of the word, and by means of which an experience of the world is determined; every successful ideational structure has its own landscape, its own way of *depicting*, in addition to propositionally specifying, how things are.[69] Thus at least part of the (by Nietzsche's lights, properly philosophical) significance of the conception of the world as will to power and as recurring eternally lies in the particular aspectual shape, the shading, affective colouring or 'feel' that it gives to the world conceived in its conceptual light. One may correctly speak of these doctrines as continuous, in terms of their position and role in Nietzsche's project, with Greek tragedy, Wagner's music drama, and the prose of *Zarathustra*. It is thus no accident that when, in a lengthy passage in the late

[68] Some remarks in these later writings are clearly continuous with those of the positivist phase: compare *GM*, Essay III, §5, on the ascetic function of art, with *HAH* II: 148.

[69] In a way that Nietzsche's richly sensuous portraits of intellectual positions illustrate: see for example Nietzsche's description of the 'soft, good-natured, silver-glistening' ideational landscape, 'the dull lustre, the enigmatic Milky-Way shimmer', of German Idealism, in *D*190 [V.1: 163–4]. The notion that conceptual items may have aesthetic force goes right back to Nietzsche's early writings: see *Nachlaß* 1872, N3, esp. no. 53, p. 19 [III.4: 27]: 'Philosophy is a form of artistic invention [*eine Form der Dichtkunst*]'; though it uses the 'same means as science [*Wissenschaft*]', namely 'conceptual representation', it is 'invention beyond the limits of experience; it is the continuation of the *mythical drive*. It is thus essentially pictorial [*auch wesentlich in Bildern*]'. As shown by *Nachlaß* 1872, N3, nos. 54–5, pp. 19–20 [III.4: 28–9], this claim is bound up at that period with Nietzsche's theory of concepts as derived from images: the 'productivity of the intellect' can be 'a life in images [*ein Bilderleben*]' (*Nachlaß* 1872, N3, no. 62, p. 23 [III.4: 33]); the value of philosophy, despite the fact that 'it cannot prove itself as a scientific [*wissenschaftlicher*] construction', is that 'it continues to exist as a *work of art* [*Es ist als* **Kunstwerk** *noch vorhanden*]'—the 'aesthetic consideration is decisive, not the pure *knowledge drive* [*es entscheidet nicht der reine* **Erkenntnißtrieb**, *sondern der* **aesthetische**]'; 'the aesthetic value of such philosophizing, in its beauty and sublimity [*aesthetischen Werthe eines solchen Philosophirens, d.h. durch Schönheit und Erhabenheit*]'; the 'philosophy of Heraclitus possesses much more artistic value than do all the propositions of Aristotle' (*Nachlaß* 1872, N3, no. 61, p. 23 [III.4: 32]). Nietzsche tells us that the 'new [artist's] metaphysics' will 'rearrange the world for you with images' (*Nachlaß* 1872, N3, no. 56, p. 21 [III.4: 3]). After the *Critique of Pure Reason*, Nietzsche says, it is unlikely that belief in any mythological construction can be reawakened, but one can 'imagine a totally new type of *philosopher-artist* who fills the empty space with a *work of art*, possessing aesthetic value' (*Nachlaß* 1872, N3, no. 44, pp. 14–15 [III.4: 19]). On Nietzsche's pictorial characterization of belief systems, see Pippin 2010: ch. 3.

Nachlaß, Nietzsche gives us his answer to the question 'And do you know what "the world" is to me?'—namely: '*This world is will to power—and nothing besides!*', 'my Dionysian world'— he employs exactly the description given in *BT* of the Dionysian (*Nachlaß* 1885, N4, §1067, pp. 549–50 [VII.3: 338–9].),[70] and that, in another note from the same late period, eternal recurrence should be described as effecting the same vision of the world as Apollonian art, 'the most extreme *approximation of the world of becoming to one of being: pinnacle of contemplation*', 'eternalization' in illusion (*Nachlaß* 1886–7, N5, 7 [54], p. 138 [VIII.1: 320–1]).[71] The conjunction of will to power with eternal recurrence recapitulates, at the level of philosophical doctrine, the union of the Dionysian and Apollonian in *BT*'s artist's metaphysics.

9 CONCLUSION

The late development just described draws attention to an important respect in which Nietzsche's philosophical aestheticism is open to challenge from the standpoint of more orthodox post-Kantian aesthetic theory.

Nietzsche's decision to transfer the role of realizing the Aesthetic State from art to philosophy draws attention to the implausibility of his original supposition, in *BT*, that the role of transforming modern, theory-saturated subjectivity could be performed by anything as lightly freighted in conceptual respects as art. This leads in turn to a doubt concerning the Aesthetic State itself. Nietzsche offers little by way of positive reassurance that it is in fact possible for us to achieve the Aesthetic State, considered as the *all-encompassing* condition of life which his anti-Schopenhauerian purposes require it to be, and which he, in opposition to Schopenhauer, supposes that it can be. It may be replied that this lies in the nature of the case that Nietzsche is making, and that the actual achievability of the Aesthetic State depends on psychological contingencies which it is not Nietzsche's job to document. What might equally be inferred, however, is that, *if* forms of aesthetic experience have the transformative potential supposed by Nietzsche, then this can only be because they contain within themselves—as Nietzsche comes close to conceding—some incipient conception of how things are, which philosophical reflection of the appropriate kind can make

[70] See also, regarding the aesthetic significance of the theory of Will to Power, the account of Heraclitus's thought in *PTG* 5–6. An alternative interpretative possibility, which should be mentioned although there is no space to explore it properly here, is that Nietzsche regards the theory of will to power as a new *Naturphilosophie*, a product of unassisted theoretical reason able to *dissolve* the conflict of theoretical and practical reason. It seems to me plausible that Nietzsche entertained this possibility but doubtful that he was ever convinced by it: he does not advertise will to power as the proper culmination of the will to truth, and the supposition that the doctrine, taken as possessing plain truth, could survive his own objections to metaphysics encounters obvious difficulty.

[71] Confirming the identification just made, of the Apollonian with 'redemption from *becoming*' and eternalization, is *Nachlaß* 1885–6, N5, no. 2 [110], pp. 80–1 [VIII.1: 113]. Eternal recurrence is envisaged as dependent on and subordinate to will to power, in just the way that the Apollonian has the Dionysian as its substrate: to '*imprint* upon becoming the character of being' is 'the highest' will to power. That Nietzsche is in the late *Nachlaß*, particularly in 1888, consciously retrieving and reactivating ideas from *BT*, often reworking them in the light of will to power, is clear from for example *Nachlaß* 1888, N4, §798, p. 419 [VIII.3: 27–8], §800, pp. 420–1 [VIII.3: 86–7], §803, p. 422 [VIII.1: 266], §811, p. 428 [VIII.3: 148], §821, p. 434 [VIII.3: 33], §851, p. 449 [VIII.3: 203–4].

discursively explicit and validate as a *theoretical structure*, something of the nature of a phil-osophical standpoint, or at any rate, that has greater epistemological significance than the conceptual 'light-images' of Nietzsche's artist's metaphysics. The orthodox post-Kantian will want to add that any such metaphysics teased out of life-affirmative aesthetic experience would allow itself to be employed to help dissolve the conflict of theoretical and practical reason which Nietzsche regards as a final fact about philosophical reason.[72]

Nietzsche's vulnerability to criticism of this type reflects the distinctiveness of the place which he occupies on the field of post-Kantian theory of art, which in turn reflects the dis-tinctive, exceptional character of his philosophical project. Insofar as nineteenth-century philosophy comprises various attempts either to salvage the legacy of classical German phi-losophy, or to re-ally philosophy with natural science while repudiating the idealist concep-tion of nature, or to coordinate the idealist legacy with the progressive naturalistic trajectory, Nietzsche belongs in the third category. What specifically distinguishes Nietzsche is his con-viction—absent from others in that category, such as Hartmann and Lotze, who aim not merely to confront idealist teleology with inductive, mechanistic theory of nature but hold out the possibility of their synthesis—that theoretical reason is drawn irresistibly to mod-ern naturalism and yet that naturalism is unable to meet the demands of our practical rea-son: practical reason needs idealism, but theoretical reason can supply only naturalism—at which point, Nietzsche takes his aesthetic turn. Nietzsche's philosophical aestheticism can-not be appreciated, or measured, without bringing this broader background into focus.

BIBLIOGRAPHY

Works by Nietzsche

References to writings by Nietzsche are given by the following abbreviations. References are given first to the English translation (where available) listed below, from which quotations are taken, and then in square brackets (in the form, e.g., '[III.2: 3]', referring to Abteilung III, Band 2, and Seite 3) to Nietzsche, *Werke: Kritische Gesamtausgabe*, ed. Giorgio Colli and Mazzino Montinari (Berlin: De Gruyter, 1967–).

BGE   *Beyond Good and Evil: Prelude to a Philosophy of the Future (1886)*, trans. Walter Kaufmann. New York: Vintage, 1966.

CW   *The Case of Wagner (1888)*, trans. Walter Kaufmann. New York: Vintage, 1966.

BT   *The Birth of Tragedy Out of the Spirit of Music (1872)*, ed. Michael Tanner, trans. Shaun Whiteside. Harmondsworth: Penguin, 1993.

D   *Daybreak: Thoughts on the Prejudices of Morality (1881)*, trans. R. J. Hollingdale. Cambridge: Cambridge University Press, 1982.

DW   'Die dionysische Weltanschauung' (Summer 1870), in *Nachlaß* III 2: 43–70.

---

[72] There is a large and impressive literature on Nietzsche's philosophy of art. Of particular interest, in addition to the works referred to above, are Came 2006, Figal 2000, Gerhardt 1988a and 1988b, Han-Pile 2006, Richardson 2004: chapter 4, Ridley 2007, the appendix of Staten 1990, Young 1992, and the essays in Kemal, Gaskell, and Conway 1998. I am grateful to Bernard Reginster and others at the History of Modern Philosophy conference on aesthetic judgement at New York University in November 2007 for responses to an early version of this paper, and to Ken Gemes and Christoph Menke for extremely helpful comments on a later draft.

EH   *Ecce Homo* (1888), trans. R. J. Hollingdale. Harmondsworth: Penguin, 1979.

GM   *On the Genealogy of Morals* (1887), ed. Keith Ansell-Pearson, trans. Carol Diethe. Cambridge: Cambridge University Press, 1994.

GS   *The Gay Science* (1882), trans. Walter Kaufmann. New York: Vintage, 1974.

GTG   'Die Geburt des tragischen Gedankens' (June 1870), in *Nachlaß III* 2: 71–91; 'The Birth of Tragic Thought', trans. Ursula Bernis, *Graduate Faculty Philosophy Journal (New School for Social Research)* 9.2 (Fall 1983): 3–15.

HAH   *Human, All Too Human: A Book for Free Spirits* (1878), trans. R. J. Hollingdale. Cambridge: Cambridge University Press, 1986.

N1   [*Nachlaß 1869–75*] *Friedrich Nietzsche on Rhetoric and Language*, trans. and ed. Sander L. Gilman, Carole Blair, and David J. Parent. Oxford: Oxford University Press, 1989.

N2   [*Nachlaß 1872–3*] *Unpublished Writings from the Period of 'Unfashionable Investigations'*, trans. Richard T. Gray. Stanford, Calif.: Stanford University Press, 1999.

N3   [*Nachlaß 1872–6*] *Philosophy and Truth: Selections from Nietzsche's Notebooks of the Early 1870s*, ed. and trans. Daniel Breazeale. Atlantic Highlands, NJ: Humanities Press, 1979.

N4   [*Nachlaß 1883–8*] *The Will to Power*, ed. Walter Kaufmann, trans. Walter Kaufmann and R. J. Hollingdale. New York: Vintage Books, 1968.

N5   [*Nachlaß 1885–8*] *Writings from the Late Notebooks*, ed. Rüdiger Bittner, trans. Kate Sturge. Cambridge: Cambridge University Press, 2003.

OS   'On Schopenhauer: Notes 1868', in *Willing and Nothingness: Schopenhauer as Nietzsche's Educator*, ed. Christopher Janaway. Oxford: Oxford University Press, 1998, 258–65.

PTG   *Philosophy in the Tragic Age of the Greeks* (1873), trans. Marianne Cowan. Chicago: Regnery/Gateway, 1962.

ST   'Sokrates und die griechische Tragödie' (June 1871), *Nachlaß III* 2: 93–132.

TI   *Twilight of the Idols: or How to Philosophize with a Hammer* [with *The Anti-Christ*] (1889), trans. R. J. Hollingdale. Harmondsworth: Penguin, 1968.

UM   *Untimely Meditations* (1876), trans. R. J. Hollingdale. Cambridge: Cambridge University Press, 1983.

Z   *Thus Spoke Zarathustra: A Book for Everyone and No One* (1883–5), trans. R. J. Hollingdale. Harmondsworth: Penguin, 1969.

ZVT1   'Zwei öffentliche Vorträge über die griechische Tragödie. Erster Vortrag: Das griechische Musikdrama' (Jan.–Feb. 1870), *Nachlaß III* 2: 1–22.

ZVT2   'Zwei öffentliche Vorträge über die griechische Tragödie: Zweiter Vortrag: Sokrates und die Tragoedie' (Jan.–Feb. 1870), *Nachlaß III* 2: 23–41.

Other Primary Works

WWR   Schopenhauer, Arthur. 1969. *The World as Will and Representation*, trans. E. F. J. Payne (2 vols). New York: Dover.

Other Works Cited

Benjamin, Walter. 1998. *The Origin of German Tragic Drama*, trans. John Osborne. London: Verso/New Left Books.

Came, Daniel. 2006. 'The Aesthetic Justification of Existence', in Keith Ansell-Pearson (ed.), *A Companion to Nietzsche*. Oxford: Blackwell, 41–57.

Clark, Maudemarie. 1990. *Nietzsche on Truth and Philosophy*. Cambridge: Cambridge University Press.

Croce, Benedetto. 1972/1902. *Aesthetic: As Science of Expression and General Linguistic*, trans. Douglas Ainslie. London: Peter Owen.

Faas, Ekbert. 2002. *The Genealogy of Aesthetics*. Cambridge: Cambridge University Press.

Ferry, Luc. 1993. *Homo Aestheticus: The Invention of Taste in the Democratic Age*, trans. Robert de Loaiza. Chicago: University of Chicago Press.

Figal, Günter. 2000. 'Aesthetically Limited Reason', in Miguel de Beistegui and Simon Sparks (eds), *Philosophy and Tragedy*. London Routledge, 139–51.

Fink, Eugen. 2003. *Nietzsche's Philosophy*, trans. Goetz Richter. London: Continuum.

Gerhardt, Volker. 1988a. 'Nietzsches ästhetische Revolution', in *Pathos und Distanz: Studien zur Philosophie Friedrich Nietzsches*. Stuttgart: Reclam, 12–45.

Gerhardt, Volker. 1988b. 'Artisten-Metaphysik', in *Pathos und Distanz: Studien zur Philosophie Friedrich Nietzsches*. Stuttgart: Reclam, 46–71.

Habermas, Jürgen. 1987. *The Philosophical Discourse of Modernity: Twelve Lectures*, trans. Frederick Lawrence. Cambridge: Polity.

Hammermeister, Kai. 2002. *The German Aesthetic Tradition*. Cambridge: Cambridge University Press.

Han-Pile, Béatrice. 2006. 'Nietzsche's Metaphysics in *The Birth of Tragedy*', *European Journal of Philosophy* 14: 373–403.

Hegel, Georg Wilhelm Friedrich. 1975/1823-9. *Aesthetics: Lectures on Fine Art*, trans. T. M. Knox (2 vols). Oxford: Clarendon.

Heidegger, Martin. 1991/1936. *Nietzsche, Volume I: The Will to Power as Art*, trans. David Farrell Krell. New York: HarperCollins.

Hill, R. Kevin. 2003. *Nietzsche's Critiques: The Kantian Foundations of His Thought*. Oxford: Oxford University Press.

Hussain, Nadeem J. Z. 2007. 'Honest Illusion: Valuing for Nietzsche's Free Spirits', in Brian Leiter and Neil Sinhababu (eds), *Nietzsche and Morality*. Oxford: Oxford University Press, 157–91.

Kant, Immanuel. 2000/1790. *Critique of the Power of Judgement*, ed. Paul Guyer, trans. Paul Guyer and Eric Matthews. Cambridge: Cambridge University Press.

Kemal, Salim, Ivan Gaskell, and Daniel W. Conway (eds). 1998. *Nietzsche, Philosophy and the Arts*. Cambridge: Cambridge University Press.

Lange, Frederick Albert. 1950/1873-5. *The History of Materialism: And Criticism of its Present Importance*, 2nd edn, trans. Ernest Chester Thomas, 3rd edn, with introduction by Bertrand Russell. London: Routledge & Kegan Paul.

Megill, Allan. 1985. *Prophets of Extremity: Nietzsche, Heidegger, Foucault, Derrida*. Berkeley: University of California Press.

Menke, Christoph. 1998. *The Sovereignty of Art: Aesthetic Negativity in Adorno and Derrida*, trans. Neil Solomon. Cambridge, Mass.: MIT Press.

Pippin, Robert. 2003. 'Love and Death in Nietzsche', in Mark A. Wrathall (ed.), *Religion After Metaphysics*. Cambridge: Cambridge University Press, 7–28.

Pippin, Robert. 2010. *Nietzsche, Psychology, and First Philosophy*. Chicago: University of Chicago Press.

Poellner, Peter. 1998. 'Myth, Art and Illusion in Nietzsche', in Matthew Bell and Peter Poellner (eds), *Myth and the Making of Modernity: The Problem of Grounding in Early Twentieth-Century Literature*. Atlanta: Rodopi, 61–80.

Poellner, Peter. 2007. 'Affect, Value, and Objectivity', in Brian Leiter and Neil Sinhababu (eds), *Nietzsche and Morality*. Oxford: Oxford University Press, 227–61.

Porter, James I. 2000. *The Invention of Dionysus: An Essay on 'The Birth of Tragedy'*. Stanford, Calif.: Stanford University Press.

Richardson, John. 1996. *Nietzsche's System*. Oxford: Oxford University Press.

Richardson, John. 2004. *Nietzsche's New Darwinism*. Oxford: Oxford University Press.

Ridley, Aaron. 2007. *Nietzsche on Art*. London: Routledge.

Schacht, Richard. 2001. 'Making Life Worth Living: Nietzsche on Art in *The Birth of Tragedy*', in John Richardson and Brian Leiter (eds), *Nietzsche*. Oxford: Oxford University Press, 186–209.

Schaeffer, Jean-Marie. 2000. *Art of the Modern Age: Philosophy of Art from Kant to Heidegger*, trans. Steven Rendall. Princeton, NJ: Princeton University Press.

Schiller, Friedrich. 1982/1793–5. *On the Aesthetic Education of Man: In a Series of Letters*, trans. Elizabeth M. Wilkinson and L. A. Willoughby. Oxford: Clarendon.

Staten, Henry. 1990. *Nietzsche's Voice*. Ithaca: Cornell University Press.

Sweet, Dennis. 1999. 'The Birth of *The Birth of Tragedy*', *Journal of the History of Ideas* 60: 345–59.

Vaihinger, Hans. 1924/1911. *The Philosophy of 'As If': A System of the Theoretical, Practical and Religious Fictions of Mankind*, trans. C. K. Ogden. London: Routledge & Kegan Paul.

Young, Julian. 1992. *Nietzsche's Philosophy of Art*. Cambridge: Cambridge University Press.

CHAPTER 27

BEING, BECOMING, AND TIME IN NIETZSCHE

ROBIN SMALL

NIETZSCHE's thinking about being and becoming is bound up with his lifelong preoccupation with the relation between knowledge and life. It is part of his attempt to uncover the errors that have led to the predicament of modern humanity, challenged to find confidence in forms of knowledge whose conceptual foundations have fallen apart, and to find meaning in lives that have no higher authority to guide them. Once, knowledge and life were coordinated through their common relation to a reality beyond that of human experience. This has been exposed as an illusion by the will to truth that it made an imperative and that remains as a legacy to those who must come to terms with a world of becoming rather than being and of appearance rather than reality.

For knowledge, the problem of becoming is just that it is ungraspable. 'Knowledge and becoming exclude each other', Nietzsche remarks (*KSA* 12: 9 [89].382 [*WP* 517]). Or rather, the human attempt to grasp becoming operates through denial. That is, it relies on an incapacity or refusal to acknowledge the absence of both discontinuities and ongoing identities in the ceaseless flow of becoming both within and outside the mind. Knowledge looks for being and invents it to satisfy its own demand. The outcome is a conceptualization of becoming which defines it as a succession of states of affairs which, taken by themselves, lack any essential coming to be or passing away. In other words, an attempt is made to reconstruct becoming on the basis of its negation. As one might expect, this is a failure. The problems that it creates were first identified by Zeno of Elea and have never been satisfactorily resolved by later thinkers. For philosophy, this is an issue that needs renewed attention.

If becoming is a problem for knowledge, it is even more so for life. The ancient Greeks, Nietzsche says, assumed awareness of the contradictoriness of reality to have a shattering effect: 'The Greek knew and felt the terror and horror of existence' (*BT* 3). The satyr Silenus had revealed the bitter truth to King Midas: that it was better not to be born or, as a second best, to die soon. It was this recognition that motivated the attempts of Greek culture to create cultural forms that would make it possible to live at all. In order to endure such an insight, they created the Olympian world of myth and imagery, an expression of the quest for order and measure that Nietzsche calls the 'Apollonian' drive. Seen in the mirror of beautiful illusion, human life becomes supportable. Even so, the reaffirmation of ceaseless creation and destruction that Nietzsche labels 'Dionysian' makes its presence known in disruptive outbreaks that can be repressed only for a while. The Greek artists had their own answers, Nietzsche suggests in his first book, *The Birth of Tragedy*. The outcome was the emergence of tragedy as an art form enabling an affirmation of reality coded in and controlled by the 'Apollonian' forms of appearance.

Yet if becoming is problematical for both knowledge and life, so is being. Its claims to validity are not borne out by closer investigation of nature or, for that matter, more careful introspection. Not only do these fail to confirm its factual status but, just as alarmingly, inconsistencies are uncovered within the conceptual scheme that centres upon being. Moreover, the values that go with belief in a 'true world' are seen to damage the interests of life in the present world, since they promote weakness and decline rather than health and strength. With both sides so problematical, we are left with a quandary, one that for Nietzsche is not just philosophical but also deeply historical in character.

THE HISTORICAL APPROACH

This last consideration serves as a starting point for looking into his own approach to being and becoming. One striking feature of Nietzsche's thought is the way that it situates itself historically. His 'historical method' demands that anything be understood in terms of its origin, including his own philosophical thinking. Hence, his attack on being is also a historical account of Western thought, starting with the ancient Greek thinkers who, he claims, between themselves represented all the essential philosophical positions.

The first *philosophical* answer to the question of becoming is that of Anaximander, reported by Simplicius as locating the origin of all existing things in the 'indefinite' (*apeiron*), and asserting that they must in due course return to this source, 'according to necessity, for they pay penalty and retribution to each other for their injustice according to the assessment of Time' (Kirk and Raven 1957: 117). In quoting this text, Nietzsche omits the words 'to each other', which suggest that the injustice committed is against other existing things, since each individual comes into being only through the passing away of others. In his version, the wrong consists in separating oneself from the 'unlimited' and laying claim to a distinct existence. He comments: 'All becoming is an emancipation from eternal being: hence an injustice, and hence subject to the punishment of perishing' (*KGW* II.4: 241).[1] Nietzsche notes that this is the view taken by Schopenhauer. He calls it a moral interpretation of the world, since it makes the categories of responsibility, guilt, and punishment applicable not just to human beings but to everything that exists. It is also a pessimistic view, since it makes guilt inescapable and redemption impossible.

In his Basel lectures, Nietzsche summarizes the history of pre-Platonic philosophy as a development from this starting point. The key figure here is Heraclitus, as he explains:

> One must compare Heraclitus with Anaximander, to determine the advance. The *apeiron* and the world of becoming were placed alongside each other in an ungraspable way, as a sort of immediate dualism. Heraclitus denies the world of Being altogether and affirms only the

---

[1] The fragment appears in Greek in the original. See *PPP* 33. He makes the same omission in *PTG* 4.

world of becoming; Parmenides does the reverse in order to resolve Anaximander's problem. Both seek to destroy this dualism, but in opposing ways: consequently, Parmenides also struggles most vigorously against Heraclitus. Both Heraclitus and the Eleatics are necessary conditions for Anaxagoras, Empedocles, and Democritus: in general, they are clearly familiar with Anaximander and take him as their presupposition. In this sense we may speak of a development. (*KGW* II.4: 253–4)[2]

Nietzsche often associates himself with Heraclitus, in whose company, he says, he feels 'altogether warmer and better than anywhere else' (*EH*: 'The Birth of Tragedy' 3). He declares his allegiance to the Heraclitean principle that the only reality is becoming: that is, continual change with no beginning or end, and no pause in its course.[3] He supports this bold claim by a destructive critique of all notions of stability and permanence, but at times also appeals to the direct experience that we have of our own ideas and their continual flow. 'This is the sole certainty we have in our hands to serve as a corrective to a great host of world hypotheses possible in themselves' (*KSA* 13: 14 [188].375 [*WP* 1066]). At the same time, he is well aware of the difficulties that this doctrine poses for philosophical thinking. Plato and Aristotle both raised what they took to be a strong objection: that the doctrine of absolute becoming leads to descriptions of reality which attribute opposite properties to the same thing. According to Aristotle, the most extreme believer in universal change was Cratylus, 'who finally did not think it right to say anything but only moved his finger, and criticised Heraclitus for saying that it is impossible to step twice into the same river; for *he* thought that one could not do so even once' (Aristotle 1984: vol. 2, *Metaphysics*, IV.5. 1010a).[4]

Nietzsche's presentation of the doctrine of absolute becoming appears not only in his lectures but also in an essay aimed at a broader audience, *Philosophy in the Tragic Age of the Greeks*. This survey centres upon a contrast between Heraclitus and Parmenides. Nietzsche treats them as contemporaries and dramatizes their relation as one of direct antagonism. The outcome of the dispute starting with their rival answers to the issue posed by Anaximander is taken to be the philosophical atomism of Democritus and Epicurus, the most consistent system in ancient thought, according to Nietzsche (*KGW* II.4: 334). Atomism is, in fact, a compromise solution. Becoming is admitted, but as the motion of particles that do not change and only alter in their configurations in relation to each other. Still, this is claimed as enough to give rise to changing properties and to the qualities perceived by sentient beings.

Nietzsche gives Democritus a privileged place: 'He is the only philosopher that still lives' (*KGW* II.4: 334). The elimination of teleology is the key to modern natural science. It is seen most strikingly in the Darwinian revolution in biology, as Nietzsche's preferred authority on scientific matters F. A. Lange emphasizes. In the systems coming immediately before Democritus there are still vestiges of this element. Anaxagoras makes *nous* the basic premise of his whole theory of the development of the world, while Empedocles appeals to concepts of love and hate in explaining the combining and separating of elements. In contrast, Democritus speaks only of processes which are visible and tangible, and explained by cause and effect. He is thus the founder of a scientific tradition which has continued and

---

[2] See *PPP* 44 (translation modified).
[3] See e.g. *KSA* 11: 36 [15].556 and 38 [12].610 (*WP* 1062 and 1067) and *KSA* 13: 11 [73].36 (*WP* 708).
[4] Cf. *UM* II: 1.

still exists. Atomism is the dominant model for physical science. Even if solid atoms are, as Nietzsche thinks, on the basis of reading R. J. Boscovich, to be replaced by 'centres of force', the basic idea is still much the same.

Even so, this success story is about to change. The model of being that it depends on has undergone a dramatic reversal in modern philosophy. Nietzsche provides an overview in *Twilight of the Idols* under the heading 'How the "True World" Finally Became a Fable: The History of An Error'. The first three stages of his account bring us from ancient Greece to the modern world.

1. The true world—attainable for the sage, the pious, the virtuous man; he lives in it, *he is it*.
    (The oldest form of the idea, relatively sensible, simple, and persuasive. A circumlocution for the sentence, 'I, Plato, am the truth'.

2. The true world—unattainable for now, but promised for the sage, the pious, the virtuous man ('for the sinner who repents').
    (Progress of the idea; it becomes more subtle, insidious, incomprehensible—*it becomes female*, it becomes Christian.)

3. The true world—unattainable, indemonstrable, unpromisable; but the very thought of it—a consolation, an obligation, an imperative.
    (At bottom, the old sun, but seen through mist and scepticism. The idea has become elusive, pale, Nordic, *Königsbergian*.)

The philosophies that Nietzsche has in mind are evidently Platonism, Christianity, and Kantianism respectively. Yet even though we have reached the nineteenth century, this is only the halfway point of his complete history. What follows? Nietzsche becomes less specific as he approaches the present day and what lies beyond it, the future direction of thinking that he wants to claim as his own discovery.

4. The true world—unattainable? At any rate, unattained. And being unattained, also *unknown*. Consequently, not consoling, redeeming, or obligating: how could something unknown obligate us?
    (Gray morning. The first yawn of reason. The cockcrow of positivism.)

A central theme so far has been the *normative* function of the concept of being. This authority is both epistemological and ethical. Hence, a retreat from Kantianism implies an abandonment of any moral philosophy that presupposes an intelligible will determined only by its own rational freedom. The next stage is not much different, but listed separately because Nietzsche has in mind the sceptical doctrine of neo-Kantians such as Otto Liebmann, who dispensed with the 'thing-in-itself' as an empty concept, superfluous to transcendental idealism.[5] He praises contemporary thinkers in *Beyond Good and Evil* for the 'extravagant and adventurous courage' that they show in giving up even the oldest and most well-established assumptions (*BGE* 10). If their choice is a loss, it also makes possible a new beginning:

---

[5] See Liebmann 1865: 69 and 205.

5. The 'true' world—an idea which is no longer good for anything, not even obligating—
   an idea which has become useless and superfluous—*consequently* a refuted idea: let us
   abolish it!
   (Bright day; breakfast; return of *bon sens* and cheerfulness; Plato's embarrassed blush;
   pandemonium of all free spirits.)

These writers were not all hostile to a reality beyond the world of experience. On the contrary,
some were idealists who wanted to vindicate the concept of a real world by discarding anything
for which absolute certainty could not be claimed. Nietzsche's favourite contemporary metaphysician was A. Spir, who took the law of identity to rule out change and plurality, as well as any
relation of conditionality between the real world and that of appearance. As with Parmenides,
the outcome was an absolute with no describable properties other than self-identity.

So it is that Nietzsche comes to his final stage, reached only when this metaphysical tradition has completed the path to its ultimate conclusion, the point of completion at which
whatever develops passes beyond itself and turns into something else.

6. The true world—we have abolished. What world has remained? The apparent one
   perhaps? But no! *With the true world we have also abolished the apparent one.*
   (Noon: moment of the briefest shadow; end of the longest error; high point of
   humanity; INCIPIT ZARATHUSTRA.)

The passage ends with a stage instruction: now the teachings of Nietzsche's own Zarathustra
can be introduced. However, since the metaphysical distinction between reality and
appearance coincides with a distinction between being and becoming, the story has also
been about the replacement of being by becoming. According to Nietzsche, the nineteenth
century had experienced this shift in the advance of the 'historical sense', which sets out to
understand everything by uncovering its origins. While natural scientists such as Darwin
had made some contributions, Nietzsche felt that special credit should go to the Germans,
who 'instinctively attribute a deeper meaning and greater value to becoming and development than to what "is"' (*GS* 357). Turning that instinct into an explicit account is a main
task for his own philosophical thinking.

Relatively few commentators on Nietzsche's thought have thematized this reconceptual-
ization of becoming. In his book *Nietzsche's System*, John Richardson treats it as a dialogue
with Plato, finding an 'underlying affinity' that makes Nietzsche's rejection of Platonism less
straightforward than his wording often suggests (Richardson 1996: 76). Richardson's further development of Nietzsche's thought emphasizes its naturalistic orientation. This has the
advantage of building on Nietzsche's frequent attempts to outline an evolutionary epistemology, as well as his sympathy for a quasi-Darwinian model in which selection for survival
and reproduction (along with what Nietzsche supposes to be its premise, the will to live) is
replaced by a parallel selection for exceptionality, driven by a will to power. The becoming of
values and perspectives now appears as a process of the living organism: a drive toward goals
that is also an overcoming of the past and, in effect, a repression and forgetting (Richardson
2006: 219).[6] And this, with the further contributions of self-awareness and social influence,
gives rise to the human experience of time.

---

[6] See also Richardson 2004: 69.

Here I intend to adopt a somewhat different approach, beginning with Nietzsche's hints about a possible awareness of becoming that, strictly speaking, might be ruled out by his wholesale rejection of our conceptual vocabulary. From that starting point, the task is to see how the problem of becoming turns into the problem of time (a phrase that is also the title of Joan Stambaugh's important work *The Problem of Time in Nietzsche*, 1959). This in turn will lead us toward Nietzsche's most profound and challenging ideas, including the thought of eternal return.

FROM BECOMING TO TIME

If we were able to gain access to becoming in its original and authentic form, as an absolutely continuous flow, how would we experience it? Nietzsche writes: 'Only succession produces the idea of time. Assuming we did not sense causes and effects but a continuum, we would not believe in time' (*KSA* 9: 11 [281].549). This sounds like speculation on a counterfactual hypothesis. Yet there is one part of life in which such opportunities do arise: in sleep and dreaming, and especially on the borderline between sleep and waking. Nietzsche specifies the hours after midnight as the period during which the 'over-awake' individual experiences anomalies of time: it seems 'too short' or 'too long' (*KSA* 12: 4 [5].178). The feeling that time in its usual form is suspended is, he speculates, a substitute for the 'time chaos' of the dreaming state that we would otherwise be in. This is a fluctuation that lacks the linear order of temporality as normally experienced. The absence of the familiar structures of time in these states of awareness allows us an authentic sense of becoming. We glimpse what the elaborations of waking life are designed to cover up, a flow of intensities that vary without any context of regular forms.

Further clues are provided by musical experience. In considering the elements that make up music—melody, rhythm, and harmony—we see different relations to becoming. Rhythm is a patterning that provides a structure for experience in general. As Nietzsche puts it in his Basel lectures: 'Rhythm is the form of becoming, and in general the form of the world of appearance' (*KGW* II.3: 338).[7] Harmony, in contrast, is the element in music that enables us to apprehend what lies beneath the forms of appearance. In his 1870 essay 'Beethoven', written during the period of closest friendship with Nietzsche, Wagner holds up harmony, 'belonging to neither space nor time', as the essential element of music, while allowing that it can enter the world of appearance, with the help of the creative musician, only as a rhythmic sequence of sounds, that is, as a temporal phenomenon (Wagner 1913: vol. 9, p. 76). He cites the music of Palestrina as one in which 'rhythm is perceptible only through the changing of harmonic sequences, and apart from these, as a symmetrical succession by itself, does not exist at all' (Wagner 1913: vol. 9, p. 79).[8] Nietzsche's own example of a music dominated by harmony is undoubtedly the final act of Wagner's *Tristan und Isolde*. He even suggests that 'so-called melody' is only an abbreviation for harmonic sequences.[9] This privileging of harmony is sharply diminished in Nietzsche's later writing on music. In *The Wagner Case* he takes the opportunity to satirize Wagner's stated views: '*Principle*: melody is immoral.

---

[7] Cf. *KSA* 8: 528.   [8] Cf. Wagner 1913: vol. 7, pp. 106–7.   [9] *KSA* 1: 557 and 585.

Proof: Palestrina. *Practical application*: *Parsifal*' (*WC* 7). Now he criticizes Wagner for an absence of rhythmic regularity, accusing him of posing 'a danger to music which cannot be exaggerated: the complete degeneration of rhythmic feeling, *chaos* in place of rhythm' (*NCW*: 'Wagner as a Danger').[10]

It is not just Wagner's music that preoccupies Nietzsche's thinking about becoming and time during the period of *The Birth of Tragedy*. He owes just as much to Wagner's writings. A case in point is Wagner's idea of a translation of the dreaming state of deep sleep into another, 'allegorical' form of dreaming, closer to waking and serving as an intermediary by making use of images that resemble the language of waking life (Wagner 1913: vol. 9, p. 73).[11] In his early forays into epistemology, Nietzsche suggests that a translation of what is originally given into the language of experience requires 'a freely inventive intermediate sphere and mediating force' (*TL* 1). It is here that structures of temporality find their origin.

The role of rhythm in transforming becoming into time is elaborated in Nietzsche's Basel lectures with special emphasis on the Aristotelian theorist Aristoxenus, who identified the alternation of motion and rest as the key to a patterning of time (Aristoxenus 1990: 23).[12] This is consistent with Nietzsche's own view that the basic operation of human thinking is the introduction of 'gaps' into becoming, supported by 'intermittence forms of the will' (*DW* 4 [*KSA* 1: 574]) but giving rise to a belief in stable and enduring things that undergo both motion and qualitative change. While becoming is not time, it is the original ground from which time is able to emerge through a conceptual construction that starts with these constancies and breaks. A similarity is taken as an identity, while differences in degree are turned into oppositions: for example, a slower rate of change is taken to be a period of rest. Hence, some of the variations in becoming are overlooked, while others are replaced by discontinuities. Often Nietzsche describes these as errors caused by the incapacity of the human mind to grasp the full content of the flow of becoming. Yet he is aware that this seeming weakness is also a strength, in that it makes us more capable of dealing with our environment. 'Our senses have a definite quantum as a mean within which they function; i.e., we sense bigness and smallness in relation to the conditions of our existence. If we sharpened or blunted our senses tenfold, we should perish' (*KSA* 12: 5 [36].197 [*WP* 563]).

The resulting conceptual scheme is one that separates things from their varying properties, so that Plato and Aristotle's objection to the doctrine of becoming is avoided: a thing can have opposing properties, but only at different times. The relation of earlier and later in turn gives rise to definite intervals of time, whose boundaries are transitions between one state and another. The introduction of supposed constancies gives rise to a distinction between an enduring thing and its varying properties and qualities. We now think of the world as a succession of states of affairs which are located before and after one another in time. But where is becoming in this model? It must consist in the transition from one state of affairs to another. Accordingly, one could say that it is not perceived directly but inferred from comparisons between successive states. This sounds like a makeshift solution, and it is. The Eleatic school revealed its vulnerability to logical attack through paradoxes such as the 'Arrow', which shows that motion cannot be reconstituted from states of rest. Yet whatever the philosophical objections, Nietzsche would comment that there is one important point in

---

[10]   A less hostile version of this section had appeared in *HAH* II: 134.

[11]   Cf. Schopenhauer 1974: vol. 1, p. 255.

[12]   Cf. *KGW* II.3: 104.

favour of this conceptualization: it enables us to cope with our environment and to achieve practical aims in life.

The transition from becoming in its reconstituted version to temporality needs to be explored in more detail. Nietzsche sees it as bound up with the concept of causality. The separation of things and their properties is also a separation of things and their actions. Yet it becomes hard to see how any necessity can be attributed to the process of cause and effect. One solution is to postulate 'laws of nature' which stand over the world of agents much as the laws of society compel individuals to behave in certain ways rather than others. The problem here is the same one already encountered with becoming in general: the task of regaining what has been negated is difficult and even, on Nietzsche's view, impossible. One major problem with cause and effect concerns succession. Why should an effect be later than its cause? After all, if the cause is a sufficient condition, should not the effect occur at once? Yet the finitude of temporal intervals is supposed to be determined by some such property of causal processes. These issues show the problem in acknowledging becoming within a conceptual scheme that is dominated by a privileging of being. Once things are separated from one another, the task of characterizing the transitions between them and accounting for the necessity of these successions becomes impossible.

Nietzsche's solution is a return to becoming in its genuine form. Instead of things, he wants to refer to the processes or occurrences (*Geschehen*) which take time, but cannot be divided into a beginning and end connected through the relation of causality. Two important aspects of this concept of *Geschehen* should be noted. The first that it involves continual conflict. This characteristic is, in fact, what accounts for temporal intervals.

> Every conflict—every occurrence is a conflict—*takes time (Aller Kampf—alles Geschehen ist ein Kampf—braucht Dauer)*. What we call 'cause' and 'effect' leaves out the conflict and consequently does not correspond to the occurrence. It is consistent to deny time in cause and effect. (*KSA* 12: 1 [92].33)

Or rather, it is *in*consistent to affirm time between cause and effect. As we have noted, a sufficient condition ought to produce its consequence straight away. Worse still, if there is any delay then the effect cannot be guaranteed, since the interval allows the possibility of some factor that prevents it from occurring. In any case, Nietzsche thinks that the notion of action at a distance in time is simply incoherent: 'Two successive states: the one cause, the other effect, is false. The first state has nothing to effect, the second has been effected by nothing' (*KSA* 13: 14 [95].273 [*WP* 633]).

What does a definition of becoming as conflict involve, though? Nietzsche refers to it in terms of force and power, in turn identified with a 'will to power' which, he says, 'expresses itself in the interpretation, in the manner in which force is used up' (*KSA* 12: 535 [*WP* 639]). Interpreters who take the will to power, prominent in Nietzsche's later writing, as central to his thought, emphasize his distinction between active and reactive forces, and extend this well beyond the realm of human motivation to the world in general, amounting to an ontology, insofar as one can apply such a term to Nietzsche's thought.[13] If we focus on his descriptions of conflict between forces, however, a further characterization of becoming as *Geschehen* must be that processes are 'entangled' or 'intertwined' with one

---

[13] See Deleuze 1983: 39–42 and Richardson 1996: 39–44.

another.[14] These two descriptions are strikingly combined in his summary of the teaching of Heraclitus: 'Ordinary people fancy they see something rigid, complete and permanent; in truth, however, light and dark, bitter and sweet are attached to each other and interlocked at any given moment like wrestlers of whom sometimes the one, sometimes the other is on top' (*PTG* 5, 54). Thus, it is precisely in these continuing conflicts between opposing forces that the entanglements occur which provide the basis for belief in subsisting things.

These two descriptions lead to a third characterization of becoming, involving the idea of *accidentality*. Arguing against the moral concepts of responsibility and blame, Nietzsche suggests that those who adopt this interpretation of the world have 'robbed of its innocence the wholly pure accidentality [*Zufälligkeit*] of occurrence' (*D* 13). But what is that? An accident is a particular kind of event: a collision between processes that up until then had proceeded separately, but whose interaction produces consequences that can be said to express their 'entanglement'. Nietzsche says that 'Accident is itself only *the collision of the creative impulses*' (*KSA* 10: 24 [28].662 [*WP* 673]). In everyday language, an accident is an event for which there is no explanation. We can say *how* it happens, but not *why*, so to speak. An example of Aristotle's is finding a buried treasure when one is digging a hole for some other purpose, such as planting a tree (Aristotle 1984: vol. 2, *Nicomachean Ethics*, III.3, 1112b). We may be able to explain how the treasure came to be in that place and we can also say why someone is engaging in digging the hole, but these are entirely separate accounts. Hence, the finding of the treasure, considered as a new event, cannot be assigned a particular cause (Aristotle 1984: vol. 2, *Metaphysics*, VI.3, 1027b). For that reason, people are normally not held responsible for genuine accidents, unless there is behaviour such as negligence which would be culpable in any case.

Evidently Nietzsche wants to generalize this model to cover the entire range of occurrences, even those we would not ordinarily regard as accidental. Hence, his view that this doctrine will eliminate the moral interpretation of the world once and for all. The word *Zufall* could also be translated as 'chance', but that has links with the notion of probability that are out of place here. Nothing is more or less probable in Nietzsche's conception. It is true that he often compares the world to a dice game, but that is simply to illustrate the continual presence of chance in the course of becoming. Zarathustra explains that this is a liberation from 'bondage under purpose' and a regaining of innocence and childlike playfulness (*Z* III: 'Before Sunrise'). Elsewhere Nietzsche calls it his 'Dionysian' conception of the world and expresses it in imagery largely drawn from natural science:

> a sea of forces flowing and rushing together, eternally changing, eternally flooding back, with tremendous years of recurrence, with an ebb and flow of its forms; out of the simplest forms striving toward the most complex, out of the stillest, most rigid, coldest forms toward the hottest, most turbulent, most self-contradictory, and then again returning out of this abundance, out of the play of contradictions back to the joy of concord...(*KSA* 11: 38 [12].610–11 [*WP* 1067])

This is more a vision than a straightforward description. In contrast, the world of everyday experience is largely stable, within a framework of space and time that makes regularities

---

[14] See e.g. *KSA* 10: 5 [1].239, 215 and 12 [8].401.

and 'laws' readily identifiable. Nevertheless, inherent conflict makes a dramatic reappear-
ance in one of the most important passages of *Thus Spoke Zarathustra*. Nietzsche approaches
the theme of time through an elaborate imagery. In a narrated episode, Zarathustra finds
himself at a gateway that stands between two long lanes, and remarks that 'no one has yet
followed either to its end'. The name of the gateway is written above: 'Moment'. From this
indication it appears that the gateway and lanes represent what Plato calls the 'forms' of
time: past, present, and future (*Parmenides*: 141). They are often associated with images of
motion. A time that consists of past, present, and future is one that brings things from the
future into the present and then carries them away into the past.

So far, nothing very startling has been said. But we are told something more about the
lanes and the gateway: 'They contradict each other, these lanes; they offend each other face
to face [*sie stossen sich gerade vor dem Kopf*]'. Nietzsche's wording suggests a head-on collision. Hence, his metaphor means that past and future are engaged in some violent struggle
over possession of the ground that each is trying to occupy. This is not just the 'moment' by
itself but goes beyond that to time as a whole and whatever is in time. If whatever occupies
the present always becomes a part of what is past, then it seems that the winner in this contest is past time. Yet there is no complete victory achieved here, but only a continual and
endlessly renewed contest over each new moment, as the previous one is taken into what
has been.

I have been arguing that time, for Nietzsche, is an interpretation of becoming.[15] In
consequence, any conflict between future and past must be understood as a particular
interpretation of the conflicts present within absolute becoming. Here they are simplified as two powerful forces. This has much to do with the human experience of temporality as Nietzsche understands it. As willing beings we are essentially oriented toward
the future. But if the past has a greater power, our hope of overcoming what has been is
doomed to failure. Zarathustra makes it clear that human temporality is a *predicament*.
The prospect of liberation from our weaknesses and discontents is provided by the creative will which builds a new future on the basis of the fragments of the past. Yet the power
of the past remains a problem which in turn gives rise to a new suffering, worse than the
others because of its apparent inescapability. 'Powerless against what has been done, he
is an angry spectator of all that is past. the will cannot will backwards; and that he cannot break time and time's covetousness, that is the will's loneliest melancholy' (*Z* II: 'On
Redemption').

The response of the will is the reactive feeling that Nietzsche calls *revenge*: an anger that
seeks to make others suffer in the hope that this act will relieve its suffering. And from this he
thinks arise all the rationalizations of the 'spirit of revenge': responsibility, guilt, and punishment. The elaborate conceptual structure of morality supports this strategy. Nietzsche identifies causality as a case in point: a cause is accountable, and the drive to identify a culprit is
the source of this concept, not a need for explanation. Similarly, the distinction between the
'doer' and the 'deed' supports the concept of responsibility, while personal identity serves to
identify the past wrongdoer with someone now at hand and available for revenge, understood as punishment.

[15] See Small 2010: 2 and 34.

Nietzsche's solution to the predicament is a radical reconstruction of thinking from the ground up. Modifications of familiar concepts will not be enough, for our conventional conceptual scheme is linked so comprehensively with the spirit of revenge that the only way out is its complete destruction. But what can replace it? Here we return to the problem of knowledge and life. While Nietzsche is violently opposed to traditional morality, he has a lot to say about what human beings may or should become, and the task that this process of becoming will typically involve. Once again his theme is the concept of becoming, but with a focus on the conditions required for the individual person's liberation from morality and realization of a form of life that affirms both becoming and appearance. Let us now turn to this prospect as he presents it.

'BECOMING WHAT YOU ARE'

In a very early text Nietzsche writes: 'Schopenhauer's ethics is criticised for not having an imperative form. The thing the philosophers call character is an incurable disease. An imperative ethics is one that deals with the symptoms of the disease and, in fighting against them, believes that it is getting rid of the single root, the original evil' (*KGW* I.5: 75 [45].276). Whether Nietzsche is referring to any particular critic of Schopenhauer is unclear. More probably he has in mind Schopenhauer's own repudiation of Kantian ethics, which suggests that its reliance on imperatives is inspired by the model of the Ten Commandments (Schopenhauer 1965: 56–7). Nietzsche's own refusal of imperatives is seen more clearly when he attributes a similar idea to Heraclitus:

> Who could possibly demand from such a philosophy an ethic with its necessary imperatives "thou shalt," or, worse yet, accuse Heraclitus of lacking such! Man is necessity down to his last fibre, and totally "unfree," that is, if one means by freedom the foolish demand to be able to change one's *essentia* arbitrarily, like a garment—a demand which every serious philosophy has rejected with the proper scorn. (*PTG* 7)

On this view, imperatives are made absurd by the fact that all our actions arise from a character that is unchangeable. There are certainly passages in which Nietzsche endorses such a claim: 'Learning changes us; it does what all nourishment does which also does not merely "preserve"—as physiologists know. But at the bottom of us, really "deep down," there is, of course, something unteachable, some granite of spiritual fatum, of predetermined decision and answer to predetermined selected questions' (*BGE* 231). Yet the idea that character is unchangeable is hard to reconcile with his interest in Darwinism and his acceptance of the Lamarckian principle that acquired characteristics can be transmitted to offspring. Darwin himself was sympathetic to this idea, since it enabled the process of evolutionary change to proceed much faster than reliance on random mutations. But it implies that individual characteristics cannot be taken as inborn and unchangeable. Similarly, Paul Rée's model of moral development relies on the transmission of acquired habits to new generations to explain why our associations of ideas—for example, of 'bad' with selfishness and 'good' with actions that benefit others—seem so natural, even though the only real explanation lies in the practices of upbringing and training that society establishes to maintain its own existence.[16]

In *Human, All Too Human* Nietzsche suggests a compromise: character does change, but the rate is too slow for us to observe. 'That the character is unalterable is not in the strict sense true; this favourite proposition means rather no more than that, during the brief lifetime of a man, the effective motives are unable to scratch deeply enough to erase the imprinted script of many millennia' (*HAH* I: 41). Later he confronts the issue in a formulation which more than any other in his writings embodies the tension between being and becoming. This is the injunction introduced in *The Gay Science* as the voice of conscience and repeated elsewhere: 'Become what you are' (*GS* 270).[17] At first sight, the expression looks best suited to an ethics concerned with the realization of an essential character within the world of experience. Yet Nietzsche's rejection of the metaphysical leaves the concept of 'what one is' problematical. What makes becoming authentic in this context cannot be its directedness toward a predetermined goal, but only the character of the process itself.

Here the notion of 'self-overcoming' is an essential clue. In *Beyond Good and Evil* Nietzsche writes: 'The German himself *is* not, he *becomes*, he "develops" ["*entwickelt sich*"]' (*BGE* 244). This is intended to characterize the way that Germans present themselves: Nietzsche accuses them of passing off as 'profundity' what is just confusion and obscurity. Hence, his further comment that 'development' is 'the truly German find and hit in the great realm of philosophical formulas' is at least ambiguous. Even so, it recalls his earlier claims for the historical approach to philosophy pioneered by *Human, All Too Human* along with Paul Rée's *Origin of the Moral Sensations*. In this sense, the concept of development is his own as well and an elaboration of the implications of 'becoming'.

Another link between becoming and development occurs in a late notebook entry that describes several ways in which different drives and passions may behave toward one another within the individual person. In some people one passion takes on a dominant role, while in others continual conflict prevails. The first case, Nietzsche says, is 'almost the definition of health', whereas the second is a painful and unhealthy state, at least while it lasts. A third possibility is a coexistence without antagonism or, it seems, any real interaction between these forces:

> The most interesting people, the chameleons, belong here; they are not in contradiction with themselves, they are happy and secure, but they have no development [*Entwicklung*]—their states lie juxtaposed, even if they are separated sevenfold. They change [*wechseln*], they do not become. (*KSA* 13: 14 [157].342 [*WP* 778])

Here becoming is clearly identified with a particular kind of change, more radical than the outer alterations of the 'chameleons' who take on the colour of their environment. The last statement could perhaps be glossed as: 'they do not *become what they are*'. But to get closer to the full meaning of this formula, we need to see it in relation to the most problematical of Nietzsche's doctrines, the thought of eternal return.

The eternal return is introduced in *The Gay Science* as the prediction made by a 'demon': 'This life as you live it and have lived it, you will have to live once more and

---

[16] See Rée 2003: 89–99.

[17] The subtitle to *Ecce Homo* is: 'How One Becomes What One Is'.

innumerable times more' (*GS* 341). In *Thus Spoke Zarathustra* it becomes a challenge posed by Zarathustra at the gateway 'Moment': 'Must not whatever can walk have walked on this lane before? Must not whatever can happen have happened, have been done, have passed by before'? (*Z* III: 'On the Vision and the Riddle' 2) Both texts hint that accepting or 'incorporating' the thought will have dramatic consequences for the individual person. The outcome may be catastrophic, and this uncertainty adds to the message's unsettling impact. A large later literature has arisen around this text, as well as the thought itself. According to some commentators, the eternal return is not to be understood in any 'literal' sense. Rather, it serves as a symbol corresponding to a particular form of life that is Nietzsche's real concern. Bernd Magnus puts forward this view in an influential discussion:

> The attitude toward life which the doctrine is designed to capture is the expression of active and passive nihilism already overcome. That form of life is the opposite of decadence, decline of life, worldweariness. The attitude portrayed is that of affirmation, overfulness; the attitude which expresses ascending life; life in and as celebration. (Magnus 1979: 369–70)[18]

Related to this approach is Alexander Nehamas's judgement that the doctrine is 'not a theory of the world but a view of the ideal life' (Nehamas 1985: 7). Nehamas argues that the eternal return provides an opportunity to construct (or reconstruct) one's life through a thoughtful reinterpretation of whatever has already been, as well as further action in accordance with the 'self' that has emerged from this activity (Nehamas 1985: 168). A number of more recent writers could be mentioned as well. For instance, Maudemarie Clark (1990: 270) and Lawrence J. Hatab (2005: 92–3) both see the thought as primarily a vehicle and measure of life affirmation, although the latter wants to allow it a 'literal' meaning that he nevertheless insists does not imply any factual status.

Despite the wide appeal of this approach, there are also interpretations in which the concerns of human life have no special claims. Often these draw attention to the doctrine's intractable and subversive character, which prevents its serving as any kind of practical resource for the enquiring reader. This undermining power extends to representation in general: the possibility of any symbolism suited for human purposes is placed in question here, as it is by the doctrine of becoming itself.[19] In an unusually provocative text, Pierre Klossowski argues that the doctrine destroys personal identity, writing: 'At the moment the Eternal Return is revealed to me, I cease to be myself *hic et nunc* and am susceptible to becoming innumerable others, knowing that I shall forget this revelation once I am outside the memory of myself' (Klossowski 1997: 58). But what does the doctrine have to say about the issue of being and becoming? On the face of things, the eternal return is simply a further determination of the doctrine of becoming. In some places, especially in his notebooks, Nietzsche seems to treat it as a kind of pre-Socratic cosmological doctrine, according to which the universe undergoes cycles of organization and disorganization. This is consistent with the account of becoming that emphasizes continual conflict and accidental episodes of entangling and disentangling.

On the other hand, one text describes the doctrine as something like a reinstatement of being: 'That everything recurs is the closest approximation of a world of becoming to a world of being: high point of the meditation' (*KSA* 12: 7 [54].312 [*WP* 617]). What does

---

[18] Cf. Magnus 1978: 155.   [19] See e.g. Stegmaier 2006: 20–41.

such an 'approximation' amount to, though? Do not becoming and being remain irreducibly different? In the same note Nietzsche writes: 'To impose [*aufzuprägen*] upon becoming the character of being—that is the highest *will to power*'. A similar image is found in an earlier note: 'Let us stamp [*Drücken wir*] the image of eternity on *our* life! This thought contains more than all religions that condemn this life as fleeting and teach us to look to an indefinite *other* life' (*KSA* 9: 11 [159].503). This notion of 'stamping' is the key to the approximation of becoming to being that the eternal return is supposed to accomplish.

The expression 'image of eternity' repeats the characterization of time in the *Timaeus* as 'a moving image of eternity' (Plato, *Timaeus* 37). This, according to Plato, is the creator's way of making a world as perfect as possible, even though it lacks the timeless perfection of a true reality. We can find a related image in the key passage of *The Gay Science* in which the thought is first introduced. There Nietzsche speculates that one might be able to accept the eternal return as an 'ultimate, eternal confirmation and sealing [*Besiegelung*]' (*GS* 341). Here again one finds the image of an imprint, in this case an exercise of authority that places a formal confirmation on record.[20] Martin Heidegger suggests that this stamping is a 'recoining' that restores the value that has been lost over time (1979–82: vol. 2, p. 202). He may have in mind Nietzsche's description of truth in 'On Truth and Lies in a Non-moral Sense' as a collection of worn-out metaphors, like 'coins which have lost their embossing and are now considered as metal and no longer as coins' (*TL* 1).[21] Certainly the issue of value is what matters here. Nietzsche's central objection to religion and metaphysics is that they devalue the world that we live in. His solution to the predicament of nihilism is to discover new sources of worth that will support a revaluation of all values. The eternal return is supposed to enable an affirmation of both life and the world.

Still, just how it does this remains unclear. One possible answer is that the eternal return makes a human life something that is not conditioned by what comes before and after. Nietzsche agrees with the claim that life cannot serve as a standard of value if it is 'fleeting'. Accordingly, he separates himself from the secularism that attaches value to such lives, and teaches people to look for happiness in their present existence, which he assumes is intended to be reached by social reform. To this extent, he is in accord with the religious impulse that refuses to be satisfied with this aim, even assuming it to be achievable. Yet having repudiated the notion of a world of being over and above that of becoming, what version of the religious alternative is available to him? Despite Nietzsche's talk of the eternal return as an 'approximation' to a world of being, any affirmation of life must be an affirmation of becoming, and this is also true of the doctrine. The commentator who pursues this point the furthest is Gilles Deleuze, who warns against understanding the eternal return 'of the same' as approximating to being through a reinstatement of the identities that Nietzsche has already denied.

> We misinterpret the expression 'eternal return' if we understand it as 'the return of the same'. It is not being that returns but rather the returning itself that constitutes being insofar as it is affirmed of becoming and of that which passes. It is not some one thing which returns but rather returning itself is the one thing which is affirmed of diversity or multiplicity. (Deleuze 1983: 48)[22]

---

[20] Cf. e.g. *BGE* 206.   [21] *TL*, ed. Breazeale 1979: 84.   [22] Cf. Deleuze 1994: 41.

It is returning itself that enables us to understand what becomes and cannot begin or end its becoming. He concludes: 'Returning is the being of that which returns'.

The problem that Nietzsche poses, as I noted at the beginning, is that of deciding between being and becoming, where each option presents difficult challenges for both knowledge and life. In terms of temporality, it is the predicament of human beings who are caught between a past and future at odds with one another. If we make this our starting point, his solution can only be a different mode of time providing reconciliation, in which past and future 'dwell together' and provide a home for the individual person.[23] In that case, a human life is not just a brief interval within a world-time that has no beginning or end, but rather a self-contained, individual time that provides an 'image of eternity' (Small 2010: 161–6). Alcmaeon of Croton is said to have taught that 'Men die for this reason, that they cannot join the beginning to the end' (Kirk and Raven 1957: 235). The thought of eternal return, if it promises a new mode of temporality, may be a fulfilment of his enigmatic formulation. Hence, perhaps, Nietzsche's equally cryptic words: 'This life—your eternal life!' (*KSA* 9: 11 [183].513).

BIBLIOGRAPHY

(A) Works by Nietzsche

PPP   *The Pre-Platonic Philosophers*, ed. and trans. G. Whitlock. Urbana and Chicago: University of Illinois Press, 2001.

PTG   *Philosophy in the Tragic Age of the Greeks*, trans. Marianne Cowan. South Bend, Ind.: Gateway Editions, 1962.

TL   'On Truth and Lies in a Non-Moral Sense', in *Philosophy and Truth*, ed. Daniel Breazeale. Atlantic Highlands, NJ: Humanities Press, 1979.

In quoting from Nietzsche's published works and from texts included in *The Will to Power*, I have used the English translations of Walter Kaufmann and R. J. Hollingdale, with occasional modifications. Other translations are my own unless otherwise stated.

(B) Other Works Cited

Aristotle. 1984. *The Complete Works of Aristotle*, ed. J. Barnes. Princeton: Princeton University Press.

Aristoxenus. 1990. *Elementa Rhythmica*, ed. and trans. Lionel Pearson. Oxford: Clarendon Press.

Clark, Maudemarie. 1990. *Nietzsche on Truth and Philosophy*. Cambridge: Cambridge University Press.

Deleuze, Gilles. 1983. *Nietzsche and Philosophy*, trans. Hugh Tomlinson. London: Athlone Press.

Deleuze, Gilles. 1994. *Difference and Repetition*, trans. Paul Patton. New York: Columbia University Press.

Hatab, Lawrence J. 2005. *Nietzsche's Life Sentence: Coming To Terms With Eternal Recurrence*. New York and London: Routledge.

Heidegger, Martin. 1979–82. *Nietzsche*, trans. D. F. Krell. San Francisco: Harper and Row.

---

[23] See Small 2010: 160.

Kirk, G. S. and Raven, J. E. 1957. *The Presocratic Philosophers: A Critical History with a Selection of Texts.* Cambridge: Cambridge University Press.

Klossowski, Pierre. 1997. *Nietzsche and the Vicious Circle*, trans. Daniel W. Smith. London: Athlone Press.

Liebmann, Otto. 1865. *Kant und die Epigonen: Eine kritische Abhandlung.* Stuttgart: Carl Schober.

Magnus, Bernd. 1978. *Nietzsche's Existential Imperative.* Bloomington and London: Indiana University Press.

Magnus, Bernd. 1979. 'Eternal Recurrence', *Nietzsche-Studien* 8: 369–70.

Nehamas, Alexander. 1985. *Nietzsche: Life As Literature.* Cambridge, Mass.: Harvard University Press.

Plato. 1937. *The Dialogues of Plato*, trans. B. Jowett. New York: Random House.

Rée, Paul. 2003. *Basic Writings*, ed. and trans. Robin Small. Urbana-Chicago: University of Illinois Press.

Richardson, John. 1996. *Nietzsche's System.* New York: Oxford University Press.

Richardson, John. 2004. *Nietzsche's New Darwinism.* New York: Oxford University Press.

Richardson, John. 2006. 'Nietzsche on Time and Becoming', in Keith Ansell-Pearson (ed.), *A Companion to Nietzsche.* Oxford: Basil Blackwell, 208–29.

Schopenhauer, Arthur. 1965. *On the Basis of Morality*, trans. E. F. J. Payne. Indianapolis: The Bobbs-Merrill Company.

Schopenhauer, Arthur. 1974. *Parerga and Paralipomena*, trans. E. F. J. Payne. Oxford: Clarendon Press.

Small, Robin. 2010. *Time and Becoming in Nietzsche's Thought.* London and New York: Continuum.

Stambaugh, Joan. 1987/1959. *The Problem of Time in Nietzsche*, trans. John F. Humphrey. Lewisburg: Bucknell University Press.

Stegmaier, Werner. 2006. 'Nietzsche's Doctrines, Nietzsche's Signs', *Journal of Nietzsche Studies* 31: 20–41.

Wagner, Richard. 1913. *Gesammelte Schriften und Dichtungen*, ed. Wolfgang Golther. Berlin: Deutsches Verlagshaus Bong & Co.

CHAPTER 28

....

ETERNAL RECURRENCE

....

PAUL S. LOEB

INTRODUCTION

....

MY goal in this essay is to offer a critical evaluation of the state of the debate regarding Nietzsche's doctrine of eternal recurrence. A key assumption governing my evaluation is that we should heed Nietzsche's own advice for interpreting his doctrine—especially his claim that this was the most consequential discovery of his career. Since contemporary scholars would probably rank eternal recurrence as his most puzzling and least compelling idea, I am led to the provisional conclusion that the current debate is overlooking the most important features of Nietzsche's doctrine.[1]

The chief reason, I think, is that the philosophical participants are avoiding the poetic work that Nietzsche said was the key to understanding his doctrine—*Thus Spoke Zarathustra*. Certainly this has something to do with the historical tension between philosophy and poetry and with the associated presumption that a philosopher will always choose to communicate and argue for his claims in his own voice. It is ironic that this tension can be traced back to Plato, since his own dialogues do not conform to this presumption. This is relevant, I will argue, because Nietzsche's *Zarathustra* is modeled upon Plato's invention of philosophical literature (*BT* 14), and because his doctrine of recurrence has many points of contact with Plato's doctrine of reincarnation in the *Phaedo*. Like Plato, that is, Nietzsche decided to communicate his most valued idea through a fictional narrative.

Although there is a lot of interesting debate today about Plato's use of philosophical drama, most scholars would agree that he wrote the *Phaedo* with the expectation that his appropriate readers would examine, test, and hopefully become convinced of his reasons for believing in the truth of reincarnation. Similarly, I think, Nietzsche wrote *Zarathustra* with

---

[1] Throughout this essay I am referring for the most part to Anglophone scholars. I should note, however, that scholars have been dismissive of Nietzsche's doctrine since they first began examining his philosophy. Indeed, as I mention below, Georg Simmel's 1907 critique has influenced most of the scholarly response during the last half century.

the expectation that his appropriate readers would come to share his belief in the truth of eternal recurrence.

Scholars today argue that Nietzsche could not have expected this, but their reasons have little to do with what he says. Rather, they themselves are convinced that there could not be any evidence to support this belief; that science has no room for such a bizarre cosmological theory; and that such a belief is irrelevant to his ideal of life affirmation. Following Nietzsche's suggestion that his doctrine may be traced back to the Stoics (*EH*: "The Birth of Tragedy" 3), I will categorize these objections as pertaining to the logic, physics, and ethics of eternal recurrence. Against these objections, and against the supposed principle of charity being invoked on Nietzsche's behalf, I will offer the following rebuttals: the first begs the question against Nietzsche's doctrine; the second depends upon an impoverished understanding of the scientific cosmology in Nietzsche's time and ours; and the third degrades Nietzsche's doctrine into a life-denying thought experiment. Once we get past these tendentious and dismissive approaches, we will be in a better position to understand why Nietzsche regarded eternal recurrence as his most significant contribution to philosophy and to conduct an informed debate about these reasons.

The Primary Text

Recent scholarly discussion of Nietzsche's doctrine of eternal recurrence usually begins and ends with the details of its presentation in *GS* 341. But this presentation leads into the next section and thus into the start of Nietzsche's next book, *Thus Spoke Zarathustra*. This book, he tells us, is his best and most important work, and is entirely informed and organized by the thought of eternal recurrence. His clear instruction, then, is that we are to think of *GS* 341 as a kind of preview of his next book. The single-paragraph introduction of eternal recurrence in *Gay Science* was supposed to provoke his readers into investigating the full-blown treatment of this concept in his subsequent book. Indeed, since the *Gay Science* treatment is so compressed and obscure, Nietzsche probably did not expect his readers to be able to understand it until they had studied his next book. I think he would have been astonished to find contemporary scholars devoting such intense attention to this single section while virtually ignoring the *magnum opus* for which it was an advertisement. To take a comparable example, we would be dismayed and suspect scholarly sloth, if a Kant scholar chose to ignore the first *Critique* and study only the *Prolegomena*. Yet contemporary Nietzsche scholars typically rely on far less when discussing his doctrine of eternal recurrence.

To be more specific, a close reading of the two sections framing *GS* 341 shows that Nietzsche's first presentation of eternal recurrence is carefully constructed so as to anticipate the conclusion of his three-part published *Zarathustra*. In this conclusion, and in contrast to Socrates' curse on life in *GS* 340, Zarathustra ends his journey by affirming and blessing life's recurrence. But *GS* 342 contains only the very start of *Zarathustra* in which the protagonist begins to descend from his mountain. Thus, in *GS* 342 and *GS* 341 we can see Nietzsche's preview of the start and finish of his next published book. Everything in between still remained to be written. Since Nietzsche informs us that eternal recurrence is the conceptual underpinning of the entire *Zarathustra*, this means that *GS* 341 only conveys those aspects of eternal recurrence that inform the last few pages of the published *Zarathustra*.

As we might expect from a mere paragraph-long invitation, then, *GS* 341 includes a very limited treatment of Nietzsche's doctrine of eternal recurrence. Some of what is left out can be discerned once we note that the second chapter of Part 3 of *Zarathustra*, entitled "On the Vision and the Riddle," anticipates the ending of the published book. *GS* 341 also previews the "Vision and Riddle" chapter, and indeed Nietzsche uses parallel concepts and language in both texts: a special moment (*Augenblick*) that includes an experience of the most solitary solitude; a hushed interrogation regarding life's eternal recurrence; and a vision of moonlight between the trees with a crawling spider. We can infer, then, that Nietzsche intended students of *GS* 341 to transfer their interpretive attention to the expanded version of this section in the "Vision and Riddle" chapter and its immediate context. If they did so, they would notice three crucial respects in which the *GS* 341 treatment of eternal recurrence is amplified in the later *Zarathustra*.

First, whereas *GS* 341 only refers to life's eternal recurrence in the future, the "Vision and Riddle" chapter also refers to this recurrence in the past and even implies the possibility of remembering aspects of the present life as having already been lived. And since this past recurrence is identical to the future recurrence, the "Vision and Riddle" chapter includes the additional and startling implication that it may be possible to have a prospective memory of life's future recurrence and of aspects of life that have not yet been experienced in the current iteration. Second, whereas *GS* 341 simply includes a revelation of eternal recurrence, the "Vision and Riddle" chapter offers a dialectical and deductive proof of eternal recurrence that assumes relational time and causal entanglement and that closely resembles the proofs Nietzsche sketched in his notes. And, third, whereas *GS* 341 concentrates on querying the reader's transformational response to the revelation of his life's eternal recurrence, the "Vision and Riddle" chapter links this transformation to Zarathustra's prevision of himself as advancing beyond the human. In short, Nietzsche's fuller treatment of eternal recurrence in *Zarathustra* involves mnemonic evidence, cosmological proof, and the *Übermensch*. But since most scholars ignore this book when they examine Nietzsche's doctrine, they do not notice or discuss these additional points. Or worse yet, they assume that Nietzsche deliberately omitted them.

After the publication of *Zarathustra*, Nietzsche very rarely writes about eternal recurrence in his own voice, and when he does so, he always refers the matter back to his book *Zarathustra*. In section 56 of *Beyond Good and Evil*, he describes his ideal figure, obviously referring back to Zarathustra, as someone who will shout *da capo* to the whole spectacle of life and as someone who is perhaps best described as a *circulus vitiosus deus*. In *Twilight of the Idols*, Nietzsche appears to take ownership of the doctrine when he concludes by describing himself as the teacher of eternal recurrence. But in fact this self-description is couched between, on the one side, another self-description of himself as the last disciple of the philosopher Dionysus, and on the other side, a concluding quote from *Zarathustra* entitled, "The Hammer Speaks." Since Nietzsche identifies the philosopher Dionysus with Zarathustra (*EH*: "Thus Spoke Zarathustra" 6–8), the phrase "I, the teacher of eternal recurrence" is therefore bracketed on both sides by Zarathustra's teaching. In his later autobiography, *Ecce Homo*, Nietzsche explicitly describes eternal recurrence as belonging to Zarathustra (*EH*: "The Birth of Tragedy" 3) and discusses this doctrine in the context of discussing the origin and merits of his earlier book *Zarathustra*. Contemporary scholars often interpret these various post-*Zarathustra* passages as showing Nietzsche's disinclination to endorse the doctrine of eternal recurrence. But he himself explains at the end of the second essay of *Genealogy of Morals* that he is a product of his decadent age and is therefore not strong or healthy enough to teach and affirm this mightiest of all thoughts. The best he can do, he says, is poetically to imagine some future stronger and healthier philosopher who will be able to do so. Nietzsche even makes a show of censoring himself so that he will not interfere with this future teacher's rightful task (*GM* II: 24–5). And the only place where he envisions this teacher and his task is in the fictional and poetic narrative of his primary text, *Thus Spoke Zarathustra*.

Truth in Fiction

Scholars hoping to avoid *Zarathustra*, as well as any consideration of Nietzsche's belief in the truth of eternal recurrence, find in *GS* 341 an ideal *locus classicus*. This is because the section posits a merely hypothetical scenario as the context for introducing eternal recurrence, and only enquires about the possible responses to this scenario as indications of the extent to which life is affirmed. The section characterizes eternal recurrence as an overpowering thought with transformative potential, but does not seem to claim the truth of this thought or to offer any evidence or demonstration in support of it. Indeed, Nietzsche seems to have devised a fantastical scenario that would minimize any such considerations: what if, some day or night, at a moment when you are all alone, and when the moonlight shines between the trees and a spider crawls by, a demon steals after you to tell that you that your life must eternally recur?

Unfortunately, these supposed advantages of *GS* 341 are gained at the expense of careful exegesis. Scholars today invariably read, quote, and debate the details of *GS* 341 as if it were a self-contained and isolated section. But a close examination of the text shows that *GS* 341 is actually a narrative bridge between the two sections that frame it. Having hypothesized in *GS* 340 that Socrates' dying words revealed his hatred of life, Nietzsche enquires in *GS* 341 as to whether the reader would be inclined to offer a similar response. Or, he asks, would the reader instead respond in a way that discloses the love of life that *GS* 342 anticipates will be revealed by Zarathustra as he finishes going under?

Nietzsche's triptych design thus sets quite rigorous constraints on any interpretation of the middle section. In particular, and contrary to scholarly consensus today, the hypothetical phrase at the start of the section, "What if [*Wie, wenn*]," is not a device for suspending the question whether eternal recurrence is true, but rather a means of extending the hypothesis about the dying Socrates that was posited in the preceding section. And what appears to be a fantastical scene when *GS* 341 is read in isolation is actually a detailed continuation of this same hypothesis:

- The moment (*Augenblick*) in which the demon speaks refers back to the last moment (*Augenblick*) of Socrates' life, the same moment (*Augenblick*) in which he loosened his tongue.
- The day or night setting that is accompanied by moonlight suggests the midnight moment of death that could arrive at any moment (*Z* IV: "The Intoxicated Song").
- The demon's announcement itself, concerning the reliving of the life that is now

being lived and has been lived—but not the life that remains to be lived in the future—implies that this announcement arrives at the end of this life.

- The longing for a last (*letzten*) eternal confirmation and seal refers back to Socrates' last word (*letzte Wort*) and last judgment (*letztes Urtheil*) and implies again that this is a dying revelation.
- The most solitary solitude in which one hears a secret and hushed voice alludes to the poetic idea that everyone dies alone, and also to the silence and secrecy that Socrates should have kept in the last moment of his life.
- The spider and dust allude to common death imagery of cobwebs, ashes, and tombs (*Z* IV: "The Intoxicated Song").
- The demon refers to Socrates' *daimon*, and the auditory and prophetic aspects of the demon's revelation allude to Socrates' *daimonion*.
- The crushing effect of this announcement alludes back to the list of possible causes of Socrates' breaking his silence as he died.
- The cursing of the demon, as opposed to the blessing of the god, refers back to Socrates' blasphemous dying words in the guise of a tribute to the god Asclepius.
- The throwing oneself down and gnashing of one's teeth allude back to Socrates' suffering from life and his taking revenge on life (*Z* II: "Of Redemption").

Taken together, all these close links between *GS* 340 and *GS* 341 show that Nietzsche's questions for the reader are therefore much more precise and concrete than the ones usually attributed to him in today's debate: "What if, in the last moment of your life, it were revealed to you, as perhaps it was revealed to Socrates, that you would have to eternally relive your identical life? Would you not curse this revelation, as perhaps Socrates did? Or do you love yourself and life enough to long for nothing more than this dying revelation?"

These questions take their departure from Plato's conceit in the *Phaedo* that Socrates died happy believing that his immortal soul was about to be released from the wheel of reincarnation in order to take its place among the gods. According to Plato's interpretation, Socrates' last words, in which he asks for a sacrifice to be made to the god of health, demonstrated his dying belief that he had been cured from the illness that is life. But Nietzsche contests Plato's interpretation and claims that Socrates' last words actually expressed his sudden and overwhelming despair. All of his life, Nietzsche writes, Socrates had kept a cheerful demeanor that concealed his true pessimistic judgment, but at the very last moment something happened that finally loosened his tongue and revealed his lifelong suffering. Although in *GS* 340 Nietzsche mentions death, poison, piety, and malice as possible causes, his allusions in *GS* 341 to Socrates' *daimon* and *daimonion* suggest the real cause. For Plato characterizes Socrates' *daimon* as his appointed guide to Hades (*Phaedo* 107d–e; see Plato 1993) and Socrates' *daimonion* as the sign that assured him death would be a good thing (*Apology* 40a–41d; see Plato 2002). Nietzsche thus speculates, against Plato's interpretation, that the dying Socrates could not have believed that he had been cured from the sickness of life or escaped to some better afterlife. Instead, Nietzsche suggests, Socrates' *daimon* must have revealed to him that he would have to return after all, and indeed to the exact same life that caused him such suffering. In fact, Nietzsche's title for *GS* 341, "The Greatest Heavy Weight," and his depiction of eternal recurrence as a crushing revelation that causes the listener to throw himself down, both allude to Plato's claim in the *Phaedo* that the soul's reincarnation is a process of being dragged back down to earth and back into the body by its heavy corporeal burdens.

On this properly contextualized reading of GS 341, and as befits a doctrine that concerns life's eternal repetition, Nietzsche presents eternal recurrence as a reality that is revealed at the moment of death. Through a re-enactment and reinterpretation of Plato's fictional portrayal of the dying Socrates, Nietzsche communicates his belief in the truth of his doctrine and also his understanding of the way in which this truth comes to be known. Although some scholars (cf. Clark 1990: 251–2) emphasize the unreliability of the demon figure in GS 341, a properly contextual reading shows that Nietzsche actually chose this figure so as to convey truth, revelation, and certainty. Skeptical scholars also often import the first words of GS 341, "Wie, wenn" into the demon's announcement itself so as to find there only a hypothetical question about eternal recurrence—"what if eternal recurrence were true?" (cf. Parkes 2005: xxiii–xxv). But in fact the demon flatly asserts the reality of eternal recurrence and even implies that this is a necessary reality. These same scholars project their own skepticism onto Nietzsche when they argue that he must not have believed in the truth of his doctrine because he did not choose to introduce it in his own voice. But since Nietzsche stages a dramatic scene in which the reality of eternal recurrence has a dramatic effect upon Socrates, he actually displays a commitment to his doctrine that lies outside the scope of the demon's announcement. By using poetic fiction to show truth, and by implicitly endorsing the metanarrative reality of eternal recurrence, Nietzsche aims to follow Plato in motivating his doctrine better than he could with traditional philosophical exposition.

However, Nietzsche does not just reimagine the dramatic ending of Plato's *Phaedo*. Because GS 341 is a narrative bridge between GS 340 and GS 342, Nietzsche is also setting up a new dramatic scene in which his own protagonist Zarathustra will experience a dying revelation of his life's eternal recurrence. This protagonist will be the antipode of Plato's Socrates, and GS 341 lets us know that he will be so well disposed to himself and to life that he will long for nothing more fervently than for this last eternal confirmation and seal. Zarathustra will be compelled by his dying revelation to respond to his own *daimon* as a god and to bless his own *daimon*'s announcement as divine.

Although GS 342 does not show this deathbed scene, it does depict Zarathustra's overflowing bliss as he begins his descent from his mountain to communicate his accumulated wisdom. Moreover, this physical descent is framed as the start of a protracted perishing or downfall (*Untergang*) that will culminate with Zarathustra setting like the sun and metaphorically descending into the underworld (*der Unterwelt*). This culmination is fulfilled nearly two years later in the conclusion of Nietzsche's published book—in the chapter at the end of Part 3 where Zarathustra's soul joyfully sings to himself of his lust for the wedding ring of recurrence that transforms his beloved life into eternity.[2] There are many clues in this chapter and the immediately preceding chapters that this song is a response to his deathbed revelation of eternal recurrence:

- The spiritually convalescing Zarathustra is bedridden, weary, sick, and unable to recover from his crucifying struggle with his most abysmal thought.

---

[2] For an account of the fourth part that Nietzsche wrote later but chose not to publish, see Loeb 2010: 85ff.

- Zarathustra's animals spoke of his impending deathbed speech in which he would announce the end of his *Untergang* and his eternal return.
- Zarathustra's soul is an overripe vine and longingly awaits his harvester in the golden death-bark.
- Zarathustra's soul has confirmed that he wants to leave life when the ancient bell tolls midnight.
- Zarathustra's soul sings his last song just as the bell tolls midnight, a song that concludes by announcing his bird-like flight into the sky.
- The published book then ends without the signature line that is common to every other chapter of the book in which Zarathustra has been speaking or singing ("Thus spoke (or sang) Zarathustra" or some variation of this).

The "Vision and Riddle" chapter in *Zarathustra* is the other key evidence that Nietzsche ended his published book with Zarathustra's joyful response to the deathbed revelation of his life's eternal recurrence. For in this chapter Zarathustra recounts a vision-riddle that has as its centerpiece a gateway inscribed "*Augenblick*." We have already seen that this term alludes back to the midnight *Augenblick* of death in *GS* 340–1 and that in these sections Nietzsche includes the death imagery of solitude, silence, secrecy, spider, and moonlight. Nietzsche repeats this same exact death imagery in Zarathustra's recounted vision-riddle and adds a death-saturated atmosphere of gloominess, corpse-colored twilight, sleep-interrupting wicked dreams, stillest midnight, deathly silence, ghosts, thieves, desolation, and an overhanging full moon that terrifies a howling dog. Also, just after invoking a courage that slays even death itself, Zarathustra sees a gateway just where he comes to a stop in his climb upward. Nietzsche thus alludes to the poetic images of death as a kind of door, threshold, or portal (*HAH* I: 113) and of the transition from life to death as taking place in an instant or *Augenblick* (*Z* III: "The Convalescent" 2). He also alludes to the ancient symbol, used by Plato in the *Phaedo*, of the gateway to Hades that is guarded by a Cerberus-like dog. Since Zarathustra says that his vision-riddle was actually a prevision (*Vorhersehn*), and since this prevision is fulfilled in the concluding chapters of the published book, Nietzsche leads us to infer that Zarathustra is recounting his prevision of the moment when he will die as the ancient bell tolls midnight at the end of the published book.

In his depiction of Zarathustra's vision-riddle, Nietzsche also fulfills his *GS* 340–2 promise of a deathbed contest between Socrates and Zarathustra as to who is better disposed toward life. First of all, he stages a dialectical confrontation between Zarathustra and his Socratic archenemy at the site of this gateway-*Augenblick*. This time, however, Zarathustra assumes the role of the demon, and after eleven deductive steps (divided by Nietzsche into eleven separate paragraphs), he communicates his most abysmal thought and proves to his Socratic archenemy what he is unable to bear—namely, that he will have to eternally return into his identical life. At this point, Zarathustra suddenly hears a dog howling nearby and recalls hearing and seeing this very same howling dog in the earliest days of his childhood. More specifically, he remembers that the terrified dog was howling in the stillest midnight and that he was howling at the full moon that was passing overhead in deathly silence and stopping to rest like a ghost or a thief above the roof of the dog's house. Zarathustra then notices that the gateway and his archenemy have vanished and he wonders whether he has just woken from a dream. Nietzsche's implication is that Zarathustra has just crossed the gateway of death and in an *Augenblick* returned into his qualitatively identical life so as to awaken into the first awareness of his early childhood. Since this is a prevision of his midnight-tolling moment of death at the end of the published book, Nietzsche leads us to infer that his dying protagonist experiences a revelation of his eternally recurring life and that his final song of joy and affirmation is a response to just this revelation.

This, then, is what Nietzsche means when he instructs us that eternal recurrence is the organizing concept (*Grundconception*) of his most important book (*EH*: "Thus Spoke Zarathustra" 1). Like Plato, Nietzsche aims to communicate the truth of a doctrine about death and therefore designs a narrative centered around the event of his protagonist's death. But Plato structured the narrative of the *Phaedo* so that it would exhibit the release of Socrates' disembodied, purified, and immortal soul from the eternal cycle of reincarnation. Against this influential plot, Nietzsche poses an alternative narrative structure that displays the eternal return of the embodied Zarathustra into his qualitatively identical life. Like Plato, Nietzsche shows his protagonist experiencing a deathbed revelation of his life after death. But against Plato, Nietzsche posits that his protagonist's life after death will be qualitatively identical to his present life, so that his deathbed response to his revelation serves to demonstrate his devotion to himself and to his life. Nevertheless, both Plato and Nietzsche are committed to the truth of their doctrines at a metanarrative level and their design of these poetic and mythical works invites us to examine and debate this commitment.

The Logic of Eternal Recurrence

Because Nietzsche's doctrine of eternal recurrence claims that I am reliving a life that I have already lived before, the question of evidence or warrant would seem to be obviously answered by an appeal to memory. If I am asked why I believe that I am now reliving a life that I have already lived, the most natural reply would seem to be that I remember having lived this life before. This kind of reply is familiar to us from the concept of déjà vu, and it is certainly more compelling on a personal level than any abstract cosmological proof. So it makes sense that this is precisely Zarathustra's testimony as he crosses the *Augenblick*-gateway of death and begins to relive the life he has just finished living. Just after having unveiled a cosmological proof that shows he will have to eternally return, he hears a dog howling and his thoughts run back to the time in his most distant childhood when he heard and saw a dog howling exactly like this. Nietzsche's clear implication is that the reason Zarathustra comes to believe that he will now be reliving his qualitatively identical life is that he *remembers* having already lived the qualitatively identical childhood moment that he is experiencing now just after having died. Like Plato, that is, Nietzsche shows his protagonist recollecting knowledge from his past life (in this case, the life he has just finished living as he crossed the gateway of death). But unlike Plato, Nietzsche posits that his protagonist's past life was qualitatively identical to his present life, so that his recollection of this past life enables him to foresee what his present life will look like prior to living it.

There are of course many questions that arise at this point, especially regarding the nature, source, and reliability of this kind of memory. But it is remarkable that contemporary scholars do not debate the obvious idea, and Nietzsche's own suggestion, that his doctrine is supportable by direct mnemonic evidence.³ There are two main reasons for this omission. The first I have already mentioned and criticized—namely, that these scholars are simply not interested in a careful study of *Zarathustra* and its literary aspects. The second is more philosophical and has its source in Ivan Soll's development of Georg Simmel's influential critique of Nietzsche's doctrine of eternal recurrence. According to Soll, "[a] person can have no direct memories of earlier recurrences" for "[i]f he did, the increment of his mental life would make him different from his predecessors and hence not an identical recurrence of them" (1973: 340). Accordingly, Soll adds, we should view the above passage in which Zarathustra cites his memory of his most distant childhood as "aberrant and ill-considered" (1973: 335).

Soll's argument has been accepted without question by three generations of scholars, and it has led them all to claim that there could not possibly be any *mnemonic* evidence to support Nietzsche's doctrine. To this, some have added a more general claim against evidence *of any kind*, because such evidence would have to distinguish what is by definition indistinguishable. As Arthur Danto argues: "When two things are so exactly alike that they cannot in principle be told apart, nothing is to count as evidence that there are two things to be told apart" (1965: 204). Citing Leibniz's principle of the identity of indiscernibles, these scholars have followed Bernd Magnus in concluding that Nietzsche cannot establish any meaningful concept of recurrence: "if we take seriously the suggestion that 'recurrences' are literally identical with 'their' occurrences" then "we can say simply that 'recurrence' misleadingly identifies a numerically identical 'occurrence'" (1978: 107).

Thus, scholars do not argue merely that Nietzsche did not offer any evidence to support his doctrine, or that he did not offer enough evidence, or that there is not in fact any such evidence. Instead, many argue the much more radical thesis that Nietzsche's doctrine is by definition insupportable and incoherent. Indeed, in a supposedly charitable extension of this thesis, some scholars add that Nietzsche himself knew this, which is why he never raised questions of evidence or truth with respect to his doctrine. Or, if he ever did raise such questions, we should just ignore these instances as aberrant and ill-considered.

Despite this nearly universal consensus among talented and otherwise careful scholars, it is easy to show that the above critique begs the question against Nietzsche's doctrine. This is because Soll and those who follow him simply presuppose that earlier predecessors do not themselves have the same memories of earlier recurrences. They presuppose, that is, that recurrence is not of the same. But Nietzsche has Zarathustra explicitly deduce the earlier recurrence of his deduction of eternal recurrence, thus implying his predecessor's memory of having made this same deduction before. And even in *GS* 341 Nietzsche has the demon explicitly emphasize the recurrence of his announcement of eternal recurrence, thus implying a later memory of having heard this same announcement before.

Conversely, Danto and Magnus, and those who follow them, simply presuppose that qualitative indiscernibility entails numerical identity. They presuppose, that is, that the same cannot recur. But in *GS* 341 Nietzsche has both the demon and the narrator explicitly say that I will have to live my qualitatively indiscernible life once more and innumerable times more ("*noch einmal und noch unzählige Male*"). And in the "Convalescent" chapter of *Zarathustra*, Nietzsche has Zarathustra's animals explain that according to his doctrine

³ For a recent exception, see Small 2010: 133–9.

they have already been there an eternal number of times ("*ewige Male*") and that there is a great year of becoming that runs down ever anew such that all these numerically distinct years are qualitatively indiscernible in the greatest and even smallest respects ("*—so dass alle diese Jahre sich selber gleich sind, im Grössten und auch im Kleinsten*") and such that in every great year they themselves are qualitatively indiscernible in the greatest and even smallest respects ("*—so dass wir selber in jedem grossen Jahre uns selber gleich sind, im Grössten und auch im Kleinsten*"). In a preparatory note for this same chapter, Nietzsche has Zarathustra himself say that his doctrine of being reborn into a same and selfsame life ("*einem gleichen und selbigen Leben*") has not yet been taught on earth—that is, not on this earth and not in this great year ("*auf der diesmaligen Erde und im diesmaligen grossen Jahre*") (KSA 11: 25 [7]). Nietzsche's reason for adding this qualification is that he imagines the obvious objection that Zarathustra has already taught his doctrine an eternal number of times. Against this potential objection, Nietzsche has Zarathustra cite the numerically distinct but qualitatively indiscernible earths and great years—thus showing that an appeal to Leibniz's principle begs the question against his doctrine of eternal recurrence.

The right kind of evidence for Nietzsche's doctrine should therefore simultaneously show qualitative identity and numerical difference. But this is precisely the primitive role Nietzsche assigns to memory in his most extensive and explicit published presentation of eternal recurrence. It is thus noteworthy that Nietzsche shows Zarathustra recounting a *prevision* of himself as dying and recurring into his most distant childhood. The reason Zarathustra is able to do this, Nietzsche suggests, is that his most distant childhood includes within it a memory of just having crossed the gateway, that is, of having died and recurred. So when this childhood memory finally surfaces into the older Zarathustra's conscious awareness, he is in effect having a prevision—that is, a prospective memory—of the death and recurrence that he has yet to experience in this particular iteration of his life.

However, against this interpretation of Zarathustra's vision-riddle, it might be argued that the conclusion of Nietzsche's published book does not explicitly show Zarathustra crossing a gateway or recurring into his early childhood. So we need to look at the very next scene in Zarathustra's vision-riddle for additional support of this interpretation. Having just wondered if he has woken from a dream, Zarathustra now sees the same howling dog notice his approach and start to scream for help. The dog is jumping around a young shepherd (presumably his owner) who is lying on the ground and choking on a serpent that has crawled down his throat. In contrast with his previous certainty that he had previously heard and seen a dog howling just like this, Zarathustra now asks himself whether he had ever heard a dog screaming for help like this. His answer seems to be no, because his very next assertion is that he has never before seen the like of the young shepherd choking on the serpent ("*Und, wahrlich, was ich sah, desgleichen sah ich nie*"). Nietzsche's implication, then, is that Zarathustra is now recalling a memory of his previous life that was *not* included in his childhood and that, indeed, had never surfaced to his conscious awareness until the moment when he was having this vision. And when we turn to the concluding "Convalescent" chapter of the published book, we notice that Nietzsche has constructed the narrative in such a way that Zarathustra himself undergoes precisely the experience of the young shepherd in his vision—that is, the serpent crawls into his throat and chokes him until he is able to bite its head off. So when Nietzsche has Zarathustra ask his listeners to guess who is the shepherd in his vision-riddle, he is thereby asking his readers to notice that Zarathustra was recounting an accurate prevision—that is, a prospective memory—of the moment later in his life when he awakens his most abysmal thought and (as he tells his animals) is then choked by the serpent-monster that he identifies as the eternally recurring small human (*Z*: III: "The Convalescent"). According to Nietzsche, traumatic experiences are remembered best (*GM* II: 4), and we are told that Zarathustra is unable to forget this shattering experience (*Z* III: "The Convalescent" 2). Nietzsche thus shows us that Zarathustra's dying memory of this fateful struggle is communicated to his awakening consciousness as he returns into his identical life but is repressed until he is older and strong enough finally to recall it in his vision-riddle.

Thus, what is especially novel about the role of memory in Nietzsche's doctrine of eternal recurrence is not the phenomenon of déjà vu, but rather the possibility of prospective memory.[4] Indeed, this is the point of the second section of the "Vision and Riddle" chapter—to relate Zarathustra's accurate prospective memory of certain crucial experiences that he himself will undergo in the chronological conclusion of the book. There are many other places in Nietzsche's book where he depicts and emphasizes his protagonist's prophetic powers. But contemporary scholars miss all these references to mnemonic evidence because they do not take Nietzsche's most valued idea seriously enough to work out its implications and because they are not interested in studying the poetic ways in which he embeds this doctrine in the narrative structure of the book that he regarded as his most important.

The Physics of Eternal Recurrence

Most of the debate concerning the cosmological aspect of Nietzsche's doctrine has involved a contrast between the ideas Nietzsche set out in notes that he never published and the ideas he prepared for publication. All scholars today agree that Nietzsche's unpublished notes from 1881 to 1888 show a sustained interest in eternal recurrence as a true cosmological theory that can be proved with assumptions derived in part from contemporaneous scientific theory and speculation. In the last four decades, however, a consensus has emerged that Nietzsche did not express a similar interest in the works he prepared for publication and that he restricted himself in these works to presenting eternal recurrence as a kind of test, diagnosis, formula, imperative, or ideal of life affirmation. This is a good thing, scholars argue, since Nietzsche's unpublished cosmological theories and proofs have no scientific merit or plausibility. Indeed, they argue further, it is likely that Nietzsche himself understood the inadequacy of these thought experiments and this is why he kept them out of those works he published or prepared for publication.

There is no need to enter here into the vexed and long-debated question concerning the relation between Nietzsche's published and unpublished writings. For the recent consensus that his published writings show no interest in cosmological eternal recurrence, or in proving such a doctrine, is actually grounded in a selective and tendentious reading of the key texts. In the first place, although Nietzsche retrospectively emphasizes *GS* 341 as the

---

[4] There is of course a great deal of scientific skepticism regarding the psychological phenomenon of déjà vu, and naturally even more so regarding the recent claim by Daryl J. Bem (2011) to have offered experimental evidence for the phenomenon of prospective memory.

656 PAUL S. LOEB

place where he introduces eternal recurrence as the fundamental thought of Zarathustra (*EH*: "Thus Spoke Zarathustra" 1), he actually refers to eternal recurrence for the first time in *GS* 109 and he mentions eternal recurrence by name for the first time in *GS* 285. Section 109 of *The Gay Science* is of course one of the most important passages in Nietzsche's corpus, since it follows his first formulation that God is dead. This is the passage in which Nietzsche sets out his programmatic call for completely de-deifying nature in such a way that nature will be pure, newly discovered, and newly redeemed (and hence a means for us humans to begin naturalizing ourselves).

A deified nature, Nietzsche explains, is a nature into which we humans have projected our theological concepts. But these concepts are themselves projections of our anthropocentric, biocentric, and geocentric needs and properties. Thus, completely de-deifying nature, or removing the shadows of God which still darken the human mind, means extracting all such projections from nature, the world, the universe. These projections include: the needs of humans (for novelty, for permanence), the properties of humans (rational, aesthetic, and moral qualities), the properties of human communities (laws), the properties of human machines (functions, purposes), the properties of organic creatures (life, nutrition, growth, self-preservation), and the properties of our astral system (cyclical movement). All of these projections, Nietzsche explains further in *GS* 110, are life-preserving erroneous articles of faith, and when they are finally doubted and denied, truth emerges. The truth, he asserts, is that the total character of the world is in all eternity chaos, lacking order, arrangement, form, beauty, or wisdom—and that "the whole music box eternally repeats its tune—a tune which may never be called a melody" ("*das ganze Spielwerk wiederholt ewig seine Weise, die nie eine Melodie heissen darf*"). Although this conclusion does not include Nietzsche's usual terms, "*ewige Wiederkehr*" or "*ewige Wiederkunft*," he employs a similar phrase when later describing Zarathustra's doctrine of the "endlessly repeated" circular course of all things ("*unendlich wiederholten Kreislauf aller Dinge*") (*EH*: "The Birth of Tragedy" 3). The truth, that is, is eternal recurrence, and the ultimate question, the ultimate experiment, is to what extent we can live in accordance with this truth, to what extent we can incorporate this truth as a condition of life.

Thus, in his very first published reference to eternal recurrence, which is located in *GS* 109 and not in *GS* 341, we find Nietzsche writing in his own voice, characterizing eternal recurrence as both true and cosmological, and even offering a kind of *via negativa* argument on its behalf that is allied to what he regards as the naturalistic project of de-deifying the cosmos. Nowhere in this presentation does he suggest that eternal recurrence is some kind of thought experiment or merely hypothetical claim, and nowhere does he link it to some kind of test, diagnosis, or ideal of life affirmation. For these reasons, an influential scholar like Maudemarie Clark acknowledges that this presentation presents a problem for her anti-cosmological interpretation. Yet she immediately dismisses the passage, because Nietzsche's image of the whole music box eternally repeating its tune "is easily interpreted as a metaphor, and by itself, certainly provides no basis for a cosmological construal of eternal recurrence" (1990: 254). This is an odd gloss though, since Nietzsche argues throughout his whole career that human language simply cannot be rid of metaphor. More precisely, Nietzsche's image is actually a synecdoche, because the finite temporal duration of the music box's tune represents the immeasurably greater, but still finite, temporal duration of the course of the cosmos. Just as a music box will repeat its identical tune once this has been played to the end, so too will the universe repeat its identical course once this has come to an end. Clark also ignores Nietzsche's implicit claim here that music is a particularly useful way for human beings to understand time and eternal recurrence (cf. Cohen 2008; Higgins 1987: 179–84)—a claim that he exemplifies later by invoking song, dance, and musical accompaniment when broaching eternal recurrence in *Zarathustra*. Indeed, his later emphasis on the musical instructions "*Noch Einmal!*" (*Z* III: "Of the Vision and the Riddle" 1; IV: "The Intoxicated Song" 1, 12) and "*da capo*" (*BGE* 56) continues the theme of musical repetition first presented in *GS* 109.

Most importantly, Clark ignores Nietzsche's allusion to the ancient Pythagorean tradition of using music to explain the cosmos—an allusion that is anticipated by Nietzsche's earlier explicit discussion of the Pythagorean cosmological theory of eternal recurrence (*UM* II: 2). And she overlooks as well Nietzsche's allusion to Heraclitus's cosmological interest in eternal recurrence when he describes the cosmos as a "*Spielwerk*"—a reference to Heraclitus's image of the universe as a child's plaything (*BT* 24; *BGE* 57; *GM* II: 16). This last allusion is reinforced in *GS* 285 when Nietzsche includes a Heraclitean mention of the eternal recurrence of war and peace ("*die ewige Wiederkunft von Krieg und Frieden*"). In his later *Ecce Homo*, Nietzsche explicitly traces eternal recurrence back to the cosmological theories of the ancient Greeks when he writes that Zarathustra's doctrine of the unconditional and endlessly repeated circular course of all things might have already been taught by Heraclitus and the Stoics (*EH*: "The Birth of Tragedy" 3). Still, none of these allusions to previous cosmologists should lead us to dismiss Nietzsche's insistence on the novelty of his doctrine (cf. Reginster 2006: 206). For in a note from 1881 Nietzsche warns explicitly against the false analogy, drawn by all these previous philosophers, between the cosmology of eternal recurrence and the cyclical movements obtaining *within* this cosmology, for example, that of the stars, or the tidal flow and ebb, or day and night, or the seasons (*KSA* 9: 11 [157]). Indeed, in *GS* 109 Nietzsche implicitly warns us not to understand the eternal repetition of the cosmos through a projection of the cyclical movements in our own astral system.

Certainly, then, *GS* 109 provides ample basis for a cosmological interpretation of eternal recurrence. Indeed, as Paolo D'Iorio (2006) has demonstrated, Nietzsche's preparatory notes and book annotations show that he composed this section in direct and detailed response to the contemporaneous cosmological debates among prominent figures like Otto Caspari, William Thomson, Eduard von Hartmann, and Eugen Dühring. When we turn next to *GS* 341, which is usually taken to be the clearest evidence and which is usually the only text cited, we find Nietzsche replacing his *GS* 109 cosmological image of the eternally repeating music box with the new, but more explicitly time-centered, cosmological image of a perpetually revolving eternal hourglass of being. For the demon concludes his announcement with this categorical assertion: "The eternal hourglass of being is turned over again and again—and you with it, speck of dust!" ("*Die ewige Sanduhr des Daseins wird immer wieder umgedreht—und du mit ihr, Stäubchen vom Staube!*").

Although routinely ignored or even suppressed by commentators (cf. Clark 1990: 248), this categorical assertion actually motivates the argument of the entire section. According to this argument, the cosmos may be likened to an eternal hourglass of being which is perpetually turned over. Again, Nietzsche here employs a synecdoche in which the amount of finite time it takes for the hourglass to run down represents the immeasurably greater, but still finite, time it takes for the course of the cosmos to reach an end and start over again exactly as before. Since any single human being is merely a grain of sand in this hourglass-cosmos, it follows that he is also perpetually turned over—that is, dies and is then reborn so as to live a qualitatively identical life. Hence, so is the particular human being who is hearing the demon's announcement. There thus arise questions concerning the different kinds of responses to this fact and concerning the different kinds of dispositions to life that yield these responses. The revealed truth of cosmological eternal recurrence is therefore the basis for asking diagnostic questions regarding life affirmation and for suggesting an ideal of life affirmation.

Finally, when we turn to Nietzsche's primary text on eternal recurrence, *Thus Spoke Zarathustra*, we find Nietzsche revisiting this *GS* 341 image of the revolving eternal hourglass of being and expanding upon it in a way that emphasizes the cosmological aspect and amplifies the Platonic background that was introduced in *GS* 340. This time, however, Nietzsche places the image inside the speech of Zarathustra's animals. These animals say that they know what he teaches about eternal recurrence, and Zarathustra agrees that they do indeed know this: [5]

> that all things eternally recur and we ourselves with them, and that we have already been here an eternity of times, and all things with us. You teach that there is a great year of becoming, a monster of a great year: that like an hourglass it must turn itself over anew, again and again [*einer Sanduhr gleich, immer wieder von Neuem umdrehn*] so that it may run down and run out anew:—so that all these years are the same as each other, in what is greatest and also in what is smallest,—so that we ourselves in every great year are the same, in what is greatest and also in what is smallest. (Z III: "The Convalescent" 2)

In this passage, Nietzsche follows Plato's *Timaeus* (39c–d) and introduces a new synecdoche, in which our ordinary temporal measure of a year represents the concept of a cosmological great year of becoming, a monster of a great year ("*ein grosses Jahr des Werdens, ein Ungeheuer von grossem Jahre*"). And he now suggests that his previous image of the cosmological hourglass was a metaphor for this more precise and literal concept. The reason seems to be that this new concept allows for an elaboration of internal temporal structure in a way that his previous images did not. Although he could suggest the time it takes for a cosmic music box to play its tune or for the grains of sand to run out in a cosmic hourglass, he could not describe any other kinds of temporal durations within this cosmic music box or hourglass. Now, however, Nietzsche is able to distinguish between the single great, monstrous cosmic year, on the one hand, and all the small, ordinary years that are contained within this great year, on the other. In this way, he is able to offer a more literal account of the span of eternal recurrence as consisting in a monstrously great number of the kinds of years that we already use to measure time.

In this *Zarathustra* passage, as in *GS* 341, Nietzsche deduces from his cosmological theory of eternal recurrence the recurrence of living beings such as Zarathustra's animals: "so that we ourselves in every great year are the same, in what is greatest and also in what is smallest." In the rest of their speech, Zarathustra's animals further deduce the recurrence of Zarathustra himself when they claim to know the deathbed speech he would give to himself:

[5] Some scholars have claimed that Nietzsche has Zarathustra repudiate his animals' statements regarding eternal recurrence, but in his preparatory notes Nietzsche has Zarathustra himself teach all of what his animals say they know he teaches (*KSA* 11: 25 [7]). See also Loeb 2010: 51–2, n. 18.

"Now I die and vanish," you would say, "and in an instant I am a nothing. Souls are as mortal as bodies.

But the knot of causes in which I am entangled recurs,—it will create me again! I myself belong to the causes of eternal recurrence.

I come again, with this sun, with this earth, with this eagle, with this serpent—not to a new life or a better life or a similar life:

—I eternally come again to this identical and selfsame life, in the greatest and even in the smallest, so that I again teach the eternal recurrence of all things—" (Z III: "The Convalescent" 2)

Here Nietzsche alludes back to his GS 341 image of reliving a life that has nothing new in it and that is identical in everything great and small and all in the same succession and sequence. He also alludes to his image in the earlier "Vision and Riddle" chapter of Zarathustra experiencing the *Augenblick* of death and recognizing that he has returned into his identical life. More importantly, Nietzsche adds here a couple of important points to his previous expositions of cosmological eternal recurrence in GS 109 and GS 341. First, he introduces the concept of the knot of causes (*"der Knoten von Ursachen"*), and he uses this concept to link the recurrence of the cosmos to the recurrence of Zarathustra: Zarathustra is entangled in the knot of causes, the knot of causes recurs, hence the knot of causes creates Zarathustra again. This point is important because it supports Nietzsche's claim, first made in GS 341, of identical succession and sequence (*"und Alles in der selben Reihe und Folge"*). Second, Zarathustra adds that he himself belongs to the causes of the recurrence, which means that he has some part in his own re-creation. This second point is important because it directs us toward Nietzsche's additional claim that nothing causes the recurrence of the knot of causes outside of those causes themselves, and that the cosmos is therefore self-re-creating—or, as Zarathustra's animals put it, "the same house of being builds itself eternally" (*"ewig baut sich das gleiche Haus des Seins"*). Thus, whereas Nietzsche had written in GS 341 that the hourglass of being is turned over again and again (*"die ewige Sanduhr des Daseins wird immer wieder umgedreht"*), he now writes in Zarathustra that the great year of becoming must, like an hourglass, turn *itself* over again and again (*"das muss sich, einer Sanduhr gleich, immer wieder von Neuem umdrehn"*).[6]

As I have said, it is part of the scholarly consensus today that Nietzsche never offered a proof of his doctrine of eternal recurrence in any of his published works, and that the most likely reason for this is that he was not satisfied with the many inadequate proofs he tried out in his unpublished notes. I have already disputed this consensus by pointing to Nietzsche's de-deification argument in his first published presentation of eternal recurrence in GS 109. But Nietzsche points us to a second published argument when he has the dying Zarathustra say that he will recur because he is entangled in an eternally recurring knot of causes. This concept of the entangling knot is first introduced in the "Vision and Riddle" chapter where Zarathustra presents a deductive proof to show his archenemy that they both must eternally return. This proof is more direct, positive, and elaborate than the argument in GS 109, and rests upon two explicit assumptions and one implicit assumption: that the past and future are eternities; that everything is causally entangled; and that time is relational, that is, exists

[6] Together, both these points help to show that Nietzsche thinks recurrence memory is grounded in a causal process and can therefore be counted as evidential (cf. Small 2010: 138).

only as a relation among events. From the first assumption, Zarathustra deduces that everything that can happen must have already happened in the past and must happen once again in the future. But since time is relational, the present moment in which he is speaking must have already obtained in the past and must obtain once again in the future. His second assumption then guarantees an identical sequence in the past and future recurrence of everything, and therefore also in the past and future recurrence of the present moment in which he is speaking. But this means that the present moment in which he is speaking is both preceded and followed by itself—indeed, as Zarathustra concludes, that it draws itself after itself. Thus, although the limited perspective of the present moment shows past and the future as distinct, linear, and infinitely extended; the longer and superior perspective invoked in this proof shows past and future as eventually curving together into a single circular course that is finite but unbounded.

The reason this proof is important is that it shows how Nietzsche's doctrine of eternal recurrence, like that of the Pythagoreans and the Stoics (Long 1985: 26–30), entails the recurrence of time itself. In GS 341, Nietzsche has the demon simply assert that even the present moment in which he is speaking will return in the same succession and sequence. Here, however, Nietzsche has Zarathustra provide a proof as to why the present moment in which he is whispering will return in the same succession and sequence. This proof shows that the qualitative identity of Zarathustra's innumerable recurring lives must include even their temporal properties. In whatever interval of cosmic time Zarathustra lives his life, this is precisely the same interval in which he has eternally lived his identical life before and will eternally relive his identical life again. Thus, when Zarathustra dies, he does not return to begin reliving his identical life at some distant future point in cosmic time, but rather at precisely the same *past* moment when he first began (re)living this life. This is why Nietzsche shows Zarathustra crossing the gateway of death and returning *back* to the exact same moment in his most distant childhood when he heard the howling dog.

Scholars (cf. Small 2010: 137; Krell 1986: 158–76) have often wondered how Nietzsche's doctrine of the eternal recurrence of *the same* could be compatible with his argument elsewhere that the interrelatedness of all things excludes the possibility of any sameness in the world (Richardson 1996: 105). The proof I have just outlined above shows how: the entangled knot of causes guarantees that all interrelations, including those of time, are the same. Scholars (cf. Heidegger 1977: 74–6) have also wondered how Nietzsche's doctrine of eternal *repetition* could be compatible with his argument elsewhere that the world is flux and becoming and that everything is constantly changing over time (Richardson 1996: 76–89). Again, this proof shows how: time itself recurs, and so everything is changing over recurring time.

There are of course many questions that need to be answered about this proof. We need to know more, for example, about Nietzsche's theory of time: whether he is entitled to begin by assuming that past and future are eternal, why he holds a conception of time as relational, and how we should make sense of his paradoxical conclusion that time itself recurs in a circular fashion (Loeb 2010: 24–31, 54–61). We also need to know why Nietzsche helps himself here to the concept of causality when he seems skeptical about this concept elsewhere in his writings (cf. Hill 2007: 77–81). But this is my point: scholars need to admit that Nietzsche did publish a detailed proof of eternal recurrence before this kind of debate can begin (cf. Loeb 2010: 49–63; Small 2010: 124–9). Indeed, besides BGE 36, this may be the only place in his later writings where Nietzsche offers what looks like a traditional deductive proof. A few commentators (cf. Lampert 1986: 165–6, Abel 1998: 249–53) have pointed out that this proof resembles some of the demonstrations sketched in Nietzsche's unpublished notes, and I think this shows that he was confident of this particular proof as his very best effort.[7] The fact that he does not present this proof anywhere else in his published works does not diminish its significance in any way. Scholars too often dismiss Nietzsche's singular and exceptional presentation of his most important ideas as an indication that they are not important at all. But Nietzsche's persistent promotion of *Zarathustra*, his emphasis on the book's doctrine of eternal recurrence, and the various ways in which he points the reader's attention to the "Vision and Riddle" chapter all show that he wanted his readers to give this proof their most close and careful attention.

Another important question regarding this proof concerns its relation to the kind of direct evidence suggested by the demon's revelation in *GS* 341 and by Zarathustra's recollection of his most distant childhood as he crosses the gateway. Why is a proof needed in addition to this direct evidence? Here we need to recall Nietzsche's distinction, explained in *Beyond Good and Evil*, between the context of discovery and the context of proof (*BGE* 5–6). Usually, he writes, philosophers pretend to have discovered their metaphysical claims through pure reason instead of showing the inspiring spirits and demons (*Dämonen*) that actually led them to their discoveries and even to the proofs they construct after the fact. So in *GS* 341 Nietzsche shows us the demon—that is, the subconscious recurrence memory—that inspired his own discovery of eternal recurrence, while in *Zarathustra* he shows us in addition the proof of eternal recurrence that his inspiring demon led him to seek after the fact of this discovery. It is noteworthy that Nietzsche emphasizes the *elenctic* style of this proof and identifies Zarathustra's archenemy-interlocutor with the dying Socrates. Although Nietzsche disparages Socratic reasoning in *Twilight of the Idols*, he also explains how it became victorious among the ancient Greeks and hence dominant in all later Western thinking. So in *Zarathustra* he appropriates dialectical reasoning on behalf of his most important discovery, and he uses Plato's own method to refute his vastly influential counter-theory that death affords an escape into a better afterlife.

Perhaps the most important question for contemporary scholars who are interested in Nietzsche's naturalism is whether *Zarathustra*'s cosmological theory and proof are compatible with modern science. As I have said, the chief reason these scholars hope to interpret away Nietzsche's interest in the physics of eternal recurrence is that they themselves find it bizarre and unscientific. But how is eternal recurrence more peculiar than an inflationary universe, black holes, and dark matter? Nor is it absurd to suggest that the kind of scientific evidence that currently supports these recent cosmological discoveries might eventually come to support a further and all-embracing discovery of eternal recurrence.[8] On the other hand, if by "naturalistic" we mean more precisely, "continuous with the method and substance of *contemporaneous* science," then certainly Nietzsche's *Zarathustra* proof was

---

[7] For most scholars, of course, this resemblance is a problem, since Georg Simmel is thought to have refuted Nietzsche's unpublished demonstrations long ago. But see Moles 1990: 305–10 and Rogers 2001: 86, 89–90, for a convincing account of how Simmel's critique relies on an uncharitable or tendentious reading of these demonstrations.

[8] See for example the recent controversial announcement by V. G. Gurzadyan and Roger Penrose that they have discovered empirical evidence (a pattern of concentric circles in the cosmic microwave background radiation) to support Penrose's conformal cyclic cosmology.

grounded in the most advanced cosmological thinking of his day. This thinking included, for example, Friedrich Zöllner's physical application of Riemannian geometry (Moles 1989; Small 2001: 65–7) and also perhaps Ernst Mach's positivistic critique of Newtonian absolute time (Brobjer 2008: 94–5). Both of these scientific breakthroughs were crucial influences in Einstein's construction of the relativity theory that is the foundation of all cosmological physics today.[9] This is why a few pioneering scholars like Alistair Moles (1990: 329–32) have argued for the compatibility of Nietzsche's doctrine of eternal recurrence with the prevailing Big Bang theory. I would argue further that Nietzsche's *Zarathustra* proof anticipates the current scientific and philosophical debate about Gödel's cosmology and global closed timelike curves (Horwich 1987: 111–28; Earman 1995; Gott 2001: 90–2; Dowe 2009).

THE ETHICS OF ETERNAL RECURRENCE

Everyone agrees that Nietzsche's ethics of eternal recurrence has something to do with his recommended ideal of life affirmation. Scholars usually support this connection with his remark in *Ecce Homo* that eternal recurrence is the highest attainable formula of affirmation (*EH*: "Thus Spoke Zarathustra" 1); and with his concluding question in *GS* 341 as to how well disposed you would have to become to life in order to crave nothing more fervently than its eternal recurrence. On the contextualized reading I have offered above, this connection is supported as well by Nietzsche's hypothesis in *GS* 340–1 that Socrates suffered from life and was therefore crushed by the deathbed revelation of its eternal recurrence. Scholars also often cite the following unpublished remark as evidence of Nietzsche's associated ethical imperative: "My doctrine says: the task is to live in such a way that you must wish live again—you will anyway!" (*KSA* 9: 11 [163]). Together, these passages suggest the following reasoning: we should affirm life; hence we should live in such a way that we are led to affirm life; but affirming life means wanting to relive it eternally in exactly the same way; therefore we should live in such a way that we want our lives to eternally recur.[10]

The difficulties with this fairly minimal and uncontroversial account begin when contemporary scholars attempt to explain why Nietzsche thinks the appeal to eternal recurrence adds anything to his ideal of life affirmation. Why, that is, does Nietzsche think that affirming life means desiring its eternal recurrence? On the reading I have offered in this essay, his reasoning is perfectly straightforward. He takes himself to have made the fundamental discovery that life does in fact eternally recur and indeed necessarily so. He therefore

[9] Notice that both of these breakthroughs, and indeed Einstein's revolutionary thought experiments, were of an a priori nature and appealed to a priori considerations that only later received experimental confirmation. This shows that we should reject the argument of scholars like Clark (1990: 247) who dismiss Nietzsche's cosmological proofs on the grounds that their a priori nature renders them unscientific. Clark's further claim, that Nietzsche's mature philosophy rejects the pursuit of metaphysical truths (such as cosmological eternal recurrence), has been amply rebutted by more recent studies (Richardson 1996; Poellner 2000; Doyle 2009).

[10] The first premise in this argument might seem to conflict with Nietzsche's observation in the *Twilight of the Idols* that the value of life cannot be evaluated, not even affirmatively (*TI*: "The Problem of Socrates" 2, "Morality as Anti-Nature" 5). But a proper reading of this observation (cf. Richardson's essay in this volume) shows that there is no conflict.

concludes that the affirmation of life must include the affirmation of its eternal recurrence.[11] To be crushed by the prospect of life's eternal recurrence is to be crushed by life itself, and to prefer that life would not recur is simply to deny life itself. So the reason I should design my life in such a way that I want to relive it in exactly the same way is that I will in fact be doing just that. This reading explains why, in the unpublished remark above, Nietzsche exclaims at the end, "you will anyway!"

But scholars today, as we have seen, dismiss as absurd the idea that life eternally recurs, ignore or misread those places in which Nietzsche claims to have discovered this, and argue that Nietzsche's published writings show no interest in the truth, warrant, or cosmological aspects of eternal recurrence. Applying what they regard as the principle of hermeneutic charity on Nietzsche's behalf, these scholars are then led to argue that he himself considered any such interest to be completely irrelevant to his ideal of life affirmation. Instead, they claim, Nietzsche devised eternal recurrence as a kind of thought experiment whereby his ideal of life affirmation could be tested, diagnosed, and implemented. One such influential interpreter is Bernard Williams, who writes: "This is an entirely hypothetical question, a thought-experiment. It is not a matter, as I read him, of Nietzsche's believing in a theory of eternal recurrence.... There are some places in which it is treated as a theoretical idea, but they are largely confined to his unpublished notes..." (2001: xvi; see also Parkes 2005: xxiii–xxv).

Two kinds of problems arise straightway for this interpretive consensus. The first has to do with the difficulty in motivating anyone to conduct such a thought experiment, much less to live in accordance with it. Although scholars argue that this thought experiment should leave us crushed, elevated, or transformed, isn't simple indifference the more appropriate response? As Williams asks: "But if the idea of Eternal Recurrence is a thought-experiment, how can answering its question lie on our actions 'as the heaviest weight'? If it is a mere fantasy, then how can 'willing' the Eternal Recurrence cost one anything at all?" (2001: xvi; cf. also Hill 2007: 90–1). The second problem has to do with the contrived and artificial nature of this thought experiment: Why should we imagine that life recurs? Why identically, so that there is no room for even trivial and insignificant changes? And why should we imagine that life recurs eternally? As Williams asks, for example: "If there is anything in this test at all, why would willing one recurrence not be enough?" (2001: xvi).

These two problems have been the subject of vigorous debate for nearly four decades now, and in response scholars have offered ingenious, but exegetically flawed, variations of the thought experiment they attribute to Nietzsche. In the first stage of this response, Ivan Soll argued that Nietzsche believed eternal recurrence could have a profound effect on us even when considered as a mere possibility (1973: 324–5). But in both *The Gay Science* and in *Zarathustra*, Nietzsche indicates the necessity of eternal recurrence. Moreover, in the single unpublished fragment Soll cites as support, Nietzsche is not discussing eternal recurrence, but other circular theories of repetition which, while only probable or possible, have had a tremendous effect in the past: "Let us examine how the thought that something repeats itself has up to now had an effect (the year, e.g. or periodic illnesses, waking and sleeping, etc.). Even if the circular repetition is only a probability or possibility, even the thought of a

---

[11] This is the source of Nietzsche's identification of life and eternity at the end of the published *Zarathustra* (*Z* III: "The Seven Seals" 16)—an identification that has often puzzled commentators on this book (cf. Seung 2005: 227ff.).

possibility can move and transform us, not just perceptions or definite expectations! What an effect the possibility of eternal damnation has had!" (*KSA* 9: 11 [203]).

A few years later, Bernd Magnus proposed that Nietzsche intended eternal recurrence as an eternalistic myth that would counter the transience-devaluing influence of the dominant Platonic and Christian myths (1978: xiv–xv, 159–85). However, in support of his proposal, Magnus argued—incorrectly, as we have seen—that in his published writings Nietzsche always presented his doctrine in allegorical disguise (1978: 162, 179). So in fact Magnus's only evidence is the Platonically inspired allegorical style of *Zarathustra*, and I have argued that Nietzsche intended this style to convey his belief in the truth of eternal recurrence. In a similar vein, Lawrence Hatab—although disagreeing with the idea of eternal recurrence as thought experiment—has more recently cited the "myth-as-story" style of *Zarathustra* to argue for Nietzsche's interest in eternal recurrence as a conceptual myth (2005: 99). But he has no additional textual evidence for this claim other than Nietzsche's early remarks about the ancient Greek interest in myth and mimetic psychology (2005: 9–10, 95–101).

The second stage of scholarly response to these two problems began with Alexander Nehamas's proposal that Nietzsche was only interested in eternal recurrence as the asser- tion of a conditional: "If anything in the world recurred, including an individual life or even a single moment within it, then everything in the world would recur in exactly identical fashion" (1985: 156). Besides the hypothetical start of *GS* 341, Nehamas cites as support this remark from Part 4 of *Zarathustra*: "All things are entangled, ensnared, enamored; if ever you wanted one thing twice, if ever you said 'You please me, happiness! Abide, moment!' then you wanted all back" (*Z* IV: "The Intoxicated Song" 10; 1985: 155). Nehamas rightly emphasizes this remark's background assumption of universal causal entanglement. And he also rightly notes that this background assumption helps to explain why Nietzsche thinks that affirming life requires that we imagine life recurring identically. But according to Nehamas this background assumption is itself supposed to be a cosmological truth, and so eternal recurrence turns out to be more than a mere thought experiment. More impor- tantly, Nehamas ignores Nietzsche's use of this same assumption to support a categorical assertion of the eternal recurrence of the identical in the two key Zarathustra passages I have discussed above—Zarathustra's "Vision and Riddle" proof, and the animals' account of Zarathustra's dying words.

A few years later, Maudemarie Clark set out to improve upon all these previous approaches by arguing that Nietzsche intended us "to imagine eternal recurrence in an uncritical or pre- analytical manner, suspending all doubts concerning its truth or conceivability" (1990: 270). This was a surprising and strange idea: hypercritical Nietzsche was now being interpreted as advising his readers to suspend all their critical faculties when considering what he regarded as his best and most important discovery. This interpretation is surely contradicted by remarks like the following in Nietzsche's notes: "You must have lived through every degree of skepticism and bathed voluptuously in ice-cold streams—otherwise, you have no right to this thought [of eternal recurrence]: I want to guard my thought well against the credu- lous and the enthusiasts!" (*KSA* 9: 11 [339]). But Clark argued that her interpretation was supported by the situation Nietzsche describes in *GS* 341 wherein a demon sneaks into one's loneliest loneliness to proclaim the eternal recurrence—"a situation of vulnerability to suggestions one would otherwise dismiss, a situation in which critical powers are at a minimum" (1990: 251). Against this, however, I have shown above that the demon is a very specific allusion back to *GS* 340 and to Socrates' *daimon* and that Nietzsche intended this allusion to convey truth, certainty, and revelation. In addition, Nietzsche's phrase "*einsamste Einsamkeit*" is more naturally translated as the most solitary solitude, which he explicitly distinguishes from loneliness or desolation (*Verlassenheit*) (*Z* III: "The Home-Coming") and indeed commends as the best possible state for maximizing one's critical powers (*BGE* 44). More recently, and in a similar vein as Clark, Hatab has argued that Nietzsche intended us to experience a theatrical, mimetic reception of eternal recurrence that requires a suspension of disbelief (2005: 99). But, again, he has no additional support for this claim besides the theatrical aspects of *Zarathustra*, Nietzsche's tenuous association of theatre and eternal recurrence in *BGE* 56, and Nietzsche's early discussion of Greek tragedy.

Finally, and most recently, Bernard Reginster has offered to supplement Clark's interpretation by directly addressing the problem of contrivance noted above: if eternal recurrence is not true, why does Nietzsche's ideal of affirming life require that we imagine it as recurring and as eternal? Reginster's answer is that since a life could not recur if it were infinite, the first feature "invites us to think of our life as finite." And since an eternal life must be an only life, the second feature "implies living under the assumption that we have only one life." In this way, Nietzsche's doctrine "expresses the thought that our only life is also a finite life." Hence "willing the eternal recurrence of our earthly life is to welcome its finitude, since it acknowledges, and affirms, the ineluctability of death" (2006: 223). As support for this interpretation, Reginster cites this passage from *Zarathustra*: "Living on earth is worthwhile: one day, one festival with Zarathustra, taught me to love the earth. 'Was that life?' I want to say to death. 'Well then! Once more!'" (*Z* IV: "The Intoxicated Song"). However, what Reginster misses in this analysis is the implication in Nietzsche's ideal of affirmation that we should *not* welcome the finality of death. For the phrase "eternal" qualifies the recurrence of life, not the life itself: the demon announces that we will have to live our same finite life once more and innumerable times more. In terms of qualitative identity, it is true, we have only one finite life; but in terms of numerical identity, we have innumerable finite lives. And although a life cannot recur unless death is unavoidable, it also cannot recur unless death is not final. This is why the ugliest man expresses his love of earthly life by wanting to repeat it, that is, by refusing to welcome the finality of death. Indeed, Zarathustra says that courage slays death itself when it says, "Was that life? Well then! Once more!" (*Z* III: "Of the Vision and the Riddle" 1). Reginster himself concedes this point when he notes that the desire for eternal recurrence, as he has explained it, "is compatible with the desire for life to go on indefinitely" (2006: 226).

Although Reginster's analysis evades the issue of death's finality, this issue has played an important background role in the scholarly debate since it was first raised abstractly by Heidegger in his 1954 essay, "Who is Nietzsche's Zarathustra?" I want to conclude, then, by discussing this role and by showing that this single issue dooms any attempt to interpret Nietzsche's doctrine as a life-affirming counterfactual thought experiment. According to Heidegger, Nietzsche aimed to liberate the will from its aversion to time, transience, and ceasing to be, by introducing a metaphysical doctrine that would have transience abide:

> Only in such a way that, as transience, it does not just constantly pass, but always comes to be. It would abide only in such a way that transience and what ceases to be return as the selfsame in its coming. But this recurrence is itself abiding only if it is eternal. (1977/1954: 74)

The problem, Heidegger writes, is that Nietzsche aims to thereby "represent transience as a fixed becoming within the eternal recurrence of the same, and so to render it secure and stable" (1977/1954: 75). But this means that within this doctrine itself "there is nonetheless concealed an aversion to mere transience" and in this way "even Nietzsche's thinking moves within the spirit of reflection-to-date" (1977/1954: 76).

I think we can sort out two different kinds of criticisms that Heidegger is here making of Nietzsche's doctrine that the ceaseless flux eventually, and eternally, turns back into itself (*KSA* 10: 4 [85], 10: 5 [1].160). The first is that this doctrine, which is supposed to eulogize and justify all transience (*Z* II: "On the Blissful Islands"), actually represents flux as fixed and therefore not as flux at all. But this is clearly a misreading of Nietzsche's doctrine, and Heidegger himself seems to admit this when he writes that for Nietzsche the permanence does not consist in something static, but in a recurrence of the same (1977/1954: 69). Hence his second and more important criticism is that there is an aversion to mere transience concealed within the doctrine's claim that the transient recurs as the same, and indeed does so eternally. But here Heidegger simply assumes that Nietzsche's doctrine is false, and that the transient does not in fact ever recur as the same. If Heidegger is right, then Nietzsche's doctrine certainly projects recurrence and eternity where they do not exist and thereby devalues the true reality of mere transience. But if Nietzsche is right, then it is Heidegger who has projected mere transience and thus degraded the true reality of eternal recurrence (see e.g. *KSA* 9: 11 [163]; 13: 11 [94]). In short, Heidegger's second criticism simply begs the question against Nietzsche's doctrine, and he in no way shows that Nietzsche's doctrine is a self-contradictory attempt to degrade the very transience it aims to enshrine.

By insisting that Nietzsche was only interested in eternal recurrence as a countermyth to Platonism and Christianity, Bernd Magnus introduced Heidegger's criticism into the contemporary debate in a way that avoided this charge of question-begging. According to Magnus, the eternalistic aspect of Nietzsche's countermyth is based upon his own inescapable human *chronophobia* and he therefore stands squarely within the metaphysical tradition he opposed (1978: 190–5). At the same time, Magnus emphasized a consequence of Heidegger's criticism that he did not explicitly address: namely, the idea that Nietzsche's doctrine conceals within itself an inability to confront and accept the inescapability and finality of death (1978: 190). Magnus thus proposed what Clark later called an alternative "finitude test": "If we have no reason to believe our life recurs, why isn't our affirmation of life best tested by reaction to a demon who tells us that we will live and die, and that will be it for us? (1990: 278; see also May 1999: 120–1, 125–6). According to Magnus, "internalizing this question would also weigh upon our actions as the greatest stress," for "[i]f I genuinely believe that this life is all there is, it might help me to sort out the trivial from the important, what sustains me from what merely distracts me" (1978: 190).

It is important to notice that this revised Heideggerian criticism is harmless for Nietzsche if, as I have argued, he actually believes that life eternally recurs. For then he also believes that death, although still inescapable, is not final.[12] So there is no need for him to include within his ideal of life affirmation any acceptance of the finality of death. Instead, this new criticism is harmful only for those commentators who dismiss the cosmological idea of eternal recurrence and hope to interpret away Nietzsche's belief in this idea. For they also attribute to Nietzsche the life-affirming ideal of wanting to return to life after death and, indeed, of wanting to do so eternally. Thus, there is a deep inconsistency in the scholarly

---

[12] As we have seen, Zarathustra's death is not final because his dying consciousness returns to his most distant childhood. But death is inescapable because his eternally recurring life has a strict sequence and death is always the final moment in that sequence.

consensus that we affirm our *non*recurring lives by craving their eternal recurrence.[13] And although Magnus attributed this inconsistency to Nietzsche, it was actually an artefact of his own interpretive strategy.

Clark attempted to avoid this problem by arguing that Magnus's finitude test does not necessarily show life affirmation, but she did not answer the question as to how Nietzsche's recurrence test could possibly show affirmation of what she herself believes is a nonrecurring life.[14] Instead, Clark persisted in claiming, falsely as we have seen, that "Nietzsche attempts to formulate what it is to find intrinsic value in a temporal, finite, life, a life that will come to an end." She then simply asserted, implausibly and without explanation, that eternal recurrence helps him to articulate "what it is to accept death in a way that does not vitiate one's affirmation of life" (1990: 278–9). Indeed, although there has been much discussion of Clark's "marriage test" model for Nietzsche's recurrence test (1990: 269–70), no one has pointed out the fundamental disanalogy introduced by her background assumption that life does not recur: wanting to marry again does not mean wanting marriage to be other than it is, but wanting to live again certainly means wanting nonrecurring life to be other than it is.

Although he does not cite Heidegger or Magnus, Aaron Ridley has recently offered a stronger version of their objection to Nietzsche's doctrine. Ridley agrees with Magnus that Nietzsche was not offering eternal recurrence as a cosmological hypothesis but only as a thought experiment designed to test how well one has learned "how to value transience, contingency, embodiment, all the other facts about living immanently" (1997: 20). And he agrees with Magnus as well that eternal recurrence is "Nietzsche's attempt to invent a non-transcendental successor to Christianity—something which will do pretty much the same job as Christianity and will even do it in something like the same way" (1997: 22–3). But Ridley invokes two other themes in Nietzsche, tragic wisdom and *amor fati*, to show why such an attempt is a "philosophical and moral embarrassment" (1997: 25). According to Ridley, Nietzsche's tragic wisdom is that life is fundamentally and ineliminably tragic because the facts of immanent life—for example, that death is inevitable and final—"may not square at all with what, in our heart of hearts, we would dearly love to be the case" (1997: 24). And *amor fati* means for Nietzsche saying Yes to just these "ugly" and inescapable truths about nontranscendental living (1997: 24). Thus, by proposing the "fantasy" of eternal recurrence, Nietzsche seeks, as the Christian seeks, "to transcendentalize the present" and he is thereby "as false as he well could be to his own 'tragic wisdom': he finds himself, in a very blatant way, denying the real character of the fate which, under the sign of *amor fati*, he is committed to loving, to saying Yes to" (1997: 24).

I hope it is clear by now that Ridley's stronger criticism still does not touch Nietzsche if he actually believes that he has discovered the truth of eternal recurrence and indeed formulated his ideal of affirmation in *response* to this discovery. According to this belief, the finality

[13] Nor does it help to suggest that we affirm the cherished moments in our nonrecurring lives by wanting them eternally repeated, since a genuine affirmation of such moments should embrace their essential transience. Similarly, to imagine the painful moments in our nonrecurring lives as eternally repeated does not help us to confront them and overcome them, but rather distorts and inflates their transient significance. Milan Kundera expresses both these points well in his novelistic treatment of Nietzsche's doctrine (Kundera 2009).

[14] For an alternative response, see Del Caro 1989: 223–32. For my criticism of this alternative response, see Loeb 2011: 109–13.

of death is not a fact about life at all and therefore does not need to be affirmed. Instead, what Nietzsche shows Zarathustra discovering is the necessary, ugly, and tragic truth that life eternally recurs and that when we die (which is inevitable) we must always return to our identical lives (Z III: "The Convalescent"). Indeed, Nietzsche tells us, he himself was not strong or healthy enough to affirm this fate (EH "Why I Am So Wise" 3; KSA 10: 4 [81]), and so he had to imagine a future philosopher who would be able to do what he could not do (GM II: 24–5). This is the reason why Nietzsche would argue that his doctrine of eternal recurrence is not a product of the kind of wishful thinking or comforting self-deception he criticizes in GS 277. Moreover, although Ridley does not mention it, Nietzsche's final definition of amor fati in Ecce Homo actually includes eternity: "not wanting anything to be different, not forwards, not backwards, not for all eternity [in alle Ewigkeit nicht]" (EH: "Why I Am So Clever" 10).[15] Nor does Ridley mention Nietzsche's account of Hellenic tragic wisdom at the conclusion of the Twilight of the Idols: "Eternal life, the eternal recurrence of life; the future heralded and consecrated in the past, the triumphant yes to life over and above death and change [über Tod und Wandel hinaus]" (TI: "What I Owe to the Ancients" 4–5).

What Ridley's stronger criticism does show, however, is that his own interpretive approach and that of like-minded scholars is doomed to failure. For he is the one who believes that life is nonrecurring and then interprets eternal recurrence as a counterfactual thought experiment that is supposed to test life affirmation but actually (according to his own lights) demonstrates life denial. Thus, Ridley designs a life-denying test of life affirmation, attributes it to Nietzsche, and then condemns Nietzsche's philosophical embarrassment. Ridley is of course entitled to criticize Nietzsche's belief in eternal recurrence as a fantasy that is inspired by chronophobia and life denial. But in that case, as I have said with Heidegger, he will simply be begging the question against Nietzsche's doctrine. According to Nietzsche, as I have interpreted him in this essay, Heidegger, Magnus, and Ridley are all themselves inspired by recurrence phobia and life denial. The eternal recurrence of life, he would argue, does not square with what they, in their heart of hearts, would dearly love to be the case. Indeed, he would add, one profound consequence of his discovery is recognizing that the ascetic ideal and the will to nothingness continue to guide all those who believe in the finality of death and who aim to affirm life as something that has a final end. Commentators have long identified Nietzsche's conception of the ascetic ideal with the ancient and dominant belief in an afterlife, but they have not yet noticed that this conception must also include the belief that death is final. Certainly modern science instructs us at every moment that death is final, but according to Nietzsche modern science is actually the best ally the ascetic ideal has at present, and precisely because it is the most unconscious, involuntary, hidden, and subterranean ally (GM III: 25). Returning to the themes in GS 340–1, Nietzsche would recall that when Socrates explains in the Apology why he is hopeful that death may be a blessing, he replies that he imagines it would be a great blessing for his soul to relocate to Hades and continue his interrogations among the illustrious ancestors of the Athenians. But Socrates also replies that if death is a complete lack of perception, like a dreamless sleep, then death would be a great advantage: "For I think that if one had to pick out that night during which a man slept soundly and did not dream, put it beside the other nights and days of his life, and then see how many days and nights had been better and more pleasant than that night, not only

15 See Loeb 2013 for my interpretation of Nietzsche's concept of amor fati.

a private person but the great king would find them easy to count compared with the other days and nights" (40c–e).[16]

BIBLIOGRAPHY

(A) Works by Nietzsche

BGE   *Beyond Good and Evil*, trans. Walter Kaufmann, in *Basic Writings of Nietzsche*, ed. Walter Kaufmann. New York: Random House, 1968, 191–427.

EH   *Ecce Homo*, trans. Walter Kaufmann, in *Basic Writings of Nietzsche*, ed. Walter Kaufmann. New York: Random House, 1968, 657–800.

GS   *The Gay Science*, trans. Walter Kaufmann. New York: Vintage, 1974.

KSA   *Sämtliche Werke: Kritische Studienausgabe in 15 Einzelbänden*, ed. G. Colli and M. Montinari. Berlin: Walter de Gruyter, 1988.

Twilight of the Idols, trans. Walter Kaufmann, in *The Portable Nietzsche*, ed. Walter Kaufmann. New York: Viking Penguin, 1954, 463–563.

Z   *Thus Spoke Zarathustra*, trans. Walter Kaufmann. New York: Penguin, 1978.

(B) Other Works Cited

Abel, Günter. 1998. *Nietzsche: Die Dynamik der Willen zur Macht und die ewige Wiederkehr*, 2nd edn. Berlin: Walter de Gruyter.

Bem, Daryl J. 2011. "Feeling the Future: Experimental Evidence for Anomalous Retroactive Influences on Cognition and Affect," *Journal of Personality and Social Psychology* 100: 407–25.

Brobjer, Thomas. 2008. *Nietzsche's Philosophical Context: An Intellectual Biography*. Urbana: University of Illinois Press.

Clark, Maudemarie. 1990. *Nietzsche on Truth and Philosophy*. New York: Cambridge University Press.

Cohen, Jonathan. 2008. "Nietzsche's Musical Conception of Time," in Manuel Dries (ed.), *Nietzsche on Time and History*. New York: Walter de Gruyter, 291–307.

Danto, Arthur C. 1965. *Nietzsche as Philosopher*. New York: Macmillan.

Del Caro, Adrian. 1989. *Nietzsche Contra Nietzsche: Creativity and the Anti-Romantic*. Baton Rouge: Louisiana State University Press.

D'Iorio, Paolo. 2006. "Das Gespräch zwischen Büchern und Handschriften am Beispiel der ewigen Wiederkehr des Gleichen," in Michael Knoche, Justus H. Ulbricht, and Jürgen Weber (eds.), *Zur unterirdischen Wirkung von Dynamit. Vom Umgang Nietzsches mit Büchern zum Umgang mit Nietzsches Büchern*. Wiesbaden: Harrassowitz Verlag, 93–113.

Dowe, Phil. 2009. "Every Now and Then: A-Theory and Loops in Time," *Journal of Philosophy* 12: 641–65.

Doyle, Tsarina. 2009. *Nietzsche on Epistemology and Metaphysics: The World in View*. Edinburgh: Edinburgh University Press.

Earman, John. 1995. "Recent Work on Time Travel," in Steven F. Savitt (ed.), *Time's Arrows Today: Recent Physical and Philosophical Work on the Direction of Time*. Cambridge: Cambridge University Press, 268–310.

[16] I am grateful to Keith Ansell Pearson, Ken Gemes, Scott Jenkins, Ian Schnee, and especially John Richardson for their helpful comments and suggestions on earlier drafts of this essay.

Gott, J. Richard. 2001. *Time Travel in Einstein's Universe*. New York: Houghton Mifflin.

Hatab, Lawrence J. 2005. *Nietzsche's Life Sentence: Coming to Terms with Eternal Recurrence*. New York: Routledge.

Heidegger, Martin. 1977/1954. "Who is Nietzsche's Zarathustra?" trans. Bernd Magnus, in David B. Allison (ed.), *The New Nietzsche: Contemporary Styles of Interpretation*. Cambridge, Mass.: MIT Press, 64–79.

Higgins, Kathleen M. 1987. *Nietzsche's Zarathustra*. Philadelphia: Temple University Press.

Hill, R. Kevin. 2007. *Nietzsche: A Guide for the Perplexed*. London: Continuum.

Horwich, Paul. 1987. *Asymmetries in Time: Problems in the Philosophy of Science*. Cambridge, Mass.: MIT Press.

Kundera, Milan. 2009. *The Unbearable Lightness of Being*. New York: Harper & Row.

Lampert, Laurence. 1986. *Nietzsche's Teaching: An Interpretation of Thus Spoke Zarathustra*. New Haven: Yale University Press.

Loeb, Paul S. 2010. *The Death of Nietzsche's Zarathustra*. Cambridge: Cambridge University Press.

Loeb, Paul S. 2011. "*Zarathustra* Hermeneutics," *Journal of Nietzsche Studies* 41: 94–114.

Loeb, Paul S. 2013. "Ecce Superhomo: How Zarathustra became what Nietzsche was not," in Duncan Large and Nicholas Martin (eds.), Nietzsche's "*Ecce Homo*." Berlin: Walter de Gruyter. Forthcoming.

Long, A. A. 1985. "The Stoics on World-Conflagration and Everlasting Recurrence," *Southern Journal of Philosophy* 23: 13–38.

Krell, David Farrell. 1986. *Postponements: Woman, Sensuality and Death in Nietzsche*. Bloomington: Indiana University Press.

Magnus, Bernd. 1978. *Nietzsche's Existential Imperative*. Bloomington: Indiana University Press.

May, Simon. 1999. *Nietzsche's Ethics and his War on "Morality."* Oxford: Clarendon Press.

Moles, Alistair. 1989. "Nietzsche's Eternal Recurrence as Riemannian Cosmology," *International Studies in Philosophy* 21: 21–35.

Moles, Alistair. 1990. *Nietzsche's Philosophy of Nature and Cosmology*. New York: Peter Lang.

Nehamas, Alexander. 1985. *Nietzsche: Life as Literature*. Cambridge, Mass.: Harvard University Press.

Parkes, Graham. 2005. "Introduction," in Friedrich Nietzsche, *Thus Spoke Zarathustra: A Book for Everyone and Nobody*. Oxford: Oxford University Press, ix–xxxiv.

Plato. 1993. *Phaedo*, trans. David Gallop. Oxford: Oxford University Press.

Plato. 2002. *Apology*, in *Five Dialogues*, trans. G. M. A. Grube, revised John M. Cooper, 2nd edn. Indianapolis: Hackett, 21–44.

Poellner, Peter. 2000. *Nietzsche and Metaphysics*. Oxford: Oxford University Press.

Reginster, Bernard. 2006. *The Affirmation of Life: Nietzsche on Overcoming Nihilism*. Cambridge, Mass.: Harvard University Press.

Richardson, John. 1996. *Nietzsche's System*. Oxford: Oxford University Press.

Ridley, Aaron. 1997. "Nietzsche's Greatest Weight," *Journal of Nietzsche Studies* 14: 19–25.

Rogers, Peter. 2001. "Simmel's Mistake: The Eternal Recurrence as a Riddle about the Intelligible Form of Time as a Whole," *Journal of Nietzsche Studies* 21: 77–95.

Small, Robin. 2001. *Nietzsche in Context*. London: Palgrave.

Small, Robin. 2010. *Time and Becoming in Nietzsche's Thought*. London: Continuum.

Seung, T. K. 2005. *Nietzsche's Epic of the Soul: Thus Spoke Zarathustra*. New York: Lexington Books.

Soll, Ivan. 1973. "Reflections on Recurrence: A Re-examination of Nietzsche's Doctrine, *die ewige Wiederkehr des Gleichen*," in Robert C. Solomon (ed.), *Nietzsche: A Collection of Critical Essays*. Garden City, NY: Doubleday, 322–42.
Williams, Bernard. 2001. "Introduction," in Friedrich Nietzsche, *The Gay Science*. Cambridge: Cambridge University Press, vii–xxii.

PART VI

DEVELOPMENTS OF WILL TO POWER

CHAPTER 29

NIETZSCHE'S METAPHYSICAL SKETCHES: CAUSALITY AND WILL TO POWER

PETER POELLNER

ONE of the interpretive issues that has traditionally divided interpreters of Nietzsche's philosophy is whether Nietzsche is, fundamentally or at least among other things, a metaphysician. In asking this question, I take it that we are asking whether Nietzsche asserts a view about the basic characteristics or properties of reality, or of all entities. Some prominent commentators have given an affirmative response to this question, while others have resisted that answer.[1] The disagreements on this issue tend to correlate with different views readers take on a textual-philological issue, namely the status of Nietzsche's notebooks from the 1880s, selections from which were first published in 1901, one year after Nietzsche's death, by his sister under the title *The Will to Power*. A somewhat expanded version of this selection of notes, under the same title, has been in print and has found widespread circulation since its first publication in 1906. It has often been treated as a 'work' of Nietzsche's, although this is true, at best, in a highly qualified sense. In fact, Nietzsche seems to have abandoned the project for which those notes were originally written in the final years of his active life. The dispute over the question of whether these notebooks contain by and large Nietzsche's final, albeit unpolished views or whether his jettisoning of the *Will to Power* project indicates his eventual rejection of the content of much of this notebook material is no mere philological pedantry. For these notebooks, as well as other notes from the same period but not included in *The Will to Power*, prominently contain many apparent positive claims and reflections on metaphysical issues, while such claims are

---

[1] Representatives of the first group – interpreting Nietzsche as a metaphysician—include Heidegger (1979–87/1961), Schacht (1983, esp. 187–202), and Richardson (1996). Aligned against this reading we find, among others, Jaspers (1936, e.g. 194–5), Nehamas (1985, e.g. 80), Rorty (1989), and Clark (1990: 205–27). Kaufmann (1968, esp. 203–7, 239) and Leiter (2002, e.g. 252) seem to acknowledge a metaphysical dimension in some of Nietzsche's claims but suggest that it is both peripheral to his main concerns and not worth taking seriously.

very largely—some would say entirely—absent from the writings published by Nietzsche himself during his 'mature' period, conventionally dated as beginning after *Daybreak* (1881).

In this essay I shall adopt a two-stage approach. In sections 1 to 4, I shall explicate and assess the *content* of Nietzsche's apparently metaphysical reflections, focusing mostly on the notebooks and bypassing the debate about his own final verdict about this material. Nietzsche's metaphysical ideas, unusual and exotic as they are by contemporary mainstream standards, either deserve to be taken seriously or they do not, and whether they do so is clearly not determined by Nietzsche's own final judgement on them, but above all by their inherent rational merits or flaws, and these can only be assayed by actually engaging with them. Only in section 5 shall I be concerned with Nietzsche's own considered attitude towards these ideas. This attitude raises perplexing questions quite independently of his final judgement on his notebooks. For many of his metaphysical meditations were written simultaneously with or even *later* than statements in the published works which are either sceptical or dismissive of metaphysics for other reasons.

1 FORCES

The following remarks from the concluding notes of *The Will to Power* are often cited as a general and gestural summing-up of the results of Nietzsche's metaphysical reflections:

> And do you know what 'the world' is to me? [...] This world: a monster of energy, without beginning, without end [...] set in a definite space as a definite force, and not a space that might be 'empty' here or there, but rather as force throughout, as a play of forces and waves of forces, at the same time one and many, increasing here and at the same time decreasing here; [...]—*This world is the will to power—and nothing besides!* And you yourselves are also this will to power—and nothing besides! (*WP* 1067)

The world is 'a play of forces' and 'will to power'. What does this mean? I want to explicate the ideas expressed by these phrases in turn. Nietzsche's talk about forces in this passage is partly motivated by reflections on causation and on physical science which occupied him intermittently throughout his active life.[2] What do we commonly want to say when we speak of causes and causal relations? In part, Nietzsche suggests, we mean to say that 'something can be constituted in such a way that when it is posited, thereby something else must also necessarily be posited' (*KGW* VII.3: 34 [70]). A cause, or at least a complete cause, is an item the presence of which is a sufficient condition for another, separately identifiable item. But what needs to be added to distinguish causal relations from other relations of dependence such as logical ones is the notion of a spatiotemporal particular, an 'effective thing' (*WP* 552b) whose 'capacity to produce effects' (*WP* 551) is released in certain kinds of circumstances, thereby necessitating, by producing, various further changes—'complexes of events' (*WP* 552d)—in other things or in the thing itself. By Nietzsche's lights, the pre-philosophical notion of a cause therefore involves the idea of a particular with an efficacious nature,

---

[2] Still useful on this are Schlechta and Anders 1962 and Mittasch 1952. See also Brobjer 2008.

such that in suitable conditions it manifests a force or necessitating 'compulsion' (*WP* 552), 'producing' (*WP* 552c) those events we call its effects.

This naive, pre-philosophical notion of causation was influentially challenged by David Hume, whose criticisms were to shape philosophical orthodoxy for much of the twentieth century. Hume's central argument against it relies on the premise that if there were a necessary connection between two independently identifiable and describable events *a* and *b*—say, a particular throwing of a stone at a glass pane and the breaking of the glass—that necessary relation would itself have to be experienceable in any single instance of A-type events and B-type events jointly occurring in suitable spatiotemporal contiguity. It would have to be possible to 'perceive' the productive, necessitating relation itself on observing such a sequence for the first time, analogously to the way in which we can appreciate the necessary relation between the premises of a valid deductive argument and its conclusion even on being presented with the argument for the first time, if we understand all the terms involved in it. Indeed, Hume seems to think that if there was a necessary connection between *a* and *b*, it would have to be registered in what are standardly regarded as ideal observational or imaginative conditions, such that we could not 'conceive'—imagine—an A without a B, just as we cannot conceive an object being coloured without being extended. But in the case of causation there is no such inconceivability. We only feel that *b has* to follow upon *a* after repeated observation of A-type and B-type events. The idea of natural necessity is thus derived from the psychological compulsion to expect a B to occur once an A has occurred, after repeated exposure to similar sequences. The belief in natural necessity in the objective world is, according to this line of thought, an illegitimate projection of that 'inner impression' onto the objects.

There are affinities with Hume in Nietzsche's thinking on these matters, but also important differences:

> We have no 'sense for the *causa efficiens*': here Hume was right; habit (but not only that of the individual!) makes us expect that a certain often-observed occurrence will follow another […] That which gives the extraordinary firmness to our belief in causality is not the habit of seeing one occurrence following another but our inability to interpret events otherwise than as events caused by intentions. It is belief in the living and thinking as the only effective force—in will, in intention—it is belief that every event is a deed, that every deed presupposes a doer, it is belief in the 'subject'. (*WP* 550)

Like Hume, Nietzsche has a projectivist explanation of the everyday belief in causal efficacy, but what is projected onto the objects, according to him, is not an associative compulsion, but volitional efficacy. Before considering just what this involves, it is worth setting out the main options open to a philosopher who holds, like Nietzsche, that the common concept of causality is based in some way on the idea of volitional agency. Such a philosopher might claim that (1) this idea is just as mistaken as the idea of objective causal efficacy itself. Causal relations as they are in the world do not involve efficacious, necessitating powers. A second option would be to say that (2) there is indeed some kind of epistemic dependence between the concept of causation and that of volitional agency, but that this does not imply an existential dependence. One might hold, for example, that we gain our grasp of causation, as opposed to symmetrical functional dependence, in some way from the experience of intentional interaction with the world, but that this experience acquaints us with causal powers or forces which are themselves not necessarily experiential. Causal forces are discovered by us in experienced intentional interactions with the world, but these forces are not essentially experience-involving. Finally, one might hold that (3) causal relations essentially involve forces, but these are necessarily agencies and thus materially analogous to our volitional agency. Unlike (2) and (3), (1) is an error theory of causation as it is ordinarily understood according to both Hume and Nietzsche. The most popular versions of this error theory have tended to favour revisionist accounts of causation in terms of lawlike regularities. An event sequence is an instance of causation if it is derivable from a lawlike (nomic) regularity of the form 'all As are Bs' in conjunction with a statement of the relevant initial conditions (with appropriate modifications for probabilistic laws). Nomic regularities, unlike acciden- tal ones, can support the counterfactuals that are essentially involved in causal explanations and that evidently stand in need of ontological grounding ('if that stone had been thrown at this window pane with such-and-such velocity, all else being equal, then the window would have broken'). But what is a lawlike regularity? An influential view used to be that laws, at least at the basic level, are not spatiotemporally restricted and that the evidence for them is not identical with their scope of predication and is open to further extension (Nagel 1961: 59–63). An alternative view, which goes back to J. S. Mill and also has contemporary advocates, is that laws are contingent regularities which owe their status as nomic to state- ments describing them figuring as axioms or theorems in an ideal deductive system of our knowledge of the world.[3] Aside from the issue of causal asymmetry and various technical problems, perhaps the most powerful intuitive objection to reductionist accounts of cau- sation according to which there is, ontologically, nothing to causation other than contin- gent regularities is that this seems to make the 'lawful' behaviour of an astronomically large number of supposedly 'distinct existences'—the particulars populating this world, however these are precisely individuated—in principle not amenable to further explanation. The immeasurably complex web of actual regularities making up this world then seems miracu- lous, since nothing is supposed to ground or produce them—according to the (ontologi- cal) regularity view the lawlike regularities are brute, inexplicable, ultimate facts (Strawson 1989: 20–31). It may be said that this is not so since higher-order regularities are explicable by more fundamental ones—ultimately perhaps, by those obtaining at the level of funda- mental physical elements and by various contingent relations of supervenience. But if many of these relations are themselves brute regularities among ontologically unconnected dis- tinct existences, the objector is likely to continue feeling dissatisfied with this explanation. The regularity theorist may insist, of course, that explanation has to terminate somewhere, and that even the friends of necessitating forces sit in the same boat here, since they will be at a loss to explain why there are precisely those very forces which, according to them, ground the causal regularities in the actual world. But this defence seems to overlook an important difference. The opponent of the regularity view is likely to reply that the problem with that view lies in its combination of ontological atomism ('distinct existences') and brute regularities in the behaviour of those supposedly atomic constituents of reality—whether thought of as particular events, timeslices of objects, or whatever. Explanation therefore ends for the regularity theorist at an intuitively deeply unpromising and unsatisfactory ter- minus: brute persistent regularities, pervasive synchronic and diachronic similarity patterns in the behaviour of innumerable putatively unconnected, particular, ontological 'atoms', for which no further reason can or *could* be given even by an omniscient being because, it is

---

[3] See Psillos 2002, esp. chapter 5.

claimed, there *is* no reason. His opponent, by contrast, is not committed to such a counter-intuitive view of where explanation has to terminate because there is allegedly nothing more to explain, while acknowledging that of course it has to end somewhere. An ontology of necessitating powers is, for example, compatible with some form of in principle self-explanatory entity monism (perhaps in Spinozist vein), although (contra Spinoza) *we* may not be able to grasp its 'sufficient reason'.

Nietzsche expresses very similar reservations about whether explanations in terms of contingent regularities provide the kind of explanation we rightly expect:

> *Cause and effect.*—'Explanation' is what we call it: but it is 'description' that distinguishes us from older stages of knowledge and science. Our descriptions are better—but we do not explain any more than our predecessors. [...] In every case the series of causes stands before us much more completely, and we reason: first this and this has to precede if that is to follow—but thereby we have comprehended nothing. In every chemical process, for example, the quality appears now as ever as a 'miracle', just as any locomotion does; no one has yet 'explained' impact. (*GS* 112)

> In fact science has emptied the concept of causality of its content and retained of it only equation formulae, where it is basically irrelevant on which side we place the cause or the effect (*KGW* VIII.3: 14 [98]; also *WP* 688).

> It is an illusion that something is *known* when we possess a mathematical formula for an event: it is only designated, described, nothing more (*WP* 628; also *WP* 624).

> Causality is created by thinking compulsion into the process. A certain 'comprehension' is the result, i.e. we have made the process more human, 'more familiar': the familiar is the familiar human habit of human compulsion associated with the feeling of force (*WP* 664).

The conception of comprehension and its correlative, explanation, broached in these and many similar passages (e.g. *GS* 335; *KGW* VII.3: 34 [246]; *KGW* VIII.1: 5 [10]) is more demanding than that which governs modern scientific practice, namely the subsumption of individual event sequences under laws—contingent correlations stated in the form of functional equations whose variables are interpreted by means of correspondence rules as standing in for quantitative indices of real physical properties. Adequate explanation, Nietzsche suggests, would require an understanding of the 'qualities' responsible for the 'compulsion' involved in individual causal sequences, and these qualities would only be understood by us if we were acquainted with them or at least with materially analogous qualities. It is evident that Nietzsche here takes the untenability of ontological regularity accounts of causation for granted. The qualities he has in mind are clearly those which would constitute actualizations of necessitating forces, forces which the everyday picture of causation—rightly, he thinks—takes to be essentially involved in individual causal relations. Without an understanding of these forces, causal explanation is incomplete or, as he hyperbolically puts it, merely descriptive.

But why is Nietzsche so confident that our acquaintance ('familiarity') with force is to be found, if anywhere, in volitional agency (*WP* 550) rather than in the observation of individual mechanical interactions among objects such as impact and pressure ('no one has yet "explained" impact')? A well-known series of experiments by Albert Michotte shows that observers actually claim to *see* certain kinematic patterns apparently involving contact between moving shapes as causal interactions, in contradistinction to mere successions of events: 'the observers see object A bump into object B [...], *give it a push*. The impression is clear; it is the blow given by A which *makes* B go, which *produces* B's movement' (Michotte 1963/1945: 20). But even if one accepts that this apparent perception of productive causality in this and similar cases is neither the result of Humean association nor inferentially based, this does not show that the subjects actually experience or even take themselves to perceive *efficacy* or force in the apparent interaction, but at best that they have an ability—possibly innate—of perceptually distinguishing event sequences of a visual type that normally involves causation 'by contact' from others which are standardly non-causal successions. Consider, as an analogy: even if it is the case that we can in favourable circumstances literally perceive another person's phenomenally conscious mental states in her expressive behaviour, this obviously does not entail that we perceive the experiential properties of these states (their what-it-is-likeness from the subject's perspective), which are yet essential to their being the conscious states that they are.

But what if we shift the perspective from observation to actual *involvement* in mechanical interactions? When a solid object bumps into me it is surely plausible to say that I experience its efficacy in the tactile pressure exerted on me. And one might then argue—analogously to (2) above—that efficacious force in the objects is what manifests itself in these experiences without being existentially dependent on them (Fales 1990: chapter 1, especially pp. 15–25, 39–46). Nietzsche's reflections suggest two lines of argument against this kind of approach. The first takes its departure from his rejection of mechanist physics. Nietzsche takes Boscovich to have 'refuted' (*BGE* 12) the mechanist conception of nature found in Boyle, Locke, and—leaving aside the mechanically irreducible force of gravitation—Newton. The Lockeans thought of the physical world as constituted by aggregates of particles characterized by the intrinsic primary properties of size, shape, and solidity, the latter taken to be a non-dispositional space-filling property which grounds, but is distinct from, an object's powers—its secondary and tertiary properties, the latter including the dispositional property of impenetrability, although this was not consistently distinguished from solidity by Locke. The details of Boscovich's case against the corpuscularians' absolutely impenetrable extended particles need not concern us here: what matters is that he ends up with a dynamist conception—a predecessor of modern field theory—of the physical world as constituted by real, attractive and repulsive, forces centred on unextended physical points (Boscovich 1966/1763). Matter for him consists intrinsically of forces which are not grounded in any primary, non-dynamical, non-geometrical properties such as Lockean solidity. Independently of Boscovich's arguments, another source of Nietzsche's views on this matter, F. A. Lange, had noted that *if* one locates the causal properties of objects in forces, such as Newtonian gravitational attraction or Boscovichean repulsive forces ('impenetrability'), then non-geometrical and non-dynamical intrinsic physical properties such as Lockean solidity become explanatorily redundant (Lange 1866: 359–73).[4] Nietzsche accepts this general dynamist approach (*KGW* VII.2: 26 [432]), although he does not regard Boscovich's proto-field theory of the physical world as itself adequately explanatory:

---

[4] It has sometimes been objected that physical pan-dynamism is viciously regressive, since forces have nothing to manifest themselves on, unless there are substantial space-occupants 'with an intrinsic nature independent of [their] causal powers' (Foster 1982: 69). If one is impressed by this line of argument and if one also accepts what it surely plausible, namely that scientific explanation has nothing to say about such non-dynamic qualitative intrinsic natures as opposed to forces and their phenomenal (observed or in principle observable) effects, then these intrinsic natures, while not dispensable, become from the perspective of science *opaque*, to use Foster's term: unknown we-know-not-whats.

One cannot 'explain' pressure and impact themselves, one cannot get free of the *actio in distans*:—one has lost the belief in being able to explain at all, and admits with a wry expression that description and not explanation is all that is possible, that the dynamic interpretation of the world with its denial of 'empty space' and its little clumps of atoms, will shortly come to prevail among physicists [...] (*WP* 618)

On the 'dynamic interpretation', the forces which constitute the physical world act in locations not occupied by solid particles, hence without mechanical contact ('at a distance') and it thus becomes evident—as it was not to Locke and the mechanists—that pressure and impact cannot acquaint us with the intrinsic qualitative nature of causal efficacy. For Locke, it seemed obvious—mistakenly—that experiences of tactile pressure transparently reveal the nature of the subject-independent ground of causal efficacy, ultimately the solidity of space-filling objects. On the dynamist picture, this apparent obviousness is revealed as patently erroneous. Feelings of strain or tactile pressure *evidently* cannot be thought of as 'like' actualizations of non-substantial, intrinsically non-experiential, gravitational or repulsive forces themselves, in the way that felt impenetrability was thought of by Locke (1959/1690: book II, chapter 4) as 'resembling' solidity as it is in the objects. Hence Nietzsche: 'has a [physical] *force* ever been shown? No, only *effects* translated into a completely foreign language' (*WP* 620). The realist about physical forces may of course insist that feelings of tactile pressure and the like *indicate* forces (Broad 1923: 162–3), but Nietzsche's point remains that these indications would leave the quality of the supposed physical (non-mental) forces—their efficacy—opaque: they cannot reveal the nature of such actualized forces *themselves*.[5] Not only do feelings of tactile pressure not reveal the nature of alleged intrinsic, non-dynamical, non-geometrical, physical properties of matter—Nietzsche thinks there are none—they cannot reveal the qualitative character of the fundamental causal properties, if these are thought of as actualized physical forces, either. There is therefore no prospect that feelings of tactile pressure might acquaint us with the nature of efficacy as it is in itself in putative causal transactions among inanimate bodies.

Nietzsche's second line of argument against the idea that 'pressure and impact' might provide us with an intuitive grasp of force independent of volitional agency is that, *by itself*, the complex of tactile sensations felt when I experience a hard object striking me does not even constitute an experience as of efficacious force. Some of his remarks about the experiences involved in taking a sensed item as real are relevant here. He suggests that, at the level of perception, 'being is grasped by us as that which acts on us, which *proves itself through its efficacy*' (*KGW* VIII.1: 5 [19]). But this causal content of perceptual experience is constitutively linked to 'performances' on our part: 'degrees of performance [...] awaken belief in the [...] reality of the object' (*WP* 533), 'an object is the sum of experienced *obstructions*'

---

[5] Since Newton's refusal to 'feign hypotheses' about the 'causes' of gravitation, the question of the qualitative nature of forces has been—very successfully—bypassed by science, which contents itself with measuring their quantitative indices (Eddington's schedule of pointer readings). Newton did not think that there was no legitimate question to be asked here, but only that answers to it are irrelevant to the predictive task of natural science. Nietzsche agrees: science 'desires nothing but quantities; but force is to be found in quality' (*WP* 660). Nietzsche is likely to have been influenced here by Schopenhauer, who observed that what remains beyond the reach and concerns of modern physical science is 'the definite mode of operation of things, the quality, the character of every phenomenon', 'in other words, the very manner of its existence, its being or true essence' (Schopenhauer 1969/1819: vol. I, pp. 121, 124).

(*KGW* VIII.1: 2 [77]). His point seems to be that the efficacy of objects which we take ourselves to experience in sensory, including tactile, encounters with them depends on our experience of ourselves as having powers (*WP* 485) manifested in agentive 'performances'. The experience of objects as efficacious depends on experiencing them as 'obstructions', as resistant to the will. This need not commit Nietzsche to the implausible view, suggested in the hyperbolical formulation of *KGW* VIII.1: 2 [77], that every perceptual experience with any causal content involves an experienced obstruction to an actual attempted action. His main point is rather that, unless we sometimes experienced ourselves as volitional agents, no sensations, tactile or otherwise, could be taken by us as manifestations of an object's efficacy.[6] If we have an acquaintance with force, the content of this acquaintance *constitutively* depends on actual experiences of willing. Any extrapolation of the content of these experiences into a putatively inanimate physical world devoid of them is therefore illegitimate projection.[7]

2 WILLING

The upshot of Nietzsche's reflections so far is as follows. The everyday concept of causation includes the idea of compulsion or efficacious force. This idea is one that we cannot rationally let go in our thought about what causation actually is in the world (as opposed to what we know about it). A full comprehension or explanation of causal relations would require acquaintance with the inherent qualitative character of actualizations of causal force. Science has no concern with this question and is, to that extent, not explanatory. Neither the observation of mechanical phenomena nor participant sensory registerings of such phenomena in tactile experience and the like acquaint us, by themselves, with efficacy. So Nietzsche at this stage might be tempted by the conclusion that while (a) we can justifiably claim that there *are* forces in the world and even that the physical world is *constituted* by forces, (b) we have no intuitively contentful conception of what these forces inherently are when they 'act'—the qualitative character of force, and thus of the world itself, is in this sense opaque or *mysterious*. There are some places (*TI*: 'The Four Great Errors' 3; *WP* 664) where Nietzsche does seem to assert (b). But as we have seen, he often claims in other passages that our acquaintance with efficacy is somehow based on the experience of 'willing'. However, in the two places just referred to he maintains that we merely *believe* that the will is efficacious while not actually *experiencing* its efficacy. Nietzsche, then, seems to take different positions in different places on this central issue, and his vacillations and evident hesitation on it are one of the

---

[6] For similar arguments, see Dilthey 1923: 101–5; Scheler 1977/1926: 238–48. William James (1983/1880) makes a similar point against the allegedly force-revealing character of kinaesthetic sensations associated with muscular tension (pp. 120–3).

[7] For Nietzsche, therefore, the fundamental causal properties we encounter in experience can be construed neither as primary properties (i.e. as conceptually and existentially mind-independent) nor as secondary properties (if these are conceptually mind-dependent but existentially mind-independent), *pace* some contemporary philosophers who agree with him at a general level about the centrality of agency for an understanding of causation. See Searle 1983: chapter 4 for a combination of an agentist epistemology of causation with a primary-property ontology of it. For a secondary-property agentist account, see Menzies and Price 1993: 187–203.

main reasons for interpretive disagreements concerning the will to power. This hesitation and uncertainty is strikingly present in the most important passage on the will to power in the published works (*BGE* 36), about which more later. In any case, opposed to the few unequivocally sceptical passages (*TI*: 'The Four Great Errors' 3; *WP* 664) stand many others in the notebooks in which he asserts or implies that we do have genuine acquaintance with efficacy in connection with willing: 'if we translate the concept 'cause' back to the only sphere known to us, from which we have derived it, we cannot imagine any change that does not involve a will to power' (*WP* 689; also *WP* 490, 533, 658; *KGW* VII. 2: 25 [436], *KGW* VIII.1: 2 [77], *KGW* VIII.1: 5 [19]). The ideas broached in these notes are foundational for his metaphysical sketches. It is therefore important to obtain some clarity on where exactly the experience of force in or dependent on willing is to be located according to Nietzsche's statements in these anti-sceptical notes.

Phenomenologically, what is a conscious volition? Nietzsche distinguishes a number of constituents in a paradigmatic episode of willed action (*BGE* 19):[8] first, a number of 'feelings', including kinaesthetic sensations, the precise nature of which need not concern us here; second, a thought or image of the end that is willed or of some aspect of the bodily movements through which that goal is to be attained (*WP* 671, 692). Thirdly, there is what he calls an 'affect of command': '*willing t[hat is] commanding*: but commanding is a particular *affect* (this affect is a sudden explosion of force)' (*KGW* VII. 2: 25 [436]). In another note (*WP* 490) he reiterates that force is to be found in this last ingredient. This seems not very illuminating. There is a temptation to think of the 'command' in question as something like a Jamesian assent to the thought or image component, transforming it into an unqualified belief about what will happen (James 1983/1880: 101–7). But this is not what Nietzsche wants to say. Rather, he initially explicates the nature and efficacy of the command in terms of what it is to be the *recipient* of a demand or the addressee of a norm which one acknowledges as authoritative, as to-be-obeyed: 'we can grasp what is required for maintaining the organism as a *moral* demand: there is a "thou shalt" for the individual organs which comes down to them from the commanding organ' (*KGW* VII.2: 25 [432]). The apparent panpsychist implications of this remark shall occupy us later. For now, we may note that the first model Nietzsche proposes in this passage for genuinely comprehending, in his sense, what force is, is the *experience of being compelled by one's acknowledgement of a norm or value*. In such cases, Nietzsche suggests, efficacy is actually experienced. While this experience is not one of the efficacy of the will itself, it is essentially linked to intentional action: I can only experience myself as compelled by a norm which I acknowledge—'I must do X'—if I take myself to be able to act on it.

A second type of case suitable for giving empirical content to the idea of force is adumbrated in the same passage: 'some tasks are commanded that cannot be fully performed (because the strength is insufficient). But often the most extreme tension [...]—an *exertion* of the will, as we know this in ourselves with difficult tasks'. Since Nietzsche has already denied that muscular effort or tension provides an experience of efficacy (*WP* 551), one may perhaps interpret his thought here as being very similar to William James's notion of a 'mental effort', a 'force of consciousness' by which in certain situations of psychic conflict we sometimes experience ourselves as spontaneously maintaining an anticipatory idea of an action or movement against

---

[8] Nietzsche need not of course hold that all these ingredients are present at the conscious personal level in all cases of voluntary action.

countervailing ideas, which in such cases of inner conflict is claimed to be necessary for enabling the former idea to become a conscious belief and to result in the appropriate action. The force, according to James, is not experienced in the relation between idea and bodily movement, which on his ideo-motor theory is merely an experience of succession (Nietzsche agrees: WP 664), but in the relation between 'spontaneous psychic effort' and the prevailing in consciousness of one anticipatory idea over its rivals (James 1983/1880: 110–17).

A third type of situation in which Nietzsche suggests we are acquainted with force is in the *resistance* of phenomenal objects to our agency, already referred to above (KGW VIII.1: 5 [19]; KGW VIII.1: 2 [77]). We need not think of this (*pace* Dilthey 1923) as always involving bodily agency or tactile pressure. Even in a case such as a voluntary shift of attention in perception because we dislike what we see and desire it to be otherwise, we discover that there are limits to our ability to control the contents of experience. I may try to stop seeing a distasteful scene by averting my attention, but I remain aware of its continued presence and its refractoriness to volitional control, which distinguishes it from an imagined scene and from many of my own trains of thought and bodily movements. As Nietzsche puts it, the phenomenal object or state of affairs in perception 'proves itself through its efficacy' which, he suggests, is genuinely experienced through its uncontrollability, its resistance to desire and willing. This experience essentially depends on a contrast with the awareness of our ability to control some events 'at will', and thus requires that we are aware of some events as happening because they are willed by us, although it does not require that the will's efficacy is itself experienced. Nevertheless, an acquaintance with phenomenal objects *as* efficacious would not be possible without the availability of a first-personal awareness of some of our behaviours as willed.

The result of these analyses of the phenomenology of willing in the notes we have considered is that we do have experiences as of efficacious force or 'compulsion' in some types of volitional activity and in other kinds of awareness—of the resistance of phenomenal objects and of normative force—which depend on our being aware of ourselves as volitional agents. Since there are no other plausible candidates for an acquaintance with force, Nietzsche concludes that the nature of causation is either fundamentally mysterious—'force we cannot imagine is an empty word' (WP 621)—or that it essentially involves something similar to human will and intention: ' "attraction" and "repulsion" in a purely mechanistic sense are complete fictions: a word. We cannot think of an attraction divorced from an intention' (WP 626). In his metaphysical sketches, he develops this latter option, which, if one is persuaded his arguments so far, is not a *rival* to a 'scientific conception' of the world, since that conception is constitutively incomplete and has nothing to say on these issues; its only real alternative is scepticism or mysterianism. But why does Nietzsche in these metaphysical sketches almost invariably qualify the will as will *to power*? Here a further aspect of his thought on the volitional life comes into play.

3 THE PSYCHOLOGY OF THE WILL TO POWER

Nietzsche originally develops his concept of the will to power as a psychological explanation of human behaviour, gradually expanding the scope of this explanation.[9] What is the

---

[9] See Kaufmann 1968: 159–80.

will to power, understood as a psychological phenomenon? While interpretations abound, most commentators agree that 'will' in this context has a broad extension, as it does in Schopenhauer, referring more generally to appetitive and conative acts or processes. Clark (1990: 210–12) has proposed that 'will to power' in a psychological context refers to a second- or higher-order desire for the *ability to satisfy* one's lower-order desires. Such a desire is only plausibly ascribed to human beings if they have lower-order desires for something other than power, however 'power' is to be precisely understood. The interpretation recommended by Clark, then, suggests an *instrumental* reading of the will to power in a human psychological context: we desire the ability to attain the ends of our other desires, as a means towards those ends. As other commentators have noted (Richardson 1996: 24–6; Reginster 2006: 128), this makes the psychological doctrine plausible and uncontroversial from a common-sense perspective, but at the cost of leaving unaccounted for Nietzsche's insistence that the will to power is not *in principle* satisfiable by any stable end state at which it would come to rest (cf. *WP* 689, 696). Nevertheless, Clark's idea of the will to power as a higher-order desire seems important and insightful and has been taken up by others.

Richardson (1996, especially 21–39) argues that the will to power is an explanatory concept intended to apply most fundamentally at the level of *drives*, which Nietzsche takes to constitute the mind. He claims that Nietzschean drives have a telic intentional structure: they inherently aim at ends which they represent as desirable or valuable, albeit in most cases not consciously. Drives thus might be said to have, or to be, perspectival viewpoints on the world, which are representational, evaluative, and conative. Richardson agrees with Clark that it makes little sense to think of power as a specific self-standing end towards which drives aim, because he takes it that power is conceptually parasitic on other ends—we cannot think of power as a separable component of a state or condition in the way we can (perhaps) think of a pleasurable sensation. Hence, 'to be a will to power, [a drive] must already want something other than power' (Richardson 1996: 23). Therefore we also cannot think of power as an end for the attainment of which the internal ends of drives are merely the means. Rather, what Nietzsche wants to say when he says that the drives manifest a will to power is that they ceaselessly aim to increase their activity patterns, to raise their pattern of effort 'to a higher level'. So the will to power is fundamentally a desire for 'growth' in a drive's distinctive telic activity. For Nietzsche, the most important example of such growth is not the striving for more of the same kind of thing—such as striving for ever more material possessions—but the transformation of the drive's internal end and of the associated activity itself through refinement and enrichment in 'sublimation', for example, the transformation of sexual activity into *amour-passion* (*WP* 312). Richardson's interpretation is subtle and worked out in great detail. His analysis of the structure of Nietzschean drives as intentional and representational, and related aspects of his reading, seem to me to capture central ingredients of Nietzsche's metapsychology, to which we shall need to return. From the perspective of our present concerns, however, we must ask whether Nietzsche's metaphysical ideas concerning a subpersonal level of drives can help us in specifying the intrinsic nature of the will qua empirically accessible phenomenon. Insofar as the psychological will to power is an unconscious feature of subpersonal drives, it clearly cannot serve as epistemic basis for metaphysical claims, since it is itself the (inferential) content of such a claim, and as such in need of appropriate evidential backing. Nietzsche himself would seem to accept this requirement when he specifies as his epistemological starting point the 'only sphere known to us' (*WP* 689), where 'desires and passions' are '"*given*" as real' (*BGE* 36;

italics mine). Several commentators have therefore argued that, at least in its epistemically fundamental use, the concept of will to power applies to conscious intentional phenomena at the personal level.

Perhaps the most promising interpretation of the *conscious* will to power is due to Bernard Reginster (2006: 124–47). According to Reginster, Nietzsche starts from Schopenhauer's insight that no achievement of any determinately specifiable end can lastingly satisfy human desire. Nietzsche explains this by what he takes to be a fundamental phenomenological fact about human desire: we desire not only various first-order ends, but also that some of these ends be attained through our own successful activity against resistances or obstacles, and that the successful overcoming of resistances should be consciously registered by us. Nietzsche calls an agent's conscious awareness of her own successful activity against resistances the 'feeling of power', and he thinks of this as having a positive hedonic character: 'It is not the satisfaction of the will that causes pleasure [...] but rather the will's forward thrust and again and again becoming master over that which stands in its way. The feeling of pleasure lies precisely [...] in the fact that the will is never satisfied unless it has opponents and resistance' (*WP* 696). The athlete does not—or not only—desire a certain end result of his activity (the state of affairs of his having won the race), but the awareness of his successful endeavour as it unfolds; the mathematician or the novelist desires not only a certain result—having solved the problem or completed the novel—but the awareness of his overcoming of the intellectual difficulties along the way. A correct psychological analysis shows, according to Nietzsche, that the 'feeling of power' is not desired as a means, but 'for its own sake'. This makes possible an explanation of the constitutive incompleteness of the human being, which, if we accept Nietzsche's analysis, is seen to have its ground in the essentially dynamic, change-involving character of the feeling of power. If what we desire constitutively includes an experienced successful struggle against resistances, then we cannot in principle attain a final, stable, satisfaction of desire, and this explains Nietzsche's talk about the 'endlessness' or 'goallessness' of the will to power—it needs and hence desires ever new resistances to be overcome (*WP* 695, 696, 1067). Reginster agrees with Clark and Richardson that the will to power cannot be an autonomous motivation, logically independent of desires for other ends. His thought here is that it is only possible to experience a feeling of power in successfully pursuing an activity if the internal goal of that activity (winning the race, solving the mathematical puzzle, completing the novel) independently matters to me. Hence 'the will to power cannot be satisfied unless the agent has a desire for something else than power' (Reginster 2006: 132). Since the will to power therefore cannot be sufficient to characterize all of an agent's desires, Nietzsche's talk about its being the *essential* human drive should not be understood literally, but as an expression of Nietzsche's own values: from Nietzsche's evaluative perspective, the will to power is what is most important about human beings. This qualification arguably renders Nietzsche's psychology more plausible, but it entails that his extrapolations from the conscious human will to the character of the moving forces in non-human agency and in human subpersonal drives, have a weak basis in his psychology. If willing, in humans, is not *invariably* a willing of 'power', in Nietzsche's specific sense, then it seems that he has not even prima facie grounds for the thesis that 'life as a special case (hypothesis based upon it applied to the total character of being—) strives after a *maximal feeling of power*, essentially a striving for more power; striving is *nothing other* than striving for power' (*WP* 689; italics mine).

There are passages, such as the one just cited, in which Nietzsche suggests that all human desires are *reducible* to the will to power, i.e. the desire for the feeling of power (also *A* 2, *BGE* 36, *KGW* VII.3: 40 [61], *KGW* VIII.1: 1 [30]), and where he concludes that 'all events that result from intention are reducible to the intention to increase power' (*WP* 663). Poellner (1995: 165–9, 207–8) argues that the later Nietzsche is, at least officially, committed to such a reducibility thesis, and criticizes it as *empirically* inadequate to the complexity and variety of human desire (1995: 238–43). Like Reginster, he takes the will to power at the conscious level to be a desire for the 'feeling of power', the latter being a 'cognitive state consisting in the awareness by a given agent of an obstacle or opponent as being overcome, assimilated, shaped or transformed by him according to his will' (1995: 168). But Poellner (1995) does not construe the will to power as necessarily a second- or higher-order desire; thus, on his interpretation there is nothing *incoherent* in the reducibility thesis—it just happens not to do justice to the variety of human desire. While Reginster's construal of the conscious will to power as a second-order desire is arguably the most philosophically attractive reading—not least because it renders the will to power doctrine compatible with the fundamental variegatedness of desire—it does not seem forced on Nietzsche by logical considerations. It seems perfectly consistent for Nietzsche in his reductionist mood to say that 'will to power' is a generic description of a vast multiplicity of specific kinds of first-order desires which all have in common that their ends involve some species of the feeling of power. The reductive claim would then be that these ends would not be desired unless they involved the element which Nietzsche calls *Machtgefühl*. This need not be taken to mean that the feeling of power is an in principle separable component, for the realization of which the desire's specific end—winning the race, completing the novel, etc.—would be merely instrumental. But it also need not commit Nietzsche to the view (attributed to him by Clark, Richardson, and Reginster) that the desire's specific aim *without* the feeling of power needs to be valued for its own sake, if that feeling is to be possible. Compare the case of pleasure as ordinarily conceived: when you desire to listen to a favourite piece of music, it might truly be said that you desire this because the experience is pleasurable. But the pleasure here is not some kind of additional sensation which could be thought of as separable from the performance-as-heard of the music, and for the production of which the music is merely a means. And yet you would not desire to hear the music unless experiencing it had that generic hedonic character we call 'pleasurable'.[10] Pleasure here is an essential feature of the end of a *first-order* desire, and Nietzsche might consistently conceive of the feeling of power analogously. I conclude that the reducibility thesis is not incoherent. If Nietzsche can show that all conscious human desires, and therefore also those effective desires we call volitions, are reducible to the will to power, he will have demonstrated that all causal efficacy, insofar as have acquaintance with it, either is or depends on will to power. Nietzsche himself thinks, at least some of the time (*BGE* 36; *WP* 663, 689), that the many psychological analyses which make up a large part of his work give us good reasons for taking the antecedent to be true.

---

[10] The example is taken from Sprigge 1990: 146–8.

4 THE WILL TO POWER IN NATURE

In the notes we are considering and, more ambiguously, in a few passages in the published works (*BGE* 19, 36), Nietzsche concludes that we are acquainted with the nature of efficacy only in experiences that either are or are dependent on 'willing', and that human desires and volitions are reducible to the will to power in the sense outlined above. If one rejects scepticism,

> one [therefore] must venture the hypothesis that wherever 'effects' are recognized, will is oper-ating upon will—and that all mechanical occurrences, in so far as a force is active in them, are force of will, effects of will. Granted finally that one succeeded in explaining our entire life of drives as the development and ramification of *one* basic form of will—as will to power, as is *my* theory—[...] one would have acquired the right to define *all* efficacious force unequivocally as: *will to power*. The world seen from within, the world described and defined according to its 'intelligible character' it would be 'will to power' and nothing else.— (*BGE* 36)
>
> [...] we cannot imagine any change that does not involve a will to power. [...] Should we not be permitted to assume this will as a motive cause in chemistry, too?—and in the cosmic order? [...] the only reality is the will to grow stronger of every centre of force—(*WP* 689; also *KGW* VIII.1: 1 [30]).
>
> The victorious concept 'force', by means of which our physicists have created God and the world, still needs to be supplemented: an inner will must be ascribed to it which I designate as 'will to power' [...] There is nothing for it: one is obliged to understand all motion, all 'appear-ances', all 'laws', only as a symptom of an inner event and to employ man as an analogy to this end. (*WP* 619)

Nietzsche's argument here is clearly not a deductive one from a priori premises, but is touted as an inference to the best explanation, and is reminiscent of arguments found in other panpsychist thinkers.[11] It is arguably weaker than those arguments, due to the rela-tive specificity of Nietzsche's characterization. He is not merely saying that we should think of force—and hence, granted the truth of dynamism, all of reality—as somehow involving mentality or a 'will', but that this will is will to power. This is questionable even if one has no animadversions about the general form of this kind of argument, since, even if all our effective desires are in fact specifications of the will to power, it does not follow that 'we cannot imagine' (*WP* 689) a will with different ends. In the final section, I shall return to the question of how seriously Nietzsche himself may have taken this argument. For now, let us see where it takes him. He claims that will can operate only on will (*BGE* 36; *WP* 658), and this conclusion may seem unwarranted by his account of the human will, which rather suggests that the will cannot operate on, or be affected by, anything that does not have *phe-nomenal properties*. We saw that one of his analyses of efficacy involved the recalcitrance of some presentational contents—objects as perceived—to volitional agency. While it makes no sense to think of those phenomenal properties *as they are perceived* being instantiated independently of perceiving 'subjects' with volitional agency, might they not, when unper-ceived, be dispositional, unactualized physical powers? Nietzsche presumably rejects this

---

[11]   Cf. Schopenhauer 1969/1819: vol. I, pp. 99–105. Also Eddington 1928: chapter 13.

idea for the same reason he considers physical dynamism more generally as incomplete. The putative dispositional physical powers would have to manifest themselves as efficacious phenomenal objects or occurrences when they are suitably acted on—when they enter another 'field of force'—but Nietzsche has argued that we can only concretely make sense of ('imagine') *being acted on* in terms of either a *phenomenal content* being acted on by a will (the Jamesian picture of volitional effort), or in terms of a will being acted on by a phenomenal content (a normative sense necessarily mediated by some phenomenal vehicle, or the 'resistance' of external phenomenal reality). It follows that the 'inner', 'intelligible' character of *both* of the terms in a genuine interaction between two existents—'centres of force'—has to involve representing and willing, if it is to be 'comprehensible' at all. The ultimate constituents of reality, the centres of force, sometimes also called 'power quanta' by Nietzsche, are therefore to be conceived as representing, willing, and affective entities, 'just as real as our willing feeling thinking is—but as a primitive form of these' (*KGW* VII.3: 40 [37]; cf. *KGW* VII.2: 27 [19]). Mentality is the basic intrinsic character of the real. Nietzsche's talk about 'a primitive form' of it might be taken as intended to deflect—not very satisfactorily—objections like the following: we have good reasons to think that the kind of mentality we are familiar with in humans and animals requires as its supervenience base a vastly complex systems of functions, described in physical vocabulary in terms of neuronal structures, electrical impulses, and so forth. It strains credulity to accept that each of the centres of force which are supposed to be the 'inner' realities informing or appearing as the ultimate physical entities (elementary particles?) constituting that supervenience base should itself be characterized by anything intelligibly continuous with human mentality.

Among the other questions raised by Nietzsche's conception, one concerns the status of spatial extension in it. Are the centres of force essentially *embodied wills* such that both mental and physical predicates apply to them at the basic level of description, and a fully adequate grasp of their nature would have to make reference to their spatial extendedness? Some of Nietzsche's formulations suggest this (*WP* 619, 636, 1067). A development of this version of the theory clearly would have to conceptualize the interactions between the centres of force as, at least in part, spatial interactions between phenomenal, animated bodies, situated in common space.[12] Some passages more ambiguously speak of the relation between the mental and apparent physical properties of the force centres as one of *expression* (*KGW* VIII.1: 1 [30]); in other places he suggests a metaphysics rather closer to the later Leibniz's view—except for the interactionism, which is of course denied by Leibniz at least for finite substances. According to these passages, the centres of force are 'willing, feeling, thinking' entities which are not themselves moving in physical space and hence presumably not intrinsically extended—like Leibniz's monads, they only appear to themselves (and other centres) as extended and in spatial motion (*WP* 634, 635; *KGW* VII.3: 37 [4]). On this view, the relation between the apparent extension-involving properties of centres of force and their 'inner', 'intelligible' properties is one of analogy (*Gleichnis*), which in this context is probably best understood in terms of a quasi-Leibnizian isomorphism, conferring

---

[12] The requirement that the bodies of the centres of force need to have *phenomenal* properties derives from Nietzsche's constraints on any adequate understanding of causation. It is of course compatible with acknowledging that the phenomenal properties of the bodies of the ultimate constituents of reality are quite different from the macroscopic phenomenal properties—colours as perceived, etc.—which we are acquainted with.

on bodies the status of well-founded phenomena. Which of these views is Nietzsche's?[13] His sketches are inconclusive, but, given his premises, the most promising of them would seem to be the first. It is very difficult to see how finite, particular force centres could *represent* anything, how they could interact with what they represent, and how a plurality of them could even exist contemporaneously, unless they had an essential dimension of phenomenal *objectivity*, and were situated in a space which made objective (i.e. non-egocentrically individuated) simultaneous co-presence possible.

A second question concerning Nietzsche's metaphysical picture concerns the role in it of consciousness. The force centres have mental properties—they will, feel, and represent—but are they also phenomenally conscious? Here, too, Nietzsche's statements are not without ambiguities, indeed, some would say that this is *the* central area of ambiguity in his philosophy. The issue is perhaps best discussed with reference to his remarks on complex organisms like the human individual. He proposes that such an organism should be thought of as a sociality of centres of force, which in this context he also calls 'drives', corresponding to the constituents of the organic structures of the body. These organic constituents are hierarchically related to each other in a way which involves mutual felt influence and value-governed relations of sub- and superordination ('command' and 'obedience'; KGW VII.3: 37 [4]). Each drive has an end-directed structure analogous to the will to power in human personal consciousness: it acts for the sake of the 'feeling of power'. If it is asked what should induce drives to enter into and, for some time, to remain in relations of subordination to others, Nietzsche's answer is, as one would expect, no different from his explanation of analogous relations at the interpersonal level. Humans, for Nietzsche in his reductionist mood, enter into such relations either through being forced into them—being 'assimilated' or 'appropriated'—or voluntarily for the sake of the power of a larger whole with which they come to identify (as, for example, in nationalist self-identifications at the social macro-level). A human individual's actions, like the actions of any hierarchical collective, require a division of labour and the mutual adjustment and cooperation of the various sub-agencies:

> Commands have to be given (and obeyed) time after time down to the smallest detail, and only then, when the command has been divided up into a multitude of low-level sub-commands, can the movement take place [...] Here it is presupposed that the whole organism thinks, and that all organic things participate in thinking, feeling, willing— (KGW VII.2: 27 [19])

The dominant drive which manifests itself as the individual's consciousness specifies, as it were, only the broad objective of the collective's action, the achievement of which requires interpretation and implementation by many subordinate agencies in terms of more basic actions and sub-objectives, and this is why Nietzsche often stresses the relative impotence of conscious motives and of our consciousness of ends *by itself* (GS 335) and surmises that frequently the ends pursued by the organism may not be those which the person is conscious of (WP 676), our consciousness in these cases resembling an ornamental monarch kept in the dark about policies really determined by scheming nominal subordinates. While it is largely uncontested among commentators that Nietzsche accords a more limited directive

---

[13] Poellner (1995: 276–81) interprets Nietzsche's sketches in terms of the Leibnizian view, plus interactionism and minus the latter's substance ontology. That reading now seems to me to be insufficiently sensitive to the ambiguities in Nietzsche's formulations.

role to consciousness than much of the philosophical tradition, it is disputed whether he gives any essential role to it at all in action. The question can be put like this: when Nietzsche says that 'we would also be able to "act" in every sense of that word: and yet none of all this would have to "enter our consciousness"' (*GS* 354), is he merely making the point about the limited role of the *person's* consciousness, or is he claiming that the mentality of the constituent centres of force themselves should be thought of as unconscious to *them*?[14] Most of Nietzsche's deflationary remarks about the place of consciousness are clearly compatible with the first, more conservative reading. Even the published passages most frequently cited in support of his purported approval of the idea of (phenomenally) unconscious mentality are, on closer inspection, not unambiguous. When Nietzsche says that 'the whole of life would be possible without, as it were, seeing itself in a mirror' (*GS* 354), he is literally asserting not the inessentiality of consciousness *tout court*, but the dispensability of objectifying *self*-consciousness. This reading would seem to be confirmed by his statement in the same text that phenomenality ('what-it-is-likeness') is of the essence: 'what is "appearance" for me now? Certainly not the opposite of some essence [...] Certainly not a dead mask that one could place on an unknown x or remove from it! Appearance is for me that which lives and is effective' (*GS* 54). Elsewhere he explicitly ascribes consciousness to the centres of force— 'living beings'—collectives of which constitute or appear as human organisms, while the full intrinsic phenomenal character of these consciousnesses is said to be largely, and for many of them entirely, inaccessible to the consciousness of the person (*KGW* VII.3: 37 [4]).

While the direct textual evidence on Nietzsche's position concerning the role of consciousness in the mentality of the centres of force is, overall, ambivalent, his ideas on causality, the point of departure for his metaphysical reflections, would seem to commit him attributing conscious intentionality to them. The whole point of these reflections is to offer a conception of reality in terms of forces that are 'comprehensible'—and any such comprehension in Nietzsche's sense (by 'acquaintance' or 'imagining') needs to make reference to *conscious* volition. Talk about so-called intrinsically unconscious occurrent representings, willings, or feelings, does not explain efficacy in his sense, but offers merely functional descriptions of the kind he considers incomplete at the basic, metaphysical level of inquiry.

The general Nietzschean account of the human organism is intended to apply, *mutatis mutandis*, also to other organic beings and even to apparently inanimate entities (*BGE* 36; *WP* 689; *KGW* VIII.1: 1 [30]). Unlike Leibniz, Nietzsche has only some cursory remarks on the question of what differences might correspond at the 'intelligible' level to the distinction between the organic and the inorganic (*KGW* VII.3: 35 [35], *KGW* VII.3: 41 [11], *KGW* VIII.1: 1 [105]), but it is not difficult to see how his theory might be expanded to accommodate these—for example, in terms of degrees of hierarchical integration of the 'projects' of force centres with appropriately similar intentional perspectives. The individuation of an organism essentially involves the continuity of such hierarchically structured and mutually integrated projects. And the distinctness of organisms from each other seems ultimately, for Nietzsche, a matter of degree. While what we normally consider to be distinct organisms may evince a high measure of integration in their projects—as in political and other kinds of sustained cooperation—this is much weaker than at the intra-individual level; if it were not, there would be no warrant for regarding the organisms as distinct.

---

[14] Among notable interpreters of Nietzsche's metaphysics, Richardson (1996) takes the latter view (pp. 36–8).

The outlines of Nietzsche's metaphysics of the will to power as presented so far offer clues on how to interpret three further metaphysical theses found in his writings: (1) First, the idea that reality is fundamentally *perspectival* and that there is no true (or even coherent) absolute conception of the world (*WP* 556, 560, 567). If everything that concretely exists are interacting 'willing, thinking, feeling' centres of force, then reality is itself constituted by perspectives and all objectivity is relative, or better, relational. I shall not directly engage here with all the specifics of this 'perspectivism', which of course has not only metaphysical, but also (perhaps more centrally) epistemological and ethical-aesthetic dimensions, but some of my remarks below are pertinent to it.[15] (2) Secondly, there is Nietzsche's claim that 'there is no "thing in itself"' (*WP* 557); and (3) finally, his thought that all reality is 'becoming'. In the remainder of this section, I shall focus on claims (2) and (3) in light of the arguments already discussed.

It is clear that when Nietzsche denies that there are things in themselves, he is not only rejecting Kantian noumena 'in the positive sense'—non-spatiotemporal entities knowable only by intellectual intuition—but also, and more often, the idea of finite particulars with *fully intrinsic properties*, that is, with existentially non-relational properties, the instantiation of which by a particular X is compatible with the non-existence of anything other than X: 'The properties of a thing are effects on other "things": [. . .] i.e., there is no thing without other things, i.e. there is no "thing in itself"' (*WP* 557; also *WP* 558, 559, 583a). In some passages, he takes this to imply that all the properties of finite particulars are extrinsic, like the property 'being seen by Y' is extrinsic to X's consciousness, if X is entirely unaware of it or its consequences—if there is nothing in X's consciousness that might count as having that property or as a result or component of that property being instantiated (*WP* 556). If it was Nietzsche's considered view that all properties are extrinsic in this sense, it would be clearly incoherent. Relations require relata, and there can only be such if they have some non-extrinsic properties. But Nietzsche's attribution of conscious mentality to the centres of force suggests a weaker and less obviously problematic interpretation of his denial that any finite particular has a 'constitution in itself'. Arguably, what he wants to say is that what a particular is cannot be characterized in terms of fully intrinsic properties. Its 'constitution' is rather a matter of its relations to what are conventionally regarded as 'other things', so that no finite particular is an ontologically independent existent: its relations to alterity are internal to what it is (*WP* 558, 635).[16] The case of personal consciousness serves well to illustrate this point. What I am, qua consciousness, at this moment in time, is very largely a matter of actual, conscious relations to particulars that I am aware of *as other* than myself-at-this-time: relations to external objects and 'affordances' in my environment, to other people, and to people whom I am conscious of as having affected me in various ways in the past. But my consciousness is also essentially characterized by non-actual ('ideal') relations to possible future particulars and states of affairs which, with various degrees

[15] For discussions of perspectivism, see Gemes's essay in this volume and Poellner 2001.
[16] My treatment of this topic is indebted to John Richardson's groundbreaking discussion of it in Richardson 1996: 102–9, 159–63. The point that the 'centres of force' can have no *fully* intrinsic constitution in the sense defined above follows from the fact that—as Nietzsche predominantly seems to think of them—they are actual manifestations of force. A real actualized force has to have intrinsic (non-extrinsic) qualitative properties, but these are also relational, since the force is essentially exercised on other particulars. 'Intrinsic' (= non-extrinsic) and (existentially) 'relational', as used here, are therefore not mutually exclusive. See also Doyle 2009: chapter 6 for a good discussion of these issues.

of explicitness, I expect to encounter or to bring about, and which I am also aware of as other than myself-at-this-time. If I were to subtract all these actual and 'ideal' relations from my current consciousness, none of it would remain as it is, and hence all the intrinsic properties of my conscious self at this time involve relations. (It might be objected that the truth-makers of statements about ideal relations are themselves fully intrinsic properties. The right response to this objection is a version of 'content externalism' according to which ideal relations are ontologically dependent on the mind's real relations to a world phenomenally external to it.) We may conclude, then, that if we take seriously Nietzsche's account of the qualitative nature of the ultimate constituents of reality in terms of mentality and phenomenal properties, his denial of ontologically independent, fully intrinsic properties to them is well-founded.

One of Nietzsche's most frequently articulated (and cited) claims, also in the published writings, is that reality is fundamentally 'becoming', an idea that is often conjoined, or even conflated, with a denial of enduring 'things' and of 'substances' (GS 110; GM I: 13; WP 517, 538). This is not merely to be understood as a rejection of substrata in which properties 'inhere' and of ontologically independent particulars (see above), but also of relatively enduring property instances (WP 517, 520). I shall call this Nietzsche's *strong becoming thesis*. In Kantian language, reality is one of continual change—replacement of one item by another—which is not alteration: it is not change in some respect taking place in something which, in another respect, remains strictly self-identical throughout the change. Nietzsche's particulars are non-discrete events or processes (WP 635) involving qualitative modifications from 'instant to instant', the earlier phases causing later ones in such a way that no phase, however finely grained we may think of it, can meaningfully be identified as being only a cause without also being an effect (GS 112). These event sequences (processes) are, more strictly, *actings* which are not grounded in agents—'subjects', in one sense—remaining strictly self-identical throughout the process (GM I: 13). No doubt this claim is partly motivated by Nietzsche's idea that the centres of force are manifestations of will to power and therefore 'at any moment' striving to transcend their current condition. But his thesis is again most readily intelligible by recalling that the centres of force are supposed to be analogous to personal conscious mentality. Consciousness is aware of itself as what is often metaphorically described as a continuous flow or stream in which there are no extended, enduring, temporal atoms, and this seems to be a necessary condition of the experience of phenomenal time as continuously 'moving' from past to future. Even when there is no change in the intentional *content* during an interval of time—when, for example, one looks at a painting on a wall for some time—there is an awareness of change, since one's consciousness in the later phases of the contemplative project differs from the consciousness in the earlier phases: in a later phase one is conscious of having looked at the same scene *for some time*. However, does the example not precisely tell *against* Nietzsche's assertion in some places that there are no relatively enduring instantiations of fully determinate properties (the strong becoming thesis)? Surely the phenomenal properties of the painting as one looks at it may, and sometimes do, remain exactly the same over an extended period. Those impressed by transcendental arguments in the Kantian tradition may even argue that the representation of some determinate qualitative property instances as remaining qualitatively identical through time is a necessary condition of the possibility of representation *überhaupt*.

Nietzsche sometimes counters such considerations by moving to the fundamental level of the constituent centres of force (drives, etc.). Enduring determinate properties at the personal level of representation are said to be simplifications and, strictly, falsifications of what, in that underlying domain, is exclusively 'becoming'. And, although he does not address 'Kantian' transcendental objections directly, he might rejoin that the conditions of representation they impute are too rigoristic: conscious representation does not require strict cross-temporal identity, but at most a degree of regularity in the changes of representational contents. But these responses, while deflecting the charges of, respectively, empirical inadequacy and incoherence, still leave Nietzsche open to the accusation of epistemic arbitrariness. He seems to have no persuasive reasons for the strong claim that there is *no* relative permanence, no strict self-identity across time, at the metaphysically fundamental level. Nor would an appeal to post-corpuscularian physics help him here, for its ultimates—assuming that they are legitimately thought of as corresponding to Nietzsche's centres of force—are conceptualized as having some enduring determinate properties (e.g. a determinate electric charge). An additional problem with the strong becoming thesis is that it makes the evident prevalence of phenomenal patterns of relative persistence and 'lawlike' regularity at the macro-level somewhat miraculous. If *everything* that has concrete, particular being changes from one instant to another, it seems a surprising fluke that all these changes should produce a world in which such patterns are omnipresent. Nietzsche himself sometimes seems to recognize the problem without satisfactorily addressing it: 'there must [...] be [...] a kind of becoming [which] must itself create the deception of beings' (*WP* 517). Perhaps a weaker version of the becoming thesis would capture Nietzsche's basic intuition more appealingly than the strong version sometimes articulated by him: if all particular reality involves consciousness, and if all consciousness is essentially a process or 'flow', then all particular reality involves a dimension of radical becoming while not necessarily being exhaustively constituted by it.

Let me conclude this discussion with brief remarks on two further anticipated criticisms. Does not Nietzsche's characterization of the will to power require that entities instantiating it are strictly self-identical over time, since they desire their *own* successful activity? The answer is: no, for that characterization is compatible with holding that what a centre-of-force-at-a-time (C_1t_1) aims at is the awareness of a successful agency against resistances, an awareness which may be constituted by a succession of such centres C_2t_2, C_3t_3, ..., suitably internally related to C_1t_1 in causal-experiential respects. A second, more vague worry is that Nietzsche's approach is vitiated by a systematic ambiguity in his concept of force. Are Nietzschean forces ('powers') categorical manifestations, or real dispositions, or both? Does his account even have really informative content without clarity on this issue? In defence of Nietzsche, one might say that he is primarily interested in forces insofar as they are exercised. Sometimes he seems to suggest that powers which are latent at a time at the macroscopic level consist in relations between forces simultaneously actualized at deeper, constituent levels (*WP* 561; *KGW* VII.3: 37 [4]). But the Boscovichean background of his metaphysics would seem to commit him to the existence of dispositional powers, since force fields, if interpreted realistically, are real dispositions. An acknowledgement of unconscious, irreducible dispositional powers would of course be inconsistent with his demand that the efficacy of powers be 'comprehensible', but Nietzsche can countenance conscious dispositional abilities irreducible to non-dispositional properties, abilities which would need to change 'from moment to moment' if the strong becoming thesis were to be insisted upon.

5 THE PLACE OF METAPHYSICS IN
NIETZSCHE'S PHILOSOPHY

Nietzsche's metaphysical ideas are no doubt outlandish by the standards of the contemporary mainstream. This circumstance by itself would of course not trouble him—quite the contrary, given his general attitude to received opinions and established orthodoxies. Insofar as resistance to his ideas is motivated primarily by 'common-sense', 'intuitive' reservations about panpsychism more generally, one may surmise that he would regard it as meriting not so much further argumentative rejoinders, as rather psycho-sociological ('genealogical') diagnosis and explanation. As far as Nietzsche is concerned, once his premises—the constitutive incompleteness of the scientific enterprise and the unacceptability of ontological regularity accounts of causation—are granted, there are no serious alternatives to his general approach other than metaphysically more extravagant ones (Platonism, theistic occasionalism), or sceptical-mysterian hand-waving. However, there are at least three core propositions in his metaphysical picture and its epistemic background which, Nietzsche's texts suggest, he himself knew to be neither rationally mandatory nor even in possession of less absolute but still persuasive rational warrant: (1) that the fundamental nature of reality should be adequately comprehensible to us in terms of generic properties with which we are 'acquainted' or can 'imagine'; (2) that we cannot imagine a will that is not a will to power; (3) that there are no strictly enduring entities or determinate property instances. As Clark (1990: 218–27) rightly says, there is therefore every reason to think that Nietzsche included his own metaphysical forays among the targets of the second half of his remark, apropos of metaphysicians, that:

> they pose as having discovered and attained their real opinions through the self-evolution of a cold, pure, divinely unperturbed dialectic [...]: while what happens at bottom is that a prejudice, a notion, an 'inspiration', generally a desire of the heart sifted and made abstract, is defended by them with reasons sought after the event— (*BGE* 5; cf. *BGE* 6)

Clark concludes that we should interpret Nietzsche's apparently metaphysical exercises as performative illustrations of the futility of metaphysics—of its inevitable rational failures and of metaphysicians' inevitable susceptibility to the sway of non-rational 'prejudice' and ultimately 'moral' commitments (*BGE* 6) whenever they attempt to venture beyond the truth claims of the best empirical science. This kind of reading enlists Nietzsche's apparent metaphysics as a pedagogical or rhetorical device in the service of a fundamentally *anti*-metaphysical philosophical project. There is much in Nietzsche's texts that can be taken to support this approach, and yet it seems to me to leave a lingering hermeneutic dissatisfaction. Could such a pedagogical project not have been pursued much more effectively, one wonders, by Nietzsche's confining himself consistently to identifying the rational lacunae in established metaphysical projects and to genealogically diagnosing the 'moral'—e.g. religious or anti-religious—commitments among their proponents and the 'prejudices' underwriting what seems 'intuitively plausible' within their broader sociocultural milieux? And why does Nietzsche trouble himself with fairly detailed descriptive developments of the conclusions from his contestable premises, evidently striving for both consistency and

empirical adequacy—doing most of this explicative work, up until the final year of his philosophical activity, in private notebooks not designed for publication and hence incapable of
having any public pedagogical effect?

Are the metaphysical ideas in the notebooks perhaps simply thought experiments, pursuing a particular line of inquiry to see where it leads, with Nietzsche nonetheless remaining
uncommitted about its contents?[17] While this reading is not ruled out by the textual facts, by
itself it does not really allay our hermeneutic puzzlement. Why does Nietzsche only pursue
one such line of inquiry in any detail, unless it holds some special attraction for him? And
why should he engage in any metaphysical thought 'experiments' at all, given what he says
elsewhere about the dispensability of metaphysics?

The metaphysical sketches read, to a reasonably unprejudiced reader, like the record of
a suppressed desire (the 'bad conscience'?) of a philosopher who, in the published writings of the final period, predominantly argues for *metaphysical indifferentism*. What might
motivate this desire? Explanations of it are bound to remain to some extent conjectural, but
here is one hypothesis. At the centre of Nietzsche's metaphysical indifferentism in (most of)
the later published writings lies the idea that most metaphysical disputes are disputes about
purely theoretical propositions, that is, about propositions which have no predictive consequences and cannot in principle be assessed by our techniques of empirical confirmation or
disconfirmation. No conceivable evidence-gathering or experiment of the kind we employ
in everyday practical life or in the sciences can settle standard metaphysical questions such
as: whether there are absolute, non-perspectival objects; whether mentality is a basic property of some or all existents; whether the putative strong supervenience relations between
sets of phenomenal and physical properties are best explained by some kind of token-iden-
tity theory, or by a version of dualism, or occasionalism, or idealism. Nor can empirical tests
decide the issue which agitates Nietzsche in his metaphysical reflections in the notebooks
concerning the intrinsic qualitative nature of actualized force—the methods of science since
Newton have been devised precisely to permit this question to be disregarded in a scientific
context, without ipso facto impugning its legitimacy (unless scientific practice is supplemented by instrumentalist or positivist philosophy of science, neither of which is—to put
it no stronger than this—required by the practice). Not only are there no really available
empirical tests by which we could decide these questions, Nietzsche also clearly thinks that
there are no a priori arguments, compelling to any sufficiently well-informed and rationally
competent human investigator, which could settle them—this is one of his main points in
BGE 5–6, BGE 11, and in many notebook passages (e.g. WP 473; KGW VII.3: 36 [30]). The
fact of ongoing debate and widespread disagreement among competent inquirers on each
of these questions, after more than two millennia of philosophical inquiry, renders this particular view of his as convincing as anything is likely to be.

Now, the distinctive, radical, and 'strangest' (*BGE* 4) thought, dominating Nietzsche's
later published writings, on the *relevance* of answers to these metaphysical questions, is that
even if compelling a priori arguments on these matters were available, we should be, in an
important sense, *indifferent* to them (*GM* III: 24; *BGE* 4, 34; *TI*: 'How the "Real World" at
last Became a Myth'; *A* 56; *WP* 583; *KGW* VIII.3: 15 [19]). In particular, if the conclusions
of such arguments were logically incompatible with 'judgements' implicated in our deep

---

[17] My thanks to Ken Gemes for this suggestion.

practical commitments, this should not count for us as a sufficient reason to revise those commitments: 'the [metaphysical] falsity of a judgement is to us not necessarily an objection to a judgement: [...] The question is to what extent it is life-advancing' (*BGE* 4)—the implicit assumption being that the latter question can be settled without appeal to metaphysics, as opposed to the systematic appearances constituting the phenomenal life-world. I have argued elsewhere that this is the central meaning of Nietzsche's rhetorical question 'why should the world *which is of any concern to us*—not be a fiction?' (*BGE* 34; cf. *BGE* 4) and that it is a core component of his ideal of the 'free spirit'.[18] The heart of Nietzsche's 'critique of the will to truth' is that the free spirit is not beholden to purely theoretical synthetic truths, even if such truths were rationally attainable; he would not permit his practical orientation to the world to be undermined by them if they conflicted with 'judgements' indispensably involved in his practical commitments. But is metaphysical indifferentism, thus interpreted, really a defensible stance? To get clear about this, here is an example of the kind of cognitive conflict Nietzsche might have in mind. It may turn out that our aesthetic practices only really make sense to us on the assumption ('judgement') that we can be, literally, causally affected by aesthetic properties such as the beauty of a painting; or that one's ethical practices depend on the judgement that the conscious apprehension of some morally relevant value can itself make one act in certain ways—that the conscious awareness, as such, *itself* has causal powers. Call such judgements collectively the *efficacy of phenomenal properties thesis* or EPPT for short. Nietzsche's advice to the free spirit, taken literally, is then that, even if it were demonstrable on a priori grounds, and on such grounds alone, that EPPT is false, this should not be taken to constitute a weighty reason for abandoning the practices depending (*ex hypothesi*) on the belief of EPPT being true. But this seems problematic, indeed incoherent, for one cannot 'judge' to be the case what one simultaneously and self-transparently believes to be false. The very fact that the free spirit can, without mental division, retain his commitments in the face of a belief supposedly incompatible with them (the belief that EPPT is false) shows that these commitments must be logically independent of EPPT.

But perhaps there is another, less problematic way of taking Nietzsche's point. Consider, for illustration, the familiar philosophical fiction scenarios of wholesale illusion, from Descartes's evil demon to its updated versions—brains or human organisms passively kept alive in vats of nutrients, their collective experiential life being globally manipulated and mutually adjusted through suitable electrical stimulation by superscientists or non-human agents such as to produce in them the thoroughgoing experiential illusion of being human individuals interacting in a common world very much like our own. Assume that there were no techniques actively deployable by the victims that could lift the illusion, and that it could be removed only by external, super-scientific intervention. There seems nothing unintelligible in the idea that such cognitively manipulated subjects, once apprised of their condition by revelation or a priori reasoning, might prefer to remain in their illusory experiential world if that world contained much that was of value to them (which, given Nietzsche's account of value, would have to include ever-renewed occasions for apparent successful activity). But Nietzsche in *BGE* 4 and 34 seems to imply something stronger: that it is not unintelligible, indeed that it may be commendable, for such subjects to prefer wholesale collective experiential

---

[18] For more detail on Nietzsche's metaphysical indifferentism, see Poellner 2011: 170–7.

illusion—including importantly the illusion of their own conscious efficacy—*while knowing* that it is illusion. This stance would be incoherent if the manipulated subjects are construed, in line with the phrasing of *BGE* 4, as literally accepting a *judgement* which they know to be false. But there is no incoherence if one replaces 'the falsity of a judgement' in that passage by 'the non-veridicality of experiential content'. The subjects in the global illusion scenario might intelligibly prefer their collective illusory world including experiences as of interaction and conscious agency, knowing the content of these experiences to be non-veridical, to the disappearance of the illusion. And if it were known to be the case that—unlike in these global deception narratives—*all* apparent conscious efficacy were illusory, then such a preference for illusion might well seem even more attractive—for dispelling the illusion, if it were really possible, would result in the disappearance of both full-blown subjectivity and its correlate, significance-laden 'worldhood' (Nietzsche's point in *WP* 485, 488, 533).[19]

While Nietzsche's 'free-spirited' metaphysical indifferentism, construed in this way, is therefore coherent, it remains debatable whether the attitude it recommends is desirable. Perhaps the best way to make sense of the metaphysical sketches discussed in this essay is therefore to read them as recording Nietzsche's own residual unease with his 'official' meta-physical indifferentism. At least in some of his moods, he seems to have been dissatisfied with that stance and to have been attracted, not by an interest in metaphysical knowledge for its own sake, but by the traditional idea that one's practical commitments ought to be in harmony with 'the nature of things'. The metaphysics of the will to power is an interpreta-tion of reality which Nietzsche seems to have accepted at least some of the time, and which inscribes in the nature of the world at large that which he—again, some of the time—values above all: the conscious will to power. It seems to me that this reading makes sense of two facts which jointly need to be explained by any adequate interpretation of this material: that Nietzsche takes considerable trouble with elaborating some of the details of his metaphysical vision until the very last year of his philosophical activity, and that he confines these labours almost entirely to his notebooks. He explicitly concedes the 'interpretive' nature of these metaphysical ideas (*BGE* 22)—their failure to compel assent on purely rational grounds. But I suspect he would add that in this respect they do not differ unfavourably from their rivals. I have suggested, by contrast, that while several of Nietzsche's reflections in this con-text deserve to be taken rather more seriously than they sometimes are, there are at least three central claims underpinning or co-constituting the metaphysics of the will to power for which there are not only no grounds that are not reasonably contestable—a circumstance one expects in metaphysics—but no discernible justification at all: that human effective desires are reducible to the will to power (*BGE* 36; *WP* 663); that we 'cannot imagine any change that does not involve a will to power' (*WP* 689); and the strong becoming thesis.

References

(A) Works by Nietzsche

A   *The Anti-Christ* (1889), in *Twilight of the Idols and The Anti-Christ*, trans. R. J. Hollingdale. Harmondsworth: Penguin, 1990.

---

[19] For more extensive discussion of this point, see Poellner 2001: 100–6.

BGE   *Beyond Good and Evil* (1886), trans. R. J. Hollingdale. Harmondsworth: Penguin, 1982.
GM   *On the Genealogy of Morals* (1887), in *On the Genealogy of Morals and Ecce Homo*, trans. W. Kaufmann and R. J. Hollingdale. New York: Vintage, 1989.
GS   *The Gay Science* (1882–7), trans. W. Kaufmann. New York: Vintage, 1974.
KGW   *Werke: Kritische Gesamtausgabe*, ed. G. Colli, M. Mntinari, et al. Berlin: De Gruyter, 1967–.
TI   *Twilight of the Idols* (1889), in *Twilight of the Idols and The Anti-Christ*, trans. R. J. Hollingdale. Harmondsworth: Penguin, 1990.
WP   *The Will to Power* (1906), ed. W. Kaufmann, trans. W. Kaufmann and R. J. Hollingdale. New York: Vintage, 1968.

(B) Other Works Cited

Boscovich, R. J. 1966/1763. *A Theory of Natural Philosophy*. Boston: MIT Press.
Broad, C. D. 1923. *Scientific Thought*. London: Kegan Paul.
Brobjer, T. 2008. *Nietzsche's Philosophical Context*. Urbana and Chicago: University of Illinois Press.
Clark, M. 1990. *Nietzsche on Truth and Philosophy*. Cambridge: Cambridge University Press.
Dilthey, W. 1923. 'Beiträge zur Lösung der Frage vom Ursprung unseres Glaubens an die Realität der Außenwelt', in W. Dilthey, *Gesammelte Schriften*, vol. V. Stuttgart: Teubner, 90–138.
Doyle, T. 2009. *Nietzsche on Epistemology and Metaphysics*. Edinburgh: Edinburgh University Press.
Eddington, A. S. 1928. *The Nature of the Physical World*. Cambridge: Cambridge University Press.
Fales, E. 1990. *Causation and Universals*. London: Routledge.
Foster, J. 1982. *The Case for Idealism*. London: Routledge & Kegan Paul.
Heidegger, M. 1979–87/1961. *Nietzsche* (4 vols). San Francisco: Harper & Row.
James, W. 1983/1880. 'The Feeling of Effort', in *Essays in Psychology*. Cambridge, Mass.: Harvard University Press.
Jaspers. K. 1936. *Nietzsche—Einführung in das Verständnis seines Philosophierens*. Berlin and Leipzig: De Gruyter.
Kaufmann, W. 1968. *Nietzsche—Philosopher, Psychologist, Antichrist*. Princeton: Princeton University Press.
Lange, F. A. 1866. *Geschichte des Materialismus*. Iserlohn: Baedeker.
Leiter, B. 2002. *Nietzsche on Morality*. London: Routledge.
Locke, J. 1959/1690. *An Essay Concerning Human Understanding*. New York: Dover.
Menzies, P. and Price, H. 1993. 'Causation as a Secondary Quality', *British Journal for the Philosophy of Science* 44: 187–203.
Michotte, A. 1963/1945. *The Perception of Causality*. London: Methuen.
Mittasch, A. 1952. *Friedrich Nietzsche als Naturphilosoph*. Stuttgart: Kroener.
Nagel, E. 1961. *The Structure of Science*. New York: Harcourt.
Nehamas, A. 1985. *Nietzsche: Life as Literature*. Cambridge, Mass.: Harvard University Press.
Poellner, P. 1995. *Nietzsche and Metaphysics*. Oxford: Clarendon Press.
Poellner, P. 2001. 'Perspectival Truth', in B. Leiter and J. Richardson (eds), *Nietzsche*. Oxford: Oxford University Press, 85–117.
Poellner, P. 2011. 'Nietzschean Freedom', in K. Gemes and S. May (eds), *Nietzsche on Freedom and Autonomy*. Oxford: Oxford University Press, 125–52.
Psillos, S. 2002. *Causation and Explanation*. Chesham: Acumen.

Reginster, B. 2006. *The Affirmation of Life: Nietzsche on Overcoming Nihilism.* Cambridge, Mass.: Harvard University Press.

Richardson, J. 1996. *Nietzsche's System.* New York and Oxford: Oxford University Press.

Rorty, R. 1989. 'Self-Creation and Affiliation: Proust, Nietzsche, and Heidegger', in *Contingency, Irony, and Solidarity.* Cambridge: Cambridge University Press, 96–121.

Schacht, R. 1983. *Nietzsche.* London: Routledge & Kegan Paul.

Scheler, M. 1977/1926. *Erkenntnis und Arbeit.* Frankfurt am Main: Klostermann.

Schlechta, K. and Anders, A. 1962. *Friedrich Nietzsche—Von den verborgenen Anfängen seines Philosophierens.* Stuttgart-Bad Cannstatt: Frommann.

Schopenhauer, A. 1969/1819. *The World as Will and Representation* (2 vols). New York: Dover.

Searle, J. 1983. *Intentionality.* Cambridge: Cambridge University Press.

Sprigge, T. L. S. 1990. *The Rational Foundations of Ethics.* London: Routledge.

Strawson, G. 1989. *The Secret Connexion.* Oxford: Clarendon Press.

CHAPTER 30

THE PSYCHOLOGY OF CHRISTIAN MORALITY: WILL TO POWER AS WILL TO NOTHINGNESS

BERNARD REGINSTER

NIETZSCHE is widely regarded as one of the great masters of moral psychology and *On the Genealogy of Morals* has a strong claim to being his most important contribution to that form of inquiry. In this paper, I attempt to circumscribe Nietzsche's conception of moral psychology and to describe the actual psychological account he develops in that work for the predominant, Christian morality. A chief distinction of his conception of moral psychology is the controversial role it is assigned in the *critique* of morality. The three essays of the *Genealogy* are "studies by a psychologist for a revaluation of all values" (*EH*: "The Genealogy of Morality"), which suggests that uncovering the psychological origins of moral values is supposed to play a role in their critique. And the central concept of his actual psychological account of morality is the *will to power*, the vicissitudes of which go a long way toward explaining the emergence and character of that morality.

PSYCHOLOGY AND CRITIQUE

Determining the precise critical role Nietzsche assigns to his inquiry into the psychological "origins" of morality is a delicate matter since he emphatically declares that "the inquiry into the *origins of our evaluations* and tables of the good is in absolutely no way identical with a critique of them" (*WP* 254; *GS* 345). Nietzsche supplies a clue in *Beyond Good and Evil* when he observes that most philosophers have "wanted to supply a *rational foundation* for morality—and every philosopher so far has believed that he has provided such a foundation. Morality itself, however, was accepted as 'given.' How remote from their clumsy pride was that task which they considered insignificant and left in dust and must—the task of description—although the subtlest fingers and senses can scarcely be subtle enough for it." (*BGE* 186)

Philosophers are here reproached for taking for granted not simply (as is usually assumed) the value, but the *description* of morality. In their eagerness to ratify the "prevalent morality," they have neglected the "task of description," a negligence that has led them astray. This preoccupation with *description* is central to the *Genealogy*, the "project" of which, Nietzsche writes in the preface, "is to traverse with quite novel questions, and as though with new eyes, the enormous, distant, and so well hidden land of morality—of morality that has actually existed, actually been lived; and does this not mean virtually to *discover* this land for the first time?" (*GM* Preface 7).

Moral psychology is usually defined as the discipline concerned with the psychology of the kind of agency we exercise in acting morally. It asks what characteristics agents must possess in order to act morally and be subject to moral appraisal and to moral attitudes, such as the feeling of guilt. Nietzsche frequently worries that moral psychology has too often proven to be little more than an expression of "the common *faith* in the prevalent morality" (*BGE* 186), by presenting as mere "description" the view of moral agency actually implied by a conception of morality uncritically taken as "given" or "factual" (e.g., *GM* I: 2; *A* 14–15; *TI*: "The Four Great Errors"). Instead of starting out with a "given" moral theory and spelling out its psychological implications, he believes we should start with human psychology as it can actually be observed, and then ask what psychological significance morality could have.

This approach leads him to develop a *naturalistic* account of morality: it is a reflection of an agent's "drives" (*BGE* 6; cf. *GS* 335) and "affects" (*BGE* 187), which have themselves ultimately "physiological" causes (*WP* 254; see *D* 199, 542; *GM* I: 15);[1] moral agents lack (contra-causal) free will, a notion he finds incoherent (*BGE* 21; *TI*: "The Four Great Errors" 7), and their moral behavior is determined by largely immutable physiological and psychic traits (*D* 109; *BGE* 5, 6, 231; *GM* Preface 2), among which *conscious* mental states are causally secondary or confined to epiphenomenal insignificance (*D* 116; *GS* 333; *TI*: "The Four Great Errors" 3; *WP* 478, 666).[2] This naturalistic account has an obvious critical function: it deflates the grandiose self-image of the "prevalent morality" (as supra-natural, as evidence of human exceptionalism) still widespread among many of his predecessors: "We have learned better. We have become more modest in every respect. We no longer trace the origin of man in the 'spirit', in 'divinity', we have placed him back among the animals." (*A* 14; *BGE* 230)[3] And it implies that the moral

---

[1] In *GM* I: 15, Nietzsche distinguishes a "*physiological* investigation and interpretation" of morality from a "psychological one," and associates the former with a consideration of morality's bearing on the "survival of a race" or the production of "a stronger type." But the characterizations he offers for either the "herd" or this "stronger type" are virtually always in moral-psychological terms. And it certainly is the moral-psychological profiles of these types that form the object of his critical assessment. Physiological factors may well underwrite psychological states, but it is in virtue of underwriting such states that they appear to matter to Nietzsche's critique of morality.

[2] Knobe and Leiter (2007: 90) summarize Nietzschean moral psychology as follows: "individuals are simply born with a certain psycho-physical package of traits (the person's distinctive type-facts); these type-facts play a powerful (but not exclusive) role in determining one's behavior and values, though a far more powerful role than education or upbringing or conscious choice; indeed, a person's crucial conscious choices and values are themselves explicable in terms of these type-facts."

[3] The deflationary character of Nietzsche's moral psychology has been widely acknowledged in the scholarly literature (see Williams 1994, Leiter 2002, Janaway 2007, and others). Nietzsche's naturalistic psychology of moral phenomena deflates the non-naturalistic moral psychology articulated by the Christians or the Kantians by combining an explanation of these phenomena, which is as coherent and compelling as its non-naturalistic alternative, with additional desiderata for good explanations, such

psychology that remains subservient to the "prevalent morality" is nothing but "an imaginary *psychology*" (*A* 15), or a "falsification *in psychologicis*" (*TI*: "The Four Great Errors" 7).

However, the significance of the psychological critique Nietzsche deploys in the *Genealogy* cannot be limited to such naturalistic deflation, for the object of this book is not simply to show that the allegedly non-natural characteristics of morality can in fact be reduced to pieces of natural psychology, but to ask why they were so misrepresented in the first place.[4] And there is one obvious reason for raising this question: it is not enough to show that moral judgment, moral attitudes, and moral agency are not as they are represented both in non-naturalistic *theories* of morality and in the *phenomenology* of moral life—after all, people do feel "guilty" or "sinful" (*GM* III: 16) or take values that express their drives and affects to transcend them (*GM* Preface 5; *BGE* 2, 230)—one must also explain why they are represented in this way, or what "drives" or "affects" such representations themselves express. One must do so not only for the purpose of *explanation*—insofar as a naturalistic account of morality would be incomplete without an explanation of the "falsification *in psychologicis*" it exposes[5] —but also for the purpose of *criticism*. For, as Nietzsche supposes, this falsification is not an innocent mistake, but the *symptom* of a certain *affective* condition:

> Even apart from the value of such claims as 'there is a categorical imperative in us', one can still always ask: what does such a claim tell us about the man who makes it? There are moralities which are meant to justify their creator before others. Other moralities are meant to calm him and lead him to be satisfied with himself. With yet others he wants to crucify himself and humiliate himself. With others he wants to wreak revenge, with others conceal himself, with others transfigure himself and place himself way up, at a distance. This morality is used by its creator to forget, that one to have others forget him or something about him. Some moralists want to vent their power and creative whims on humanity; some others, perhaps including Kant, suggest with their morality: 'What deserves respect in me is that I can obey—and you *ought* not to be different from me'.—In short, moralities are also merely a *sign language of the affects*. (*BGE* 187; see *TI*: "'Improving' Humanity" 1)

Merely showing that the categorical imperative lacks "value," by which Nietzsche means here "rational foundations" (*BGE* 186), will have little critical efficacy—in actually changing minds—if, as he believes, it represents the rationalization of certain affects or "a desire of the heart that has been filtered and made abstract" (*BGE* 5). For such affects will not necessarily respond to purely philosophical arguments and the very possibility of their successful alteration therefore requires that they themselves be fully understood (see *GS* 347).[6]

---

as ontological parsimony and explanatory minimalism, to establish the superiority of the naturalistic alternative. Some of Nietzsche's objections to the non-naturalistic moral psychology of many of his predecessors are more direct and consist in exposing the incoherence of some of its fundamental concepts (e.g., the concept of free will, *BGE* 21). On all this, see Leiter 2001, 2002.

[4] I will not consider here construals of Nietzsche's genealogical critique that present it as aiming to debunk or destabilize ordinary moral beliefs, for example by exposing their contingent origins (for a good recent example, see Kail 2011). I believe these views underestimate Nietzsche's critical ambitions to a considerable degree, but I cannot argue for this here.

[5] On the necessity of such an explanation, see Scheffler 1992: 52–72.

[6] Janaway (2007) is particularly sensitive to this issue, but focuses more on the nonphilosophical means Nietzsche employs in order to touch and possibly unsettle the affective underpinnings of traditional morality than on the characterization of these underpinnings themselves.

However, even this qualification cannot suffice to circumscribe the critical project of the *Genealogy*. For to be anxious to change the minds of those who view morality as more than a piece of natural psychology, Nietzsche would have to regard the falseness of the view as reason enough to debunk it. But he notoriously does not: "The falseness of a judgment is for us not necessarily an objection to a judgment. [...] The question is to what extent it is life-promoting" (*BGE* 4). And the central claim of the *Genealogy* is not simply that morality is only a piece of natural psychology, but rather that it is (or promotes) psycho*pathology* or "sickness." Nietzsche's focus on feelings of power and self-esteem suggests that he has in mind the role of what is understood today as *narcissistic* pathologies in the development of moral phenomena. Narcissistic pathologies may be present, for example, when an individual holds himself to exceedingly demanding standards, which underwrite illusions of his own grandiosity or, alternatively, debilitating feelings of inferiority or worthlessness. So long as the critique of this individual's condition is limited, for example, to the "rational foundations" of the standards that govern his self-assessment or to the epistemic credentials of that assessment, it misses the point by *describing* its object inadequately. For the issue surely is not simply that his standards are excessively demanding, but what his holding himself to them tells about the individual, or what *affective* role they play in his psychological economy.

In insisting, in the Preface to the *Genealogy*, that his target is the morality that has "actually been lived," Nietzsche indicates that he is talking not simply of an abstract assortment of normative claims (about principles and values) and metaphysical claims (about the ontological status of these values and the character of moral agency), but of a lived experience in which these normative and metaphysical claims take on particular *affective* meanings. This suggests that, in his view, the "value" of a moral life is not exhausted by the extent to which it is lived in conformity with moral values and ideals, and by the extent to which these values and ideals are justified. Quite "apart from" the "rational foundations" of these values and ideals, then, is the question of their affective meanings for the agent who holds himself to them, which has a bearing on the "value" of those values, not insofar as it touches on the question of their rationality, but insofar as it concerns what Nietzsche often calls the "health" of the agent. So, even if the standards in terms of which the narcissist assesses himself proved to be reasonable, we would still have to determine their affective significance for him, and through it, their impact on his health.[7]

Most commentators have supposed that Nietzsche understands his genealogical critique of moral values to be a challenge to their *rational legitimacy*. They have accordingly been at pains to find a way in which an inquiry into the psychological origins of moral values could have a bearing on their rational legitimacy. However, this common supposition about the character of Nietzsche's genealogical critique overlooks a crucial distinction he draws repeatedly between two ways of evaluating moral values. On the one hand, evaluating moral values may be a matter of examining their "rational foundations" (*BGE* 186) or the justification of beliefs about them, including beliefs about their "religious sanction" or about the "free will" required for their application (*GS* 345). On the other hand, evaluating moral values may be a matter of determining the *psychological significance* of adopting and living

---

[7] This suggests that Nietzsche might have considered relations between affects and values that differ from the prevailing view that he takes values to be simply expressions or rationalizations of affects (e.g., Janaway 2007: 46–7; Poellner 2007).

in accordance with such values. Nietzsche draws this contrast explicitly in the section of *Beyond Good and Evil* I quoted earlier, where the psychological investigation of the categorical imperative takes place "apart from" questions about its "rational foundations," but also in *The Gay Science*, where he distinguishes between the *truth value* of moral beliefs and their *medical value*, so to speak:

> Even if a morality has grown out of an error, the realization of this fact would not as much as touch the problem of its value. Thus nobody up to now has examined the *value* of that most famous of all medicines which is called morality; and the first step would be—for once to *question* it. Well then, precisely this is our task.— (*GS* 345)

We might accordingly venture the following conjecture about the critical significance of a psychological genealogy of morality. Regardless of whether or not the normative and metaphysical claims that constitute the dominant Christian morality rest on solid "rational foundations," they can be recruited to express pathological configurations of affects. Nietzsche's claim would be that the distinctive normative and metaphysical claims of Christian morality are so uniquely well suited to express certain narcissistic pathologies that one (and, in some cases, the best) explanation of their origin must be found there.

Such a critique of Christian morality is pressing business for Nietzsche on two grounds. First, he takes most human beings to be liable to the pathologies Christian morality is so well suited to express, in virtue of basic and (fairly) uncontroversial features of the human condition—namely, a will to power, together with more or less severe limitations in the ability to satisfy it. Second, he takes Christian morality to be well suited not only to express, but also to *worsen* these pathologies and render them considerably more destructive. Thus, the chief critical claim the *Genealogy* makes about morality is not, for the most part, that its normative and metaphysical claims lack adequate "rational foundations," but that the psychological ("affective") outlook they frame is *dangerous*, indeed "the danger of dangers" (*GM* Preface 6).

RESSENTIMENT AND WILL TO POWER

Nietzsche presents genealogy as a *psychological* inquiry. And he defines psychology as a "morphology and the *doctrine of the development of the will to power*" (*BGE* 23). In other words, psychology is the study of the *forms* and *patterns of development* of the will to power.[8] Whatever we may think of this characterization, it unequivocally indicates that Nietzsche

---

[8] Pippin (2009: 73) has argued that for psychology to be the "queen of the sciences," it must be "quite foreign to any notion of systematic thought or metaphysical or epistemological foundations." Although there is something undeniably true in the claim that Nietzsche's remarkably broad-ranging psychological observations operate free from such constraints, it is also true that some themes emerge from these observations and eventually become firm enough to induce him to identify the will to power as central to human motivational psychology. In fact, I believe along with others that the concept of the will to power operates throughout the *Genealogy*, where it figures as ubiquitous principle of explanation (e.g., Soll 1994; Owen 2007: 84, 106, 116).

considers the will to power as a *fundamental* and *essential* feature of human motivational psychology.

A motivation is fundamental, as I use the term here, if it is not derivative from or dependent on other motives: it must be an independent or self-standing source of motivation. In the *Genealogy*, the will to power operates as an independent drive, which can compete with and "dominate" other drives: for example, it is "the dominating instinct" of the sovereign individual (*GM* II: 2). A motivation counts as essential if a motivational repertoire that does not include it would no longer be recognizably human. In the *Genealogy*, the will to power is presented as "the will of life," that is to say, as the defining component of the motivational equipment of all animals, including human beings: "every animal [...] instinctively strives for an optimum of favorable conditions under which it can expend all its strength and achieve its maximum feeling of power" (*GM* III: 7; cf. *BGE* 13, 259).

The inquiries of the *Genealogy* invite the following analysis of the concept of will to power. It is the drive for *effective agency*, that is to say, the capacity to govern oneself and shape one's environment in accordance with one's will. It is "ambition" or what Nietzsche sometimes calls a desire for "proficiency" (*A* 2). He often presents the "feeling of power," and not simply power, as the aim of the will to power: we want not only effective agency, but also the *experience* of effective agency (e.g., *A* 2). This is intended to reflect a simple but significant fact about the satisfaction of desires. Presumably, a desire the agent wants to satisfy will not stop exercising its motivational pressure until he *knows* that it is satisfied. For this reason, when we talk of the satisfaction of a desire, we often mean at once the objective fact of possession of the object of desire and the subjective consciousness of this fact. The desire for power understood as effective agency will therefore count as satisfied only if the agent has an *experience* of effective agency.

This explains the peculiar fact that the satisfaction of the will to power requires that there be "resistance" to its satisfaction. Thus, in the *Genealogy*, Nietzsche characterizes it as "a desire to overcome, a desire to throw down, a desire to become master, a thirst for enemies and resistances and triumphs" (*GM* I: 13).[9] An agent's will to power counts as satisfied only if he has an *experience* of effective agency. The mere satisfaction of determinate needs or wishes cannot suffice to elicit this experience, because it might not necessarily be a consequence of his effective agency, but could just as well be the product of luck or of an accommodating environment. Hence, it is only when the environment resists his will, and he manages to overcome this resistance, that he can experience a feeling of power or effective agency: "the will to power can manifest itself only against resistances; therefore it seeks that which resists it" (*WP* 656; cf. 696).

Nietzsche's first psychological thesis is that the will to power is an *independent* source of motivation. If, as I proposed, we understand it as the desire for effective agency, for the power to make my environment hospitable to the satisfaction of the desires I choose to pursue, the will to power initially appears not to stand on its own: it rather seems dependent on those other desires, insofar as I would be motivated to seek effective agency only insofar as it is instrumentally or prudentially required for their satisfaction. What, then, are Nietzsche's grounds for claiming that we have an interest in effective agency that is independent from those needs and desires such agency would be effective in satisfying?

---

[9] This "thirst for enemies and resistances" is a feature of the will to power left unaccounted for in the otherwise illuminating accounts developed in Clark 1990: 210–12 and Richardson 1996: 18–28.

It is relatively easy to think of non-instrumental instances of the will to power. Young children will sometimes badger their parents for a piece of candy, in which they lose interest as soon as it is given to them. This suggests that the badgering was not motivated by hunger or by a desire for sweets: it was rather motivated by the desire to test the effectiveness of their agency in their (social) environment. Naturally, we might suppose that they did so out of prudence: their desire to test the effectiveness of their agency could have been motivated by the implicit recognition that a desire for food or sweets, or indeed any other desire for the satisfaction of which they have to rely on their parents' cooperation, might arise in the future. Nietzsche's fundamental insight is that the will to power can stand apart even from such prudential motivations.

The *Genealogy* offers two kinds of consideration in support of the motivational independence of the will to power. The first kind of consideration is essentially *phenomenological*. Nietzsche observes that we are frequently motivated to engage in activity not—or not just—in order to realize some particular end, but simply to *discharge energy*; and he identifies this peculiar motivation as will to power: "A living being seeks above all to *discharge* its energy [*seine Kraft*]—life itself is *will to power*." (*BGE* 13; see *GM* I: 10, 13) We should think of "energy" in this context very precisely in the sense in which overactive children are said to have "too much energy," that is to say, in the sense in which energy is conceived as something that essentially seeks expression in activity—as *vitality*. This is the sense in which the strong masters, for example, are "rounded men replete with energy [*mit Kraft überladene*] and therefore *necessarily* active" (*GM* I: 10: see also the claim that it is of the essence of "strength [*Stärke*]" to "express itself as strength," *GM* I: 13). Thus, a child full of "energy" who tests the effectiveness of his agency against all kinds of obstacles even when no pressing desire requires their overcoming could be thought to develop the abilities necessary for the satisfaction of possible future desires. But this thought, for Nietzsche, would not be in keeping with the facts, for what the child most evidently seeks in such bursts of activity is "to *discharge* its energy" (or to exercise his effective agency), not to build it up or harness it in preparation for the future. Indeed, far from being a kind of long-range prudence, "the really fundamental instinct of life […] aims at the *expansion of power*, and, wishing for that frequently risks and even sacrifices self-preservation" (*GS* 349).

The second kind of consideration is, so to speak, *transcendental*. We must suppose the will to power to be an independent source of motivation in order to account for the human susceptibility to *ressentiment*. While there is disagreement among scholars over the character of *ressentiment*, there is agreement that it is a response to *suffering*.[10] Following Schopenhauer, Nietzsche conceives of suffering as the experience of *frustration*, of an obstacle or resistance to the satisfaction of a desire: "all suffering is nothing but unfulfilled and thwarted willing" (*WWR* I: 65, p. 363). We should note that Schopenhauer speaks here not of unfulfilled *desire*, but unfulfilled *willing*. I may have many desires that will not necessarily elicit suffering when they go unsatisfied. It is only when I *will* to satisfy a desire that I experience its going unsatisfied as *suffering*.

---

[10] The disagreement concerns primarily the question of whether *ressentiment* is, as Wallace puts it, a "social sentiment," essentially directed at others, or a more impersonal feeling that can be directed at things (such as "time" or "the world"). On this issue, see Bittner 1994, Wallace 2007, and Poellner 2011. I will not pursue this question here.

I will to satisfy a desire, presumably, when I consider its object *good*. This might suggest that suffering is distinct from other forms of pain and discomfort by virtue of registering the loss of a good.[11] The experience of suffering has another dimension, however: it registers not only the loss of a desired good, but also one's inability to secure its possession. The non-satisfaction of a desire I did not will to satisfy may cause a painful sense of deprivation, but since it did not engage my agency, it cannot affect my sense of its *effectiveness*. In Nietzsche's terminology, it does not elicit a "feeling of impotence." If I will to satisfy a desire, by contrast, I engage the effectiveness of my agency in its pursuit. In this case, its going unsatisfied will elicit an experience of *frustration*, which denotes thwarted effort and involves a feeling of incapacity.

Ressentiment responds precisely to the feeling of impotence or ineffectiveness constitutively involved in the experience of suffering.[12] Thus, the *ressentiment* of the "priests" is aroused by the frustration of their aspiration for political and social supremacy. Common responses to the loss of something valued include regret or disappointment, or distinctively moral emotions when circumstances make them appropriate, such as resentment or indignation. *Ressentiment* is distinct from all these responses. Regret and disappointment are responses that focus on the *value of the lost object*, and resentment and indignation are responses that focus on the agent's *entitlement* to it. *Ressentiment* clearly differs from these, in my view, in virtue of being focused on the agent's *inability* to get what he wants. In other words, *ressentiment* is a response not to the loss of a good or to the violation of a right, but to a lack of power: it bears an essential connection to the "feeling of impotence" (*GM* I: 7, 10, 13, 14). *Ressentiment* is thus a response to suffering experienced as *an injury to the feeling of power*. Nietzsche describes it as "the gnawing worm of injured ambition" (*GM* III: 8).

Two facts about *ressentiment* show that we have an interest in being effective agents that is independent of our interest in any particular good such agency would be effective at securing. First, if our interest in effective agency were dependent on our interest in these goods, its frustration could elicit only regret or indignation, but not *ressentiment*. Our very *susceptibility* to *ressentiment* would be left unexplained. Second, the motivational independence of the will to power is particularly evident in a frequent consequence of *ressentiment*, to which Nietzsche devotes much of his attention in the *Genealogy*, namely the fact that it motivates a *devaluation* of the goods, specifically a devaluation of the *value* we formerly attributed to them. Such devaluation would make no sense if the interest in effective agency manifested in *ressentiment* were dependent on our interest in those goods.

It is important to note that Nietzsche regards *ressentiment* as a *normal* response to frustration. The strong, noble type of man is also liable to *ressentiment*, although in his case, it "consummates and exhausts itself in an immediate reaction, and therefore does not *poison*" (*GM* I: 10). It is only when it is experienced by "the weak and impotent" that *ressentiment* becomes "poison," precisely because it cannot be consummated in "an immediate reaction." In this case, *ressentiment* becomes a persistent and dominant trait of the individual, who

[11] In the case of Schopenhauer, this aspect of the distinction between willing and (merely) desiring is blurred by his view that "good" designates whatever satisfies our desires: "we call everything good that is just as we want it to be" (*WWR* I: 65, p. 360). However, my focus here is on the *other* aspect of the distinction between willing and desiring.

[12] Although not explicitly thematized, the connection between *ressentiment* and impotence figures clearly in the treatment offered in Scheler 1961.

then deserves the characterization of "man of *ressentiment*." Consider Nietzsche's example of the priest. It is because he wills, and therefore values, political or social supremacy that the priest's defeat at the hands of the stronger "warriors" arouses his *ressentiment*. Unable to regain political and social supremacy, he is then compelled to "an act of the most spiritual revenge": he revaluates his values. The purpose of this revaluation, as I will argue shortly, is to restore his injured feeling of power: he devalues his own values because they have become intolerable reminders of his impotence.

The conception of will to power as will for effective agency invites a comparison with Kant's famous claim about the relation between willing ends and willing means. By presenting this relation as "analytical" (Kant, *Foundations of the Metaphysics of Morals*, Ak. 417), Kant indicates that the relation of willing ends to willing means is one of identity: the concept of willing the means is already contained in the concept of willing the end so that, in a sense, willing an end just *is* willing the means necessary to it. Nietzsche makes a seemingly similar claim: "To have purposes, aims, intentions, *willing* in general, is the same thing as willing to be stronger, willing to grow—and, in addition, willing the means to this." (*WP* 675) Like Kant, he appears to claim that "*willing* in general" just *is* willing power.

But there are some significant differences. In particular, by distinguishing willing power from willing means, Nietzsche indicates that willing power is not just a matter of willing the means necessary to the realization of one's ends; it is willing the *independent end* of *power* or effective agency. Moreover, Nietzsche assimilates willing power to "willing to be stronger, willing to grow": in contrast, willing the means necessary to one's ends does not always require becoming stronger or growing. If the strength one already possesses is instrumentally sufficient to realize one's end, *growing stronger* is not necessary. Presumably, this is a consequence of the self-standing character of the will to power: not conditioned by other particular desires, the will to power is not restricted to the determinate amount of power demanded by their satisfaction.

Finally, whereas for Kant the relation between willing ends and willing means is one of rational necessity, the relation Nietzsche identifies between "*willing* in general" and willing power appears to be descriptive and contingent. Like Schopenhauer, Nietzsche believes that *suffering* is a ubiquitous condition of life: this means that human beings live in an environment not perfectly ordained for the satisfaction of their will. The experience of suffering, as we saw, is at least in part the experience by human agents of a challenge to the effectiveness of their agency. It is therefore plausible to suppose that the repeated challenges to this effectiveness would eventually spawn an independent interest in it, or that beings with such an interest would be more likely to thrive in such an environment (see *BGE* 13). This would explain why, in addition to caring about the realization of their chosen ends, human beings also care about being effective agents, about competence or "proficiency" (cf. *A* 2), and why this interest would be an essentially vital drive: "the will of life" (*BGE* 259), "life itself" (*BGE* 13), or the "strongest, most life-affirming drive" (*GM* III: 18).

THE SLAVE REVOLT IN MORALITY

"The slave revolt in morality begins when *ressentiment* itself becomes creative and gives birth to values: the *ressentiment* of natures that are denied the true reaction, that of deeds, and compensate themselves with an imaginary revenge." (*GM* I: 10) *Ressentiment* is a reaction to suffering, experienced as a challenge to one's feeling of power, which motivates a desire for "revenge" understood as aiming to restore the threatened feeling of power. When it is experienced by the weak and impotent, this vengefulness is denied "an immediate reaction" in physical action. As a consequence, it becomes "submerged" or "repressed," and thus gains in intensity (*GM* I: 7; see 8).[13] It also gains in "cleverness" and find eventual expression in a "revaluation of all values" (*GM* I: 8, 10).

It is tempting to give a *strategic* interpretation of this *ressentiment* revaluation (Wallace 2007), which goes as follows. Oppressed by the strong, and unable to defeat them in the usual physical way, they resort to revaluation—"an act of *the most spiritual revenge*" (*GM* I: 7)—to regain the advantage over the strong masters. Thus, they represent the traits and states of affairs valued by their opponents as "evil." To persuade the strong to embrace the new values, they must claim *objective authority* for them: they are "unconditional" norms. And to get their opponents to be troubled by their failure to live up to those values, they contrive the fiction of *free will*, to induce their opponents to think that they are to be *blamed* for such a failure.

Nietzsche's writings occasionally invite this strategic interpretation. For instance, he observes that "the 'neighbor' praises selflessness *because it brings him advantages*" (*GS* 21). And in the *Genealogy*, he once describes this revaluation as a "bait," which the "men of *ressentiment*" set up for their oppressors (*GM* I: 8), so that the following would count for them as "the ultimate, subtlest, sublimest triumph of revenge": "Undoubtedly if they succeeded in *poisoning the consciences* of the fortunate with their own misery, with all misery, so that one day the fortunate began to be ashamed of their good fortune and perhaps said to one another: 'it is disgraceful to be fortunate: *there is too much misery!*'" (*GM* III 14).

However, Wallace (2007) has raised strong objections against this strategic interpretation. One objection is that it leaves the *effectiveness* of the revaluation in altering the mindset of the strong a complete mystery: why would they buy into the values (and metaphysical assumptions) of the weak at all?[14] Moreover, Nietzsche suggests that the man of *ressentiment* benefits from the invention of new values only by *endorsing* them himself—by *deceiving himself* about their legitimacy—and not simply by pretending to endorse them to fool his enemies. Although the priests themselves sometimes seem to engage in such pretense, appeasing the *ressentiment* of the members of the "herd" apparently requires inducing them to endorse the new values (see *GM* III: 15–16). But such an endorsement is not required for their strategic use, and is in fact incompatible with it.[15]

---

[13] There is a strong analogy between the *ressentiment* of "the weak and impotent" and the phenomenon of narcissistic rage, the response to an experience of loss of control or power by individuals who have developed such a pressing need to feel powerful that this experience is simply intolerable. The pressing need to feel powerful is itself a defensive reaction to the anxiety generated by a deep and pervasive feeling of impotence. Narcissism, which is understood as a drive for power, is also taken to represent a self-standing drive, with its independent line of development, apart from other drives (such as sex and hunger). See, e.g., Kohut 1971.

[14] Some commentators have recognized this difficulty but their attempts to resolve it remain very speculative: e.g., Migotti 2006: 113–16; Owen 2007: 120–3; Hatab 2011.

[15] This incompatibility comes in two forms. First, a genuine endorsement of the values of compassion and equality is arguably incompatible with the cynical preaching of these values to further the objective of political superiority; indeed, a genuine endorsement of these values is arguably incompatible with the

To resolve these difficulties, Wallace puts forth an *expressive* interpretation, according to which the revaluation of values by the man of *ressentiment* is not a strategic means to harm those who possess the goods he wants for himself, but rather an expression of his hatred for them. In Wallace's view, the weak is in the grip of a "psychic tension": his emotional life is dominated by negative affects directed at individuals whom he also regards as worthy of admiration. The revaluation of noble values provides a resolution for this psychic tension. If the strong masters come to be seen as "evil," then the hatred the man of *ressentiment* harbors toward them becomes an intelligible response, and the psychic tension vanishes. In other words, the purpose of this revaluation is "self-vindication," that is to say, the rationalization by the weak of their hatred of the strong masters. In this view, the invention of new values is supposed to benefit the man of *ressentiment* by eliminating an inner "psychic tension," and it manages to do so only if he actually endorses them.

However, this appealing interpretation crucially underestimates the role of the feeling of impotence in *ressentiment* revaluation. According to Wallace's expressive interpretation, the invention of new values is intended to resolve a psychic tension created by emotional attitudes that conflict with existing evaluative commitments. In this interpretation, the "feeling of impotence" of the weak refers only to his experience of defeat and oppression at the hands of the strong masters: it explains how he comes to hate and admire his masters at the same time, and therefore how a psychic tension arises in him, but it does not supply the *motivation* for resolving it. The tension created by the conflicting attitudes is itself the motivating factor. Indeed, this feeling of impotence becomes a purely accidental feature of the case as we can imagine other instances of the same type of psychic tension, calling for the same sort of self-vindicating revaluation, in which no such experience of defeat or oppression is involved (for example, feeling attracted to someone one also despises).

But Nietzsche insists that *ressentiment* revaluation is a "self-deception of impotence" (*GM* I: 13; see 7, 10, 14). In other words, the feeling of impotence of the weak, and not simply the need to "make sense" of his attitudes, motivates his revaluation. The purpose of the revaluation of "aristocratic" values is to alleviate the feeling of impotence, which his inability to live up to them continuously elicits.[16] Thus, Nietzsche offers the following characterizations of what motivates the men of *ressentiment* to engage in revaluation:

pursuit of such an objective in the first place. Second, if this revaluation were part of a strategy to recover that superiority, it would be singularly ill suited for it, for a genuine endorsement of the devaluation of political superiority would undermine the ability to *enjoy* the recovery of it (see Reginster 1997).

[16] As I argued in Reginster 1997, only priestly *ressentiment* is "capable of creating values": Nietzsche describes the hatred of the "Jewish priestly people" as "the profoundest and sublimest kind of hatred, capable of creating ideals and reversing values, *the like of which has never existed on earth before*" (*GM* I: 8). Although *ressentiment* may well be a reaction to oppression, *ressentiment revaluation* must be more, for it would otherwise be far more common and widespread than Nietzsche maintains. Moreover, it is a distinctive characteristic of the slave type that he simply accepts his masters' values (*BGE* 261) and so resigns himself to his inferiority. It must presumably be that the need to feel powerful is especially pressing for the priest: his weak constitution, which Nietzsche identifies as the central causal factor of this type, must have spawned in him early on a deep and pervasive feeling of impotence, for which he compensated by contriving fantasies of power so necessary to his psychological equilibrium that he responds with "brooding and emotional explosions" to anyone or anything that threatens its maintenance. In his meticulous analysis, Ridley (1998: 44–62) argues that the priest does not share the slave's impotent *ressentiment*, but is particularly apt to understand and exploit it; but he does not explain why the priest possesses this particular aptitude, and this suggests an immediate acquaintance with that emotion.

These failures [...] what do they really want? At least to *represent* justice, love, wisdom, supe-riority—that is the ambition of the 'lowest', the sick. And how skillful such an ambition makes them! Admire above all the forger's skill with which the stamp of virtue, even the ring, the golden-sounding ring of virtue, is here counterfeited. They monopolize virtue, these weak, hopelessly sick people, there is no doubt of it: 'we alone are the good and the just', they say, 'we alone are *homines bonae voluntatis*'. [...] The will of the weak to represent *some* form of superiority, their instinct for devious paths of tyranny over the healthy—where can it not be discovered, this will to power of the weakest! (*GM* III: 14)[17]

There is a human being who has turned out badly, [...] who is fundamentally ashamed of his existence [...]; such a human being who has become poisoned through and through [...] eventually ends up in a state of habitual revenge, will to revenge. What do you suppose he finds necessary, absolutely necessary, to give himself *in his own eyes* the appearance of superiority over more spiritual people and to attain the pleasure of an *accomplished revenge* at least in his own imagination? Always *morality*; you can bet on that. Always big moral words. Always the rub-a-dub of justice, wisdom, holiness, virtue. (*GS* 359; first emphasis mine)

It might be tempting to suppose that the motivation behind this revaluation is to alleviate the feelings of regret or disappointment that accompany the failure to realize certain values and ideals. Such feelings would be alleviated by means of a self-deceptive strategy similar to "sour grapes": the man of *ressentiment* would act as if he does not really care about the values and ideals that elude him (see Scheler 1961; Reginster 1997). However, both of these pas-sages indicate that the motivation of the man of *ressentiment* is instead the alleviation of his "feeling of impotence," which his inability to realize his ideals and values is bound to arouse in him. He disparages these values and ideals, not because he seeks to spare himself regret over the loss or lack of the goods they represent, but because he wants to feel "superior": he seeks to restore his damaged "feeling of power."

This view that *ressentiment* revaluation is motivated by the "will to power of the weak-est" circumvents the problems that afflict the strategic interpretation. If the purpose of revaluation is to restore the "feeling of power" of the weak, then it is not susceptible to the objection that the strong have no reason to buy into the new values contrived by the weak, since on this interpretation, only the weak has to buy into these values.[18] Furthermore, this view is not susceptible to the objection that the instrumental use of the new values is not compatible with a true *invention* of new values, since the instrumental effective-ness of the new values in restoring the weak's feeling of power actually requires him to endorse them.

---

[17] Poellner (2011) relies on passages such as this one to develop a subtle version of the strategic interpretation, which avoids the problems exposed by Wallace. The aim of the revaluation is for the weak to elicit in themselves a feeling of "moral superiority" over the strong, whom they blame for their suffering, and to find in the enjoyment of this feeling of superiority a measure of relief from their suffering. Poellner does not explain, however, why the weak choose *this* particular way of seeking relief from suffering, as opposed to a number of conceivable others. The passage makes the importance of the will to power clear.

[18] This interpretation is compatible with Nietzsche's claim that the man of *ressentiment* might also wish to poison the "conscience" of his oppressors (*GM* III: 14). It simply assumes that this is no more necessary to the success of his enterprise of regaining a feeling of power or superiority than persuading another of a sound philosophical position is required to feel intellectually powerful or superior to him.

THE INVENTION OF "GOOD AND EVIL"

The view that the revaluation of values aims at restoring a feeling of power to the weak can readily be inferred from Nietzsche's account of the invention of "good and evil" and of "free will" in the *Genealogy*'s first essay. These two concepts are closely related, since free will is a condition of application for the concepts of good and evil: an action can be deemed morally "good" or "evil" only if it was done freely. In Nietzsche's view, when the weak devaluate aristocratic values (such as war and superiority) as "evil" and adopt opposite values (such as compassion and equality) as "good," "this, listened to calmly and without previous bias, really amounts to no more than: 'we weak ones are, after all, weak; it would be good if we did nothing *for which we are not strong enough*'" (*GM* I: 13; cf. *GM* III: 18).

He takes the invention of the concept of free will, which he believes to be incoherent (*BGE* 21), to result from the exploitation of a metaphysical prejudice fostered by a certain linguistic structure for psychological purposes. The syntactic form "subject–predicate" encourages the metaphysical prejudice that the agent and the action (the "doer" and the "deed") are distinct. The addition of the concept of free will to this distinction allows the weak to represent any action as the result of a free, deliberate choice by the agent, a move for which Nietzsche offers the following explanation:

> This type of man *needs* to believe in a neutral independent 'subject', prompted by an instinct for self-preservation and self-affirmation in which every lie is sanctified. The subject (or, to use a more popular expression, the *soul*) has perhaps been believed in hitherto more firmly than anything else on earth because it makes it possible to the majority of mortals, the weak and oppressed of every kind, the sublime self-deception that interprets weakness as freedom, and their being thus-and-thus as a *merit*. (*GM* I: 13)

Contrary to what many commentators maintain (e.g., recently Leiter 2002: 215–16 and Janaway 2007: 112–14), the primary purpose of the invention of free will is not to make *the strong* feel as though their political dominance is "evil" and as though they are "free" to refrain from it and therefore "guilty" for not doing so. As the passage clearly indicates, the invention of free will is designed by the weak to change not the attitudes of the strong, but *their own* attitudes. It is the weak *themselves* who "need" to "believe" in freedom, so that their "weakness is being lied into something *meritorious*" (*GM* I: 14). If the weak do not retaliate against the strong, in this moral fantasy, it is *not* because they are impotent and incapable of it, but because they simply *choose* not to, and show themselves able to govern their conduct in accordance with their will. The invention of free will allows them to pass off their weakness as power.

Moreover, the new morality also claims a distinctive normative standing for the things it values: "the things of the highest value must have another, *proper* source [*eigene Ursprung*]—[...] from the lap of Being, the intransitory, the hidden God, the 'thing-in-itself'—there must be their basis, and nowhere else." (*BGE* 2) The authority of the new morality is therefore at once objective and overriding (*GM* Preface 5; see *GM* III: 23; *BGE* 202). This is in contrast to the "noble type of man" who "experiences *itself* as determining values" (*BGE* 260). The "man of *ressentiment*" cannot experience himself as "determining values," as the noble does, presumably because doing so would require him to recognize that his values were contrived to suit his capacities, which means that he could not derive a feeling of power from their realization—much as it becomes impossible to feel proud of an achievement if one believes that one values the achievement only in order to feel proud of it.

IMAGINATION AND REACTION

The interpretation of the slave revolt in morality as aiming to restore a feeling of power to the weak also offers a simple way of understanding two perplexing features of this revolt: it is *imaginary* and it is *reactive*. First, Nietzsche describes the weak's revenge on the strong as "imaginary," which suggests that he merely *represents* the strong masters' aggressiveness as blameworthy or "evil" and his own nonviolent pacifism as meritorious or "good" (see *GM* III: 14). It is thus only *"in effigie"* (*GM* I: 10) or "in his own imagination" (*GS* 359), not in reality, that he achieves some "superiority" over the strong masters, but this act of imagination satisfies his challenged will to power anyway.

Nietzsche might be taken to draw here on the idea that fantasy and make-believe can be sources of great satisfaction, so that the mere imagining of his own superior merit (and of the punishments awaiting his oppressors for their evil ways) suffices to satisfy him (see *GM* I: 15). If the mere fantasy of revenge sufficed to satisfy the desire for it, however, one might wonder why the weak did not simply choose to fantasize themselves of a higher political standing than the "knightly-aristocratic" masters, and spare themselves the complications of a full-blown revaluation of aristocratic values.

The solution to this difficulty is suggested by Nietzsche's description of the revaluation as a "spiritual revenge [*geistigen Rache*]": this revenge is "spiritual" (or "mental") not only insofar as it is a mental act, rather than a physical one, but also insofar it turns revenge itself and its conditions of success into something spiritual or mental. The fantasy that one is of a higher social or political standing than others is quite difficult to sustain because there are highly visible (physical) markers of such superiority. By contrast, fantasizing oneself stronger or superior *in spirit*—for instance, by way of possessing the "moral" strength involved in deliberately refraining from doing something one considers evil—is much easier to sustain since it is not so dependent on *observable* facts. The weak favor this sort of fantasy because it seems immune to the test of reality: *"their 'kingdom'"* is not of this world (*GM* I: 15; see III: 20).

The full significance of Nietzsche's claim that the weak's revenge is "imaginary" may be found in an apt observation Sartre offers in his *Psychology of Imagination*:

> To prefer the imaginary is not only to prefer a richness, a beauty, an imaginary luxury to the existing mediocrity *in spite of* their unreal nature. It is also to adopt 'imaginary' feelings and actions for the sake of their imaginary nature. It is not only this or that image that is chosen, but the imaginary state with everything it implies; it is not only an escape from the content of the real (poverty, frustrated love, failure of one's enterprise, etc.), but from the form of the real itself, its character of *presence*, the sort of response it demands of us, the adaptation of our

actions to the object, the inexhaustibility of perception, their independence, the very way our feelings have of developing themselves. (1950: 165–6)

Part of what motivates the man of *ressentiment*'s escape into imagination is not just frustration with the particular content of his real predicament (for example, the fact that some particular aspiration of his has been repeatedly frustrated), but frustration with what Sartre calls "the form of the real itself," namely the fact that it resists, impinges, frustrates—that it demands "adaptation," or that it remains obstinately "independent" from his control. To the man of *ressentiment*, in other words, the form of the real itself can become an intolerable challenge to his feeling of power, so that to restore it he must *deny* the form of the real by adopting " 'imaginary' feelings and actions *for the sake of their imaginary nature*."[19]

The second perplexing feature of *ressentiment* revaluation is the primacy of negation in it, or what Nietzsche calls its "reactive" nature:

> While every noble morality develops from a triumphant affirmation of itself, slave morality from the outset says No to what is 'outside', what is 'different', what is 'not itself': and *this* No is its creative deed. This inversion of the value-positing eye—this *need* to direct one's view outward instead of back to oneself—is of the essence of *ressentiment*: in order to exist, slave morality always first needs a hostile external world; it needs, physiologically speaking, external stimuli in order to act at all—its action is fundamentally reaction. [...] He has conceived 'the evil enemy', 'the Evil One', and this in fact is his basic concept, from which he then evolves, as an afterthought and pendant, a 'good one'—himself! (*GM* I: 10)

In this passage, Nietzsche appears to make two distinct claims: first, the original act of *ressentiment* revaluation is to deny the value of what one is not, and to affirm the value of what one is only "as an afterthought"; and second, any action motivated by *ressentiment*, including the act of revaluation, is in fact a "reaction." If we suppose, as I have been urging, that the driving motivation of *ressentiment* revaluation is the desire of the weak to feel powerful, both of these puzzling claims become intelligible.

It makes sense that the weak would *begin* with a devaluation of the values he feels unable to realize, since it is the endorsement of these values that elicited a feeling of impotence in the first place, and only *then*, having found out what ends he is actually able to realize, represent *these* as valuable. Understanding the "reactive" character of *ressentiment* revaluation requires closer analysis. The concepts of *active* and *reactive* are among the new psychological categories Nietzsche introduces in his analysis of morality. The *active* type is also the *strong* type, while *reactivity* is a characteristic of *weakness*. The weak type needs "external stimuli" to engage in activity, including evaluative activity, and this is why "its action is fundamentally reaction," whereas the strong type does not.

---

[19] It is worth pointing out another respect in which the revaluation motivated by *ressentiment* has an "imaginary" character. As Nietzsche insists, it does not simply consist of a mere *inversion* of an existing order of value (what was "bad" becomes "good," and vice versa); it also involves a change in the *character* of the values. One difference between the "good/bad" and the "good/evil" kinds of evaluation is that the former denotes "clearly visible signs" of superior or inferior "station" (*GM* I: 5) whereas the latter no longer refers to station or "political superiority," but to something *not observable* by its very nature ("intentions," "superiority of soul") (*GM* I: 6). I must defer an exploration of this point to another occasion.

We should begin our analysis of this distinction by recalling a crucial aspect of Nietzsche's characterization of "strength": it is of its very essence to "express itself as strength" (*GM* I: 13). We gain a better understanding of this peculiar notion if, following Nietzsche, we think of strength in terms not only of *capacity*, but also of *disposition* to act (or *energy* in the sense in which energy is conceived as something that essentially seeks expression in activity, *GM* I: 10). These two characteristics are connected: insofar as he has a will to power, every individual agent begins with a "spontaneous" disposition to activity, but the expression of this disposition is conditioned by his feeling of *capacity*; thus, the feeling of impotence elicited by repeated experiences of defeat or failure would "inhibit" this disposition to activity, and so deprive it of its spontaneity.[20] Having lost spontaneity, the weak would be prompted into action only by external stimulation, so that his action would become "fundamentally reaction." By contrast, not beset by any such feeling of impotence, the strong retain their spontaneous disposition to activity.[21]

GUILT

Christian guilt, which is the object of the second essay, results from the exploitation of the feeling of "indebtedness" by "bad conscience." In contrast to a dominant line of interpretation, I take Nietzsche's genealogy of guilt to provide an account not of how human agents became susceptible to the ordinary feeling of guilt, but of how Christianity perverted this susceptibility by exploiting it as an instrument of self-directed cruelty, so as to offer the weak a way to feel powerful.[22]

Nietzsche's analysis begins with the etymological connection between "guilt" and "indebtedness" ("*Schuld*" refers to both), which he takes to suggest a conceptual one (*GM* II: 6). The feeling of indebtedness does not originally amount to a feeling of guilt because the debtor regards his debt as a merely *prudential* obligation, which does not engage his worth *as a person*.[23] It follows that the feeling of guilt is the feeling of indebtedness when my worth as a person is taken to be at stake in the repayment of the debt. Thus, Nietzsche describes the feeling of guilt as a feeling of "personal obligation [*persönlichen Verpflichtung*]" (*GM* II: 8): the failure to discharge a contractual obligation arouses a feeling of *guilt* only when it takes on a *personal*, as opposed to a merely *prudential*, significance.

An obligation becomes "personal" in this sense when the agent who has undertaken it takes his status as a "responsible" agent or a "sovereign individual" to be at stake in its fulfillment. A "responsible" agent, as Nietzsche employs the term, is an individual who can

---

[20] This loss of spontaneity is part of the phenomenon Nietzsche calls "the *internalization* of man," which is itself a consequence of the feeling of impotence. Under conditions in which his desires are frequently frustrated, the agent can no longer trust that their pursuit will not cause him suffering, and so must trade spontaneity for "the whole somber thing called reflection" (*GM* II: 3; see 16).

[21] On the relations between the feeling of power and spontaneity, see Winnicott 1965: 37–55 and 140–52.

[22] This section summarizes the detailed account I develop in Reginster 2011.

[23] E.g., "the debtor's attitude toward the fact is primarily prudential; he may regard it as inconvenient, but he does not regard himself as a worse person for his indebtedness" (Ridley 1998: 32; see May 1999: 62; Risse 2001: 65; Leiter 2002: 241; Janaway 2007: 132).

be "trusted" to keep his promises because he cares about promise-keeping *as such*, that is, not because he fears the consequences of violation, or takes an interest in the particular content of his promises. He so cares about promise-keeping because it gratifies his will to power by demonstrating his ability to overcome the resistance opposed by conflicting impulses. The feeling of guilt is elicited by the violation of commitments he has undertaken when he considers his standing as a "responsible" agent—a "person"—to be at stake in his honoring them.

His worth as a person is thus, following a long tradition, his worth as a "responsible" or "autonomous" or "free" agent, which Nietzsche reinterprets in his concept of the "sovereign individual." A sovereign individual has the power to conduct his life in accordance with the commitments he has undertaken, which means that he is master of his impulses and feelings. His motivation to keep his commitments is no longer conditioned by the fear of bad consequences—such as losing the benefits of communal life—but, at least in part, by his desire to preserve his "free," "autonomous" agency—"the proud awareness [...] of this rare freedom, this power over himself and over fate" (*GM* II: 2). The central motivation of the sovereign individual—"his dominating instinct"—is therefore the will to *power*, understood as effective agency. For effective agency requires not only the ability to transform the external environment, but also the ability to shape and control the internal environment constituted by his own impulses and feelings. And an individual's worth as a *person*, Nietzsche suggests, lies in his being an *effective agent*, capable of shaping or controlling his impulses.[24]

Nietzsche then turns to "bad conscience," which he describes as the "internalization" of the will to power (the "instinct for freedom") under the pressure of forced socialization (*GM* II: 16): "This *instinct for freedom* forcibly made latent—we have seen it already—this instinct for freedom pushed back and repressed, incarcerated within and finally able to discharge and vent itself only on itself: that, and that alone, is what the *bad conscience* is in its beginnings." (*GM* II: 17) Here, Nietzsche singles out *cruelty* as a paradigmatic manifestation of the will to power, for it consists in overcoming the resistance others necessarily oppose to the prospect of suffering by "*making* [them] suffer" (*GM* II: 6).[25] Unable to vent his cruelty freely on others, the socialized individual turns this cruelty against itself.

The "animals' 'bad conscience'" refers to "self-directed cruelty" (*GM* III: 20), through which the individual satisfies his will to power by overcoming the resistance that the prospect of suffering necessarily arouses in himself. This bad conscience can be the source either of "an abundance of strange new beauty and affirmation" (*GM* II: 18; see 16), or of "the most terrible sickness that has ever raged in man" (*GM* II: 22). In the first case, it manifests the spontaneous "activity" of the artist who takes his own self as material, and it can for example be the source of "sovereignty." The sovereign individual does not turn his will to power inward because it is denied discharge outward. He rather exercises mastery over his impulses and feelings because he understands that his effective agency is as likely to be challenged by them as by external obstacles. As an expedient of *ressentiment* (*GM* II: 11), by contrast, bad conscience can also manifest the will to power of the weak: unable to overcome

---

[24] Gemes (2009) also interprets sovereignty in terms of agency, but downplays the role of the will to power in Nietzsche's account.

[25] Nietzsche observes that "*making* someone suffer" is taking part "in a *right of the masters*" (*GM* II: 5). And bad conscience, where this someone is oneself, consists of the "delight in imposing a form upon oneself as a hard, recalcitrant, suffering matter, and in burning a will [...] into it" (*GM* II: 18; see *BGE* 230; *D* 18). Soll (1994) also emphasizes the essential connection between cruelty and the will to power.

the pressures of socialization, the individual can gratify his will to power only by turning it against itself.[26]

Most commentators suppose that the "moralization" of indebtedness refers to the process whereby it becomes a feeling of guilt by being associated with "bad conscience," understood as self-directed cruelty (*GM* II: 21).[27] However, this cannot be right: the association of indebtedness with bad conscience does not suffice to produce a feeling of guilt. For the feeling of indebtedness can be used as an instrument of self-directed cruelty without altering its prudential character: I could imagine that harboring cruel impulses is a breach of contract (say, with God) and torment myself with thoughts of terrific "punishments" for harboring them. But if such a feeling of indebtedness produces no diminution in my estimation of myself as a person, it is hard to see how it could be marshaled to produce *moral* bad conscience or a feeling of *guilt*.[28] Emphasizing indebtedness *toward God*, as some commentators propose to do (Risse 2001: 65), will not help. If the feeling of indebtedness itself does not decrease my worth as a person, it is hard to see how making it indebtedness toward God could have this effect.

This difficulty invites an alternative line of interpretation, according to which the feeling of indebtedness would involve, *prior* to its "moralization," a belief in the non-prudential "personal" character of the obligations I have undertaken, such that the failure to repay my debts would cause me to experience a decrease in my worth as a person.[29] This interpretation explains how "pushing back" indebtedness into bad conscience could produce a distinctively *moral* bad conscience, namely, self-directed cruelty manifested under the distinctive guise of *guilt* or reproach of myself *as a person*. Self-directed cruelty could not assume this guise by making use of the feeling of indebtedness, unless I already took my worth as a person to be at stake in my indebtedness.

This interpretation faces an obvious challenge: if the feeling of indebtedness is already a feeling of guilt, it becomes unclear what the "moralization" of the concepts of guilt and duty could accomplish. The answer to this challenge is hinted in Nietzsche's insistence on the fact that, as a consequence of their "moralization," the concepts of guilt and duty become the exclusive property of "*bad* conscience" (*GM* II: 21). This indicates that "moralized" guilt and duty can only evoke a *diminished* self-esteem in the agent who experiences them. It is easy to see how the association of bad conscience with the concept of God, particularly in the notion of indebtedness toward God, could accomplish this: the notion of indebtedness toward God is, in effect, the notion of an *inexpiable guilt*, and the contractual obligation that cannot be fulfilled therefore represents a normative standard—a "duty"—designed only to make man "feel the palpable certainty of his own absolute unworthiness" (*GM* II: 22).

[26] The contrast between two forms of "bad conscience," which appears to anticipate the contrast between "philosophical" and "priestly" asceticism in the third essay, is a complex matter, to which my brief remarks hardly do justice. I am only interested in the "moralized" forms of both bad conscience and asceticism. For more on the ambiguity of "bad conscience" and "asceticism," see Ridley (1998: 16–26) and especially May (1999: chapters 4 and 5).

[27] Ridley (1998: 32), Risse (2001: 56), Leiter (2002: 240), Janaway (2007: 134), to mention a few influential examples.

[28] It is worth noting that even Freud's famous 1930 account, with which Nietzsche's second essay is often compared, does not quite succeed. For a recent critique, see Velleman 2006.

[29] May (1999: 74–6) proposes this interpretation, but says little about the notion of "personal accountability" at work here.

Christian guilt is inexpiable because the debt we owe God is of such "transcendence" and "holiness" that "it cannot be discharged" (*GM* II: 21) by such finite animal beings as we are. We would be justified in feeling indebted only if we believed that God has in fact delivered the goods for the possession of which we feel indebted to Him (*GM* II: 19), and the loss of that belief would have to result in a loss of guilt (*GM* II: 20). But this is precisely *not* what happens (*GM* II: 21), and this leads Nietzsche to surmise that what is at work in Christian guilt is not answerability to existing norms of self-assessment, but their corruption out of self-directed cruelty:

> In this psychical cruelty there resides a madness of the will which is absolutely unexampled: the *will* of man to find himself guilty and reprehensible to a degree than can never be atoned for; his *will* to think himself punished, without any possibility of the punishment ever becoming equal to the guilt; his *will* to infect and poison the fundamental ground of things with the problem of punishment and guilt so as to cut off once and for all his own exit from this labyrinth of 'fixed ideas'; his *will* to erect an ideal—that of the 'holy God'—and in the face of it to feel the palpable certainty of his own absolute unworthiness. (*GM* II: 22)

It is not, in other words, because he happens to believe in a "holy God" to whom he owes more than he can repay that the Christian feels guilty. It is rather because of his "*will* to find himself guilty" that he believes in such a God (see *EH*: "Why I am a Destiny" 8). The motivation for this relentless self-reproach is cruelty when, deprived of an "outer" outlet, it is directed "inwardly."

The connection between guilt and freedom of will is all but ignored in the second essay of the *Genealogy*.[30] But it figures prominently in both the first and the third essays. In the first essay, freedom of will—the fact that he could have acted otherwise—was invoked to allow the weak to feel powerful for not doing something he is unable to do anyway, but by way of making him feel "meritorious," rather than "guilty." In the third essay, the same concept serves the same aim, though this time by way of making him feel "guilty." The feeling of guilt is, in this case, a defense against the shame of impotence: it represents the failure to fulfill obligations as the result of free choice, rather than impotence. This explains, in particular, why the "sickly sheep" would be so amenable to the priest's explanation of his suffering: "you alone are to blame for it—*you alone are to blame for yourself!*" (*GM* III: 15; 20) Through the notion of "sin" and the whole metaphysical fantasy associated with it (God the judge, Hell, and so on), the weak regains at least a sense of mastery over his fate, a fresh feeling of power.[31]

The feeling of guilt can thus be used to satisfy the will to power in two ways. In the second essay, in which the connection with bad conscience is emphasized and the connection with free will downplayed, the agent derives a feeling of power from his continual self-reproach. His very ability to endure the pain caused by the acknowledgment of his own sinfulness is a demonstration of his fortitude. In the first and third essays, in which the connection with

---

[30] It is conceivable that Nietzsche thinks of guilt in this context as a sense of indebtedness in which one's worth as a person is at stake. For instance, Scheffler (1992: 68) notes the existence of a moral "sense of indebtedness." And freedom of will does not seem to be a condition of it: I will feel bad for failing to repay a debt I owe regardless of whether or not I was free to do so. Guilt properly so-called presupposes freedom of will, a contrivance that allows the weak to trade impotence for sinfulness.

[31] Piers (1953: 26) offers a crisp description of the "guilt defense against shame": " 'What the other one has seen was not a real deficiency after all, since it was manufactured by myself.' Thus, the real catastrophic shame is prevented. The clown who makes others laugh at himself never feels humiliated—since *he* has *made* them laugh."

free will is highlighted, guilt elicits a feeling of power by transforming weakness into power. The guilty no longer derives satisfaction from having the fortitude to torment himself with the acknowledgment of his own sinfulness, but now represents this sinfulness, not as weakness but as free choice, and therefore as an expression of power since it supposes intact his ability to have done otherwise.

ASCETICISM AND SICKNESS

The third essay raises the question, "What is the meaning of the ascetic ideal?" In the most general terms, the ascetic ideal is the valuation of "voluntary deprivation" or "self-sacrifice," most notably in the form of a denial of the sensual pleasures associated with the gratification of natural "instincts." Nietzsche progressively sharpens the question's focus and concludes that only when "we behold the *ascetic priest* do we seriously come to grips with our problem" (*GM* III: 11). With the priest, the valuation of ascetic denial is based no longer on considerations of prudence (as it was with the "philosopher" who eschews sensual pleasures not because they are "evil" but because they are incompatible with the "spiritual" pleasures he favors, *GM* III: 7–8), but on an absolute condemnation of the life being denied (*GM* III: 11). This priestly asceticism is thus not a matter of renouncing one kind of life in favor of another (*GM* III: 7), but a matter of pitting "life *against* life" (*GM* III: 13):

> For an ascetic life is a self-contradiction: here rules a *ressentiment* without equal, that of an insatiable instinct and power-will that wants to become master not over something in life but over life itself, over its most profound, powerful, and basic conditions; here an attempt is made to employ energy [*Kraft*] to block up the wells of energy; here physiological well-being itself is viewed askance, and especially the outward expression of this well-being, beauty and joy; while pleasure is felt and *sought* in ill-constitutedness, decay, pain, mischance, ugliness, voluntary deprivation, self-mortification, self-flagellation, self-sacrifice. All this is in the highest degree paradoxical: we stand before a discord that *wants* to be discordant, that *enjoys* itself in this suffering and even grows more self-confident and triumphant the more its own presupposition, its physiological capacity for life, *decreases*. (*GM* III: 11)

The ascetic ideal is the expression of a "*ressentiment* without equal" because it is *life* itself, and not just the "knightly-aristocratic" way of life of the first essay, that is devaluated. The physiological debility under consideration in this context not only makes the weak and impotent unable to achieve aristocratic ends, it makes them generally inept at *living*, that is to say, at securing the satisfaction of their most basic natural "instincts." Motivated by this *ressentiment*, these individuals adopt the ascetic devaluation of these basic natural instincts: they now value voluntary deprivation and self-sacrifice. Nietzsche surmises that this ascetic "self-contradiction" must be an appearance, and proposes to explain it in the following terms: '*the ascetic ideal springs from the protective instinct of a degenerating life* which tries by all means to sustain itself and to fight for its existence; it indicates a partial physiological inhibition [*Hemmung*] and exhaustion against which the deepest instincts of life, which have remained intact, continually struggle with new expedients and devices' (*GM* III: 13).

However, this explanation does not so much resolve the contradiction as bring it into sharper focus. In particular, it reveals that the contradiction has two aspects. In the first place, how can the force driving the ascetic "denial" of life count "among the greatest and yes-creating forces of life" (*GM* III: 13)—in other words, how can asceticism be a contradiction of life *by itself*?[32] In the second place, if the force driving asceticism is life-affirming and life-preserving, how can its chief consequence be to have "ruined health" (*GM* III: 23)—in other words, how can asceticism be a *contradiction* of life by itself?

Let us begin with the first aspect of the "self-contradiction" of asceticism. In an unwelcoming environment, the "physiological inhibition or exhaustion" characterizing the "weak" is bound to result in the chronic frustration of their will, including the will to satisfy their basic instinctual needs. Under extreme conditions, this produces a generalized feeling of impotence that threatens them with a sense of "disgust with life" or "weariness," and a "desire for the 'end'" (*GM* III: 13). In these circumstances, the "deepest instincts" of life, most prominently the will to power, resort to "new expedients and devices" to achieve satisfaction. The ascetic ideal is such an expedient: by restoring a feeling of power to the weak, it overcomes their disgust with life and their desire for the "end" (*GM* III: 20).

The ascetic ideal aims to restore the feeling of power to the weak by enacting each of the strategies described in the first two essays. The first and official strategy, so to speak, consists in placing "all suffering under the perspective of *guilt*" (*GM* III: 28). According to one explicit suggestion, this implies that the agent "must understand his suffering as a *punishment*" (*GM* III: 20; II: 7). This interpretation has the merit of restoring a measure of feeling of power, for this suffering now represents something the agent *brought on himself*, insofar as he had the power to act otherwise, rather than something he passively undergoes or is powerless to prevent. Thanks to the ascetic ideal, "the invalid has been transformed into 'the sinner'" (*GM* III: 20). This ascetic interpretation is not only a *representation* of suffering as an expression of the agent's power, it is also an *exercise* of that power: it a piece of self-directed cruelty, insofar as it "brought fresh suffering with it" (*GM* III: 28). I assert power over myself by "making [myself] suffer" with the torments of self-reproach.[33]

However, there can be no guilt without a fundamental *norm*, the violation of which elicits this feeling of guilt. This norm is supplied by the ascetic ideal itself, in the notion that *this* life *ought* to be repudiated. In circumstances of chronic frustration, in other words, the will to power arouses *ressentiment* in the weak, which produces the ascetic devaluation of life, particularly of the sensual pleasures derived from the satisfaction of natural instincts (*GM* III: 11). The second strategy is therefore a *devaluation* of those basic vital instinctual needs the weak prove unable to satisfy.

> The idea at issue here is the *valuation* the ascetic priest places on our life: he juxtaposes it (along with what pertains to it: 'nature', 'world', the whole sphere of becoming and transitoriness) with

---

[32] This is the aspect of the contradiction most often emphasized: see, e.g., Welshon 2004: 28 and Hussain 2011: 164.

[33] In Nietzsche's view, to "interpret" or assign a "meaning" to something is a way of "subduing and becoming master" of it (*GM* II: 12) (Owen 1995: 65; Ridley 1998: 39–40). Precisely what this means is unclear: as I am assuming here, I can "become master" of my suffering by offering an interpretation that represents it as an expression of my power; or the interpretation I give of my suffering is itself an exercise of this power.

> a quite different mode of existence which it opposes and excludes, *unless* it turn against itself, *deny itself:* in that case, the case of the ascetic life, life counts as a bridge to that other mode of existence. The ascetic treats life as a ... mistake that is put right by deeds—that we *ought* to put right. (*GM* III: 11)

Inept at living, the weak deny the value of "this" "natural" life and contrives the fantasy of "another" *better* ("moral") mode of existence, in which they do not have to "work" or "struggle," at least in the particular ways in which they have demonstrated their ineptitude in this life (*GM* III: 11; WP 224). This devaluation allows them to represent their frustration as "voluntary deprivation" or "self-sacrifice": it makes "virtue" out of their weakness (*GM* I: 14).

We now understand how the ascetic life is a contradiction of life *by itself.* But how, then, is the ascetic life also a *contradiction* of life by itself? How, can the ascetic ideal also be responsible for having "ruined health" (*GM* III: 23)? Nietzsche's precise claim is that the ascetic ideal "makes the sick sicker" (GM III: 20; see 15, 17). To understand Nietzsche's claim, we first need to take a look at his conception of the very character of pathology. The concepts of the "normal" and the "pathological" undergo a radical transformation in nineteenth-century medical science, particularly in the works of Auguste Comte and Claude Bernard. Prior to this transformation, the normal and the pathological were considered radically different or heterogeneous phenomena: pathology was the consequence of organs functioning abnormally or not at all, perhaps as a result of being invaded by destructive foreign entities.

The new view, crisply articulated by Bernard, is that the normal and the pathological are in fact identical and homogeneous phenomena:

> Health and sickness are not essentially different, as the ancient physicians and some practitioners even today suppose. One must not make of them distinct principles or entities that fight over the living organism and turn it into their arena. That is silly nonsense and chatter that is no good any longer. In fact, there are only differences in degree between these two kinds of existence: the exaggeration, the disproportion, the disharmony of the normal phenomena constitute the pathological state. (1876: 391)

To illustrate this view, Bernard observes that the hyperglycemia of the diabetic is not the consequence of the abnormal functioning of the kidneys, but only of an essentially quantitative alteration in the organism's relation to its environment (for instance, an unusual quantity of sugar in the blood stream).

This new conception of pathology faces a basic problem, however: what are the normative standards that determine when otherwise normal functioning becomes pathological. If the pathological is a purely quantitative variation or variation in "degree" of the normal, it seems difficult to avoid arbitrariness in the determination of when so much is actually *too much.* In his influential treatment of this issue, Canguilhem discusses a suggestion offered in relation to the question of what is pathological in gastric ulcer:

> [C]oncerning the very case of ulcer, we must say that what is essential to the sickness does not consist of the hyperchlorhydria, but of the fact that the stomach is digesting itself [...]. A function could be said to be normal so long as it is independent of its effects. The stomach is normal so long as it digests without digesting itself. (1966: 45)

In other words, the otherwise normal functioning of an organ is pathological when it takes place in circumstances in which such functioning contradicts or undermines itself. The stomach's function is to digest food by secreting gastric acid; the quantity of such secretion becomes pathological when it undermines this function by causing the stomach to "digest itself."

Nietzsche was sufficiently impressed by his reading of Bernard's *Lectures on Animal Heat*, for example, that he quotes verbatim its most essential lessons—the passage quoted above—in his notes (*WP* 47). And he takes these lessons to heart in his own understanding of sickness. Thus, in describing it as "an artifice for the *preservation* of life" (*GM* III: 13), he indicates that asceticism does not make the sick sicker by disrupting normal functioning in otherwise normal circumstances, but on the contrary, by perpetuating *normal* functioning—most prominently, in this case, the "instinctive" striving "for an optimum of favorable conditions under which it can expend all its strength and achieve its maximal feeling of power" (*GM* III: 7)—in circumstances in which such functioning becomes pathological, because "*self-contradicting.*"

Under conditions in which their weakness has made them unable to overcome the resistance a hostile and oppressive environment opposes to the satisfaction of their natural instincts, asceticism induces those debilitated by "physiological inhibition or exhaustion" to gratify their will to power by turning it against themselves, in the form of "voluntary deprivation, self-mortification, self-flagellation, self-sacrifice." As a consequence of this operation, they are bound to experience a "decrease" in their "physiological capacity for life," which is the very "presupposition" not only of the *pursuit* and *achievement* of power, but also of its "enjoyment." They attempt to satisfy their will to power essentially by destroying the very "energy" that makes such satisfaction possible in the first place (*GM* III: 11). [34]

This idea underwrites Nietzsche's "most fundamental objection" to priestly asceticism: it "combats only the suffering itself, the discomfiture of the sufferer, *not* its cause, *not* the real sickness" (*GM* III: 17; see 20). The "discomfiture of the sufferer" or his "depression" is the "disgust with life" brought about by his experience of impotence or ineffectiveness. The "cause" of the suffering, the "real sickness" is a depletion of the "physiological capacity for life," that is, the physiological fragility that undermines his effective agency. The ascetic ideal enables him to avoid disgust with life by restoring his feeling of power, but in a way that necessarily further depletes his "physiological capacity for life" and so in effect "makes the sick sicker."

Nietzsche famously opens and closes the third essay of the *Genealogy* with the claim that "man would rather will *nothingness* than *not* will" (*GM* III: 28; see 1). The condition of "not willing" designates *nihilism*. At first glance, nihilism is meaninglessness: the lack of something *to* will. This lack of something to will, of worthwhile goals to pursue, is troubling because of "the basic fact of the human will, its *horror vacui: it needs a goal*" (*GM* III: 1). The point seems to be that since any willing is necessarily the expression of *values*; the absence of values reduces the agent to a condition of "not willing." But the "*horror vacui*" of the human will cannot suffice to explain why it would "will *nothingness*." Nihilism—"*not* willing"—can also be the consequence of *impotence*. The inability to satisfy one's will can also breed "depression" or "disgust with life," in other words, "suicidal nihilism."[35] They

---

[34] In a related but different way, Owen (2007) and Katsafanas (2011) also argue that Nietzsche's objection to the ascetic ideal is that it conflates the *perception* of power with *actual* power in a way detrimental to agency.

[35] The distinction I draw here between two forms of nihilism corresponds to the distinction between *disorientation* and *despair* I drew in Reginster 2006: chapter 1.

reduce the individual to a condition of "*not* willing," not because there is nothing *to* will, but because willing appears pointless insofar as it is *ineffective.* By adopting the ascetic ideal, the individual can avoid the condition of "*not* willing," not just because he now has something *to* will, but also because it restores effectiveness to his agency: it makes him feel powerful again.

The ascetic ideal restores the possibility of willing, by breeding the "will to *nothingness.*" But this restoration of willing, by which nihilism is avoided, comes at an exorbitant price: it constitutes in effect "a rebellion against the most fundamental presuppositions of life" (*GM* III: 28), a rebellion that simply cannot be sustained without a dramatic and "life-destructive" decrease in energy and vitality. It is the last resort of the *ressentiment* of "the weak and impo-tent": rather deny one's natural instincts—"the most fundamental presuppositions of life"—than admit one's impotence to satisfy them.[36] Insofar as it is motivated by *ressentiment,* the "will to *nothingness*" underwritten by the ascetic ideal is a *sickness* precisely because it is a "self-contradictory" form of the will to power.[37]

BIBLIOGRAPHY

(A) Works by Nietzsche

Reference edition of Nietzsche's works: *Friedrich Nietzsche: Sämtliche Werke, Kritische Studienausgabe,* ed. G. Colli and M. Montinari. Berlin: De Gruyter, 1967–77.

A   *The Anti-Christ,* trans. R. J. Hollingdale. Harmondsworth: Penguin, 1968.
BGE   *Beyond Good and Evil,* trans. W. Kaufmann. New York: Random House, 1966.
D   *Daybreak,* trans. R. J. Hollingdale. Cambridge: Cambridge University Press, 1982.
EH   *Ecce Homo,* trans. W. Kaufmann. New York: Random House, 1969.
GM   *On the Genealogy of Morality,* trans. C. Diethe. Cambridge: Cambridge University Press.
GS   *The Gay Science,* trans. W. Kaufmann. New York: Random House, 1974.
HAH   *Human, All Too Human,* trans. R. J. Hollingdale. Cambridge: Cambridge University Press, 1986.
TI   *Twilight of the Idols,* trans. R. J. Hollingdale. Harmondsworth: Penguin, 1968.
WP   *The Will to Power,* trans. W. Kaufmann and R. J. Hollingdale. New York: Random House, 1968.
Z   *Thus Spoke Zarathustra,* trans. W. Kaufmann. Harmondsworth: Penguin Books, 1978.

[36] Rosenfeld (1971) shows how the narcissistic hankering for power can lead the individual to repudiate even those basic vital needs and wishes the pursuit of which would expose his impotence or inadequacy, and so it can become a "death instinct." In the *Genealogy,* Nietzsche argues that the "*kernel*" of the ascetic ideal is the will to truth, an association in which he sees the operation of "a concealed will to death" (*GS* 344).

[37] I owe a debt of gratitude to Ken Gemes and John Richardson, who both offered detailed comments on an earlier draft of this paper, as well as to the participants to the Workshop on Nietzsche, Genealogy, and Revaluation at the University of Southampton in December 2009, and to a Department Colloquium at Haverford College in March 2012.

(B) Other Primary Works

WWR   Schopenhauer, Arthur. 1969. *The World as Will and Representation*, trans. E. E. F. J. Payne (2 vols). New York: Dover.

(C) Other Works Cited

Bernard, Claude. 1876. *Leçons sur la chaleur animale*. Paris: J.-B. Baillière & Fils.

Bittner, Rüdiger. 1994. "Ressentiment," in R. Schacht (ed.), *Nietzsche, Genealogy, Morality*. Berkeley: University of California Press, 127–38.

Canguilhem, George. 1966. *Le normal et le pathologique*. Paris: Presses Universitaires de France.

Clark, Maudemarie.1990. *Nietzsche on Truth and Philosophy* Cambridge: Cambridge University Press.

Freud, Sigmund. 1914. "On Narcissism: An Introduction," in J. Strachey (ed. and trans.), *The Standard Edition of the Complete Psychological Works of Sigmund Freud*, vol. 14. London: Hogarth Press, 67–102.

Freud, Sigmund. 1930. *Civilization and its Discontents*, in J. Strachey (ed. and trans.), *The Standard Edition of the Complete Psychological Works of Sigmund Freud*, vol. 21. London: Hogarth Press, 59–148.

Gemes, Ken. 2009. "Nietzsche on Free Will, Autonomy, and the Sovereign Individual," in K. Gemes and S. May (eds), *Nietzsche on Freedom and Autonomy*. Oxford: Oxford University Press, 33–50.

Hatab, Lawrence. 2011. "Why Would Master Morality Surrender its Power?" in S. May (ed.), *Nietzsche's "On the Genealogy of Morality": A Critical Guide* Cambridge: Cambridge University Press, 193–213.

Hussain, Nadeem. 2011. "The Role of Life in the *Genealogy*," S. May (ed.), *Nietzsche's "On the Genealogy of Morality": A Critical Guide* Cambridge: Cambridge University Press, 142–69.

Janaway, Christopher. 2007. *Beyond Selflessness. Reading Nietzsche's "Genealogy."* Oxford: Oxford University Press.

Kail, Peter. 2011. "'Genealogy' and the *Genealogy*," in S. May (ed.), *Nietzsche's "On the Genealogy of Morality": A Critical Guide* Cambridge: Cambridge University Press, 214–33.

Katsafanas, Paul. 2011. "The Relevance of History for Moral Philosophy: A Study of Nietzsche's *Genealogy*," in S. May (ed.), *Nietzsche's "On the Genealogy of Morality": A Critical Guide* Cambridge: Cambridge University Press, 170–92.

Kohut, Heinz. 1972. "Thoughts on Narcissism and Narcissistic Rage," *The Psychoanalytic Study of the Child* 27: 360–400.

Knobe, Joshua and Leiter, Brian. 2007. "The Case for Nietzschean Moral Psychology," in B. Leiter and N. Sinhababu (eds), *Nietzsche and Morality* Oxford: Oxford University Press, 83–109.

Kohut, Heinz. 1972. "Thoughts on Narcissism and Narcissistic Rage," *The Psychoanalytic Study of the Child* 27: 360–400.

Leiter, Brian. 2001. "Moral Facts and Best Explanations," *Social Philosophy and Policy* 18: 79–101.

Leiter, Brian. 2002. *Nietzsche on Morality*. London: Routledge.

Owen, David. 1995. *Nietzsche, Politics, and Modernity* London: Sage.

Owen, David. 2007. *Nietzsche's "Genealogy of Morality."* Stockfield: Acumen.

May, Simon. 1999. *Nietzsche's Ethics and his "War on Morality."* Oxford: Clarendon Press.

Migotti, Mark. 2006. "Slave Morality, Socrates, and the Bushmen: A Critical Introduction to *On the Genealogy of Morality, Essay I*," in C. D. Acampora (ed.), *Nietzsche's "On the Genealogy of Morals."* Oxford: Rowan & Littlefield Publishers, 109–29.

Piers, Gerhart and Singer, Milton. 1953. *Shame and Guilt: A Psychoanalytic and Cultural Study* Springfield, Ill.: Charles Thomas Publisher.

Pippin, Robert. 2006. *Nietzsche, moraliste français: La conception nietzschéenne d'une psychologie philosophique* Paris: Odile Jacob.

Pippin, Robert. 2009. "How to Overcome Oneself: Nietzsche on Freedom," in K. Gemes and S. May (eds), *Nietzsche on Freedom and Autonomy* Oxford: Oxford University Press, 69–88.

Poellner, Peter. 2007. "Affect, Value, and Objectivity," in B. Leiter and N. Sinhababu (eds), *Nietzsche and Morality* Oxford: Oxford University Press, 227–61.

Poellner, Peter. 2011. "*Ressentiment* and Morality," in S. May (ed.), *Nietzsche's "On the Genealogy of Morality": A Critical Guide* Cambridge: Cambridge University Press, 120–41.

Reginster, Bernard. 1997. "Nietzsche on *Ressentiment* and Valuation," *Philosophy and Phenomenological Research* 57: 291–305.

Reginster, Bernard. 2003. "What is a Free Spirit? Nietzsche on Fanaticism," *Archiv für Geschichte der Philosophie* 85: 51–85.

Reginster, Bernard. 2006. *The Affirmation of Life: Nietzsche on Overcoming Nihilism* Cambridge, Mass.: Harvard University Press.

Reginster, Bernard. 2010. "The Genealogy of Guilt," in S. May (ed.), *Cambridge Critical Guide to Nietzsche's "On the Genealogy of Morality."* Cambridge: Cambridge University Press, 56–77.

Richardson, John. 1996. *Nietzsche's System* Oxford: Oxford University Press.

Ridley, Aaron. 1998. *Nietzsche's Conscience: Six Character Studies from the Genealogy.* Ithaca: Cornell University Press.

Risse, Mathias. 2001. "The Second Treatise in *On the Genealogy of Morality*: Nietzsche on the Origin of Bad Conscience," *European Journal of Philosophy* 9: 55–81.

Rosenfeld, Herbert. 1971. "A Clinical Approach to the Psychoanalytic Theory of the Life and Death Instinct: An Investigation Into the Aggressive Aspects of Narcissism," *International Journal of Psychoanalysis* 52: 169–78.

Sartre, Jean-Paul. 1950. *L'Imagination.* Paris: PUF.

Scheffler, Samuel. 1992. *Human Morality.* Oxford: Oxford University Press.

Scheler, Max. 1961. *Ressentiment*, trans. W. W. Holdheim. New York: Schocken Books.

Soll, Ivan. 1994. "Nietzsche on Cruelty, Asceticism, and the Failure of Hedonism," in R. Schacht (ed.), *Nietzsche, Genealogy, Morality*. Berkeley: University of California Press, 168–92.

Taylor, Gabriele. 1985. *Pride, Shame, and Guilt: Emotions of Self-Assessment.* Oxford: Clarendon Press.

Velleman, David. 2006. "A Rational Superego," in *Self to Self: Selected Essays* Cambridge: Cambridge University Press, 129–55.

Wallace, R. Jay. 2007. "Ressentiment, Value, and Self-Understanding: Making Sense of Nietzsche's Slave Revolt," in B. Leiter and N. Sinhababu (eds), *Nietzsche and Morality* Oxford: Oxford University Press, 110–37.

Welshon, Rex. 2004. *The Philosophy of Nietzsche.* Chesham: Acumen Publishing.

Williams, Bernard. 1994. "Nietzsche's Minimalist Moral Psychology," in R. Schacht (ed.), *Nietzsche, Genealogy, Morality*. Berkeley: University of California Press, 237–47.

Winnicott, Donald. W. 1965. *The Maturational Processes and the Facilitating Environment.* New York: International Universities Press.

CHAPTER 31

NIETZSCHE'S PHILOSOPHICAL PSYCHOLOGY

PAUL KATSAFANAS

FREUD claimed that the concept of *drive* is "at once the most important and the most obscure element of psychological research" ("Beyond the Pleasure Principle," 1957: vol. 18, p. 34). It is hard to think of a better proof of Freud's claim than the work of Nietzsche, which provides ample support for the idea that the drive concept is both tremendously important and terribly obscure.

Nietzsche tells us that psychology is "the path to the fundamental problems" (*BGE* 23). Included among these "fundamental problems" are the nature of agency, freedom, selfhood, morality, and evaluation. The psychological concept that is the key to these notions, Nietzsche's principal explanatory token within psychology, is the *drive* (*Trieb, Instinkt*).[1] For example, Nietzsche tells us that the self is a relation of drives (*BGE* 6, 9, 12), and he claims that willing should be understood in terms of the operations of drives (*BGE* 19). If we are to understand these central elements of Nietzsche's thought, we will need an account of his concept of drive.

However, it is far from clear what exactly a drive is. Talk of drives conjures up images of very basic motivational states, such as urges or cravings; it can also bring to mind physiological states. Thus, *The Oxford English Dictionary* tells us that a drive is "any internal mechanism which sets an organism moving or sustains its activity in a certain direction, or causes it to pursue a certain satisfaction...*esp.* one of the recognized physiological tensions or conditions of need, such as hunger and thirst." Hunger and thirst are indeed what spring to mind when we think of drives. Many commentators assume that Nietzsche has the same

---

[1] Nietzsche seems to regard *Instinkt* and *Trieb* as terminological variants; he will sometimes alternate between the two in the same sentence (see, for example, *GS* 1). Here, I will simply use the term *drive* to translate both *Instinkt* and *Trieb*. (I use *drive* instead of *instinct* because, we will soon see, the English term "instinct" has misleading connotations.) Daniel Conway claims that Nietzsche distinguishes *Instinkt* and *Trieb* beginning in his works of 1888. According to Conway, beginning in *Twilight*, *Instinkt* refers to a *Trieb* that has been "organized" or "trained to discharge" in a specific way (1997: 30–4). I find Conway's textual evidence for this alleged distinction unpersuasive; however, we need not resolve the issue here, for this distinction would not affect the points that I make in the text.

understanding of drives, and consequently treat drives either as simple urges and cravings or as purely physiological states.

But these interpretations cannot be correct. Nietzsche does not identify drives with physiological states or simple causal forces. On the contrary, he explicitly *contrasts* his drive psychology with certain "materialistic" explanations of human behavior (*BGE* 12).[2] Moreover, he tells us that drives "adopt perspectives," "interpret the world," and "evaluate."[3] Clearly, physiological states and urges do not do *that*.

The language of valuing, interpreting, and adopting perspectives is ordinarily used only with regard to *agents*. So Nietzsche sometimes seems to be treating drives as agents-within-agents, homunculi with ends of their own. Some commentators have taken this at face value, interpreting drives as homunculi. For example, Peter Poellner writes that "Nietzsche ultimately treats drives not as attributes of agents (like desires) but as agents themselves" (1995: 174). Yet this proposed interpretation encounters its own set of problems. It is difficult to see how there could be any theoretical advantage in explaining agency and selfhood by appealing to entities that already possess the properties of full-fledged agents and selves. Moreover, it would be rather incongruous for Nietzsche, who so vociferously argues against the superfluous positing of subjects, to multiply the number of subjects beyond measure by splintering each human being into a host of homunculi.

Another puzzle arises when we ask how drives *operate*. How does a drive move a self-conscious organism to act? Nietzsche claims that drives operate beneath the level of consciousness. He argues that we are typically ignorant of both what drives we harbor and how these drives move us (*D* 119). This raises the question of how the influence of drives relates to the workings of reflective thought. Consider an example to which Nietzsche often returns: he claims that Wagner's development can be understood in terms of one drive's becoming dominant (*CW* Epilogue). Of course, Wagner himself understood his own actions quite differently. After all, Wagner was engaged in some highly reflective activities: he was composing music, self-consciously attempting to inaugurate a new form of culture, and so on. Presumably, Nietzsche is not suggesting that these self-conscious thoughts bear *no* relation to Wagner's actions. So there is a puzzle concerning the way in which we reconcile claims about the activities of drives with claims about the agent's reflective thoughts and choices.

Accordingly, Nietzsche's drive psychology seems to involve an uneasy and possibly incoherent assembly of claims. Drives appear to be at times physiological states and at other times homunculi; moreover, the drive psychology seems to discount the agent's self-conscious thoughts and choices in ways that are difficult to understand. Yet it would be decidedly odd if Nietzsche's principal psychological concept bore such obvious inconsistencies. These are not arcane or deeply hidden inconsistencies of the sort that a philosopher might overlook; the tensions are palpable. Could a "psychologist without equal," a philosopher who regards psychology as the "path to the fundamental problems," really be this deeply confused about his foundational psychological concept?[4]

---

[2] In particular, Nietzsche contrasts his drive psychology with the accounts of "clumsy naturalists who can hardly touch on 'the soul' without immediately losing it" (*BGE* 12).

[3] For some examples, see *KSA* 12: 1 [58]; *WP* 481, 260, 567.

[4] "That a psychologist without equal speaks from my writings, is perhaps the first insight reached by a good reader" (*EH*: "Why I Write Such Good Books" 5).

In this essay, I will argue that Nietzsche in fact has a coherent and philosophically fruitful account of drives. In order to explicate this account, I will focus on three central questions: first, what is a drive? Second, what type of awareness do we have when we are being moved by a drive? Third, what is the relationship between being moved by a drive and reflectively choosing to perform an action?

Section 1 surveys existing attempts to answer the first and second questions. I argue that these attempts encounter textual and philosophical difficulties, so we need a new account. Section 2 lays some groundwork for this new account, by examining the history of the drive concept. With this historical backdrop in place, Section 3 offers a new account of the nature of drives and the type of awareness that is present in drive-motivated actions. Section 4 then examines the relationship between reflectively choosing to perform an action and being caused by one's drives to perform an action.

1 INTERPRETATIONS OF NIETZSCHEAN DRIVES

1.1 First Interpretive Strategy: Drives as Homunculi

We can start with a simple question: what is a drive? To answer this question, let's consider the types of properties that Nietzsche attributes to drives. Nietzsche frequently claims that drives reason, evaluate, interpret, and adopt perspectives. To cite just two examples:

> Anyone who considers the basic drives of man to see to what extent they may have been at play... will find that all of them have done philosophy at some time—and that every single one of them would like only too well to represent just *itself* as the ultimate purpose of existence and the legitimate *master* of all the other drives. For every drive wants to be master—and it attempts to philosophize in *that spirit*. (BGE 6)

> It is our needs that interpret the world; our drives and their For and Against. Every drive is a kind of lust to rule; each one has its perspective that it would like to compel all the other drives to accept as a norm. (WP 481)

In the above passages, Nietzsche characterizes drives in agential terms. Philosophizing, representing oneself in a certain way, interpreting, and adopting perspectives are typically understood as activities that are performed by full-fledged agents, not by parts of an agent.

Poellner draws attention to this aspect of Nietzsche's view, writing: "It is sometimes not sufficiently appreciated in the literature that, when it comes to specifying the actual mode of operation or agency of these drives, which he in fact seems to conceive as the ultimate agents, Nietzsche invariably uses intentional-mechanistic terms" (1995: 215). Among these terms are "desiring, interpreting, willing, commanding, and obeying" (1995: 216). Poellner notes that "these terms, in their ordinary meanings, imply the presence of consciousness. Can one be said, for example, to be 'interpreting' a text... unless one is aware of there being a text to be interpreted?" (1995: 215).

This raises an interpretive question: just how literally does Nietzsche intend this language? Does he mean to suggest that drives are agents?

Poellner takes the agential language quite literally, interpreting drives as homunculi, or agents-within-agents. Clark and Dudrick endorse a similar interpretation. They point out that Nietzsche speaks of drives "commanding and obeying" other drives, and argue that drives therefore "exhibit agency of a sort" (2009: 265). As they put it, Nietzschean drives are "homunculi" or "proto-persons" (2009: 264).[5] Similarly, Thiele attributes a robust form of agency to drives, including even the idea that drives have "political relations" with one another (1990: 57). He claims that each drive "has its will to dominate and exploit its competitors…the ruling drive(s) provides its own agenda and worldview…The individual…is a battleground of competing drives, each with its own perspective" (1990: 57–8).

These homuncular readings of drives do have an obvious advantage: they fit quite well with Nietzsche's use of agential language in describing drives. Additionally, Nietzsche sometimes does seem to suggest that drives are agents, as in WP 270, where he writes that "the assumption of one single subject is perhaps unnecessary; perhaps it is just as permissible to assume a multiplicity of subjects, whose interaction and struggle is the basis of our thought and consciousness in general."

That said, there are compelling philosophical and textual reasons for rejecting the homuncular reading of drives. First, some proponents of the homuncular view fail to appreciate just how radical their thesis is. Some of these readings attribute to drives properties that imply the presence of *self-consciousness*. For example, Thiele speaks of drives having agendas, perspectives, worldviews, and political relations with other drives, but taken literally this implies that drives are aware of one another, communicate with one another, and reason with one another. Thus, Thiele's interpretation would require that each drive have perceptual capacities, communicative capacities, and reasoning capacities. This seems scarcely conceivable.[6]

A second problem arises when we ask how the homuncular view of drives could have any explanatory power. It is difficult to see how there could be any theoretical advantage in explaining agency and selfhood by appealing to entities that already possess the properties of full-fledged agents and selves. For example, take Nietzsche's efforts to explain conscious agency in terms of drives. If drives are themselves conscious agents, what exactly is being explained here? We want an explanation of conscious agency, and we are told to understand a person's conscious agency as a manifestation of the conscious agency of various drives. This is hardly informative. Rather than explaining agency and selfhood, it simply shifts the problematic terms about, from the level of persons to the level of drives.[7]

---

[5] While Clark and Dudrick provide some intriguing remarks about drives in this article, their primary focus is elsewhere: they attempt an analysis of the notion of the will. For this reason, it is not entirely clear whether the remarks on drives constitute their considered view.

[6] Though Poellner interprets drives as agents, he is quite sensitive to this problem. He notes that certain passages in Nietzsche's work suggest that drives should *not* be understood "as themselves conscious of their activity—of their desiring, interpreting, willing, commanding, and obeying" (1995: 216). Accordingly, he seeks an explanation of how drives could be non-conscious agents. Failing to find a satisfactory explanation, he concludes, with admirable candor, that Nietzsche's remarks on unconscious drives are ultimately indefensible (1995: 215–29). Clark and Dudrick also address this problem; see the next note.

[7] Arguably, there could be some advantage in explaining agency in terms of simpler, less complex sub-agents. Thus, if we could understand drives as less complex agents, perhaps the drive psychology would have some explanatory power. Clark and Dudrick (2009) give an interesting argument in favor of this point. They claim that if we interpret drives as simple sub-agents, capable of commanding and obeying one another, then we can make sense of more complex agential phenomena such as valuing and resisting temptation. While this proposal is intriguing, I think there are grounds for objection. First, it

This brings us to a more fundamental problem with attributing the homuncular view to Nietzsche: it is hard to reconcile this interpretation with Nietzsche's other commitments. Nietzsche makes it quite clear that he wants to rethink our notion of the self:

> And as for the *Ego*! That has become a fable, a fiction, a play on words: it has altogether ceased to think, feel, or will! (*TI*: 'The Four Great Errors' 3)

> To babble about "unity," "soul," "person," this we have forbidden: with such hypotheses one only complicates the problem. (*KSA* 11: 37 [4])

These passages question our ordinary understanding of the self. As noted above, Nietzsche argues that once we recognize that the self harbors multiple drives, we must reconceptualize the conscious self. But if drives are homunculi, then Nietzsche's rethinking of the self is a rather modest affair: Nietzsche would simply be claiming that there are many *more* selves than we thought. In other words, the homuncular interpretation assumes that we already have a coherent concept of selfhood, and are simply mistaken as to which entities instantiate this concept: we thought that whole persons instantiated selfhood, but we find that parts of persons—drives—instantiate selfhood.

This interpretation seems dubious. Nietzsche seems to be claiming, not simply that we have applied the concept of selfhood to the wrong entity (person rather than drive), but that we do not even possess a coherent concept of selfhood. In other words, Nietzsche is not simply claiming that there are *more* selves than we think there are; instead, he is claiming that we have a mistaken conception of selfhood. He wants to transform our notion of selfhood, not simply to apply the notion in a more profligate fashion.

1.2 Second Interpretive Strategy: Drives as Dispositions

The homuncular interpretations take the agential language that Nietzsche employs when describing drives quite literally. At the other extreme, there are interpretations that ignore or downplay this language, assimilating drives to mere urges. For example, Janaway claims that a drive is simply "a relatively stable tendency to activate behavior of some kind" (2007: 214). Indeed, he suggests that drives may be identical to affects, which "are glossed as inclinations and aversions or fors and againsts" (2007: 214). Thus, "we may wonder whether drives and affects are even properly distinguishable kinds" (2007: 213). With Janaway, we have traveled very far from the idea that drives are self-conscious agents; drives are now described as nothing more than inclinations or tendencies.

This minimalist reading of drives is quite common in the Nietzsche literature. For example, Cox suggests that all of the following terms are roughly analogous: drives, desires, instincts, forces, impulses, and passions (1999: 126–7). Schacht claims that the term "drive" or "instinct" applies "to all firmly established dispositions of any significant degree of specificity, however acquired" (1983: 279–80). Hales and Welshon treat drives as "functional states and dispositions" (2000: 159). Leiter seems to identify drives with urges (2007: 99). These interpretations,

---

is not clear that commanding and obeying are simpler activities than valuing and resisting temptation. Moreover, commanding and obeying require, at the very least, the presence of consciousness. So the type of agency attributed to drives is still quite robust. Thus, while Clark and Dudrick's proposal is certainly an improvement upon the other homuncular views, it still faces certain problems.

which I will call dispositional views, agree in their description of drives as members of familiar psychological categories: drives are simply urges, dispositions, or tendencies.

An advantage of the dispositional interpretation is that it renders drives philosophically unproblematic, thereby avoiding the difficulties that plague the homuncular view. However, the dispositional interpretation faces significant problems of its own. First and most obviously, many of these views offer no real explanation of the agential language that Nietzsche uses when he appeals to drives. For example, if Schacht is correct in claiming that a drive is simply a firmly established disposition, what can it mean to say that drives evaluate and interpret? Suppose I have a firmly established disposition to scratch my head when I am thinking; on Schacht's view, this should count as a drive. But in what sense could this disposition to scratch be said to evaluate or interpret? Or suppose I am firmly disposed to forget my keys every morning. Can this disposition to forget my keys be regarded as adopting a perspective? The questions seem almost nonsensical: the answer seems to be an obvious no. If the dispositional view is to succeed, it will need to explain how drives are appropriate candidates for agential language.

The philosopher who has done the most to address this issue is John Richardson. Richardson emphasizes that Nietzsche employs agential language in describing drives, but Richardson seeks an interpretation of this language that does not require drives themselves to be conscious agents: "when [Nietzsche] says that a drive 'aims' at certain ends, 'views' the world in a consequent way, and 'experiences' certain values within it, none of this is supposed to entail that the drive is conscious" (1996: 38).[8] Rather, "a Nietzschean drive is a disposition that was selected for a certain result; this result is its individuating goal, which explains its presence and its character" (2004: 39). Drives are simply a certain sort of disposition. Accordingly, Richardson endeavors to make sense of the way in which a disposition can be an appropriate candidate for agential language. Focusing on Nietzsche's claim that drives *evaluate*, Richardson argues that we can identify values with the ends at which drives aim: "a drive's values are precisely the goals it drives towards" (2004: 13).

I think Richardson's approach is illuminating: we should ask whether Nietzsche's agential language can be applied to dispositions. However, the connection that Richardson draws between being disposed, as a result of selection, toward some end E and valuing E does not seem fully convincing. There are cases in which values and selected dispositions appear to diverge. For example, a typical ascetic who regards sexual activity as disvaluable will nonetheless be strongly disposed, as a result of natural selection, to engage in sexual activity.[9] Despite the fact that the agent is strongly disposed toward sexual activity, we would typically say that the agent does not value sexual activity. There are also cases of the opposite sort, in which the agent regards an end E as valuable, but is not disposed toward E. For example, the aforementioned ascetic would view celibacy as valuable, but would be strongly disposed, as a result of selection, not to be celibate.

As these examples indicate, being disposed as a result of selection toward an end E and valuing E can come apart. So the identification of values with selected dispositions seems

---

[8] Richardson addresses the same question in a later work, asking whether Nietzsche has "a viable notion of drives... At issue, in particular, will be how Nietzsche can attribute the *end-directed* character he clearly does to these drives and wills, without illicitly anthropomorphizing an implausible mentality into them." (2004: 13)

[9] I say a "typical" ascetic because natural selection may not have disposed *every* agent toward sexual activity.

problematic.[10] Perhaps, though, we can tie valuing to having a *specific kind* of disposition. In an earlier work, Richardson makes a suggestive comment:

> Value lies in the way the world is 'polarized' for each will and not in any theories or beliefs about value. It lies in how things 'matter' to the will and so depends on that deep receptiveness of will that Nietzsche calls 'affect' [*Affekt*] or 'feeling' [*Gefühl*]. (Richardson 1996: 37)

Here, Richardson suggests that valuing an end E isn't simply being disposed to E; in addition, valuing E involves having certain affects or feelings. Although Richardson doesn't pursue the suggestion at length, I think it is the key to unraveling Nietzsche's remarks about drives. In sections 2 and 3, I will explore this point in detail, arguing that Nietzschean drives are dispositions that induce affective orientations in the agent. Moreover, I will argue that these affective orientations can be understood as *evaluative* orientations.

1.3 Drives and Self-awareness in Action

Before continuing our analysis of the nature of drives, we will need to gain clarity on another aspect of the drive psychology: the way in which drives cause agents to act. Seeing how drives *operate* will help us to understand what drives *are*. Accordingly, in this section I will examine Nietzsche's characterization of the type of awareness that is present in drive-motivated actions.

When Nietzsche discusses drives, he often emphasizes that agents are ignorant of the way in which drives move them.

> However far a man may go in self-knowledge, nothing however can be more incomplete than his image of the totality of drives which constitute his being. He can scarcely name even the cruder ones: their number and strength, their ebb and flood, their play and counterplay among one another, and above all the laws of their nutriment remain wholly unknown to him. (*D* 119)

---

[10] Richardson does anticipate this form of objection, and responds as follows:

> We should bear in mind that this valuing need not—and principally does not—occur in a conscious act… We suppose that "our values" are those we put into *language* and *consciousness*… But according to Nietzsche… the really effective or influential values are not those conscious ones… Values are built into our bodies, and their conscious and linguistic expression is something quite secondary. (2004: 73–4)

Part of Richardson's point, here, is that Nietzsche might reject my characterization of the ascetic, above. In particular, Nietzsche might deny that the ascetic's conscious thoughts about the disvalue of sex and the value of celibacy actually count as *values*. Nietzsche might, instead, take the fact that the ascetic is disposed toward sex to indicate that he values it. I agree with Richardson that this is one way of interpreting the texts: we could read Nietzsche as departing from our ordinary conception of value, and introducing this novel conception of value, according to which values are identified with selected dispositions. However, I think there is some reason to resist this interpretation. Arguably, it is an essential feature of our concept of value that values can conflict with motivations in general and dispositions in particular. In the following sections, I will argue that there is another way of interpreting Nietzsche's remarks about drives' valuing, which preserves a distinction between being disposed to E and valuing E.

For this reason, Nietzsche claims that "actions are *never* what they appear to be ... all actions are essentially unknown" (*D* 116). But puzzles arise when we ask what Nietzsche means by these claims about self-ignorance in action.

Commentators often interpret Nietzsche as arguing that our actions can proceed independently of conscious monitoring and deliberation. For example, Schacht interprets Nietzsche in this way, illustrating his point with an example of a pianist. Schacht points out that a *novice* pianist may need to consciously attend to his activity, focusing on the positions of the keys, keeping in mind the notes that he wants to play, consciously monitoring his performance, and so on. An *expert* pianist, by contrast, is able "to dispense with the mediation of conscious deliberation and reckoning at each step of the way" (1983: 281). The expert can simply play, without needing to deliberate or consciously attend to his movements. This example of skilled action draws attention to the fact that once we acquire a disposition to perform some activity A-ing, we can A without deliberating on or attending to our A-ing. According to Schacht, Nietzsche is claiming that *all* of our drive-motivated actions have an analogous form, proceeding independently of conscious monitoring.

Now, it certainly is true that many actions occur without conscious monitoring. However, this cannot be the full point of Nietzsche's claim that agents are ignorant of drive-motivated actions. After all, the piano player is not ignorant of his action in any strong sense: he can attend to his movements at any moment, without difficulty. Even when he is not explicitly attending to his movements, he certainly *knows* that he is playing the piano. In fact, his playing is exactly analogous to everyday actions such as walking: when I walk to my office, I rarely attend to or reflect on the movements of my legs; indeed, I often walk about in a kind of daze, thoughts occupied with other matters. Nevertheless, I know that I am walking, and my walking is an intentional action.[11] If this humdrum type of inattentiveness were all that Nietzsche had in mind when he claims that "all actions are essentially unknown" (*D* 116), then he would be grossly exaggerating a familiar, uncontroversial feature of action.

Moreover, Nietzsche claims that even paradigmatically self-conscious actions are in some sense unknown to us. We should distinguish two claims:

(1) An agent can perform an action A without self-consciously attending to her A-ing.
(2) An agent who *does* self-consciously attend to her A-ing can in some sense remain ignorant of her A-ing.

Schacht's analysis illustrates (1), yet Nietzsche more often focuses upon (2). For example, Nietzsche writes, "everything about [an action] that can be seen, known, 'conscious,' still belongs to its surface and skin—which, like every skin, betrays something but conceals even more" (*BGE* 32). Here, Nietzsche is not claiming that we can act without monitoring our act; he is claiming that even if we do monitor our act, we will in some sense be ignorant of it. Schacht's point about the dispensability of conscious monitoring seems unable to account for this aspect of Nietzsche's view.

---

[11] Many contemporary philosophers accept Anscombe's thesis that if an agent intentionally As, then the agent knows that she is A-ing (Anscombe 2000). But this should not be mistaken for the claim that if an agent intentionally A-s, then the agent's A-ing is an object of explicit attention. Just as I can know straightforward factual matters, such as my birth date, without explicitly attending to them at all times, so too I can know that I am walking to my office without attending to the movements of my legs.

Consider, then, an alternative interpretation of Nietzsche's remarks on self-ignorance in action: perhaps Nietzsche is arguing that we cannot know our true *motives* for action. As Leiter puts it, "we do not have epistemic access to what the causally effective motives really are" (2002: 104). This interpretation fits the texts somewhat better: passages such as *BGE* 32 and *D* 116, quoted above, certainly suggest that we are mistaken about our true motives.

However, I think this interpretation also falls short of capturing the full truth. While Nietzsche does claim that we are often mistaken about our causally effective motives, this can hardly be the centerpiece of his analysis of reflective agency. The claim that we lack epistemic access to our causally effective motives is widely accepted; indeed, one could argue that even in Nietzsche's day it was a commonplace. After all, even Kant, whose model of agency Nietzsche wanted to attack, emphasized that we can *never* be certain which motives we are acting upon (*Groundwork* 4: 407; see Kant 1998).[12]

So we are left with a problem. While Schacht is certainly correct to claim that conscious monitoring is not a necessary condition for action, and while Leiter is undeniably right in claiming that we are often ignorant of our motives for action, neither of these points is controversial. If these are the only points that Nietzsche makes about conscious awareness in action, then his account is in no way revolutionary.

1.4 Summary

The prior sections have addressed two central questions about drives: what is a drive, and what type of awareness do we have when acting under the influence of a drive?

The first question led to some problems: the homuncular view of drives seems philosophically and textually problematic, whereas the dispositional view of drives has difficulty accounting for Nietzsche's use of agential language in describing drives. The second question was also puzzling: Nietzsche emphasizes that we are ignorant of our own actions, but it is difficult to find an interpretation of this claim that renders it philosophically significant. If Nietzsche is simply claiming that action does not require attention, no one will disagree; if he is merely pointing out that we are often mistaken about our motives, then he is belaboring a truism.

2 A HIGHLY ABBREVIATED HISTORY OF

THE DRIVE CONCEPT

We can gain clarity on the questions of what drives are and how drives engender self-ignorance by situating Nietzsche's account in its historical context. Nietzsche's drive psychology did not develop in a vacuum; the concept of instinct or drive was much discussed in the eighteenth and nineteenth centuries. In a debate spanning several generations, a diverse group of scientists, philosophers, and theologians attempted to explain what instincts

---

[12] In addition, the idea that we lack epistemic access to our causally effective motives (at least in ordinary circumstances) is a frequently voiced theme in Augustine, La Rochefoucauld, Montaigne, Spinoza, and Schopenhauer, to name but a few.

are, how they arise, and how they move organisms.[13] Here I will examine just one aspect of this debate: the question of how the unreflective nature of drives should be understood. Answering this question will enable us to illuminate Nietzsche's view of drives.

During the eighteenth and nineteenth centuries, the concept of instinct was typically contrasted with the concept of *learned behavior*. There are marvelous examples of the distinction between learned and instinctive behavior in the animal kingdom, many of which fascinated the thinkers of this time. Reimarus, in his *Allgemeine Betrachtungen über die Triebe der Thiere* (1760), draws our attention to the caterpillar, which weaves its elaborate cocoon without having witnessed anything similar. Henry Lord Brougham discusses a species of solitary wasp that gathers grubs and stores them beside its eggs, then departs before the eggs hatch. The grubs serve as food for the larvae that will hatch from the eggs, but the wasp cannot possibly know this. For "this wasp never saw an egg produce a worm [i.e., a larva]—nor ever saw a worm—nay, is to be dead long before the worm can be in existence—and moreover she never has in any way tasted or used these grubs, or used the hole she made, except for the prospective benefit of the unknown worm she will never see" (Brougham, *Dissertations on Subjects of Science concerned with Natural Theology* (1839): I: 17–18; quoted in Richards 1987: 136). These highly complex behaviors are directed at an end of which the animal simply cannot be cognizant.

These complex, unlearned behaviors are attributed to instincts. Thus, in an early treatise on the notion of instinct, we read of Frédéric Cuvier's distinction between instinct and intelligence:

> The wolf and the fox who recognize the traps in which they have been caught, and who avoid them, the dog and the horse, who understand the meaning of several of our words and who obey us, thereby show *intelligence*. The dog who hides the remains of his dinner, the bee who constructs his cell, the bird who builds his nest, act only from *instinct*. (Flourens, *Analytical Summary of the Observations of Frédéric Cuvier* (1839); quoted in Proudhon 1994)

Charles Darwin concurs:

> An action, which we ourselves require experience to enable us to perform, when performed by an animal, more especially by a very young one, without experience, and when performed by many individuals in the same way, without their knowing for what purpose it is performed, is usually said to be instinctive. (Darwin 1993: 317–18)

So the writers of this time period operate with the following dichotomy: some animal behaviors are learned, and therefore require the animal to have awareness of the goal at which the behavior is directed; other behaviors, the instinctive ones, are not learned, and the animal

---

[13] Some principal figures in the debate were Le Roy, Reimarus, Condillac, Erasmus Darwin, Cabanis, Cuvier, Flourens, Lamarck, and Charles Darwin. On the more philosophical side, instinct was discussed by Schiller, Hegel, and Schopenhauer. Turning to literature, the most obvious influences on Nietzsche are Hölderlin and Emerson, both of whom frequently employed the notion of instinct. For useful discussions of the history of the instinct concept, see Richards 1987, Thorpe 1956, and Wilm 1925. Boring 1929 and Lowry 1971 provide more general discussions of the history of psychology. In regard to Nietzsche, Moore 2002, Parkes 1996 and Assoun 2000 are particularly helpful.

performing these behaviors lacks awareness of the goal it is pursuing.[14] Thus, the central characteristic of instinctual behavior is that it is in some sense *unknown* or *unreflective*.

Although thinkers of this time agree that instinctual behavior is unreflective, they disagree about what this means. Some thinkers advance a very strong thesis about the lack of awareness in instinct. Consider movements that, though they look purposive, are mere mechanism. A clock is set up so that it ticks away the hours; a car's engine is set up so that it produces movement when stimulated by a depressed pedal. Of course, the clock and car do not in any sense know what they are doing. We might think that organisms are exactly analogous: instincts operate in a purely mechanical fashion, with stimulus S causing behavior B.

Schopenhauer believed that some instincts operate in this way. At several points throughout his work, he compares the animal acting instinctively with the sleepwalker: he writes that instinctive actions have "a remarkable similarity to those of somnambulists" and claims that "insects are to a certain extent natural somnambulists" (*WWR* II: 344). And of course the Cartesians, as well as some German Materialists of the nineteenth century, claimed that non-human animals were mere mechanisms: Descartes writes that "the actions of beasts are similar only to those which we perform without the help of our minds" (Letter to More (1649); quoted in Huxley, "On the hypothesis that animals are automata, and its history" (1874)) and his followers notoriously compared the screams of an animal to the ringing of a bell.[15]

These thinkers suggest that the animal acting instinctively is completely unaware of its action. So we have a very strong claim about the unreflective character of instinctive actions:

(1) If an organism instinctively *A*-s, then the organism is not aware[16] that it is *A*-ing.

Claim (1) seems accurate with respect to certain organisms. For example, it is hard to imagine that an amoeba oozing toward its prey is doing anything more than acting mechanically, in response to determinate stimuli; it is not as if there can be mediation by thought here. But some writers argue that (1) mischaracterizes the nature of instinctive actions in more complex animals. For example, imagine a wolf that is instinctively hunting a moose. It is difficult to imagine the wolf pursuing the moose, tracking scents, coordinating with other members of the pack, and so on, all the while being ignorant of its actions. It is more plausible to assume that the wolf has some rudimentary awareness of its actions, which enables it intelligently to adjust the means to the fulfillment of its instincts.

How might this work? To employ a somewhat anachronistic source, consider William James, who writes:

> We may conclude that, to the animal which obeys it, every impulse and every step of every instinct shines with its own sufficient light... What voluptuous thrill may not shake a fly, when she at last discovers the one particular leaf, or carrion, or bit of dung, that out of all the world can stimulate

---

[14] The claim that learned behaviors require awareness of the action's goal is perhaps most plausible when we are considering isolated animals that engage in highly original behaviors. Otherwise, we can imagine one animal simply copying or imitating the behavior of another, in much the way that an infant might imitate the gestures of its parents without understanding their purpose. See also note 17.

[15] See, for example, Fontaine's account of the Port Royal experimenters: "they said the animals were clocks; that the cries they emitted when struck were only the noise of a little spring that had been touched, but that the whole body was without feeling" (*Mémoires pour servir à l'historie de Port-Royal*, 1738, quoted in Rosenfield 1968: 54).

[16] In place of "is not aware," we might substitute "does not know," "does not believe," "is not cognizant of the fact," and so on. I intend (1) to be neutral among these formulations.

her ovipositor to its discharge? Does not the discharge seem to her the only fitting thing? And need she care or know anything about the future maggot and its food? (James 1890: vol. II, pp. 387–8)

Or, to choose an example from a book that was in Nietzsche's personal library: Schneider, in *Der Thierische Wille* (1880), writes, "it might easily appear" that the cuckoo "acted with full consciousness of the purpose" when it laid its eggs in another bird's nest. But no: "the cuckoo is simply excited by the perception of quite determinate sorts of nest, which already contain eggs, to drop her own into them, and throw the others out, because this perception is a direct stimulus to these acts. It is impossible that she should have any notion of the other bird coming and sitting on her egg" (quoted in James 1890: vol. II, p. 389). These quotations suggest that instincts operate by presenting the animal with a compelling motive to act in a certain way: the fly experiences a voluptuous thrill in the presence of a bit of dung; the cuckoo is excited by the perception of a certain kind of nest.

In short, an instinct might operate purely mechanically, by producing a series of behaviors; or it might operate at one remove, by producing internal states, such as emotions, desires, and urges, which then strongly dispose the organism to pursue some end. The animal acting on these internal states may be aware of its progress toward the nest, its pursuit of its prey, and so forth. But it remains ignorant of something else: the purpose of the action, or the ultimate *end* at which its action is directed. For example, the cuckoo knows that it is laying eggs in a nest, but does not know that it is doing so in order that another bird might care for its young. Or, the female wasp knows that it is collecting grubs, but does not know that it is doing so in order to provide food for its future offspring. So we have a second characterization of the unreflective character of instinct:

(2) If an organism instinctively A-s in order to G, then the organism may know that it is A-ing, but does not know that it is A-ing *in order to G*.

To put (2) in a more colloquial form: the organism may know *what* it is doing, but it doesn't know *why* it is doing what it is doing.[17, 18]

So we have two different views on the unreflective character of instinct. Instinctive actions might be unreflective in the sense that they involve no awareness whatsoever (1),

[17] Brian Leiter and Ken Gemes (personal communication) point out that some philosophers may find these characterizations of animal awareness problematic. Why is the cuckoo's excitement at the perception of a nest a *motive*, rather than a mere *cause*? Why say that the cuckoo has thoughts involving *nests*—and indeed, can it even have the concept of a nest? While these questions are important, for present purposes we can set them aside. I am here discussing the way in which certain eighteenth- and nineteenth-century thinkers characterized animal thought and motivation. Some thinkers—those embracing claim (1)—would deny that the cuckoo has motives, is aware of nests, and so forth. Other thinkers—those embracing claim (2)—wish to describe these animal actions in terms of more advanced mental processes. My task at this stage of the essay is not to *assess* these competing claims, but simply to *distinguish* them.
[18] To clarify what proponents of (2) have in mind, it is worth noting that there are relatively straightforward ways of testing whether an animal knows that it is A-ing in order to G: we can break the connection between A-ing and G-ing, and see whether the animal continues to A. The rat that learns to press a lever a certain number of times in order to acquire a food pellet will cease to do so, if the lever-pressing fails to yield food consistently. The wasp which collects grubs and stores them beside its eggs will *not* cease to do so if, for example, its eggs are clearly destroyed. So the rat seems to know that it is pressing the lever in order to obtain food, whereas the wasp seems not to know that it is collecting grubs in order to feed its offspring.

or in the sense that they involve no awareness of the ultimate goal of the action (2). We will have to determine which of these views Nietzsche adopts.

2.2 An Interpretive Clue: Schopenhauer on Drives

Before turning to Nietzsche, let's briefly examine one of the greatest influences on Nietzsche's work: Schopenhauer. Schopenhauer discusses drives at some length and endorses a view of type (2). In a wonderful chapter entitled "The Metaphysics of Sexual Love," Schopenhauer examines the workings of the reproductive drive. He claims that the reproductive drive leads human beings to pursue sexual partners, not by blindly impelling them to this end, but by fostering a *distorted orientation* toward the world. The reproductive drive "creates illusions [*Illusionen schafft*]" (*WWR* II: 566) or a "delusion [*Wahn*]" (*WWR* II: 541):

> Here then, as in the case of all instinct, truth assumes the form of delusion, in order to act on the will. [*Also nimmt hier, wie bei allem Instinkt, die Wahrheit die Gestalt des Wahnes an, um auf den Willen zu wirken.*] It is a voluptuous delusion which leads a man to believe that he will find greater pleasure in the arms of a woman whose beauty appeals to him than in those of any other, or which, exclusively directed to a *particular* individual, firmly convinces him that her possession will afford him boundless happiness... The character of instinct is here so completely present, namely an action as though in accordance with the conception of an end and yet entirely without such a conception, that whoever is urged by that delusion often abhors it and would like to prevent the end, procreation, which alone guides it... (*WWR* II: 540)

Schopenhauer here reasons as follows. The human reproductive drive aims at reproduction. But when we are in the grip of this drive, we do not believe that we are pursuing reproduction. We believe we are pursuing happiness, or pleasure, or possession of a particular individual. Schopenhauer claims that this belief—or, as he puts it, this *delusion*—is produced by the drive itself. In other words, the reproductive drive manifests itself by leading a person to conceive of his potential sexual partners as supremely alluring, capable of providing him with great happiness and pleasure. The reproductive drive moves us not by generating a blind urge or disposition to copulate, but by producing desires and other emotions, by influencing the way in which the person perceives potential partners, and so on.

Thus, "in all sexual love, instinct holds the reins, and creates illusions [*bei aller Geschlechtsliebe der Instinkt die Zügel führt und Illusionen schafft*]" (*WWR* II: 566). But the phenomenon is not restricted to the sexual: Schopenhauer believes that all instincts work in this fashion. Accordingly, he claims that animals acting on instinct "are urged not so much by an objective, correct apprehension, as by subjective representations which stimulate the desire... and that accordingly they are urged by a certain *delusion*...." (*WWR* II: 541).

Schopenhauer holds that drives typically move a person not by blindly impelling him to act, but by structuring his affects, thoughts, and perceptual orientation toward the world.[19]

---

[19] To be precise, Schopenhauer does seem to allow that in some cases, drives move a person by blindly impelling him to act. Schopenhauer's claim that certain instinctive actions bear "a remarkable similarity to those of somnambulists" (*WWR* II: 344) seems to make this point. However, when Schopenhauer offers extended discussions of the operations of drives, he typically treats them as operating *through*, rather than *independently of*, the agent's reflective thoughts.

Crucially, it follows that the agent's actions—though they may be highly reflective and deliberate, though they may occupy the agent's attention, though the agent may think of nothing else—are in one sense *unreflective*: the person being moved by the drive is not aware of his ultimate purpose in acting. Thus, the person being moved by his reproductive drive knows that he is pursuing a particular partner; he knows that he is planning a date; he devotes all of his attention to his actions. Yet the deeper purpose of these actions eludes him. While he thinks that he wants his love because she will provide him with immeasurable happiness, Schopenhauer claims that the deeper purpose is less grandiose: reproduction.[20]

In sum, we can see that Schopenhauer endorses a view of type (2). The claim that a person is being moved by a drive does not entail that the person cannot be acting reflectively, attending to his action, and so forth. Rather, it implies that the agent's conscious reflection and thought is in the service of a goal of which the agent is ignorant. The drive manifests itself by generating an affective orientation, which then inclines the agent to pursue the drive's end. So a drive is a disposition that induces an affective orientation.

3 The Nature of Nietzschean Drives

3.1 Drives are Dispositions that Induce Evaluative Orientations

Schopenhauer treats drives as dispositions that induce affective orientations. In this section, I argue that Nietzsche has an exactly analogous understanding of drives. Ultimately, I am going to argue that this account of drives enables us to make sense of Nietzsche's claim that drives evaluate and interpret. For the affective orientation induced by a drive can be understood as an *evaluative* orientation.

To make sense of these ideas, let's start with the most obvious way in which having an end or harboring an affect can influence an agent's view of the world: it can make certain features *salient*. This is easiest to see with the manifestations of simple feelings, such as hunger. When one is hungry, the presence of food is salient: I notice each restaurant, my attention is drawn to each piece of food eaten by passers-by. When I am not hungry, the presence of food recedes: it is often mere background, barely noticed.

---

[20] There are, however, two potential problems with this claim. First, it is not clear what criteria Schopenhauer employs in order to determine that reproduction is the true purpose of the action, rather than, say, romantic love. To be sure, reproduction is what the action was *selected* for; but it is not obvious why the selected purpose of the instinctual activity should be identified with the true purpose. Second, it is worth noting that the agent is not straightforwardly *wrong* about his actions: it may well be true that his love will provide him with immense happiness. His descriptions of his own actions need not be false, but they are *incomplete*. This raises a question: what if the agent simply doesn't care that his knowledge is incomplete? After all, knowledge is always incomplete; why should knowledge of one's own actions be any different? In short, why should Schopenhauer's remarks trouble us? For the moment, I want to bypass this question; what concerns us here is not the particular purpose that Schopenhauer singles out, but rather the *structure* of the action that Schopenhauer discusses. That is, what concerns us is not the claim that an agent is actually pursuing reproduction, but the more general claim that an agent takes himself to be pursuing A, whereas "pursuing B" is a more apt description.

With more complex affects and drives, the influences are of course more complex. Hatred is an instructive case. Hating affects perceptual saliences: if you hate someone, you tend to experience everything about him as despicable, focusing on all of his flaws and ignoring all of his virtues. In other words, hatred typically manifests itself by inducing a certain orientation toward the object of hatred: it leads one to find certain features (the despicable ones) salient and others (the redeeming ones) peripheral.

In each of these cases, the affect influences the perceptual saliences, causing certain features to stand out and others to recede into the background.[21] This is why Nietzsche is concerned with the role of the emotions and other attitudes in deliberation. In deliberation, the presentation of the facts—the selection of some features as salient and others as peripheral—is, at least in part, a function of the attitudes. This is particularly clear in the case of extreme emotions, but Nietzsche believes that it happens in subtler ways with every attitude. Here he follows Schopenhauer, who claims that "every inclination or disinclination twists, colors, and distorts not merely the judgment but even the original perception of things" (*WWR* II: 373).[22]

So the first point is that perceptions are selective, and the particular ways in which they are selective is, in part, a function of our drives and affects. But the effects of drives are not limited to selectivity. Nietzsche believes that there is a sense in which drives influence the *content* of experience itself.

Daybreak 119 offers an extended discussion of this phenomenon. Nietzsche starts with a discussion of dreams:

> Why was the dream of yesterday full of tenderness and tears, that of the day before yesterday humorous and exuberant, an earlier dream adventurous and involved in a continuous gloomy searching? Why do I in this dream enjoy indescribable joys of music, why do I in another soar and fly with the joy of an eagle up to distant mountain peaks? These inventions, which give scope and discharge to our drives to tenderness or humorousness or adventurousness or to our desire for music and mountains ... are interpretations of nervous stimuli we receive while asleep, *very free*, very arbitrary interpretations of the motions of the blood and intestines, of the pressure of the arm and the bedclothes, of the sounds made by church bells, weatherclocks, night-revelers and other things of the kind. That this text, which is in general much the same on one night as on another, is commented upon in such varying ways, that the inventive reasoning faculty *imagines* today a *cause* for the nervous stimuli so very different from the cause it imagined yesterday, though the stimuli are the same: the explanation of this is that today's prompter of the reasoning faculty was different from yesterday's—a different *drive* wanted to gratify itself, to be active, to exercise itself, to refresh itself, to discharge itself ... (*D* 119)

Nietzsche is interested in the fact that the sensory stimuli present from night to night remain relatively constant, while the dreams vary enormously. He attributes the variation in dreams to the activities of different drives: the same sensory stimuli give rise to quite different dreams, depending upon which drives are most active.

The full point of the discussion of dreams is revealed a few lines later:

> Waking life does not have this *freedom* of interpretation possessed by the life of dreams, it is less inventive and unbridled—but do I have to add that when we are awake our drives likewise

[21] For a related discussion, see Clark 1998: §3.
[22] Schopenhauer also discusses this idea throughout chapter XIX of *WWR* II. For contemporary discussions of related ideas, see for example Stampe 1987 and Brewer 2002.

do nothing but interpret nervous stimuli and, according to their requirements, posit their 'causes'? that there is no *essential* difference between waking and dreaming? (*D* 119)

Nietzsche claims that just as drives influence the content of dreams, so too drives influence the content of waking experience. The same sensory stimuli can give rise to quite different perceptual experiences, depending upon which drives are active. This is clearest in the case of dreams; but Nietzsche believes that the same phenomenon occurs, in a more restricted way, in waking life. He provides the following example: "Take some trifling experience. Suppose we were in the market place one day and we noticed someone laughing at us as we went by." He claims that different agents will experience this stimulus in different ways, depending upon which drives are active. Thus, one person will scarcely notice the laughter, another will be angered by it, another will worry over it, another will be led to reflect on the nature of laughter itself, another will be happy. The selfsame stimulus is experienced in quite different ways.

Of course, Nietzsche is not claiming that drives manifest themselves in *exactly* the same way in dreams and in waking life. In dreaming, there is only the slightest connection between sensory stimuli and experience: the sounds of distant clocks might lead to dreams of beautiful music; the murmurs of night-revelers might lead to thoughts of soaring through the air; the entanglement in blankets might lead to dreams of continuous searching. The effects of drives on waking experience are not this dramatic: while the stimulus of laughter can be experienced in a variety of ways—angrily, happily, contemplatively, and so forth—there is clearly less room for creative interpretation than in the case of dreams. So, when Nietzsche says, "there is no *essential* difference between waking and dreaming," he does not mean that facts about the world play as little role in determining waking experiences as they do in determining dreams. Rather, he means that in waking, as in dreaming, our experiences are determined not by facts about the world alone, but also by facts about which drives are active. Thus, Nietzsche will speak of affects and drives as "coloring," "gilding," "lighting," and "staining" the world; these terms suggest that affects and drives highlight or even alter aspects of an experience, but not that they *create* the experience in the way that they create dreams (see for example *GS* 7, 139, 152, 301; *BGE* 186). Thus, Nietzsche is seeking to undermine the intuitively plausible thought that our perceptual experiences of the world are determined by nothing other than the nature of the world itself.[23]

In order to make Nietzsche's idea more precise, it will be helpful to work with a more detailed example. A famous passage from Iris Murdoch provides an excellent illustration:

> A mother, whom I shall call M, feels hostility to her daughter-in-law, whom I shall call D. M finds D quite a good-hearted girl, but while not exactly common yet certainly unpolished and lacking in dignity and refinement. D is inclined to be pert and familiar, insufficiently ceremonious, brusque, sometimes positively rude, always tiresomely juvenile ...
>
> Thus much for M's first thoughts about D. Time passes, and it could be that M settles down with a hardened sense of grievance and a fixed picture of D, imprisoned (if I may use a question-begging word) by the cliché: my poor son has married a silly vulgar girl. However, the M of the example is an intelligent and well-intentioned person, capable of self-criticism, capable of giving careful and just *attention* to an object which confronts her. M tells herself: 'I am old-fashioned and conventional. I may be prejudiced and narrow-minded. I may be snobbish.

---

[23] Nietzsche must have regarded this point as extremely important, for he discusses it in nearly identical fashion in several of his major works. For example, *Twilight* contains a virtually identical passage, in which nothing but the example has changed (*TI*: "The Four Great Errors" 4).

I am certainly jealous. Let me look again.' Here, I assume that M observes D or at least reflects deliberately about D, until gradually her vision of D alters. If we take D to be now absent or dead this can make it clear that the change is not in D's behavior but in M's mind. D is discovered not to be vulgar but refreshingly simple, not undignified but spontaneous, not noisy but gay, not tiresomely juvenile but delightfully youthful, and so on. (Murdoch 1985: 17–18)

There are several important features of this example. First, notice that the *situation itself* remains constant: D's behavior does not change at all. Nevertheless, M's *view of the situation* changes dramatically. M initially sees D's behavior as brusque, rude, juvenile, and pert; later, she sees the same behavior as spontaneous, simple, delightfully youthful, and gay. M achieves this latter view by engaging in critical self-assessment, examining the effects of her motives on her perceptions and judgments.

This passage reveals the way in which affects can influence the content of experience: the selfsame situation can be viewed in exceedingly different ways. M's jealousy not only makes certain features of the situation salient, but also influences the very content of M's experience. For example, M's jealousy not only causes D's hand gestures to be salient; in addition, it leads M to perceive these gestures as juvenile, whereas later they will be perceived as delightfully youthful. In short, the attitude leads the agent to conceptualize the situation in a certain way. (Here it is important to notice that M is not first experiencing a neutral movement of the hand and then interpreting it as brusque; rather, she immediately sees the hand movement as brusque. In this way, drives and affects influence the content of experience itself.)[24]

I have quoted this passage at length because it provides a detailed, realistic illustration of the phenomenon in which Nietzsche is interested: the way in which motivational states influence the content of experience. Drives manifest themselves by coloring our view of the world, by generating perceptual saliences, by influencing our emotions and other attitudes, by fostering desires. Thus, Nietzsche's idea is that the way in which one experiences the world is, in general, determined by one's drives in a way that one typically does not grasp.[25]

3.2 This Account of Drives Avoids Problematic Theoretical Commitments and Explains Nietzsche's Use of Evaluative Language

This account of drives and affects enables us to make sense of Nietzsche's claim that drives "interpret the world," generate "evaluations," and "adopt perspectives." Section 1.1 pointed out

[24] For a discussion of Nietzsche's remarks on conceptualized experiences, see Katsafanas 2005.

[25] The role that Murdoch gives to self-scrutiny and self-criticism is roughly analogous to the role that Nietzsche gives to self-understanding and genealogy: in both cases, the agent discovers the impact of hidden or unnoticed motives, and thereby puts herself in a position to counteract them. Murdoch's account is, however, somewhat simpler and more straightforward than Nietzsche's. For example, notice that Murdoch simply assumes that M's latter view is in some way *better* than the earlier one—that the latter view is *correct* in a way that the former view is not. As Nietzsche would point out, there is no reason to take this as obvious. The earlier view was motivated by jealousy; the latter view might be motivated by a desire to please her son. The mere fact that a view changes in such a way that it presents its object in a more appealing light does not imply that the new view is more adequate; the reverse could be the case. While Nietzsche does think that there are better and worse views, he recognizes that the question of whether a given view is better or worse than others is always difficult, and cannot always be determined.

that these claims have led to some extravagant interpretations of Nietzsche's drive psychology, tempting some commentators to treat Nietzschean drives as homunculi. Evaluation and interpretation are normally understood as highly reflective acts performed by self-conscious beings. I interpret a book or a poem by reflecting on its meaning; I evaluate an action or a trait of character by reflecting on a moral principle. Unless each drive is a self-conscious center of agency, it is difficult to see how drives could do *that*.

However, we can now see that the homuncular view looks appealing only when we have a restricted view of the available options. Poellner and Thiele seem to assume that there are only two options: either drives, considered as isolated entities, have agential properties or they do not. If these were the only two possibilities, the homuncular view would indeed be preferable. After all, Nietzsche certainly does employ agential language with respect to drives, and it stretches the imagination to claim that these are nothing more than colorful metaphors. So the former possibility seems better, despite its air of paradox.

Yet there is another option: we can deny that drives, *considered in isolation*, can reason, evaluate, and interpret, while maintaining that *embodied drives*—drives considered as part of a whole organism—can reason, evaluate, and interpret. Suppose we accept Nietzsche's claim that our views of the world are selective, emphasizing certain features at the expense of others, presenting objects as oriented toward ends of ours, presenting situations in affectively charged ways. This selective, affectively charged orientation can be understood as an *evaluative* orientation. For example, if Murdoch's M has an immediate view of D as vulgar, brusque, and rude, this view can be understood as constituting a negative evaluation of D.[26, 27]

Nietzsche often directs our attention to this point, emphasizing the way in which values are manifested in sensory experiences:

> The extent of moral evaluations: they play a part in almost every sense impression. Our world is *colored* by them. (*WP* 260)

> There is no doubt that all sense perceptions are wholly permeated with value-judgments...(*WP* 505)

The visual language in this passage is revealing: Nietzsche's point is that we experience the world in evaluative terms. The world does not present itself as an indifferent array of inert facts. The world tempts and repulses, threatens and charms; certain features impress themselves upon us, others recede into the periphery, unnoticed. Our experience of the world is fundamentally value-laden.[28, 29]

[26] Thus, embodied drives can reason/evaluate/interpret in the sense that they can induce in agents affective dispositions that constitute reasonings/evaluations/interpretations.

[27] Notice that even non-self-conscious animals could be said to reason, evaluate, and interpret, in the above sense. That is, if Nietzsche's talk of reasoning, evaluating, and interpreting is intended to express the fact that many animals have affective orientations, then it makes perfectly good sense.

[28] I have discussed this point in Katsafanas 2012.

[29] It is important to note that an organism need not and typically will not be aware of the evaluative outlook manifested in its orientation toward its environment. A self-conscious animal, such as a human being, *can* become aware of the partiality and selectivity in its orientation, as Murdoch's example demonstrates. But this takes work. Typically, agents will be largely ignorant of their own evaluative outlooks.

Thus, the link between drives and values is this: drives generate affectively charged, selective responses to the world, which incline the agent to experience situations in evaluative terms. We can summarize this point by saying that drives are dispositions that generate evaluative orientations. Accordingly, Nietzsche writes, "from each of our basic drives there is a different perspectival assessment [*perspektivische Abschätzung*] of all events and experiences" (*KSA* 12: 1 [58]); in plainer language, each drive generates an evaluative orientation. Thus, we can make sense of Nietzsche's evaluative language without treating drives as homunculi.[30]

This interpretation also enables us to see what Nietzsche means when he claims that drives induce a form of self-ignorance. Drives influence an agent's behavior by structuring the agent's view of his environment. This structuring has dramatic effects on behavior: consider the difference in the way that M will act prior to and after the change in her view. Or consider Schopenhauer's remarks on sexual love. The lover believes that he desires his love because she is beautiful, because she will please him like no other, because she will complete his very being. Schopenhauer explains why the lover sees her this way, why he has these thoughts, why he so ardently desires his love, by appealing to a reproductive urge which colors the lover's mental economy. The lover, if Schopenhauer is right, is acting for reasons that he does not grasp. Thus, drives engender self-ignorance in the sense that agents are typically unaware of the way in which their drives direct their thoughts, affects, and perceptions.

3.3 Drives as Psychic Forces

The above interpretation enables us to make sense of both Nietzsche's evaluative language and his claim that drives induce a form of self-ignorance. However, another aspect of Nietzsche's view remains to be explicated. Nietzsche speaks of the "ebb and flood" of our drives, their "play and counterplay among one another," their "growth and nourishment" (*D* 119; *BGE* 6 et passim). This language is familiar to us; drives are almost inevitably associated with active *forces*, *impulsions*, and *pressures seeking discharge*. Although vague and metaphorical, these colorful terms are suggestive; they are capturing something important about the concept of drives. Drives are not simply *responses* to external stimuli; on the contrary, drives seek to manifest themselves. But again, I will argue that this needn't lead us to interpret drives as agents.

We can begin by considering simpler psychic states: desires. Some desires arise as responses to the perception of external stimuli. Walking down the street on a hot summer day, I see an ice cream shop, and this sight creates a desire for ice cream. Walking through the forest, I see a shape lurching out of the trees, and I desire to get away. These desires are affectively charged responses to external stimuli.

But other desires arise in a different way, seeming to have a life of their own. Consider a habitually aggressive, combative person. Part of what it is to be habitually aggressive is to have a recurrent tendency to seek out opportunities for aggression, regardless of whether

---

[30] Ken Gemes defends a related claim about drives in his contribution to this volume. See especially section 2.1. There, Gemes argues that Nietzsche's claims about drives "interpreting" phenomena and generating "perspectives" are best understood as claims about drives leading agents to interact with their environments in determinate ways.

the circumstances merit aggressive responses. The aggressive person will typically distort circumstances in order to find these kinds of outlets. He will interpret ordinary, inoffensive behavior as offensive, raging at the driver who cuts in front of him or the cashier who seems distracted. This aggressive tendency consists, in part, in the tendency to see aspects of his environment as *warranting* aggression. Nietzschean drives are supposed to have an analogous form. They have a psychic life of their own: drives do not *await* occasions for expression, but *create* them, by inclining the agent to see certain actions as warranted.

Freud, no doubt influenced by Nietzsche's conception of drives, suggested a similar model of drives. In "Drives and their Vicissitudes," Freud asks what the relation is between the notions *drive* and *stimulus*.[31] "Stimulus" here serves as Freud's most general term for a motivational state; it is analogous to the contemporary use of terms such as "pro-attitude" or "desire." So Freud is asking whether drives are just desires. He answers with a qualified "yes." Drives can be understood as a type of stimulus (or desire), but if we do group them in this way it is important not to think that all stimuli function in the same way. For there are two differences between drives and other stimuli. First, "a drive stimulus does not arise from the external world but from within the organism itself." Second, many stimuli operate with

> a single impact, so that [they] can be disposed of by a single expedient action. A typical instance of this is motor flight from the source of stimulation. These impacts may, of course, be repeated and summated, but that makes no difference to our notion of the process and to the conditions for the removal of the stimulus. A drive, on the other hand, never operates as a force giving a *momentary* impact but always as a *constant* one. (Freud 1957: vol. 14, p. 118)

Summarizing these points, Freud writes that the essential nature of drives is "their origination in sources of stimulation within the organism and their appearance as a constant force" (Freud 1957: vol. 14, p. 119). So drives have two features: drives do not await external stimuli, but manifest themselves independently of external stimuli; moreover, drives are not momentary occurrences, but are relatively constant.

Start with the second point. Drives need not be constant in the literal sense of being active at each moment; rather, they are constant in the sense that they arise, with some regularity, throughout the individual's life. Hunger provides a good example: although we are not *always* hungry, there is a sense in which hunger is a constant motive. For hunger cannot be eliminated once and for all; it can only be put into abeyance. Likewise, drives cannot be eliminated, but only temporarily sated.

Turn now to the first point. When a drive is active, it leads the agent to engage in behavior that satisfies the drive. The drive does not await appropriate stimuli or occasions for discharge. Again, take hunger. Though hunger is sometimes roused by external stimuli, such as the sight or smell of food, hunger can also arise independently of any external stimuli. Presumably brought about by physiological conditions, hunger can arise at the most inopportune times, and will not slacken until it is, to some extent, satisfied by the acquisition of some object.

---

[31] The Standard Edition translates the title *Triebe und Triebschicksale* as "Instincts and their Vicissitudes." I think *Trieb* is better translated as *drive* in this context. In the quotations from Freud above, I follow the Standard Edition, but translate all occurrences of *Trieb* as drive.

When Nietzsche writes of drives being active, ebbing and flooding, and seeking discharge, he has something similar in mind. Drives arise independently of external stimuli, and once they have become active, they will seek discharge. The fact that drives are active and do not arise in response to external stimuli creates a problem. In many cases, a drive will be active in conditions that do not provide the agent with appropriate objects with which to satisfy the drive. Just as we can be hungry when there are no opportunities to eat, we can be angry when there are no occasions for anger. For example, suppose the aggressive drive is active in a situation in which the individual has not been threatened or provoked. Nietzsche tells us that the drive will *seek* outlets—seek objects on which to vent itself.

To clarify this point, it will be helpful to draw on a useful distinction that Freud introduces. Freud distinguishes between the *aim* [*Ziel*] and the *object* [*Objekt*] of the drive. The aim of the drive is its characteristic goal, in terms of which it is individuated from other drives. The aim of the sex drive is sexual activity; the aim of the ascetic drive is ascetic activity; and so on. Freud remarks "although the ultimate aim of each drive remains unchangeable, there may yet be different paths leading to the same ultimate aim" (Freud 1957: vol. 14, p. 118). Thus, he introduces the notion of the drive's object.

> The object of a drive is the thing in regard to which or through which the drive is able to achieve its aim. It is what is most variable about a drive and is not originally connected with it, but becomes assigned to it only in consequence of being peculiarly fitted to make satisfaction possible... It may be changed any number of times in the course of the vicissitudes which the drive undergoes during its existence... (Freud 1957: vol. 14, p. 118)

The aim of a drive is its characteristic form of activity. The sexual drive aims at sexual activity; the aggressive drive aims at aggressive activity. In order for a drive to be expressed, one needs an object. The drive itself is indifferent to the object; the drive simply seeks expression. So the aggressive drive will seek to vent itself on whatever object happens to be present.

We have already seen that drives do not just blindly impel an agent to act. Rather, drives operate by influencing the agent's perception and reflective thought, so that the agent sees a certain activity as warranted. With this in mind, suppose a drive is active, and seeks expression. If an appropriate object is unavailable, the drive will seek expression on whatever object happens to be present. The aggressive drive would most naturally be expressed upon things worthy of aggression. But, if there are no such objects, the drive will lead the agent to *seek* objects. So, a neutral stimulus may be interpreted as worthy of aggression, as *warranting* aggression. For example, the cashier's distraction may be seen as a personal snub, worthy of a rude remark. The driver's pulling in front of the car may be seen as an aggressive attack, worthy of horn play and rage. I take it that this is a familiar phenomenon: anyone who has been in the grip of rage, jealousy, or any other strong affect can understand the sense in which these affects *seek* objects.

In this way, drives affect the agent's perceptions of reasons. The aggressive drive does not just produce a blind urge that causes the agent to act aggressively. Rather, the aggressive drive manifests itself by producing desires, affects, and perceptual saliences that jointly incline the agent to see aggression as warranted by the circumstances. This is why Nietzsche writes that a drive will "emphasize certain features and lines in what is foreign, in every piece of the 'external world', retouching and falsifying the whole to suit itself" (*BGE* 230).

We can now put some points together. In the preceding section, we saw that drives manifest themselves by generating evaluative orientations. In this section, we have seen that when a drive is active it will induce a particular *kind* of orientation; it will induce an orientation that inclines the agent to take steps toward fulfilling the drive, by making it appear as if taking these steps is *warranted* by the situation at hand. For example, when the aggressive drive seeks to discharge itself, it will generate evaluative orientations that lead the agent to see aggressiveness as warranted by the situation at hand. So a drive manifests itself by impacting the agent's rational capacities.

And now we can begin to see something interesting: being moved by a drive and being moved by reflective thought are not distinct processes. Drives move us by directing and influencing our reflective thought.[32] The next section examines this point in detail.

4 Drives and Reflective Agency

This essay began by posing three questions about drives. First, we asked what a drive is. We have seen that drives are a particular type of disposition, which manifests itself by generating an evaluative orientation. Second, we asked what type of awareness an agent has when she is being moved by a drive. We have seen that the agent typically lacks awareness of the end at which the drives dispose her to aim. With these claims in place, we can now turn to the third question: how should this understanding of drives impact our conception of reflective agency?

Nietzsche is notoriously skeptical of reflective agency. He explains paradigmatically reflective phenomena, such as self-conscious episodes of choice, as precipitates of drives. He tells us that reflection does not enable one to escape the influence of drives, arguing that an agent who acts reflectively is still "secretly guided and channeled" by his drives (*BGE* 3). In addition, he claims that whenever an agent steps back from and reflects upon a drive, the agent's "intellect is only the blind instrument of *another drive*" (*D* 109). These passages certainly seem designed to call into question our ordinary understanding of agency. In the following sections, I will ask how these passages should be understood.

4.1 Recent Interpretations of Nietzsche on Choice

We need an explanation of what Nietzsche means when he tells us that choice and reflective thought are guided or channeled by drives. Moreover, this explanation should make it clear why Nietzsche thinks the claim has implications for our understanding of the role of choice and reflective thought in agency.

---

[32] Although I lack the space to argue for this point here, Nietzsche seems to embrace the following claims: (1) drives *always* exert some influence upon reflective thought, but (2) the *extent* of this influence differs from case to case, and, perhaps most importantly, (3) the drives' influence *often*, but *not always*, undermines the agent's claim to being in control of the action. I return to the third point, briefly, in the final paragraphs of this essay. For an extended defense of the third point, see Katsafanas 2011.

There seems to be a consensus within the Nietzsche literature on two points about choice. First, Nietzsche clearly denies that choice is a necessary condition for action. As we saw in section 1.3, Nietzsche claims that many actions occur without the agent's engaging in an episode of choice, indeed without the agent's even attending to her action. Second, it is by now a commonplace that Nietzsche rejects the *libertarian* conception of choice, according to which an agent's choices are undetermined by prior events. As Gemes puts it, Nietzsche rejects "the notion of a will autonomous from the causal order, an uncaused cause" (2006: 325).

Of course, this leaves open a vast range of possible views about the nature of choice: few philosophers have claimed that choice is a necessary condition for action, and non-libertarian accounts of choice are legion. So these two claims about choice do not make Nietzsche's account seem particularly original.

A third claim, which has been defended by Brian Leiter, would make Nietzsche's account quite revolutionary. According to Leiter, Nietzsche argues that choice is epiphenomenal: "there is no causal link between the experience of willing and the resulting action" (2007: 13). On this interpretation, the agent's drives and other non-conscious factors[33] cause action, while the agent's reflective choices are simply idle.

Although Leiter's epiphenomenalist interpretation of choice would have dramatic implications, several commentators have argued on both textual and philosophical grounds that Nietzsche is not an epiphenomenalist.[34] I lack the space to examine these arguments here, but I do wish to register my agreement with them and to make one further point: Leiter's interpretation has textual costs. There are a number of passages in which Nietzsche appears to rely on the idea that choice can be causally efficacious, and Leiter's interpretation forces us to explain away these passages. For example, Nietzsche praises the "sovereign" or "autonomous" individual, who is distinguished by the fact that he "has his own independent, protracted will" (*GM* II: 2). Elsewhere, Nietzsche develops these ideas, claiming that "strong" agents have the power "not to react at once to a stimulus, but to gain control of all the inhibiting, excluding instincts...the essential feature is precisely not to 'will', to be able to suspend decision. All unspirituality, all vulgar commonness, depend on an inability to resist a stimulus: one must react, one follows every impulse" (*TI*: "What the Germans Lack" 6). In the same work, Nietzsche defines weakness as the "inability *not* to respond to a stimulus" (*TI*: "Morality as Anti-Nature" 2). The weak individual's actions are determined by whatever impulse or stimulus happens to arise; he possesses no capacity to direct his own behavior. By contrast, the strong individual is able to check his impulses and resist stimuli.[35]

---

[33] In particular, Leiter claims that actions are caused by "type-facts" about the person, where "type-facts, for Nietzsche, are either *physiological* facts about the person or facts about the person's unconscious drives or affects" (2007: 7).

[34] See, for example, Clark and Dudrick 2009, Gemes 2006, and Janaway 2006. I discuss this issue in Katsafanas 2005.

[35] There are a number of similar passages, both in the notebooks and in the published works. In *WP* 95, Nietzsche condemns nineteenth-century thinkers for being "deeply convinced of the rule of cravings. (Schopenhauer spoke of 'will'; but nothing is more characteristic of his philosophy than the absence of all genuine willing)." *WP* 928 speaks of great individuals controlling their affects: "Greatness of character does not consist in not possessing these affects—on the contrary, one possesses them to the highest degree—but in having them under control." *WP* 933 makes a similar point: "*In summa: domination* of the passions, *not* their weakening or extirpation!—The greater the dominating power of a will, the more freedom may the passions be allowed. The 'great man' is great owing to the free play and scope of his

In these passages, Nietzsche claims that some individuals have the capacity to control their behavior. Leiter's epiphenomenalist interpretation must treat these passages as rhetorical excesses or clumsy phrasings.[36] This is certainly possible: Nietzsche may have inadvertently invoked images of a causally efficacious capacity for choice, or his texts may be inconsistent. However, it would be preferable to find an interpretation of Nietzsche's views on choice that does not require us to discount any published passages. In the next section, I will show that such an interpretation is available.[37]

4.2 Choice and the Possibility of Reflective Detachment

I am going to argue that Nietzsche is not primarily interested in questioning the causal connection between *choice* and *action*. Rather, Nietzsche's drive psychology problematizes the connection between *the agent* and *choice*.

To begin, let's consider the model of reflective choice that Nietzsche is attacking. I take it that Nietzsche is attacking a very influential model of agency, which is associated with Locke and Kant. The central claim of this model is that self-conscious reflection enables a deliberative suspension of motives. Locke writes that the mind has "a power to *suspend* the execution and satisfaction of any of its desires." The mind can "consider the objects of [these desires]; examine them on all sides and weigh them with others. In this lies the liberty that man has" (1975: 263). Kant endorses a similar model of deliberation, writing that human choice "can indeed be *affected* but not *determined* by impulses . . . *Freedom* of choice is this independence from being determined by sensible impulses" (*Metaphysics of Morals* 6: 213–14; see Kant 1996). Christine Korsgaard describes the Kantian model of deliberation as follows:

> Our capacity to turn our attention to our own mental activities is also a capacity to distance ourselves from them, to call them into question . . . I desire and I find myself with a powerful impulse to act. But I back up and bring that impulse into view and then I have a certain distance. Now the impulse doesn't dominate me and now I have a problem. Shall I act? Is this desire really a *reason* to act? (Korsgaard 1996: 93)

The Lockean/Kantian claim about deliberative suspension can be broken into two parts. First, there is a claim about motivation: self-conscious reflection enables us to distance ourselves from our motives, thereby making these motives cease to "dominate" us or

---

desires and to the yet greater power than knows how to press these magnificent monsters into service." *WP* 962 claims that a great individual "has the ability to extend his will across great stretches of his life." For an example from a published work, consider *Zarathustra*. In Z II: "Of Redemption" and elsewhere, Zarathustra claims that the *past* is a source of dissatisfaction because it cannot be modified by the will: "powerless against what has been, the will is an angry spectator of all that is past. The will cannot will backwards . . . that is the will's loneliest melancholy." If the will could not will *forward*, either—if acts of will had no causal impact on the agent's actions—then this claim would be unintelligible. The future would be just as inaccessible as the past.

   [36] And indeed, Leiter attempts to deflate these passages in Leiter 2011.
   [37] To be clear, we should distinguish two claims: (1) Nietzsche's account of the relationship between drives and conscious thought is compatible with the claim that conscious thought is causally efficacious; (2) Nietzsche maintains that conscious thought is causally efficacious. I think both (1) and (2) are

"suspending" these motives.[38] Second, there is a claim about normativity: once we have suspended a motive, we "consider" the motive, "weigh" it, ask if it is "really a reason to act." In other words, once I have begun reflecting on the motive, what I do is look for a reason to act on the motive.

Of course, Locke and Kant do think that choice is causally efficacious; they believe that choice results in action. But they view choice as philosophically significant not simply because it results in action, but because in choosing, the agent suspends and rationally assesses her motives. So, one way of attacking this model would be to argue that choice doesn't cause action. But another way, which I think Nietzsche pursues, is to grant that choice causes action and attack the claim that in choosing, the agent suspends his motives.

For an illustration of the way in which Nietzsche is attacking this point, recall Murdoch's example, discussed in section 2.2. This example involves a mother, M, and a daughter-in-law, D. M initially sees D's behavior as brusque, rude, pert, and juvenile; later, she sees the same behavior as spontaneous, simple, gay, and delightfully youthful. A slight modification of Murdoch's example can be used to illustrate the complex way in which attempts at reflective detachment can fail. Let us imagine M at a somewhat earlier stage of her relationship with D, before M investigates the connections between her jealousy and her perceptions of D. Imagine that, at this earlier stage, M reflects on her dislike of D. Reasons for this dislike are forthcoming: D is vulgar and brusque. So reflection on the dislike apparently vindicates the dislike. But notice that the perception of D's behavior as vulgar and brusque is, in part, a result of M's jealousy. So the apparent detachment from her dislike of D, the reflective scrutiny of that dislike, the assessment of the dislike in light of evidence from observation, is influenced by another aspect of the very attitude from which M is attempting to detach.[39]

M is acting reflectively, and her choice does result in action. Yet M is in the thrall of attitudes that operate in the background. I suggest that this is what Nietzsche has in mind when he claims that reflection does not enable one to escape the influence of drives. The reflective agent is, in one sense, different from the unreflective agent: after all, the reflective agent deliberates, thinks about reasons for acting, and examines her motives, whereas the unreflective agent does none of this. But in another sense, the reflective agent is not so different from the unreflective agent: while the reflective agent supposes that she is escaping the influence of her drives, she is mistaken. The influence of the drive has simply become more covert.[40]

---

true—this, I submit, is the most natural reading of the passages cited above. However, in this essay I argue only for claim (1). For defenses of claim (2), see Katsafanas 2005 and the works cited in note 34.

[38] To be precise, Kant and Locke seem to maintain that for any motive, I can self-consciously suspend its influence. We should distinguish this claim from the much stronger claim that I can, at any moment, suspend the influence of *all* of my motives. (Compare the analogous point about belief: we can, at any moment, self-consciously reflect on and critically assess any given belief; but we cannot, at one moment, self-consciously reflect on and critically assess *all* of our beliefs. For we assess given beliefs in light of other beliefs, which are held fixed.)

[39] Of course, in Murdoch's original example M eventually does achieve a reflective detachment from her jealous motives. However, achieving this reflective detachment requires hard, self-critical work: M needs to engage in an extended investigation of the effects of various attitudes on her perceptions.

[40] Although I lack the space to argue for this point here, I think Nietzsche maintains that reflection and self-understanding enable an agent to counteract the effects of particular drives. Murdoch's original example illustrates this point: by coming to understand the way in which her jealousy influences her reflection, M manages to counteract its effects. Indeed, this seems to be one reason why Nietzsche

If this is correct, then we needn't interpret Nietzsche as claiming that conscious choice is epiphenomenal. As mundane events such as choosing what to eat for breakfast indicate, our choices result in action all the time. But the causal connection between choice and action is not sufficient to demonstrate that we self-consciously control our actions, for self-conscious choice and the reflective assessment of motives are determined by drives that operate in the background. Reflectively choosing to A, and being caused to A by one's drives, are not distinct phenomena. *This* is the problem that Nietzsche's drive psychology raises: choice may control action, but agents do not control choice.[41]

5 CONCLUSION

A drive is a disposition that induces an evaluative orientation. Drives manifest themselves by structuring the agent's perceptions, affects, and reflective thought. Moreover, drives do not simply arise in response to external stimuli; they actively seek opportunities for expression, sometimes distorting the agent's perception of the environment in order to incline the agent to act in ways that give the drives expression.

This account of drives requires us to rethink our notion of deliberative or reflective agency. An agent who deliberates seems to enjoy a certain detachment from her motivational states. The deliberating agent experiences herself as capable of suspending the effects of her motivational states, and determining her action by choice. The drive psychology complicates this account. While it may be true that the agent who deliberates is not immediately compelled to act by her motivational states, her drives and other motives do continue to operate, in a subterranean fashion, even as the agent reflects on them. In many cases, the drives appear to decisively guide the agent's reflective choice in ways that she does not recognize.

This raises a potential problem. If the deliberating agent's thoughts and actions are guided, sometimes decisively, by her drives, can the actions that issue from her genuinely be regarded as *her* doings? Nietzsche sometimes suggests not:

emphasizes the importance of self-understanding: self-understanding enables one to counteract the effects of certain drives, and thereby renders the agent increasingly in control of her action. See note 32. For a related discussion of the role of self-understanding, see Richardson 2004 (especially 95–103).

    41 Section 4.1 noted that Leiter interprets Nietzsche as an epiphenomenalist about willing. However, Leiter acknowledges that there is some evidence for a different reading of Nietzsche, according to which "the will is, indeed, causal, but it is not the *ultimate* cause of an action: something *causes* the experience of willing and then the will causes the action" (Leiter 2007: 13). Leiter calls this the "Will as Secondary Cause" interpretation. The interpretation that I have defended, above, is in some respects similar to Leiter's Will as Secondary Cause reading. However, there are two potential disagreements that merit attention. First, the Will as Secondary Cause reading suggests a unidirectional causal path between drives and choice: drives determine conscious choices, which then determine actions. On my interpretation, however, there is a bidirectional causal path: drives causally influence conscious thoughts, but conscious thoughts (including choices) also causally influence drives (see Katsafanas 2005 for the details). Second, we should distinguish two readings of the relationship between drives and conscious thoughts. According to the strong reading, drives *determine* conscious thoughts: if two agents' drives (and circumstances) are identical, then their conscious thoughts must be identical. According to the weak reading, drives merely *influence* conscious thought: two agents' drives (and circumstances) could

'I have no idea what I am *doing*! I have no idea what I *ought to do!*'—you are right, but be sure of this: *you are being done! [du wirst gethan!]* at every moment! Mankind has in all ages confused the active and the passive: it is their everlasting grammatical blunder. (*D* 120)

In this quotation, Nietzsche argues that many appearances of agency are illusory: what looks like a case of the agent's activity is better described as a case of the agent's being acted upon, presumably by her own drives. Echoing this point in another disconcerting passage, he writes, "Nothing is rarer than a *personal* action. A class, a rank, a race, an environment, an accident—everything expresses itself sooner in a work or deed, than a 'person' " (*WP* 866).

However, Nietzsche does not appear to believe that *every* action has this structure. After all, Nietzsche repeatedly speaks of "self-determination," "taking responsibility for oneself," and being a "sovereign individual" (*HAH* I: Preface 3; *TI*: "Skirmishes of an Untimely Man" 38; *GM* II: 2). This suggests that Nietzsche does have some conception of genuine agency, which contrasts with the degenerate forms of agency manifested by most individuals.[42]

Thus, there is some sense in which the agent acting under the influence of drives may be a passive conduit for the drives; however, Nietzsche also suggests that there is some way of acting that avoids this problem. Although I lack the space to address these topics here, my hope is that the analysis of drive psychology offered in this essay will bring us closer to understanding them.[43]

BIBLIOGRAPHY

(A) Works by Nietzsche

Reference edition of Nietzsche's works:

KSA   *Sämtliche Werke: Kritische Studienausgabe in 15 Einzelbänden*, ed. G. Colli and M. Montinari. Berlin: De Gruyter, 1988.

List of abbreviations of Nietzsche's works:
A   *The Antichrist*, trans. W. Kaufmann. New York: Viking, 1954.
BGE   *Beyond Good and Evil*, trans. W. Kaufmann. New York: Modern Library, 1968.
CW   *The Case of Wagner*, trans. W. Kaufmann. New York: Random House, 1967.
D   *Daybreak*, trans. R. J. Hollingdale. Cambridge: Cambridge University Press, 1982.
EH   *Ecce Homo*, trans. W. Kaufmann. New York: Modern Library, 1968.
GM   *On the Genealogy of Morality*, trans. W. Kaufmann. New York: Modern Library, 1968.
GS   *The Gay Science*, trans. W. Kaufmann. New York: Vintage, 1974.
HC   "Homer's Contest," trans. W. Kaufmann. New York: Viking, 1954.

be identical, and yet they could have different conscious thoughts. I accept the weak reading, whereas Leiter's Will as Secondary Cause interpretation seems to be premised upon the strong reading. For a defense of these points, see Katsafanas 2005 and 2011.
   [42] Katsafanas 2011 provides an argument for the claim that Nietzsche has a conception of genuine agency.
   [43] For helpful discussions of the material in this essay, I owe great thanks to Lanier Anderson, Ken Gemes, Christine Korsgaard, Brian Leiter, Richard Moran, Bernard Reginster, John Richardson, Mathias Risse, and Danielle Slevens.

HAH   *Human, All Too Human*, trans. R. J. Hollingdale. Cambridge: Cambridge University Press, 1986.

NCW   *Nietzsche Contra Wagner*, trans. W. Kaufmann. New York: Viking, 1954.

TI   *Twilight of the Idols*, trans. W. Kaufmann. New York: Viking, 1954.

UM   *Untimely Meditations*, trans. R. J. Hollingdale. New York: Cambridge, 1997.

WP   *The Will to Power*, trans. W. Kaufmann and R. J. Hollingdale. New York: Vintage, 1967.

Z   *Thus Spoke Zarathustra*, trans. W. Kaufmann. New York: Viking, 1954.

(B) Other Primary Works

WWR   Schopenhauer, Arthur. 1969. *The World as Will and Representation*, trans. E. E. F. J. Payne (2 vols). New York: Dover.

(C) Other Works Cited

Anscombe, G. E. M. 2000. *Intention*. Cambridge, Mass.: Harvard University Press.

Assoun, Paul-Laurent. 2000. *Freud and Nietzsche*, trans. R. L. Collier. New Brunswick: Athlone Press.

Boring, Edwin G. 1929. *A History of Experimental Psychology*. New York: D. Appleton-Century Company.

Brewer, Talbot. 2002. "Maxims and Virtues," *Philosophical Review* 111: 539–72.

Clark, Maudemarie. 1998. "On Knowledge, Truth, and Value: Nietzsche's Debt to Schopenhauer and the Development of his Empiricism," in C. Janaway (ed.), *Willing and Nothingness: Schopenhauer as Nietzsche's Educator*. Oxford: Oxford University Press, 37–78.

Clark, Maudemarie and Dudrick, David. 2009. "Nietzsche on the Will: An Analysis of BGE 19," in Ken Gemes and Simon May (eds), *Nietzsche on Freedom and Autonomy*. Oxford: Oxford University Press, 247–68.

Conway, Daniel. 1997. *Nietzsche's Dangerous Game: Philosophy in the "Twilight of the Idols."* Cambridge: Cambridge University Press.

Cox, Christoph. 1999. *Nietzsche: Naturalism and Interpretation*. Berkeley and Los Angeles: University of California Press.

Darwin, Charles. 1993. *On the Origin of Species*. New York: Modern Library.

Darwin, Charles. 2004. *The Descent of Man*. London: Penguin.

Freud, Sigmund. 1957. *The Standard Edition of the Complete Psychological Works of Sigmund Freud*, ed. J. Strachey. London: Hogarth Press.

Gemes, Ken. 2001. "Post-Modernism's Use and Abuse of Nietzsche," *Philosophy and Phenomenological Research* 52: 337–60.

Gemes, Ken. 2006. "Nietzsche on Free Will, Autonomy and the Sovereign Individual," *Proceedings of the Aristotelian Society* 80 (supp. vol.): 321–38.

Hales, Steven and Welshon, Rex. 2000. *Nietzsche's Perspectivism*. Champaign, Ill.: University of Illinois Press.

Huxley, T. H. 1874. "On the Hypothesis that Animals are Automata, and its History," *Fortnightly Review* 95: 555–80.

James, William. 1890. *The Principles of Psychology*. New York: Dover.

Janaway, Christopher. 2006. "Nietzsche on Free Will, Autonomy and the Sovereign Individual," *Proceedings of the Aristotelian Society* 80 (supp. vol.): 339–57.

Janaway, Christopher. 2007. *Beyond Selflessness: Reading Nietzsche's Genealogy*. New York: Oxford University Press.

Kant, Immanuel. 1996. *The Metaphysics of Morals*, ed. Mary Gregor. New York: Cambridge University Press.

Kant, Immanuel. 1998. *Groundwork of the Metaphysics of Morals*, ed. Mary Gregor. New York: Cambridge University Press.

Katsafanas, Paul. 2005. "Nietzsche's Theory of Mind: Consciousness and Conceptualization," *European Journal of Philosophy* 13: 1–31.

Katsafanas, Paul. 2011. "The Concept of Unified Agency in Nietzsche, Plato, and Schiller," *Journal of the History of Philosophy* 49.1: 87–113.

Katsafanas, Paul. 2012. "Nietzsche on Agency and Self-Ignorance," *Journal of Nietzsche Studies* 43.1: 5–17.

Korsgaard, Christine. 1996. *The Sources of Normativity*. New York: Cambridge University Press.

Leiter, Brian. 2002. *Nietzsche on Morality*. London: Routledge.

Leiter, Brian. 2007. "Nietzsche's Theory of the Will," *Philosophers Imprint* 7.7: 1–15.

Leiter, Brian. 2011. "Who is the Sovereign Individual? Nietzsche on Freedom," in Simon May (ed.), *Nietzsche's "On the Genealogy of Morality": A Critical Guide*. Cambridge: Cambridge University Press, 101–19.

Locke, John. 1975. *An Essay Concerning Human Understanding*. New York: Oxford University Press.

Lowry, Richard. 1971. *The Evolution of Psychological Theory*. Hawthorne, NY: Aldine Publishing.

Moore, Gregory. 2002. *Nietzsche, Biology, and Metaphor*. New York: Cambridge University Press.

Murdoch, Iris. 1985. *The Sovereignty of Good*. New York: Routledge.

Parkes, Graham. 1996. *Composing the Soul*. Chicago: University of Chicago Press.

Poellner, Peter. 1995. *Nietzsche and Metaphysics*. New York: Oxford University Press.

Proudhon, Pierre-Joseph. 1994. *What is Property?* New York: Cambridge University Press.

Richards, Robert. 1987. *Darwin and the Emergence of Evolutionary Theories of Mind and Behavior*. Chicago: University of Chicago Press.

Richardson, John. 1996. *Nietzsche's System*. New York: Oxford University Press.

Richardson, John. 2004. *Nietzsche's New Darwinism*. New York: Oxford University Press.

Rosenfield, Lenora. 1968. *From Beast-Machine to Man-Machine: Animal Soul in French Letters from Descartes to La Mettrie*. New York: Columbia University Press.

Schacht, Richard. 1983. *Nietzsche*. New York: Routledge.

Schopenhauer, Arthur. 1969. *The World as Will and Representation*, trans. E. F. J. Payne. New York: Dover.

Stampe, Dennis. 1987. "The Authority of Desire," *Philosophical Review* 96: 335–81.

Thiele, Leslie Paul. 1990. *Friedrich Nietzsche and the Politics of the Soul*. Princeton: Princeton University Press.

Thorpe, W. H. 1956. *Learning and Instinct in Animals*. London: Methuen.

Wilm, E. C. 1925. *The Theories of Instinct*. New Haven: Yale University Press.

CHAPTER 32

....

NIETZSCHE ON LIFE'S ENDS

....

JOHN RICHARDSON

1 INTRODUCTION

....

MY overall topic is Nietzsche's notion of life [*Leben*], and in particular how he uses it to guide or correct his and our values. I'll try to say what Nietzsche means by "life" and by "value"—and will examine how he relates them. An obvious answer, and the start of a more adequate answer, is that he means *many* things by "life" and even by "value." So there is an unavoidable complexity to the topic. The challenge will be to bring this multiplicity into some kind of perspicuous order.

Now I think life is one of the topics those working on Nietzsche in an analytic way tend to avoid. There are, after all, some topics and arguments in Nietzsche that are noticed better by beginning readers. Those who go on to treat him philosophically, i.e., argumentatively, tend to discount these topics and place them on the periphery of his thought, either because (a) these views look like embarrassing weaknesses, or (b) they at least look useless *as arguments*—they seem *dead weight* in his theory. Life is one such topic—and in particular the way Nietzsche so often uses it to support or justify his evaluations.

I think beginning readers better notice the importance of this argument. Indeed I think it is Nietzsche's *principal* justification for his values: life gives the main criterion by which he carries out his "revaluation of values," and the fact that life supplies it is what justifies that criterion. "Life" is the clear fulcrum of *most* of his defenses of his values, and only such judgments as (a) and (b) can explain the widespread neglect of the topic.[1] Moreover, contra those judgments, I think that this argument has some *merit*—or (backing off a long ways) at the very least some *interest*. Although early readers can't well say quite why, I think they aptly

---

[1] Hunt (1991: 111–30) is one exception who stresses and examines Nietzsche's argument from life to values. See also Conway 2006. May 1999 develops how "life-enhancement" is Nietzsche's standard for evaluating values, but doesn't examine just what life is. The same is true of Reginster 2006, despite his focus on "the affirmation of life." Schacht (1983: 232–53) treats at length Nietzsche's notion of life, and more briefly the role of life in supporting values (354–6, 395–8).

feel some force in this argument. So it shouldn't embarrass us as much as we (sympathetic) interpreters might think.

Given its key role in supporting his values, it's not surprising that the idea of life is constantly present in Nietzsche's writing. It appears again and again at crucial points. The most dramatic of these is at the climax of *Thus Spoke Zarathustra*, when Zarathustra marries Life, with the aid of his thought of eternal return; I'll review these passages shortly. But the idea of life already plays an important role near the start of his first book, *The Birth of Tragedy*, which develops how art "made life possible and worth living" for the Greeks, in the face of their tragic view that it's "better never to have been born." The way tragedy is life-affirming despite this negative judgment is a crucial point of the book. This is confirmed in the later-added "Attempt at a Self-Criticism," which famously says that the book's task was "to look at science in the optic of the artist, but at art in that of life" (*BT*: "Attempt at a Self-Criticism" 2); it adds later that the book was burdened with the question "What, seen in the optic of *life*, is the significance of morality?" (*BT*: "Attempt at a Self-Criticism" 4)

The idea of life remains important in the middle, "positivist" works[2] and then all through Nietzsche's maturity. He counts himself among the "advocates of life" (*Fürsprecher des Lebens*) (*WP* 116 [1888]).[3] The idea that life is/gives the standard for his revaluation is quite standardly presumed and relied on.[4] We'll look at many quotations as we go. Indeed Nietzsche even composed music for a "Hymn to Life," to words by Lou Salomé (as he mentions in *EH*: "Thus Spoke Zarathustra" 1). Of course our main interest will be in the arguments he wants to turn on life. But I also want to do some justice to his poetic and affective relation to it.

Why is this idea of life so easy to discount, despite its omnipresence? Chiefly I think because it seems hopelessly vague and as such quite unable to do the work Nietzsche wants it for. When he tells us that he "takes the side of life," we remember how wide a spectrum of viewpoints can call themselves "pro-life." Moreover, it seems that every viewpoint, just insofar as it values, can claim (if it wants) a right to so count itself. For inasmuch as values render a judgment *how to live*, all of them are (in this way) for the sake of life. Any values—including the Christian—purport to tell how to live life best; each is a strategy *for* life. Nietzsche remarks this all-inclusiveness when he says of the advice " 'live according to life'—how could you *not*? Why make a principle of what you yourselves are and must be?" (*BGE* 9) These impressions of vagueness and indeterminacy are reinforced by the way his most conspicuous mentions of life are those poetic personifications of "her." If he is so loose and metaphorical here, we may suspect him to be just a little less so elsewhere too. And indeed even in

---

[2] Life as criterion is embedded in the title of the second *Untimely Meditation*: *On the Uses and Disadvantages of History for Life*: "[I] demand that the human should above all learn to live and should use history only in *the service of the life [he has] learned [to live]*" (*UM* II: 10). In *Human, All Too Human* he continues to mull the question whether truth is harmful to life; e.g., *HAH* I: 34. Notice the important role of life at the beginning of *The Gay Science*, *GS* 1.

[3] This is Zarathustra's role too: Z II: "The Prophet," III: "The Convalescent." Nietzsche also says that he belongs to the "friends of life" (*KSA* 10: 2 [4] [1882], 10: 4 [1] [1882–3]).

[4] *WP* 266 (1886–7) is a sketch of a book about morality's relation to life: "*opposition* of life and *morality*: morality judged and condemned from life." It lists ways morality has been detrimental to life—but also ways it has been useful. *BGE* 2: "For all the value that the true, the truthful, the selfless may deserve: it would be possible that a higher and more fundamental value for all life must be ascribed to appearance, the will to deception, selfishness, and lust." See also *BGE* 4, 19, 23.

places where he's not actually personifying life, he sometimes seems to be treating it as a "thing" in ways that can only be metaphorical.

I will try to show that Nietzsche's idea of life is not so much indefinite as multiple, and that we can profitably examine and sort out this multiplicity. I want to think about the relations in which Nietzsche's different notions of life stand to one another, including which might have priority. And I want to say something about those personifications of life, and their relation to any arguments.

Now it might seem that the second main term, "values," is much less problematic. But I think there's also an ambiguity here that we need to expose. And I think we especially need clarity here because we miss out on a large part of Nietzsche's point if we take the term "values" for granted—if we hear it, say, in the way the term is used in contemporary ethics. Much of the interest of Nietzsche's thought lies in the ways it is hard to align with prevailing debates; I'll try to bring out this recalcitrance.

Nietzsche's idea of "values" is complicated by, first, his strong *naturalism* regarding values. Values are naturally occurring entities; they occur in or by virtue of real acts of valuing; genealogy studies how they evolve. Here in this naturalism Nietzsche takes an external or third-personal view of values. However he also "posits values" in a quite different way: by valuing, first-personally, himself. Our key question will be the relation between these two ways of "positing values": how—if at all—does his naturalistic study of them guide and support the values he himself proposes?

Nietzsche's idea of values is further complicated by the way his naturalism leads to a certain *critique* of the very faculty of reflecting on, choosing, and abiding by values, which it is the point of ethics to develop and improve in us. He questions whether we have such a faculty, and whether (if we do) it's in fact desirable. This critique is often interpreted as bearing especially against "free will." But I think it's much broader than this; it attacks our confidence in our agency, and in our "agential" way of valuing. It calls into question the importance and value of what we *usually* call "valuing," the kind of values we're aware of and put into words. I'll argue that this attack, though not meant to be fatal, points a lesson to change how agency and its values work in us—their role in our personal economy.

After talking first about life, then about values, I'll turn finally to the question how the former are used to correct/guide the latter. Nietzsche faces three challenges here, and we must see how he meets them. First, he must give reasons or arguments for appealing to life—justifications of its authority to correct our values. Second he must extract from life some determinate criterion to serve as a standard to revalue values. And third he must show that this criterion can actually be used to generate new values we might plausibly practice.

There is a large philosophical difficulty in meeting these challenges. In extracting from life a "criterion" for revaluing values, Nietzsche is extracting a value—a value offered as authoritative for revising other values. But any argument from life to such a value seems to (try to) derive a value from a fact, which is often taken as an outright mistake. How, from the premise that life *is* so and so, could any evaluative conclusions follow as to how we should be? We must study Nietzsche's prospects for using life to support his values in a way that can deflect this obvious retort.

Before looking at some passages, I want to offer a very quick partition of some senses in which Nietzsche (or anyone) *might* use "life."[5] We will hold these options in mind when we look at the passages. Which of the following—or which combination of them—does

5 Compare Schacht's partition (1983: 234–6) of the "biological-scientific" and "experiential-psychological" ways in which Nietzsche regards life.

Nietzsche mean? When he counsels us, for example, to "say Yes to life," which sense of life is intended? And similarly with his claim that "life is will to power": what kind of life does he so characterize?

1. Biological. Life = all organisms, or what it is to be an organism. So either (a) life is the sum total of living things, as when one says, "So far as we know, life is confined to this planet." Or (b) life is the property (being-alive) that all of these organisms possess, as when one says "Life is what they all have in common." If meant biologically, "saying Yes to life" would be affirming or valuing all organic life, or that property of aliveness that all of it has. And if meant biologically, "life is will to power" would say that organisms' aliveness either is or involves willing power. If it's life in this sense that underlies his values, Nietzsche's biology would play a crucial role indeed.

2. Human. Life = all humans, or what it is to be a human being. There can be the same distinction here between referring to the whole set of humans, or to their property of being-alive (or being-humanly-alive). In this case life is to be studied not by biology but by anthropology—yet in the same scientific fashion. If meant in this sense, "saying Yes to life" would mean affirming or valuing human life, and the claim that "life is will to power" would apply only to human life.

3. Phenomenal. Life = the experience of living, what it's like to live (either as an organism or as a human). When we say "Life is hard," I think we mean life in this sense. Meant so, "life" always involves a point of view, an intentionality that has this experience. And—looking ahead—this is how Nietzsche thinks of not just human life, but biological life in general. To understand organisms we must see them not as mechanical systems but as wills or drives, with perspectives and aims. (So life is something "lived," i.e., experienced, a sense captured in the German *erlebt*.) This is indeed part of what is meant by the claim that "life is will to power." If meant the same way, "saying Yes to life" would be affirming the (first-personal) effort or experience of living.

4. Personal. Life = that which a person is aware of living through. Each of us understands him/herself as living *a* life, *my* life between birth and death. Perhaps this is the special character of phenomenal life in the case of humans: the life recognizes about itself that it is this interval, before death, of first-personal effort and feeling. If I say "Life teaches me...," I probably mean life in this sense. And if Nietzsche advocates in this sense "saying Yes to life," he means affirming or valuing *my* life, my experience of living a life. The claim "life is will to power" would attribute this will to the standpoint that has this personal life in view.

5. Poetic. Life = (no definition is feasible; the term isn't a concept denoting a certain descriptive content). Let's distinguish two ways life might be meant poetically.

(a) "Life" is a metaphorical stand-in for something else. The most obvious case is *Zarathustra*'s personification of Life as a woman—although here we may suspect that Life represents life in one of the four prior senses. But it's also possible that Nietzsche *everywhere* uses "life" metaphorically and not in those senses—even where he doesn't explicitly personify it. Perhaps when he says Yes to life, it stands for that particular *way* of living he promotes to us. In this light, we might hear "life is will to power" as Nietzsche's announcement of what he'll be using "life" as a metaphor *for*: will to power.

b) "Life" is used not to communicate any content at all, even indirectly by metaphor, but to attune our feelings a certain way. It's used only emotively, not to designate or refer (even as metaphor). In this case the expression "life is will to power" might mean just "you should will power." Then Nietzsche would not really use life to justify his values, but to attach certain feelings to them. The term would function not as part of an argument, but in his rhetorical selling of his values.

These poetic uses of "life" thus pose a threat to my project: if *all* his uses are really poetic, especially in that emotive way, then he wouldn't mean them as arguments for his values after all. As we'll see though, there are many places Nietzsche clearly uses "life" to designate—in the biological, human, phenomenal, and personal senses—and to count as justifying his values. If he is tricking us here, and these arguments are also meant in that rhetorical spirit, there would be very little we could trust him on. I think we must assume that he does not cynically give arguments he knows are bad, just for their power to persuade.

On the other hand I do think that Nietzsche's poetic uses of "life" are extremely important to him. An adequate account must do justice to the strong affective force he gives it, in particular by embedding it in certain dramatic scenarios. These poetic uses express ideas about life that don't show up in the argument that runs through the biological and other senses. We must see how to connect the argumentative and affective uses of the term.

2 PASSAGES AND ISSUES

Let's start though with Nietzsche's most poetic and dramatic treatments of life, his personifications of her in *Thus Spoke Zarathustra*. What these mean, and also *whether* they mean some point about life we can formulate, will be ultimate issues for us. These passages open up another dimension of problems for us, and give us a fuller sense of Nietzsche's topic of life. Is there any argument in (or behind) this drama with "Life"? In which of the above senses is life here represented?

The personification of Life in *Zarathustra* begins in Z II: "The Dance-Song," where Zarathustra's song begins: "Into your eye I looked lately, O Life! And into the unfathomable [*Unergründliche*] I seemed then to be sinking. | But you pulled me out with a golden fishing-rod; mockingly you laughed when I called you unfathomable. | 'So runs the talk of all fishes,' you said; 'what *they* do not fathom is unfathomable. | But changeable am I only and wild and in all things a woman, and not a virtuous one…'"

Note here the image of *depth*, of life as an encompassing medium one sinks down into towards no bottom, no place to find ground. This lack of ground is *epistemic*: we can't find the explanation or truth about life, we can't see to the bottom of it. We can't see to the bottom, above all, of what it's *for*, of its purpose or meaning. (To life in which sense do these thoughts apply?) Notice also that Life implies that she *has* a ground, even if people can't find it.[6]

"The Dance-Song" then introduces a second female, his "wild Wisdom," and depicts the two of them jealous over him. Zarathustra sums the situation: "Thus it stands, then, among us three.

---

[6] Regarding the image of Life drawing him out of herself (*mit goldner Angel*): does this mean he leaves the medium or perspective of life? Nietzsche elsewhere denies this is possible, we'll see.

From the ground up I love only Life—and verily, most of all when I hate her! | But that I am good to Wisdom and often too good: that is because she reminds me so much of Life!"

Zarathustra's love for life belongs to a great host of passages in which Nietzsche promotes "saying Yes to life"; we'll examine these later. Notice here how the idea of ground (*Grund*) returns, in Zarathustra's striking statement that he loves only life "from the ground up." Now is this life's ground, or Zarathustra's? If he loves life from its own ground up, this would seem to mean loving it *as it is*, and hence knowing what it is—and knowing in particular what it's for, its ground as its purpose or meaning. So does Zarathustra think he has fathomed it after all? Or is it rather that he loves life "from the bottom of himself," i.e., wholeheartedly?

We should also remark the competition between his love for/by life, with that for/by wisdom. As his two loves they represent Zarathustra's (and Nietzsche's) ultimate ends. The second, "wisdom," is ambiguous: does it refer to Zarathustra's effort at truth, i.e., his will to truth, or to his achievement of it (the truth he knows)? In any case this attachment to truth stands in tension with his love of life, even though he cares about truth because it reminds him of life. We'll examine this conflict between life and truth.

Life as persona reappears soon in Z II: "On Self-Overcoming," to which I'll return. But let's jump first to Z III: "The Other Dance-Song," where Zarathustra's romance with life is resumed, again in a song sung by Zarathustra's soul to Life: "'Into your eye I looked lately, O Life: gold I saw in your night-eye glinting,—my heart stood still from this delight: | —a golden boat I saw glinting on nocturnal waters: a sinking, drinking, ever-winking golden rocking-boat!'" Note that life is again depicted as a sea. Now there's a boat, but a "sinking" boat that doesn't keep one out of life's depths. This is presumably the boat of Dionysus, bringing the new ideal.

After the song there is a conversation between Zarathustra and Life, in which she tells him: "'And even if we do not love each other from the ground up—, must one then be cross, because one does not love from the ground up? | And that I am good to you and often too good, that you know: and the reason [*Grund*] is that I am jealous of your Wisdom. Ah, that crazy old madwoman Wisdom! | If your Wisdom should ever desert you, ah! then my love too would desert you just as swiftly.'"

The idea of "loving from the ground up" returns, with the same ambiguity (whose ground?) we noted. Life doubts that they so love one another, but seems to reject that requirement. Is it full insight, or full devotion, that's not required? And she says that she is "good" to him from jealousy of his wisdom, which is indeed all that sustains her love of him. Once again: in which of the above senses of "life" might it make sense to think that love for it is in this kind of conflict with love of truth?

There then follows the climax of the book, rich with significance: "Thereupon Life looked pensively behind her and about her and said softly: 'O Zarathustra, you are not true enough to me! | You have long not loved me as much as you say you do; I know you are thinking that you will to leave me soon....| 'Yes,' I answered hesitantly, 'but you also know that—' And I said something into her ear, right through her tangled yellow crazy locks of hair. | 'You *know* that, O Zarathustra? No one knows that. — —'" Presumably Zarathustra has said that he knows he will eternally return. He then marries Life with the "ring" of eternal return, and she changes her name to Eternity in the final chapter of Part III.[7]

---

[7] See the illuminating account of the drama of Z in Lampert 1986.

What's the meaning of these dramatic events at the climax of the book Nietzsche valued most? Is there any philosophical *claim* or *argument* in this drama with Life? Or can we at least find hints or indications of what Nietzsche means to claim and argue elsewhere? And there is still the challenge to say what "Life" stands for here: biological life, or human life, or phenomenal aliveness, or Zarathustra's own life? Or does the personification function "just" poetically or rhetorically, to affect us?

This device of personifying some abstraction as a woman is used elsewhere by Nietzsche. *Zarathustra*'s "Wisdom" is echoed in the famous opening of the Preface to *Beyond Good and Evil*, "Supposing truth is a woman." And *Zarathustra*'s "Life" is anticipated in *GS* 339, entitled "*Vita femina*," which concludes: "But perhaps that is the strongest magic of life: a gold-worked veil of beautiful possibilities lies over it, promising, resisting, bashful, mocking, compassionate, seductive. Yes, life is a woman!"

Obviously enough, these "femalizations" are adopted where the abstract entity is something that Nietzsche loves or strains towards. Woman is Nietzsche's personification of endhood, of what one wants, loves, wills. This personification gives to this willing a specifically *erotic* character. Is there any larger significance to this? What is it, to stand in an erotic relation to life—and again, to life in what sense?

Now I've skipped over one important section in *Zarathustra* using this personification of life: *Z* II: "On Self-Overcoming." It has a somewhat different character than the others. For here, Nietzsche explicitly relates the character Life to a discussion of the (kind of) life that is being personified. He partly does this by having Life describe herself. Hence he offers much more content about life than in the other personifications. The content he announces, of course, is that life is will to power.

Notice that Zarathustra first seems to derive the point from third-personal observation: "Where I found the living, there I found will to power; and even in the will of one who serves I found a will to be master." But he then presents this as something told him by Life: "And this secret did Life herself tell to me. 'Behold,' she said, 'I am that *which must always overcome itself.* | Indeed, you call it will to procreate or drive towards an end, towards the higher, farther, more manifold: but all this is one and one secret.'"

A bit later, Life gives Nietzsche's famous expression: "'He surely missed the truth who shot at it the words "will to existence [*Dasein*]": this will—does not exist! | For: what is not cannot will; but what is in existence, how could that still will to exist! | Only, where Life is, there too is will: though not will to life, but—thus I teach you—will to power! | Much is valued by the living more highly than life itself; but out of this very valuing there speaks—will to power!'— | Thus did Life once teach me: and with this, you who are wisest, I go on to solve the riddle of your hearts." He solves the riddle of their hearts, because he sees their deepest aim, at power.

3   LIFE'S ENDS

Let's now begin to address these two sets of puzzles about Nietzsche's use of "life": over its abstract role in his justification of his values and its exotic presentation in a sexual scenario. Since it is the account of life as will to power that gives his most obvious ground for his values, let's begin there.[8] This claim that life is will to power appears to be a *biological* point, an account of the life of all organisms. Nietzsche purports to uncover life as such scientifically—not of course so much by his own observations of other organisms, as by reflection on the biological literature he read so attentively.

WP 641 (1883–4) gives this definition: "A multiplicity of forces, connected by a common nutrition-procedure, we call 'life'. To this nutrition-procedure, as a means of making it possible, belong all so-called feelings, representations, thoughts, i.e. (1) a striving-against all other forces, (2) a preparation for this by form and rhythm, (3) an evaluation in regard to incorporation or separation." This presents forces as accruing around a "nutrition-procedure," i.e., a certain metabolic mechanism. This might suggest that nutrition and the aim to eat is our deepest project, and that the intentional "striving" against others is a secondary means.

But elsewhere Nietzsche insists that nutrition and eating are themselves expressions of life's basic directedness, its will to power. The organism aims to "incorporate" other organisms not for the sake of sustaining itself (nor reproducing itself) but in order to grow by overcoming.[9] WP 681 (1886–7): "life is *not* adaptation of inner conditions to outer, but will to power, which, [working] from within, subdues and incorporates ever more 'outer.'" And WP 656 (1887): "Appropriation and incorporation is above all a willing to overwhelm, a forming, shaping and reshaping until finally the overwhelmed has gone completely over into the power of the attacker and has increased it."[10]

So although Nietzsche is critical of "teleology," his main claim about life attributes this particular aim or purpose to it. It's by virtue of this aiming that organisms have perspectives and interpret. WP 643 (1885–6): "The will to power *interprets*: the formation of an organ is a matter of interpretation; it defines limits, determines degrees, variations of power. Mere variations of power could not feel themselves to be such: there must be present something that wills to grow, that interprets the value of whatever else wants to grow.... (*The organic process constantly presupposes interpretations.*)" Note that the thesis of will to power is not a metaphysical or (universal) ontological claim, but a biological one: its principal application is to *life*, and Nietzsche sees the extension to inorganic nature as speculative and dispensable.[11]

These passages have all come from Nietzsche's notebooks, but the main points are made in the published works too. Here are three prominent passages. BGE 13: "Physiologists should think twice before putting down the self-preservation drive as the cardinal drive of an organic being. A living thing [*etwas Lebendiges*] wills above all to *discharge* its strength— life itself is *will to power* —: self-preservation is only one of the indirect and most frequent *results*."[12] GS 349: "The struggle for existence [*Dasein*] is only an *exception*, a temporary restriction of the life-will [*Lebenswillens*]; the great and small struggle revolves everywhere around preponderance, around growth and expansion, around power, in accordance with

---

[8] I give much fuller accounts of will to power in Richardson 1996: §1.1 and 2004: chapter 1, §5; the latter, neo-Darwinian account is more consonant with the one I sketch here.

[9] WP 702 (1888): "Let us take the simplest case, that of primitive nourishing: the protoplasm stretches its pseudopods out, in search of something that opposes it—not out of hunger, but will to power." Also WP 657 (1886–7), WP 651 (1887–8), WP 652 (1888). Nietzsche argues similarly that procreation is a derivative project in WP 654 (1885–6). WP 658 (1885) makes the general point: "the organic functions translated back into the basic will, the will to power,—and splitting off from it."

[10] Compare the definition of life in WP 642 (1885).

[11] E.g., BGE 36; WP 689 (1888).

[12] This is echoed later in BGE, in 259: "life simply *is* will to power [*Leben eben Wille zur Macht ist*]."

the will to power which is simply [*eben*] the will of life [*Wille des Lebens*, mistranslated in the Cambridge edition as 'will to life')." And *GM* II: 12 says that in making "adaptation" basic, Darwinists like Spencer "mistake the essence [*Wesen*] of life, its *will to power*; thereby the fundamental priority of the spontaneous, attacking, infringing, reinterpreting, reordering, and formative forces is overlooked."

As these show, Nietzsche often puts this point in opposition to an alternative he thinks is widespread, shared diversely by Spinoza, Schopenhauer, and Darwinists: that life strives to survive, to exist.[13] So *WP* 688 (1888): "It can be shown most clearly for every living thing, that it does everything, *not* in order to preserve itself, but to become *more*." And *GS* 349 again: "To will to preserve oneself is the expression of distress, of a limitation of the genuinely basic drive of life [*Lebens-Grundtriebes*] which aims at *the expansion of power* and in this willing frequently puts in question and even sacrifices self-preservation."

What is this "power" that life is distinctively towards? I suggest that we understand it as a "growth by control." The rough picture is of organisms—and even their organic parts— as competing to subordinate and control one another, to grow by taking power over one another. In particular, organisms are bodies distinguished by their particular sets of *drives*, which are behavioral dispositions directed at particular acts or outcomes. And Nietzsche's claim about will to power is that these manifold drives all aim, not just at their distinguishing ends (sex for the sex drive, eating for the hunger drive), but at the more ultimate end of such growth and control. Eating is perhaps the most obvious (and brutal) way of growing by overcoming: the organism "incorporates" another's tissue. But there are many other ways of incorporating other living things by subordinating their activity to one's own (including our efforts with Nietzsche now).

And yet, when Nietzsche attributes will to power to "life," it may seem he *couldn't*, or at least *shouldn't*, mean life biologically. For how can it be plausible to attribute this end-directedness, with its associated intentionality, to all living things? Doesn't this involve attributing mental or cognitive powers to them? And how can we seriously suppose that the amoeba or "protoplasm" (which Nietzsche often speaks of this way[14]) has "drives" thus aimed at power?

In *Nietzsche's New Darwinism* I try to show how Nietzsche can (and sometimes does) fully naturalize this biological notion of will to power by presenting it as a directedness designed into organisms by natural selection. So life values in (by virtue of) its selected plasticity towards outcomes. The amoeba's hunger drive is its dispositional responsiveness to the conditions around it, by which it identifies and assimilates food. It thereby uses these environmental resources for its own growth, i.e., the enhancement of its powers. This outcome "power" is the end of this disposition not because there is any "preview" of that outcome within the amoeba, but because that's what the disposition was selected to do (that's what gave it selective advantage).[15] So the outcome (power) explains why the disposition is there in the amoeba, and this explanatory structure is what it is, for an outcome to be an end.

By naturalizing end-directedness in this way, Nietzsche can (perhaps) naturalize a biological intentionality or perspectivity as well. Science—at least science so far—has tried

---

[13] Earlier Nietzsche often speaks of the end as preservation, however; see, e.g., *GS* 1.

[14] E.g., *WP* 656 (1887), *WP* 651 (1887–8), *WP* 702 (1888).

[15] Here I lean on the "etiological" analysis of functions pioneered by Wright, e.g., in his 1973; I develop this in Richardson 2004: chapter 1, §3.

to reduce nature to "a *happening* arranged *for sight and touch*, consequently as motions" (*WP* 640 [1883–4]).[16] So it treats them simply as mechanisms. Nietzsche insists we must go beyond science-so-far by introducing "will," i.e., directed effort. In being responsively directed towards certain ends, organisms have "perspectives" or "views"—as even the amoeba does in its differential responsiveness to environmental cues. He can argue this without sacrificing his naturalism, by taking this directedness to be constituted by selection. Hence, as hinted already, all biological life is also phenomenal.

Still, even if Nietzsche does think of all biological life as willing power in this way, it may seem that this view can't be that important to him, given that his attention is overwhelmingly focused on one particular kind of organism, the *human*. Isn't all that matters that he thinks of humans as willing power in this way? So aren't his biological claims about life quite aside from the main point?

But I think it's important to Nietzsche that "life" also refers to something *wider* than the human—yet something that is represented and accessible *within* us. For he thinks that the wills or drives of other kinds of life are built into us, by the way evolution works: our genetic line passed through the simpler modes of life, which has built their dispositions and aims into each of us. So Nietzsche shares, for his own reasons, Aristotle's view of life as forming a *hierarchy*, and of the human as containing "lower" forms of life within it. Here "lower" simply means capable of less diverse and effective control, i.e., with fewer and simpler power drives.

This means that "life's ends," the ends of biological life, are to an important extent built into me individually. Life is not just the largest genus to which I belong, but my inner constitution.[17] More precisely, a range of other members of this genus are represented in me: I bear parts of their aims and perspectives. So I also bear samples from the stances of earlier stages of *human* life. This persistence of evolutionarily earlier traits is a very important idea for Nietzsche; he harps on it especially in *Human, All Too Human*.

Nietzsche thinks of each human life as opening out into biological life generally. It is a medium we enter at our own point, but in which we communicate with all the rest. Here are a few characteristic passages (there are many others like these): "The human is *not* only an individual [*Individuum*], but the on-living collective-organic [*Fortlebende Gesammt-Organische*] in one particular line" (*WP* 678 [1886–7]). And "The *ego* is a hundred times more than just a unit in the chain of members; it is this *chain* itself, entirely" (*WP* 682 [1887]).[18]

This reveals in turn another way Nietzsche thinks he has access to (biological) life's essence: by experiencing or feeling it within himself. The reason is not metaphysical (as in Schopenhauer) but naturalistic and biological: these other levels of life are built into us, are elements within us. (Recall *Zarathustra*'s depiction of life as a sea—its depths reach down within us.) The inevitable image is of them as lower strata in our dispositional set. What's built into us are layers of "directed efforts," tendencies plastic towards outcomes or ends. Inasmuch as these dispositions are responsive and intentional, we can experience them, even deep and primordial ones, ourselves.

---

[16] Also *WP* 634 (1888), *WP* 625 (1888).
[17] *BGE* 258: "the foundation of the affects, which is called 'life.'"
[18] Also *WP* 687 (1887), *WP* 785 (1887), *WP* 379 (1887), *WP* 373 (1888).

As Nietzsche often thinks of it, these lower strata of life's willing are built into us in our *bodies*. Here he uses "body" in a way that *distinguishes* it from our spirit, from our conscious-linguistic intentionality (our agency). Elsewhere, to be sure, he emphasizes that we are *just* our bodies, and that spirit is just a fact about the body. So *Z* I: "Of the Despisers of the Body": "Body am I entirely, and nothing more; and soul is only the name of something of the body." Still he continues to use "body" to refer to this *subset* of the body's capacities, those made not by social history but by a more ancient, prehuman genetic evolution.

Because these deep projects are intentional, they are part of an individual human's stance and are accessible in a first-personal attitude. It's possible to make explicit, to bring to awareness, the end-directedness in our body. We can notice better than we usually do "what it's like" to will as these bodily drives do. And I think this is another kind of access Nietzsche thinks he has to the truth that biological (and human) life is will to power. It's not just by those studies of biological works, but also by a kind of phenomenology—of course Nietzsche doesn't have this term—that he thinks he can see this truth. By "living" his body more alertly, he can see the biological will at work in it.

So what's most important to Nietzsche is the *human* way of encountering this level of *biological* life within us—understanding both of these as something *phenomenal*. But what about the fourth sense for "life"—what I called the personal? Does Nietzsche give any importance to our awareness of "living a life," of being in a single passage between birth and death? Not surprisingly there are many discussions of life in this sense in *Ecce Homo*. But they also occur in many places outside that explicit autobiography; thus *GS* 324: "*In media vita*. No! Life has not disappointed me! From year to year I find it much truer, more desirable and more mysterious,—since the day the great liberator overcame me, the thought that life could be an experiment for the knowledge-seeker." Here I believe "life" refers to his individual life as he has it to live—he shows here his reflection on just how to live it.

It is a part of this individual life that he lives it in this body that bears as it does many strata of drives—dispositions and projects—laid down in the social and evolutionary past. "Life" in a biological sense is represented in the deepest layers of this bodily end-directedness; this is something generic, built as well into all the other descendants since its first fixing by selection. We live this personal life, before death, in a body whose biological wills must be given their due, as we so live it. We'll see later how this relation to a personal life is the real center of Nietzsche's own values.

4 Values: In Our Bodies and as Agents

Having sorted some of the multiplicity in Nietzsche's idea of "life," let's now turn our attention to the "values" he's going to use this idea of life to correct. What *are* values, according to Nietzsche? *Werth* is another of his favorite, indispensable terms.

I've said that it's crucial to distinguish between two *ways* in which Nietzsche speaks about values—two ways he "posits" values. (Later I'll add that he also posits two *kinds* of values, cutting across this first distinction.) (a) On the one hand he studies, in his special naturalistic way, different kinds of values, as the intentional objects of particular acts of valuing—in particular by groups of persons. (b) But on the other hand he values certain things, himself: i.e., he makes value judgments, he expresses that these things are valuable *to him*.

In this section let's focus on his naturalistic study of values. Here he makes, of course, no commitment to valuing these things himself; indeed he most often studies values he clearly does *not* share in. In section 5 we'll look at the way he tries to move from this study of values (and life) to his own values, which he commends to us.

Now familiarly enough, Nietzsche is in one sense an anti-realist about values; they arise *only* through intentional acts of valuing. Z I: "Of the Thousand and One Goals": "First through esteeming [*Schätzen*] is there value." But he's certainly a realist about these acts of valuing: there's a fact to the matter, what values what.

Moreover it's crucial to notice that he thinks that these real acts of valuing extend far more widely than we suppose. He attributes valuing to all biological life: "'Alive': that means already *esteeming*:—| In all willing is *esteeming*—and will is there in the organic" (*KSA* 11: 25 [433]); "Valuations [*Werthschätzungen*] lie in all functions of the organic being" (*KSA* 11: 26 [72]).

We've already seen how all organisms have had directedness (teleology) designed into them, in their plastic (responsive) drives. And now it's easy to add, that Nietzsche thinks of this directedness, this willing, as already a valuing: its ends are values, as are the means it is responsive to: "But willing: = willing an end. End contains a valuation." (*WP* 260 [1883–4]) Once again this is *not* a matter of attributing minds or cognitive-representational powers to organisms and their parts. Organisms value power not by having a concept of power, but by having been selected to be responsive towards outcomes that enhance their power or control. So even the amoeba values power by its responsive disposition, designed into it by selection, to appropriate other organisms into itself as food; this disposition "wills power" inasmuch as it was selected because it brings about this "growth by control."

Thus Nietzsche thinks that all biological life—every organism—values. But he also thinks that this biological life is built into each of us, in our underlying bodily drives. So these are a way in which each of *us* values, as well. And although Nietzsche cares not at all about how an amoeba or a cat or a chimp values, he thinks that an "animal" kind of valuing operates in us all the time, in the "part" of us we call our body. I'll refer to this lower level of valuing in us as *body values*; these are the ends in us that we share with other living things. Nietzsche speaks of this valuing whenever he speaks of our *drives*.

But of course this isn't what we usually call our "values," which are the values we're aware of and put into words, the principles we refer to in order to steer our actions. They are our ethics or morality. By contrast with body values, I'll call these *agent values*. These are *conscious* and *linguistic*, the rules or ideals we formulate and then refer to in "moments of decision." Making a decision is, in many cases at least, precisely a matter of acting on the basis of such reference. What does Nietzsche say about values in this ordinary sense?

We greatly pride ourselves on this agency; we claim to be "sovereign individuals" in it. It's a main mark of distinction for the human. Such valuing seems to involve a very different kind of teleology than we've seen holds for biological values. The amoeba "aims" at power insofar as this is the outcome its responsive dispositions were selected to effect. The outcome explains insofar as ancestral achievements of it gave selective advantage explaining the disposition now. But when we "value" a certain outcome in our ordinary sense this is because we represent it to ourselves in advance, desire it, and act accordingly; this is what we call "agency." So here the outcome explains as "represented in advance," which can seem to be the only real kind of teleology.

But Nietzsche raises strong doubts against this agency. He thinks we should be far more suspicious of it than we are. He questions, that is, not just the particular rules and ideals— the *content*—we value in this way. He also questions *this very way of valuing*, this very way of deciding our behavior. His critiques of "what" and "how" we value are of course linked; they express a common diagnosis of our agent values.

Nietzsche makes two kinds of attacks on agency (and agent values).[19] They may seem inconsistent. (a) On the one hand he belittles agency as epiphenomenal, as not really effective. Things are quite thoroughly settled elsewhere in us—in our bodily drives in particular—and our "decisions" based on conscious values merely express those real forces. (b) But on the other hand he decries our agency as harmful, as all too effective *against* our real interests.

(a) Take first the claim that agency is epiphenomenal. Sometimes the point is that the entire causal process works elsewhere, in the body, and our conscious choices are after-effects that change nothing themselves. But more commonly the point is that those choices, and the agent values they're steered by, are *tools* of bodily drives. So they're effective indeed, but only as instruments for the real "deciders" beneath them, the body values. So Z I: "Of the Despisers of the Body": "Behind your thoughts and feelings, my brother, stands a mighty commander, an unknown wise man—his name is Self. In your body he dwells, he is your body. |...The creating body created spirit for itself as a hand of its will."[20] And *WP* 254 (1885–6): "*what is the meaning of evaluating* [*Werthschätzen*] *itself?*...Answer: moral evaluating is an *exegesis*, a way of interpreting. The exegesis itself is a *symptom* of certain physiological conditions, likewise of a particular spiritual level of ruling judgments: *Who interprets?*—our *affects*." *WP* 314 (1887–8): "Our most sacred convictions, the unchangeable in regard to supreme values, are *judgments of our muscles*."

This is the first way agency is a sham. It is not as distinct and independent from that biological way of valuing as it claims. The representation may indeed explain the behavior in some of these cases—it does indeed do some work—yet this explanation is incomplete unless we see what explains the representation. And when we do, we see how agent values rest on the other kind of teleology after all, and so have their fuller significance in that same body value way. When Nietzsche thinks of our agent values this way he finds them for the most part benign: as instruments for body-valuing, they serve the latter's largely healthy ends.

(b) But Nietzsche also has a second story. This makes agency not only effective but also *harmful*, by the way it works *against* the interests in our body. In this light Nietzsche sees agency as favoring interests foreign to the body. In particular, agency is a "secret agent" on behalf of *society*, understood to require a very strong *homogeneity* and likeness among its members. And we will only be sufficiently homogeneous if we very strongly *want* to be like one another, want to "do as one does." Agency and its agent values were designed—in the same extended sense in which natural selection designs—by prehistorical cultural processes

---

[19] I give a fuller account of Nietzsche's genealogy for agency in Richardson 2009.
[20] Z I: "Of the Afterworldsmen" says that even belief in an "other world" is rooted in the body—in a body's despair of itself.

to "tame" and "domesticate" the human animal. Nietzsche tells this story in the famous second essay of the *Genealogy*.

Agency is the "ability to promise," above all the ability to promise to obey the social rules. This involves the capacity to *remember* the rules in the heat of the moment when drives are engaged—when the urge to take the marketplace fruit is strongest. One becomes conscious of a linguistic formula such as "don't steal," and this awareness has a crucially *inhibitive* effect: one *refrains* from acting as the drive pushes.[21] This ability to promise—to act not by one's immediate drives but by conscious reference to principles—is deeply designed to subordinate us to social rules—to turn us into "herd animals."

So the key feature of agent values—uppermost in Nietzsche's mind—is that they're designed not in my interest (not for my personal life) but for social purposes, by a kind of "group selection." So values are the "tablet of things held good" that "hangs over every people" (Z I: "Of the Thousand and One Goals"). *WP* 275 (1886–7) answers the question "who speaks in our values?" (which used to be answered "God"): "My answer, taken not from metaphysics but from animal physiology: *the herd-instinct speaks*. It wills to be master: hence its 'thou shalt!'(:) it will allow the individual to matter only in the sense of the whole, for the good of the whole."[22]

So agent values are not individual but social; to be a value is to hang over a society this way. And the agent's *impression* of sovereignty, of choosing in his/her valuing, is false—is indeed designed into agency as a refinement of social control. I have my values not by choice, but by their seduction of me—a seduction the social process has designed them for. I think I'm free in my valuing, but this is the better to steer me to a socializing end. I think I'm doing what I decide, but it was decided long ago, in the social process, that so doing serves that end.

How can we reconcile (a) and (b)? How can agent values express both bodily drives, but also these interests foreign to the body? As I've noted, Nietzsche uses "body" elastically, and here too. For there is a way in which those foreign interests—the social purpose to herd and homogenize me—*are* built into my body.[23] They are there in the form of a "herd instinct," the deposit in my body of that long, prehistorical domesticating of my ancestors. Still, in another light Nietzsche regards this instinct as not quite so "bodily" as the drives and dispositions settled by genetic selection in our deeper past.

5 LIFE'S END AS CORRECTIVE CRITERION

Having surveyed some of the complexities in Nietzsche's notions of life and of value, let's come back now to his argument from life to values. This might be considered his strategy for getting from a *fact* to a *value*: for persuading us that because life *is* so and so, such and such is *good*. We'll see that this argument from life to a criterial value takes two forms. Sometimes

---

[21] This is why our agent values are deeply *ascetic*; GM III claims that all (human) values so far have promoted "the ascetic ideal."

[22] *WP* 276 (1886–7): "The whole of E(uropean) morality is based upon what is useful for the herd."

[23] Z I: "Of the Bestowing Virtue": "In a hundred ways up to now has spirit as well as virtue flown away and made mistakes. Ah, in our bodies all this delusion and mistaking still dwell: body and will it has become there."

the point seems to be that life itself *is* the ultimate good.[24] But elsewhere, and principally I think, the point is that life essentially *values* a certain good, and by doing so makes that good ultimate. We can separate three main questions.

1. First, what *authority* does life have? Nietzsche should give us a reason to accept its standing, to determine a criterion for values.
2. Next, what *criterion* does life supply? What basic value does it provide, to be used as a standard in the revaluation of values?
3. Third, what *correction* does this criterion make? What are the consequences of applying it? This is a question of results, of how this revaluation will change our values.

A. I'll begin by addressing these questions with respect to the *biological* idea of life and examining how this idea supports a redesign of our *agent* values. This is the way I addressed these questions in *Nietzsche's New Darwinism*, and I think it is the most obvious way to think of Nietzsche's argument from life to values. But I'll eventually (in **B**) suggest that it is crucially incomplete, and that to get the full scope of his point we need to bring in the *personal* idea of life and see how it requires us to redesign more than just our agent values. To afford space for these further ideas—which will let us address those "poetic" treatments of life in *Zarathustra*—I will have to present this very rich first argument very compactly.

1. Consider first the authority of life—its authority to give (assign) a lesson or standard to us. What's the proof that life itself is good, much less the ultimate good? Or, why should what life values be thereby the ultimate good? Life needs authority, and it needs this authority, we should bear in mind, for *each* of us (his readers) individually. Nietzsche would want us each to ask: why should *I* care about life, or what it aims at? If there's an end built into biological life, why should it matter to me? This authority in life must give me a reason to revalue my values, and in particular my agent values—those I put into words and cite to myself in my deliberations and decisions.

Now Nietzsche has a long-standing interest in the question of the "value of life" (*Werth des Lebens*).[25] He initially poses his disagreement with Schopenhauer in this way: he replaces the latter's negative judgment on life with a positive one. In this early period he thinks it is the philosopher's main task to make a judgment on this question.[26] He discusses the conditions required for such a judgment to be just or correct.[27] Even as late as *BGE* 205 he suggests (without criticism) that the philosopher "demands of himself a judgment, a Yes or No, not about the sciences but about life and the value of life."

[24] Hunt (1991: 212) so reads him.
[25] Notice his very lengthy notes on Dühring's *The Value of Life* preserved as *KSA* 8: 9 [1] (1875).
[26] *KSA* 8: 3 [63] (1875) says that the philosopher uses the philologist's labors "to make a statement about the *value of life.*" *KSA* 8: 20 [12] (1876–7): "It is perhaps the most important goal of humanity, that the value of life be measured, and the reason [*Grund*] why it is there be correctly determined. It awaits for this the appearance of the highest intellect; for only this can settle the value or disvalue of life conclusively." (Cf. *KSA* 8: 5 [188] [1875], which adds the requirement of "the warmest heart.")
[27] *UM* III: 3: "The verdict of the philosophers of ancient Greece on the value of existence [*Daseins*] says so much more than a modern verdict does because they had life itself before and around them in luxuriant perfection"; see how the section ends.

However Nietzsche also has doubts from early on whether the project is feasible.[28] And he eventually comes to think there is something incoherent in the effort to state the value of life. *TI* "The Problem of Socrates" 2: "Judgments, value-judgments on life, for or against, can ultimately never be true: they have value only as symptoms, they can be taken seriously only as symptoms,—in themselves, judgments like these are stupidities. One must stretch out one's fingers and make an effort to grasp this amazing subtlety [*finesse*], *that the value of life cannot be evaluated* [*abgeschätzt*]." Judgments about the value of life will be crucially used as symptoms of whether a person "says Yes to life."

But the reason these judgments can't be true—Nietzsche here thinks[29]—is that life is the source or precondition for all values, so that it stands before and beyond them. He means biological life, understood as something phenomenal; it is the "source" of all values in an intentional way: it *means* them. Values arise only by and in (biological) life's end-direct-edness and the valuing this involves. They are the intentional objects of the valuing life engages in. "The viewpoint of 'value' is the viewpoint of *preservation-enhancement conditions* with respect to complex forms of relative duration of life within becoming" (*WP* 715 [1887–8]).

So the argument that it makes no sense to speak of the "value of life" still gives life a certain authority. Life is not the ultimate value (good), but it is the ultimate valuer. And Nietzsche tries to use this authority to pick out *what* it values as the ultimate good; this will be, of course, power. He has several reasons for denying that life is itself the good. One is the transcendental point behind *TI*: "The Problem of Socrates" 2 and "Morality as Anti-Nature" 5. Another is his idea that to make "life" the good is to value merely "staying-alive" or survival; it's to suppose that the end is "more life" in the sense of *longer* life, and perhaps of *more numerous* life (we know how little these matter to Nietzsche). Making "life" the good flattens the differences between levels or degrees of life, and pro-motes those efforts at more of a merely generic life. Life is not a consequentialist good we're to maximize.

On the other hand, life, as what values, is the source of all values. And its valuing takes a form that gives life a presence in the ultimate value after all. For although life does not essen-tially value life,[30] it does so value power, and power is *life's own growth*. This reflexive character of life's valuing brings itself into its valuing: life wants *more of itself*. But the character of this "more" is (as it were) qualitative: it's not longer life or more numerous life, but this life brought to a higher level of capacity and control. So it is life's own essential valuing that sets the dimen-sion in which life becomes more or better, and specifies the sense in which life—its qualitative increase—is indeed "the good."

2. Let's look more closely at Nietzsche's way of extracting a criterial value from life. The rough lines of the argument seem pretty evident. Life—biological life—has as its "essence"

---

[28] *HAH* I: 32: "All judgments as to the value of life have evolved illogically and are therefore unjust." *KSA* 10: 6 [1] (1882–3): "all estimates [*Ansätze*] about the value of life (are) false."

[29] The passage continues: "Not by the living, who are an interested party, even a bone of contention [*Streitobjekt*], and not judges; not by the dead for other reasons." We can't step out of life's perspective, and still evaluate. The point is put most directly later in *TI*: "Morality as Anti-Nature" 5. See how Schacht (1983: 395–8) and Reginster (2006: 82–3) develop the point.

[30] This is the difference Nietzsche thinks he has with Darwin: life doesn't live in order to stay alive, i.e., to survive or preserve itself. The will *of* life is not a will *to* life, but to power.

will to power, i.e., a kind of directedness at power. So power is life's essential end, and this licenses it as the criterion for revaluing values.

Obviously the argument turns crucially on the notion of essence. That is, it turns not so much on this term—though Nietzsche does repeatedly use it (*Wesen*)[31]—but on the idea that willing power is somehow *central* or *crucial* to life in a way that requires an allegiance or respect for it. Nietzsche would want "essence" to carry as little metaphysical weight as possible, but he does need some way to privilege will to power, among the other properties living things have, so that it can have the authority over values he wants for it.

Without so singling out some particular aspect of life as "essential," it seems that life *couldn't* supply a criterion, since in that case it would apply to *everything* we do or will. This is the problem of all-inclusiveness we noticed near the start; we saw there how Nietzsche remarks this problem in *BGE* 9: "'live according to life'—how could you *not* do that? Why make a principle of what you yourselves are and must be?" If *all* values come from life, why don't they all have the same status—each thing we will just as worthy as anything else? Specifying some values as essential privileges them, and lets them serve as correctives to other values—those we hold as agents, in particular.

So what's essential is a directedness at an end. This end can be achieved or realized to a greater or lesser degree. So there is a scale, running from lower/worse to higher/better, along which all living things can be ranked—are ranked by their own essential aiming.[32] Individual organisms move up or down on it, as ascending or declining life. Importantly, Nietzsche tends to conflate these degrees of achievement of the aim with degrees of the *directedness*: an organism ranking high in power is also a more complete or adequate *will* to power. Because will to power likewise occurs in degrees, life's essence is differentially realized. Higher life, in more adequately willing power, is also "more alive."[33] But what is it about will to power that can make it, in this special way, life's essence?

The obvious suggestion is *generality*: will to power is the most widespread characteristic of living things, what they all have in common. So all living things will—and value—power, even though they may value other nonuniversal ends besides. But now why should this generality of will to power make it matter to me? Obviously, as a living thing myself it follows that I value this common end, as well as all my particular ends. But what reason do I have to prioritize the common over the particular? Why should the common or shared valuing give me reason to revalue the agent values I now steer by?

Rather than its generality, I think it is will to power's *depth* that makes it essential for Nietzsche. Will to power lies "beneath" all our other willing and aiming. This depth has chiefly a teleological character: will to power sets the first end, which functions as the "final"

<hr/>

[31] E.g., *BGE* 259; *GM* II: 12.

[32] *WP* 592 (1886–7) says that the struggle between "sickly, despairing life" and "richer, less degenerate life" is "one kind of life in struggle with another....Here the argument must settle that a rank-order is necessary,—that the first problem is that of the *rank-order of kinds of life*." Notice *EH* I: 1's expression "ladder of life."

[33] See *EH*: "Maxims and Arrows" 2 on *Mehr-leben*.

end for all our other values. Other aimings all arise for the sake of, or as a means to, this power. And the organism persists in them due to an implicit judgment that they serve its own strengthening. So it is the effort at power that gives the ultimate point to our other values, including our explicit agent values. This primary willing is our most persistent effort, even ineliminable and inescapable. So will to power is "essential" not because of external relations of similarity I bear by it to other living things, but because it is embedded in a special way in me, so as to be inescapably and basically motivating. This makes essence biological more than metaphysical, we might say.

Now notice that in leaning on the idea that life's deep aim is inescapable for us, Nietzsche faces a dilemma. His use of life's essence as corrective criterion depends on two ideas that seem in tension: (i) we can't help but will (value) power (because it's essential to life, hence our deepest viewpoint); (ii) yet we *do* will things incompatible with power, which is why that criterion is needed as *corrective*. The advice to aim at power only occurs, we've seen, because it happens that we often *do not* aim at power. So this essence (willing power) is not completely compelling: we can "fall away from it." What kind of essence is this? And what kind of grip can it then have?

We fall away from willing power in our agent values, in particular—that is, in the conscious aims and principles we try to live by. Nietzsche argues that these have come unhooked from the deep pursuit of power, and aim us at quite different and incompatible things. For agent values are mainly set by *morality*, which aims them often directly *against* life as will to power. And yet Nietzsche also thinks that deep effort at power is somehow still operative even here: "When we talk about values we are under the inspiration, under the optic, of life: life itself forces us to posit values, life itself evaluates through us, *when* we posit values" (*TI*: "Morality as Anti-Nature" 5). How can he have it both ways?

I suggest that Nietzsche relies here on a commonplace idea: the organism's deep directedness at power can support (motivate) agent values that are hostile and damaging to power, because those values can *seem* to serve its power (though really they don't). So he posits an epistemic error, but posits it in an implicit and bodily will that judges quite unconsciously in us and sometimes judges wrong. Morality appears, to this implicit will, as if it furthers my life, but in fact it doesn't. By exposing how our agent values conflict with that deep aim in us, he shows that we only hold them by an error.

Why do life-hostile values arise in the first place, if our deep aim is for "more life"? Nietzsche has several complicated stories to tell here. But his principal idea, I think, is that values always *originate* in a person or people whose power they express (are meant to serve). However, these values can then be transmitted to other kinds of life for which they are decidedly *not* the means to grow. This transmission can happen by simple inheritance, or copying, or by compulsion or seduction. All our values originated as means to power, but the question is *whose* power. Our usual error lies in living by values designed in the interest of different kinds of persons than ourselves.

Even herd morality develops as a means to power—but it's the power of the social group. Selection favors societies that best subordinate members into an effective large group. It is because they favor the power of the group, that agent values are settled as they are. Moreover, we should notice that it is in each case a particular group, a group organized on behalf of a particular kind of person. So Nietzsche's famous story about master and slave moralities describes how these two systems of agent values express the interests (and will to power) of two different kinds and sets of individuals. It may often be that agent values favor the power of a very different kind of person than myself.

Hence seeing life's essence as will to power reveals the underlying end, which all others were adopted as means to—though the latter's status as means has been missed or forgotten. Nietzsche puts the point so: "Humanity has always repeated the same mistake: it has made a means to life into a *standard* of life | : so that instead of finding the measure in the highest enhancement of life itself,...it has used the *means* to a quite particular life to the exclusion of other forms of life, in short for the critique and selection of life | : i.e. the human finally loves the means for their own sake and *forgets* they are means: so that they enter his consciousness as goals, as standards for ends | : i.e. *a particular species of human* treats the conditions for its existence as conditions which ought to be imposed as a law" (*WP* 354 [1888]).[34]

The most basic types for whom values are designed are ascending and declining life; which of these values makes the crucial difference. When declining life values, it might seem *not* to aim at growth but at the decrease, decline, and even extinction of life. And sometimes Nietzsche puts it so. In *TI*: "Morality as Anti-Nature" 5 he says that "the anti-natural in morality" is the value judgment "of declining, of weakened, of exhausted, of condemned life"; it is "the *décadence-instinct* itself that makes an imperative of itself: it says '*be destroyed* [*geh zu Grunde*]!'" Yet Nietzsche elsewhere insists that even these values that seem so starkly to deny and devalue life are made in the interest of life: "It must be some necessity of the first rank that makes this species [the ascetic priest] that is *hostile to life* grow and prosper again and again,—it must be an *interest of life itself* that this type of self-contradiction should not die out" (*GM* III: 11). Ascetic values make declining life bearable—help it to sustain itself, the next-best to growing; they let it cope with the pain associated with that decline.[35]

So in general moral values have evolved because they favor the power of the group, and the power of particular groups, groups of particular kinds of persons. There's still the question why *I*, if so "deeply" motivated by will to power, would adopt or go along with these values if they don't serve *my* power. And the answer must be, I think, that I—or this deep judge in me—simply err. I judge (in my body) that the way to my progress must lie on the road I see all around me take—that my best chance to rise is to sign onto the shared norms too. Moreover these social values are even designed to seduce the individual to think they *are* in his/her interest. They "infect" a population in the way today attributed to "memes."[36]

---

[34] *WP* 707 (1887): "This is my *basic objection*...against all *Whys* and *highest values* in previous philosophy and religion-philosophy. *A kind of means has been misunderstood as end; conversely life and its power-enhancement has been* reduced to *means*."

[35] *GM* III: 13: "*the ascetic ideal springs from the protective and healing instincts of a degenerating life* that seeks with every means to hold its ground and is fighting for its existence; it points to a partial physiological hindrance and tiredness against which the deepest instincts of life, which have remained intact, fight incessantly with new means and inventions." So "the ascetic ideal is an artifact for the *preservation* of life." It is the mark of a declining life that it values preservation—as a second-best to growth, currently denied it. So *GS* 349: "The wish to preserve oneself is an expression of distress."

[36] *TI*: "Expeditions of an Untimely Man" 5 says that life-denying morality "is very dangerous, it is infectious,—it quickly grows in society's morbid soil."

This, I suggest, is Nietzsche's principal account how will to power is "essential" to life—an account that shows how we can will things contrary to power, but also criticizes such contrary willing as resting on *error*. So what, in a nutshell, is his argument from life to values? What reason does he give me to revalue my agent values by the criterion of power?

Nietzsche claims there is a bottom to my system of motives, and at this bottom an aim that invents and sustains all my further motives. But this deep aim—which is implicit and bodily—is subject to error in its selection of means. It is without words itself, and can choose the wrong words (agent values) to express itself. It misjudges morality as its best strategy for improvement. Nietzsche appeals to us to side with this underlying will and to free it of the errors that make morality appealing to it.[37]

In what sense does this amount to an argument from facts to values? Nietzsche does indeed make a transition in his argument from a descriptive to a valuative way of "positing values" (see the distinction at the beginning of section 4). He describes a deep valuing in us of power; power is, in real fact, a value—for this valuing. He then uses this description to justify and promote his own values, and in particular his advice that we revalue our agent values by the criterion of (whether they enhance our) power. What status does this argument give to his values and that criterion in particular? Is it subject to the "open question" objection?

Clearly the value of power depends on the (purported) fact that it *is* valued by this deep will. Power is not valuable "in itself" or apart from that valuing; *nothing* is valuable in that way. I think Nietzsche's firm anti-realism saps the open question argument of much of its usual force. If the question "agreed that x is valued, but is it valuable?"[38] is asking whether x has such intrinsic value, Nietzsche would reject it as incoherent. There's no value to anything independent of its being valued—by some living things or other. So the question must instead suppose that whether x is valuable depends on some *different* valuing than this which values it. To apply this to Nietzsche's argument: "agreed that power is valued in this deep way, but is it valuable?" asks why we should not instead privilege those viewpoints that do *not* value power, for example our moral principles. Nietzsche's answer is as above: those moral agent values only matter to us because we deeply—but mistakenly—suppose they serve our power. When the anti-realism reduces the question to a choice between these viewpoints, he thinks the decision will favor that underlying will.

3. Now given this sketched argument from biological life to values, let's look more closely at how these values get applied. Surprisingly, I think, Nietzsche draws two quite different kinds of lessons. The first is obvious from what we've just seen: we're to revalue our (agent) values using the standard of will to power, taken as the essence of life. But there's a second way he makes values from life, which is probably even more prominent in his texts: we're to judge values by whether they "say Yes to life," i.e. by whether they're life-affirming. This seems like a quite different point, and it may be puzzling to see how much weight Nietzsche puts on it. I want to examine these two points and give an account how they operate together.

---

[37] Hunt (1991) develops a related line: "all moralities are fundamentally vitalistic in the intentions that lie behind them" (120–1).

[38] Similarly for "agreed that x is valued, but *should* it be valued?"

a) Let's start with the injunction to try to live so as to "say Yes to life"—and to judge a person or viewpoint or values by whether they affirm or deny life.[39] So *TI*: "What I Owe to the Ancients" 5: "Saying-yes to life [*Jasagen zum Leben*] even in its strangest and hardest problems; the will to life rejoicing in its own inexhaustibility in the *sacrifice* of its highest types—*that* I named Dionysian." And *EH*: "The Birth of Tragedy" 4: "a new party in favor of life" will make possible a "surplus of life on earth"; tragedy is the "highest art of saying-yes to life." Conversely Nietzsche attacks morality because it "*negates* life" (*CW* Preface) and Christianity as "*the denial of the will to life* become religion" (*EH*: "The Case of Wagner" 2).[40]

This lesson seems to belong to that simpler way of arguing from life to values, via the claim that life itself (rather than what it deeply values) is the good. It appears quite independent of the thesis that life is essentially will to power, since it seems one could judge whether x affirms life, no matter what life might essentially be. But I think this independence vanishes as we look more closely.

Affirming (saying yes to) life is of course an attitude or perspective, but in Nietzsche's rich sense. It involves not just seeing or thinking, but also feeling and most of all willing. Adequately affirming life must engage all these aspects, in an overall intending of life *as good*. It must view and "think" life as good, but it must also feel it as good, i.e., take pleasure in it, as well as will it as good, i.e., pursue or promote it as an end. So "saying Yes" doesn't happen in a cold or contemplative judgment, but only when the person's full faculties are engaged—engaged positively towards life.

But this overall pro-attitude must be towards *life*: for Nietzsche it's crucial that one "say Yes" to life *as it actually is*. It's not enough to announce oneself "on the side of life"—as we've seen that can mean almost anything. If you're in favor of "life," by which you mean the eternal life of Christianity, you're not really "life-affirming" according to Nietzsche. One needs to be at least approximately right about what life is. And life affirmation is fuller to the extent one more adequately faces life as it is. Hence this point, to be applied, depends on a specification of "how life is" and this can only be, for Nietzsche, the specification of it as will to power. Surely it is *as such* that one must "say Yes" to life, to do so in the fullest sense.[41]

Because affirming life involves both (a) seeing it accurately as it is, and (b) effort on behalf of life, it is natural that this attitude should tend to *be effective*, i.e., actually promote or enhance life. Nietzsche, we may notice, tends to treat the life-affirming attitude as indeed furthering life and the life-denying attitude as indeed harming it: "as soon one wills to carry this principle [refraining mutually from injury, violence, and exploitation and placing one's will on a par with that of someone else] further, even as *basic principle of society*, it immediately proves to be what it really is: a will to the *denial* of life, a principle of disintegration and decay" (*BGE* 259).[42]

---

[39] I treat this affirmation of life more thoroughly in "Nietzsche's Value Monism" (Richardson n.d.).

[40] Re morality, see also *WP* 343 (1886–7) and re Christianity, see *WP* 1052 (1888).

[41] Notice how life affirmation involves insight in *EH*: "The Birth of Tragedy" 2: "This ultimate, most joyous, most abundantly playful Yes to life is not only the highest insight, it is also the *deepest*, the most strictly confirmed and supported by truth and science."

[42] *EH* "Why I Am a Destiny" 7: "This, the only morality that has been taught so far, the unselfing-morality, betrays a will to the end, it *negates* life in its lowest ground....*Definition of morality*: morality—the idiosyncrasy of *décadents*, with the ulterior motive of revenging *themselves on life*—and successfully. I attach value to *this* definition."

Because affirming life is both (somewhat) *accurate* in its idea of life and (probably) *effective* in furthering life, the notion cannot in the end be separated from the essential truth—Nietzsche claims—*about* life, that it is will to power. The latter is needed to specify or determine (a) what life-affirming must view life as, and (b) how it really does advance life. Without this privileging of *one* of life's manifold aims (and values), the idea of affirming or advancing life loses content—or its content is dispersed into the all-inclusive multiplicity of life: every attitude says Yes to life in its way, and every event advances it to some view. So Nietzsche's lesson to "say Yes to life" leans hard on the will to power specification of life after all.

b) Let's turn now to this primary way Nietzsche uses life as corrective criterion, the straightforward route of judging by the standard of will to power, as the essence of life. This standard asks whether values advance/empower life, i.e., advance it in its essential end, which is power. Power gives the criterion for marking *levels* of life, higher and lower forms, and life that is ascending vs life that is declining.

So WP 254 (1885–6), after saying that study of the origin of values "in no way coincides with a critique of them": "what are our evaluations and moral tables of goods themselves worth [*werth*]? *What is the outcome of their rule? For whom? In relation to what?—* Answer: for life. But *what is life?* Here we need a new, more definite formulation of the concept 'life'. My formula for it is: Life is will to power."[43]

The lesson—at least part of it—must be to adopt life's end of power as our ultimate agent value, as our conscious guide or criterion. We bring our agency into deliberate service of this end; we take power as our "principle." We think what to do by what will maximize power/growth; we operate with some kind of utility-calculus maximizing power. And *whose* power? It sometimes seems we're called to further the power of life generally, or of those we care about. But I think Nietzsche's dominant answer is that I am to aim at *my own* power.

What are the more particular implications of this? When Nietzsche stresses that it's power rather than survival that is life's end, one lesson seems to be that we should risk ourselves. Life's end is not to live as long as possible; the good isn't quantity of life in that sense. Indeed Nietzsche wants us to learn the Dionysian lesson that all growth involves destruction: life is self-overcoming. So GS 26: "*What is life?*—Life—that is: continually shedding something that wills to die; life—that is: being cruel and inexorable against anything that is becoming weak and old in us, and not just in us."

I am to see that the point to life is growth, growth by overcoming previous states of myself. I am to set my sights explicitly on this meta-project, which subjects all my existing projects to a critical eye, under the aim to transform them. I now review and rethink all my practical rules and principles, asking whether they help or hinder this self-overcoming. I "revalue" my values by asking whether they serve this ultimate task. I design myself a new set of values promoting this new end. Nietzsche's view again looks like a kind of consequentialism, with power—the individual's own power—as the good to be maximized.

---

[43] *A* 2: "What is good?—Everything that enhances people's feeling of power, will to power, power itself."

B. And yet—I think this leaves out a whole side to Nietzsche's view of life and its bearing on values. Our focus on the biological(-phenomenal) notion of life, and our assumption that the lesson must be to revise our agent values, have closed off a main side of his thought here. In this side he reaches out from debates over principles like the various consequentialisms (maximize pleasure vs maximize power), to commend a different kind of stance altogether. This different stance is his answer to the conflict between his loves for life and for truth: it's what lets him subordinate the latter to the former. We can see this side by retrieving a different set (than in **A**) of the points made in sections 3–4, and applying them to our questions about the authority, criterion, and results by which Nietzsche argues from life to values.

1. Let's return to the authority of life. In **A** we located this in the way life—biological life, understood as phenomenal or intentional—is the transcendental source of all valuing; since its basic valuing is of its *own* growth or power, life is in an extended sense the ultimate value itself. So the "Life" that teaches Zarathustra would be the point of view at the bottom of all organisms: she speaks for and as them all. However, this reading fails to take account of two important points in section 3's account of life.

The first point is the role of the *body*: more specifically the way biological life is built into each of our bodies. Earlier and simpler forms of life are deposited in my body, as the drives operating all my physiological processes; my body is made up of these. So my body bears "biological life" in a narrower sense, in which it means life that is *merely* biological (and not also agential). And this more narrowly biological life has a different kind of "authority" in me, by this presence in my body. It has authority by its "depth," we'll see.

The second overlooked point is that "life" can also mean *personal* life—the sense in which each of us lives "a life." Many of Nietzsche's references to life are to *his own* life. And, I suggest, in the two dancing songs of *Zarathustra* (though not perhaps in *Z* II: "On Self-Overcoming"), the "Life" that's personified is meant to be Zarathustra's own life. It's this that he is in this intimate relation with, and not biological life in the abstract or generality. She stands for his own life as he knows he has it to live.

So notice just how Zarathustra engages with Life in these climactic passages. He engages with her in terms of his personal life—over the "existential questions" in which he confronts the main character of his life. He thinks about his relation to (his) life in connection with his dominant passion, his ideal of wisdom or truth. And he thinks about his relation to life in connection with his death, the end of his life ("you think that you want to leave me soon"). Both of these (death, his will to truth) pose challenges to his love of (his) life, but he is able to reconcile both with it.

Now does this mean that the biological sense of "life," in which it applies to all organisms, is irrelevant here at the heart of his point? For presumably it's only humans that have such "personal" lives—mean themselves to be living a life[44]—so that if it's only the latter that count, broader life would drop out of the picture. Yet we've just seen how a

---

[44] Or might Nietzsche suppose that all organisms have a rudimentary sense of themselves as living a life? They all will, after all, their growth/control, and might be sensitive too that some things will kill them. To be sure it's implausible to suppose them to "look ahead" so as to see their living as bounded into a (finite) life. But we should bear in mind that they indeed are designed—by selection—to live through a life cycle, and are sensitive, physiologically, to "where they are" in this cycle (life). So there may be a rudimentary "personal life" in simple organisms.

personal life involves biological life for Nietzsche: it's built into each of us, in our body. This life I have to live is lived as or in a body, and in my body I will as biological life generally wills.

2. But to see better how such personal and bodily life might have authority, we need to turn (again) to the criterion it supplies. This is of course power or growth, as **A** has shown. But our personal and bodily life supplies this criterion in a different way than there appeared. To be sure, I suggested that Nietzsche promotes this criterion because of its "depth" in us, but I didn't develop how this depth reaches into our bodies, nor how the criterion comes to us *from* our bodies. We need to rethink *how* life "supplies" this criterion.

We've supposed the criterion of power to have been extracted by philosophical argument from observation of life generally, via the claim that life's "essential" aim at power is "inescapably determining"—i.e., such that all values originate as means to it. Life gives the criterion as an object of our study: we examine her and ourselves, and infer that power has this ultimacy; we then deliberately review the ethics and practical rules we've accepted, and revise them in view of that clarified end.

But this is too cold-blooded to be Nietzsche's point (—there's not enough life in it). Life isn't passive object in his "argument," but has a speaking role, and delivers her will to us more forcefully than via our study and inference. The way biological life is built into our bodies gives it a voice in them, and most of the trick will be to let it speak. We get the criterion not so much by inferences taken from our bodies and applied in our deliberations, as by giving the body more place in our lives—and principle-driven deliberation less.

The biological (in the narrow sense) life built into my body speaks with special authority because it has its principal allegiance to the power of the organism I am. As we've seen, my agent values have been constructed for different purposes—especially for the power of groups, and often groups of people very unlike myself. By contrast my drives, and the body values they involve, are more reliably aimed at my power, growth, health. Of course they were laid down in the ancient past within organisms and in environments extremely different from my own. Still they preserve, even if very deep-buried, my organism's aim at *its own* power. So these wills in my body—"life" there—speak in me for me, by contrast with the inherited "value tables" generally expressing the power interests of others.

Indeed it is by this judgment in my strong bodily drives that I finally identify what "power" is. Definitions like "growth in control" need to be replaced by that judgment: its unstudied taste is the compass for this power. And so "I," as a deliberative agent consciously choosing for worded reasons, learn to submit to the "self" that values and judges in my body.[45] I learn to defer to a taste in my body, a taste Nietzsche often represents as a sense of smell. I encourage my passions, trusting their judgment better than the most careful conclusions of moral reasoning—suspicious as I now am of the design of that reasoning power: "Listen rather, my brothers, to the voice of the healthy body: a more honest and purer voice is this" (*Z* I: "Of

---

[45] See this contrast between "I" and "self" in *Z* I: "Of the Despisers of the Body"; *WP* 343 (1886–7): "My insight: all the forces and drives by virtue of which there are life and growth, are covered by the *ban of morality*: morality as instinct of the denial of life. One must destroy morality, in order to free life."

the Afterworldsmen"); "There is more reason in your body than in your best wisdom" (Z I: "Of the Despisers of the Body"). And "That one gives back to humans the *courage* to their natural drives [*Naturtrieben*]" (*WP* 124 [1887]).[46]

This is not to say that agent values can play no role. The body may *not* be healthy—may have no sound taste for its interests. Or it may express a "declining" line and lack vigor to grow. In some such cases, maybe even in most, Nietzsche is convinced that nothing can be done. But most of us are mixtures, healthy in some drives (or moods) but not in others, sometimes feeling the way to grow, to be more alive, but other times not. For most of us our *deepest* drives and aims are healthy, and track power. Indeed I think Nietzsche supposes that if one goes deep enough one will always find a healthy will, a will that does aim at power. This was one of the points we saw he meant by will to power's "depth"—its ineliminability.

If there are enough such resources in the body, agency can help to realize them— once it learns (is trained) to set itself to that task. But to learn this is very hard, because it goes quite against the grain of agency's long-standing design. Our agency has a designed-in bias against the drives; its first instinct is to distrust and suppress them. I—the agent—need to use this insight about life's essence to identify what's healthy in my (bodily) self, and to exert whatever effective force my agency can have to favor it. This is why Nietzsche addresses us—in part at least—as agents, giving reasons that are to work in our deliberating: in the expectation that his explicit lessons for us can help us where it counts. Persuaded by his argument from life, we can use the concept of power to favor the right side, and build up our more-aiming drives. Still, it's only in the working of those drives themselves, and not grasp of the concept, that we truly see what life's end is.

This reconfiguration of the relation between our agency and our bodily drives is Nietzsche's response to the problem we've seen he was long obsessed with: the conflict between his will to truth, and his life or living. It is the adjustment that allows the will to truth, with its inherent asceticism, to function helpfully in the person. This will gives up the reins. It grants authority to the drives, but can do so willingly because it sees that even its own aim, truth—above all the truth about life—needs to be accomplished in these drives.

3. We can see the results of applying this criterion, so supplied, by returning to the idea of life affirmation. We concluded above that this had little to contribute to Nietzsche's argument from life to values. But this was due to our focus on agent values: we presumed that the argument meant to change our principles. I think the idea of life affirmation works in that other personal and bodily side to Nietzsche's thought; this is why it's needed as complement to the arguments about will to power. Filling out this life affirmation brings us to the bottom of his points.[47]

---

[46] *EH*: "Why I Am So Clever" 9: "That one becomes what one is presupposes that one is furthest from suspecting *what* one is.... One must keep the whole surface of consciousness—consciousness *is* a surface—clean of all great imperatives." *TI*: "The Problem of Socrates" 11: "so long as life is *ascending*, happiness equals instinct."

[47] Here I agree with Reginster (2006: 228): "We truly 'understand' him only when we understand what the affirmation of life amounts to."

Even though the lesson "say Yes to life" relies on and runs into the lesson to agent-value power, it includes an emotive or affective aspect not present in agent-valuing—and also not present in the agent principle to maximize power. I suggest this is the key reason Nietzsche so often puts the point this way. Saying Yes to life is a matter not just of a positive judgment, but of (something much like) *loving* it. It shows that the lesson must be learned in a personal and bodily way.

It is to stress the engagement with personal life that Nietzsche so often describes the revaluative process in his own case—as he has managed it in the living of his own life.[48] This personalizing of his ideas of course culminates in *Ecce Homo*, which presents the new ideal as it is found and embraced within an individual life. The point of this personalizing is not to relativize the ideal to Nietzsche himself, but to display how the ideal needs to be appropriated: not propositionally, and not just consciously and deliberatively, but in a way that engages the whole organism, drives and all.

This is also one reason Nietzsche wrote *Zarathustra* as he did. The drama about Zarathustra sets our attention on the personal: the ideas are events in an individual's life, and are, in their crucial points, responses to his awareness of living his own one life. Although this character is of course a rather distant persona, we are invited to enter into it, and to experience the drama and teachings first-personally. Similarly, we may take the book's poetizing as an effort to speak to the body—to feeling and to primitive effort. It appeals to the judgment of the deep will in our body, whose taste is sensitive to a different kind of argument or evidence.

Nietzsche expresses this affective point most dramatically in those culminating passages of *Zarathustra* describing the hero's love for (personified) Life. This love is much more than the kind of "affirmation" involved in believing that life is good. We've already seen how the drama emphasizes the personal sense of "life": Zarathustra is engaged reflectively with *his own* life, before death and in the light of his dominant project and passion (towards truth). He *loves* this his life in a way that contains and guides that passion: he pursues it out of this love for his life. This love is itself a passion, as it were, a meta-passion, a passion for passions. As a passion, it belongs to his body.

The drama presents Zarathustra's love for life as *erotic*. It is inspired by and directed at life's beauty, not its truth or moral rightness. So this love of life involves an *aesthetic* sensibility and judgment.[49] We apply this artistic sensibility, as artists themselves usually don't, to our lives, so that as Nietzsche famously puts it in *GS* 299: "*we*, however, will to be the poets of our lives, first of all in the smallest and most everyday things." This poetic work on one's life is carried out not in a deliberate way—it's not a precious effort to be picturesque. Rather it's run by that passion for life aimed at enhancement, that judges and arranges the other passions, including that for truth. It arranges them into a life it favors by its own inarticulate taste.[50]

Zarathustra's embrace of eternal return, the ultimate saying-Yes to life, takes place only in confrontation with the existential structure of his own life: it's *this* life whose return he

---

[48] Conway 2006: 539: "most of his specific references to self-overcoming pertain to the developmental trajectory of his own life."

[49] In Richardson 2004: chapter 4, I try to show that Nietzsche thinks of sexuality as the evolutionary root of our aesthetic responsiveness.

[50] *GS* 290: "To 'give style' to one's character: a great and rare art!" Nehamas (1985: 185–99) treats this idea famously.

affirms.[51] And he only accomplishes this embrace by a struggle fought in his body and suffered physiologically, as described in Z III: "The Convalescent."[52] So Nietzsche's test for life affirmation—whether one can will this return—needs to be met with regard to one's personal life and at the level of one's body values.

Although *Zarathustra* makes the point about life "just" metaphorically, it locates the point where Nietzsche felt it most strongly. The personification of Life as the object of sexual love stresses both the existential-personal sense of life, and the need to respond to it in one's bodily taste and feeling. It expresses the emotive relation to one's living that Nietzsche principally advocates. We can't simply apply these lessons about life's ends to our values "from outside": we need to uncover and activate these life-ends in ourselves (in our bodies), and arrange a cooperation between them and our agential valuing.

In sum: I've tried first to *analyze* the elements in Nietzsche's notion of life—biological, human, phenomenal, personal, poetic—then to show (a) how these elements are *synthesized* in his complex notion, and also (b) how the different parts function together in the crucial *argument* he makes, that "life" supports or justifies his values.

We saw how the claim that 'life is will to power' seems to make the argument depend on a quasi-metaphysical claim about all biological life. But the weight of Nietzsche's point runs at a more personal level: biological life is important not so much for its generality as for its depth in each of us. Biological life is represented in our bodies, by our drives, which ultimately aim us at power. Such life (aiming at power) has authority, as criterion for judging values, because of this bodily presence in each of us. It is the undermost valuing in us, aimed at our individual good, which is growth.

Our agent-valuing, by contrast, was shaped by social processes whose aim is to tame and herd us (turn us into good citizens). It pretends to be our freedom, the better to so socialize us. We should revalue these agent values by diagnosing this hidden design. But the point of this revaluation is not just to change the content of our agent values, but to change the role of agency in us—its own relation to body values. This is the role of the poetic personification of Life in *Zarathustra* and its insertion in a sexual drama.

BIBLIOGRAPHY

(A) Works by Nietzsche

I have retranslated most passages, so they do not generally follow any particular English editions. The exception is that I have mostly retained Parkes's rendering of *Zarathustra*.

KSA   *Sämtliche Werke: Kritische Studienausgabe in 15 Einzelbänden*, ed. G. Colli and M. Montinari. Berlin: De Gruyter, 1988.

Z   *Thus Spoke Zarathustra*, trans. Graham Parkes. Oxford: Oxford University Press, 2005.

[51] The focus is also on personal life in GS 341: "What, if some day or night a demon were to steal after you in your loneliest loneliness and say to you: 'This life as you now live it and have lived it you will have to live once more and innumerable times more; and there will be nothing new in it . . . .' "

[52] "(H)e collapsed like a dead man and lay for a long time like one dead. But when he came to himself again, he was pale and trembling and remained lying down, and for a long time he wanted neither food nor drink." Nietzsche thought of himself as having undergone a decisive illness and then convalescence in his "middle," positivist period.

(B) Other Works Cited

Conway, D. W. 2006. "Nietzsche and Self-Overcoming," in K. Ansell-Pearson (ed.), *A Companion to Nietzsche*. Oxford: Blackwell, 532–47.

Hunt, L. H. 1991. *Nietzsche and the Origin of Virtue*. London: Routledge.

Lampert, L. 1986. *Nietzsche's Teaching: An Interpretation of "Thus Spoke Zarathustra."* New Haven, Conn.: Yale University Press.

May, S. 1999. *Nietzsche's Ethics and his War on "Morality."* Oxford: Clarendon Press.

Nehamas, A. 1985. *Nietzsche: Life as Literature*. Cambridge, Mass.: Harvard University Press.

Reginster, B. 2006. *The Affirmation of Life: Nietzsche on Overcoming Nihilism*. Cambridge, Mass.: Harvard University Press.

Richardson, J. 1996. *Nietzsche's System*. New York: Oxford University Press.

Richardson, J. 2004. *Nietzsche's New Darwinism*. New York: Oxford University Press.

Richardson, J. 2009. "Nietzsche's Freedoms," in K Gemes and S. May (eds), *Nietzsche on Freedom and Autonomy*. Oxford: Oxford University Press, 127–49.

Richardson, J. n.d. "Nietzsche's Value Monism: Saying Yes to Everything." Unpublished ms.

Schacht, R. 1983. *Nietzsche*. London: Routledge & Kegan Paul.

Wright, L. 1973. "Functions," *Philosophical Review* 82: 139–68.

Subject Index

Note: This subject index is selective: it tries to pick out, from the many more places a term (or its cognate) occurs, those where the author pays direct attention to what the term names. So passing uses or mentions are excluded, as are places the term occurs only in a quotation from Nietzsche, or in a bibliography or page-heading.

Name Index

Note: This name index (unlike the topic index) aims to be complete, recording all occurrences of the name or its derivative forms (e.g. Platonic, Cartesian, Darwinism) though only occurrences in the papers themselves, not in their bibliographies or page-headings.

Lightning Source UK Ltd.
Milton Keynes UK
UKHW030800120421
381799UK00003B/7